STUDENT'S *t* CRITICAL VALUES

This table shows the *t*-value that defines the area for the stated degrees of freedom (ν).

	Confidence Level						Confidence Level			
	.80	.90	.95	.98	.99		.80	.90	.95	.98	.99
	Significance Level for Two-Tailed Test						Significance Level for Two-Tailed Test				
	.20	.10	.05	.02	.01		.20	.10	.05	.02	.01
	Significance Level for One-Tailed Test						Significance Level for One-Tailed Test				
ν	.10	.05	.025	.01	.005	ν	.10	.05	.025	.01	.005
1	3.078	6.314	12.706	31.821	63.656	36	1.306	1.688	2.028	2.434	2.719
2	1.886	2.920	4.303	6.965	9.925	37	1.305	1.687	2.026	2.431	2.715
3	1.638	2.353	3.182	4.541	5.841	38	1.304	1.686	2.024	2.429	2.712
4	1.533	2.132	2.776	3.747	4.604	39	1.304	1.685	2.023	2.426	2.708
5	1.476	2.015	2.571	3.365	4.032	40	1.303	1.684	2.021	2.423	2.704
6	1.440	1.943	2.447	3.143	3.707	41	1.303	1.683	2.020	2.421	2.701
7	1.415	1.895	2.365	2.998	3.499	42	1.302	1.682	2.018	2.418	2.698
8	1.397	1.860	2.306	2.896	3.355	43	1.302	1.681	2.017	2.416	2.695
9	1.383	1.833	2.262	2.821	3.250	44	1.301	1.680	2.015	2.414	2.692
10	1.372	1.812	2.228	2.764	3.169	45	1.301	1.679	2.014	2.412	2.690
11	1.363	1.796	2.201	2.718	3.106	46	1.300	1.679	2.013	2.410	2.687
12	1.356	1.782	2.179	2.681	3.055	47	1.300	1.678	2.012	2.408	2.685
13	1.350	1.771	2.160	2.650	3.012	48	1.299	1.677	2.011	2.407	2.682
14	1.345	1.761	2.145	2.624	2.977	49	1.299	1.677	2.010	2.405	2.680
15	1.341	1.753	2.131	2.602	2.947	50	1.299	1.676	2.009	2.403	2.678
16	1.337	1.746	2.120	2.583	2.921	55	1.297	1.673	2.004	2.396	2.668
17	1.333	1.740	2.110	2.567	2.898	60	1.296	1.671	2.000	2.390	2.660
18	1.330	1.734	2.101	2.552	2.878	65	1.295	1.669	1.997	2.385	2.654
19	1.328	1.729	2.093	2.539	2.861	70	1.294	1.667	1.994	2.381	2.648
20	1.325	1.725	2.086	2.528	2.845	75	1.293	1.665	1.992	2.377	2.643
21	1.323	1.721	2.080	2.518	2.831	80	1.292	1.664	1.990	2.374	2.639
22	1.321	1.717	2.074	2.508	2.819	85	1.292	1.663	1.988	2.371	2.635
23	1.319	1.714	2.069	2.500	2.807	90	1.291	1.662	1.987	2.368	2.632
24	1.318	1.711	2.064	2.492	2.797	95	1.291	1.661	1.985	2.366	2.629
25	1.316	1.708	2.060	2.485	2.787	100	1.290	1.660	1.984	2.364	2.626
26	1.315	1.706	2.056	2.479	2.779	110	1.289	1.659	1.982	2.361	2.621
27	1.314	1.703	2.052	2.473	2.771	120	1.289	1.658	1.980	2.358	2.617
28	1.313	1.701	2.048	2.467	2.763	130	1.288	1.657	1.978	2.355	2.614
29	1.311	1.699	2.045	2.462	2.756	140	1.288	1.656	1.977	2.353	2.611
30	1.310	1.697	2.042	2.457	2.750	150	1.287	1.655	1.976	2.351	2.609
31	1.309	1.696	2.040	2.453	2.744	∞	1.282	1.645	1.960	2.326	2.576
32	1.309	1.694	2.037	2.449	2.738						
33	1.308	1.692	2.035	2.445	2.733						
34	1.307	1.691	2.032	2.441	2.728						
35	1.306	1.690	2.030	2.438	2.724						

Note: As *n* increases, critical values of Student's *t* approach the *z*-values in the last line of this table. A common rule of thumb is to use *z* when *n* > 30, but that is *not* conservative.

STANDARD NORMAL AREAS

This table shows the normal area between 0 and z. Example: $P(0 < z < 1.96) = .4750$

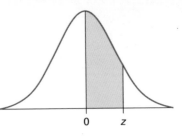

z	.00	.01	.02	.03	.04	.05	**.06**	.07	.08	.09
0.0	.0000	.0040	.0080	.0120	.0160	.0199	.0239	.0279	.0319	.0359
0.1	.0398	.0438	.0478	.0517	.0557	.0596	.0636	.0675	.0714	.0753
0.2	.0793	.0832	.0871	.0910	.0948	.0987	.1026	.1064	.1103	.1141
0.3	.1179	.1217	.1255	.1293	.1331	.1368	.1406	.1443	.1480	.1517
0.4	.1554	.1591	.1628	.1664	.1700	.1736	.1772	.1808	.1844	.1879
0.5	.1915	.1950	.1985	.2019	.2054	.2088	.2123	.2157	.2190	.2224
0.6	.2257	.2291	.2324	.2357	.2389	.2422	.2454	.2486	.2517	.2549
0.7	.2580	.2611	.2642	.2673	.2704	.2734	.2764	.2794	.2823	.2852
0.8	.2881	.2910	.2939	.2967	.2995	.3023	.3051	.3078	.3106	.3133
0.9	.3159	.3186	.3212	.3238	.3264	.3289	.3315	.3340	.3365	.3389
1.0	.3413	.3438	.3461	.3485	.3508	.3531	.3554	.3577	.3599	.3621
1.1	.3643	.3665	.3686	.3708	.3729	.3749	.3770	.3790	.3810	.3830
1.2	.3849	.3869	.3888	.3907	.3925	.3944	.3962	.3980	.3997	.4015
1.3	.4032	.4049	.4066	.4082	.4099	.4115	.4131	.4147	.4162	.4177
1.4	.4192	.4207	.4222	.4236	.4251	.4265	.4279	.4292	.4306	.4319
1.5	.4332	.4345	.4357	.4370	.4382	.4394	.4406	.4418	.4429	.4441
1.6	.4452	.4463	.4474	.4484	.4495	.4505	.4515	.4525	.4535	.4545
1.7	.4554	.4564	.4573	.4582	.4591	.4599	.4608	.4616	.4625	.4633
1.8	.4641	.4649	.4656	.4664	.4671	.4678	.4686	.4693	.4699	.4706
1.9	.4713	.4719	.4726	.4732	.4738	.4744	**.4750**	.4756	.4761	.4767
2.0	.4772	.4778	.4783	.4788	.4793	.4798	.4803	.4808	.4812	.4817
2.1	.4821	.4826	.4830	.4834	.4838	.4842	.4846	.4850	.4854	.4857
2.2	.4861	.4864	.4868	.4871	.4875	.4878	.4881	.4884	.4887	.4890
2.3	.4893	.4896	.4898	.4901	.4904	.4906	.4909	.4911	.4913	.4916
2.4	.4918	.4920	.4922	.4925	.4927	.4929	.4931	.4932	.4934	.4936
2.5	.4938	.4940	.4941	.4943	.4945	.4946	.4948	.4949	.4951	.4952
2.6	.4953	.4955	.4956	.4957	.4959	.4960	.4961	.4962	.4963	.4964
2.7	.4965	.4966	.4967	.4968	.4969	.4970	.4971	.4972	.4973	.4974
2.8	.4974	.4975	.4976	.4977	.4977	.4978	.4979	.4979	.4980	.4981
2.9	.4981	.4982	.4982	.4983	.4984	.4984	.4985	.4985	.4986	.4986
3.0	.49865	.49869	.49874	.49878	.49882	.49886	.49889	.49893	.49896	.49900
3.1	.49903	.49906	.49910	.49913	.49916	.49918	.49921	.49924	.49926	.49929
3.2	.49931	.49934	.49936	.49938	.49940	.49942	.49944	.49946	.49948	.49950
3.3	.49952	.49953	.49955	.49957	.49958	.49960	.49961	.49962	.49964	.49965
3.4	.49966	.49968	.49969	.49970	.49971	.49972	.49973	.49974	.49975	.49976
3.5	.49977	.49978	.49978	.49979	.49980	.49981	.49981	.49982	.49983	.49983
3.6	.49984	.49985	.49985	.49986	.49986	.49987	.49987	.49988	.49988	.49989
3.7	.49989	.49990	.49990	.49990	.49991	.49991	.49992	.49992	.49992	.49992

Essential Statistics

in Business and Economics

Second Edition

THE McGRAW-HILL/IRWIN SERIES
Operations and Decision Sciences

BUSINESS STATISTICS

Aczel and Sounderpandian, **Complete Business Statistics,** *Seventh Edition*

ALEKS Corporation, **ALEKS for Business Statistics,** *First Edition*

Alwan, **Statistical Process Analysis,** *First Edition*

Bowerman, O'Connell, and Murphree, **Business Statistics in Practice,** *Fifth Edition*

Bowerman, O'Connell, Orris, and Murphree, **Essentials of Business Statistics,** *Third Edition*

Bryant and Smith, **Practical Data Analysis: Case Studies in Business Statistics, Volumes I, II, and III***

Cooper and Schindler, **Business Research Methods,** *Tenth Edition*

Doane, Mathieson, and Tracy, **Visual Statistics,** *Second Edition, 2.0*

Doane and Seward, **Applied Statistics in Business and Economics,** *Second Edition*

Doane and Seward, **Essential Statistics in Business and Economics,** *Second Edition*

Gitlow, Oppenheim, Oppenheim, and Levine, **Quality Management,** *Third Edition*

Kutner, Nachtsheim, Neter, and Li, **Applied Linear Statistical Models,** *Fifth Edition*

Kutner, Nachtsheim, and Neter, **Applied Linear Regression Models,** *Fourth Edition*

Lind, Marchal, and Wathen, **Basic Statistics for Business and Economics,** *Sixth Edition*

Lind, Marchal, and Wathen, **Statistical Techniques in Business and Economics,** *Fourteenth Edition*

Merchant, Goffinet, and Koehler, **Basic Statistics Using Excel for Office XP,** *Fourth Edition*

Olson and Shi, **Introduction to Business Data Mining,** *First Edition*

Orris, **Basic Statistics Using Excel and MegaStat,** *First Edition*

Siegel, **Practical Business Statistics,** *Fifth Edition*

Wilson, Keating, and John Galt Solutions, Inc., **Business Forecasting,** *Fifth Edition*

Zagorsky, **Business Information,** *First Edition*

QUANTITATIVE METHODS AND MANAGEMENT SCIENCE

Hillier and Hillier, **Introduction to Management Science,** *Third Edition*

Stevenson and Ozgur, **Introduction to Management Science with Spreadsheets,** *First Edition*

Kros, **Spreadsheet Modeling for Business Decisions,** *First Edition*

*Available only through McGraw-Hill's PRIMIS Online Assets Library.

Essential Statistics

in Business and Economics

Second Edition

David P. Doane
Oakland University

Lori E. Seward
University of Colorado

McGraw-Hill Irwin

Boston   Burr Ridge, IL   Dubuque, IA   New York   San Francisco   St. Louis
Bangkok   Bogotá   Caracas   Kuala Lumpur   Lisbon   London   Madrid   Mexico City
Milan   Montreal   New Delhi   Santiago   Seoul   Singapore   Sydney   Taipei   Toronto

The McGraw·Hill Companies

ESSENTIAL STATISTICS IN BUSINESS AND ECONOMICS

Published by McGraw-Hill/Irwin, a business unit of The McGraw-Hill Companies, Inc., 1221 Avenue of the Americas, New York, NY, 10020. Copyright © 2010, 2008 by The McGraw-Hill Companies, Inc. All rights reserved. No part of this publication may be reproduced or distributed in any form or by any means, or stored in a database or retrieval system, without the prior written consent of The McGraw-Hill Companies, Inc., including, but not limited to, in any network or other electronic storage or transmission, or broadcast for distance learning.

Some ancillaries, including electronic and print components, may not be available to customers outside the United States.

This book is printed on acid-free paper.

1 2 3 4 5 6 7 8 9 0 WCK/WCK 0 9

ISBN 978-0-07-337365-2
MHID 0-07-337365-6

Vice president and editor-in-chief: *Brent Gordon*
Editorial director: *Stewart Mattson*
Executive editor: *Steve Schuetz*
Senior developmental editor: *Wanda J. Zeman*
Marketing manager: *Scott Bishop*
Lead project manager: *Pat Frederickson*
Full service project manager: *Siddhartha Ghosh, Macmillan Publishing Solutions*
Production supervisor: *Gina Hangos*
Designer: *Matt Diamond*
Senior photo research coordinator: *Jeremy Cheshareck*
Photo researcher: *Ira C. Roberts*
Senior media project manager: *Greg Bates*
Typeface: *10/12 Times New Roman*
Compositor: *Macmillan Publishing Solutions*
Printer: *Quebecor World Versailles Inc.*

Library of Congress Cataloging-in-Publication Data

Doane, David P.
    Essential statistics in business and economics / David P. Doane, Lori E. Seward.—2nd ed.
        p. cm.—(The McGraw-Hill/Irwin series : operations and decision sciences)
    Includes index.
    ISBN-13: 978-0-07-337365-2 (alk. paper)
    ISBN-10: 0-07-337365-6 (alk. paper)
    1. Commercial statistics. 2. Economics—Statistical methods. I. Seward, Lori Welte,
1962– II. Title.
HF1017.D553 2010
519.5—dc22
                                                                    2008042158

www.mhhe.com

ABOUT THE AUTHORS

David P. Doane

David P. Doane is Professor of Quantitative Methods in Oakland University's Department of Decision and Information Sciences. He earned his Bachelor of Arts degree in mathematics and economics at the University of Kansas and his PhD from Purdue University's Krannert Graduate School. His research and teaching interests include applied statistics, forecasting, and statistical education. He is co-recipient of three National Science Foundation grants to develop software to teach statistics and to create a computer classroom. He is a long-time member of the American Statistical Association and INFORMS, serving in 2002 as President of the Detroit ASA chapter, where he remains on the board. He has consulted with government, health care organizations, and local firms. He has published articles in many academic journals and is the author of *LearningStats* (McGraw-Hill, 2003, 2007) and co-author of *Visual Statistics* (McGraw-Hill, 1997, 2001).

Lori E. Seward

Lori E. Seward is an Instructor in the Decisions Sciences Department in the College of Business at The University of Colorado at Denver and Health Sciences Center. She earned her Bachelor of Science and Master of Science degrees in Industrial Engineering at Virginia Tech. After several years working as a reliability and quality engineer in the paper and automotive industries, she earned her PhD from Virginia Tech. She served as the Chair of the INFORMS Teachers' Workshop for the annual 2004 meeting. Prior to joining UCDHSC in 2008, Dr. Seward served on the faculty at the Leeds School of Business at CU–Boulder for ten years. Her teaching interests focus on developing pedagogy that uses technology to create a collaborative learning environment in both large undergraduate and MBA statistics courses. Her most recent article was published in *The International Journal of Flexible Manufacturing Systems,* (Kluwer Academic Publishers, 2004).

DEDICATION

To Robert Hamilton Doane-Solomon

David

To all my students who challenged me to make statistics relevant to their lives.

Lori

"How often have you heard people/students say about a particular subject, 'I'll never use this in the real world?' I thought statistics was a bit on the 'math-geeky' side at first. Imagine my horror when I saw α, R^2, and correlations on several financial reports at my current job (an intern position at a financial services company). I realized then that I had better try to understand some of this stuff."

—Jill Odette (an introductory statistics student)

As recently as a decade ago our students used to ask us, "**How** do I use statistics?" Today we more often hear, "**Why** should I use statistics?" *Applied Statistics in Business and Economics* has attempted to provide real meaning to the use of statistics in our world by using real business situations and real data and appealing to your need to know *why* rather than just *how*.

With over 50 years of teaching statistics between the two of us, we feel we have something to offer. Seeing how students have changed as the new century unfolds has required us to adapt and seek out better ways of instruction. So we wrote *Applied Statistics in Business and Economics* to meet four distinct objectives.

Objective 1: Communicate the Meaning of Variation in a Business Context Variation exists everywhere in the world around us. Successful businesses know how to measure variation. They also know how to tell when variation should be responded to and when it should be left alone. We'll show how businesses do this.

Objective 2: Use Real Data and Real Business Applications Examples, case studies, and problems are taken from published research or real applications whenever possible. Hypothetical data are used when it seems the best way to illustrate a concept. You can usually tell the difference by examining the footnotes citing the source.

Objective 3: Incorporate Current Statistical Practices and Offer Practical Advice With the increased reliance on computers, statistics practitioners have changed the way they use statistical tools. We'll show the current practices and explain why they are used the way they are. We will also tell you when each technique should *not* be used.

Objective 4: Provide More In-Depth Explanation of the Why and Let the Software Take Care of the How It is critical to understand the importance of communicating with data. Today's computer capabilities make it much easier to summarize and display data than ever before. We demonstrate easily mastered software techniques using the common software available. We also spend a great deal of time on the idea that there are risks in decision making and those risks should be quantified and directly considered in every business decision.

Our experience tells us that students want to be given credit for the experience they bring to the college classroom. We have tried to honor this by choosing examples and exercises set in situations that will draw on students' already vast knowledge of the world and knowledge gained from other classes. Emphasis is on thinking about data, choosing appropriate analytic tools, using computers effectively, and recognizing limitations of statistics.

What's New in This Second Edition?

In this second edition we have listened to you and have made many changes that you asked for. We sought advice from students and faculty who are currently using the textbook, objective reviewers at a variety of colleges and universities, and participants in focus groups on teaching statistics with technology. There are many improvements in this second edition, some of which are highlighted below:

- Better nontechnical motivation of chapter topics.
- Improved transitions between concepts within chapters.
- More and updated mini cases on topics that will interest students.
- Revisions to graphic illustrations and tables in order to provide a better "picture" of the concept for students.
- More large real data sets for student assignment projects, included on Student CD.

AUTHORS

- New exercises and examples using real data from Noodles & Company, a rapidly growing casual dining chain whose success is based on a customer-driven business model and decision making using statistical analysis.

- Updated examples and updated data sets used in exercises.

- Enlarged and improved test bank for instructors.

- Compatibility with Excel 2007 as well as Excel 2003.

- Section exercises for review before exams, with complete solutions (Appendix H).

Software

There are different types of software for statistical analysis, ranging from Excel's functions to stand-alone packages. Excel is used throughout this book because it is available everywhere. But calculations are illustrated using *MegaStat,* an Excel add-in whose Excel-based menus and spreadsheet format offer more capability than Excel's Data Analysis Tools. MINITAB menus and examples are also included to point out similarities and differences of these tools. To assist students who need extra help or "catch up" work, the text website (www.mhhe.com/doaness2e) contains tutorials or demonstrations on using Excel, MINITAB, or *MegaStat* for the tasks of each chapter. At the end of each chapter is a list of *LearningStats* and Visual Statistics demonstrations, case studies, and applications that illustrate the concepts from the chapter.

Math Level

The assumed level of mathematics is pre-calculus, though there are rare references to calculus where it might help the better-trained reader. All but the simplest proofs and derivations are omitted, though key assumptions are stated clearly. The learner is advised what to do when these assumptions are not fulfilled. Worked examples are included for basic calculations, but the textbook does assume that computers will do all calculations after the statistics class is over. Thus, *interpretation* is paramount. End-of-chapter references and suggested Web sites are given so that interested readers can deepen their understanding.

Exercises

Simple practice exercises are placed within each section. End-of-chapter exercises tend to be more integrative or to be embedded in more realistic contexts. The end-of-chapter exercises encourage the learner to try alternative approaches and discuss ambiguities or underlying issues when the statistical tools do not quite "fit" the situation. Many exercises invite mini-essays (at least a sentence or two) rather than just quoting a formula. Answers to odd-numbered exercises are in the back of the book (all answers are in the instructor's manual).

LearningStats

LearningStats is intended to let students explore data and concepts at their own pace, ignoring material they already know and focusing on things that interest them. *LearningStats* includes explanations on topics that are not covered in other software packages, such as writing effective reports, how to perform calculations, how to make effective charts, or how the bootstrap method works. It also includes some topics that did not appear prominently in the textbook (e.g., stem-and-leaf plots, finite population correction factor, bootstrap simulation techniques). Instructors can use *LearningStats* PowerPoint presentations in the classroom, but students can also use them for self-instruction. No instructor can "cover everything," but students can be encouraged to explore *LearningStats* data sets and/or demonstrations perhaps with an instructor's guidance, or even as an assigned project.

David P. Doane
Lori E. Seward

Chapter Contents

Each chapter begins with a short list of section Topics that are covered in the chapter.

Chapter Learning Objectives

Each chapter includes a list of learning Objectives students should be able to attain upon reading and studying the chapter material. Learning objectives give students an overview of what is expected and identify the goals for learning.

Section Exercises · connect

Multiple section exercises are found throughout the chapter so that students can focus on material just learned.

Mini Cases

Every chapter includes two or three mini cases, which are solved applications. They show and illlustrate the analytical application of specific statistical concepts at a deeper level than the examples.

Chapter Contents	
	1.1 What Is Statistics?
	1.2 Why Study Statistics?
	1.3 Uses of Statistics
	1.4 Statistical Challenges
	1.5 Writing and Presenting Reports
	1.6 Critical Thinking
	1.7 Statistics: An Evolving Field

Chapter Learning Objectives	

When you finish this chapter you should be able to

- Define statistics and explain some of its uses in business.
- List reasons for a business student to study statistics.
- State the common challenges facing data analysts.
- Explain why written communication is important.
- Know the basic rules for effective writing and oral presentations.

SECTION EXERCISES

4.1 For each data set, find the mean, median, and mode. Discuss anything about the data that affects the usefulness of each statistic as a measure of central tendency.

a. Class absences (12 students)	0, 0, 0, 0, 0, 1, 2, 3, 3, 5, 5, 15
b. Exam scores (9 students)	40, 40, 65, 71, 72, 75, 76, 78, 98
c. GPAs (8 students)	2.25, 2.55, 2.95, 3.02, 3.04, 3.37, 3.51, 3.66

4.2 Prof. Hardtack gave four Friday quizzes last semester in his 10-student senior tax accounting class. (a) Without using Excel, find the mean, median, and mode for each quiz. (b) Do these measures of central tendency agree? Explain. (c) For each data set, note strengths or weaknesses of each statistic of central tendency. (d) Are the data symmetric or skewed? If skewed, which direction? (e) Briefly describe and compare student performance on each quiz. **Quizzes**

Quiz 1: 60, 60, 60, 60, 71, 73, 74, 75, 88, 99

Quiz 2: 65, 65, 65, 65, 70, 74, 79, 79, 79, 79

Quiz 3: 66, 67, 70, 71, 72, 72, 74, 74, 95, 99

Mini Case   **1.2**

How Do You Sell Noodles with Statistics?

"The best answer starts with a thorough and thoughtful analysis of the data." Aaron Kennedy, founder and chairman of Noodles & Company.

(Visit www.noodles.com to find a Noodles & Company restaurant near you.)

Noodles & Company is the new model for the *quick casual* restaurant concept. They are setting the standard for modern casual dining here in the United States in the 21st century. Noodles & Company first opened in Colorado in 1995 and has not stopped growing since. As of

Figures and Tables

Throughout the text, there are hundreds of charts, graphs, tables, and spreadsheets to illustrate statistical concepts being applied. These visuals help stimulate student interest and clarify the text explanations.

TABLE 4.7	100 ATM Deposits (dollars)		ATMDeposits								
3	10	15	15	20	20	20	22	23	25	26	26
30	30	35	35	36	39	40	40	40	40	47	50
50	50	50	53	55	60	60	60	67	75	78	86
90	96	100	100	100	100	100	103	105	118	125	125
130	131	139	140	145	150	150	153	153	156	160	163
170	176	185	198	200	200	200	220	232	237	252	259
260	268	270	279	295	309	345	350	366	375	431	433
450	450	474	484	495	553	600	720	777	855	960	987
1,020	1,050	1,200	1,341								

Source: Michigan State University Federal Credit Union.

Examples

Examples of interest to students are taken from published research or real applications to illustrate the statistics concept. For the most part, examples are focused on business but there are also some that are more general and don't require any prerequisite knowledge. And, there are some that are based on student projects.

Figure 3.17 shows the U.S. balance of trade. The arithmetic scale shows that growth has been exponential. Yet, although exports and imports are increasing in absolute terms, the log graph suggests that the *growth rate* in both series may be slowing, because the log graph is slightly concave. On the log graph, the recently increasing trade deficit is not *relatively* as large. Regardless how it is displayed, the trade deficit remains a concern for policymakers, for fear that foreigners may no longer wish to purchase U.S. debt instruments to finance the trade deficit (see *The Wall Street Journal*, July 24, 2005, p. C1).

EXAMPLE

U.S. Trade
USTrade

FIGURE 3.17

Comparison of Arithmetic and Log Scales   USTrade

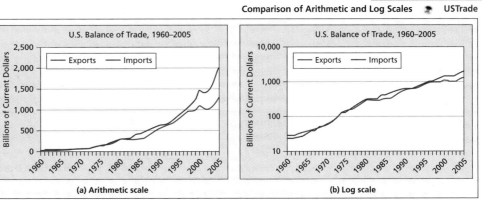

(a) Arithmetic scale   (b) Log scale

Source: *Economic Report of the President, 2007.*

Data Set Icon

A data set icon is used throughout the text to identify data sets used in the figures, examples, and exercises that are included on the Student CD packaged with the text.

USTrade

Chapter Summary

Chapter summaries provide an overview of the material covered in the chapter.

CHAPTER SUMMARY For a set of observations on a single numerical variable, a **dot plot** displays the individual data values, while a **frequency distribution** classifies the data into classes called **bins** for a **histogram** of **frequencies** for each bin. The number of bins and their limits are matters left to your judgment, though **Sturges' Rule** offers advice on the number of bins. The **line chart** shows values of one or more **time series** variables plotted against time. A **log scale** is sometimes used in time series charts when data vary by orders of magnitude. The **bar chart** shows a **numerical** data value for each category of an **attribute.** However, a bar chart can also be used for a time series. A **scatter plot** can reveal the association (or lack of association) between two variables X and Y. The **pie chart** (showing a **numerical** data value for each category of an **attribute** if the data values are parts of a whole) is common but should be used with caution. Sometimes a **simple table** is the best visual display. Creating effective visual displays is an acquired skill. Excel offers a wide range of charts from which to choose. Deceptive graphs are found frequently in both media and business presentations, and the consumer should be aware of common errors.

Key Terms

Key terms are highlighted and defined within the text. They are also listed at the ends of chapters, along with chapter page references, to aid in reviewing.

KEY TERMS

Central Tendency
geometric mean, *126*
mean, *116*
median, *117*
midhinge, *145*
midrange, *127*
mode, *118*
trimmed mean, *127*

Dispersion
Chebyshev's
   Theorem, *136*
coefficient of
   variation, *132*
Empirical Rule, *136*
mean absolute

population
   variance, *130*
range, *129*
sample variance, *130*
standard deviation, *130*
standardized
   variable, *137*

two-sum formula,
   131Shape
bimodal
   distribution, *120*
multimodal
   distribution *120*

Commonly Used Formulas

Some chapters provide a listing of commonly used formulas for the topic under discussion.

Commonly Used Formulas in Descriptive Statistics ●

Sample mean: $\bar{x} = \dfrac{1}{n}\sum_{i=1}^{n} x_i$

Geometric mean: $G = \sqrt[n]{x_1 x_2 \cdots x_n}$

Range: $\text{Range} = x_{max} - x_{min}$

Midrange: $\text{Midrange} = \dfrac{x_{min} + x_{max}}{2}$

Sample standard deviation: $s = \sqrt{\dfrac{\sum_{i=1}^{n}(x_i - \bar{x})^2}{n-1}}$

Chapter Review

Each chapter has a list of questions for student self-review or for discussion.

CHAPTER REVIEW

1. What are descriptive statistics? How do they differ from visual displays of data?
2. Explain each concept: (a) central tendency, (b) dispersion, and (c) shape.
3. (a) Why is sorting usually the first step in data analysis? (b) Why is it useful to begin a data analysis by thinking about how the data were collected?
4. List strengths and weaknesses of each measure of central tendency and write its Excel function: (a) mean, (b) median, and (c) mode.
5. (a) Why must the deviations around the mean sum to zero? (b) What is the position of the median in the data array when n is even? When n is odd? (c) Why is the mode of little use in continuous data? For what type of data is the mode most useful?
6. (a) What is a bimodal distribution? (b) Explain two ways to detect skewness.
7. List strengths and weaknesses of each measure of central tendency and give its Excel function (if any): (a) midrange, (b) geometric mean, and (c) 10 percent trimmed mean.
8. (a) What is dispersion? (b) Name five measures of dispersion. List the main characteristics (strengths, weaknesses) of each measure.

STUDENT LEARNING?

Chapter Exercises

Exercises give students an opportunity to test their understanding of the chapter material. Exercises are included at the ends of sections and at the ends of chapters. Some exercises contain data sets, identified by data set icons, that can be accessed on the Student CD and used to solve problems in the text.

12.52 Below are percentages for *annual sales growth* and *net sales attributed to loyalty card usage* at 74 Noodles & Company restaurants. (a) Make a scatter plot. (b) Find the correlation coefficient and interpret it. (c) Test the correlation coefficient for significance, clearly stating the degrees of freedom. (d) Does it appear that loyalty card usage is associated with increased sales growth? **LoyaltyCard**

Annual Sales Growth (%) and Loyalty Card Usage (% of Net Sales) (n = 74 restaurants)

Store	Growth%	Loyalty%
1	−8.3	2.1
2	−4.0	2.5
3	−3.9	1.7
⋮	⋮	⋮
72	20.8	1.1
73	25.5	0.6
74	28.8	1.8

Source: Noodles & Company

12.15 These data are for a sample of 10 different vendors in a large airport. (a) Fit an "eyeball" regression equation to this scatter plot of Y = bottles of Evian water sold and X = price of the water. (b) Interpret the slope. (c) Interpret the intercept. Would the intercept have meaning in this example?

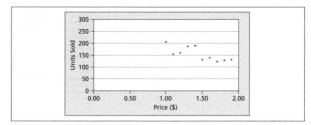

Related Readings

For the instructor or student interested in further content on a particular topic, the related readings provide a listing of some additional resources the authors recommend.

RELATED READING

Barnett, Vic; and Toby Lewis. *Outliers in Statistical Data.* 3rd ed. John Wiley and Sons, 1994.

Blyth, C. R. "Minimizing the Sum of Absolute Deviations." *The American Statistician* 44, no. 4 (November 1990), p. 329.

Freund, John E.; and Benjamin M. Perles. "A New Look at Quartiles of Ungrouped Data." *The American Statistician* 41, no. 3 (August 1987), pp. 200–203.

Hoaglin, David C.; Frederick Mosteller; and John W. Tukey. *Understanding Robust and Exploratory Data Analysis.* John Wiley and Sons, 1983.

LearningStats Unit

Learning Stats, included on the Student CD, provides a means for students to explore data and concepts at their own pace. Applications that relate to the material in the chapter are identified at the ends of chapters.

LearningStats Unit 02   Manipulating Data   LS

LearningStats Unit 02 introduces data types, sampling, random numbers, and surveys. Modules are designed for self-study, so you can proceed at your own pace, concentrate on material that is new, and pass quickly over things that you already know. Your instructor may assign specific modules, or you may decide to check them out because the topic sounds interesting. In addition to helping you learn about statistics, they may be useful as references later on.

Topic	LearningStats Modules
Data types	Level of Measurement
Sampling	Sampling Methods—Overview
	Sampling Methods—Worksheet
	Who Gets Picked?
	Randomizing a File
	Sampling a Large Database*
	Excel's RANDBETWEEN Function
Surveys	Survey Methods
Data sources	Web Data Sources

Key: = PowerPoint = Word = Excel
*Denotes a specialized topic.

Exam Review Questions

At the end of a group of chapters, students can review the material they covered in the group of chapters. This provides them with an opportunity to test themselves on their grasp of the material.

EXAM REVIEW QUESTIONS FOR CHAPTERS 1–4

1. Which type of statistic (descriptive, inferential) is each of the following?
   a. Estimating the default rate on all U.S. mortgages from a random sample of 500 loans.
   b. Reporting the percent of students in your statistics class who use Verizon.
   c. Using a sample of 50 iPhones to predict the average battery life in typical usage.

2. Which is *not* an ethical obligation of a statistician? Explain.
   a. To know and follow accepted procedures.
   b. To ensure data integrity and accurate calculations.
   c. To support client wishes in drawing conclusions from the data.

3. "Driving without a seat belt is not risky. I've done it for 25 years without an accident." This *best* illustrates which fallacy?
   a. Unconscious bias.

There are three software tools included on the Student CD that are referred to in the text: *LearningStats, MegaStat for Excel 2007,* and *Visual Statistics 2.2.*

LearningStats

LearningStats allows students to explore data and concepts at their own pace. It includes demonstrations, simulations, tutorials, and hundreds of data files that can be imported into any statistical package.

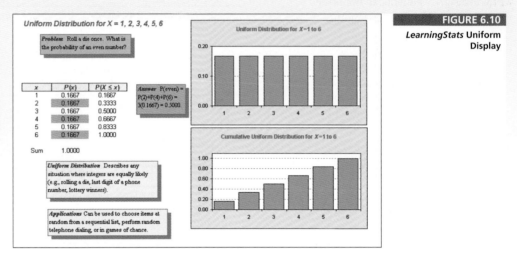

FIGURE 6.10

LearningStats Uniform Display

MegaStat®

MegaStat is a full-featured Excel add-in that is included on the Student CD with this text. It performs statistical analyses within an Excel workbook. It does basic functions such as descriptive statistics, frequency distributions, and probability calculations as well as hypothesis testing, ANOVA, and regression.

MegaStat output is carefully formatted and ease-of-use features include Auto Expand for quick data selection and Auto Label detect. Since *MegaStat* is easy to use, students can focus on learning statistics without being distracted by the software. MegaStat is always available from Excel's main menu. Selecting a menu item pops up a dialog box. Regression analysis is shown here. MegaStat works with all recent versions of Excel including Excel 2007.

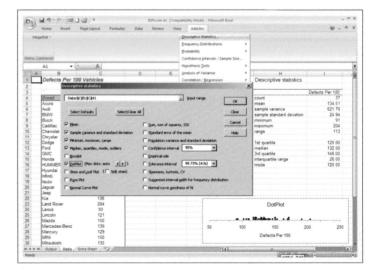

Visual Statistics

Visual Statistics 2.2 by Doane, Mathieson, and Tracy is a software program for teaching and learning statistics concepts. It is unique in that it allows students to learn the concepts through interactive experimentation and visualization. There is a Visual Statistics (VS) icon included in the margins in some chapters to point out topics where the student can enrich his or her learning by looking at the related material in the Visual Statistics chapter.

FIGURE 6.18

Visual Statistics Binomial Display

Chapter 4

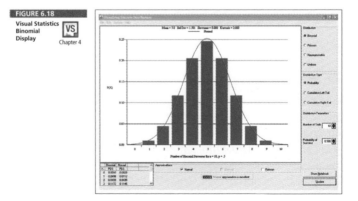

MINITAB® / SPSS® / JMP®

MINITAB® Student Version 14, SPSS® Student Version 15, and JMP Student Edition 6 are software tools that are available to help students solve the business statistics exercises in the text. Each is available in the student version and can be packaged with any McGraw-Hill business statistics text.

|BUSINESS STATISTICS

|BUSINESS STATISTICS

McGraw-Hill Connect™ Business Statistics

McGraw-Hill *Connect Business Statistics* is an online assignment and assessment system customized to the text and available as an option for students. With *Connect Business Statistics*, instructors can deliver assignments, quizzes, and tests online. The system utilizes the exercises from the text both in a static one-problem-at-a-time fashion as well as algorithmically where problems generate multiple data possibilities and answers. In addition, instructors can edit existing questions and author entirely new problems.

You choose or create the problems. Assignments are graded automatically, and the results are stored in your private gradebook. You can track individual student performance by question, assignment, or in comparison to the rest of the class. Detailed grade reports are easily integrated with Learning Management Systems, such as WebCT and Blackboard.

McGraw-Hill Connect Business Statistics is also available with the interactive online version of the text—*Connect Plus Business Statistics*. Like *Connect Business Statistics*, *Connect Plus Business Statistics* provides students with online assignments and assessments, plus 24/7 online access to an eBook, an identical, online edition of the printed text, to aid them in successfully completing their work, wherever and whenever they choose.

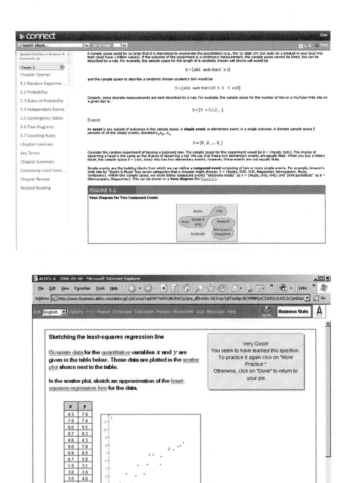

ALEKS®

ALEKS is an assessment and learning system that provides individualized instruction in Business Statistics. Available from McGraw-Hill/Irwin over the World Wide Web, ALEKS delivers precise assessments of students' knowledge, guides them in the selection of appropriate new study material, and records their progress toward mastery of goals.

ALEKS interacts with students much as a skilled human tutor would, moving between explanation and practice as needed, correcting and analyzing errors, defining terms and changing topics on request. By accurately assessing their knowledge, ALEKS focuses precisely on what to learn next, helping them master the course content more quickly and easily.

Save money. Go Green. McGraw-Hill eBooks

Green . . . it's on everybody's mind these days. It's not only about saving trees, it's also about saving money. At 55% of the bookstore price, McGraw-Hill eBooks are an eco-friendly and cost-saving alternative to the traditional printed textbook. So, you do some good for the environment and . . . you do some good for your wallet.

CourseSmart

CourseSmart is a new way to find and buy eTextbooks. CourseSmart has the largest selection of eTextbooks available anywhere, offering thousands of the most commonly adopted textbooks from a wide variety of higher education publishers. CourseSmart eTextbooks are available in one standard online reader with full text search, notes and highlighting, and email tools for sharing notes between classmates. Visit www.CourseSmart.com for more information on ordering.

Online Learning Center: www.mhhe.com/doaneess2e

The online Learning Center (OLC) is the text website with online content for both students and instructors.

Instructor Content

- Instructor's Manual
- Test Bank
- PowerPoint
- Image Library
- LearningStats Walkthrough
- Visual Statistics Walkthrough
- MegaStat User's Guide
- Instructor Updates and Errata

Student Content

- Quizzes
- PowerPoint
- Data Sets
- MegaStat User's Guide
- Screencam Tutorials
- ipod videos
- Appendices
- Updates and Errata

WebCT / Blackboard / eCollege

All of the material in the Online Learning Center is also available in portable WebCT, Blackboard, or e-College content "cartridges" provided free to adopters of this text.

Business Statistics Center (BSC): www.mhhe.com/bstat/

The BSC contains links to statistical publications and resources, software downloads, learning aids, statistical websites and databases, and McGraw-Hill/Irwin product websites, and online courses.

Instructor's Resource CD-ROM (ISBN: 0073364657)

This resource allows instructors to conveniently access the Instructor's Solutions Manual, Test Bank in Word and EZ Test formats, Instructor PowerPoint slides, and data sets.

Online Learning Center:
www.mhhe.com/doaneess2e

The Online Learning Center (OLC) provides the instructor with a complete Instructor's Manual in Word format, the complete Test Bank in both Word files and computerized EZ Test format, Instructor PowerPoint slides, text art files, an introduction to ALEKS®, an introduction to McGraw-Hill Connect business Statistics™, access to the eBook, and more.

All test bank questions are available in an EZ Test electronic format. Included are a number of multiple-choice, true-false, and short-answer questions and problems. The answers to all questions are given, along with a rating of the level of difficulty, chapter goal the question tests, Bloom's taxonomy question type, and AACSB knowledge category.

AACSB Statement

The McGraw-Hill Companies is a proud corporate member of AACSB International. Understanding the importance and value of AACSB accreditation, Doane/Seward *Essential Statistics in Business & Economics 2e* has connected questions in the test bank to the six general knowledge and skill guidelines found in the AACSB standards.

Student CD-ROM

The Student CD-ROM packaged with each copy of the text includes software resources for student self-study and tools for working the exercises in the text. These resources include:

- Visual Statistics,
- LearningStats
- MegaStat® for Excel 2007
- Data sets

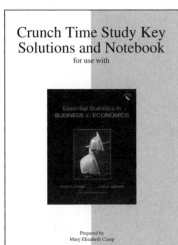

Student Study Guide (ISBN: 007336469X)

This supplement has been created to help students master the course content. It highlights the important ideas in the text and provides opportunities for students to review the worked-out solutions, review terms and concepts, and practice.

ACKNOWLEDGMENTS

The authors would like to acknowledge some of the many people who have helped with this book. Dorothy Duffy permitted use of the chemistry lab for the experiments on Hershey Kisses, Brach's jelly beans, and Sathers gum drops. Nainan Desai and Robert Edgerton explained the proper use of various kinds of engineering terminology. Thomas W. Lauer and Floyd G. Willoughby permitted quotation of a case study. Richard W. Hartl of Memorial Hospital and Kathryn H. Sheehy of Critten-ton Hospital provided data for case studies. Morgan Elliott, Karl Majeske, Robin McCutcheon, Kevin Murphy, John Sase, T. J. Wharton, and Kenneth M. York permitted questionnaires to be administered in their classes. Ian S. Bradbury, Winson-Taam, and especially RonTracy and Robert Kushler gave generously of their time as expert statistical consultants. Don Smith and Dana Cobb contributed greatly to the *LearningStats* databases. Jonathan G. Koomey of E.O. Lawrence Berkeley National Laboratory offered valuable suggestions on visual data presentation.

Mark Isken has reliably provided Excel expertise and has suggested health care applications for examples and case studies. John Seeley and Jeff Whitbey provided regression databases. John Savio and the Michigan State Employees Credit Union provided ATM data. The Siena Research Institute has made its poll results available. The Public Interest Research Group of Michigan (PIRGIM) has generously shared data from its field survey of prescription drug prices.

We owe special thanks to Aaron Kennedy and Dave Boenninghausen of Noodles & Company for providing suggestions and access to data for minicases and examples.

We are grateful for the careful proofreading and suggestions offered by students Frances J. Williams, William G. Knapp, John W. Karkowski, Nirmala Ranganathan, Thomas H. Miller, Clara M. Michetti, Fielder S. Lyons, Catherine L. Tatem, Anup D. Karnalkar, Richard G. Taylor, Ian R. Palmer, Rebecca L. Curtiss, Todd R. Keller, Emily Claeys, Tom Selby, and Jun Moon. Dozens of other individuals have provided examples and cases which are cited in the text and *LearningStats* software.

For reviewing the material on quality, we wish to thank Kay Beauregard, Administrative Director at William Beaumont Hospital, and Ellen Barnes and Karry Roberts of Ford Motor Company. Reviewers of the *LearningStats* software have made numerous suggestions for improvement, which we have tried to incorporate. In particular, we wish to thank Lari H. Arjomand of Clayton College & State University, Richard P. Gebhart of the University of Tulsa, Kieran Mathieson of Oakland University, Vincent F. Melfi of Michigan State University, J. Burdeane Orris of Butler University, Joe Sullivan of Mississippi State University, and Donald L. Westerfield of Webster University.

A special debt of gratitude is due to Carol Rose and Richard Wright for careful copyediting and editorial suggestions, Steve Schuetz for his direction and support, Wanda Zeman for coordinating the project, and especially Dick Hercher for guiding us at every step, solving problems, and encouraging us along the way. We are grateful to Ardith Baker of Oral Roberts University for her timely and detailed suggestions for improving the manuscript. Thanks to Loren Maray John for helping with the Instructor's Manual and Lloyd Jasingh, Morehead State University, for updating the PowerPoint slides. Special thanks to the accuracy checkers, Scott Bailey, Troy University, Terry Dalton, University of Denver and Don Gren, Salt Lake Community College. Gary W. Smith of Florida State University offered many detailed, thoughtful suggestions. Thanks to the many reviewers who provided such valuable feedback including criticism which made the book better, some of whom reviewed several drafts of the manuscript. Any remaining errors or omissions are the authors' responsibility.

Charles Apigian	*Middle Tennessee State University*	Lillian Fok	*University of New Orleans*
Lari H. Arjomand	*Clayton College & State University*	James C. Ford	*SAS Institute, North America*
Ardith Baker	*Oral Roberts University*	Ellen Fuller	*Arizona State University*
Kay Ballard	*University of Nebraska-Lincoln*	Richard P. Gebhart	*University of Tulsa*
Bruce Barrett	*University of Alabama*	Robert Gillette	*University of Kentucky—Lexington*
Mary Beth Camp	*Indiana University—Bloomington*	Betsy Greenberg	*University of Texas—Austin*
Timothy Butler	*Wayne State University*	Don Gren	*Salt Lake Community College*
Alan R. Cannon	*University of Texas—Arlington*	Alfred L. Guiffrida	*Kent State University*
Alan S. Chesen	*Wright State University*	Kemal Gursoy	*Long Island University*
Chia-Shin Chung	*Cleveland State University*	Rhonda Hensley	*North Carolina A&T State University*
Susan Cohen	*University of Illinois—Champaign/Urbana*	Mickey A. Hepner	*University of Central Oklahoma*
Teresa Dalton	*University of Denver*	Johnny C. Ho	*University of Texas—El Paso*
Bernard Dickman	*Hofstra University*	Tom Innis	*University of Cincinnati*

Kishen Iyenger	University of Colorado—Boulder	Don R. Robinson	Illinois State University
Mark G. Kean	Boston University	Farhad Saboori	Albright College
Belayet Khandoker	Northeastern University	Sue Schou	Idaho State University
Jerry LaCava	Boise State University	Bill Seaver	University of Tennessee—Knoxville
Carl Lee	Central Michigan University	Gary W. Smith	Florida State University
Jun Liu	Georgia Southern University	William E. Stein	Texas A&M University
Salvador Martinez	Weber State University	Stanley Stephenson	Southwest Texas State University
Ralph May	Southwestern Oklahoma State University	Joe Sullivan	Mississippi State University
Mary Ruth McRae	Appalachian State University	Patrick Thompson	University of Florida
Glenn Milligan	The Ohio State University	Elizabeth Trybus	California State University—Tallahassee
Robert M. Nauss	University of Missouri—St. Louis	Geetha Vaidyanathan	University of North Carolina—Greensboro
Cornelius Nelan	Quinnipiac University	Raja P. Velu	Syracuse University
J. B. Orris	Butler University	Charles Wilf	Duquesne University
Dane K. Peterson	Southwest Missouri State University	Janet Wolcutt	Wichita State University
Stephen Pollard	California State University—Los Angeles	Jack Yurkiewicz	Pace University
Michael Polomsky	Cleveland State University	Zhen Zhu	University of Central Oklahoma
Priya Rajagopalan	Purdue—West Lafayette		

Thanks to the participants in our focus groups and symposia on teaching business statistics in Burr Ridge, LaJolla, Pasadena, Sante Fe, Atlanta, and Las Vegas, who provided so many teaching ideas and insights into their particular students and courses. We hope you will be able to see in the book and the teaching package consideration of those ideas and insights.

Sung Ahn	Washington State University	Susanne Currier	University of Central Oklahoma
Mostafa Aminzadeh	Towson University	Nit Dasgupta	University of Wisconsin—Eau Claire
Charlie Apigian	Middle Tennessee State University	Ron Davis	San Jose State University
Scott Bailey	Troy University	Brent Eagar	Utah State University—Logan
Michael Bendixen	Nova Southeastern University	Kathy Ernstberger	Indiana University—Southeast
Imad Benjelloun	Delaware Valley College	Zek Eser	Eastern Kentucky University
Carl Bodenschatz	University of Pittsburgh	Soheila Fardanesh	Towson University
Ted Bos	University of Alabama—Birmingham	Gail Gemberling	University of Texas—Austin
Dave Bregenzer	Utah State University	John Grandzol	Bloomsburg University of Pennsylvania
Scott Callan	Bentley College	Betsy Greenberg	University of Texas—Austin
Greg Cameron	Brigham Young University—Idaho	Don Gren	Salt Lake City Community College
Mary Beth Camp	Indiana University	Kemal Gursoy	Long Island University
Alan Cannon	University of Texas—Arlington	Ping-Hung Hsieh	Oregon State University
James Carden	University of Mississippi	Patrick Johanns	Purdue University—West Lafayette
Priscilla Chaffe-Stengel	California State University—Fresno	Allison Jones-Farmer	Auburn University
Alan Chesen	Wright State University	Belayet Khandoker	Northeastern University
Chia-Shin Chung	Cleveland State University	Ron Klimberg	Saint Joseph's University
Susan Cohen	University of Illinois—Champaign/Urbana	Supriya Lahiri	University of Massachusetts—Lowell

John Landry	Metro State College of Denver	Victor Raj	Murray State University
John Lawrence	California State University—Fullerton	Don Robinson	Illinois State University
Andy Liu	Youngstown State University	Anne Royalty	Indiana University Perdue University—Indianapolis
Carol Markowski	Old Dominion University	David Rubin	University of North Carolina—Chapel Hill
Ed Markowski	Old Dominion University		
Rutilio Martinez	University of Northern Colorado	Said Said	East Carolina University
Salvador Martinez	Weber State University	James Schmidt	University of Nebraska—Lincoln
Brad McDonald	Northern Illinois University	Sue Schou	Idaho State University
Elaine McGivern	Duquesne University	Pali Sen	University of North Florida
Herb McGrath	Bowling Green State University	Robert Setaputra	Shippensburg University
Larry McRae	Appalachian State University	Murali Shanker	Kent State University—Kent
Edward Melnick	New York University	Charlie Shi	Diablo Valley College
Khosrow Moshirvaziri	California State University—Long Beach	Harvey Singer	George Mason University
		Gary Smith	Florida State University
Gary Newkirk	Clemson University	Debbie Stiver	University of Nevada—Reno
Patrick Noonan	Emory University	Debbie Tesch	Xavier University
Quinton Nottingham	Virginia Polytechnic Institute and State University	Sue Umashankar	University of Arizona
		Geetha Vaidyanathan	University of North Carolina—Greensboro
Cliff Nowell	Weber State University		
Maureen O'Brien	University of Minnesota—Duluth	Bill Verdini	Arizona State University
Rene Ordonez	Southern Oregon University	Avinash Waikar	Southeastern Louisiana University
Deane Orris	Butler University	Rachel Webb	Portland State University
Edward Pappanastos	Troy State University	Al Webster	Bradley University
Norm Pence	Metropolitan State College of Denver	Jeanne Wendel	University of Nevada—Reno
		Donald Westerfield	Webster University
Dennis Petruska	Youngstown State University	Kathleen Whitcomb	University of South Carolina
Michael Polomsky	Cleveland State University	Mary Whiteside	University of Texas—Arlington
Janet Pol	University of Nebraska—Omaha	Blake Whitten	University of Iowa—Iowa City
Dawn Porter	University of Southern California—Los Angeles	Janet Wolcutt	Wichita State University
		Gary Yoshimoto	St. Cloud State University
B. K. Rai	University of Massachusetts—Dartmouth	William Younkin	University of Miami—Coral Gables
Priya Rajagopalan	Purdue University—West Lafayette	Zhiwei Zhu	University of Louisiana—Lafayette

BRIEF CONTENTS

CONTENTS

Essential Statistics

in Business and Economics

Second Edition

Overview of Statistics

Chapter Learning Objectives

When you finish this chapter you should be able to

- Define statistics and explain some of its uses in business.
- List reasons for a business student to study statistics.
- State the common challenges facing data analysts.
- Explain why written communication is important.
- Know the basic rules for effective writing and oral presentations.
- Tell what an executive summary is and why it's important.
- List and explain common statistical pitfalls.

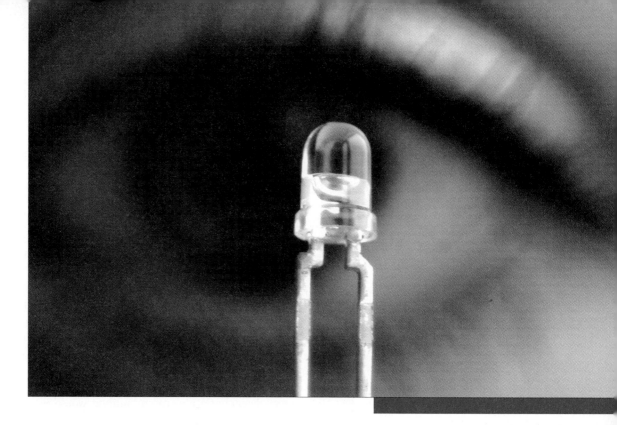

Prelude ●

When managers are well informed about a company's internal operations (e.g., sales, production, inventory levels, time to market, warranty claims) and competitive position (e.g., market share, customer satisfaction, repeat sales) they can take appropriate actions to improve their business. Managers need reliable, timely information so they can analyze market trends and adjust to changing market conditions. Better data can also help a company decide which types of strategic information they should share with trusted business partners to improve their supply chain. *Statistics* and *statistical analysis* permit *data-based decision making* and reduce managers' need to rely on guesswork.

Statistics is a key component of the field of *business intelligence,* which encompasses all the technologies for collecting, storing, accessing, and analyzing data on the company's operations in order to make better business decisions. Statistics helps convert unstructured "raw" data (e.g., point-of-sale data, customer spending patterns) into *useful information* through online analytical processing (OLAP) and data mining, terms that you may have encountered in your other business classes. Statistical analysis focuses attention on key problems and guides discussion toward issues, not personalities or territorial struggles. While powerful database software and query systems are the key to managing a firm's data warehouse, relatively small Excel spreadsheets are often the focus of discussion among managers when it comes to "bottom line" decisions. That is why Excel is featured prominently in this textbook.

In short, companies increasingly are using business analytics to support decision making, recognize anomalies that require tactical action, or to gain strategic insight to align business processes with business objectives. Businesses that combine managerial judgment with statistical analysis are more successful.

1.1
WHAT IS STATISTICS?

Statistics is the science of collecting, organizing, analyzing, interpreting, and presenting data. Some experts prefer to call statistics *data science,* a trilogy of tasks involving data modeling, analysis, and decision making. Here are some alternative definitions.

Statistics

"I like to think of statistics as the science of learning from data . . ."
   Jon Kettenring, ASA President, 1997

"The mathematics of the collection, organization, and interpretation of numerical data, especially the analysis of population characteristics by inference from sampling."
   American Heritage Dictionary®*

"Statistical analysis involves collecting information, evaluating it, drawing conclusions, and providing guidance in what information is reliable and which predictions can be trusted."
   American Statistical Association

In contrast, a **statistic** is a single measure, reported as a number, used to summarize a sample data set. Many different measures can be used to summarize data sets. You will learn throughout this textbook that there can be different measures for different sets of data and different measures for different types of questions about the same data set. Consider, for example, a sample data set that consists of heights of students in a university. There could be many different uses for this data set. Perhaps the manufacturer of graduation gowns wants to know how long to make the gowns; the best *statistic* for this would be the *average* height of the students. But an architect designing a classroom building would want to know how high the doorways should be, and would base measurements on the *maximum* height of the students. Both the average and the maximum are examples of a *statistic.*

You may not have a trained statistician in your organization, but any college graduate is expected to know something about statistics, and anyone who creates graphs or interprets data is "doing statistics" without an official title.

1.2
WHY STUDY STATISTICS?

A recent *BusinessWeek* article called statistics and probability "core skills for businesspeople" in order to know when others are dissembling, to build financial models, or to develop a marketing plan. This same report also said that "B-school grads with strong calculus will find far more opportunities." Each year, *The Wall Street Journal* asks corporate recruiters to rate U.S. business schools on various attributes. In a recent *WSJ* survey, recruiters said that the top five attributes were: (1) communication and interpersonal skills; (2) ability to work well within a team; (3) personal ethics and integrity; (4) analytical and problem-solving skills; and (5) work ethic. (See "Why Math Will Rock Your World," *BusinessWeek,* January 23, 2006, p. 60; and *The Wall Street Journal,* Sept. 20, 2006.)

Knowing statistics will make you a better consumer of other people's data. You should know enough to handle everyday data problems, to feel confident that others cannot deceive you with spurious arguments, and to know when you've reached the limits of your expertise. Statistical knowledge gives your company a competitive advantage against organizations that cannot understand their internal or external market data. And mastery of basic statistics gives you, the individual manager, a competitive advantage as you work your way through the promotion process, or when you move to a new employer. Here are some more reasons to study statistics.

Communication   The language of statistics is widely used in science, social science, education, health care, engineering, and even the humanities. In all areas of business (accounting, finance, human resources, marketing, information systems, operations management), workers use statistical jargon to facilitate communication. In fact, statistical terminology has reached the highest corporate strategic levels (e.g., "Six Sigma" at GE and Motorola). And in the multinational environment, the specialized vocabulary of statistics permeates language barriers to improve problem solving across national boundaries.

---

* *American Heritage Dictionary of the English Language,* 4th Ed. Copyright © 2000 by Houghton Mifflin Company. Used with permission.

Computer Skills   Whatever your computer skill level, it can be improved. Every time you create a spreadsheet for data analysis, write a report, or make an oral presentation, you bring together skills you already have, and learn new ones. Specialists with advanced training design the databases and decision support systems, but you must expect to handle daily data problems *without* experts. Besides, you can't always find an "expert," and, if you do, the "expert" may not understand your application very well. You need to be able to analyze data, use software with confidence, prepare your own charts, write your own reports, and make electronic presentations on technical topics.

Information Management   Statistics can help you handle either too little or too much information. When insufficient data are available, statistical surveys and samples can be used to obtain the necessary market information. But most large organizations are closer to drowning in data than starving for it. Statistics can help summarize large amounts of data and reveal underlying relationships. You've heard of data mining? Statistics is the pick and shovel that you take to the data mine.

Technical Literacy   Many of the best career opportunities are in growth industries propelled by advanced technology. Marketing staff may work with engineers, scientists, and manufacturing experts as new products and services are developed. Sales representatives must understand and explain technical products like pharmaceuticals, medical equipment, and industrial tools to potential customers. Purchasing managers must evaluate suppliers' claims about the quality of raw materials, components, software, or parts.

Career Advancement   Whenever there are customers to whom services are delivered, statistical literacy can enhance your career mobility. Multi-billion-dollar companies like Blue Cross, Citibank, Microsoft, and Wal-Mart use statistics to control cost, achieve efficiency, and improve quality. Without a solid understanding of data and statistical measures, you may be left behind.

Quality Improvement   Large manufacturing firms like Boeing or General Motors have formal systems for continuous quality improvement. The same is true of insurance companies and financial service firms like Vanguard or Fidelity, and the federal government. Statistics helps firms oversee their suppliers, monitor their internal operations, and identify problems. Quality improvement goes far beyond statistics, but every college graduate is expected to know enough statistics to understand its role in quality improvement.

Mini Case 1.1

Can Statistics Predict Airfares?

When you book an airline ticket online, does it annoy you when the next day you find a cheaper fare on exactly the same flight? Or do you congratulate yourself when you get a "good" fare followed by a price rise? This ticket price volatility led to the creation of an Internet start-up company called Farecast, that examines over 150 billion "airfare observations" and tries to use the data to predict whether or not the fare for a given ticket is likely to rise. The company's prediction accuracy so far is estimated at 61 percent (in independent tests) and 75 percent (the company's tests). In this case, the benchmark is a coin toss (50 percent). The company offers price rise insurance for a small price. If you travel a lot and like to play the odds, such predictions could save money. With online air bookings at $44 billion, a few dollars saved here and there can add up. (See *Budget Travel,* February, 2007, p. 37; and *The New York Times,* "An Insurance Policy for Low Airfares," January 22, 2007, p. C10.)

1.3
USES OF STATISTICS

There are two primary kinds of statistics:

- **Descriptive statistics** refers to the collection, organization, presentation, and summary of data (either using charts and graphs or using a numerical summary).
- **Inferential statistics** refers to generalizing from a sample to a population, estimating unknown parameters, drawing conclusions, and making decisions.

Figure 1.1 identifies the tasks and the text chapters for each.

FIGURE 1.1
Overview of Statistics

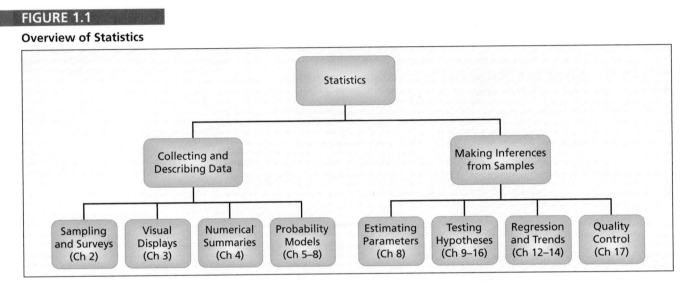

Now let's look at some of the ways statistics is used in business.

Auditing   A large firm pays over 12,000 invoices to suppliers every month. The firm has learned that some invoices are being paid incorrectly, but they don't know how widespread the problem is. The auditors lack the resources to check all the invoices, so they decide to take a sample to estimate the proportion of incorrectly paid invoices. How large should the sample be for the auditors to be confident that the estimate is close enough to the true proportion?

Marketing   A marketing consultant is asked to identify likely repeat customers for Amazon.com, and to suggest co-marketing opportunities based on a database containing records of 5 million Internet purchases of books, CDs, and DVDs. How can this large database be mined to reveal useful patterns that might guide the marketing strategy?

Health Care   An outpatient cognitive retraining clinic for victims of closed-head injuries or stroke evaluates 100 incoming patients using a 42-item physical and mental assessment questionnaire. Each patient is evaluated independently by two experienced therapists. From their evaluations, can we conclude that the therapists agree on the patient's functional status? Are some assessment questions redundant? Do the initial assessment scores accurately predict the patients' lengths of stay in the program?

Quality Control   A manufacturer of rolled copper tubing for radiators wishes to improve its product quality. It initiates a triple inspection program, sets penalties for workers who produce poor-quality output, and posts a slogan calling for "zero defects." The approach fails. Why?

Purchasing   A retailer's shipment of 200 DVD players reveals 4 with defects. The supplier's historical defect rate is .005. Has the defect rate really risen, or is this simply a "bad" batch?

Medicine   An experimental drug to treat asthma is given to 75 patients, of whom 24 get better. A placebo is given to a control group of 75 volunteers, of whom 12 get better. Is the new drug better than the placebo, or is the difference within the realm of chance?

Forecasting   The Home Depot carries 50,000 different products. To manage this vast inventory, it needs a weekly order forecasting system that can respond to developing patterns in consumer demand. Is there a way to predict weekly demand and place orders from suppliers for every item, without an unreasonable commitment of staff time?

Product Warranty   A major automaker wants to know the average dollar cost of engine warranty claims on a new hybrid engine. It has collected warranty cost data on 4,300 warranty claims during the first 6 months after the engines are introduced. Using these warranty claims as an estimate of future costs, what is the margin of error associated with this estimate?

Mini Case   1.2

How Do You Sell Noodles with Statistics?

"The best answer starts with a thorough and thoughtful analysis of the data." Aaron Kennedy, founder and chairman of Noodles & Company.

(Visit www.noodles.com to find a Noodles & Company restaurant near you.)

Noodles & Company is the new model for the *quick casual* restaurant concept. They are setting the standard for modern casual dining here in the United States in the 21st century. Noodles & Company first opened in Colorado in 1995 and has not stopped growing since. As of June 2007, they had over 150 restaurants all across the United States from Portland and Encinitas to Alexandria and Silver Spring with stops in cities such as Omaha and Naperville.

Noodles & Company has achieved this success with a customer driven business model and fact-based decision making. Their widespread popularity and high growth rate have been supported by careful consideration of data and thorough statistical analysis which provide answers to questions such as:

- Should we offer continuity/loyalty cards for our customers?
- How can we increase the use of our extra capacity during the dinner hours?
- Which new city should we open in?
- Which location should we choose for the new restaurant?
- How do we determine the effectiveness of a marketing campaign?
- Which meal maximizes the chance that a new customer will return?
- Are Rice Krispies related to higher sales?
- Does reducing service time increase sales?

Aaron Kennedy, founder and chairman of Noodles & Company, says that "using data is the strongest way to inform good decisions. By assessing our internal and external environments on a continuous basis our Noodles management team has been able to plan and execute our vision."

"I had no idea as a business student that I'd be using statistical analysis as extensively as I do now," says Dave Boennighausen, director of finance at Noodles & Company. In the coming chapters, as you learn about the statistical tools businesses use today, look for the Noodles logo next to examples and exercises that show how Noodles uses data and statistical methods in its business functions.

1.4
STATISTICAL CHALLENGES

Business professionals who use statistics are not mere number crunchers who are "good at math." As Jon Kettenring succinctly said, "Industry needs holistic statisticians who are nimble problem solvers" (www.amstat.org). Consider the criteria listed below:

The ideal data analyst

- Is technically current (e.g., software-wise).
- Communicates well.
- Is proactive.
- Has a broad outlook.
- Is flexible.
- Focuses on the main problem.
- Meets deadlines.
- Knows his/her limitations and is willing to ask for help.
- Can deal with imperfect information.
- Has professional integrity.

Clearly, many of these characteristics would apply to any *business* professional.

Working with Imperfect Data

In mathematics, exact answers are expected. But statistics lies at the messy interface between theory and reality. For instance, suppose a new air bag design is being tested. Is the new air bag design safer for children? Test data indicate the design may be safer in some crash situations, but the old design appears safer in others. The crash tests are expensive and time-consuming, so the sample size is limited. A few observations are missing due to sensor failures in the crash dummies. There may be random measurement errors. If you are the data analyst, what can you do? Well, you can know and use generally accepted statistical methods, clearly state any assumptions you are forced to make, and honestly point out the limitations of your analysis. You can use statistical tests to detect unusual data points or to deal with missing data. You can give a range of answers under varying assumptions. But occasionally, you need the courage to say, "No useful answer can emerge from this data."

Dealing with Practical Constraints

You will face constraints on the type and quantity of data you can collect. Automobile crash tests can't use human subjects (*too risky*). Telephone surveys can't ask a female respondent whether or not she has had an abortion (*sensitive question*). We can't test everyone for HIV (*the world is not a laboratory*). Survey respondents may not tell the truth or may not answer all the questions (*human behavior is unpredictable*). Every analyst faces constraints of time and money (*research is not free*).

Upholding Ethical Standards

Safeguards are in place not only to protect professional integrity but also to minimize ethical breaches. All data analysts must

- Know and follow accepted procedures.
- Maintain data integrity.
- Carry out accurate calculations.
- Report procedures faithfully.
- Protect confidential information.
- Cite sources.
- Acknowledge sources of financial support.

Further, because legal and ethical issues are intertwined, there are specific ethical guidelines for statisticians concerning treatment of human and animal subjects, privacy protection, obtaining informed consent, and guarding against inappropriate uses of data. For further information about ethics, see the American Statistical Association's ethical guidelines (www.amstat.org), which have been extensively reviewed by the statistics profession.

Ethical dilemmas for a nonstatistician are likely to involve conflicts of interest or competing interpretations of the validity of a study and/or its implications. For example, suppose a market research firm is hired to investigate a new corporate logo. The CEO lets you know that she strongly favors a new logo, and it's a big project that could earn you a promotion. Yet, the market data have a high error margin and could support either conclusion. As a manager, you will face such situations. Statistical practices and statistical data can clarify your choices.

Using Consultants

Someone once said the main thing you need to know about statisticians is when to call for one. An hour with an expert at the *beginning* of a project could be the smartest move a manager can make. When should a consultant be hired? When your team lacks certain critical skills, or when an unbiased or informed view cannot be found inside your organization. Expert consultants can handle domineering or indecisive team members, personality clashes, fears about adverse findings, and local politics. Large and medium-sized companies may have in-house statisticians, but smaller firms only hire them as needed. If you hire a statistical expert, you can make better use of the consultant's time by learning how consultants work. Read books about statistical consulting. If your company employs a statistician, take him or her to lunch!

SECTION EXERCISES

connect

1.1   Select *two* of the following scenarios. Explain why you selected each, and give an example of how statistics might be useful to the person in the scenario.
   a. An auditor is looking for inflated broker commissions in stock transactions.
   b. An industrial marketer is representing her firm's compact, new low-power LCD screens to the military.
   c. A plant manager is studying absenteeism at assembly plants in three states.
   d. An automotive purchasing agent is comparing defect rates in steel shipments from three vendors of steel.
   e. A personnel executive is examining job turnover by gender in a fast-food chain.
   f. An intranet manager is studying e-mail usage rates by employee job classification.
   g. A retirement planner is studying mutual fund performance for six different types of asset portfolios.
   h. A hospital administrator is studying surgery scheduling to improve facility utilization rates.

1.2   (a) How much statistics does a student need in *your* chosen field of study? Why not more? Why not less? (b) How can you tell when the point has been reached where you should call for an expert statistician? List some costs and some benefits that would govern this decision.

1.3   (a) Should the average business school graduate expect to use computers to manipulate data, or is this a job better left to specialists? (b) What problems arise when an employee is weak in quantitative skills? Based on your experience, is that common?

1.4   "Many college graduates will not use very much statistics during their 40-year careers, so why study it?" (a) List several arguments for and against this statement. Which position do you find more convincing? (b) Replace the word "statistics" with "accounting" or "foreign language" and repeat this exercise. (c) On the Internet, look up the Latin phrase *reductio ad absurdum*. How is this phrase relevant here?

1.5   How can statistics help organizations deal with (a) information overload? (b) insufficient information? Give an example from a job you have held where statistics might have been useful.

Mini Case   1.3

Lessons from NASA

Former President Lyndon Baines Johnson observed, "A President's hardest task is not to *do* what is right, but to *know* what is right." What's missing is wisdom, not courage. Given incomplete or contradictory data, people have trouble making decisions (remember *Hamlet*?). Sometimes the correct choice is obvious in retrospect, as in NASA's space shuttle disasters. On January 28, 1986, *Challenger* exploded shortly after takeoff, due to erosion of O-rings that had become brittle in freezing overnight temperatures at Cape Canaveral. The crux of the matter was a statistical relationship between brittleness and temperature. Data on O-ring erosion were available for 22 prior shuttle flights. The backup O-rings (there were two layers of O-rings) had suffered no erosion in 9 prior flights at launch temperatures in the range 72°F–81°F, but significant erosion in 4 of 13 prior flights at temperatures in the range 53°F–70°F. However, the role of temperature was by no means clear. NASA and Morton-Thiokol engineers had debated the erratic data inconclusively, including the night before the launch.

After the *Challenger* accident, it was clear that the risk was underestimated. Two *statistical* issues were the degree to which backup layer O-rings provided redundant protection and the correct way to predict O-ring erosion at the *Challenger* launch temperature of 36°F when the lowest previous launch temperature had been 53°F. Two possible *ethical* issues were that NASA officials did not scrub the launch until they understood the problem better and that the astronauts, as participants in a dangerous experiment, had insufficient opportunity for informed consent. NASA's 100 percent previous success record was undoubtedly a factor in everyone's self-confidence, including the astronauts'.

On February 1, 2003, space shuttle *Columbia* burned on re-entry. The heat shield failure was apparently due to tiles damaged by falling foam insulation from the fuel tanks, loosened by vibration during launch. Prior to the *Columbia* disaster in 2003, foam-damaged tiles had been noted 70 times in 112 flights. In retrospect, review of the data showed that some previous flights may have come close to *Columbia*'s fate. This is a *statistical* issue because the heat shield had worked 70 times despite being damaged. Is it surprising that NASA officials believed that the tiles were resistant to foam damage? The statistical and ethical issues are similar to those in the *Challenger* disaster. Organizational inertia and pressure to launch have been blamed in both cases, favoring a risky interpretation of the data.

These disasters remind us that decisions involving data and statistics are always embedded in organizational culture. NASA's evaluation of risk differs from most businesses, due to the dangers inherent in its cutting-edge exploration of space. At the time of the *Challenger* launch, the risk of losing a vehicle was estimated at 1 in 30. At the time of the *Columbia* re-entry accident, the risk was estimated at 1 in 145. For nonhuman launches the risk is about 1 in 50 (2 percent) compared with 2 space shuttle losses in 113 flights (1.8 percent). By comparison, the risk of losing a commercial airline flight is about 1 in 2,000,000.

Sources: yahoo.com; www.nasa.gov; *The New York Times*, February 2, 2003.

1.5 WRITING AND PRESENTING REPORTS

Business recruiters say that written and oral communication skills are critical for success in business. Susan R. Meisinger, President and CEO of the Society for Human Resource Management, says that "In a knowledge-based economy a talented workforce with communication and critical thinking skills is necessary for organizations and the United States to be successful." Yet a survey of 431 human-resource officials in corporate America found a need for improvement in writing (www.conference-board.org). Table 1.1 lists the key business skills needed for *initial* and *long-range* success, as well as some common *weaknesses*.

For Initial *Job Success*	*For* Long-Range *Job Success*	*Common* Weaknesses
Report writing	Managerial accounting	Communication skills
Accounting principles	Managerial economics	Writing skills
Mathematics	Managerial finance	Immaturity
Statistics	Oral communication	Unrealistic expectations

TABLE 1.1

Skills Needed for Success in Business

Mini Case 1.4

Can You Read a Company Annual Report?

Many people say that company annual reports are hard to read. To investigate this claim, Prof. Feng Li of the University of Michigan's Ross School of Business analyzed the readability of more than 50,000 annual reports. One of his readability measures was the Gunning-Fog Index (GFI) which estimates how many years of formal education would be needed in order to read and understand a block of text. For company annual reports, the average GFI was 19.4. Since a college graduate will have 16 years of education, almost a Ph.D. level of education is apparently required to read a typical firm's annual report. Li also found that annual reports of firms with lower earnings were harder to read. (See http://accounting.smartpros.com/x53453.xml; and *Detroit Free Press,* June 7, 2006, p. E1.)

Rules for "Power" Writing

Why is writing so important? Because someone may mention your report on warranty repairs during a meeting of department heads, and your boss may say "OK, make copies of that report so we can all see it." Next thing you know, the CEO is looking at it! Wish you'd taken more care in writing it? To avoid this awkward situation, set aside 25 percent of your allotted project time to *write* the report. You should always outline the report *before* you begin. Then complete the report in sections. Finally, ask trusted peers to review the report, and make revisions as necessary. Keep in mind that you may need to revise more than once. If you have trouble getting started, consult a good reference on technical report-writing.

While you may have creative latitude in how to organize the flow of ideas in the report, it is essential to answer the assigned question succinctly. Describe what you did and what conclusions you reached, listing the most important results first.

Use section headings to group related material and avoid lengthy paragraphs. Your report is your legacy to others who may rely on it. They will find it instructive to know about difficulties you encountered. Provide clear data so others will not need to waste time checking your data and sources. Consider placing technical details in an appendix to keep the main report simple.

If you are writing the report as part of a team, an "editor-in-chief" must be empowered to edit the material so that it is stylistically consistent, has a common voice, and flows together. Allow enough lead time so that all team members can read the final report and give their comments and corrections to the editor-in-chief.

Avoid Jargon Experts use jargon to talk to one another, but outsiders may find it obscure or even annoying. Technical concepts must be presented so that others can understand them. If you can't communicate the importance of your work, your potential for advancement will be limited. Even if your ideas are good and hundreds of hours went into your analysis, readers up the food chain will toss your report aside if it contains too many cryptic references like SSE, MAPE, or 3-Sigma Limits.

Make It Attractive Reports should have a title page, descriptive title, date, and author names. It's a good idea to use footers with page numbers and dates (e.g., Page 7 of 23—Draft of 10/8/06) to distinguish revised drafts.

Use wide margins so readers can take notes or write comments. Select an appropriate typeface and point size. Times Roman, Garamond, and Arial are widely accepted.

Call attention to your main points by using subheadings, bullets, **boldfaced type,** *italics,* large fonts, or **color,** but use special effects sparingly.

Watch Your Spelling and Grammar   To an educated reader, incorrect grammar or spelling errors are conspicuous signs of sloppy work. You don't recognize your errors—that's why you make them. Get someone you trust to red-pencil your work. Study your errors until you're sure you won't repeat them. Your best bet? Keep a dictionary handy! You can refer to it for both proper spelling and grammatical usage. Remember that Microsoft specializes in software, not English, so don't rely on spelling and grammar checkers. Here are some examples from student papers that passed the spell-checker, but each contains two errors. Can you spot them quickly?

Original	*Correction*
• "It's effects will transcend our nation's boarders."	(its, borders)
• "We cannot except this shipment on principal."	(accept, principle)
• "They seceded despite there faults."	(succeeded, their)
• "This plan won't fair well because it's to rigid."	(fare, too)
• "The amount of unhappy employees is raising."	(number, rising)

Organizing a Technical Report

Report formats vary, but a business report usually begins with an *executive summary* limited to a *single page*. Attach the full report containing discussion, explanations, tables, graphs, interpretations, and (if needed) footnotes and appendices. Use appendices for backup material. There is no single acceptable style for a business report but the following would be typical:

- Executive Summary (1 page maximum)
- Introduction (1 to 3 paragraphs)
  - Statement of the problem
  - Data sources and definitions
  - Methods utilized
- Body of the Report (as long as necessary)
  - Discussion, explanations, interpretations
  - Tables and graphs, as needed
- Conclusions (1 to 3 paragraphs)
  - Statement of findings (in order of importance)
  - Limitations (if necessary)
  - Future research suggestions
- Bibliography and Sources
- Appendices (if needed for lengthy or technical material)

Writing an Executive Summary

The goal of an **executive summary** is to permit a busy decision maker to understand what you did and what you found out *without reading the rest of the report*. In a statistical report, the executive summary *briefly* describes the task and goals, data and data sources, methods that were used, main findings of the analysis, and (if necessary) any limitations of the analysis. The main findings will occupy most of the space in the executive summary. Each other item may only rate a sentence or two. The executive summary is limited to a single page (maybe only two or three paragraphs) and should avoid technical language.

An excellent way to evaluate your executive summary is to hand it to a peer. Ask him/her to read it and then tell you what you did and what you found out. If the peer cannot answer precisely, then your summary is deficient. The executive summary must make it *impossible to miss your main findings*. Your boss may judge you and your team by the executive summary alone. S/he may merely leaf through the report to examine key tables or graphs, or may assign someone to review your full report.

	1999	2000	2001	2002	2003	2004	2005
Applications Filed	328.6	361.8	277.3	264.1	271.7	304.5	334.7
Trademarks Issued	191.9	115.2	142.9	176.0	166.6	146.0	154.8

TABLE 1.2

U.S. Trademarks, 1999–2005 (thousands)

Source: U.S. Census Bureau, *Statistical Abstract of the United States, 2007*, p. 507. A trademark (identified with ®) is a name or symbol identifying a product, registered with the U.S. Patent and Trademark Office and restricted by law to use by its owner.

Tables and Graphs

Tables should be embedded in the narrative (*not* on a separate page) near the paragraph in which they are cited. Each table should have a number and title. Graphs should be embedded in the narrative (*not* on a separate page) near the paragraph in which they are discussed. Each table or graph should have a title and number. A graph may make things clearer. For example, compare Table 1.2 and Figure 1.2. Which is more helpful in understanding U.S. trademark activity in recent years?

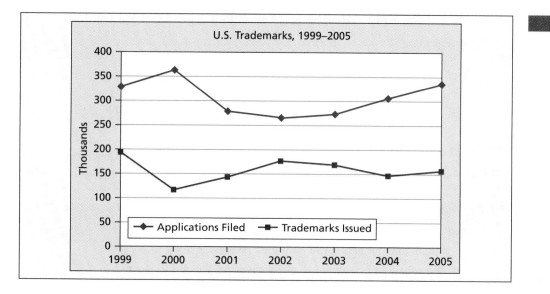

FIGURE 1.2

U.S. Trademarks, 1999–2005

Rules for Presenting Oral Reports

The goals of an oral report are *not the same* as those of a written report. Your oral presentation must only *highlight* the main points. If your presentation does not provide the answer to an audience question, you can say, "Good question. We don't have time to discuss that further here, but it's covered in the full report. I'll be happy to talk to you about it at the end of the presentation." Or, give a brief answer so they know you did consider the matter. Keep these tips in mind while preparing your oral presentation:

- Select just a few key points you most want to convey.
- Use simple charts and diagrams to get the point across.
- Use **color** and *fonts* creatively to **emphasize a point.**
- Levity is nice on occasion, but avoid gratuitous jokes.
- Have backup slides or transparencies just in case.
- Rehearse to get the timing right (don't go too long).
- Refer the audience to the written report for details.
- Imagine yourself in the audience. Don't bore yourself!

The Three Ps

Pace Many presenters speak too rapidly—partly because they are nervous and partly because they think it makes them look smarter.

FIGURE 1.3

Pictures Help Make the Point

Source: Copyright © 2005 Stuart Rojstaczer. Used with permission.

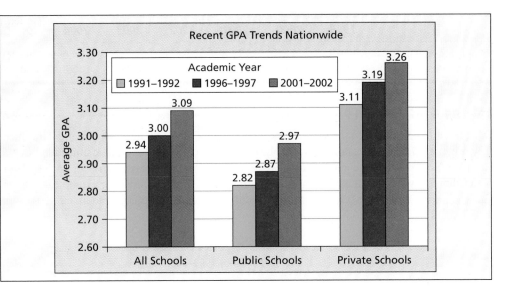

Slow down! Take a little time to introduce yourself, introduce your data, and explain what you are trying to do. If you skip the basic background and definitions, many members of the audience will not be able to follow the presentation and will have only a vague idea what you are talking about.

Planning   Create an outline to organize the ideas you want to discuss. Remember to keep it simple! You'll also need to prepare a verbal "executive summary" to tell your audience what your talk is about. Before you choose your planned opening words, "*Our team correlated robbery with income,*" you should ask yourself:

- Is the audience familiar with correlation analysis?
- Should I explain that our data came from the FBI and the 2000 U.S. Census?
- Will they know that our observations are averages for the 50 U.S. states?
- Will they know that we are talking about per capita robbery rates (not total robberies)?
- Will they know that we are using per capita personal income (not median family income)?
- Should I show them a few data values to help them visualize the data?

Don't bury them in detail, but make the first minute count. If you ran into problems or made errors in your analysis, it's OK to say so. The audience will sympathize.

Check the raw data carefully—you may be called on to answer questions. It's hard to defend yourself when you failed to catch serious errors or didn't understand a key definition.

Practice   Rehearse the oral presentation to get the timing right. Maybe your employer will send you to training classes to bolster your presentation skills. Otherwise consider videotaping yourself or practicing in front of a few peers for valuable feedback. Technical presentations may demand skills different from the ones you used in English class, so don't panic if you have a few problems.

SECTION EXERCISES

connect

1.6   Discuss and criticize each of these two executive summaries from student reports, noting both good and bad points. Is the summary succinct? Was the purpose of the investigation clear? Were the methods explained? Are the main findings stated clearly? Were any limitations of the study noted? Is jargon a problem? How might each summary be improved?

a. "We weighed 10 Tootsie Rolls chosen randomly without replacement from a finite population of 290. The sample mean was calculated at 3.3048 grams and the sample standard deviation was 0.1320 grams. A 95 percent confidence interval using Student's *t* without FPCF was 3.2119 grams to 3.3977 grams."

b. "The November issue of *Money* magazine contained an estimated proportion of pages with advertisements of between 53 percent and 67 percent with an estimated mean advertisements per page between 0.5 and 1.3. The November issue consisted of 222 pages, and the sample consisted of the first 100 even-numbered pages."

1.7 (a) Which of these two displays (table or graph) is more helpful in describing the salad sales by Noodles & Company? Why? (b) Write a one-sentence summary of the data. (*Source:* Noodles & Company) **NoodlesSalad**

2005 Average Daily Salads Sold by Month, Noodles & Company

Month	Salads	Month	Salads
Jan	2847	Jul	2554
Feb	2735	Aug	2370
Mar	2914	Sep	2131
Apr	3092	Oct	1990
May	3195	Nov	1979
Jun	3123	Dec	1914

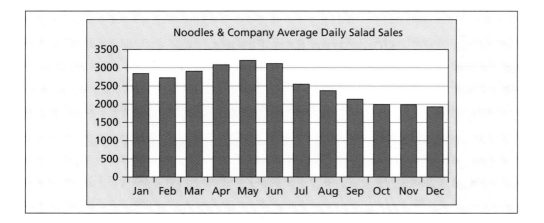

1.8 Go to the Web and use your favorite search engine to look up key words like "technical writing" or "scientific reports." Print one or two excerpts from Web sites that you found particularly interesting or useful, and write a few sentences explaining why you liked them.

1.9 Cite a situation from your work, daily life, or general reading where numerical facts could be presented in more than one way. What were the ethical implications for each alternative? How was it resolved? What was the result?

1.6 CRITICAL THINKING

Statistics is an essential part of **critical thinking**, because it allows us to test an idea against empirical evidence. Random occurrences and chance variation inevitably lead to occasional outcomes that could support one viewpoint or another. But the science of statistics tells us whether the sample evidence is convincing. In this book, you will learn how to use statistics correctly in accordance with professional standards to make the best decision.

"Critical thinking means being able to evaluate evidence, to tell fact from opinion, to see holes in an argument, to tell whether cause and effect has been established, and to spot illogic."
The Wall Street Journal, October 20, 2006.

We use statistical tools to compare our prior ideas with **empirical data** (data collected through observations and experiments). If the data do not support our theory, we can reject or revise our theory. In *The Wall Street Journal,* in *Money* magazine, and on CNN you see stock market experts with theories to "explain" the current market (bull, bear, or pause). But each year brings new experts and new theories, and the old ones vanish. Logical pitfalls abound in both the data collection process and the reasoning process. Let's look at some.

Pitfall 1: Conclusions from Small Samples

"My Aunt Harriet smoked all her life and lived to 90. Smoking doesn't hurt you." Good for her. But does one case prove anything? Five customers are asked if the new product design is an improvement. If three say yes, should the company implement the new design? If 10 patients try a new asthma medication and one gets a rash, can we conclude that the medication caused the rash? How large a sample is needed to make reliable conclusions? Fortunately statisticians have developed clear rules about sample sizes. Until you learn them, it's OK to raise your pennant hopes when your favorite baseball team wins five games in a row.

Pitfall 2: Conclusions from Nonrandom Samples

"Rock stars die young. Look at Buddy Holly, Jimi Hendrix, Janis Joplin, Jim Morrison, John Lennon, and Kurt Cobain." But we are looking only at those who *did* die young. What about the thousands who are alive and well or who lived long lives? Similarly, we should be careful about generalizing from retrospective studies of people who have heart attacks, unless we also study those who do not have heart attacks. (From Arnold Barnett, "How Numbers Can Trick You," *Technology Review,* October 1994, p. 40.)

Pitfall 3: Conclusions from Rare Events

Unlikely events happen if we take a large enough sample. Yet some people draw strong inferences from events that are not surprising when looking at the entire population.

- "Mary in my office won the lottery. Her system must have worked." Millions of people play the lottery. Someone will eventually win.
- "Bill's a sports genius. He predicted every Notre Dame football win last season." Millions of sports fans make predictions. A few of them will call every game correctly.
- "Tom's SUV rolled over. SUVs are dangerous." Millions of people drive SUVs, so some will roll over.

Pitfall 4: Poor Survey Methods

Did your instructor ever ask a question like "How many of you remember the simplex method from your math class?" One or two timid hands (or maybe none) are raised, even though the topic was covered. Did the math department not teach the simplex method? Or did students not "get it"? More likely, the instructor has used a poor sampling method and a vaguely worded question. It's difficult for students to respond to such a question in public, for they assume (often correctly) that if they raise a hand the instructor is going to ask them to explain it, or that their peers will think they are showing off. An anonymous survey or a quiz on the simplex method would provide better insight.

Pitfall 5: Assuming a Causal Link

In your economics class, you may have learned about the **post hoc fallacy** (the mistaken conclusion that if *A* precedes *B* then *A* is the *cause* of *B*). For example, the divorce rate in Mississippi fell in 2005 after Hurricane Katrina. Did the hurricane cause couples to stay together? A little research reveals that the divorce rate had been falling for the previous two years, so Hurricane Katrina could hardly be credited.

The *post hoc fallacy* is a special case of the general fallacy of *assuming causation* anytime there is a *statistical association* between events. For example, there is the "curse of the ballfield," which says that teams who play in named ballparks (e.g., Citi Field for the New York Mets) tend to lose more games than they win (see *The New York Times,* November 15, 2006, p. C16). Perhaps in a statistical sense this may be true. But it is actually the players and managers who determine whether a team wins. Association does not prove causation. You've probably heard that. But many people draw unwarranted conclusions when no cause-and-effect link exists. Consider anecdotes like these:

- "Murder rates were higher during the full moon in Miami last year. I guess the moon makes people crazy." But what about cities that saw a *decrease* in murders during the same full moon?

- "Most shark attacks occur between 12 P.M. and 2 P.M. Sharks must be hungrier then." Maybe it's just that more people go swimming near midday. If a causal link exists, it would have to be shown in a carefully controlled experiment.

On the other hand, association may warrant further study when common sense suggests a potential causal link. For example, many people believed that smoking was harmful decades before scientists showed *how* smoking leads to cancer, heart disease, and emphysema. A cell phone user who develops cancer might blame the phones, yet almost everyone uses cell phones, and very few get cancer. A statistical analysis should consider factors like occupation, smoking, alcohol use, birth control pills, diet, and exercise.

Pitfall 6: Generalizations about Individuals

"Men are taller than women." Yes, but only in a statistical sense. Men are taller *on average,* but many women are taller than many men. "Japanese cars have high quality." Yes, but not all of them. We should avoid reading too much into **statistical generalizations**. Instead, ask how much *overlap* is in the populations that are being considered. Often, the similarities transcend the differences.

Pitfall 7: Unconscious Bias

Without obvious fraud (tampering with data), researchers can unconsciously or subtly allow bias to color their handling of data. For example, for many years it was assumed that heart attacks were more likely to occur in men than women. But symptoms of heart disease are usually more obvious in men than women and so doctors tend to catch heart disease earlier in men. Studies now show that heart disease is the number one cause of death in women over the age of 25. (See Lori Mosca et al., "Evidence-based Guidelines for Cardio-vascular Disease Prevention in Women," *American Heart Association* 109, no. 5 (February 2004), pp. 672–93.)

Pitfall 8: Significance versus Importance

Statistically significant effects may lack practical importance. A study published in *The American Statistician* of over 500,000 Austrian military recruits showed that those born in the spring averaged 0.6 cm taller than those born in the fall (J. Utts, vol. 57, no. 2 (May 2003), pp. 74–79). But who would notice? Would prospective parents change their timing in hopes of having a child 0.6 cm taller? Cost-conscious businesses know that some product improvements cannot support a valid business case. Consumers cannot perceive small improvements in durability, speed, taste, and comfort if the products already are "good enough." For example, Seagate's Cheetah 147GB disk drive already has a mean time between failure (MTBF) rating of 1.4 million hours (about 160 years in continuous use). Would a 10 percent improvement in MTBF matter to anyone?

SECTION EXERCISES

connect

1.10 "Radar detector users have a lower accident rate than nonusers. Moreover, detector users seem to be better citizens. The study found that detector users wear their seat belts more and even vote more than nonusers." (a) Assuming that the study is accurate, do you think there is cause-and-effect? (b) If everyone used radar detectors, would voting rates and seat-belt usage rise?

1.11 A lottery winner told how he picked his six-digit winning number (5-6-8-10-22-39): number of people in his family, birth date of his wife, school grade of his 13-year-old daughter, sum of his birth date and his wife's, number of years of marriage, and year of his birth. He said, "I try to pick numbers that mean something to me." The State Lottery Commissioner called this method "the screwiest I ever heard of . . . but apparently it works." (a) From a statistical viewpoint, do you agree that this method "works"? (b) Based on your understanding of how a lottery works, would someone who picks 1-2-3-4-5-6 because "it is easy to remember" have a lower chance of winning?

1.12 "Smokers are much more likely to speed, run red lights, and get involved in car accidents than nonsmokers." (a) Can you think of reasons why this statement might be misleading? *Hint:* Make a list of six factors that you think would cause car accidents. Is smoking on your list? (b) Can you suggest a causal link between smoking and car accidents?

1.13 An ad for a cell phone service claims that its percent of "dropped calls" was significantly lower than its main competitor. In the fine print, the percents were given as 1.2 percent versus 1.4 percent. Is this reduction likely to be *important* to customers (as opposed to being *significant*)?

1.14 What logical or ethical problems do you see in these hypothetical scenarios?
   a. Dolon Privacy Consultants concludes that its employees are not loyal because a few random samples of employee e-mails contained comments critical of the company's management.
   b. Calchas Financial Advisors issues a glowing report of its new stock market forecasting system, based on testimonials of five happy customers.
   c. Five sanitation crew members at Malcheon Hospital are asked to try a new cleaning solvent to see if it has any allergic or other harmful side effects.
   d. A consumer group rates a new personal watercraft from Thetis Aquatic Conveyances as "Unacceptable" because two Ohio teens lost control and crashed into a dock.

1.7
STATISTICS: AN EVOLVING FIELD

Statistics is a relatively young field, having been developed mostly during the 20th century, although its roots hark back several centuries to early mathematicians in China and India. Its mathematical frontiers continue to expand, aided by the power of computers. Major developments of the late 20th century include exploratory data analysis (EDA), computer-intensive statistics, design of experiments, robust product design, advanced Bayesian methods, graphical methods, and data mining. In this book you will only get a glimpse of statistical methods and applications. But you can find many reference works that tell the story of statistics and famous statisticians (see Related Reading). The Web has many resources, including college statistics Web sites and biographies of famous statisticians.

CHAPTER SUMMARY

Statistics is the science of collecting, organizing, analyzing, interpreting, and presenting data. A **statistician** is an expert with at least a master's degree in mathematics or statistics, while a **data analyst** is anyone who works with data. **Descriptive statistics** is the collection, organization, presentation, and summary of data with charts or numerical summaries. **Inferential statistics** refers to generalizing from a sample to a population, estimating unknown parameters, drawing conclusions, and making decisions. Statistics is used in all branches of business. **Statistical challenges** include imperfect data, practical constraints, and ethical dilemmas. Effective **technical report writing** requires attention to style, grammar, organization, and proper use of tables and graphs. Business data analysts must learn to write a good **executive summary** and learn the *3 Ps* for oral presentations: pace, planning, and practice. Statistical tools are used to test theories against empirical data. Pitfalls include nonrandom samples, incorrect sample size, and lack of causal links. The field of statistics is relatively new and continues to grow as mathematical frontiers expand.

KEY TERMS

critical thinking, *15*	executive summary, *12*	statistic, *4*
descriptive statistics, *6*	inferential statistics, *6*	statistics, *4*
empirical data, *15*	post hoc fallacy, *16*	statistical generalization, *17*

CHAPTER REVIEW

1. Define (a) statistic; (b) statistics.
2. List three reasons to study statistics.
3. List three applications of statistics.
4. List four skills needed by statisticians. Why are these skills important?

5. List five rules for good writing. Why are good writing skills important?

6. (a) List some typical components of a technical report. (b) What does an executive summary include? What is its purpose?

7. (a) List three rules for using tables and graphs. (b) List three tips for making effective oral reports.

8. List three challenges faced by statisticians.

9. List five pitfalls or logical errors that may ensnare the unwary statistician.

1.15 A survey of beginning students showed that a majority strongly agreed with the statement, "I am afraid of statistics." Why might this attitude exist among students who have not yet taken a statistics class? Would a similar attitude exist toward an ethics class? Explain your reasoning.

1.16 Under a recent U.S. Food and Drug Administration (FDA) standard for food contaminants, 3.5 ounces of tomato sauce can have up to 30 fly eggs, and 11 ounces of wheat flour can contain 450 insect fragments. How could statistical sampling be used to see that these standards of food hygiene are not violated by producers?

1.17 A statistical consultant was retained by a linen supplier to analyze a survey of hospital purchasing managers. After looking at the data, she realized that the survey had missed several key geographic areas and included some that were outside the target region. Some survey questions were ambiguous. Some respondents failed to answer all the questions or gave silly replies (one manager said he worked 40 hours a day). Of the 1,000 surveys mailed, only 80 were returned. (a) What alternatives are available to the statistician? (b) Might an imperfect analysis be better than none? (c) If you were the consultant, how might you respond to the supplier?

1.18 Ergonomics is the science of making sure that human surroundings are adapted to human needs. How could statistics play a role in the following:
a. Choosing the height of an office chair so that 95 percent of the employees (male and female) will feel it is the "right height" for their legs to reach the floor comfortably.
b. Designing a drill press so its controls can be reached and its forces operated by an "average employee."
c. Defining a doorway width so that a "typical" wheelchair can pass through without coming closer than 6 inches from either side.
d. Setting the width of a parking space to accommodate 95 percent of all vehicles at your local Wal-Mart.
e. Choosing a font size so that a highway sign can be read in daylight at 100 meters by 95 percent of all drivers.

1.19 A research study showed that 7 percent of "A" students smoke, while nearly 50 percent of "D" students do. (a) List in rank order six factors that you think affect grades. Is smoking on your list? (b) If smoking is not a likely cause of poor grades, can you suggest reasons why these results were observed? (c) Assuming these statistics are correct, would "D" students who give up smoking improve their grades?

1.20 A research study by the Agency for Healthcare Research Quality showed that adolescents who watched more than 4 hours of TV per day were more than five times as likely to start smoking as those who watched less than 2 hours a day. The researchers speculate that TV actors' portrayals of smoking as personally and socially rewarding were an effective indirect method of tobacco promotion (*Note:* Paid television tobacco ads are illegal). List in rank order six factors that you think cause adolescents to start smoking. Did TV portrayals of attractive smokers appear on your list? (Data are from the *AHRQ Newsletter,* no. 269, January 2003, p. 12.)

1.21 The Graduate Management Admission Test (GMAT) is used by many graduate schools of business as one of their admission criteria. GMAT scores for selected undergraduate majors are shown below. Using your own reasoning and concepts in this chapter, criticize each of the following statements.
a. "Philosophy majors must not be interested in business since so few take the GMAT."
b. "More students major in engineering than in English."
c. "If marketing students majored in physics, they would score better on the GMAT."
d. "Physics majors would make the best managers."

GMAT Scores and Undergraduate Major, 1984–1989   GMAT

Major	Average GMAT Score	Number Taking Test
Accounting	483	25,233
Computer Science	508	7,573
Economics	513	16,432
Engineering	544	29,688
English	507	3,589
Finance	489	20,001
Marketing	455	15,925
Philosophy	546	588
Physics	575	1,223

Source: Graduate Management Admission Council, *Admission Office Profile of Candidates,* October 1989, pp. 27–30.

1.22   (a) Which of these two displays (table or graph) is most helpful in visualizing the relationship between restaurant size and interior seating for 74 Noodles restaurants? Explain your reasoning. (b) Do you see anything unusual in the data? (*Source:* Noodles & Company)   **NoodlesSqFt**

Number of Restaurants in Each Category (*n* = 74 restaurants)

Interior Seats	Square Feet Inside Restaurant				Row Total
	1000 < 1750	1750 < 2500	2500 < 3250	3250 < 4000	
105 < 130	0	0	0	3	3
80 < 105	0	4	17	0	21
55 < 80	0	21	24	0	45
30 < 55	1	4	0	0	5
Col Total	1	29	41	3	74

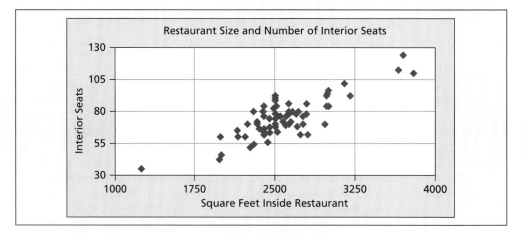

1.23   Each of the following is an actual writing sample, mostly from student projects. In each, find as many errors of spelling and/or grammar as you can, and correct them.
   a. "Its' R^2 value is quite close to 1 indicating it is a good fit to the actual data. I feel that G.E., one of the most respected corporations in the world, because of its' strong management and name recognition, not to mention its' valuable assets, is poised for steady growth over the next decade."
   b. "If a countries unemployment rate is to high it could cause a down swing in their economics structure."
   c. "This forecast is very unlikely, because you cannot have a negative amount of people unemployed."
   d. "It is not a well designed graph because it's title is too long and there isn't any axis labels."

e. "This graph has no clear concise boarder to give it a sense of containment. With this graph especially since it is dealing with actually three seperate pieces of information. In this graph, the same data is presented but in a deceptive manor. Its sources weren't as specific as they should of been."

1.24   Choose *three* of the following statisticians and use the Web to find out a few basic facts about them (e.g., list some of their contributions to statistics, when they did their work, whether they are still living, etc.).

Florence Nightingale	John Wilder Tukey	Genichi Taguchi
Gertrude Cox	William Cochran	Helen Walker
Sir Francis Galton	Siméon Poisson	George Box
W. Edwards Deming	S. S. Stevens	Sam Wilks
The Bernoulli family	R. A. Fisher	Carl F. Gauss
Frederick Mosteller	George Snedecor	William S. Gosset
William H. Kruskal	Karl Pearson	Thomas Bayes
Jerzy Neyman	C. R. Rao	Bradley Efron
Egon Pearson	Abraham De Moivre	
Harold Hotelling	Edward Tufte	

RELATED READING

Practical Guides

Coleman, S.; T. Greenfield; R. Jones; C. Morris; and I. Puzey. *The Pocket Statistician*. Wiley, 1996.

Dodge, Yadolah. *The Concise Encyclopedia of Statistics*. Springer, 2008.

Everitt, B. S. *The Cambridge Dictionary of Statistics*. 2nd ed. Cambridge University Press, 2002.

John, J. A.; and D. Whitaker. *Statistical Thinking in Business*. 2nd ed. Chapman and Hall, 2005.

Kanji, Gopal K. *100 Statistical Tests*. Sage Publications, 1999.

Newton, Rae R.; and Kjell Erik Rudestam. *Your Statistical Consultant*. Sage Publications, 1999.

Sahei, Hardeo; and Anwer Khurshid. *Pocket Dictionary of Statistics*. McGraw-Hill, 2002.

Utts, Jessica. "What Educated Citizens Should Know About Statistics and Probability." *The American Statistician* 57, no. 2 (May 2003), pp. 74–79.

Effective Writing

Harris, Robert A. *Writing with Clarity and Style*. Pyrczak Publishing, 2003.

May, Claire B.; and Gordon S. May. *Effective Writing: Handbook for Accountants*. Prentice Hall, 2006.

Pyrczak, Fred; and Randall Bruce. *Writing Empirical Research Reports*. 4th ed. Pyrczak Publishing, 2003.

Radke-Sharpe, N. "Writing as a Component of Statistics Education." *The American Statistician* 45, November 1991, pp. 292–93.

Sabin, William A. *The Gregg Reference Manual*. 9th ed. Glencoe/McGraw-Hill, 2000.

Sides, Charles H. *How to Write and Present Technical Information*. 3rd ed. Cambridge University Press, 1999.

Strunk, William J.; and E. B. White. *The Elements of Style*. Prentice-Hall, 1999.

Tichy, H. J. *Effective Writing for Engineers, Managers, and Scientists*. 2nd ed. Wiley, 1988.

Ethics

Nash, Laura L. *Good Intentions Aside: A Manager's Guide to Resolving Ethical Problems*. Harvard University Press, 1990.

Vardeman, Stephen B.; and Max D. Morris. "Statistics and Ethics: Some Advice for Young Statisticians." *The American Statistician* 57, February 2003, pp. 21–26.

History of Statistics

Gani, J. *The Making of Statisticians*. Springer-Verlag, 1982.

Heyde, C. C.; and E. Seneta. *Statisticians of the Centuries*. Springer-Verlag, 2001.

Johnson, Norman L.; and Samuel Kotz. *Leading Personalities in Statistical Science from the Seventeenth Century to the Present*. Wiley, 1997.

Statistics: Uses and Misuses

Almer, Ennis C. *Statistical Tricks and Traps*. Pyrczak Publishing, 2000.

Barnett, Arnold. "How Numbers Can Trick You." *Technology Review,* October 1994, pp. 38–45.

Gould, Stephen Jay. *The Mismeasure of Man*. W. W. Norton, 1996.

Nash, J. C. "Spreadsheets in Practice—Another Look." *The American Statistician* 60, no. 3 (August 2006), pp. 287–89.

LearningStats Unit 00   Basic Skills

Even if you already know how to use Microsoft® Office tools (Excel, Word, PowerPoint), there may be features that you have never tried or skills you can improve. One objective of *LearningStats* is to show you how to use software applications (especially Excel) *in the context of statistics* for calculations, reports, and presentations. Excel is emphasized but there are also helpful tips on statistical reports using Word and PowerPoint. At your own pace, you should examine each demonstration. Some material will already be familiar to you, but you may pick up a few new tips. If you don't know anything about Excel, Word, or PowerPoint, you should consult additional sources, but you can still use *LearningStats*.

Topic	LearningStats Modules
Microsoft® Office	Excel Tips Word Tips PowerPoint Tips Checklist of Office Skills
Excel	Excel Basics Excel Features Excel Functions Excel Advanced Features
Math Review	Math Review Using Symbols in Word Significant Digits

Key: = PowerPoint   = Word   = Excel

LearningStats Unit 01   Overview of Statistics

LearningStats Unit 01 introduces statistics, report writing, and professional ethical guidelines. Modules are designed for self-study, so you can proceed at your own pace, concentrate on material that is new, and pass quickly over things that you already know. Your instructor may assign specific modules, or you may decide to check them out because the topic sounds interesting. In addition to helping you learn about statistics, they may be useful as references later on.

Topic	LearningStats Modules
Overview	What Is Statistics?
	Web Resources
	Statistics Software
Report writing	Effective Writing
	Technical Report Writing
	The Executive Summary
	The Oral Presentation
	Common Errors
	Writing Self-Test 1
	Writing Self-Test 2
	Writing Self-Test 3
	Fog Index Project
Ethics	Ethical Guidelines

Key: = PowerPoint   = Word   = Excel

Data Collection

Chapter Learning Objectives

When you finish this chapter you should be able to

- Use basic terminology for describing data and samples.

- Explain the distinction between numerical and categorical data.

- Recognize levels of measurement in data and ways of coding data.

- Recognize a Likert scale and know how to use it.

- Explain the difference between time series and cross-sectional data.

- Use the correct terminology for samples and populations.

- Explain the common sampling methods and how to implement them.

- Find everyday print or electronic data sources.

- Describe basic elements of survey design, survey types, and sources of error.

In scientific research, data arise from experiments whose results are recorded systematically. In business, data usually arise from accounting transactions or management processes (e.g., inventory, sales, payroll). Much of the data that statisticians analyze were recorded without explicit consideration of their statistical uses, yet important decisions may depend on the data. How many pints of type A blood will be required at Mt. Sinai Hospital next Thursday? How many dollars must State Farm keep in its cash account to cover automotive accident claims next November? How many yellow three-quarter sleeve women's sweaters will Lands' End sell this month? To answer such questions, we usually look at historical data.

Data: Singular or Plural?

Data is the plural of the Latin *datum* (a "given" fact). This traditional usage is preferred in Britain, and especially in scientific journals, where over 90 percent of the references use data as a plural ("These data show a correlation . . ."). But in the popular press (newspapers, magazines) you will often see "data" used synonymously with "information" and hence as a singular ("The compressed data is stored on a CD . . ."). The singular usage is especially common in the United States and is becoming more common in the United Kingdom, rather to the chagrin of the educated populace.

Subjects, Variables, and Data Sets

A **subject** or **individual** is a single member of a collection of items that we want to study, such as persons, firms, or regions. An example of a subject is an employee or an invoice mailed last month. A **variable** is a characteristic of the subject or individual, such as an employee's income or an invoice amount. The **data set** consists of all the values of all of the variables for all of the individuals we have chosen to observe. In this book, we will use **data** as a plural, and data set to refer to a collection of **observations** taken as a whole. Table 2.1 shows a small data set with eight subjects, five variables, and 40 observations (eight subjects times five variables).

Subject	Name	Age	Income	Position	Gender
1	Frieda	45	$67,100	Personnel director	F
2	Stefan	32	56,500	Operations analyst	M
3	Barbara	55	88,200	Marketing VP	F
4	Donna	27	59,000	Statistician	F
5	Larry	46	36,000	Security guard	M
6	Alicia	52	68,500	Comptroller	F
7	Alec	65	95,200	Chief executive	M
8	Jaime	50	71,200	Public relations	M

TABLE 2.1

A Small Multivariate Data Set (5 variables, 8 subjects)
   SmallData

A data set may consist of many variables. The questions that can be explored and the analytical techniques that can be used will depend upon the data type and the number of variables. This textbook starts with **univariate data sets** (one variable), then moves to **bivariate data sets** (two variables) and **multivariate data sets** (more than two variables), as illustrated in Table 2.2.

TABLE 2.2

Number of Variables and Typical Tasks

Data Set	Variables	Example	Typical Tasks
Univariate	One	Income	Histograms, basic statistics
Bivariate	Two	Income, Age	Scatter plots, correlation
Multivariate	More than two	Income, Age, Gender	Regression modeling

Data Types

A data set may contain a mixture of *data types*. Two broad categories are **categorical data** and **numerical data,** as shown in Figure 2.1.

Categorical Data   *Categorical* data (also called *qualitative*) have values that are described by words rather than numbers. For example:

   Structural lumber type (e.g., $X =$ fir, hemlock, pine).

   Automobile style (e.g., $X =$ full, midsize, compact, subcompact).

   Mutual fund type (e.g., $X =$ load, no-load).

You might imagine that categorical data would be of limited statistical use, but in fact there are many statistical methods that can handle categorical data.

FIGURE 2.1

Data Types

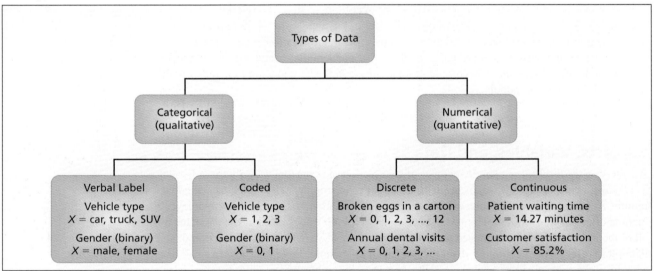

Using numbers to represent categories to facilitate statistical analysis is called **coding**. For example, a database might classify movies using numerical codes:

1 = Action, 2 = Classic, 3 = Comedy, 4 = Horror,

5 = Romance, 6 = Science Fiction, 7 = Western, 8 = Other

But coding a category as a number does *not* make the data numerical. Movie codes are assigned arbitrarily, and the codes generally do not imply a ranking. However, sometimes codes do imply a ranking:

1 = Bachelor's, 2 = Master's, 3 = Doctorate

Rankings may exist if we are measuring an underlying continuum, such as political orientation:

1 = Liberal, 2 = Moderate, 3 = Conservative

A **binary variable** has only two values, indicating the presence (1) or absence (0) of a characteristic of interest. For example, for an individual:

Employment	*Education*	*Marital status*
1 = employed	1 = college graduate	1 = currently married
0 = not employed	0 = not college graduate	0 = not currently married

The codes are arbitrary. A variable like gender could be coded in many ways:

Like This	*Or Like This*	*Or Like This*
1 = female	0 = female	1 = female
0 = male	1 = male	2 = male

Here again the coding itself has no numerical meaning, so binary variables are *categorical* data.

Numerical Data   *Numerical* or *quantitative* data arise from counting, measuring something, or from some kind of mathematical operation. For example:

Number of auto insurance claims filed in March (e.g., $X = 114$ claims).

Sales for last quarter (e.g., $X = \$4{,}920$).

Percent of mortgage applicants who are retired (e.g., $X = 22.7$ percent).

Most accounting data, economic indicators, and financial ratios are quantitative, as are physical measurements (length, weight, time, speed).

Numerical data can be further broken down into two types. A variable with a countable number of distinct values is **discrete**. Often, such data are integers. You can recognize integer data because their description begins with "number of." For example:

Number of Medicaid patients in a hospital waiting room (e.g., $X = 2$).

Number of takeoffs at Chicago's O'Hare Airport in a given hour (e.g., $X = 37$).

We express such data as integer variables because we cannot observe a fractional number of patients or takeoffs.

A numerical variable that can have any value within an interval is **continuous.** This would include things like physical measurements (e.g., length, weight, time, speed) and financial variables (e.g., sales, assets, price/earnings ratios, inventory turns). For example:

Weight of a package of Sun-Maid raisins (e.g., $X = 427.31$ grams).

Hourly fuel flow in a Cessna Citation V (e.g., $X = 1390.67$ pounds).

These are continuous variables because any interval (e.g., $422 < X < 428$) contains infinitely many possible values.

Apparent ambiguity between *discrete* and *continuous* is introduced when we round continuous data to whole numbers (e.g., your weight this morning). However, the underlying measurement scale is continuous. That is, a package of Sun-Maid raisins is labeled 425 grams, but on an accurate scale its weight would be a noninteger (e.g., 427.31). Precision depends on the instrument we use to measure the continuous variable. We generally treat financial data (dollars, euros, pesos) as continuous even though retail prices go in discrete steps of .01 (i.e., we go from $1.25 to $1.26). The FM radio spectrum is continuous, but only certain discrete values are observed (e.g., 104.3) because of Federal Communications Commission rules. Conversely, we sometimes treat discrete data as continuous when the range is very large (e.g., SAT scores) and when small differences (e.g., 604 or 605) aren't of much importance. This topic will be discussed in later chapters. If in doubt, just think about how X was measured and whether or not its values are countable.

SECTION EXERCISES

connect™

2.1   Explain the difference between an observation and a variable.

2.2   Give an example of (a) categorical data, (b) discrete numerical data, and (c) continuous numerical data.

2.3   What type of data (categorical, discrete numerical, or continuous numerical) is each of the following variables? If there is any ambiguity about the data type, explain why the answer is unclear.
a. The manufacturer of your car.
b. Your college major.
c. The number of college credits you are taking.
d. Your GPA.
e. The miles on your car's odometer.
f. The fat grams you ate for lunch yesterday.
g. Your dog's age.

2.4   What type of data (categorical, discrete numerical, or continuous numerical) is each of the following variables? If there is any ambiguity, explain why the answer is unclear.
a. Length of a TV commercial.
b. Number of peanuts in a can of Planter's Mixed Nuts.
c. Occupation of a mortgage applicant.
d. Flight time from London Heathrow to Chicago O'Hare.
e. Name of the airline with the cheapest fare from New York to London.
f. Blouse size purchased by a Marks and Spencer customer.

2.5   (a) Give three original examples of discrete data. (b) Give three original examples of continuous data. In each case, explain and identify any ambiguities that might exist. *Hint:* Do not restrict yourself to published data. Consider data describing your own life (e.g., your sports performance, financial data, or academic data). You need *not* list all the data, merely describe them and show a few typical data values.

2.6   Look at data sets in LearningStats under Cross-Sectional Data > Cars. Find an example of (a) a univariate data set, (b) a bivariate data set, and (c) a multivariate data set.

2.2
LEVEL OF MEASUREMENT

Statisticians sometimes refer to four levels of measurement for data: *nominal, ordinal, interval,* and *ratio* (see Table 2.3). This typology was proposed over 60 years ago by psychologist S. S. Stevens. The allowable statistical tests depend on the measurement level. The criteria are summarized in Table 2.3 and Figure 2.2.

Nominal Measurement

Nominal measurement is the weakest level of measurement and the easiest to recognize. **Nominal data** (from Latin *nomen* meaning "name") merely identify a *category*. "Nominal" data are the same as "qualitative," "categorical," or "classification" data. For example, the following survey questions yield nominal data:

Did you file an insurance claim last month?

1. Yes   2. No

Which kind of laptop do you own?

1. Acer	2. Apple	3. Compaq	4. Dell	5. Gateway	6. HP
7. IBM	8. Micron	9. Sony	10. Toshiba	11. Other	12. None

TABLE 2.3

Levels of Measurement

Characteristic	Level of Measurement			
	Nominal	*Ordinal*	*Interval*	*Ratio*
Do data values indicate the natural order of something?	No	Yes	Yes	Yes
Are differences between data values meaningful?	No	No	Yes	Yes
Is there a natural zero point that indicates the absence of something?	No	No	No	Yes
Operations allowed	Only counting allowed (e.g., frequency tally, finding the mode)	Counting and order statistics allowed (e.g., mode, median, rank tests)	Statistics that use sums or differences allowed (e.g., mean, standard deviation)	All statistical operations allowed, including ratios of numbers
Example	Eye color (blue, brown, green, hazel)	Bond ratings (Aaa, Baa1, C1, etc.)	Temperature on Celsius scale (e.g., 17° C)	Accounts payable ($21.7 million)

FIGURE 2.2

Measurement Level Illustrated

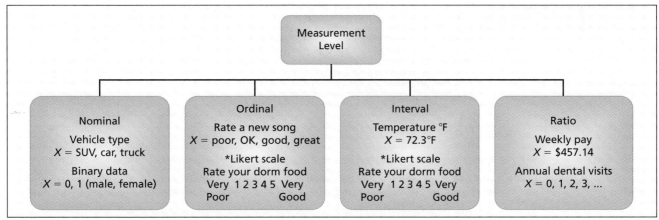

*You can treat a Likert scale as interval data if distances between scale points have meaning (otherwise, it's ordinal).

We usually code nominal data numerically. However, the codes are arbitrary placeholders with no numerical meaning, so it is improper to perform mathematical analysis on them. For example, we would not calculate an average using the laptop data (1 through 12). This may seem obvious, yet people have been known to do it. Once the data are in the computer, it's easy to forget that the "numbers" are only categories. With nominal data, the only permissible mathematical operations are counting (e.g., frequencies) and a few simple statistics such as the mode.

Ordinal Measurement

Ordinal data codes connote a *ranking* of data values. For example:

What size automobile do you usually drive?

1. Full-size   2. Compact   3. Subcompact

How often do you use Microsoft Access?

1. Frequently   2. Sometimes   3. Rarely   4. Never

Thus, a 2 (Compact) implies a larger car than a 3 (Subcompact). Like nominal data, these ordinal numerical codes lack the properties that are required to compute many statistics, such as the average. Specifically, there is no clear meaning to the *distance* between 1 and 2, or between 2 and 3, or between 3 and 4 (what would be the distance between "Rarely" and "Never"?). Other examples of ordinal scales can be found in a recruiter's rating of job candidates (outstanding, good, adequate, weak, unsatisfactory), S&P credit ratings (AAA, AA+, AA, AA−, A+, A, A−, B+, B, B−, etc.) or job titles (president, group vice-president, plant manager, department head, clerk). Ordinal data can be treated as nominal, but not vice versa. Ordinal data are especially common in social sciences, marketing, and human resources research. There are many useful statistical tests for ordinal data.

Interval Measurement

The next step up the measurement scale is **interval data,** which not only is a rank but also has meaningful intervals between scale points. Examples are the Celsius or Fahrenheit scales of temperature. The interval between 60°F and 70°F is the same as the interval between 20°F and 30°F. Since intervals between numbers represent *distances,* we can do mathematical operations such as taking an average. But because the zero point of these scales is arbitrary, we can't say that 60°F is twice as warm as 30°F, or that 30°F is 50 percent warmer than 20°F. That is, ratios are not meaningful for interval data. The absence of a meaningful zero is a key characteristic of interval data.

Likert Scales   The **Likert scale** is a special case that is frequently used in survey research. You have undoubtedly seen such scales. Typically, a statement is made and the respondent is asked to indicate his or her agreement/disagreement on a five-point or seven-point scale using verbal anchors. The *coarseness* of a Likert scale refers to the number of scale points (typically 5 or 7). For example:

"College-bound high school students should be required to study a foreign language." (check one)

❑	❑	❑	❑	❑
Strongly Agree	Somewhat Agree	Neither Agree Nor Disagree	Somewhat Disagree	Strongly Disagree

A neutral midpoint ("Neither Agree Nor Disagree") is allowed if we use an *odd* number of scale points (usually 5 or 7). Occasionally, surveys may omit the neutral midpoint to force the respondent to "lean" one way or the other. Likert data are coded numerically (e.g., 1 to 5) but any equally spaced values will work, as shown in Table 2.4.

But do Likert data qualify as interval measurements? By choosing the verbal anchors carefully, many researchers believe that the *intervals* are the same (e.g., the distance from 1 to 2 is "the same" as the *interval,* say, from 3 to 4). However, ratios are not meaningful (i.e., here 4 is not twice 2). The assumption that Likert scales produce interval data justifies a wide range of statistical calculations, including averages, correlations, and so on. Researchers use many Likert-scale variants.

"How would you rate your marketing instructor?" (check one)

❑ Terrible   ❑ Poor   ❑ Adequate   ❑ Good   ❑ Excellent

TABLE 2.4		
Examples of Likert-Scale Coding: "How will a change in inflation affect the investment climate?"	*Likert Coding: 1 to 5 scale*	*Likert Coding: −2 to +2 scale*
	5 = Will help a lot	+2 = Will help a lot
	4 = Will help a little	+1 = Will help a little
	3 = No effect on investment climate	0 = No effect on investment climate
	2 = Will hurt a little	−1 = Will hurt a little
	1 = Will hurt a lot	−2 = Will hurt a lot

Respondents may prefer having verbal labels for each category but researchers who are uncomfortable with the labels can put verbal anchors only on the end points, where 1 = "very poor" and 5 = "very good."

"How would you rate your marketing instructor?" (check one)

Very Bad ❑ ❑ ❑ ❑ ❑ Very Good

This avoids intermediate scale labels and permits any number of scale points, but lacks a concrete interpretation (what does a "3" mean?). Likert data usually are discrete, but some Web surveys now use a continuous response scale that allows the respondent to position a "slider" anywhere along the scale to produce continuous data (actually the number of positions is finite but very large). For example:

Likert (using scale points)

Very Poor 1 2 3 4 5 6 7 Very Good

Likert (using a slider)

Very Poor _____▼___ Very Good

Ratio Measurement

Ratio measurement is the strongest level of measurement. **Ratio data** have all the properties of the other three data types, but in addition possess a *meaningful zero* that represents the absence of the quantity being measured. Because of the zero point, ratios of data values are meaningful (e.g., $20 million in profit is twice as much as $10 million). Balance sheet data, income statement data, financial ratios, physical counts, scientific measurements, and most engineering measurements are ratio data because zero has meaning (e.g., a company with zero sales sold nothing). Having a zero point does *not* restrict us to positive data. For example, profit is a ratio variable (e.g., $4 million is twice $2 million) yet firms can have negative profit.

Zero does *not* have to be observable in the data. Newborn babies, for example, cannot have zero weight, yet baby weight clearly is ratio data (i.e., an 8-pound baby is 33 percent heavier than a 6-pound baby). What matters is that the zero is an absolute reference point. The Kelvin temperature scale is a ratio measurement because its absolute zero represents the absence of molecular vibration, while zero on the Celsius scale is merely a convenience (note that 30° C is not "twice as much temperature" as 15° C).

Lack of a true zero is often the quickest test to defrock variables masquerading as ratio data. For example, a Likert scale (+2, +1, 0, −1, −2) is *not* ratio data despite the presence of zero because the zero (neutral) point does not connote the absence of anything. As an acid test, ask yourself whether 2 (strongly agree) is twice as much "agreement" as 1 (slightly agree). Some classifications are debatable. For example, college GPA has a zero, but does it represent the absence of learning? Does 4.00 represent "twice as much" learning as 2.00? Is there an underlying reality ranging from 0 to 4 that we are measuring? Most people seem to think so, although the conservative procedure would be to limit ourselves to statistical tests that assume only ordinal data.

Although beginning statistics textbooks usually emphasize interval or ratio data, there are textbooks that emphasize other kinds of data, notably in behavioral research (e.g., psychology, sociology, marketing, human resources).

Changing Data by Recoding

We can recode ratio measurements *downward* into ordinal or nominal measurements (but not conversely). For example, doctors may classify systolic blood pressure as "normal" (under 130), "elevated" (130 to 140), or "high" (140 or over). The recoded data are ordinal, since the ranking is preserved. Intervals may be unequal. For example, U.S. air traffic controllers classify planes as "small" (under 41,000 pounds), "large" (41,001 to 254,999 pounds), and "heavy" (255,000 pounds or more). Such recoding is done to simplify the data when the exact data magnitude is of little interest; however, it discards information by mapping stronger measurements into weaker ones.

2.7   Which type of data (nominal, ordinal, interval, ratio) is each of the following variables? Explain.
    a. Number of hits in Game 1 of the next World Series.
    b. Baltimore's standing in the American League East (among five teams).
    c. Field position of a baseball player (catcher, pitcher, etc.).
    d. Temperature on opening day (Celsius).

SECTION EXERCISES

connect

e. Salary of a randomly chosen American League pitcher.

f. Freeway traffic on opening day (light, medium, heavy).

2.8 Which type of data (nominal, ordinal, interval, ratio) is each of the following variables? Explain.

a. Number of employees in the Wal-Mart store in Hutchinson, Kansas.

b. Number of merchandise returns on a randomly chosen Monday at a Wal-Mart store.

c. Temperature (in Fahrenheit) in the ice-cream freezer at a Wal-Mart store.

d. Name of the cashier at register 3 in a Wal-Mart store.

e. Manager's rating of the cashier at register 3 in a Wal-Mart store.

f. Social security number of the cashier at register 3 in a Wal-Mart store.

2.9 Give an original example of each type of data (nominal, ordinal, interval, ratio) from your own life (e.g., your finances, sporting activities, education).

2.10 Which type of data (nominal, ordinal, interval, ratio) is the response to each question? If you think that the level of measurement is ambiguous, explain why.

a. How would you describe your level of skill in using Excel? (check one)

❑ Low   ❑ Medium   ❑ High

b. How often do you use Excel? (check one)

❑ Rarely   ❑ Often   ❑ Very Often

c. Which version of Excel do you use? (check one)

❑ 2000   ❑ XP   ❑ 2003   ❑ 2007   ❑ Other

d. I spend _____ hours a day using Excel.

2.3
TIME SERIES VERSUS CROSS-SECTIONAL DATA

Time Series Data

If each observation in the sample represents a different equally spaced point in time (years, months, days) we have **time series data.** The *periodicity* is the time between observations. It may be annual, quarterly, monthly, weekly, daily, hourly, etc. Examples of *macroeconomic* time series data would include national income (GDP, consumption, investment), economic indicators (Consumer Price Index, unemployment rate, Standard & Poor's 500 Index), and monetary data (M1, M2, M3, prime rate, T-bill rate, consumer borrowing, federal debt). Examples of *microeconomic* time series data would include a firm's sales, market share, debt/equity ratio, employee absenteeism, inventory turnover, and product quality ratings. For time series, we are interested in *trends and patterns over time* (e.g., annual growth in consumer debit card use from 2001 to 2008).

Cross-Sectional Data

If each observation represents a different individual unit (e.g., a person, firm, geographic area) at the same point in time, we have **cross-sectional data.** Thus, traffic fatalities in the 50 U.S. states for a given year, debt/equity ratios for the Fortune 500 firms in the last quarter of a certain year, last month's Visa balances for a bank's new mortgage applicants, or GPAs of students in a statistics class would be cross-sectional data. For cross-sectional data, we are interested in *variation among observations* (e.g., collection period for accounts receivable in 10 Subway franchises) or in *relationships* (e.g., whether collection period correlates with sales volume in 10 Subway franchises).

Some variables (such as unemployment rates) could be either time series (monthly data over each of 60 months) or cross-sectional (January's unemployment rate in 50 different largest cities). We can combine the two (e.g., monthly unemployment rates for the 13 Canadian provinces or territories for the last 60 months) to obtain *pooled cross-sectional and time series data.*

SECTION EXERCISES

2.11 Which type of data (cross-sectional or time series) is each variable?

a. Scores of 50 students on a midterm accounting exam last semester.

b. Bob's scores on 10 weekly accounting quizzes last semester.

c. Average score by all takers of the state's CPA exam for each of the last 10 years.

d. Number of years of accounting work experience for each of the 15 partners in a CPA firm.

2.12 Which type of data (cross-sectional or time series) is each variable?

a. Value of Standard & Poor's 500 stock price index at the close of each trading day last year.

b. Closing price of each of the 500 stocks in the S&P 500 index on the last trading day this week.

c. Dividends per share paid by General Motors common stock for the last 20 quarters.

d. Latest price/earnings ratios of 10 stocks in Bob's retirement portfolio.

2.13 Which type of data (cross-sectional or time series) is each variable?

a. Mexico's GDP for each of the last 10 quarters.

b. Unemployment rates in each of the 31 states in Mexico at the end of last year.

c. Unemployment rate in Mexico at the end of each of the last 10 years.

d. Average home value in each of the 10 largest Mexican cities today.

2.14 Give an original example of a time series variable and a cross-sectional variable. Use your own experience (e.g., your sports activities, finances, education).

There are almost 2 million retail businesses in the United States. It is unrealistic for market researchers to study them all or in a timely way. But since 2001, a new firm called Shopper-Trak RCT (www.shoppertrak.com) has been measuring purchases at a sample of 45,000 mall-based stores, and using this information to advise clients quickly of changes in shopping trends. This application of sampling is part of the relatively new field of *retail intelligence*. In this section, you will learn the differences between a **sample** and a **population**, and why sometimes a sample is necessary or desirable.

2.4 SAMPLING CONCEPTS

Population All of the items that we are interested in. May be either finite (e.g., all of the passengers on a particular plane) or effectively infinite (e.g., all of the Cokes produced in an ongoing bottling process).

Sample A subset of the population that we will actually analyze.

Sample or Census?

A *sample* involves looking only at some items selected from the population but a **census** is an examination of all items in a defined population. The accuracy of a census can be illusory. For example, the U.S. decennial census cannot locate every individual in the United States (the 1990 census is thought to have missed 8 million people while the 2000 census is believed to have overcounted 1.3 million people). Reasons include the extreme mobility of the U.S. population and the fact that some people do not want to be found (e.g., illegal immigrants) or do not reply to the mailed census form. Further, budget constraints make it difficult to train enough census field workers, install data safeguards, and track down incomplete responses or nonresponses. For these reasons, U.S. censuses have long used sampling in certain situations. Many statistical experts advised using sampling more extensively in the 2000 decennial census, but the U.S. Congress decided that an actual headcount must be attempted.

When the quantity being measured is volatile, there cannot be a census. For example, The Arbitron Company tracks American radio listening habits using over 2.6 million "Radio Diary Packages." For each "listening occasion," participants note start and stop times for each station. Panelists also report their age, sex, and other demographic information. Table 2.5 outlines some situations where a sample rather than a census would be preferred, and vice versa.

Parameters and Statistics

From a sample of n items, chosen from a population, we compute **statistics** that can be used as estimates of **parameters** found in the population. To avoid confusion, we use different symbols for each parameter and its corresponding statistic. Thus, the population mean is denoted μ (the Greek letter mu) while the sample mean is $\bar{x}$. The population proportion is denoted π (the Greek letter pi) while the sample proportion is p. Figure 2.3 illustrates this idea.

Parameter A measurement or characteristic of the population (e.g., a mean or proportion). Usually unknown since we can rarely observe the entire population. Usually (but not always) represented by a Greek letter (e.g., μ or π).

Statistic A numerical value calculated from a sample (e.g., a mean or proportion). Usually (but not always) represented by a Roman letter (e.g., $\bar{x}$ or p).

TABLE 2.5

Sample or Census?

Situations Where a Sample May Be Preferred:	*Situations Where a Census May Be Preferred*
Infinite Population No census is possible if the population is of indefinite size (an assembly line can keep producing bolts, a doctor can keep seeing more patients).	**Small Population** If the population is small, there is little reason to sample, for the effort of data collection may be only a small part of the total cost.
Destructive Testing The act of measurement may destroy or devalue the item (battery life, vehicle crash tests).	**Large Sample Size** If the required sample size approaches the population size, we might as well go ahead and take a census.
Timely Results Sampling may yield more timely results (checking wheat samples for moisture content, checking peanut butter for aflatoxin contamination).	**Database Exists** If the data are on disk, we can examine 100% of the cases. But auditing or validating data against physical records may raise the cost.
Accuracy Instead of spreading resources thinly to attempt a census, budget might be better spent to improve training of field interviewers and improve data safeguards.	**Legal Requirements** Banks must count *all* the cash in bank teller drawers at the end of each business day. The U.S. Congress forbade sampling in the 2000 decennial population census.
Cost Even if a census is feasible, the cost, either in time or money, may exceed our budget.	
Sensitive Information A trained interviewer might learn more about sexual harassment in an organization through in-depth interviews of a small sample of employees and confidentiality may also be improved.	

FIGURE 2.3

Population versus Sample

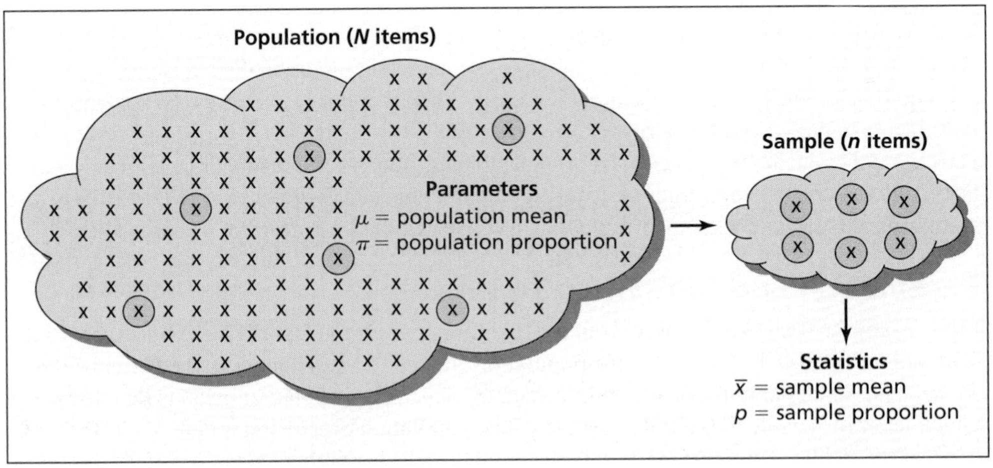

For example, suppose we want to know the mean (average) repair cost for auto air-conditioning warranty claims, or the proportion (percent) of 25-year-old concert-goers who have permanent hearing loss. Since a census is impossible, these parameters would be estimated using a sample. For the sample statistics to provide good estimates of the population parameters, the population must be carefully specified and the sample must be drawn scientifically so the sample items are representative of the population.

Target Population

A population may be defined either by a list (e.g., the names of the passengers on Flight 234) or by a rule (e.g., the customers who eat at Noodles & Company). The **target population** is the population in which we are interested. Suppose we wish to estimate the proportion of potential consumers who would purchase a $20 Harley-Davidson desk calendar. Is the target population all drivers? Only male drivers over age 16? Only drivers with incomes over $25,000? Only motorcycle owners? By answering questions such as these, we not only identify the target population but also are forced to define our business goals more clearly. The **sampling frame** is the group from which we take the sample. If the frame differs from the target population, then our estimates will be of little use. Examples of frames are phone directories, voter registration lists, alumni association mailing lists, or marketing databases. Other examples might be:

- Names and addresses of all registered voters in Colorado Springs, Colorado.
- Names and addresses of all vehicle owners in Ventura County, California.
- E-mail addresses of all L. L. Bean customers who have placed online orders.

EXAMPLE

Gasoline Price Survey

The sample for the U.S. Energy Information Administration's survey of gasoline prices is drawn from a frame of approximately 115,000 retail gasoline outlets, constructed from purchased private commercial sources and EIA sources, combined with zip codes from private lists. Individual frames are mapped to the county level by using zip codes, and outlets are assigned to standard metropolitan statistical areas from Census Bureau definitions. (For details, see www.eia.doe.gov.)

Finite or Infinite?

A population is *finite* if it has a definite size, N, even if its size is unknown. For example, the number of cars in a McDonald's parking lot or the number of MBA students enrolled at the University of Kansas will be finite. A population is treated as *infinite* if it is of arbitrarily large size. For instance, assembly lines can produce indefinitely large numbers of M&Ms, aspirin tablets, or loaves of bread. Thus, quality process control samples of n items usually come from *effectively infinite* populations. But if a sample comes from a particular batch and we wish to make inferences about that specific batch, we might regard the batch as a finite population. When a population is known to be very large relative to the sample, a statistician may treat the population as infinite.

Rule of Thumb

A population may be treated as infinite when N is at least 20 times n (i.e., when $N/n \geq 20$).

Mini Case
2.1

College Students—You Have a Voice in TV Ratings!

Nielsen Media Research (see www.nielsenmedia.com) conducts random sampling using a panel of 10,000 television households in order to provide viewing information to advertisers and broadcast companies. Advertising agencies use the viewing ratings to decide which programs are best for airing their commercials. Broadcast companies make decisions on advertising rates, which nights to run which shows, and which shows to keep on the air.

In 2006, Nielsen decided to add college students living in dorms to their National People Meter Sample. After monitoring their viewing habits, Nielsen estimated that 636,000 women age 18–24, living in dorms, viewed *Grey's Anatomy* during November 2006. This implied a 50 percent jump in the program ranking and elevated *Grey's Anatomy* to a top spot in the TV rankings. But to calculate their estimates, Nielsen is extrapolating from the viewing habits of *just 130 students* around the country who have agreed to have electronic monitors installed in their dorm rooms. That means that a handful of students can lead to a huge swing in ratings. For example, an estimated 163,000 jump in viewers for *Drawn Together* was based on only 12 people in the survey group who tuned in to the show. Later in this text-book, you will learn how to estimate the *margin of error* in a sample like this. But advertis-ers clearly believe that the information is reliable enough to use in making their decisions (for a discussion of Nielson's margin of error, see *The New York Times,* April 8, 2007, p. 10).

Does Nielsen accept volunteers in their National People Meter Sample? No. According to the Nielsen Web site, the firm draws its samples in a way that offers every American household with a television an equal chance of being selected. They go on to say that "To include volunteers would violate basic laws of random sampling practice and skew our results. A truly representative sample of the population can only be generated using statis-tical methods of selection."

SECTION EXERCISES

connect

2.15 Would you use a sample or a census to measure each of the following? Why? If you are uncertain, explain the issues.
a. The model years of the cars driven by each of your five closest friends.
b. The model years of the cars driven by each student in your statistics class.
c. The model years of the cars driven by each student in your university.
d. The model years of the cars driven by each professor whose classes you are taking.

2.16 Is each of the following a parameter or a statistic? If you are uncertain, explain the issues.
a. The average price/earnings ratio for all 500 stocks in the S&P index.
b. The proportion of all stocks in the S&P 500 index that had negative earnings last year.
c. The proportion of energy-related stocks in portfolios owned by 50 investors.
d. The average rate of return for stock portfolios recommended by 50 brokers.

2.17 Would you use a sample or a census to measure each of the following? Why? If you are uncertain, explain the issues.
a. The mean time battery life of your laptop computer in continuous use.
b. The number of students in your statistics class who brought laptop computers to class today.
c. The average price paid for a laptop computer by students at your university.
d. The percentage of disk space available on laptop computers owned by your five closest friends.

2.18 The target population is all students in your university. You wish to estimate the average current Visa balance for each student. How large would the university student population have to be in order to be regarded as effectively infinite in each of the following samples?
a. A sample of 10 students.
b. A sample of 50 students.
c. A sample of 100 students.

2.5 SAMPLING METHODS

There are two main categories of sampling methods. In **random sampling** items are chosen by randomization or a chance procedure. **Non-random sampling** is less scientific but is sometimes used for expediency. Seven common sampling methods are shown in Table 2.6.

TABLE 2.6	**Seven Sampling Methods**		
Random Samples		**Non-Random Samples**	
Simple Random Sample	Use random numbers to select items from a list (e.g., Visa cardholders).	Judgment Sample	Use expert knowledge to choose "typical" items (e.g., which employees to interview).
Systematic Sample	Select every *k*th item from a list or sequence (e.g., restaurant customers).	Convenience Sample	Use a sample that happens to be available (e.g., ask co-worker opinions at lunch).
Stratified Sample	Select randomly within defined strata (e.g., by age, occupation, gender).	Focus Groups	In-depth dialog with a representative panel of individuals (e.g., iPod users).
Cluster Sample	Like stratified sampling except strata are geographical areas (e.g., zip codes).		

Simple Random Sample

We denote the population size by N and the sample size by n. In a **simple random sample**, every item in the population of N items has the same chance of being chosen in the sample of n items. A physical experiment to accomplish this would be to write each of the N data values on a poker chip, and then to draw n chips from a bowl after stirring it thoroughly. But we can accomplish the same thing if the N population items appear on a numbered list, simply by choosing n integers at random between 1 and N. But we must take care not to allow any bias to creep into the selection process.

A simple random sample is easy to obtain if the population items are in a list or table. For example, suppose we want to select one student at random from a list of 48 students (see Figure 2.4). If you were asked to "use your judgment," you would probably pick a name in the middle, thereby biasing the draw against those individuals at either end of the list. Instead, we rely on **random numbers**. In this example, we used Excel's function =RANDBETWEEN(1,48) to pick a random integer between 1 and 48. The number was 44, so Stephanie was selected. There is no bias since all values from 1 to 48 are *equiprobable* (i.e., equally likely to occur).

FIGURE 2.4

Picking on Stephanie

Random person **44**

1	Adam	17	Haitham	33	Moira
2	Addie	18	Jackie	34	Nathan
3	Anne	19	Jennie	35	Oded
4	Aristo	20	Joel	36	Pablo
5	Balaji	21	Judy	37	Pat
6	Dean	22	Kay	38	Peter
7	Dennis	23	Kristina	39	Randy
8	Diana	24	LaDonna	40	Rick
9	Don	25	Latrice	41	Sarah
10	Ellen	26	Laura	42	Shamel
11	Erik	27	Leah	43	Sid
12	Floyd	28	Lindsay	**44**	**Stephanie**
13	Frances	29	Loretta	45	Stephen
14	Gadis	30	Lou	46	Sylvia
15	Ginnie	31	Majda	47	Tara
16	Giovanni	32	Mario	48	Tim

Random Number Tables   Another method (somewhat obsolete) to select random numbers between 1 and N is to use a table of random digits. A table of random digits has the property that, no matter how we pick our digits (up, down, diagonally, etc.) each digit 0 through 9 is equally likely. Table 2.7 shows 1,000 random digits arranged in 10 columns and 20 rows of five-digit blocks. All we need is a consistent rule for picking the digits.

TABLE 2.7

1,000 Random Digits
RandomDigits

82134	14458	66716	54269	31928	46241	03052	00260	32367	25783
07139	16829	76768	11913	42434	91961	92934	18229	15595	02566
45056	43939	31188	43272	11332	99494	19348	97076	95605	28010
10244	19093	51678	63463	85568	70034	82811	23261	48794	63984
12940	84434	50087	20189	58009	66972	05764	10421	36875	64964
84438	45828	40353	28925	11911	53502	24640	96880	93166	68409
98681	67871	71735	64113	90139	33466	65312	90655	75444	30845
43290	96753	18799	49713	39227	15955	46167	63853	03633	19990
96893	85410	88233	22094	30605	79024	01791	38839	85531	94576
75403	41227	00192	16814	47054	16814	81349	92264	01028	29071
78064	92111	51541	76563	69027	67718	06499	71938	17354	12680
26246	71746	94019	93165	96713	03316	75912	86209	12081	57817
98766	67312	96358	21351	86448	31828	86113	78868	67243	06763
37895	51055	11929	44443	15995	72935	99631	18190	85877	31309
27988	81163	52212	25102	61798	28670	01358	60354	74015	18556
19216	53008	44498	19262	12196	93947	90162	76337	12646	26838
28078	86729	69438	24235	35208	48957	53529	76297	41741	54735
34455	61363	93711	68038	75960	16327	95716	66964	28634	65015
53510	90412	70438	45932	57815	75144	52472	61817	41562	42084
30658	18894	88208	97867	30737	94985	18235	02178	39728	66398

For example, suppose that NilCo wants to award cash "customer loyalty" prizes to 10 of its customers from a list of 875 who made purchases last month. To get 10 three-digit random numbers between 001 and 875, we define *any consistent rule* for moving through the table. For example, we can point a finger at random to choose a starting point. In Table 2.7, we started in the second column in the third row. Our rule is to choose the first three digits of this five-digit block, move to the right one column, down one row, and repeat. When we reach the end of a line, we wrap around to the other side of the table and continue. We discard any number greater than 875 and move on. If we get a duplicate, we continue on. The chosen 10 three-digit random numbers are highlighted in the table:

439, 516, 201, 119, 334, 461, 388, 010, 126, 262

By chance, no number greater than 516 was selected. Without random numbers, you might have an unconscious tendency to try to "cover" the range from 1 to 875 "evenly," but that would *not* be random.

With or Without Replacement?   The same number could occur more than once. If we allow duplicates, we are **sampling with replacement**. Using the bowl analogy, if we throw each chip back in the bowl and stir the contents before the next draw, an item can be chosen again. Duplicates are unlikely when the sample size n is much smaller than the population size N. People instinctively prefer **sampling without replacement** because drawing the same item more than once seems to add nothing to our knowledge. However, using the same sample item more than once does not introduce any *bias* (i.e., no systematic tendency to over- or underestimate whatever parameter we are trying to measure).

Computer Methods   Because computers are easier, we rarely use random number tables. Table 2.8 shows a few alternative ways to choose 10 integers between 1 and 875. All are based on a software algorithm that creates uniform decimal numbers between 0 and 1. Excel's function

TABLE 2.8

Some Ways to Get 10 Random Integers between 1 and 875

Excel—Option A	Enter the Excel function =RANDBETWEEN(1,875) into 10 spreadsheet cells. Press F9 to get a new sample.
Excel—Option B	Enter the function =INT(1+875*RAND()) into 10 spreadsheet cells. Press F9 to get a new sample.
Internet	The Web site www.random.org will give you many kinds of excellent random numbers (integers, decimals, etc).
MINITAB	Use MINITAB's Random Data menu with the Integer option.

=RAND( ) does this, and many pocket calculators have a similar function. We call these *pseudo-random* generators because even the best algorithms eventually repeat themselves (after a cycle of millions of numbers). Thus, a software-based random data encryption scheme could conceivably be broken. To enhance data security, Intel and other firms are examining hardware-based methods (e.g., based on thermal noise or radioactive decay) to prevent patterns or repetition. Fortunately, most applications don't require that degree of randomness. For example, the iPod Shuffle's song choices are not strictly random because its random numbers are generated by an algorithm from a "seed number" that eventually repeats. However, the repeat period is so great that an iPod user would never notice. Excel's and MINITAB's random numbers are good enough for most purposes.

Row/Column Data Arrays   When the data are arranged in a rectangular array, we can choose an item at random by picking a row and column at random. For example, here is a 4 × 3 array containing the names of 12 large general merchandise companies in the United States. We select a random column between 1 and 3 and a random row between 1 and 4, so that every company has the same chance of being chosen. In this case, we used Excel's =RANDBETWEEN function to select row 3 and column 2 (Macy's).

	Col 1	*Col 2*	*Col 3*
Row 1	Big Lots	Fred's	Penney, J.C.
Row 2	Bon-Ton	Kohl's	Sears
Row 3	Dillards	Macy's	Target
Row 4	Dollar Tree	Nordstrom	Tuesday Morning

Randomizing a List   To randomize a list (assuming it is in a spreadsheet) we can insert the Excel function =RAND( ) beside each row. This creates a column of random decimal numbers between 0 and 1. Copy the random numbers and paste them in the same column using Paste Special > Values to "fix" them (otherwise they will keep changing). Then sort all the columns by the random number column, and *voilà*—the list is now random! Figure 2.5 uses this method to randomize an alphabetized list of 12 students. The first *n* items on the randomized list can now be used as a random sample. This method is especially useful when the list is very long (perhaps millions of lines). The first *n* items are a random sample of the entire list, for they are as likely as any others.

Names in Alphabetical Order					Names in Random Order			
Rand	*Name*	*Major*	*Gender*		*Rand*	*Name*	*Major*	*Gender*
0.382091	Claudia	Accounting	F		0.143539	Dave	Human Res	M
0.730061	Dan	Economics	M		0.229854	Marcia	Accounting	F
0.143539	Dave	Human Res	M		0.334449	Ryan	MIS	M
0.906060	Kalisha	MIS	F		0.382091	Claudia	Accounting	F
0.624378	LaDonna	Finance	F		0.402726	Victor	Marketing	M
0.229854	Marcia	Accounting	F		0.431740	Rachel	Oper Mgt	F
0.604377	Matt	Undecided	M		0.604377	Matt	Undecided	M
0.798923	Moira	Accounting	F		0.624378	LaDonna	Finance	F
0.431740	Rachel	Oper Mgt	F		0.730061	Dan	Economics	M
0.334449	Ryan	MIS	M		0.798923	Moira	Accounting	F
0.836594	Tammy	Marketing	F		0.836594	Tammy	Marketing	F
0.402726	Victor	Marketing	M		0.906060	Kalisha	MIS	F

FIGURE 2.5

Randomizing a List
RandomNames

Systematic Sample

Another method of random sampling is to choose every *k*th item from a sequence or list, starting from a randomly chosen entry among the first *k* items on the list. This is called **systematic sampling**. Figure 2.6 shows how to sample every fourth item, starting from item 2, resulting in a sample of *n* = 20 items.

FIGURE 2.6

Systematic Sampling

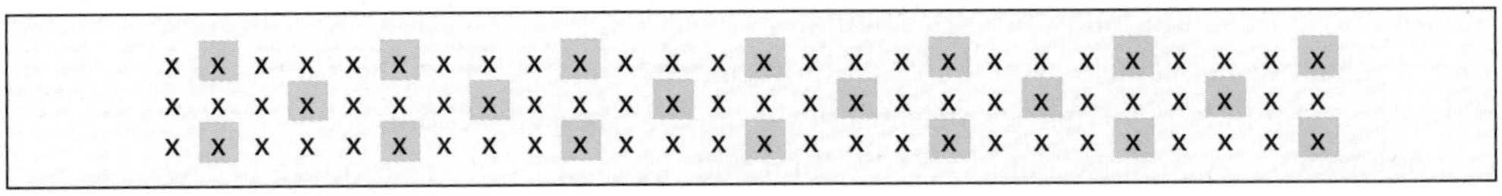

An attraction of systematic sampling is that it can be used with unlistable or infinite populations, such as production processes (e.g., testing every 5,000th light bulb) or political polling (e.g., surveying every tenth voter who emerges from the polling place). Systematic sampling is also well-suited to linearly organized physical populations (e.g., pulling every tenth patient folder from alphabetized filing drawers in a veterinary clinic).

A systematic sample of n items from a population of N items requires that periodicity k be approximately N/n. For example, to choose 25 companies from a list of 501 companies in Mini Case 2.2 (Table 2.9), we chose every twentieth stock ($k = 501/25 \approx 20$). Systematic sampling should yield acceptable results unless patterns in the population happen to recur at periodicity k. For example, weekly pay cycles ($k = 7$) would make it illogical to sample bank

Mini Case   2.2

CEO Compensation

To sample the compensation of the CEOs of the 501 largest companies in the United States listed in *Forbes'* annual survey, take every twentieth company in the alphabetized list, starting (randomly) with the thirteenth company. The starting point (the thirteenth company) is chosen at random. This yields the sample of 25 CEOs, shown in Table 2.9. While it would be very time-consuming to examine all 501 executives, this sample should provide a representative cross-section.

TABLE 2.9	CEO Compensation in 25 Large U.S. Firms*	CEOComp	
Observation	**Firm**	**CEO**	**One-Year Total ($000)**
1	Allegheny Energy	Alan J. Noia	$ 1,530
2	Analog Devices	Jerald G. Fishman	16,550
3	AutoNation	Michael J. Jackson	1,898
4	BJ Services	J. W. Stewart	23,354
5	Cendant	Henry R. Silverman	40,472
6	Coca-Cola Enterprises	Lowry F. Kline	8,725
7	Costco Wholesale	James D. Sinegal	6,078
8	DST Systems	Thomas A. McDonnell	29,644
9	EOG Resources	Mark G. Papa	785
10	Fleming Cos.	Mark S. Hansen	4,476
11	Gillette	James M. Kilts	2,840
12	Hibernia	J. Herbert Boydstun	1,231
13	ITT Industries	Louis J. Giuliano	3,022
14	Laboratory Corp. Amer.	Thomas P. Mac Mahon	10,385
15	Marshall & Ilsley	Dennis J. Kuester	6,510
16	Micron Technology	Steven R. Appleton	949
17	Noble Drilling	James C. Day	5,066
18	Park Place Entertain.	Thomas E. Gallagher	975
19	Principal Financial	J. Barry Griswell	2,321
20	RJ Reynolds Tobacco	Andrew J. Schindler	5,552
21	Smurfit-Stone	Patrick J. Moore	1,549
22	Synovus Financial	James H. Blanchard	1,800
23	Union Pacific	Richard K. Davidson	1,681
24	Visteon	Peter J. Pestillo	1,366
25	Wm. Wrigley, Jr.	William Wrigley, Jr.	1,697

Source: CEO Compensation, *Forbes*, May 13, 2002, pp. 116–38. Copyright © 2005 Forbes Inc. Reprinted by permission.

*Compensation is for the latest fiscal year.

check cashing volume every Friday. A less obvious example would be a machine that stamps a defective part every twelfth cycle due to a bad tooth in a 12-tooth gear, which would make it misleading to rely on a sample of every twelfth part ($k = 12$). But periodicity coincident with k is not typical or expected in most situations.

Stratified Sample

Sometimes we can improve our sample efficiency by utilizing prior information about the population. This method is applicable when the population can be divided into relatively homogeneous subgroups of known size (called *strata*). Within each *stratum,* a simple random sample of the desired size could be taken. Alternatively, a random sample of the whole population could be taken, and then individual strata estimates could be combined using appropriate weights. This procedure, called **stratified sampling**, can reduce cost per observation and narrow the error bounds. For a population with L strata, the population size N is the sum of the stratum sizes: $N = N_1 + N_2 + \cdots + N_L$. The weight assigned to stratum j is $w_j = N_j/N$ (i.e., each stratum is weighted by its known proportion of the population).

To illustrate, suppose we want to estimate smallpox vaccination rates among employees in state government, and we know that our target population (those individuals we are trying to study) is 55 percent male and 45 percent female. Suppose our budget only allows a sample of size 200. To ensure the correct gender balance, we could sample 110 males and 90 females. Alternatively, we could just take a random sample of 200 employees. Although our random sample probably will not contain *exactly* 110 males and 90 females, we can get an overall estimate of vaccination rates by *weighting* the male and female sample vaccination rates using $w_M = 0.55$ and $w_F = 0.45$ to reflect the known strata sizes.

Stratified sampling is widely used in marketing and economic surveys. For example, the Consumer Price Index is a stratified sample of 90,000 items from 364 categories, chosen from about 20,000 retail stores in 85 geographically distributed areas (strata) that are chosen to be as homogeneous as possible. Similarly, to estimate the unemployment rate each month, the Bureau of Labor Statistics conducts a survey of 50,000 households in about 2,000 counties and cities in all 50 states. Data are *stratified* using known weights for factors such as occupation, race, and gender. To ensure continuity yet to allow the panel to rotate, a household is kept in the panel for 4 consecutive months, is out of the survey for 8 months, is included for 4 more months, and finally is replaced by a new household.

Mini Case 2.3

Sampling for Safety

To help automakers and other researchers study the causes of injuries and fatalities in vehicle accidents, the U.S. Department of Transportation developed the National Accident Sampling System (NASS) Crashworthiness Data System (CDS). Because it is impractical to investigate every accident (there were 6,159,000 police-reported accidents in 2005), detailed data is collected in a common format from 24 primary sampling units, chosen to represent all serious police-reported motor vehicle accidents in the United States during the year. Selection of sample accidents is done in three stages: (1) The country is divided into 1,195 geographic areas called Primary Sampling Units (PSUs) grouped into 12 strata based on geographic region. Two PSUs are selected from each stratum using weights roughly proportional to the number of accidents in each stratum. (2) In each sampled PSU, a second stage of sampling is performed using a sample of Police Jurisdictions (PJs) based on the number, severity, and type of accidents in the PJ. (3) The final stage of sampling is the selection of accidents within the sampled PJs. Each reported accident is classified into a stratum based on type of vehicle, most severe injury, disposition of the injured, tow status of the vehicles, and model year of the vehicles. Each team is assigned a fixed number of accidents to investigate each week, governed by the number of researchers on a team. Weights for the strata are assigned to favor a larger percentage of higher severity accidents while ensuring that accidents in the same stratum have the same probability of being selected, regardless of the PSU. The NASS CDS database is administered by the National Center for Statistics and Analysis (NCSA) of the National Highway Traffic Safety Administration (NHTSA). These data are currently helping to improve the government's "5 Star" crashworthiness rating system for vehicles. (*Source:* www-nrd.nhtsa.dot.gov/Pubs/NASS94.PDF)

Cluster Sample

Cluster samples are taken from strata consisting of geographical regions. We divide a region (say, a city) into subregions (say, blocks, subdivisions, or school districts). In one-stage cluster sampling, our sample consists of all elements in each of *k* randomly chosen subregions (or clusters). In two-stage cluster sampling, we first randomly select *k* subregions (clusters) and then choose a random sample of elements within each cluster. Figure 2.7 illustrates how four elements could be sampled from each of three randomly chosen clusters using two-stage cluster sampling.

Because elements within a cluster are proximate, travel time and interviewer expenses are kept to a minimum. Cluster sampling is useful when:

- Population frame and stratum characteristics are not readily available.
- It is too expensive to obtain a simple or stratified sample.
- The cost of obtaining data increases sharply with distance.
- Some loss of reliability is acceptable.

Although cluster sampling is cheap and quick, it is often reasonably accurate because people in the same neighborhood tend to be similar in income, ethnicity, educational background, and so on. Cluster sampling is useful in political polling, surveys of gasoline pump prices, studies of crime victimization, vaccination surveys, or lead contamination in soil. A hospital may contain clusters (floors) of similar patients. A warehouse may have clusters (pallets) of inventory parts. Forest sections may be viewed as clusters to be sampled for disease or timber growth rates.

FIGURE 2.7

Two-Stage Cluster Sampling

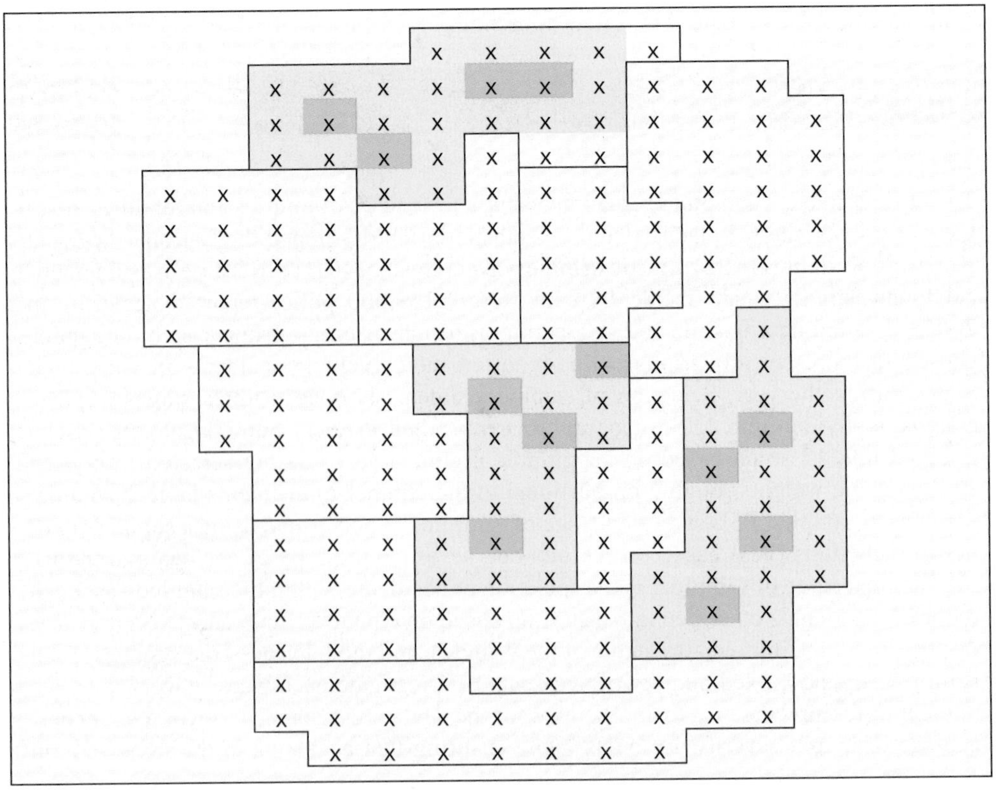

Judgment Sample

Judgment sampling is a nonprobability sampling method that relies on the expertise of the sampler to choose items that are representative of the population. For example, to estimate the corporate spending on research and development (R&D) in the medical equipment industry, we might ask an industry expert to select several "typical" firms. Unfortunately, subconscious biases can affect experts, too. In this context, "bias" does not mean prejudice, but rather *nonrandomness* in the choice. Judgment samples may be the best alternative in some cases, but we can't be sure whether the sample was random. *Quota sampling* is a special kind of judgment sampling, in which the interviewer chooses a certain number of people in each category (e.g., men/women).

Convenience Sample

The sole virtue of **convenience sampling** is that it is quick. The idea is to grab whatever sample is handy. An accounting professor who wants to know how many MBA students would take a summer elective in international accounting can just survey the class she is currently teaching. The students polled may not be representative of all MBA students, but an answer (although imperfect) will be available immediately. A newspaper reporter doing a story on perceived airport security might interview co-workers who travel frequently. An executive might ask department heads if they think nonbusiness Web surfing is widespread.

You might think that convenience sampling is rarely used or, when it is, that the results are used with caution. However, this does not appear to be the case. Since convenience samples often sound the first alarm on a timely issue, their results have a way of attracting attention and have probably influenced quite a few business decisions. The mathematical properties of convenience samples are unknowable, but they do serve a purpose and their influence cannot be ignored.

Focus Groups

A **focus group** is a panel of individuals chosen to be representative of a wider population, formed for open-ended discussion and idea gathering about an issue (e.g., a proposed new product or marketing strategy). Typically 5–10 people are selected, and the interactive discussion lasts 1–2 hours. Participants are usually individuals who do not know each other, but who are prescreened to be broadly compatible yet diverse. A trained moderator guides the focus group's discussion and keeps it on track. Although not a random sampling method, focus groups are widely used, both in business and in social science research, for the insights they can yield beyond "just numbers."

Mini Case   2.4

Scanner Accuracy

Kmart was the first retailer fined in 1997 under Wisconsin's scanner accuracy law because the wrong prices were charged at some stores. A scanner reads a bar code, and then rings up the prices on the cash register. Nine of the 32 Kmart scanners failed random sampling tests. Samples of 50 items per store were taken, and failure was defined as 3 or more scanned at the wrong price. Although the number of overcharges and undercharges were nearly equal, the average overcharge ($2.85) exceeded the average undercharge ($1.00).

In Michigan, the Attorney General's office performs random scanner accuracy tests in 25 stores that represent six national chains. Over time, scanner accuracy has improved, as the error rate declined from 15.2 percent in 1998 to only 3.2 percent in 2001. Scanner errors ranged from zero percent in Target and Mervyn's to 1.8 percent in Sears, 3 percent in Kmart, 5.3 percent in Marshall Field's, and 6 percent in J. C. Penney. When a census is impossible, sampling is an essential tool in enforcing consumer protection laws.

Source: *Detroit Free Press,* October 23, 1997, p. 1E, and November 30, 2001, p. 1C.

Sample Size

The necessary sample size depends on the inherent variability of the quantity being measured and the desired precision of the estimate. For example, the caffeine content of Mountain Dew is fairly consistent because each can or bottle is filled at the factory, so a small sample size would suffice to estimate the mean. In contrast, the amount of caffeine in an individually brewed cup of Bigelow Raspberry Royale tea varies widely because people let it steep for varying lengths of time, so a larger sample would be needed to estimate the mean. The purposes of the investigation, the costs of sampling, the budget, and time constraints are also taken into account in deciding on sample size. Setting the sample size is worth a detailed discussion, found in later chapters.

Sources of Error

No matter how careful you are when conducting a survey, you will encounter potential sources of error. Let's briefly review a few, summarized in Table 2.10.

Nonresponse bias occurs when those who respond have characteristics different from those who don't respond. For example, people with caller ID, answering machines, blocked or unlisted numbers, or cell phones are likely to be missed in telephone surveys. Since these are generally more affluent individuals, their socioeconomic class may be underrepresented in the poll. A special case is **selection bias**, a self-selected sample. For example, a talk show host who invites viewers to take a Web survey about their sex lives will attract plenty of respondents. But those who are willing to reveal details of their personal lives (and who have time to complete the survey) are likely to differ substantially from those who dislike nosy surveys or are too busy (and probably weren't watching the show anyway).

Further, it is easy to imagine that hoax replies will be common to such a survey (e.g., a bunch of college dorm students giving silly answers on a Web survey). **Response error** occurs when respondents deliberately give false information to mimic socially acceptable answers, to avoid embarrassment, or to protect personal information.

Next, **coverage error** occurs when some important segment of the target population is systematically missed. For example, a survey of Notre Dame University alumni will fail to represent noncollege graduates or those who attended public universities. And **measurement error** results when the survey questions do not accurately reveal the construct being assessed, as discussed previously. When the interviewer's facial expressions, tone of voice, or appearance influences the responses data are subject to **interview error**.

Finally, **sampling error** is uncontrollable random error that is inherent in any survey. Even using a probability sampling method, it is possible that the sample will contain unusual responses. This cannot be prevented and is generally undetectable.

TABLE 2.10	Source of Error	Characteristics
Potential Sources of Survey Error	Nonresponse bias	Respondents differ from nonrespondents
	Selection bias	Self-selected respondents are atypical
	Response error	Respondents give false information
	Coverage error	Incorrect specification of frame or population
	Measurement error	Survey instrument wording is biased or unclear
	Interviewer error	Responses influenced by interviewer
	Sampling error	Random and unavoidable

SECTION EXERCISES

connect

2.19 Suppose you want to know the ages of moviegoers who attend *Spiderman III*. What kind of sample is it if you (a) survey the first 20 persons to emerge from the theater, (b) survey every tenth person to emerge from the theater, and (c) survey everyone who is wearing an earring?

2.20 (a) Referring to the previous question, would a simple random sample be possible? Explain. (b) Identify possible flaws and/or strengths in each of the sampling methods suggested in the previous problem. (c) Why might a survey not work at all?

2.21   Below is a 6 × 8 array containing the ages of moviegoers (see file 🎬 **HarryPotter**). Treat this as a population. Select a random sample of 8 moviegoers' ages by using (a) simple random sampling with a random number table, (b) simple random sampling with Excel's =RANDBETWEEN( ) function, (c) systematic sampling, (d) judgment sampling, and (e) convenience sampling. Explain your methods.

32	34	33	12	57	13	58	16
23	23	62	65	35	15	17	20
14	11	51	33	31	13	11	58
23	10	63	34	12	15	62	13
40	11	18	62	64	30	42	20
21	56	11	51	38	49	15	21

2.22   (a) In the previous problem, what was the proportion of all 48 moviegoers who were under age 30? (b) For each of the samples of size $n = 8$ that you took, what was the proportion of moviegoers under age 30? (c) If your samples did not resemble the population, can you suggest why?

2.23   In Excel, type a list containing names for 10 of your friends into cells B1:B10. Choose three names at random by randomizing this list. To do this, enter =RAND( ) into cells A1:A10, copy the random column and paste it using **Paste > Special > Values** to fix the random numbers, and then sort the list by the random column. The first three names are the random sample.

One goal of a statistics course is to help you learn where to find data that might be needed. Fortunately, many excellent sources are widely available, either in libraries or through private purchase. Table 2.11 summarizes a few of them.

The *Statistical Abstract of the United States* is the largest, most general, and widely available annual compendium of facts and figures from public sources. You can purchase it at government bookstores in major cities, order it by mail, or use it for free on the Web. It covers a wide range of cross-sectional data (e.g., states, cities) as well as time series data. Subjects include population, vital statistics, immigration, health, nutrition, education, law enforcement, geography, environment, parks, recreation, elections, government, national defense, social insurance, human services, labor force, income, prices, banking, finance, insurance, communications, energy, science, transportation, agriculture, forests, fisheries, mining, construction, housing, manufactures, and international statistics. No business statistician should be without this reference.

For annual and monthly time series economic data, try the *Economic Report of the President* (*ERP*), which is published every February. The tables in the *ERP* can be downloaded for free in Excel format. Data on cities, counties, and states can be found in the *State and Metropolitan Area Data Book*, published every few years by the Bureau of the Census and available on CD-ROM in many libraries.

Annual almanacs from several major publishers are sold at most bookstores. These include data reprinted from the above sources, but also information on recent events, sports, stock market, elections, Congress, world nations, states, and higher education. One of these almanacs should be on every informed citizen's shelf.

2.6 DATA SOURCES

TABLE 2.11

Useful Data Sources

Type of Data	Examples
U.S. general data	*Statistical Abstract of the United States*
U.S. economic data	*Economic Report of the President*
Almanacs	*World Almanac, Time Almanac*
Periodicals	*Economist, BusinessWeek, Fortune*
Indexes	*The New York Times, The Wall Street Journal*
Databases	Compustat, Citibase, U.S. Census
World data	*CIA World Factbook*
Web	Google, Yahoo!, MSN

Annual surveys of major companies, markets, and topics of business or personal finance are found in magazines such as *BusinessWeek, Consumer Reports, Forbes, Fortune,* and *Money.* Indexes such as the *Business Periodical Index, The New York Times Index,* and *The Wall Street Journal Index* are useful for locating topics. Libraries have Web search engines that can access many of these periodicals in abstract or full-text form.

Specialized computer databases (e.g., CRSP, Compustat, Citibase, U.S. Census) are available (at a price) for research on stocks, companies, financial statistics, and census data. An excellent summary of sources is F. Patrick Butler's *Business Research Sources: A Reference Navigator.* The Web allows us to use search engines (e.g., Google, Yahoo!, MSN) to find information. Sometimes you may get lucky, but Web information is often undocumented, unreliable, or unverifiable. Better information is available through private companies or trade associations, though often at a steep price. Related Reading and Web Data Sources are listed at the end of this chapter.

Often overlooked sources of help are your university librarians. University librarians understand how to find databases and how to navigate databases quickly and accurately. Librarians can help you distinguish between valid and invalid Internet sources and then help you put the source citation in the proper format when writing reports.

2.7
SURVEY RESEARCH

Most survey research follows the same basic steps. These steps may overlap in time:

- Step 1:   State the goals of the research.
- Step 2:   Develop the budget (time, money, staff).
- Step 3:   Create a research design (target population, frame, sample size).
- Step 4:   Choose a survey type and method of administration.
- Step 5:   Design a data collection instrument (questionnaire).
- Step 6:   Pretest the survey instrument and revise as needed.
- Step 7:   Administer the survey (follow up if needed).
- Step 8:   Code the data and analyze it.

Survey Types

Surveys fall into five general categories: mail, telephone, interview, Web, and direct observation. They differ in cost, response rate, data quality, time required, and survey staff training requirements. Table 2.12 lists some common types of surveys and a few of their salient strengths/weaknesses.

Response Rates

Consider the *cost per valid response*. A telephone survey might be cheapest to conduct, but bear in mind that over half the households in some metropolitan areas have unlisted phones, and many have answering machines or call screening. The sample you get may not be very useful in terms of reaching the target population. Telephone surveys (even with random dialing) do lend themselves nicely to cluster sampling (e.g., using each three-digit area code as a cluster and each three-digit exchange as a cluster) to sample somewhat homogeneous populations. Similarly, mail surveys can be clustered by zip code, which is a significant attraction. Web surveys are cheap, but rather uncontrolled. Nonresponse bias is a problem with all of these. Interviews or observational experiments are expensive and labor-intensive, but they may provide higher quality data. Large-scale national research projects (e.g., mental health status of U.S. household members) offer financial incentives to encourage participants who otherwise would not provide information. Research suggests that adjustments can be made for whatever biases may result from such incentives. Table 2.13 offers some tips to conduct successful surveys.

TABLE 2.12

Common Types of Surveys

Type of Survey	Characteristics
Mail	You need a well-targeted and current mailing list (people move a lot). Expect low response rates and nonresponse bias (nonrespondents differ from those who respond). Zip code lists (often costly) are an attractive option to define strata of similar income, education, and attitudes. To encourage participation, a cover letter should clearly explain the uses to which the data will be put. Plan for follow-up mailings.
Telephone	Random dialing yields very low response and is poorly targeted. Purchased phone lists help reach the target population, though a low response rate still is typical (disconnected phones, caller screening, answering machines, work hours, no-call lists). Other sources of nonresponse bias include the growing number of non-English speakers and distrust caused by scams and spams.
Interviews	Interviewing is expensive and time-consuming, yet a trade-off between sample size for high-quality results may still be worth it. Interviewers must be well-trained—an added cost. But interviewers can obtain information on complex or sensitive topics (e.g., gender discrimination in companies, birth control practices, diet and exercise habits).
Web	Web surveys are growing in popularity but are subject to nonresponse bias because they miss those who feel too busy, don't own computers, or distrust your motives (scams and spam). This type of survey works best when targeted to a well-defined interest group on a question of self-interest (e.g., views of CPAs on new Sarbanes-Oxley accounting rules, frequent flyer views on airline security).
Direct Observation	Observation can be done in a controlled setting (e.g., psychology lab) but requires informed consent, which can change behavior. Unobtrusive observation is possible in some nonlab settings (e.g., what percentage of airline passengers carry on more than two bags, what percentage of SUVs carry no passengers, what percentage of drivers wear seat belts).

TABLE 2.13

Survey Guidelines

Planning	What is the purpose of the survey? What do you really need to know? What staff expertise is available? What skills are best obtained externally? What degree of precision is required? How is your budget best spent?
Design	To ensure a good response and useful data, you must invest time and money in designing the survey. Take advantage of many useful books and references so that you do not make unnecessary errors.
Quality	Care in preparation is needed. Glossy printing and advertising have raised people's expectations about quality. A scruffy questionnaire will be ignored. Some surveys (e.g., Web-based) may require special software.
Pilot Test	Questions that are clear to you may be unclear to others. You can pretest the questionnaire on friends or co-workers, but using a small test panel of naive respondents who don't owe you anything is best.
Buy-In	Response rates may be improved by clearly stating the purpose of the survey, offering a token of appreciation (e.g., discount coupon, free gift) or paving the way with endorsements (e.g., from a trusted professional group).
Expertise	Consider working with an outside (or internal) consultant at the early stages, even if you plan to carry out the data collection and tabulation on your own. Early consultation is more cost-effective than waiting until you get in trouble.

Questionnaire Design

You should consider hiring a consultant, at least in the early stages, to help you get your survey off the ground successfully. Alternatively, resources are available on the Web to help you plan a survey. The American Statistical Association (www.amstat.org) offers brochures *What Is a Survey* and *How to Plan a Survey*. Additional materials are available from the Research Industry Coalition, Inc., (www.researchindustry.org) and the Council of American Survey Research Organizations (www.casro.org). Entire books have been written to help you design and administer your own survey (see Related Reading).

The layout must not be crowded (use lots of white space). Begin with very short, clear instructions, stating the purpose, assuring anonymity, and explaining how to submit the completed survey. Questions should be numbered. Divide the survey into sections if the topics fall naturally into distinct areas. Let respondents bypass sections that aren't relevant to them (e.g., "If you answered no to Question 7, skip directly to Question 15"). Include an "escape option" where it seems appropriate (e.g., "Don't know or Does not apply"). Use wording and response scales that match the reading ability and knowledge level of the intended respondents. Pretest and revise. Keep the questionnaire as short as possible. Table 2.14 lists a few common question formats and response scales.

Question Wording

The way a question is asked has a profound influence on the response. For example, in a *Wall Street Journal* editorial, Fred Barnes tells of a *Reader's Digest* poll that asked two similar questions:

Version 1:   I would be disappointed if Congress cut its funding for public television.

Version 2:   Cuts in funding for public television are justified to reduce federal spending.

The same 1,031 people were polled in both cases. Version 1 showed 40 percent in favor of cuts, while version 2 showed 52 percent in favor of cuts. The margin of error was ±3.5 percent (in "How to Rig a Poll," June 14, 1995, p. A18). To "rig" the poll, emotional overlays or

---

TABLE 2.14

Question Format and Response Scale

Type of Question	Example
Open-ended	Briefly describe your job goals.
Fill-in-the-blank	How many times did you attend formal religious services during the last year? _____ times
Check boxes	Which of these statistics packages have you used? ❑ SAS ❑ Visual Statistics ❑ SPSS ❑ MegaStat ❑ Systat ❑ MINITAB
Ranked choices	Please evaluate your dining experience: |	Excellent	Good	Fair	Poor
Food	❑	❑	❑	❑
Service	❑	❑	❑	❑
Ambiance	❑	❑	❑	❑
Cleanliness	❑	❑	❑	❑
Overall	❑	❑	❑	❑	
Pictograms	What do you think of the president's economic policies? (circle one) ☺ ☺ ☺ ☹ ☹
Likert scale	Statistics is a difficult subject. Strongly Agree / Slightly Agree / Neither Agree Nor Disagree / Slightly Disagree / Strongly Disagree ❑ ❑ ❑ ❑ ❑

"loaded" mental images can be attached to the question. In fact, it is often difficult to ask a neutral question without any context. For example:

Version 1:   Shall state taxes be cut?

Version 2:   Shall state taxes be cut, if it means reducing highway maintenance?

Version 3:   Shall state taxes be cut, if it means firing teachers and police?

An unconstrained choice (version 1) makes tax cuts appear to be a "free lunch," while versions 2 and 3 require the respondent to envision the consequences of a tax cut. An alternative is to use version 1 but then ask the respondent to list the state services that should be cut to balance the budget after the tax cut.

Another problem in wording is to make sure you have covered all the possibilities. For example, how does a widowed independent voter answer questions like these?

Are you married?	What is your party preference?
❑ Yes	❑ Democrat
❑ No	❑ Republican

Overlapping classes or unclear categories are a problem. What if your father is deceased or is 45 years old?

How old is your father?

❑ 35–45   ❑ 45–55   ❑ 55–65   ❑ 65 or older

Coding and Data Screening

Survey responses usually are coded numerically (e.g., 1 = male, 2 = female) although some software packages can also tabulate text variables (nominal data) and use them in certain kinds of statistical tests. Most packages require you to denote missing values by a special character (e.g., blank, period, or asterisk). If too many entries on a given respondent's questionnaire are flawed or missing, you may decide to discard the entire response.

Other data screening issues include multiple responses (i.e., the respondent chose two responses where one was expected), outrageous replies on fill-in-the-blank questions (e.g., a respondent who claims to work 640 hours a week), "range" answers (e.g., 10–20 cigarettes smoked per day), or inconsistent replies (e.g., a 55-year-old respondent who claims to receive Medicare benefits). Sometimes a follow-up is possible, but in anonymous surveys you must make the best decisions you can about how to handle anomalous data. Be sure to document your data-coding decisions—not only for the benefit of others but also in case you are asked to explain how you did it (it is easy to forget after a month or two, when you have moved on to other projects).

Data File Format

Data usually are entered into a spreadsheet or database. A "flat file" is an $n \times m$ matrix. Specifically, each column is a variable (m columns) and each row is a subject (n rows).

Subject	Variable 1	Variable 2	...	Variable m
1	XXX	XXX	...	XXX
2	XXX	XXX	...	XXX
3	XXX	XXX	...	XXX
...	...	...	...	...
n	XXX	XXX	...	XXX

Spreadsheets may offer enough statistical power to handle your needs (particularly if you have an add-in like MegaStat for Excel). But spreadsheets are a general tool with limited features. You may prefer to use a professional statistical package that is designed for statistical analysis (e.g., MINITAB, SPSS, SyStat, SAS, etc.). You can copy your spreadsheet data and paste it into columns in the statistical software package, which will store the data in its own proprietary format.

Advice on Copying Data

If your data set contains commas (e.g., 42,586), dollar signs (e.g., $14.88), or percents (e.g., 7.5%) your statistics package (e.g., MINITAB or SPSS) may treat the data as text. A numerical variable may only contain the digits 0–9, a decimal point, and a minus sign. Format the data column as plain numbers with the desired number of decimal places *before* you copy the data to whatever package you are using. Excel can display a value such as 32.8756 as 32.9 if you set only one decimal digit, but it is the *displayed* number that is copied, so your Excel statistics may not agree with the package you are using.

SECTION EXERCISES

connect

2.24   What sources of error might you encounter if you want to know (a) about the dating habits of college men, so you go to a dorm meeting and ask students how many dates they have had in the last year; (b) how often people attend religious services, so you stand outside a particular church on Sunday and ask entering individuals how often they attend; (c) how often people eat at McDonald's, so you stand outside a particular McDonald's and ask entering customers how often they eat at McDonald's?

2.25   What kind of survey (mail, telephone, interview, Web, direct observation) would you recommend for each of the following purposes, and why? What problems might be encountered?
a. To estimate the proportion of students at your university who would prefer a Web-based statistics class to a regular lecture.
b. To estimate the proportion of students at your university who carry backpacks to class.
c. To estimate the proportion of students at your university who would be interested in taking a two-month summer class in international business with tours of European factories.
d. To estimate the proportion of U.S. business graduates who have taken a class in international business.

2.26   What kind of survey (mail, telephone, interview, Web, direct observation) would you recommend that a small laundry and dry cleaning business use for each of the following purposes, and why? What problems might be encountered?
a. To estimate the proportion of customers preferring opening hours at 7 A.M. instead of 8 A.M.
b. To estimate the proportion of customers who have only laundry and no dry cleaning.
c. To estimate the proportion of residents in the same zip code who spend more than $20 a month on dry cleaning.
d. To estimate the proportion of its seven employees who think it is too hot inside the building.

2.27   What would be the difference in student responses to the two questions shown?

Version 1:   I would prefer that tuition be reduced.

Version 2:   Cuts in tuition are a good idea even if some classes are canceled.

2.28   What problems are evident in the wording of these two questions?

What is your race?	What is your religious preference?
❑ White	❑ Christian
❑ Black	❑ Jewish

Mini Case   2.5

Roles of Colleges

A survey of public opinion on the role of colleges was conducted by *The Chronicle of Higher Education*. The survey utilized 1,000 telephone interviews of 20 minutes each, using a random selection of men and women aged 25 through 65. It was conducted February 25, 2004. The survey was administered by TMR Inc. of Broomall, Pennsylvania. Data were collected and analyzed by GDA Integrated Services, a market research firm in Old Saybrook, Connecticut. Table 2.15 shows selected results.

The Likert-type scale labels are weighted toward the positive, which is common when the survey items (roles for colleges in this case) are assumed to be potentially important and there is little likelihood of a strong negative response. Respondents were also asked for demographic information. Fifty-eight percent were women and 42 percent were men, coming from all states except Alaska and Hawaii. Eleven percent were African American (similar to the national average) but only 6 percent were Hispanic (about 8 percent below the national average). The under-representation of Hispanics was due to language barriers, illustrating one difficulty faced by surveys. However, the respondents' incomes, religious affiliations, and political views were similar to the general U.S. population. The random selection method was not specified. Note that firms that specialize in survey sampling generally have access to commercial lists and use their own proprietary methods.

TABLE 2.15	**Important Roles for a College to Perform (*n* = 1,000 interviews)**				
Role	*Very Important*	*Important*	*Somewhat Important*	*Not Important*	*No Answer*
Top three roles (percent of respondents)					
Prepare its undergraduate students for a career	70	22	7	1	0
Prepare students to be responsible citizens	67	18	11	3	0
Provide education for adults so they qualify for better jobs	66	21	11	2	0

Source: *The Chronicle of Higher Education,* May 7, 2004. Copyright © 2004. Reprinted with permission. Percents may not sum to 100 due to rounding.

CHAPTER SUMMARY

A **data set** is an array with *n* rows and *m* columns. Data sets may be **univariate** (one variable), **bivariate** (two variables), or **multivariate** (three or more variables). There are two basic data types: **categorical data** (categories that are described by labels) or **numerical** (meaningful numbers). Numerical data are **discrete** if the values are integers or can be counted or **continuous** if any interval can contain more data values. **Nominal** measurements are names, **ordinal** measurements are ranks, **interval** measurements have meaningful distances between data values, and **ratio** measurements have meaningful ratios and a zero reference point. **Time series** data are observations measured at *n* different points in time or over sequential time intervals, while **cross-sectional** data are observations among *n* entities such as individuals, firms, or geographic regions. Among **probability samples, simple random** samples pick items from a list using random numbers, **systematic** samples take every *k*th item, **cluster** samples select geographic regions, and **stratified** samples take into account known population proportions. **Nonprobability** samples include convenience or judgment samples, gaining time but sacrificing randomness. **Focus groups** give in-depth information. **Survey design** requires attention to question **wording** and **scale definitions**. **Survey techniques** (mail, telephone, interview, Web, direct observation) depend on time, budget, and the nature of the questions and are subject to various sources of error.

KEY TERMS

binary variable, *27*
bivariate data sets, *26*
categorical data, *26*
census, *33*
cluster sample, *42*
coding, *27*
continuous data, *27*
convenience sampling, *43*
coverage error, *44*
cross-sectional data, *32*
data, *25*
data set, *25*
discrete data, *27*
focus group, *43*
individual, *25*
interval data, *30*
interviewer error, *44*

judgment sampling, *43*
Likert scale, *30*
measurement error, *44*
multivariate data sets, *26*
nominal data, *28*
non-random sampling, *36*
nonresponse bias, *44*
numerical data, *26*
observation, *25*
ordinal data, *29*
parameter, *33*
population, *33*
random numbers, *37*
random sampling, *36*
ratio data, *31*
response error, *44*
sample, *33*

sampling error, *44*
sampling frame, *35*
sampling with replacement, *38*
sampling without replacement, *38*
selection bias, *44*
simple random sample, *37*
statistics, *33*
stratified sampling, *41*
subject, *25*
systematic sampling, *39*
target population, *35*
time series data, *32*
univariate data sets, *26*
variable, *25*

CHAPTER REVIEW

1. Define (a) data, (b) data set, (c) subject, and (d) variable.

2. How do business data differ from scientific experimental data?

3. Distinguish (a) univariate, bivariate, and multivariate data; (b) discrete and continuous data; (c) numerical and categorical data.

4. Define the four measurement levels and give an example of each.

5. Explain the difference between cross-sectional data and time series data.

6. (a) List three reasons why a census might be preferred to a sample; (b) List three reasons why a sample might be preferred to a census.

7. (a) What is the difference between a parameter and a statistic? (b) What is a target population?

8. (a) List four methods of random sampling. (b) List two methods of non-random sampling. (c) Why would we ever use non-random sampling? (d) Why is sampling usually done without replacement?

9. List five (a) steps in a survey, (b) issues in survey design, (c) survey types, (d) question scale types, and (e) sources of error in surveys.

10. List advantages and disadvantages of the different types of surveys.

CHAPTER EXERCISES

DATA TYPES

connect

2.29 Which type of data (categorical, discrete numerical, continuous numerical) is each of the following variables? Explain. If there is ambiguity, explain why.
a. Age of a randomly chosen tennis player in the Wimbledon tennis tournament.
b. Nationality of a randomly chosen tennis player in the Wimbledon tennis tournament.
c. Number of double-faults in a randomly chosen tennis game at Wimbledon.
d. Number of spectators at a randomly chosen Wimbledon tennis match.
e. Water consumption (liters) by a randomly chosen Wimbledon player during a match.

2.30 Which type of data (nominal, ordinal, interval, ratio) is each of the following variables? Explain.
a. "Seed" (e.g., 20 of 128) of a randomly chosen tennis player in the Wimbledon tournament.
b. Noise level 100 meters from the Dan Ryan Expressway at a randomly chosen moment.
c. Number of occupants in a randomly chosen commuter vehicle on the San Diego Freeway.
d. Number of annual office visits by a particular Medicare subscriber.
e. Daily caffeine consumption by a 6-year-old child.

2.31 (a) Give *two* original examples of discrete data. (b) Give *two* original examples of continuous data. In each case, explain and identify any ambiguities that might exist. *Hint:* Do not restrict yourself to published data. Consider data describing your own life (e.g., your sports performance or financial or academic data). You need *not* list all the data, merely describe them and show a few typical data values.

2.32 (a) Give *two* original examples of time series data. (b) Give *two* original examples of cross-sectional data. In each case, identify the unit of observation carefully. If the data are both cross-sectional and time series, explain why. *Hint:* Do not restrict yourself to published data, and consider data describing your own life (e.g., sports performance or financial data). You need *not* list any data, merely describe them and perhaps show a few typical data values.

2.33 Below are 15 questions from a survey that was administered to a sample of MBA students (see *LearningStats,* Cross-Sectional Data, Surveys). Answers were recorded on paper in the blank at the left of each question. For each question, state the data type (categorical, discrete numerical, or continuous numerical) and measurement level (nominal, ordinal, interval, ratio). Explain your reasoning. If there is doubt, discuss the alternatives.

_____	Q1	What is your gender? (Male = 0, Female = 1)
_____	Q2	What is your approximate undergraduate college GPA? (1.0 to 4.0)
_____	Q3	About how many hours per week do you expect to work at an outside job this semester?
_____	Q4	What do you think is the ideal number of children for a married couple?
_____	Q5	On a 1 to 5 scale, which best describes your parents? 1 = Mother clearly dominant ↔ 5 = Father clearly dominant
_____	Q6	On a 1 to 5 scale, assess the current job market for your undergraduate major. 1 = Very bad ↔ 5 = Very good
_____	Q7	During the last month, how many times has your schedule been disrupted by car trouble?

_____ Q8   About how many years of college does the more-educated one of your parents have? (years)

_____ Q9   During the last year, how many traffic tickets (excluding parking) have you received?

_____ Q10   Which political orientation most nearly fits you? (1 = Liberal, 2 = Middle-of-Road, 3 = Conservative)

_____ Q11   What is the age of the car you usually drive? (years)

_____ Q12   About how many times in the past year did you attend formal religious services?

_____ Q13   How often do you read a daily newspaper? (0 = Never, 1 = Occasionally, 2 = Regularly)

_____ Q14   Can you conduct simple transactions in a language other than English? (0 = No, 1 = Yes)

_____ Q15   How often do you exercise (aerobics, running, etc)? (0 = Not At All, 1 = Sometimes, 2 = Regularly)

SAMPLING METHODS

2.34 Would you use a sample or a census to measure each of the following? Why? If you are uncertain, explain the issues.
a. The number of cans of Campbell's soup on your local supermarket's shelf today at 6:00 P.M.
b. The proportion of soup sales last week in Boston that was sold under the Campbell's brand.
c. The proportion of Campbell's brand soup cans in your family's pantry.
d. The number of workers currently employed by Campbell Soup Company.

2.35 Is each of the following a parameter or a statistic? If you are uncertain, explain the issues.
a. The number of cans of Campbell's soup sold last week at your local supermarket.
b. The proportion of all soup in the United States that was sold under the Campbell's brand last year.
c. The proportion of Campbell's brand soup cans in the family pantries of 10 students.
d. The total earnings of workers employed by Campbell Soup Company last year.

2.36 You can test Excel's algorithm for selecting random integers with a simple experiment. Enter =RANDBETWEEN(1,2) into cell A1 and then copy it to cells A1:E20. This creates a data block of 100 cells containing either a one or a two. In cell G1 type =COUNTIF(A1:E20,"=1") and in cell G2 type =COUNTIF(A1:E20,"=2"). Highlight cells G1 and G2 and use Excel's Chart Wizard to create a bar chart. Click on the vertical axis scale and set the lower limit to 0 and upper limit to 100. You will see something like the example shown below. Then hold down the F9 key and observe the chart. Are you convinced that, on average, you are getting about 50 ones and 50 twos? *Ambitious Students:* Generalize this experiment to integers 1 through 5.   **RandBetween**

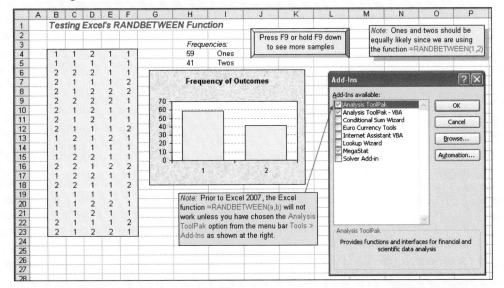

2.37 (a) To study profitability, which variables in the Fortune 1000 data set following could be used to *stratify* the sample? Name the strata for each. (b) Why might stratification be important if we wanted to study average profitability for both industries combined? (c) The Fortune 1000 list had 11 apparel companies and 39 chemical companies. If we just used the 20 companies here to estimate average profitability, what errors might we commit?

Profitability of 20 Selected Companies from the 2003 Fortune 1000   🐝   20Firms

Company	Profit as % of Revenue	Industry	Employees (000)
Ashland	1	Chemicals	15 and Up
Cabot	4	Chemicals	Under 15
Dow Chemical	5	Chemicals	15 and Up
DuPont	4	Chemicals	15 and Up
Jones Apparel Group	8	Apparel	15 and Up
Kellwood	3	Apparel	15 and Up
Levi Strauss	−9	Apparel	Under 15
Liz Claiborne	7	Apparel	15 and Up
Lubrizol	4	Chemicals	Under 15
Nike	4	Apparel	15 and Up
Phillips Van Heusen	1	Apparel	Under 15
Polo Ralph Lauren	7	Apparel	Under 15
PPG Industries	6	Chemicals	15 and Up
Reebok International	5	Apparel	Under 15
Rohm & Haas	4	Chemicals	15 and Up
Scotts	5	Chemicals	Under 15
Terra Industries	−1	Chemicals	Under 15
VF	8	Apparel	15 and Up
W.R. Grace	−3	Chemicals	Under 15
Warnaco Group	159	Apparel	Under 15

2.38   The General Accounting Office conducted random testing of retail gasoline in Michigan, Missouri, Oregon, and Tennessee. The study concluded that 49 percent of gasoline nationwide is mislabeled by more than one-half of an octane point. (a) What kind of sampling technique was most likely to have been used in this study? Why not the others? (b) Is the population finite or infinite? (Data are from *Detroit Free Press,* April 27, 1990, p. 1A.)

2.39   What sampling method would you use to estimate the percent of automobile owners who have radar detectors nationwide? Suggest several alternative methods, and discuss the strengths and weaknesses of each. Is a census possible?

2.40   Aflatoxin is the generic name for a family of natural poisons produced by the mold *aspergillus flavus,* which grows on peanuts and grains. Lab tests show that aflatoxin is a potent carcinogen. (a) What sampling method would you use to estimate the aflatoxin in brand-name and fresh-ground peanut butter sold in grocery stores nationwide to see whether the samples violate the U.S. Food and Drug Administration guidelines of 20 parts per billion (ppb)? (b) What is the sampling frame? Is the population finite or infinite? (c) Is a census possible? (See *Consumer Reports* 55, no. 9 [September 1990], p. 591.)

2.41   Arsenic (a naturally occurring, poisonous metal) in home water wells is a common threat. (a) What sampling method would you use to estimate the arsenic levels in wells in a rural county to see whether the samples violate the EPA limit of 10 parts per billion (ppb)? (b) Is the population finite or infinite? (c) Is a census possible? (See *Popular Science,* February 2002, p. 24.)

2.42   In the aftermath of the 2003 SARS outbreak in Toronto, a survey firm Wirthlin Worldwide of Reston, Virginia, found that 95 percent of men and 97 percent of women using restrooms at Toronto International Airport during August 2003 washed their hands with soap and water. At the other airports studied (O'Hare in Chicago, Kennedy in New York, Dallas/Ft. Worth, Miami, and San Francisco) the percentages of hand-washers ranged from 62 to 80 percent for men and from 59 to 92 for women. (a) Could a census have been used for this type of study? (b) Is the population finite or infinite? (c) Discuss what kind of sampling was probably used to study these questions. (d) How do you think the data were collected? (e) What biases or difficulties might be encountered? (Data are from *Science News* 164, no. 14 [October 2003], p. 222.)

2.43   How often are "fresh wild salmon" really farm-bred? Newspaper reporters visited eight stores in New York City and brought samples of salmon sold as "wild" to a laboratory. The results showed that 6 of the 8 samples were actually farm-bred, based on analysis of pigments known as carotenoids. (a) What kind of sampling method would you suppose was used? (b) If it was not a true random sample, does this invalidate the conclusion? (See *The New York Times,* April 10, 2005.)

2.44   The average American male wears a size 10 shoe and spends 4 hours a year tying a tie. The average American female college student owns 3.5 pairs of jeans. The average American laughs 15 times daily, swallows 215 aspirin tablets a year, and has a dog weighing 32 pounds. (a) Choose one of these estimates. How do you suppose it was derived? (b) What sampling method would *you* use to update each of these statistics? What problems would you anticipate? (c) Could a census be used? (d) Are the populations finite or infinite? (Data are from Mike Feinsilber and William B. Mead, *American Averages: Amazing Facts of Everyday Life* [Doubleday-Dolphin, 1980].)

2.45 Would you expect Noodles & Company to use a sample or census to measure each of the following? Explain.

a. The annual average weekly revenue of each Noodles restaurant.

b. The average number of weekly lunch visits by customers.

c. The customer satisfaction rating of a new dessert.

d. The number of weeks in a year that a restaurant sells more bottled beverages than fountain drinks.

2.46 *Money Magazine* published an annual list of major stock funds. In 2003, the list contained 1,699 funds. What method would you recommend to obtain a sample of 20 stock funds to estimate the 10-year percent return? If more than one method is acceptable, discuss the strengths and weaknesses of each. (Data are from *Money* 32, no. 2 [February 2003], p. 166.)

2.47 Examine each of the following statistics. Which sampling method was most likely to have been used and why? What degree of accuracy would you imagine for each statistic? Why?

a. A survey showed that 30 percent of U.S. businesses have fired an employee for inappropriate Web surfing, such as gambling, watching porn, or shopping (*Popular Science,* January 2007, p. 37).

b. Surveyed doctors report that 59 percent of patients do not follow their prescribed treatment (*Consumer Reports* 72, no. 2 [February 2007] p. 35).

c. The Internal Revenue Service reports that, based on a sample of individual taxpayers, 80 percent of those who failed to pay what they owed did so through honest errors or misinterpretation of the tax code (*The Wall Street Journal,* October 23, 2006, p. A4).

d. In Spain, per capita consumption of cigarettes is 2,274 compared with 1,230 in the United States (*The Wall Street Journal,* March 23, 2006, p. B1).

e. The estimated number of illegal immigrants who are not working is 3.9 million (*The New York Times,* April 2, 2006, p. 3).

2.48 According to a recent study, radar detector users have a lower accident rate than non-users. Moreover, detector users seem to be better citizens. The study found that detector users wear their seatbelts more and even vote more than non-users. (a) Can you suggest potential sources of coverage error? Nonresponse bias? Measurement error? (b) Do you agree with the conclusion that radar detector users are better citizens? Explain.

2.49 Prior to starting a recycling program, a city decides to measure the quantity of garbage produced by single-family homes in various neighborhoods. This experiment will require weighing garbage on the day it is set out. (a) What sampling method would you recommend, and why? (b) Why not the others? (c) What would be a potential source of sample error?

2.50 As a statistics project, a student examined every cigarette butt along the sidewalk and curb along one block near his home. Of 47 identifiable butts, 22 were Marlboro. (a) What sampling method is this (if any)? (b) Is it correct to infer that 47 percent of all smokers prefer Marlboro? (c) What inferences *would* be appropriate? (d) What potential sources of error are present in this sample?

2.51 Devise a practical sampling method (not necessarily one of those mentioned in this chapter) to collect data to estimate each parameter.

a. Mean length of TV commercials during Monday night NFL games.

b. Percentage of peanuts in cans of Planter's Mixed Nuts.

c. Percentage of bank mortgages issued to first-time borrowers.

d. Mean winner-loser margin in NCAA Division I regular season games.

e. Percentage of institutional holdings of publicly traded stocks in the United States.

2.52 Devise a practical sampling method (not necessarily one of those mentioned in this chapter) to collect data to estimate each parameter.

a. Percentage of an HMO's patients who make more than five office visits per year.

b. Percentage of commuters on your local freeway who drive alone.

c. Noise level (decibels) in neighborhoods 100 meters from a certain freeway.

d. Average flight departure delay for Northwest Airlines in Minneapolis.

e. Average price of gasoline in your area.

2.53 (a) If the goal is to estimate the price of a particular brand of soft drink at various stores in your county, suggest several strata that might be relevant to choose the stores. (b) Suggest a feasible sampling method (not necessarily one of the standard ones).

2.54   What kind of bugs are killed by "mosquito zappers"? Prof. Douglas Tallamy, an entomologist at the University of Delaware, suspected that most of the carcasses were not mosquitoes. With the help of high school student volunteers, he analyzed 13,789 dead insects from six zappers from people's houses in suburban Newark, Delaware. The final count was only 18 mosquitoes and 13 other biting flies, or about 0.002 of the total. (a) Is there any alternative to sampling in this case? (b) What kind of stratification might be needed to generalize this experiment to the United States as a whole? (Data are from *Scientific American* 276, no. 6 [June 1997], p. 30.)

2.55   To protect baby scallops and ensure the survival of the species, the U.S. Fisheries and Wildlife Service requires that an average scallop must weigh at least 1/36 pound. The harbormaster at a Massachusetts port randomly selected 18 bags of scallops from 11,000 bags on an arriving vessel. From each bag, agents took a large scoop of scallops, separated and weighed the meat, and divided by the number of scallops in the scoop, finding a mean weight of 1/39 pound. (a) Is there any alternative to sampling in this case? (b) What kind of sampling method do you suppose was used to select the 18 bags? (Data are from *Interfaces* 25, no. 2 [March-April 1995], p. 18.)

2.56   *U.S. News & World Report* (March 17, 2003) reports that the U.S. Food and Drug Administration (FDA) estimates that swordfish contains an average of 1.00 parts per million (ppm) of mercury, which exceeds the FDA guideline of 0.20 ppm. What kind of sampling method do you suppose was used to arrive at the swordfish estimate? Would more than one method be appropriate? Could a census be done? Explain.

2.57   A survey of 500 potential customers for new vehicles across the United States indicated that 37 percent expected their next vehicle to be an SUV. What kind of sampling method do you suppose was used to arrive at this estimate? Why not the others? (Data are from *Detroit Free Press,* April 3, 2002, p. 3F.)

2.58   Blood lead levels exceeding 10 micrograms per deciliter have been shown to be harmful to mental and physical development in children. The U.S. Centers for Disease Control and Prevention in Atlanta say that about 500,000 children in the U.S. have blood concentrations of lead higher than this level. (a) Which sampling method do you suppose was used to measure blood levels of lead in U.S. children to reach this conclusion? (b) Which sampling methods would be infeasible in this case?

2.59   Households can sign up for a telemarketing "no-call list." How might households who sign up differ from those who don't? What biases might this create for telemarketers promoting (a) financial planning services, (b) carpet cleaning services, and (c) vacation travel packages?

2.60   "When we were kids, nobody wore seat belts or bike helmets. We used lead-based paint and didn't install ground-fault circuit protectors in our electrical circuits. Yet we survived." What kind of sampling bias(es) does this statement illustrate?

SURVEYS AND SCALES

2.61   Insurance companies are rated by several rating agencies. The Fitch 20-point scale is AAA, AA+, AA, AA−, A+, A, A−, BBB+, BBB, BBB−, BB+, BB, BB−, B+, B, B−, CCC+, CCC, CCC−, DD. (a) What level of measurement does this scale use? (b) To assume that the scale uses interval measurements, what assumption is required? (Scales are from *Weiss Ratings Guide to HMOs and Health Insurers,* Summer 2003, p. 15.)

2.62   Suggest response check boxes for these questions. In each case, what difficulties do you encounter as you try to think of appropriate check boxes?
a. Where are you employed?
b. What is the biggest issue facing the next U.S. president?
c. Are you happy?

2.63   Suggest both a Likert scale question and a response scale to measure the following:
a. A student's rating of a particular statistics professor.
b. A voter's satisfaction with the president's economic policy.
c. An HMO patient's perception of waiting time to see a doctor.

2.64   A survey by the National Abortion Rights Action League showed that 68 percent favored keeping abortion legal. A survey by the National Right to Life found that 53 percent opposed abortion. (a) How could these contradictory results be reconciled? (b) Write a question on abortion that favors a "yes" reply. Then write a question on abortion that favors a "no" reply. (c) Try to write a "neutral" question on abortion. (Data are from *Detroit Free Press,* February 18, 1992, p. 1C.)

2.65   A Web-based poll on newsweek.com asked *Newsweek* readers the question shown below. Do you consider the wording of the responses to be neutral? Can you suggest alternative response wording? (From *Newsweek,* May 8, 2002, p. 6.)

Should the Boy Scouts be allowed to exclude gays?
1. No, it is wrong to discriminate.
2. No, but they should have a "don't ask, don't tell" policy regarding gays.
3. Yes, as a private group, they can determine whom they want to admit.
4. Yes, gays compromise the Scouts' moral code.

2.66   What level of measurement (nominal, ordinal, interval, ratio) is appropriate for the movie rating system that you see in *TV Guide* (☆, ☆☆, ☆☆☆, ☆☆☆☆)? Explain your reasoning.

2.67   A survey by the American Automobile Association is shown below. (a) What kind of response scale is this? (b) Suggest an alternative response scale. (Survey question from *Michigan Living,* December 1994. Copyright © Automobile Association of America. Used with permission.)

New drivers under 18 should be required to complete additional hours of supervised driving beyond that provided in driver education.
❑ Strongly agree   ❑ Strongly disagree
❑ Agree   ❑ Undecided
❑ Disagree

2.68   A tabletop survey by a restaurant asked the question shown below. (a) What kind of response scale is this? (b) Suggest an alternative response scale that would be more sensitive to differences in opinion. (c) Suggest possible sources of bias in this type of survey.

Were the food and beverage presentations appealing?
❑ Yes
❑ No

SAMPLING EXPERIMENTS

2.69   Below are 64 names of employees at NilCo. Colors denote different departments (finance, marketing, purchasing, engineering). Sample eight names from the display shown by using (a) simple random sampling, (b) sequential sampling, and (c) cluster sampling. Try to ensure that every name has an equal chance of being picked. Which sampling method seems most appropriate?
🐚   **PickEight**

Floyd	Sid	LaDonna	Tom	Mabel	Nicholas	Bonnie	Deepak
Nathan	Ginnie	Mario	Claudia	Dmitri	Kevin	Blythe	Dave
Lou	Tim	Peter	Jean	Mike	Jeremy	Chad	Doug
Loretta	Erik	Jackie	Juanita	Molly	Carl	Buck	Janet
Anne	Joel	Moira	Marnie	Ted	Greg	Duane	Amanda
Don	Gadis	Balaji	Al	Takisha	Dan	Ryan	Sam
Graham	Scott	Lorin	Vince	Jody	Brian	Tania	Ralph
Bernie	Karen	Ed	Liz	Erika	Marge	Gene	Pam

2.70   From the display below pick five cards (without replacement) by using random numbers. Explain your method. Why would the other sampling methods not work well in this case?

A ♠	A ♥	A ♣	A ♦
K ♠	K ♥	K ♣	K ♦
Q ♠	Q ♥	Q ♣	Q ♦
J ♠	J ♥	J ♣	J ♦
10 ♠	10 ♥	10 ♣	10 ♦
9 ♠	9 ♥	9 ♣	9 ♦
8 ♠	8 ♥	8 ♣	8 ♦
7 ♠	7 ♥	7 ♣	7 ♦
6 ♠	6 ♥	6 ♣	6 ♦
5 ♠	5 ♥	5 ♣	5 ♦
4 ♠	4 ♥	4 ♣	4 ♦
3 ♠	3 ♥	3 ♣	3 ♦
2 ♠	2 ♥	2 ♣	2 ♦

2.71   Treating this textbook as a population, select a sample of 10 pages at random by using (a) simple random sampling, (b) systematic sampling, (c) cluster sampling, and (d) judgment sampling. Explain your methodology carefully in each case. (e) Which method would you recommend to estimate the mean number of formulas per page? Why not the others?

2.72   Photocopy the exhibit below (omit these instructions) and show it to a friend or classmate. Ask him/her to choose a number at random and write it on a piece of paper. Collect the paper. Repeat for *at least* 20 friends/classmates. Tabulate the results. Were all the numbers chosen equally often? If not, which were favored or avoided? Why? *Hint:* Review section 2.6.   ✎ **PickOne**

0	11	17	22
8	36	14	18
19	28	6	41
12	3	5	0

2.73   Ask each of 20 friends or classmates to choose a whole number between 1 and 5. Tabulate the results. Do the results seem random? If not, can you think of any reasons?

Web Data Sources

Source	Web Site
Bureau of Economic Analysis	www.bea.gov
Bureau of Justice Statistics	www.ojp.usdoj.gov/bjs
Bureau of Labor Statistics	www.bls.gov
Central Intelligence Agency	www.cia.gov
Economic Report of the President	www.gpoaccess.gov/eop
Environmental Protection Agency	www.epa.gov
Federal Reserve System	www.federalreserve.gov
Financial Forecast Center	www.forecasts.org
National Agricultural Statistics Service	www.usda.gov/nass
National Center for Education Statistics	www.nces.ed.gov
National Center for Health Statistics	www.cdc.gov/nchs
National Science Foundation	www.nsf.gov
Population Reference Bureau	www.prb.org
State and Metropolitan Area Data Book	www.census.gov/statab/www/smadb.html
Statistical Abstract of the United States	www.census.gov/statab
Statistics Canada	www.statcan.ca
U.N. Dept of Economic and Social Affairs	www.un.org/depts/unsd
U.S. Bureau of the Census	www.census.gov
U.S. Federal Statistics	www.fedstats.gov
U.S. Government Printing Office	www.gpo.gov
World Bank	www.worldbank.org
World Demographics	www.demographia.com
World Health Organization	www.who.int/en

RELATED READING   *Guides to Data Sources*

Butler, F. Patrick. *Business Research Sources: A Reference Navigator.* Irwin/McGraw-Hill, 1999.

Clayton, Gary E.; and Martin Giesbrecht. *A Guide to Everyday Economic Statistics.* 6th ed. Irwin/McGraw-Hill, 2003.

Sampling and Surveys

Cantwell, Patrick J.; Howard Hogan; and Kathleen M. Styles. "The Use of Statistical Methods in the U.S. Census: *Utah v. Evans.*" *The American Statistician* 58, no. 3 (August 2004), pp. 203–12.

Cochran, William G. *Sampling Techniques*. 3rd ed. Wiley, 1990.

Cooper, Donald R.; and Pamela S. Schindler. *Business Research Methods*. 9th ed. Irwin/McGraw-Hill, 2005.

Cox, Eli P. "The Optimal Number of Response Alternatives for a Scale: A Review." *Journal of Marketing Research* 17 (1980), pp. 407–22.

Dillman, Don A. *Mail and Internet Surveys*. 2nd ed. Wiley, 1999.

Fowler, Floyd J. *Survey Research Methods*. 3rd ed. Sage, 2001.

Groves, Robert M. et al. *Survey Methodology*. Wiley, 2004.

Groves, Robert M.; Paul P. Biemer; and Lars E. Lyberg. *Telephone Survey Methodology*. Wiley, 2001.

Hahn, Gerald J.; and William Q. Meeker. "Assumptions for Statistical Inference." *The American Statistician* 47, no. 1 (February 1993), pp. 1–11.

Levy, Paul S.; and Stanley Lemeshow. *Sampling of Populations*. 3rd ed. Wiley, 2003.

Lyberg, Lars; and Paul Blemer. *Introduction to Survey Quality*. Wiley Europe, 2003.

Mathieson, Kieran; and David P. Doane. "Using Fine-Grained Likert Scales in Web Surveys." *Alliance Journal of Business Research* 1, no. 1 (2006), pp. 27–34.

Peterson, Ivars. "Sampling and the Census: Improving the Accuracy of the Decennial Count." *Science News* 152 (October 11, 1997), pp. 238–39.

Scheaffer, Richard L.; William Mendenhall; and R. Lyman Ott. *Elementary Survey Sampling*. 6th ed. Duxbury, 2006.

Singh, Ravindra; and Naurang Singh Mangat. *Elements of Survey Sampling*. Kluwer, 1996.

Som, R. K. *Practical Sampling Techniques*. 2nd ed. Marcel Dekker, 1996.

Thompson, Steven K. *Sampling*. 2nd ed. Wiley, 2002.

Velleman, Paul F.; and Leland Wilkinson. "Nominal, Ordinal, Interval, and Ratio Typologies Are Misleading." *The American Statistician* 47, no. 1 (February 1993), pp. 65–72.

LearningStats Unit 02 Manipulating Data LS

LearningStats Unit 02 introduces data types, sampling, random numbers, and surveys. Modules are designed for self-study, so you can proceed at your own pace, concentrate on material that is new, and pass quickly over things that you already know. Your instructor may assign specific modules, or you may decide to check them out because the topic sounds interesting. In addition to helping you learn about statistics, they may be useful as references later on.

Topic	LearningStats Modules
Data types	Level of Measurement
Sampling	Sampling Methods—Overview
	Sampling Methods—Worksheet
	Who Gets Picked?
	Randomizing a File
	Sampling a Large Database*
	Excel's RANDBETWEEN Function
Surveys	Survey Methods
Data sources	Web Data Sources

Key: = PowerPoint   = Word   = Excel
*Denotes a specialized topic.

Describing Data Visually

Chapter Learning Objectives

When you finish this chapter you should be able to

- Make a dot plot by hand or by computer.
- Create a frequency distribution for a data set.
- Make a histogram by hand or by computer.
- Recognize skewness, modes, and outliers in a histogram.
- Make and interpret a scatter plot by using the computer.
- Use line charts, bar charts, and pie charts appropriately.
- Use Excel to make effective charts.
- Recognize deceptive graphing techniques.
- Define the characteristics of good graphs in general.

Managers need information that can help them identify trends and adjust to changing conditions. But it is hard to assimilate piles of raw data. How can a business analyst convert raw data into useful information? Statistics offers many methods that can help organize, explore, and summarize data in a succinct way. The methods may be *visual* (charts and graphs) or *numerical* (statistics or tables). In this chapter, you will see how visual displays can provide insight into the characteristics of a data set *without* using mathematics. We begin with a set of n observations $x_1, x_2, \ldots, x_n$ on one variable (univariate data). Such data can be discussed in terms of three characteristics: **central tendency**, **dispersion**, and **shape**. Table 3.1 summarizes these characteristics as *questions* that we will be asking about the data.

3.1
VISUAL DESCRIPTION

Characteristic	Interpretation
Measurement	What are the units of measurement? Are the data integer or continuous? Any missing observations? Any concerns with accuracy or sampling methods?
Central Tendency	Where are the data values concentrated? What seem to be typical or middle data values?
Dispersion	How much variation is there in the data? How spread out are the data values? Are there unusual values?
Shape	Are the data values distributed symmetrically? Skewed? Sharply peaked? Flat? Bimodal?

TABLE 3.1

Characteristics of Univariate Data

EXAMPLE

Price/Earnings Ratios

Price/earnings (P/E) ratios—current stock price divided by earnings per share in the last 12 months—show how much an investor is willing to pay for a stock based on the stock's earnings. P/E ratios are also used to determine how optimistic the market is for a stock's growth potential. Investors may be willing to pay more for a lower earning stock than a higher earning stock if they see potential for growth. Table 3.2 shows P/E ratios for a random sample of companies ($n = 57$) from Standard & Poor's 500 index. We might be interested in learning how the P/E ratios of the companies in the S&P 500 compare to each other and what the overall distribution of P/E ratios looks like within the S&P 500. Visual displays can help us describe and summarize the main characteristics of this sample.

TABLE 3.2		P/E Ratios for 57 Companies 🐟 PERatios			
Company	**P/E Ratio**	**Company**	**P/E Ratio**	**Company**	**P/E Ratio**
Ace Ltd	8	Family Dollar Stores	19	Nike Inc B	18
AFLAC Inc	14	Fed Natl Mtg Corp	11	Northrop Grumman	14
Allied Waste Inc	21	FirstEnergy Corp	14	Nucor Corp	11
AutoNation Inc	12	Fluor Corp	22	Occidental Petroleum	11
Baker Hughes Inc	13	Freeport-Mcmor-B	11	PPG Industries	13
Bank New York	16	General Electric	16	Principal Financial	16
Bank of America	11	Genzyme-Genl Div	23	Progress Energy	17
Baxter International	20	Goldman-Sachs Group	10	Radioshack Corp	24
Bear Stearns Cos	11	Hilton Hotels Co	28	Rohm & Haas Co	15
Bed Bath & Beyond	20	Ingersoll-Rand-A	12	Sara Lee Corp	25
Bemis Co	17	Jones Apparel	13	Staples Inc	20
BMC Software Inc	27	KB Home	14	Starwood Hotels	25
Burlington/Santa	14	KeySpan Corp	16	Stryker Corp	25
Chevron Corp	9	Leggett & Platt	13	Symantec Corporation	21
ConocoPhillips	8	Lexmark Intl A	17	Tribune Co	14
Constellation Energy	16	Limited Brands	16	Union Pacific Corp	15
Disney (Walt) Co	20	Mellon Financial	17	Wendy's Intl Inc	24
Electronic Data	17	Moody's Corp	29	Whirlpool Corp	18
Emerson Elec Co	17	New York Times A	19	Yum! Brands Inc	18

Source: Standard & Poor's, *Security Owner's Stock Guide*, February 2007.

Measurement

Before calculating any statistics or drawing any graphs, it is a good idea to *look at the data* and try to visualize how it was collected. Because the companies in the S&P 500 index are publicly traded, they are required to publish verified financial information, so the accuracy of the data is not an issue. Since the intent of the analysis is to study the S&P 500 companies at a *point in time,* these are *cross-sectional* data. (Financial analysts also study time series data on P/E ratios, which vary daily as stock prices change.) Although rounded to integers, the measurements are continuous. For example, a stock price of $43.22 divided by earnings per share of $2.17 gives a P/E ratio $(43.22)/(2.17) = 19.92$, which would be rounded to 20 for convenience. Since there is a true zero, we can speak meaningfully of ratios and can perform any standard mathematical operations. Finally, since the analysis is based on a sample (not a census), we must allow for the possibility of *sampling error,* that is, the possibility that our sample is not representative of the population of all 500 S&P 500 firms, due to the nature of random sampling.

Sorting

As a first step, it is helpful to sort the data. This is a visual display, although a very simple one. From the sorted data, we can see the range, the frequency of occurrence for each data value, and the data values that lie near the middle and ends.

8	8	9	10	11	11	11	11	11	11
12	12	13	13	13	13	14	14	14	14
14	14	15	15	16	16	16	16	16	16
17	17	17	17	17	17	18	18	18	19
19	20	20	20	20	21	21	22	23	24
24	25	25	25	27	28	29			

When the number of observations is large, a sorted list of data values is difficult to analyze. Further, a simple list of numbers may not reveal very much about central tendency, dispersion, and shape. To see broader patterns in the data, analysts often prefer a *visual display* of the data. This chapter explains various types of visual displays, offers guidelines for effective graphs, and warns you of ways that visual displays can be deceptive.

A **dot plot** is a simple graphical display of *n* individual values of numerical data. The basic steps in making a dot plot are to (1) make a scale that covers the data range, (2) mark axis demarcations and label them, and (3) plot each data value as a dot above the scale at its approximate location. If more than one data value lies at approximately the same *X*-axis location, the dots are piled up vertically. Figure 3.1 shows a dot plot for 57 P/E ratios.

Dot plots are an attractive tool for data exploration because they are easy to understand. A dot plot shows *dispersion* by displaying the range of the data. It shows *central tendency* by revealing where the data values tend to cluster and where the midpoint lies. A dot plot can also reveal some things about the *shape* of the distribution if the sample is large enough. For the P/E ratios, the dot plot in Figure 3.1 shows that:

- The range is from 8 to 29.
- All but a few data values lie between 10 and 25.
- A typical "middle" data value would be around 15 or 16.
- The sample is not quite symmetric due to a few large P/E ratios.

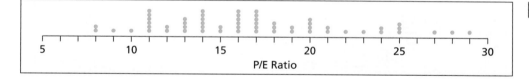

FIGURE 3.1

Dot Plot of 57 P/E Ratios
       PERatios

You can make a dot plot yourself (if the sample is small) using a straightedge and a pencil. Excel doesn't offer dot plots, but you can get them from MegaStat or Visual Statistics or MINITAB. Figure 3.2 shows the dot plot menus and check box for MegaStat > Descriptive Statistics for the chosen data range on a spreadsheet.

Comparing Groups

A **stacked dot plot** can be used to compare two or more groups. For example, Figure 3.3 shows a stacked dot plot for median home prices for 150 U.S. cities in four different regions. A common *X*-axis scale is used for all four dot plots. This stacked dot plot shows the range of data values and gives an idea of typical home values within each region. (MegaStat doesn't offer stacked dot plots, but MINITAB does.) Could a table show this amount of information as clearly?

While they are easy to understand, dot plots have limitations. They don't reveal very much information about the data set's shape when the sample is small, but they become awkward to plot when the sample is large (what if you have 100 dots at the same point?). The next section of this textbook explains some widely used methods for creating visual displays that work for any sample size.

FIGURE 3.2

MegaStat Menus for Dot Plot

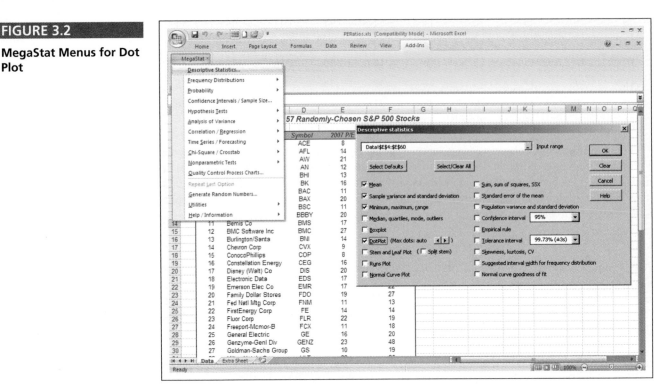

FIGURE 3.3

Stacked Dot Plot (n = 150 cities)
🐟 **HomePrices**

Source: www.realtor.org

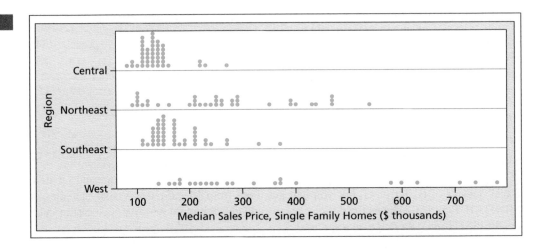

SECTION EXERCISES

3.1 (a) Without using a computer, make a dot plot for these 32 observations on the number of customers to use a downtown CitiBank ATM during the noon hour on 32 consecutive workdays. (b) Describe its appearance. 🐟 **CitiBank**

25	37	23	26	30	40	25	26
39	32	21	26	19	27	32	25
18	26	34	18	31	35	21	33
33	9	16	32	35	42	15	24

3.2 Without using a computer, make a dot plot for the number of defects per 100 vehicles for these 37 brands. Describe its appearance. 🐟 **JDPower**

Defects per 100 Vehicles (alphabetical by brand)

Brand	Defects	Brand	Defects	Brand	Defects
Acura	120	Infiniti	117	Nissan	121
Audi	130	Isuzu	191	Pontiac	133
BMW	142	Jaguar	109	Porsche	91
Buick	134	Jeep	153	Saab	163
Cadillac	117	Kia	136	Saturn	129
Chevrolet	124	Land Rover	204	Scion	140
Chrysler	120	Lexus	93	Subaru	146
Dodge	132	Lincoln	121	Suzuki	169
Ford	127	Mazda	150	Toyota	106
GMC	119	Mercedes-Benz	139	Volkswagen	171
Honda	110	Mercury	129	Volvo	133
HUMMER	171	MINI	150		
Hyundai	102	Mitsubishi	135		

Source: J. D. Power and Associates 2006 Initial Quality Study™. Used with permission.

3.3 Sarah and Bob share a 1,000-minute cell phone calling plan. Without using a computer, make a *stacked dot plot* to compare the lengths of cell phone calls by Sarah and Bob during the last week. Describe what the dot plots tell you.   **PhoneCalls**

Sarah's calls: 1, 1, 1, 1, 2, 3, 3, 3, 5, 5, 6, 6, 7, 8, 8, 12, 14, 14, 22, 23, 29, 33, 38, 45, 66

Bob's calls: 5, 8, 9, 14, 17, 21, 23, 23, 24, 26, 27, 27, 28, 29, 31, 33, 35, 39, 41

Mini Case   3.1

U.S. Business Cycles

Although many businesses anticipated the 2001 recession that followed the long boom and stock market bubble of the 1990s, they needed to anticipate its probable length to form strategies for debt management and future product releases. Fortunately, good data are available from the National Bureau of Economic Research, which keeps track of business cycles. The length of a contraction is measured from the peak of the previous expansion to the beginning of the next expansion based on the real Gross Domestic Product (GDP). Table 3.3 shows the durations, in months, of 32 U.S. recessions.

TABLE 3.3   U.S. Business Contractions, 1857–2001 (*n* = 32)   Recessions

Peak	Trough	Months	Peak	Trough	Months
Jun 1857	Dec 1858	18	Jan 1920	Jul 1921	18
Oct 1860	Jun 1861	8	May 1923	Jul 1924	14
Apr 1865	Dec 1867	32	Oct 1926	Nov 1927	13
Jun 1869	Dec 1870	18	Aug 1929	Mar 1933	43
Oct 1873	Mar 1879	65	May 1937	Jun 1938	13
Mar 1882	May 1885	38	Feb 1945	Oct 1945	8
Mar 1887	Apr 1888	13	Nov 1948	Oct 1949	11
Jul 1890	May 1891	10	Jul 1953	May 1954	10
Jan 1893	Jun 1894	17	Aug 1957	Apr 1958	8
Dec 1895	Jun 1897	18	Apr 1960	Feb 1961	10
Jun 1899	Dec 1900	18	Dec 1969	Nov 1970	11
Sep 1902	Aug 1904	23	Nov 1973	Mar 1975	16
May 1907	Jun 1908	13	Jan 1980	Jul 1980	6
Jan 1910	Jan 1912	24	Jul 1981	Nov 1982	16
Jan 1913	Dec 1914	23	Jul 1990	Mar 1991	8
Aug 1918	Mar 1919	7	Mar 2001	Nov 2001	8

Source: U.S. Business Contractions found at www.nber.org. Copyright © 2005 National Bureau of Economic Research, Inc. Used with permission.

From the dot plot in Figure 3.4, we see that the 65-month contraction (1873–1879) was quite unusual, although four recessions did exceed 30 months. Most recessions have lasted less than 20 months. Only 7 of 32 lasted less than 10 months. The 8-month 2001 recession was therefore among the shortest, although its recovery phase was sluggish and inconsistent compared to most other recessions.

FIGURE 3.4   **Dot Plot of Business Cycle Duration ($n = 32$)**

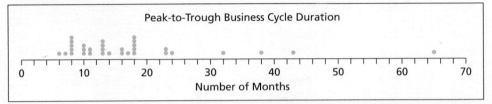

Still, the table supplies information that the dot plot cannot. For example, during the 1930s there were actually *two* major contractions (43 months from 1929 to 1933, 13 months from 1937 to 1938) which is one reason why that period seemed so terrible to those who lived through it. The Great Depression of the 1930s was so named because it lasted a long time and the economic decline was deeper than in most recessions.

3.3
FREQUENCY DISTRIBUTIONS AND HISTOGRAMS

Bins and Bin Limits

A **frequency distribution** is a table formed by classifying n data values into k classes called *bins* (we adopt this terminology from Excel). The *bin limits* define the values to be included in each bin. Usually, all the bin widths are the same. The table shows the *frequency* of data values within each bin. Frequencies can also be expressed as *relative frequencies* or *percentages* of the total number of observations.

Frequency Distribution

A tabulation of n data values into k classes called *bins,* based on values of the data. The *bin limits* are cutoff points that define each bin. Bins generally have equal widths and their limits cannot overlap.

The basic steps for constructing a frequency distribution are to (1) sort the data in ascending order, (2) choose the number of bins, (3) set the bin limits, (4) put the data values in the appropriate bin, and (5) create the table. Let's walk through these steps.

Constructing a Frequency Distribution

Step 1: Find Smallest and Largest Data Values

8	8	9	10	11	11	11	11	11	11
12	12	13	13	13	13	14	14	14	14
14	14	15	15	16	16	16	16	16	16
17	17	17	17	17	17	18	18	18	19
19	20	20	20	20	21	21	22	23	24
24	25	25	25	27	28	29			

For the P/E data, we get $x_{min} = 8$ and $x_{max} = 29$. You might be able to find x_{min} and x_{max} without sorting the entire data set, but it is easier to experiment with bin choices if you have already sorted the data.

Sample Size (n)	Suggested Number of Bins (k)
16	5
32	6
64	7
128	8
256	9
512	10
1,024	11

TABLE 3.4

Sturges' Rule

Note: Sturges said that the number of classes to tabulate n items should be approximately $1 + 3.3 \log_{10}(n)$.

Step 2: Choose Number of Bins Since a frequency distribution seeks to condense many data points into a small table, we expect the number of bins k to be much smaller than the sample size n. When you use *too many* bins some bins are likely to be sparsely populated, or even empty. With *too few* bins, dissimilar data values are lumped together. Left to their own devices, people tend to choose similar bin limits for a given data set. Generally, larger samples justify more bins. According to **Sturges' Rule**, a guideline proposed by statistician Herbert Sturges, every time we double the sample size, we should add one bin, as shown in Table 3.4.

For the sample sizes you are likely to encounter, Table 3.4 says that you would expect to use from $k = 5$ to $k = 11$ bins. Sturges' Rule can be expressed as a formula:

$$\text{Sturges' Rule:} \quad k = 1 + 3.3 \log(n) \tag{3.1}$$

For the P/E data ($n = 57$) Sturges' Rule says:

$$k = 1 + 3.3 \log(n) = 1 + 3.3 \log(57) = 1 + 3.3(1.7559) = 6.79 \text{ bins}$$

Using either Table 3.4 or Sturges' formula, we would consider using 6 or 7 bins for the P/E data. But to get "nice" bin limits you may choose more or fewer bins. Picking attractive bin limits is often an overriding consideration (not Sturges' Rule).

Step 3: Set Bin Limits Just as choosing the number of bins requires judgment, setting the bin limits also requires judgment. For guidance, find the approximate width of each bin by dividing the data range by the number of bins:

$$\text{Bin width} \approx \frac{x_{\max} - x_{\min}}{k} \tag{3.2}$$

Round the bin width *up* to an appropriate value, then set the lower limit for the first bin as a multiple of the bin width. What does "appropriate" mean? If the data are discrete, then it makes sense to have a width that is an integer value. If the data are continuous, then setting a bin width equal to a fractional value may be appropriate. Experiment until you get bins that cover the data range.

For example, for this data set, the smallest P/E ratio was 8 and the largest P/E ratio was 29, so if we want to use $k = 6$ bins, we calculate the approximate bin width as:

$$\text{Bin width} \approx \frac{29 - 8}{6} = \frac{21}{6} = 3.50$$

To obtain "nice" limits, we can round the bin width up to 4 and start the first bin at 8 to get bin limits 8, 12, 16, 20, 24, 28, 32. Usually "nice" bin limits are 2, 5, or 10 multiplied by an appropriate integer power of 10. As a starting point for the lowest bin, we choose the largest multiple of the bin width smaller than the lowest data value. For example, if bin width is 5 and the smallest data value is 23, the first bin would start at 20.

Step 4: Put Data Values in Appropriate Bins In general, the lower limit is *included* in the bin, while the upper limit is *excluded*. MegaStat and MINITAB follow this convention. However, Excel's histogram option *includes* the upper limit and *excludes* the lower limit. There are advantages to either method. Our objective is to make sure that none of the bins overlap and that data values are counted in only one bin.

TABLE 3.5

Frequency Distribution of P/E Ratios Using Six Bins
🐾 **PERatios**

Bin Limits			Frequency	Relative Frequency	Cumulative Frequency	Cumulative Relative Frequency
From		To				
8	<	12	10	.1754	10	.1754
12	<	16	14	.2456	24	.4210
16	<	20	17	.2982	41	.7193
20	<	24	8	.1404	49	.8596
24	<	28	6	.1053	55	.9649
28	<	32	2	.0351	57	1.0000
	Total:		57	1.0000		

Step 5: Create Table   You can choose to show only the absolute frequencies, or counts, for each bin or also include the relative frequencies and the cumulative frequencies. Relative frequencies are calculated as the absolute frequency for a bin divided by the total number of data values. Cumulative relative frequencies accumulate relative frequency values as the bin limits increase. Table 3.5 shows the frequency distribution we've created for the P/E ratio data. Sometimes the relative frequencies do not sum to 1 due to rounding.

Histograms

A **histogram** is a graphical representation of a frequency distribution. A histogram is a bar chart whose *Y*-axis shows the number of data values (or a percentage) within each bin of a frequency distribution and whose *X*-axis ticks show the end points of each bin. There should be no gaps between bars (except when there are no data in a particular bin) as shown in Figure 3.5.

FIGURE 3.5

Histogram of P/E Ratios (6 bins) 🐾 **PERatios**

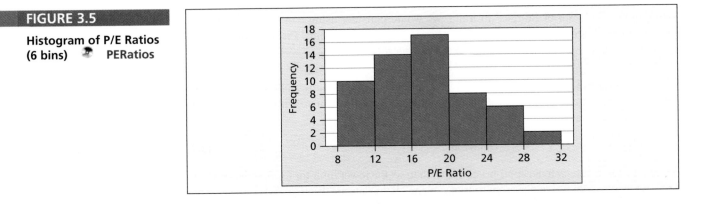

As we discussed earlier, choosing the number of bins and bin limits requires judgment on our part. The process of creating a histogram is often an iterative process. Our first choice of bins and limits may not be our final choice for presentation. Figure 3.6 shows histograms for the P/E ratio sample using three different bin definitions. Our perception of the shape of the distribution depends on how the bins are chosen. The 5-bin histogram is too coarse to give a precise view of the data. The 8-bin histogram clearly shows concentration between 11 and 20. The 11-bin histogram reveals more detail in the right tail. You can use your own judgment to determine which histogram you would ultimately include in a report.

Excel Histograms

Excel will produce histograms. Click on the menu bar Data tab (if you don't see Data Analysis on the Data tab, you must click Add-Ins and check Analysis Tool Pak). You can specify a range containing the bin limits (cells E4:E60 in Figure 3.7) or accept Excel's default. The result, shown in Figure 3.7, is not very attractive. Modifying an Excel histogram is possible, but you may prefer using software designed for drawing histograms.

FIGURE 3.6

Three Histograms for P/E Ratios   **PERatios**

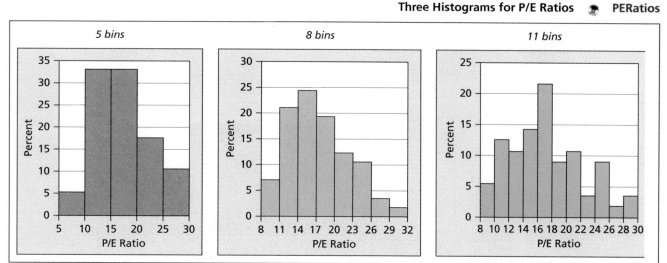

FIGURE 3.7

Excel's Histogram
PERatios

MegaStat Histograms

Figure 3.8 shows MegaStat's menu for a frequency distribution and histogram for the P/E ratios using six bins. MegaStat shows percents on the *Y*-axis instead of frequencies. You can specify the bins with two numbers (interval width and lower limit of the first interval) or you can let MegaStat make its own decisions. MegaStat also provides a frequency distribution, including *cumulative* frequencies.

FIGURE 3.8

MegaStat Frequency Distribution and Histogram 🖳 **PERatios**

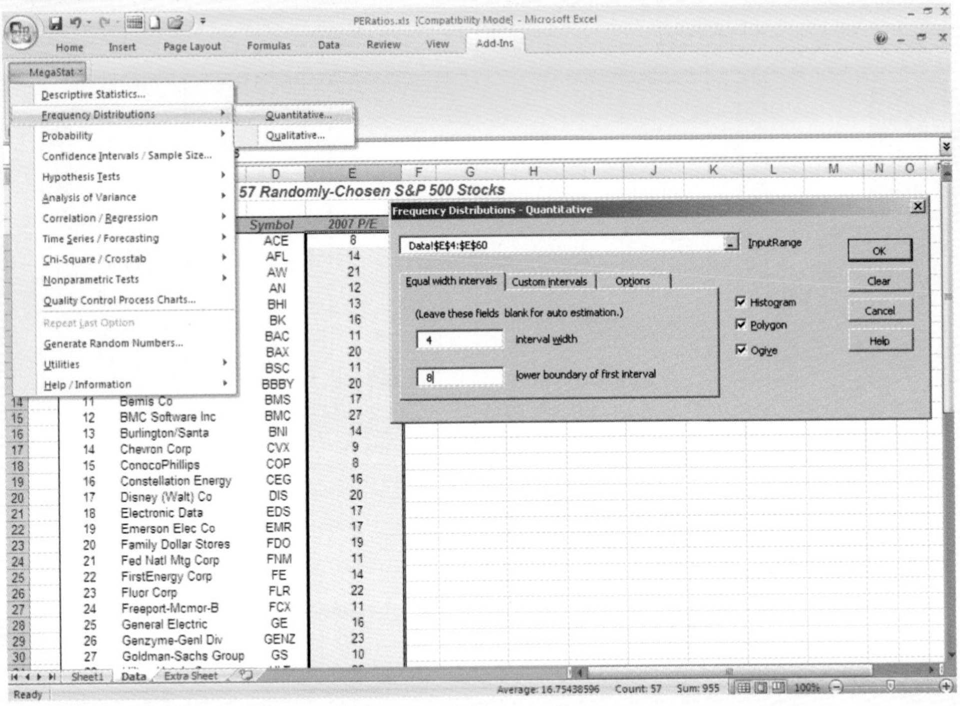

Frequency Distribution - Quantitative

2007 P/E						cumulative	
lower	upper	midpoint	width	frequency	percent	frequency	percent
8 <	12	10	4	10	17.5	10	17.5
12 <	16	14	4	14	24.6	24	42.1
16 <	20	18	4	17	29.8	41	71.9
20 <	24	22	4	8	14.0	49	86.0
24 <	28	26	4	6	10.5	55	96.5
28 <	32	30	4	2	3.5	57	100.0
				57	100.0		

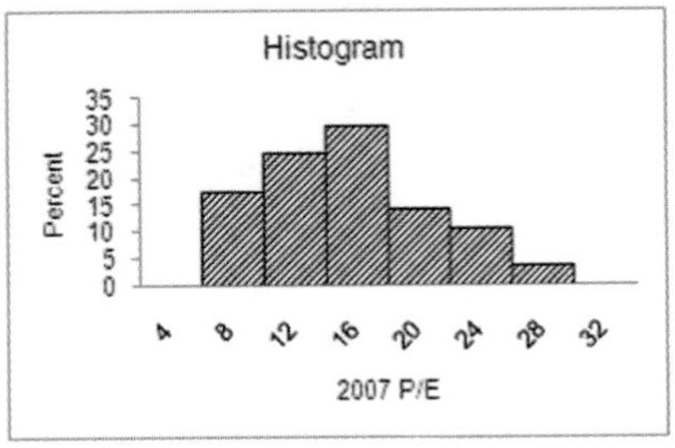

MINITAB Histograms

Figure 3.9 shows how MINITAB creates a histogram for the same data. Copy the data from the spreadsheet and paste it into MINITAB's worksheet, then choose Graphs > Histogram from the top menu bar. Let MINITAB use its default options. Once the histogram has been created, you can right-click the *X*-axis to adjust the bins, axis tick marks, and so on.

A **modal class** is a histogram bar that is higher than those on either side. A histogram with a single modal class is *unimodal,* one with two modal classes is *bimodal,* and one with more than two modes is *multimodal.* However, modal classes may be artifacts of the way the bin limits are chosen. It is wise to experiment with various ways of binning and to make cautious inferences about modality unless the modes are strong and invariant to binning. Figure 3.9 shows a single modal class for P/E ratios between 16 and 20.

Shape

A histogram suggests the *shape* of the population we are sampling, but, unless the sample is large, we must be cautious about making inferences. Our perception is also influenced by the number of bins and the way the bin limits are chosen. The following terminology is helpful in discussing shape.

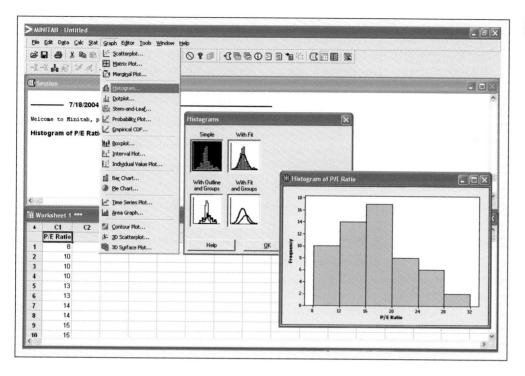

FIGURE 3.9

**MINITAB Histogram
PERatios**

A histogram's *skewness* is indicated by the direction of its longer tail. If neither tail is longer, the histogram is **symmetric**. A **right-skewed** (or positively skewed) histogram has a longer right tail, with most data values clustered on the left side. A **left-skewed** (or negatively skewed) histogram has a longer left tail, with most data values clustered on the right side. Few histograms are exactly symmetric. Business data tend to be right-skewed because they are often bounded by zero on the left but are unbounded on the right (e.g., number of employees). You may find it helpful to refer to the templates shown in Figure 3.10.

FIGURE 3.10

Prototype Distribution Shapes

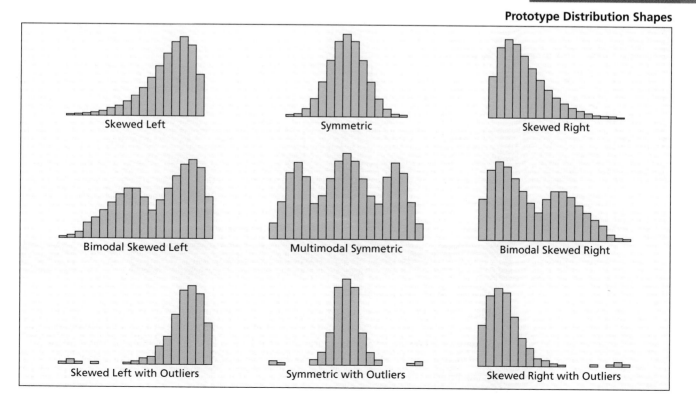

An **outlier** is an extreme value that is far enough from the majority of the data that it probably arose from a different cause or is due to measurement error. We will define outliers more precisely in the next chapter. For now, think of outliers as unusual points located in the histogram tails. None of the histograms shown so far has any obvious outliers.

Tips for Effective Frequency Distributions

Here are some general tips to keep in mind when making frequency distributions and histograms.

1. Check Sturges' Rule first, but only as a suggestion for the number of bins.
2. Choose an appropriate bin width.
3. Choose bin limits that are multiples of the bin width.
4. Make sure that the range is covered, and add bins if necessary.

Frequency Polygon and Ogive

Figure 3.11 shows two more graphs offered by MegaStat (look at the three check boxes in the MegaStat menu in Figure 3.8). A **frequency polygon** is a line graph that connects the midpoints of the histogram intervals, plus extra intervals at the beginning and end so that the line will touch the *X*-axis. It serves the same purpose as a histogram, but is attractive when you need to compare two data sets (since more than one frequency polygon can be plotted on the same scale). An **ogive** (pronounced "oh-jive") is a line graph of the cumulative frequencies. It is useful for finding percentiles or in comparing the shape of the sample with a known benchmark such as the normal distribution (that you will be seeing in the next chapter).

FIGURE 3.11

MegaStat's Frequency Polygon and Ogive (embellished)   PERatios

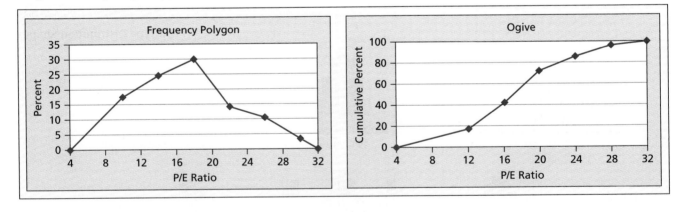

Mini Case   3.2

Duration of U.S. Recessions

Table 3.6 shows four "nice" ways to bin the data on the duration of 32 U.S. recessions (for details, see **Mini Case 3.1**). Most observers would think that $k = 2$ or $k = 4$ would be too few bins while $k = 13$ might be considered too many bins. Sturges would recommend using six bins, which suggests that seven bins would be the best choice of these four ways. However, you can think of other valid possibilities.

TABLE 3.6			Some Ways to Tabulate 32 Business Contractions			🐝	Recessions				
k = 2 bins			**k = 4 bins**			**k = 7 bins**			**k = 13 bins**		
From	*To*	*f*	*From*	*To*	*f*	*From*	*To*	*f*	*From*	*To*	*f*
0	35	29	0	20	25	0	10	7	5	10	7
35	70	3	20	40	5	10	20	18	10	15	10
			40	60	1	20	30	3	15	20	8
Total		32	60	80	1	30	40	2	20	25	3
						40	50	1	25	30	0
			Total		32	50	60	0	30	35	1
						60	70	1	35	40	1
									40	45	1
						Total		32	45	50	0
									50	55	0
									55	60	0
									60	65	0
									65	70	1
									Total		32

All four histograms in Figure 3.12 suggest right-skewness (long right tail, most values cluster to the left). Each histogram has a single modal class, although $k = 7$ and $k = 13$ reveal modality more precisely (e.g., the $k = 7$ bin histogram says that a recession most often lasts between 10 and 20 months). The long recession of 1873–79 (65 months) can be seen as a possible outlier in the right tail of the last two histograms.

FIGURE 3.12	Histograms for 2, 4, 7, and 13 Bins

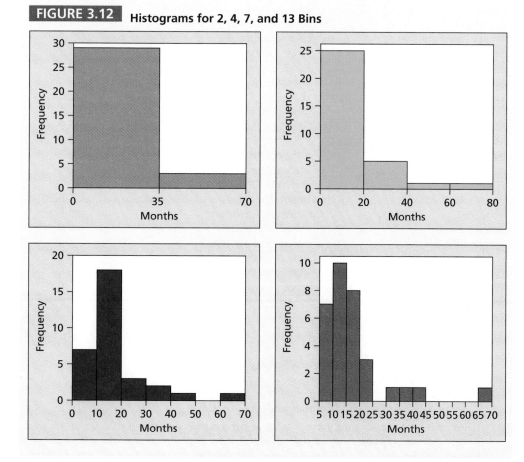

SECTION EXERCISES   **3.4**   (a) Without using a computer, make a frequency distribution and histogram (using appropriate bins) for these 28 observations on the amount spent for dinner for four in downtown Chicago on Friday night. (b) Repeat the exercise, using a different number of bins. Which is preferred? Why?

Dinner

95	103	109	170	114	113	107
124	105	80	104	84	176	115
69	95	134	108	61	160	128
68	95	61	150	52	87	136

3.5   (a) Without using a computer, make a frequency distribution and histogram for the monthly off-campus rent paid by 30 students. (b) Repeat the exercise, using a different number of bins. Which is preferred? Why?   **Rents**

730	730	730	930	700	570
690	1030	740	620	720	670
560	740	650	660	850	930
600	620	760	690	710	500
730	800	820	840	720	700

3.6   (a) Without using a computer, make a frequency distribution and histogram for the 2003 annual compensation of these 20 randomly chosen CEOs from a list of 200 top CEOs. (b) Repeat the exercise, using a different number of bins. Which is preferred? Why?   **CEOComp**

2003 Compensation for 20 Randomly Chosen CEOs ($ millions)

Company	CEO	Compensation ($ millions)
Aetna	John W. Rowe	16.9
Allstate	Edward M. Liddy	14.3
American Electric Power	E. Linn Draper, Jr.	2.1
Baxter International	H. M. Jansen Kraemer, Jr.	4.5
Bear Stearns	James E. Cayne	39.5
Cardinal Health	Robert D. Walter	13.4
Cooper Tire & Rubber	Thomas A. Dattilo	2.0
Family Dollar Stores	Howard R. Levine	2.1
Fifth Third Bancorp	George A. Schaefer, Jr.	6.0
Merrill Lynch	E. Stanley O'Neal	28.1
Harley-Davidson	Jeffrey L. Bleustein	6.7
NCR	Mark V. Hurd	2.6
PG&E	Robert D. Glynn, Jr.	20.1
Praxair	Dennis H. Reilley	5.6
Sara Lee	C. Steven McMillan	10.5
Sunoco	John G. Drosdick	8.6
Temple-Inland	Kenneth M. Jastrow II	2.5
U.S. Bancorp	Jerry A. Grundhofer	10.3
Union Pacific	Richard K. Davidson	18.6
Whirlpool	David R. Whitwam	6.6

Source: *The New York Times*, April 4, 2004, p. 8.

3.7   For each frequency distribution, suggest "nice" bins. Did your choice agree with Sturges' Rule? If not, explain.
a. Last week's MPG for 35 student vehicles ($x_{min} = 9.4$, $x_{max} = 38.7$).
b. Ages of 50 airplane passengers ($x_{min} = 12$, $x_{max} = 85$).
c. GPAs of 250 first-semester college students ($x_{min} = 2.25$, $x_{max} = 3.71$).
d. Annual rates of return on 150 mutual funds ($x_{min} = .023$, $x_{max} = .097$).

3.8   Below are sorted data showing average spending per customer (in dollars) at 74 Noodles & Company restaurants. (a) Construct a frequency distribution. Explain how you chose the number of bins and the bin limits. (b) Make a histogram and describe its appearance. (c) Repeat, using a larger number of bins and different bin limits. (d) Did your visual impression of the data change when you increased the number of bins? Explain. *Note:* You may use MegaStat or MINITAB if your instructor agrees.   **NoodlesSpending**

6.54	6.58	6.58	6.62	6.66	6.70	6.71	6.73	6.75	6.75	6.76	6.76
6.76	6.77	6.77	6.79	6.81	6.81	6.82	6.84	6.85	6.89	6.90	6.91
6.91	6.92	6.93	6.93	6.94	6.95	6.95	6.95	6.96	6.96	6.98	6.99
7.00	7.00	7.00	7.02	7.03	7.03	7.03	7.04	7.05	7.05	7.07	7.07
7.08	7.11	7.11	7.13	7.13	7.16	7.17	7.18	7.21	7.25	7.28	7.28
7.30	7.33	7.33	7.35	7.37	7.38	7.45	7.56	7.57	7.58	7.64	7.65
7.87	7.97										

Simple Line Charts

A *simple line chart* like the one shown in Figure 3.13 is used to display a time series, to spot trends, or to compare time periods. Line charts can be used to display several variables at once. If two variables are displayed, the right and left scales can differ, using the right scale for one variable and the left scale for the other. Excel's *two-scale line chart,* illustrated in Figure 3.14, lets you compare variables that *differ in magnitude* or are measured in *different units*. But keep in mind that someone who only glances at the chart may mistakenly conclude that both variables are of the same magnitude.

How many variables can be displayed at once on a line graph? Too much clutter ruins any visual display. If you try to display half a dozen time series variables at once, no matter how cleverly you choose symbols and graphing techniques, the result is likely to be unsatisfactory. You will have to use your judgment.

3.4
LINE CHARTS

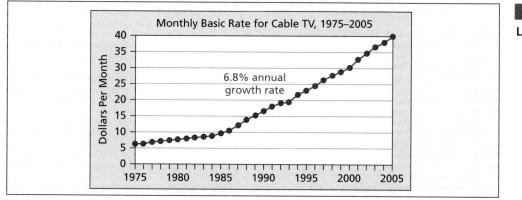

FIGURE 3.13

Line Chart   CableTV

Source: *Statistical Abstract of the U.S., 2007,* p. 717.

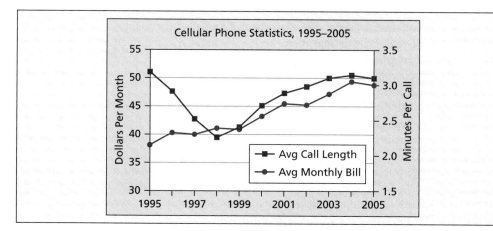

FIGURE 3.14

Two Scales
 CellPhones

Source: *Statistical Abstract of the U.S., 2007,* p. 720.

FIGURE 3.15

Effect of Grid Lines: (a) Many Heavy Lines; (b) Fewer, Lighter Lines 🐝 **Utilities**

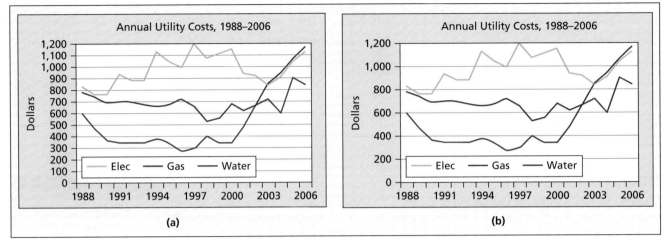

Source: Author's utility bills.

Grid Lines 🐝 Utilities

A line graph usually has no vertical grid lines. What about horizontal grid lines? While grid lines do add background clutter, they make it easier to establish the *Y* value for a given year. One compromise is to use lightly colored dashed or dotted grid lines to minimize the clutter, and to increase grid line spacing, as illustrated in Figure 3.15. If the intent is to convey only a general sense of the data magnitudes, grid lines may be omitted.

Bar charts can also be used to portray time series data. Bars add a feeling of solidity and may hold the reader's attention, particularly if the reader is accustomed to bar charts. However, when you are displaying more than one time series, bar charts make it harder to see individual data values, so a line chart usually is preferred. In Section 3.5 we discuss rules for bar charts. Exercise judgment to decide which type of display is most effective for the audience you are addressing.

Log Scales 🐝 BobsFunds

On the customary **arithmetic scale**, distances on the *Y*-axis are proportional to the magnitude of the variable being displayed. But on a **logarithmic scale**, equal distances represent equal *ratios* (for this reason, a log scale is sometimes called a *ratio scale*). When data vary over a wide range, say, by more than an order of magnitude (e.g., from 6 to 60), we might prefer a *log scale* for the vertical axis, to reveal more detail for small data values. For example, Figure 3.16 shows the value of an investment over a 30-year period. The data vary roughly from $50,000 to $500,000. The log scale reveals that there were substantial *relative* fluctuations in the first decade, which might go unnoticed on the arithmetic scale. The log scale also shows that the larger *absolute* fluctuations in the most recent decade are actually similar to those in the first decade in *relative* terms.

A log graph reveals whether the quantity is growing at an *increasing percent* (convex function), *constant percent* (straight line), or *declining percent* (concave function). On the arithmetic scale, Bob's investment appears to grow at an increasing rate, but on the log scale it is roughly a straight line. Thus, Bob's investment seems to be growing at a *constant percent rate* (the yearly average rate is actually 7.25 percent). On a log scale, *equal distances* represent *equal ratios*. That is, the distance from 10,000 to 100,000 is the same as the distance from 100,000 to 1,000,000. Since logarithms are undefined for negative or zero values (try it on your calculator), a log scale is only suited for positive data values.

FIGURE 3.16

Same Data on Different Y-Axis Scales   BobsFunds

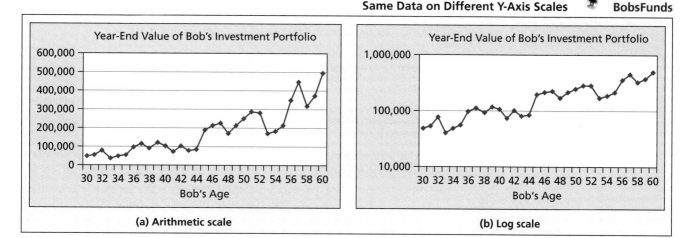

(a) Arithmetic scale   **(b) Log scale**

When to Use Log Scales   A log scale is useful for time series data that might be expected to grow at a compound annual percentage rate (e.g., GDP, the national debt, or your future income). Log scales are common in financial charts that cover long periods of time or for data that grow rapidly (e.g., revenues for a start-up company). Some experts feel that corporate annual reports and stock prospectuses should avoid ratio scales, on the grounds that they may be misleading to uninformed individuals. But then how can we fairly portray data that vary by orders of magnitude? Should investors become better informed? The bottom line is that business students must understand log scales, because they are sure to run into them.

Figure 3.17 shows the U.S. balance of trade. The arithmetic scale shows that growth has been exponential. Yet, although exports and imports are increasing in absolute terms, the log graph suggests that the *growth rate* in both series may be slowing, because the log graph is slightly concave. On the log graph, the recently increasing trade deficit is not *relatively* as large. Regardless how it is displayed, the trade deficit remains a concern for policymakers, for fear that foreigners may no longer wish to purchase U.S. debt instruments to finance the trade deficit (see *The Wall Street Journal,* July 24, 2005, p. C1).

EXAMPLE

U.S. Trade
   USTrade

FIGURE 3.17

Comparison of Arithmetic and Log Scales   USTrade

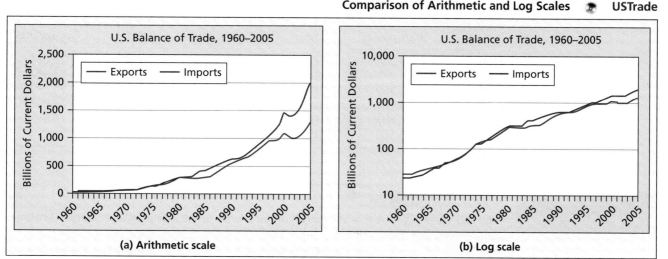

(a) Arithmetic scale   **(b) Log scale**

Source: *Economic Report of the President, 2007.*

Tips for Effective Line Charts

Here are some general tips to keep in mind when creating line charts:

1. Line charts are used for *time series data* (never for cross-sectional data).

2. The numerical variable is shown on the *Y*-axis, while the time units go on the *X*-axis with time increasing from left to right. Business audiences expect this rule to be followed.

3. Except for log scales, use a zero origin on the *Y*-axis (this is the default in Excel) unless more detail is needed. The zero-origin rule is mandatory for a corporate annual report or investor stock prospectus.

4. To avoid graph clutter, numerical labels usually are *omitted* on a line chart, especially when the data cover many time periods. Use gridlines to help the reader read data values.

5. Data markers (squares, triangles, circles) are helpful. But when the series has many data values or when many variables are being displayed, they clutter the graph.

6. If the lines on the graph are too thick, the reader can't ascertain graph values.

SECTION EXERCISES

3.9 Use Excel to prepare a line chart to display the lightning death data. Modify the default colors, fonts, etc., as you judge appropriate to make the display effective.

U.S. Deaths by Lightning, 1940–2005   Lightning

Year	Deaths	Year	Deaths
1940	340	1975	91
1945	268	1980	74
1950	219	1985	74
1955	181	1990	74
1960	129	1995	85
1965	149	2000	51
1970	122	2005	38

Sources: *Statistical Abstract of the United States, 2007*, p. 228; and www.nws.noaa.gov.

3.10 Use Excel to prepare a line chart to display the following transplant data. Modify the default colors, fonts, etc., to make the display effective.

California Living Organ Transplants, 1988–2004   Transplants

Year	Transplants	Year	Transplants	Year	Transplants
1988	12,786	1994	18,170	2000	23,004
1989	13,471	1995	19,264	2001	23,942
1990	15,462	1996	19,566	2002	24,552
1991	15,687	1997	20,093	2003	25,083
1992	16,043	1998	21,313	2004	26,539
1993	17,533	1999	21,824		

Source: www.gsds.org.

3.5
BAR CHARTS

Plain Bar Charts   Tires

The **bar chart** is probably the most common type of data display in business. Attribute data is typically displayed using a bar chart. Each bar represents a category or attribute. The length of each bar reflects the frequency of that category. Each bar has a label showing

FIGURE 3.18

Same Data Displayed Two Ways

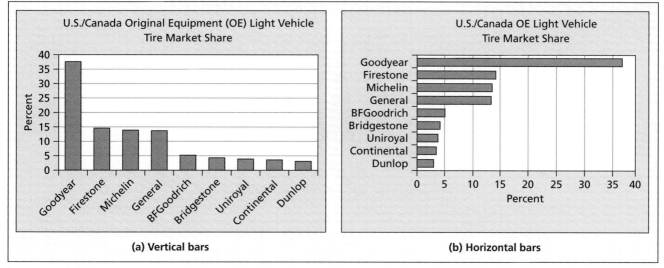

(a) Vertical bars   (b) Horizontal bars

Source: www.mtdealer.com.

a category or time period. Figure 3.18 shows simple bar charts comparing market shares among tire manufacturers. Each bar is separated from its neighbors by a slight gap to improve legibility (you can control gap width in Excel). *Vertical* bar charts are the most common, but *horizontal* bar charts can be useful when the axis labels are long or when there are many categories.

3-D and Novelty Bar Charts   Tires

This same data can be displayed in a *3-D bar chart,* shown in Figure 3.19. Many observers feel that the illusion of depth adds to the visual impact. The depth effect is mostly harmless in terms of bar proportions, but it does introduce ambiguity in bar height. Do we measure from the back of the bar or from the front? For a general readership (e.g., *USA Today*) 3-D charts are common, but in business they are rare. Novelty bar charts like the **pyramid chart** in Figure 3.20 are charming but should be avoided because they distort the bar volume and make it hard to measure bar height.

FIGURE 3.19

3-D Bar Chart

Source: www.mtdealer.com.

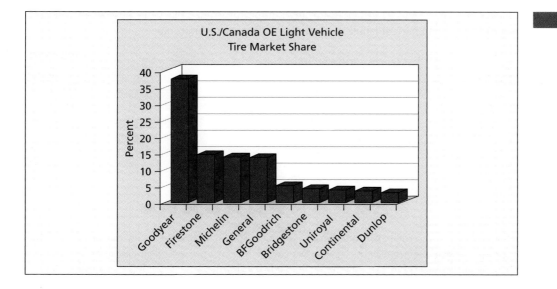

FIGURE 3.20

Pyramid Chart (avoid it)

Source: www.mtdealer.com.

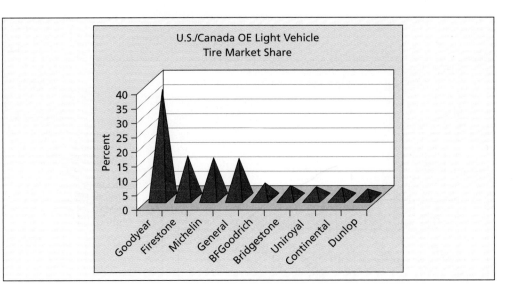

Pareto Charts

A special type of bar chart used frequently in business is the **Pareto chart**. Pareto charts are used in quality management to display the *frequency* of defects or errors of different types. Categories are displayed in descending order of frequency, so that the most common errors or defects appear first. This helps managers focus on the *significant few* (i.e., only a few categories typically account for most of the defects or errors).

Figure 3.21 shows a Pareto chart for paint and body defects in a sample of 50 new vehicles that were inspected. Defects were recorded by body location (e.g., right front door) using a checklist of 60 possible body locations. There were 38 defects altogether (many of them minor). The "top 9" locations accounted for 95 percent of the total defects (36 out of the 38 defects). The company can concentrate its quality improvement efforts on the "top 9" body locations. The Pareto chart is attractive because it is easy to understand and is directly relevant to business tasks.

Stacked Bar Chart

In a **stacked bar chart** like Figure 3.22, the bar height is the sum of several subtotals. Areas may be compared by color to show patterns in the subgroups, as well as showing the total. Stacked bar charts can be effective for any number of groups but work best when you have only a few. Use numerical labels if exact data values are of importance.

FIGURE 3.21

Pareto Chart
Pareto

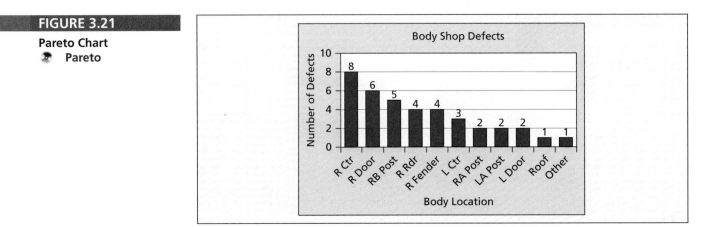

FIGURE 3.22

Stacked Bar Chart
🐟 **MedSchool**

Source: www.aamc.org.

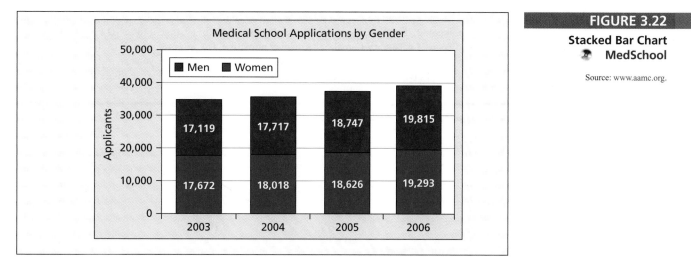

FIGURE 3.23

Same Data on: (a) Line Chart and (b) Bar Chart   🐟   CableTV

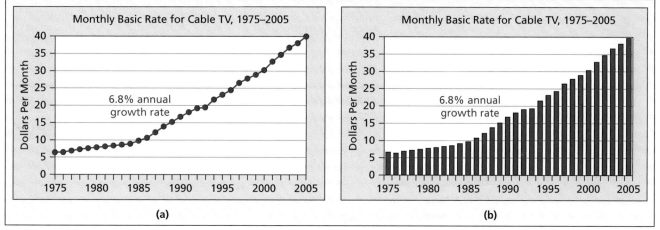

Source: *Statistical Abstract of the United States, 2007*, p. 717.

You can use a bar chart for time series data. Figure 3.23 shows the same data, first in a line chart, and then in a bar chart. Some people feel that the solid bars give a clearer sense of the trend. However, if you have more than one time series, it is harder to compare trends on a bar chart.

Tips for Effective Bar Charts

The following guidelines will help you to create the most effective bar charts:

1. The numerical variable of interest usually is shown with vertical bars on the *Y*-axis, while the category labels go on the *X*-axis.

2. If the quantity displayed is a time series, the category labels (e.g., years) are displayed on the horizontal *X*-axis with time increasing from left to right.

3. The height or length of each bar should be proportional to the quantity displayed. This is easy, since most software packages default to a zero origin on a bar graph. The zero-origin rule is essential for a corporate annual report or investor stock prospectus (e.g., to avoid overstating earnings). However, nonzero origins may be justified to reveal sufficient detail.

4. Put numerical values at the top of each bar, except when labels would impair legibility (e.g., lots of bars) or when visual simplicity is needed (e.g., for a general audience).

SECTION EXERCISES   **3.11**   (a) Use Excel to prepare a line chart to display the following gasoline price data. Modify the default colors, fonts, etc., to make the display effective. (b) Change it to a *2-D bar chart*. Modify the display if necessary to make the display attractive. Do you prefer the line chart or bar chart? Why? *Hint:* Use years as *X*-axis labels. After the chart is completed, you can right-click the chart, choose Select Data, Select Horizontal AxisLabels, and then click Edit to insert the range for the years.

Average U.S. Retail Price of Gasoline (dollars per gallon) 🐝 **GasPrice**

Year	Price	Year	Price
1950	0.27	1980	1.25
1955	0.29	1985	1.20
1960	0.31	1990	1.16
1965	0.31	1995	1.15
1970	0.36	2000	1.51
1975	0.57	2005	2.30

Source: www.fueleconomy.gov. Pre-1980 prices are for unleaded gas.

3.12   (a) Use Excel to prepare a *2-D vertical bar chart* for television sales by year. Modify the colors, fonts, etc., to make the display effective. (b) Change your graph to a *2-D horizontal bar chart*. Modify the chart if necessary to make it attractive. Do you prefer the vertical or horizontal bar chart? Why? (c) Change your graph to a *3-D vertical bar chart*. Modify the chart if necessary to make it attractive. Is 3-D better than 2-D? Why? (d) Right-click the data series, choose Chart Tools, and add labels to the data. Do the labels help?

U.S. Television Sales, 2002–2005 ($ thousands) 🐝 **TVSales**

Year	Projection TV	LCD TV	Plasma TV
2002	3,574	246	515
2003	4,351	664	1,590
2004	6,271	1,579	2,347
2005	5,320	3,295	4,012

Source: *Statistical Abstract of the United States, 2007*, p. 643.

3.13   (a) Use Excel to prepare a *stacked bar chart* for in-car use and noncar use of cell phones. Modify the colors, fonts, etc., to make the display effective. (b) Right-click the data series, choose Format Data Series, and add labels to the data. Do the labels help? *Hint:* Use only the first two data columns (not the total).

Annual U.S. Wireless Phone Usage (billions of minutes) 🐝 **Wireless**

Year	In-Car Use	NonCar Use	Total
2000	187	87	274
2001	312	191	503
2002	324	346	670
2003	400	512	912

Source: © Dow Jones & Co., Inc. Used with permission.

3.6
SCATTER PLOTS

A **scatter plot** shows *n* pairs of observations (x_1, y_1), (x_2, y_2), . . . , (x_n, y_n) as dots (or some other symbol) on an *X-Y* graph. This type of display is so important in statistics that it deserves careful attention. A scatter plot is a starting point for bivariate data analysis. We create scatter plots to investigate the relationship between two variables. Typically, we would like to know if there is an *association* between two variables and if so, what kind of association exists. As we did with univariate data analysis, let's look at a scatter plot to see what we can observe.

Table 3.7 shows the *birth rate* and *life expectancy* for nine randomly selected nations. Figure 3.24 shows a scatter plot with life expectancy on the *X*-axis and birth rates on the *Y*-axis. In this illustration, there seems to be an association between *X* and *Y*. That is, nations with higher birth rates tend to have lower life expectancy (and vice versa). No cause-and-effect relationship is implied, since in this example both variables could be influenced by a third variable that is not mentioned (e.g., GDP per capita). As with a dot plot, comments can be added. Here, nations with the lowest and highest life expectancy have been labeled. It is impractical to label all the data points.

EXAMPLE

Birth Rates and Life Expectancy

TABLE 3.7	**Birth Rates and Life Expectancy (*n* = 9 nations)**	**LifeExp**
Nation	*Birth Rate (per 1,000)*	*Life Expectancy (years)*
Afghanistan	41.03	46.60
Canada	11.09	79.70
Finland	10.60	77.80
Guatemala	34.17	66.90
Japan	10.03	80.90
Mexico	22.36	72.00
Pakistan	30.40	62.70
Spain	9.29	79.10
United States	14.10	77.40

Source: *The CIA World Factbook 2003*, www.cia.gov.

FIGURE 3.24	**Scatter Plot of Birth Rates and Life Expectancy (*n* = 9)**

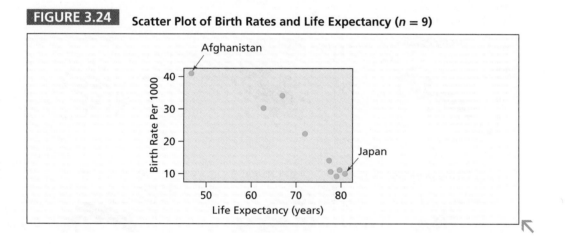

Table 3.8 shows five observations on flight time and fuel consumption for a twin-engine Piper Cheyenne aircraft. This time, a causal relationship between these two variables is assumed, since longer flights would consume more fuel.

EXAMPLE

Aircraft Fuel Consumption

TABLE 3.8	**Flight Time and Fuel Consumption**	**Cheyenne**
Trip Leg	*Flight Time (hours)*	*Fuel Used (pounds)*
1	2.3	145
2	4.2	258
3	3.6	219
4	4.7	276
5	4.9	283

Source: *Flying* 130, no. 4 (April 2003), p. 99.

The pattern in Figure 3.25 appears to be linear. The linear pattern shows that, as flight time increases, fuel consumption increases, so we say that the slope is positive. Later, you will learn about describing this relationship mathematically.

FIGURE 3.25   **Scatter Plot of Fuel Consumption and Flight Time**

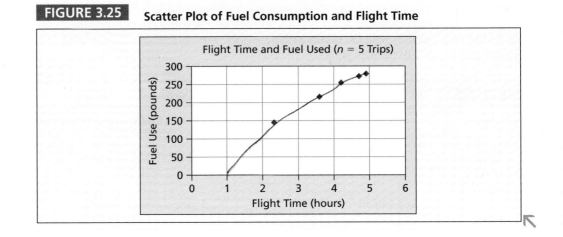

Figure 3.26 shows some scatter plot patterns similar to those that that you might observe when you have a sample of (X, Y) data pairs. A scatter plot can convey patterns in data pairs that would not be apparent from a table. Compare Figures 3.27 through 3.30 with the prototypes, and use your own words to describe the patterns that you see.

FIGURE 3.26

Prototype Scatter Plot Patterns

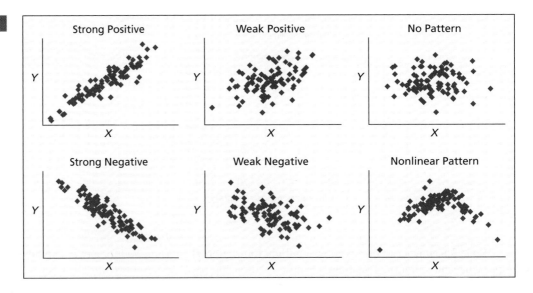

FIGURE 3.27

Very Strong Positive Association

Source: *National Center for Education Statistics.*

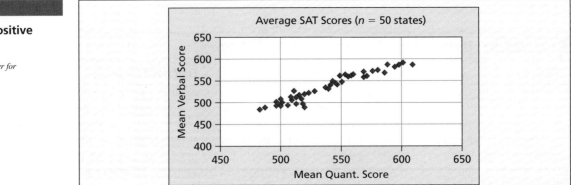

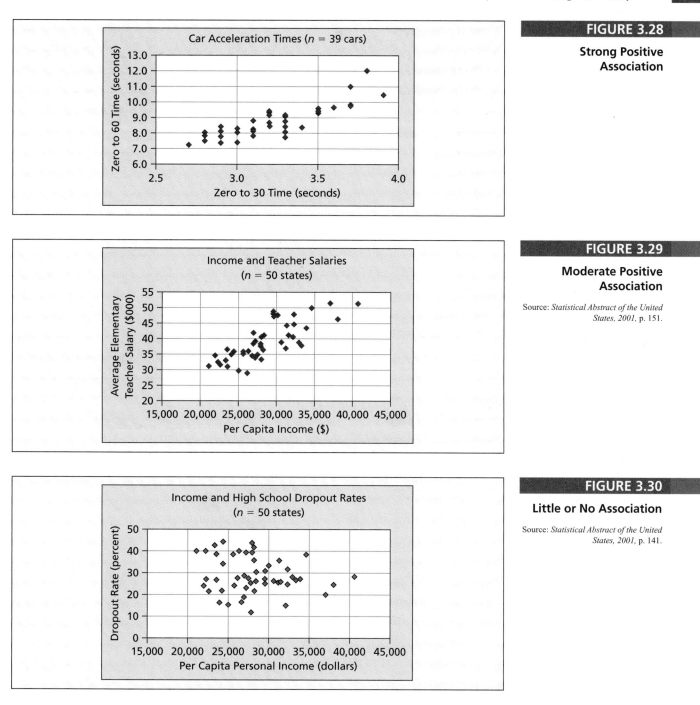

FIGURE 3.28

Strong Positive Association

FIGURE 3.29

Moderate Positive Association

Source: *Statistical Abstract of the United States, 2001,* p. 151.

FIGURE 3.30

Little or No Association

Source: *Statistical Abstract of the United States, 2001,* p. 141.

Making a Scatter Plot in Excel   LifeExp

Highlight the two data columns. Then click the Insert tab in the top menu bar. Select the Scatter icon, and choose the first template, as shown in Figure 3.31. Excel assumes that the first column is X and the second column is Y, but you can change this after the graph is created, if you wish.

The resulting scatter plot is rather plain. However, you can embellish it, as illustrated in Figure 3.32 (e.g., to add labels, change colors, try different fonts). To embellish an Excel chart, click on the chart (a border will appear to show that you have selected the chart). Above the menu bar, a Chart Tools tab will appear. Click on the Chart Tools tab and choose one of the three tabs. The Design tab will let you edit the data (e.g., select new markers or change colors for the data points). The Format tab lets you select different templates for the graph. The Layout tab is probably the one you will use most often (e.g., to add a title or axis labels; edit gridlines; or annotate the graph with a text box, arrows, or shapes). Exploring these Excel menus is a "hands-on"

FIGURE 3.31

Setting Up the Excel Scatter Plot

🐾 **LifeExp**

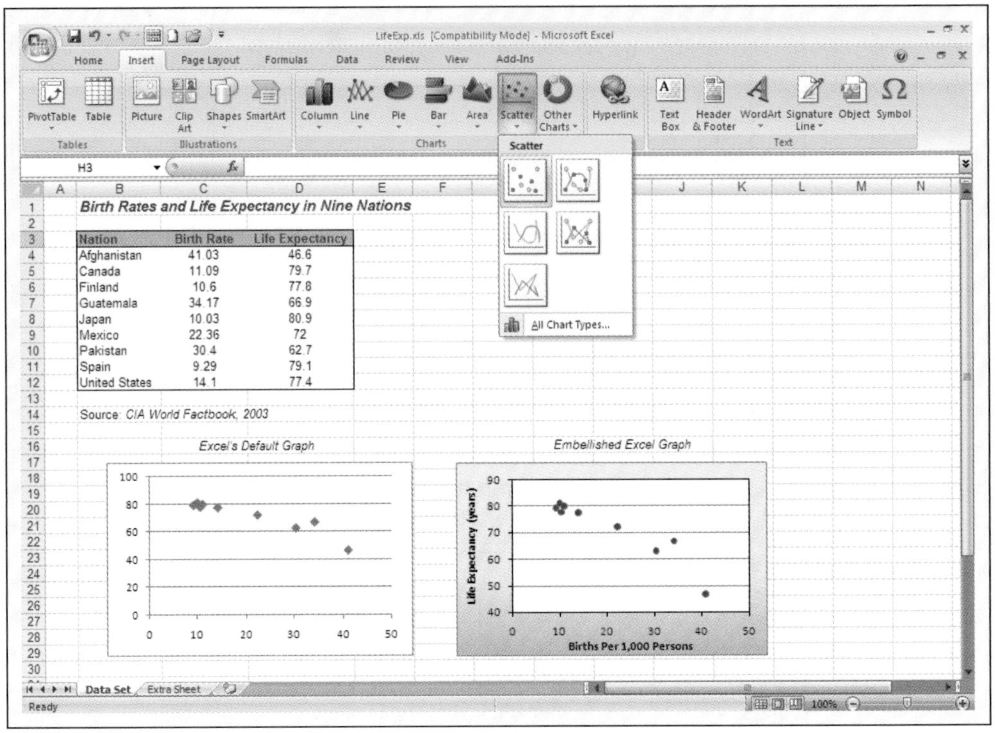

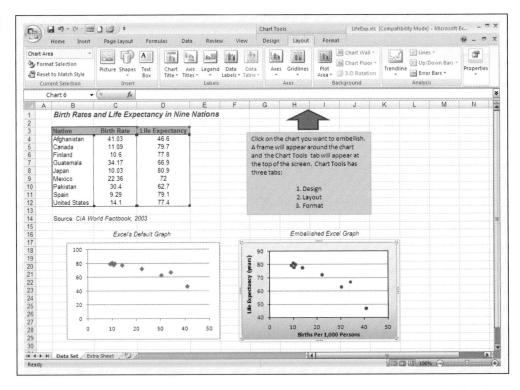

FIGURE 3.32

Using Chart Tools **to Embellish a Chart**

🐾 **LifeExp**

experience that you will have to try for yourself. At first, the proliferation of menus in Excel can be daunting, but as you gain experience you will begin to find shortcuts for the tasks that you are most likely to do. Soon, you will find ways to get what you want.

Excel's Fitted Trend Line   Excel makes it easy to fit a line to data on a scatter plot. Just click on the data, choose Add Trendline, choose the Options tab, and check Display equation on chart. This assumes a linear relationship between X and Y. For example, Figure 3.33 shows Excel's fitted trend for X = total gross leasable area and Y = total retail sales for a sample of 28 states. The slope of the line (0.2594) suggests that a unit change in X (each "unit" is

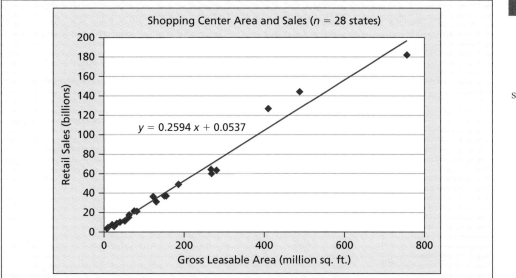

FIGURE 3.33

Excel Scatter Plot with Fitted Trend Line ($n = 28$ states)
RetailSales

Source: *Statistical Abstract of the United States, 2007*, p. 660.

one million square feet) is associated with an extra 0.2594 billion dollars in retail sales, on average. The intercept is near zero, suggesting that a shopping center with no leasable area would have no sales. Later (in Chapter 12) you will learn how Excel fits a **trend line**, how to interpret it, and when such a line is meaningful. But since almost every student discovers this option the first time he or she makes a scatter plot, we must mention Excel's fitted trend line here purely as a *descriptive tool* that may help you find patterns in (X, Y) data.

3.14 (a) Use Excel to make a scatter plot of these vehicle data, placing Weight on the X-axis and City MPG on the Y-axis. Add titles and modify the default colors, fonts, etc., as you judge appropriate to make the scatter plot effective. (b) Describe the relationship (if any) between X and Y. Weak? Strong? Negative? Positive? Linear? Nonlinear?

SECTION EXERCISES

connect

Weight and MPG for 20 Randomly Selected Vehicles CityMPG

Vehicle	City MPG	Weight (lbs.)
Acura TSX	23	3,320
BMW 3-Series	19	3,390
Chevrolet Corvette	19	3,255
Chevrolet Silverado 1500	14	4,935
Chrysler Pacifica	17	4,660
Dodge Caravan	18	4,210
Ford Focus	26	2,760
Infiniti FX	16	4,295
Jaguar XJ8	18	3,805
Lexus IS300	18	3,390
Lincoln Aviator	13	5,000
Mazda 6	19	3,355
Land Rover Freelander	17	3,640
Mercedes-Benz S-Class	17	4,195
Nissan 350Z	20	3,345
Nissan Xterra	16	4,315
Pontiac Vibe	28	2,805
Pontiac Grand Am	25	3,095
Toyota Sienna	19	4,120
Volvo C70	20	3,690

Source: © 2003 by Consumers Union of U.S., Inc. Yonkers, NY, a nonprofit organization. From *Consumer Reports New Car Buying Guide, 2003–2004*. Used with permission.

3.15 (a) Use Excel to make a scatter plot of the following exam score data, placing Midterm on the X-axis and Final on the Y-axis. Add titles and modify the default colors, fonts, etc., as you judge appropriate to make the scatter plot effective. (b) Describe the relationship (if any) between X and Y. Weak? Strong? Negative? Positive? Linear? Nonlinear?

Exam Scores for 18 Statistics Students   **ExamScores**

Name	Midterm Score	Final Score	Name	Midterm Score	Final Score
Aaron	50	30	Joe	68	83
Angela	95	83	Lisa	75	58
Brandon	75	90	Liz	70	83
Buck	60	83	Michele	60	73
Carole	60	75	Nancy	88	78
Cecilia	63	45	Ryan	93	100
Charles	90	100	Tania	73	83
Dmitri	88	90	Ursula	33	53
Ellie	75	68	Xiaodong	60	70

3.16 (a) Use Excel to make a scatter plot of the data, placing Floor Space on the X-axis and Weekly Sales on the Y-axis. Add titles and modify the default colors, fonts, etc., as you judge appropriate to make the scatter plot effective. (b) Describe the relationship (if any) between X and Y. Weak? Strong? Negative? Positive? Linear? Nonlinear?   **FloorSpace**

Floor Space (sq. ft.)	Weekly Sales (dollars)
6,060	16,380
5,230	14,400
4,280	13,820
5,580	18,230
5,670	14,200
5,020	12,800
5,410	15,840
4,990	16,610
4,220	13,610
4,160	10,050
4,870	15,320
5,470	13,270

3.17 (a) Use Excel to make a scatter plot of the data for bottled water sales for 10 weeks, placing Price on the X-axis and Units Sold on the Y-axis. Add titles and modify the default colors, fonts, etc., as you judge appropriate to make the scatter plot effective. (b) Describe the relationship (if any) between X and Y. Weak? Strong? Negative? Positive? Linear? Nonlinear?   **WaterSold**

Unit Price	Units Sold
1.15	186
0.94	216
1.04	173
1.05	182
1.08	183
1.33	150
0.99	190
1.25	165
1.16	190
1.11	201

Tables are the simplest form of data display, yet creating effective tables is an acquired skill. By arranging numbers in rows and columns, their meaning can be enhanced so it can be understood at a glance.

Table 3.9 is a *compound table* that contains time series data (going down the columns) on seven variables (going across the rows). The data can be viewed in several ways. We can focus on the time pattern (going down the columns) or on comparing public and private spending (between columns) for a given school level (elementary/secondary or college/university). Or we can compare spending by school level (elementary/secondary or college/university) for a given type of control (public or private). Figures are rounded to three or four significant digits to make it easier for the reader. Units of measurement are stated in the footnote to keep the column headings simple. Columns are grouped using merged heading cells (blank columns could be inserted to add vertical separation). Presentation tables can be linked dynamically to spreadsheets so that slides can be updated quickly, but take care that data changes do not adversely affect the table layout.

TABLE 3.9 School Expenditures by Control and Level, 1960–2000   Schools

Year	All Schools	Elementary and Secondary			Colleges and Universities		
		Total	*Public*	*Private*	*Total*	*Public*	*Private*
1960	142.2	99.6	93.0	6.6	42.6	23.3	19.3
1970	317.3	200.2	188.6	11.6	117.2	75.2	41.9
1980	373.6	232.7	216.4	16.2	140.9	93.4	47.4
1990	526.1	318.5	293.4	25.1	207.6	132.9	74.7
2000	691.9	418.2	387.8	30.3	273.8	168.8	105.0

Source: U.S. Census Bureau, *Statistical Abstract of the United States, 2002*, p. 133.
Note: All figures are in billions of constant 2000–2001 dollars.

Tips for EffectiveTables

Here are some tips for creating effective tables:

1. Keep the table simple, consistent with its purpose. Put summary tables in the *main body* of the written report and detailed tables in an *appendix*. In a slide presentation, the main point of the table should be clear to the reader within *10 seconds*. If not, break the table into parts or aggregate the data.

2. Display the data to be compared in columns rather than rows. Research shows that people find it easier to compare across rather than down.

3. For presentation purposes, round off to three or four significant digits (e.g., 142 rather than 142.213). People mentally round numbers anyway. Exceptions: when accounting requirements supersede the desire for rounding or when the numbers are used in subsequent calculations.

4. Physical table layout should guide the eye toward the comparison you wish to emphasize. Spaces or shading may be used to separate rows or columns. Use lines sparingly.

5. Row and column headings should be simple yet descriptive.

6. Within a column, use a consistent number of decimal digits. Right-justify or decimal-align the data unless all field widths are the same within the column.

Pivot Tables   PivotTable

One of Excel's most popular and powerful features is the **pivot table**, which provides interactive analysis of a data matrix. The simplest kind of pivot table has rows and columns. Each of its cells shows a statistic for a row and column combination. The row and column variables must be either *categorical* or *discrete numerical* and the variable for the table cells must be *numerical* (review Chapter 2 if you do not remember these terms). After the table is created, you can change the table by dragging variable names from the list specified in your data matrix. You can change the displayed statistic in the cells (sum, count, average, maximum, minimum, product) by right-clicking the display and selecting from the *field settings* menu. We show here the steps needed to create a pivot table for a small data matrix (25 homes, 3 variables). The first table shows the *frequency count* of homes for each cell (you can pick any cell and verify the count of the number of homes in that cell). The second table was created by copying the first table and then changing the cells to display the *average* square feet of homes in that cell.

Step 1: Select the Insert tab and specify the data range.

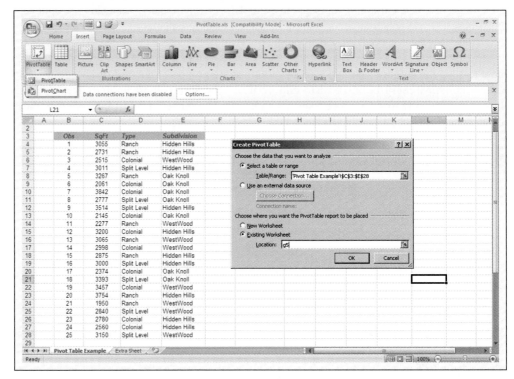

Step 2: Drag and drop desired fields for rows, columns, and the table body.

Step 3: Now you can format the table or right-click to choose desired field setting.

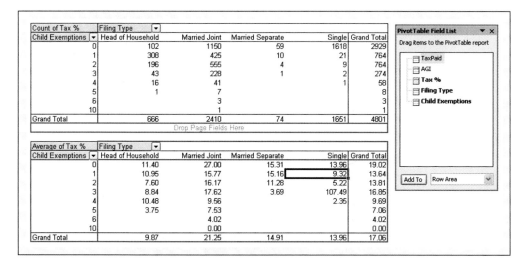

LearningStats has a more detailed step-by-step guide to creating a pivot table (see the end of this chapter list of *LearningStats* demonstrations). A pivot table is especially useful when you have a large data matrix with several variables. For example, Figure 3.34 shows two pivot tables based on tax return data for $n = 4,801$ U.S. taxpayers. The first pivot table shows the number of taxpayers by filing type (single, married joint, married separate, head of household) cross-tabulated against the number of child exemptions (0, 1, 2, . . . , 10). The second pivot table shows average tax rate (percent) for each cell in the cross-tabulation. Note that some of the averages are based on small cell counts.

Count of Tax %	Filing Type				
Child Exemptions	Head of Household	Married Joint	Married Separate	Single	Grand Total
0	102	1150	59	1618	2929
1	308	425	10	21	764
2	196	555	4	9	764
3	43	228	1	2	274
4	16	41		1	58
5	1	7			8
6		3			3
10		1			1
Grand Total	666	2410	74	1651	4801

Average of Tax %	Filing Type				
Child Exemptions	Head of Household	Married Joint	Married Separate	Single	Grand Total
0	11.40	27.00	15.31	13.96	19.02
1	10.95	15.77	15.16	9.32	13.64
2	7.60	16.17	11.28	5.22	13.81
3	8.84	17.62	3.69	107.49	16.85
4	10.48	9.56		2.35	9.69
5	3.75	7.53			7.06
6		4.02			4.02
10		0.00			0.00
Grand Total	9.87	21.25	14.91	13.96	17.06

PivotTable Field List

Drag items to the PivotTable report

- TaxPaid
- AGI
- Tax %
- Filing Type
- Child Exemptions

Add To   Row Area

FIGURE 3.34

Two Pivot Tables for U.S. Income Tax Returns ($n = 4,801$)   Taxes

An Oft-Abused Chart   PieCharts

Many statisticians feel that a table or bar chart is a better choice than a **pie chart** for several reasons. But, because of their visual appeal, pie charts appear daily in company annual reports and the popular press (e.g., *USA Today, The Wall Street Journal, Scientific American*) so you must understand their uses and misuses. A pie chart can only convey a *general idea of the data*

3.8

PIE CHARTS

because it is hard to assess areas precisely. It should have only a few slices (e.g., two or three) and the slices should be labeled with data values or percents. The only correct use of a pie chart is to *portray data which sum to a total* (e.g., percent market shares). A simple 2-D pie chart is best, as in Figure 3.35. A bar chart (Figure 3.36) could be used to display the same data.

Pie Chart Options   PieCharts ————————————————————————•

Exploded and *3-D pie charts* (Figures 3.37 and 3.38) add visual interest, but the sizes of pie slices are even harder to assess. Nonetheless, you will see 3-D charts in business publications because of their strong visual impact. Black-and-white charts may be used internally in business, but color is typically preferred for customers, stockholders, or investors. Practices may change as color copiers become more cost-effective.

FIGURE 3.35

2-D Pie with Labels
 Textbook

Source: Web survey of 269 students at two large public universities in 2007.

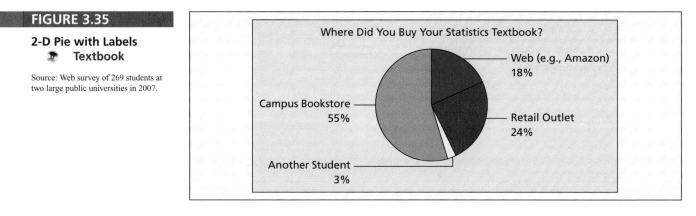

FIGURE 3.36

Bar Chart Alternative
 Textbook

Source: Web survey of 269 students at two large public universities in 2007.

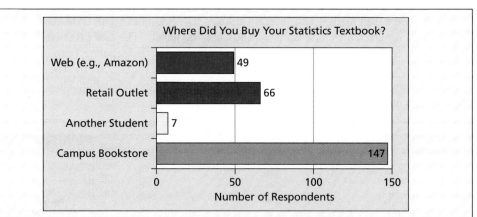

FIGURE 3.37

Exploded Pie Chart

Source: *PC Magazine* 22, no. 4 (March 11, 2003).

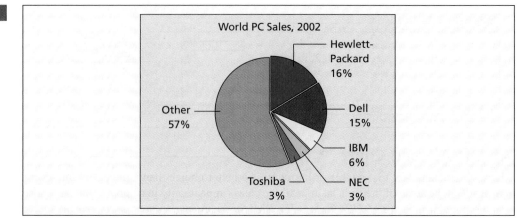

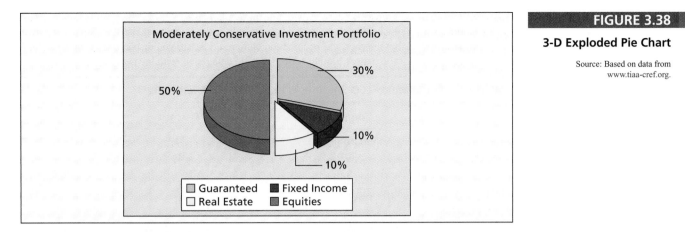

FIGURE 3.38

3-D Exploded Pie Chart

Source: Based on data from
www.tiaa-cref.org.

Common Errors in Pie Chart Usage

- Pie charts can only convey a general idea of the data values.
- Pie charts are ineffective when they have too many slices.
- Pie chart data must represent *parts of a whole* (e.g., percent market share).

SECTION EXERCISES

3.18 (a) Use Excel to prepare a *2-D pie chart* for these Web-surfing data. Modify the default colors, fonts, etc., as you judge appropriate to make the display effective. (b) Right-click the chart area, select Chart Type, and change to an *exploded 2-D pie chart*. (c) Right-click the chart area, select Chart Type, and change to a *bar chart*. Which do you prefer? Why? *Hint:* Include data labels with the percent *values*.

Are You Concerned About Being Tracked While Web Surfing? WebSurf	
Level of Concern	*Percent*
Very/extreme concern	68
Somewhat concerned	23
No/little concern	9
Total	100

Source: *PC Magazine* 21, no. 11 (November 2003), p. 146.

3.19 (a) Use Excel to prepare a *2-D pie chart* for the following Pitney-Bowes data. Modify the default colors, fonts, etc., as you judge appropriate to make the display effective. (b) Right-click the chart area, select Chart Type, and change to a *3-D pie chart*. (c) Right-click the chart area, select Chart Type, and change to a *bar chart*. Which do you prefer? Why? *Hint:* Include data labels with the percent *values*.

Pitney-Bowes Medical Claims in 2003 PitneyBowes	
Spent On	*Percent of Total*
Hospital services	47.5
Physicians	27.0
Pharmaceuticals	19.5
Mental health	5.0
Other	1.0
Total	100.0

Source: *The Wall Street Journal,* July 13, 2004, p. A10. © Dow Jones & Co., Inc. Used with permission.

3.20   (a) Use Excel to prepare a *2-D pie chart* for these LCD (liquid crystal display) shipments data. Modify the default colors, fonts, etc., as you judge appropriate to make the display effective. (b) Do you feel that the chart has become too cluttered (i.e., are you displaying too many slices)? Would a bar chart be better? Explain. *Hint:* Include data labels with the percent *values.*

World Market Share of LCD Shipments in 2004   LCDMarket

Company	Percent
Sharp	34.6
Zenith	10.9
Sony	10.5
Samsung	9.6
Panasonic	8.7
Phillips	8.5
Others	17.3
Total	100.0

Source: *The Wall Street Journal,* July 15, 2004, p. B1. © Dow Jones & Co., Inc. Used with permission.

May not add to 100 due to rounding.

3.9
EFFECTIVE EXCEL CHARTS

You've heard it said that a picture is worth a thousand words. Effective visual displays help you get your point across and persuade others to listen to your point of view. Good visuals help your employer make better decisions, but they also make *you* a more desirable employee and help *you* see the facts more clearly. Powerful graphics stand out in business reports, to the career benefit of those who know how to create them. This means knowing which visual displays to use in different situations. If you can make complex data comprehensible, you stand to gain a reputation for clear thinking.

The good news is that it's fun to make Excel graphs. The skills to make good displays can be learned, and the information provided here builds on the basics of Excel graphical displays that you have already learned. Excel is used widely throughout business primarily because of its excellent graphics capabilities. You say you already know all about Excel charts? That would be surprising. Professionals who make charts say that they learn new things every day.

Excel offers a vast array of charts. Although only a few of them are likely to be used in business, it is a good idea to review the whole list and to become familiar with their uses (and abuses). For example, Figure 3.39 shows data on fractional shares of aircraft ownership from

FIGURE 3.39

Inserting a Chart
    Fractional

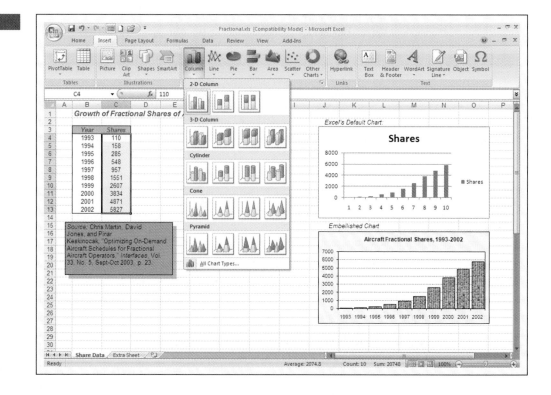

1993 to 2002 in cells C4:C13. Use the mouse to select the data you want to plot, so the data are highlighted. Click the *Insert* tab on Excel's upper menu bar, and select the icon for the type of chart you want. The appropriate chart type depends on the data. A simple bar chart is appropriate for the fractional shares time series.

Embellished Charts

Excel's default charts tend to be very plain. (See Excel's default bar chart in Figure 3.39). But business charts need not be dull. You can customize any graph to your taste. Figures 3.40 and 3.41 show embellished bar charts for the same data. After the chart is created in Excel, you can edit the graph to:

- Improve the titles (main, *X*-axis, *Y*-axis).
- Change the axis scales (minimum, maximum, demarcations).
- Display the data values (on top of each bar).
- Add a data table underneath the graph.
- Change color or patterns in the plot area or chart area.
- Format the decimals (on the axes or data labels).
- Edit the gridlines (color, dotted or solid, patterns).
- Alter the appearance of the bars (color, pattern, gap width).

To alter a chart's appearance, click on any chart object (plot area, *X*-axis, *Y*-axis, gridlines, title, data series, chart area) to select the object, and then right-click to see a menu showing the *properties* that you can change. *LearningStats* Unit 03 gives a step-by-step explanation of how to make and edit charts in Excel. Just don't let your artistic verve overwhelm the data.

Excel offers many other types of specialized charts. When data points are connected and the area is filled with color or shading, the result is an *area chart* (or *mountain chart*). This is basically a line chart. Its appeal is a feeling of solid dimensionality, which might make trends

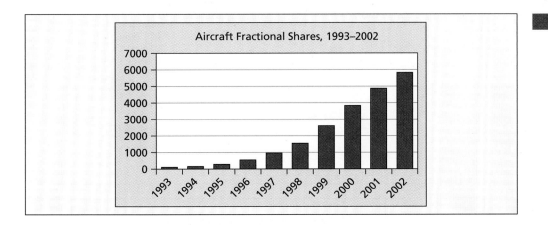

FIGURE 3.40

Embellished Bar Chart

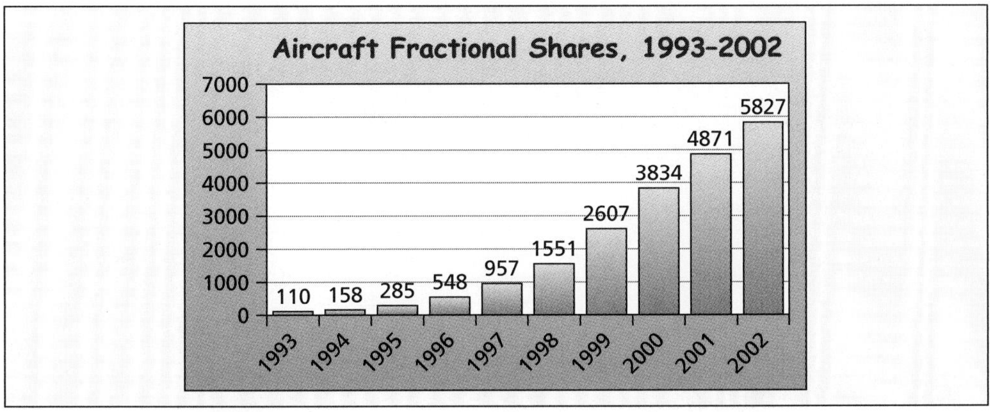

FIGURE 3.41

Over-Embellished Chart?

or patterns clearer to the reader. Figure 3.42 shows an example. A drawback is that, when plotting more than one variable (e.g., especially time series data), we can distinguish variables only if the data values "in back" are larger than the data values "in front." We might be better off using a multiple bar chart as in Figure 3.43 (or a line chart if we were showing time series data).

Excel offers other specialized charts, including:

- *Bubble* charts (to display three variables on a 2-dimensional scatter plot).
- *Stock* charts (for high/low/close stock prices).
- *Radar* or *spider* charts (to compare individual performance against a benchmark).

Although **radar charts** (spider charts) are visually attractive, statisticians have reservations about them because they distort the data by emphasizing *areas*. In Figure 3.44, MedMax HMO seems farther below the industry benchmark on most criteria, because the eye sees *areas*.

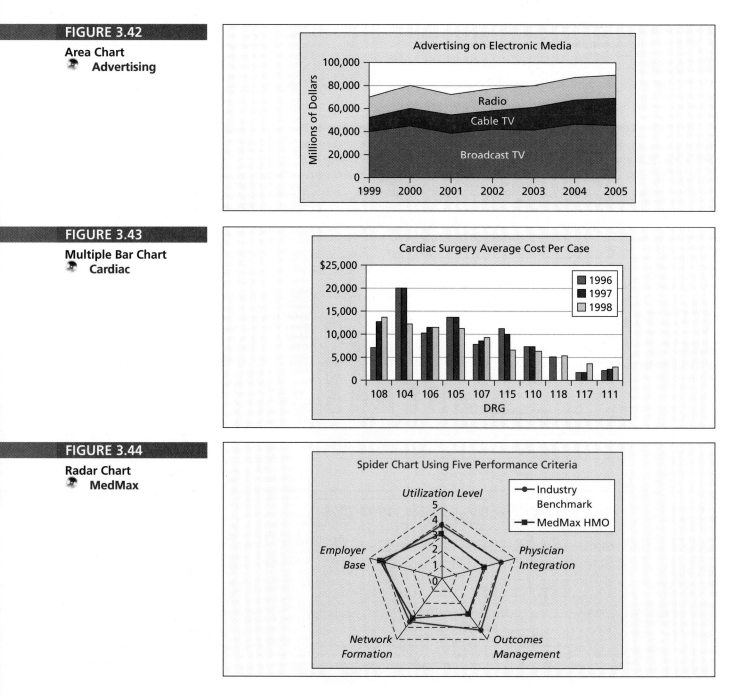

FIGURE 3.42

Area Chart
🌀 **Advertising**

FIGURE 3.43

Multiple Bar Chart
🌀 **Cardiac**

FIGURE 3.44

Radar Chart
🌀 **MedMax**

We have explained how to create *good* graphs. Now, let's turn things around. As an impartial consumer of information, you need a checklist of errors to beware. Those who want to slant the facts may do these things deliberately, although most errors occur through ignorance. Use this list to protect yourself against ignorant or unscrupulous practitioners of the graphical arts.

Error 1: Nonzero Origin   NonZero

A nonzero origin will exaggerate the trend. Measured distances do not match the stated values or axis demarcations. The accounting profession is particularly aggressive in enforcing this rule. Although zero origins are preferred, sometimes a nonzero origin is needed to show sufficient detail. Here are two charts of the same data. The first chart (non-zero origin) exaggerates the trend.

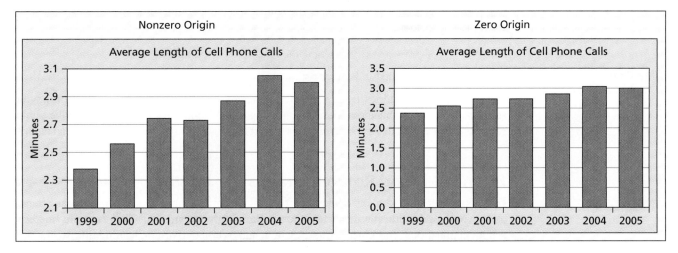

Error 2: Elastic Graph Proportions   Elastic

By shortening the *X*-axis in relation to the *Y*-axis, vertical change is exaggerated. For a time series (*X*-axis representing time) this can make a sluggish sales or profit curve appear steep. Conversely, a wide *X*-axis and short *Y*-axis can downplay alarming changes (recalls, industrial accidents). Keep the *aspect ratio* (width/height) below 2.00. Excel graphs use a default aspect ratio of about 1.8. The Golden Ratio you learned in art history suggests that 1.62 is ideal. Older TV screens use a 1:33 ratio as do older PCs (640 × 480 pixels). Movies use a wide-screen format (up to 2.55) but VHS tapes and DVDs may crop it to fit on a television screen. HDTV and multimedia computers use a 16:9 aspect ratio (about 1.78). Charts whose height exceeds their width don't fit well on pages or computer screens. These two charts show the same data. Which seems to be growing faster?

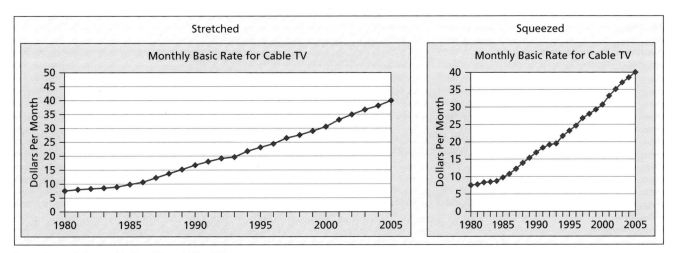

Source: *Statistical Abstract of the United States, 2007*, p. 717.

Error 3: Dramatic Title

The title often is designed more to grab the reader's attention than to convey the chart's content (Criminals on a Spree, Deficit Swamps Economy). Sometimes the title attempts to draw your conclusion for you (Inflation Wipes Out Savings, Imports Dwarf Exports). A title should be short but adequate for the purpose.

Error 4: Distracting Pictures

To add visual pizzazz, artists may superimpose the chart on a photograph (e.g., a gasoline price chart atop a photo of Middle East warfare) or add colorful cartoon figures, banners, or drawings. This is mostly harmless, but can distract the reader or impart an emotional slant (e.g., softening bad news about the home team's slide toward the cellar by drawing a sad-face team mascot cartoon).

Error 5: Authority Figures

Advertisements sometimes feature mature, attractive, conservatively attired actors portraying scientists, doctors, or business leaders examining scientific-looking charts. Because the public respects science's reputation, such displays impart credibility to self-serving commercial claims.

Error 6: 3-D and Rotated Graphs 🖱 MedSchool

By making a graph 3-dimensional and/or rotating it through space, the author can make trends appear to dwindle into the distance or loom alarmingly toward you. This example (medical school applications) combines errors 1, 3, 4, 5, and 6 (nonzero origin, leading title, distracting picture, vague source, rotated 3-D look).

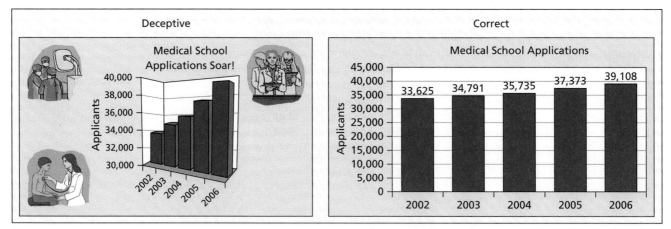

Source: www.aamc.org.

Error 7: Missing Axis Demarcations

Without "tick" marks on the axis, the reader cannot identify individual data values. Grid lines help the viewer compare magnitudes but are often omitted for clarity. For maximum clarity in a bar graph, label each bar with its numerical value, unless the scale is clearly demarcated and labeled.

Error 8: Missing Measurement Units or Definitions

Missing or unclear units of measurement (dollars? percent?) can render a chart useless. Even if the vertical scale is in dollars, we must know whether the variable being plotted is sales, profits, assets, or whatever. If percent, indicate clearly *percentage of what.*

Error 9: Vague Source

Large federal agencies or corporations employ thousands of people and issue hundreds of reports per year. Vague sources like "Department of Commerce" may indicate that the author lost the citation, didn't know the data source, or mixed data from several sources. Scientific publications insist on complete source citations. Rules are less rigorous for publications aimed at a general audience.

Error 10: Complex Graphs

Complicated visual displays make the reader work harder. Keep your main objective in mind. Omit "bonus" detail or put it in the appendix. Apply the *10-second rule* to graphs. If the message really is complex, can it be broken into smaller parts? This example (surgery volume) combines errors 3, 4, 7, 8, 9, and 10 (silly subtitle, distracting pictures, no data labels, no definitions, vague source, too much information).

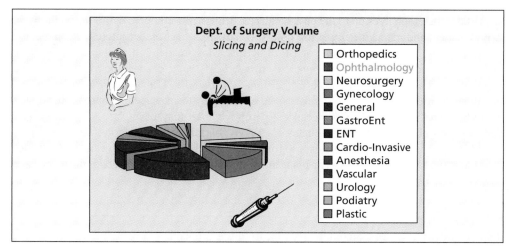

Source: Hospital reports.

Error 11: Gratuitous Effects

Slide shows often use color and special effects (sound, interesting slide transitions, spinning text, etc.) to attract attention. But once the novelty wears off, audiences may find special effects annoying.

Error 12: Estimated Data

In a spirit of zeal to include the "latest" figures, the last few data points in a time series are often estimated. Or perhaps a couple of years were missing or incompatible, so the author had to "fill in the blanks." At a minimum, estimated points should be noted.

Error 13: Area Trick 🐁 AreaTrick

One of the most pernicious visual tricks is simultaneously enlarging the width of the bars as their height increases, so the bar area misstates the true proportion (e.g., by replacing graph bars with figures like human beings, coins, or gas pumps). As figure height increases, so does width, distorting the area. This example (physician salaries) illustrates this distortion.

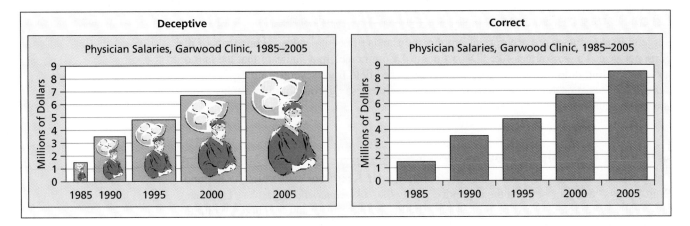

Final Advice

Can you trust any visual display (unless you created it yourself)? Be a skeptic, and be pleasantly surprised if the graph lives up to the best standards. Print media compete with TV and the Web, so newspapers and magazines must use colorful charts to attract reader interest. People enjoy visual displays, so we accept some artistic liberties. Mass-readership publications like *U.S. News & World Report, Maclean's, Time, Newsweek, USA Today,* or even the more specialized business-oriented publications like *Forbes, Fortune, BusinessWeek,* and *The Wall Street Journal* should not be judged by the same standards you would apply to an academic journal. Businesses want charts that follow the rules, because a deceptive chart may have serious consequences. Decisions may be made about products or services that affect lives, market share, and jobs (including yours). So know the rules, try to follow them, and expect your peers and subordinates to do the same. Catchy graphics have a place in selling your ideas but shouldn't dominate the data.

Further Challenges

If you enjoy playing with computers, try to learn these skills on your own:

- Copy and paste Excel charts into Word or PowerPoint.
- Copy and paste charts from other software (MINITAB, Visual Statistics).
- Use screen captures and edit the results in Paint if necessary.
- Use presentation software (e.g., PowerPoint) with transition effects.
- Know how (and when) to link Excel charts to spreadsheets.
- Use clip art and create your own simple graphics.

CHAPTER SUMMARY

For a set of observations on a single numerical variable, a **dot plot** displays the individual data values, while a **frequency distribution** classifies the data into classes called **bins** for a **histogram** of **frequencies** for each bin. The number of bins and their limits are matters left to your judgment, though **Sturges' Rule** offers advice on the number of bins. The **line chart** shows values of one or more **time series** variables plotted against time. A **log scale** is sometimes used in time series charts when data vary by orders of magnitude. The **bar chart** shows a **numerical** data value for each category of an **attribute.** However, a bar chart can also be used for a time series. A **scatter plot** can reveal the association (or lack of association) between two variables *X* and *Y.* The **pie chart** (showing a **numerical** data value for each category of an **attribute** if the data values are parts of a whole) is common but should be used with caution. Sometimes a **simple table** is the best visual display. Creating effective visual displays is an acquired skill. Excel offers a wide range of charts from which to choose. Deceptive graphs are found frequently in both media and business presentations, and the consumer should be aware of common errors.

CHAPTER REVIEW

1. (a) What is a dot plot? (b) Why are dot plots attractive? (c) What are their limitations?

2. (a) What is a frequency distribution? (b) What are the steps in creating one?

3. (a) What is a histogram? (b) What does it show?

4. (a) What is a bimodal histogram? (b) Explain the difference between left-skewed, symmetric, and right-skewed histograms. (c) What is an outlier?

5. (a) What is a scatter plot? (b) What do scatter plots reveal? (c) Sketch a scatter plot with a moderate positive correlation. (d) Sketch a scatter plot with a strong negative correlation.

6. For what kind of data would we use a bar chart? List three tips for creating effective bar charts.

7. For what kind of data would we use a line chart? List three tips for creating effective line charts.

8. (a) List the three most common types of charts in business, and sketch each type (no real data, just a sketch). (b) List three specialized charts that can be created in Excel, and sketch each type (no real data, just a sketch).

9. (a) For what kind of data would we use a pie chart? (b) Name two common pie chart errors. (c) Why are pie charts regarded with skepticism by some statisticians?

10. Which types of charts can be used for time series data?

11. (a) When might we need a log scale? (b) What do equal distances on a log scale represent? (c) State one drawback of a log scale graph.

12. (a) When might we use a stacked bar chart? An area chart? A radar chart? (b) Sketch one of each (no real data, just a sketch).

13. List six deceptive graphical techniques.

14. What is a pivot table? Why is it useful?

CHAPTER EXERCISES

Note: In these exercises, you may use a software package. Use MegaStat's Descriptive Statistics for dot plots or Frequency Distributions for histograms. Use MINITAB's Graphs or a similar software package to create the dot plot or histogram.

connect

3.21 A study of 40 U.S. cardiac care centers showed the following ratios of nurses to beds. (a) Prepare a dot plot. (b) Prepare a frequency distribution and histogram (you may either specify the bins yourself or use automatic bins). (c) Describe the distribution, based on these displays.
  Nurses

1.48	1.16	1.24	1.52	1.30	1.28	1.68	1.40	1.12	0.98	0.93	2.76
1.34	1.58	1.72	1.38	1.44	1.41	1.34	1.96	1.29	1.21	2.00	1.50
1.68	1.39	1.62	1.17	1.07	2.11	2.40	1.35	1.48	1.59	1.81	1.15
1.35	1.42	1.33	1.41								

3.22 The first Rose Bowl (football) was played in 1902. The next was not played until 1916, but a Rose Bowl has been played every year since then. The margin of victory in each of the 87 Rose Bowls from 1902 through 2003 is shown below (0 indicates a tie). (a) Prepare a dot plot. (b) Prepare a frequency distribution and histogram (you may either specify the bins yourself or use automatic bins). (c) Describe the distribution, based on these displays. (Data are from *Sports Illustrated 2004 Sports Almanac,* and www.cbs.sportsline.com.)
  RoseBowl

49	14	14	1	28	0	11	0	17	1	0
1	1	33	24	9	35	7	16	7	21	13
4	14	8	4	9	29	25	20	31	49	6
3	8	33	7	8	13	3	16	3	26	36
10	18	5	10	27	2	1	11	11	7	10
1	25	21	1	13	8	7	7	1	17	28
10	36	3	17	7	3	8	7	12	20	7
5	18	9	3	5	7	8	10	23	20	

3.23 An executive's telephone log showed the following data for the length of 65 calls initiated during the last week of July. (a) Prepare a dot plot. (b) Prepare a frequency distribution and histogram (you may either specify the bins yourself or use automatic bins). (c) Describe the distribution, based on these displays. 🦇 **CallLength**

1	2	10	5	3	3	2	20	1	1
6	3	13	2	2	1	26	3	1	3
1	2	1	7	1	2	3	1	2	12
1	4	2	2	29	1	1	1	8	5
1	4	2	1	1	1	1	6	1	2
3	3	6	1	3	1	1	5	1	18
2	13	13	1	6					

3.24 Below are batting averages of the New York Yankees players who were at bat five times or more in 2006. (a) Construct a frequency distribution. Explain how you chose the number of bins and the bin limits. (b) Make a histogram and describe its appearance. (c) Repeat, using a different number of bins and different bin limits. (d) Did your visual impression of the data change when you changed the number of bins? Explain. *Note:* You may use MegaStat or MINITAB if your instructor agrees. 🦇 **Yankees**

Batting Averages for the 2006 New York Yankees

Player	Avg	Player	Avg	Player	Avg
Derek Jeter	0.343	Miguel Cairo	0.239	Sal Fasano	0.143
Johnny Damon	0.285	Bobby Abreu	0.330	Terrence Long	0.167
Alex Rodriguez	0.290	Hideki Matsui	0.302	Kevin Thompson	0.300
Robinson Cano	0.342	Gary Sheffield	0.298	Kevin Reese	0.417
Jorge Posada	0.277	Craig Wilson	0.212	Andy Cannizaro	0.250
Melky Cabrera	0.280	Bubba Crosby	0.207	Randy Johnson	0.167
Jason Giambi	0.253	Aaron Guiel	0.256	Wil Nieves	0.000
Bernie Williams	0.281	Kelly Stinnett	0.228		
Andy Phillips	0.240	Nick Green	0.240		

Source: www.thebaseballcube.com/statistics/2006/.

3.25 Concerned about a possible threat of hearing loss due to cockpit noise, airline pilots took measurements of cockpit noise levels in several aircraft during various flight phases (climb, cruise, descent). Is the cockpit noise level related to airspeed? Use the CD data set ($n = 61$) to prepare a scatter plot of X = airspeed (knots) and Y = cockpit noise level (decibels). Describe what the scatter plot tells you. *Hint:* You may need to rescale the X and Y axes to see more detail. 🦇 **CockpitNoise**

3.26 (a) What kind of display is this? (b) Identify its strengths and weaknesses, using the tips and checklists shown in this chapter. (c) Can you suggest any improvements? Would a different type of display be better? 🦇 **WomenPilots**

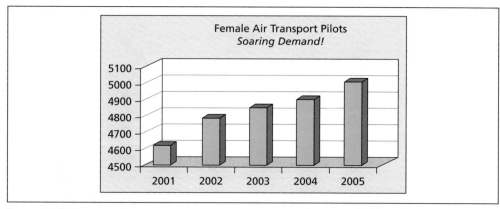

Source: www.faa.gov.

3.27 (a) What kind of display is this? (b) Identify its strengths and weaknesses, using the tips and checklists shown in this chapter. (c) Can you suggest any improvements? Would a different type of display be better?   **MedError**

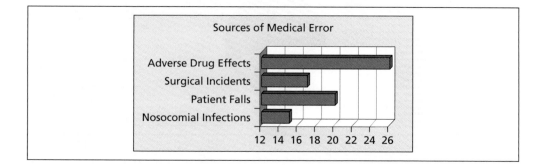

3.28 (a) What kind of display is this? (b) Identify its strengths and weaknesses, using the tips and checklists shown in this chapter. (c) Can you suggest any improvements? Would a different type of display be better?   **Oxnard**

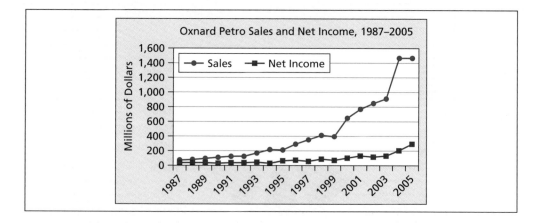

3.29 (a) What kind of display is this? (b) Identify its strengths and weaknesses, using the tips and checklists shown in this chapter. (c) Can you suggest any improvements? Would a different type of display be better?   **Bankruptcies**

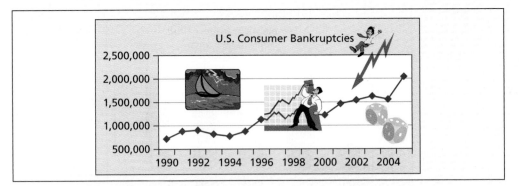

Source: American Bankruptcy Institute, www.abiworld.org.

3.30 (a) What kind of display is this? (b) Identify its strengths and weaknesses, using the tips and checklists shown in this chapter. (c) Can you suggest any improvements? Would a different type of display be better? **Advertising**

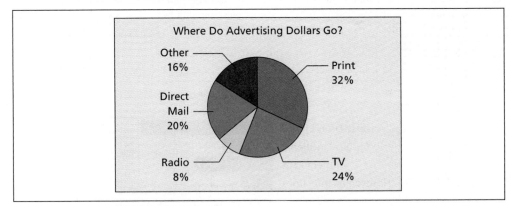

Source: *Statistical Abstract of the United States, 2002*, p. 772.

3.31 (a) What kind of display is this? (b) Identify its strengths and weaknesses, using the tips and checklists shown in this chapter. (c) Can you suggest any improvements? Would a different type of display be better?

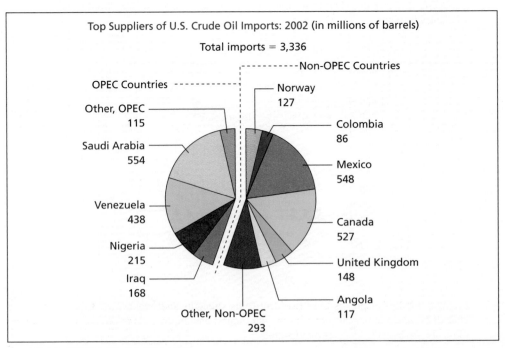

Source: *Statistical Abstract of the United States, 2003*.

3.32 (a) What kind of display is this? (b) Identify its strengths and weaknesses, using the tips and checklists shown in this chapter. (c) Can you suggest any improvements? Would a different type of display be better? **BirthRate**

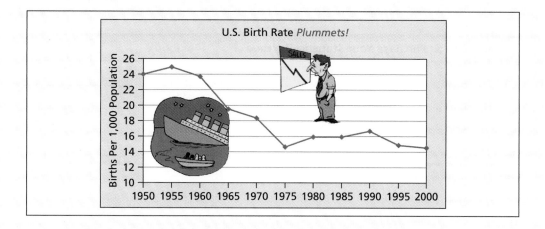

3.33 (a) What kind of display is this? (b) Identify its strengths and weaknesses, using the tips and checklists shown in this chapter. (c) Can you suggest any improvements? Would a different type of display be better?

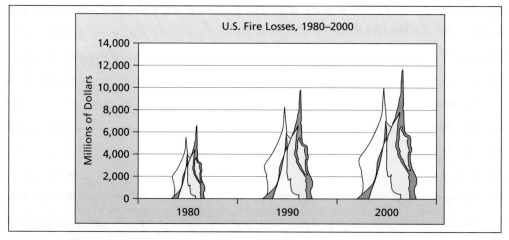

Source: *Statistical Abstract of the United States, 2001*, p. 340.

3.34 (a) What kind of display is this? (b) Identify its strengths and weaknesses, using the tips and checklists shown in this chapter. (c) Can you suggest any improvements? Would a different type of display be better?

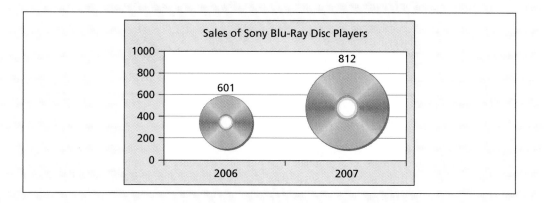

3.35 (a) Use Excel to prepare an appropriate type of chart (bar, line, pie, scatter) to display the following data. Modify the default colors, fonts, etc., as you judge appropriate to make the display effective. (b) Would more than one kind of display be acceptable? Why or why not?

Where Did You Purchase Your Statistics Textbook? 🐝 **Textbook**

Response	Count
Campus Bookstore	147
Retail Outlet	66
Web (e.g., Amazon)	49
Another Student	7
Total	269

Source: Survey of statistics students in 2007 at two large public universities.

3.36 (a) Use Excel to prepare an appropriate type of chart (bar, line, pie, scatter) to display the following data. Modify the default colors, fonts, etc., as you judge appropriate to make the display effective. (b) Would more than one kind of display be acceptable? Why or why not?

How Often Do You Use an Advanced Calculator? 🐝 **Calculator**

Response	Count
Frequently	75
Rarely	172
Never	44
Total	291

Source: Survey of statistics students in 2007 at two large public universities.

3.37 (a) Use Excel to prepare an appropriate type of chart (bar, line, pie, scatter) to display the following data. Modify the default colors, fonts, etc., as you judge appropriate to make the display effective. (b) Would more than one kind of display be acceptable? Why or why not?

How Confident Are You That You Have Saved Enough to Retire in Comfort? 🐝 **Retirement**

Confidence Level	1993 (%)	2003 (%)
Very confident	18	21
Somewhat confident	55	45
Not very confident	25	33
Don't know	2	1
Total	100	100

Source: *Detroit Free Press*, November 3, 2003.

3.38 (a) Use Excel to prepare an appropriate type of chart (bar, line, pie, scatter) to display the following data. Modify the default colors, fonts, etc., as you judge appropriate to make the display effective. (b) Would more than one kind of display be acceptable? Why or why not?

New Car Color Preferences for U.S. Buyers   CarColor

Color	Percent
Blue	12
Green	7
Natural	12
Red	13
Silver/Grey	24
White	16
Black	13
Other	3
Total	100

Source: *Detroit Auto Scene,* 24 (2006), no. 1, p. 1.

3.39 (a) Use Excel to prepare an appropriate type of chart (bar, line, pie, scatter) to display the following data. Modify the default colors, fonts, etc., as you judge appropriate to make the display effective. (b) Would more than one kind of display be acceptable? Why or why not?

Domestic Market Share, Ten Largest U.S. Airlines   AirlineMkt

Airline	Percent
Alaska	2.6
America West	3.8
American	15.4
Continental	7.7
Delta	11.2
JetBlue	4.0
Northwest	7.0
Southwest	11.8
United	12.1
US Airways	4.7
Other	19.7
Total	100.0

Source: www.transtats.bts.gov. Data are for 2006.

3.40 (a) Use Excel to prepare an appropriate type of chart (bar, line, pie, scatter) to display the following data. Modify the default colors, fonts, etc., as you judge appropriate to make the display effective. (b) Would more than one kind of display be acceptable? Why or why not?

U.S. and World Petroleum Usage (millions of barrels per day)   Petroleum

	1995	1996	1997	1998	1999	2000	2001	2002	2003	2004
United States	17.7	18.3	18.6	18.9	19.5	19.7	19.6	19.8	20.0	20.7
Rest of World	52.2	53.2	54.7	55.1	56.1	57.0	57.8	58.4	59.8	61.9

Source: www.eia.doe.gov.

3.41 (a) Use Excel to prepare an appropriate type of chart (bar, line, pie, scatter) to display the following data. Modify the default colors, fonts, etc., as you judge appropriate to make the display effective. (b) Would more than one kind of display be acceptable? Why or why not?

Operating Expenses per Seat Mile for U.S. Airlines (cents)   SeatMile

Carrier	Cost	Carrier	Cost
AirTran	9.9	Frontier	11.1
Alaska	12.3	JetBlue	7.9
America West	14.1	Northwest	13.6
American	12.6	Southwest	8.7
ATA	9.5	Spirit	11.7
Continental	13.4	United	13.0
Delta	13.6	US Airways	15.7

Source: www.bts.gov. Data are for 3rd quarter 2006.

3.42 (a) Use Excel to prepare an appropriate type of chart (bar, line, pie, scatter) to display the following data. Modify the default colors, fonts, etc., as you judge appropriate to make the display effective. (b) Would more than one kind of display be acceptable? Why or why not?

Licensed Drivers and Fatal Accidents in the U.S.   Fatal

Age Group	Percent of Drivers	Percent of Fatal Crashes
15–19	4.7	11.0
20–24	8.5	14.3
25–34	18.2	18.1
35–44	20.5	16.5
45–54	19.7	15.6
55–64	13.8	9.8
65–74	8.2	6.3
75 and over	6.4	8.4
Total	100.0	100.0

Source: *Statistical Abstract of the United States, 2007*, p. 696.

3.43 (a) Use Excel to prepare an appropriate type of chart (bar, line, pie, scatter) to display the following data. Modify the default colors, fonts, etc., as you judge appropriate to make the display effective. (b) Would more than one kind of display be acceptable? Why or why not?

U.S. Market Share for Search Engines   WebSearch

Search Engine	Percent
Google	45.4
Yahoo	28.2
Microsoft	11.7
Ask	5.8
AOL/Time Warner	5.4
All Others	3.5
Total	100.0

Source: *The New York Times*, December 4, 2006, p. C1.

3.44 (a) Use Excel to prepare an appropriate type of chart (bar, line, pie, scatter) to display the following data. Modify the default colors, fonts, etc., as you judge appropriate to make the display effective. (b) Would more than one kind of display be acceptable? Why or why not?

Survey of 282,549 Freshmen at 437 Colleges and Universities Freshmen		
Year	Percent Who Study at Least 6 Hours/Week	Percent Who Plan to Major in Business
1995	31.6	17.6
1996	31.6	18.2
1997	32.7	17.0
1998	30.9	16.0
1999	28.9	16.2
2000	26.1	16.3
2001	21.8	15.6
2002	21.9	15.8

Source: *Chronical of Higher Education,* January 27, 2003; and UCLA's Higher Education Research Institute.

3.45 (a) Use Excel to prepare an appropriate type of chart (bar, line, pie, scatter) to display the following data. Modify the default colors, fonts, etc., as you judge appropriate to make the display effective. (b) Would more than one kind of display be acceptable? Why or why not?

Average Wedding Expenses in 2002 Wedding	
Expense	$ Amount
Rings (engagement, wedding)	4,877
Photos	1,814
Flowers	967
Reception	7,630
Attire (except bride)	1,656
Bride's attire, makeup, hair	1,523
Rehearsal dinner	875
Music	900
Other	2,118

Source: *The New York Times,* July 13, 2003, p. 17.

DO-IT-YOURSELF

3.46 (a) On the Web, look up "geographical information systems" or "GIS." Do you find many references? (b) Suggest some potential applications of GIS (e.g., marketing, health care, government, military).

3.47 (a) Clip an example of a deceptive visual data presentation from a recent magazine or newspaper (if it is from a library, make a photocopy instead). Try to choose an outrageous example that violates many principles of ideal graphs. (b) Cite the exact source where you found the display. (c) What do you think is its presumed purpose? (d) Write a short, critical evaluation of its strengths and weaknesses. Be sure to attach the original clipping (or a good photocopy) to your analysis.

3.48 (a) Make a hand-drawn graph that presents some numerical data of your own (e.g., your GPA, earnings, work hours, golf scores) in a visual manner designed to dramatize or slant the facts. Violate the principles of ideal graphs *without actually changing any of the numbers*. (b) List each violation you tried to illustrate. (c) Now present the same data in an objective visual display that violates as few rules as possible. (d) Which took more time and effort, the deceptive display or the objective one?

RELATED READING   *Visual Displays*

Chambers, J. M.; W. S. Cleveland; B. Kleiner; and P. A. Tukey. *Graphical Methods for Data Analysis.* Duxbury, 1983.

Cleveland, William S. *The Elements of Graphing Data.* Hobart Press, 1994.

Cleveland, William S. *Visualizing Data.* Hobart Press, 1993.

Ehrenberg, A.S.C. "The Problem of Numeracy." *The American Statistician* 35, no. 2 (May 1981), pp. 67–71.

Huff, Darrell; and Irving Geiss. *How to Lie with Statistics.* W. W. Norton, 1954.

Jones, Gerald E. *How to Lie with Charts.* Sybex, 1995.

Monmonier, Mark. *How to Lie with Maps.* University of Chicago Press, 1996.

Steinbart, John P. "The Auditor's Responsibility for the Accuracy of Graphs in Annual Reports: Some Evidence of the Need for Additional Guidance." *Accounting Horizons* 3, no. 3 (1989), pp. 60–70.

Taylor, Barbara G.; and Lane K. Anderson. "Misleading Graphs: Guidelines for the Accountant." *Journal of Accountancy,* October 1986, pp. 126–35.

Tufte, Edward R. *The Visual Display of Quantitative Information.* Graphics Press, 1995.

Wilkinson, Leland. *The Grammar of Graphics.* Springer, 2005.

Zelazny, Gene. *Say It with Charts: The Executive's Guide to Visual Communication.* Irwin Professional Publishers, 1995.

Zweig, Jason. "Chart Burn: The Mountain Charts in Fund Ads Can Be Confusing." *Money* 29, no. 4 (April 2000), pp. 67–68.

LearningStats Unit 03   Visual Displays

LearningStats Unit 03 introduces tables, charts, and rules for visual displays. Modules are designed for self-study, so you can proceed at your own pace, concentrate on material that is new, and pass quickly over things that you already know. Your instructor may assign specific modules, or you may decide to check them out because the topic sounds interesting. In addition to helping you learn about statistics, they may be useful as references later on.

Topic	LearningStats Modules
Effective visual displays	Presenting Data—I Presenting Data—II EDA Graphics
How to make an Excel chart	Excel Charts: Step-by-Step Pivot Tables Using MegaStat Using Visual Statistics Using MINITAB
Types of Excel charts	Excel Charts: Bar, Pie, Line Excel Charts: Scatter, Pareto, Other Excel Charts: Histograms Wrong Chart Type? Gallery of Charts—1 Gallery of Charts—2 Gallery of Charts—3 Gallery of Charts—4
Applications	Adult Heights Bimodal Data Data Format Sturges' Rule Stem and Leaf Plots

Key: = PowerPoint   = Word   = Excel

Descriptive Statistics

Chapter Learning Objectives

When you finish this chapter you should be able to

- Explain the concepts of central tendency, dispersion, and shape.
- Use Excel to obtain descriptive statistics and visual displays.
- Calculate and interpret common descriptive statistics.
- Identify the properties of common measures of central tendency.
- Calculate and interpret common measures of dispersion.
- Transform a data set into standardized values.
- Apply the Empirical Rule and recognize outliers.
- Calculate quartiles and other percentiles.
- Make and interpret box plots.
- Calculate and interpret a correlation coefficient.

The last chapter explained *visual* descriptions of data (e.g., histograms, dot plots, scatter plots). This chapter explains *numerical* descriptions of data. Descriptive measures derived from a sample (*n* items) are *statistics,* while for a population (*N* items or infinite) they are *parameters*. For a sample of numerical data, we are interested in three key characteristics: central tendency, dispersion, and shape. Table 4.1 summarizes the questions that we will be asking about the data.

Chapter 1

TABLE 4.1

Characteristics of Numerical Data

Characteristic	Interpretation
Central Tendency	Where are the data values concentrated? What seem to be typical or middle data values?
Dispersion	How much variation is there in the data? How spread out are the data values? Are there unusual values?
Shape	Are the data values distributed symmetrically? Skewed? Sharply peaked? Flat? Bimodal?

Every year, J.D. Power and Associates issues its initial vehicle quality ratings. These ratings are of interest to consumers, dealers, and manufacturers. Table 4.2 shows defect rates for a sample of 37 vehicle brands. We will demonstrate how numerical statistics can be used to summarize a data set like this. The brands represented are a random sample that we will use to illustrate certain calculations.

EXAMPLE

Vehicle Quality

113

TABLE 4.2	Number of Defects per 100 Vehicles, 2006 Model Year				JDPower
Brand	**Defects**	**Brand**	**Defects**	**Brand**	**Defects**
Acura	120	Infiniti	117	Nissan	121
Audi	130	Isuzu	191	Pontiac	133
BMW	142	Jaguar	109	Porsche	91
Buick	134	Jeep	153	Saab	163
Cadillac	117	Kia	136	Saturn	129
Chevrolet	124	Land Rover	204	Scion	140
Chrysler	120	Lexus	93	Subaru	146
Dodge	132	Lincoln	121	Suzuki	169
Ford	127	Mazda	150	Toyota	106
GMC	119	Mercedes-Benz	139	Volkswagen	171
Honda	110	Mercury	129	Volvo	133
HUMMER	171	MINI	150		
Hyundai	102	Mitsubishi	135		

Source: J.D. Power and Associates 2006 Initial Quality Study™. Used with permission.

NOTE: Ratings are intended for educational purposes only, and should not be used as a guide to consumer decisions.

Preliminary Analysis

Before calculating any statistics, we consider how the data were collected. A Web search reveals that J.D. Power and Associates is a well-established independent company whose methods are widely considered to be objective. Data on defects are obtained by inspecting randomly chosen vehicles for each brand, counting the defects, and dividing the number of defects by the number of vehicles inspected. J.D. Power multiplies the result by 100 to obtain defects per 100 vehicles, rounded to the nearest integer. However, the underlying measurement scale is continuous (e.g., if 4 defects were found in 3 Saabs, the defect rate would be 1.333333, or 133 defects per 100 vehicles). Defect rates would vary from year to year, and perhaps even within a given model year, so the timing of the study could affect the results. Since the analysis is based on sampling, we must allow for the possibility of sampling error. With these cautions in mind, we look at the data. The dot plot, shown in Figure 4.1, offers a visual impression of the data. A dot plot can also reveal extreme data values.

FIGURE 4.1

Dot Plot of J.D. Power Data (*n* = 37 brands)
JDPower

Defects Per 100 Vehicles

Sorting   A good first step is to sort the data. Except for tiny samples, this would be done in Excel, as illustrated in Figure 4.2. Highlight the data array (including the headings), right click, choose Sort > Custom Sort, choose the column to sort on, and click OK. Table 4.3 shows the sorted data for all 37 brands.

Chapter 1

Visual Displays   The sorted data in Table 4.3 provide insight into central tendency and dispersion. The values range from 91 (Porsche) to 204 (Land Rover) and the middle values seem to be around 130. The next visual step is a histogram, shown in Figure 4.3. Sturges' Rule suggests 5 bins, but we use 7 and 12 bins to show more detail. Both histograms are roughly symmetric (maybe slightly right-skewed) with no extreme values. Both show modal classes near 130.

FIGURE 4.2

Sorting Data in Excel
JDPower

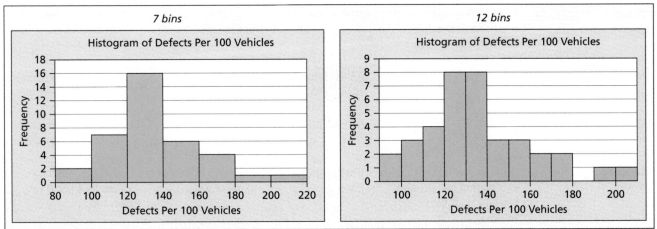

TABLE 4.3

Number of Defects per 100 Vehicles (2006 Model Year) Ranked Lowest to Highest   JDPower

Source: J.D. Power and Associates 2006 Initial Quality Study™. Used with permission.

Brand	Defects	Brand	Defects	Brand	Defects
Porsche	91	Chevrolet	124	BMW	142
Lexus	93	Ford	127	Subaru	146
Hyundai	102	Mercury	129	Mazda	150
Toyota	106	Saturn	129	MINI	150
Jaguar	109	Audi	130	Jeep	153
Honda	110	Dodge	132	Saab	163
Cadillac	117	Pontiac	133	Suzuki	169
Infiniti	117	Volvo	133	HUMMER	171
GMC	119	Buick	134	Volkswagen	171
Acura	120	Mitsubishi	135	Isuzu	191
Chrysler	120	Kia	136	Land Rover	204
Lincoln	121	Mercedes-Benz	139		
Nissan	121	Scion	140		

FIGURE 4.3

Histograms of J.D. Power Data (*n* = 37 brands)   JDPower

4.2
CENTRAL TENDENCY

Chapter 1

When we speak of *central tendency* we are trying to describe the middle or typical values of a distribution. You can assess central tendency in a general way from a dot plot or histogram, but numerical statistics allow more precise statements. Table 4.4 lists six common measures of central tendency. Each has strengths and weaknesses. We need to look at several of them to obtain a clear picture of central tendency.

Mean

The most familiar statistical measure of central tendency is the **mean**. It is the sum of the data values divided by number of data items. For a population we denote it μ, while for a sample we call it $\bar{x}$. We use equation 4.1 to calculate the mean of a population:

$$\textbf{(4.1)} \qquad \mu = \frac{\sum_{i=1}^{N} x_i}{N} \qquad \text{(population definition)}$$

Since we rarely deal with populations, the sample notation of equation 4.2 is more commonly seen:

$$\textbf{(4.2)} \qquad \bar{x} = \frac{\sum_{i=1}^{n} x_i}{n} \qquad \text{(sample definition)}$$

We calculate the mean by using Excel's function =AVERAGE(Data) where Data is an array containing the data. So for the sample of $n = 37$ car brands:

$$\bar{x} = \sum_{i=1}^{n} x_i = \frac{91 + 93 + 102 + \cdots + 171 + 191 + 204}{37} = \frac{4977}{37} = 134.51$$

Characteristics of the Mean

The arithmetic mean is the "average" with which most of us are familiar. The mean is affected by every sample item. It is the balancing point or fulcrum in a distribution if we view the X-axis as a lever arm and represent each data item as a physical weight, as illustrated in Figure 4.4 for the J.D. Powers data.

TABLE 4.4		Six Measures of Central Tendency		
Statistic	**Formula**	**Excel Formula**	**Pro**	**Con**
Mean	$\frac{1}{n}\sum_{i=1}^{n} x_i$	=AVERAGE(Data)	Familiar and uses all the sample information.	Influenced by extreme values.
Median	Middle value in sorted array	=MEDIAN(Data)	Robust when extreme data values exist.	Ignores extremes and can be affected by gaps in data values.
Mode	Most frequently occurring data value	=MODE(Data)	Useful for attribute data or discrete data with a small range.	May not be unique, and is not helpful for continuous data.
Midrange	$\frac{x_{min} + x_{max}}{2}$	=0.5*(MIN(Data) +MAX(Data))	Easy to understand and calculate.	Influenced by extreme values and ignores most data values.
Geometric mean (G)	$\sqrt[n]{x_1 x_2 \cdots x_n}$	=GEOMEAN(Data)	Useful for growth rates and mitigates high extremes.	Less familiar and requires positive data.
Trimmed mean	Same as the mean except omit highest and lowest k% of data values (e.g., 5%)	=TRIMMEAN(Data, Percent)	Mitigates effects of extreme values.	Excludes some data values that could be relevant.

FIGURE 4.4

Mean as Fulcrum
($n = 37$ vehicles)
🐦 **JDPower**

The mean is the balancing point because it has the property that distances from the mean to the data points *always* sum to zero:

$$\sum_{i=1}^{n} (x_i - \bar{x}) = 0 \tag{4.3}$$

This statement is true for *any* sample or population, regardless of its shape (skewed, symmetric, bimodal, etc.). Even when there are extreme values, the distances below the mean are *exactly* counterbalanced by the distances above the mean. For example, Bob's scores on five quizzes were 42, 60, 70, 75, 78. His mean is pulled down to 65, mainly because of his poor showing on one quiz, as illustrated in Figure 4.5. Although the data are asymmetric, the three scores above the mean exactly counterbalance the two scores below the mean:

$$\sum_{i=1}^{n} (x_i - \bar{x}) = (42 - 65) + (60 - 65) + (70 - 65) + (75 - 65) + (78 - 65)$$
$$= (-23) + (-5) + (5) + (10) + (13) = -28 + 28 = 0$$

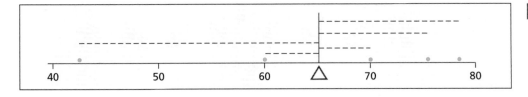

FIGURE 4.5

Bob's Quiz Scores
($n = 5$ quizzes)

Median

The **median** (denoted M) is the 50th percentile or midpoint of the *sorted* sample data set $x_1, x_2, \ldots, x_n$. It separates the upper and lower half of the sorted observations:

The median is the middle observation in the sorted array if n is odd, but is the average of the middle two observations if n is even, as illustrated in Figure 4.6. For example, if we have an even n, say $n = 6$,

Median

11   12   15 ↓ 17   21   32

then the median is halfway *between* the third and fourth observation in the sorted array:

$$M = (x_3 + x_4)/2 = (15 + 17)/2 = 16$$

But for an odd n, say $n = 7$,

the median is the fourth observation in the sorted array:

$$M = x_4 = 25$$

The *position* of the median in the sorted array is $(n + 1)/2$ so we can write:

$$\text{Median} = x_{(n+1)/2} \quad \text{for } odd\ n \quad \text{and} \quad \text{Median} = \frac{x_{n/2} + x_{(n/2+1)}}{2} \quad \text{for even } n \tag{4.4}$$

Excel's function for the median is =MEDIAN(Data) where Data is the data array. For the 37 vehicle quality ratings (odd n) the *position* of the median is $(n + 1)/2 = (37 + 1)/2 = 19$ so the median is:

$$M = x_{(n+1)/2} = x_{(37+1)/2} = x_{19} = 132$$

It is tempting to imagine that half the observations are less than the median, but this is not necessarily the case. For example, here are 11 exam scores in ascending order:

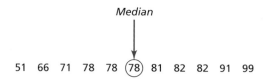

Their median is 78. But only three data values are *below* 78, while five data values are *above* 78. This median did not provide a clean "50-50 split" in the data, because there were several identical exam scores clustered at the middle of the distribution. This situation is not so unusual. In fact, we might expect it when there is strong central tendency in a data set.

FIGURE 4.6

Illustration of the Median

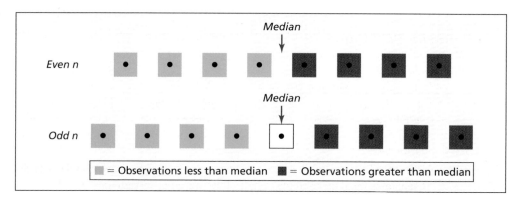

Characteristics of the Median

The median is especially useful when there are extreme values. For example, government statistics use the median income, because a few very high incomes will render the mean atypical. The median's insensitivity to extremes may seem advantageous or not, depending on your point of view. Consider three students' scores on five quizzes:

Tom's scores: 20, 40, 70, 75, 80   Mean = 57, Median = 70

Jake's scores: 60, 65, 70, 90, 95   Mean = 76, Median = 70

Mary's scores: 50, 65, 70, 75, 90   Mean = 70, Median = 70

Each student has the same median quiz score (70). Tom, whose mean is pulled down by a few low scores, would rather have his grade based on the median. Jake, whose mean is pulled up by a few high scores, would prefer the mean. Mary is indifferent, since her measures of central tendency agree (she has symmetric scores).

The median lacks some of the mean's useful mathematical properties. For example, if we multiply the mean by the sample size, we always get the total of the data values. But this is not true for the median. For instance, Tom's total points on all five quizzes (285) are the product of the sample size times his mean ($5 \times 57 = 285$). But this is not true for his median ($5 \times 70 = 350$). That is one reason why instructors tend to base their semester grades on the mean. Otherwise, the lowest and highest scores would not "count."

Mode

The **mode** is the most frequently occurring data value. It may be similar to the mean and median, if data values near the center of the sorted array tend to occur often. But it may also be quite different from the mean and median. A data set may have multiple modes or no mode at all. For example, consider these four students' scores on five quizzes:

Lee's scores: 60, 70, 70, 70, 80   Mean = 70, Median = 70, Mode = 70

Pat's scores: 45, 45, 70, 90, 100   Mean = 70, Median = 70, Mode = 45

Sam's scores: 50, 60, 70, 80, 90   Mean = 70, Median = 70, Mode = none

Xiao's scores: 50, 50, 70, 90, 90   Mean = 70, Median = 70, Modes = 50, 90

Each student has the same mean (70) and median (70). Lee's mode (70) is the same as his mean and median, but Pat's mode (45) is nowhere near the "middle." Sam has no mode, while Xiao has two modes (50, 90). These examples illustrate some quirks of the mode.

The mode is easy to define, but is *not* easy to calculate (except in very small samples), because it requires tabulating the frequency of occurrence of every distinct data value. For example, the sample of $n = 37$ brands has six modes (117, 121, 129, 133, 150, 171), each occurring twice:

91	93	102	106	109	110	**117**	**117**	119	120
120	**121**	**121**	124	127	**129**	**129**	130	132	**133**
133	134	135	136	139	140	142	146	**150**	**150**
153	163	169	**171**	**171**	191	204			

Excel's function =MODE(Data) will return #N/A if there is no mode. If there are multiple modes, =MODE(Data) will return the first one it finds. In this example, since our data are already sorted, =MODE(Data) will return 117 as the mode. But if the data were in alphabetical order by car brand (as in Table 4.2) Excel would return 120 as the mode. Sometimes the mode is far from the "middle" of the distribution and may not be at all "typical." Indeed, for the car defects data, one has the feeling that the modes are merely a statistical fluke. For *continuous* data, the mode generally isn't useful, because continuous data values rarely repeat. To assess central tendency in continuous data, we would rely on the mean or median.

But the mode is good for describing central tendency in *categorical data* such as gender (male, female) or college major (accounting, finance, etc.). Indeed, the mode is the *only* useful measure of central tendency for categorical data. The mode is also useful to describe a *discrete* variable with a *small range* (e.g., responses to a five-point Likert scale).

Tip   The mode is most useful for discrete or categorical data with only a few distinct data values. For continuous data or data with a wide range, the mode is rarely useful.

EXAMPLE

Price/Earnings Ratios and Mode

Table 4.5 shows P/E ratios (current stock price divided by the last 12 months' earnings) for a random sample of 68 Standard & Poor's 500 stocks. Although P/E ratios are continuous data, *The Wall Street Journal* rounds the data to the nearest integer.

TABLE 4.5		P/E Ratios for 68 Randomly Chosen S&P 500 Stocks								PERatios2						
7	8	8	10	10	10	10	12	13	13	13	13	13	13	13	14	14
14	15	15	15	15	15	16	16	16	17	18	18	18	18	19	19	19
19	19	20	20	20	21	21	21	22	22	23	23	23	24	25	26	26
26	26	27	29	29	30	31	34	36	37	40	41	45	48	55	68	91

Source: *The Wall Street Journal*, July 31, 2003.

Note: The data file has company names and ticker symbols.

Excel's Descriptive Statistics for this sample are:

Mean:	22.7206	Minimum:	7
Median:	19	Maximum:	91
Mode:	13	Sum:	1545
Range:	84	Count:	68

For these 68 observations, 13 is the mode (occurs 7 times) suggesting that it actually is somewhat "typical." However, the dot plot in Figure 4.7 also shows local modes at 10, 13, 15, 19, 23, 26, and 29 (a local mode is a "peak" with "valleys" on either side). These multiple "mini-modes" suggest that the mode is not a stable measure of central tendency for this data set, and that these modes may not be very likely to recur if we took a different sample.

FIGURE 4.7   **Dot Plot for P/E Ratios (*n* = 68 stocks)**   PERatios2

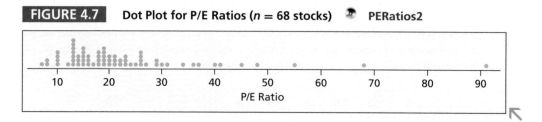

There may be a logical reason for the existence of modes. For example, points scored by winning college football teams on a given Saturday will tend to have modes at multiples of 7 (e.g., 7, 14, 21, etc.) because each touchdown yields 7 points (counting the extra point). Other mini-modes in football scores reflect commonly occurring combinations of scoring events. Figure 4.8 shows a dot plot of the points scored by the winning team in the first 87 Rose Bowl games (one game was a scoreless tie). The mode is 14, but there are several other local modes. If you are a football fan, you can figure out, for example, why 20 points occur so often.

FIGURE 4.8

Dot Plot of Rose Bowl Winners' Points (*n* = 87 games)
RoseBowl

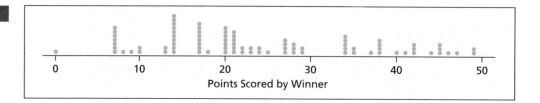

FIGURE 4.9

Frequency Polygons of Heights of 1,000 Men and Women   Heights

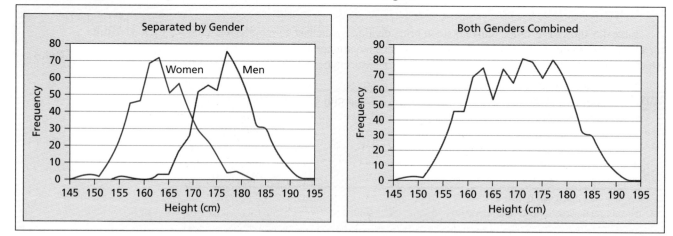

A **bimodal distribution** or a **multimodal distribution** occurs when dissimilar populations are combined into one sample. For example, if heights of 500 adult men and 500 adult women are combined into a single sample of 1,000 adults, we would get something like the second polygon in Figure 4.9.

In such a case, the mean of all 1,000 adults would not represent central tendency for either gender. When heterogeneity is known to exist, it would be better to create separate histograms or frequency polygons and carry out the analysis on each group separately. Unfortunately, we don't always know when heterogeneous populations have been combined into one sample.

Shape

Chapter 3

The shape of a distribution may be judged by looking at the histogram or by comparing the mean and median. In **symmetric data**, the mean and median are about the same. When the data are **skewed right** (or **positively skewed**) the mean exceeds the median. When the data are **skewed left** (or **negatively skewed**) the mean is below the median. Figure 4.10 shows prototype population shapes showing varying degrees of **skewness**.

FIGURE 4.10

Skewness Prototype Populations

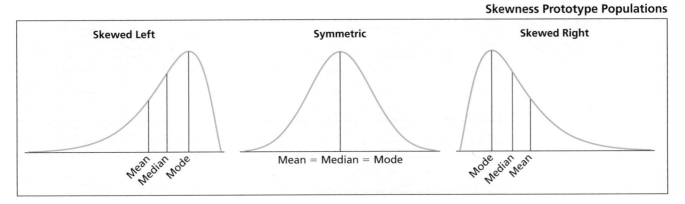

Table 4.6 summarizes the symptoms of skewness in a sample. Since few data sets are exactly symmetric, skewness is a matter of degree. Due to the nature of random sampling, the mean and median may differ, even when a symmetric population is being sampled. Small differences between the mean and median may not indicate significant skewness and may lack practical importance.

TABLE 4.6

Symptoms of Skewness

Distribution's Shape	Histogram Appearance	Statistics
Skewed left (negative skewness)	Long tail of histogram points left (a few low values but most data on right)	Mean < Median
Symmetric	Tails of histogram are balanced (low/high values offset)	Mean ≈ Median
Skewed right (positive skewness)	Long tail of histogram points right (most data on left but a few high values)	Mean > Median

For example, in Figure 4.11 the average spending per customer at 74 Noodles & Company restaurants appears somewhat right-skewed, so we would expect the mean to exceed the median. Actually, the difference is slight (using the spreadsheet raw data, the mean is $7.04 and the median is $7.00). The student GPA histogram in Figure 4.11 appears left-skewed, so we would expect the mean to be lower than the median. But again, the difference is slight (using the spreadsheet raw data, the mean is 3.17 and the median is 3.20). Since a histogram's appearance is affected by the way its bins are set up, its shape offers only a rough guide to skewness.

For the sample of J.D. Power quality ratings, the mean (134.51) exceeds the median (132), which suggests right-skewness. However, this small difference between the mean and median may lack practical importance. The histograms in Figure 4.3 suggest that the skewness is minimal. In Section 4.8, we will introduce more precise tests for skewness.

Business data tend to be right-skewed because financial variables often are unlimited at the top but are bounded from below by zero (e.g., salaries, employees, inventory). This is also true for engineering data (e.g., time to failure, defect rates) and sports (e.g., scores in soccer). Even in a Likert scale (1, 2, 3, 4, 5) a few responses in the opposite tail can skew the mean if most replies are clustered toward the top or bottom of the scale.

FIGURE 4.11

Histograms to Illustrate Skewness

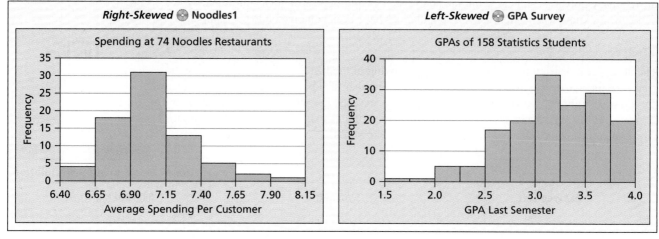

Descriptive Statistics in Excel

As shown in Figure 4.12, select the Data tab and click the Data Analysis icon (on the far right side of the top menu). When the Data Analysis menu appears, select Descriptive Statistics. On the Descriptive Statistics menu form, click anywhere inside the Input Range field, then highlight the data block (in this case C4:C41). Specify a destination cell for the upper left corner of the output range (cell K1 in this example). Notice that we checked the Labels in first row box, since cell C4 is actually a column heading that will be used to label the output in cell K1. Check the Summary Statistics box and then click OK. The resulting statistics are shown in Figure 4.12. You probably recognize some of them (e.g., mean, median, mode) and the others will be covered later in this chapter.

FIGURE 4.12

Excel's Data Analysis and Descriptive Statistics
   JDPower

Note: If Data Analysis does not appear on the upper right of the Data tab, click the multicolored Office icon in the extreme upper left corner, select Add-Ins, and then check the box for Analysis ToolPak.

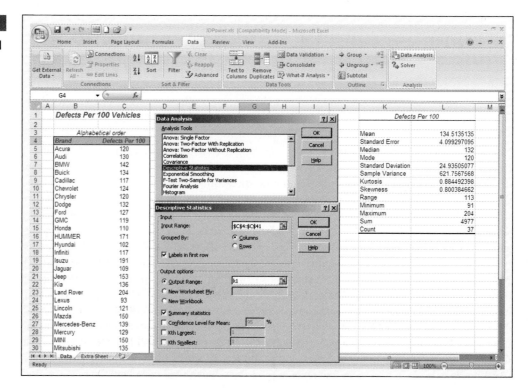

Descriptive Statistics Using MegaStat

You can get similar statistics (and more) from MegaStat as illustrated in Figure 4.13. Click the Add-Ins tab on the top menu, and then click on the MegaStat icon (left side of the top menu in this example). On the list of MegaStat procedures, click Descriptive Statistics. On the new menu, enter the data range (in this case C4:C41) in the Input range field (or highlight the data block on the worksheet. You can see that MegaStat offers you many statistics, plus some visual displays such as a dot plot, stem-and-leaf, and other graphs. We have only chosen a few of them for this illustration. MegaStat output normally appears on a separate worksheet, but the results have been copied to the data worksheet so that everything can be seen in one picture. Try using both Excel and MegaStat to see the similarities and differences in their interfaces and results. *LearningStats* has PowerPoint demonstrations with more detailed explanations of how to use Excel and MegaStat for statistical data description.

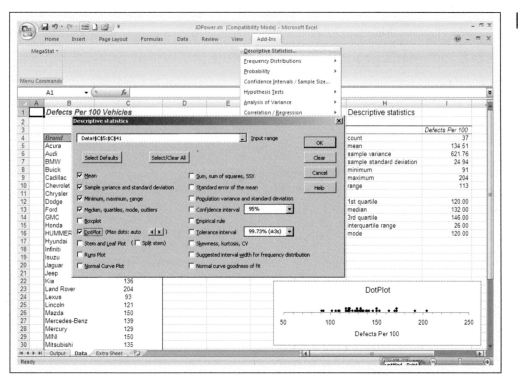

FIGURE 4.13

MegaStat's Descriptive Statistics JDPower

Note: MegaStat is on your textbook CD. You will be prompted to install it when you insert the CD in your computer. If MegaStat does not appear on the Add-Ins tab, click the multicolored Office icon in the extreme upper left corner, select Add-Ins, and then check the box for MegaStat.

Descriptive Statistics Using MINITAB

MINITAB is a comprehensive software system for statistical analysis. It has nothing to do with Excel, although you can copy data from Excel to MINITAB's worksheet (and vice versa). You can get a wide range of statistics and attractive graphs from MINITAB. Although MINITAB is not on the textbook CD, it is widely available at colleges and universities. This textbook emphasizes Excel and MegaStat, but it is wise to learn about other software that may give you just the result you want (or in a more attractive form) so we will show MINITAB results when they are appropriate. Also, *LearningStats* has a PowerPoint demonstration with more detailed explanations of how to use MINITAB. Figure 4.14 shows MINITAB's menus and a graphical summary of descriptive statistics for the J.D. Powers data.

FIGURE 4.14

MINITAB's Basic Statistics > Graphical Summary

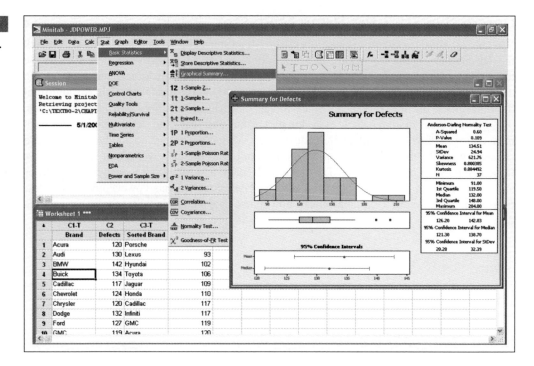

SECTION EXERCISES

connect

4.1 For each data set, find the mean, median, and mode. Discuss anything about the data that affects the usefulness of each statistic as a measure of central tendency.

a. Class absences (12 students)   0, 0, 0, 0, 0, 1, 2, 3, 3, 5, 5, 15
b. Exam scores (9 students)   40, 40, 65, 71, 72, 75, 76, 78, 98
c. GPAs (8 students)   2.25, 2.55, 2.95, 3.02, 3.04, 3.37, 3.51, 3.66

4.2 Prof. Hardtack gave four Friday quizzes last semester in his 10-student senior tax accounting class. (a) Without using Excel, find the mean, median, and mode for each quiz. (b) Do these measures of central tendency agree? Explain. (c) For each data set, note strengths or weaknesses of each statistic of central tendency. (d) Are the data symmetric or skewed? If skewed, which direction? (e) Briefly describe and compare student performance on each quiz.   **Quizzes**

Quiz 1: 60, 60, 60, 60, 71, 73, 74, 75, 88, 99

Quiz 2: 65, 65, 65, 65, 70, 74, 79, 79, 79, 79

Quiz 3: 66, 67, 70, 71, 72, 72, 74, 74, 95, 99

Quiz 4: 10, 49, 70, 80, 85, 88, 90, 93, 97, 98

4.3 CitiBank recorded the number of customers to use a downtown ATM during the noon hour on 32 consecutive workdays. (a) Use Excel or MegaStat or MINITAB to find the mean, median, and mode. (b) Do these measures of central tendency agree? Explain. (c) Make a histogram and dot plot. (d) Are the data symmetric or skewed? If skewed, which direction? (e) Note strengths or weaknesses of each statistic of central tendency for the data.   **CitiBank**

25	37	23	26	30	40	25	26
39	32	21	26	19	27	32	25
18	26	34	18	31	35	21	33
33	9	16	32	35	42	15	24

4.4 On Friday night, the owner of Chez Pierre in downtown Chicago noted the amount spent for dinner for 28 four-person tables. (a) Use Excel or MegaStat or MINITAB to find the mean, median, and mode. (b) Do these measures of central tendency agree? Explain. (c) Make a histogram and dot plot. (d) Are the data symmetric or skewed? If skewed, which direction? (e) Note strengths or weak-nesses of each statistic of central tendency for the data.   **Dinner**

95	103	109	170	114	113	107
124	105	80	104	84	176	115
69	95	134	108	61	160	128
68	95	61	150	52	87	136

4.5   An executive's telephone log showed the lengths of 65 calls initiated during the last week of July. (a) Sort the data. (b) Use Excel or MegaStat or MINITAB to find the mean, median, and mode. (c) Do the measures of central tendency agree? Explain. (d) Make a histogram and dot plot. (e) Are the data symmetric or skewed? If skewed, which direction?   **CallLength**

1	2	10	5	3	3	2	20	1	1
6	3	13	2	2	1	26	3	1	3
1	2	1	7	1	2	3	1	2	12
1	4	2	2	29	1	1	1	8	5
1	4	2	1	1	1	1	6	1	2
3	3	6	1	3	1	1	5	1	18
2	13	13	1	6					

Mini Case   4.1

ATM Deposits

Table 4.7 shows a sorted random sample of 100 deposits at an ATM located in the student union on a college campus. The sample was selected at random from 1,459 deposits in one 30-day month. Deposits range from $3 to $1,341. The dot plot shown in Figure 4.15 indi-cates a right-skewed distribution with a few large values in the right tail and a strong clus-tering on the left (i.e., most ATM deposits are small). Excel's Descriptive Statistics indicate a very skewed distribution, since the mean (233.89) greatly exceeds the median (135). The mode (100) is somewhat "typical," occurring five times. However, 40 and 50 each occur four times (mini-modes).

TABLE 4.7	**100 ATM Deposits (dollars)**					**ATMDeposits**					
3	10	15	15	20	20	20	22	23	25	26	26
30	30	35	35	36	39	40	40	40	40	47	50
50	50	50	53	55	60	60	60	67	75	78	86
90	96	100	100	100	100	100	103	105	118	125	125
130	131	139	140	145	150	150	153	153	156	160	163
170	176	185	198	200	200	200	220	232	237	252	259
260	268	270	279	295	309	345	350	366	375	431	433
450	450	474	484	495	553	600	720	777	855	960	987
1,020	1,050	1,200	1,341								

Source: Michigan State University Federal Credit Union.

FIGURE 4.15   **Dot Plot for ATM Deposits (*n* = 100)**

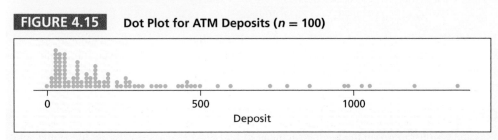

Figure 4.16 shows one possible histogram for this severely skewed data. Using seven equal bins (Sturges' Rule) with a nice bin width of 200, we don't get very much detail for the first bin. Figure 4.17 shows that even doubling the number of bins still does not show much detail in the first bin. This example illustrates some of the difficulties in making good frequency tabulations when the data are skewed (a very common situation in business and economic data).

FIGURE 4.16   Histogram with 7 Bins

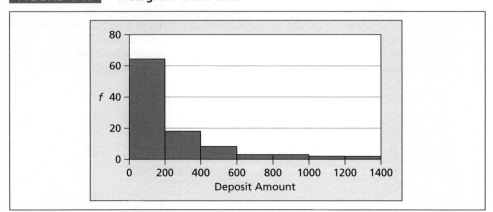

FIGURE 4.17   Histogram with 14 Bins

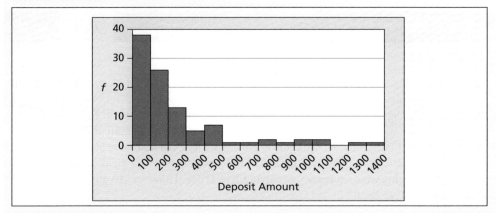

Geometric Mean

The **geometric mean** (denoted G) is a multiplicative average, obtained by multiplying the data values and then taking the nth root of the product. This is a measure of central tendency used when all the data values are positive (greater than zero).

(4.5) $$G = \sqrt[n]{x_1 x_2 \cdots x_n} \quad \text{for the geometric mean}$$

For example, the geometric mean for $X = 2, 3, 7, 9, 10, 12$ is:

$$G = \sqrt[6]{(2)(3)(7)(9)(10)(12)} = \sqrt[6]{45,360} = 5.972$$

The product of n numbers can be quite large. For the J.D. Power quality data:

$$G = \sqrt[37]{(91)(93)\cdots(201)(204)} = \sqrt[37]{3.21434 \times 10^{78}} = 132.38$$

The calculation is easy using Excel's function =GEOMEAN(Data). Scientific calculators have a y^x key whose inverse permits taking the nth root needed to calculate G. However, if the data values are large the product can exceed the calculator's capacity. The geometric mean tends to mitigate the effects of high outliers.

Growth Rates

We can use a variation on the geometric mean to find the *average growth rate* for a time series (e.g., sales in a growing company):

$$GR = \sqrt[n-1]{\frac{x_n}{x_1}} - 1 \quad \text{(average growth rate of a time series)} \quad \textbf{(4.6)}$$

For example, from 2002 to 2006, JetBlue Airlines' revenues grew dramatically, as shown in Table 4.8.

Year	Revenue (mil)
2002	635
2003	998
2004	1265
2005	1701
2006	2363

TABLE 4.8

JetBlue Airlines Revenue
    JetBlue

Source: http://moneycentral.msn.com

The *average growth rate* is given by taking the geometric mean of the ratios of each year's revenue to the preceding year. However, due to cancellations, only the first and last years are relevant:

$$GR = \sqrt[4]{\left(\frac{998}{635}\right)\left(\frac{1265}{998}\right)\left(\frac{1701}{1265}\right)\left(\frac{2363}{1701}\right)} - 1 = \sqrt[4]{\frac{2363}{635}} - 1 = 1.389 - 1 = .389$$

    or 38.9% per year

In Excel, we could use the formula =(2363/635)^(1/4)−1 to get this result.

Midrange

The **midrange** is the point halfway between the lowest and highest values of X. It is easy to calculate, but is not a robust measure of central tendency because it is sensitive to extreme data values. It is useful when you only have x_{min} and x_{max}.

$$\text{Midrange} = \frac{x_{min} + x_{max}}{2} \quad \textbf{(4.7)}$$

For the J.D. Power data:

$$\text{Midrange} = \frac{x_1 + x_{37}}{2} = \frac{91 + 204}{2} = 147.5$$

In this example, the midrange is higher than the mean (134.51) or median (132).

Trimmed Mean

The **trimmed mean** is calculated like any other mean, except that the highest and lowest k percent of the observations are removed. For the 68 P/E ratios (Table 4.5), the 5 percent trimmed mean will remove the three smallest and three largest ($0.05 \times 68 = 3.4$ observations). Excel's function for a 5 percent trimmed mean would be =TRIMMEAN(Data, 0.10) since $.05 + .05 = .10$. As shown below, the trimmed mean mitigates the effects of extremely high values, but still exceeds the median. The midrange is a poor measure of central tendency for the P/E data because of the high outlier ($x_{min} = 7$, $x_{max} = 91$).

Mean: 22.72	=AVERAGE(Data)
Median: 19.00	=MEDIAN(Data)
Mode: 13.00	=MODE(Data)
Geo Mean: 19.85	=GEOMEAN(Data)
Midrange: 49.00	=(MIN(Data)+MAX(Data))/2
5% Trim Mean: 21.10	=TRIMMEAN(Data,0.1)

The Federal Reserve uses a 16 percent trimmed mean to mitigate the effect of extremes in its analysis of trends in the Consumer Price Index, as illustrated in Figure 4.18. In this example,

FIGURE 4.18

16 Percent Trimmed-Mean for CPI

🐝 **TrimmedMean**

Source: Federal Reserve Bank of
Cleveland, www.clevelandfed.org

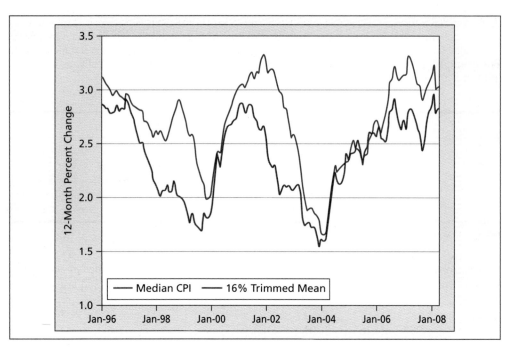

because a fairly high number of values are trimmed (the highest 8 percent and the lowest 8 percent of the price changes) the result is that the trimmed mean typically is lower than the median and is less volatile.

SECTION EXERCISES

connect

4.6   For each data set, find the median, midrange, and geometric mean. Are they reasonable measures of central tendency? Explain.
a. Exam scores (9 students)   42, 55, 65, 67, 68, 75, 76, 78, 94
b. GPAs (8 students)   2.25, 2.55, 2.95, 3.02, 3.04, 3.37, 3.51, 3.66
c. Class absences (12 students)   0, 0, 0, 0, 0, 1, 2, 3, 3, 5, 5, 15

4.7   (a) Write the Excel function for the 10 percent trimmed mean of a data set in cells A1:A50. (b) How many observations would be trimmed in each tail? (c) How many would be trimmed overall? (d) What ambiguity would arise in this case if you wanted a 5 percent trimmed mean?

4.8   Spirit Airlines kept track of the number of empty seats on flight 308 (DEN-DTW) for 10 consecutive trips on each weekday. (a) Sort the data for each weekday. (b) Without using Excel, find the mean, median, mode, midrange, geometric mean, and 10 percent trimmed mean (i.e., dropping the first and last sorted observation) for each weekday. (c) Do the measures of central tendency agree? Explain. (d) Note strengths or weaknesses of each statistic of central tendency for the data. (e) Briefly describe and compare the number of empty seats on each weekday.   🐝 **EmptySeats**

Monday: 6, 1, 5, 9, 1, 1, 6, 5, 5, 1

Tuesday: 1, 3, 3, 1, 4, 6, 9, 7, 7, 6

Wednesday: 6, 0, 6, 0, 6, 10, 0, 0, 4, 6

Thursday: 1, 1, 10, 1, 1, 1, 1, 1, 1, 1

4.9   CitiBank recorded the number of customers to use a downtown ATM during the noon hour on 32 consecutive workdays. (a) Use Excel or MegaStat to find the mean, midrange, geometric mean, and 10 percent trimmed mean (i.e., dropping the first three and last three observations). (b) Do these measures of central tendency agree? Explain.   🐝 **CitiBank**

25	37	23	26	30	40	25	26
39	32	21	26	19	27	32	25
18	26	34	18	31	35	21	33
33	9	16	32	35	42	15	24

4.10 On Friday night, the owner of Chez Pierre in downtown Chicago noted the amount spent for dinner at 28 four-person tables. (a) Use Excel or MegaStat to find the mean, midrange, geometric mean, and 10 percent trimmed mean (i.e., dropping the first three and last three observations). (b) Do these measures of central tendency agree? Explain. **Dinner**

95	103	109	170	114	113	107
124	105	80	104	84	176	115
69	95	134	108	61	160	128
68	95	61	150	52	87	136

4.11 An executive's telephone log showed the lengths of 65 calls initiated during the last week of July. (a) Use Excel to find the mean, midrange, geometric mean, and 10 percent trimmed mean (i.e., dropping the first seven and last seven observations). (b) Do the measures of central tendency agree? Explain. (c) Are the data symmetric or skewed? If skewed, which direction? (d) Note strengths or weaknesses of each statistic of central tendency for the data. **CallLength**

1	2	10	5	3	3	2	20	1	1
6	3	13	2	2	1	26	3	1	3
1	2	1	7	1	2	3	1	2	12
1	4	2	2	29	1	1	1	8	5
1	4	2	1	1	1	1	6	1	2
3	3	6	1	3	1	1	5	1	18
2	13	13	1	6					

4.12 The number of Internet users in Latin America grew from 15.8 million in 2000 to 60.6 million in 2004. Use the geometric mean to find the mean annual growth rate. (Data are from George E. Belch and Michael A. Belch, *Advertising and Promotion* [Irwin, 2004], p. 488.)

We can use a statistic such as the mean to describe the *center* of a distribution. But it is just as important to look at how individual data values are dispersed around the mean. For example, if two *NYSE* stocks A and B have the same mean return over the last 100 trading days, but A has more day-to-day variation, then the portfolio manager who wants a stable investment would prefer B. Consider possible sample distributions of study time spent by several college students taking an economics class:

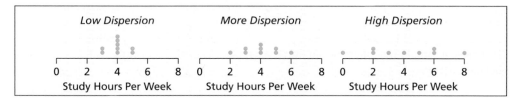

Each diagram has the same mean, but they differ in dispersion around the mean. The problem is: how do we *describe* dispersion in a sample? Since different variables have different means and different units of measurements (dollars, pounds, yen) we are looking for measures of dispersion that can be applied to many situations.

Histograms and dot plots tell us something about variation in a data set (the "spread" of data points about the center) but formal measures of dispersion are needed. Table 4.9 lists several common measures of dispersion. All formulas shown are for sample data sets.

Range

The **range** is the difference between the largest and smallest observation:

$$\text{Range} = x_{\max} - x_{\min} \tag{4.8}$$

For the P/E data the range is:

$$\text{Range} = 91 - 7 = 84$$

A drawback of the range is that it only considers the two extreme data values. It seems desirable to seek a broad-based measure of dispersion that is based on *all* the data values $x_1, x_2, \ldots, x_n$.

TABLE 4.9		Five Measures of Dispersion for a Sample		
Statistic	**Formula**	**Excel**	**Pro**	**Con**
Range	$x_{max} - x_{min}$	=MAX(Data)-MIN(Data)	Easy to calculate.	Sensitive to extreme data values.
Sample variance (s^2)	$\dfrac{\sum\limits_{i=1}^{n}(x_i - \bar{x})^2}{n-1}$	=VAR(Data)	Plays a key role in mathematical statistics.	Nonintuitive meaning.
Sample standard deviation (s)	$\sqrt{\dfrac{\sum\limits_{i=1}^{n}(x_i - \bar{x})^2}{n-1}}$	=STDEV(Data)	Most common measure. Same units as the raw data ($, £, ¥, grams, etc.).	Nonintuitive meaning.
Coefficient of variation (CV)	$100 \times \dfrac{s}{\bar{x}}$	None	Expresses relative variation in *percent* so can compare data sets with different units of measurement.	Requires nonnegative data.
Mean absolute deviation (MAD)	$\dfrac{\sum\limits_{i=1}^{n}|x_i - \bar{x}|}{n}$	=AVEDEV(Data)	Easy to understand.	Lacks "nice" theoretical properties.

Variance and Standard Deviation

If we calculate the differences between each data value x_i and the mean, we would have both positive and negative differences. Since the mean is the balancing point of the distribution, if we just sum these differences and take the average, we will always get zero, which obviously doesn't give us a useful measure of dispersion. One way to avoid this is to *square* the differences before we find the average. Following this logic, the **population variance** (denoted σ^2) is defined as the sum of squared deviations from the mean divided by the population size:

$$(4.9) \qquad \sigma^2 = \frac{\sum\limits_{i=1}^{N}(x_i - \mu)^2}{N}$$

If we have a sample (i.e., most of the time), we replace μ with $\bar{x}$ to get the **sample variance** (denoted s^2):

$$(4.10) \qquad s^2 = \frac{\sum\limits_{i=1}^{n}(x_i - \bar{x})^2}{n-1}$$

A variance is basically a mean squared deviation. But why then do we divide by $n-1$ instead of n when using sample data? This question perplexes many students. A sample contains n pieces of information, each of which can have any value, independently from the others. But once you have calculated the sample mean (as you must in order to find the variance) there are only $n-1$ pieces of independent information left (since the sample values must add to a fixed total that gives the mean). We divide the sum of squared deviations by $n-1$ instead of n because otherwise s^2 would tend to underestimate the unknown population variance σ^2.

In describing dispersion, we most often use the **standard deviation** (the square root of the variance). The standard deviation is a single number that helps us understand how individual values in a data set vary from the mean. Because the square root has been taken, its units of measurement are the same as X (e.g., dollars, kilograms, miles). To find the standard deviation of a population we use:

$$(4.11) \qquad \sigma = \sqrt{\frac{\sum\limits_{i=1}^{N}(x_i - \mu)^2}{N}}$$

and for the standard deviation of a sample:

$$s = \sqrt{\frac{\sum_{i=1}^{n}(x_i - \bar{x})^2}{n-1}} \qquad \text{(4.12)}$$

Many inexpensive calculators have built-in formulas for the standard deviation. To distinguish between the population and sample formulas, some calculators have one function key labeled σ_x and another labeled s_x. Others have one key labeled σ_n and another labeled σ_{n-1}. The only question is whether to divide the numerator by the number of data items or the number of data items minus one. Computers and calculators don't know whether your data are a sample or a population. They will use whichever formula you request. It is up to you to know which is appropriate for your data. Excel has built-in functions for these calculations:

Statistic	Excel population formula	Excel sample formula
Variance	=VARP(Data)	=VAR(Data)
Standard deviation	=STDEVP(Data)	=STDEV(Data)

Calculating a Standard Deviation

Table 4.10 illustrates the calculation of a standard deviation using Stephanie's scores on five quizzes (40, 55, 75, 95, 95). Her mean is 72. Notice that the deviations around the mean (column three) sum to zero, an important property of the mean. Because the mean is rarely a "nice" number, such calculations typically require a spreadsheet or a calculator. Stephanie's sample standard deviation is:

$$s = \sqrt{\frac{\sum_{i=1}^{n}(x_i - \bar{x})^2}{n-1}} = \sqrt{\frac{2,380}{5-1}} = \sqrt{595} = 24.39$$

The **two-sum formula** can also be used to calculate the standard deviation:

$$s = \sqrt{\frac{\sum_{i=1}^{n}x_i^2 - \frac{\left(\sum_{i=1}^{n}x_i\right)^2}{n}}{n-1}} \qquad \text{(4.13)}$$

This formula avoids calculating the mean and subtracting it from each observation. Many calculators use this formula and also give the sums $\sum_{i=1}^{n}x_i$ and $\sum_{i=1}^{n}x_i^2$. For Stephanie's five quiz scores, using the sums shown in Table 4.10, we get the same result as from the definitional formula:

$$s = \sqrt{\frac{\sum_{i=1}^{n}x_i^2 - \frac{\left(\sum_{i=1}^{n}x_i\right)^2}{n}}{n-1}} = \sqrt{\frac{28,300 - \frac{(360)^2}{5}}{5-1}} = \sqrt{\frac{28,300 - 25,920}{5-1}} = \sqrt{595} = 24.39$$

Because it is less intuitive (and because we usually rely on spreadsheets, calculators, statistical software) some textbooks omit the two-sum formula, which is sensitive to rounding of sums in some situations. However, the definitional formula can also give inaccurate results if you round off the mean before subtracting (a common error). For business data, either formula should be OK.

i	x_i	$x_i - \bar{x}$	$(x_i - \bar{x})^2$	x_i^2
1	40	$40 - 72 = -32$	$(-32)^2 = 1,024$	$40^2 = 1,600$
2	55	$55 - 72 = -17$	$(-17)^2 = 289$	$55^2 = 3,025$
3	75	$75 - 72 = +3$	$(3)^2 = 9$	$75^2 = 5,625$
4	95	$95 - 72 = +23$	$(23)^2 = 529$	$95^2 = 9,025$
5	95	$95 - 72 = +23$	$(23)^2 = 529$	$95^2 = 9,025$
Sum	360	0	2,380	28,300
Mean	72			

TABLE 4.10

Worksheet for Standard Deviation Stephanie

Characteristics of the Standard Deviation

The standard deviation is nonnegative because the deviations around the mean are squared. When every observation is exactly equal to the mean, then the standard deviation is zero (i.e., there is no variation). For example, if every student received the same score on an exam, the numerators of formulas 4.9 through 4.13 would be zero because every student would be at the mean. At the other extreme, the greatest dispersion would be if the data were concentrated at x_{min} and x_{max} (e.g., if half the class scored 0 and the other half scored 100).

But the standard deviation can have any nonnegative value, depending on the unit of measurement. For example, yields on n randomly chosen investment bond funds (e.g., Westcore Plus at 0.052 in 2004) would have a small standard deviation compared to annual revenues of n randomly chosen Fortune 500 corporations (e.g., Wal-Mart at $259 billion in 2003).

Standard deviations can be compared *only* for data sets measured in the same units. For example, prices of hotel rooms in Tokyo (yen) cannot be compared with prices of hotel rooms in Paris (euros). Also, standard deviations should not be compared if the means differ substantially, even when the units of measurement are the same. For instance, weights of apples (ounces) have a smaller mean than weights of watermelons (ounces).

Coefficient of Variation

To compare dispersion in data sets with dissimilar units of measurement (e.g., kilograms and ounces) or dissimilar means (e.g., home prices in two different cities) we define the **coefficient of variation** (*CV*), which is a unit-free measure of dispersion:

(4.14)
$$CV = 100 \times \frac{s}{\bar{x}}$$

The *CV* is the standard deviation expressed as a percent of the mean. In some data sets, the standard deviation can actually exceed the mean so the *CV* can exceed 100 percent. The *CV* is useful for comparing variables measured in different units. For example:

Defect rates: $s = 24.94$, $\bar{x} = 134.51$ $CV = 100 \times (24.94)/(134.51) = 19\%$

ATM deposits: $s = 280.80$, $\bar{x} = 233.89$ $CV = 100 \times (280.80)/(233.89) = 120\%$

P/E ratios: $s = 14.08$, $\bar{x} = 22.72$ $CV = 100 \times (14.08)/(22.72) = 62\%$

Despite the different units of measurement, we can say that ATM deposits have much greater relative dispersion (120 percent) than either defect rates (18 percent) or P/E ratios (62 percent). The chief weakness of the *CV* is that it is undefined if the mean is zero or negative, so it is appropriate only for positive data.

Mean Absolute Deviation

An additional measure of dispersion is the **mean absolute deviation** (*MAD*). This statistic reveals the average distance from the center. Absolute values must be used since otherwise the deviations around the mean would sum to zero.

(4.15)
$$MAD = \frac{\sum_{i=1}^{n} |x_i - \bar{x}|}{n}$$

The *MAD* is appealing because of its simple, concrete interpretation. Using the lever analogy, the *MAD* tells us what the average distance is from an individual data point to the fulcrum. Excel's function =AVEDEV(Data) will calculate the *MAD*.

Mini Case   4.2

Bear Markets

Investors know that stock prices have extended cycles of downturns ("bear markets") or upturns ("bull markets"). But how long must an investor be prepared to wait for the cycle to end? Table 4.11 shows the duration of 14 bear markets since 1929 and the decline in the S&P 500 stock index.

TABLE 4.11   Duration of Bear Markets   BearMarkets

Peak	Trough	Duration (months)	S&P Loss (%)
Sep 1929	Jun 1932	34	83.4
Jun 1946	Apr 1947	11	21.0
Aug 1956	Feb 1957	7	10.2
Aug 1957	Dec 1957	5	15.0
Jan 1962	Jun 1962	6	22.3
Feb 1966	Sep 1966	8	15.6
Dec 1968	Jun 1970	19	29.3
Jan 1973	Sep 1974	21	42.6
Jan 1977	Feb 1978	14	14.1
Dec 1980	Jul 1982	20	16.9
Sep 1987	Nov 1987	3	29.5
Jun 1990	Oct 1990	5	14.7
Jul 1998	Aug 1998	2	15.4
Sep 2000	Mar 2003	31	42.0

Source: TIAA/CREF, *Balance,* Summer 2004, p. 15. Downturns are defined as a loss in value of 10 percent or more. Standard & Poor's 500 stock index and S&P 500 are registered trademarks.

Figure 4.19 shows that bear markets typically are short-lived (under 1 year) but may last nearly 3 years. S&P losses generally are in the 10–40 percent range, with one notable exception (the 1929 crash).

Table 4.12 shows that both duration (months) and S&P loss (percent) are right-skewed (mean substantially exceeding median) and have similar coefficients of variation. The other measures of central tendency and disperson cannot be compared because the units of measurement differ.

FIGURE 4.19   Dot Plots of Bear Market Measurements

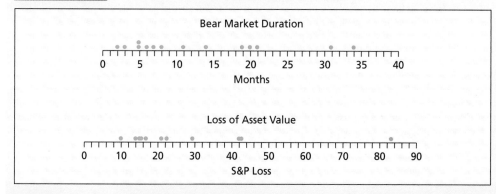

TABLE 4.12   Statistical Summary of Bear Markets

Statistic	Duration (months)	S&P Loss (%)
Count	14	14
Mean	13.29	26.57
Median	9.5	18.95
Standard deviation	10.29	19.27
Minimum	2	10.2
Maximum	34	83.4
Range	32	73.2
Coefficient of variation	77.4%	72.5%
Mean absolute deviation	8.47	13.42

SECTION EXERCISES

4.13 Without using Excel: (a) Find the mean and standard deviation for each sample. (b) What does this exercise show?

> *Sample A:* 6, 7, 8
>
> *Sample B:* 61, 62, 63
>
> *Sample C:* 1000, 1001, 1002

4.14 Without using Excel, for each data set: (a) Find the mean. (b) Find the standard deviation, treating the data as a sample. (c) Find the standard deviation, treating the data as a population. (d) What does this exercise show?

> *Data Set A:* 6, 7, 8
>
> *Data Set B:* 4, 5, 6, 7, 8, 9, 10
>
> *Data Set C:* 1, 2, 3, 4, 5, 6, 7, 8, 9, 10, 11, 12, 13

4.15 Find the coefficient of variation for prices of these three stocks. (a) Which stock has the greatest relative variation? (b) To measure variability, why not just compare the standard deviations?

> *Stock A:* $\bar{x} = \$24.50$, $s = 5.25$
>
> *Stock B:* $\bar{x} = \$147.25$, $s = 12.25$
>
> *Stock C:* $\bar{x} = \$5.75$, $s = 2.08$

4.16 Prof. Hardtack gave four Friday quizzes last semester in his 10-student senior tax accounting class. (a) Using Excel, find the sample mean, standard deviation, and coefficient of variation for each quiz. (b) How do these data sets differ in terms of central tendency and dispersion? (c) Briefly describe and compare student performance on each quiz. **Quizzes**

> *Quiz 1:* 60, 60, 60, 60, 71, 73, 74, 75, 88, 99
>
> *Quiz 2:* 65, 65, 65, 65, 70, 74, 79, 79, 79, 79
>
> *Quiz 3:* 66, 67, 70, 71, 72, 72, 74, 74, 95, 99
>
> *Quiz 4:* 10, 49, 70, 80, 85, 88, 90, 93, 97, 98

4.17 An executive's telephone log showed the lengths of 65 calls initiated during the last week of July. Use Excel to find the sample standard deviation and mean absolute deviation. **CallLength**

1	2	10	5	3	3	2	20	1	1
6	3	13	2	2	1	26	3	1	3
1	2	1	7	1	2	3	1	2	12
1	4	2	2	29	1	1	1	8	5
1	4	2	1	1	1	1	6	1	2
3	3	6	1	3	1	1	5	1	18
2	13	13	1	6					

Mini Case   4.3

What Is the DJIA? DJIA

The Dow Jones Industrial Average (commonly called the DJIA) is the oldest U.S. stock market price index, based on the prices of 30 large, widely held, and actively traded "blue chip" public companies in the United States (e.g., Coca-Cola, Microsoft, Wal-Mart, Walt Disney). Actually, only a few of its 30 component companies are "industrial." The DJIA is measured in "points" rather than dollars. Originally, a simple mean of stock prices, the DJIA now is the sum of the 30 stock prices divided by a "divisor" to compensate for stock splits and other changes over time. The divisor is revised as often as necessary (see www.djindexes.com/mdsidx or www.cbot.com for the latest value). Since high-priced stocks comprise a larger proportion of the sum, the DJIA is more strongly affected by changes in high-priced stocks. That is, a 10 percent price increase in a $10 stock would have less effect than a 10 percent price increase in a $50 stock, even if both companies have the same total market capitalization (the total number of shares times the price per share; often referred to as "market cap"). Broad-based market price indexes (e.g., NSDQ, AMEX, NYSE, S&P 500, Russ 2K) are widely used by fund managers, but the venerable "Dow" is still the one you see first on CNN or MSNBC.

Central Tendency versus Dispersion

Figure 4.20 shows histograms of hole diameters drilled in a steel plate during a manufacturing process. The desired distribution is shown in red. The samples from Machine *A* have the desired *mean* diameter (5 mm) but too much *variation* around the mean. It might be an older machine whose moving parts have become loose through normal wear, so there is greater variation in the holes drilled. Samples from Machine *B* have acceptable *variation* in hole diameter, but the *mean* is incorrectly adjusted (less than the desired 5 mm). To monitor quality, we would take frequent samples from the output of each machine, so that the process can be stopped and adjusted if the sample statistics indicate a problem.

FIGURE 4.20

Central Tendency versus Dispersion

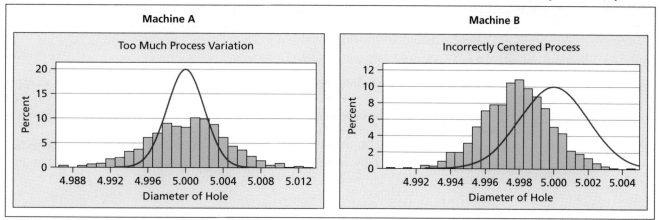

Similarly, Table 4.13 shows how four professors were rated by students on eight teaching attributes (on a 10-point scale). Jones and Wu have identical means but different standard deviations. Smith and Gopal have different means but identical standard deviations. In teaching, a high mean (better rating) and a low standard deviation (more consistency) would presumably be preferred. How would *you* describe these professors?

Attribute	Same Mean, Different Variance		Different Mean, Same Variance	
	Prof. Wu	**Prof. Jones**	**Prof. Smith**	**Prof. Gopal**
1. Challenging	8.4	5.1	6.5	8.8
2. Approachable	6.7	9.4	5.4	9.8
3. Enthusiastic	7.5	5.9	7.3	8.1
4. Helps students	7.0	9.2	5.8	8.3
5. Fair exams	7.4	7.8	6.3	8.8
6. Knowledge	6.9	8.3	6.3	7.9
7. Lecture ability	7.6	6.4	5.6	9.0
8. Organized	6.1	5.5	4.8	7.3
Mean	7.20	7.20	6.00	8.50
Std Dev	0.69	1.69	0.77	0.77
CV	9.6%	23.5%	12.8%	9.0%

TABLE 4.13

Average Teaching Ratings for Four Professors
FourProfs

4.4
STANDARDIZED DATA

The standard deviation is an important measure of dispersion because of its many roles in statistics. One of its main uses is to gauge the position of items within a data array.

Chebyshev's Theorem

The French mathematician Jules Bienaymé (1796–1878) and the Russian mathematician Pafnuty Chebyshev (1821–1894) proved that, for any data set, no matter how it is distributed, the percentage of observations that lie within k standard deviations of the mean (i.e., within $\mu \pm k\sigma$) must be at least $100 [1 - 1/k^2]$. Commonly called **Chebyshev's Theorem**, it says that for *any population* with mean μ and standard deviation σ:

$k = 2$ at least 75.0% will lie within $\mu \pm 2\sigma$.

$k = 3$ at least 88.9% will lie within $\mu \pm 3\sigma$.

Although applicable to any data set, these limits tend to be rather wide.

The Empirical Rule

More precise statements can be made about data from a normal or Gaussian distribution, named for its discoverer Karl Gauss (1777–1855). The Gaussian distribution is the well-known bell-shaped curve. Commonly called the **Empirical Rule**, it says that for data from a *normal distribution* we expect the interval $\mu \pm k\sigma$ to contain a known percentage of the data:

$k = 1$ about 68.26% will lie within $\mu \pm 1\sigma$.

$k = 2$ about 95.44% will lie within $\mu \pm 2\sigma$.

$k = 3$ about 99.73% will lie within $\mu \pm 3\sigma$.

The Empirical Rule is illustrated in Figure 4.21. The Empirical Rule does *not* give an upper bound, but merely describes what is *expected*. Rounding off a bit, we say that in samples from a normal distribution we expect 68 percent of the data within 1 standard deviation, 95 percent within 2 standard deviations, and virtually all of the data within 3 standard deviations. The last statement is imprecise, since 0.27 percent of the observations are expected outside 3 standard deviations, but it correctly conveys the idea that data values outside $\mu \pm 3\sigma$ are rare in a normal distribution.

EXAMPLE

Exam Scores

Suppose 80 students take an exam. How many students will score within 2 standard deviations of the mean? Assuming that exam scores follow a normal or bell-shaped curve, we might be willing to rely on the Empirical Rule, which predicts that 95.44% × 80 or approximately 76 students will score within 2 standard deviations from the mean. Since a normal distribution is symmetric about the mean, we further expect that about 2 students will score more than 2 standard deviations above the mean, and 2 below the mean. Using the Empirical Rule, we can further say that it is unlikely that any student will score more than 3 standard deviations from the mean (99.73% × 80 = 79.78 ≈ 80).

FIGURE 4.21

The Empirical Rule for a Normal Population

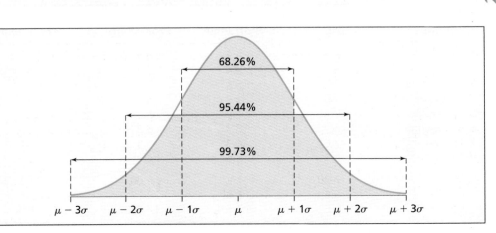

Term	Criterion
Unusual	2 or more standard deviations from the mean
Outlier	3 or more standard deviations from the mean

TABLE 4.14

Detecting Unusual Observations

Note: For a large sample like $n = 1,000$ it would *not* be surprising to see a few data values outside the 3 standard deviation range, since 99.73% of 1,000 is only 997.

Unusual Observations

The Empirical Rule suggests criteria for detecting *unusual* observations (beyond $\mu \pm 2\sigma$) or **outliers** (beyond $\mu \pm 3\sigma$). Many variations on the criteria in Table 4.14 are possible.

The P/E data set contains several large data values. Would we classify them as unusual or as outliers?

EXAMPLE

Unusual Observations

7	8	8	10	10	10	10	12	13	13	13	13
13	13	13	14	14	14	15	15	15	15	15	16
16	16	17	18	18	18	18	19	19	19	19	19
20	20	20	21	21	21	22	22	23	23	23	24
25	26	26	26	26	27	29	29	30	31	34	36
37	40	41	45	48	55	68	91				

For the P/E data, $\bar{x} = 22.72$ and $s = 14.08$. From these sample statistics, the Empirical Rule says that *if the sample came from a normal distribution:*

$\bar{x} \pm 1s$: $22.72 \pm 1(14.08)$ 68.26% of the P/E ratios would be within the interval 8.6 to 36.8.

$\bar{x} \pm 2s$: $22.72 \pm 2(14.08)$ 95.44% of the P/E ratios would be within the interval -5.4 to 50.9.

$\bar{x} \pm 3s$: $22.72 \pm 3(14.08)$ 99.73% of the P/E ratios would be within the interval -19.5 to 65.0.

We can ignore the negative lower limits, since negative P/E ratios are impossible. By these criteria, we have one *unusual* data value (55) and two *outliers* (68 and 91). In fact, our calculations suggest that the sample probably *isn't* from a normal population, because it does not match the Empirical Rule very well, as shown in Table 4.15. However, unless the sample is fairly large (say, 50 or more) comparing the tabulated sample frequencies with a normal distribution would not be very informative.

TABLE 4.15   **P/E Sample versus Normal ($n = 68$)   PERatios2**

Data Range	Sample	If Normal
Within $\bar{x} \pm 1s$	57/68, or 83.8%	68.26%
Within $\bar{x} \pm 2s$	65/68, or 95.59%	95.44
Within $\bar{x} \pm 3s$	66/68, or 97.06%	99.73

Defining a Standardized Variable

Another approach is to redefine each observation in terms of its distance from the mean in standard deviations. We call this a **standardized variable** and denote it by the letter Z. We get the standardized variable Z by transforming each value of the random variable X:

$$z_i = \frac{x_i - \mu}{\sigma} \quad \text{for a population} \tag{4.16}$$

$$z_i = \frac{x_i - \bar{x}}{s} \quad \text{for a sample} \tag{4.17}$$

Chapter 5

FIGURE 4.22

Empirical Rule Using MegaStat ($n = 37$ cars)

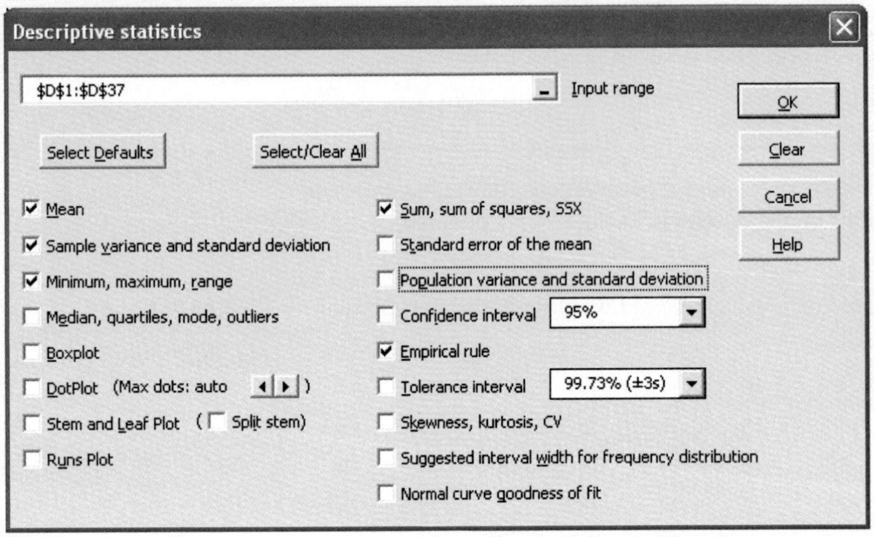

Descriptive statistics	⊠
$D$1:$D$37 ⏷ Input range	OK
Select Defaults Select/Clear All	Clear
	Cancel
☑ Mean ☑ Sum, sum of squares, SSX	Help
☑ Sample variance and standard deviation ☐ Standard error of the mean	
☑ Minimum, maximum, range ☐ Population variance and standard deviation	
☐ Median, quartiles, mode, outliers ☐ Confidence interval 95% ⏷	
☐ Boxplot ☑ Empirical rule	
☐ DotPlot (Max dots: auto ◀▶) ☐ Tolerance interval 99.73% (±3s) ⏷	
☐ Stem and Leaf Plot (☐ Split stem) ☐ Skewness, kurtosis, CV	
☐ Runs Plot ☐ Suggested interval width for frequency distribution	
☐ Normal curve goodness of fit	

Defects per 100 Vehicles	
count	37
mean	134.51
sample variance	621.76
sample standard deviation	24.94
minimum	91
maximum	204
range	113
sum	4,977.00
sum of squares	691,857.00
deviation sum of squares (SSX)	22,383.24
empirical rule	
mean − 1s	109.58
mean + 1s	159.45
percent in interval (68.26%)	70.3%
mean − 2s	84.64
mean + 2s	184.38
percent in interval (95.44%)	94.6%
mean − 3s	59.71
mean + 3s	209.32
percent in interval (99.73%)	100.0%

By looking at z_i we can tell at a glance how far away from the mean each observation lies. For the P/E data the standardized values are:

−1.12	−1.05	−1.05	−0.90	−0.90	−0.90	−0.90	−0.76	−0.69	−0.69	−0.69	−0.69
−0.69	−0.69	−0.69	−0.62	−0.62	−0.62	−0.55	−0.55	−0.55	−0.55	−0.55	−0.48
−0.48	−0.48	−0.41	−0.34	−0.34	−0.34	−0.34	−0.26	−0.26	−0.26	−0.26	−0.26
−0.19	−0.19	−0.19	−0.12	−0.12	−0.12	−0.05	−0.05	0.02	0.02	0.02	0.09
0.16	0.23	0.23	0.23	0.23	0.30	0.45	0.45	0.52	0.59	0.80	0.94
1.01	1.23	1.30	1.58	1.80	2.29	3.22	4.85				

The standardizing calculations for the four largest data points (48, 55, 68, 91) are shown:

$$z_i = \frac{x_i - \bar{x}}{s} = \frac{48 - 22.72}{14.08} = 1.80 \qquad \text{Within 2 standard deviations (not unusual)}$$

$$z_i = \frac{x_i - \bar{x}}{s} = \frac{55 - 22.72}{14.08} = 2.29 \qquad \text{Beyond 2 standard deviations (unusual)}$$

$$z_i = \frac{x_i - \bar{x}}{s} = \frac{68 - 22.72}{14.08} = 3.22 \qquad \text{Beyond 3 standard deviations (outlier)}$$

$$z_i = \frac{x_i - \bar{x}}{s} = \frac{91 - 22.72}{14.08} = 4.85 \qquad \text{Beyond 4 standard deviations (extreme outlier)}$$

Excel's function =STANDARDIZE(XValue, Mean, StDev) makes it easy to calculate standardized values from a column of data. Visual Statistics calculates standardized values, sorts the data, checks for outliers, and tabulates the sample frequencies so you can apply the Empirical Rule. MegaStat does the same thing, as seen in Figure 4.22 for the J.D. Powers data.

Outliers

Extreme values of a variable are vexing, but what do we do about them? It is tempting to discard unusual data points. Discarding an outlier would be reasonable if we had reason to suppose it is erroneous data. For example, a blood pressure reading of 1200/80 seems impossible (probably was supposed to be 120/80). Perhaps the lab technician was distracted by a conversation while marking down the reading. An outrageous observation is almost certainly invalid. But how do we guard against self-deception? More than one scientist has been convinced to disregard data that didn't fit the pattern, when in fact the weird observation was trying to say something important. At this stage of your statistical training, it suffices to *recognize* unusual data points and outliers and their potential impact, and to know that there are entire books that cover the topic of outliers (see Related Reading).

Estimating Sigma

Since for a normal distribution essentially all the observations lie within $\mu \pm 3\sigma$, the range is approximately 6σ (from $\mu - 3\sigma$ to $\mu + 3\sigma$). Therefore, if you know the range R, you can estimate the standard deviation as $\sigma = R/6$. This rule can come in handy for approximating the standard deviation when all you know is the range. For example, the caffeine content of a cup of tea depends on the type of tea and length of time the tea steeps, with a range of 20 to 90 mg. Knowing only the range, we could estimate the standard deviation as $s = (90 - 20)/6$, or about 12 mg. This estimate assumes that the caffeine content of a cup of tea is normally distributed.

Mini Case   4.4

Presidential Ages

Table 4.16 shows the sorted ages at inauguration of the first 43 U.S. Presidents. There are two modes (age 51 and age 54) sorted that occur five times each. However, there are several other ages that occur four times (age 55 and age 57). In such data, the mean (54.86) or median (55.0) would give a better indication of central tendency.

| TABLE 4.16 | Ages at Inauguration of 43 U.S. Presidents (sorted) | Presidents |

President	Age	President	Age	President	Age
T. Roosevelt	42	Lincoln	52	Washington	57
Kennedy	43	Carter	52	Jefferson	57
Grant	46	Van Buren	*54*	Madison	57
Cleveland	47	Hayes	*54*	J. Q. Adams	57
Clinton	47	McKinley	*54*	Monroe	58
Pierce	48	Hoover	*54*	Truman	60
Polk	49	G. W. Bush	*54*	J. Adams	61
Garfield	49	B. Harrison	55	Jackson	61
Fillmore	50	Cleveland	55	Ford	61
Tyler	*51*	Harding	55	Eisenhower	62
Arthur	*51*	L. Johnson	55	Taylor	64
Taft	*51*	A. Johnson	56	G. H. W. Bush	64
Coolidge	*51*	Wilson	56	Buchanan	65
F. Roosevelt	*51*	Nixon	56	W. H. Harrison	68
				Reagan	69

Source: Ken Parks, *The World Almanac and Book of Facts 2002*, p. 545. Copyright © 2005 The World Almanac Education Group, Inc.

The dot plot in Figure 4.23 shows the mode and several mini-modes. It also reveals the extremes on either end (Theodore Roosevelt and John Kennedy were the youngest presidents, while William Henry Harrison and Ronald Reagan were the oldest presidents).

| FIGURE 4.23 | Dot Plot of Presidents' Ages at Inauguration |

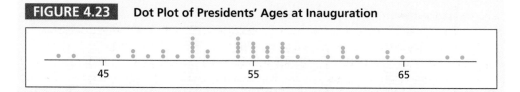

A histogram is more useful for revealing modality. Using six classes, based on Sturges' Rule, Figure 4.24 shows that the modal class is 50 to 55 (13 presidents are in that class). However, since the next higher class has almost as many observations, it might be more helpful to say that presidents tend to be between 50 and 59 years of age upon inauguration (25 presidents are within this range). *Question:* In which histogram interval does the 2008 president's age fall?

FIGURE 4.24   **Histogram of Presidents' Ages at Inauguration**

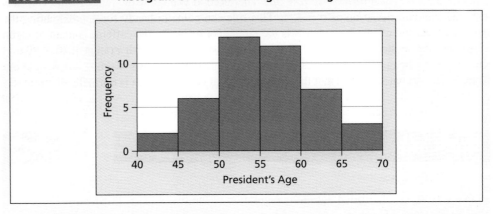

SECTION EXERCISES

connect

4.18 (a) By Chebychev's Theorem, at least how many students in a class of 200 would score within the range $\mu \pm 2\sigma$? (b) By the Empirical Rule, how many students in a class of 200 would score within the range $\mu \pm 2\sigma$? (c) What assumption is required in order to apply the Empirical Rule?

4.19 Convert each individual X data value to a standardized Z value and interpret it.
   a. Class exam: $\mu = 79$, $\sigma = 5$, John's score is 91.
   b. Student GPA: $\mu = 2.87$, $\sigma = 0.31$, Mary's GPA is 3.18.
   c. Weekly study hours: $\mu = 15.0$, $\sigma = 5.0$, Jaime studies 18 hours

4.20 CitiBank recorded the number of customers to use a downtown ATM during the noon hour on 32 consecutive workdays. (a) Use Excel or MegaStat to sort and standardize the data. (b) Based on the Empirical Rule, are there outliers? Unusual data values? (c) Compare the percent of observations that lie within 1 and 2 standard deviations of the mean with a normal distribution. What is your conclusion? (d) Do you feel the sample size is sufficient to assess normality? **CitiBank**

25	37	23	26	30	40	25	26
39	32	21	26	19	27	32	25
18	26	34	18	31	35	21	33
33	9	16	32	35	42	15	24

4.21 An executive's telephone log showed the lengths of 65 calls initiated during the last week of July. (a) Use Excel or MegaStat to sort and standardize the data. (b) Based on the Empirical Rule, are there outliers? Unusual data values? (c) Compare the percent of observations that lie within 1 and 2 standard deviations of the mean with a normal distribution. What is your conclusion? (d) Do you feel the sample size is sufficient to assess normality? **CallLength**

1	2	10	5	3	3	2	20	1	1
6	3	13	2	2	1	26	3	1	3
1	2	1	7	1	2	3	1	2	12
1	4	2	2	29	1	1	1	8	5
1	4	2	1	1	1	1	6	1	2
3	3	6	1	3	1	1	5	1	18
2	13	13	1	6					

Percentiles

You are familiar with percentile scores of national educational tests such as ACT, SAT, and GMAT, which tell you where you stand in comparison with others. For example, if you are in the 83rd percentile, then 83 percent of the test-takers scored below you, and you are in the top 17 percent of all test-takers. However, only when the sample is large can we meaningfully divide the data into 100 groups (*percentiles*). Alternatively, we can divide the data into 10 groups (*deciles*), 5 groups (*quintiles*), or 4 groups (*quartiles*).

In health care, manufacturing, and banking, selected percentiles (e.g., 5, 25, 50, 75, and 95 percent) are calculated to establish *benchmarks* so that any firm can compare itself with similar firms (i.e., other firms in the same industry) in terms of profit margin, debt ratio, defect rate, or any other relevant performance measure. In finance, quartiles (25, 50, and 75 percent) are commonly used to assess financial performance of companies and stock portfolio performances. In human resources, percentiles are used in employee merit evaluations and salary benchmarking. The number of groups depends on the task at hand and the sample size, but quartiles deserve special attention because they are meaningful even for fairly small samples.

Quartiles

The **quartiles** (denoted Q_1, Q_2, Q_3) are scale points that divide the sorted data into four groups of approximately equal size, that is, the 25th, 50th, and 75th percentiles, respectively.

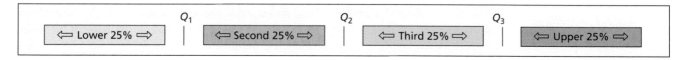

The second quartile Q_2 is the *median*. Since equal numbers of data values lie below and above the median, it is an important indicator of *central tendency*.

The first and third quartiles Q_1 and Q_3 indicate *central tendency* because they define the boundaries for the middle 50 percent of the data. But Q_1 and Q_3 also indicate *dispersion,* since the *interquartile range* Q_3–Q_1 measures the degree of spread in the data (the middle 50 percent).

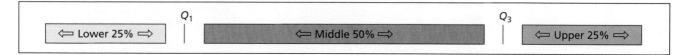

Conceptually, the first quartile Q_1 is the median of the data values below Q_2, and the third quartile Q_3 is the median of the data values above Q_2. Depending on n, the quartiles Q_1, Q_2, Q_3 may be members of the data set or may lie *between* two of the sorted data values. Figure 4.25 shows four possible situations.

Method of Medians

For small data sets, you can find the quartiles using the **method of medians**, as illustrated in Figure 4.26.

- Step 1:   Sort the observations.
- Step 2:   Find the median Q_2.
- Step 3:   Find the median of the data values that lie below Q_2.
- Step 4:   Find the median of the data values that lie above Q_2.

This method is attractive because it is quick and logical (see Freund 1987 in Related Reading). However, Excel uses a different method.

FIGURE 4.25

Possible Quartile Positions

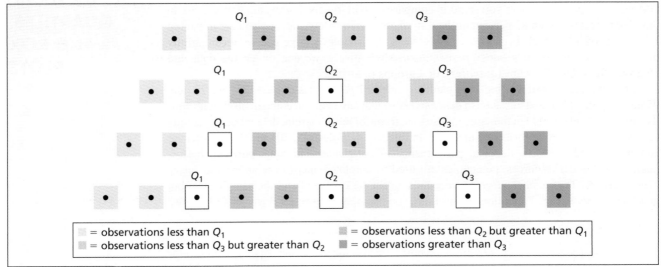

= observations less than Q_1
= observations less than Q_3 but greater than Q_2
= observations less than Q_2 but greater than Q_1
= observations greater than Q_3

EXAMPLE

Method of Medians

A financial analyst has a portfolio of 12 energy equipment stocks. She has data on their recent price/earnings (P/E) ratios. To find the quartiles, she sorts the data, finds Q_2 (the median) halfway between the middle two data values, and then finds Q_1 and Q_3 (medians of the lower and upper halves, respectively) as illustrated in Figure 4.26.

FIGURE 4.26   **Method of Medians**

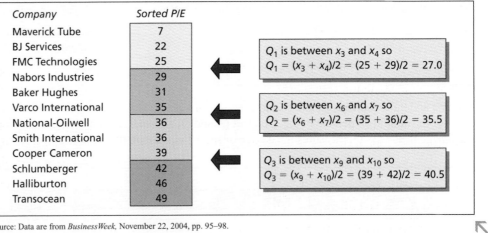

Company	Sorted P/E
Maverick Tube	7
BJ Services	22
FMC Technologies	25
Nabors Industries	29
Baker Hughes	31
Varco International	35
National-Oilwell	36
Smith International	36
Cooper Cameron	39
Schlumberger	42
Halliburton	46
Transocean	49

Q_1 is between x_3 and x_4 so
$Q_1 = (x_3 + x_4)/2 = (25 + 29)/2 = 27.0$

Q_2 is between x_6 and x_7 so
$Q_2 = (x_6 + x_7)/2 = (35 + 36)/2 = 35.5$

Q_3 is between x_9 and x_{10} so
$Q_3 = (x_9 + x_{10})/2 = (39 + 42)/2 = 40.5$

Source: Data are from *BusinessWeek,* November 22, 2004, pp. 95–98.

Formula Method

Statistical software (e.g., Excel, MegaStat, MINITAB) will not use the method of medians, but instead will use a formula to calculate the quartile positions.* There are several possible ways of calculating the quartile positions. The two that you are most likely to use are:

	Method A (MINITAB)	*Method B (Excel or MegaStat)*
Position of Q_1	$0.25n + 0.25$	$0.25n + 0.75$
Position of Q_2	$0.50n + 0.50$	$0.50n + 0.50$
Position of Q_3	$0.75n + 0.75$	$0.75n + 0.25$

Q_2 is the same using either method, but Q_1 and Q_3 generally are not. It depends on the gap between data values when interpolation is necessary. Most textbooks prefer MINITAB's method, so it will be illustrated here.

---

*The quartiles (25th, 50th, and 75th percentiles) are a special case of percentiles. *Method A* defines the Pth percentile position as $P(n + 1)/100$ while *Method B* defines it as $1 + P(n - 1)/100$. See Eric Langford, "Quartiles in Elementary Statistics," *Journal of Statistics Education* 14, no. 3, November, 2006.

Figure 4.27 illustrates the quartile calculations for the same sample of P/E ratios using *Method A*. The resulting quartiles are similar to those using the method of medians.

EXAMPLE

Formula Method

FIGURE 4.27

Formula Interpolation Method

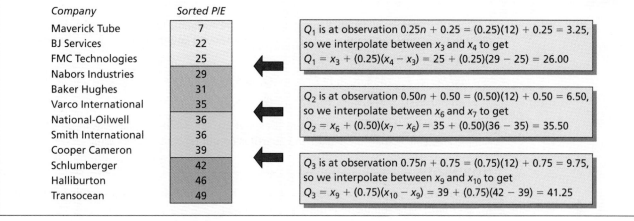

Source: Data are from *BusinessWeek*, November 22, 2004, pp. 95–98.

Excel Quartiles

Excel's function =QUARTILE(Data, k) returns the *k*th quartile, so =QUARTILE(Data, 1) would return Q_1 and =QUARTILE(Data, 3) would return Q_3. Excel treats quartiles as a special case of percentiles, so you could get the same results by using the function =PERCENTILE(Data, Percent). For example, =PERCENTILE(Data, 0.75) would return the 75th percentile or Q_3.

A financial analyst has a diversified portfolio of 68 stocks. Their recent P/E ratios are shown. She wants to use the quartiles to define benchmarks for stocks that are low-priced (bottom quartile) or high-priced (top quartile).   **PERatios2**

EXAMPLE

P/E Ratios and Quartiles

7	8	8	10	10	10	10	12	13	13	13	13	13	13	13	14	14
14	15	15	15	15	15	16	16	16	17	18	18	18	18	19	19	19
19	19	20	20	20	21	21	21	22	22	23	23	23	24	25	26	26
26	26	27	29	29	30	31	34	36	37	40	41	45	48	55	68	91

Using Excel's method of interpolation (*Method B*), the quartile *positions* are:

Q_1 position: $0.25(68) + 0.75 = 17.75$ (interpolate between $x_{17} + x_{18}$)

Q_2 position: $0.50(68) + 0.50 = 34.50$ (interpolate between $x_{34} + x_{35}$)

Q_3 position: $0.75(68) + 0.25 = 51.25$ (interpolate between $x_{51} + x_{52}$)

The quartiles are:

First quartile: $Q_1 = x_{17} + 0.75(x_{18} - x_{17}) = 14 + 0.75(14 - 14) = 14$

Second quartile: $Q_2 = x_{34} + 0.50(x_{35} - x_{34}) = 19 + 0.50(19 - 19) = 19$

Third quartile: $Q_3 = x_{51} + 0.25(x_{52} - x_{51}) = 26 + 0.25(26 - 26) = 26$

The median stock has a P/E ratio of 19. A stock with a P/E ratio below 14 is in the bottom quartile, while a stock with a P/E ratio above 26 is in the upper quartile. These statements are easy to understand, and convey an impression both of central tendency *and* dispersion in the sample. But notice that the quartiles do not provide clean cut-points between groups of observations because of clustering of identical data values on either side of the quartiles (a common occurrence). Since stock prices vary with the stage of the economic cycle, portfolio analysts must revise their P/E benchmarks continually and would actually use a larger sample (perhaps even *all* publicly traded stocks).

Tip

Whether you use the method of medians or Excel, your quartiles will be about the same. Small differences in calculation techniques typically do not lead to different conclusions in business applications.

Quartiles are robust statistics that generally resist outliers. However, quartiles do not always provide clean cutpoints in the sorted data, particularly in small samples or when there are repeating data values. For example:

Data Set A: 1, 2, 4, 4, 8, 8, 8, 8 $Q_1 = 3, Q_2 = 6, Q_3 = 8$
Data Set B: 0, 3, 3, 6, 6, 6, 10, 15 $Q_1 = 3, Q_2 = 6, Q_3 = 8$

These two data sets have identical quartiles, but are not really similar. Because of the small sample size and "gaps" in the data, the quartiles do not represent either data set well.

Box Plots

A useful tool of *exploratory data analysis* (EDA) is the **box plot** (also called a *box-and-whisker plot*) based on the **five-number summary**:

$$x_{min}, Q_1, Q_2, Q_3, x_{max}$$

The box plot is displayed visually, like this.

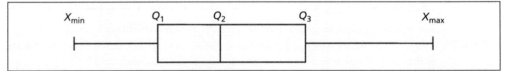

Below the box plot there is a well-labeled scale showing the values of X. A box plot shows *central tendency* (position of the median Q_2). A box plot shows *dispersion* (width of the "box" defined by Q_1 and Q_3 and the range between x_{min} and x_{max}). A box plot shows *shape* (skewness if the whiskers are of unequal length and/or if the median is not in the center of the box). For example, the five number summary for the 68 P/E ratios is:

7, 14, 19, 26, 91

Figure 4.28 shows a box plot of the P/E data. The vertical lines that define the ends of the box are located at Q_1 and Q_3 on the X-axis. The vertical line within the box is the median (Q_2). The "whiskers" are the horizontal lines that connect each side of the box to x_{min} and x_{max} and their length suggests the length of each tail of the distribution. The long right whisker suggests right-skewness in the P/E data, a conclusion also suggested by the fact that the median is to the left of the center of the box (the center of the box is the average of Q_1 and Q_3).

FIGURE 4.28

Simple Box Plot of P/E Ratios ($n = 68$ stocks) (Visual Statistics)

PERatios2

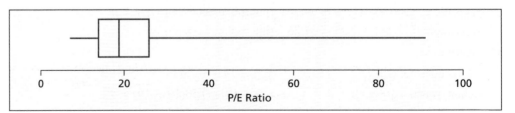

Fences and Unusual Data Values

We can use the quartiles to identify unusual data points. The idea is to detect data values that are far below Q_1 or far above Q_3. The *fences* are based on the **interquartile range** $Q_3 - Q_1$:

		Inner fences	*Outer fences*
(4.18)	Lower fence:	$Q_1 - 1.5(Q_3 - Q_1)$	$Q_1 - 3.0(Q_3 - Q_1)$
(4.19)	Upper fence:	$Q_3 + 1.5(Q_3 - Q_1)$	$Q_3 + 3.0(Q_3 - Q_1)$

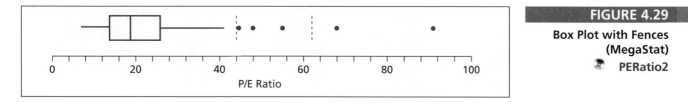

FIGURE 4.29

**Box Plot with Fences
(MegaStat)**
PERatio2

Observations outside the inner fences are *unusual* while those outside the outer fences are *outliers*. For the P/E data:

	Inner fences	*Outer fences*
Lower fence:	$14 - 1.5(26 - 14) = -4$	$14 - 3.0(26 - 14) = -22$
Upper fence:	$26 + 1.5(26 - 14) = +44$	$26 + 3.0(26 - 14) = +62$

In this example, we can ignore the lower fences (since P/E ratios can't be negative) but in the right tail there are three unusual P/E values (45, 48, 55) that lie above the *inner* fence and two P/E values (68, 91) that are outliers because they exceed the *outer* fence. Unusual data points are shown on a box plot by truncating the whisker at the fences and displaying the unusual data points as dots or asterisks, as in Figure 4.29.

Midhinge

Quartiles can be used to define an additional measure of central tendency that has the advantage of not being influenced by outliers. The **midhinge** is the average of the first and third quartiles:

$$\text{Midhinge} = \frac{Q_1 + Q_3}{2} \tag{4.20}$$

The name "midhinge" derives from the idea that, if the "box" were folded at its halfway point, it would resemble a hinge:

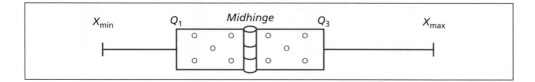

Since the midhinge is always exactly *halfway* between Q_1 and Q_3 while the median Q_2 can be *anywhere* within the "box," we have a new way to describe skewness:

$Q_2 <$ Midhinge $\Rightarrow$ Skewed right (longer right tail)
$Q_2 \cong$ Midhinge $\Rightarrow$ Symmetric (tails roughly equal)
$Q_2 >$ Midhinge $\Rightarrow$ Skewed left (longer left tail)

SECTION EXERCISES

4.22 CitiBank recorded the number of customers to use a downtown ATM during the noon hour on 32 consecutive workdays. (a) Use Excel to find the quartiles. What do they tell you? (b) Find the midhinge. What does it tell you? (c) Make a box plot and interpret it.   **CitiBank**

25	37	23	26	30	40	25	26
39	32	21	26	19	27	32	25
18	26	34	18	31	35	21	33
33	9	16	32	35	42	15	24

4.23 An executive's telephone log showed the lengths of 65 calls initiated during the last week of July. (a) Use Excel to find the quartiles. What do they tell you? (b) Find the midhinge. What does it tell you? (c) Make a box plot and interpret it.   **CallLength**

1	2	10	5	3	3	2	20	1	1
6	3	13	2	2	1	26	3	1	3
1	2	1	7	1	2	3	1	2	12
1	4	2	2	29	1	1	1	8	5
1	4	2	1	1	1	1	6	1	2
3	3	6	1	3	1	1	5	1	18
2	13	13	1	6					

Mini Case   4.5

Airline Delays   UnitedAir

In 2005, United Airlines announced that it would award 500 frequent flier miles to every traveler on flights that arrived more than 30 minutes late on all flights departing from Chicago O'Hare to seven other hub airports (see *The Wall Street Journal,* June 14, 2005). What is the likelihood of such a delay? On a randomly chosen day (Tuesday, April 26, 2005) the Bureau of Transportation Statistics Web site (www.bts.gov) showed 278 United Airlines departures from O'Hare. The mean arrival delay was -7.45 minutes (i.e., flights arrived early, on average). The quartiles were $Q_1 = -19$ minutes, $Q_2 = -10$ minutes, and $Q_3 = -3$ minutes. While these statistics show that most of the flights arrive early, we must look further to estimate the probability of a frequent flier bonus.

In the box plot with fences (Figure 4.30) the "box" is entirely below zero. In the right tail, one flight was slightly above the inner fence (unusual) and eight flights were above the outer fence (outliers). An empirical estimate of the probability of a frequent flier award is 8/278 or about a 3% chance. A longer period of study might alter this estimate (e.g., if there were days of bad winter weather or traffic congestion).

FIGURE 4.30   **Box Plot of Flight Arrival Delays**

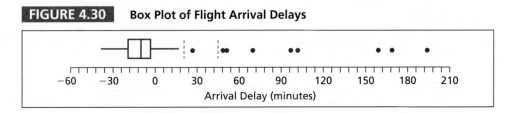

The dot plot (Figure 4.31) shows that the distribution of arrival delays is rather bell-shaped, except for the unusual values in the right tail. This is consistent with the view that "normal" flight operations are predictable, with only random variation around the mean. While it is impossible for flights to arrive much earlier than planned, unusual factors could delay them by a lot.

FIGURE 4.31   **Dot Plot of Flight Arrival Delays**

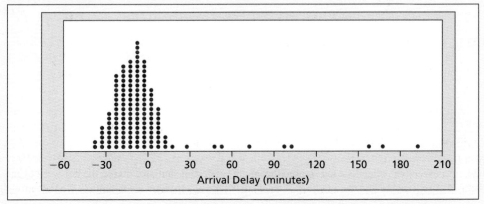

You often hear the term "significant correlation" in casual use, often imprecisely or incorrectly. Actually, the **sample correlation coefficient** is a well-known statistic that describes the degree of linearity between *paired* observations on two quantitative variables X and Y. The data set consists of n pairs (x_i, y_i) that are usually displayed on a *scatter plot* (review Chapter 3 if you need to refresh your memory about making scatter plots). The formula for the sample correlation coefficient is:

$$r = \frac{\sum_{i=1}^{n}(x_i - \bar{x})(y_i - \bar{y})}{\sqrt{\sum_{i=1}^{n}(x_i - \bar{x})^2}\sqrt{\sum_{i=1}^{n}(y_i - \bar{y})^2}} \tag{4.21}$$

Its range is $-1 \leq r \leq +1$. When r is near 0 there is little or no linear relationship between X and Y. An r value near $+1$ indicates a strong positive relationship, while an r value near -1 indicates a strong negative relationship.

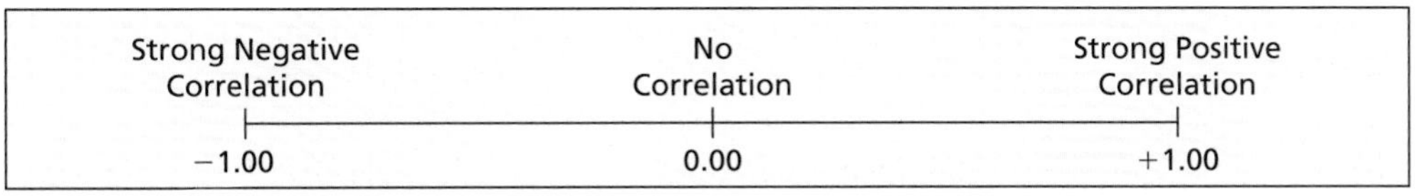

Strong Negative Correlation	No Correlation	Strong Positive Correlation
−1.00	0.00	+1.00

Excel's formula =CORREL(XData,YData) will return the sample correlation coefficient for two columns (or rows) of paired data. In fact, many cheap scientific pocket calculators will calculate r. The diagrams in Figure 4.32 will give you some idea of what various correlations look like. The correlation coefficient is a measure of the *linear relationship*—so take special note of the last scatter plot, which shows a relationship but not a *linear* one.

FIGURE 4.32

Illustration of Correlation Coefficients

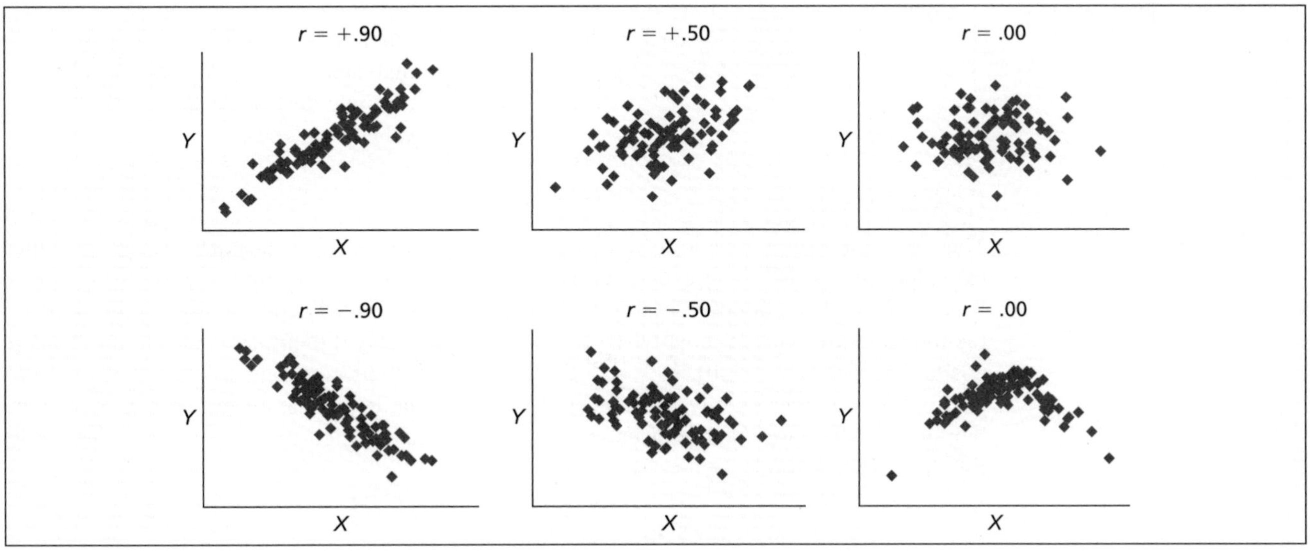

Figure 4.33 shows a scatter plot and correlation coefficient ($r = 0.9890$) for $X =$ gross leasable area (millions of square feet) and $Y =$ total retail sales (billions of dollars) for retail shopping malls in 28 states. Clearly, this is a very strong linear relationship, as you would expect (more square feet of shopping area would imply more sales). In Chapter 12, you will learn how to determine when a correlation is "significant" in a statistical sense (i.e., significantly different than zero) but for now it is enough to recognize the correlation coefficient as a *descriptive statistic*.

FIGURE 4.33

**Mall Area and Sales
Correlation**

🐾 **RetailSales**

Source: U.S. Census Bureau, *Statistical
Abstract of the United States, 2007,*
p. 660.

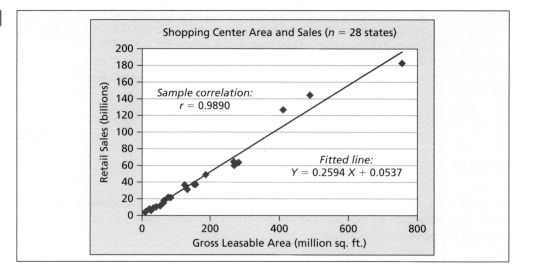

If you right-click on the data in the Excel scatter plot and select Add Trendline, Excel will fit a line to your (X, Y) data, as shown in Figure 4.33. The slope and intercept of this line are *descriptive statistics*. We can interpret Excel's fitted trend line ($Y = 0.2594\ X + 0.0537$) as follows:

Statistic	Value	Mathematical Meaning	Interpretation
Slope	0.2594	Expected change in Y for a one-unit change in X	For each extra million square feet of leasable space (since the X units are in millions) we would expect an increase in retail sales of $0.2594 billion.
Intercept	0.0537	Expected value of Y when $X = 0$.	We would expect only $0.0537 billion in retail sales in a state with no leasable mall area ($X = 0$). The intercept has meaning only if the data set has X values near zero.

Covariance

The **covariance** of two random variables X and Y (denoted σ_{XY}) measures the degree to which the values of X and Y change together. This concept is particularly important in financial portfolio analysis. For example, if the prices of two stocks X and Y tend to move in the same direction their covariance is positive ($\sigma_{XY} > 0$), and conversely if their prices tend to move in opposite directions ($\sigma_{XY} < 0$). If X and Y are unrelated, their covariance is zero ($\sigma_{XY} = 0$). A portfolio manager can apply this concept to reduce volatility in the overall portfolio, by combining stocks in a way that reduces variation. To estimate the covariance, we would generally use the sample formula.

$$(4.22) \qquad \sigma_{XY} = \frac{\sum_{i=1}^{N}(x_i - \mu_X)(y_i - \mu_Y)}{N} \qquad \textit{for a population}$$

$$(4.23) \qquad s_{XY} = \frac{\sum_{i=1}^{n}(x_i - \bar{x})(y_i - \bar{y})}{n - 1} \qquad \textit{for a sample}$$

Because the units of measurement for the covariance are unpredictable (since the means and/or units of measurement of X and Y may differ) analysts generally prefer the correlation

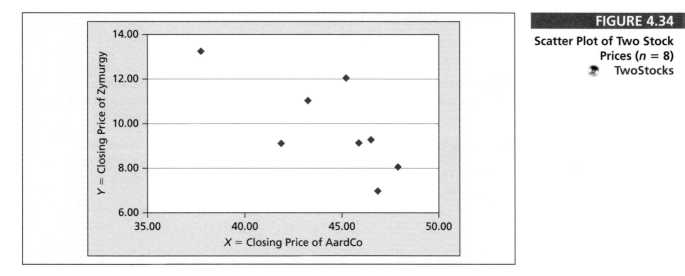

FIGURE 4.34

**Scatter Plot of Two Stock
Prices (*n* = 8)**
TwoStocks

coefficient, which is a standardized value of the covariance. As you have already learned, the correlation coefficient always lies between -1 and $+1$. Conceptually, a correlation coefficient is the covariance divided by the product of the standard deviations of X and Y. For a population, the correlation coefficient is indicated by the Greek letter ρ (rho), while for a sample we use the Roman letter r (as you saw in equation 4.21 in the previous section).

$$\rho = \frac{\sigma_{XY}}{\sigma_X \sigma_Y} \qquad \textit{for a population} \qquad \textbf{(4.24)}$$

$$r = \frac{s_{XY}}{s_X s_Y} \qquad \textit{for a sample} \qquad \textbf{(4.25)}$$

Application: Stock Prices

The prices of two stocks are recorded at the close of trading each Friday for 8 weeks, as displayed in Figure 4.34.

Closing Price for Week (*n* = 8 weeks)

Company	1	2	3	4	5	6	7	8
X (AardCo)	41.87	47.87	43.26	37.76	45.86	45.22	46.83	46.49
Y (Zymurgy)	9.11	8.07	11.02	13.24	9.14	12.04	6.96	9.27

We can see that these two stock prices tend to move in opposite directions, so we anticipate a negative covariance (and a negative correlation). We can do the calculations using Excel functions with named data ranges. Because Excel's =COVAR function uses the population formula, we must make an adjustment to get a *sample* covariance (since we have only a sample of stock prices).

Statistic	Result	Excel Formula
Sample covariance:	$s_{XY} = -5.0890$	=COVAR(XData, YData)*(n/(n − 1)
Std. dev. of X:	$s_X = 3.3146$	=STDEV(XData)
Std. dev. of Y:	$s_Y = 2.0896$	=STDEV(YData)
Sample correlation:	$r = -0.7347$	=CORREL(Xdata, YData)
Sample size:	$n = 8$ weeks	=COUNT(XData)

Applying equation 4.25:

$$r = \frac{s_{XY}}{s_X s_Y} = \frac{-5.0890}{(3.3146)(2.0896)} = -0.7347$$

This is the same value for the correlation coefficient that we would get from equation 4.21. Using this information, a financial analyst can arrange the portfolio whose total value is more stable, knowing that these stock prices tend to move in opposite directions.

SECTION EXERCISES

4.24 For each X-Y data set ($n = 12$) make a scatter plot and find the sample correlation coefficient. Is there a linear relationship between X and Y? If so, describe it. *Note:* Use Excel or MegaStat or MINITAB if your instructor permits.   🕸 **XYDataSets**

Data Set (a)

X	64.7	25.9	65.6	49.6	50.3	26.7	39.5	56.0	90.8	35.9	39.9	64.1
Y	5.8	18.1	10.6	11.9	11.4	14.6	15.7	4.4	2.2	15.4	14.7	9.9

Data Set (b)

X	55.1	59.8	72.3	86.4	31.1	41.8	40.7	36.8	42.7	28.9	24.8	16.2
Y	15.7	17.5	15.2	20.6	7.3	8.2	9.8	8.2	13.7	11.2	7.5	4.5

Data Set (c)

X	53.3	18.1	49.8	43.8	68.3	30.4	18.6	45.8	34.0	56.7	60.3	29.3
Y	10.2	6.9	14.8	13.4	16.8	9.5	16.3	16.4	1.5	11.4	10.9	19.7

4.25 Make a scatter plot of the following data on $X =$ home size and $Y =$ selling price (thousands of dollars) for new homes ($n = 20$) in a suburb of an Eastern city. Find the sample correlation coefficient. Is there a linear relationship between X and Y? If so, describe it. *Note:* Use Excel or MegaStat or MINITAB if your instructor permits.   🕸 **HomePrice**

Square Feet	Selling Price (thousands)	Square Feet	Selling Price (thousands)
3,570	861	3,460	737
3,410	740	3,340	806
2,690	563	3,240	809
3,260	698	2,660	639
3,130	624	3,160	778
3,460	737	3,310	760
3,340	806	2,930	729
3,240	809	3,020	720
2,660	639	2,320	575
3,160	778	3,130	785

Excel Hints

Hint 1: Formats When You Copy Data from Excel
Excel's dollar format (e.g., $214.07) or comma format (e.g., 12,417) will cause many statistical packages (e.g., MINITAB or Visual Statistics) to interpret the pasted data as text (because "$" and "," are not numbers). For example, in MINITAB a column heading C1-T indicates that the data column is text. Text cannot be analyzed numerically, so you can't get means, medians, etc. Check the format before you copy and paste.

Hint 2: Decimals When You Copy Data from Excel
Suppose you have adjusted Excel's decimal cell format to display 2.4 instead of 2.35477. When you copy this cell and paste it into MINITAB, the pasted cell contains 2.4 (not 2.35477). Thus, Excel's statistical calculations (based on 2.35477) will not agree with MINITAB (likewise for Visual Statistics). If you copy several columns of data (e.g., for a regression model), the differences can be serious.

The **mean** and **median** describe a sample's **central tendency** and also indicate **skewness**. The **mode** is useful for discrete data with a small range. The **trimmed mean** eliminates extreme values. The **geometric mean** mitigates high extremes but fails when zeros or negative values are present. The **midrange** is easy to calculate but is sensitive to extremes. Dispersion is typically measured by the **standard deviation** while **relative dispersion** is given by the **coefficient of variation** for nonnegative data. **Standardized data** reveal **outliers** or unusual data values, and the **Empirical Rule** offers a comparison with a normal distribution. In measuring dispersion, the **mean absolute deviation** or **MAD** is easy to understand, but lacks nice mathematical properties. **Quartiles** are meaningful even for fairly small data sets, while **percentiles** are used only for large data sets. **Box plots** show the quartiles and data range. The **sample correlation coefficient** measures the degree of linearity between two variables.

CHAPTER SUMMARY

KEY TERMS

Central Tendency	*Dispersion*	*Shape*	*Other*
geometric mean, *126*	Chebyshev's	bimodal	box plot, *144*
mean, *116*	Theorem, *136*	distribution, *120*	covariance, *148*
median, *117*	coefficient of	multimodal	five-number
midhinge, *145*	variation, *132*	distribution *120*	summary, *144*
midrange, *127*	Empirical Rule, *136*	negatively skewed, *121*	interquartile
mode, *118*	mean absolute	positively skewed, *121*	range, *144*
trimmed mean, *127*	deviation, *132*	skewed left, *121*	method of
	outliers, *137*	skewed right, *121*	medians, *141*
	population	skewness, *121*	quartiles, *141*
	variance, *130*	symmetric data, *121*	sample correlation
	range, *129*		coefficient, *147*
	sample variance, *130*		
	standard deviation, *130*		
	standardized		
	variable, *137*		
	two-sum formula, *131*		

Commonly Used Formulas in Descriptive Statistics

Sample mean: $\bar{x} = \dfrac{1}{n} \sum\limits_{i=1}^{n} x_i$

Geometric mean: $G = \sqrt[n]{x_1 x_2 \cdots x_n}$

Range: $\text{Range} = x_{max} - x_{min}$

Midrange: $\text{Midrange} = \dfrac{x_{min} + x_{max}}{2}$

Sample standard deviation: $s = \sqrt{\dfrac{\sum\limits_{i=1}^{n} (x_i - \bar{x})^2}{n-1}}$

Coefficient of variation: $CV = 100 \times \dfrac{s}{\bar{x}}$

Standardized variable: $z_i = \dfrac{x_i - \mu}{\sigma}$ or $z_i = \dfrac{x_i - \bar{x}}{s}$

Midhinge: $\text{Midhinge} = \dfrac{Q_1 + Q_3}{2}$

Sample correlation coefficient: $r = \dfrac{\sum\limits_{i=1}^{n}(x_i - \bar{x})(y_i - \bar{y})}{\sqrt{\sum\limits_{i=1}^{n}(x_i - \bar{x})^2}\sqrt{\sum\limits_{i=1}^{n}(y_i - \bar{y})^2}}$ or $r = \dfrac{s_{XY}}{s_X s_Y}$

CHAPTER REVIEW

1. What are descriptive statistics? How do they differ from visual displays of data?

2. Explain each concept: (a) central tendency, (b) dispersion, and (c) shape.

3. (a) Why is sorting usually the first step in data analysis? (b) Why is it useful to begin a data analysis by thinking about how the data were collected?

4. List strengths and weaknesses of each measure of central tendency and write its Excel function: (a) mean, (b) median, and (c) mode.

5. (a) Why must the deviations around the mean sum to zero? (b) What is the position of the median in the data array when n is even? When n is odd? (c) Why is the mode of little use in continuous data? For what type of data is the mode most useful?

6. (a) What is a bimodal distribution? (b) Explain two ways to detect skewness.

7. List strengths and weaknesses of each measure of central tendency and give its Excel function (if any): (a) midrange, (b) geometric mean, and (c) 10 percent trimmed mean.

8. (a) What is dispersion? (b) Name five measures of dispersion. List the main characteristics (strengths, weaknesses) of each measure.

9. (a) Which standard deviation formula (population, sample) is used most often? Why? (b) When is the coefficient of variation useful? When is it useless?

10. (a) To what kind of data does Chebyshev's Theorem apply? (b) To what kind of data does the Empirical Rule apply? (c) What is an outlier? An unusual data value?

11. (a) In a normal distribution, approximately what percent of observations are within 1, 2, and 3 standard deviations of the mean? (b) In a sample of 10,000 observations, about how many observations would you expect beyond 3 standard deviations of the mean?

12. (a) Write the mathematical formula for a standardized variable. (b) Write the Excel formula for standardizing a data value in cell F17 from an array with mean Mu and standard deviation Sigma.

13. (a) Why is it dangerous to delete an outlier? (b) When might it be acceptable to delete an outlier?

14. (a) Explain how quartiles can measure both centrality and dispersion. (b) Why don't we calculate percentiles for small samples?

15. (a) Explain the method of medians for calculating quartiles. (b) Write the Excel formula for the first quartile of an array named XData.

16. (a) What is a box plot? What does it tell us? (b) What is the role of fences in a box plot? (c) Define the midhinge and interquartile range.

17. What does a correlation coefficient measure? What is its range?

CHAPTER EXERCISES

Note: Unless otherwise instructed, you may use any desired statistical software for calculations and graphs in the following problems.

connect

DESCRIBING DATA

4.26 Below are monthly rents paid by a sample of 30 students who live off campus. (a) Find the mean, median, mode, standard deviation, and quartiles. (b) Describe the "typical" rent paid by a student. (c) Do the measures of central tendency agree? Explain. (d) Sort and standardize the data. (e) Are there outliers or unusual data values? (f) Using the Empirical Rule, do you think the data could be from a normal population? **Rents**

730	730	730	930	700	570
690	1,030	740	620	720	670
560	740	650	660	850	930
600	620	760	690	710	500
730	800	820	840	720	700

4.27 How many days in advance do travelers purchase their airline tickets? Below are data showing the advance days for a sample of 28 passengers on United Airlines Flight 815 from Chicago to Los Angeles. (a) Prepare a dot plot and discuss it. (b) Calculate the mean, median, mode, and midrange. (c) Calculate the quartiles, midhinge, and interquartile range. (d) Why can't you use the geometric mean for this data set? (e) Which is the best measure of central tendency? Why? (Data are from *The New York Times,* April 12, 1998.) **Days**

11	7	11	4	15	14	71	29	8	7	16	28	17	249
0	20	77	18	14	3	15	52	20	0	9	9	21	3

4.28 In a particular week, the cable channel TCM (Turner Classic Movies) showed seven movies rated ****, nine movies rated ***, three movies rated **, and one movie rated *. Which measure of central tendency would you use to describe the "average" movie rating on TCM (assuming that week was typical)? (Data are from *TV Guide*.)

4.29 The "expense ratio" is a measure of the cost of managing the portfolio. Investors prefer a low expense ratio, all else equal. Below are expense ratios for 23 randomly chosen stock funds and 21 randomly chosen bond funds. (a) Calculate the mean, median, and mode for each sample. (b) Succinctly compare central tendency in expense ratios for stock funds and bond funds. (c) Calculate the standard deviation and coefficient of variation for each sample. Which type of fund has more variability? Explain. (d) Calculate the quartiles and midhinge. What do they tell you? (Data are from *Money* 32, no. 2 [February 2003]. Stock funds were selected from 1,699 funds by taking the 10th fund on each page in the list. Bond funds were selected from 499 funds by taking the 10th, 20th, and 30th fund on each page in the list.)   **Funds**

23 Stock Funds

1.12	1.44	1.27	1.75	0.99	1.45	1.19	1.22	0.99	3.18	1.21	1.89
0.60	2.10	0.73	0.90	1.79	1.35	1.08	1.28	1.20	1.68	0.15	

21 Bond Funds

1.96	0.51	1.12	0.64	0.69	0.20	1.44	0.68	0.40	0.94	0.75	1.77
0.93	1.25	0.85	0.99	0.95	0.35	0.64	0.41	0.90			

4.30 Statistics students were asked to fill a one-cup measure with raisin bran, tap the cup lightly on the counter three times to settle the contents, if necessary add more raisin bran to bring the contents exactly to the one-cup line, spread the contents on a large plate, and count the raisins. The 13 students who chose Kellogg's Raisin Bran obtained the results shown below. (a) Use Excel to calculate the mean, median, mode, and midrange. (b) Which is the best measure of central tendency, and why? (c) Calculate the standard deviation and coefficient of variation. (d) Why is there variation in the number of raisins in a cup of raisin bran? Why might it be difficult for Kellogg to reduce variation?   **Raisins**

23	33	44	36	29	42	31	33	61	36	34	23	24

4.31 The table below shows estimates of the total cost of repairs in four bumper tests (full frontal, front corner, full rear, rear corner) on 17 cars. (a) Make a dot plot for the data. (b) Calculate the mean and median. (c) Would you say the data are skewed? (d) Why is the mode not useful for these data? (Data are from Insurance Institute for Highway Safety, *Detroit Free Press*, March 1, 2007, p. 2E).   **CrashDamage**

Car Tested	Damage	Car Tested	Damage	Car Tested	Damage
Chevrolet Malibu	6,646	Mazda 6	4,961	Suburu Legacy	7,448
Chrysler Sebring	7,454	Mitsubishi Galant	4,277	Toyota Camry	4,911
Ford Fusion	5,030	Nissan Altima	6,459	Volkswagen Jetta	9,020
Honda Accord	8,010	Nissan Maxima	9,051	Volkswagen Passat	8,259
Hyundai Sonata	7,565	Pontiac G6	8,919	Volvo S40	5,600
Kia Optima	5,735	Saturn Aura	6,374		

4.32 Salt-sensitive people must be careful of sodium content in foods. The sodium content (milligrams) in a 3-tablespoon serving of 33 brands of peanut butter is shown below. (a) Prepare a dot plot and discuss it. (b) Calculate the mean, median, mode, and midrange. (c) Which is the best measure of central tendency? The worst? Why? (d) Why would the geometric mean not work here? (e) Sort and standardize the data. (f) Are there outliers? Unusual data values? (Data are from *Consumer Reports* 67, no. 5.)   **Sodium**

98	225	225	225	23	0	210	0	210	225	210	165	180	240
225	8	375	225	270	285	180	210	180	195	195	188	173	
165	165	180	180	0	300								

4.33 Below are the lengths (in yards) of 27 18-hole golf courses in Oakland County, Michigan. (a) Prepare a dot plot and discuss it. (b) Calculate the mean, median, mode, and midrange.

(c) Which is the best measure of central tendency? The worst? Why? (d) Why would the geometric mean pose a problem for this data set? (Data are from *Detroit Free Press*, April 13, 1995.)
🐝 **Golf**

5646	5767	5800	5820	6005	6078	6100	6110	6179
6186	6306	6366	6378	6400	6470	6474	6494	6500
6500	6554	6555	6572	6610	6620	6647	6845	7077

4.34 A false positive occurs when a radiologist who interprets a mammogram concludes that cancer is present, but a biopsy subsequently shows no breast cancer. False positives are unavoidable because mammogram results often are ambiguous. Below are false positive rates (percent) for 24 radiologists who interpreted a total of 8,734 mammograms. (a) Prepare a dot plot and interpret it. (b) Calculate the mean, median, mode, and midrange. (c) Which is the best measure of central tendency? The worst? Why? (Data are from Joann G. Elmore et al., "Screening Mammograms by Community Radiologists: Variability in False Positive Rates," *Journal of the National Cancer Institute* 94, no. 18 [September 18, 2002], p. 1376.) 🐝 **Cancer**

8.5	4.9	12.5	2.6	7.6	15.9	5.6	9.0	9.0	10.8	10.2	12.2
4.0	6.9	6.0	6.7	6.5	9.5	2.7	5.3	4.4	3.5	11.9	4.2

4.35 The table below shows percentiles of height (in cm) for 20-year-old males and females. (a) Calculate the midhinge and interquartile range. Why are these statistics appropriate to measure centrality and dispersion in this situation? (b) Choose a 20 year old whose height you know and describe that person's height (*Note:* 1 in. = 2.54 cm) in comparison with these percentiles. (c) Do you suppose that height percentiles change over time for the population of a specified nation? Explain. (Data are from the National Center for Health Statistics, www.fedstats.gov.)

Selected Percentiles for Heights of 20 Year Olds (cm)

Gender	5%	25%	50%	75%	95%
Male	165	172	177	182	188
Female	153	159	163	168	174

4.36 Grace took a random sample of the number of steps per minute from the electronic readout of her aerobic climbing machine during a 1-hour workout. (a) Calculate the mean, median, and mode. (b) Which is the best measure of central tendency? The worst? Why? (Data are from a project by Grace Obringer, MBA student.) 🐝 **Steps**

90	110	97	144	54	60	156	86	82	64	100	47	80	164	93

4.37 How much revenue does it take to maintain a cricket club? The following table shows annual income for 18 first-class clubs that engage in league play. (a) Calculate the mean, median, and mode. Show your work carefully. (b) Describe a "typical" cricket club's income. (Data are from *The Economist* 367, no. 8329 [June 21, 2003], p. 47.)

Annual Income of First-Class Cricket Clubs in England   🐝 Cricket

Club	Income (£000)	Club	Income (£000)
Lancashire	5,366	Durham	3,009
Surrey	6,386	Worcestershire	2,446
Derbyshire	2,088	Gloucestershire	2,688
Middlesex	2,280	Northamptonshire	2,416
Somerset	2,544	Glamorgan	2,133
Nottinghamshire	3,669	Essex	2,417
Kent	2,894	Warwickshire	4,272
Leicestershire	2,000	Yorkshire	2,582
Sussex	2,477	Hampshire	2,557

4.38 A plumbing supplier's mean monthly demand for vinyl washers is 24,212 with a standard deviation of 6,053. The mean monthly demand for steam boilers is 6.8 with a standard deviation of 1.7. Compare the dispersion of these distributions. Which demand pattern has more relative variation? Explain.

4.39 The table below shows average daily sales of Rice Krispies in the month of June in 74 Noodles & Company restaurants. (a) Make a histogram for the data. Would you say the distribution is skewed? (b) Calculate the mean, median, and mode. Which best describes central tendency, and why? (c) Find the standard deviation. (d) Are there any outliers? **RiceKrispies**

32	8	14	20	28	19	37	31	16	16
16	29	11	34	31	18	22	17	27	16
24	49	25	18	25	21	15	16	20	11
21	29	14	25	10	15	8	12	12	19
21	28	27	26	12	24	18	19	24	16
17	20	23	13	17	17	19	36	16	34
25	15	16	13	20	13	13	23	17	22
11	17	17	9						

4.40 Analysis of portfolio returns over the period 1981–2000 showed the statistics below. (a) Calculate and compare the coefficients of variation. (b) Why would we use a coefficient of variation? Why not just compare the standard deviations? (c) What do the data tell you about risk and return at that time period? **Returns**

Comparative Returns on Four Types of Investments

Investment	Mean Return	Standard Deviation	Coefficient of Variation
Venture funds (adjusted)	19.2	14.0	
All common stocks	15.6	14.0	
Real estate	11.5	16.8	
Federal short term paper	6.7	1.9	

Source: Dennis D. Spice and Stephen D. Hogan, "Venture Investing and the Role of Financial Advisors," *Journal of Financial Planning* 15, no. 3 (March 2002), p. 69. These statistics are for educational use only and should not be viewed as a guide to investing.

4.41 Analysis of annualized returns over the period 1991–2001 showed that prepaid tuition plans had a mean return of 6.3 percent with a standard deviation of 2.7 percent, while the Standard & Poor's 500 stock index had a mean return of 12.9 percent with a standard deviation of 15.8 percent. (a) Calculate and compare the coefficients of variation. (b) Why would we use a coefficient of variation? Why not just compare the standard deviations? (c) What do the data say about risk and return of these investments at that time? (Data are from Mark C. Neath, "Section 529 Prepaid Tuition Plans: A Low Risk Investment with Surprising Applications," *Journal of Financial Planning* 15, no. 4 [April 2002], p. 94.)

4.42 Caffeine content in a 5-ounce cup of brewed coffee ranges from 60 to 180 mg, depending on brew time, coffee bean type, and grind. (a) Use the midrange to estimate the mean. (b) Why is the assumption of a normal, bell-shaped distribution important in making these estimates? (c) Why might caffeine content of coffee *not* be normal? (Data are from *Popular Science* 254, no. 5 [May 1999].)

4.43 Chlorine is added to all city water to kill bacteria. In 2001, chlorine content in water from the Lake Huron Water Treatment plant ranged from 0.79 ppm (parts per million) to 0.92 ppm. (a) Use the midrange to estimate the mean. (b) Why is it reasonable to assume a normal distribution in this case? (Data are from City of Rochester Hills, Michigan, *2002 Water Quality Report*.)

THINKING ABOUT DISTRIBUTIONS

4.44 At the Midlothian Independent Bank, a study shows that the mean ATM transaction takes 74 seconds, the median 63 seconds, and the mode 51 seconds. (a) Sketch the distribution, based on these statistics. (b) What factors might cause the distribution to be like this?

4.45 At the Eureka library, the mean time a book is checked out is 13 days, the median is 10 days, and the mode is 7 days. (a) Sketch the distribution, based on these statistics. (b) What factors might cause the distribution to be like this?

4.46 On Professor Hardtack's last cost accounting exam, the mean score was 71, the median was 77, and the mode was 81. (a) Sketch the distribution, based on these statistics. (b) What factors might cause the distribution to be like this?

4.47 (a) Sketch the histogram you would expect for the number of DVDs owned by n randomly chosen families. (b) Describe the expected relationship between the mean, median, and mode. How could you test your ideas about these data?

4.48 (a) Sketch the histogram you would expect for the price of regular gasoline yesterday at n service stations in your area. (b) Guess the range and median. (c) How could you test your ideas about these data?

4.49 The median life span of a mouse is 118 weeks. (a) Would you expect the mean to be higher or lower than 118? (b) Would you expect the life spans of mice to be normally distributed? Explain. (Data are from *Science News* 161, no. 3 [January 19, 2002].)

4.50 The median waiting time for a liver transplant in the U.S. is 1,154 days for patients with type O blood (the most common blood type). (a) Would you expect the mean to be higher or lower than 1,154 days? Explain. (b) If someone dies while waiting for a transplant, how should that be counted in the average? (Data are from *The New York Times,* September 21, 2003.)

4.51 A small suburban community agreed to purchase police services from the county sheriff's department. The newspaper said, "In the past, the charge for police protection from the Sheriff's Department has been based on the median cost of the salary, fringe benefits, etc. That is, the cost per deputy was set halfway between the most expensive deputy and the least expensive." (a) Is this the median? If not, what is it? (b) Which would probably cost the city more, the midrange or the median? Why?

4.52 A company's contractual "trigger" point for a union absenteeism penalty is a certain distance above the *mean* days missed by all workers. Now the company wants to switch the trigger to a certain distance above the *median* days missed for all workers. (a) Visualize the distribution of missed days for all workers (symmetric, skewed left, skewed right). (b) Discuss the probable effect on the trigger point of switching from the mean to the median. (c) What position would the union be likely to take on the company's proposed switch?

EXCEL PROJECTS

4.53 (a) Use Excel functions to calculate the mean and standard deviation for weekend occupancy rates (percent) in nine resort hotels during the off-season. (b) What conclusion would a casual observer draw about centrality and dispersion, based on your statistics? (c) Now calculate the median for each sample. (d) Make a dot plot for each sample. (e) What did you learn from the medians and dot plots that was not apparent from the means and standard deviations? 🐟 **Occupancy**

Observation	Week 1	Week 2	Week 3	Week 4
1	32	33	38	37
2	41	35	39	42
3	44	45	39	45
4	47	50	40	46
5	50	52	56	47
6	53	54	57	48
7	56	58	58	50
8	59	59	61	67
9	68	64	62	68

4.54 (a) Enter the Excel function =ROUND(NORMINV(RAND(),70,10),0) in cells B1:B100. This will create 100 random data points from a normal distribution using parameters $\mu = 70$ and $\sigma = 10$. Think of these numbers as exam scores for 100 students. (b) Use the Excel functions =AVERAGE(B1:B100) and =STDEV(B1:B100) to calculate the sample mean and standard deviation for your data array. (c) Every time you press F9 you will get a new sample. Watch the sample statistics and compare them with the desired parameters $\mu = 70$ and $\sigma = 10$. Do Excel's random samples have approximately the desired characteristics? (d) Use Excel's =MIN(B1:B100) and =MAX(B1:B100) to find the range of your samples. Do the sample ranges look as you would expect from the Empirical Rule?

DO-IT-YOURSELF SAMPLING

4.55 (a) Record the points scored by the winning team in 50 college football games played last weekend (if it is not football season, do the same for basketball or another sport of your choice). If you can't find 50 scores, do the best you can. (b) Make a dot plot. What does it tell you? (c) Make a frequency distribution and histogram. Describe the histogram. (d) Calculate the mean, median, and mode. Which is the best measure of central tendency? Why? (e) Calculate standard deviation and coefficient of variation. (f) Standardize the data. Are there any outliers? (g) Find the quartiles. What do they tell you? (h) Make a box plot. What does it tell you?

4.56 (a) Record the length (in minutes) of 50 movies chosen at random from a movie guide (e.g., Leonard Maltin's *Movie and Video Guide*). Include the name of each movie. (b) Make a dot plot. What does it tell you? (c) Make a frequency distribution and histogram. Describe the histogram. (d) Calculate the mean, median, and mode. Which is the best measure of central tendency? Why? (e) Calculate the standard deviation and coefficient of variation. (f) Standardize the data. Are there any outliers? (g) Find the quartiles and interquartile range. What do they tell you? (h) Make a box plot. What does it tell you?

SCATTER PLOTS AND CORRELATION

Note: Exercises 4.57 and 4.58 refer to data sets on the CD.

4.57 (a) Make an Excel scatter plot of $X = 1990$ assault rate per 100,000 population and $Y = 2004$ assault rate per 100,000 population for the 50 U.S. states. (b) Use Excel's =CORREL function to find the correlation coefficient. (c) What do the graph and correlation coefficient say about assault rates by state for these two years? (d) Use MegaStat or Excel to find the mean, median, and standard deviation of assault rates in these two years. What does this comparison tell you?
🌩 **Assault**

4.58 (a) Make an Excel scatter plot of $X =$ airspeed (nautical miles per hour) and $Y =$ cockpit noise level (decibels) for 61 aircraft flights. (b) Use Excel's =CORREL function to find the correlation coefficient. (c) What do the graph and correlation coefficient say about the relationship between airspeed and cockpit noise? Why might such a relationship exist? *Optional:* Fit an Excel trend line to the scatter plot and interpret it. 🌩 **CockpitNoise**

MINI-PROJECTS

4.59 (a) Choose a data set and prepare a brief, descriptive report. You may use any computer software you wish (e.g., Excel, MegaStat, Visual Statistics, MINITAB). Include relevant worksheets or graphs in your report. If some questions do not apply to your data set, explain why not. (b) Discuss any possible weaknesses in the data. (c) Sort the data. (d) Make a dot plot. What does it tell you? (e) Make a histogram. Describe its shape. (f) Calculate the mean, median, and mode(s) and use them to describe central tendency for this data set. (g) Calculate the standard deviation and coefficient of variation. (h) Standardize the data and check for outliers. (i) Compare the data with the Empirical Rule. Discuss. (j) Calculate the quartiles and interpret them. (k) Make a box plot. Describe its appearance.

DATA SET A	Advertising Dollars as Percent of Sales in Selected Industries ($n = 30$) 🌩 Ads		
Industry	**Percent**	**Industry**	**Percent**
Accident and health insurance	0.9	Jewelry stores	4.6
Apparel and other finished products	5.5	Management services	1.0
Beverages	7.4	Millwork, veneer, and plywood	3.5
Cable and pay TV services	1.3	Misc. furniture and fixtures	2.3
Computer data processing	1.1	Mortgage bankers and loans	4.9
Computer storage devices	1.8	Motorcycles, bicycles, and parts	1.7
Cookies and crackers	3.5	Paints, varnishes, lacquers	3.1
Drug and proprietary stores	0.9	Perfume and cosmetics	11.9
Electric housewares and fans	6.4	Photographic equipment	4.3
Equipment rental and leasing	2.0	Racing and track operations	2.5
Footwear except rubber	4.5	Real estate investment trusts	3.8
Greeting cards	3.5	Shoe stores	3.0
Grocery stores	1.1	Steel works and blast furnaces	1.9
Hobby, toy, and games shops	3.0	Tires and inner tubes	1.8
Ice cream and frozen desserts	2.0	Wine, brandy, and spirits	11.3

DATA SET B   Maximum Rate of Climb for Selected Piston Aircraft (n = 54)
ClimbRate

Manufacturer/Model	Year	Climb (ft./min.)	Manufacturer/Model	Year	Climb (ft./min.)
AMD CH 2000	2000	820	Diamond C1 Eclipse	2002	1,000
Beech Baron 58	1984	1,750	Extra Extra 400	2000	1,400
Beech Baron 58P	1984	1,475	Lancair Columbia 300	1998	1,340
Beech Baron D55	1968	1,670	Liberty XL-2	2003	1,150
Beech Bonanza B36 TC	1982	1,030	Maule Comet	1996	920
Beech Duchess	1982	1,248	Mooney 231	1982	1,080
Beech Sierra	1972	862	Mooney Eagle M205	1999	1,050
Bellanca Super Viking	1973	1,840	Mooney M20C	1965	800
Cessna 152	1978	715	Mooney Ovation 2 M20R	2000	1,150
Cessna 170B	1953	690	OMF Aircraft Symphony	2002	850
Cessna 172 R Skyhawk	1997	720	Piper 125 Tri Pacer	1951	810
Cessna 172 RG Cutlass	1982	800	Piper Archer III	1997	667
Cessna 1825 Skylane	1997	865	Piper Aztec F	1980	1,480
Cessna 182Q Skylane	1977	1,010	Piper Dakota	1979	965
Cessna 310 R	1975	1,662	Piper Malibu Mirage	1998	1,218
Cessna 337G Skymotor II	1975	1,100	Piper Malibu Mirage	1989	1,218
Cessna 414A	1985	1,520	Piper Saratoga II TC	1998	818
Cessna 421B	1974	1,850	Piper Saratoga SP	1980	1,010
Cessna Cardinal	1970	840	Piper Seneca III	1982	1,400
Cessna P210	1982	945	Piper Seneca V	1997	1,455
Cessna T210K	1970	930	Piper Seneca V	2002	1,455
Cessna T303 Crusader	1983	1,480	Piper Super Cab	1975	960
Cessna Turbo Skylane RG	1979	1,040	Piper Turbo Lance	1979	1,000
Cessna Turbo Skylane T182T	2001	1,060	Rockwell Commander 114	1976	1,054
Cessna Turbo Stationair TU206	1981	1,010	Sky Arrow 650 TC	1998	750
Cessna U206H	1998	1,010	Socata TB20 Trinidad	1999	1,200
Cirrus SR20	1999	946	Tiger AG-5B	2002	850

Source: *Flying Magazine* (various issues from 1997 to 2002).

DATA SET C   December Heating Degree-Days for Selected U.S. Cities (n = 35)
Heating

City	Degree-Days	City	Degree-Days	City	Degree-Days
Albuquerque	911	El Paso	639	Omaha	1,172
Baltimore	884	Hartford	1,113	Philadelphia	915
Bismarck	1,538	Honolulu	0	Phoenix	368
Buffalo	1,122	Indianapolis	1,039	Providence	1,014
Charleston	871	Jackson	513	Salt Lake City	1,076
Charlotte	694	Los Angeles	255	San Francisco	490
Cheyenne	1,107	Miami	42	Seattle	744
Chicago	1,156	Mobile	382	Sioux Falls	1,404
Cleveland	1,051	Nashville	747	St. Louis	955
Concord	1,256	New Orleans	336	Washington, D.C.	809
Detroit	1,132	Norfolk	667	Wichita	949
Duluth	1,587	Oklahoma City	778		

Source: U.S. Bureau of the Census, *Statistical Abstract of the United States*.

Note: A degree-day is the sum over all days in the month of the difference between 65 degrees Fahrenheit and the daily mean temperature of each city.

DATA SET D   Commercial Bank Profit as Percent of Revenue, 2003   Banks

Bank	Percent	Bank	Percent
AmSouth Bancorp	21	Mellon Financial Group	15
Bank of America Corp.	22	National City Corp.	22
Bank of New York Co.	18	National Commerce Finan	20
Bank One Corp.	16	North Fork Bancorp	31
BankNorth Group	22	Northern Trust Corp.	16
BB&T Corp.	17	PNC Financial Services Group	17
Charter One Financial	22	Popular	18
Citigroup	19	Provident Financial Group	6
Comerica	20	Providian Financial	7
Compass Bancshares	19	Regions Financial	18
Fifth Third Bancorp	27	SouthTrust Corp.	23
First Tenn. Natl. Corp.	18	State St. Corp.	13
FleetBoston	18	SunTrust Banks	19
Hibernia Corp.	20	Synovus Financial Corp.	16
Huntington Bancshares	16	U.S. Bancorp	24
J. P. Morgan Chase	15	Union Planters Corp.	21
KeyCorp	16	Wachovia Corp.	19
M&T Bank Corp.	19	Wells Fargo	20
Marshall & Ilsley Corp.	20	Zions Bancorp	18
MBNA	20		

Source: *Fortune* 149, no. 7 (April 5, 2004). Copyright © 2004 Time Inc. All rights reserved.

Note: These banks are in the Fortune 1000 companies.

DATA SET E   Caffeine Content of Randomly Selected Beverages (*n* = 32)   Caffeine

Company/Brand	mg/oz.	Company/Brand	mg/oz.
Barq's Root Beer	1.83	Mountain Dew	4.58
Coca-Cola Classic	2.83	Mr. Pibb	3.33
Cool from Nestea	1.33	Nestea Earl Grey	4.17
Cool from Nestea Rasberry Cooler	0.50	Nestea Peach	1.33
Diet A&W Cream Soda	1.83	Nestea Rasberry	1.33
Diet Ale 8	3.67	Nestea Sweet	2.17
Diet Code Red	4.42	Pepsi One	4.58
Diet Dr. Pepper	3.42	RC Edge	5.85
Diet Inca Kola	3.08	Royal Crown Cola	3.60
Diet Mountain Dew	4.58	Snapple Diet Peach Tea	2.63
Diet Mr. Pibb	3.33	Snapple Lemon Tea	2.63
Diet Pepsi-Cola	3.00	Snapple Lightning (Black Tea)	1.75
Inca Kola	3.08	Snapple Sun Tea	0.63
KMX (Blue)	0.00	Snapple Sweet Tea	1.00
Mello Yello Cherry	4.25	Sunkist Orange Soda	3.42
Mello Yello Melon	4.25	Vanilla Coke	2.83

Source: National Soft Drink Association (www.nsda.org).

DATA SET F   Super Bowl Scores 1967–2008 (*n* = 42 games)   SuperBowl

Year	Teams and Scores	Year	Teams and Scores
1967	Green Bay 35, Kansas City 10	1988	Washington 42, Denver 10
1968	Green Bay 33, Oakland 14	1989	San Francisco 20, Cincinnati 16
1969	NY Jets 16, Baltimore 7	1990	San Francisco 55, Denver 10
1970	Kansas City 23, Minnesota 7	1991	NY Giants 20, Buffalo 19
1971	Baltimore 16, Dallas 13	1992	Washington 37, Buffalo 24
1972	Dallas 24, Miami 3	1993	Dallas 52, Buffalo 17
1973	Miami 14, Washington 7	1994	Dallas 30, Buffalo 13
1974	Miami 24, Minnesota 7	1995	San Francisco 49, San Diego 26
1975	Pittsburgh 16, Minnesota 6	1996	Dallas 27, Pittsburgh 17
1976	Pittsburgh 21, Dallas 17	1997	Green Bay 35, New England 21
1977	Oakland 32, Minnesota 14	1998	Denver 31, Green Bay 24
1978	Dallas 27, Denver 10	1999	Denver 34, Atlanta 19
1979	Pittsburgh 35, Dallas 31	2000	St. Louis 23, Tennessee 16
1980	Pittsburgh 31, LA Rams 19	2001	Baltimore 34, New York 7
1981	Oakland 27, Philadelphia 10	2002	New England 20, St. Louis 17
1982	San Francisco 26, Cincinnati 21	2003	Tampa Bay 48, Oakland 21
1983	Washington 27, Miami 17	2004	New England 32, Carolina 29
1984	LA Raiders 38, Washington 9	2005	New England 24, Philadelphia 21
1985	San Francisco 38, Miami 16	2006	Pittsburgh 21, Seattle 10
1986	Chicago 46, New England 10	2007	Indianapolis 29, Chicago 17
1987	NY Giants 39, Denver 20	2008	NY Giants 17, New England 14

Source: *Sports Illustrated 2004 Sports Almanac, Detroit Free Press*, and www.cbs.sportsline.com.

DATA SET G   Property Crimes Per 100,000 Residents (*n* = 68 cities)   Crime

City and State	Crime	City and State	Crime	City and State	Crime
Albuquerque, NM	8,515	Honolulu, HI	4,671	Phoenix, AZ	6,888
Anaheim, CA	2,827	Houston, TX	6,084	Pittsburgh, PA	5,246
Anchorage, AK	4,370	Indianapolis, IN	4,306	Portland, OR	6,897
Arlington, TX	5,615	Jacksonville, FL	6,118	Raleigh, NC	6,327
Atlanta, GA	10,759	Kansas City, MO	9,882	Riverside, CA	3,610
Aurora, CO	5,079	Las Vegas, NV	4,520	Sacramento, CA	5,859
Austin, TX	6,406	Lexington, KY	5,315	San Antonio, TX	6,232
Birmingham, AL	7,030	Long Beach, CA	3,407	San Diego, CA	3,405
Boston, MA	4,986	Los Angeles, CA	3,306	San Francisco, CA	4,859
Buffalo, NY	5,791	Louisville, KY	5,102	San Jose, CA	2,363
Charlotte, NC	7,484	Memphis, TN	6,958	Santa Ana, CA	3,008
Chicago, IL	6,333	Mesa, AZ	5,590	Seattle, WA	8,397
Cincinnati, OH	5,694	Miami, FL	8,619	St. Louis, MO	11,765
Cleveland, OH	5,528	Milwaukee, WI	6,886	St. Paul, MN	6,215
Colorado Springs, CO	4,665	Minneapolis, MN	7,247	Stockton, CA	5,638
Columbus, OH	8,247	Nashville, TN	7,276	Tampa, FL	8,675
Corpus Christi, TX	6,266	New Orleans, LA	6,404	Toledo, OH	6,721
Dallas, TX	8,201	New York, NY	2,968	Tucson, AZ	8,079
Denver, CO	4,685	Newark, NJ	6,068	Tulsa, OK	6,234
Detroit, MI	8,163	Oakland, CA	6,820	Virginia Beach, VA	3,438
El Paso, TX	5,106	Oklahoma City, OK	8,464	Washington, DC	6,434
Fort Worth, TX	6,636	Omaha, NE	5,809	Wichita, KS	5,733
Fresno, CA	6,145	Philadelphia, PA	5,687		

Source: *Statistical Abstract of the United States, 2002.*

DATA SET H   Size of Whole Foods Stores (*n* = 171)   🐝 WholeFoods

Location (Store Name)	Sq. Ft.
Albuquerque, NM (Academy)	33,000
Alexandria, VA (Annandale)	29,811
Ann Arbor, MI (Washtenaw)	51,300
⋮	⋮
Winter Park, FL	20,909
Woodland Hills, CA	28,180
Wynnewood, PA	14,000

Source: www.wholefoodsmarket.com/stores/. *Note:* 165 stores omitted for brevity - see data file.

Barnett, Vic; and Toby Lewis. *Outliers in Statistical Data.* 3rd ed. John Wiley and Sons, 1994.

Blyth, C. R. "Minimizing the Sum of Absolute Deviations." *The American Statistician* 44, no. 4 (November 1990), p. 329.

Freund, John E.; and Benjamin M. Perles. "A New Look at Quartiles of Ungrouped Data." *The American Statistician* 41, no. 3 (August 1987), pp. 200–203.

Hoaglin, David C.; Frederick Mosteller; and John W. Tukey. *Understanding Robust and Exploratory Data Analysis.* John Wiley and Sons, 1983.

Pukelsheim, Friedrich. "The Three Sigma Rule." *The American Statistician* 48, no. 2 (May 1994), pp. 88–91.

Roderick, J. A.; A. Little; and Donald B. Rubin. *Statistical Analysis with Missing Data.* 2nd ed. John Wiley and Sons, 2002.

Tukey, John W. *Exploratory Data Analysis.* Addison-Wesley, 1977.

RELATED READING

LearningStats Unit 04   Describing Data

LearningStats Unit 04 uses interesting data sets, samples, and simulations to illustrate the tools of data analysis. Your instructor may assign a specific project, but you can work on the others if they sound interesting.

Topic	LearningStats Modules
Overview	Describing Data Using MegaStat Using Visual Statistics Using MINITAB
Descriptive statistics	Basic Statistics Quartiles Box Plots Coefficient of Variation Grouped Data Stacked Data Skewness and Kurtosis
Case studies	Brad's Bowling Scores Aircraft Cockpit Noise Batting Averages Bridget Jones's Diary Sample Variation Sampling NYSE Stocks
Sampling methods	Simple Random Sampling Systematic Sampling Cluster Sampling
Student projects	College Tuition Per Capita Income
Formulas	Table of Formulas Significant Digits

Key: = PowerPoint   = Word   = Excel

Visual Statistics

Visual Statistics is a software tool that is included on your CD, to be installed on your own computer. The CD will guide you through the installation process. Visual Statistics consists of 21 learning modules. Its purpose is to help you learn *concepts* on your own, through experimentation, individual learning exercises, and team projects. It consists of software with graphical displays, customized experiments, well-indexed help files (definitions, formulas, examples), and a complete textbook (in .PDF format). Each chapter has learning exercises (basic, intermediate, advanced), learning projects (individual, team), a self-evaluation quiz, a glossary of terms, and solutions.

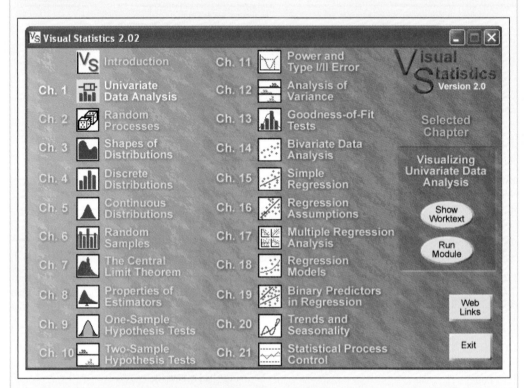

Visual Statistics modules 1, 3, and 6 are designed to help you

- Recognize and interpret different types of histograms (frequency, cumulative, relative).
- Realize how histogram setup can affect one's perception of the data.
- Be able to visualize common shape measures (centrality, dispersion, skewness, kurtosis).
- Recognize discrete and continuous random variables.
- Learn to infer a population's shape, mean, and standard deviation from a sample.
- See how outliers affect histograms.

Visual Statistics Modules on Describing Data

Module	Module Name	
1	VS	Univariate Data Analysis
3	VS	Shapes of Distributions
6	VS	Random Samples

MegaStat for Excel by J. B. Orris of Butler University is an Excel add-in that is included on the CD, to be installed on your own computer. The CD will guide you through the installation process. MegaStat goes beyond Excel's built-in statistical functions to offer a full range of statistical tools to help you analyze data, create graphs, and perform calculations. MegaStat examples are shown throughout this textbook.

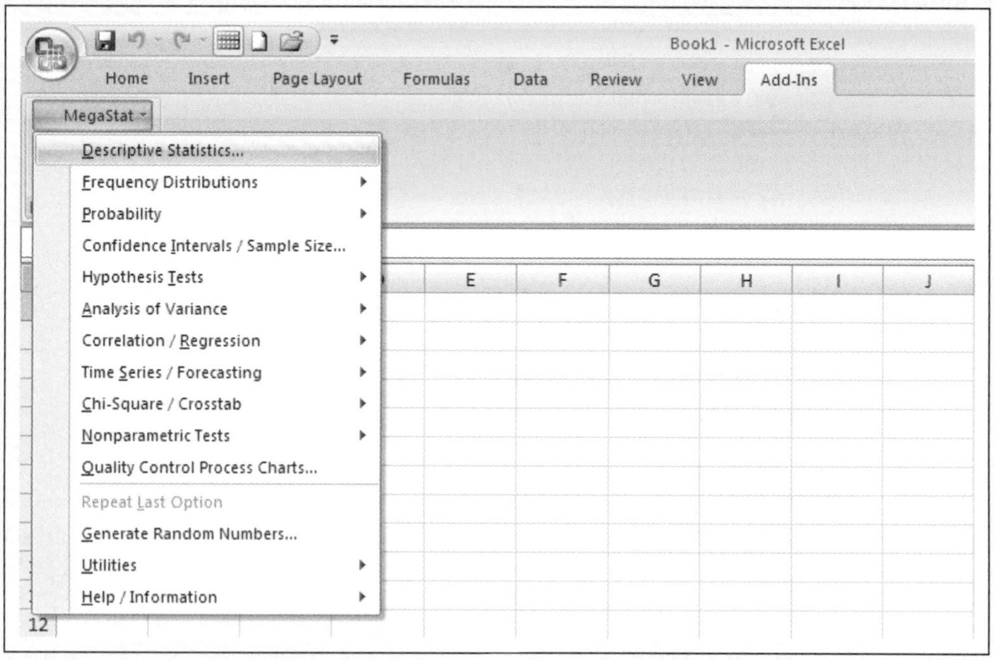

After installing MegaStat, you should see MegaStat appear on the left when you click the Add-Ins tab on the top menu bar (right side in the illustration above). If not, click the Office icon in the upper left and then click the Excel Options button (yellow highlight in the illustration below). At the bottom, find Manage Excel Add-Ins, click the Go button, and check the MegaStat add-in box. The CD includes further instructions.

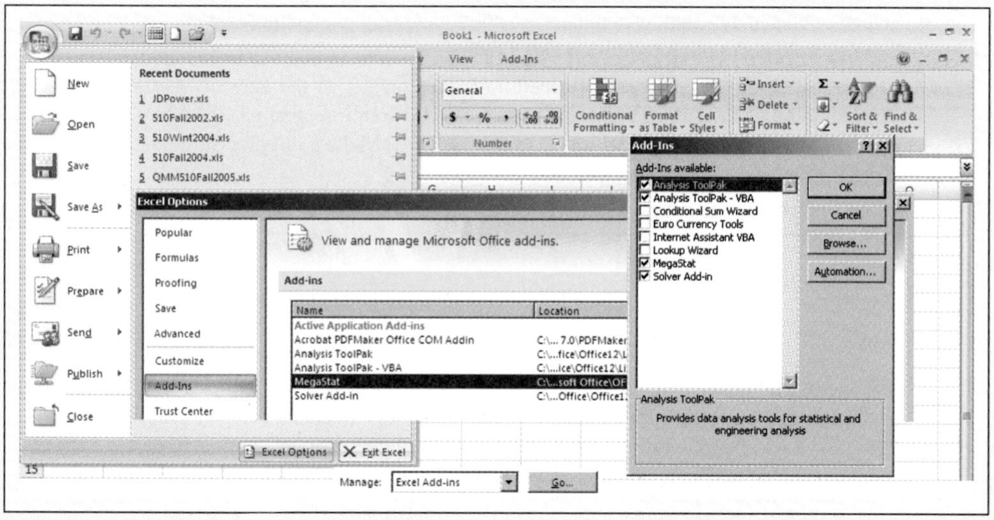

1. Which type of statistic (descriptive, inferential) is each of the following?
   a. Estimating the default rate on all U.S. mortgages from a random sample of 500 loans.
   b. Reporting the percent of students in your statistics class who use Verizon.
   c. Using a sample of 50 iPhones to predict the average battery life in typical usage.

2. Which is *not* an ethical obligation of a statistician? Explain.
   a. To know and follow accepted procedures.
   b. To ensure data integrity and accurate calculations.
   c. To support client wishes in drawing conclusions from the data.

3. "Driving without a seat belt is not risky. I've done it for 25 years without an accident." This *best* illustrates which fallacy?
   a. Unconscious bias.
   b. Conclusion from a small sample.
   c. *Post hoc* reasoning.

4. Which data type (categorical, numerical) is each of the following?
   a. Your current credit card balance.
   b. Your college major.
   c. Your car's odometer mileage reading today.

5. Give the type of measurement (nominal, ordinal, interval, ratio) for each variable.
   a. Length of time required for a randomly-chosen vehicle to cross a toll bridge.
   b. Student's ranking of five cell phone service providers.
   c. The type of charge card used by a customer (Visa, MasterCard, AmEx, Other).

6. Tell if each variable is continuous or discrete.
   a. Tonnage carried by an oil tanker at sea.
   b. Wind velocity at 7 o'clock this morning.
   c. Number of text messages you received yesterday.

7. To choose a sample of 12 students from a statistics class of 36 students, which type of sample (simple random, systematic, cluster, convenience) is each of these?
   a. Picking every student who was wearing blue that day.
   b. Using Excel's =RANDBETWEEN(1,36) to choose students from the class list.
   c. Selecting every 3rd student starting from a randomly-chosen position.

8. Which of the following is *not* a reason for sampling? Explain.
   a. The destructive nature of some tests.
   b. High cost of studying the entire population.
   c. Bias inherent in Excel's random numbers.

9. Which statement is *correct*? Why not the others?
   a. Likert scales are interval if scale distances are meaningful.
   b. Cross-sectional data are measured over time.
   c. A census is always preferable to a sample.

10. Which statement is *false*? Explain.
    a. Sampling error can be reduced by using appropriate data coding.
    b. Selection bias means that respondents are not typical of the target population.
    c. Simple random sampling requires a list of the population.

11. The management of a theme park obtained a random sample of the ages of 36 riders of its Space Adventure Simulator. (a) Make a nice histogram. (b) Did your histogram follow Sturges' Rule? If not, why not? (c) Describe the distribution of sample data. (d) Make a dot plot of the data. (e) What can be learned from each display (dot plot and histogram)?

39	46	15	38	39	47	50	61	17
40	54	36	16	18	34	42	10	16
16	13	38	14	16	56	17	18	53
24	17	12	21	8	18	13	13	10

12. Which one of the following is *true*? Why not the others?
    a. Histograms are useful for visualizing correlations.
    b. Pyramid charts are generally preferred to bar charts.
    c. A correlation coefficient can be negative.

13. Which data would be most suitable for a pie chart? Why not the others?
    a. Presidential vote in the last election by party (Democratic, Republican, Other).
    b. Retail prices of six major brands of color laser printers.
    c. Labor cost per vehicle for ten major world automakers.

14. Find the mean, standard deviation, and coefficient of variation for $X = 5, 10, 20, 10, 15$.

15. Here are the ages of a random sample of 20 CEOs of Fortune 500 U.S. corporations. (a) Find the mean, median, and mode. (b) Discuss advantages and disadvantages of each of these measures of central tendency for this data set. (c) Find the quartiles and interpret them. (d) Sketch a boxplot and describe it. Source: http://www.forbes.com

57	56	58	46	70	62	55	60	59	64
62	67	61	55	53	58	63	51	52	77

16. A consulting firm used a random sample of 12 CIOs (Chief Information Officers) of large businesses to examine the relationship (if any) between salary and years of service in the firm. (a) Make a scatter plot and describe it. (b) Calculate a correlation coefficient and interpret it.

Years (X)	4	15	15	8	11	5	5	8	10	1	6	17
Salary (Y)	133	129	143	132	144	61	128	79	140	116	88	170

17. Which statement is *true*? Why not the others?
    a. We expect the median to exceed the mean in positively-skewed data.
    b. The geometric mean is not helpful when there are negative data values.
    c. The midrange is resistant to outliers.

18. Which statement is *false*? Explain.
    a. If $\mu = 52$ and $\sigma = 15$, then $X = 81$ would be an outlier.
    b. If the data are from a normal population, about 68% of the values will be within $\mu \pm \sigma$.
    c. If $\mu = 640$ and $\sigma = 128$ then the coefficient of variation is 20 percent.

19. Which is *not* a characteristic of using a log scale to display time series data? Explain.
    a. A log scale helps if we are comparing changes in two time series of dissimilar magnitude.
    b. General business audiences find it easier to interpret a log scale.
    c. If you display data on a log scale, equal distances represent equal ratios.

Probability

Chapter Contents

Chapter Learning Objectives

When you finish this chapter you should be able to

- Describe the sample space of a random experiment.
- Distinguish among the three views of probability.
- Apply the definitions and rules of probability.
- Calculate odds from given probabilities.
- Determine when events are independent.
- Apply the concepts of probability to contingency tables.
- Apply counting rules to calculate possible event arrangements.

You've learned that a statistic is a measurement that describes a sample data set of observations. Descriptive statistics allow us to describe a business process that we have already observed. But how will that process behave in the future? Nothing makes a business person more nervous than not being able to anticipate customer demand, supplier delivery dates, or their employees' output. Businesses want to be able to quantify the *uncertainty* of future events. What are the chances that revenue next month will exceed last year's average? How likely is it that our new production system will help us decrease our product defect rate? Businesses also want to understand how they can increase the chance of positive future events (increasing market share) and decrease the chance of negative future events (failing to meet forecasted sales.) The field of study called *probability* allows us to understand and quantify the uncertainty about the future. We use the rules of probability to bridge the gap between what we know now and what is unknown about the future.

Sample Space

A **random experiment** is an observational process whose results cannot be known in advance. For example, when a customer enters a Lexus dealership, will the customer buy a car or not? How much will the customer spend? The set of all possible *outcomes* (denoted S) is the **sample space** for the experiment. A sample space with a countable number of outcomes is *discrete*. Some discrete sample spaces can be enumerated easily, while others may be immense or impossible to enumerate. For example, when CitiBank makes a consumer loan, we might define a sample space with only two outcomes:

$$S = \{\text{default, no default}\}$$

The sample space describing a Wal-Mart customer's payment method might have four outcomes:

$$S = \{\text{cash, debit card, credit card, check}\}$$

The sample space to describe rolling a die has six outcomes:

$$S = \{\quad,\quad,\quad,\quad,\quad,\quad\}$$

When two dice are rolled, the sample space consists of 36 outcomes, each of which is a pair:

	Second Die					
First Die	(1,1)	(1,2)	(1,3)	(1,4)	(1,5)	(1,6)
	(2,1)	(2,2)	(2,3)	(2,4)	(2,5)	(2,6)
	(3,1)	(3,2)	(3,3)	(3,4)	(3,5)	(3,6)
	(4,1)	(4,2)	(4,3)	(4,4)	(4,5)	(4,6)
	(5,1)	(5,2)	(5,3)	(5,4)	(5,5)	(5,6)
	(6,1)	(6,2)	(6,3)	(6,4)	(6,5)	(6,6)

A sample space could be so large that it is impractical to enumerate the possibilities (e.g., the 12-digit UPC bar code on a product in your local Wal-Mart could have 1 trillion values). If the outcome of the experiment is a *continuous* measurement, the sample space cannot be listed, but can be described by a rule. For example, the sample space for the length of a randomly chosen cell phone call would be

$$S = \{\text{all } X \text{ such that } X \geq 0\}$$

and the sample space to describe a randomly chosen student's GPA would be

$$S = \{\text{all } X \text{ such that } 0.00 \leq X \leq 4.00\}$$

Similarly, some discrete measurements are best described by a rule. For example, the sample space for the number of hits on a YouTube Web site on a given day is:

$$S = \{X = 0, 1, 2, \ldots\}$$

Event

An **event** is any subset of outcomes in the sample space. A **simple event**, or *elementary event*, is a single outcome. A discrete sample space S consists of all the simple events, denoted $E_1, E_2, \ldots, E_n$.

(5.1) $$S = \{E_1, E_2, \ldots, E_n\}$$

Consider the random experiment of tossing a balanced coin. The sample space for this experiment would be $S = \{\text{heads, tails}\}$. The chance of observing a head is the same as the chance of observing a tail. We say that these two elementary events are *equally likely*. When you buy a lottery ticket, the sample space $S = \{\text{win, lose}\}$ also has two elementary events; however, these events are not equally likely.

Simple events are the building blocks from which we can define a **compound event** consisting of two or more simple events. For example, Amazon's Web site for "Books & Music" has seven categories that a shopper might choose: $S = \{\text{Books, DVD, VHS, Magazines, Newspapers, Music, Textbooks}\}$. Within this sample space, we could define compound events "electronic media" as $A = \{\text{Music, DVD, VHS}\}$ and "print periodicals" as $B = (\text{Newspapers, Magazines})$. This can be shown in a **Venn diagram** like Figure 5.1.

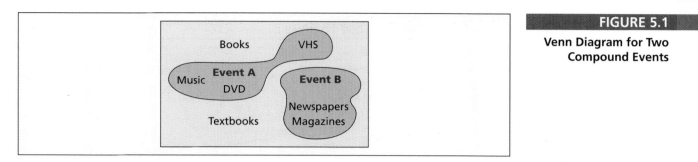

FIGURE 5.1

Venn Diagram for Two Compound Events

SECTION EXERCISES

connect

5.1   A credit card customer at Border's can use Visa (V), MasterCard (M), or American Express (A). The merchandise may be books (B), electronic media (E), or other (O). (a) Enumerate the elementary events in the sample space describing a customer's purchase. (b) Would each elementary event be equally likely? Explain.

5.2   A survey asked tax accounting firms their business form (S = sole proprietorship, P = partnership, C = corporation) and type of risk insurance they carry (L = liability only, T = property loss only, B = both liability and property). (a) Enumerate the elementary events in the sample space. (b) Would each elementary event be equally likely? Explain.

5.3   A baseball player bats either left-handed (L) or right-handed (R). The player either gets on base (B) or does not get on base (B'). (a) Enumerate the elementary events in the sample space. (b) Would these elementary events be equally likely? Explain.

5.4   A die is thrown (1, 2, 3, 4, 5, 6) and a coin is tossed (H, T). (a) Enumerate the elementary events in the sample space for the die/coin combination. (b) Are the elementary events equally likely? Explain.

The concept of probability is so familiar to most people that it can easily be misused. Therefore, we begin with some precise definitions and a few rules.

5.2

PROBABILITY

Definitions

The **probability** of an event is a number that measures the relative likelihood that the event will occur. The probability of an event A, denoted $P(A)$, must lie within the interval from 0 to 1:

$$0 \leq P(A) \leq 1 \tag{5.2}$$

$P(A) = 0$ means the event cannot occur (e.g., a naturalized citizen becoming president of the United States) while $P(A) = 1$ means the event is certain to occur (e.g., rain occurring in Hilo, Hawaii, sometime this year). In a discrete sample space, the probabilities of all simple events must sum to 1, since it is certain that one of them will occur:

$$P(S) = P(E_1) + P(E_2) + \cdots + P(E_n) = 1 \tag{5.3}$$

For example, if 32 percent of purchases are made by credit card, 15 percent by debit card, 35 percent by cash, and 18 percent by check, then:

$$P(\text{credit card}) + P(\text{debit card}) + P(\text{cash}) + P(\text{check}) = .32 + .15 + .35 + .18 = 1$$

What Is "Probability"?

There are three distinct ways of assigning probability, listed in Table 5.1. Many people mix them up or use them interchangeably; however, each approach must be considered separately.

TABLE 5.1

Three Views of Probability

Approach	Example
Empirical	There is a 2 percent chance of twins in a randomly chosen birth.
Classical	There is a 50 percent chance of heads on a coin flip.
Subjective	There is a 75 percent chance that England will adopt the euro currency by 2010.

CLOSE TO HOME By John McPherson

WELL, THAT'S PRETTY CONCLUSIVE. 182 CARTS HIT THE CORVETTE, 11 HIT THE PINTO, AND 7 WENT STRAIGHT UP THE MIDDLE.

Researchers at MIT prove that rolling shopping carts will almost invariably hit the most expensive car in their vicinity.

Empirical Approach

Sometimes we can collect empirical data through observations or experiments. We can use the **empirical** or **relative frequency approach** to assign probabilities by counting the frequency of observed outcomes (f) defined in our experimental sample space and dividing by the number of observations (n). For example, we could estimate the reliability of a bar code scanner:

$$P(\text{a missed scan}) = \frac{\text{number of missed scans}}{\text{number of items scanned}}$$

or the default rate on student loans:

$$P(\text{a student defaults}) = \frac{\text{number of defaults}}{\text{number of loans}}$$

Empirical estimation is necessary when we have no prior knowledge of the events. As we increase the number of observations (n) or the number of times we perform the experiment, our estimate will become more and more accurate. We use the ratio f/n to represent the probability. Here are some examples of empirical probabilities:

- An industrial components manufacturer in Pennsylvania interviewed 280 production workers before hiring 70 of them. (See *The Wall Street Journal,* September 25, 2006.)

  A = event that a randomly chosen interviewee is hired

  $$P(A) = \frac{70}{280} = .25$$

- Over 20 years, a medical malpractice insurer saw only one claim for "wrong-site" surgery (e.g., amputating the wrong limb) in 112,994 malpractice claims. (*Source:* AHRQ, *Research Activities,* no. 308, April 2006, p. 1.)

  A = event that malpractice claim is for wrong-site surgery

  $$P(A) = \frac{1}{112,994} = .00000885$$

- On average, 2,118 out of 100,000 Americans live to age 100 or older. (*Source:* www.cdc.gov/nchs/data/.)

  A = event that a randomly chosen American lives to 100 or older

  $$P(A) = \frac{2,118}{100,000} = .02118$$

Law of Large Numbers   An important probability theorem is the **law of large numbers**. Imagine flipping a coin 50 times. You know that the proportion of heads should be near .50. But in any finite sample it will be some ratio such as 1/3, 7/13, 10/22, or 28/50. Coin flip experiments show that a large *n* may be needed to get close to .50. As you can see in Figure 5.2, even after many flips, the ratio is likely to still differ from .50.

The law of large numbers says that as the number of trials increases, the empirical probability approaches its theoretical limit. Gamblers are aware of this principle, although they sometimes misconstrue it to imply that a streak of bad luck is "bound to change." But the probability of rolling a seven is always 6/36, even if you have rolled the dice 20 times previously without getting a seven.

Practical Issues for Actuaries   You may know that **actuarial science** is a high-paying career that involves estimating empirical probabilities. Actuaries help companies calculate payout rates on life insurance, pension plans, and health care plans. Actuaries created the tables that guide IRA withdrawal rates for individuals from age 70 to 99. Here are a few challenges that actuaries face:

• Is *n* "large enough" to say that f/n has become a good approximation to the probability of the event of interest? Data collection costs money, and decisions must be made. The sample should be large enough but not larger than necessary for a given level of precision.

• Was the experiment repeated identically? Subtle variations may exist in the experimental conditions and data collection procedures.

• Is the underlying process invariant over time? For example, default rates on 1997 student loans may not apply in 2007, due to changes in attitudes and interest rates.

• Do nonstatistical factors override data collection? Drug companies want clinical trials of a promising AIDS treatment to last long enough to ascertain its adverse side effects, yet ethical considerations forbid withholding a drug that could be beneficial.

FIGURE 5.2

Results of 10, 20, 50, and 500 Coin Flips   CoinFlips

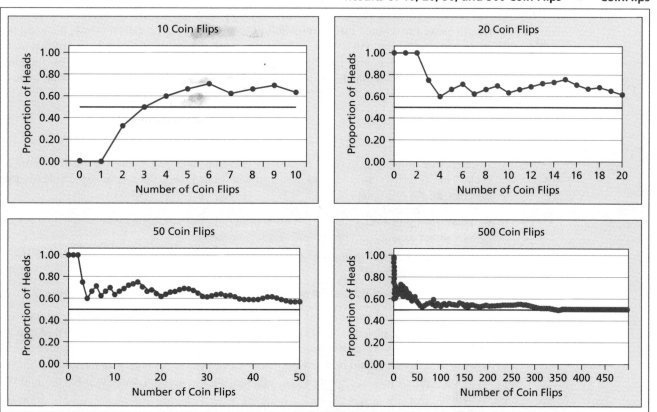

FIGURE 5.3

FIGURE 5.3

Venn Diagram for Two Dice   DiceRolls

(1,1)	(1,2)	(1,3)	(1,4)	(1,5)	**(1,6)**
(2,1)	(2,2)	(2,3)	(2,4)	**(2,5)**	(2,6)
(3,1)	(3,2)	(3,3)	**(3,4)**	(3,5)	(3,6)
(4,1)	(4,2)	**(4,3)**	(4,4)	(4,5)	(4,6)
(5,1)	**(5,2)**	(5,3)	(5,4)	(5,5)	(5,6)
(6,1)	(6,2)	(6,3)	(6,4)	(6,5)	(6,6)

- What if repeated trials are impossible? A good example occurred when Lloyd's of London was asked to insure a traveling exhibition of Monet paintings that was sent on a tour of the United States. Such an event only occurs once, so we have no f/n to help us.

Classical Approach

When flipping a coin or rolling a pair of dice, we do not actually have to perform an experiment, because the nature of the process allows us to envision the entire sample space as a collection of equally likely outcomes. We can use deduction to determine $P(A)$. Statisticians use the term *a priori* to refer to the process of assigning probabilities *before* we actually observe the event. For example, the two dice experiment shown in Figure 5.3 has 36 equally likely simple events, so the probability of rolling a seven is:

$$P(A) = \frac{\text{number of outcomes with 7 dots}}{\text{number of outcomes in sample space}} = \frac{6}{36} = .1667$$

The probability is obtained *a priori* without actually doing an experiment. This is the **classical approach** to probability. Such calculations are rarely possible in business situations.

We can apply pure reason to cards, lottery numbers, and roulette. Also, in some physical situations we can assume that the probability of an event such as a defect (leak, blemish) occurring in a particular unit of area, volume, or length is proportional to the ratio of that unit's size to the total area, volume, or length. Examples would be pits on rolled steel, stress fractures in concrete, or leaks in pipelines. These are *a priori* probabilities if they are based on logic or theory, not experience.

Subjective Approach

A *subjective* probability reflects someone's personal judgment about the likelihood of an event. The **subjective approach** to probability is needed when there is no repeatable random experiment. For example:

- What is the probability that GM's new supplier of plastic fasteners will be able to meet the September 23 shipment deadline?
- What is the probability that a new truck product program will show a return on investment of at least 10 percent?
- What is the probability that the price of GM stock will rise within the next 30 days?

In such cases, we rely on personal judgment or expert opinion. However, such a judgment is not random, because it is typically based on experience with similar events and knowledge of the underlying causal processes. Assessing the New York Knicks's chances of an NBA title next year would be an example. Thus, subjective probabilities have something in common with empirical probabilities, although their empirical basis is informal and not quantified.

Instructions for Exercises 5.5 – 5.10: (a) Which kind of probability is it (empirical, classical, subjective)? (b) How do you think it would have been derived?

5.5 "There is a 20% chance that a new stock offered in an initial public offering (IPO) will reach or exceed its target price on the first day."

5.6 "There is a 50% chance that AT&T Wireless and Cingular will merge."

5.7 "Commercial rocket launches have a 95% success rate."

5.8 "The probability of rolling three sevens in a row with dice is .0046."

5.9 On a given day, there is about 1 chance in 100,000 that the International Space Station will be critically damaged by a piece of orbiting debris. (See *The New York Times,* May 9, 2007, p. A-15.)

5.10 More than 30 percent of the results from major search engines for the keyword phrase "ring tone" are fake pages created by spammers. (See *The New York Times,* March 19, 2007, p. C-4.)

The field of probability has a distinct vocabulary that is important to understand. This section reviews the definitions of probability terms and illustrates how to use them.

**5.3
RULES OF
PROBABILITY**

Complement of an Event

The **complement** of an event A is denoted A' and consists of everything in the sample space S except event A, as illustrated in the Venn diagram in Figure 5.4.

Since A and A' together comprise the sample space, their probabilities sum to 1:

$$P(A) + P(A') = 1 \qquad (5.4)$$

The probability of the complement of A is found by subtracting the probability of A from 1:

$$P(A') = 1 - P(A) \qquad (5.5)$$

For example, *The Wall Street Journal* reports that about 33 percent of all new small businesses fail within the first 2 years (July 12, 2004). From this we can determine that the probability that a new small business will survive at least 2 years is:

$$P(\text{survival}) = 1 - P(\text{failure}) = 1 - .33 = .67, \text{ or } 67\%$$

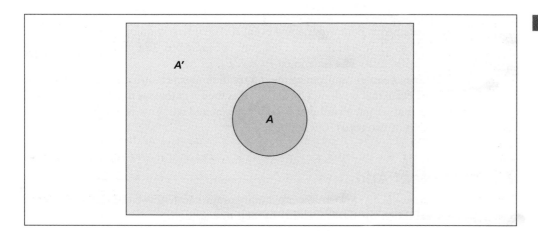

FIGURE 5.4

Complement of Event *A*

Union of Two Events

The **union** of two events consists of all outcomes in the sample space S that are contained either in event A or in event B or in both. The union of A and B is sometimes denoted $A \cup B$ or "A or B" as illustrated in the Venn diagram in Figure 5.5. The symbol $\cup$ may be read "or" since it means that either or both events occur. For example, when we choose a card at random from a deck of playing cards, if Q is the event that we draw a queen and R is the event that we draw a red card, $Q \cup R$ consists of getting *either* a queen (4 possibilities in 52) *or* a red card (26 possibilities in 52) or *both* a queen and a red card (2 possibilities in 52).

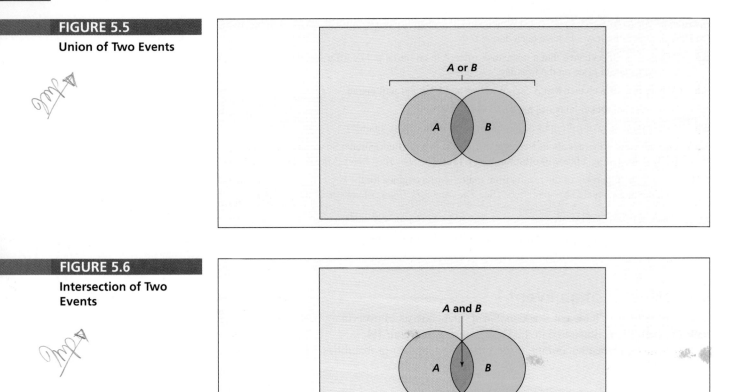

FIGURE 5.5

Union of Two Events

FIGURE 5.6

Intersection of Two Events

Intersection of Two Events

The **intersection** of two events A and B is the event consisting of all outcomes in the sample space S that are contained in both event A and event B. The intersection of A and B is denoted $A \cap B$ or "A and B" as illustrated in a Venn diagram in Figure 5.6. The probability of $A \cap B$ is called the **joint probability** and is denoted $P(A \cap B)$.

The symbol $\cap$ may be read "and" since the intersection means that both events occur. For example, if Q is the event that we draw a queen and R is the event that we draw a red card, then, $Q \cap R$ is the event that we get a card that is both a queen and red. That is, the intersection of sets Q and R consists of two cards (Q♥ and Q♦).

General Law of Addition

The **general law of addition** says that the probability of the union of two events A and B is the sum of their probabilities less the probability of their intersection:

(5.6)
$$P(A \cup B) = P(A) + P(B) - P(A \cap B)$$

The rationale for this formula is apparent from an examination of Figure 5.6. If we just add the probabilities of A and B, we would count the intersection twice, so we must subtract the probability of $A \cap B$ to avoid overstating the probability of $A \cup B$. For the card example:

$$\text{Queen: } P(Q) = 4/52 \qquad \text{(there are 4 queens in a deck)}$$

$$\text{Red: } P(R) = 26/52 \qquad \text{(there are 26 red cards in a deck)}$$

$$\text{Queen and Red: } P(Q \cap R) = 2/52 \qquad \text{(there are 2 red queens in a deck)}$$

Therefore,

$$\text{Queen or Red:} \quad P(Q \cup R) = P(Q) + P(R) - P(Q \cap R)$$

$$= 4/52 + 26/52 - 2/52$$

$$= 28/52 = .5385, \text{ or a } 53.85\% \text{ chance}$$

This result, while simple to calculate, is not obvious.

A survey of introductory statistics students showed that 29.7 percent have AT&T wireless service (event A), 73.4 percent have a Visa card (event B), and 20.3 percent have both (event $A \cap B$). The probability that a student uses AT&T *or* has a Visa card is:

$$P(A \cup B) = P(A) + P(B) - P(A \cap B) = .297 + .734 - .203 = .828$$

EXAMPLE

Cell Phones and Credit Cards   **WebSurvey**

Mutually Exclusive Events

Events A and B are **mutually exclusive** (or **disjoint**) if their intersection is the **null set** (a set that contains no elements). In other words, one event precludes the other from occurring. The null set is denoted ϕ.

$$\text{If } A \cap B = \phi, \text{ then } P(A \cap B) = 0 \quad\quad (5.7)$$

As illustrated in Figure 5.7, the probability of $A \cap B$ is zero when the events do not overlap. For example, if A is the event that an Applebee's customer finishes her lunch in less than 30 minutes and B is the event that she takes 30 minutes or more, then $P(A \cap B) = P(\phi) = 0$. Here are examples of events that are mutually exclusive (cannot be in both categories):

- *Customer age:* $A =$ under 21, $B =$ over 65
- *Purebred dog breed:* $A =$ border collie, $B =$ golden retriever
- *Business form:* $A =$ corporation, $B =$ sole proprietorship

These events may not cover all of the possibilities (e.g., a business could also be a partnership or S-corporation). The only issue is whether the categories overlap. Here are examples of events that are *not* mutually exclusive (can be in both categories):

- *Student's major:* $A =$ marketing major, $B =$ economics major
- *Bank account:* $A =$ Bank of America, $B =$ J.P. Morgan Chase Bank
- *Credit card held:* $A =$ Visa, $B =$ MasterCard, $C =$ American Express

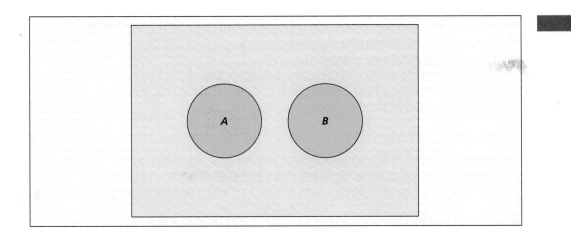

FIGURE 5.7

Mutually Exclusive Events

FIGURE 5.8

Binary Events

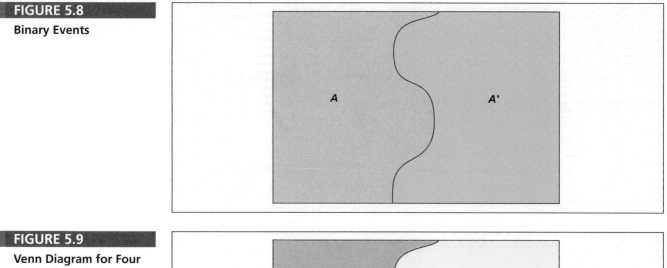

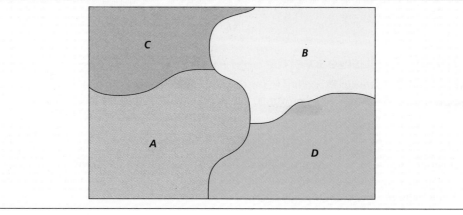

Special Law of Addition

If A and B are mutually exclusive events, then $P(A \cap B) = 0$ and the addition law reduces to

(5.8) $P(A \cup B) = P(A) + P(B)$ (addition law for mutually exclusive events)

For example, if we look at a person's age, then $P(\text{under } 21) = .28$ and $P(\text{over } 65) = .12$, so $P(\text{under } 21 \text{ } or \text{ over } 65) = .28 + .12 = .40$ since these events do not overlap.

Collectively Exhaustive Events

Events are **collectively exhaustive** if their union is the entire sample space S (i.e., all the events that can possibly occur). Two mutually exclusive, collectively exhaustive events are **binary** (or *dichotomous*) **events**, as illustrated in Figure 5.8. For example, a car repair is either covered by the warranty (A) or is not covered by the warranty (A'): There can be more than two mutually exclusive, collectively exhaustive events, as illustrated in Figure 5.9. For example, a Wal-Mart customer can pay by credit card (A), debit card (B), cash (C), or check (D).

Categorical data (e.g., freshman, sophomore, junior, senior) can be collapsed into binary events by defining the second category as everything *not* in the first category. For example, a college student either *is* a senior (A) or *isn't* a senior (A'). Table 5.2 shows examples of multiple outcomes events that have been "binarized" into dichotomous events. In statistics, it is often useful to assign a numerical value (0 or 1) to each binary event.

Conditional Probability

The probability of event A *given* that event B has occurred is a **conditional probability**, denoted $P(A \mid B)$ which is read "the probability of A given B." The vertical line is read as "given." The conditional probability is the joint probability of A and B divided by the probability of B.

(5.9) $$P(A \mid B) = \frac{P(A \cap B)}{P(B)} \quad \text{for } P(B) > 0$$

Categorical Data	Binary (Dichotomous) Variable
Vehicle type (SUV, sedan, truck, motorcycle)	$X = 1$ if SUV, 0 otherwise
A randomly chosen NBA player's height	$X = 1$ if height exceeds 7 feet, 0 otherwise
Tax return type (single, married filing jointly, married filing separately, head of household, qualifying widower)	$X = 1$ if single, 0 otherwise

TABLE 5.2

Collapsing to a Binary

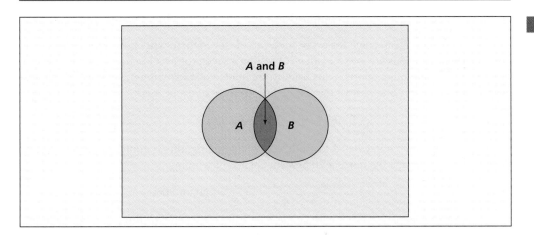

FIGURE 5.10

Conditional Probability

The logic of formula 5.9 is apparent by looking at the Venn diagram in Figure 5.10. The sample space is restricted to B, an event that we know has occurred (the lightly shaded circle). The intersection, $A \cap B$, is the part of B that is also in A (the heavily shaded area). The ratio of the relative size of set $A \cap B$ to set B is the conditional probability $P(A \mid B)$.

Of the population aged 16–21 and not in college, 13.50 percent are unemployed, 29.05 percent are high school dropouts, and 5.32 percent are unemployed high school dropouts. What is the conditional probability that a member of this population is unemployed, given that the person is a high school dropout? To answer this question, define:

EXAMPLE

High School Dropouts

U = the event that the person is unemployed

D = the event that the person is a high school dropout

This "story problem" contains three facts:

$$P(U) = .1350 \qquad P(D) = .2905 \qquad P(U \cap D) = .0532$$

So by formula 5.9 the conditional probability of an unemployed youth given that the person dropped out of high school is:

$$P(U \mid D) = \frac{P(U \cap D)}{P(D)} = \frac{.0532}{.2905} = .1831, \text{ or } 18.31\%$$

The *conditional* probability of being unemployed is $P(U \mid D) = .1831$ (18.31 percent), which is greater than the *unconditional probability* of being unemployed $P(U) = .1350$ (13.50 percent). In other words, knowing that someone is a high school dropout alters the probability that the person is unemployed.

Odds of an Event

Statisticians usually speak of probabilities rather than odds, but in sports and games of chance, we often hear **odds** quoted. We define the *odds in favor* of an event A as the ratio of the probability that event A will occur to the probability that event A will not occur. Its reciprocal is the *odds against* event A.

Odds *in favor* of A:

$$\frac{P(A)}{P(A')} = \frac{P(A)}{1 - P(A)}$$

Odds *against* A:

$$\frac{P(A')}{P(A)} = \frac{1 - P(A)}{P(A)}$$

For a pair of fair dice, the probability of rolling a seven is 6/36 or 1/6, so the odds in favor of rolling a seven would be:

$$Odds = \frac{P(\text{rolling seven})}{1 - P(\text{rolling seven})} = \frac{1/6}{1 - 1/6} = \frac{1/6}{5/6} = \frac{1}{5}$$

This means that on the average for every time we roll seven there will be five times that we do not roll seven. The odds are 1 to 5 *in favor* of rolling a seven (or 5 to 1 *against* rolling a seven). In horse racing and other sports, odds usually are quoted *against* winning. If the odds against event A are quoted as b to a, then the implied probability of event A is:

$$P(A) = \frac{a}{a + b}$$

For example, if a race horse has 4 to 1 odds *against* winning, this is equivalent to saying that the odds-makers assign the horse a 20 percent chance of winning:

$$P(\text{win}) = \frac{a}{a + b} = \frac{1}{4 + 1} = \frac{1}{5} = .20, \text{ or } 20\%$$

If a probability is expressed as a percentage, you can easily convert it to odds. For example, the IRS tax audit rate is 1.41 percent among taxpayers earning between \$100,000 and \$199,999 (*The Wall Street Journal,* April 15, 2006, p. A5). Let $A = $ the event that the taxpayer is audited and set $P(A) = .0141$. The odds against an audit are:

$$\frac{P(\text{no audit})}{P(\text{audit})} = \frac{1 - P(A)}{P(A)} = \frac{1 - .0141}{.0141} = 70 \text{ to } 1 \text{ } against \text{ being audited}$$

SECTION EXERCISES

connect

5.11 Are these characteristics of a student at your university mutually exclusive or not? Explain.
a. $A = $ works 20 hours or more, $B = $ majoring in accounting
b. $A = $ born in the United States, $B = $ born in Canada
c. $A = $ owns a Toyota, $B = $ owns a Honda

5.12 Are these events collectively exhaustive or not? Explain.
a. $A = $ college grad, $B = $ some college, $C = $ no college
b. $A = $ born in the United States, $B = $ born in Canada, $C = $ born in Mexico
c. $A = $ full-time student, $B = $ part-time student, $C = $ not enrolled as a student

5.13 Given $P(A) = .40$, $P(B) = .50$, and $P(A \cap B) = .05$, find (a) $P(A \cup B)$, (b) $P(A \mid B)$, and (c) $P(B \mid A)$. (d) Sketch a Venn diagram.

5.14 Given $P(A) = .70$, $P(B) = .30$, and $P(A \cap B) = .00$, find (a) $P(A \cup B)$ and (b) $P(A \mid B)$. (c) Sketch a Venn diagram and describe it in words.

5.15 Samsung ships 21.7 percent of the liquid crystal displays (LCDs) in the world. Let S be the event that a randomly selected LCD was made by Samsung. Find (a) $P(S)$, (b) $P(S')$, (c) the odds *in favor* of event S, and (d) the odds *against* event S. (Data are from *The Economist* 372, no. 8385 [July 24, 2004], p. 59.)

5.16 In 1997, the probability of an IRS audit was 1.7 percent for U.S. taxpayers who filed form 1040 and who earned \$100,000 or more. (a) What are the odds that such a taxpayer will be audited? (b) What are the odds *against* such a taxpayer being audited? (Data are from *The New York Times,* April 12, 1998, p. I-17.)

5.17 List *two* binary events that describe the possible outcomes of each situation.
a. A pharmaceutical firm seeks FDA approval for a new drug.
b. A baseball batter goes to bat.
c. A woman has a mammogram test.

5.18 List *more than two* events (i.e., categorical events) that might describe the outcome of each situation.
  a. A student applies for admission to Oxnard University.
  b. A football quarterback throws a pass.
  c. A bank customer makes an ATM transaction.

5.19 Let S be the event that a randomly chosen female aged 18–24 is a smoker. Let C be the event that a randomly chosen female aged 18–24 is a Caucasian. Given $P(S) = .246$, $P(C) = .830$, and $P(S \cap C) = .232$, find each probability and express the event in words. (Data are from *Statistical Abstract of the United States, 2001.*)
  a. $P(S')$.
  b. $P(S \cup C)$.
  c. $P(S \mid C)$.
  d. $P(S \mid C')$.

Event A is **independent** of event B if the conditional probability $P(A \mid B)$ is the same as the unconditional probability $P(A)$, that is, if the probability of event A is the same whether event B occurs or not. For example, if text messaging among high school students is *independent* of gender, this means that knowing whether a student is a male or female does not *change* the probability that the student uses text messaging. To check for independence, we apply this test:

Event A is *independent* of event B if and only if $P(A \mid B) = P(A)$.   **(5.10)**

Another way to check for independence is to ask whether the product of the event probabilities equals the probability of their intersection:

Event A is *independent* of event B if and only if $P(A \cap B) = P(A)P(B)$.   **(5.11)**

This is so because, if $P(A \cap B) = P(A)P(B)$, then by the definition of conditional probability in formula 5.9

$$P(A \mid B) = \frac{P(A \cap B)}{P(B)} = \frac{P(A)P(B)}{P(B)} = P(A).$$

The target audience is 2,000,000 viewers. Ad A reaches 500,000 viewers, ad B reaches 300,000 viewers, and both ads reach 100,000 viewers. That is:

$$P(A) = \frac{500{,}000}{2{,}000{,}000} = .25 \quad P(B) = \frac{300{,}000}{2{,}000{,}000} = .15 \quad P(A \cap B) = \frac{100{,}000}{2{,}000{,}000} = .05$$

Applying the definition of conditional probability from formula 5.11, the conditional probability that ad A reaches a viewer *given* that ad B reaches the viewer is:

$$P(A \mid B) = \frac{P(A \cap B)}{P(B)} = \frac{.05}{.15} = .3333 \text{ or } 33.3\%$$

We see that A and B are not independent because $P(A) = .25$ is not equal to $P(A \mid B) = .3333$. That is, knowing that ad B reached the viewer raises the probability that ad A reached the viewer from $P(A) = .25$ to $P(A \mid B) = .3333$. Alternatively, since $P(A)P(B) = (.25)(.15) = .0375$ is not equal to $P(A \cap B) = .05$, we know that events A and B are not independent.

EXAMPLE

Television Ads

Dependent Events

When $P(A)$ differs from $P(A \mid B)$ the events are **dependent**. You can easily think of examples of dependence. For example, cell phone text messaging is more common among young people, while arteriosclerosis is more common among older people. Therefore, knowing a person's age would affect the *probability* that the individual uses text messaging or has arteriosclerosis, but causation would have to be proven in other ways. Dependent events may be causally related, but statistical dependence does *not* prove cause-and-effect. It only means that knowing that event B has occurred will affect the *probability* that event A will occur.

Using Actuarial Data

Banks and credit unions know that the probability that a customer will default on a car loan is dependent on his/her past record of unpaid credit obligations. That is why lenders consult credit bureaus (e.g., Equifax, Experian, and TransUnion) before they make a loan. Your credit score is based on factors such as the ratio of your credit card balance to your credit limit, length of your credit history, number of accounts with balances, and frequency of requests for credit. Your score can be compared with actuarial data and national averages to see what percentile you are in. The lender can then decide whether your loan is worth the risk.

Automobile insurance companies (e.g., AAA, Allstate, State Farm) know that the probability that a driver will be involved in an accident depends on the driver's age, past traffic convictions, and similar factors. This actuarial information is used in deciding whether to accept you as a new customer and to set your insurance premium. The situation is similar for life insurance. Can you think of factors that might affect a person's life insurance premium?

In each of these loan and insurance examples, knowing *B* will affect our estimate of the likelihood of *A*. Obviously, bankers and insurance companies need to quantify these conditional probabilities precisely. An *actuary* studies conditional probabilities empirically, using accident statistics, mortality tables, and insurance claims records. Although few people undergo the extensive training to become actuaries, many businesses rely on actuarial services, so a business student needs to understand the concepts of conditional probability and statistical independence.

EXAMPLE

Restaurant Orders

Based on past data, the probability that a customer at a certain Noodles & Company restaurant will order a dessert (event *D*) with the meal is .08. The probability that a customer will order a bottled beverage (event *B*) is .14. The joint probability that a customer will order both a dessert *and* a bottled beverage is .0112. Is ordering a dessert independent of ordering a bottled beverage? Since $P(D) \times P(B) = .08 \times .14 = .0112 = P(D \text{ and } B)$, we see that *D* and *B* are independent of each other. If we know that a customer has ordered a bottled beverage, does this information change the probability that he or she will also order a dessert? No, because the events are independent.

Multiplication Law for Independent Events

The probability of several independent events occurring simultaneously is the product of their separate probabilities, as shown in formula 5.12 for *n* independent events $A_1, A_2, \ldots, A_n$.

(5.12) $P(A_1 \cap A_2 \cap \cdots \cap A_n) = P(A_1)P(A_2) \cdots P(A_n)$ if the events are independent

The **multiplication law** for independent events can be applied to system reliability. To illustrate, suppose a Web site has two independent file servers (i.e., no shared power or other components). Each server has 99 percent reliability (i.e., is "up" 99 percent of the time). What is the total system reliability? Let F_1 be the event that server 1 fails, and F_2 be the event that server 2 fails. Then

$$P(F_1) = 1 - 0.99 = .01$$
$$P(F_2) = 1 - 0.99 = .01$$

Applying the rule of independence:

$$P(F_1 \cap F_2) = P(F_1)P(F_2) = (.01)(.01) = .0001$$

The probability that at least one server is up is 1 minus the probability that both servers are down, or $1 - .0001 = .9999$. Dual file servers dramatically improve reliability to 99.99 percent.

When individual components have a low reliability, high reliability can still be achieved with massive redundancy. For example, a Teramac supercomputer has over 7 million components. About 3 percent are defective (nanodevices are extremely difficult to manufacture). Yet programs can run reliably because there is significant redundancy in the interconnect circuitry, so that a valid path can almost always be found (see *Scientific American* 293, no. 5 [November 2005], p. 75).

↘   **Redundancy** can increase system reliability even when individual component reliability is low. For example, the NASA space shuttle has three flight computers. Suppose that they function independently but that each has an unacceptable .03 chance of failure (3 failures in 100 missions). Let F_j = event that computer j fails. Then

$$P(\text{all 3 fail}) = P(F_1 \cap F_2 \cap F_3)$$
$$= P(F_1)P(F_2)P(F_3) \quad \text{(presuming that failures are independent)}$$
$$= (.03)(.03)(.03)$$
$$= .000027, \text{ or 27 in } 1,000,000 \text{ missions}$$

Triple redundancy can reduce the probability of computer failure to .000027 (27 failures in 1,000,000 missions). Of course, in practice, it is very difficult to have truly independent computers, since they may share electrical buses or cables. On one shuttle mission, two of the three computers actually did fail, which proved the value of redundancy. Another example of space shuttle redundancy is the four independent fuel gauges that prevent the shuttle's main engines from shutting down too soon. Initial launch rules allowed the shuttle to fly as long as two of them were functional, but after the *Challenger* launch explosion, the rules were modified to require that 3 of 4 be functional, and were modified again after the *Columbia* accident to require that all 4 be functional (see http://aolsvc.news.aol.com).   ↖

The Five Nines Rule

How high must reliability be? Prime business customers expect public carrier-class telecommunications data links to be available 99.999 percent of the time. This so-called five nines rule implies only 5 minutes of downtime per year. Such high reliability is needed not only in telecommunications but also for mission-critical systems such as airline reservation systems or banking funds transfers. Table 5.3 shows some expected system reliabilities in contemporary applications.

Type of System	Typical Reliability (%)
Commercial fiber-optic cable systems	99.999
Cellular-radio base stations with mobile switches connected to public-switched telephone networks	99.99
Private-enterprise networking (e.g., connecting two company offices)	99.9
Airline luggage systems	99
Excellent student exam-taking	90

TABLE 5.3

Typical System Reliabilities in Various Applications

See *Scientific American* 287, no. 1 (July 2002), p. 52, and 288, no. 6, p. 56.

How Much Redundancy Is Needed?

Suppose a certain network Web server is up only 94 percent of the time (i.e., its probability of being down is .06). How many independent servers are needed to ensure that the system is up at least 99.99 percent of the time? This is equivalent to requiring that the probability of all the servers being down is .0001 (i.e., $1 - .9999$). Four servers will accomplish the goal*:

2 servers: $P(F_1 \cap F_2) = (.06)(.06) = .0036$

3 servers: $P(F_1 \cap F_2 \cap F_3) = (.06)(.06)(.06) = .000216$

4 servers: $P(F_1 \cap F_2 \cap F_3 \cap F_4) = (.06)(.06)(.06)(.06) = .00001296$

*In general, if p is the probability of failure, we can set $p^k = .0001$, plug in $p = .06$, take the log of both sides, and solve for k. In this case, $k = 3.27$, so we can then round up to the next higher integer.

5.20 Given $P(A) = .40$, $P(B) = .50$. If A and B are independent, find $P(A \cap B)$.

5.21 Given $P(A) = .40$, $P(B) = .50$, and $P(A \cap B) = .05$. (a) Find $P(A \mid B)$. (b) In this problem, are A and B independent? Explain.

5.22 Which pairs of events are independent?
a. $P(A) = .60$, $P(B) = .40$, $P(A \cap B) = .24$.
b. $P(A) = .90$, $P(B) = .20$, $P(A \cap B) = .18$.
c. $P(A) = .50$, $P(B) = .70$, $P(A \cap B) = .25$.

5.23 The probability that a student has a Visa card (event V) is .73. The probability that a student has a MasterCard (event M) is .18. The probability that a student has both cards is .03. (a) Find the probability that a student has either a Visa card or a MasterCard. (b) In this problem, are V and M independent? Explain.

5.24 Bob sets two alarm clocks (battery-powered) to be sure he arises for his Monday 8:00 A.M. accounting exam. There is a 75 percent chance that either clock will wake Bob. (a) What is the probability that Bob will oversleep? (b) If Bob had three clocks, would he have a 99 percent chance of waking up?

5.25 A hospital's backup power system has three independent emergency electrical generators, each with uptime averaging 95 percent (some downtime is necessary for maintenance). Any of the generators can handle the hospital's power needs. Does the overall reliability of the backup power system meet the five nines test?

5.5
CONTINGENCY TABLES

In Chapter 4, you saw how Excel's pivot tables can be used to display the frequency of co-occurrence of data values (e.g., how many taxpayers in a sample are filing as "single" and also have at least one child?). Since a probability usually is estimated as a *relative frequency,* we can use tables of relative frequencies to learn about relationships (e.g., dependent events or conditional probabilities) that are extremely useful in business planning. Data for the table may be from a survey or from actuarial records.

What Is a Contingency Table?

To better understand dependent events and conditional probability, let's look at some real data. A **contingency table** is a cross-tabulation of frequencies into rows and columns. The intersection of each row and column is a *cell* that shows a frequency. A contingency table is like a frequency distribution for a single variable, except it has *two* variables (rows and columns). A contingency table with r rows and c columns has rc cells and is called an $r \times c$ table. Contingency tables often are used to report the results of a survey.

Table 5.4 shows a cross-tabulation of tuition cost versus 5-year net salary gains for MBA degree recipients at 67 top-tier graduate schools of business. Here, salary gain is compensation after graduation, minus the sum of tuition and forgone compensation. Are large salary gains more likely for graduates of high-tuition MBA programs?

TABLE 5.4

Contingency Table of Frequencies ($n = 67$ MBA programs)
🐾 MBASalary

Tuition	Salary Gain			Row Total
	Small (S_1) *Under $50K*	*Medium (S_2)* *$50K–$100K*	*Large (S_3)* *$100K+*	
Low (T_1) *Under $40K*	5	10	1	16
Medium (T_2) *$40K–$50K*	7	11	1	19
High (T_3) *$50K+*	5	12	15	32
Column Total	17	33	17	67

Source: Data are from *Forbes* 172, no. 8 (October 13, 2003), p. 78. Copyright © 2005 Forbes, Inc. Reprinted with permission.

Inspection of this table reveals that MBA graduates of the high-tuition schools do tend to have large salary gains (15 of the 67 schools) and that about half of the top-tier schools charge high tuition (32 of 67 schools). We can make more precise interpretations of this data by applying the concepts of probability.

Marginal Probabilities

The **marginal probability** of an event is found by dividing a row or column total by the total sample size. For example, using the column totals, 33 out of 67 schools had medium salary gains, so the marginal probability of a medium salary gain is $P(S_2) = 33/67 = .4925$. In other words, salary gains at about 49 percent of the top-tier schools were between $50,000 and $100,000. This calculation is shown in Table 5.5.

TABLE 5.5

Marginal Probability of Event S_2

| Tuition | Salary Gain | | | |
	Small (S_1)	Medium (S_2)	Large (S_3)	Row Total
Low (T_1)	5	10	1	16
Medium (T_2)	7	11	1	19
High (T_3)	5	12	15	32
Column Total	17	33	17	67

Using the row totals, for example, we see that 16 of the 67 schools had low tuition so the marginal probability of low tuition is $P(T_1) = 16/67 = .2388$. In other words, there is a 24 percent chance that a top-tier school's MBA tuition is under $40,000. This calculation is illustrated in Table 5.6.

TABLE 5.6

Marginal Probability of Event T_1

| Tuition | Salary Gain | | | |
	Small (S_1)	Medium (S_2)	Large (S_3)	Row Total
Low (T_1)	5	10	1	16
Medium (T_2)	7	11	1	19
High (T_3)	5	12	15	32
Column Total	17	33	17	67

Joint Probabilities

Each of the nine main cells is used to calculate a *joint probability* representing the intersection of *two* events. For example, the upper right-hand cell is the joint event that the school has low tuition (T_1) *and* has large salary gains (S_3). We can write this event either as $P(T_1$ and $S_3)$ or as $P(T_1 \cap S_3)$. Since only 1 out of 67 schools is in this category, the joint probability is $P(T_1$ and $S_3) = 1/67 = .0149$. In other words, there is less than a 2 percent chance that a top-tier school has *both* low tuition *and* high salary gains. This calculation is illustrated in Table 5.7.

TABLE 5.7

Joint Probability of Event $T_1 \cap S_3$

| Tuition | Salary Gain | | | |
	Small (S_1)	Medium (S_2)	Large (S_3)	Row Total
Low (T_1)	5	10	1	16
Medium (T_2)	7	11	1	19
High (T_3)	5	12	15	32
Column Total	17	33	17	67

Conditional Probabilities

Conditional probabilities may be found by *restricting* ourselves to a single row or column (the *condition*). For example, suppose we know that a school's MBA tuition is high (T_3). When we restrict ourselves to the 32 schools in the third row (those with high tuition) the conditional probabilities of any event may be calculated. For example, Table 5.8 illustrates the calculation of the conditional probability that salary gains are small (S_1) *given* that the MBA tuition is large (T_3). This conditional probability may be written $P(S_1 \mid T_3)$. We see that $P(S_1 \mid T_3) = 5/32 = .1563$, so there is about a 16 percent chance that a top-tier school's salary gains will be small despite its high tuition because there were 5 small-gain schools out of the 32 high-tuition schools.

TABLE 5.8

Conditional Probability $P(S_1 \mid T_3)$

Tuition	Salary Gain			Row Total
	Small (S_1)	Medium (S_2)	Large (S_3)	
Low (T_1)	5	10	1	16
Medium (T_2)	7	11	1	19
High (T_3)	5	12	15	32
Column Total	17	33	17	67

Here are some other conditional probabilities and their interpretations:

Low Tuition MBA Program

$P(S_1 \mid T_1) = 5/16 = .3125$ — There is a 31 percent probability that schools whose tuition is low will have small MBA salary gains.

$P(S_2 \mid T_1) = 10/16 = .6250$ — There is a 63 percent probability that schools whose tuition is low will have medium MBA salary gains.

$P(S_3 \mid T_1) = 1/16 = .0625$ — There is a 6 percent probability that schools whose tuition is low will have large MBA salary gains.

High Tuition MBA Program

$P(S_1 \mid T_3) = 5/32 = .1563$ — There is a 16 percent probability that schools whose tuition is high will have small MBA salary gains.

$P(S_2 \mid T_3) = 12/32 = .3750$ — There is a 38 percent probability that schools whose tuition is high will have medium MBA salary gains.

$P(S_3 \mid T_3) = 15/32 = .4688$ — There is a 47 percent probability that schools whose tuition is high will have large MBA salary gains.

Caveat   Conditional probabilities show, as we would expect, that higher tuition is associated with higher MBA salary gains (and conversely). But these results pertain only to a set of elite universities at a particular point in time, and few MBA students actually have access to such schools. Data from different universities or at a different point in time might show a different pattern.

Independence

To check whether events in a contingency table are independent, we can look at *conditional probabilities*. For example, if large salary gains (S_3) were independent of low tuition (T_1), then the conditional probability $P(S_3 \mid T_1)$ would be the same as the marginal probability $P(S_3)$. But this is not the case:

Conditional
$P(S_3 \mid T_1) = 1/16 = .0625$

Marginal
$P(S_3) = 17/67 = .2537$

Thus, large salary gains (S_3) is *not* independent of low tuition (T_1). Alternatively, we could ask whether $P(S_3 \text{ and } T_1) = P(S_3) P(T_1)$ is a necessary condition for independence. But

$$P(S_3)P(T_1) = (17/67)(16/67) = .0606$$

which is *not* equal to the observed joint probability

$$P(S_3 \text{ and } T_1) = 1/67 = .0149$$

Therefore, large salary gains (S_3) are *not* independent of low tuition (T_1).

Relative Frequencies

To facilitate probability calculations, we can divide each cell frequency f_{ij} by the total sample size ($n = 67$) to get the *relative frequencies* f_{ij}/n shown in Table 5.9. For example, the upper left-hand cell becomes $5/67 = .0746$.

TABLE 5.9

**Relative Frequency Table
Each Cell Is f_{ij}/n**

Tuition	Salary Gains Small (S_1)	Medium (S_2)	Large (S_3)	Row Total
Low (T_1)	.0746	.1493	.0149	.2388
Medium (T_2)	.1045	.1642	.0149	.2836
High (T_3)	.0746	.1791	.2239	.4776
Column Total	.2537	.4926	.2537	1.0000

The nine joint probabilities sum to 1.0000 since these are all the possible intersections:

$$.0746 + .1045 + .0746 + .1493 + .1642 + .1791 + .0149 + .0149 + .2239 = 1.0000$$

Except for rounding, summing the joint probabilities across a row or down a column gives *marginal* (or *unconditional*) probabilities for the respective row or column:

Adding across rows

.0746 + .1493 + .0149 = .2388
.1045 + .1642 + .0149 = .2836
.0746 + .1791 + .2239 = .4776

Adding down columns

.0746	.1493	.0149
+ .1045	+ .1642	+ .0149
+ .0746	+ .1791	+ .2239
= .2537	= .4926	= .2537

The marginal row and column probabilities sum to 1.0000 (except for rounding):

Columns (Salary): $P(S_1) + P(S_2) + P(S_3) = .2537 + .4926 + .2537 = 1.0000$

Rows (Tuition): $P(T_1) + P(T_2) + P(T_3) = .2388 + .2836 + .4776 = 1.0000$

Table 5.9 may be written in symbolic form as shown in Table 5.10.

TABLE 5.10

Symbolic Notation for Relative Frequencies

Tuition	Salary Gains			Row Total
	Small (S_1)	Medium (S_2)	Large (S_3)	
Low (T_1)	$P(T_1$ and $S_1)$	$P(T_1$ and $S_2)$	$P(T_1$ and $S_3)$	$P(T_1)$
Medium (T_2)	$P(T_2$ and $S_1)$	$P(T_2$ and $S_2)$	$P(T_2$ and $S_3)$	$P(T_2)$
High (T_3)	$P(T_3$ and $S_1)$	$P(T_3$ and $S_2)$	$P(T_3$ and $S_3)$	$P(T_3)$
Column Total	$P(S_1)$	$P(S_2)$	$P(S_3)$	1.0000

EXAMPLE

Payment Method and Purchase Quantity

Payment

A small grocery store would like to know if the number of items purchased by a customer is independent of the type of payment method the customer chooses to use. Having this information can help the store manager determine how to set up his/her various checkout lanes. The manager collected a random sample of 368 customer transactions. The results are shown in Table 5.11.

TABLE 5.11 **Contingency Table for Payment Method by Number of Items Purchased**

Number of Items Purchased	Payment Method			Row Total
	Cash	Check	Credit/ Debit Card	
1–5	30	15	43	88
6–9	46	23	66	135
10–19	31	15	43	89
20+	19	10	27	56
Column Total	126	63	179	368

Looking at the frequency data presented in the table we can calculate the marginal probability that a customer will use cash to make the payment. Let C be the event that the customer chose cash as the payment method.

$$P(C) = \frac{126}{368} = .3424$$

Is $P(C)$ the same if we condition on number of items purchased?

$$P(C \mid 1{-}5) = \frac{30}{88} = .3409 \qquad P(C \mid 6{-}10) = \frac{46}{135} = .3407$$

$$P(C \mid 10{-}20) = \frac{31}{89} = .3483 \qquad P(C \mid 20{+}) = \frac{19}{56} = .3393$$

Notice that there is little difference in these probabilities. If we perform the same type of analysis for the next two payment methods we find that *payment method* and *number of items purchased* are essentially independent. Based on this study, the manager might decide to offer a cash-only checkout lane that is *not* restricted to the number of items purchased.

How Do We Get a Contingency Table?

Contingency tables do not just "happen" but require careful data organization and forethought. They are created from raw data. In this example, numerical values were mapped into discrete codes, as shown in Table 5.12. If the data were already categorical (e.g., a survey with discrete responses) this step would have been unnecessary. Once the data are coded, we tabulate the frequency in each cell of the contingency table. The tabulation would be done using Excel's Pivot Table or another software package (e.g., MINITAB's Stat > Tables > Cross Tabulation).

School	Original Data ($000)		Coded Data	
	Tuition	Gain	Tuition	Gain
Alabama (Manderson)	67	21	T_3	S_1
Arizona (Eller)	69	42	T_3	S_1
Arizona State (Carey)	70	41	T_3	S_1
Auburn	46	18	T_2	S_1
Babson (Olin)	22	53	T_1	S_2
$\vdots$	$\vdots$	$\vdots$	$\vdots$	$\vdots$
Wake Forest (Babcock)	91	50	T_3	S_2
Washington U.—St. Louis (Olin)	120	61	T_3	S_2
William & Mary	94	45	T_3	S_1
Wisconsin—Madison	81	48	T_3	S_1
Yale	137	65	T_3	S_2

TABLE 5.12

Data Coding for MBA Data 🐭 MBASalary

Note: S_1 is salary gain under $50K, $S_2 =$ salary gain $50K–$100K, and S_3 is salary gain $100K+. T_1 is tuition under $40K, T_2 is tuition from $40K–$50K, and T_3 is tuition of $50K+. Data are provided for educational purposes and not as a guide to financial gains.

Source: *Forbes* 172, no. 8 (October 13, 2003), p. 78. Copyright © 2005 Forbes, Inc. Reprinted by permission of Forbes magazine.

Mini Case 5.1

Smoking and Gender

Table 5.13 shows that the proportion of women over age 65 who have never smoked is much higher than for men, that a higher proportion of men than women used to smoke but have quit, and that the number of current smokers over 65 is about the same for men and women.

TABLE 5.13 **Smoking and Gender for Persons Age 65 and Over (Thousands) 🐭 Smoking1**

Gender	Never Smoked (N)	Former Smoker (R)	Current Smoker (S)	Total
Male (M)	3,160	5,087	2,320	10,567
Female (F)	10,437	2,861	2,007	15,305
Total	13,597	7,948	4,327	25,872

Source: U.S. Department of Commerce, *Statistical Abstract of the United States, 1986,* p. 119.

Conditional probabilities may be found from Table 5.13 by restricting ourselves to a single row or column (the *condition*). For example, for males we get:

$P(N \mid M) = 3,160/10,567 = .2990$ There is a 29.9% probability that an individual never smoked *given* that the person is male.

$P(R \mid M) = 5,087/10,567 = .4814$ There is a 48.1% probability that an individual is a former smoker *given* that the person is male.

$P(S \mid M) = 2,320/10,567 = .2196$ There is a 22.0% probability that an individual currently smokes *given* that the person is male.

On the other hand, for females we get:

$P(N \mid F) = 10,437/15,305 = .6819$ There is a 68.2% probability that an individual never smoked *given* that the person is female.

$P(R \mid F) = 2,861/15,305 = .1869$ There is an 18.7% probability that an individual is a former smoker *given* that the person is female.

$P(S \mid F) = 2,007/15,305 = .1311$ There is a 13.1% probability that an individual currently smokes *given* that the person is female.

These conditional probabilities show that a female is over twice as likely as a male never to have smoked. However, the number of *former* smokers is higher among males (you can't be a former smoker unless you once smoked).

Table 5.14 shows the *relative frequencies* obtained by dividing each table frequency by the sample size ($n = 25,872$).

TABLE 5.14 Smoking and Gender for Persons Age 65 and Over (Proportion)

Gender	Never Smoked (N)	Former Smoker (R)	Current Smoker (S)	Total
Male (M)	.1221	.1966	.0897	0.4084
Female (F)	.4034	.1106	.0776	0.5916
Total	.5255	.3072	.1673	1.0000

For example, the joint probability $P(M \cap N)$ is .1221 (i.e., about 12.2 percent of the sample were males who had never smoked). The six joint probabilities sum to 1.0000, as they should.

SECTION EXERCISES

connect

5.26 A survey of 158 introductory statistics students showed the following contingency table. Find each event probability. **WebSurvey**
   a. $P(V)$ b. $P(A)$ c. $P(A \cap V)$
   d. $P(A \cup V)$ e. $P(A \mid V)$ f. $P(V \mid A)$

Cell Phone Provider	Visa Card (V)	No Visa Card (V′)	Row Total
AT&T (A)	32	15	47
Other (A′)	84	27	111
Column Total	116	42	158

5.27 A survey of 156 introductory statistics students showed the following contingency table. Find each event probability. **WebSurvey**
   a. $P(D)$ b. $P(R)$ c. $P(D \cap R)$
   d. $P(D \cup R)$ e. $P(R \mid D)$ f. $P(R \mid P)$

	Living Where?			
Newspaper Read	Dorm (D)	Parents (P)	Apt (A)	Row Total
Never (N)	13	6	6	25
Occasionally (O)	58	30	21	109
Regularly (R)	8	7	7	22
Column Total	79	43	34	156

5.28 This contingency table describes 200 business students. Find each probability and interpret it in words. **GenderMajor**
   a. $P(A)$ b. $P(M)$ c. $P(A \cap M)$ d. $P(F \cap S)$
   e. $P(A \mid M)$ f. $P(A \mid F)$ g. $P(F \mid S)$ h. $P(E \cup F)$

	Major			
Gender	Accounting (A)	Economics (E)	Statistics (S)	Row Total
Female (F)	44	30	24	98
Male (M)	56	30	16	102
Column Total	100	60	40	200

5.29 Based on the previous problem, is major independent of gender? Explain the basis for your conclusion.

5.30 This contingency table shows average yield (rows) and average duration (columns) for 38 bond funds. For a randomly chosen bond fund, find the probability that:
a. The bond fund is long duration.
b. The bond fund has high yield.
c. The bond fund has high yield given that it is of short duration.
d. The bond fund is of short duration given that it has high yield.

Yield	Average Portfolio Duration			Row Total
	Short (D₁)	Intermediate (D₂)	Long (D₃)	
Small (Y₁)	8	2	0	10
Medium (Y₂)	1	6	6	13
High (Y₃)	2	4	9	15
Column Total	11	12	15	38

Source: Data are from *Forbes* 173, no. 2 (February 2, 2004). **BondFunds**

Mini Case 5.2

Can Amazon Read Your Mind?

You go to Amazon.com to purchase a copy of *Eugenie Grandet* by Honore de Balzac. Amazon offers you 714 online choices (new, used, various vendors). But Amazon also recommends that you consider buying a copy of *Hedda Gabler* by Henrik Ibsen or *Madame Bovary* by Gustave Flaubert. How did they decide on these suggestions? The answer is that Amazon has a matrix (like an Excel pivot table) that keeps track of the frequency of *copurchased* items (e.g., books, music, DVDs) for Web shoppers. Probabilities derived from the cells in this contingency table are used to recommend products that are likely to be of interest to you, assuming that you are "like" other buyers. While such predictions of your behavior are only probabilistic, even a modest chance of landing extra sales can make a difference in bottom-line profit. There are even more sophisticated logic engines that can track your Web clicks. Is this an invasion of your privacy? Does it bother you to think that you may be predictable? Interestingly, many consumers don't seem to mind, and actually find value in this kind of statistical information system.

5.6 COUNTING RULES

Fundamental Rule of Counting

If event A can occur in n_1 ways and event B can occur in n_2 ways, then events A and B can occur in $n_1 \times n_2$ ways. In general, the number of ways that m events can occur is $n_1 \times n_2 \times \cdots \times n_m$.

EXAMPLE

Stock-Keeping Labels

How many unique stock-keeping unit (SKU) labels can a chain of hardware stores create by using two letters (ranging from *AA* to *ZZ*) followed by four numbers (digits 0 through 9)? For example:

AF1078: hex-head 6 cm bolts—box of 12

RT4855: Lime-A-Way cleaner—16 ounce

LL3119: Rust-Oleum Professional primer—gray 15 ounce

This problem may be viewed as filling six empty boxes, as shown in Figure 5.11.

FIGURE 5.11   Creating SKU Labels

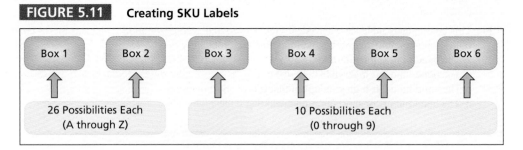

There are 26 ways (letters A through Z) to fill either the first or second box. There are 10 ways (digits 0 through 9) to fill the third through sixth boxes. The number of unique inventory labels is therefore $26 \times 26 \times 10 \times 10 \times 10 \times 10 = 6{,}760{,}000$. Such a system should suffice for a moderately large retail store.

EXAMPLE

Shirt Inventory

The number of possibilities can be large, even for a very simple counting problem. For example, the L.L. Bean men's cotton chambray shirt comes in six colors (blue, stone, rust, green, plum, indigo), five sizes (*S, M, L, XL, XXL*), and two styles (short sleeve, long sleeve). Their stock, therefore, might include $6 \times 5 \times 2 = 60$ possible shirts. The number of shirts of each type to be stocked will depend on prior demand experience. Counting the outcomes is easy with the counting formula, but even for this simple problem, a tree diagram would be impossible to fit on one page, and the enumeration of them all would be tedious (but necessary for L.L. Bean).

Factorials

The number of unique ways that *n* items can be arranged in a particular order is *n* **factorial**, the product of all integers from 1 to *n*.

(5.13) $$n! = n(n - 1)(n - 2) \cdots 1$$

This rule is useful for counting the possible arrangements of any *n* items. There are *n* ways to choose the first item, $n - 1$ ways to choose the second item, and so on until we reach the last item, as illustrated in Figure 5.12. By definition, $0! = 1$.

FIGURE 5.12

Choosing *n* Items

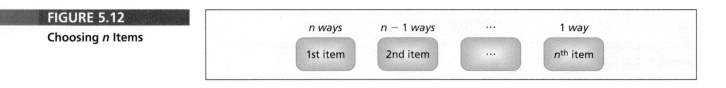

EXAMPLE

Truck Routing

In very small problems we can actually count the possibilities. For example, a home appliance service truck must make three stops (*A, B, C*). In how many ways could the three stops be arranged? There are six possible arrangements: {*ABC, ACB, BAC, BCA, CAB, CBA*}. But if all we want is the *number of possibilities* without listing them all:

$$3! = 3 \times 2 \times 1 = 6$$

Even in moderate-sized problems, listing all the possibilities is not feasible. For example, the number of possible arrangements of nine baseball players in a batting order rotation is:

$$9! = 9 \times 8 \times 7 \times 6 \times 5 \times 4 \times 3 \times 2 \times 1 = 362{,}880$$

Permutations

Choose r items at random without replacement from a group of n items. In how many ways can the r items be arranged, treating each arrangement as a different event (i.e., treating the three-letter sequence XYZ as different from the three-letter sequence ZYX)? A **permutation** is an arrangement of the r sample items *in a particular order*. The number of possible permutations of n items taken r at a time is denoted nPr.

$$_nP_r = \frac{n!}{(n-r)!} \tag{5.14}$$

Permutations are used when we are interested in finding how many possible arrangements there are when we select r items from n items, when each possible arrangement of items is a distinct event.

EXAMPLE

Appliance Service Calls

Five home appliance customers (A, B, C, D, E) need service calls, but the field technician can service only three of them before noon. The order in which they are serviced is important (to the customers, anyway) so each possible arrangement of three service calls is different. The dispatcher must assign the sequence. The number of possible permutations is

$$_nP_r = \frac{n!}{(n-r)!} = \frac{5!}{(5-3)!} = \frac{5 \cdot 4 \cdot 3 \cdot 2 \cdot 1}{2!} = \frac{120}{2} = 60$$

This may seem a surprisingly large number, but it can be enumerated. There are 10 distinct groups of three customers (two customers must be omitted):

   ABC ABD ABE ACD ACE ADE BCD BCE BDE CDE

In turn, each group of three customers can be arranged in six possible orders. For example, the first distinct set of customers $\{A, B, C\}$ could be arranged in six distinct ways:

   ABC ACB CAB CBA BAC BCA

We could do the same for each of the other nine groups of three customers. Since there are 10 distinct groups of three customers and six possible arrangements per group, there are $10 \times 6 = 60$ permutations. Clearly, we would prefer not to enumerate sequences like this very often.

Combinations

A **combination** is a collection of r items chosen at random without replacement from n items where the order of the selected items is *not* important (i.e., treating the three-letter sequence XYZ as being the same as the three-letter sequence ZYX). The number of possible combinations of r items chosen from n items is denoted $_nC_r$.

$$_nC_r = \frac{n!}{r!(n-r)!} \tag{5.15}$$

We use combinations when the only thing that matters is which r items are chosen, regardless of how they are arranged.

EXAMPLE

Appliance Service Calls Revisited

Suppose that five customers (A, B, C, D, E) need service calls and the maintenance worker can only service three of them this morning. The customers don't care when they are serviced as long as it's before noon, so the dispatcher does not care who is serviced first, second, or third. In other words, the dispatcher regards ABC, ACB, BAC, BCA, CAB, or CBA as being the same event because the same three customers (A, B, C) get serviced. The number of combinations is:

$$_nC_r = \frac{n!}{r!(n-r)!} = \frac{5!}{3!(5-3)!} = \frac{5 \cdot 4 \cdot 3 \cdot 2 \cdot 1}{(3 \cdot 2 \cdot 1)(2 \cdot 1)} = \frac{120}{12} = 10$$

This is much smaller than the number of permutations in the previous example where order was important. In fact, the possible combinations can be enumerated easily since there are only 10 distinct groups of three customers:

ABC ABD ABE ACD ACE ADE BCD BCE BDE CDE

Permutations or Combinations?

Permutations and combinations both calculate the number of ways we could choose r items from n items. But in permutations *order is important* while in combinations *order does not matter*. The number of permutations $_nP_r$ always is at least as great as the number of combinations $_nC_r$ in a sample of r items chosen at random from n items.

MegaStat offers computational assistance with factorials, permutations, and combinations. It is exceptionally fast and accurate, even for very large factorials.

SECTION EXERCISES

connect

5.31 (a) Find 7! without a calculator. Show your work. (b) Use your calculator to find 14! (c) Type 70! in the Google search window and record the answer (d) Which method, do you prefer? Why?

5.32 In the Minnesota Northstar Cash Drawing you pick five different numbers between 1 and 31. What is the probability of picking the winning combination (order does not matter)? *Hint:* Count how many ways you could pick the first number, the second number, and so on, and then divide by the number of permuations of the five numbers.

5.33 American Express Business Travel uses a six-letter record locator number (RLN) for each client's trip (e.g., KEZLFS). (a) How many different RLNs can be created using capital letters (A–Z)? (b) What if they allow any mixture of capital letters (A–Z) and digits (0–9)? (c) What if they allow capital letters and digits but exclude the digits 0 and 1 and the letters O and I because they look too much alike?

5.34 At Oxnard University, a student ID consists of two letters (26 possibilities) followed by four digits (10 possibilities). (a) How many unique student IDs can be created? (b) Would one letter followed by three digits suffice for a university with 40,000 students? (c) Why is extra capacity in student IDs a good idea?

5.35 Until 2005, the UPC bar code had 12 digits (0–9). The first six digits represent the manufacturer, the next five represent the product, and the last is a check digit. (a) How many different manufacturers could be encoded? (b) How many different products could be encoded? (c) In 2005, the EAN bar code replaced the UPC bar code, adding a 13th digit. If this new digit is used for product identification, how many different products could now be encoded?

5.36 Bob has to study for four final exams: accounting (*A*), biology (*B*), communications (*C*), and drama (*D*). (a) If he studies one subject at a time, in how many different ways could he arrange them? (b) List the possible arrangements in the sample space.

5.37 (a) In how many ways could you arrange seven books on a shelf? (b) Would it be feasible to list the possible arrangements?

5.38 Find the following permutations $_nP_r$:
   a. $n = 8$ and $r = 3$.
   b. $n = 8$ and $r = 5$.
   c. $n = 8$ and $r = 1$.
   d. $n = 8$ and $r = 8$.

5.39 Find the following combinations $_nC_r$:
   a. $n = 8$ and $r = 3$.
   b. $n = 8$ and $r = 5$.
   c. $n = 8$ and $r = 1$.
   d. $n = 8$ and $r = 8$.

5.40 A real estate office has 10 sales agents. Each of four new customers must be assigned an agent. (a) Find the number of agent arrangements where order *is* important. (b) Find the number of agent arrangements where order is *not* important. (c) Why is the number of combinations smaller than the number of permutations?

The **sample space** for a **random experiment** describes all possible outcomes. **Simple events** in a **discrete** sample space can be enumerated, while outcomes of a **continuous** sample space can only be described by a rule. An **empirical** probability is based on relative frequencies, a **classical** probability can be deduced from the nature of the experiment, and a **subjective** probability is based on judgment. An event's **complement** is every outcome except the event. The **odds** are the ratio of an event's probability to the probability of its complement. The **union** of two events is all outcomes in either or both, while the intersection is only those events in both. **Mutually exclusive** events cannot both occur, and **collectively exhaustive** events cover all possibilities. The **conditional probability** of an event is its probability given that another event has occurred. Two events are **independent** if the conditional probability of one is the same as its **unconditional** probability. The **joint probability** of independent events is the product of their probabilities. A **contingency table** is a cross-tabulation of frequencies for two variables with categorical outcomes and can be used to calculate probabilities. The number of arrangements of sampled items drawn from a population is found with the formula for **permutations** (if order is important) or **combinations** (if order does not matter).

actuarial science, *171*
binary events, *176*
classical approach, *172*
collectively exhaustive, *176*
combination, *191*
complement, *173*
compound event, *168*
conditional probability, *176*
contingency table, *182*
dependent, *179*
disjoint, *175*
empirical approach, *170*

event, *168*
factorial, *190*
general law of addition, *174*
independent, *179*
intersection, *174*
joint probability, *174*
law of large numbers, *171*
marginal probability, *183*
multiplication law, *180*
mutually exclusive, *175*
null set, *175*
odds, *177*

permutation, *191*
probability, *169*
random experiment, *167*
redundancy, *181*
relative frequency approach, *170*
sample space, *167*
simple event, *168*
subjective approach, *172*
union, *173*
Venn diagram, *168*

Commonly Used Formulas in Probability ————————•

	Odds for A	**Odds against A**
Odds:	$\dfrac{P(A)}{1 - P(A)}$	$\dfrac{1 - P(A)}{P(A)}$

General Law of Addition: $P(A \cup B) = P(A) + P(B) - P(A \cap B)$

Conditional probability: $P(A \mid B) = \dfrac{P(A \cap B)}{P(B)}$

Independence property: $P(A \cap B) = P(A)P(B)$

Permutation: $_nP_r = \dfrac{n!}{(n - r)!}$

Combination: $_nC_r = \dfrac{n!}{r!(n - r)!}$

1. Define (a) random experiment, (b) sample space, (c) simple event, and (d) compound event.

2. What are the three approaches to determining probability? Explain the differences among them.

3. Sketch a Venn diagram to illustrate (a) complement of an event, (b) union of two events, (c) intersection of two events, (d) mutually exclusive events, and (e) dichotomous events.

4. Define *odds*. What does it mean to say that odds are usually quoted against an event?

5. (a) State the additive law. (b) Why do we subtract the intersection?

6. (a) Write the formula for conditional probability. (b) When are two events independent?

7. (a) What is a contingency table? (b) How do we convert a contingency table into a table of relative frequencies?

8. In a contingency table, explain the concepts of (a) marginal probability and (b) joint probability.

9. Define (a) fundamental rule of counting, (b) factorial, (c) permutation, and (d) combination.

CHAPTER EXERCISES

Note: Explain answers and show your work clearly. Problems marked * are more difficult.

connect

EMPIRICAL PROBABILITY EXPERIMENTS

5.41 (a) Make your own empirical estimate of the probability that a car is parked "nose first" (as opposed to "backed in"). Choose a local parking lot, such as a grocery store. Let A be the event that a car is parked nose first. Out of n cars examined, let f be the number of cars parked nose first. Then $P(A) = f/n$. (b) Do you feel your sample is large enough to have a reliable empirical probability? (c) If you had chosen a different parking lot (such as a church or a police station) would you expect the estimate of $P(A)$ to be similar? That is, would $P(A \mid \text{church}) = P(A \mid \text{police station})$? Explain.

5.42 (a) Make your own empirical estimate of the probability that a page in this book contains a figure. For n pages sampled (chosen using random numbers or some other random method) let f be the number of pages with a figure. Then $P(A) = f/n$. (b) Do you feel your sample is large enough to have a reliable empirical probability? (c) If you had chosen a different textbook (such as a biology book or an art history book), would you expect $P(A)$ to be similar? That is, would $P(A \mid \text{biology}) = P(A \mid \text{art history})$? Explain.

5.43 (a) Make your own empirical estimate of the probability that a DVD movie from your collection is longer than 2 hours (120 minutes). For the n DVDs in your sample, let f be the number that exceed 2 hours. Then $P(A) = f/n$. (b) Do you feel your sample is large enough to have a reliable empirical probability? (c) If you had chosen a different DVD collection (say, your best friend's), would you expect $P(A)$ to be similar? Explain.

5.44 M&Ms are blended in a ratio of 13 percent brown, 14 percent yellow, 13 percent red, 24 percent blue, 20 percent orange, and 16 percent green. Suppose you choose a sample of two M&Ms at random from a large bag. (a) Show the sample space. (b) What is the probability that both are brown? (c) Both blue? (d) Both green? (e) Find the probability of one brown and one green M&M. (f) Actually take 100 samples of two M&Ms (with replacement) and record the frequency of each outcome listed in (b) and (c) above. How close did your empirical results come to your predictions? (g) Which definition of probability applies in this situation? (Data are from www.mmmars.com.)

PROBLEMS

5.45 A survey showed that 44 percent of online Internet shoppers experience some kind of technical failure at checkout (e.g., when submitting a credit card) after loading their shopping cart. (a) What kind of probability is this? Explain. (b) What are the odds *for* a technical failure? (See J. Paul Peter and Jerry C. Olson, *Consumer Behavior and Marketing Strategy,* 7th ed. [McGraw-Hill-Irwin], p. 278.)

5.46 A Johnson Space Center analysis estimated a 1 in 71 chance of losing the International Space Station to space debris or a meteoroid hit. (a) What kind of probability is this? Explain. (b) What is the probability of losing the station in this way? (See *Aviation Week & Space Technology* 149, no. 16 [October 19, 1998], p. 11.)

5.47 Baseball player Tom Brookens once commented on his low batting average of .176: "I figure the law of averages has got to come into play sooner or later." A batting average is the ratio of hits to times at bat. Do you think the law of large numbers can be counted on to save Tom's batting average?

5.48 Bob says he is 50 percent sure he could swim across the Thames River. (a) What kind of probability is this? (b) On what facts might Bob have based his assertion?

5.49 In the first year after its release, 83 percent of emergency room doctors were estimated to have tried Dermabond glue (an alternative to sutures in some situations). (a) What kind of probability is this? (b) How was it probably estimated? (c) Why might the estimate be inaccurate? (Data are from *Modern Healthcare* 29, no. 32 [August 9, 1999], p. 70.)

5.50 The U.S. Cesarean section delivery rate in a recent year was estimated at 20.6 percent. (a) What kind of probability is this? (b) How was it probably estimated? (c) How accurate would you say this estimate is? (Data are from *Modern Healthcare* 27, no. 40 [October 6, 1997], p. 60.)

5.51 A recent article states that there is a 2 percent chance that an asteroid 100 meters or more in diameter will strike the earth before 2100. (a) What kind of probability is this? (b) How was it probably estimated? (c) How accurate would you say this estimate is? (Data are from *Scientific American* 289, no. 5 [November 2003], p. 56.)

5.52   If Punxsutawney Phil sees his shadow on February 2, then legend says that winter will last 6 more weeks. In 118 years, Phil has seen his shadow 104 times. (a) What is the probability that Phil will see his shadow on a randomly chosen Groundhog Day? (b) What kind of probability is this? (Data are from www.groundhog.org.)

5.53   "On Los Angeles freeways during the rush hour, there is an 18 percent probability that a driver is using a hand-held cell phone." (a) What kind of probability would you say this is? (b) How might it have been estimated? (c) How might the estimate be inaccurate?

5.54   Bob owns two stocks. There is an 80 percent probability that stock A will rise in price, while there is a 60 percent chance that stock B will rise in price. There is a 40 percent chance that both stocks will rise in price. Are the stock prices independent?

5.55   To run its network, the Ramjac Corporation wants to install a system with dual independent servers. Employee Bob grumbled, "But that will double the chance of system failure." Is Bob right? Explain your reasoning with an example.

5.56   A study showed that trained police officers can detect a lie 65 percent of the time, based on controlled studies of videotapes with real-life lies and truths. What are the odds that a lie will be detected? (*Source: Science News* 166, no. 5 [July 31, 2004] p. 73.)

5.57   During 2002, the theft probability of an Acura Integra was estimated as 1.3 percent. Find the odds against an Acura Integra being stolen. (Data are from *Popular Science* 261, no. 3 [September 2002], p. 30.)

5.58   A person hit by lightning has a 33 percent chance of being killed (event K). (a) Find the odds that a person will be killed if struck by lightning. (b) Find the odds *against* a person being killed if struck by lightning (event K'). (Data are from Martin A. Uman, *Understanding Lightning* [Bek Technical Publications, 1971], p. 19.)

5.59   During the 2003 NBA playoffs, the Caesar's Palace Race and Sports Book gave the Detroit Pistons 50–1 odds against winning the NBA championship, and the New Jersey Nets 5–1 odds against winning the NBA championship. What is the implied probability of each team's victory? (Data are from *Detroit Free Press,* May 22, 2003, p. 1E.)

5.60   A certain model of remote-control Stanley garage door opener has nine binary (off/on) switches. The homeowner can set any code sequence. (a) How many separate codes can be programmed? (b) A newer model has 10 binary switches. How many codes can be programmed? (c) If you try to use your door opener on 1,000 other garages, how many times would you expect to succeed? What assumptions are you making in your answer?

5.61   (a) In a certain state, license plates consist of three letters (A–Z) followed by three digits (0–9). How many different plates can be issued? (b) If the state allows any six-character mix (in any order) of 26 letters and 10 digits, how many unique plates are possible? (c) Why might some combinations of digits and letters be disallowed? *(d) Would the system described in (b) permit a unique license number for every car in the United States? For every car in the world? Explain your assumptions. *(e) If the letters O and I are not used because they look too much like the numerals 0 and 1, how many different plates can be issued?

5.62   Bob, Mary, and Jen go to dinner. Each orders a different meal. The waiter forgets who ordered which meal, so he randomly places the meals before the three diners. Let C be the event that a diner gets the correct meal and let N be the event that a diner gets an incorrect meal. Enumerate the sample space and then find the probability that:
a. No diner gets the correct meal.
b. Exactly one diner gets the correct meal.
c. Exactly two diners get the correct meal.
d. All three diners get the correct meal.

5.63   An MBA program offers seven concentrations: accounting (A), finance (F), human resources (H), information systems (I), international business (B), marketing (M), and operations management (O). Students in the capstone business policy class are assigned to teams of three. In how many different ways could a team contain exactly one student from each concentration?

5.64   A certain airplane has two independent alternators to provide electrical power. The probability that a given alternator will fail on a 1-hour flight is .02. What is the probability that (a) both will fail? (b) Neither will fail? (c) One or the other will fail? Show all steps carefully.

5.65   There is a 30 percent chance that a bidding firm will get contract A and a 40 percent chance they will get contract B. There is a 5 percent chance that they will get both. Are the events independent?

5.66   A couple has two children. What is the probability that both are boys, given that the first is a boy?

5.67   On July 14, 2004, a power outage in the Northwest Airlines operations center near Minneapolis forced the airline's computer systems to shut down, leading to cancellation of 200 flights and delays in scores of other flights. (a) Explain how the concept of statistical independence might be applicable here. (b) How would the airline decide whether, say, expenditure of $100,000 would be justified for a backup system to prevent future occurrences? (Data are from *The Wall Street Journal,* July 15, 2004.)

5.68   Which are likely to be independent events? For those you think are not, suggest reasons why.
a. Gender of two consecutive babies born in a hospital.
b. Car accident rates and the driver's gender.
c. Phone call arrival rates at a university admissions office and time of day.

5.69   In child-custody cases, about 70 percent of the fathers win the case if they contest it. In the next three custody cases, what is the probability that all three win? What assumption(s) are you making?

5.70   RackSpace-managed hosting advertises 99.999 percent guaranteed network uptime. (a) How many independent network servers would be needed if each has 99 percent reliability? (b) If each has 90 percent reliability? (Data are from www.rackspace.com.)

5.71   Four students divided the task of surveying the types of vehicles in parking lots of four different shopping malls. Each student examined 100 cars in each of three large suburban Detroit malls and one suburban Jamestown, New York, mall, resulting in the 5×4 contingency table shown below. (a) Calculate each probability (i–ix) and explain in words what it means. (b) Do you see evidence that vehicle type is not independent of mall location? Explain. (c) Do the row-total vehicle percentages correspond roughly to your experience in your own city and state? If not, discuss possible reasons for the difference. (Data are from an independent project by MBA students Steve Bennett, Alicia Morais, Steve Olson, and Greg Corda.)   **Malls**

i. $P(C)$	ii. $P(G)$	iii. $P(T)$
iv. $P(V \mid S)$	v. $P(C \mid J)$	vi. $P(J \mid C)$
vii. $P(C$ and $G)$	viii. $P(T$ and $O)$	ix. $P(M$ and $J)$

Number of Vehicles of Each Type in Four Shopping Malls

Vehicle Type	Somerset (S)	Oakland (O)	Great Lakes (G)	Jamestown, NY (J)	Row Total
Car (C)	44	49	36	64	193
Minivan (M)	21	15	18	13	67
Full-size van (F)	2	3	3	2	10
SUV (V)	19	27	26	12	84
Truck (T)	14	6	17	9	46
Column Total	100	100	100	100	400

5.72   Refer to the contingency table shown below. (a) Calculate each probability (i–vi) and explain in words what it means. (b) Do you see evidence that smoking and race are *not* independent? Explain. (c) Do the smoking rates shown here correspond to your experience? (d) Why might public health officials be interested in this type of data? (Data are from *Statistical Abstract of the United States, 2001,* pp. 12 and 16. Note: Actual statistics are applied to a hypothetical sample of 1,000.)   **Smoking2**

i. $P(S)$	ii. $P(W)$	iii. $P(S \mid W)$
iv. $P(S \mid B)$	v. $P(S$ and $W)$	vi. $P(N$ and $B)$

Smoking by Race for Males Aged 18–24

	Smoker (S)	Nonsmoker (N)	Row Total
White (W)	290	560	850
Black (B)	30	120	150
Column Total	320	680	1,000

5.73 Analysis of forecasters' interest rate predictions over the period 1982–1990 was intended to see whether the predictions corresponded to what actually happened. The 2×2 contingency table below shows the frequencies of actual and predicted interest rate movements. (a) Calculate each probability (i–vi) and explain in words what it means. (b*) Do you think that the forecasters' predictions were accurate? Explain. (Data are from R. A. Kolb and H. O. Steckler, "How Well Do Analysts Forecast Interest Rates?" *Journal of Forecasting* 15, no. 15 [1996], pp. 385–394.)   **Forecasts**

i. $P(F-)$	ii. $P(A+)$	iii. $P(A- \mid F-)$
iv. $P(A+ \mid F+)$	v. $P(A+ \text{ and } F+)$	vi. $P(A- \text{ and } F-)$

Interest Rate Forecast Accuracy

	Actual Change		
Forecast Change	Decline (A−)	Rise (A+)	Row Total
Decline (F−)	7	12	19
Rise (F+)	9	6	15
Column Total	16	18	34

5.74 High levels of cockpit noise in an aircraft can damage the hearing of pilots who are exposed to this hazard for many hours. Cockpit noise in a jet aircraft is mostly due to airflow at hundreds of miles per hour. This 3×3 contingency table shows 61 observations of data collected by an airline pilot using a handheld sound meter in a Boeing 727 cockpit. Noise level is defined as "low" (under 88 decibels), "medium" (88 to 91 decibels), or "high" (92 decibels or more). There are three flight phases (climb, cruise, descent). (a) Calculate each probability (i–ix) and explain in words what it means. (b) Do you see evidence that noise level depends on flight phase? Explain. (c) Where else might ambient noise be an ergonomic issue? (*Hint*: search the Web.) (Data are from Capt. Robert E. Hartl, retired.)   **Cockpit**

i. $P(B)$	ii. $P(L)$	iii. $P(H)$
iv. $P(H \mid C)$	v. $P(H \mid D)$	vi. $P(D \mid L)$
vii. $P(L \text{ and } B)$	viii. $P(L \text{ and } C)$	ix. $P(H \text{ and } C)$

Cockpit Noise

	Flight Phase			
Noise Level	Climb (B)	Cruise (C)	Descent (D)	Row Total
Low (L)	6	2	6	14
Medium (M)	18	3	8	29
High (H)	1	3	14	18
Column Total	25	8	28	61

RELATED READING   Albert, James H. "College Students' Conceptions of Probability." *The American Statistician* 57, no. 1 (February 2001), pp. 37–45.

LearningStats Unit 05   Probability   LS

LearningStats Unit 05 reviews set notation, introduces probability concepts, illustrates decision trees and Bayes' Theorem, and explains counting rules. Modules are designed for self-study, so you can proceed at your own pace, concentrate on material that is new, and pass quickly over things that you already know. Your instructor may assign specific modules, or you may decide to check them out because the topic sounds interesting. In addition to helping you learn about statistics, they may be useful as references later on.

Topic	*LearningStats Modules*
Events and probability	Probability Basics Empirical Probability
Contingency tables	Contingency Tables Cross-Tabulations Independent Events
Life tables and expected value	Mortality Rates Using Life Tables Survival Curves Retirement Planning
Independent events	Birthday Problem Four-Leaf Clover System Reliability Organ Transplants
Random processes	Law of Large Numbers Dice Rolls Pick a Card Random Names
Bayes' Theorem	Bayes' Theorem
Life insurance	Life Insurance Terminology

Key: = PowerPoint   = Word   = Excel

Visual Statistics

Visual Statistics Module on Probability

Module	Module Name
2	VS Visualizing a Random Process

Visual Statistics Module 2 is designed to help you

- Recognize that outcomes of a random process exhibit regularity even though the process is random.
- Learn through experimentation how the parameters affect the outcomes of an experiment.
- Learn how a histogram can summarize the results of an experiment.
- Visualize data-generating processes that give rise to common probability distributions.
- Understand how relative frequencies can be used to estimate the probability of an event.

The worktext chapter (included on the CD as a .PDF file) contains a list of concepts, objectives of the module, overview of concepts, illustration of concepts, orientation to module features, learning exercises (basic, intermediate, advanced), learning projects (individual, team), self-evaluation quiz, glossary of terms, and solutions to the self-evaluation quiz.

Discrete Probability Distributions

Chapter Learning Objectives

When you finish this chapter you should be able to

- Define a discrete random variable and a probability distribution.

- Solve problems by using the concepts of expected value and variance.

- Explain common discrete probability models and their parameters.

- Recognize the appropriate discrete model to use from the problem context.

- Find event probabilities for discrete models by using Excel, formulas, or tables.

This chapter shows how probability can be used to analyze *random processes* and to understand business processes. A random process is also called a **stochastic process** and is defined as a repeatable random experiment. Almost any business process can be thought of as a stochastic process. For example, consider cars being serviced in a quick oil change shop or calls arriving at the L.L. Bean order center. Think of each car or call as a random experiment. The variable of interest associated with the car might be service time. The variable of interest associated with the call might be amount of order.

A **probability model** is a mathematical equation that assigns a probability to each outcome in the sample space defined by a random process. We use probability models to depict the essential characteristics of a stochastic process, to guide decisions or make predictions. How many service technicians do we need from noon to 1 P.M. on Friday afternoon? To answer this we need to model the process of servicing cars during the lunch hour. Can L.L. Bean predict its total order amount from the next 50 callers? To answer this question L.L. Bean needs to model the process of call orders to its call center. Probability models must be reasonably realistic yet simple enough to be analyzed.

Many stochastic processes can be described by using common probability models whose properties are well known. To correctly use these probability models it is important that you understand their development. In the following sections we will explain how probability models are developed and describe several commonly used models.

Random Variables

A **random variable** is a function or rule that assigns a numerical value to each outcome in the sample space of a random experiment. We use X when referring to a random variable in general, while specific values of X are shown in lowercase (e.g., x_1). The random variable often is a direct result of an observational experiment (e.g., counting the number of takeoffs in a given hour at O'Hare Airport). A **discrete random variable** has a countable number of distinct values. Some random variables have a clear upper limit (e.g., number of absences in a class of 40 students) while others do not (e.g., number of text messages you receive in a given hour). Here are some examples of decision problems involving discrete random variables.

Decision Problem

- Oxnard University has space in its MBA program for 65 new students. In the past, 75 percent of those who are admitted actually enroll. The decision is made to admit 80 students. What is the probability that more than 65 admitted students will actually enroll?

- On the late morning (9 to 12) work shift, L.L. Bean's order processing center staff can handle up to 5 orders per minute. The mean arrival rate is 3.5 orders per minute. What is the probability that more than 5 orders will arrive in a given minute?

- Rolled steel from a certain supplier averages 0.01 defects per linear meter. Toyota will reject a shipment of 500 linear meters if inspection reveals more than 10 defects. What is the probability that the order will be rejected?

Discrete Random Variable

- $X =$ number of admitted MBA students who actually enroll ($X = 0, 1, 2, \ldots, 80$)

- $X =$ number of phone calls that arrive in a given minute at the L.L. Bean order processing center ($X = 0, 1, 2, \ldots$)

- $X =$ number of defects in 500 meters of rolled steel ($X = 0, 1, 2, \ldots$)

Probability Distributions

A **discrete probability distribution** assigns a probability to each value of a discrete random variable X. The distribution must follow the rules of probability defined in Chapter 5. If there are n distinct values of X ($x_1, x_2, \ldots, x_n$):

(6.1) $0 \leq P(x_i) \leq 1$ (the probability for any given value of X)

(6.2) $\displaystyle\sum_{i=1}^{n} P(x_i) = 1$ (the sum over all values of X)

Both X and $P(x)$ follow the rules of functions. More than one sample space outcome can be assigned to the same number, but you cannot assign one outcome to two different numbers. Likewise, more than one random variable value can be assigned to the same probability, but one random variable value cannot have two different probabilities. The probabilities must sum to 1. Figure 6.1 illustrates the relationship between the sample space, the random variable, and the probability distribution function for a simple experiment of rolling a die.

FIGURE 6.1

Random Experiment: Rolling a Die

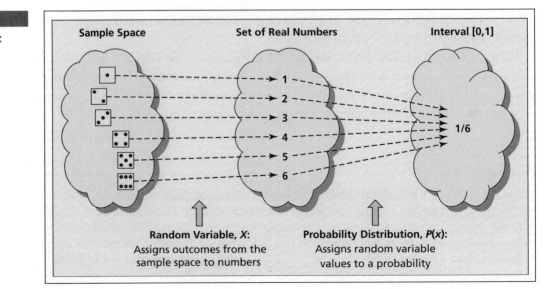

EXAMPLE

Coin Flips
🐭 **ThreeCoins**

When you flip a fair coin three times, the sample space has eight equally likely simple events: {HHH, HHT, HTH, THH, HTT, THT, TTH, TTT}. If X is the number of heads, then X is a random variable whose probability distribution is shown in Table 6.1 and Figure 6.2.

TABLE 6.1   **Probability Distribution for Three Coin Flips**

Possible Events	x	P(x)
TTT	0	1/8
HTT, THT, TTH	1	3/8
HHT, HTH, THH	2	3/8
HHH	3	1/8
Total		1

The values of X need not be equally likely. In this example, $X = 1$ and $X = 2$ are more likely than $X = 0$ or $X = 3$. However, the probabilities sum to 1, as in any probability distribution.

FIGURE 6.2   **Probability Distribution for Three Coin Flips**

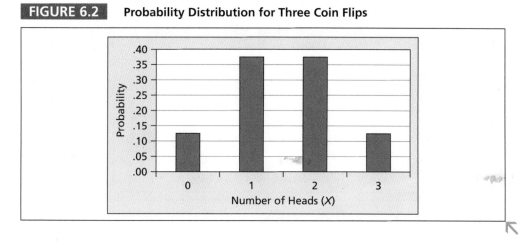

Expected Value

As shown in Figure 6.2, a discrete probability distribution is defined only at specific points on the X-axis. The **expected value** $E(X)$ of a discrete random variable is the sum of all X-values weighted by their respective probabilities. It is a measure of *central tendency*. If there are n distinct values of X ($x_1, x_2, \ldots, x_n$), the expected value is

$$E(X) = \mu = \sum_{i=1}^{n} x_i P(x_i) \tag{6.3}$$

The expected value is a weighted average because outcomes can have different probabilities. We usually call $E(X)$ the *mean* and use the symbol μ.

EXAMPLE

Service Calls
🐭 **ServiceCalls**

The distribution of Sunday emergency service calls by Ace Appliance Repair is shown in Table 6.2. The probabilities sum to 1, as must be true for any probability distribution.

TABLE 6.2   **Probability Distribution of Service Calls**

x	P(x)	xP(x)
0	.05	0.00
1	.10	0.10
2	.30	0.60
3	.25	0.75
4	.20	0.80
5	.10	0.50
Total	1.00	2.75

The mode (most likely value of X) is 2, but the *expected* number of service calls $E(X)$ is 2.75, that is, $\mu = 2.75$. In other words, the "average" number of service calls is 2.75 on Sunday:

$$E(X) = \mu = \sum_{i=1}^{5} x_i P(x_i) = 0P(0) + 1P(1) + 2P(2) + 3P(3) + 4P(4) + 5P(5)$$

$$= 0(.05) + 1(.10) + 2(.30) + 3(.25) + 4(.20) + 5(.10) = 2.75$$

In Figure 6.3, we see that this particular probability distribution is not symmetric around the mean $\mu = 2.75$. However, the mean $\mu = 2.75$ is still the balancing point, or fulcrum.

Note that $E(X)$ need not be an observable event. For example, you could have 2 service calls or 3 service calls, but not 2.75 service calls. This makes sense because $E(X)$ is an *average*. It is like saying that "the average American family has 2.1 children" (even though families come only in integer sizes) or "Barry Bonds's batting average is .275" (even though the number of hits by Bonds in a particular game must be an integer).

FIGURE 6.3   **Probability Distribution for Service Calls**

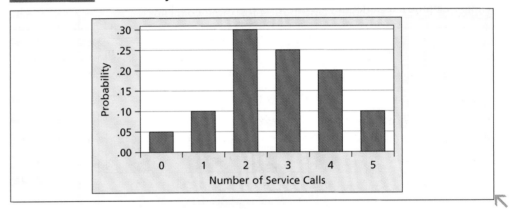

Application: Life Insurance   Expected value is the basis of life insurance, a purchase that almost everyone makes. For example, based on U.S. mortality statistics, the probability that a 30-year-old white female will die within the next year is .00059 (see *LearningStats* Unit 05) so the probability of living another year is $1 - .00059 = .99941$. What premium should a life insurance company charge to break even on a $500,000 1-year term insurance policy (that is, to achieve zero expected payout)? This situation is shown in Table 6.3. Let X be the amount paid by the company to settle the policy. The expected payout is $295, so the premium should be $295 plus whatever return the company needs to cover its administrative overhead and profit.

TABLE 6.3

Expected Payout for a 1-Year Term Life Policy

Source: Centers for Disease Control and Prevention, *National Vital Statistics Reports* 47, no. 28 (1999).

Event	x	P(x)	xP(x)
Live	0	.99941	.00
Die	500,000	.00059	295.00
Total		1.00000	295.00

The mortality rate shown here is for *all* 30-year-old women. An insurance quote (e.g., from the Web) is likely to yield a lower premium, as long as you are a healthy, educated, nonsmoker in a nonrisky occupation. Insurance companies make money by knowing the actuarial probabilities and using them to set their premiums. The task is difficult because actuarial probabilities must be revised as life expectancies change over time.

Application: Raffle Tickets   Expected value can be applied to raffles and lotteries. If it costs $2 to buy a ticket in a raffle to win a new luxury automobile worth $55,000 and 29,346 raffle tickets are sold, the expected value of a lottery ticket is

$$E(X) = (\text{value if you win})P(\text{win}) + (\text{value if you lose})P(\text{lose})$$

$$= (55,000)\left(\frac{1}{29,346}\right) + (0)\left(\frac{29,345}{29,346}\right)$$

$$= (55,000)(.000034076) + (0)(.999965924) = \$1.87$$

The raffle ticket is actually worth $1.87. So why would you pay $2.00 for it? Partly because you hope to beat the odds, but also because you know that your ticket purchase helps the charity. Since the idea of a raffle is to raise money, the sponsor tries to sell enough tickets to push the expected value of the ticket below its price (otherwise, the charity would lose money on the raffle). If the raffle prize is donated (or partially donated) by a well-wisher, the break-even point may be much less than the full value of the prize.

Actuarial Fairness   Like a lottery, an **actuarially fair** insurance program must collect as much in overall revenue as it pays out in claims. This is accomplished by setting the premiums to reflect empirical experience with the insured group. Individuals may gain or lose, but if the pool of insured persons is large enough, the total payout is predictable. Of course, many insurance policies have exclusionary clauses for war and natural disaster (e.g., Hurricane Katrina), to deal with cases where the events are not independent. Actuarial analysis is critical for corporate pension fund planning. Group health insurance is another major application.

Variance and Standard Deviation

The **variance** $V(X)$ of a discrete random variable is the sum of the squared deviations about its expected value, weighted by the probability of each X-value. If there are n distinct values of X, the variance is

$$V(X) = \sigma^2 = \sum_{i=1}^{n} [x_i - \mu]^2 P(x_i) \tag{6.4}$$

Just as the expected value $E(X)$ is a weighted average that measures *central tendency,* the variance $V(X)$ is a weighted average that measures *dispersion* about the mean. And just as we interchangeably use μ or $E(X)$ to denote the mean of a distribution, we use either σ^2 or $V(X)$ to denote its variance.

The *standard deviation* is the square root of the variance and is denoted σ:

$$\sigma = \sqrt{\sigma^2} = \sqrt{V(X)} \tag{6.5}$$

The Bay Street Inn is a seven-room bed-and-breakfast in the sunny California coastal city of Santa Theresa. Demand for rooms generally is strong during February, a prime month for tourists. However, experience shows that demand is quite variable. The probability distribution of room rentals during February is shown in Table 6.4 where $X =$ the number of rooms rented ($X = 0, 1, 2, 3, 4, 5, 6, 7$). The worksheet shows the calculation of $E(X)$ and $V(X)$.

EXAMPLE

Bed and Breakfast   Airbnb
  RoomRent

TABLE 6.4	Worksheet for E(X) and V(X) for February Room Rentals				
x	**P(x)**	**xP(x)**	**x − μ**	**[x − μ]²**	**[x − μ]²P(x)**
0	.05	0.00	−4.71	22.1841	1.109205
1	.05	0.05	−3.71	13.7641	0.688205
2	.06	0.12	−2.71	7.3441	0.440646
3	.10	0.30	−1.71	2.9241	0.292410
4	.13	0.52	−0.71	0.5041	0.065533
5	.20	1.00	+0.29	0.0841	0.016820
6	.15	0.90	+1.29	1.6641	0.249615
7	.26	1.82	+2.29	5.2441	1.363466
Total	1.00	$\mu = 4.71$			$\sigma^2 = 4.225900$

The formulas are:

$$E(X) = \mu = \sum_{i=1}^{7} x_i P(x_i) = 4.71$$

$$V(X) = \sigma^2 = \sum_{i=1}^{7} [x_i - \mu]^2 P(x_i) = 4.2259$$

$$\sigma = \sqrt{4.2259} = 2.0557$$

This distribution is skewed to the left and bimodal. The mode (most likely value) is 7 rooms rented, but the average is only 4.71 room rentals in February. The standard deviation of 2.06 indicates that there is considerable variation around the mean, as seen in Figure 6.4.

FIGURE 6.4   **Probability Distribution of Room Rentals**

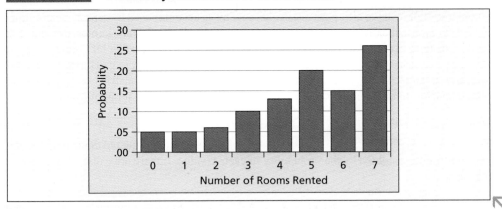

What Is a PDF or a CDF?

A known distribution can be described either by its **probability distribution function** (PDF) or by its **cumulative distribution function** (CDF). The PDF and CDF are mathematical equations. A discrete PDF shows the probability of each *X*–value, while the CDF shows the cumulative sum of probabilities, adding from the smallest to the largest *X*–value. Figure 6.5 illustrates a discrete PDF and Figure 6.6 illustrates the corresponding CDF. Notice that the CDF approaches 1.

Recall from Chapter 2 that a parameter is a number that describes a population. A random process generates a population of outcomes. Random variables and their distributions are described by their parameters. The equations for the PDF, the CDF, and the characteristics of the distribution (such as the mean and standard deviation) will depend on the parameters of the process. The rest of this chapter explains several well-known discrete distributions and their applications. Many random business processes can be described by these common distributions.

FIGURE 6.5

PDF = *P*(*X* = *x*)

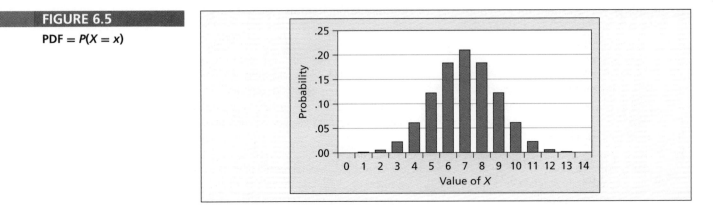

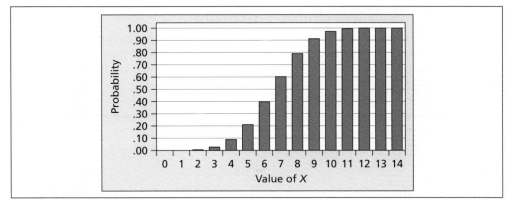

FIGURE 6.6

CDF = $P(X \leq x)$

6.1 Which of the following could *not* be probability distributions? Explain.

SECTION EXERCISES

connect

Example A		Example B		Example C	
x	P(x)	x	P(x)	x	P(x)
0	.80	1	.05	50	.30
1	.20	2	.15	60	.60
		3	.25	70	.40
		4	.40		
		5	.10		

6.2 On hot, sunny, summer days, Jane rents inner tubes by the river that runs through her town. Based on her past experience, she has assigned the following probability distribution to the number of tubes she will rent on a randomly selected day. (a) Calculate the expected value and standard deviation of this random variable X by using the PDF shown. (b) Describe the shape of this distribution.

x	25	50	75	100	Total
P(x)	.20	.40	.30	.10	1.00

6.3 On the midnight shift, the number of patients with head trauma in an emergency room has the probability distribution shown below. (a) Calculate the mean and standard deviation. (b) Describe the shape of this distribution.

x	0	1	2	3	4	5	Total
P(x)	.05	.30	.25	.20	.15	.05	1.00

6.4 Pepsi and Mountain Dew products sponsored a contest giving away a Lamborghini sports car worth $215,000. The probability of winning from a single bottle purchase was .00000884. Find the expected value. Show your calculations clearly. (Data are from J. Paul Peter and Jerry C. Olson, *Consumer Behavior and Marketing Strategy,* 7th ed. [McGraw-Hill/Irwin, 2005], p. 226.)

6.5 Student Life Insurance Company wants to offer a $1,000 student personal property plan for dorm students to cover theft of certain items. Past experience suggests that the probability of a total loss claim is .01. What premium should be charged if the company wants to make a profit of $25 per policy (assume total loss with no deductible)? Show your calculations clearly.

6.6 A lottery ticket has a grand prize of $28 million. The probability of winning the grand prize is .000000023. Based on the expected value of the lottery ticket, would you pay $1 for a ticket? Show your calculations and reasoning clearly.

6.7 Oxnard Petro Ltd. is buying hurricane insurance for its off-coast oil drilling platform. During the next 5 years, the probability of total loss of only the above-water superstructure ($250 million) is .30, the probability of total loss of the facility ($950 million) is .30, and the probability of no loss is .40. Find the expected loss.

6.2
UNIFORM DISTRIBUTION

Characteristics of the Uniform Distribution

The **uniform distribution** is one of the simplest discrete models. It describes a random variable with a finite number of consecutive integer values from a to b. That is, the entire distribution depends only on the two parameters a and b. Each value is equally likely. Table 6.5 summarizes the characteristics of the uniform discrete distribution.

TABLE 6.5

Uniform Discrete Distribution

Parameters	a = lower limit b = upper limit
PDF	$P(x) = \dfrac{1}{b - a + 1}$
Domain	$X = a, a + 1, a + 2, \ldots, b$
Mean	$\dfrac{a + b}{2}$
Standard deviation	$\sqrt{\dfrac{[(b - a) + 1]^2 - 1}{12}}$
Random data generation in Excel	=a+INT((b-a+1)*RAND( ))
Comments	Used mainly as a benchmark, to generate random integers, or to create other distributions.

EXAMPLE

Rolling a Die

DieRoll

When you roll one die, the number of dots forms a uniform discrete random variable with six equally likely integer values 1, 2, 3, 4, 5, 6, shown in the PDF in Figure 6.7. The CDF is shown in Figure 6.8.

FIGURE 6.7 $P(X = x)$ **for One Die**

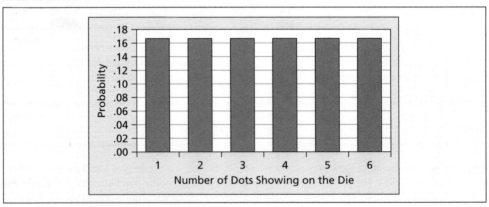

For this example, the mean and standard deviation are:

$$\text{PDF} = P(x) = \frac{1}{b - a + 1} = \frac{1}{6 - 1 + 1} = \frac{1}{6} \quad \text{for } x = 1, 2, \ldots, 6$$

$$\text{Mean} = \frac{a + b}{2} = \frac{1 + 6}{2} = 3.5$$

$$\text{Std. Dev.} = \sqrt{\frac{[(b - a) + 1]^2 - 1}{12}} = \sqrt{\frac{[(6 - 1) + 1]^2 - 1}{12}} = 1.708$$

FIGURE 6.8 $P(X \le x)$ **for One Die**

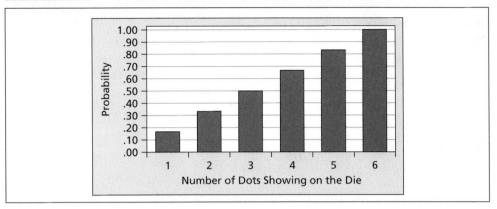

You can see that the mean (3.5) must be halfway between 1 and 6, but there is no way you could anticipate the standard deviation without using a formula. Try rolling a die many times, or use Excel to simulate the rolling of a die by generating random integers from 1 through 6. Compare the mean and standard deviation from your random experiment to the values we calculated above.

Application: Pumping Gas   **Petrol**   The last two digits (pennies) showing on a fill-up will be a uniform random integer (assuming you don't "top off" but just let the pump stop automatically) ranging from $a = 00$ to $b = 99$. Figure 6.9 shows the PDF for this uniform distribution. You could verify the predicted mean and standard deviation shown here by looking at a large sample of fill-ups on your own car:

$$\text{PDF} = P(x) = \frac{1}{b - a + 1} = \frac{1}{99 - 0 + 1} = \frac{1}{100} = .010 \quad \text{for all } x$$

$$\text{Mean} = \frac{a + b}{2} = \frac{0 + 99}{2} = 49.5$$

$$\text{Std. Dev.} = \sqrt{\frac{[(b - a) + 1]^2 - 1}{12}} = \sqrt{\frac{[(99 - 0) + 1]^2 - 1}{12}} = 28.87$$

FIGURE 6.9

Uniform PDF and CDF with $a = 00$ and $b = 99$

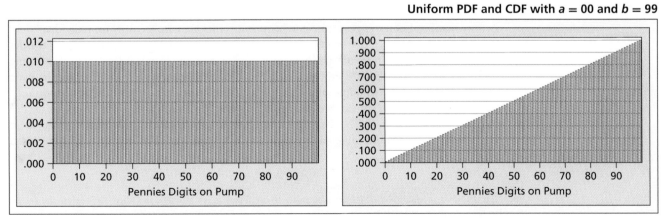

Mini Case 6.1

The "Daily 3" Lottery

Many states have a "daily 3" lottery. The daily 3 is a uniformly distributed discrete random variable whose values range from 000 through 999. There are 1,000 equally likely outcomes, so the probability of any given three-digit number is $1/1,000$. The theoretical characteristics of this lottery are:

$$P(x) = \frac{1}{b - a + 1} = \frac{1}{999 - 0 + 1} = \frac{1}{1,000} = .001$$

$$\mu = \frac{a + b}{2} = \frac{0 + 999}{2} = 499.5$$

$$\sigma = \sqrt{\frac{(b - a + 1)^2 - 1}{12}} = \sqrt{\frac{(999 - 0 + 1)^2 - 1}{12}} = 288.67$$

In a large sample of three-digit lottery numbers, you would expect the sample mean and standard deviation to be very close to 499.5 and 288.67, respectively. For example, in Michigan's daily three-digit lottery, from January 1, 1999, through October 5, 2002, there were 1,180 evening drawings. The mean of all the three-digit numbers drawn over that period was 502.1 with a standard deviation of 287.6. These sample results are extremely close to what would be expected. It is the nature of random samples to vary, so no sample is expected to yield statistics identical with the population parameters.

In Michigan, randomization is achieved by drawing a numbered ping-pong ball from each of three bins. Within each bin, the balls are agitated using air flow. Each bin contains 10 ping-pong balls. Each ball has a single digit (0, 1, 2, 3, 4, 5, 6, 7, 8, 9). The drawing is televised, so there is no possibility of bias or manipulation. Lotteries are studied frequently to make sure that they are truly random, using statistical comparisons like these, as well as tests for overall shape and patterns over time.

Uniform Random Integers   To generate random integers from a discrete uniform distribution we can use the Excel function =a+INT((b-a+1)*RAND( )). For example, to generate a random integer from 5 through 10, the Excel function would be =5+INT((10-5+1)*RAND( )). To create random integers 1 through N, set $a = 1$ and $b = N$ and use the Excel function =1+INT(N*RAND( )). The same integer may come up more than once, so to obtain n distinct random integers you would have to generate a few extras and then eliminate the duplicates. This method is useful in accounting and auditing (e.g., to allow the auditor to choose numbered invoices at random).*

Application: Copier Codes   The finance department at Zymurgy, Inc., has a new digital copier that requires a unique user ID code for each individual user. The department has 37 employees. The department head considered using the last four digits of each employee's social security number, but it was pointed out to her that it is illegal to use the SSN for individual identification (and more than one employee could have the same last four digits). Instead, the department generated unique four-digit uniform random integers from 1000 to 9999 by copying the function =1000+INT(9000*RAND( )) into 50 cells on an Excel spreadsheet. The 50 cells were copied and pasted to two adjacent columns using Paste Special (so the value would not keep changing every time the spreadsheet was updated). The first column was sorted to check for duplicates (none was found). The first 37 random integers in the second (unsorted) column were assigned to the employees in alphabetical order. The remaining 13 copier codes were retained for future employees.

---

*Excel's function =RANDBETWEEN(a,b) is even easier to use, but it is not available in Office 2003 unless the Analysis ToolPak Add-In is installed. If not, go to Tools > Add-In and check the box for Analysis ToolPak.

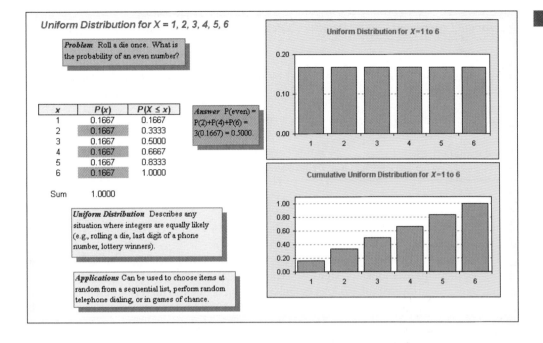

FIGURE 6.10

LearningStats Uniform
Display

Uniform Model in *LearningStats*

Figure 6.10 shows the *uniform distribution* for one die from *LearningStats*. The distribution is visually apparent. The uniform distribution is so simple that you really don't need a spreadsheet. *LearningStats* also has demonstrations of uniform random number generation.

SECTION EXERCISES

connect

6.8   Find the mean and standard deviation of four-digit uniformly distributed lottery numbers (0000 through 9999).

6.9   The ages of Java programmers at SynFlex Corp. range from 20 to 60. (a) If their ages are uniformly distributed, what would be the mean and standard deviation? (b) What is the probability that a randomly selected programmer's age is at least 40? At least 30? *Hint:* Treat employee ages as integers.

6.10   An auditor for a medical insurance company selects a random sample of prescription drug claims for evaluation of correct payment by company experts. The claims were selected at random from a database of 500,000 claims by using uniform random numbers between 1 and 500,000. To verify that the random numbers really were from a uniform distribution, the auditor calculated the mean and standard deviation of the random numbers. What should the mean and standard deviation be if these were uniformly distributed random integers?

6.11   (a) If the birthdays of students born in January are uniformly distributed, what would be their expected mean and standard deviation? (b) Do you think that birthdays in January really are uniformly distributed?

6.12   Use Excel to generate 100 random integers from (a) 1 through 2, inclusive; (b) 1 through 5, inclusive; and (c) 0 through 99, inclusive. (d) In each case, write the Excel formula. (e) In each case, calculate the mean and standard deviation of the sample of 100 integers you generated, and compare them with their theoretical values. *Hint:* Table 6.5 shows the Excel function.

Bernoulli Experiments

6.3

BERNOULLI DISTRIBUTION

A random experiment that has only two outcomes is called a **Bernoulli experiment**, named after Jakob Bernoulli (1654–1705). We arbitrarily call one outcome a "success" (denoted $X = 1$) and the other a "failure" (denoted $X = 0$). The probability of success is denoted π (the Greek letter "pi", *not* to be confused with the mathematical constant 3.14159).* The probability of

---

*Some textbooks denote the probability of success p. However, in this textbook, we prefer to use Greek letters for population parameters. Later, p will be used to denote a sample estimate of π.

TABLE 6.6

Examples of Bernoulli Experiments

Bernoulli Experiment	Possible Outcomes	Probability of "Success"
Flip a coin	1 = heads 0 = tails	$\pi = .50$
Inspect a jet turbine blade	1 = crack found 0 = no crack found	$\pi = .001$
Purchase a tank of gas	1 = pay by credit card 0 = do not pay by credit card	$\pi = .78$
Do a mammogram test	1 = positive test 0 = negative test	$\pi = .0004$

failure is $1 - \pi$, so the probabilities sum to 1, that is, $P(0) + P(1) = (1 - \pi) + \pi = 1$. The probability of success, π, remains the same for each trial.

The examples in Table 6.6 show that a success ($X = 1$) may in fact represent something undesirable. Metallurgists look for signs of metal fatigue. Auditors look for expense voucher errors. Bank loan officers look for loan defaults. A success, then, is merely an event of interest.

The probability of success π can be any value between 0 and 1. In flipping a fair coin, π is .50. But in other applications π could be close to 1 (e.g., the probability that a customer's Visa purchase will be approved) or close to 0 (e.g., the probability that an adult male is HIV positive). Table 6.6 is only intended to suggest the possibilities. The definitions of success and failure are arbitrary and can be switched, although we usually define success as the less likely outcome so that π is less than .5.

The only parameter needed to define a Bernoulli process is π. A Bernoulli experiment has mean π and variance $\pi(1 - \pi)$ as we see from the definitions of $E(X)$ and $V(X)$:

(6.6) $$E(X) = \sum_{i=1}^{2} x_i P(x_i) = (0)(1 - \pi) + (1)(\pi) = \pi \qquad \text{(Bernoulli mean)}$$

$$V(X) = \sum_{i=1}^{2} [x_i - E(X)]^2 P(x_i)$$

(6.7) $$= (0 - \pi)^2(1 - \pi) + (1 - \pi)^2(\pi) = \pi(1 - \pi) \qquad \text{(Bernoulli variance)}$$

A Bernoulli process is a very simplistic probability model. There are many business applications that can be described by the Bernoulli model and it is an important building block for more complex models. We will use the Bernoulli to develop the next model.

SECTION EXERCISES

connect

6.13 Define a Bernoulli variable for (a) guessing on a true-false exam question; (b) checking to see whether an ER patient has health insurance; (c) dialing a talkative friend's cell phone; (d) going on a 10-day diet.

6.14 (a) In the previous exercise, suggest the approximate probability of success in each scenario. (b) Is success a desirable or undesirable thing in each of these scenarios?

6.4

BINOMIAL DISTRIBUTION

VS

Chapter 4

Characteristics of the Binomial Distribution

Bernoulli experiments lead to an important and more interesting model. The **binomial distribution** arises when a Bernoulli experiment is repeated n times. Each Bernoulli trial is independent so that the probability of success π remains constant on each trial. In a binomial experiment, we are interested in $X =$ the number of successes in n trials, so the binomial random variable X is the sum of n independent Bernoulli random variables:

$$X = X_1 + X_2 + \cdots + X_n$$

We can add the n identical Bernoulli means ($\pi + \pi + \cdots + \pi$) to get the binomial mean $n\pi$. Since the n Bernoulli events are independent, we can add the n identical Bernoulli variances

TABLE 6.7

Binomial Distribution

Parameters	n = number of trials
	π = probability of success
PDF	$P(x) = \dfrac{n!}{x!(n-x)!}\pi^{x}(1-\pi)^{n-x}$
Excel function	=BINOMDIST(x, n, π, 0)
Domain	$X = 0, 1, 2, \ldots, n$
Mean	$n\pi$
Standard deviation	$\sqrt{n\pi(1-\pi)}$
Random data generation in Excel	=CRITBINOM(n, π, RAND()) or use Excel's **Tools > Data Analysis**
Comments	Skewed right if $\pi < .50$, skewed left if $\pi > .50$, and symmetric if $\pi = .50$.

$\pi(1-\pi) + \pi(1-\pi) + \cdots + \pi(1-\pi)$ to obtain the binomial variance $n\pi(1-\pi)$ and hence its standard deviation $\sqrt{n\pi(1-\pi)}$. The range of the binomial is $X = 0, 1, 2, \ldots, n$. The binomial probability of a particular number of successes $P(x)$ is determined by the two parameters n and π. The characteristics of the binomial distribution are summarized in Table 6.7. The binomial probability function is shown:

$$P(X = x) = \frac{n!}{x!(n-x)!}\pi^{x}(1-\pi)^{n-x}, \text{ for } X = 0, 1, 2, 3, 4, \ldots, n. \qquad \textbf{(6.8)}$$

EXAMPLE

Servicing Cars at a Quick Oil Change Shop

Consider a shop that specializes in quick oil changes. It is important to this type of business to ensure that a car's service time is not considered "late" by the customer. Therefore, to study this process, we can define service times as being either *late* or *not late* and define the random variable X to be the number of cars that are late out of the total number of cars serviced. We further assume that cars are independent of each other and the chance of a car being late stays the same for each car. Based on our knowledge of the process we know that $P(\text{car is late}) = \pi = .10$.

Now, think of each car as a Bernoulli experiment and let's apply the binomial distribution. Suppose we would like to know the probability that exactly 2 of the next 12 cars serviced are late. In this case, $n = 12$, and we want to know $P(X = 2)$:

$$P(X = 2) = \frac{12!}{2!(12-2)!}(.10)^{2}(1-.10)^{12-2} = .2301$$

Alternatively, we could calculate this by using the Excel function =BINOMDIST(2,12,.1,0). The fourth parameter, 0, means that we want Excel to calculate $P(X = 2)$ rather than $P(X \le 2)$.

Binomial Shape

A binomial distribution is skewed right if $\pi < .50$, skewed left if $\pi > .50$, and symmetric only if $\pi = .50$. However, skewness decreases as n increases, regardless of the value of π, as illustrated in Figure 6.11. Notice that $\pi = .20$ and $\pi = .80$ have the same shape, except reversed from left to right. This is true for any values of π and $1 - \pi$.

Binomial Shape

$\pi < .50$	skewed right
$\pi = .50$	symmetric
$\pi > .50$	skewed left

FIGURE 6.11

Binomial Distributions

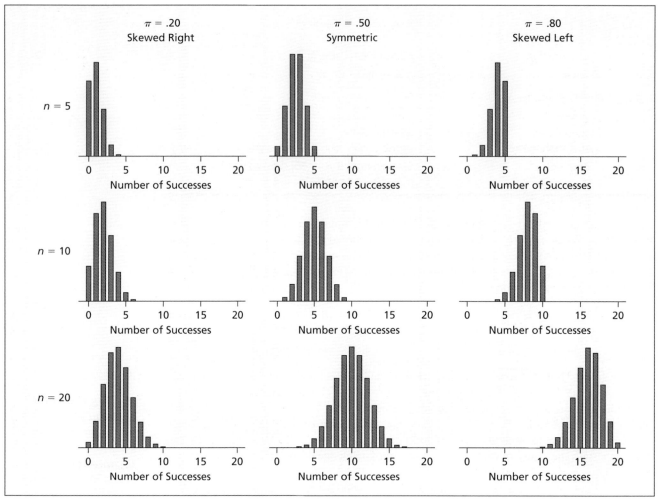

Application: Uninsured Patients   Uninsured   On average, 20 percent of the emergency room patients at Greenwood General Hospital lack health insurance. In a random sample of four patients, what is the probability that two will be uninsured? Define X = number of uninsured patients and set $\pi = .20$ (i.e., a 20 percent chance that a given patient will be uninsured) and $1 - \pi = .80$ (i.e., an 80 percent chance that a patient will be insured). The range is $X = 0, 1, 2, 3, 4$ patients. Applying the binomial formulas, the mean and standard deviation are:

$$\text{Mean} = \mu = n\pi = (4)(.20) = 0.8 \text{ patients}$$

$$\text{Standard deviation} = \sigma = \sqrt{n\pi(1 - \pi)} = \sqrt{(4)(.20)(1 - .20)} = 0.8 \text{ patients}$$

Using the Binomial Formula

The PDF is shown in Table 6.8. We can calculate binomial probabilities by using Excel's binomial formula =BINOMDIST(x, n, π, cumulative) where cumulative is 0 (if you want a PDF) or 1 (if you want a CDF). We can also use a calculator to work it out from the mathematical

TABLE 6.8

Binomial Distribution for
$n = 4$, $\pi = .20$

x	PDF	CDF
0	.4096	.4096
1	.4096	.8192
2	.1536	.9728
3	.0256	.9984
4	.0016	1.0000

formula with $n = 4$ and $\pi = .20$. For example:

PDF Formula   *Excel Function*

$$P(0) = \frac{4!}{0!(4-0)!}(.20)^0(1-.20)^{4-0} = 1 \times .20^0 \times .80^4 = .4096 \qquad \text{=BINOMDIST(0,4,.20,0)}$$

$$P(1) = \frac{4!}{1!(4-1)!}(.20)^1(1-.20)^{4-1} = 4 \times .20^1 \times .80^3 = .4096 \qquad \text{=BINOMDIST(1,4,.20,0)}$$

$$P(2) = \frac{4!}{2!(4-2)!}(.20)^2(1-.20)^{4-2} = 6 \times .20^2 \times .80^2 = .1536 \qquad \text{=BINOMDIST(2,4,.20,0)}$$

$$P(3) = \frac{4!}{3!(4-3)!}(.20)^3(1-.20)^{4-3} = 4 \times .20^3 \times .80^1 = .0256 \qquad \text{=BINOMDIST(3,4,.20,0)}$$

$$P(4) = \frac{4!}{4!(4-4)!}(.20)^4(1-.20)^{4-4} = 1 \times .20^4 \times .80^0 = .0016 \qquad \text{=BINOMDIST(4,4,.20,0)}$$

As for any discrete probability distribution, the probabilities sum to unity. That is, $P(0) + P(1) + P(2) + P(3) + P(4) = .4096 + .4096 + .1536 + .0256 + .0016 = 1.0000$. Figure 6.12 shows the PDF. Since $\pi < .50$, the distribution is right-skewed. The mean $\mu = n\pi = 0.8$ would be the balancing point or fulcrum of the PDF. Figure 6.13 shows the corresponding CDF.

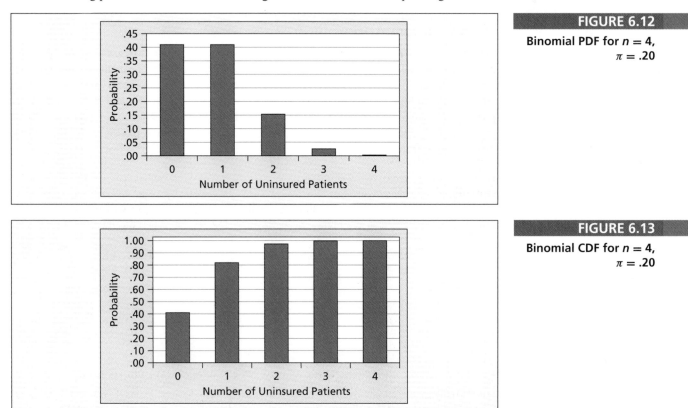

FIGURE 6.12

Binomial PDF for $n = 4$,
$\pi = .20$

FIGURE 6.13

Binomial CDF for $n = 4$,
$\pi = .20$

Compound Events

We can add the individual probabilities to obtain any desired event probability. For example, the probability that the sample of four patients will contain *at least* two uninsured patients is

$$P(X \geq 2) = P(2) + P(3) + P(4) = .1536 + .0256 + .0016 = .1808$$

The probability that *fewer than 2* patients have insurance is

$$P(X < 2) = P(0) + P(1) = .4096 + .4096 = .8192$$

Since $P(X \geq 2)$ and $P(X < 2)$ are complementary events, we could also obtain $P(X < 2)$:

$$P(X < 2) = 1 - P(X \geq 2) = 1 - .1808 = .8192$$

Choose whichever calculation method offers the shortest sum. To interpret phrases such as "more than," "at most," or "at least," it is helpful to sketch a diagram, as illustrated in Figure 6.14.

FIGURE 6.14

Diagrams to Illustrate Events

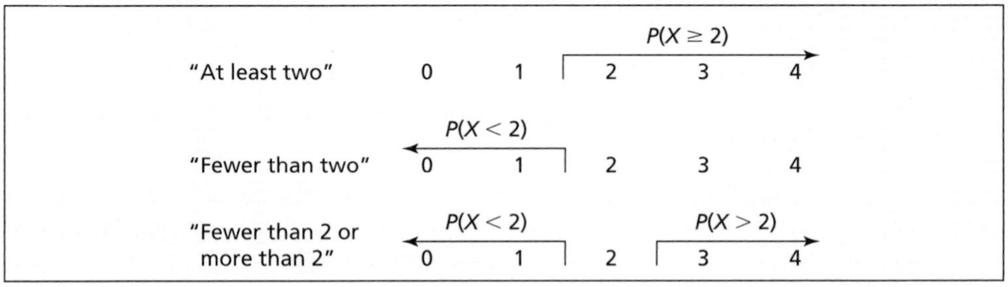

Using Tables: Appendix A

The binomial formula is cumbersome, even for small n, so we prefer to use a computer program (Excel, MINITAB, MegaStat, Visual Statistics, or *LearningStats*) or a calculator with a built-in binomial function. When you have no access to a computer (e.g., taking an exam) you can use Appendix A to look up binomial probabilities for selected values of n and π. An abbreviated portion of Appendix A is shown in Figure 6.15. The probabilities for $n = 4$ and $\pi = .20$ are highlighted. Probabilities in Appendix A are rounded to 4 decimal places so the values may differ slightly from Excel.

FIGURE 6.15

Binomial Probabilities from Appendix A

n	X	.01	.02	.05	.10	.15	.20	.30	.40	.50	.60	.70	.80	.85	.90	.95	.98	.99
2	0	.9801	.9604	.9025	.8100	.7225	.6400	.4900	.3600	.2500	.1600	.0900	.0400	.0225	.0100	.0025	.0004	.0001
	1	.0198	.0392	.0950	.1800	.2550	.3200	.4200	.4800	.5000	.4800	.4200	.3200	.2550	.1800	.0950	.0392	.0198
	2	.0001	.0004	.0025	.0100	.0225	.0400	.0900	.1600	.2500	.3600	.4900	.6400	.7225	.8100	.9025	.9604	.9801
3	0	.9703	.9412	.8574	.7290	.6141	.5120	.3430	.2160	.1250	.0640	.0270	.0080	.0034	.0010	.0001	—	—
	1	.0294	.0576	.1354	.2430	.3251	.3840	.4410	.4320	.3750	.2880	.1890	.0960	.0574	.0270	.0071	.0012	.0003
	2	.0003	.0012	.0071	.0270	.0574	.0960	.1890	.2880	.3750	.4320	.4410	.3840	.3251	.2430	.1354	.0576	.0294
	3	—	—	.0001	.0010	.0034	.0080	.0270	.0640	.1250	.2160	.3430	.5120	.6141	.7290	.8574	.9412	.9703
4	0	.9606	.9224	.8145	.6561	.5220	.4096	.2401	.1296	.0625	.0256	.0081	.0016	.0005	.0001	—	—	—
	1	.0388	.0753	.1715	.2916	.3685	.4096	.4116	.3456	.2500	.1536	.0756	.0256	.0115	.0036	.0005	—	—
	2	.0006	.0023	.0135	.0486	.0975	.1536	.2646	.3456	.3750	.3456	.2646	.1536	.0975	.0486	.0135	.0023	.0006
	3	—	—	.0005	.0036	.0115	.0256	.0756	.1536	.2500	.3456	.4116	.4096	.3685	.2916	.1715	.0753	.0388
	4	—	—	—	.0001	.0005	.0016	.0081	.0256	.0625	.1296	.2401	.4096	.5220	.6561	.8145	.9224	.9606

FIGURE 6.16

Excel's Binomial Function

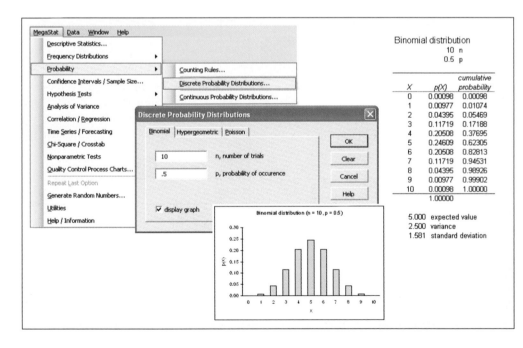

Using Software

Excel   Figure 6.16 shows Excel's Insert > Function menu to calculate the probability of $x = 67$ successes in $n = 1,024$ trials with success probability $\pi = .048$. Alternatively, you could just enter the formula =BINOMDIST(67,1024,0.048,0) in the spreadsheet cell.

MegaStat   MegaStat will compute an entire binomial PDF (not just a single point probability) for any n and π that you specify, as illustrated in Figure 6.17 for $n = 10$, $\pi = .50$. Optionally, you can see a graph of the PDF. This is even easier than entering your own Excel functions.

FIGURE 6.17

MegaStat's Binomial Distribution

Binomial distribution
10 n
0.5 p

X	p(X)	cumulative probability
0	0.00098	0.00098
1	0.00977	0.01074
2	0.04395	0.05469
3	0.11719	0.17188
4	0.20508	0.37695
5	0.24609	0.62305
6	0.20508	0.82813
7	0.11719	0.94531
8	0.04395	0.98926
9	0.00977	0.99902
10	0.00098	1.00000
	1.00000	

5.000 expected value
2.500 variance
1.581 standard deviation

Visual Statistics   Figure 6.18 shows a binomial distribution for $n = 10$, $\pi = .50$ from *Visual Statistics* **Module 4.** Numerical probabilities are shown in a table in the lower left (both PDF and CDF). The graph can be copied and pasted as a bitmap, and the tab-delimited table probabilities can be copied and pasted into Excel. An attractive feature of Visual Statistics is that you can "spin" both n and π and can superimpose a normal curve on your binomial distribution to see if it is bell-shaped.

VS

Chapter 4

FIGURE 6.18

Visual Statistics Binomial Display

Chapter 4

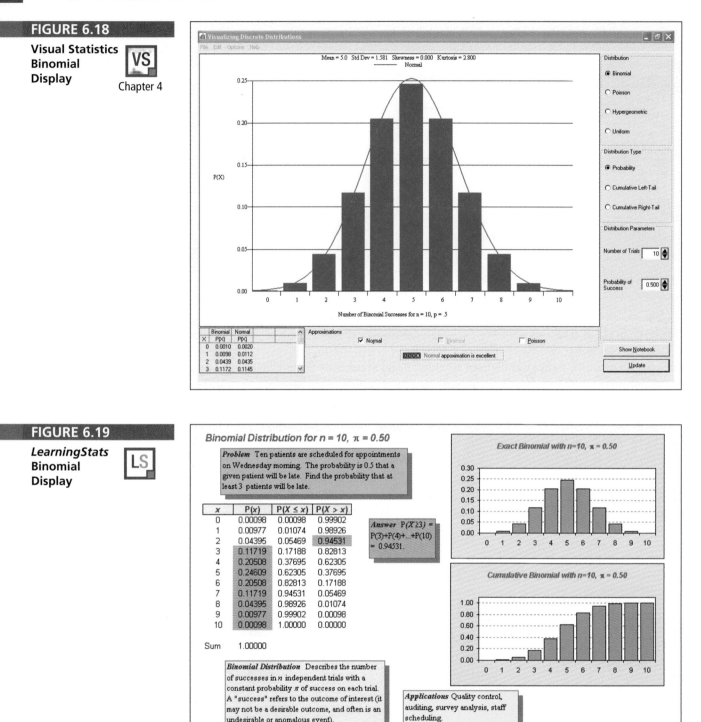

FIGURE 6.19

LearningStats **Binomial Display**

LearningStats   Figure 6.19 shows a *LearningStats* binomial screen using $n = 50$ and $\pi = .095$ with graphs and a table of probabilities. The spin buttons let you vary n and π.

Binomial Random Data   You could generate a single binomial random number by summing n Bernoulli random variables (0 or 1) created with Excel's function =IF(RAND( )<, 0.5, 0). However, that only creates a single random data value and is tedious. Why not rely on Excel's Tools > Data Analysis to generate binomial random data? Figure 6.20 shows how to use the Excel menu to generate 20 binomial random data values using $n = 4$ and $\pi = .20$. A third option is to use the function =CRITBINOM(4, .20, RAND()) to create a binomial random variable value.

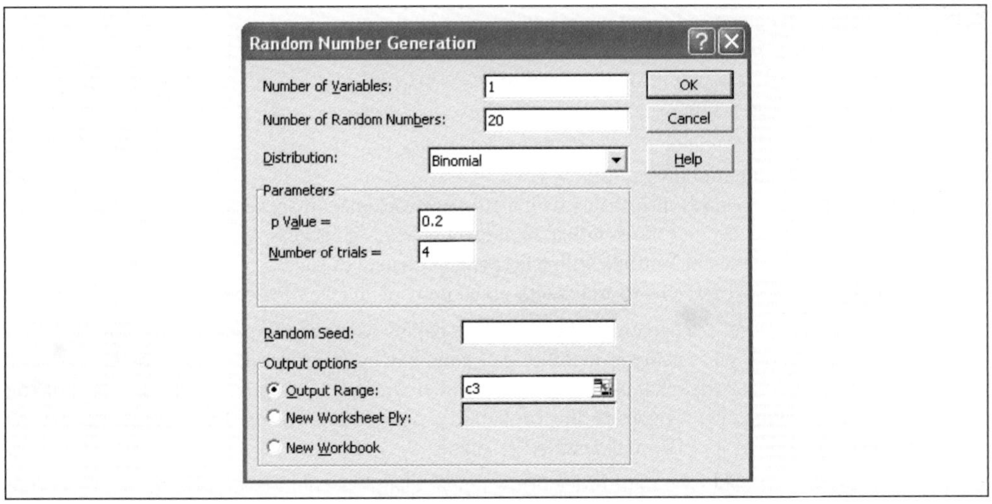

FIGURE 6.20

Excel's Binomial Random Number Menu

Recognizing Binomial Applications

Can you recognize a binomial situation? The binomial distribution has four main characteristics.

- There is a fixed number of trials: n.
- There are only two outcomes for each trial: *success* or *failure*.
- There is a constant probability of success for each trial: π.
- The trials are independent of each other.

Ask yourself if the four characteristics above make sense in the following examples.
In a sample of 20 friends:

- How many are left-handed?
- How many have ever worked on a factory floor?
- How many own a motorcycle?

In a sample of 50 cars in a parking lot:

- How many are parked end-first?
- How many are blue?
- How many have hybrid engines?

In a sample of 10 emergency patients with chest pain:

- How many will be admitted?
- How many will need bypass surgery?
- How many will be uninsured?

Even if you don't know π, you may have a binomial experiment. In practice, the value of π would be estimated from experience, but in this chapter it will be given.

SECTION EXERCISES

connect

6.15 Find the mean and standard deviation for each binomial random variable:
a. $n = 8, \pi = .10$ b. $n = 10, \pi = .40$ c. $n = 12, \pi = .50$
d. $n = 30, \pi = .90$ e. $n = 80, \pi = .70$ f. $n = 20, \pi = .80$

6.16 Calculate each binomial probability:
a. $X = 2, n = 8, \pi = .10$
b. $X = 1, n = 10, \pi = .40$
c. $X = 3, n = 12, \pi = .70$
d. $X = 5, n = 9, \pi = .90$

6.17 Calculate each compound event probability:
a. $X \leq 3$, $n = 8$, $\pi = .20$
b. $X > 7$, $n = 10$, $\pi = .50$
c. $X < 3$, $n = 6$, $\pi = .70$
d. $X \leq 10$, $n = 14$, $\pi = .95$

6.18 Calculate each binomial probability:
a. Fewer than 4 successes in 12 trials with a 10 percent chance of success.
b. At least 3 successes in 7 trials with a 40 percent chance of success.
c. At most 9 successes in 14 trials with a 60 percent chance of success.
d. More than 10 successes in 16 trials with an 80 percent chance of success.

6.19 In the Ardmore Hotel, 20 percent of the customers pay by American Express credit card. (a) Of the next 10 customers, what is the probability that none pay by American Express? (b) At least two? (c) Fewer than three? (d) What is the expected number who pay by American Express? (e) Find the standard deviation. (f) Construct the probability distribution (using Excel or Appendix A). (g) Make a graph of its PDF, and describe its shape.

6.20 Historically, 5 percent of a mail-order firm's repeat charge-account customers have an incorrect current address in the firm's computer database. (a) What is the probability that none of the next 12 repeat customers who call will have an incorrect address? (b) One customer? (c) Two customers? (d) Fewer than three? (e) Construct the probability distribution (using Excel or Appendix A), make a graph of its PDF, and describe its shape.

6.21 At a Noodles & Company restaurant, the probability that a customer will order a nonalcoholic beverage is .38. Use Excel to find the probability that in a sample of 5 customers (a) none of the five will order a nonalcoholic beverage, (b) at least 2 will, (c) fewer than 4 will, (d) all five will order a nonalcoholic beverage.

6.22 J.D. Power and Associates says that 60 percent of car buyers now use the Internet for research and price comparisons. (a) Find the probability that in a sample of 8 car buyers, all 8 will use the Internet; (b) at least 5; (c) more than 4. (d) Find the mean and standard deviation of the probability distribution. (e) Sketch the PDF (using Excel or Appendix A) and describe its appearance (e.g., skewness). (Data are from J. Paul Peter and Jerry C. Olson, *Consumer Behavior and Marketing Strategy,* 7th ed. [McGraw-Hill/Irwin, 2005], p. 188.)

6.5
POISSON DISTRIBUTION

Poisson Processes

Named for the French mathematician Siméon-Denis Poisson (1781–1840), the **Poisson distribution** describes the number of occurrences within a randomly chosen unit of time (e.g., minute, hour) or space (e.g., square foot, linear mile). For the Poisson distribution to apply, the events must occur randomly and independently over a continuum of time or space, as illustrated in Figure 6.21. We will call the continuum "time" since the most common Poisson application is modeling **arrivals** *per unit of time.* Each dot (•) is an occurrence of the event of interest.

FIGURE 6.21

Poisson Events Distributed over Time

One Unit of Time	One Unit of Time	One Unit of Time

Flow of Time ⟶

Let X = the number of events per unit of time. The value of X is a random variable that depends on when the unit of time is observed. Figure 6.21 shows that we could get $X = 3$ or $X = 1$ or $X = 5$ events, depending on where the randomly chosen unit of time happens to fall.

We often call the Poisson distribution the *model of arrivals* (customers, defects, accidents). Arrivals can reasonably be regarded as Poisson events if each event is **independent** (i.e., each event's occurrence has no effect on the probability of other events occurring). Some situations lack this characteristic. For example, computer users know that a power interruption often presages another within seconds or minutes. But, as a practical matter, the Poisson assumptions often are met sufficiently to make it a useful model of reality. For example:

- X = number of customers arriving at a bank ATM in a given minute.
- X = number of file server virus infections at a data center during a 24-hour period.
- X = number of asthma patient arrivals in a given hour at a walk-in clinic.
- X = number of Airbus 330 aircraft engine shutdowns per 100,000 flight hours.
- X = number of blemishes per sheet of white bond paper.

The Poisson model has only one parameter denoted λ (the Greek letter "lambda") representing the *mean number of events per unit of time or space*. The unit of time should be short enough that the mean arrival rate is not large (typically $\lambda < 20$). For this reason, the Poisson distribution is sometimes called the *model of* **rare events**. If the mean is large, we can reformulate the time units to yield a smaller mean. For example, $\lambda = 90$ events per hour is the same as $\lambda = 1.5$ events per minute.

Characteristics of the Poisson Distribution

All characteristics of the Poisson model are determined by its mean λ, as shown in Table 6.9. The constant e (the base of the natural logarithm system) is approximately 2.71828 (to see a more precise value of e, use your calculator's e^x function with $x = 1$). The mean of the Poisson distribution is λ, and its standard deviation is the square root of the mean. The simplicity of the Poisson formulas makes it an attractive model (easier than the binomial, for example). Unlike the binomial, X has no obvious limit, that is, the number of events that can occur in a given unit of time is not bounded. However, Poisson probabilities taper off toward zero as X increases, so the effective range is usually small.

Table 6.10 shows some Poisson PDFs. Going down each column, the probabilities must sum to 1.0000 (except for rounding, since these probabilities are only accurate to four decimals). The Poisson probability function is:

$$P(X = x) = \frac{\lambda^x e^{-\lambda}}{x!}, \text{ for } X = 1, 2, 3, 4, \ldots \tag{6.9}$$

Poisson distributions are always right-skewed (long right tail) but become less skewed and more bell-shaped as λ increases, as illustrated in Figure 6.22.

Chapter 4

TABLE 6.9
Poisson Distribution

Parameters	λ = mean arrivals per unit of time or space
PDF	$P(x) = \frac{\lambda^x e^{-\lambda}}{x!}$
Excel function	=POISSON(X, λ, 0)
Domain	$X = 0, 1, 2, \ldots$ (no obvious upper limit)
Mean	λ
Standard deviation	$\sqrt{\lambda}$
Comments	Always right-skewed, but less so for larger λ.

TABLE 6.10
Poisson Probabilities for Various Values of λ

x	$\lambda = 0.1$	$\lambda = 0.5$	$\lambda = 0.8$	$\lambda = 1.6$	$\lambda = 2.0$
0	.9048	.6065	.4493	.2019	.1353
1	.0905	.3033	.3595	.3230	.2707
2	.0045	.0758	.1438	.2584	.2707
3	.0002	.0126	.0383	.1378	.1804
4	—	.0016	.0077	.0551	.0902
5	—	.0002	.0012	.0176	.0361
6	—	—	.0002	.0047	.0120
7	—	—	—	.0011	.0034
8	—	—	—	.0002	.0009
9	—	—	—	—	.0002
Sum	1.0000	1.0000	1.0000	1.0000	1.0000

Note: Probabilities less than .0001 have been omitted. Columns may not sum to 1 due to rounding.

FIGURE 6.22

Poisson Becomes Less Skewed for Larger λ

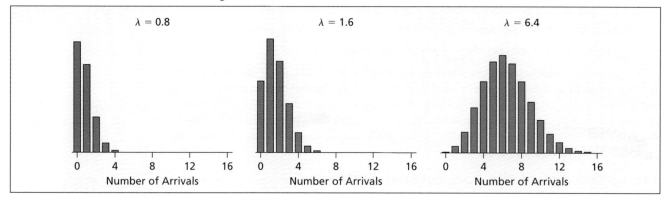

EXAMPLE

Credit Union Customers

CreditUnion

On Thursday morning between 9 A.M. and 10 A.M. customers arrive at a mean rate of 1.7 customers per minute at the Oxnard University Credit Union and enter the queue (if any) for the teller windows. Using the Poisson formulas with $\lambda = 1.7$, the equations for the PDF, mean, and standard deviation are:

$$\text{PDF: } P(x) = \frac{\lambda^x e^{-\lambda}}{x!} = \frac{(1.7)^x e^{-1.7}}{x!}$$

$$\text{Mean: } \lambda = 1.7$$

$$\text{Standard deviation: } \sigma = \sqrt{\lambda} = \sqrt{1.7} = 1.304$$

TABLE 6.11

Probability Distribution for λ = 1.7

x	P(X = x)	P(X ≤ x)
0	.1827	.1827
1	.3106	.4932
2	.2640	.7572
3	.1496	.9068
4	.0636	.9704
5	.0216	.9920
6	.0061	.9981
7	.0015	.9996
8	.0003	.9999
9	.0001	1.0000

Using the Poisson Formula

Table 6.11 shows the probabilities for each value of X. The probabilities for individual X-values can be calculated by inserting $\lambda = 1.7$ into the Poisson PDF or by using Excel's Poisson function =POISSON(x, λ, cumulative) where cumulative is 0 (if you want a PDF) or 1 (if you want a CDF).

PDF Formula   *Excel Function*

$$P(0) = \frac{1.7^0 e^{-1.7}}{0!} = .1827 \qquad \text{=POISSON(0,1.7,0)}$$

$$P(1) = \frac{1.7^1 e^{-1.7}}{1!} = .3106 \qquad \text{=POISSON(1,1.7,0)}$$

$$P(2) = \frac{1.7^2 e^{-1.7}}{2!} = .2640 \qquad \text{=POISSON(2,1.7,0)}$$

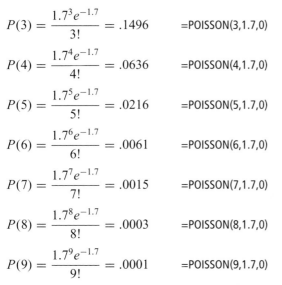

$$P(3) = \frac{1.7^3 e^{-1.7}}{3!} = .1496 \qquad \text{=POISSON(3,1.7,0)}$$

$$P(4) = \frac{1.7^4 e^{-1.7}}{4!} = .0636 \qquad \text{=POISSON(4,1.7,0)}$$

$$P(5) = \frac{1.7^5 e^{-1.7}}{5!} = .0216 \qquad \text{=POISSON(5,1.7,0)}$$

$$P(6) = \frac{1.7^6 e^{-1.7}}{6!} = .0061 \qquad \text{=POISSON(6,1.7,0)}$$

$$P(7) = \frac{1.7^7 e^{-1.7}}{7!} = .0015 \qquad \text{=POISSON(7,1.7,0)}$$

$$P(8) = \frac{1.7^8 e^{-1.7}}{8!} = .0003 \qquad \text{=POISSON(8,1.7,0)}$$

$$P(9) = \frac{1.7^9 e^{-1.7}}{9!} = .0001 \qquad \text{=POISSON(9,1.7,0)}$$

Poisson probabilities must sum to 1 (except due to rounding) as with any discrete probability distribution. Beyond $X = 9$, the probabilities are below .0001. Graphs of the PDF and CDF are shown in Figures 6.23 and 6.24. The most likely event is one arrival (probability .3106, or a

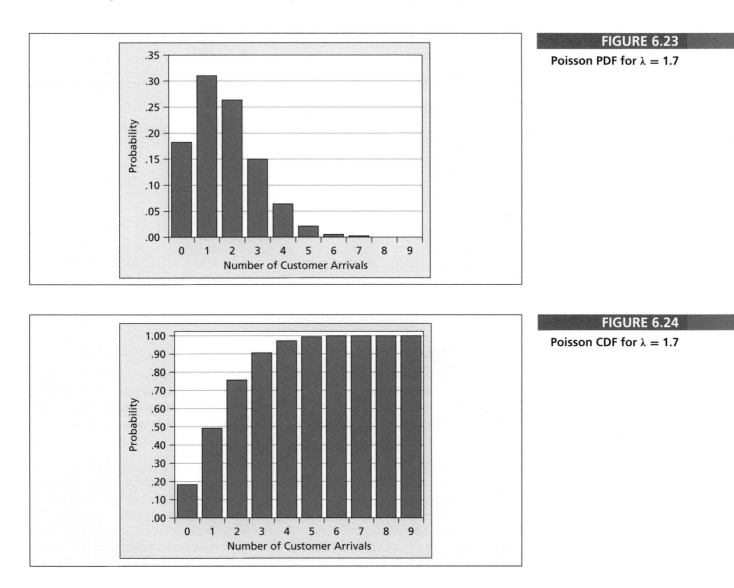

FIGURE 6.23

Poisson PDF for $\lambda = 1.7$

FIGURE 6.24

Poisson CDF for $\lambda = 1.7$

31.1 percent chance), although two arrivals is almost as likely (probability .2640, or a 26.4 percent chance). This PDF would help the credit union schedule its tellers for the Thursday morning work shift.

Compound Events

Cumulative probabilities can be evaluated by summing individual X probabilities. For example, the probability that two or fewer customers will arrive in a given minute is the sum of probabilities for several events:

$$P(X \le 2) = P(0) + P(1) + P(2)$$
$$= .1827 + .3106 + .2640 = .7573$$

We could then calculate the probability of at least three customers (the complementary event):

$$P(X \ge 3) = 1 - P(X \le 2) = 1 - [P(0) + P(1) + P(2)]$$
$$= 1 - [.1827 + .3106 + .2640] = 1 - .7573 = .2427$$

The cumulative probability $P(X \le 2)$ can also be obtained by using the Excel function =POISSON(2,1.7,1).

Using Tables (Appendix B)

Appendix B facilitates Poisson calculations, as illustrated in Figure 6.25 with highlighted probabilities for the terms in the sum for $P(X \ge 3)$. Appendix B doesn't go beyond $\lambda = 20$, partly because the table would become huge, but mainly because we have Excel.

FIGURE 6.25

Poisson Probabilities for $P(X \ge 3)$ from Appendix B

			λ			
X	1.6	1.7	1.8	1.9	2.0	2.1
0	.2019	.1827	.1653	.1496	.1353	.1225
1	.3230	.3106	.2975	.2842	.2707	.2572
2	.2584	.2640	.2678	.2700	.2707	.2700
3	.1378	.1496	.1607	.1710	.1804	.1890
4	.0551	.0636	.0723	.0812	.0902	.0992
5	.0176	.0216	.0260	.0309	.0361	.0417
6	.0047	.0061	.0078	.0098	.0120	.0146
7	.0011	.0015	.0020	.0027	.0034	.0044
8	.0002	.0003	.0005	.0006	.0009	.0011
9	—	.0001	.0001	.0001	.0002	.0003
10	—	—	—	—	—	.0001
11	—	—	—	—	—	—

Using Software

Tables are helpful for taking statistics exams (when you may not have access to Excel). However, tables contain only selected λ values, and in real-world problems, we cannot expect λ always to be a nice round number. Excel's menus are illustrated in Figure 6.26. In this example, Excel calculates =POISSON(11,17,0) as .035544812, which is more accurate than Appendix B.

Visual Statistics   Figure 6.27 shows *Visual Statistics Module 4* using $\lambda = 1.7$. A table of probabilities is in the lower left. You can also display cumulative probabilities from either tail. The Visual Statistics graph can be copied and pasted into a report, and its table probabilities can be copied and pasted into Excel (they are tab-delimited, so they will paste nicely into Excel columns). An advantage of Visual Statistics is that you can "spin" λ and can display a normal overlay. In this example, the Poisson distribution does not resemble a normal because λ is too small.

Chapter 4

FIGURE 6.26

Excel's Poisson Function

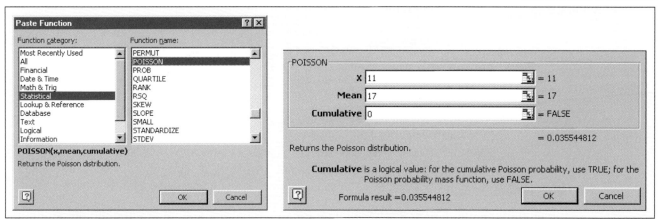

FIGURE 6.27

Visual Statistics Poisson Display

Chapter 4

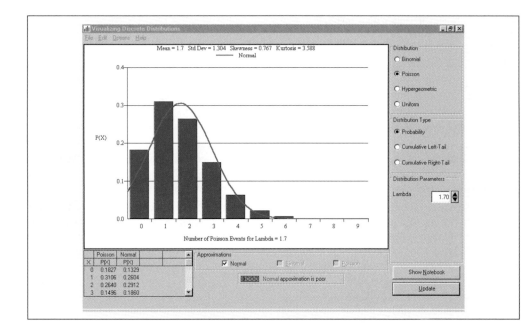

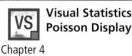

Recognizing Poisson Applications

Can you recognize a Poisson situation? The Poisson distribution has three main characteristics.

- Potentially, there is an unlimited number of arrivals in a fixed time period.
- The arrivals occur randomly.
- The arrivals are independent of each other.

Ask yourself if the three characteristics above make sense in the following examples.

- In the last week, how many credit card applications did you receive by mail?
- In the last week, how many checks did you write?
- In the last week, how many e-mail viruses did your firewall deflect?

It may be a Poisson process, even if you don't know the mean (λ). In business applications, the value of λ would have to be estimated from experience, but in this chapter λ will be given.

SECTION EXERCISES

connect

6.23 Find the mean and standard deviation for each Poisson:
a. $\lambda = 1.0$
b. $\lambda = 2.0$
c. $\lambda = 4.0$
d. $\lambda = 9.0$
e. $\lambda = 12.0$

6.24 Calculate each Poisson probability:
a. $X = 2, \lambda = 0.1$
b. $X = 1, \lambda = 2.2$
c. $X = 3, \lambda = 1.6$
d. $X = 6, \lambda = 4.0$
e. $X = 10, \lambda = 12.0$

6.25 Calculate each compound event probability:
a. $X \leq 3, \lambda = 4.3$
b. $X > 7, \lambda = 5.2$
c. $X < 3, \lambda = 2.7$
d. $X \leq 10, \lambda = 11.0$

6.26 Calculate each Poisson probability:
a. Fewer than 4 arrivals with $\lambda = 5.8$.
b. At least 3 arrivals with $\lambda = 4.8$.
c. At most 9 arrivals with $\lambda = 7.0$.
d. More than 10 arrivals with $\lambda = 8.0$.

6.27 According to J.D. Power and Associates' 2006 Initial Quality Study, consumers reported on average 1.7 problems per vehicle with new 2006 Volkswagens. In a randomly selected new Volkswagen, find the probability of (a) at least one problem; (b) no problems; (c) more than three problems. (d) Construct the probability distribution using Excel or Appendix B, make a graph of its PDF, and describe its shape. (Data are from J.D. Power and Associates 2006 Initial Quality Study[SM].)

6.28 At an outpatient mental health clinic, appointment cancellations occur at a mean rate of 1.5 per day on a typical Wednesday. Let X be the number of cancellations on a particular Wednesday. (a) Justify the use of the Poisson model. (b) What is the probability that no cancellations will occur on a particular Wednesday? (c) One? (d) More than two? (e) Five or more?

6.29 The average number of items (such as a drink or dessert) ordered by a Noodles & Company customer in addition to the meal is 1.4. These items are called *add-ons*. Define X to be the number of add-ons ordered by a randomly selected customer. (a) Justify the use of the Poisson model. (b) What is the probability that a randomly selected customer orders at least 2 add-ons? (c) No add-ons? (d) Construct the probability distribution using Excel or Appendix B, make a graph of its PDF, and describe its shape.

6.30 (a) Why might the number of yawns per minute by students in a warm classroom not be a Poisson event? (b) Give two additional examples of events per unit of time that might violate the assumptions of the Poisson model, and explain why.

Poisson Approximation to Binomial (Optional)

The binomial and Poisson are close cousins. The Poisson distribution may be used to approximate a binomial by setting $\lambda = n\pi$. This approximation is helpful when the binomial calculation is difficult (e.g., when n is large) and when Excel is not available. For example, suppose 1,000 women are screened for a rare type of cancer that has a nationwide incidence of 6 cases per 10,000 (i.e., $\pi = .0006$). What is the probability of finding two or fewer cases? The number of cancer cases would follow a binomial distribution with $n = 1,000$ and $\pi = .0006$. However, the binomial formula would involve awkward factorials. To use a Poisson approximation, we set the Poisson mean (λ) equal to the binomial mean ($n\pi$):

$$\lambda = n\pi = (1000)(.0006) = 0.6$$

To calculate the probability of x successes, we can then use Appendix B or the Poisson PDF $P(x) = \lambda^x e^{-\lambda}/x!$ which is simpler than the binomial PDF $P(x) = \dfrac{n!}{x!(n-x)!}\pi^x(1-\pi)^{n-x}$.

The Poisson approximation of the desired probability is $P(X \leq 2) = P(0) + P(1) + P(2) = .5488 + .3293 + .0988 = .9769$.

Poisson Approximation   *Actual Binomial Probability*

$$P(0) = 0.6^0 e^{-0.6}/0! = .5488$$ $$P(0) = \frac{1000!}{0!(1000-0)!}.0006^0(1-.0006)^{1000-0} = .5487$$

$$P(1) = 0.6^1 e^{-0.6}/1! = .3293$$ $$P(1) = \frac{1000!}{1!(1000-1)!}.0006^1(1-.0006)^{1000-1} = .3294$$

$$P(2) = 0.6^2 e^{-0.6}/2! = .0988$$ $$P(2) = \frac{1000!}{2!(1000-2)!}.0006^2(1-.0006)^{1000-2} = .0988$$

The Poisson calculations are easy and (at least in this example) the Poisson approximation is accurate. The Poisson approximation does a good job in this example, but when is it "good enough" in other situations? The general rule is that n should be "large" and π should be "small." A common rule of thumb says the approximation is adequate if $n \geq 20$ and $\pi \leq .05$.

6.31   An experienced order taker at the L.L. Bean call center has a .003 chance of error on each keystroke (i.e., $\pi = .003$). In 500 keystrokes, find the approximate probability of (a) at least two errors and (b) fewer than four errors. (c) Why not use the binomial? (d) Is the Poisson approximation justified?

6.32   The probability of a manufacturing defect in an aluminum beverage can is .00002. If 100,000 cans are produced, find the approximate probability of (a) at least one defective can and (b) two or more defective cans. (c) Why not use the binomial? (d) Is the Poisson approximation justified? (See *Scientific American* 271, no. 3 [September 1994], pp. 48–53.)

6.33   Three percent of the letters placed in a certain postal drop box have incorrect postage. Suppose 200 letters are mailed. (a) For this binomial, what is the expected number with incorrect postage? (b) For this binomial, what is the standard deviation? (c) What is the approximate probability that at least 10 letters will have incorrect postage? (d) Fewer than five? (e) Why not use the binomial? (f) Is the Poisson approximation justified?

6.34   In a string of 100 Christmas lights, there is a .01 chance that a given bulb will fail within the first year of use (if one bulb fails, it does not affect the others). Find the approximate probability that two or more bulbs will fail within the first year.

6.35   The probability that a passenger's bag will be mishandled on a U.S. airline is .0046. During spring break, suppose that 500 students fly from Minnesota to various southern destinations. (a) What is the expected number of mishandled bags? (b) What is the approximate probability of no mishandled bags? More than two? (c) Would you expect the approximation to be accurate (cite a rule of thumb)? Is the approximation attractive in this case? (See *The New York Times*, November 12, 2006, p. 21.)

CHAPTER SUMMARY

A **random variable** assigns a numerical value to each outcome in the sample space of a **stochastic process**. A **discrete random variable** has a countable number of distinct values. Probabilities in a **discrete probability distribution** must be between zero and one, and must sum to one. The **expected value** is the mean of the distribution, measuring central tendency, and its **variance** is a measure of dispersion. A known distribution is described by its **parameters**, which imply its **probability distribution function** (PDF) and its **cumulative distribution function** (CDF).

As summarized in Table 6.12 the **uniform distribution** has two parameters (a, b) that define its range $a \leq X \leq b$. The **Bernoulli distribution** has one parameter (π, the probability of success) and two outcomes (0 or 1). The **binomial distribution** has two parameters (n, π). It describes the sum of n independent Bernoulli random experiments with constant probability of success. It may be skewed left ($\pi > .50$) or right ($\pi < .50$) or symmetric ($\pi = .50$) but becomes less skewed as n increases. The **Poisson distribution** has one parameter (λ, the mean arrival rate). It describes arrivals of independent events per unit of time or space. It is always right-skewed, becoming less so as λ increases. Unlike the binomial, the Poisson has no obvious upper limit on the number of events. If we set $\lambda = n\pi$, the binomial may be approximated by the Poisson, with greatest accuracy when n is large and π is small, as illustrated in Figure 6.28.

TABLE 6.12   **Comparison of Models**

Model	Parameters	Mean E(X)	Variance V(X)	Characteristics
Bernoulli	π	π	$\pi(1 - \pi)$	Used to generate the binomial.
Binomial	n, π	$n\pi$	$n\pi(1 - \pi)$	Skewed right if $\pi < .50$, left if $\pi > .50$.
Poisson	λ	λ	λ	Always skewed right.
Uniform	a, b	$(a + b)/2$	$[(b - a + 1)^2 - 1]/12$	Always symmetric.

FIGURE 6.28

Relationships among Three Discrete Models

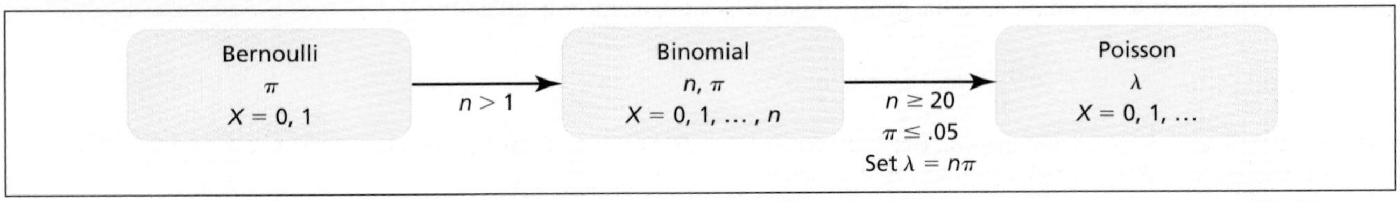

Bernoulli π $X = 0, 1$ → $n > 1$ → Binomial n, π $X = 0, 1, \ldots, n$ → $n \geq 20$ $\pi \leq .05$ Set $\lambda = n\pi$ → Poisson λ $X = 0, 1, \ldots$

KEY TERMS

actuarially fair, *205*
arrivals (Poisson), *220*
Bernoulli experiment, *211*
binomial distribution, *212*
cumulative distribution
   function, *206*
discrete probability
   distribution, *202*

discrete random
   variable, *201*
expected value, *203*
independent, *220*
Poisson distribution, *220*
probability distribution
   function, *206*
probability model, *201*

random variable, *201*
rare events (Poisson), *221*
stochastic process, *201*
uniform distribution, *208*
variance, *205*

Commonly Used Formulas in Discrete Distributions

Total probability: $\displaystyle\sum_{i=1}^{n} P(x_i) = 1$

Expected value: $E(X) = \mu = \displaystyle\sum_{i=1}^{n} x_i P(x_i)$

Variance: $V(X) = \sigma^2 = \displaystyle\sum_{i=1}^{n} [x_i - \mu]^2 P(x_i)$

if there are n distinct values $x_1, x_2, \ldots, x_n$

Uniform PDF: $P(x) = \dfrac{1}{b - a + 1} \qquad X = a, a + 1, \ldots, b$

Binomial PDF: $P(x) = \dfrac{n!}{x!(n - x)!} \pi^x (1 - \pi)^{n-x} \qquad X = 0, 1, 2, \ldots, n$

Poisson PDF: $P(x) = \dfrac{\lambda^x e^{-\lambda}}{x!} \qquad X = 0, 1, 2, \ldots$

CHAPTER REVIEW

1. Define (a) stochastic process; (b) random variable; (c) discrete random variable; and (d) probability distribution.

2. Without using formulas, explain the meaning of (a) expected value of a random variable; (b) actuarial fairness; and (c) variance of a random variable.

3. What is the difference between a PDF and a CDF? Sketch a picture of each.

4. (a) What are the two parameters of a uniform distribution? (b) Why is the uniform distribution the first one considered in this chapter?

5. (a) Describe a Bernoulli experiment and give two examples. (b) What is the connection between a Bernoulli experiment and a binomial distribution?

6. (a) What are the parameters of a binomial distribution? (b) What is the mean of a binomial distribution? The standard deviation? (c) When is a binomial skewed right? Skewed left? Symmetric? (d) Suggest a data-generating situation that might be binomial.

7. (a) What are the parameters of a Poisson distribution? (b) What is the mean of a Poisson distribution? The standard deviation? (c) Is a Poisson ever symmetric? (d) Suggest a data-generating situation that might be Poisson.

8. In the binomial and Poisson models, why is the assumption of independent events important?

9. (a) When are we justified in using the Poisson approximation to the binomial? (b) Why would we want to do this approximation?

CHAPTER EXERCISES

connect

6.36 The probability that a 30-year-old white male will live another year is .99842. What premium would an insurance company charge to break even on a 1-year $1 million term life insurance policy? (Data are from National Center for Health Statistics, *National Vital Statistics Reports* 47, no. 28 [December 13, 1999], p. 8.)

6.37 If a fair die rolled once comes up 6 you win $100. Otherwise, you lose $15. Would a rational person play this game? Justify your answer, using the definition of $E(X)$.

6.38 As a birthday gift, you are mailing a new personal digital assistant (PDA) to your cousin in Toledo. The PDA cost $250. There is a 2 percent chance it will be lost or damaged in the mail. Is it worth $4 to insure the mailing? Explain, using the concept of expected value.

6.39 A large sample of two-digit lottery numbers between 01 and 44 shows a mean of 29.22 and a standard deviation of 18.71. (a) To what extent do these results differ from a uniform distribution? (b) What else would you want to know to decide whether the random number generator was working correctly?

6.40 Use Excel to generate 1,000 random integers in the range 1 through 5. (a) What is the expected mean and standard deviation? (b) What is your sample mean and standard deviation? (c) Is your sample consistent with the uniform model? Discuss. (d) Show the Excel formula you used.

6.41 Consider the Bernoulli model. What would be a typical probability of success (π) for (a) free throw shooting by a good college basketball player? (b) Hits by a good baseball batter? (c) Passes completed by a good college football quarterback? (d) Incorrect answers on a five-part multiple choice exam if you are guessing? (e) Can you suggest reasons why independent events might not be assumed in some of these situations? Explain.

6.42 There is a 14 percent chance that a Noodles & Company customer will order bread with the meal. Use Excel to find the probability that in a sample of 10 customers (a) more than five will order bread; (b) no more than two will; (c) none of the 10 will order bread; (d) Is the distribution skewed left or right?

6.43 In a certain year, on average 10 percent of the vehicles tested for emissions failed the test. Suppose that five vehicles are tested. (a) What is the probability that all pass? (b) All but one pass? (c) Sketch the probability distribution and discuss its shape.

6.44 The probability that an American CEO can transact business in a foreign language is .20. Ten American CEOs are chosen at random. (a) What is the probability that none can transact business in a foreign language? (b) That at least two can? (c) That all 10 can? (d) Sketch the probability distribution and discuss its appearance. (See Lamalie Associates, *The Lamalie Report on Top Executives of the 1990's,* p. 11.)

6.45 In a certain Kentucky Fried Chicken franchise, half of the customers typically request "crispy" instead of "original." (a) What is the probability that none of the next four customers will request "crispy?" (b) At least two? (c) At most two? (d) Construct the probability distribution (Excel or Appendix A), make a graph of its PDF, and describe its shape.

6.46 On average, 40 percent of U.S. beer drinkers order light beer. (a) What is the probability that none of the next eight customers who order beer will order light beer? (b) That one customer will? (c) Two customers? (d) Fewer than three? (e) Construct the probability distribution (Excel or Appendix A), make a graph of its PDF, and describe its shape. (See George E. Belch and Michael A. Belch, *Advertising & Promotion,* 6th ed. [McGraw-Hill, 2004], p. 43.)

6.47 Write the Excel binomial formula for each probability.
a. Three successes in 20 trials with a 30 percent chance of success.
b. Seven successes in 50 trials with a 10 percent chance of success.

c. Six or fewer successes in 80 trials with a 5 percent chance of success.

d. At least 30 successes in 120 trials with a 20 percent chance of success.

6.48   Tired of careless spelling and grammar, a company decides to administer a test to all job applicants. The test consists of 20 sentences. Applicants must state whether each sentence contains any grammar or spelling errors. Half the sentences contain errors. The company requires a score of 14 or more. (a) If an applicant guesses randomly, what is the probability of passing? (b) What minimum score would be required to reduce the probability "passing by guessing" to 5 percent or less?

6.49   The default rate on government-guaranteed student loans at a certain private 4-year institution is 7 percent. The college extends 10 such loans. (a) What is the probability that none of them will default? (b) That at least three will default? (c) What is the expected number of defaults?

6.50   Experience indicates that 8 percent of the pairs of men's trousers dropped off for dry cleaning will have an object in the pocket that should be removed before cleaning. Suppose that 14 pairs of pants are dropped off and the cleaner forgets to check the pockets. What is the probability that none have an object in the pocket?

6.51   A study by the Parents' Television Council showed that 80 percent of movie commercials aired on network television between 8 and 9 P.M. (the prime family viewing hour) were for R-rated films. (a) Find the probability that in 16 commercials during this time slot at least 10 will be for R-rated films. (b) Find the probability of fewer than 8 R-rated films.

6.52   Write the Excel formula for each Poisson probability, using a mean arrival rate of 10 arrivals per hour.
a. Seven arrivals.   b. Three arrivals.   c. Fewer than five arrivals.   d. At least 11 arrivals.

6.53   A small feeder airline knows that the probability is .10 that a reservation holder will not show up for its daily 7:15 A.M. flight into a hub airport. The flight carries 10 passengers. (a) If the flight is fully booked, what is the probability that all those with reservations will show up? (b) If the airline overbooks by selling 11 seats, what is the probability that no one will have to be bumped? (c) That more than one passenger will be bumped? *(d) The airline wants to overbook the flight by enough seats to ensure a 95 percent chance that the flight will be full, even if some passengers may be bumped. How many seats would it sell?

6.54   Although television HDTV converters are tested before they are placed in the installer's truck, the installer knows that 20 percent of them still won't work properly. The driver must install eight converters today in an apartment building. (a) Ten converters are placed in the truck. What is the probability that the driver will have enough working converters? *(b) How many boxes should the driver load to ensure a 95 percent probability of having enough working converters?

6.55   (a) Why might the number of calls received per minute at a fire station not be a Poisson event? (b) Name two other events per unit of time that might violate the assumptions of the Poisson model.

6.56   The U.S. mint, which produces billions of coins annually, has a mean daily defect rate of 5.2 coins. Let X be the number of defective coins produced on a given day. (a) Justify the use of the Poisson model. (b) On a given day, what is the probability of exactly five defective coins? (c) More than 10? (d) Construct the probability distribution (Excel or Appendix B) and make a graph of its PDF. (Data are from *Scientific American* 271, no. 3 [September 1994], pp. 48–53.)

6.57   Lunch customers arrive at a Noodles & Company restaurant at an average rate of 2.8 per minute. Define X to be the number of customers to arrive during a randomly selected minute during the lunch hour and assume X has a Poisson distribution. (a) Calculate the probability that exactly five customers will arrive in a minute during the lunch hour. (b) Calculate the probability that no more than five customers will arrive in a minute. (c) What is the average customer arrival rate for a 5 minute interval? (d) What property of the Poisson distribution did you use to find this arrival rate?

6.58   In the U.K. in a recent year, potentially dangerous commercial aircraft incidents (e.g., near collisions) averaged 1.2 per 100,000 flying hours. Let X be the number of incidents in a 100,000-hour period. (a) Justify the use of the Poisson model. (b) What is the probability of at least one incident? (c) More than three incidents? (d) Construct the probability distribution (Excel or Appendix B) and make a graph of its PDF. (Data are from *Aviation Week and Space Technology* 151, no. 13 [September 27, 1999], p. 17.)

6.59   At an outpatient mental health clinic, appointment cancellations occur at a mean rate of 1.5 per day on a typical Wednesday. Let X be the number of cancellations on a particular Wednesday. (a) Justify the use of the Poisson model. (b) What is the probability that no cancellations will occur on a particular Wednesday? (c) That one will? (d) More than two? (e) Five or more?

6.60   Car security alarms go off at a mean rate of 3.8 per hour in a large Costco parking lot. Find the probability that in an hour there will be (a) no alarms; (b) fewer than four alarms; and (c) more than five alarms.

6.61   In a certain automobile manufacturing paint shop, paint defects on the hood occur at a mean rate of 0.8 defects per square meter. A hood on a certain car has an area of 3 square meters. (a) Justify the use of the Poisson model. (b) If a customer inspects a hood at random, what is the probability that there will be no defects? (c) One defect? (d) Fewer than two defects?

6.62   In the manufacture of gallium arsenide wafers for computer chips, defects average 10 per square centimeter. Let X be the number of defects on a given square centimeter. (a) Justify the use of the Poisson model. (b) What is the probability of fewer than five defects? (c) More than 15 defects? (d) Construct the probability distribution (Excel or Appendix B) and make a graph of its PDF. (Data are from *Scientific American* 266, no. 2 [February 1992], p. 102.)

6.63   A "rogue wave" (one far larger than others surrounding a ship) can be a threat to ocean-going vessels (e.g., naval vessels, container ships, oil tankers). The European Centre for Medium-Range Weather Forecasts issues a warning when such waves are likely. The average for this rare event is estimated to be .0377 rogue waves per hour in the South Atlantic. Find the probability that a ship will encounter at least one rogue wave in a 5-day South Atlantic voyage (120 hours). (See *Science News,* November 18, 2006, pp. 328–329)

6.64   In Northern Yellowstone Lake, earthquakes occur at a mean rate of 1.2 quakes per year. Let X be the number of quakes in a given year. (a) Justify the use of the Poisson model. (b) What is the probability of fewer than three quakes? (c) More than five quakes? (d) Construct the probability distribution (Excel or Appendix B) and make a graph of its PDF. (Data are from *Scientific American* 288, no. 3 [March 2003], p. 33.)

6.65   On New York's Verrazano Narrows bridge, traffic accidents occur at a mean rate of 2.0 crashes per day. Let X be the number of crashes in a given day. (a) Justify the use of the Poisson model. (b) What is the probability of at least one crash? (c) Fewer than five crashes? (d) Construct the probability distribution (Excel or Appendix B), make a graph of its PDF, and describe its shape. (Data are from *New Yorker,* December 2, 2002, p. 64.)

APPROXIMATIONS

6.66   Leaks occur in a pipeline at a mean rate of 1 leak per 1,000 meters. In a 2,500-meter section of pipe, what is the probability of (a) no leaks? (b) Three or more leaks? (c) Sketch the probability distribution. (d) What is the expected number of leaks? (e) Why not use the binomial? (f) Will the approximation be good?

6.67   Among live deliveries, the probability of a twin birth is .02. (a) In 200 live deliveries, how many would be expected to have twin births? (b) What is the probability of no twin births? (c) One twin birth? (d) Calculate these probabilities both with and without an approximation. (e) Is the approximation justified? Discuss fully.

6.68   The probability is .03 that a passenger on American Airlines flight 2458 is a Platinum flyer (50,000 miles per year). If 200 passengers take this flight, use Excel to find the binomial probability of (a) no Platinum flyers. (b) One Platinum flyer. (c) Two Platinum flyers. (d) Calculate the same probabilities using a Poisson approximation. (e) Is the Poisson approximation justified? Explain.

6.69   In 2006, the probability of being "bumped" (voluntarily or involuntarily) on a U.S. airline was .00128. In August, 5,000 accountants traveled from various cities to the annual American Accounting Association meeting in Washington, D.C. (a) What is the expected number of bumped passengers? (b) What is the *approximate* probability of fewer than ten bumped passengers? More than five? (c) Would you expect the approximation likely to be accurate (cite a rule of thumb)? Is the approximation attractive in this case? (See *The Wall Street Journal*, October 10, 2006, p. D4.)

6.70   On average, 2 percent of all persons who are given a breathalyzer test by the State Police pass the test (blood alcohol under .08 percent). Suppose that 500 breathalyzer tests are given. (a) What is the expected number who pass the test? (b) What is the approximate Poisson probability that 5 or fewer will pass the test?

Evans, Merran; Nicholas Hastings; and Brian Peacock. *Statistical Distributions.* 3rd ed. John Wiley & Sons, 2000.   **RELATED READING**

LearningStats Unit 06   Discrete Distribution

LS

LearningStats Unit 06 covers expected value and discrete distributions. Modules are designed for self-study, so you can proceed at your own pace, concentrate on material that is new, and pass quickly over things that you already know. Your instructor may assign specific modules, or you may decide to check them out because the topic sounds interesting.

Topic	LearningStats Modules
Discrete distributions	Distributions: An Overview
	Discrete Distributions
	Discrete Distributions: Examples
	Probability Calculator
	Random Discrete Data
Expected value	Life Insurance
Approximations	Binomial/Poisson Approximation
Equations	Discrete Models: Characteristics
Tables	Table A—Binomial Probabilities
	Table B—Poisson Probabilities
Applications	Hypergeometric Probabilities
	Covariance Explained
	Covariance in Asset Portfolios: A Simulation

Key: = PowerPoint   = Word   = Excel

Visual Statistics

Visual Statistics Modules on Discrete Distributions

Module	Module Name
2	Visualizing a Random Process
4	Visualizing Discrete Distributions

Visual Statistics Modules 2 and 4 (included on your CD) are designed to help you

- Recognize that outcomes of a stochastic process may exhibit regularity even though the process is random.
- Learn through experimentation how changing the parameters can affect the outcomes of an experiment.
- Visualize data-generating situations that give rise to common probability distributions.
- Recognize common discrete distributions and their cumulative distribution functions.
- Identify the parameters of common discrete distributions and how they affect their shape.
- Understand when to apply approximations and learn to assess their accuracy.

The worktext chapter (included on the CD in .PDF format) contains a list of concepts covered, objectives of the module, overview of concepts, illustration of concepts, orientation to module features, learning exercises (basic, intermediate, advanced), learning projects (individual, team), self-evaluation quiz, glossary of terms, and solutions to the self-evaluation quiz.

CHAPTER

7

Continuous Probability Distributions

Chapter Learning Objectives

When you finish this chapter you should be able to

- Distinguish between discrete and continuous random variables.

- State the parameters and uses of the uniform, normal, and exponential distributions.

- Select, in a problem context, the appropriate continuous distribution.

- Sketch uniform, normal, and exponential probability density functions and areas.

- Use a table or spreadsheet to find uniform, normal, or exponential areas for a given X.

- Solve for X for a given area from a uniform, normal, or exponential model.

- Know how and when a normal distribution can approximate a binomial or a Poisson.

I n Chapter 6, you learned about probability models and discrete random variables. We will now expand our discussion of probability models to include models that describe **continuous random variables**. Recall that a discrete random variable usually arises from *counting* something such as the number of customer arrivals in the next minute. In contrast, a continuous random variable usually arises from *measuring* something such as the waiting time until the next customer arrives. Unlike a discrete variable, a continuous random variable can have noninteger (decimal) values.

Probability for a discrete variable is defined at a point such as $P(X = 3)$ or as a sum over a series of points such as $P(X \leq 2) = P(0) + P(1) + P(2)$. But when X is a continuous variable (e.g., waiting time) it does not make sense to speak of probability "at" a particular X value (e.g., $X = 54$ seconds) because the values of X are not a set of discrete points. Rather, probabilities are defined as *areas under a curve* called the *probability density function* (PDF). Probabilities for a continuous random variable are defined on intervals such as $P(53.5 \leq X \leq 54.5)$ or $P(X < 54)$ or $P(X \geq 53)$. Figure 7.1 illustrates the differences between discrete and continuous random variables. This chapter explains how to recognize data-generating situations that produce continuous random variables, how to calculate event probabilities, and how to interpret the results.

Discrete Variable: Defined at Each Point

0 1 2 3 4 5

Continuous Variable: Defined over an Interval

53   53.5   54   54.5   55

FIGURE 7.1

Discrete and Continuous Events

7.1
DESCRIBING A CONTINUOUS DISTRIBUTION

PDFs and CDFs

A probability distribution can be described either by its **probability density function (PDF)** or by its **cumulative distribution function (CDF)**. For a continuous random variable, the PDF is an equation that shows the height of the curve $f(x)$ at each possible value of X. Any continuous PDF must be nonnegative and the area under the entire PDF must be 1. The mean, variance, and shape of the distribution depend on the PDF and its *parameters*. The CDF is denoted $F(x)$ and shows $P(X \leq x)$, the cumulative *area* to the left of a given value of X. The CDF is useful for probabilities, while the PDF reveals the *shape* of the distribution. There are Excel functions for most common PDFs or CDFs.

For example, Figure 7.2 shows a hypothetical PDF for a distribution of freeway speeds. It is a smooth curve showing the probability density at points along the X-axis. The CDF in Figure 7.3 shows the *cumulative* proportion of speeds, gradually approaching 1 as X approaches 90. In this illustration, the distribution is symmetric and bell-shaped (Normal or Gaussian) with a mean of 75 and a standard deviation of 5.

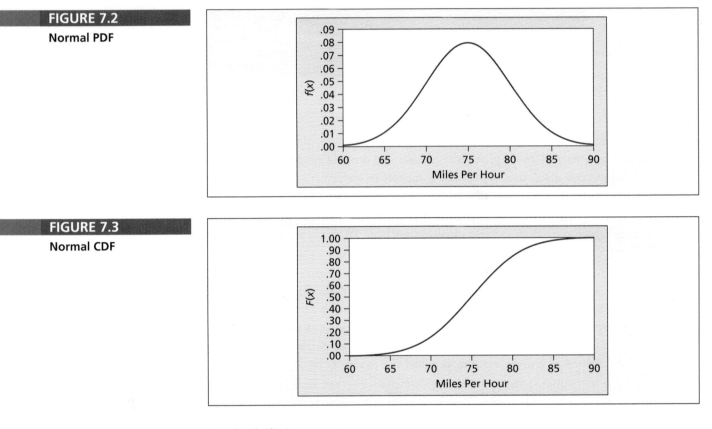

FIGURE 7.2
Normal PDF

FIGURE 7.3
Normal CDF

Probabilities as Areas

With discrete variables, we take sums of probabilities over groups of points. But continuous probability functions are smooth curves, so the area *at* any point would be zero. Instead of taking sums of probabilities, we speak of *areas under curves*. In calculus terms, we would say that $P(a < X < b)$ is the **integral** of the probability density function $f(x)$ over the interval from a to b. Because $P(X = a) = 0$ the expression $P(a < X < b)$ is equal to $P(a \leq X \leq b)$. Figure 7.4 shows the area under a continuous PDF. The entire area under any PDF must be 1.

Expected Value and Variance

The mean and variance of a continuous random variable are analogous to $E(X)$ and $V(X)$ for a discrete random variable, except that the integral sign $\int$ replaces the summation sign Σ. Integrals are taken over all X-values. The mean is still the balancing point or fulcrum for the entire distribution, and the variance is still a measure of dispersion about the mean. The mean is still the average of all X-values weighted by their probabilities, and the variance is still the

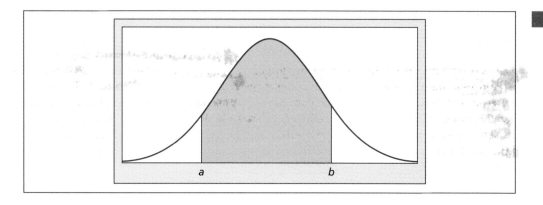

FIGURE 7.4

Probability as an Area

weighted average of all squared deviations around the mean. The standard deviation is still the square root of the variance.

	Continuous Random Variable	*Discrete Random Variable*	
Mean	$E(X) = \mu = \displaystyle\int_{-\infty}^{+\infty} x f(x)\, dx$	$E(X) = \mu = \displaystyle\sum_{\text{all } x} x P(x)$	**(7.1)**
Variance	$V(X) = \sigma^2 = \displaystyle\int_{-\infty}^{+\infty} (x - \mu)^2 f(x)\, dx$	$V(X) = \sigma^2 = \displaystyle\sum_{\text{all } x} [x - \mu]^2 P(x)$	**(7.2)**

Oh My, Calculus?

Calculus notation is used occasionally for the benefit of those who have studied it. But statistics can be taught without calculus, if you are willing to accept that others have worked out the details by using calculus. If you decide to become an actuary, you *will* use calculus (so don't sell your calculus book). However, in this chapter, the means and variances are presented *without* proof for the distributions that you are most likely to see applied to business situations.

7.1 Flight 202 is departing Los Angeles. Is each random variable discrete (D) or continuous (C)?
a. Number of airline passengers traveling with children under age 3.
b. Proportion of passengers traveling without checked luggage.
c. Weight of a randomly chosen passenger on Flight 202.

7.2 It is Saturday morning at Starbucks. Is each random variable discrete (D) or continuous (C)?
a. Temperature of the coffee served to a randomly chosen customer.
b. Number of customers who order only coffee with no food.
c. Waiting time before a randomly chosen customer is handed the order.

7.3 Which of the following could *not* be probability density functions for a continuous random variable? Explain. *Hint:* Find the area under the function $f(x)$.
a. $f(x) = .25$ for $0 \le x \le 1$
b. $f(x) = .25$ for $0 \le x \le 4$
c. $f(x) = x$ for $0 \le x \le 2$

7.4 For a continuous PDF, why can't we sum the probabilities of all x-values to get the total area under the curve?

SECTION EXERCISES

connect

Characteristics of the Uniform Distribution

7.2

UNIFORM CONTINUOUS DISTRIBUTION

The **uniform continuous distribution** is perhaps the simplest model one can imagine. If X is a random variable that is uniformly distributed between a and b, its PDF has constant height, as shown in Figure 7.5. The uniform continuous distribution is sometimes denoted $U(a, b)$ for short. Its mean and standard deviation are shown in Table 7.1.

Since the PDF is rectangular, you can easily verify that the area under the curve is 1 by multiplying its base $(b - a)$ by its height $1/(b - a)$. Its CDF increases linearly to 1, as shown in

FIGURE 7.5

Uniform PDF

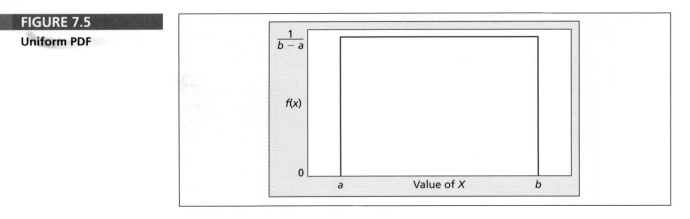

TABLE 7.1

Uniform Continuous Distribution

Parameters	a = lower limit b = upper limit
PDF	$f(x) = \dfrac{1}{b-a}$
CDF	$P(X \le x) = \dfrac{x-a}{b-a}$
Domain	$a \le X \le b$
Mean	$\dfrac{a+b}{2}$
Standard deviation	$\sqrt{\dfrac{(b-a)^2}{12}}$
Shape	Symmetric with no mode.
Random data in Excel	=a+(b−a)*RAND()
Comments	Used as a conservative what-if benchmark.

FIGURE 7.6

Uniform CDF

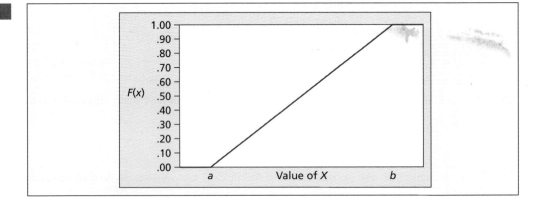

Figure 7.6. Since events can easily be shown as rectangular areas, we rarely need to refer to the CDF, whose formula is just $P(X \le x) = (x - a)/(b - a)$.

The continuous uniform distribution is similar to the discrete uniform distribution if the x values cover a wide range. For example, three-digit lottery numbers ranging from 000 to 999 would closely resemble a continuous uniform with $a = 0$ and $b = 999$.

An oral surgeon injects a painkiller prior to extracting a tooth. Given the varying characteristics of patients, the dentist views the time for anesthesia effectiveness as a uniform random variable that takes between 15 minutes and 30 minutes. In short notation, we could say that X is $U(15, 30)$. Setting $a = 15$ and $b = 30$ we obtain the mean and standard deviation:

$$\mu = \frac{a+b}{2} = \frac{15+30}{2} = 22.5 \text{ minutes}$$

$$\sigma = \sqrt{\frac{(b-a)^2}{12}} = \sqrt{\frac{(30-15)^2}{12}} = 4.33 \text{ minutes}$$

An event probability is simply an interval width expressed as a proportion of the total. Thus, the probability of taking between c and d minutes is

$$P(c < X < d) = (d-c)/(b-a) \qquad \text{(area between } c \text{ and } d \text{ in a uniform model)} \quad \textbf{(7.3)}$$

For example, the probability that the anesthetic takes between 20 and 25 minutes is

$$P(20 < X < 25) = (25 - 20)/(30 - 15) = 5/15 = 0.3333, \text{ or } 33.3\%.$$

This situation is illustrated in Figure 7.7.

EXAMPLE

Anesthesia Effectiveness

FIGURE 7.7   **Uniform Probability *P*(20 < *X* < 25)**

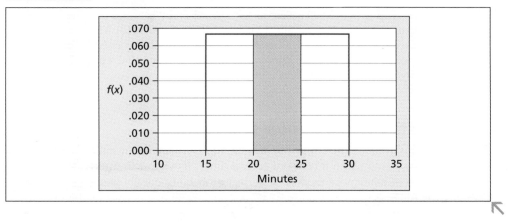

Special Case: Unit Rectangular

The **unit rectangular distribution**, denoted $U(0, 1)$, has limits $a = 0$ and $b = 1$, as shown in Figure 7.8. Using the formulas for the mean and standard deviation, you can easily show that this distribution has $\mu = 0.5$ and $\sigma = 0.2887$. This special case is important because Excel's function =RAND() uses this distribution. If you create random numbers by using =RAND() you know what their mean and standard deviation should be. This important distribution is discussed in more detail in later chapters on simulation and goodness-of-fit tests.

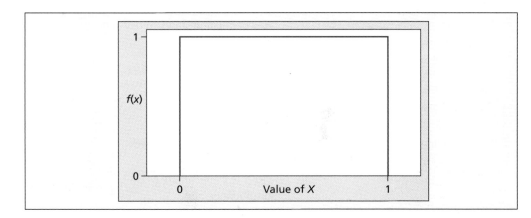

FIGURE 7.8

Unit Rectangular Distribution

Uses of the Uniform Model

The uniform model $U(a, b)$ is used only when you have no reason to imagine that any X values are more likely than others. In reality, this would be a rare situation. However, the uniform distribution can be useful in business for what-if analysis, in situations where you know the "worst" and "best" range, but don't want to make any assumptions about the distribution in between. That may sound like a conservative approach. But bear in mind that if the data-generating situation has any central tendency at all, the assumption of a uniform distribution would lead to a higher standard deviation than might be appropriate. Still, the uniform is often used in business planning, partly because it is easy to understand.

SECTION EXERCISES

connect

7.5   Find the mean and standard deviation for each uniform continuous model.
a. $U(0, 10)$ b. $U(100, 200)$ c. $U(1, 99)$

7.6   Find each uniform continuous probability and sketch a graph showing it as a shaded area.
a. $P(X < 10)$ for $U(0, 50)$
b. $P(X > 500)$ for $U(0, 1{,}000)$
c. $P(25 < X < 45)$ for $U(15, 65)$

7.7   For a continuous uniform distribution, why is $P(25 < X < 45)$ the same as $P(25 \leq X \leq 45)$?

7.8   Assume the weight of a randomly chosen American passenger car is a uniformly distributed random variable ranging from 2,500 pounds to 4,500 pounds. (a) What is the mean weight of a randomly chosen vehicle? (b) The standard deviation? (c) The quartiles? (d) What is the probability that a vehicle will weigh less than 3,000 pounds? (e) More than 4,000 pounds? (f) Between 3,000 and 4,000 pounds? (Data are from *Popular Science* 254–258 [selected issues]. Parameters are based on actual weights of 1997 through 2002 vehicles.)

7.3

NORMAL DISTRIBUTION

VS

Chapter 5

Characteristics of the Normal Distribution

The **normal** or **Gaussian distribution**, named for German mathematician Karl Gauss (1777–1855), has already been mentioned several times. Its importance gives it a major role in our discussion of continuous models. A normal probability distribution is defined by two parameters, μ and σ. It is often denoted $N(\mu, \sigma)$. The domain of a normal random variable is $-\infty < X < +\infty$; however, as a practical matter, $\mu - 3\sigma < X < \mu + 3\sigma$ includes almost all the area (as you know from the Empirical Rule in Chapter 4). Besides μ and σ, the normal probability density function $f(x)$ depends on the constants e (approximately 2.71828) and π (approximately 3.14159). It may be shown that the expected value of a normal random variable is μ and that its variance is σ^2. The normal distribution is always symmetric. Table 7.2 summarizes its main characteristics.

TABLE 7.2

Normal Distribution

Parameters	μ = population mean σ = population standard deviation
PDF	$f(x) = \dfrac{1}{\sigma\sqrt{2\pi}} e^{-\frac{1}{2}\left(\frac{x-\mu}{\sigma}\right)^2}$
Domain	$-\infty < X < +\infty$
Mean	μ
Std. Dev.	σ
Shape	Symmetric and bell-shaped.
Random data in Excel	=NORMINV(RAND(),μ,σ)
Comment	Used as a benchmark to compare other distributions.

The normal probability density function $f(x)$ reaches a maximum at μ and has points of inflection* at $\mu \pm \sigma$ as shown in the left chart in Figure 7.9. Despite its appearance, $f(x)$ does not reach the X-axis beyond $\mu \pm 3\sigma$, but is merely asymptotic to it. Its single peak and symmetry cause some observers to call it "mound-shaped" or "bell-shaped." Its CDF has a "lazy-S" shape, as shown in the right chart in Figure 7.9. It approaches, but never reaches, 1.

FIGURE 7.9

Normal PDF and CDF

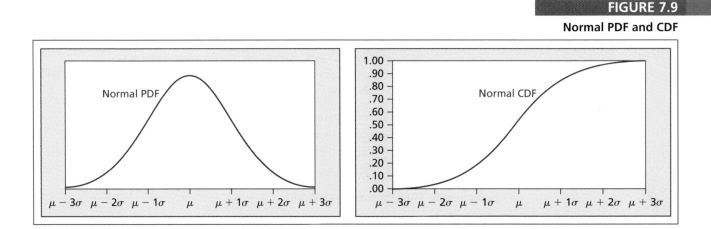

A normal distribution with mean μ and standard deviation σ is sometimes denoted $N(\mu, \sigma)$ for short. All normal distributions have the same shape, differing only in the axis scales. For example, the left chart in Figure 7.10 shows the distribution of diameters of golf balls from a manufacturing process that produces normally distributed diameters with a mean diameter of $\mu = 42.70$ mm and a standard deviation $\sigma = 0.01$ mm, or $N(42.70, 0.01)$ in short notation. The right chart in Figure 7.10 shows the distribution of scores on the CPA theory exam, assumed to be normal with a mean of $\mu = 70$ and a standard deviation $\sigma = 10$, or $N(70, 10)$ in short notation. Although the shape of each PDF is the same, notice that the horizontal and vertical axis scales differ.

FIGURE 7.10

All Normal Distributions Look Alike Except for Scaling

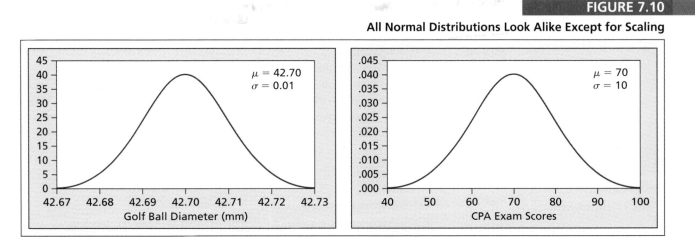

It is a common myth that $f(x)$ must be smaller than 1, but in the left chart in Figure 7.10 you can see that this is not the case. Because the area under the entire curve must be 1, when X has a small range (e.g., the golf ball diameter range is about 0.06 mm), the height of $f(x)$ is large

---

*For those who have studied calculus, $f'(\mu) = 0$ and $f''(\mu \pm \sigma) = 0$.

(about 40 for the golf ball diameters). Conversely, the right chart in Figure 7.10, when X has a large range (e.g., the CPA exam range is about 60 points), the height of $f(x)$ is small (about 0.04 for the exam scores). You could roughly verify that the area under each curve is 1 by treating them as triangles (area = ½ base × height).

What Is Normal?

Many physical measurements in engineering and the sciences resemble normal distributions. Normal random variables can also be found in economic and financial data, behavioral measurement scales, marketing research, and operations analysis. The normal distribution is especially important as a sampling distribution for estimation and hypothesis testing. To be regarded as a candidate for normality, a random variable should:

- Be measured on a continuous scale.
- Possess clear central tendency.
- Have only one peak (unimodal).
- Exhibit tapering tails.
- Be symmetric about the mean (equal tails).

When the range is large, we often treat a discrete variable as continuous. For example, exam scores are discrete (range from 0 to 100) but are often treated as continuous data. Here are some variables that *might* be expected to be approximately normally distributed:

- X = quantity of beverage in a 2-liter bottle of Diet Pepsi.
- X = absentee percent for skilled nursing staff at a large urban hospital on Tuesday.
- X = cockpit noise level in a Boeing 777 at the captain's left ear during cruise.
- X = diameter in millimeters of a manufactured steel ball bearing.

Each of these variables would tend toward a certain mean but would exhibit random variation. For example, even with excellent quality control, not every bottle of a soft drink will have exactly the same fill (even if the variation is only a few milliliters). The mean and standard deviation depend on the nature of the data-generating process. Precision manufacturing can achieve very small σ in relation to μ (e.g., steel ball bearing diameter) while other data-generating situations produce relatively large σ in relation to μ (e.g., your driving fuel mileage). Thus, each normally distributed random variable may have a different coefficient of variation, even though they may share a common shape.

There are statistical tests to see whether a sample came from a normal population. In Chapter 4, for example, you saw that a histogram can be used to assess normality. Visual tests suffice to detect gross departures from normality. More precise tests will be discussed later. For now, our task is to learn more about the normal distribution and its applications.

SECTION EXERCISES

connect

7.9 If all normal distributions have the same shape, how do they differ?

7.10 (a) Where is the maximum of a normal distribution $N(75,5)$? (b) Does $f(x)$ touch the X-axis at $\mu \pm 3\sigma$?

7.11 State the Empirical Rule for a normal distribution (see Chapter 4).

7.12 Discuss why you would or would not expect each of the following variables to be normally distributed. *Hint:* Would you expect a single central mode and tapering tails? Would the distribution be roughly symmetric? Would one tail be longer than the other?
a. Shoe size of adult males.
b. Years of education of 30-year-old employed women.
c. Days from mailing home utility bills to receipt of payment.
d. Time to process insurance claims for residential fire damage.

Characteristics of the Standard Normal

Since there is a different normal distribution for every pair of values of μ and σ, we often transform the variable by subtracting the mean and dividing by the standard deviation to produce a *standardized variable,* just as in Chapter 4, except that now we are talking about a population distribution instead of sample data. This important transformation is shown in formula 7.4.

$$z = \frac{x - \mu}{\sigma}$$ (transformation of each x-value to a z-value)   **(7.4)**

If X is normally distributed $N(\mu, \sigma)$, the standardized variable Z has a **standard normal distribution** with mean 0 and standard deviation 1, denoted $N(0, 1)$. The maximum height of $f(z)$ is at 0 (the mean) and its points of inflection are at ± 1 (the standard deviation). The shape of the distribution is unaffected by the z transformation. Table 7.3 summarizes the main characteristics of the standard normal distribution.

7.4

STANDARD NORMAL DISTRIBUTION

VS

Chapter 5

TABLE 7.3

Standard Normal Distribution

Parameters	μ = population mean σ = population standard deviation
PDF	$f(z) = \dfrac{1}{\sqrt{2\pi}} e^{-z^2/2}$ where $z = \dfrac{x - \mu}{\sigma}$
Domain	$-\infty < Z < +\infty$
Mean	0
Standard deviation	1
Shape	Symmetric and bell-shaped.
Random data in Excel	=NORMSINV(RAND())
Comment	There is no simple formula for a normal CDF, so we need normal tables or Excel to find areas.

Notation

Use an uppercase variable name like Z or X when speaking in general, and a lowercase variable name like z or x to denote a particular value of Z or X.

Since every transformed normal distribution will look the same, we can use a common scale, usually labeled from -3 to $+3$, as shown in Figure 7.11. Since $f(z)$ is a probability density function, the entire area under the curve is 1, as you can approximately verify by treating it

FIGURE 7.11

Standard Normal PDF and CDF

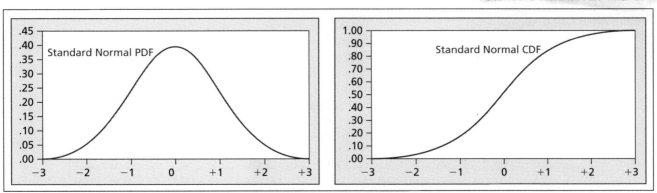

as a triangle (area $=$ ½ base $\times$ height). As a rule, we are not interested in the height of the function $f(z)$ but rather in areas under the curve (although Excel will provide either). The probability of an event $P(z_1 < Z < z_2)$ is a definite integral of $f(z)$. Although there is no simple integral for $f(z)$, a normal area can be approximated to any desired degree of accuracy using various methods (e.g., covering the area from 0 to $f(z)$ with many narrow rectangles and summing their areas). You do not need to worry about this, because tables or Excel functions are available.

Normal Areas from Appendix C-1

Tables of normal probabilities have been prepared so you can look up any desired normal area. Such tables have many forms. Table 7.4 illustrates Appendix C-1 which shows areas from 0 to z using increments of 0.01 from $Z = 0$ to $Z = 3.79$ (beyond this range, areas are very small). For example, to calculate $P(0 < Z < 1.96)$, you select the row for $z = 1.9$ and the column for 0.06 (since $1.96 = 1.90 + 0.06$). This row and column are shaded in Table 7.4. At the intersection of the shaded row and column, we see $P(0 < Z < 1.96) = .4750$. This area is illustrated in Figure 7.12. Since half the area lies to the right of the mean, we can find a right-tail area by subtraction. For example, $P(Z > 1.96) = .5000 - P(0 < Z < 1.96) = .5000 - .4750 = .0250$ as illustrated in Figure 7.12.

TABLE 7.4

Normal Area from 0 to z (from Appendix C-1)

z	0.00	0.01	0.02	0.03	0.04	0.05	0.06	0.07	0.08	0.09
0.0	.0000	.0040	.0080	.0120	.0160	.0199	.0239	.0279	.0319	.0359
0.1	.0398	.0438	.0478	.0517	.0557	.0596	.0636	.0675	.0714	.0753
0.2	.0793	.0832	.0871	.0910	.0948	.0987	.1026	.1064	.1103	.1141
⋮	⋮	⋮	⋮	⋮	⋮	⋮	⋮	⋮	⋮	⋮
1.6	.4452	.4463	.4474	.4484	.4495	.4505	.4515	.4525	.4535	.4545
1.7	.4554	.4564	.4573	.4582	.4591	.4599	.4608	.4616	.4625	.4633
1.8	.4641	.4649	.4656	.4664	.4671	.4678	.4686	.4693	.4699	.4706
1.9	.4713	.4719	.4726	.4732	.4738	.4744	.4750	.4756	.4761	.4767
2.0	.4772	.4778	.4783	.4788	.4793	.4798	.4803	.4808	.4812	.4817
2.1	.4821	.4826	.4830	.4834	.4838	.4842	.4846	.4850	.4854	.4857
2.2	.4861	.4864	.4868	.4871	.4875	.4878	.4881	.4884	.4887	.4890
2.3	.4893	.4896	.4898	.4901	.4904	.4906	.4909	.4911	.4913	.4916
⋮	⋮	⋮	⋮	⋮	⋮	⋮	⋮	⋮	⋮	⋮
3.6	.49984	.49985	.49985	.49986	.49986	.49987	.49987	.49988	.49988	.49989
3.7	.49989	.49990	.49990	.49990	.49991	.49991	.49992	.49992	.49992	.49992

FIGURE 7.12

Finding Areas Using Appendix C-1

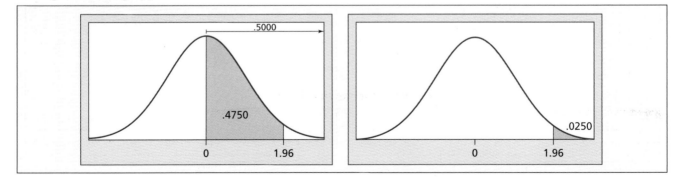

Suppose we want a middle area such as $P(-1.96 < Z < +1.96)$. Because the normal distribution is symmetric, we also know that $P(-1.96 < Z < 0) = .4750$. Adding these areas, we get

$$P(-1.96 < Z < +1.96) = P(-1.96 < Z < 0) + P(0 < Z < 1.96)$$
$$= .4750 + .4750 = .9500$$

So the interval $-1.96 < Z < 1.96$ encloses 95 percent of the area under the normal curve. Figure 7.13 illustrates this calculation. Since a point has no area in a continuous distribution, the probability $P(-1.96 \le Z \le +1.96)$ is the same as $P(-1.96 < Z < +1.96)$, so, for simplicity, we omit the equality.

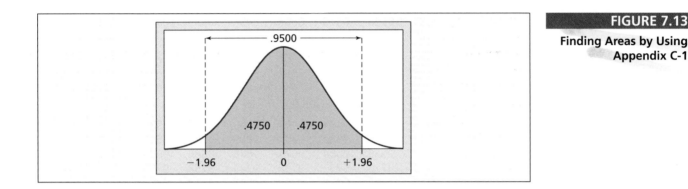

FIGURE 7.13

Finding Areas by Using Appendix C-1

Basis for the Empirical Rule

From Appendix C-1 we can see the basis for the Empirical Rule, illustrated in Figure 7.14. These are the "k-sigma" intervals mentioned in Chapter 4 and used by statisticians for quick reference to the normal distribution. Thus, it is *approximately* correct to say that a "2-sigma interval" contains 95 percent of the area (actually $z = 1.96$ would yield a 95 percent area):

$$P(-1.00 < Z < +1.00) = 2 \times P(0 < Z < 1.00) = 2 \times .3413 = .6826, \text{ or } 68.26\%$$

$$P(-2.00 < Z < +2.00) = 2 \times P(0 < Z < 2.00) = 2 \times .4772 = .9544, \text{ or } 95.44\%$$

$$P(-3.00 < Z < +3.00) = 2 \times P(0 < Z < 3.00) = 2 \times .49865 = .9973, \text{ or } 99.73\%$$

FIGURE 7.14

Normal Areas within $\mu \pm k\sigma$

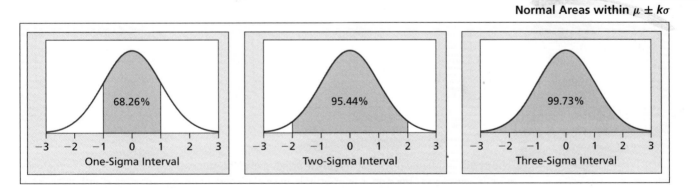

Normal Areas from Appendix C-2

Table 7.5 illustrates another kind of table. Appendix C-2 shows cumulative normal areas from the left to z. This second table corresponds to the way Excel calculates normal areas. Using this approach, we see that $P(Z < -1.96) = .0250$ and $P(Z < +1.96) = .9750$. By subtraction, we get

$$P(-1.96 < Z < +1.96) = P(Z < +1.96) - P(Z < -1.96) = .9750 - .0250 = .9500$$

TABLE 7.5

Cumulative Normal Area from Left to z (from Appendix C-2)

z	0.00	0.01	0.02	0.03	0.04	0.05	0.06	0.07	0.08	0.09
−3.7	.00011	.00010	.00010	.00010	.00009	.00009	.00008	.00008	.00008	.00008
−3.6	.00016	.00015	.00015	.00014	.00014	.00013	.00013	.00012	.00012	.00011
⋮	⋮	⋮	⋮	⋮	⋮	⋮	⋮	⋮	⋮	⋮
−2.3	.0107	.0104	.0102	.0099	.0096	.0094	.0091	.0089	.0087	.0084
−2.2	.0139	.0136	.0132	.0129	.0125	.0122	.0119	.0116	.0113	.0110
−2.1	.0179	.0174	.0170	.0166	.0162	.0158	.0154	.0150	.0146	.0143
−2.0	.0228	.0222	.0217	.0212	.0207	.0202	.0197	.0192	.0188	.0183
−1.9	.0287	.0281	.0274	.0268	.0262	.0256	.0250	.0244	.0239	.0233
−1.8	.0359	.0351	.0344	.0336	.0329	.0322	.0314	.0307	.0301	.0294
−1.7	.0446	.0436	.0427	.0418	.0409	.0401	.0392	.0384	.0375	.0367
−1.6	.0548	.0537	.0526	.0516	.0505	.0495	.0485	.0475	.0465	.0455
⋮	⋮	⋮	⋮	⋮	⋮	⋮	⋮	⋮	⋮	⋮
0.0	.5000	.5040	.5080	.5120	.5160	.5199	.5239	.5279	.5319	.5359
0.1	.5398	.5438	.5478	.5517	.5557	.5596	.5636	.5675	.5714	.5753
0.2	.5793	.5832	.5871	.5910	.5948	.5987	.6026	.6064	.6103	.6141
⋮	⋮	⋮	⋮	⋮	⋮	⋮	⋮	⋮	⋮	⋮
1.6	.9452	.9463	.9474	.9484	.9495	.9505	.9515	.9525	.9535	.9545
1.7	.9554	.9564	.9573	.9582	.9591	.9599	.9608	.9616	.9625	.9633
1.8	.9641	.9649	.9656	.9664	.9671	.9678	.9686	.9693	.9699	.9706
1.9	.9713	.9719	.9726	.9732	.9738	.9744	.9750	.9756	.9761	.9767
2.0	.9772	.9778	.9783	.9788	.9793	.9798	.9803	.9808	.9812	.9817
2.1	.9821	.9826	.9830	.9834	.9838	.9842	.9846	.9850	.9854	.9857
2.2	.9861	.9864	.9868	.9871	.9875	.9878	.9881	.9884	.9887	.9890
2.3	.9893	.9896	.9898	.9901	.9904	.9906	.9909	.9911	.9913	.9916
⋮	⋮	⋮	⋮	⋮	⋮	⋮	⋮	⋮	⋮	⋮
3.6	.99984	.99985	.99985	.99986	.99986	.99987	.99987	.99988	.99988	.99989
3.7	.99989	.99990	.99990	.99990	.99991	.99991	.99992	.99992	.99992	.99992

FIGURE 7.15

Finding Areas by Using Appendix C-2

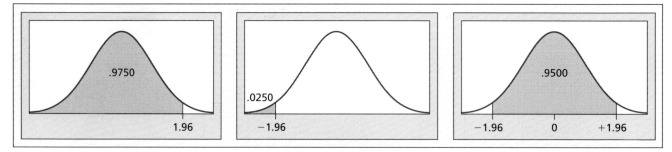

The result is identical to that obtained previously. The interval −1.96 < Z < 1.96 encloses 95 percent of the area under the normal curve. This calculation is illustrated in Figure 7.15.

Since Appendix C-1 and Appendix C-2 yield identical results, you should use whichever table is easier for the area you are trying to find. Appendix C-1 is often easier for "middle areas." It also has the advantage of being more compact (it fits on one page) which is one reason why it has traditionally been used for statistics exams and in other textbooks (e.g., marketing). But Appendix C-2 is easier for left-tail areas and some complex areas. Further, Appendix C-2 corresponds to the way Excel calculates normal areas. When subtraction is required for a right-tail or middle area, either table is equally convenient.

Note: Use Appendix C-1 or C-2 for these exercises.

7.13 Find the standard normal area for each of the following, showing your reasoning clearly and indicating which table you used.
a. $P(0 < Z < 0.50)$ b. $P(-0.50 < Z < 0)$ c. $P(Z > 0)$ d. $P(Z = 0)$

7.14 Find the standard normal area for each of the following, showing your reasoning clearly and indicating which table you used.
a. $P(1.22 < Z < 2.15)$ b. $P(2.00 < Z < 3.00)$ c. $P(-2.00 < Z < 2.00)$ d. $P(Z > 0.50)$

7.15 Find the standard normal area for each of the following, showing your reasoning clearly and indicating which table you used.
a. $P(-1.22 < Z < 2.15)$ b. $P(-3.00 < Z < 2.00)$ c. $P(Z < 2.00)$ d. $P(Z = 0)$

7.16 Daily output of Marathon's Garyville, Lousiana, refinery is normally distributed with a mean of 232,000 barrels of crude oil per day with a standard deviation of 7,000 barrels. (a) What is the probability of producing at least 232,000 barrels? (b) Between 232,000 and 239,000 barrels? (c) Less than 239,000 barrels? (d) Less than 245,000 barrels? (e) More than 225,000 barrels?

7.17 Assume that the number of calories in a McDonald's Egg McMuffin is a normally distributed random variable with a mean of 290 calories and a standard deviation of 14 calories. (a) What is the probability that a particular serving contains fewer than 300 calories? (b) More than 250 calories? (c) Between 275 and 310 calories? Show all work clearly. (Data are from McDonalds.com)

7.18 The weight of a miniature Tootsie Roll is normally distributed with a mean of 3.30 grams and standard deviation of 0.13 grams. (a) Within what weight range will the middle 95 percent of all miniature Tootsie Rolls fall? (b) What is the probability that a randomly chosen miniature Tootsie Roll will weigh more than 3.50 grams? (Data are from a project by MBA student Henry Scussel.)

7.19 The pediatrics unit at Carver Hospital has 24 beds. The number of patients needing a bed at any point in time is $N(19.2, 2.5)$. What is the probability that the number of patients needing a bed will exceed the pediatric unit's bed capacity?

7.20 The cabin of the Hawker 850XP business jet has a cabin height 5 feet 9 inches high. If height is $N(5'10", 2.7")$, what percentage of the business travelers will have to stoop? (See *Flying* 133, no. 11, 2006, p. 83.)

Finding *z* for a Given Area

We can also use the tables to find the *z*-value that corresponds to a given area. For example, what *z*-value defines the top 1 percent of a normal distribution? Since half the area lies above the mean, an upper area of 1 percent implies that 49 percent of the area must lie between 0 and *z*. Searching Appendix C-1 for an area of .4900 we see that $z = 2.33$ yields an area of .4901. Without interpolation, that is as close as we can get to 49 percent. This is illustrated in Table 7.6 and Figure 7.16.

TABLE 7.6

Normal Area from 0 to *z* (from Appendix C-1)

z	0.00	0.01	0.02	0.03	0.04	0.05	0.06	0.07	0.08	0.09
0.0	.0000	.0040	.0080	.0120	.0160	.0199	.0239	.0279	.0319	.0359
0.1	.0398	.0438	.0478	.0517	.0557	.0596	.0636	.0675	.0714	.0753
0.2	.0793	.0832	.0871	.0910	.0948	.0987	.1026	.1064	.1103	.1141
⋮	⋮	⋮	⋮	⋮	⋮	⋮	⋮	⋮	⋮	⋮
1.6	.4452	.4463	.4474	.4484	.4495	.4505	.4515	.4525	.4535	.4545
1.7	.4554	.4564	.4573	.4582	.4591	.4599	.4608	.4616	.4625	.4633
1.8	.4641	.4649	.4656	.4664	.4671	.4678	.4686	.4693	.4699	.4706
1.9	.4713	.4719	.4726	.4732	.4738	.4744	.4750	.4756	.4761	.4767
2.0	.4772	.4778	.4783	.4788	.4793	.4798	.4803	.4808	.4812	.4817
2.1	.4821	.4826	.4830	.4834	.4838	.4842	.4846	.4850	.4854	.4857
2.2	.4861	.4864	.4868	.4871	.4875	.4878	.4881	.4884	.4887	.4890
2.3	.4893	.4896	.4898	.4901	.4904	.4906	.4909	.4911	.4913	.4916
⋮	⋮	⋮	⋮	⋮	⋮	⋮	⋮	⋮	⋮	⋮
3.6	.49984	.49985	.49985	.49986	.49986	.49987	.49987	.49988	.49988	.49989
3.7	.49989	.49990	.49990	.49990	.49991	.49991	.49992	.49992	.49992	.49992

FIGURE 7.16

Finding Areas by Using Appendix C-1

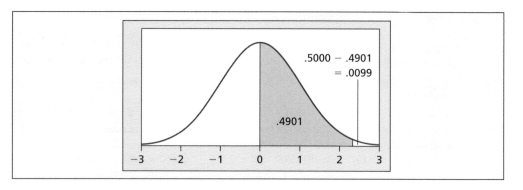

We can find other important areas in the same way. Since we are often interested in the top 25 percent, 10 percent, 5 percent, 1 percent, etc., or the middle 50 percent, 90 percent, 95 percent, 99 percent, etc., it is convenient to record these important z-values for quick reference. Table 7.7 summarizes some important normal areas. For greater accuracy, these z-values are shown to three decimals (they were obtained from Excel).

TABLE 7.7

Some Important Normal Areas

Upper Tail Areas		Middle Areas	
z	Upper Tail Area	Z Range	Middle Area
0.675	0.25, or 25%	$-0.675 < Z < 0.675$	0.50, or 50%
1.282	0.10, or 10%	$-1.282 < Z < 1.282$	0.80, or 80%
1.645	0.05, or 5%	$-1.645 < Z < 1.645$	0.90, or 90%
1.960	0.025, or 2.5%	$-1.960 < Z < 1.960$	0.95, or 95%
2.326	0.01, or 1%	$-2.326 < Z < 2.326$	0.98, or 98%
2.576	0.005, or 0.5%	$-2.576 < Z < 2.576$	0.99, or 99%

SECTION EXERCISES

connect

7.21 The time required to verify and fill a common prescription at a neighborhood pharmacy is normally distributed with a mean of 10 minutes and a standard deviation of 3 minutes. Find the time for each event. Show your work.
a. Highest 10 percent
b. Highest 50 percent
c. Highest 5 percent
d. Highest 80 percent
e. Lowest 10 percent
f. Middle 50 percent
g. Lowest 93 percent
h. Middle 95 percent
i. Lowest 7 percent

7.22 The weight of a small Starbucks coffee is a normally distributed random variable with a mean of 360 grams and a standard deviation of 9 grams. Find the weight that corresponds to each event. Show your work.
a. Highest 10 percent
b. Highest 50 percent
c. Highest 5 percent
d. Highest 80 percent
e. Lowest 10 percent
f. Middle 50 percent
g. Lowest 90 percent
h. Middle 95 percent
i. Highest 4 percent

7.23 The weight of newborn babies in Foxboro Hospital is normally distributed with a mean of 6.9 pounds and a standard deviation of 1.2 pounds. (a) How unusual is a baby weighing 8.0 pounds or more? (b) What would be the 90th percentile for birth weight? (c) Within what range would the middle 95 percent of birth weights lie?

7.24 The credit score of a 35 year old applying for a mortgage at Ulysses Mortgage Associates is normally distributed with a mean of 600 and a standard deviation of 100. (a) Find the credit score that defines the upper 5 percent. (b) Seventy-five percent of the customers will have a credit score higher than what value? (c) Within what range would the middle 80 percent of credit scores lie?

7.25 The number of patients needing a bed at any point in time in the pediatrics unit at Carver Hospital is $N(19.2, 2.5)$. Find the middle 50 percent of the number of beds needed (round to the next higher integer since a "bed" is indivisible).

7.26 High-strength concrete is supposed to have a compressive strength greater than 6,000 pounds per square inch (psi). A certain type of concrete has a mean compressive strength of 7,000 psi, but due to variability in the mixing process it has a standard deviation of 420 psi, assuming a normal distribution. What is the probability that a given pour of concrete from this mixture will fail to meet the high-strength criterion? In your judgment, does this mixture provide an adequate margin of safety?

Finding Normal Areas with Excel

Table 7.8 and Figure 7.17 show four Excel functions that provide normal areas or *z*-values. Excel is more accurate than a table; however, you still have to be careful of syntax. It is a good idea to *visualize* the answer you expect, so that you will recognize if you are getting the wrong answer from Excel.

TABLE 7.8

Four Excel Functions for Normal Areas

Syntax of Function	Example	What It Does
=NORMDIST(x,μ,σ,cumulative)	=NORMDIST(80,70,10,1) = 0.84134475	Area to the left of *x* for given μ and σ. Here, 84.13% of the CPA exam-takers score 80 or less if $\mu = 70$ and $\sigma = 10$.
=NORMINV(area,μ,σ)	=NORMINV(0.99,70,10) = 93.2634699	Value of *x* corresponding to a given left-tail area. Here, the 99th percentile for CPA exam-takers is a score of 93.26 or 93 to nearest integer.
=NORMSDIST(*z*)	=NORMSDIST(1.96) = 0.975002175	Area to the left of *z* in a standard normal. Here, we see that 97.50% of the area is to the left of $z = 1.96$.
=NORMSINV(area)	=NORMSINV(0.75) = 0.674489526	Value of *z* corresponding to a given left-tail area. Here, the 75th percentile (third quartile) of a standard normal is at $z = 0.675$.

FIGURE 7.17

Four Useful Normal Functions in Excel

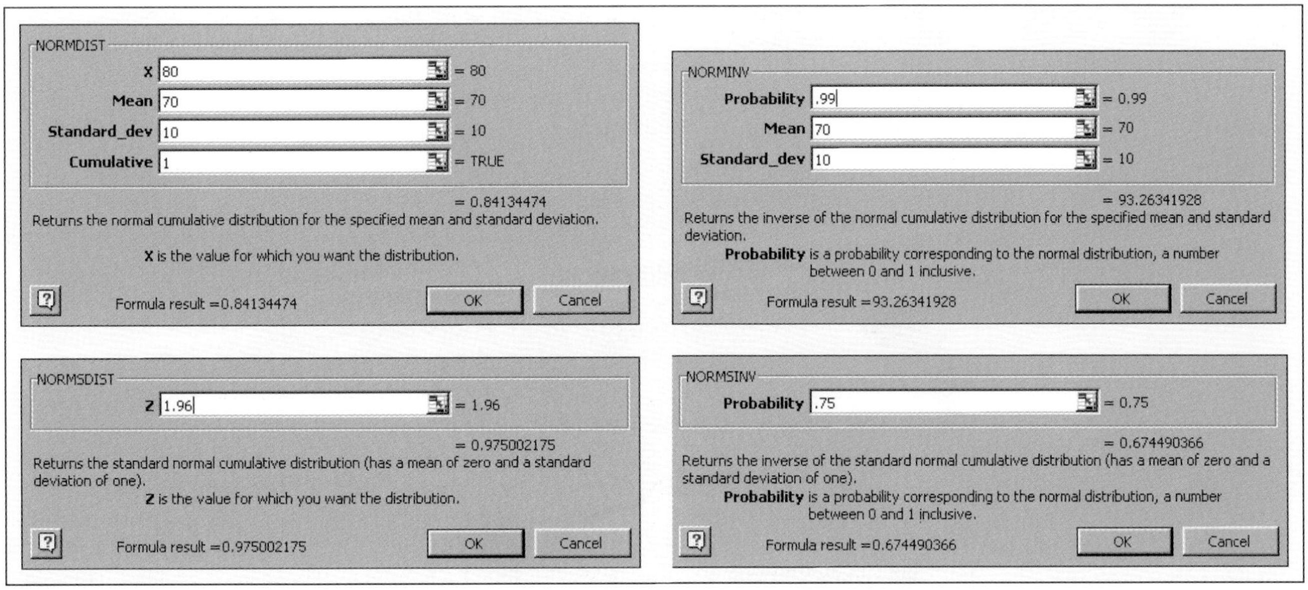

Finding Areas by Using Standardized Variables ●

John took an economics exam and scored 86 points. The class mean was 75 with a standard deviation of 7. What percentile is John in? That is, what is $P(X < 86)$? We need first to calculate John's standardized Z-score:

$$z_{John} = \frac{x_{John} - \mu}{\sigma} = \frac{86 - 75}{7} = \frac{11}{7} = 1.57$$

This says that John's score is 1.57 standard deviations above the mean. From Appendix C-2 we get $P(X < 86) = P(Z < 1.57) = .9418$, so John is approximately in the 94th percentile. That means that his score was better than 94 percent of the class, as illustrated in Figures 7.18 and 7.19. The table gives a slightly different value from Excel due to rounding.

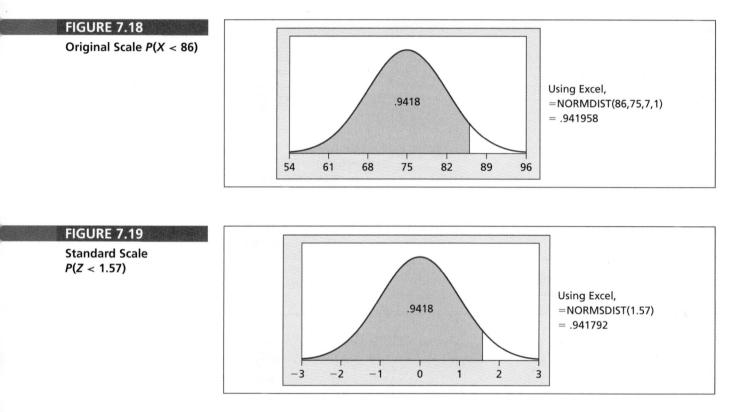

FIGURE 7.18

Original Scale $P(X < 86)$

.9418

Using Excel,
=NORMDIST(86,75,7,1)
= .941958

54 61 68 75 82 89 96

FIGURE 7.19

Standard Scale $P(Z < 1.57)$

.9418

Using Excel,
=NORMSDIST(1.57)
= .941792

−3 −2 −1 0 1 2 3

On this exam, what is the probability that a randomly chosen test-taker would have a score of at least 65? We begin by standardizing:

$$z = \frac{x - \mu}{\sigma} = \frac{65 - 75}{7} = \frac{-10}{7} = -1.43$$

Using Appendix C-1 we can calculate $P(X \geq 65) = P(Z \geq -1.43)$ as

$$P(Z \geq -1.43) = P(-1.43 < Z < 0) + .5000$$
$$= .4236 + .5000 = .9236, \text{ or } 92.4\%$$

Using Appendix C-2 we can calculate $P(X \geq 65) = P(Z \geq -1.43)$ as

$$P(Z \geq -1.43) = 1 - P(Z < -1.43) = 1 - .0764 = .9236, \text{ or } 92.4\%$$

Using either method, there is a 92.4 percent chance that a student scores 65 or above on this exam. These calculations are illustrated in Figures 7.20 and 7.21.

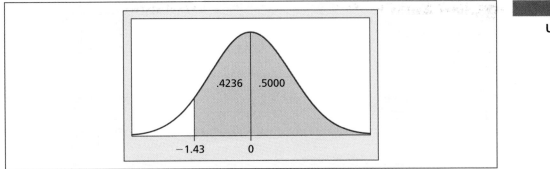

FIGURE 7.20

Using Appendix C-1

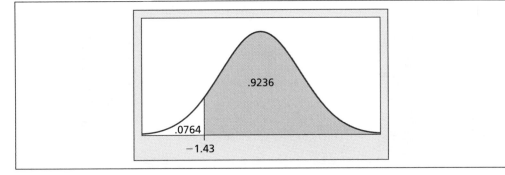

FIGURE 7.21

Using Appendix C-2

Inverse Normal

How can we find the various normal percentiles (5th, 10th, 25th, 75th, 90th, 95th, etc.) known as the **inverse normal**? That is, how can we find X for a given area? We simply turn the standardizing transformation around:

$$x = \mu + z\sigma \qquad \left(\text{solving for } x \text{ in } z = \frac{x - \mu}{\sigma} \right) \qquad (7.5)$$

Using Table 7.7 (or looking up the areas in Excel) we obtain the results shown in Table 7.9. Note that to find a lower tail area (such as the lowest 5 percent) we must use negative Z-values.

Percentile	z	$x = \mu + z\sigma$	x (to nearest integer)
95th (highest 5%)	1.645	$x = 75 + (1.645)(7)$	86.52, or 87 (rounded)
90th (highest 10%)	1.282	$x = 75 + (1.282)(7)$	83.97, or 84 (rounded)
75th (highest 25%)	0.675	$x = 75 + (0.675)(7)$	79.73, or 80 (rounded)
25th (lowest 25%)	−0.675	$x = 75 - (0.675)(7)$	70.28, or 70 (rounded)
10th (lowest 10%)	−1.282	$x = 75 - (1.282)(7)$	66.03, or 66 (rounded)
5th (lowest 5%)	−1.645	$x = 75 - (1.645)(7)$	63.49, or 63 (rounded)

TABLE 7.9

Percentiles for Desired Normal Area

Normal Random Data (Optional)

You can generate random data from a normal distribution $N(\mu, \sigma)$ by using Excel's function =NORMINV(RAND(),μ,σ). Copy this formula to n cells to get a sample of n random data values. Every time you press F9 you will get a different sample. For example, =NORMINV(RAND(),25,3) will generate a random data point from a normal distribution with mean $\mu = 25$ and standard deviation $\sigma = 3$. This technique is useful in what-if simulation experiments.

FIGURE 7.22

Excel's *P(X < 2.039)*

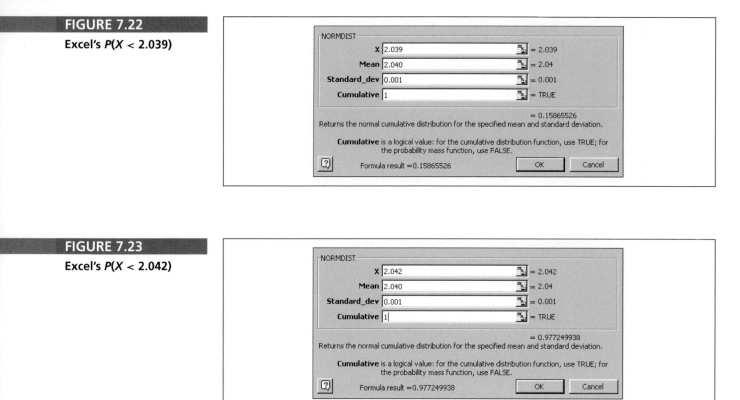

FIGURE 7.23

Excel's *P(X < 2.042)*

FIGURE 7.24

Cumulative Areas from Excel's NORMDIST

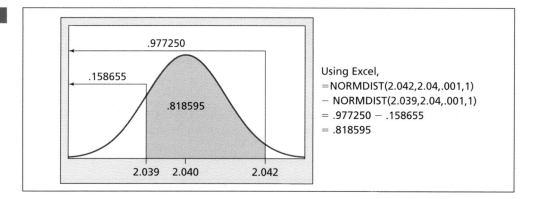

Using Excel without Standardizing

Excel's NORMDIST and NORMINV functions let us evaluate areas and inverse areas *without* standardizing. For example, let *X* be the diameter of a manufactured steel ball bearing whose mean diameter is $\mu = 2.040$ cm and whose standard deviation $\sigma = .001$ cm. What is the probability that a given steel bearing will have a diameter between 2.039 and 2.042 cm? We use Excel's function =NORMDIST(x,μ,σ,cumulative) where cumulative is TRUE.

Since Excel gives left-tail areas, we first calculate $P(X < 2.039)$ and $P(X < 2.042)$ as in Figures 7.22 and 7.23. We then obtain the area between by subtraction, as illustrated in Figure 7.24. The desired area is approximately 81.9 percent. Of course, we could do exactly the same thing by using Appendix C-2:

$$P(2.039 < X < 2.042) = P(X < 2.042) - P(X < 2.039)$$

$$= .9773 - .1587 = .8186, \text{ or } 81.9\%$$

After studying the process of changing oil, the shop's manager has found that the distribution of service times, X, is normal with a mean $\mu = 28$ minutes and a standard deviation $\sigma = 5$ minutes, that is, $X \sim N(28, 5)$. This information can now be used to answer questions such as "What proportion of cars will be finished in less than half an hour?," "What is the chance that a randomly selected car will take longer than 40 minutes to service?," or "What service time corresponds to the 90th percentile?"

To answer these types of questions it is helpful to follow a few basic steps. (1) Draw a picture and label the picture with the information you know. (2) Shade in the area that will answer your question. (3) Standardize the random variable. (4) Find the area by using one of the tables or Excel.

What proportion of cars will be finished in less than half an hour?

- **Steps 1 and 2:**   Draw a picture and shade the desired area.

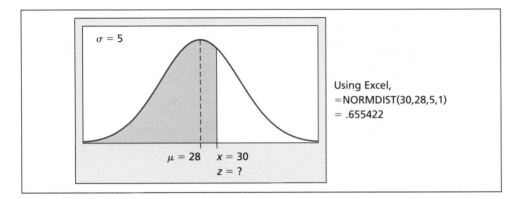

Using Excel,
=NORMDIST(30,28,5,1)
= .655422

$\sigma = 5$

$\mu = 28$ $x = 30$
        $z = ?$

- **Step 3:** $z = \dfrac{30 - 28}{5} = 0.40$

- **Step 4:**   Using Appendix C-2 or Excel we find that $P(Z < 0.40) = .6554$.

Approximately 66 percent of the cars will be finished in less than half an hour.

What is the chance that a randomly selected car will take longer than 40 minutes to complete?

- **Steps 1 and 2:**   Draw a picture and shade the desired area.

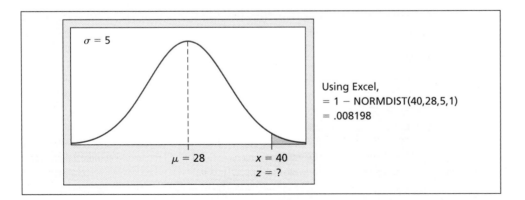

Using Excel,
= 1 − NORMDIST(40,28,5,1)
= .008198

$\sigma = 5$

$\mu = 28$ $x = 40$
            $z = ?$

- **Step 3:** $z = \dfrac{40 - 28}{5} = 2.4$

- **Step 4:**   Using Appendix C-2 or Excel we find that $P(Z > 2.4) = 1 - P(Z \le 2.4) = 1 - .9918 = .0082$.

There is less than a 1 percent chance that a car will take longer than 40 minutes to complete.

What service time corresponds to the 90th percentile?

Steps 1 and 2:   Draw a picture and shade the desired area.

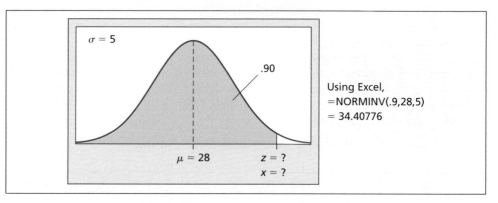

In this case, steps 3 and 4 need to be reversed.

- **Step 3:**   Find $z = 1.28$ by using the tables or Excel.

- **Step 4:** $1.28 = \dfrac{x - 28}{5}$, so $x = 28 + 5(1.28) = 34.4$ minutes.

Ninety percent of the cars will be finished in 34.4 minutes or less.

SECTION EXERCISES

connect

7.27   Use Excel to find each probability.
     a. $P(X < 110)$ for $N(100, 15)$ b. $P(X < 2.00)$ for $N(0, 1)$
     c. $P(X < 5{,}000)$ for $N(6000, 1000)$ d. $P(X < 450)$ for $N(600, 100)$

7.28   Use Excel to find each probability.
     a. $P(80 < X < 110)$ for $N(100, 15)$ b. $P(1.50 < X < 2.00)$ for $N(0, 1)$
     c. $P(4{,}500 < X < 7{,}000)$ for $N(6000, 1000)$ d. $P(225 < X < 450)$ for $N(600, 100)$

7.29   The weight of a small Starbucks coffee is a random variable with a mean of 360 g and a standard deviation of 9 g. Use Excel to find the weight corresponding to each percentile of weight.
     a. 10th percentile   b. 32nd percentile   c. 75th percentile
     d. 90th percentile   e. 99.9th percentile   f. 99.99th percentile

7.30   A study found that the mean waiting time to see a physician at an outpatient clinic was 40 minutes with a standard deviation of 28 minutes. Use Excel to find each probability. (a) What is the probability of more than an hour's wait? (b) Less than 20 minutes? (c) At least 10 minutes. (Data are from J. C. Bennett and D. J. Worthington, "An Example of Good but Partially Successful OR Engagement: Improving Outpatient Clinic Operations," *Interfaces* 28, no. 5 [September-October 1998], pp. 56–69.)

7.31   (a) Write an Excel formula to generate a random normal deviate from $N(0, 1)$ and copy the formula into 10 cells. (b) Find the mean and standard deviation of your sample of 10 random data values. Are you satisfied that the random data have the desired mean and standard deviation? (c) Press F9 to generate 10 more data values and repeat question (b).

7.32   (a) Write an Excel formula to generate a random normal deviate from $N(4000, 200)$ and copy the formula into 100 cells. (b) Find the mean and standard deviation of your sample of 100 random data values. Are you satisfied that the random data have the desired mean and standard deviation? (c) Make a histogram of your sample. Does it appear normal?

**7.5
NORMAL
APPROXI-
MATIONS**

Normal Approximation to the Binomial

We have seen that (unless we are using Excel) binomial probabilities may be difficult to calculate when n is large, particularly when many terms must be summed. Instead, we can use a normal approximation. The logic of this approximation is that as n becomes large, the discrete binomial bars become more like a smooth, continuous, normal curve.

As a rule of thumb, when $n\pi \geq 10$ and $n(1 - \pi) \geq 10$ it is appropriate to use the normal approximation to the binomial, setting the normal μ and σ equal to the binomial mean and standard deviation:

$$\mu = n\pi \tag{7.6}$$

$$\sigma = \sqrt{n\pi(1 - \pi)} \tag{7.7}$$

VS

Chapter 4

What is the probability of more than 17 heads in 32 flips of a fair coin? In binomial terms, this would be $P(X \geq 18) = P(18) + P(19) + \cdots + P(32)$, which would be a tedious sum even if we had a table. Could the normal approximation be used? With $n = 32$ and $\pi = .50$ we clearly meet the requirement that $n\pi \geq 10$ and $n(1 - \pi) \geq 10$. However, when translating a discrete scale into a continuous scale we must be careful about individual points. The event "more than 17" actually falls halfway *between* 17 and 18 on a discrete scale, as shown in Figure 7.25.

EXAMPLE

Coin Flips

FIGURE 7.25   **Normal Approximation to $P(X \geq 18)$**

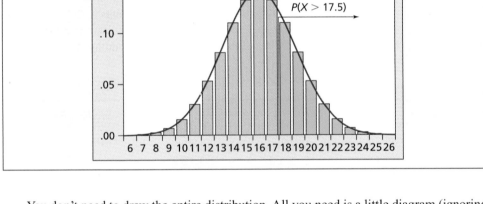

You don't need to draw the entire distribution. All you need is a little diagram (ignoring the low and high ends of the scale since they are not relevant) to show the event "more than 17" visually:

... 14   15   16   17   *18   19   20   21   22   23* ...

If you make a diagram like this, you can *see* the correct cutoff point. Since the cutoff point for "more than 17" is halfway between 17 and 18, the normal approximation is $P(X > 17.5)$. The 0.5 adjustment is called the **continuity correction**. The normal parameters are

$$\mu = n\pi = (32)(0.5) = 16$$

$$\sigma = \sqrt{n\pi(1 - \pi)} = \sqrt{(32)(0.5)(1 - 0.5)} = 2.82843$$

We then perform the usual standardizing transformation with the continuity-corrected X-value:

$$z = \frac{x - \mu}{\sigma} = \frac{17.5 - 16}{2.82843} = .53$$

From Appendix C-1 we find $P(Z > .53) = .5000 - P(0 < Z < .53) = .5000 - .2019 = .2981$. Alternately, we could use Appendix C-2 to get $P(Z > .53)$ which, by the symmetry of the normal distribution, is the same as $P(Z < -.53) = .2981$. The calculations are illustrated in Figure 7.26.

FIGURE 7.26   Normal Area for $P(Z > .53)$

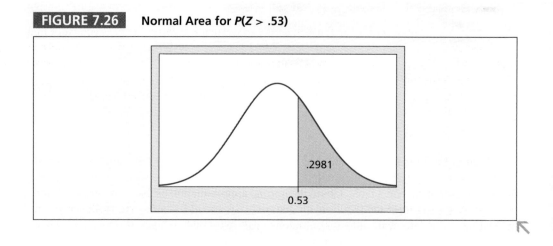

How accurate is this normal approximation to the binomial $P(X \geq 18)$ in our coin flip example? We can check it by using Excel. Since Excel's function is cumulative to the left, we find $P(X \leq 17)$ with the Excel function =BINOMDIST(17,32,0.5,1) and then subtract from 1:

$$P(X \geq 18) = 1 - P(X \leq 17) = 1 - .7017 = .2983$$

In this case, the normal approximation (.2981) is very close to the binomial probability.

To be sure you understand the continuity correction, consider the events in the table below. We sketch a diagram to find the correct cutoff point to approximate a discrete model with a continuous one. The 0.5 adjustment may be added or subtracted, depending on the event of interest.

Event	Relevant Range of X	Normal Cutoff
At least 17	. . . 14 15 16 *17 18 19 20* . . .	Use $x = 16.5$
More than 15	. . . 14 15 *16 17 18 19 20* . . .	Use $x = 15.5$
Fewer than 19	. . . *14 15 16 17 18* 19 20 . . .	Use $x = 18.5$

SECTION EXERCISES

connect

Note: Use Appendix C-2 for these exercises.

7.33   The default rate on government-guaranteed student loans at a certain public 4-year institution is 7 percent. (a) If 1,000 student loans are made, what is the probability of fewer than 50 defaults? (b) More than 100? Show your work carefully.

7.34   In a certain store, there is a .03 probability that the scanned price in the bar code scanner will not match the advertised price. The cashier scans 800 items. (a) What is the expected number of mismatches? The standard deviation? (b) What is the probability of at least 20 mismatches? (c) What is the probability of more than 30 mismatches? Show your calculations clearly.

7.35   The probability that a vending machine in the Oxnard University Student Center will dispense the desired item when correct change is inserted is .90. If 200 customers try the machine, find the probability that (a) at least 175 will receive the desired item and (b) that fewer than 190 will receive the desired item. Explain.

7.36   When confronted with an in-flight medical emergency, pilots and crew can consult staff physicians at MedAire, an emergency facility in Tempe, Arizona. If MedAire is called, there is a 4.8 percent chance that the flight will be diverted for an immediate landing. (a) If MedAire is called 8,465 times (as it was in 2002), what is the expected number of diversions? (b) What is the probability of at least 400 diversions? (c) Fewer than 450 diversions? Show your work carefully. (Data are from *Popular Science* 263, no. 5 [November 2003], p. 70.)

Normal Approximation to the Poisson

The normal approximation for the Poisson works best when λ is fairly large. If you can't find λ in Appendix B (which only goes up to $\lambda = 20$), you are reasonably safe in using the normal approximation. Some textbooks allow the approximation when $\lambda \geq 10$, which is comparable to the rule that the binomial mean must be at least 10. To use the normal approximation to the Poisson we set the normal μ and σ equal to the Poisson mean and standard deviation:

$$\mu = \lambda \tag{7.8}$$

$$\sigma = \sqrt{\lambda} \tag{7.9}$$

EXAMPLE

Utility Bills

On Wednesday between 10 A.M. and noon, customer billing inquiries arrive at a mean rate of 42 inquiries per hour at Consumers Energy. What is the probability of receiving more than 50 calls? Call arrivals presumably follow a Poisson model, but the mean $\lambda = 42$ is too large to use Appendix B. The formula would entail an infinite sum $P(51) + P(52) + \cdots$ whose terms gradually become negligible (recall that the Poisson has no upper limit) but the calculation would be tedious at best. However, the normal approximation is simple. We set

$$\mu = \lambda = 42$$

$$\sigma = \sqrt{\lambda} = \sqrt{42} = 6.48074$$

The continuity-corrected cutoff point for $X \geq 51$ is $X = 50.5$ (halfway between 50 and 51):

$$\ldots 46 \ \ 47 \ \ 48 \ \ 49 \ \ 50 \ \ \boldsymbol{51 \ \ 52 \ \ 53} \ldots$$

The standardized Z-value for the event "more than 50" is $P(X > 50.5) = P(Z > 1.31)$ since

$$z = \frac{x - \mu}{\sigma} = \frac{50.5 - 42}{6.48074} \cong 1.31$$

Using Appendix C-2 we look up $P(Z < -1.31) = .0951$, which is the same as $P(Z > 1.31)$ because the normal distribution is symmetric. We can check the actual Poisson probability by using Excel's cumulative function =POISSON(50,42,1) and subtracting from 1:

$$P(X \geq 51) = 1 - P(X \leq 50) = 1 - .9025 = .0975$$

In this case, the normal approximation comes fairly close to the actual Poisson result. This example gives us confidence in the approximation. Of course, if you have access to Excel, you don't need the approximation at all.

SECTION EXERCISES

Note: Use Appendix C-2 for these exercises.

7.37 On average, 28 patients per hour arrive in the Foxboro 24-Hour Walk-in Clinic on Friday between 6 P.M. and midnight. (a) What is the approximate probability of more than 35 arrivals? (b) What is the approximate probability of fewer than 25 arrivals? (c) Is the normal approximation justified? Show all calculations. (d) Use Excel to calculate the actual Poisson probabilities. How close were your approximations?

7.38 For a large Internet service provider (ISP), Web virus attacks occur at a mean rate of 150 per day. (a) Estimate the probability of at least 175 attacks in a given day. (b) Estimate the probability of fewer than 125 attacks. (c) Is the normal approximation justified? Show all calculations. (d) Use Excel to calculate the actual Poisson probabilities. How close were your approximations?

Characteristics of the Exponential Distribution

Back in Chapter 6 we introduced the idea of a *random process*. For example, consider the process of customers arriving at a Noodles & Company restaurant, illustrated in Figure 7.27. There are two different variables that could be used to describe this process. We could count the number of customers who arrive in a randomly selected minute, or we could measure the

7.6

EXPONENTIAL DISTRIBUTION

FIGURE 7.27

Customer Arrival Process at a Noodles & Company Restaurant

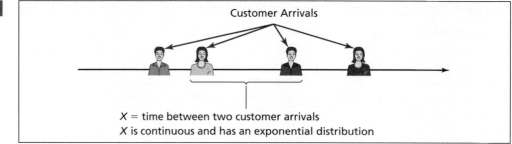

Customer Arrivals

X = time between two customer arrivals
X is continuous and has an exponential distribution

time between two customer arrivals. As you learned in Chapter 6, the *count* of customer arrivals is a discrete random variable and typically has a Poisson distribution. When the count of customer arrivals has a Poisson distribution, the distribution of the time between two customer arrivals, will have an **exponential distribution**, detailed in Table 7.10. In the exponential model, the focus is on the waiting time until the next event, a continuous variable. The exponential probability function approaches zero as x increases, and is very skewed, as shown in Figures 7.28 and 7.29.

We are usually not interested in the height of the function $f(x)$ but rather in areas under the curve. Fortunately, the CDF is simple; no tables are needed, just a calculator that has the e^x function key. The probability of waiting more than x units of time until the next arrival is $e^{-\lambda x}$, while the probability of waiting x units of time or less is $1 - e^{-\lambda x}$.

(7.10)   Right-tail area: $P(X > x) = e^{-\lambda x}$ (probability of waiting *more* than x)

(7.11)   Left-tail area: $P(X \leq x) = 1 - e^{-\lambda x}$ (probability of waiting x or less)

TABLE 7.10

Exponential Distribution

Parameters	λ = mean arrival rate per unit of time or space (same as Poisson mean)
PDF	$f(x) = \lambda e^{-\lambda x}$
CDF	$P(X \leq x) = 1 - e^{-\lambda x}$
Domain	$X \geq 0$
Mean	$1/\lambda$
Standard deviation	$1/\lambda$
Shape	Always right-skewed.
Comments	Waiting time is exponential when arrivals follow a Poisson model. Often $1/\lambda$ is given (mean time between events) rather than λ.

FIGURE 7.28

Right-Tail Exponential Area

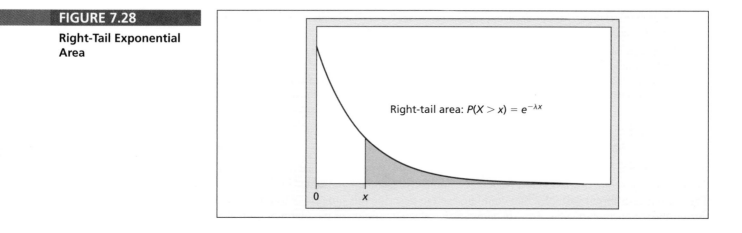

Right-tail area: $P(X > x) = e^{-\lambda x}$

0   x

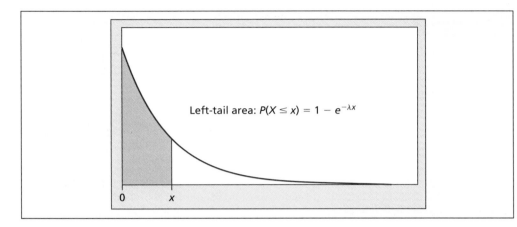

FIGURE 7.29

**Left-Tail Exponential
Area**

Left-tail area: $P(X \leq x) = 1 - e^{-\lambda x}$

Recall that $P(X \leq x)$ is the same as $P(X < x)$ since the point x has no area. For this reason, we could use either $<$ or $\leq$ in formula 7.11.

EXAMPLE

Customer Waiting Time

Between 2 P.M. and 4 P.M. on Wednesday, patient insurance inquiries arrive at Blue Choice insurance at a mean rate of 2.2 calls per minute. What is the probability of waiting more than 30 seconds for the next call? We set $\lambda = 2.2$ events per minute and $x = 0.50$ minutes. Note that we must convert 30 seconds to 0.50 minutes since λ is expressed in minutes, and the units of measurement must be the same. We have

$$P(X > 0.50) = e^{-\lambda x} = e^{-(2.2)(0.50)} = .3329, \text{ or } 33.29\%$$

There is about a 33 percent chance of waiting more than 30 seconds before the next call arrives. Since $x = 0.50$ is a *point* that has no area in a continuous model, $P(X \geq 0.50)$ and $P(X > 0.50)$ refer to the same event (unlike, say, a binomial model, in which a point *does* have a probability). The probability that 30 seconds or less (0.50 minutes) will be needed before the next call arrives is

$$P(X \leq 0.50) = 1 - e^{-(2.2)(0.50)} = 1 - .3329 = .6671$$

These calculations are illustrated in Figures 7.30 and 7.31.

FIGURE 7.30 $P(X > 0.50)$ for $\lambda = 2.2$

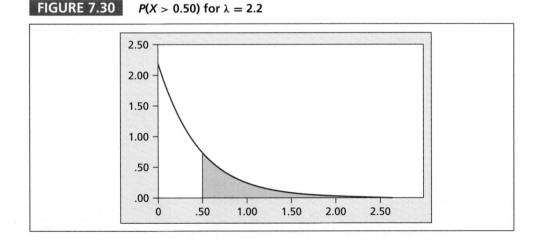

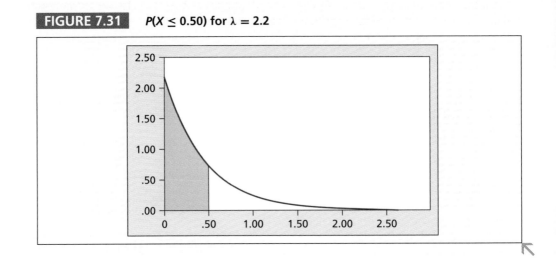

FIGURE 7.31 $P(X \leq 0.50)$ for $\lambda = 2.2$

SECTION EXERCISES

connect

noodles
& company

7.39   In Santa Theresa, false alarms are received at the downtown fire station at a mean rate of 0.3 per day. (a) What is the probability that more than 7 days will pass before the next false alarm arrives? (b) Less than 2 days? (c) Explain fully.

7.40   Between 11 P.M. and midnight on Thursday night, Mystery Pizza gets an average of 4.2 telephone orders per hour. Find the probability that (a) at least 30 minutes will elapse before the next telephone order; (b) less than 15 minutes will elapse; and (c) between 15 and 30 minutes will elapse.

7.41   A passenger metal detector at Chicago's Midway Airport gives an alarm 2.1 times a minute. What is the probability that (a) less than 60 seconds will pass before the next alarm? (b) More than 30 seconds? (c) At least 45 seconds?

7.42   The Johnson family uses a propane tank for cooking on their gas grill. During the summer they need to replace their tank on average every 30 days. At a randomly chosen moment, what is the probability that they can grill out (a) at least 40 days before they need to replace their tank; (b) no more than 20 days?

7.43   At a certain Noodles & Company restaurant, customers arrive during the lunch hour at a rate of 2.8 per minute. What is the probability that (a) at least 30 seconds will pass before the next customer walks in; (b) no more than 15 seconds; (c) more than 1 minute?

Inverse Exponential

We can use the exponential area formula in reverse. If the mean arrival rate is 2.2 calls per minute, we want the 90th percentile for waiting time (the top 10 percent of waiting time) as illustrated in Figure 7.32. We want to find the *x*-value that defines the upper 10 percent.

FIGURE 7.32

Finding *x* for the Upper 10 Percent

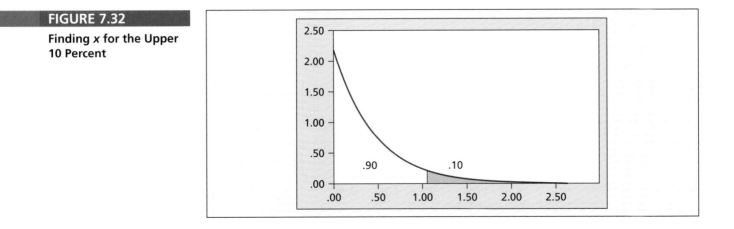

Call the unknown time x. Since $P(X \le x) = .90$ implies $P(X > x) = .10$, we set the right-tail area to .10, take the natural logarithm of both sides, and solve for x:

$$e^{-\lambda x} = .10$$
$$-\lambda x = \ln(.10)$$
$$-\lambda x = -2.302585$$
$$x = 2.302585/\lambda$$
$$x = 2.302585/2.2$$
$$x = 1.0466 \text{ minutes}$$

So 90 percent of the calls will arrive within 1.0466 minutes (or 62.8 seconds). We can find any percentile in the same way. For example, Table 7.11 illustrates similar calculations to find the quartiles (25 percent, 50 percent, 75 percent) of waiting time.

	Quartiles for Exponential with $\lambda = 2.2$	TABLE 7.11
First Quartile Q$_1$	**Second Quartile Q$_2$ (median)**	**Third Quartile Q$_3$**
$e^{-\lambda x} = .75$	$e^{-\lambda x} = .50$	$e^{-\lambda x} = .25$
$-\lambda x = \ln(.75)$	$-\lambda x = \ln(.50)$	$-\lambda x = \ln(.25)$
$-\lambda x = -0.2876821$	$-\lambda x = -0.6931472$	$-\lambda x = -1.386294$
$x = 0.2876821/\lambda$	$x = 0.6931472/\lambda$	$x = 1.386294/\lambda$
$x = 0.2876821/2.2$	$x = 0.6931472/2.2$	$x = 1.386294/2.2$
$x = 0.1308$ minutes, or 7.8 seconds	$x = 0.3151$ minutes, or 18.9 seconds	$x = 0.6301$ minutes, or 37.8 seconds

The calculations in Table 7.11 show that the mean waiting time is $1/\lambda = 1/2.2 = 0.4545$ minutes, or 27 seconds. It is instructive to note that the median waiting time (18.9 seconds) is less than the mean. Since the exponential distribution is highly right-skewed, we would expect the mean waiting time to be above the median, which it is.

Mean Time between Events

Exponential waiting times are often described in terms of the **mean time between events** *(MTBE)* rather than in terms of Poisson arrivals per unit of time. In other words, we might be given $1/\lambda$ instead of λ.

$\text{MTBE} = 1/\lambda = $ *mean time between events* (units of time per event)

$1/\text{MTBE} = \lambda = $ mean *events per unit of time* (events per unit of time)

For example, if the mean time between patient arrivals in an emergency room is 20 minutes, then $\lambda = 1/20 = 0.05$ arrivals per minute (or $\lambda = 3.0$ arrivals per hour). We could work a problem either using hours or minutes, as long as we are careful to make sure that x and λ are expressed in the same units when we calculate $e^{-\lambda x}$. For example, $P(X > 12 \text{ minutes}) = e^{-(0.05)(12)} = e^{-0.60}$ is the same as $P(X > 0.20 \text{ hour}) = e^{-(3)(0.20)} = e^{-0.60}$.

The NexGenCo color flat-panel display in an aircraft cockpit has a mean time between failures (MTBF) of 22,500 flight hours. What is the probability of a failure within the next 10,000 flight hours? Since 22,500 hours per failure implies $\lambda = 1/22,500$ failures per hour, we calculate:

EXAMPLE

Flat-Panel Displays

$$P(X < 10,000) = 1 - e^{-\lambda x} = 1 - e^{-(1/22,500)(10,000)} = 1 - e^{-0.4444} = 1 - .6412 = .3588$$

There is a 35.88 percent chance of failure within the next 10,000 hours of flight. This assumes that failures follow the Poisson model.

EXAMPLE

Warranty Period

A manufacturer of GPS navigation receivers for boats knows that their mean life under typical maritime conditions is 7 years. What warranty should be offered in order that not more than 30 percent of the GPS units will fail before the warranty expires? The situation is illustrated in Figure 7.33.

Let x be the length of the warranty. To solve this problem, we note that if 30 percent fail before the warranty expires, 70 percent will fail afterward. That is, $P(X > x) = 1 - P(X \leq x) = 1 - 0.30 = .70$.

FIGURE 7.33   **Finding *x* for the Lower 30 Percent**

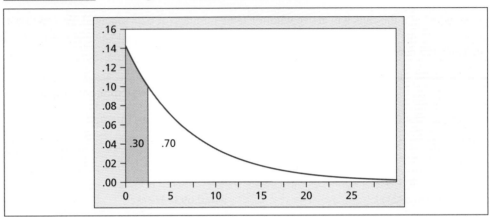

We set $P(X > x) = e^{-\lambda x} = .70$ and solve for x by taking the natural log of both sides of the equation:

$$e^{-\lambda x} = .70$$

$$-\lambda x = \ln(.70)$$

$$-\lambda x = -0.356675$$

$$x = (0.356675)/\lambda$$

But in this case, we are not given λ but rather its reciprocal MTBF $= 1/\lambda$. Seven years *mean time between failures* is the same as saying $\lambda = 1/7$ *failures per year*. So we plug in $\lambda = 1/7 = 0.1428571$ to finish solving for x:

$$x = (0.356675)/(0.142857) = 2.497 \text{ years}$$

Thus, the firm would offer a 30-month warranty.

It may seem paradoxical that such a short warranty would be offered for something that lasts 7 years. However, the right tail is very long. A few long-lived GPS units will pull up the mean. This is typical of electronic equipment, which helps explain why your laptop computer may have only a 1-year warranty when we know that laptops often last for many years. Similarly, automobiles typically outlast their warranty period (although competitive pressures have recently led to warranties of 5 years or more, even though it may result in a loss on the warranty). In general, warranty periods are a policy tool used by business to balance costs of expected claims against the competitive need to offer contract protection to consumers.

Using Excel

The Excel function =EXPONDIST(x,Lambda,1) will return the left-tail area $P(X \leq x)$. The "1" indicates a cumulative area. If you enter 0 instead of 1, you will get the height of the PDF instead of the left-tail area for the CDF.

Model	Random Variable	Parameter	Domain	Variable Type
Poisson	$X =$ number of arrivals per unit of time	$\lambda = \dfrac{\text{(mean arrivals)}}{\text{(unit of time)}}$	$X = 0, 1, 2, \ldots$	Discrete
Exponential	$X =$ waiting time until next arrival	$\lambda = \dfrac{\text{(mean arrivals)}}{\text{(unit of time)}}$	$X \geq 0$	Continuous

Relation between Exponential and Poisson Models   TABLE 7.12

Every situation with Poisson arrivals over time is associated with an exponential waiting time. Both models depend solely on the parameter $\lambda =$ mean arrival rate per unit of time. These two closely related distributions are summarized in Table 7.12.

SECTION EXERCISES

connect

7.44 The time it takes a ski patroller to respond to an accident call has an exponential distribution with an average equal to 5 minutes. (a) In what time will 90 percent of all ski accident calls be responded to? (b) If the ski patrol would like to be able to respond to 90 percent of the accident calls within 10 minutes, what does the average response time need to be?

7.45 Between 11 P.M. and midnight on Thursday night, Mystery Pizza gets an average of 4.2 telephone orders per hour. (a) Find the median waiting time until the next telephone order. (b) Find the upper quartile of waiting time before the next telephone order. (c) What is the upper 10 percent of waiting time until the next telephone order? Show all calculations clearly.

7.46 A passenger metal detector at Chicago's Midway Airport gives an alarm 0.5 times a minute. (a) Find the median waiting time until the next alarm. (b) Find the first quartile of waiting time before the next alarm. (c) Find the 30th percentile waiting time until the next alarm. Show all calculations clearly.

7.47 Between 2 A.M. and 4 A.M. at an all-night pizza parlor the mean time between arrival of telephone pizza orders is 20 minutes. (a) Find the median wait for pizza order arrivals. (b) Explain why the median is not equal to the mean. (c) Find the upper quartile.

7.48 The mean life of a certain computer hard disk in continual use is 8 years. (a) How long a warranty should be offered if the vendor wants to ensure that not more than 10 percent of the hard disks will fail within the warranty period? (b) Not more than 20 percent?

CHAPTER SUMMARY

The **probability density function (PDF)** of a **continuous random variable** is a smooth curve, and probabilities are **areas** under the curve. The area under the entire PDF is 1. The **cumulative distribution function (CDF)** shows the area under the PDF to the left of X, approaching 1 as X increases. The mean $E(X)$ and variance $V(X)$ are integrals, rather than sums, as for a discrete random variable. The **uniform continuous distribution,** denoted $U(a, b)$, has two parameters a and b that enclose the range. It is a simple what-if model with applications in simulation. The symmetric, bell-shaped **normal distribution,** denoted $N(\mu, \sigma)$, has two parameters, the mean μ and standard deviation σ. It serves as a benchmark. Because there is a different normal distribution for every possible μ and σ, we apply the transformation $z = (x - \mu)/\sigma$ to get a new random variable that follows a **standard normal distribution,** denoted $N(0, 1)$, with mean 0 and standard deviation 1. There is no simple formula for normal areas, but tables or Excel functions are available to find an area under the curve for given z-values or to find z-values that give a specified area (the "inverse normal"). As shown in Figure 7.34, a **normal approximation** for a binomial or Poisson probability is acceptable when the mean is at least 10. The **exponential distribution** describes **waiting time** until the next Poisson arrival. Its one parameter is λ (the mean arrival rate) and its right tail area is $e^{-\lambda x}$ (the probability of waiting at least x time units for the next arrival). It is strongly right-skewed and is used to predict warranty claims or to schedule facilities. Table 7.13 compares these four models.

FIGURE 7.34

Relationships among Three Models

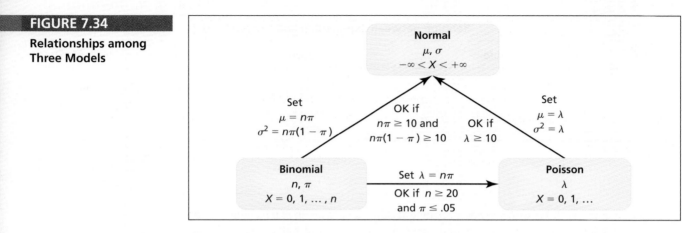

TABLE 7.13 Comparison of Models

Model	Parameters	Mean E(X)	Variance V(X)	Characteristics
Uniform	a, b	$(a+b)/2$	$(b-a)^2/12$	Always symmetric
Normal	μ, σ	μ	σ^2	Symmetric. Useful as reference benchmark.
Standard normal	μ, σ	0	1	Special case of the normal with $z = (x - \mu)/\sigma$
Exponential	λ	$1/\lambda$	$1/\lambda$	Always skewed right. Right-tail area is $e^{-\lambda x}$ for waiting times.

KEY TERMS

continuity correction, *255*
continuous random variable, *235*
cumulative distribution function, *236*
exponential distribution, *258*
Gaussian distribution, *240*

integral, *236*
inverse normal, *251*
mean time between events, *261*
normal distribution, *240*
probability density function, *236*

standard normal distribution, *243*
uniform continuous distribution, *237*
unit rectangular distribution, *239*

Commonly Used Formulas in Continuous Distributions ●

Uniform CDF: $P(X \leq x) = \dfrac{x-a}{b-a}$ for $a \leq X \leq b$

Exponential CDF: $P(X \leq x) = 1 - e^{-\lambda x}$ for $X \geq 0$

Standard Normal Random Variable: $z = \dfrac{x-\mu}{\sigma}$ for $-\infty < X < +\infty$

Normal Approximation to Binomial: $\mu = n\pi$ $\sigma = \sqrt{n\pi(1-\pi)}$ for $n\pi \geq 10$ and $n(1-\pi) \geq 10$

Normal Approximation to Poisson: $\mu = \lambda$ $\sigma = \sqrt{\lambda}$ for $\lambda \geq 10$

CHAPTER REVIEW

1. (a) Why does a point have no probability in a continuous distribution? (b) Why are probabilities areas under curves in a continuous distribution?

2. Define (a) parameter, (b) PDF, and (c) CDF.

3. For the uniform distribution: (a) tell how many parameters it has; (b) indicate what the parameters represent; (c) describe its shape; and (d) explain when it would be used.

4. For the normal distribution: (a) tell how many parameters it has; (b) indicate what the parameters represent; (c) describe its shape; and (d) explain why all normal distributions are alike despite having different μ and σ.

5. (a) What features of a stochastic process might lead you to anticipate a normal distribution? (b) Give two examples of random variables that might be considered normal.

6. (a) What is the transformation to standardize a normal random variable? (b) Why do we standardize a variable to find normal areas? (c) How does a standard normal distribution differ from any other normal distribution, and how is it similar?

7. (a) Explain the difference between Appendix C-1 and Appendix C-2. (b) List advantages of each type of table. (c) Which table do you expect to use, and why? (d) Why not always use Excel?

8. (a) Why does Excel rely on the cumulative to find normal areas? (b) Write an example of each of the four normal functions in Excel and tell what each function does.

9. List the standard normal z-values for several common areas (tail and/or middle). *You will use them often.*

10. For the exponential distribution: (a) tell how many parameters it has; (b) indicate what the parameters represent; (c) describe its shape; and (d) explain when it would be used.

11. When does the normal give an acceptable approximation (a) to a binomial and (b) to a Poisson? (c) Why might you never need these approximations? (d) When might you need them?

12. Why is calculus needed to find probabilities for continuous distributions, but not for discrete distributions?

Note: Show your work clearly.

CHAPTER EXERCISES

connect

7.49 Which of the following is a continuous random variable?
   a. Number of Honda Civics sold in a given day at a car dealership.
   b. Gallons of gasoline used for a 200-mile trip in a Honda Civic.
   c. Miles driven on a particular Thursday by the owner of a Honda Civic.

7.50 Which of the following could be probability density functions for a continuous random variable? Explain.
   a. $f(x) = .50$ for $0 \leq x \leq 2$
   b. $f(x) = 2 - x$ for $0 \leq x \leq 2$
   c. $f(x) = .5x$ for $0 \leq x \leq 2$

7.51 Applicants for a night caretaker position are uniformly distributed in age between 25 and 65. (a) What is the mean age of an applicant? (b) The standard deviation? (c) What is the probability that an applicant will be over 45? (d) Over 55? (e) Between 30 and 60?

7.52 Passengers using New York's MetroCard system must swipe the card at a rate between 10 and 40 inches per second, or else the card must be re-swiped through the card reader. Research shows that actual swipe rates by subway riders are uniformly distributed between 5 and 50 inches per second. (a) What is the mean swipe rate? (b) What is the standard deviation of the swipe rate? (c) What are the quartiles? (d) What percentage of subway riders must re-swipe the card because they were outside the acceptable range? (Data are from *The New York Times*, July 18, 2004, p. 23.)

7.53 Discuss why you would or would not expect each of the following variables to be normally distributed. *Hint:* Would you expect a single central mode and tapering tails? Would the distribution be roughly symmetric? Would one tail be longer than the other?
   a. Time for households to complete the U.S. Census short form.
   b. Size of automobile collision damage claims.
   c. Diameters of randomly chosen circulated quarters.
   d. Weight of contents of 16-ounce boxes of elbow macaroni.

7.54 Why might the following not be normally distributed? (a) The time it takes you to drive to the airport. (b) The annual income for a randomly chosen major league baseball player. (c) The annual hurricane losses suffered by homeowners in Florida.

7.55 Scores on a certain accounting exam were normally distributed with a mean of 75 and a standard deviation of 7. Find the percentile for each individual using Excel's =NORMSDIST function. (a) Bob's score was 82; (b) Phyllis's score was 93; (c) Tom's score was 63.

7.56 Chlorine concentration in a municipal water supply is a uniformly distributed random variable that ranges between 0.74 ppm and 0.98 ppm. (a) What is the mean chlorine concentration? (b) The standard deviation? (c) What is the probability that the chlorine concentration will exceed 0.80 ppm on a given day? (d) Will be under 0.85 ppm? (e) Will be between 0.80 ppm and 0.90 ppm? (f) Why is chlorine added to municipal water? What if there is too much? Too little? *Hint:* Use the Internet. (Data are from *Annual Water Quality Report,* City of Rochester Hills, MI.)

7.57 The weekly demand for Baked Lay's potato chips at a certain Subway sandwich shop is a normally distributed random variable with mean 450 and standard deviation 80. Find the value of X for each event. Show your work.

a. Highest 50 percent   b. Lowest 25 percent   c. 90th percentile

d. Highest 80 percent   e. Highest 5 percent   f. Middle 50 percent

g. 20th percentile   h. Middle 95 percent   i. Highest 1 percent

7.58 The length of a Colorado brook trout is normally distributed. (a) What is the probability that a brook trout's length exceeds the mean? (b) Exceeds the mean by at least 1 standard deviation? (c) Exceeds the mean by at least 2 standard deviations? (d) Is within 2 standard deviations?

7.59 The caffeine content of a cup of home-brewed coffee is a normally distributed random variable with a mean of 115 mg with a standard deviation of 20 mg. (a) What is the probability that a randomly chosen cup of home-brewed coffee will have more than 130 mg of caffeine? (b) Less than 100 mg? (c) A very strong cup of tea has a caffeine content of 91 mg. What is the probability that a cup of coffee will have less caffeine than a very strong cup of tea? (Data are from *Popular Science* 254, no. 5 [May 1999], p. 95.)

7.60 The fracture strength of a certain type of manufactured glass is normally distributed with a mean of 579 MPa with a standard deviation of 14 MPa. (a) What is the probability that a randomly chosen sample of glass will break at less than 579 MPa? (b) More than 590 MPa? (c) Less than 600 MPa? (Data are from *Science* 283 [February 26, 1999], p. 1296.)

7.61 Tire pressure in a certain car is a normally distributed random variable with mean 30 psi (pounds per square inch) and standard deviation 2 psi. The manufacturer's recommended correct inflation range is 28 psi to 32 psi. A motorist's tire is inspected at random. (a) What is the probability that the tire's inflation is within the recommended range? (b) What is the probability that the tire is under-inflated? *(c) The Alliance of Automotive Manufacturers has developed a microchip that will warn when a tire is 25 percent below the recommended mean, to warn of dangerously low tire pressure. How often would such an alarm be triggered? (See *The Wall Street Journal,* July 14, 2004.)

7.62 In a certain microwave oven on the high power setting, the time it takes a randomly chosen kernel of popcorn to pop is normally distributed with a mean of 140 seconds and a standard deviation of 25 seconds. What percentage of the kernels will fail to pop if the popcorn is cooked for (a) 2 minutes? (b) Three minutes? (c) If you wanted 95 percent of the kernels to pop, what time would you allow? (d) If you wanted 99 percent to pop?

7.63 Procyon Manufacturing produces tennis balls. Their manufacturing process has a mean ball weight of 2.035 ounces with a standard deviation of 0.03 ounces. Regulation tennis balls are required to have a weight between 1.975 ounces and 2.095 ounces. What proportion of Procyon's production will fail to meet these specifications? (See *Scientific American* 292, no. 4 [April 2005], p. 95.)

7.64 Manufacturers of HRT (hormone replacement therapy) drugs need to know the potential market for their products that relieve side effects of menopause. For women without hysterectomy, the average age at menopause is 51.4 years. Assume a standard deviation of 3.8 years. (a) What is the probability that menopause will occur before age 40? (b) After age 55? (c) What assumptions did you make? *(d) Among the 73.1 million American women between ages 30 and 75, how many would be potential users of HRT? *Hint:* Assume equal numbers of women in all ages from 30 to 75, and compute the $\mu \pm 3\sigma$ range for menopause age. (Data are from *Statistical Abstract of the United States, 2001.*)

7.65 In a study of e-mail consultations with physicians at the University of Virginia Children's Medical Center, the monthly average was 37.6 requests with a standard deviation of 15.9 requests. (a) What is the probability of more than 50 requests in a given month? (b) Fewer than 29? (c) Between 40 and 50 requests? (d) What assumptions did you make? (Data are from S. M. Borowitz and J. Wyatt, "The Origin, Content, and Workload of E-Mail Consultations," *Journal of the American Medical Association* 280, no. 15 [October 1998], p. 1321.)

7.66 The time it takes to give a man a shampoo and haircut is normally distributed with mean 22 minutes and standard deviation 3 minutes. Customers are scheduled every 30 minutes. (a) What is the probability that a male customer will take longer than the allotted time? *(b) If three male customers are scheduled sequentially on the half-hour, what is the probability that all three will be finished within their allotted half-hour times?

7.67 The length of a time-out during a televised professional football game is normally distributed with a mean of 84 seconds and a standard deviation of 10 seconds. If the network runs consecutive commercials totaling 90 seconds, what is the probability that play will resume before the commercials are over? What assumption(s) did you make in answering this question?

7.68 In Rivendell Memorial Hospital the time to complete surgery in a routine tubal ligation without complications is normally distributed with a mean of 30 minutes and a standard deviation of 8 minutes. The next procedure has been scheduled in the same operating room 60 minutes after the beginning of a tubal ligation procedure. Allowing 20 minutes to vacate and prepare the operating room between procedures, what is the probability that the next procedure will have to be delayed? Explain carefully.

7.69 Demand for residential electricity at 6:00 P.M. on the first Monday in October in Santa Theresa County is normally distributed with a mean of 4,905 MW (megawatts) and a standard deviation of 355 MW. Due to scheduled maintenance and unexpected system failures in a generating station the utility can supply a maximum of 5,200 MW at that time. What is the probability that the utility will have to purchase electricity from other utilities or allow brownouts?

7.70 Jim's systolic blood pressure is a random variable with a mean of 145 mmHg and a standard deviation of 20 mmHg. For Jim's age group, 140 is the cutoff for high blood pressure. (a) If Jim's systolic blood pressure is taken at a randomly chosen moment, what is the probability that it will be 135 or less? (b) 175 or more? (c) Between 125 and 165? (d) Discuss the implications of variability for physicians who are trying to identify patients with high blood pressure.

7.71 A statistics exam was given. Explain the meaning of each z-value.
a. John's z-score was -1.62.
b. Mary's z-score was 0.50.
c. Zak's z-score was 1.79.
d. Frieda's z-score was 2.48.

7.72 Are the following statements true or false? Explain your reasoning.
a. "If we see a standardized z-value beyond ± 3, the variable cannot be normally distributed."
b. "If X and Y are two normally distributed random variables measured in different units (e.g., X is in pounds and Y is in kilograms), then it is not meaningful to compare the standardized z-values."
c. "Two machines fill 2-liter soft drink bottles by using a similar process. Machine A has $\mu = 1,990$ ml and $\sigma = 5$ ml while Machine B has $\mu = 1,995$ ml and $\sigma = 3$ ml. The variables cannot both be normally distributed since they have different standard deviations."

7.73 John can take either of two routes (A or B) to LAX airport. At midday on a typical Wednesday the travel time on either route is normally distributed with parameters $\mu_A = 54$ minutes, $\sigma_A = 6$ minutes, $\mu_B = 60$ minutes, and $\sigma_B = 3$ minutes. (a) Which route should he choose if he must be at the airport in 54 minutes to pick up his spouse? (b) Sixty minutes? (c) Sixty-six minutes? Explain carefully.

7.74 The amount of fill in a half-liter (500 ml) soft drink bottle is normally distributed. The process has a standard deviation of 5 ml. The mean is adjustable. (a) Where should the mean be set to ensure a 95 percent probability that a half-liter bottle will not be underfilled? (b) A 99 percent probability? (c) A 99.9 percent probability? Explain.

7.75 The length of a certain kind of Colorado brook trout is normally distributed with a mean of 12.5 inches and a standard deviation of 1.2 inch. What minimum size limit should the Department of Natural Resources set if it wishes to allow people to keep 80 percent of the trout they catch?

7.76 Times for a surgical procedure are normally distributed. There are two methods. Method A has a mean of 28 minutes and a standard deviation of 4 minutes, while method B has a mean of 32 minutes and a standard deviation of 2 minutes. (a) Which procedure is preferred if the procedure must be completed within 28 minutes? (b) Thirty-eight minutes? (c) Thirty-six minutes? Explain your reasoning fully.

7.77 The length of a brook trout is normally distributed. Two brook trout are caught. (a) What is the probability that both exceed the mean? (b) Neither exceeds the mean? (c) One is above the mean and one is below? (d) Both are equal to the mean?

APPROXIMATIONS

7.78 Among live deliveries, the probability of a twin birth is .02. (a) In 2,000 live deliveries what is the probability of at least 50 twin births? (b) Fewer than 35? Explain carefully.

7.79   Nationwide, the probability that a rental car is from Hertz is 25 percent. In a sample of 100 rental cars, what is the probability that fewer than 20 are from Hertz? Explain.

7.80   When a needle biopsy is ordered, there is an 85 percent chance that the test will indicate no breast cancer. In a given week, 20,000 such tests are performed. Find the quartiles for the number of such biopsies that will indicate no cancer. Explain fully and show all steps. (Data are from *The Economist Technology Quarterly* 367, no. 8329 [June 21, 2003], p. 8.)

7.81   A multiple-choice exam has 100 questions. Each question has four choices. (a) What minimum score should be required to reduce the chance of passing by random guessing to 5 percent? (b) To 1 percent? (c) Find the quartiles for a guesser. Explain fully.

7.82   The probability that a certain kind of flower seed will germinate is .80. (a) If 200 seeds are planted, what is the probability that fewer than 150 will germinate? (b) That at least 150 will germinate?

7.83   On a cold morning the probability is .02 that a given car will not start. In the small town of Eureka 1,500 cars are started each cold morning. (a) What is the probability that at least 25 cars will not start? (b) More than 40?

7.84   At a certain fire station, false alarms are received at a mean rate of 0.2 per day. In a year, what is the probability that fewer than 60 false alarms are received? Explain fully and show all steps.

EXPONENTIAL DISTRIBUTION

7.85   The HP dvd1040i 20X Multiformat DVD Writer has an MTBF of 70,000 hours. (a) Assuming continuous operation, what is the probability that the DVD writer will last more than 100,000 hours? (b) Less than 50,000 hours? (c) At least 50,000 hours but not more than 80,000 hours? (Product specifications are from www.hp.com.)

7.86   Automobile warranty claims for engine mount failure in a Troppo Malo 2000 SE are rare at a certain dealership, occurring at a mean rate of 0.1 claims per month. (a) What is the probability that the dealership will wait at least 6 months until the next claim? (b) At least a year? (c) At least 2 years? (d) At least 6 months but not more than 1 year?

7.87   Suppose the average time to service a Noodles & Company customer at a certain restaurant is 3 minutes and the service time follows an exponential distribution. (a) What is the probability that a customer will be serviced in less than 3 minutes? (b) Why is your answer more than 50 percent? Shouldn't exactly half the area be below the mean?

7.88   Systron Donner Inertial manufactures inertial subsystems for automotive, commercial/industrial, and aerospace and defense applications. The sensors use a one-piece, micromachined inertial sensing element to measure angular rotational velocity or linear acceleration. The MTBF for a single axis sensor is 400,000 hours. (a) Find the probability that a sensor lasts at least 30 years, assuming continuous operation. (b) Would you be surprised to learn that a sensor has failed within the first 3 years? Explain. (Product specifications are from www.systron.com/techsupp_A.asp.)

DISCUSSION QUESTION

7.89   On a police sergeant's examination, the historical mean score was 80 with a standard deviation of 20. Four officers who were alleged to be cronies of the police chief scored 195, 171, 191, and 189, respectively, on the test. This led to allegations of irregularity in the exam. (a) Convert these four officers' scores to standardized z-values. (b) Do you think there was sufficient reason to question these four exam scores? What assumptions are you making? (Data are from *Detroit Free Press,* March 19, 1999, p. 10A.)

RELATED READING   Balakrishnan, N.; and V. B. Nevzorov. *A Primer on Statistical Distributions*. Wiley, 2003.

Evans, Merran; Nicholas Hastings; and Brian Peacock. *Statistical Distributions*. 3rd ed. Wiley, 2000.

International Organization for Standardization. *Guide to the Expression of Uncertainty in Measurement*. 1995.

LearningStats Unit 07   Continuous Distributions

LS

LearningStats Unit 07 lets you work with continuous distributions, particularly the normal distribution, demonstrating how to calculate areas and showing the shapes of the distributions. Modules are designed for self-study, so you can proceed at your own pace.

Topic	LearningStats Modules
Overview	Continuous Distributions
Calculations	Continuous Distributions: Examples Normal Areas Probability Calculator
Normal approximations	Evaluating Rules of Thumb
Random data	Random Continuous Data
Tables	Table C—Normal Probabilities
Applications	Formulas for Continuous PDFs Exponential Model and Problems Random Normal Data

Key: = PowerPoint   = Word   = Excel

Visual Statistics

VS

Visual Statistics Modules on Continuous Distributions

Module	Module Name
5	**VS** Visualizing Continuous Distributions

Visual Statistics Module 5 (included on your CD) is designed to help you

- Recognize common continuous distributions and their distribution functions.
- Identify the parameters of common continuous distributions and how they affect shape.
- Recognize shape measures for common distributions.
- Understand when common continuous distributions can be approximated by a normal.
- Understand the relation between a value of a distribution and its tail area.

The worktext chapter (included on the CD in .PDF format) contains a list of concepts covered, objectives of the module, overview of concepts, illustration of concepts, orientation to module features, learning exercises (basic, intermediate, advanced), learning projects (individual, team), self-evaluation quiz, glossary of terms, and solutions to a self-evaluation quiz.

1. Which type of probability (empirical, classical, subjective) is each of the following?
    a. On a given Friday, the probability that Flight 277 to Chicago is on time is 23.7%.
    b. Your chance of going to Disney World next year is 10%.
    c. The chance of rolling a 3 on two dice is 1/18.

2. For the following contingency table, find (a) $P(H \cap T)$; (b) $P(S \mid G)$; (c) $P(S)$

	R	S	T	Row Total
G	10	50	30	90
H	20	50	40	110
Col Total	30	100	70	200

3. If $P(A) = .30$, $P(B) = .70$, and $P(A \cap B) = .25$ are A and B independent events? Explain.

4. Which statement is *false*? Explain.
    a. If $P(A) = .05$ then the odds against event A's occurrence are 19 to 1.
    b. If A and B are mutually exclusive events then $P(A \cup B) = 0$.
    c. The number of permutations of 5 things taken 2 at a time is 20.

5. Which statement is *true*? Why not the others?
    a. The Poisson distribution has two parameters.
    b. The binomial distribution assumes dependent random trials.
    c. The uniform distribution has two parameters.

6. If the payoff of a risky investment has three possible outcomes ($1000, $2000, $5000) with probabilities .60, .30, and .10 respectively, find the expected value.
    a. $1500   b. $2300   c. $1700

7. Assuming independent arrivals with a mean of 2.5 arrivals per minute, find the probability that in a given minute there will be (a) exactly 2 arrivals; (b) at least 3 arrivals; (c) fewer than 4 arrivals. (d) Which probability distribution did you use and why?

8. If a random experiment whose success probability is .20 is repeated 8 times, find the probability of (a) exactly 3 successes; (b) more than 3 successes; (c) at most 2 successes. (d) Which probability distribution did you use and why?

9. In a random experiment with 50 independent trials with constant probability of success .30, find the mean and standard deviation of the number of successes.

10. Which probability distribution (uniform, binomial, Poisson) is most nearly appropriate to describe each situation (assuming you knew the relevant parameters)?
    a. The number of dimes older than 10 years in a random sample of 8 dimes.
    b. The number of hospital patients admitted during a given minute on Tuesday morning.
    c. The last digit of a randomly chosen student's social security number.

11. Which statement is *false*? Explain.
    a. The Poisson distribution is always right-skewed.
    b. The mean of the uniform distribution is always $(a + b)/2$.
    c. The Excel function =RAND() generates a normal random variable.

12. Which statement is *false*? Explain.
    a. To find probabilities in a continuous distribution we add up the probabilities at each point.
    b. A uniform continuous model $U(5,21)$ has mean 13 and standard deviation 4.619.
    c. A uniform PDF is constant for all values within the interval $a \leq X \leq b$.

13. Which statement is *true* for a normal distribution? Why not the others?
    a. The shape of the PDF is always symmetric regardless of μ and σ.
    b. The shape of the CDF resembles a bell-shaped curve.
    c. When no tables are available, areas may be found by a simple formula.

14. If freeway speeds are normally distributed with a mean of $\mu = 70$ mph and $\sigma = 7$ mph, find the probability that the speed of a randomly chosen vehicle (a) exceeds 78 mph; (b) is between 65 and 75 mph; (c) is less than 70 mph.

15. In the previous problem, calculate (a) the 95th percentile of vehicle speeds (i.e., 95 percent below); (b) the lowest 10 percent of speeds; (c) the highest 25 percent of speeds (3rd quartile).

16. Which of the following Excel formulas would be a correct way to calculate $P(X < 450)$ given that X is $N(500, 60)$?
    a. =NORMDIST(450, 500, 60, 1)
    b. =NORMSDIST(450, 60)
    c. =1−NORMDIST(450, 500, 60, 0)

17. If arrivals follow a Poisson distribution with mean 1.2 arrivals per minute, find the probability that the waiting time until the next arrival will be (a) less than 1.5 minutes; (b) more than 30 seconds; (c) between 1 and 2 minutes.

18. In the previous problem, find (a) the 95th percentile of waiting times (i.e., 95 percent below); (b) the first quartile of waiting times; (c) the mean time between arrivals.

19. Which statement is *correct* concerning the normal approximation? Why not the others?
    a. The normal Poisson approximation is acceptable when $\lambda \geq 10$.
    b. The normal binomial approximation is better when n is small and π is large.
    c. Normal approximations are needed since Excel lacks discrete probability functions.

Sampling Distributions and Estimation

Chapter Learning Objectives

When you finish this chapter you should be able to

- Define sampling variation, sampling error, parameter, and estimator.
- Explain why it is desirable that an estimator be unbiased, consistent, and efficient.
- State the Central Limit Theorem for a mean or proportion.
- Explain how the standard error is affected by sample size.
- Construct a 90, 95, or 99 percent confidence interval for a mean or proportion.
- Describe similarities and differences between z and Student's t.
- Find t-values in tables or Excel for a desired confidence level.
- Calculate sample size for a given precision and confidence level to estimate μ or π.

A sample statistic is a *random variable* whose value depends on which population items happen to be included in the *random sample*. Some samples may represent the population well, while other samples could differ greatly from the population (particularly if the sample size is small). To illustrate **sampling variation**, let's draw some random samples from a large population of GMAT scores for MBA applicants. The population *parameters* are $\mu = 520.78$ and $\sigma = 86.80$. Figure 8.1 shows a dot plot of the entire population ($N = 2,637$), which resembles a normal distribution.

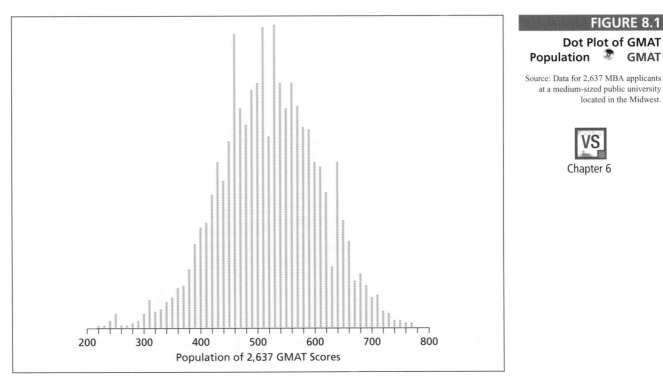

FIGURE 8.1

Dot Plot of GMAT Population 🖱 **GMAT**

Source: Data for 2,637 MBA applicants at a medium-sized public university located in the Midwest.

VS

Chapter 6

Population of 2,637 GMAT Scores

The table below shows eight random samples of $n = 5$ from this population. The samples vary because of the variability of GMAT scores in the population. Sampling variation is inevitable, yet there is a tendency for the sample means to be close to the population mean ($\mu = 520.78$), as shown in Figure 8.2. In larger samples, the sample means would tend to be even closer to μ. This phenomenon is the basis for **statistical estimation**.

Random Samples ($n = 5$) from the GMAT Score Population

Sample 1	Sample 2	Sample 3	Sample 4	Sample 5	Sample 6	Sample 7	Sample 8
490	310	500	450	420	450	490	670
580	590	450	590	640	670	450	610
440	730	510	710	470	390	590	550
580	710	570	240	530	500	640	540
430	540	610	510	640	470	650	540
$\bar{x}_1 = 504.0$	$\bar{x}_2 = 576.0$	$\bar{x}_3 = 528.0$	$\bar{x}_4 = 500.0$	$\bar{x}_5 = 540.0$	$\bar{x}_6 = 496.0$	$\bar{x}_7 = 564.0$	$\bar{x}_8 = 582.0$

FIGURE 8.2

Dot Plots of Eight Sample Means

From Figure 8.2 we see that the sample *means* (red markers) have much less variation than the *individual* sample items. This is because the mean is an *average*. This chapter describes the behavior of the sample mean and other statistical estimators of population parameters, and explains how to make *inferences* about a population that take into account four factors:

- Sampling variation (uncontrollable).
- Population variation (uncontrollable).
- Sample size (controllable).
- Desired *confidence* in the estimate (controllable).

SHOE By Jeff MacNelly

Some Terminology

An **estimator** is a statistic derived from a sample to infer the value of a population **parameter**. An **estimate** is the value of the estimator in a particular sample. Table 8.1 and Figure 8.3 show some common estimators. We usually denote a population parameter by a Greek letter (e.g., μ, σ, or π). The corresponding sample estimator is usually a Roman letter (e.g., $\bar{x}$, s, or p) or a Greek letter with a "hat" (e.g., $\hat{\mu}$, $\hat{\sigma}$, or $\hat{\pi}$). Statistics books may use different symbols for these things. That's because the science of statistics developed over many decades and its founders had various ways of expressing their ideas.

Estimator	Formula	Parameter
Sample mean	$\bar{x} = \dfrac{1}{n}\sum_{i=1}^{n} x_i$ where x_i is the ith data value and n is the sample size	μ
Sample proportion	$p = x/n$ where x is the number of successes in the sample and n is the sample size	π
Sample standard deviation	$s = \sqrt{\dfrac{\sum_{i=1}^{n} (x_i - \bar{x})^2}{n-1}}$ where x_i is the ith data value and n is the sample size	σ

TABLE 8.1

Examples of Estimators

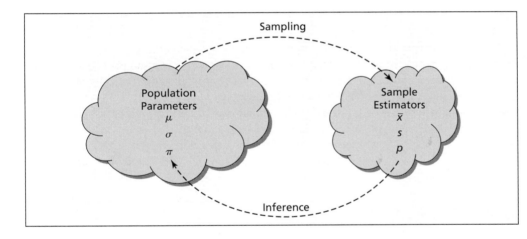

FIGURE 8.3

Sample Estimators of Population Parameters

Sampling Distributions and Sampling Error

Random samples vary, so an estimator is a *random variable*. The **sampling distribution** of an estimator is the probability distribution of all possible values the statistic may assume when a random sample of size n is taken. It has a probability distribution, mean, and variance. The **sampling error** is the difference between an estimate $\hat{\theta}$ and the corresponding population parameter θ:

$$\text{Sampling Error} = \hat{\theta} - \theta \tag{8.1}$$

Sampling error exists because different samples will yield different values for $\hat{\theta}$, depending on which population items happen to be included in the sample.

Bias

The **bias** is the difference between the expected value (i.e., the average value) of the estimator and the true parameter:

$$\text{Bias} = E(\hat{\theta}) - \theta \tag{8.2}$$

An estimator is *unbiased* if $E(\hat{\theta}) = \theta$. There can be sampling error in a particular sample, but an **unbiased estimator** neither overstates nor understates the true parameter *on average*.

Sampling error is *random* whereas bias is *systematic.* Consider an analogy with target shooting, illustrated in Figure 8.4. An expert whose rifle sights are correctly aligned will produce a target pattern like one on the left. The same expert shooting a rifle with misaligned sights might produce the pattern on the right. There is sample variation, but the unbiased estimator is correctly *aimed.*

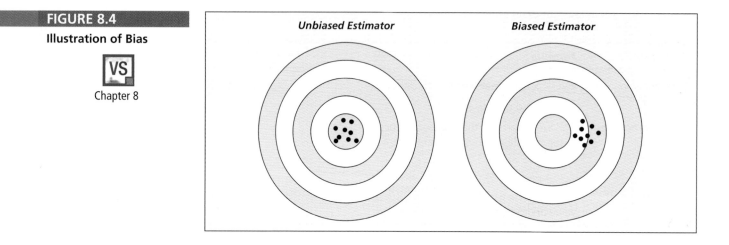

Some samples may happen to hit closer to the bull's-eye than others, but at least an unbiased estimator avoids *systematic* error. You cannot observe bias in a sample because you do not know the true population parameter, but bias can be studied mathematically or by simulation experiments (e.g., Visual Statistics). Statisticians have shown that the sample mean $\bar{x}$ and the sample proportion p are unbiased estimators for μ and π, respectively. Similarly, s^2 is an unbiased estimate of σ^2. Table 8.2 shows examples of estimates from *known* populations. It is interesting to see that some of the estimates came very close to the population

TABLE 8.2 **Sample Estimates** 🐟 **Samples3**

Estimator	True Parameter	Sample Estimate	Interpretation
Sample mean	In 2005, the average age of all *Forbes 500* top CEOs was $\mu = 55.7$ years.	A random sample of 10 of these CEOs gave a mean age of $\bar{x} = 56.3$ years.	The sample mean is an unbiased estimate of μ. The difference between $\bar{x}$ and μ is *sampling error.* A different sample could yield a different estimate of μ.
Sample proportion	In 2006, the proportion of the *Fortune 1000* companies that reported a negative profit (i.e., a loss) was $\pi = 95/1000 = .095$ or 9.5%.	In a random sample of 50 of these companies, 6 reported a negative profit, giving a sample proportion $p = 6/50 = .12$ or 12%.	The sampling error in this case is not very large. However, a different sample could yield a different estimate of π.
Sample standard deviation	In 2005, compensation (in millions) of *Forbes'* top 500 CEOs was $\mu = \$10.31$m with $\sigma = 17.95$m. σ is huge because of outliers and skewed data.	A random sample of 20 of these CEOs showed $\bar{x} = 8.90$m and $s = \$19.83$m.	Our sample included none of the 13 CEOs in the population who earned over \$50m, but did include Steven P. Jobs whose \$0 compensation lowered the mean and raised the standard deviation.

values, while others did not. While it is helpful in visualizing the process of estimation, Table 8.2 is unusual because most of the time you wouldn't *know* the true population parameters (if you had the population, why would you take a sample?). As you think about Table 8.2, you might ask yourself how *you* would take a "random sample" from each of these populations.

Bias is not a concern for the sample mean ($\bar{x}$) and sample proportion (p). But we can find examples of biased estimators. For example, you will get a slightly biased estimate of σ if you use Excel's population standard deviation formula =STDEVP(Data) instead of its sample standard deviation formula =STDEV(Data) for a sample array named Data. But why would you do that? Further, there is no reason to *worry* about sampling error, because it is an inevitable risk in statistical sampling. Anyway, you cannot *know* whether you have sampling error without knowing the population parameter (and if you knew it, you wouldn't be taking a sample). It is more important to take a large enough sample to obtain a reliable estimate and to take the sample scientifically (see Chapter 2, "Data Collection").

Efficiency

Efficiency refers to the variance of the estimator's sampling distribution. Smaller variance means a more efficient estimator. Among all unbiased estimators, we prefer the **minimum variance estimator**, referred to as MVUE (minimum variance unbiased estimator). Figure 8.5 shows two unbiased estimators. Both patterns are centered on the bull's-eye, but the estimator on the left has less variation. You cannot assess efficiency from one sample, but it can be studied either mathematically or by simulation (e.g., Visual Statistics). While an MVUE does not exist for every parameter of every distribution, statisticians have proved that, for a normal distribution, $\bar{x}$ and s^2 are minimum variance estimators of μ and σ^2, respectively (i.e., no other estimators can have smaller variance). Similarly, the sample proportion p, is an MVUE of the population proportion, π. That is one reason these statistics are widely used.

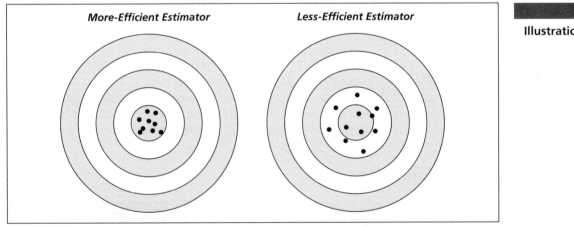

More-Efficient Estimator   *Less-Efficient Estimator*

FIGURE 8.5

Illustration of Efficiency

Consistency

A **consistent estimator** converges toward the parameter being estimated as the sample size increases. That is, the sample distribution collapses on the true parameter, as illustrated in Figure 8.6. It seems logical that in larger samples $\bar{x}$ ought to be closer to μ, p ought to be closer to π, and s ought to be closer to σ. In fact, it can be shown that the variances of these three estimators diminish as n increases, so all are consistent estimators. Figure 8.6 illustrates the importance of a large sample, because in a large sample your estimate is likely to be closer to θ.

FIGURE 8.6

Illustration of
Consistency

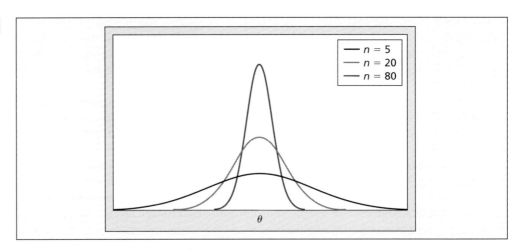

8.3

SAMPLE MEAN AND THE CENTRAL LIMIT THEOREM

Chapter 7

Consider the sample mean $\bar{X}$ used to estimate the population mean μ. Our ultimate objective is to use the sampling distribution of $\bar{X}$ to say something about the population that we are studying. To describe the sampling distribution we need to know the mean, variance, and shape of the distribution. As we've already learned, the sample mean is an unbiased estimator for μ; therefore,

(8.3) $E(\bar{X}) = \mu$ (expected value of the mean)

We've also learned that the value of $\bar{X}$ will change whenever we take a different sample. And as long as our samples are *random samples,* we should feel confident that the only type of error we will have in our estimating process is *sampling error.* The sampling error of the sample mean is described by its standard deviation. This value has a special name, the **standard error of the mean**. Notice that the standard error of the mean decreases as the sample size increases:

(8.4) $\sigma_{\bar{x}} = \dfrac{\sigma}{\sqrt{n}}$ (standard error of the mean)

Suppose the average price, μ, of a 2 GB MP3 player is $80.00 with a standard deviation, σ, equal to $10.00. What will be the mean and standard error of $\bar{x}$ from a sample of 20 MP3 players?

$$\mu_{\bar{x}} = \$80.00, \qquad \sigma_{\bar{x}} = \frac{\$10.00}{\sqrt{20}} = \$2.236$$

Furthermore, if we know that the population is exactly normal, then the sample mean follows a normal distribution for any sample size. Unfortunately, the population may not have a normal distribution, or we may simply not know *what* the population distribution looks like. What can we do in these circumstances? We can use one of the most fundamental laws of statistics, the Central Limit Theorem.

Central Limit Theorem for a Mean

Central Limit Theorem for a Mean

If a random sample of size n is drawn from a population with mean μ and standard deviation σ, the distribution of the sample mean $\bar{X}$ approaches a normal distribution with mean μ and standard deviation $\sigma_{\bar{x}} = \sigma/\sqrt{n}$ as the sample size increases.

The **Central Limit Theorem** (CLT) is a powerful result that allows us to approximate the shape of the sampling distribution of $\bar{X}$ even when we don't know what the population looks like. Here are 3 important facts about the sample mean.

1. If the population is exactly normal, the sample mean follows a normal distribution centered at μ regardless of sample size, with a standard error equal to $\sigma/\sqrt{n}$.

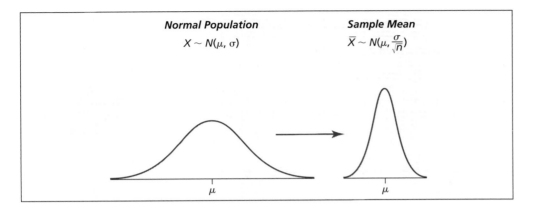

2. As sample size *n* increases, the distribution of sample means narrows in on the population mean μ (i.e., the *standard error of the mean* $\sigma_{\bar{x}} = \sigma/\sqrt{n}$ approaches zero).

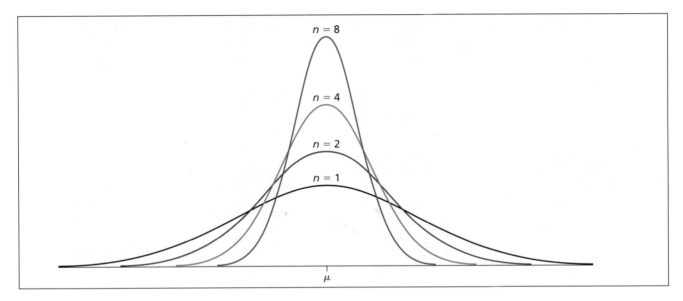

3. By the Central Limit Theorem, if the sample size is large enough, the sample means will have approximately a normal distribution even if your population is *not* normal.

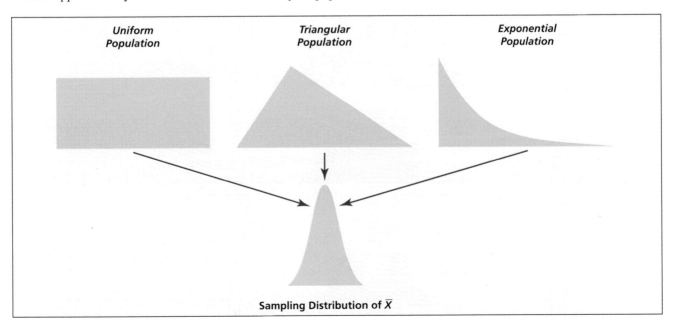

Sampling Distribution of $\bar{X}$

TABLE 8.3	Predictions for Samples from a Uniform Population		CLTPopulations	
	Predicted Sampling Distribution Parameters		**Results for 2000 Sample Means**	
Sample Size	**Mean of Means**	**Standard Error of Means**	**Mean of Means**	**Standard Deviation of Means**
$n = 1$	$\mu = 500$	$\sigma_{\bar{x}} = \sigma/\sqrt{n} = 288.7/\sqrt{1} = 288.7$	$\bar{\bar{x}} = 508.7$	$s_{\bar{x}} = 290.7$
$n = 2$	$\mu = 500$	$\sigma_{\bar{x}} = \sigma/\sqrt{n} = 288.7/\sqrt{2} = 204.1$	$\bar{\bar{x}} = 497.9$	$s_{\bar{x}} = 202.6$
$n = 4$	$\mu = 500$	$\sigma_{\bar{x}} = \sigma/\sqrt{n} = 288.7/\sqrt{4} = 144.3$	$\bar{\bar{x}} = 498.4$	$s_{\bar{x}} = 145.2$
$n = 8$	$\mu = 500$	$\sigma_{\bar{x}} = \sigma/\sqrt{n} = 288.7/\sqrt{8} = 102.1$	$\bar{\bar{x}} = 498.8$	$s_{\bar{x}} = 100.2$

Illustration: Uniform Population You may have heard the rule of thumb that $n \geq 30$ is required to ensure a normal distribution for the sample mean, but actually a much smaller n will suffice if the population is symmetric. You can demonstrate this by performing your own simulations in *LearningStats* or Visual Statistics. For example, consider a uniform population $\mu(0,1000)$ with mean $\mu = 500$ and standard deviation $\sigma = 288.7$. The Central Limit Theorem predicts that the distribution of sample means drawn from the population will approach normality. Also, the standard error of the sample mean will decrease as sample size increases. $\bar{\bar{x}}$ is the notation used to represent the average of many $\bar{x}$'s and $s_{\bar{x}}$ represents the standard deviation of many $\bar{x}$'s. This is illustrated in Table 8.3.

Figure 8.7 shows histograms of the actual means of many samples drawn from this uniform population. There is sampling variation, but the means and standard deviations of the sample

FIGURE 8.7

Illustrations of Central Limit Theorem

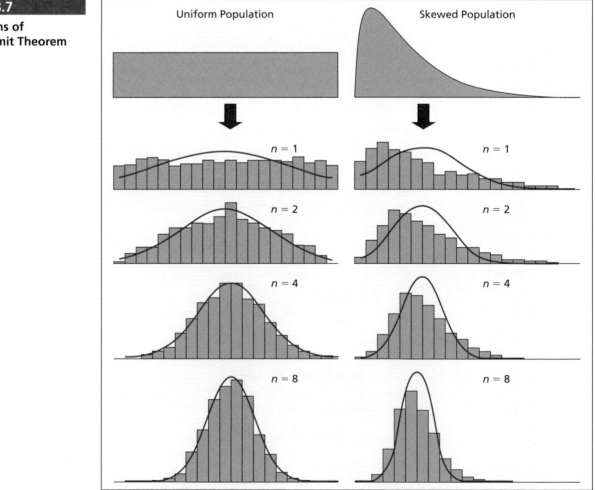

means are very close to the predictions in Table 8.3. When $n = 1$, the "means" are simply individual population items, so the histogram looks just like the population, and is not normal. For $n = 2$, the histogram of means is triangular, while for $n = 4$ and $n = 8$ we clearly see the approach to a bell shaped histogram and decreasing variance of the sample mean as sample size increases.

Illustration: Skewed Population   A symmetric, uniform population does not pose much of a challenge for the Central Limit Theorem. But what if the population is severely skewed? For example, consider a strongly skewed population (e.g., waiting times at airport security screening). The Central Limit Theorem predicts that *for any population* the distribution of sample means drawn from this population will approach normality. The standard error of the sample mean will diminish as sample size increases, as illustrated in Table 8.4.

Predictions for Samples from a Skewed Population CLTPopulations			Results for 2000 Sample Means		TABLE 8.4
	Predicted Sampling Distribution Parameters			**Results for 2000 Sample Means**	
Sample Size	**Mean of Means**	**Standard Error of Means**	**Mean of Means**	**Standard Deviation of Means**	
$n = 1$	$\mu = 3.000$	$\sigma_{\bar{x}} = \sigma/\sqrt{n} = 2.449/\sqrt{1} = 2.449$	$\bar{\bar{x}} = 3.050$	$s_{\bar{x}} = 2.517$	
$n = 2$	$\mu = 3.000$	$\sigma_{\bar{x}} = \sigma/\sqrt{n} = 2.449/\sqrt{2} = 1.732$	$\bar{\bar{x}} = 2.982$	$s_{\bar{x}} = 1.704$	
$n = 4$	$\mu = 3.000$	$\sigma_{\bar{x}} = \sigma/\sqrt{n} = 2.449/\sqrt{4} = 1.225$	$\bar{\bar{x}} = 2.973$	$s_{\bar{x}} = 1.196$	
$n = 8$	$\mu = 3.000$	$\sigma_{\bar{x}} = \sigma/\sqrt{n} = 2.449/\sqrt{8} = 0.866$	$\bar{\bar{x}} = 3.005$	$s_{\bar{x}} = 0.868$	

Figure 8.7 shows histograms of the actual means of many samples drawn from this skewed population. Despite the skewness, the means and standard deviations of the sample means are very close to the CLT's predictions. When $n = 1$, the "means" are simply individual population items, so the histogram of means looks just like the skewed parent population. In contrast to the uniform population example, $n = 2$ and $n = 4$ do *not* produce bell-shaped histograms, although the variance does decrease. When $n = 8$ the histogram begins to look normal but a larger sample might be preferable. In highly skewed populations, even $n \geq 30$ will not ensure normality, although in general it is not a bad rule. In severely skewed populations, recall that the mean is a poor measure of central tendency to begin with due to outliers.

The Central Limit Theorem permits us to define an interval within which the sample means are expected to fall. As long as the sample size n is large enough, we can use the normal distribution regardless of the population shape (or any n if the population is normal to begin with):

$$\mu \pm z \frac{\sigma}{\sqrt{n}} \qquad \text{(range of sample means according to CLT)} \qquad \textbf{(8.5)}$$

We use the familiar z-values for the standard normal distribution. If we know μ and σ, we can predict the range of sample means for samples of size n:

90% Interval   *95% Interval*   *99% Interval*

$$\mu \pm 1.645 \frac{\sigma}{\sqrt{n}} \qquad\qquad \mu \pm 1.960 \frac{\sigma}{\sqrt{n}} \qquad\qquad \mu \pm 2.576 \frac{\sigma}{\sqrt{n}}$$

For example, within what range would we expect GMAT sample means to fall for samples of $n = 5$ applicants (see Figure 8.1)? The population is approximately normal with parameters $\mu = 520.78$ and $\sigma = 86.80$, so the predicted range for 95 percent of the sample means is

$$\mu \pm 1.960 \frac{\sigma}{\sqrt{n}} = 520.78 \pm 1.960 \frac{86.80}{\sqrt{5}} = 520.78 \pm 76.08$$

Our eight sample means for $n = 5$ (see Figure 8.2) drawn from this population fall comfortably within this range (roughly 444 to 597), as predicted by the Central Limit Theorem.

EXAMPLE

Bottle Filling: Variation in $\bar{X}$

The amount of fill in a half-liter (500 ml) bottle of Diet Coke is normally distributed with mean $\mu = 505$ ml and standard deviation $\sigma = 1.2$ ml. Since the population is normal, the sample mean $\bar{X}$ will be a normally distributed random variable for any sample size. If we sample a single bottle (i.e., $n = 1$) and measure its fill, the sample "mean" is just X, which should lie within the ranges shown in Table 8.5. It appears that the company has set the mean far enough above 500 ml that essentially all bottles contain at least the advertised half-liter quantity. If we increase the sample size to $n = 4$ bottles, we expect the sample means to lie within a narrower range, as shown in Table 8.5, because when we average 4 items, we *reduce the variability* in the sample mean.

TABLE 8.5	95 Percent Range of the Mean
n = 1	**n = 4**
$\mu \pm 1.960 \dfrac{\sigma}{\sqrt{n}}$	$\mu \pm 1.960 \dfrac{\sigma}{\sqrt{n}}$
$505 \pm 1.960 \dfrac{1.2}{\sqrt{1}}$	$505 \pm 1.960 \dfrac{1.2}{\sqrt{4}}$
505 ± 2.352	505 ± 1.176
$502.6 < \bar{X} < 507.4$	$503.8 < \bar{X} < 506.2$

If this experiment were repeated a large number of times, we would expect that the sample means would lie within the limits shown above. For example, if we took 1,000 samples and computed the mean fill for each sample, we would expect that approximately 950 of the sample means would lie within the 95 percent limits. But we don't really take 1,000 samples (except in a computer simulation). We actually take only *one* sample. The importance of the CLT is that it *predicts* what will happen with that *one* sample.

Sample Size and Standard Error

Even if the population standard deviation σ is large, the sample means will fall within a narrow interval as long as n is large. The key is the *standard error of the mean:* $\sigma_{\bar{x}} = \sigma/\sqrt{n}$. The standard error decreases as n increases. Figure 8.8 illustrates how increasing n reduces the standard error (expressed in this diagram as a fraction of σ). For example, when $n = 4$ the standard error is halved. To halve it again requires $n = 16$, and to halve it again requires $n = 64$. To *halve* the standard error, you must *quadruple* the sample size (the law of diminishing returns).

Sample Size	*Standard Error*
$n = 4$	$\sigma_{\bar{x}} = \sigma/2$
$n = 16$	$\sigma_{\bar{x}} = \sigma/4$
$n = 64$	$\sigma_{\bar{x}} = \sigma/8$

FIGURE 8.8

Standard Error Declines as *n* Increases

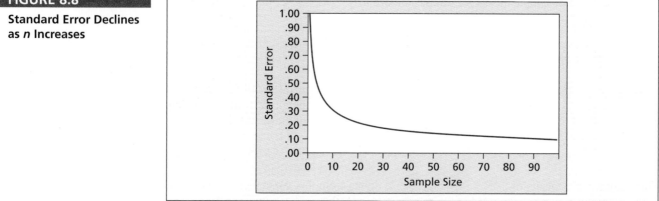

You can make the interval $\mu \pm z\sigma/\sqrt{n}$ as small as you want by increasing n. Thus, the distribution of sample means collapses at the true population mean μ as n increases.

Illustration: All Possible Samples from a Uniform Population

To help visualize the meaning of the Central Limit Theorem, consider a small discrete uniform population consisting of the integers $\{0, 1, 2, 3\}$. The population parameters are $\mu = 1.5$ and $\sigma = 1.118$ (using the population definition of σ).

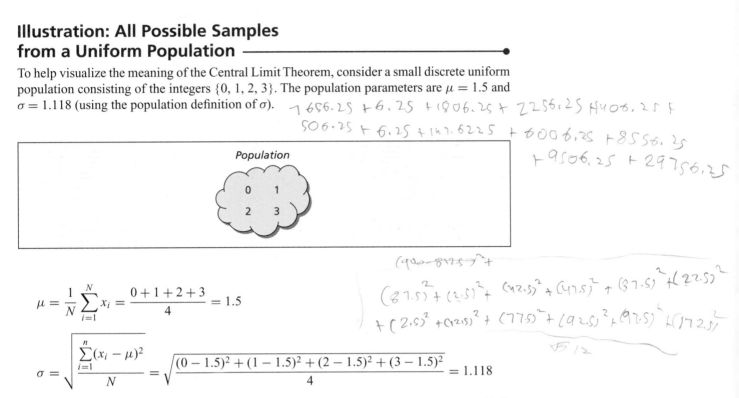

Population

$$\mu = \frac{1}{N}\sum_{i=1}^{N} x_i = \frac{0+1+2+3}{4} = 1.5$$

$$\sigma = \sqrt{\frac{\sum_{i=1}^{n}(x_i - \mu)^2}{N}} = \sqrt{\frac{(0-1.5)^2 + (1-1.5)^2 + (2-1.5)^2 + (3-1.5)^2}{4}} = 1.118$$

Take all possible random samples of $n = 2$ items *with replacement*. There are 16 equally likely outcomes (x_1, x_2). Each sample mean is $\bar{x} = (x_1 + x_2)/2$:

Possible Values of x_2	Possible Values of x_1			
	0	**1**	**2**	**3**
0	$\bar{x} = (0+0)/2 = 0.0$	$\bar{x} = (1+0)/2 = 0.5$	$\bar{x} = (2+0)/2 = 1.0$	$\bar{x} = (3+0)/2 = 1.5$
1	$\bar{x} = (0+1)/2 = 0.5$	$\bar{x} = (1+1)/2 = 1.0$	$\bar{x} = (2+1)/2 = 1.5$	$\bar{x} = (3+1)/2 = 2.0$
2	$\bar{x} = (0+2)/2 = 1.0$	$\bar{x} = (1+2)/2 = 1.5$	$\bar{x} = (2+2)/2 = 2.0$	$\bar{x} = (3+2)/2 = 2.5$
3	$\bar{x} = (0+3)/2 = 1.5$	$\bar{x} = (1+3)/2 = 2.0$	$\bar{x} = (2+3)/2 = 2.5$	$\bar{x} = (3+3)/2 = 3.0$

The population is uniform (0, 1, 2, 3 are equally likely) yet the distribution of all possible sample means has a peaked triangular shape, as shown in Table 8.6 and Figure 8.9. The distribution of sample means has distinct central tendency, as predicted by the Central Limit Theorem.

Sample Mean	Frequency	Relative Frequency
0.0	1	0.0625
0.5	2	0.1250
1.0	3	0.1875
1.5	4	0.2500
2.0	3	0.1875
2.5	2	0.1250
3.0	1	0.0625
Total	16	1.0000

TABLE 8.6

All Possible Sample Means for $n = 2$

FIGURE 8.9

Population and Sampling Distribution of Means for $n = 2$

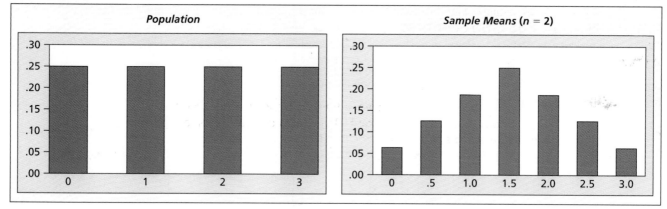

The Central Limit Theorem's predictions for the mean and standard error are

$$\mu_{\bar{x}} = \mu = 1.5 \quad \text{and} \quad \sigma_{\bar{x}} = \frac{\sigma}{\sqrt{n}} = \frac{1.118}{\sqrt{2}} = 0.7905$$

These theoretical predictions are borne out exactly for all 16 possible sample means. The mean of *means* $\bar{\bar{x}}$ is

$$\bar{\bar{x}} = \frac{1(0.0) + 2(0.5) + 3(1.0) + 4(1.5) + 3(2.0) + 2(2.5) + 1(3.0)}{16} = 1.5$$

As predicted by the CLT, the standard deviation of the *sample means* is

$$\sigma_{\bar{x}} = \sqrt{\frac{\begin{bmatrix} 1(0.0 - 1.5)^2 + 2(0.5 - 1.5)^2 + 3(1.0 - 1.5)^2 + 4(1.5 - 1.5)^2 \\ + 3(2.0 - 1.5)^2 + 2(2.5 - 1.5)^2 + 1(3.0 - 1.5)^2 \end{bmatrix}}{16}} = 0.7906$$

SECTION EXERCISES

8.1 Find the standard error of the mean for each sampling situation (assuming a normal population). What happens to the standard error each time you quadruple the sample size?
a. $\sigma = 32, n = 4$
b. $\sigma = 32, n = 16$
c. $\sigma = 32, n = 64$

8.2 Find the 95 percent range for the sample mean, assuming that each sample is from a normal population.
a. $\mu = 200, \sigma = 12, n = 36$
b. $\mu = 1,000, \sigma = 15, n = 9$
c. $\mu = 50, \sigma = 1, n = 25$

8.3 The diameter of bushings turned out by a manufacturing process is a normally distributed random variable with a mean of 4.035 mm and a standard deviation of 0.005 mm. The inspection procedure requires a sample of 25 bushings once an hour. (a) Within what range should 95 percent of the bushing diameters fall? (b) Within what range should 95 percent of the sample *means* fall? (c) What conclusion would you reach if you saw a sample mean of 4.020? A sample mean of 4.055?

8.4 For this exercise, you will use *LearningStats* Unit 08 "CLT Demonstration." (a) Use the first worksheet (uniform distribution) to complete exercises 1−4 (shown on the worksheet) to study the behavior of 100 sample means with sample sizes of $n = 1, 2, 4, 8, 16, 32, 64$. (b) Repeat, using the second worksheet (skewed distribution). (c) Do you prefer computer simulation or mathematical discussion to clarify the meaning of the Central Limit Theorem?

What Is a Confidence Interval?

A sample mean $\bar{x}$ calculated from a random sample $x_1, x_2, \ldots, x_n$ is a **point estimate** of the population mean μ. Since samples vary, we need to indicate our uncertainty about the true value of μ. Based on our knowledge of the sampling distribution (using the CLT) we create an *interval estimate* by specifying the *probability* that the interval will contain μ. The probability that the interval contains the true mean is usually expressed as a percentage, called the **confidence level** (commonly 90, 95, or 99 percent). The interval estimate is then called the **confidence interval**.

A confidence interval is constructed around the point estimate $\bar{x}$ by adding and subtracting a **margin of error**. The margin of error depends on both the sampling distribution of $\bar{X}$ and the standard error of $\bar{X}$. Given the standard deviation σ and knowing that the population is normal (or if we have a sufficiently large n for the CLT to apply), the confidence interval formula is

$$\bar{x} \pm z \frac{\sigma}{\sqrt{n}} \qquad \text{where } z \frac{\sigma}{\sqrt{n}} \text{ is the margin of error} \tag{8.6}$$

The value of z will depend on the confidence level desired. For example, if the chosen confidence level is 90 percent, then $z_{.05} = 1.645$ which is the value associated with an upper tail area of .05.

8.4
CONFIDENCE INTERVAL FOR A MEAN (μ) WITH KNOWN σ

Chapter 9

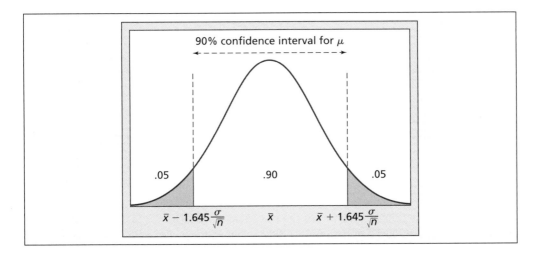

The middle area of the curve corresponds to the confidence level, .90. The remaining area is divided into two symmetrical tails each equal to $(1-.90)/2$ or .05. Table 8.7 shows z-values for common confidence levels.

You might also see the confidence interval expressed as a range $\mu_{lower} < \mu < \mu_{upper}$. The lower confidence limit is the smallest value of μ that we expect, and the upper confidence limit is the largest value of μ that we expect.

The rule of thumb that $n \geq 30$ to assume normality is sufficient for a symmetric or slightly skewed population without outliers. However, a larger n may be needed if you are sampling from a strongly skewed population or one with outliers.

Confidence Level	z
90	$z_{.05} = 1.645$
95	$z_{.025} = 1.960$
98	$z_{.01} = 2.326$
99	$z_{.005} = 2.576$

TABLE 8.7
Common z-values

Confidence Interval for μ (known σ)

$$\bar{x} - z\frac{\sigma}{\sqrt{n}} < \mu < \bar{x} + z\frac{\sigma}{\sqrt{n}}$$

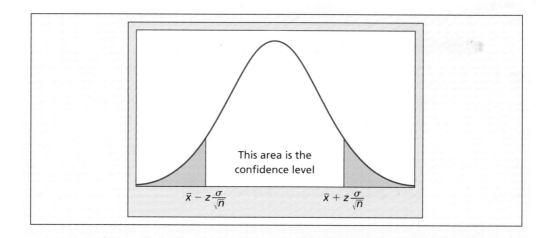

This area is the confidence level

$$\bar{x} - z\frac{\sigma}{\sqrt{n}}$$ $$\bar{x} + z\frac{\sigma}{\sqrt{n}}$$

EXAMPLE

Bottle Filling: Confidence Intervals for μ

The amount of fill in a half-liter bottle of Diet Coke is normally distributed. From past experience, the process standard deviation is known to be $\sigma = 1.20$ ml. The mean amount of fill can be adjusted. A sample of 10 bottles gives a sample mean $\bar{x} = 503.4$ ml. Since the population is normal, the sample mean is a normally distributed random variable for any sample size, so we can use the z distribution to construct a confidence interval.

For a 90 percent confidence **interval estimate** for μ, we insert $z = 1.645$ in the formula along with the sample mean $\bar{x} = 503.4$ and the known standard deviation $\sigma = 1.20$:

90% confidence interval: $\bar{x} \pm z\frac{\sigma}{\sqrt{n}} = 503.4 \pm 1.645\frac{1.20}{\sqrt{10}} = 503.4 \pm 0.62$

The 90 percent confidence interval for the true mean is $502.78 < \mu < 504.02$. An interval constructed this way has a probability of .90 of containing μ. For a 95 percent confidence interval, we would use $z = 1.960$, keeping everything else the same:

95% confidence interval: $\bar{x} \pm z\frac{\sigma}{\sqrt{n}} = 503.4 \pm 1.96\frac{1.20}{\sqrt{10}} = 503.4 \pm 0.74$

The 95 percent confidence interval for μ is $502.66 < \mu < 504.14$. There is a probability of .95 that an interval constructed this way will contain μ. For a 99 percent confidence interval, we would use $z = 2.576$ in the formula, keeping everything else the same:

99% confidence interval: $\bar{x} \pm z\frac{\sigma}{\sqrt{n}} = 503.4 \pm 2.576\frac{1.2}{\sqrt{10}} = 503.4 \pm 0.98$

The 99 percent confidence interval for μ is $502.42 < \mu < 504.38$. There is a probability of .99 that an interval created in this manner will enclose μ.

Choosing a Confidence Level

You might be tempted to assume that a higher confidence level gives a "better" estimate. However, *a higher confidence level leads to a wider confidence interval* (as shown in the preceding calculations). Thus, greater confidence implies *loss of precision* as shown in Figure 8.10. A 95 percent confidence level is often used because it is a reasonable compromise between confidence and precision.

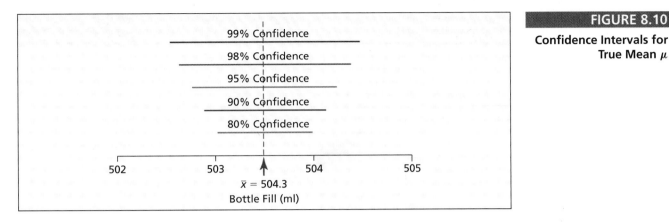

FIGURE 8.10

**Confidence Intervals for
True Mean μ**

Interpretation A confidence interval either *does* or *does not* contain μ. But the confidence level quantifies the *risk*. If 100 statisticians were to use exactly this procedure to create 95 percent confidence intervals, approximately 95 of their intervals *would* contain μ, while approximately 5 unlucky ones *would not* contain μ. Since you only do it once, you don't know if you captured the true mean or not. For the bottle-filling example, lower bounds for all five of the confidence intervals shown in Figure 8.10 are well above 500, indicating that the mean of the bottle-filling process is safely above the required minimum half-liter (500 ml).

Is σ Ever Known?

Yes, but not very often. In quality control applications with ongoing manufacturing processes, it may be reasonable to assume that σ stays the same over time. The type of confidence interval just seen is therefore important because it is used to construct *control charts* to track the mean of a process (such as bottle filling) over time. However, the case of unknown σ is more typical, and will be examined in the next section.

SECTION EXERCISES

connect

8.5 Find a confidence interval for μ assuming that each sample is from a normal population.
　　a. $\bar{x} = 14$, $\sigma = 4$, $n = 5$, 90 percent confidence
　　b. $\bar{x} = 37$, $\sigma = 5$, $n = 15$, 99 percent confidence
　　c. $\bar{x} = 121$, $\sigma = 15$, $n = 25$, 95 percent confidence

8.6 Prof. Hardtack gave three exams last semester in a large lecture class. The standard deviation $\sigma = 7$ was the same on all three exams, and scores were normally distributed. Below are scores for 10 randomly chosen students on each exam. Find the 95 percent confidence interval for the mean score on each exam. Do the confidence intervals overlap? If so, what does this suggest?
　　Exams1
　　Exam 1: 71, 69, 78, 80, 72, 76, 70, 82, 76, 76
　　Exam 2: 77, 66, 71, 73, 94, 85, 83, 72, 89, 80
　　Exam 3: 67, 69, 64, 65, 72, 59, 64, 70, 64, 56

8.7 Bob said "About 95 percent of the individual X values will lie within the 95 percent confidence interval for the mean." Explain why his statement is *incorrect*.

Student's *t* Distribution

8.5

**CONFIDENCE
INTERVAL FOR
A MEAN (μ)
WITH
UNKNOWN σ**

In situations where the population is normal but its standard deviation σ is unknown, the **Student's *t* distribution** should be used instead of the normal *z* distribution. This is particularly important when the sample size is small. When σ is unknown, the formula for a confidence interval resembles the formula for known σ except that *t* replaces *z* and *s* replaces σ:

$$\bar{x} \pm t \frac{s}{\sqrt{n}} \qquad \text{(confidence interval for } \mu \text{ with unknown } \sigma\text{)} \qquad \text{(8.7)}$$

Confidence Interval for μ (unknown σ)

$$\bar{x} - t\frac{s}{\sqrt{n}} < \mu < \bar{x} + t\frac{s}{\sqrt{n}}$$

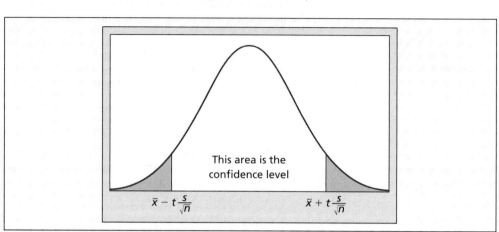

This area is the confidence level

$\bar{x} - t\dfrac{s}{\sqrt{n}}$ $\bar{x} + t\dfrac{s}{\sqrt{n}}$

The Student's t distributions were proposed by a Dublin brewer named W. S. Gossett (1876–1937) who published his research under the name "Student" because his employer did not approve of publishing research based on company data. The t distributions are symmetric and shaped very much like the standard normal distribution, except they are somewhat less peaked and have thicker tails. Note that the t distributions are a class of distributions, each of which is dependent on the size of the sample we are using. Figure 8.11 shows how the tails of the distributions change as the sample size increases. A closer look reveals that the t distribution's tails lie *above* the normal (i.e., the t distribution always has heavier tails).

FIGURE 8.11

Comparison of Normal and Student's t

$n = 3$	$n = 5$	$n = 9$

—— Student's t —— Std Normal

Degrees of Freedom

Knowing the sample size allows us to calculate a parameter called **degrees of freedom** (sometimes abbreviated d.f.). This parameter is used to determine the value of the t statistic used in the confidence interval formula. The degrees of freedom tell us how many observations we used to calculate s, the sample standard deviation, less the number of intermediate estimates we used in our calculation. Recall that the formula for s uses all n individual values from the sample and also $\bar{x}$, the sample mean. Therefore, the degrees of freedom are equal to the sample size minus 1. We will use the symbol ν (the Greek letter "nu"), to represent degrees of freedom.

$$\text{d.f.} = \nu = n - 1 \qquad \text{(degrees of freedom for a confidence interval for } \mu) \qquad \textbf{(8.8)}$$

For large degrees of freedom the t distribution approaches the shape of the normal distribution, as illustrated in Figure 8.11. However, in small samples, the difference is important. For example, in Figure 8.11 the lower axis scale range extends out to ± 4, while a range of ± 3 would cover most of the area for a standard normal distribution. We have to go out further into the tails of the t distribution to enclose a given area, so for a given confidence level, t is *always larger than z* so the confidence interval is always *wider* than if z were used.

Comparison of *z* and *t*

Table 8.8 (taken from Appendix D) shows that for very small samples the t-values differ substantially from the normal. But for a given confidence level, as degrees of freedom increase, the t-values approach the familiar normal z-values (shown at the bottom of each column corresponding to an infinitely large sample). For example, for $n = 31$, we would have degrees of freedom $\nu = 31 - 1 = 30$, so for a 90 percent confidence interval, we would use $t = 1.697$, which is only slightly larger than $z = 1.645$. It might seem tempting to use the z-values to avoid having to look up the correct degrees of freedom, but this would not be conservative (because the resulting confidence interval would be slightly too narrow).

TABLE 8.8

Student's *t*-values for Selected Degrees of Freedom

	Confidence Level				
ν	**80%**	**90%**	**95%**	**98%**	**99%**
1	3.078	6.314	12.706	31.821	63.656
2	1.886	2.920	4.303	6.965	9.925
3	1.638	2.353	3.182	4.541	5.841
4	1.533	2.132	2.776	3.747	4.604
5	1.476	2.015	2.571	3.365	4.032
10	1.372	1.812	2.228	2.764	3.169
20	1.325	1.725	2.086	2.528	2.845
30	1.310	1.697	2.042	2.457	2.750
40	1.303	1.684	2.021	2.423	2.704
60	1.296	1.671	2.000	2.390	2.660
100	1.290	1.660	1.984	2.364	2.626
∞	1.282	1.645	1.960	2.326	2.576

Note: The bottom row shows the z-values for each confidence level.

EXAMPLE

GMAT Scores, Again

GMATScores

Let's look at the random sample of GMAT scores submitted by 20 applicants to an MBA program. A dot plot of this sample is shown in Figure 8.12.

530	450	600	570	360
550	640	490	460	550
480	440	530	470	560
500	430	640	420	530

FIGURE 8.12 **Dot Plot and Confidence Interval ($n = 20$ Scores)** **GMATScores**

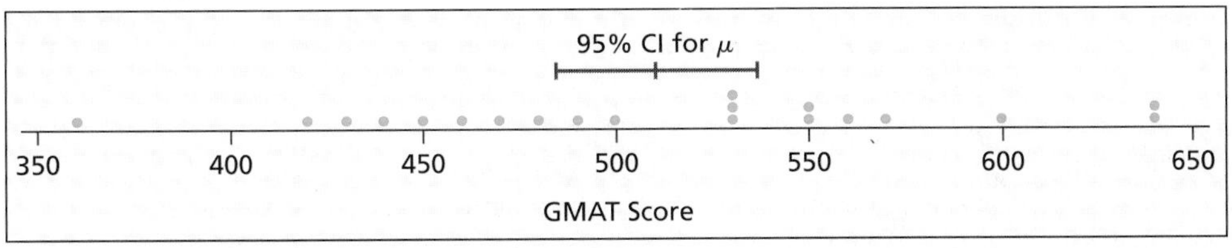

We will construct a 90 percent confidence interval for the mean GMAT score of all MBA applicants. The sample mean is $\bar{x} = 510$ and the sample standard deviation is $s = 73.77$. Since the population standard deviation σ is unknown, we will use the Student's t for our confidence interval with 19 degrees of freedom:

$$\nu = n - 1 = 20 - 1 = 19 \quad \text{(degrees of freedom for } n = 20\text{)}$$

For a 90 percent confidence interval, we consult Appendix D and find $t_{.05} = 1.729$:

	Confidence Level				
	0.80	0.90	0.95	0.98	0.99
			Upper Tail Area		
ν	0.10	0.05	0.025	0.01	0.005
1	3.078	6.314	12.706	31.821	63.656
2	1.886	2.920	4.303	6.965	9.925
3	1.638	2.353	3.182	4.541	5.841
4	1.533	2.132	2.776	3.747	4.604
5	1.476	2.015	2.571	3.365	4.032
6	1.440	1.943	2.447	3.143	3.707
7	1.415	1.895	2.365	2.998	3.499
8	1.397	1.860	2.306	2.896	3.355
9	1.383	1.833	2.262	2.821	3.250
10	1.372	1.812	2.228	2.764	3.169
11	1.363	1.796	2.201	2.718	3.106
12	1.356	1.782	2.179	2.681	3.055
13	1.350	1.771	2.160	2.650	3.012
14	1.345	1.761	2.145	2.624	2.977
15	1.341	1.753	2.131	2.602	2.947
16	1.337	1.746	2.120	2.583	2.921
17	1.333	1.740	2.110	2.567	2.898
18	1.330	1.734	2.101	2.552	2.878
19	1.328	1.729	2.093	2.539	2.861
20	1.325	1.725	2.086	2.528	2.845

The 90 percent confidence interval is

$$\bar{x} \pm t \frac{s}{\sqrt{n}} = 510 \pm (1.729)\frac{73.77}{\sqrt{20}} = 510 \pm 28.52$$

We are 90 percent confident that the true mean GMAT score is within the interval $481.48 < \mu < 538.52$ (see Figure 8.12). There is a 90 percent chance that an interval constructed in this manner contains μ (but a 10 percent chance that it does not). If we wanted a narrower confidence interval with the same level of confidence, we would need a larger sample size to reduce the right-hand side of $\bar{x} \pm t \frac{s}{\sqrt{n}}$.

EXAMPLE

Hospital Stays
🐁 **Maternity**

During a certain period of time, Balzac Hospital had 8,261 maternity cases. Each case is assigned a code called a DRG (which stands for "Diagnostic Related Group"). The most common DRG was 373 (simple delivery without complicating diagnoses), accounting for 4,409 cases during the study period. Hospital management needs to know the mean length of stay (LOS) so they can plan the maternity unit bed capacity and schedule the nursing staff. For DRG 373, a random sample of hospital records for $n = 25$ births, the mean length of stay was $\bar{x} = 39.144$ hours with a standard deviation of $s = 16.204$ hours. What is the 95 percent confidence interval for the true mean?

To justify using the Student's *t* distribution we will assume that the population is normal (we will examine this assumption later). Since the population standard deviation is unknown, we use the Student's *t* for our confidence interval with 24 degrees of freedom:

$$\nu = n - 1 = 25 - 1 = 24 \qquad \text{(degrees of freedom for } n = 25\text{)}$$

For a 95 percent confidence interval, we consult Appendix D and find $t_{.025} = 2.064$:

	Confidence Level				
	0.80	0.90	0.95	0.98	0.99
	Upper Tail Area				
ν	0.10	0.05	0.025	0.01	0.005
1	3.078	6.314	12.706	31.821	63.656
2	1.886	2.920	4.303	6.965	9.925
3	1.638	2.353	3.182	4.541	5.841
4	1.533	2.132	2.776	3.747	4.604
5	1.476	2.015	2.571	3.365	4.032
6	1.440	1.943	2.447	3.143	3.707
7	1.415	1.895	2.365	2.998	3.499
8	1.397	1.860	2.306	2.896	3.355
9	1.383	1.833	2.262	2.821	3.250
10	1.372	1.812	2.228	2.764	3.169
11	1.363	1.796	2.201	2.718	3.106
12	1.356	1.782	2.179	2.681	3.055
13	1.350	1.771	2.160	2.650	3.012
14	1.345	1.761	2.145	2.624	2.977
15	1.341	1.753	2.131	2.602	2.947
16	1.337	1.746	2.120	2.583	2.921
17	1.333	1.740	2.110	2.567	2.898
18	1.330	1.734	2.101	2.552	2.878
19	1.328	1.729	2.093	2.539	2.861
20	1.325	1.725	2.086	2.528	2.845
21	1.323	1.721	2.080	2.518	2.831
22	1.321	1.717	2.074	2.508	2.819
23	1.319	1.714	2.069	2.500	2.807
24	1.318	1.711	2.064	2.492	2.797
25	1.316	1.708	2.060	2.485	2.787

The 95 percent confidence interval is

$$\bar{x} \pm t\frac{s}{\sqrt{n}} = 39.144 \pm (2.064)\frac{16.204}{\sqrt{25}} = 39.144 \pm 6.689$$

With 95 percent confidence, the true mean LOS is within the interval $32.455 < \mu < 45.833$, so our best guess is that a simple maternity stay averages between 32.5 hours and 45.8 hours. A dot plot of this sample and confidence interval are shown in Figure 8.13.

FIGURE 8.13   **Dot Plot and Confidence Interval (*n* = 25 Births)**   **Maternity**

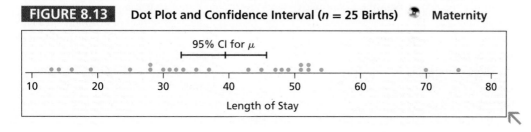

Confidence Interval Width

Our confidence interval width reflects the sample size, the confidence level, and the standard deviation. If we wanted a narrower interval (i.e., more precision) we could either increase the sample size or lower the confidence level (e.g., to 90 percent or even 80 percent). But we cannot do anything about the standard deviation, because it is an aspect of the sample. In fact, some samples could have larger standard deviations than this one.

A "Good" Sample?

Was our sample of 25 births typical? If we took a different sample, would we get a different confidence interval? Let's take a few new samples and see what happens. Figure 8.14 shows 95 percent confidence intervals using five *different* random samples of 25 births (the samples are from a very large population of $N = 4,409$ births). Samples 1 through 4 give similar results. However, sample 5 has a much higher mean and standard deviation, and a very wide confidence interval.

FIGURE 8.14

Five Sample Confidence Intervals

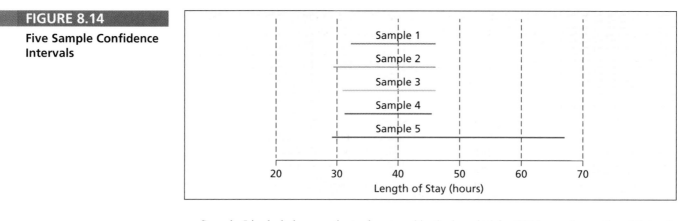

Sample 5 included one patient who stayed in the hospital for 254 hours (more than 10 days), skewing the sample severely (see Figure 8.15). Yet an observer might still conclude that a "typical" length of maternity stay is around 40 hours. It is just a matter of luck which sample you get. However, the statistician who obtains sample 5 is not helpless. He/she would know that the sample contained a severe outlier, and might suggest taking a larger sample. It would certainly be a warning that the confidence interval from sample 5 cannot be trusted. We might consider constructing a confidence interval without the outlier to see how much it is affecting our results. More importantly, the existence of an outlier reminds us that the mean is not always a good measure of the "typical" value of X.

FIGURE 8.15

Dot Plot for Sample 5 Maternity

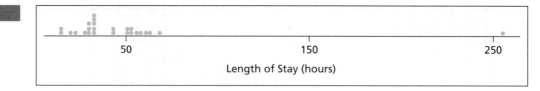

More Analysis Needed

Preoccupation with mathematics could make us forget the purpose of the research. The statistician is expected to help the client understand the problem, not to use a particular formula. We should ask: (1) Are there outliers that might invalidate the assumption of normality? (2) Is a sample of 25 cases large enough for the Central Limit Theorem to apply? (3) Is a confidence interval really needed? Figure 8.16 shows a large random sample of LOS for 200 births from the same population. Its quartiles are $Q_1 = 29.1$ hours, $Q_2 = 40.3$ hours, and $Q_3 = 54.8$ hours. Instead of constructing a confidence interval, we could simply define 55 hours or more (the third quartile) as "long" stay, 29 hours or less (the first quartile) as "short" stay, and 40 hours as "typical" stay. Maybe that's all the hospital wants to know.

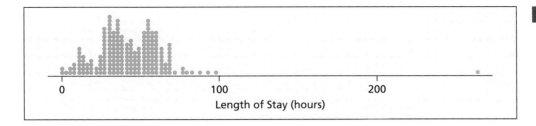

FIGURE 8.16

LOS Dot Plot for Sample of $n = 200$ Births Maternity

Yet, from the point of view of staffing, the mean *does* matter. Although outliers can render confidence intervals useless, that does not imply that the hospital can ignore them. If a handful of maternity patients stay 10 days (240 hours) instead of 2 days (48 hours), real resources will be required to treat them. What we can do (and must do) is ask some deeper questions. For example, if a length of stay exceeds 10 days, we might suspect that the diagnostic code DRG 373 (simple delivery without complicating diagnoses) was assigned incorrectly. In this example, further analysis revealed 23 cases out of 4,409 in the population with LOS greater than 240 hours (10 days). Two cases had LOS exceeding 1,000 hours, which are almost certainly errors in classification, suggesting that a different DRG should have been assigned.

Messy Data?

Yes. But also not unusual. Outliers and messy data are common. If you are thinking, Well, there are specialists who know how to deal with such data, you may be wrong. Every day, managers encounter large databases containing unruly data and rarely is there a professional statistician on call. You have just seen a typical example from a hospital database. Health care managers in hospitals, clinics, insurers, state and federal agencies all spend a lot of time working with messy data just like this. In the United States, health care spending is nearly 1/6 of the GDP, suggesting that 1 job out of every 6 (perhaps yours) is tied directly or indirectly to health care, so examples like this are not unusual. You need to be ready to deal with messy data.

Must the Population Be Normal?

The *t* distribution assumes a normal population, but in practice, this assumption can be relaxed, as long as the population is not badly skewed. Large sample size offers further protection if the normality assumption is questionable.

Using Appendix D

Beyond $v = 50$, Appendix D shows v in steps of 5 or 10. If Appendix D does not show the exact degrees of freedom that you want, use the *t*-value for the *next lower* v. For example, if $v = 54$, you would use $v = 50$. Using the next lower degrees of freedom is a conservative procedure because it overestimates the margin of error. Since *t*-values change very slowly as v rises beyond $v = 50$, rounding down will make little difference.

Can I Ever Use *z* Instead of *t*?

In large samples, *z* and *t* give similar results. But a conservative statistician always uses the *t* distribution for confidence intervals when σ is unknown because using *z* would underestimate the margin of error. Since *t* tables are easy to use (or we can get *t*-values from Excel) there isn't much justification for using *z* when σ is unknown.

Using Excel

If you have access to Excel, you don't need tables. Excel's function =TINV(probability,degrees of freedom) gives a two-tailed value of t, where probability is 1 minus the confidence level. For example, for a 95 percent confidence interval with 60 degrees of freedom, the function =TINV(0.05,60) yields $t = 2.000298$. Since Excel wants the *two-tailed area* outside the confidence interval, we would use 0.05 for 95 percent, 0.01 for 99 percent, etc. The output from Excel's Tools > Data Analysis > Descriptive Statistics does not give the confidence interval limits, but it does give the standard error and width of the confidence interval $ts/\sqrt{n}$ (the oddly labeled last line in the table). Figure 8.17 shows Excel's results for sample 1 (maternity LOS).

FIGURE 8.17

Excel's Confidence Interval

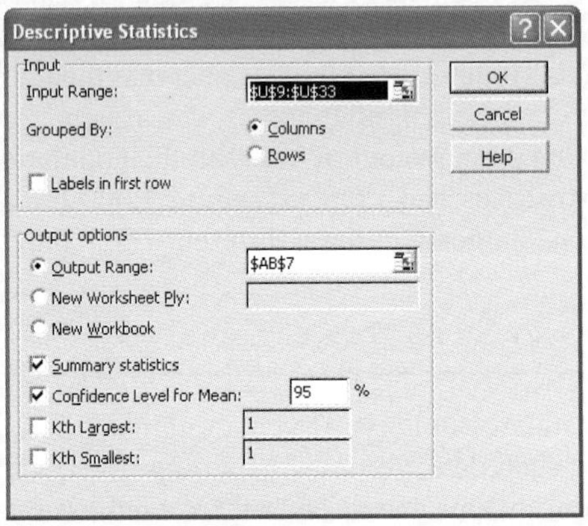

Mean	39.144
Standard Error	3.240769405
Median	37.37
Mode	#N/A
Standard Deviation	16.20384702
Sample Variance	262.5646583
Kurtosis	-0.28780002
Skewness	0.263313568
Range	61.92
Minimum	12.59
Maximum	74.51
Sum	978.6
Count	25
Confidence Level(95.0%)	6.688617936

Using MegaStat

If you really want to make the calculations easy, MegaStat gives you a choice of z or t, and does all the calculations for you, as illustrated in Figure 8.18 for sample 1 (maternity LOS). Notice the Preview button. If you click OK you will also see the t-value and other details.

FIGURE 8.18

MegaStat's Confidence Interval

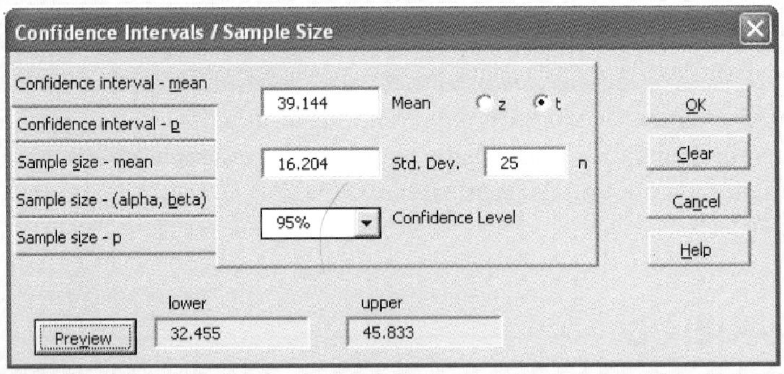

Using MINITAB

Use MINITAB's Stat > Basic Statistics > Graphical Summary to get confidence intervals, as well as a histogram and box plot. MINITAB uses the Student's t for the confidence interval for the mean. It also gives confidence intervals for the median and standard deviation. Figure 8.19 shows the MINITAB Graphical Summary for sample 1 (maternity LOS).

SECTION EXERCISES

connect

8.8 Find a confidence interval for μ assuming that each sample is from a normal population.

a. $\bar{x} = 24, s = 3, n = 7$, 90 percent confidence
b. $\bar{x} = 42, s = 6, n = 18$, 99 percent confidence
c. $\bar{x} = 119, s = 14, n = 28$, 95 percent confidence

FIGURE 8.19

MINITAB's Confidence
Interval

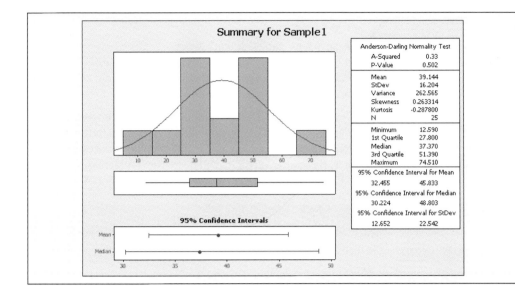

8.9   For each value of ν (degrees of freedom) look up the value of Student's t in Appendix D for the stated level of confidence. Then use Excel to find the value of Student's t to four decimal places. Which method (Appendix D or Excel) do you prefer, and why?
a. $\nu = 9$, 95 percent confidence
b. $\nu = 15$, 98 percent confidence
c. $\nu = 47$, 90 percent confidence

8.10   For each value of ν look up the value of Student's t in Appendix D for the stated level of confidence. How close is the t-value to the corresponding z-value (at the bottom of the column for $\nu = \infty$).
a. $\nu = 40$, 95 percent confidence
b. $\nu = 80$, 95 percent confidence
c. $\nu = 100$, 95 percent confidence

8.11   A sample of 21 minivan electrical warranty repairs for "loose, not attached" wires (one of several electrical failure categories the dealership mechanic can select) showed a mean repair cost of \$45.66 with a standard deviation of \$27.79. (a) Construct a 95 percent confidence interval for the true mean repair cost. (b) How could the confidence interval be made narrower? (Data are from a project by MBA student Tim Polulak.)

8.12   A random sample of 16 pharmacy customers showed the waiting times below (in minutes). Find a 90 percent confidence interval for μ, assuming that the sample is from a normal population.
   Pharmacy

| 21 | 22 | 22 | 17 | 21 | 17 | 23 | 20 |
| 20 | 24 | 9 | 22 | 16 | 21 | 22 | 21 |

8.13   A random sample of monthly rent paid by 12 college seniors living off campus gave the results below (in dollars). Find a 99 percent confidence interval for μ, assuming that the sample is from a normal population.   **Rent1**

| 900 | 810 | 770 | 860 | 850 | 790 |
| 810 | 800 | 890 | 720 | 910 | 640 |

8.14   A random sample of 10 shipments of stick-on labels showed the following order sizes. (a) Construct a 95 percent confidence interval for the true mean order size. (b) How could the confidence interval be made narrower? (c) Do you think the population is normal? (Data are from a project by MBA student Henry Olthof, Jr.)   **OrderSize**

| 12,000 | 18,000 | 30,000 | 60,000 | 14,000 | 10,500 | 52,000 | 14,000 | 15,700 | 19,000 |

8.15   Prof. SoftTouch gave three exams last semester. Scores were normally distributed on each exam. Below are scores for 10 randomly chosen students on each exam. (a) Find the 95 percent confidence interval for the mean score on each exam. (b) Do the confidence intervals overlap? What inference might you draw by comparing the three confidence intervals? (c) How is this problem different from Exercise 8.6?   **Exams2**

Exam 1: 81, 79, 88, 90, 82, 86, 80, 92, 86, 86
Exam 2: 87, 76, 81, 83, 100, 95, 93, 82, 99, 90
Exam 3: 77, 79, 74, 75, 82, 69, 74, 80, 74, 76

8.6

CONFIDENCE INTERVAL FOR A PROPORTION (π)

The Central Limit Theorem (CLT) also applies to a sample proportion, since a proportion is just a mean of data whose only values are 0 or 1. For a proportion, the CLT says that the distribution of a sample proportion $p = x/n$ tends toward normality as n increases. The distribution is centered at the population proportion π. Its standard error σ_p will decrease as n increases just as in the case of the standard error for $\overline{X}$. We say that $p = x/n$ is a *consistent* estimator of π.

Central Limit Theorem for a Proportion

As sample size increases, the distribution of the sample proportion $p = x/n$ approaches a normal distribution with mean π and standard deviation $\sigma_p = \sqrt{\dfrac{\pi(1 - \pi)}{n}}$.

Illustration: Internet Hotel Reservations   Hotel

Management of the Pan-Asian Hotel System tracks the percent of hotel reservations made over the Internet to adjust its advertising and Web reservation system. Such data are binary: either a reservation is made on the Internet (x) or not (o). Last week (2,000 reservations) the proportion of Internet reservations was 20 percent ($\pi = .20$) as you can verify if you have the time. We can visualize the week's data like this:

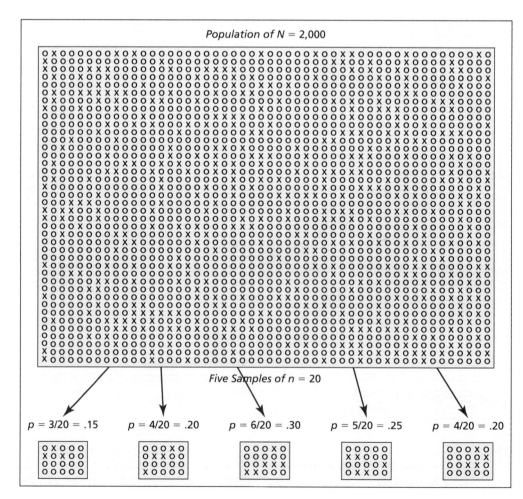

Five random samples of $n = 20$ hotel reservations are shown. Some sample proportions (p) are close to $\pi = .20$ while others are not, due to sampling variation. But each sample proportion p is a valid *point estimate* of the population proportion π:

$$p = \frac{x}{n} = \frac{\text{number of Internet reservations}}{\text{number of items in the sample}}$$

If we took many such samples, we could empirically study the *sampling distribution* of p. But even for a single sample, we can apply the CLT to *predict* the behavior of p. In Chapter 6, you learned that the binomial model describes the number of successes in a sample of n items from a population with constant probability of success π. A binomial distribution is symmetric if $\pi = .50$, and as n increases approaches symmetry even if $\pi \neq .50$. The same is true for the distribution of the sample proportion $p = x/n$. Figure 8.20 shows histograms of $p = x/n$ for 1,000 samples of various sizes with $\pi = .20$. For small n, the distribution is quite discrete. For example:

Sample Size	Possible Values of $p = x/n$
$n = 5$	0/5, 1/5, 2/5, 3/5, 4/5, 5/5
$n = 10$	0/10, 1/10, 2/10, 3/10, 4/10, 5/10, 6/10, 7/10, 8/10, 9/10, 10/10

As n increases, the statistic $p = x/n$ more closely resembles a continuous random variable and its distribution becomes more symmetric and bell-shaped.

FIGURE 8.20

Histograms of $p = x/n$ When $\pi = .20$ Hotel

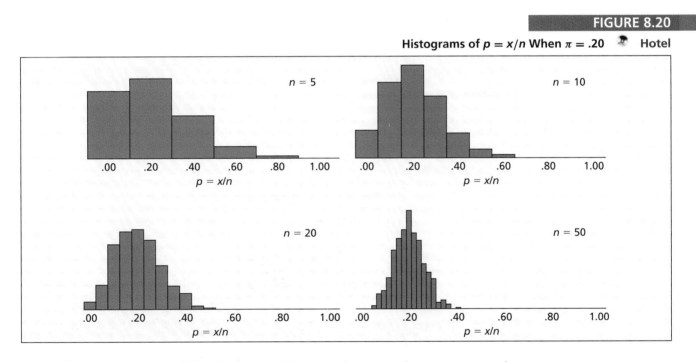

As n increases, the range of the sample proportion $p = x/n$ narrows, because n appears in the denominator of the *standard error:*

$$\sigma_p = \sqrt{\frac{\pi(1-\pi)}{n}} \qquad \text{(standard error of the sample proportion)} \qquad \textbf{(8.9)}$$

Therefore, the sampling variation can be reduced by increasing the sample size. Larger samples also help justify the use of the normal distribution.

When Is It Safe to Assume Normality?

The statistic $p = x/n$ may be assumed normally distributed when the sample is "large." How large must n be? Table 8.9 illustrates a conservative rule of thumb that normality may be assumed whenever $n\pi \geq 10$ and $n(1 - \pi) \geq 10$. By this rule, a very large sample may be needed to assume normality of the sample proportion when π differs greatly from .50.*

Rule of Thumb

The sample proportion $p = x/n$ may be assumed normal if both $n\pi \geq 10$ and $n(1 - \pi) \geq 10$.

TABLE 8.9

Sample Size to Assume Normality of $p = x/n$

π	n
.50	20
.40 or .60	25
.30 or .70	33
.20 or .80	50
.10 or .90	100
.05 or .95	200
.02 or .98	500
.01 or .99	1,000
.005 or .995	2,000
.002 or .998	5,000
.001 or .999	10,000

Standard Error of the Proportion

The **standard error of the proportion** is denoted σ_p. It depends on π, as well as on n, being largest when the population proportion is near $\pi = .50$ and becoming smaller when π is near 0 or 1. For example:

$$\text{If } \pi = .50: \quad \sigma_p = \sqrt{\frac{\pi(1 - \pi)}{n}} = \sqrt{\frac{.50(1 - .50)}{n}} = \sqrt{\frac{.25}{n}}$$

$$\text{If } \pi = .40: \quad \sigma_p = \sqrt{\frac{\pi(1 - \pi)}{n}} = \sqrt{\frac{.40(1 - .40)}{n}} = \sqrt{\frac{.24}{n}}$$

$$\text{If } \pi = .30: \quad \sigma_p = \sqrt{\frac{\pi(1 - \pi)}{n}} = \sqrt{\frac{.30(1 - .30)}{n}} = \sqrt{\frac{.21}{n}}$$

$$\text{If } \pi = .20: \quad \sigma_p = \sqrt{\frac{\pi(1 - \pi)}{n}} = \sqrt{\frac{.20(1 - .20)}{n}} = \sqrt{\frac{.16}{n}}$$

$$\text{If } \pi = .10: \quad \sigma_p = \sqrt{\frac{\pi(1 - \pi)}{n}} = \sqrt{\frac{.10(1 - .10)}{n}} = \sqrt{\frac{.09}{n}}$$

The formula is symmetric (i.e., $\pi = .20$ gives the same standard error as $\pi = .80$). Figure 8.21 shows the *relative* size of the standard error of the proportion σ_p for different values of π. Figure 8.22 shows that enlarging n reduces the standard error σ_p but at a diminishing rate (e.g., you have to *quadruple* the sample size to *halve* σ_p).

Confidence Interval for π

By the Central Limit Theorem, we can state the probability that a sample proportion will fall within a given interval. For example, there is a 95 percent chance that p will fall within the

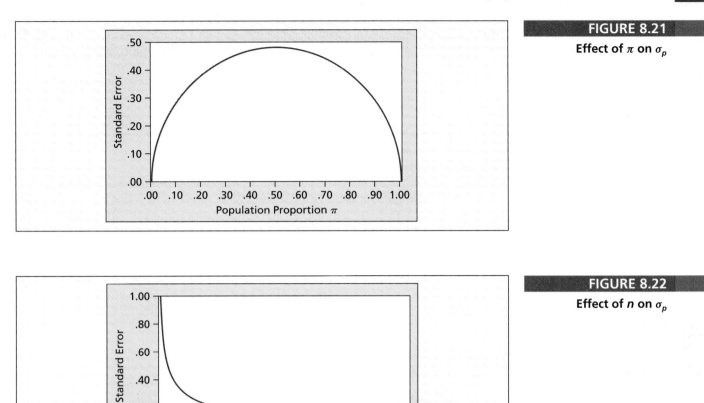

FIGURE 8.21

Effect of π on σ_p

FIGURE 8.22

Effect of n on σ_p

range $\pi \pm z_{.025}\sqrt{\frac{\pi(1-\pi)}{n}}$ where $z_{.025} = 1.96$ and similarly for other values of z. This is the basis for a confidence interval estimate of π. Replacing π with $p = x/n$ (since π is unknown) and assuming a large sample (to justify the assumption of normality), the confidence interval for π is

$$p \pm z\sqrt{\frac{p(1-p)}{n}} \qquad \text{(confidence interval for } \pi\text{)} \qquad \textbf{(8.10)}$$

We can choose z for any confidence level we want. For example:

$z_{.05} = 1.645$, for 90 percent confidence

$z_{.025} = 1.960$, for 95 percent confidence

$z_{.01} = 2.326$, for 98 percent confidence

$z_{.005} = 2.576$, for 99 percent confidence

A sample of 75 retail in-store purchases showed that 24 were paid in cash. We will construct a 95 percent confidence interval for the proportion of all retail in-store purchases that are paid in cash. The sample proportion is

$$p = x/n = 24/75 = .32 \qquad \text{(proportion of in-store cash transactions)}$$

EXAMPLE

Auditing

We can assume that p is normally distributed* since np and $n(1 - p)$ exceed 10. That is, $np = (75)(.32) = 24$ and $n(1 - p) = (75)(.68) = 51$. The 95 percent confidence interval is

$$p \pm z\sqrt{\frac{p(1 - p)}{n}} = .32 \pm 1.960\sqrt{\frac{.32(1 - .32)}{75}}$$
$$= .32 \pm .106 = .214 < \pi < .426$$

There is a 95 percent probability that an interval constructed in this way contains the true population proportion π. We think that the true proportion π is between 21.4 percent and 42.6 percent, and our best guess (point estimate) is 32 percent. Different samples could yield different estimates. *We cannot know whether the true proportion lies within the interval we have constructed.* Either it does, or it does not. What we *do* know is that the odds are very good (95 to 5 or 19 to 1) that our 95 percent confidence interval will contain the true proportion π.

Narrowing the Interval?

In this example, the confidence interval is fairly wide. The width of the confidence interval for π depends on

- Sample size
- Confidence level
- Sample proportion p

We cannot do anything about p because it is an aspect of the sample. If we want a narrower interval (i.e., more precision), we could either increase the sample size or reduce the confidence level (e.g., from 95 percent to 90 percent). If the confidence level is sacrosanct, our only choice is to increase n. Of course, larger samples are more costly (or even impossible).

EXAMPLE

Display Ads

A random sample of 200 pages from the *Ameritech Pages Plus Yellow Pages* telephone directory revealed that 30 of the selected pages contained at least one multicolored display ad (large blocks with illustrations, maps, and text). What is the 90 percent confidence interval for the proportion of all pages with at least one such display ad? The sample proportion is

$$p = x/n = 30/200 = .15 \qquad \text{(proportion of pages with at least one display ad)}$$

The normality test is easily met because $np = (200)(.15) = 30$ and $n(1 - p) = (200)(.85) = 170$. The 90 percent confidence interval requires $z = 1.645$:

$$p \pm z\sqrt{\frac{p(1 - p)}{n}} = .15 \pm 1.645\sqrt{\frac{.15(1 - .15)}{200}}$$
$$= .15 \pm .042 = .108 < \pi < .192$$

With 90 percent confidence, between 10.8 percent and 19.2 percent of the pages have multicolor display ads. This confidence interval is narrower than the previous example because the sample size is larger, this sample proportion is farther from .5, and the confidence level is lower.

An increase in confidence decreases the precision of the estimate. Further, the law of diminishing returns applies: A given increment in confidence widens the confidence interval disproportionately, as we must go farther out into the tails of the normal distribution to enclose the desired area. A wider confidence interval is less helpful in visualizing the location of the true value π. In the limit, we can be 100 percent confident that π lies somewhere between 0 and 100 percent, but such a statement is useless. Given its common use, it appears that many people feel that 95 percent confidence strikes a good balance between confidence and precision for common applications.

---

*When constructing a confidence interval, we use p instead of π in our rule of thumb to test whether n is large enough to assure normality because π is unknown. The test is therefore equivalent to asking if $x \geq 10$ and $n - x \geq 10$.

To illustrate the trade-off between *confidence* and *precision* (the interval half-width), here are some alternatives that could have been used in the display ad example:

Confidence Level	z	Interval Width
80%	$z = 1.282$	$.15 \pm .032$
90%	$z = 1.645$	$.15 \pm .042$
95%	$z = 1.960$	$.15 \pm .049$
98%	$z = 2.326$	$.15 \pm .059$
99%	$z = 2.576$	$.15 \pm .065$

Using Excel and MegaStat

Excel's Tools > Data Analysis does not offer a confidence interval for a proportion, presumably because the calculations are easy. For example:

=0.15–NORMSINV(.95)*SQRT(0.15*(1-0.15)/200)   for the lower 95% confidence limit

=0.15+NORMSINV(.95)*SQRT(0.15*(1-0.15)/200)   for the upper 95% confidence limit

However, MegaStat makes it even easier, as shown in Figure 8.23. You only need to enter p and n. A convenient feature is that, if you enter p larger than 1, MegaStat assumes that it is the *x*-value in $p = x/n$ so you don't even have to calculate p. Click the Preview button to see the confidence interval. This example verifies the Ameritech calculations shown previously (click OK for additional details). MegaStat always assumes normality, even when it is not justified, so you need to check this assumption for yourself.

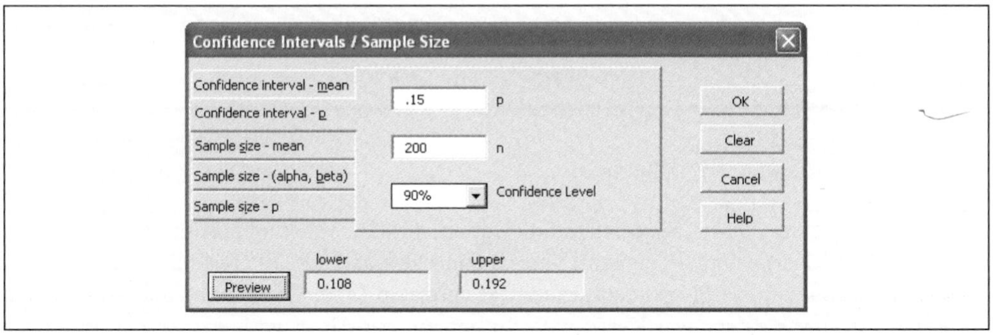

FIGURE 8.23

MegaStat's Confidence Interval

Small Samples: MINITAB

If the sample is small (i.e., if we cannot meet the requirement that $n\pi \geq 10$ and $n(1 - \pi) \geq 10$), the distribution of p may not be well approximated by the normal. Instead of assuming a continuous normal model, confidence limits around p can be constructed by using the binomial distribution. MINITAB uses this method by default, since it works for any n (you have to press the Options button to assume normality). Although the underlying calculations are a bit complex, MINITAB does all the work and the resulting interval is correct for any n and p.

For example, *The New York Times Magazine* reported that, in a sample of 14 purchasers of the *Spider-Man 2* DVD, 11 watched only the film and never even looked at the "extras" (November 14, 2004, p. 107). The sample proportion is $p = 11/14$. What is the 95 percent confidence interval for the proportion of purchasers who never viewed the "extras"? We have $np = 11$ but $n(1 - p) = 3$, which is less than 10, so we should not assume normality. Figure 8.24 shows a sample of MINITAB's confidence interval using the binomial distribution with Stat > Basic Statistics > One Proportion. MINITAB's binomial confidence interval (.492, .953) is quite different from the normal confidence interval (.571, 1.000). MINITAB includes a warning about the normal confidence interval.

FIGURE 8.24

MINITAB's Confidence Interval

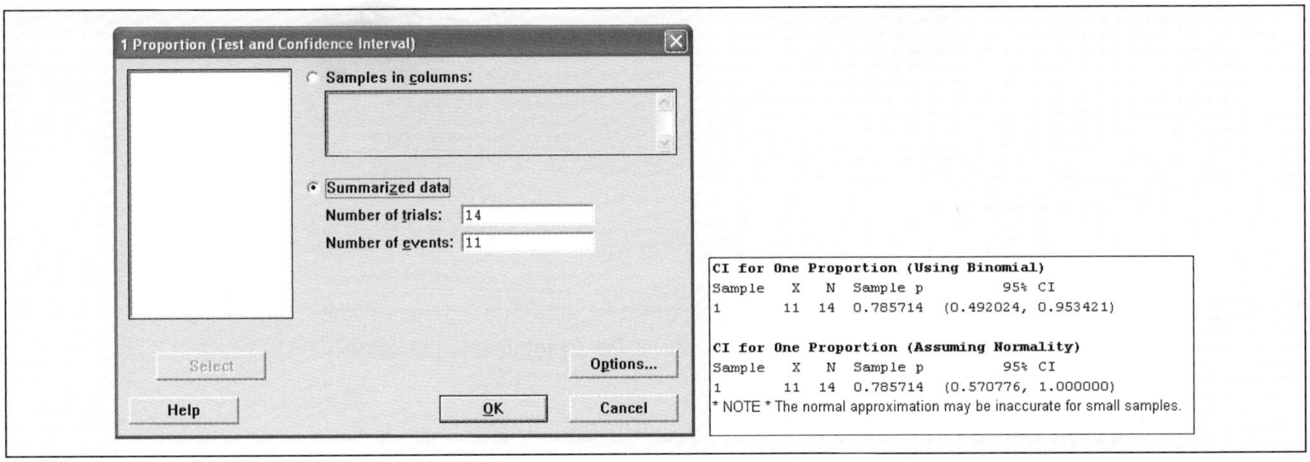

Polls and Margin of Error

In polls and survey research, the margin of error is typically based on a 95 percent confidence level and the initial assumption that $\pi = .50$. This is a conservative assumption since σ_p is at its maximum when $\pi = .50$. Table 8.10 shows the margin of error for various sample sizes. The law of diminishing returns is apparent. Greater accuracy is possible, but each reduction in the margin of error requires a disproportionately larger sample size.

TABLE 8.10

Margin of Error for 95 Percent Confidence Interval Assuming $\pi = .50$

n = 100	n = 200	n = 400	n = 800	n = 1,200	n = 1,600
± 9.8%	± 6.9%	± 4.9%	± 3.5%	± 2.8%	± 2.5%

EXAMPLE

The 2004 Election

Just before the 2004 U.S. presidential election, an ABC tracking poll showed Bush with 50 percent and Kerry with 46 percent. The sample size was 1,589 likely adult voters, and the reported accuracy was ±2.5 percent, exactly as shown in Table 8.10. At about the same time, a Reuters/Zogby poll showed Kerry with 46 percent and Bush with 45 percent, based on 1,216 likely voters, with a reported accuracy of ±2.9 percent. These are typical sample sizes for national opinion polls on major issues such as a presidential election, foreign policy, or a Supreme Court decision. Tracking polls do vary, but if several different independent polls show the same candidate ahead, and if the margin is stable over time, they usually get it right. Of course, the opinions being tracked may be changing continuously from day to day.

The margin of error is sometimes referred to as the *sample accuracy*. Popular media sometimes use statistical terminology loosely, but the idea is the same. Statewide political polls, such as a gubernatorial race, typically have 800 respondents (margin of error ±3.5 percent) while a mayoral or local political poll might have 400 respondents (margin of error ±4.9 percent). Private market research or customer mail surveys may rely on even smaller samples, while Internet surveys can yield very large samples. In spite of the large samples possible from an Internet survey, it may be important to consider nonresponse bias (see Chapter 2) when applying the survey results.

Rule of Three

A useful quick rule is the *Rule of Three*. If in n independent trials no events occur, the upper 95 percent confidence bound is approximately $3/n$. For example, if no medical complications arise in 17 prenatal fetal surgeries, the upper bound on such complications is roughly

$3/17 = .18$, or about 18 percent. This rule is sometimes used by health care practitioners when limited data are available.*

Very Quick Rule

The ubiquity of the 95 percent confidence interval has led consulting statisticians to create various quick rules.** For example, a **Very Quick Rule** (VQR) for a 95 percent confidence interval when p is near .50 is

$$p \pm \frac{1}{\sqrt{n}} \qquad \text{(very quick 95\% confidence interval if } p \text{ is near .50)} \qquad \textbf{(8.11)}$$

By trying a few values of p near .50 in Formula 8.10 you can verify the VQR. However, the VQR begins to fail when p is outside the range $.40 < p < .60$. For example, it works poorly for the Ameritech example because $p = .15$. However, the VQR may be useful in making a quick assessment.

Proportions Are Important in Business

Proportions are easy to work with, and they occur frequently in business (most often expressed as percents). In many ways, estimating π is simpler than estimating μ because you are just counting things.

8.16 Calculate the standard error. May normality be assumed?
   a. $n = 30, \pi = .50$ b. $n = 50, \pi = .20$ c. $n = 100, \pi = .10$ d. $n = 500, \pi = .005$

8.17 A car dealer is taking a customer satisfaction survey. Find the margin of error (i.e., assuming 95% confidence and $\pi = .50$) for (a) 250 respondents, (b) 125 respondents, and (c) 65 respondents.

8.18 In a sample of 500 new Web sites registered on the Internet, 24 were anonymous (i.e., they shielded their name and contact information). (a) Construct a 95 percent confidence interval for the proportion of all new Web sites that were anonymous. (b) May normality be assumed? Explain. (c) Would the *Very Quick Rule* work here? (Data are from "New Services Are Making It Easier to Hide Who Is Behind Web Sites," *The Wall Street Journal,* September 30, 2004.)

8.19 From a list of stock mutual funds, 52 funds were selected at random. Of the funds chosen, it was found that 19 required a minimum initial investment under $1,000. (a) Construct a 90 percent confidence interval for the true proportion requiring an initial investment under $1,000. (b) May normality be assumed? Explain.

8.20 Of 43 bank customers depositing a check, 18 received some cash back. (a) Construct a 90 percent confidence interval for the proportion of all depositors who ask for cash back. (b) Check the normality assumption.

8.21 A 2003 survey showed that 4.8 percent of the 250 Americans surveyed had suffered some kind of identity theft in the past 12 months. (a) Construct a 98 percent confidence interval for the true proportion of Americans who had suffered identity theft in the past 12 months. (b) May normality be assumed? Explain. (Data are from *Scientific American* 291, no. 6, p. 33.)

8.22 A sample of 50 homes in a subdivision revealed that 24 were ranch style (as opposed to colonial, tri-level, or Cape Cod). (a) Construct a 98 percent confidence interval for the true proportion of ranch style homes. (b) Check the normality assumption.

8.23 In a grocery parking lot 32 of 136 cars selected at random were white. (a) Construct a 98 percent confidence interval for the true proportion of white cars. (b) May normality be assumed? Explain.

---

*For further details, see B. D. Jovanovic and P. S. Levy, "A Look at the Rule of Three," *The American Statistician* 51, no. 2 (May 1997), pp. 137–39.
**See James R. Boen and Douglas A. Zahn, *The Human Side of Statistical Consulting* (Wadsworth, 1982), p. 171.

(c) What sample size would be needed to estimate the true proportion of white cars with an error of ± 0.06 and 90 percent confidence? With an error of ± 0.03 and 95 percent confidence? (d) Why are the sample sizes in (c) so different?

Mini Case 8.1

Airline Water Quality

Is the water on your airline flight safe to drink? It isn't feasible to analyze the water on every flight, so sampling is necessary. In August and September 2004, the Environmental Protection Agency (EPA) found bacterial contamination in water samples from the lavatories and galley water taps on 20 of 158 randomly selected U.S. flights (12.7 percent of the flights). Alarmed by the data, the EPA ordered sanitation improvements and then tested water samples again in November and December 2004. In the second sample, bacterial contamination was found in 29 of 169 randomly sampled flights (17.2 percent of the flights).

Aug./Sep. sample: $p = 20/158 = .12658$, or 12.7% contaminated
Nov./Dec. sample: $p = 29/169 = .17160$, or 17.2% contaminated

Is the problem getting worse instead of better? From these samples, we can construct confidence intervals for the true proportion of flights with contaminated water. We begin with the 95 percent confidence interval for π based on the August/September water sample:

$$p \pm z\sqrt{\frac{p(1-p)}{n}} = .12658 \pm 1.96\sqrt{\frac{.12658(1-.12658)}{158}}$$
$$= .12658 \pm .05185, \text{ or } 7.5\% \text{ to } 17.8\%$$

Next we determine the 95 percent confidence interval for π based on the November/December water sample:

$$p \pm z\sqrt{\frac{p(1-p)}{n}} = .17160 \pm 1.96\sqrt{\frac{.17160(1-.17160)}{169}}$$
$$= .17160 \pm .05684, \text{ or } 11.5\% \text{ to } 22.8\%$$

Although the sample percentage (a point estimate of π) did rise, the margin of error is a little over 5 percent in each sample. Since the confidence intervals overlap, we cannot rule out the possibility that there has been no change in water contamination on airline flights; that is, the difference could be due to sampling variation. Nonetheless, the EPA is taking further steps to encourage airlines to improve water quality.

The Wall Street Journal, November 10, 2004, and January 20, 2005.

8.7 SAMPLE SIZE DETERMINATION FOR A MEAN

A Myth

Many people feel that when the population is large, you need a larger sample to obtain a given level of precision in the estimate. This is incorrect. For a given level of precision, it is the sample size that matters, even if the population is a million or a billion. This is apparent from the confidence interval formula, which includes n but not N.*

Sample Size to Estimate μ

Suppose we wish to estimate a population mean with an allowable margin of error of ± E. What sample size is required? We start with the general form of the confidence interval:

General Form ⁄ *What We Want*

$\bar{x} \pm z\dfrac{\sigma}{\sqrt{n}}$ ⁄ $\bar{x} \pm E$

*The special case of sampling finite populations is discussed in *LearningStats*.

In this confidence interval, we use z instead of t because we are going to solve for n, and degrees of freedom cannot be determined unless we know n. Equating the allowable error E to half of the confidence interval width and solving for n,

$$E = z\frac{\sigma}{\sqrt{n}} \quad \rightarrow \quad E^2 = z^2\frac{\sigma^2}{n} \quad \rightarrow \quad n = z^2\frac{\sigma^2}{E^2}$$

Thus, the formula for the sample size can be written:

$$n = \left(\frac{z\sigma}{E}\right)^2 \qquad \text{(sample size to estimate } \mu) \qquad \textbf{(8.12)}$$

Always round n to the next higher integer to be conservative.

How to Estimate σ?

Into this formula, we can plug our desired precision E and the appropriate z for the desired confidence level. However, σ poses a problem since it is usually unknown. Table 8.11 shows several ways to approximate the value of σ. You can always try more than one method and see how much difference it makes. But until you take the sample, you will not know for sure if you have achieved your goal (i.e., the desired precision E).

TABLE 8.11

Four Ways to Estimate σ

Method 1: Take a Preliminary Sample
Take a small preliminary sample and use the sample estimate s in place of σ. This method is the most common, though its logic is somewhat circular (i.e., take a sample to plan a sample).

Method 2: Assume Uniform Population
Estimate rough upper and lower limits a and b and set $\sigma = [(b - a)^2/12]^{1/2}$. For example, we might guess the weight of a light-duty truck to range from 1,500 pounds to 3,500 pounds, implying a standard deviation of $\sigma = [(3,500 - 1,500)^2/12]^{1/2} = 577$ pounds. Since a uniform distribution has no central tendency, the actual σ is probably smaller than our guess, so we get a larger n than necessary (a conservative result).

Method 3: Assume Normal Population
Estimate rough upper and lower bounds a and b, and set $\sigma = (b - a)/4$. This assumes normality with most of the data within $\mu + 2\sigma$ and $\mu - 2\sigma$ so the range is 4σ. For example, we might guess the weight of a light truck to range from 1,500 pounds to 3,500 pounds, implying $\sigma = (3,500 - 1,500)/4 = 500$ pounds. Some books suggest $\sigma = R/6$ based on the Empirical Rule, but recent research shows that rule is not conservative enough (see Related Reading).

Method 4: Poisson Arrivals
In the special case when μ is a Poisson arrival rate, then $\sigma = \sqrt{\mu}$. For example, if you think the arrival rate is about 20 customers per hour, then you would estimate $\sigma = \sqrt{20} = 4.47$.

EXAMPLE

Onion Weight

A produce manager wants to estimate the mean weight of Spanish onions being delivered by a supplier, with 95 percent confidence and an error of ± 1 ounce. A preliminary sample of 12 onions shows a sample standard deviation of 3.60 ounces. For a 95 percent confidence interval, we will set $z = 1.96$. We use $s = 3.60$ in place of σ and set the desired error $E = 1$ to obtain the required sample size:

$$n = [(1.96)(3.60)/(1)]^2 = 49.79, \text{ or } 50 \text{ onions}$$

We would round to the next higher integer and take a sample of 50 Spanish onions. This should ensure an estimate of the true mean weight with an error not exceeding ± 1 ounce.

A seemingly modest change in E can have a major effect on the sample size because it is squared. Suppose we reduce the allowable error to $E = 0.5$ ounce to obtain a more precise estimate. The required sample size would then be

$$n = [(1.96)(3.60)/(0.5)]^2 = 199.1, \text{ or } 200 \text{ onions}$$

Using *LearningStats*

There is a sample size calculator in *LearningStats* that makes these calculations easy, as illustrated in Figure 8.25 for $E = 1$ and $E = 0.5$.

Assuming $E = \pm 1$ and $\sigma = 1$

| | **Desired Confidence Level** | | | | |
	90%	**95%**	**98%**	**99%**	**99.9%**
z	1.645	1.960	2.326	2.576	3.291
n	36	50	71	86	141

Assuming $E = \pm 1$ and $\sigma = .5$

| | **Desired Confidence Level** | | | | |
	90%	**95%**	**98%**	**99%**	**99.9%**
z	1.645	1.960	2.326	2.576	3.291
n	141	200	281	344	562

Using MegaStat

There is also a sample size calculator in MegaStat, as illustrated in Figure 8.26. The Preview button lets you change the setup and see the result immediately.

Caution 1: Units of Measure

When estimating a mean, the allowable error E is expressed in the same units as X and σ. For example, E would be expressed in dollars when estimating the mean order size for mail-order customers (e.g., $E = \$2$) or in minutes to estimate the mean wait time for patients at a clinic (e.g., $E = 10$ minutes). To estimate last year's starting salaries for MBA graduates from a university, the allowable error could be large (e.g., $E = \$2,000$) because a $2,000 error in estimating μ might still be a reasonably accurate estimate.

Caution 2: Using *z*

Using z in the sample size formula for a mean is necessary but not conservative. Since t always exceeds z for a given confidence level, your actual interval may be wider than $\pm E$ as intended. As long as the required sample size is large (say 30 or more), the difference will be acceptable.

Caution 3: Larger *n* Is Better

The sample size formulas for a mean are not conservative, that is, they tend to underestimate the required sample size.* Therefore, the sample size formulas for a mean should be

---

*See Lawrence L. Kupper and Kerry B. Hafner, "How Appropriate Are Popular Sample Size Formulas?" *The American Statistician* 43, no. 2 (May 1989), pp. 101–105.

regarded only as a minimum guideline. Whenever possible, samples should exceed this minimum.*

8.24   For each level of precision, find the required sample size to estimate the mean starting salary for a new CPA with 95 percent confidence, assuming a population standard deviation of $7,500 (same as last year).

  a. $E = \$2,000$ b. $E = \$1,000$ c. $E = \$500$

8.25   Last year, a study showed that the average ATM cash withdrawal took 65 seconds with a standard deviation of 10 seconds. The study is to be repeated this year. How large a sample would be needed to estimate this year's mean with 95 percent confidence and an error of ± 4 seconds?

8.26   The EPA city/hwy mpg range for a Saturn Vue FWD automatic 5-speed transmission is 20 to 28 mpg. If you owned this vehicle, how large a sample (e.g., how many tanks of gas) would be required to estimate your mean mpg with an error of ± 1 mpg and 90 percent confidence? Explain your assumption about σ.

8.27   Popcorn kernels are believed to take between 100 and 200 seconds to pop in a certain microwave. What sample size (number of kernels) would be needed to estimate the true mean seconds to pop with an error of ± 5 seconds and 95 percent confidence? Explain your assumption about σ.

8.28   Analysis showed that the mean arrival rate for vehicles at a certain Shell station on Friday afternoon last year was 4.5 vehicles per minute. How large a sample would be needed to estimate this year's mean arrival rate with 98 percent confidence and an error of ± 0.5?

8.29   Noodles & Company wants to estimate the mean spending per customer at a certain restaurant with 95 percent confidence and an error of $\pm \$0.25$. What is the required sample size, assuming a standard deviation of $2.50 (based on similar restaurants elsewhere)?

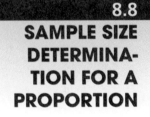

Suppose we wish to estimate a population proportion with a precision (allowable error) of $\pm E$. What sample size is required? We start with the general form of the confidence interval:

General Form   *What We Want*

$$p \pm z\sqrt{\frac{\pi(1-\pi)}{n}}$$ $$p \pm E$$

We equate the allowable error E to half of the confidence interval width and solve for n:

$$E = z\sqrt{\frac{\pi(1-\pi)}{n}} \quad \rightarrow \quad E^2 = z^2\frac{\pi(1-\pi)}{n} \quad \rightarrow \quad n = z^2\frac{\pi(1-\pi)}{E^2}$$

Thus, the formula for the sample size for a proportion can be written:

$$n = \left(\frac{z}{E}\right)^2 \pi(1-\pi) \qquad \text{(sample size to estimate } \pi) \qquad \textbf{(8.13)}$$

Always round n to the next higher integer.

  Since a proportion is a number between 0 and 1, the precision allowable error E is also between 0 and 1. For example, if we want an allowable error of ± 7 percent we would specify $E = 0.07$.

  Since π is unknown (that's why we are taking the sample) we need to make an assumption about π to plan our sample size. If we have a prior estimate of π (e.g., from last year or a comparable application), we can plug it in the formula. Or we could take a small preliminary sample. Some experts recommend using $\pi = .50$ because the resulting sample size will guarantee the desired precision for any π. However, this conservative assumption may lead to a larger sample than necessary. Sampling costs money, so if a prior estimate of π is available, it might be advisable to use it, especially if you think that π differs greatly from .50. For example, in estimating the

---

*If you are sampling a finite population without replacement and your required sample size (n) exceeds 5 percent of the population size (N), you can adjust the sample size by using $n' = \frac{nN}{n+(N-1)}$. This adjustment will guarantee that the sample size never exceeds the population size. See *LearningStats* for details.

proportion of home equity loans that result in default, we would expect π to be much smaller than .50, while in estimating the proportion of motorists who use seat belts, we would hope that π would be much larger than .50. Table 8.12 details three ways to estimate π.

TABLE 8.12	
Three Ways to Estimate π	**Method 1: Take a Preliminary Sample** Take a small preliminary sample and insert *p* into the sample size formula in place of π. This method is appropriate if π is believed to differ greatly from .50, as is often the case, though its logic is somewhat circular (i.e., we must take a sample to plan our sample). **Method 2: Use a Prior Sample or Historical Data** A reasonable approach, but how often are such data available? And might π have changed enough to make it a questionable assumption? **Method 3: Assume That π = .50** This method is conservative and ensures the desired precision. It is therefore a sound choice. However, the sample may end up being larger than necessary.

EXAMPLE

ATM Withdrawals

A university credit union wants to know the proportion of cash withdrawals that exceed $50 at its ATM located in the student union building. With an error of ± 2 percent and a confidence level of 95 percent, how large a sample is needed to estimate the proportion of withdrawals exceeding $50? The *z*-value for 95 percent confidence is $z = 1.960$. Using $E = 0.02$ and assuming conservatively that $\pi = .50$, the required sample size is

$$n = \left(\frac{z}{E}\right)^2 \pi(1 - \pi) = \left(\frac{1.960}{0.02}\right)^2 (.50)(1 - .50) = 2,401$$

We would need to examine $n = 2,401$ withdrawals to estimate π within ± 2 percent and with 95 percent confidence. In this case, last year's proportion of ATM withdrawals over $50 was 27 percent. If we had used this estimate in our calculation, the required sample size would be

$$n = \left(\frac{z}{E}\right)^2 p(1 - p) = \left(\frac{1.960}{0.02}\right)^2 (.27)(1 - .27) = 1,893 \qquad \text{(rounded to next higher integer)}$$

We would need to examine $n = 1,893$ withdrawals to estimate π within ± 0.02. The required sample size is smaller than when we make the conservative assumption $\pi = .50$.

Alternatives

Suppose that our research budget will not permit a large sample. In the previous example, we could reduce the confidence interval level from 95 to 90 percent and increase the allowable error to ± 4 percent. Assuming $\pi = .50$, the required sample size is

$$n = \left(\frac{z}{E}\right)^2 \pi(1 - \pi) = \left(\frac{1.645}{0.04}\right)^2 (.50)(1 - .50) = 423 \qquad \text{(rounded to next higher integer)}$$

These seemingly modest changes make a huge difference in the sample size.

Practical Advice

Choosing a sample size is a common problem. Clients who take samples are constrained by time and money. Naturally, they prefer the highest possible confidence level and the lowest possible error. But when a statistical consultant shows them the required sample size, they may find it infeasible. A better way to look at it is that the formula for sample size provides a structure for a dialogue between statistician and client. A good consultant can propose several possible confidence levels and errors, and let the client choose the combination that best balances the need for accuracy against the available time and budget. The statistician can offer advice about these trade-offs, so the client's objectives are met. Other issues include nonresponse rates, dropout rates from ongoing studies, and possibly incorrect assumptions used in the calculation.

Using *LearningStats*

The sample size calculator in *LearningStats* makes these calculations easy, as illustrated in Figure 8.27 for $\pi = .50$ and $E = 0.02$.

FIGURE 8.27

LearningStats
**Sample Size
for a Mean**

	Desired Confidence Level				
	90%	95%	98%	99%	99.9%
z	1.645	1.960	2.326	2.576	3.291
n	1691	2401	3383	4147	6768

Caution 1: Units of Measure

A common error is to insert $E = 2$ in the formula when you want an error of ± 2 percent. Because we are dealing with a *proportion,* a 2% error is $E = 0.02$. In other words, when estimating a proportion, E is always between 0 and 1.

Caution 2: Finite Population

If you are sampling a **finite population** without replacement and your required sample size (n) exceeds 5 percent of the population size (N), you can adjust the sample size by using $n' = \frac{nN}{n + (N - 1)}$. This adjustment will guarantee that the sample size never exceeds the population size. See *LearningStats* for details.

8.30 (a) What sample size would be required to estimate the true proportion of American female business executives who prefer the title "Ms.", with an error of ± 0.025 and 98 percent confidence? (b) What sampling method would you recommend? Explain.

8.31 (a) What sample size would be needed to estimate the true proportion of American households that own more than one DVD player, with 90 percent confidence and an error of ± 0.02? (b) What sampling method would you recommend? Why?

8.32 (a) What sample size would be needed to estimate the true proportion of students at your college (if you are a student) who are wearing backpacks, with 95 percent confidence and an error of ± 0.04? (b) What sampling method would you recommend? Why?

8.33 (a) What sample size would be needed to estimate the true proportion of American adults who know their cholesterol level, using 95 percent confidence and an error of ± 0.02? (b) What sampling method would you recommend, and why?

An **estimator** is a sample statistic $(\bar{x}, s, p)$ that is used to estimate an unknown population **parameter** (μ, σ, π). A desirable estimator is **unbiased** (correctly centered), **efficient** (minimum variance), and **consistent** (variance goes to zero as n increases). **Sampling error** (the difference between an estimator and its parameter) is inevitable, but a larger sample size yields estimates that are closer to the unknown parameter. The **Central Limit Theorem** (CLT) states that the sample mean $\bar{x}$ is centered at μ and follows a normal distribution if n is large, regardless of the population shape. A **confidence interval** for μ consists of lower and upper bounds that have a specified probability (called the **confidence level**) of enclosing μ. Any confidence level may be used, but 90, 95, and 99 percent are common. If the population variance is unknown, we replace z in the confidence interval formula for μ with **Student's t** using $n - 1$ degrees of freedom. The CLT also applies to the sample proportion (p) as an estimator of π, using a rule of thumb to decide if normality may be assumed. The **margin of error** is the half-width of the confidence interval. Formulas exist for the required **sample size** for a given level of precision in a confidence interval for μ or π, although they entail assumptions and are only approximate. Confidence intervals and sample sizes may be adjusted for finite populations, but often the adjustments are not material.

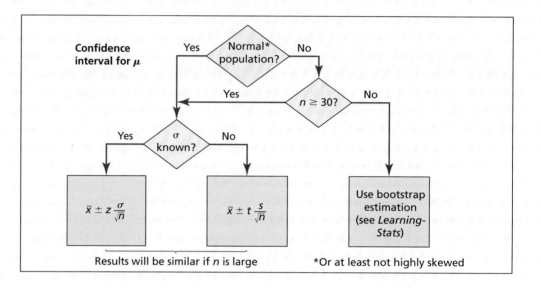

Commonly Used Formulas in Sampling Distributions and Estimation

Sample Proportion: $p = \dfrac{x}{n}$

Standard Error of the Sample Mean: $\sigma_{\bar{x}} = \dfrac{\sigma}{\sqrt{n}}$

Confidence Interval for μ, known σ: $\bar{x} \pm z \dfrac{\sigma}{\sqrt{n}}$

Confidence Interval for μ, unknown σ: $\bar{x} \pm t \dfrac{s}{\sqrt{n}}$

Degrees of Freedom: $\nu = n - 1$

Standard Error of the Sample Proportion: $\sigma_p = \sqrt{\dfrac{\pi(1-\pi)}{n}}$

Confidence Interval for π: $p \pm z \sqrt{\dfrac{p(1-p)}{n}}$

Sample Size to Estimate μ: $n = \left(\dfrac{z\sigma}{E}\right)^2$

Sample Size to Estimate π: $n = \left(\dfrac{z}{E}\right)^2 \pi(1-\pi)$

1. Define (a) parameter, (b) estimator, (c) sampling error, and (d) sampling distribution.

2. Explain the difference between sampling error and bias. Can they be controlled?

3. Name three estimators. Which ones are unbiased?

4. Explain what it means to say an estimator is (a) unbiased, (b) efficient, and (c) consistent.

5. State the main points of the Central Limit Theorem for a mean.

6. Why is population shape of concern when estimating a mean? What does sample size have to do with it?

7. (a) Define the standard error of the mean. (b) What happens to the standard error as sample size increases? (c) How does the law of diminishing returns apply to the standard error?

8. Define (a) point estimate, (b) margin of error, (c) confidence interval, and (d) confidence level.

9. List some common confidence levels. Why not use other confidence levels?

10. List differences and similarities between Student's t and the standard normal distribution.

11. Give an example to show that (a) for a given confidence level, the Student's t confidence interval for the mean is wider than if we use a z-value; and (b) it makes little difference in a large sample whether we use Student's t or z.

12. Why do outliers and skewed populations pose a problem for estimating a sample mean?

13. (a) State the Central Limit Theorem for a proportion. (b) When is it safe to assume normality for a sample proportion?

14. (a) Define the standard error of the proportion. (b) What happens to the standard error as sample size increases? (c) Why does a larger sample improve a confidence interval?

15. (a) What is the Rule of Three? (b) What is the Very Quick Rule? When does it not work well?

16. (a) Why does σ pose a problem for sample size calculation for a mean? (b) How can σ be approximated when it is unknown?

17. (a) When doing a sample size calculation for a proportion, why is it conservative to assume that $\pi = .50$? (b) When might we not want to assume that $\pi = .50$, and why?

Note: Explain answers and show your work clearly.

8.34 This is an exercise using Excel. (a) Use =RANDBETWEEN(0,99) to create 20 samples of size $n = 4$ by choosing two-digit random numbers between 00 and 99. (b) For each sample, calculate the mean. (c) Make a histogram of the 80 *individual X-values* using bins 10 units wide (i.e., 0, 10, 20, . . . , 100). Describe the shape of the histogram. (d) Make a histogram of your 20 *sample means* using bins 10 units wide. (e) Discuss the histogram shape. Does the Central Limit Theorem seem to be working? (f) Find the mean of the sample means. Was it what you would expect by the CLT? Explain. (g) Find the average standard deviation of the sample means. Was it what you would expect by the CLT?

8.35 A random sample of 21 nickels measured with a very accurate micrometer showed a mean diameter of 0.834343 inches with a standard deviation of 0.001886 inches. (a) Why would nickel diameters vary? (b) Construct a 99 percent confidence interval for the true mean diameter of a nickel. (c) Discuss any assumptions that are needed. (d) What sample size would ensure an error of ± 0.0005 inches with 99 percent confidence? (Data are from a project by MBA student Bob Tindall.)

8.36 A random sample of 10 miniature Tootsie Rolls was taken from a bag. Each piece was weighed on a very accurate scale. The results in grams were

3.087	3.131	3.241	3.241	3.270	3.353	3.400	3.411	3.437	3.477

(a) Construct a 90 percent confidence interval for the true mean weight. (b) What sample size would be necessary to estimate the true weight with an error of ± 0.03 grams with 90 percent confidence? (c) Discuss the factors which might cause variation in the weight of Tootsie Rolls during manufacture. (Data are from a project by MBA student Henry Scussel.)   **Tootsie**

8.37 Statistics students were asked to go home and fill a 1-cup measure with raisin bran, tap the cup lightly on the counter three times to settle the contents, if necessary add more raisin bran to bring the contents exactly up to the 1-cup line, spread the contents on a large plate, and count the raisins. For the 13 students who chose Kellogg's brand the reported results were

23	33	44	36	29	42	31	33	61	36	34	23	24

(a) Construct a 90 percent confidence interval for the mean number of raisins per cup. Show your work clearly. (b) Can you think of features of the sample or data-gathering method that might create problems? If so, how could they be improved? (c) Identify factors that might prevent Kellogg's from achieving uniformity in the number of raisins per cup of raisin bran. (d) How might a quality control system work to produce more uniform quantities of raisins, assuming that improvement is desired? 🐛 **Raisins**

8.38 A sample of 20 pages was taken without replacement from the 1,591-page phone directory *Ameritech Pages Plus Yellow Pages*. On each page, the mean area devoted to display ads was measured (a display ad is a large block of multicolored illustrations, maps, and text). The data (in square millimeters) are shown below:

0	260	356	403	536	0	268	369	428	536
268	396	469	536	162	338	403	536	536	130

(a) Construct a 95 percent confidence interval for the true mean. (b) Why might normality be an issue here? (c) What sample size would be needed to obtain an error of ± 10 square millimeters with 99 percent confidence? (d) If this is not a reasonable requirement, suggest one that is. (Data are from a project by MBA student Daniel R. Dalach.) 🐛 **DisplayAds**

8.39 Sixteen owners of 2005 Chrysler Pacifica 2WD vehicles kept track of their average fuel economy for a month. The results are shown below. (a) Construct a 95 percent confidence interval for the mean. (b) What factor(s) limit the conclusions that can be drawn about the true mean? (Data are from www.fueleconomy.gov.) 🐛 **MPG**

20.8	20.0	19.4	19.7	21.1	22.6	18.3	20.1
20.5	19.5	17.4	22.4	18.9	20.2	19.6	19.0

8.40 Twenty-five blood samples were selected by taking every seventh blood sample from racks holding 187 blood samples from the morning draw at a medical center. The white blood count (WBC) was measured using a Coulter Counter Model S. The mean WBC was 8.636 with a standard deviation of 3.9265. (a) Construct a 90 percent confidence interval for the true mean. (b) Why might normality be an issue here? (c) What sample size would be needed for an error of ± 1.5 with 98 percent confidence? (Data are from a project by MBA student Wendy Blomquist.)

8.41 Twenty-one warranty repairs were selected from a population of 126 by selecting every sixth item. The population consisted of "loose, not attached" minivan electrical wires (one of several electrical failure categories the dealership mechanic can select). The mean repair cost was $45.664 with a standard deviation of $27.793. (a) Construct a 95 percent confidence interval for the true mean repair cost. (b) Why might normality be an issue here? Explain. (c) What sample size would be needed to obtain an error of $\pm \$5$ with 95 percent confidence? *(d) Construct a 95 percent confidence interval for the true standard deviation. (Data are from a project by MBA student Tim Polulak.)

8.42 Dave the jogger runs the same route every day (about 2.2 miles). On 18 consecutive days, he recorded the number of steps using a pedometer. The results were

3,450	3,363	3,228	3,360	3,304	3,407	3,324	3,365	3,290
3,289	3,346	3,252	3,237	3,210	3,140	3,220	3,103	3,129

(a) Construct a 95 percent confidence interval for the true mean number of steps Dave takes on his run. (b) What sample size would be needed to obtain an error of ± 20 steps with 95 percent confidence? (c) Using Excel, plot a line chart of the data. What does the data suggest about the pattern over time? 🐛 **DaveSteps**

8.43 A pediatrician's records showed the mean height of a random sample of 25 girls at age 12 months to be 29.530 inches with a standard deviation of 1.0953 inches. (a) Construct a 95 percent confidence interval for the true mean height. (b) Could normality reasonably be assumed for this population? (c) What sample size would be needed for 95 percent confidence and an error of $\pm .20$ inch? (Data are from a project by statistics students Lori Bossardet, Shannon Wegner, and Stephanie Rader.)

8.44 During the Rose Bowl, the length (in seconds) of 12 randomly chosen commercial breaks during timeouts (following touchdown, turnover, field goal, or punt) were

65	75	85	95	80	100	90	80	85	85	60	65

(a) Assuming a normal population, construct a 90 percent confidence interval for the mean length of a commercial break during the Rose Bowl. (b) What are the limitations on your estimate? How could they be overcome?   **TimeOuts**

8.45 A sample of 40 CDs from a student's collection showed a mean length of 52.74 minutes with a standard deviation of 13.21 minutes. (a) Construct a 95 percent confidence interval for the mean. (b) Why might the normality assumption be an issue here? (c) What sample size would be needed for 95 percent confidence and an error of ± 3 minutes? (Data are from a project by statistics students Michael Evatz, Nancy Petack, and Jennifer Skladanowski.)

8.46 The Environmental Protection Agency (EPA) requires that cities monitor over 80 contaminants in their drinking water. Samples from the Lake Huron Water Treatment Plant gave the results shown here. Only the range is reported, not the mean (presumably the mean would be the midrange). (a) For each substance, estimate the *standard deviation* σ by using one of the methods shown in Table 8.11 in Section 8.7. (b) Why might an estimate of σ be helpful in planning future water sample testing?

Substance	MCLG Range Detected	Allowable MCLG	Origin of Substance
Chromium	0.47 to 0.69	100	Discharge for steel and pulp mills, natural erosion
Selenium	0 to 0.0014	50	Corrosion of household plumbing, leaching from wood preservatives, natural erosion
Barium	0.004 to 0.019	2	Discharge from drilling wastes, metal refineries, natural erosion
Fluoride	1.07 to 1.17	4.0	Natural erosion, water additive, discharge from fertilizer and aluminum factories

MCLG = Maximum contaminant level goal

8.47 In a sample of 100 Planter's Mixed Nuts, 19 were found to be almonds. (a) Construct a 90 percent confidence interval for the true proportion of almonds. (b) May normality be assumed? Explain. (c) What sample size would be needed for 90 percent confidence and an error of ± 0.03? (d) Why would a quality control manager at Planter's need to understand sampling?

8.48 Fourteen of 180 publicly traded business services companies failed a test for compliance with Sarbanes-Oxley requirements for financial records and fraud protection. (a) Assuming that these are a random sample of all publicly traded companies, construct a 95 percent confidence interval for the overall noncompliance proportion. (b) Why might this statistic not apply to all sectors of publicly traded companies (e.g., aerospace and defense)? See *The New York Times,* April 27, 2005, p. BU5.

8.49 How "decaffeinated" is decaffeinated coffee? If a researcher wants to estimate the mean caffeine content of a cup of Starbucks decaffeinated espresso with 98 percent confidence and an error of ± 0.1 mg, what is the required number of cups that must be tested? Assume a standard deviation of 0.5 mg, based on a small preliminary sample of 12 cups. (See R. R. McCusker, B. A. Goldberger, and E. J. Cone, "Caffeine Content of Decaffeinated Coffee," *Journal of Analytical Toxicology* 30, no. 7 [October 2006], pp. 611–613.)

8.50 Noodles & Company wants to estimate the percent of customers who order dessert, with 95 percent confidence and an error of ± 10%. What is the required sample size?

8.51 Junior Achievement and Deloitte commissioned a "teen ethics poll" of 787 students aged 13–18, finding that 29 percent felt inadequately prepared to make ethical judgments. (a) Assuming that this was a random sample, find the 95 percent confidence interval for the true proportion of U.S.

teens who feel inadequately prepared to make ethical judgments. (b) Is the sample size large enough to assume normality? (See ja.org/about_newsitem.asp?StoryID=376.)

8.52 A certain brand of dry noodles contains a mixture of beet, spinach, carrot, and plain. A random sample of 200 dry noodles contained 47 beet noodles. (a) Construct a 95 percent confidence interval for the true proportion of beet noodles. (b) Check the normality assumption. Show your work. (c) Does the *Very Quick Rule* work well here? Explain. (d) What sample size would be needed to obtain an error of ± 0.04 with 90 percent confidence? (e) How might a manufacturer design a quality control program to monitor the proportions of each type of noodles so as to produce a consistent mix?

8.53 NBC asked a sample of VCR owners to record "Late Night with David Letterman" on their VCRs. Of the 125 VCR owners surveyed, 83 either "gave up or screwed up" because they did not understand how to program the VCR. (a) Construct a 90 percent confidence interval for the true proportion of VCR owners who cannot program their VCRs. (b) Would viewers of this program be typical of all television viewers? Explain. (Data are from *Popular Science* 237, no. 5, p. 63.)

8.54 A survey of 4,581 U.S. households that owned a mobile phone found that 58 percent are satisfied with the coverage of their cellular phone provider. (a) Assuming that this was a random sample, construct a 90 percent confidence interval for the true proportion of satisfied U.S. mobile phone owners. (b) Why is the confidence interval so narrow? (See *The Wall Street Journal*, October 23, 2006, p. R4.)

8.55 A "teen ethics poll" was commissioned by Junior Achievement and Deloitte. The survey by Harris Interactive surveyed 787 students aged 13–18. (a) Assuming that this was a random sample of all students in this age group, find the margin of error of the poll. (b) Would the margin of error be greater or smaller for the subgroup consisting only of male students? Explain. (See ja.org/about_newsitem.asp?StoryID=376.)

8.56 Biting an unpopped kernel of popcorn hurts! As an experiment, a self-confessed connoisseur of cheap popcorn carefully counted 773 kernels and put them in a popper. After popping, the unpopped kernels were counted. There were 86. (a) Construct a 90 percent confidence interval for the proportion of all kernels that would not pop. (b) Check the normality assumption. (c) Try the *Very Quick Rule*. Does it work well here? Why, or why not? (d) Why might this sample not be typical?

8.57 A sample of 213 newspaper tire ads from several Sunday papers showed that 98 contained a low-price guarantee (offer to "meet or beat any price"). (a) Assuming that this was a random sample, construct a 95 percent confidence interval for the proportion of all Sunday newspaper tire ads that contain a low-price guarantee. (b) Is the criterion for normality met? (See *The New York Times*, January 11, 2007, p. C3.)

8.58 The U.S. Customs Service conducted a random check of Miami longshoremen and found that 36 of 50 had arrest records. (a) Construct a 90 percent confidence interval for the true proportion. (b) Is the sample size large enough to be convincing? Explain. (c) How would *you* select a random sample of longshoremen? (See *U.S. News & World Report* 123, no. 22 [December 8, 1997].)

8.59 Of 250 college students taking a statistics class, 4 reported an allergy to peanuts. (a) Is the criterion for normality met? (b) Assuming that this was a random sample, use MINITAB to construct a 95 percent confidence interval for the proportion of all college statistics students with a peanut allergy.

8.60 In a sample of 15 F/A-18E Super Hornet fighter engines inspected, 3 had cracked turbine blades. Use MINITAB to obtain a 95 percent confidence interval for the population proportion with cracked turbine blades, both assuming normality and without assuming normality. Is normality justified? (See *Aviation Week & Space Technology* 149, no. 24 [December 14, 1998], p. 18.)

8.61 Acoustomagnetic surveillance antitheft portals (the kind used to prevent shoplifting) temporarily affected the pacemakers in 48 out of 50 subjects tested. (a) Construct a 90 percent confidence interval for the proportion of all subjects whose pacemakers would be affected. (b) What problems of interpretation arise? (c) Check the normality assumption. If not met, what could we do? (d) Use MINITAB to estimate a confidence interval without assuming normality. (Data are from *Science News* 154, no. 19, p. 294.)

8.62 (a) A poll of 2,277 voters throughout Britain on the proposed EU constitution would have approximately what margin of error? (b) The poll showed that 44 percent opposed Britain's signing the proposed constitution. Construct a 90 percent confidence interval for the true proportion opposed to signing it. (c) Would you say that the percentage of all voters opposed could be 50 percent? Explain. (Data are from *The Economist* 268, no. 8331 [July 5, 2003], p. 30.)

8.63   To determine the proportion of taxpayers who prefer filing tax returns electronically, a survey of 600 taxpayers was conducted. Calculate the margin of error used to estimate this proportion. What assumptions are required to find the margin of error?

EXPERIMENTS

8.64   For 10 tanks of gas for your car, calculate the miles per gallon. (a) Construct a 95 percent confidence interval for the true mean mpg for your car. (b) Discuss the normality assumption. (c) How many tanks of gas would you need to obtain an error of ± 0.2 mpg with 95 percent confidence?

8.65   (a) Take a random sample of 50 members of the U.S. House of Representatives. Explain your sampling methodology. (b) Count the number whose surname begins with "S." (c) Construct a 95 percent confidence interval for the true proportion of U.S. representatives whose surname begins with "S." (d) Is normality assured?

8.66   (a) Look at 50 vehicles in a parking lot near you. Count the number that are SUVs (state your definition of SUV). Use any sampling method you like (e.g., the first 50 you see). (b) Construct a 95 percent confidence interval for the true population proportion of SUVs. (c) What sample size would be needed to ensure an error of ± 0.025 with 98 percent confidence? (d) Would the proportion be the same if this experiment were repeated in a university parking lot?

8.67   (a) From a sports almanac or Web site, take a random sample of 50 NBA players and calculate the proportion who are at least 7 feet in height. (b) Make a 90 percent confidence interval for the population proportion of all NBA players who are at least 7 feet tall.

RELATED READINGS

Albert, James H. "College Students' Conceptions of Probability." *The American Statistician* 57, no. 1 (February 2001), pp. 37–45.

Boos, Dennis D.; and Jacqueline M. Hughes-Oliver. "How Large Does *n* Have to be for *z* and *t* Intervals?" *The American Statistician* 54, no. 2 (May 2000), pp. 121–28.

Browne, Richard H. "Using the Sample Range as a Basis for Calculating Sample Size in Power Calculations." *The American Statistician* 55, no. 4 (November 2001), pp. 293–98.

Efron, Bradley. "The Bootstrap and Modern Statistics." *Journal of the American Statistical Association* 95, no. 452 (December 2000), pp. 1293–1300.

Efron, Bradley; and Rob Tibshirani. *An Introduction to the Bootstrap.* CRC Press, 1994.

Kupper, Lawrence L.; and Kerry B. Hafner. "How Appropriate Are Popular Sample Size Formulas?" *The American Statistician* 43, no. 2 (May 1989), pp. 101–105.

Lenth, Russell V. "Some Practical Guidelines for Effective Sample Size Determination." *The American Statistician* 55, no. 3 (August 2001), pp. 187–93.

Parker, Robert A. "Sample Size: More Than Calculations." *The American Statistician* 57, no. 3 (August 2003), pp. 166–70.

van Belle, Gerald. *Statistical Rules of Thumb.* Wiley, 2002.

LearningStats Unit 08   Estimation

LearningStats Unit 08 illustrates the idea of sample variation, the Central Limit Theorem, and confidence intervals. Your instructor may assign specific units, or you may decide to check them out because the topic sounds interesting.

Topic	LearningStats Modules
Overview	Survey Guidelines Sampling Methods Confidence Intervals Sample Size
Central Limit Theorem	CLT Demonstration: Simulation CLT Demonstration: Finite Population
Sampling distributions	Sampling Distributions Critical Values (z, t, χ^2) Sample Proportion Demonstration
Confidence intervals	Confidence Interval: Means Confidence Interval: Proportions Confidence Interval: Variances Confidence Interval: Simulation Confidence Interval: Bootstrap
Sample size	Sample Size Calculator
Student projects	Coffee Drinking Habits Office Chairs with Wheels
Applications and case studies	Sample Variation Finite Populations Bootstrap Explained
Tables	Appendix C—Normal Appendix D—Student's t Appendix E—Chi-Square
Equations	Equations: Confidence Intervals Equations: PDFs

Key: = PowerPoint   = Word   = Excel

Visual Statistics

VS

Visual Statistics Modules on Estimation

Module	Module Name
6	VS Visualizing Random Samples
7	VS Visualizing the Central Limit Theorem
8	VS Visualizing Properties of Estimators
9	VS Visualizing One-Sample Hypothesis Tests

Visual Statistics Modules 6, 7, 8, and 9 (included on your CD) are designed to help you

- Understand variability in samples.
- Learn to infer a population's shape from samples.
- Recognize outliers and their effects.
- Distinguish between the population sampled and the sampling distribution of the mean.
- Understand how sample size affects the standard error.
- Understand unbiasedness, efficiency, and consistency.
- Learn what a confidence interval represents.

The worktext (included on the CD in .PDF format) contains lists of concepts covered, objectives of the modules, overviews of concepts, illustrations of concepts, orientations to module features, learning exercises (basic, intermediate, advanced), learning projects (individual, team), self-evaluation quizzes, glossaries of terms, and solutions to self-evaluation quizzes.

One-Sample Hypothesis Tests

**Chapter Learning
Objectives**

When you finish this chapter you should be able to

- Formulate a null and alternative hypothesis for a mean or proportion.

- Define Type I error, Type II error, and power.

- List the steps in testing hypotheses.

- Do a hypothesis test for a proportion.

- Find the *p*-value for a test statistic using *z*.

- Do a hypothesis test for a mean with known or unknown σ.

- Explain similarities and differences between Student's *t* and *z*.

- Find critical values of *z* or *t* in tables or by using Excel.

- Find the *p*-value for a test statistic using *t*.

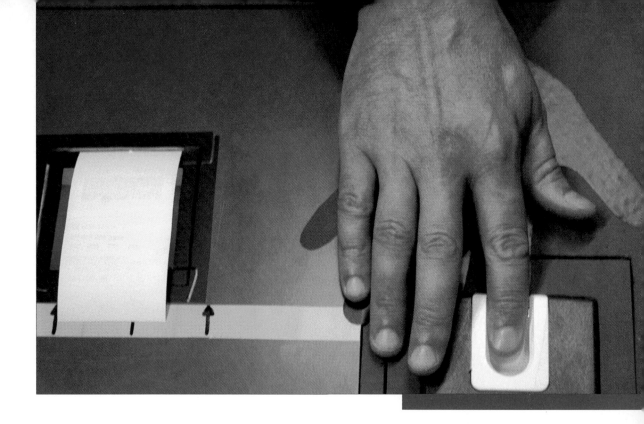

Data are used in business every day to support marketing claims, help managers make decisions, and to show business improvement. Whether the business is small or large, profit or nonprofit, the use of data allows businesses to find the best answers to their questions.

- Does a new airline mishandle fewer bags than the industry benchmark?
- Did the proportion of defective products decrease after a new manufacturing process was introduced?
- Has the average service time at a Noodles & Company restaurant decreased since last year?
- Has a ski resort decreased its average response time to accidents?
- Has the proportion of satisfied car repair customers increased after providing more training for the employees?

Savvy businesspeople use data and many of the statistical tools that you've already learned to answer these types of questions. We will build on these tools in this chapter and learn about one of the most widely used statistical tools—**hypothesis testing**. Hypothesis testing is used in both science and business to test assumptions and theories and ultimately guide managers when facing decisions. First we will explain the logic behind hypothesis testing and then show how *statistical hypothesis testing* helps businesses make decisions.

9.1 LOGIC OF HYPOTHESIS TESTING

Logical inquiry occurs when we ask questions, propose theories, make conjectures, and assume truths about the world around us. The process of inquiry requires that these theories, conjectures, and assumptions be tested rigorously and under various conditions. A theory or assumption that has not been disproved, in spite of repeated efforts to do so by testing, is a strong theory. The scientific community will often operate under the assumption that a strong theory is true, as long as they have no evidence that says otherwise. When testing a theory, a scientist states a clear assumption, called a **hypothesis**, which is then tested using a well-defined procedure that requires data collection. *Hypothesis testing* is the name of the statistical tool that compares the collected data against the assumption to determine if the data are consistent or inconsistent with the assumption. When the data are found to be inconsistent (i.e., or in conflict) with the assumption, the assumption is either discarded or the hypothesis is reformulated. As you might imagine, the process of hypothesis testing can be an iterative process.

Mini Case   9.1

Data Back New Airlines' Claims

The global air travel industry realized approximately $350 billion in revenue in 2006.*
How could a new airline be competitive in a market that is so large? One way would be to convince potential customers that they provide better customer service than the existing airlines. But not only must the airline *claim* that they are better, their statements must be *supported by data*. Flight problems and baggage problems were the number 1 and number 2 ranking complaint categories reported to the U.S. Department of Transportation by the end of 2005 and 2006. Are new airlines competitive in areas that matter to customers? JetBlue would like to think so. So would Southwest. What do the data say? Using information from the Department of Transportation, *The Wall Street Journal* issued a report card on U.S. airline customer service for 2006. Airlines were ranked in five service categories, including ontime arrivals and mishandled baggage. The top three ranking airlines were new airlines: JetBlue, Southwest, and AirTran. The number 9 and number 10 spots were held by older airlines United and Delta. The new airlines *claimed* better customer service, and the data *supported* their claims.

*IATA Industry Statistics March 2007.

Who Uses Hypothesis Testing? ●

Anyone who does research in science, engineering, social science, education, or medicine needs strong training in hypothesis testing. Furthermore, all business managers need at least a basic understanding of hypothesis testing because managers often interact with specialists and deal with technical reports. Managers in accounting, finance, and human resources must know enough not to be intimidated. Those involved in marketing, operations analysis, or quality management need somewhat stronger skills.

Why? Because the innovative vigor of our economy is largely based on technology: new materials, new manufacturing methods, new distribution systems, new information strategies. A manager must understand especially the meaning of concepts such as *significance* and *power,* because financial or strategic decisions often are required. For example, if a redesigned process could improve a truck engine's mpg rating *significantly,* but requires spending $250 million, is it worth doing? Such a decision requires clear understanding not only of **significance**, but also of the **importance** of the potential improvement: the magnitude of the effect, and its implications for product durability, customer satisfaction, budgets, cash flow, and staffing. Sound business decisions cannot be made without understanding the basic ideas of hypothesis tests.

Steps in Hypothesis Testing ●

Step1: State the assumption to be tested. This is the *hypothesis.*

Step2: Specify what level of inconsistency will lead to rejection of the hypothesis. This is called a **decision rule**.

Step3: Collect data and calculate necessary statistics to test the hypothesis.

Step4: Make a decision. Should the hypothesis be rejected or not?

Step5: Take action based on the decision. (This could include conducting a new test with a reformulated hypothesis.)

Step 1: State the Hypothesis   We formulate a pair of mutually exclusive, collectively exhaustive statements about the world. One statement or the other must be true, but they cannot both be true.

H_0: Null Hypothesis

H_1: Alternative Hypothesis

The two statements are *hypotheses* because the truth is unknown. Efforts will be made to reject the **null hypothesis** (sometimes called the *maintained hypothesis*). If H_0 happens to be a favorite theory, we might not really wish to reject it, but we try anyway. If we reject H_0, we tentatively conclude that the **alternative hypothesis** H_1 is the case. Whereas H_0 represents the *status quo* (e.g., the current state of affairs) H_1 is sometimes called the *action alternative* because action may be required if we reject H_0 in favor of H_1.

Criminal Trial   In a criminal trial, the hypotheses are:

H_0: The defendant is innocent

H_1: The defendant is guilty

Our legal system assumes a defendant is innocent *unless the evidence gathered by the prosecutor allows us to reject this assumption.*

Drug Testing   When an Olympic athlete is tested for performance-enhancing drugs like steroids, the presumption is that the athlete is in compliance with the rules. The hypotheses are:

H_0: No illegal steroid use

H_1: Illegal steroid use

Samples of urine or blood are taken as evidence and *used only to disprove the null hypothesis because we assume the athlete is free of illegal steroids.*

Biometric Security   This rapidly growing application of hypothesis testing seeks ways to identify authorized and unauthorized persons for computer access, ATM withdrawals, entry into secure facilities, and so on, using the person's physical characteristics (e.g., fingerprints, facial structure, or iris patterns). The intent is to get rid of paper and plastic IDs, which can be forged. The hypotheses are:

H_0: User is authorized

H_1: User is unauthorized

The system assumes the user is authorized and *looks for ways in which the physical characteristic being presented is inconsistent with the assumed pattern.*

Step 2: Specify the Decision Rule   Before collecting data to compare against the hypothesis, the researcher must specify *how* the evidence will be used to reach a decision about the null hypothesis. In our legal system, the evidence presented by the prosecutor must convince a jury "beyond a reasonable doubt" that the defendant is not innocent. In steroid testing, the lab that analyzes the urine or blood sample must conduct duplicate tests to decide whether the sample exceeds the agreed-upon benchmark. With biometric screening, the designer of the security system determines how many discrepancies on a fingerprint would indicate an unauthorized user.

Steps 3 and 4: Data Collection and Decision Making   Much of the critical work in hypothesis testing takes place during steps 1 and 2. Once the hypotheses and decision rule have been clearly articulated, the process of data collection, while time-consuming, is often straightforward. We compare the data against the decision rule and decide to reject or not reject the null hypothesis.

Step 5: Take Action Based on Decision   This last step—taking action—requires experience and expertise on the part of the decision maker. Suppose the evidence presented at a trial convinces a jury that the defendant is not innocent. What punishment should the judge impose? Or suppose the blood sample of an athlete shows steroid use. What fine should the athletic commission impose? Should the athlete be banned from competing? If the fingerprint presented for authentication has been rejected, should an alarm go off? Should a security breach be recorded in the system? Appropriate action for the decision should relate back to the purpose of conducting the hypothesis test in the first place.

Can a Null Hypothesis Be Proved?

No, we cannot prove a null hypothesis—we can only *fail to reject* it. A null hypothesis that survives repeated tests without rejection is "true" only in the limited sense that it has been thoroughly scrutinized. Today's "true" hypothesis could be falsified tomorrow. If we fail to reject H_0, we provisionally accept H_0. However, an "accepted" hypothesis may be retested. That is how scientific inquiry works. Einstein's theories, for example, are over 100 years old but are still being subjected to rigorous tests. Yet few scientists really think that Einstein's theories are "wrong." It's in the nature of science to keep trying to refute accepted theories, especially when a new test is possible or when new data become available. Similarly, the safety of commonly used prescription drugs is continually being studied. Sometimes, "safe" drugs are revealed to have serious side effects only after large-scale, long-term use by consumers (e.g., the Vioxx arthritis drug that was shown to be safe in clinical trials, but later showed a dangerous association with heart attack after years of use by millions of people).

Types of Error

Because our ability to collect evidence can be limited by our tools and by time and financial resources, we recognize that on occasion we will be making a decision about the null hypothesis that could be wrong. Consequently, our decision rule will be based on the levels of risk of making a wrong decision. We can allow more risk or less risk by changing the threshold of the decision rule.

It is possible to make an incorrect decision regarding the null hypothesis. How can this occur? Consider Table 9.1 below. In reality, either the null hypothesis is true or it is false. We have only two possible decisions to choose between concerning the null hypothesis. We either reject H_0 or fail to reject H_0.

TABLE 9.1

Type I and II Error

Decision	True Situation	
	H_0 is True	H_0 is False
Reject H_0	Type I error	Correct Decision
Fail to reject H_0	Correct Decision	Type II error

The true situation determines whether our decision was correct. If the decision about the null hypothesis matches the true situation, there is no error. Rejecting the null hypothesis when it is true is a **Type I error**. Failure to reject the null hypothesis when it is false is **Type II error**.

Will We Ever Know If We Made an Error? Because we rarely have perfect information about the true situation we can't know immediately when we have committed Type I or Type II errors. When constructing the decision rule we try to minimize the chance of either of these errors by collecting as much evidence as our resources allow. We also try to understand the consequences of making an error in order to be as informed as possible before taking action. Statistics lets us determine the risks of Type I or II errors, so that we can assess the *probability* of making an incorrect decision.

Consequences of Type I and Type II Errors

The consequences of these two errors are quite different, and the costs are borne by different parties. Depending on the situation, decision makers may fear one error more than the other. It would be nice if both types of error could be avoided. Unfortunately, when making a decision based on a fixed body of sample evidence, reducing the risk of one type of error often increases the risk of the other. Consider our examples of a criminal trial, drug testing, and biometric security.

Criminal Trial   Type I error is convicting an innocent defendant, so the costs are borne by the defendant. Type II error is failing to convict a guilty defendant, so the costs are borne by society if the guilty person returns to the streets. Concern for the rights of the accused and stricter rules of evidence during the 1960s and 70s led American courts to try to reduce the risk of Type I error, which probably increased the risk of Type II error. But during the 1980s and 90s, amid growing concern over the social costs of crime and victims' rights, courts began closing loopholes to reduce Type II error, presumably at the expense of Type I error. Both risks can be reduced only by devoting more effort to gathering evidence and strengthening the legal process (expediting trials, improving jury quality, increasing investigative work).

H_0: Defendant is innocent
H_1: Defendant is guilty

Drug Testing   Type I error is unfairly disqualifying an athlete who is "clean." Type II error is letting the drug user get away with it and have an unfair competitive advantage. The costs of Type I error are hard feelings and unnecessary embarrassment. The costs of Type II error are tarnishing the Olympic image and rewarding those who break the rules. Over time, improved tests have reduced the risk of both types of error. However, for a given technology, the threshold can be set lower or higher, balancing Type I and Type II error. Which error is more to be feared?

H_0: No illegal steroid use
H_1: Illegal steroid use

Biometric Security   Type I error means denying a legitimate user access to a facility or funds. Type II error is letting an unauthorized user have access to facilities or a financial account. Technology has progressed to the point where Type II errors have become very rare, though Type I errors remain a problem. The error rates depend on how much is spent on the equipment and software.

H_0: User authorized
H_1: User unauthorized

You are already halfway there, if you understand the previous chapter. A confidence interval often gives enough information to make a decision. Knowing the 95 percent range of likely values for a key decision parameter (e.g., the proportion of repeat customers under age 30) may be all you need. This chapter extends the idea of confidence intervals by showing how to test a sample against a benchmark, and how to assess the risk of incorrect decisions.

9.2 STATISTICAL HYPOTHESIS TESTING

A **statistical hypothesis** is a statement about the value of a population parameter that we are interested in (call it θ). For example, the parameter θ could be a mean, a proportion, or a variance. A **hypothesis test** is a decision between two competing, mutually exclusive, and collectively exhaustive hypotheses about the value of θ:

Left-Tailed Test	*Two-Tailed Test*	*Right-Tailed Test*
H_0: $\theta \geq \theta_0$	H_0: $\theta = \theta_0$	H_0: $\theta \leq \theta_0$
H_1: $\theta < \theta_0$	H_1: $\theta \neq \theta_0$	H_1: $\theta > \theta_0$

The *direction of the test* is indicated by H_1:

   $<$ indicates a **left-tailed test**

   $\neq$ indicates a **two-tailed test**

   $>$ indicates a **right-tailed test**

The hypothesized value θ_0 is the center of interest. If the true value of θ is θ_0, then a sample estimate should not differ greatly from θ_0. We rely on our knowledge of the *sampling distribution* and the *standard error of the estimate* to decide if the sample estimate is far enough away from θ_0 to contradict the assumption that $\theta = \theta_0$, as illustrated in Figure 9.1.

The parameter we test is typically a mean, μ, or a proportion, π. Stating the null hypothesis requires a benchmark value for μ or π that we denote with the subscript "0" as in μ_0 or π_0.

FIGURE 9.1

Outcomes in a Sampling Distribution

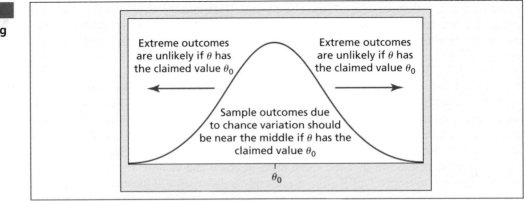

This value does not come from a sample but is based on past performance, an industry standard, or a product specification.

Where Do We Get μ_0 (or π_0)?

The value of μ_0 (or π_0) that we are testing is a *benchmark*, such as past experience, an industry standard, or a product specification. The value of μ_0 (or π_0) does *not* come from a sample.

The application will dictate which type of test we should construct. When testing a mean we choose between three tests:

Left-Tailed Test	*Two-Tailed Test*	*Right-Tailed Test*
$H_0: \mu \geq \mu_0$	$H_0: \mu = \mu_0$	$H_0: \mu \leq \mu_0$
$H_1: \mu < \mu_0$	$H_1: \mu \neq \mu_0$	$H_1: \mu > \mu_0$

EXAMPLE

Testing a Mean

The width of a sheet of standard size copier paper should be $\mu = 216$ mm (i.e., 8.5 inches). There is some variation in paper width due to the nature of the production process, so the width of a sheet of paper is a random variable. However, per strict industry standards only 34 nonconforming sheets per million would be allowable. For this reason, samples are taken from the production process, the width is measured with extreme accuracy, and the mean is calculated. Each time a sample is taken, we use its mean to test a hypothesis. Has the mean decreased? Increased? Stayed the same? The possible pairs of hypotheses are

Left-Tailed Test	*Two-Tailed Test*	*Right-Tailed Test*
$H_0: \mu \geq 216$	$H_0: \mu = 216$	$H_0: \mu \leq 216$
$H_1: \mu < 216$	$H_1: \mu \neq 216$	$H_1: \mu > 216$

If the paper is too narrow ($\mu < 216$ mm), the pages might not be well-centered in the feeder. If this is our main concern, we might choose a *left-tailed test*. If the pages are too wide ($\mu > 216$ mm), sheets could jam in the feeder or paper trays. If this is our main concern, we might choose a *right-tailed test*. Since either violation poses a quality problem ($\mu \neq 216$ mm) we would probably choose a two-tailed test. If the null hypothesis is rejected, the manufacturing process should be corrected, that is, action is required. Our decision depends on the severity of the departure from H_0, the test type, and our tolerance for making the wrong decision.

Similarly, when testing a proportion we choose between three tests:

Left-Tailed Test	*Two-Tailed Test*	*Right-Tailed Test*
$H_0: \pi \geq \pi_0$	$H_0: \pi = \pi_0$	$H_0: \pi \leq \pi_0$
$H_1: \pi < \pi_0$	$H_1: \pi \neq \pi_0$	$H_1: \pi > \pi_0$

In 2006, U.S. airlines mishandled 6 out of every 1,000 bags checked for air travel. One airline, FlyFast, found that 54 percent of their mishandled bag incidents were related to transferring baggage to a connecting flight. FlyFast recently installed an RFID (Radio Frequency Identification) system with the goal of decreasing the proportion of mistakes caused during transfer and ultimately reducing the overall proportion of lost bags. After operating their new system for several months, FlyFast would like to know if the wireless system has been effective. FlyFast could use a hypothesis test to answer this question. The benchmark for the null hypothesis is their proportion of transfer mistakes using their old system ($\pi_0 = .54$.) The possible set of statistical hypotheses would be:

Left-Tailed Test	*Two-Tailed Test*	*Right-Tailed Test*
$H_0: \pi \geq .54$	$H_0: \pi = .54$	$H_0: \pi \leq .54$
$H_1: \pi < .54$	$H_1: \pi \neq .54$	$H_1: \pi > .54$

Which set of hypotheses would be most logical for FlyFast to use? Since FlyFast believes the RFID system will reduce the proportion of transfer errors, they might use a left-tailed test. They would assume there has been no improvement, unless their evidence shows otherwise. If they can reject H_0 in favor of H_1 in a left-tailed test FlyFast would be able to say that their data provide evidence that the proportion of transfer errors has decreased since the RFID tagging system was implemented.

Decision Rule

When performing a statistical hypothesis test, we compare a sample statistic to the hypothesized value of the population parameter stated in the null hypothesis. Extreme outcomes occurring in the left tail would cause us to reject the null hypothesis in a left-tailed test; extreme outcomes occurring in the right tail would cause us to reject the null hypothesis in a right-tailed test. Extreme values in *either* the left or right tail would cause us to reject the null hypothesis in a two-tailed test.

We specify our decision rule by defining an "extreme" outcome. We rely on our knowledge of the *sampling distribution* and the *standard error of the estimate* to decide if the sample statistic is far enough away from θ_0 to contradict the assumption that $\theta = \theta_0$. The area under the sampling distribution curve that defines an extreme outcome is called the **rejection region**. For example, if we are dealing with a normal sampling distribution, we might reject H_0 if the sample statistic is more than 1.96 standard deviations from θ_0. We calculate a *test statistic* to determine how far our sample statistic is from the hypothesized population parameter. Before we collect sample data, we decide what the critical value of the test statistic would have to be, in order to reject H_0. Table 9.2 and Figure 9.2 illustrate the three test types, the rejection regions, and corresponding decision rules.

TABLE 9.2

Three Types of Decision Rules

Test Type	Decision Rule
Left-tailed	Reject H_0 if the test statistic < left-tail critical value
Two-tailed	Reject H_0 if the test statistic < left-tail critical value or if the test statistic > right-tail critical value
Right-tailed	Reject H_0 if the test statistic > right-tail critical value

In a left-tailed or right-tailed test, the inequality in H_0 comprises an *infinite* number of hypotheses. But we can only test *one* value of the hypothesized parameter at a time. To handle this problem, we test the null hypothesis H_0 *only* at the point of equality $H_0: \theta = \theta_0$. That is, we temporarily ignore the infinite possibilities in H_0. If we reject $\theta = \theta_0$ in favor of the alternative, then we implicitly reject the *entire class* of H_0 possibilities. For example, suppose we want a

FIGURE 9.2

FIGURE 9.2

Three Types of Decision Rules

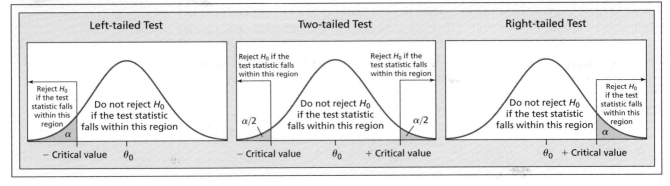

right-tailed test for the paper size problem (i.e., we are checking only for oversized paper). We take a sample of 100 sheets and measure them carefully. If the sample mean is far enough above 216 mm to cause us to reject the null hypothesis $H_0: \mu = 216$ mm in favor of the alternative hypothesis $H_1: \mu > 216$ mm, the same sample would also permit rejection of any value of μ *less than* $\mu = 216$ mm. If we reject $\mu = 216$ mm, we actually can reject $\mu \leq 216$ mm.

In quality control, any deviation from specifications indicates that something may be wrong with the process, so a two-tailed test is common. In a two-tailed test, the decision maker has no *a priori* reason to expect rejection in one direction. In such cases, it is reasonable to use a two-tailed test. As you'll soon see, rejection in a two-tailed test guarantees rejection in a one-tailed test, other things being equal.

However, when the consequences of rejecting H_0 are asymmetric, or where one tail is of special importance to the researcher, we might prefer a one-tailed test. For example, suppose that a machine is supposed to bore holes with a 3.5-mm diameter in a piece of sheet metal. Although any deviation from 3.5 mm is a violation of the specification, the consequences of rejecting H_0 may be different. Suppose an attachment pin is to be inserted into the hole. If the hole is too small, the pin cannot be inserted, but the metal piece could probably be reworked to enlarge the hole so the pin does fit. On the other hand, if the hole is too large, the pin will fit too loosely and may fall out. The piece may have to be discarded since an oversized hole cannot be made smaller. This is illustrated in Figure 9.3.

FIGURE 9.3

Asymmetric Effects of Nonconformance

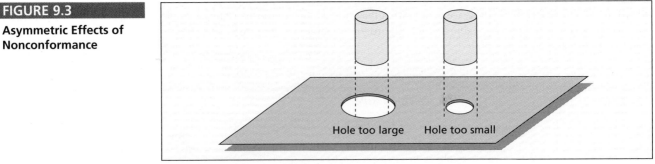

Hole too large   Hole too small

Probability of Type I and Type II Errors

Type I Error   The probability of Type I error is denoted α and is commonly called the **level of significance**. It is the risk that we will wrongly reject a true H_0: When stating the decision rule, the decision maker decides what the *level of significance* will be for the hypothesis test. Note that α is the acceptable level of risk of making a Type I error.

(9.1)
$$\alpha = P(\text{reject } H_0 \mid H_0 \text{ is true})$$

Type I Error

The probability of rejecting the null hypothesis when it is true is denoted α and is called the *level of significance*. A Type I error is sometimes called a *false positive*.

If we specify a decision rule based on a choice of $\alpha = .05$, we would expect to commit a Type I error about 5 times in 100 samples *if H_0 is true.* We would like α to be small, usually less than .10. Common choices for α are .10, .05, and .01. The level of significance is usually expressed as a percent, that is, 10, 5, or 1 percent.

Stated differently, α is the probability that the test statistic would happen to fall in the rejection region even though H_0 is true. Since we don't want to reject a true hypothesis, this would be a Type I error. This α risk is the area under the tail(s) of the sampling distribution. In a two-tailed test, the α risk is split with $\alpha/2$ in each tail, since there are two ways to reject H_0 (if the test statistic is too far above or below the expected value). Thus, in a two-tailed test using $\alpha = .10$ we would put half the risk ($\alpha/2 = .05$) in each tail. Figure 9.2 illustrates these concepts.

By choosing a small α (say $\alpha = .01$) the decision maker can make it harder to reject the null hypothesis. By choosing a larger α (say $\alpha = .05$) it is easier to reject the null hypothesis. This raises the possibility of manipulating the decision. For this reason, the choice of α should precede the calculation of the test statistic, thereby minimizing the temptation to select α so as to favor one conclusion over the other.

Type II Error   The probability of Type II error, sometimes referred to as β risk, is the probability that the test statistic falls in the acceptance region, even though the null hypothesis H_0 is actually false. It is the risk that we will wrongly accept a false H_0.

$$P(\text{fail to reject } H_0 \mid H_0 \text{ is false}) = \beta \qquad (9.2)$$

Type II Error

The probability of accepting the null hypothesis when it is false is denoted β. A Type II error is sometimes called a *false negative*.

Unlike α, we cannot choose β in advance. The reason is that β depends on several things, including our choice for α and the size of the sample. Other things being equal, we would like β to be small. However, for a given sample, there is a trade-off between α and β. We will discuss this trade-off in more detail shortly.

Power of a Test   If the null hypothesis is false, we ought to reject it. If we do so, we have done the right thing, and there is no Type II error. The **power** of a test is the probability that a false hypothesis will be rejected, as it should be. More power is good, because power is the probability of doing the right thing. Power is the complement of beta risk ($1 - \beta$). If we have low β risk, we have high power:

$$\text{Power} = P(\text{reject } H_0 \mid H_0 \text{ is false}) = 1 - \beta \qquad (9.3)$$

Power

The probability of rejecting the null hypothesis when it is false is $1 - \beta$ and is called *power*. In medicine, the power of a test to correctly detect a disease is its *sensitivity*.

More powerful tests are more likely to detect false hypotheses. For example, if a new weight-loss drug actually is effective, we would want to reject the null hypothesis that the drug has no effect. We prefer the most powerful test possible. Larger samples lead to increased power, which is why clinical trials often involve thousands of people.

Relationship between α and β

We desire tests that avoid false negatives (small β risk) yet we also want to avoid false positives (small α risk). Given two acceptable tests, we will choose the more powerful one. But for a given type of test and fixed sample size, there is a trade-off between α and β. The larger critical value needed to reduce α risk makes it harder to reject H_0, thereby increasing β risk. The proper balance between α and β can be elusive. Consider these examples:

- If your household carbon monoxide detector's sensitivity threshold is increased to reduce the risk of overlooking danger (reduced β), there will be more false alarms (increased α).

- A doctor who is conservative about admitting patients with symptoms of myocardial infarction to the ICU (reduced β) will admit more patients without myocardial infarction (increased α).

- Reducing the threshold for dangerously high blood pressure from 140/90 to 130/80 will reduce the chance of missing the diagnosis of hypertension (reduced β), but some patients may incorrectly be given medication that is not needed (increased α).

Both α and β risk can be reduced simultaneously only by increasing the sample size (gathering more evidence), which is not always feasible or cost-effective.

EXAMPLE

Consequences of Type II Error

Firms are increasingly wary of Type II error (failing to recall a product as soon as sample evidence begins to indicate potential problems):

H_0: Product is performing safely

H_1: Product is not performing safely

They may even order a precautionary product recall before the statistical evidence has become convincing (e.g., Verizon's 2004 recall of 50,000 cell phone batteries after one exploded and another caused a car fire) or even *before* anything bad happens (e.g., Intel's 2004 recall of its 915 G/P and 925X chip sets from OEMs (original equipment manufacturer), before the chips actually reached any consumers). Failure to act swiftly can generate liability and adverse publicity as with the spate of Ford Explorer rollover accidents and eventual recall of certain 15-inch Firestone radial tires. Ford and Firestone believed they had found an engineering workaround to make the tire design safe, until accumulating accident data, lawsuits, and NHTSA pressure forced recognition that there was a problem. In 2004, certain COX_2 inhibitor drugs that had previously been thought effective and safe, based on extensive clinical trials, were found to be associated with increased risk of heart attack. The makers' stock price plunged (e.g., Merck). Lawyers, of course, have an incentive to claim product defects, even when the evidence is doubtful (e.g., Dow's silicone breast implants). The courts, therefore, often must use statistical evidence to adjudicate product liability claims.

Statistical Significance versus Practical Importance

The standard error of most sample estimators approaches zero as sample size increases (if they are consistent estimators), so almost any difference between θ and θ_0, no matter how tiny, will be significant if the sample size is large enough. Researchers who deal with large samples must expect "significant" effects, even when an effect is too slight to have any *practical importance*. Is an improvement of 0.2 mpg in fuel economy *important* to Toyota buyers? Is a 0.5 percent loss of market share *important* to Hertz? Is a laptop battery life increase of 15 minutes *important* to Dell customers? Such questions depend not so much on statistics as on the cost/benefit calculation. Since resources are always scarce, a dollar spent on a quality improvement always has an opportunity cost (the foregone alternative). If we spend money to make a certain product improvement, then some other project may have to be shelved. Since we can't do everything, we must ask whether the proposed product improvement is the best use of our scarce resources. These are questions that must be answered by experts in medicine, marketing, product safety, or engineering, rather than by statisticians.

9.1   Sketch a diagram of the decision rule for each pair of hypotheses.
   a. H_0: $\mu \geq 80$ versus H_1: $\mu < 80$
   b. H_0: $\mu = 80$ versus H_1: $\mu \neq 80$
   c. H_0: $\mu \leq 80$ versus H_1: $\mu > 80$

9.2   In 1,000 samples, assuming that H_0 is true, how many times would you expect to commit Type I error if (a) $\alpha = .05$, (b) $\alpha = .01$, and (c) $\alpha = .001$.

9.3   Define Type I and Type II error for each scenario, and discuss the cost(s) of each type of error.
   a. A 25-year-old ER patient in Minneapolis complains of chest pain. Heart attacks in 25 year olds are rare, and beds are scarce in the hospital. The null hypothesis is that there is no heart attack (probably muscle pain due to shoveling snow).
   b. Approaching O'Hare for landing, a British Air flight from London has been in a holding pattern for 45 minutes due to bad weather. Landing is expected within 15 minutes. The flight crew could declare an emergency and land immediately, but an FAA investigation would be launched. The null hypothesis is that there is enough fuel to stay aloft for 15 more minutes.
   c. You are trying to finish a lengthy statistics report and print it for your evening class. Your color printer is very low on ink, and you just have time to get to Staples for a new cartridge. But it is snowing and you need every minute to finish the report. The null hypothesis is that you have enough ink.

9.4   Discuss the issues of *statistical significance* and *practical importance* in each scenario.
   a. A process for producing I-beams of oriented strand board used as main support beams in new houses has a mean breaking strength of 2,000 lbs./ft. A sample of boards from a new process has a mean breaking strength of 2,150 lbs./ft. The improvement is statistically significant, but the per-unit cost is higher.
   b. Under continuous use, the mean battery life in a certain cell phone is 45 hours. In tests of a new type of battery, the sample mean battery life is 46 hours. The improvement is statistically significant, but the new battery costs more to produce.
   c. For a wide-screen HDTV LCD unit, the mean half-life (i.e., to lose 50 percent of its brightness) is 32,000 hours. A new process is developed. In tests of the new display, the sample mean half-life is 35,000 hours. The improvement is statistically significant, though the new process is more costly.

9.5   A firm decides to test its employees for illegal drugs. (a) State the null and alternative hypotheses. (b) Define Type I and II error. (c) What are the consequences of each? Which is more to be feared, and by whom?

9.6   A hotel installs smoke detectors with adjustable sensitivity in all public guest rooms. (a) State the null and alternative hypotheses. (b) Define Type I and II error. What are the consequences of each? (c) Which is more to be feared, and by whom? (d) If the hotel decides to reduce β risk, what would be the consequences? Who would be affected?

Mini Case   9.2

Type I and Type II Error

We generally call a Type I error, rejecting a true H_0, a "false positive" or a "false rejection." A Type II error, failing to reject a false H_0, is often called a "false negative" or a "false acceptance." Technology is always changing, but this mini case shows some actual rates of Type I error and Type II error in real applications. In each application, ask: What is the cost of a false positive or a false negative? Who bears these costs? This way of thinking will help you decide whether Type I or Type II error is more to be feared, and why.

BIOMETRIC SECURITY
This is a hot area for business. If your ATM could recognize your physical characteristics (e.g., fingerprint, face, palm, iris) you wouldn't need an ATM card or a PIN. A reliable biometric ID system could also reduce the risk of ID theft, eliminate computer passwords, and speed airport security screening. The hypotheses are

   H_0: User is authorized

   H_1: User is not authorized

Fujitsu Laboratories has tested a palm ID system on 700 people, ranging from children to seniors. It achieved a false rejection rate of 1 percent and a false acceptance rate of

0.5 percent. Bank of Tokyo-Mitsubishi introduced palm-scanning at its ATM machines in 2004. DigitalPersona of Redwood City, California, has developed a fingerprint scanner (called *U.Are.U*) that is able to recognize fingerprints in 200 milliseconds with a 1 percent false rejection rate and a 0.002 percent false acceptance rate. In some high-end devices, false acceptance rates as low as 25 per million have been achieved. False rejection rates (Type I error) are higher, but merely cause user inconvenience. The low rates of false acceptance (Type II error) are encouraging, since they mean that others cannot easily impersonate you. Fingerprint scanning is the most popular because it is cheaper and easier to implement, though many experts believe that iris scanning has better long-run potential to reduce both error rates (especially important in airport security screening). Any such system requires a stored database of biometric data.

Sources: *BusinessWeek,* November 22, 2004, p. 127; *Scientific American* 290, no. 6 (June 2004), p. 108, and 289, no. 4 (April 2003), p. 74; and *PC Magazine,* April 22, 2003, p. 74.

MEDICAL TESTS

Cancer-screening tests have become routine. Unfortunately, they have fairly high rates of Type I error (unnecessary alarm, risk of biopsy) and Type II error (missed cancer). The hypotheses are

H_0: No cancer exists

H_1: Cancer exists

Consider these examples. Up to 25 percent of men with prostate cancer have normal PSA levels, while 50 percent of those with no cancer have elevated PSA levels and 70 percent of men with high PSA levels do not have cancer. Up to 33 percent of the PAP smears for cancer of the cervix give false positives—a rate that may soon be reduced by applying computer pattern recognition to the 50 million tests done every year by human technicians. MRI scanning for breast cancer detects about 80 percent of invasive growths in women (power = $1 - \beta$) compared with only 33 percent for standard mammography. In other medical testing, of the 250,000 people treated annually for appendicitis, from 15 percent to 40 percent have a healthy appendix removed, while about 20 percent of the time the appendicitis diagnosis is missed.

Sources: *Scientific American* 284, no. 12 (December 1998), p. 75; *Technology Review* 107, no. 6, p. 64; *Popular Science* 247, no. 6, p. 76; *The Wall Street Journal,* July 29, 2004; and *Science News* 153 (January 31, 1998). p. 78.

OTHER APPLICATIONS

Tests for "mad cow" disease have a 1 in 10,000 chance of a false positive. Most computer virus-detection software packages have very low rates of false positives (e.g., McAfee and Norton Antivirus had only 1 false positive in 3,700,000 files tested). But in spam detection, the results are not as good (e.g., in one test, ZoneAlarm misidentified less than 1 percent of legitimate e-mails as spam but failed to detect 4 percent of actual spam). Accuracy will improve over time in most of these applications.

Sources: www.npr.org, accessed July 3, 2004; *PC Magazine* 23, no. 10 (June 8, 2004), p. 116, and 24, no. 2 (February 8, 2005), p. 40.

9.3

TESTING A MEAN: KNOWN POPULATION VARIANCE

VS

Chapter 9

A hypothesis test tests a claim about a population parameter such as π, μ, or σ. We will first explain how to test a population mean, μ. The sample statistic used to estimate μ is $\bar{X}$. The sampling distribution for $\bar{X}$ depends on whether or not the population variance σ^2 is known. We begin with the case of known σ^2. We learned in Chapter 8 that the sampling distribution of $\bar{X}$ will be a normal distribution provided that we have a normal population (or, by the Central Limit Theorem, if the sample size is large). In Section 9.4 we will turn to the more common case when σ^2 is estimated.

Test Statistic

A decision rule is specified based on our chosen level of significance and the sampling distribution of the sample statistic. A **test statistic** measures the difference between $\bar{x}$ and μ_0 in terms of the standard error of the mean. Think of the test statistic as the "standardized score" of the sample statistic. When testing μ with a known σ, the test statistic is the z score. Once we have collected our sample, we calculate a value of the test statistic using the sample mean and then compare it against the critical value of z. We will refer to the calculated value of the test statistic as z_{calc}.

$$z_{calc} = \frac{\bar{x} - \mu_0}{\sigma_{\bar{x}}} = \frac{\bar{x} - \mu_0}{\frac{\sigma}{\sqrt{n}}} \quad \text{(test statistic for a mean with known } \sigma\text{)} \qquad \textbf{(9.4)}$$

The critical value of the test statistic will be referenced by the tail area of the rejection region. If the true mean of the population is μ_0 then the value of $\bar{x}$ calculated from our sample should be near μ_0 and therefore the test statistic should be near zero.

Critical Value

The test statistic is compared with a **critical value** from a table. The critical value is the boundary between two regions (reject H_0, do not reject H_0) in the decision rule. The critical value shows the range of values for the test statistic that would be expected by chance if the null hypothesis were true. For a two-tailed test (but *not* for a one-tailed test) the hypothesis test is equivalent to asking whether the confidence interval for μ includes zero. In a two-tailed test, half the risk of Type I error (i.e., $\alpha/2$) goes in each tail, as shown in Table 9.3, so the z-values are the same as for a confidence interval. You can verify these z-values from Excel.

Level of Significance (α)	Two-Tailed Test	Right-Tailed Test	Left-Tailed Test
.10	±1.645	1.282	−1.282
.05	±1.960	1.645	−1.645
.01	±2.576	2.326	−2.326

TABLE 9.3

Some Common z-Values

EXAMPLE

Paper Manufacturing

The Hammermill Company produces paper for laser printers. Standard paper width is supposed to be 216 mm, or 8.5 inches. Suppose that the actual width is a random variable that is normally distributed with a known standard deviation of .023 mm. This standard deviation reflects the manufacturing technology currently in use and is known from long experience with this type of equipment. The standard deviation is small, due to the company's considerable effort to maintain precise control over paper width. However, variation still arises during manufacturing because of slight differences in the paper stock, vibration in the rollers and cutting tools, and wear and tear on the equipment. The cutters can be adjusted if the paper width drifts from the correct mean. A quality control inspector chooses 50 sheets at random and measures them with a precise instrument, showing a mean width of 216.007 mm. Using a 5 percent level of significance ($\alpha = .05$), does this sample show that the product mean exceeds the specification?   **Paper**

Step1: State the Hypotheses   The question we want to answer indicates a right-tailed test, so the hypotheses would be

H_0: $\mu \leq 216$ mm (product mean does not exceed the specification)

H_1: $\mu > 216$ mm (product mean has risen above the specification)

From the null hypothesis we see that $\mu_0 = 216$ mm, which is the product specification.

Step 2: Specify the Decision Rule   We use the *level of significance* to find the *critical value* of the z statistic that determines the threshold for rejecting the null hypothesis to be

FIGURE 9.4

Right-Tailed z Test for
α = .05

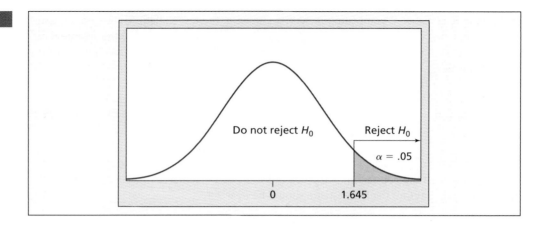

α = .05. The critical value of z that accomplishes this is $z_{.05} = 1.645$. As illustrated in Figure 9.4, the decision rule is

Reject H_0 if $z_{calc} > 1.645$

Otherwise do not reject H_0

Step 3: Collect Sample Data and Calculate the Test Statistic   If H_0 is true, then the test statistic should be near 0 because $\bar{x}$ should be near μ_0. The value of the test statistic is

$$z_{calc} = \frac{\bar{x} - \mu_0}{\frac{\sigma}{\sqrt{n}}} = \frac{216.007 - 216.000}{\frac{0.023}{\sqrt{50}}} = \frac{0.007}{0.00325269} = 2.152$$

Step 4: Make the Decision   The test statistic falls in the right rejection region, so we reject the null hypothesis H_0: $\mu \leq 216$ and conclude the alternative hypothesis H_1: $\mu > 216$ at the 5 percent level of significance. Although the difference is slight, it is statistically significant.

Step 5: Take Action   Now that we have concluded that the process is producing paper with an average width *greater* than the specification, it is time to adjust our manufacturing process to bring the average width back to specification. Our course of action could be to readjust the machine settings or it could be time to resharpen the cutting tools. At this point it is the responsibility of the process engineers to determine the best course of action.

p-Value Method

The critical value method described above requires that you specify your rejection criterion in terms of the test statistic before you take a sample. The *p*-value method is a different approach that is often preferred by statisticians over the critical value method. It requires that you express the strength of your evidence (i.e., your sample) against the null hypothesis in terms of a probability. The *p*-value answers the following question: What is the probability that we would observe our particular sample mean (or something even farther away from μ_0) if, in fact, the null hypothesis is true? The *p*-value gives us more information than a test using one particular value of α.

The *p*-value is compared to the level of significance. In order to calculate the *p*-value, we still need to find z_{calc}. For a right-tailed test, the decision rule using the *p*-value approach is stated as:

Reject H_0 if $P(Z > z_{calc}) < \alpha$, otherwise fail to reject H_0.

Whether we use the critical value approach or the *p*-value approach, our decision about the null hypothesis will be the same.

P-value

A *p*-value directly measures how well the sample agrees with H_0. The smaller the *p*-value, the stronger is the evidence for *rejecting H_0*.

The *p*-value for this test is $P(Z > 2.152)$. Note that the direction of the inequality in the *p*-value is the same as in the alternative hypothesis: H_1: $\mu > 216$ mm.

To find the *p*-value, we can use Excel's function =NORMSDIST(2.152) to obtain the left-tail area for the cumulative *Z* distribution (see Figure 9.5). Since $P(Z < 2.152) = .9843$ the right-tail area is $P(z > 2.152) = 1 - .9843 = .0157$. This is the *p*-value for the right-tailed test, as illustrated in Figure 9.5. The *p*-value diagram does not show α. The *p*-value of .0157 says that in a right-tailed test a test statistic of $z_{calc} = 2.152$ (or a more extreme test statistic) would happen by chance about 1.57 percent of the time if the null hypothesis were true.

FIGURE 9.5

***p*-Value for a Right-Tailed Test with $z_{calc} = 2.152$, Using Excel**

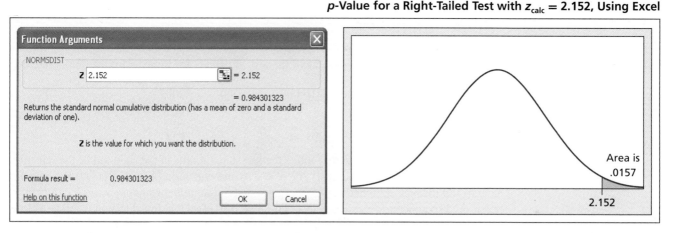

We could also obtain the *p*-value from Appendix C-2, which shows cumulative standard normal areas less than *z*, as illustrated in Table 9.4. The cumulative area is not exactly the same as Excel, because Appendix C-2 requires that we round the test statistic to two decimals ($z = 2.15$).

TABLE 9.4

Finding the *p*-Value for $z = 2.15$ in Appendix C-2

z	.00	.01	.02	.03	.04	.05	.06	.07	.08	.09
−3.7	.00011	.00010	.00010	.00010	.00009	.00009	.00008	.00008	.00008	.00008
−3.6	.00016	.00015	.00015	.00014	.00014	.00013	.00013	.00012	.00012	.00011
−3.5	.00023	.00022	.00022	.00021	.00020	.00019	.00019	.00018	.00017	.00017
⋮	⋮	⋮	⋮	⋮	⋮	⋮	⋮	⋮	⋮	⋮
2.0	.97725	.97778	.97831	.97882	.97932	.97982	.98030	.98077	.98124	.98169
2.1	.98214	.98257	.98300	.98341	.98382	*.98422*	.98461	.98500	.98537	.98574
2.2	.98610	.98645	.98679	.98713	.98745	.98778	.98809	.98840	.98870	.98899

Two-Tailed Test

What if we used a two-tailed test? This might be appropriate if the objective is to detect a deviation from the desired mean in *either* direction.

Step 1: State the Hypotheses   For a two-tailed test, the hypotheses are

H_0: $\mu = 216$ mm (product mean is what it is supposed to be)

H_1: $\mu \neq 216$ mm (product mean is not what it is supposed to be)

Step 2: Specify the Decision Rule   We will use the same $\alpha = .05$ as in the right-tailed test. But for a two-tailed test, we split the risk of Type I error by putting $\alpha/2 = .05/2 = .025$ in each tail. For $\alpha = .05$ in a two-tailed test, the critical value is $z_{.025} = \pm 1.96$ so the decision rule is

Reject H_0 if $z_{\text{calc}} > +1.96$ or if $z_{\text{calc}} < -1.96$

Otherwise do not reject H_0

The decision rule is illustrated in Figure 9.6.

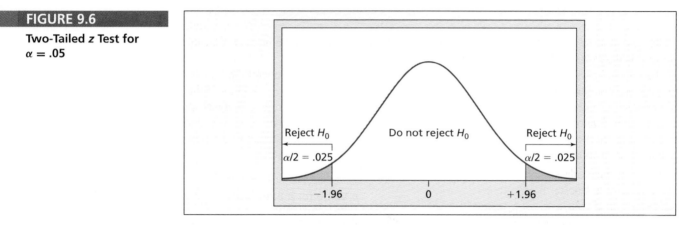

Step 3: Calculate the Test Statistic   The test statistic is *unaffected by the hypotheses or the level of significance.* The value of the test statistic is the same as for the one-tailed test:

$$z_{\text{calc}} = \frac{\bar{x} - \mu_0}{\dfrac{\sigma}{\sqrt{n}}} = \frac{216.007 - 216.000}{\dfrac{.023}{\sqrt{50}}} = \frac{.007}{.00325269} = 2.152$$

Step 4: Make the Decision   Since the test statistic falls in the right tail of the rejection region, we reject the null hypothesis H_0: $\mu = 216$ and conclude H_1: $\mu \neq 216$ at the 5 percent level of significance. Another way to say this is that the sample mean *differs significantly* from the desired specification at $\alpha = .05$ in a two-tailed test. Note that this decision is rather a close one, since the test statistic just barely falls into the rejection region.

Using the *p*-Value Approach

In a two-tailed test, the decision rule using the *p*-value is the same as in a one-tailed test.

Reject H_0 if *p*-value $< \alpha$.

The difference between a one-tailed and a two-tailed test is how we obtain the *p*-value. Because we allow rejection in either the left or the right tail in a two-tailed test, the level of significance, α, is divided equally between the two tails to establish the rejection region. In order to fairly evaluate the *p*-value against α, we must now double the tail area. The *p*-value in this two-tailed test is $2 \times P(z_{\text{calc}} > 2.152) = 2 \times .0157 = .0314$. See Figure 9.7. This says that in a two-tailed test a result as extreme as 2.152 would arise about 3.14 percent of the time by chance alone *if the null hypothesis were true.*

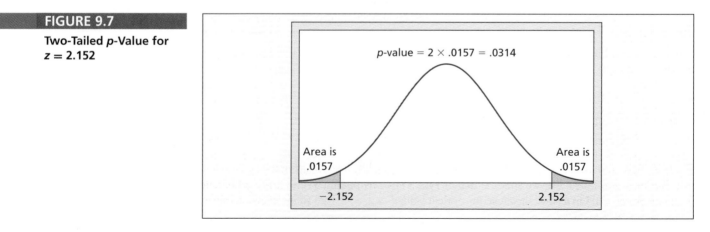

Interpretation   Although the sample mean 216.007 might seem very close to 216, it is more than two standard deviations from the desired mean. This example shows that even a small difference can be significant. It all depends on σ and n, that is, on the standard error of the mean in the denominator of the test statistic. In this case, there is a high degree of precision in the manufacturing process ($\sigma = .023$ is very small) so the standard error (and hence the allowable variation) is extremely small. Such a tiny difference in means would not be noticeable to consumers, but stringent quality control standards are applied to ensure that no shipment goes out with any noticeable nonconformance.

Our statistical tests show that there is a statistically *significant* departure from the desired mean for paper width at $\alpha = .05$. But is the difference *important*? Is 216.007 so close to 216 that nobody could tell the difference? The question of whether to adjust the process is up to the engineers or business managers, not statisticians.

Analogy to Confidence Intervals

A two-tailed hypothesis test at the 5 percent level of significance ($\alpha = .05$) is exactly equivalent to asking whether the 95 percent confidence interval for the mean includes the hypothesized mean. If the confidence interval includes the hypothesized mean H_0: $\mu = 216$, then we cannot reject the null hypothesis. In this case the 95 percent confidence interval would be

$$\bar{x} \pm z\frac{\sigma}{\sqrt{n}} = 216.007 \pm 1.96\frac{.023}{\sqrt{50}} = 216.001 < \mu < 216.013$$

Since this confidence interval does not include 216, we reject the null hypothesis H_0: $\mu = 216$. However, the decision is rather a close one as it was with the two-tailed hypothesis test, since the lower limit of the confidence interval almost includes 216.

SECTION EXERCISES

connect

9.7   Calculate the test statistic and p-value for each sample.
a. H_0: $\mu = 60$ versus H_1: $\mu \neq 60$, $\alpha = .025$, $\bar{x} = 63$, $\sigma = 8$, $n = 16$
b. H_0: $\mu \geq 60$ versus H_1: $\mu < 60$, $\alpha = .05$, $\bar{x} = 58$, $\sigma = 5$, $n = 25$
c. H_0: $\mu \leq 60$ versus H_1: $\mu > 60$, $\alpha = .05$, $\bar{x} = 65$, $\sigma = 8$, $n = 36$

9.8   Find the p-value for each test statistic.
a. Right-tailed test, $z = +1.34$ b. Left-tailed test, $z = -2.07$ c. Two-tailed test, $z = -1.69$

9.9   Procyon Mfg. produces tennis balls. Weights are supposed to be normally distributed with a mean of 2.035 ounces and a standard deviation of 0.002 ounces. A sample of 25 tennis balls shows a mean weight of 2.036 ounces. At $\alpha = .025$ in a right-tailed test, is the mean weight heavier than it is supposed to be?

9.10   The mean arrival rate of flights at O'Hare Airport in marginal weather is 195 flights per hour with a historical standard deviation of 13 flights. To increase arrivals, a new air traffic control procedure is implemented. In the next 30 days of marginal weather the mean arrival rate is 200 flights per hour. (a) Set up a right-tailed decision rule at $\alpha = .025$ to decide whether there has been a significant increase in the mean number of arrivals per hour. (b) Carry out the test and make the decision. Is it close? Would the decision be different if you used $\alpha = .01$? (c) What assumptions are you making, if any?   **Flights**

210	215	200	189	200	213	202	181	197	199
193	209	215	192	179	196	225	199	196	210
199	188	174	176	202	195	195	208	222	221

9.11   An airline serves bottles of Galena Spring Water that are supposed to contain an average of 10 ounces. The filling process follows a normal distribution with process standard deviation 0.07 ounce. Twelve randomly chosen bottles had the weights shown below (in ounces). (a) Set up a two-tailed decision rule to detect quality control violations using the 5 percent level of significance. (b) Carry out the test. (c) What assumptions are you making, if any?   **BottleFill**

10.02	9.95	10.11	10.10	10.08	10.04	10.06	10.03	9.98	10.01	9.92	9.89

9.12   The Scottsdale fire department aims to respond to fire calls in 4 minutes or less, on average. Response times are normally distributed with a standard deviation of 1 minute. Would a sample of 18 fire calls with a mean response time of 4 minutes 30 seconds provide sufficient evidence to show that the goal is not being met at $\alpha = .01$? What is the p-value? (See *Arizona Republic*, November 23, 2006, p. A10.)

9.13 The lifespan of xenon metal halide arc-discharge bulbs for aircraft landing lights is normally distributed with a mean of 3,000 hours and a standard deviation of 500 hours. If a new ballast system shows a mean life of 3,515 hours in a test on a sample of 10 prototype new bulbs, would you conclude that the new lamp's mean life exceeds the current mean life at $\alpha = .01$? What is the p-value? (For more information, see www.xevision.com.)

9.4
TESTING A MEAN: UNKNOWN POPULATION VARIANCE

If the population variance σ^2 must be estimated from the sample, the hypothesis testing procedure is modified. There is a loss of information when s replaces σ in the formulas, and it is no longer appropriate to use the normal distribution. However, the basic hypothesis testing steps are the same.

Using Student's t

When the population standard deviation σ is unknown (as it usually is) and the population may be assumed normal (or generally symmetric with no outliers) the test statistic follows the Student's t distribution with $n - 1$ degrees of freedom. Since σ is rarely known, we generally expect to use Student's t instead of z, as you saw for confidence intervals in the previous chapter.

VS

Chapter 9

$$(9.5) \qquad t_{calc} = \frac{\bar{x} - \mu_0}{\frac{s}{\sqrt{n}}} \qquad \text{if } \sigma \text{ is unknown}$$

EXAMPLE

Hot Chocolate

In addition to its core business of bagels and coffee, Bruegger's Bagels also sells hot chocolate for the noncoffee crowd. Customer research shows that the ideal temperature for hot chocolate is 142°F ("hot" but not "too hot"). A random sample of 24 cups of hot chocolate is taken at various times, and the temperature of each cup is measured using an ordinary kitchen thermometer that is accurate to the nearest whole degree.   **HotChoc**

140	140	141	145	143	144	142	140
145	143	140	140	141	141	137	142
143	141	142	142	143	141	138	139

The sample mean is 141.375 with a sample standard deviation of 1.99592. At $\alpha = .10$, does this sample evidence show that the true mean differs from 142?

Step 1: State the Hypotheses
We use a two-tailed test. The null hypothesis is in conformance with the desired standard.

$H_0: \mu = 142$ (mean temperature is correct)
$H_1: \mu \neq 142$ (mean temperature is incorrect)

Step 2: Specify the Decision Rule
For $\alpha = .10$, using Excel, the critical value for $\nu = n - 1 = 24 - 1 = 23$ degrees of freedom is =TINV(0.10,23) = 1.714 (note that Excel's inverse t assumes a two-tailed test). The same value can be obtained from Appendix D, shown here in abbreviated form:

| | | | Upper Tail Area | | |
ν	.10	.05	.025	.01	.005
1	3.078	6.314	12.706	31.821	63.657
2	1.886	2.920	4.303	6.965	9.925
3	1.638	2.353	3.182	4.541	5.841
⋮	⋮	⋮	⋮	⋮	⋮
21	1.323	1.721	2.080	2.518	2.831
22	1.321	1.717	2.074	2.508	2.819
23	1.319	*1.714*	2.069	2.500	2.807
24	1.318	1.711	2.064	2.492	2.797
25	1.316	1.708	2.060	2.485	2.787

We will reject H_0 if $t_{calc} > 1.714$ or if $t_{calc} < -1.714$, as illustrated in Figure 9.8.

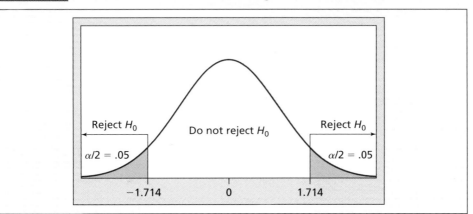

FIGURE 9.8 Two-Tailed Test for a Mean Using t for $v = 23$

Step 3: Calculate the Test Statistic
Plugging in the sample information, the test statistic is

$$t_{calc} = \frac{\bar{x} - \mu_0}{\frac{s}{\sqrt{n}}} = \frac{141.375 - 142}{\frac{1.99592}{\sqrt{24}}} = \frac{-.6250}{.40742} = -1.534$$

Step 4: Make the Decision
Since the test statistic lies within the range of chance variation, we cannot reject the null hypothesis H_0: $\mu = 142$.

Sensitivity to α   Is our conclusion sensitive to the choice of level of significance? Table 9.5 shows several critical values of Student's t. At $\alpha = .20$ we could reject H_0, but not at the other α values shown. This table is not to suggest that experimenting with various α values is desirable, but merely to illustrate that our decision may depend on the choice of α.

	$\alpha = .20$	$\alpha = .10$	$\alpha = .05$	$\alpha = .01$
Critical value	$t_{.10} = \pm1.319$	$t_{.05} = \pm1.714$	$t_{.025} = \pm2.069$	$t_{.005} = \pm2.807$
Decision	Reject H_0	Don't reject H_0	Don't reject H_0	Don't reject H_0

TABLE 9.5
Effect of α on the Decision (Two-Tailed t Test with $v = 23$)

Using the p-Value

A more general approach favored by researchers is to find the p-value. We want to determine the tail area less than $t = -1.534$ or greater than $t = +1.534$. However, from Appendix D we can only get a range for the p-value. From Appendix D, we see that the two-tail p-value must lie between .20 and .10 (it's a two-tailed test, so we double the right-tail area). It is easier and more precise to use Excel's function =TDIST(t test statistic,degrees of freedom, tails). In this case the formula =TDIST(1.534,23,2) gives the two-tailed p-value of .13867. The area of each tail is half that, or .06934, as shown in Figure 9.9. A sample mean as extreme in either tail would occur by chance about 139 times in 1,000 two-tailed tests if H_0 were true. Since the p-value $> \alpha$, we cannot reject H_0. Dave Boennighausen, VP of Finance at Noodles & Company, says "Executives at Noodles & Company may not perform a statistical analysis themselves, but they do understand the p-value associated with the results of an analysis. The p-value allows us to objectively consider the data and statistical results when we make an important strategic decision."

FIGURE 9.9

Two-Tailed *p*-Value for *t* = 1.534

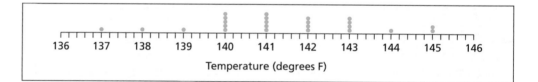

Interpretation

It is doubtful whether a consumer could tell the difference in hot chocolate temperature within a few degrees of 142°F, so a tiny difference in means might lack *practical importance* even if it were *statistically significant*. Importance must be judged by management, not by the statistician.

In the hot chocolate example, there are no outliers and something of a bell-shape, as shown in the dot plot below. The *t* test is reasonably robust to mild non-normality. However, outliers or extreme skewness can affect the test, just as when we construct confidence intervals.

Confidence Interval versus Hypothesis Test

The two-tailed test at the 10 percent level of significance is equivalent to a two-tailed 90 percent confidence interval. If the confidence interval does not contain μ_0, we reject H_0. For the hot chocolate, the sample mean is 141.375 with a sample standard deviation of 1.99592. Using Appendix D we find $t_{.05} = 1.714$ so the 90 percent confidence interval for μ is

$$\bar{x} \pm t\frac{s}{\sqrt{n}} = 141.375 \pm (1.714)\frac{1.99592}{\sqrt{24}} = 141.375 \pm .6983$$

Since $\mu = 142$ lies within the 90 percent confidence interval $140.677 < \mu < 142.073$, we cannot reject the hypothesis $H_0: \mu = 142$ at $\alpha = .10$ in a two-tailed test. Many decisions can be handled either as hypothesis tests or using confidence intervals. The confidence interval has the appeal of providing a graphic feeling for the location of the hypothesized mean within the confidence interval, as shown in Figure 9.10. We can see that 142 is near the upper end of the confidence interval, nearly (but not quite) leading to a rejection of $H_0: \mu = 142$.

Using MegaStat

You can get tests for one mean, including a confidence interval, using MegaStat. Figure 9.11 shows its setup screen and output for the test of one mean for the hot chocolate data. You enter

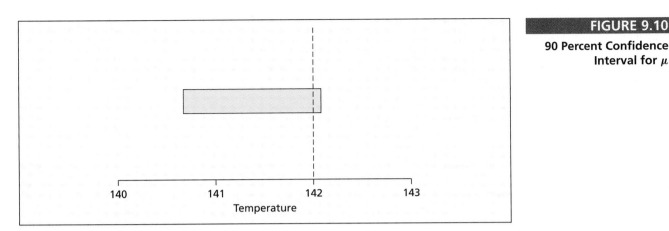

FIGURE 9.10

90 Percent Confidence Interval for μ

the data range and everything else is automatic. It gives a choice of z or t, but to use z you must know σ.

FIGURE 9.11

MegaStat Test for One Mean

Large Samples

From Appendix D you can verify that when n is large, there is little difference between critical values of t and z (the last line in Appendix D, for $v = \infty$). For this reason, it is unlikely that harm will result if you use z instead of t, as long as the sample size is not small. The test statistic is

$$z_{\text{calc}} = \frac{\bar{x} - \mu_0}{\dfrac{s}{\sqrt{n}}} \qquad \text{(large sample, unknown } \sigma\text{)} \qquad \text{(9.6)}$$

However, using z instead of t is not conservative, because it will increase Type I error somewhat. Therefore, statisticians recommend that we always apply t when σ is unknown. We then can use Excel or Appendix D to get the critical value.

SECTION EXERCISES

connect

9.14   Estimate the *p*-value *as a range* using Appendix D (*not* Excel):
a. $t = 1.457$, $v = 14$, right-tailed test
b. $t = 2.601$, $v = 8$, two-tailed test
c. $t = -1.847$, $v = 22$, left-tailed test

9.15   Find the *p*-value using Excel (*not* Appendix D):
a. $t = 1.457$, $v = 14$, right-tailed test
b. $t = 2.601$, $v = 8$, two-tailed test
c. $t = -1.847$, $v = 22$, left-tailed test

9.16   Use Excel to find the *p*-value for each test statistic.
a. Right-tailed test, $t = +1.677$, $n = 13$ b. Left-tailed test, $t = -2.107$, $n = 5$ c. Two-tailed test, $t = -1.865$, $n = 34$

9.17 Calculate the test statistic and *p*-value for each sample. State the conclusion for the specified α.
   a. H_0: $\mu = 200$ versus H_1: $\mu \neq 200$, $\alpha = .025$, $\bar{x} = 203$, $s = 8$, $n = 16$
   b. H_0: $\mu \geq 200$ versus H_1: $\mu < 200$, $\alpha = .05$, $\bar{x} = 198$, $s = 5$, $n = 25$
   c. H_0: $\mu \leq 200$ versus H_1: $\mu > 200$, $\alpha = .05$, $\bar{x} = 205$, $s = 8$, $n = 36$

9.18 The manufacturer of an airport baggage scanning machine claims it can handle an average of 530 bags per hour. (a) At $\alpha = .05$ in a left-tailed test, would a sample of 16 randomly chosen hours with a mean of 510 and a standard deviation of 50 indicate that the manufacturer's claim is overstated? (b) Why might the assumption of a normal population be doubtful? (See *Aviation Week and Space Technology* 162, no. 4 (January 24, 2005), p. 42.)

9.19 The manufacturer of Glo-More flat white interior latex paint claims one-coat coverage of 400 square feet per gallon on interior walls. A painter keeps careful track of 6 gallons and finds coverage (in square feet) of 360, 410, 380, 360, 390, 400. (a) At $\alpha = .10$ does this evidence contradict the claim? State your hypotheses and decision rule. (b) Is this conclusion sensitive to the choice of α? (c) Use Excel to find the *p*-value. Interpret it. (d) Discuss the distinction between importance and significance in this example.   **Paint**

9.20 The average weight of a package of rolled oats is supposed to be at least 18 ounces. A sample of 18 packages shows a mean of 17.78 ounces with a standard deviation of 0.41 ounces. (a) At the 5 percent level of significance, is the true mean smaller than the specification? Clearly state your hypotheses and decision rule. (b) Is this conclusion sensitive to the choice of α? (c) Use Excel to find the *p*-value. Interpret it.

9.21 According to J.D. Power & Associates, the mean wait for an airport rental car shuttle bus in 2004 was 19 minutes. In 2005, a random sample of 20 business travelers showed a mean wait of 15 minutes with a standard deviation of 7 minutes. (a) At $\alpha = .05$, has the mean wait decreased? State the hypotheses and decision rule clearly. (b) Use Excel to find the *p*-value. Interpret it.

9.22 In 2004, a small dealership leased 21 Chevrolet Impalas on 2-year leases. When the cars were returned in 2006, the mileage was recorded (see below). Is the dealer's mean significantly greater than the national average of 30,000 miles for 2-year leased vehicles, using the 10 percent level of significance?   **Mileage**

40,060	24,960	14,310	17,370	44,740	44,550	20,250
33,380	24,270	41,740	58,630	35,830	25,750	28,910
25,090	43,380	23,940	43,510	53,680	31,810	36,780

9.23 At Oxnard University, a sample of 18 senior accounting majors showed a mean cumulative GPA of 3.35 with a standard deviation of 0.25. (a) At $\alpha = .05$ in a two-tailed test, does this differ significantly from 3.25 (the mean GPA for all business school seniors at the university)? (b) Use the sample to construct a 95 percent confidence interval for the mean. Does the confidence interval include 3.25? (c) Explain how the hypothesis test and confidence interval are equivalent.

Mini Case   9.3

Beauty Products and Small Business

Lisa has been working at a beauty counter in a department store for 5 years. In her spare time she's also been creating lotions and fragrances using all natural products. After receiving positive feedback from her friends and family about her beauty products, Lisa decides to open her own store. Lisa knows that convincing a bank to help fund her new business will require more than a few positive testimonials from family. Based on her experience working at the department store, Lisa believes women in her area spend more than the national average on fragrance products. This fact could help make her business successful.

   Lisa would like to be able to support her belief with data to include in a business plan proposal that she would then use to obtain a small business loan. Lisa took a business statistics course while in college and decides to use the hypothesis testing tool she learned. After conducting research she learns that the national average spending by women on fragrance products is $59 every 3 months.

The hypothesis test is based on this survey result:

$H_0: \mu \leq \$59$

$H_1: \mu > \$59$

In other words, she will assume the average spending in her town is the same as the national average *unless she has strong evidence that says otherwise*. Lisa takes a random sample of 25 women and finds that the sample mean $\bar{x}$ is $68 and the sample standard deviation s is $15. Lisa uses a t statistic because she doesn't know the population standard deviation. Her calculated t statistic is

$$t_{\text{calc}} = \frac{68 - 59}{\dfrac{15}{\sqrt{25}}} = 3.00 \qquad \text{with 24 degrees of freedom}$$

Using the Excel formula =TDIST(3,24,1), Lisa finds that the one-tail p-value is .003103. This p-value is quite small and she can safely reject her null hypothesis. Lisa now has strong evidence to conclude that over a 3-month period women in her area spend more than $59 on average.

Lisa would also like to include an estimate for the average amount women in her area *do* spend. Calculating a confidence interval would be her next step. Lisa chooses a 95 percent confidence level and finds the t value to use in her calculations by using the Excel formula =TINV(0.05,24). The result is $t = 2.0639$. Her 95 percent confidence interval for μ is

$$\$68 \pm 2.0639\frac{15}{\sqrt{25}} = \$68 \pm \$6.19$$

Lisa's business plan proposal can confidently claim that women in her town spend more than the national average on fragrance products and that she estimates the average spending is between $62 and $74 every 3 months. Hopefully the bank will see not only that Lisa creates excellent beauty products, but she also will be a smart businessperson!

Source: For national average spending see The NPD Group press release, "New NPD Beauty Study Identifies Key Consumer Differences and Preferences," March 28, 2005.

9.5 TESTING A PROPORTION

Proportions are used frequently in business situations and collecting proportion data is straightforward. It is easier for customers to say whether they like or dislike this year's new automobile color than it is for customers to quantify their degree of satisfaction with the new color. Also, many business performance indicators such as market share, employee retention rates, and employee accident rates are expressed as proportions.

The steps we follow for testing a hypothesis about a population proportion, π, are the same as the ones we follow for testing a mean. The difference is that we now calculate a sample proportion, p, to calculate the test statistic. We know from Chapter 8 that for a sufficiently large sample the sample proportion can be assumed to follow a normal distribution. Our rule is to assume normality if $n\pi_0 \geq 10$ and $n(1 - \pi_0) \geq 10$. If we can assume a normal sampling distribution, then the test statistic would be the z-score. Recall that the sample proportion is

$$p = \frac{x}{n} = \frac{\text{number of successes}}{\text{sample size}} \qquad (9.7)$$

The test statistic, calculated from sample data, is the difference between the sample proportion p and the hypothesized proportion π_0 divided by the *standard error of the proportion* (sometimes denoted σ_p):

$$z_{\text{calc}} = \frac{p - \pi_0}{\sigma_p} = \frac{p - \pi_0}{\sqrt{\dfrac{\pi_0(1 - \pi_0)}{n}}} \qquad (9.8)$$

The value of π_0 we are testing is a **benchmark**, such as past performance, an industry standard, or a product specification. The value of π_0 does *not* come from a sample.

EXAMPLE

Return Policy

Retailers such as Guess, Staples, Sports Authority, and Limited Brands are employing new technology to crack down on "serial exchangers"—customers who abuse their return and exchange policies (*The Wall Street Journal,* November 29, 2004). For example, some customers buy an outfit, wear it once or twice, and then return it. Software called *Verify-1,* a product of a California-based company Return Exchange, tracks a shopper's record of bringing back items. The historical return rate for merchandise at department stores is 13.0 percent. At one department store, after implementing the new software, there were 22 returns in a sample of 250 purchases. At $\alpha = .05$, does this sample prove that the true return rate has fallen?

Step 1: State the Hypotheses
The hypotheses are

$H_0: \pi \geq .13$ (return rate is the same or greater than the historical rate)

$H_1: \pi < .13$ (return rate has fallen below the historical rate)

Step 2: Specify the Decision Rule
For $\alpha = .05$ in a left-tailed test, the critical value is $z_{.05} = -1.645$, so the decision rule is

Reject H_0 if $z_{calc} < -1.645$

Otherwise do not reject H_0

This decision rule is illustrated in Figure 9.12.

FIGURE 9.12   Left-Tailed *z* Test Using $\alpha = .05$

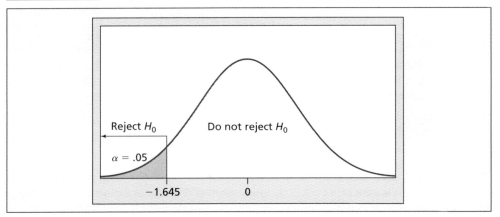

Before using *z* we should check the normality assumption. To assume normality we require that $n\pi_0 \geq 10$ and $n(1 - \pi_0) \geq 10$. Note that we use the hypothesized proportion π_0 (not *p*) to check normality, because we are assuming H_0 to be the truth about the population. Inserting $\pi_0 = .13$ and $n = 250$ we see that these conditions are easily met: $(250)(.13) = 32.5$ and $(250)(1 - .13) = 217.5$.

Step 3: Calculate the Test Statistic
Since $p = x/n = 22/250 = .088$, the sample seems to favor H_1. But we will assume that H_0 is true and see if the test statistic contradicts this assumption. We test the hypothesis at $\pi = .13$. If we can reject $\pi = .13$ in favor of $\pi < .13$, then we implicitly reject the class of hypotheses $\pi \geq .13$. The test statistic is the difference between the sample proportion $p = x/n$ and the hypothesized parameter π_0 divided by the standard error of *p*:

$$z_{calc} = \frac{p - \pi_0}{\sqrt{\frac{\pi_0(1 - \pi_0)}{n}}} = \frac{.088 - .13}{\sqrt{\frac{.13(1 - .13)}{250}}} = \frac{-.042}{.02127} = -1.975$$

Step 4: Make the Decision
Because the test statistic falls in the left-tail rejection region, we reject H_0. We conclude that the return rate is less than .13 after implementing the new software.

Calculating the *p*-Value

For our test statistic $z_{calc} = -1.975$, the *p*-value (.02413) can be obtained from Excel's cumulative standard normal =NORMSDIST(–1.975). Alternatively, if we round the test statistic to two decimals, we can use the cumulative normal table in Appendix C-2. Depending on how we round the test statistic, we might obtain two possible *p*-values, as shown in Table 9.6. Using the *p*-value, we reject H_0 at $\alpha = .05$, but the decision would be very close if we had used $\alpha = .025$. Figure 9.13 illustrates the *p*-value.

					Finding the *p*-Value for *z* = 1.975 in Appendix C-2				TABLE 9.6	
z	**.00**	**.01**	**.02**	**.03**	**.04**	**.05**	**.06**	**.07**	**.08**	**.09**
−3.7	.00011	.00010	.00010	.00010	.00009	.00009	.00008	.00008	.00008	.00008
−3.6	.00016	.00015	.00015	.00014	.00014	.00013	.00013	.00012	.00012	.00011
−3.5	.00023	.00022	.00022	.00021	.00020	.00019	.00019	.00018	.00017	.00017
⋮	⋮	⋮	⋮	⋮	⋮	⋮	⋮	⋮	⋮	⋮
−2.0	.02275	.02222	.02169	.02118	.02068	.02018	.01970	.01923	.01876	.01831
−1.9	.02872	.02807	.02743	.02680	.02619	.02559	.02500	*.02442*	*.02385*	.02330
−1.8	.03593	.03515	.03438	.03362	.03288	.03216	.03144	.03074	.03005	.02938

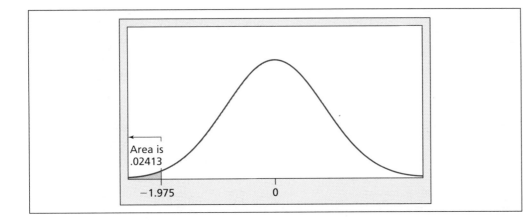

FIGURE 9.13

***p*-Value for a Left-Tailed Test with $z_{calc} = -1.975$**

The *smaller* the *p*-value, the more we want to *reject* H_0. Does this seem backward? You might think a large *p*-value would be "more significant" than a small one. But the *p*-value is a direct measure of the level of significance at which we could reject H_0, so *a smaller* p-*value is more convincing.* For the left-tailed test, the *p*-value tells us that there is a .02413 probability of getting a sample proportion of .088 or less if the true proportion is .13; that is, such a sample would arise by chance only about 24 times in 1,000 tests if the null hypothesis is true. In our left-tailed test, we would reject H_0 because the *p*-value (.02413) is smaller than α (.05). In fact, we could reject H_0 at *any* α greater than .02413.

Two-Tailed Test

What if we used a two-tailed test? This might be appropriate if the objective is to detect a change in the return rate in *either* direction. In fact, two-tailed tests are used more often, because rejection in a two-tailed test always implies rejection in a one-tailed test, other things being equal. The same sample can be used for either a one-tailed or two-tailed test. The type of hypothesis test is up to the statistician.

Step 1: State the Hypotheses   The hypotheses are

H_0: $\pi = .13$ (return rate is the same as the historical rate)

H_1: $\pi \neq .13$ (return rate is different from the historical rate)

Step 2: Specify the Decision Rule   For a two-tailed test, we split the risk of Type I error by putting $\alpha/2 = .05/2 = .025$ in each tail (as we would for a confidence interval). For $\alpha = .05$ in a two-tailed test, the critical value is $z_{.025} = 1.96$ so the decision rule is

Reject H_0 if $z_{calc} > +1.96$ or if $z_{calc} < -1.96$
Otherwise do not reject H_0

The decision rule is illustrated in Figure 9.14.

FIGURE 9.14

Two-Tailed z Test for $\alpha = .05$

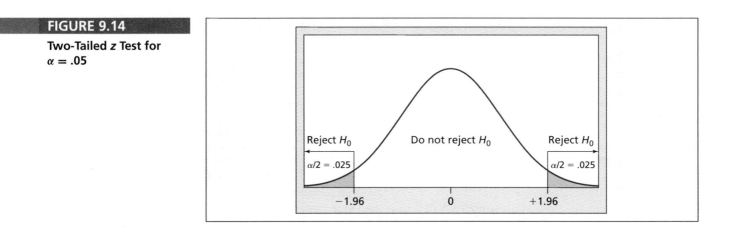

Step 3: Calculate the Test Statistic   The test statistic is *unaffected by the hypotheses or the level of significance*. The value of the test statistic is the same as for the one-tailed test:

$$z_{calc} = \frac{p - \pi_0}{\sqrt{\dfrac{\pi_0(1 - \pi_0)}{n}}} = \frac{.088 - .13}{\sqrt{\dfrac{.13(1 - .13)}{250}}} = \frac{-.042}{.02127} = -1.975$$

Step 4: Make the Decision   Since the test statistic falls in the left tail of the rejection region, we reject the null hypothesis H_0: $\pi = .13$ and conclude H_1: $\pi \neq .13$ at the 5 percent level of significance. Another way to say this is that the sample proportion *differs significantly* from the historical return rate at $\alpha = .05$ in a two-tailed test. Note that this decision is rather a close one, since the test statistic just barely falls into the rejection region.

Notice also that the rejection was stronger in a one-tailed test, that is, the test statistic is farther from the critical value. *Holding α constant, rejection in a two-tailed test always implies rejection in a one-tailed test.* This reinforces the logic of choosing a two-tailed test unless there is a specific reason to prefer a one-tailed test.

Calculating a *p*-Value for a Two-Tailed Test

In a two-tailed test, we divide the risk into equal tails, one on the left and one on the right, to allow for the possibility that we will reject H_0 whenever the sample statistic is very small or very large. With the *p*-value approach in a two-tailed test, we find the tail area associated with our sample test statistic, multiply this by two, and then compare that probability to α. Our z statistic was calculated to be -1.975. The p-value would then be

$$2 \times P(Z < -1.975) = 2 \times .02413 = .04826$$

We would reject the null hypothesis because the p-value .04826 is less than α (.05).

Effect of α

Would the decision be the same if we had used a different level of significance? Table 9.7 shows some possibilities. *The test statistic is the same regardless of α.* While we can reject the null hypothesis at $\alpha = .10$ or $\alpha = .05$, we cannot reject at $\alpha = .01$. Therefore, we would say that the current return rate differs from the historical return rate at the 10 percent and 5 percent levels of significance, but not at the 1 percent level of significance.

α	Test Statistic	Two-Tailed Critical Values	Decision
.10	$z_{calc} = -1.975$	$z_{.05} = \pm 1.645$	Reject H_0
.05	$z_{calc} = -1.975$	$z_{.025} = \pm 1.960$	Reject H_0
.01	$z_{calc} = -1.975$	$z_{.005} = \pm 2.576$	Don't reject H_0

TABLE 9.7

Effect of Varying α

Which level of significance is the "right" one? They all are. It depends on how much Type I error we are willing to allow. Before concluding that $\alpha = .01$ is "better" than the others because it allows less Type I error, you should remember that smaller Type I error leads to increased Type II error. In this case, Type I error would imply that there has been a change in return rates when in reality nothing has changed, while Type II error implies that the software had no effect on the return rate, when in reality the software did decrease the return rate.

EXAMPLE

Length of Hospital Stay

A hospital is comparing its performance against an industry benchmark that no more than 50 percent of normal births should result in a hospital stay exceeding 2 days (48 hours). Thirty-one births in a sample of 50 normal births had a length of stay (LOS) greater than 48 hours. At $\alpha = .025$, does this sample prove that the hospital exceeds the benchmark? This question requires a right-tailed test.

Step 1: State the Hypotheses
The hypotheses are

H_0: $\pi \le .50$ (the hospital is compliant with the benchmark)

H_1: $\pi > .50$ (the hospital is exceeding the benchmark)

Step 2: Specify the Decision Rule
For $\alpha = .025$ in a right-tailed test, the critical value is $z_{.025} = 1.96$, so the decision rule is

Reject H_0 if $z > 1.960$

Otherwise do not reject H_0

This decision rule is illustrated in Figure 9.15.
Before using z we should check the normality assumption. To assume normality we require that $n\pi_0 \ge 10$ and $n(1 - \pi_0) \ge 10$. Inserting $\pi_0 = .50$ and $n = 50$ we see that the normality conditions are easily met: $(50)(.50) = 25$ and $(50)(1 - .50) = 25$.

Step 3: Calculate the Test Statistic
Since $p = x/n = 31/50 = .62$, the sample seems to favor H_1. But we will assume that H_0 is true and see if the test statistic contradicts this assumption. We test the hypothesis at $\pi = .50$. If we can reject $\pi = .50$ in favor of $\pi > .50$, then we can reject the class of hypotheses

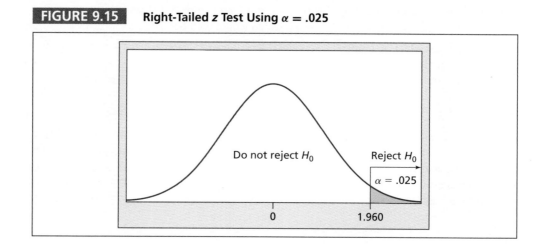

FIGURE 9.15   **Right-Tailed z Test Using α = .025**

$\pi \le .50$. The test statistic is the difference between the sample proportion $p = x/n$ and the hypothesized parameter π_0 divided by the standard error of p:

$$z_{calc} = \frac{p - \pi_0}{\sqrt{\dfrac{\pi_0(1 - \pi_0)}{n}}} = \frac{.62 - .50}{\sqrt{\dfrac{.50(1 - .50)}{50}}} = \frac{.12}{.07071068} = 1.697$$

Step 4: Make the Decision
The test statistic does not fall in the right-tail rejection region, so we cannot reject the hypothesis that $\pi \le .50$ at the 2.5 percent level of significance. In other words, the test statistic is within the realm of chance at $\alpha = .025$.

Calculating the *p*-Value

In this case, the *p*-value can be obtained from Excel's cumulative standard normal function =1−NORMSDIST(1.697)=.04485 or from Appendix C-2 (using $z = 1.70$ we get $p = 1 - .9554 = .0446$). Excel's accuracy is greater because $z = 1.697$ is not rounded to $z = 1.70$. Since we want a right-tail area, we must subtract the cumulative distribution function from 1. The *p*-value is greater than .025 so we fail to reject the null hypothesis in a right-tailed test. We could (barely) reject at $\alpha = .05$. This demonstrates that the level of significance can affect our decision. The advantage of the *p*-value is that it tells you exactly the point of indifference between rejecting or not rejecting H_0. The *p*-value is illustrated in Figure 9.16.

FIGURE 9.16

p-Value for a Right-Tailed Test with $z_{calc} = 1.697$

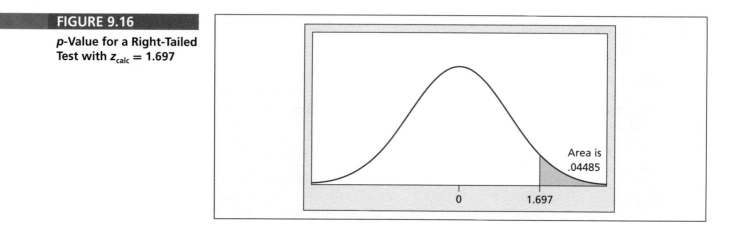

Effect of a Larger Sample

In general, a larger sample *increases power* (our ability to detect a false null hypothesis). In this case, a larger sample was possible. Fifty more births were examined, increasing the sample size to $n = 100$ births. In this new sample, 61 had an LOS exceeding 48 hours, or $p = 61/100 = .61$. The new test statistic is

$$z_{calc} = \frac{p - \pi_0}{\sqrt{\dfrac{\pi_0(1 - \pi_0)}{n}}} = \frac{.61 - .50}{\sqrt{\dfrac{.50(1 - .50)}{100}}} = \frac{.11}{.05} = 2.20$$

This time we obtain a rejection since $z = 2.20$ exceeds the critical value $z_{.025} = 1.96$. With the larger sample, the rejection is decisive. The new *p*-value ($p = .0139$) shown in Figure 9.17 indicates that such a test statistic would arise only 1.39 percent of the time by chance alone, if the true proportion were .50.

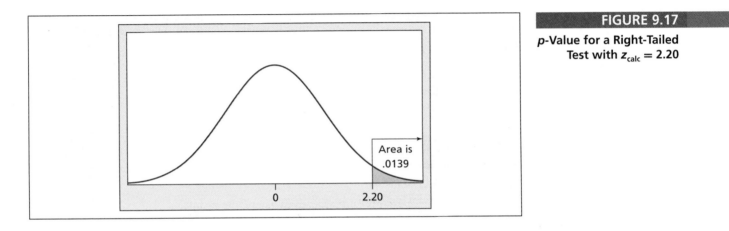

FIGURE 9.17

p-Value for a Right-Tailed Test with $z_{calc} = 2.20$

Area is .0139

0   2.20

SECTION EXERCISES

connect

9.24 Interpret each *p*-value in your own words:
   a. *p*-value $= .387$, H_0: $\pi \geq .20$, H_1: $\pi < .20$, $\alpha = .10$
   b. *p*-value $= .043$, H_0: $\pi \leq .90$, H_1: $\pi > .90$, $\alpha = .05$
   c. *p*-value $= .0012$, H_0: $\pi = .50$, H_1: $\pi \neq .50$, $\alpha = .01$

9.25 Calculate the test statistic and *p*-value for each sample.
   a. H_0: $\pi = .20$ versus H_1: $\pi \neq .20$, $\alpha = .025$, $p = .28$, $n = 100$
   b. H_0: $\pi \leq .50$ versus H_1: $\pi > .50$, $\alpha = .025$, $p = .60$, $n = 90$
   c. H_0: $\pi \leq .75$ versus H_1: $\pi > .75$, $\alpha = .10$, $p = .82$, $n = 50$

9.26 Calculate the test statistic and *p*-value for each sample.
   a. H_0: $\pi \leq .60$ versus H_1: $\pi > .60$, $\alpha = .05$, $x = 56$, $n = 80$
   b. H_0: $\pi = .30$ versus H_1: $\pi \neq .30$, $\alpha = .05$, $x = 18$, $n = 40$
   c. H_0: $\pi \geq .10$ versus H_1: $\pi < .10$, $\alpha = .01$, $x = 3$, $n = 100$

9.27 May normality be assumed? Show your work.
   a. H_0: $\pi = .30$ versus H_1: $\pi \neq .30$, $n = 20$
   b. H_0: $\pi = .05$ versus H_1: $\pi \neq .05$, $n = 50$
   c. H_0: $\pi = .10$ versus H_1: $\pi \neq .10$, $n = 400$

9.28 In a recent survey, 10 percent of the participants rated Pepsi as being "concerned with my health." PepsiCo's response included a new "Smart Spot" symbol on its products that meet certain nutrition criteria, to help consumers who seek more healthful eating options. At $\alpha = .05$, would a follow-up survey showing that 18 of 100 persons now rate Pepsi as being "concerned with my health" provide sufficient evidence that the percentage has increased? (Data are from *The Wall Street Journal*, July 30, 2004.)

9.29 In a hospital's shipment of 3,500 insulin syringes, 14 were unusable due to defects. (a) At $\alpha = .05$, is this sufficient evidence to reject future shipments from this supplier if the hospital's quality standard requires 99.7 percent of the syringes to be acceptable? State the hypotheses and decision rule. (b) May normality be assumed? (c) Explain the effects of Type I error and Type II error. (d) Find the p-value. (e) Would reducing α be a good idea? Explain the pros and cons.

9.30   The Tri-Cities Tobacco Coalition sent three underage teenagers into various stores in Detroit and Highland Park to see if they could purchase cigarettes. Of 320 stores checked, 82 sold cigarettes to teens between 15 and 17 years old. (a) If the goal is to reduce the percent to 20 percent or less, does this sample show that the goal is *not* being achieved at $\alpha = .05$ in a right-tailed test? (b) Construct a 95 percent confidence interval for the true percent of sellers who allow teens to purchase tobacco. (c) Explain how the confidence interval is equivalent to a two-tailed test at $\alpha = .05$. (Data are from *Detroit Free Press,* March 19, 2001, p. 2C.)

9.31   To encourage telephone efficiency, a catalog call center issues a guideline that at least half of all telephone orders should be completed within 2 minutes. Subsequently, a random sample of 64 telephone calls showed that 40 calls lasted over 2 minutes. (a) At $\alpha = .05$ is this a significant departure from the guideline in a right-tailed test? State your hypotheses and decision rule. (b) Find the p-value. (c) Is the difference important (as opposed to significant)?

9.32   The recent default rate on all student loans is 5.2 percent. In a recent random sample of 300 loans at private universities there were 9 defaults. (a) Does this sample show sufficient evidence that the private university loan default rate is below the rate for all universities, using a left-tailed test at $\alpha = .01$? (b) Calculate the p-value. (c) Verify that the assumption of normality is justified.

9.33   The Association of Flight Attendants/Communication Workers of America and National Consumers League conducted a poll of 702 frequent and occasional fliers and found that 442 respondents favored a ban on cell phones in flight, even if technology permits it. At $\alpha = .05$, can we conclude that more than half the sampled population supports a ban? (Data are from *Aviation Week and Space Technology* 182, no. 15 [April 11, 2005], p. 14.)

Mini Case   9.4

Every Minute Counts

As more company business is transacted by telephone or Internet, there is a considerable premium to reduce customer time spent with human operators. Verizon recently installed a new speech recognition system for its repair calls. In the old system, the user had to press keys on the numeric keypad to answer questions, which led many callers to opt to talk to an operator instead. Under the old system, 94 percent of the customers had to talk to an operator to get their needs met. Suppose that, using the new system, a sample of 150 calls showed that 120 required an operator. The hypotheses are

H_0: $\pi \geq .94$ (the new system is no better than the old system)

H_1: $\pi < .94$ (the new system has reduced the proportion of operator calls)

These hypotheses call for a left-tailed test. Using $\alpha = .01$, the left-tail critical value is $z_{.01} = -2.326$, as illustrated in Figure 9.18.

FIGURE 9.18   Decision Rule for Left-Tailed Test

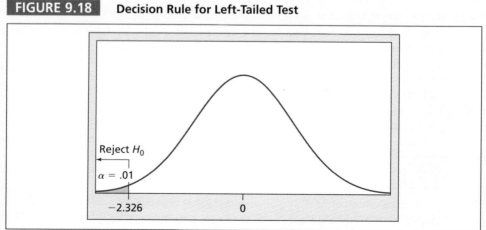

Reject H_0

$\alpha = .01$

−2.326   0

For normality, we want $n\pi_0 \geq 10$ and $n(1 - \pi_0) \geq 10$. The condition for normality is not quite met, since $(150)(.94) = 141$ but $(150)(.06) = 9$. Since this is only a rule of thumb, we will proceed, bearing in mind this possible concern. The sample proportion is $p = 120/150 = .80$ so the test statistic is

$$z_{\text{calc}} = \frac{p - \pi_0}{\sqrt{\dfrac{\pi_0(1-\pi_0)}{n}}} = \frac{.80 - .94}{\sqrt{\dfrac{.94(1-.94)}{150}}} = \frac{-.14}{.01939} = -7.22$$

The test statistic is far below the critical value, so we conclude that the percentage of customers who require an operator has declined. MINITAB verifies this calculation and also gives the p-value (.000) as shown in Figure 9.19.

Besides being significant, such savings are important. For example, Boston Financial Data Services, a company that provides record-keeping services for mutual funds, shaved a minute off the mean time to process a customer request. Since its call centers process 1.7 million calls a year, the savings are very large. See *The Wall Street Journal,* July 26, 2004.

FIGURE 9.19

MINITAB Results for One-Sample Proportion

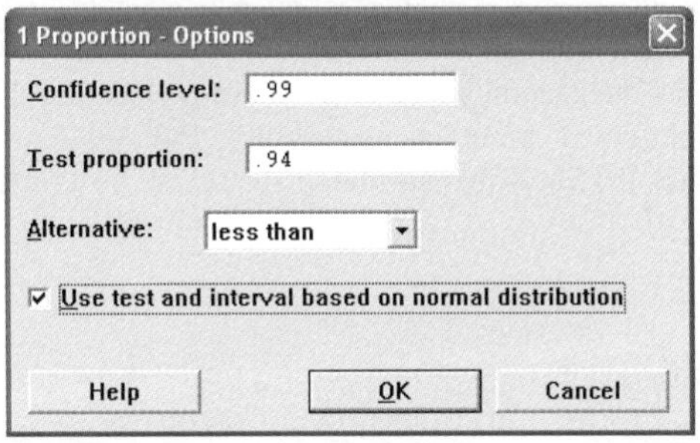

Test and CI for One Proportion

Test of p = 0.94 vs p < 0.94
99%

Sample	X	N	Sample p	Upper Bound	Z-Value	P-Value
1	120	150	0.800000	0.875978	-7.22	0.000

Small Samples and Non-Normality

In random tests by the FAA, 12.5 percent of all passenger flights failed the agency's test for bacterial count in water served to passengers (*The Wall Street Journal,* November 10, 2004, p. D1). Airlines now are trying to improve their compliance with water quality standards. Random inspection of 16 recent flights showed that only 1 flight failed the water quality test. Has overall compliance improved?

H_0: $\pi \geq .125$ (failure rate has not improved)

H_1: $\pi < .125$ (failure rate has declined)

The sample is clearly too small to assume normality since $n\pi_0 = (16)(.125) = 2$. Instead, we use MINITAB to test the hypotheses by finding the exact binomial left-tail probability of a sample proportion $p = 1/16 = .0625$ under the assumption that $\pi = .125$, as shown in Figure 9.20.

FIGURE 9.20

MINITAB Small-Sample Test of a Proportion

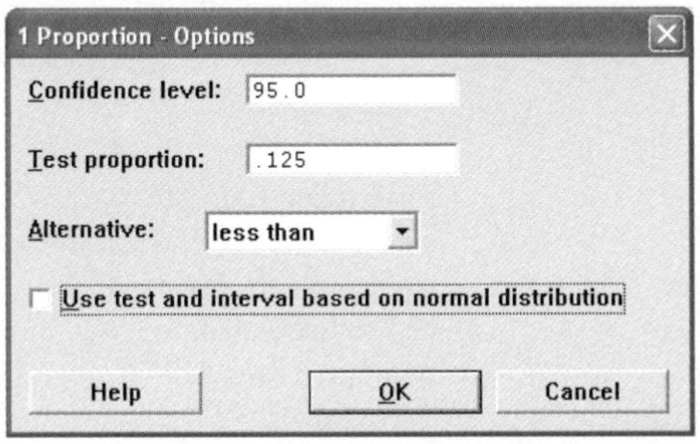

Test and CI for One Proportion

Test of p = 0.125 vs p < 0.125

Sample	X	N	Sample p	95% Upper Bound	Exact P-Value
1	1	16	0.062500	0.263957	0.388

The p-value of .388 does not permit rejection of H_0 at any of the usual levels of significance (e.g., 5 percent). The binomial test is easy and is always correct since no assumption of normality is required. Lacking MINITAB, you could do the same thing by using Excel or MegaStat to calculate the cumulative binomial probability of the observed sample result under the null hypothesis as $P(X \leq 1 \mid n = 16, \pi = .125) = .38793$.

SECTION EXERCISES

connect

9.34 A coin was flipped 12 times and came up heads 10 times. (a) Is the assumption of normality justified? Explain. (b) Calculate a p-value for the observed sample outcome, using the normal distribution. At the .05 level of significance in a right-tailed test, is the coin biased toward heads? (c) Use Excel to calculate the binomial probability $P(X \geq 10 \mid n = 12, \pi = .50) = 1 - P(X \leq 9 \mid n = 12, \pi = .50)$. (d) Why is the binomial probability not exactly the same as the p-value you calculated under the assumption of normality?

9.35 BriteScreen, a manufacturer of 19-inch LCD computer screens, requires that on average 99.9 percent of all LCDs conform to its quality standard. In a day's production of 2,000 units, 4 are defective. (a) Assuming this is a random sample, is the standard being met, using the 10 percent level of significance? *Hint:* Use MegaStat or Excel to find the binomial probability $P(X \geq 4 \mid n = 2000, \pi = .001) = 1 - P(X \leq 3 \mid n = 2000, \pi = .001)$. Alternatively, use MINITAB. (b) Show that normality should not be assumed.

9.36 Perfect pitch is the ability to identify musical notes correctly without hearing another note as a reference. The probability that a randomly chosen person has perfect pitch is .0005. (a) If 20 students at Julliard School of Music are tested, and 2 are found to have perfect pitch, would you conclude that Julliard students are more likely than the general population to have perfect pitch? *Hint:* Use MegaStat or Excel to find the right-tailed binomial probability $P(X \geq 2 \mid n = 20, \pi = .0005)$. Alternatively, use MINITAB. (b) Show that normality should not be assumed.

CHAPTER SUMMARY

The **null hypothesis (H_0)** represents the status quo or a benchmark. We try to reject H_0 in favor of the **alternative hypothesis (H_1)** on the basis of the sample evidence. The alternative hypothesis points to the tail of the test ($<$ for a left-tailed test, $>$ for a right-tailed test, $\neq$ for a two-tailed test). Rejecting a true H_0 is **Type I error,** while failing to reject a false H_0 is **Type II error.** The **power** of the test is the probability of correctly rejecting a false H_0. The probability of Type I error is denoted α (often called **the level of significance**) and can be set by the researcher. The probability of Type II error is denoted β and is dependent on the true parameter value, sample size, and α. In general, lowering α increases β, and vice versa. The **test statistic** compares the sample statistic with the hypothesized parameter. For a mean, the **decision rule** tells us whether to reject H_0 by comparing the test statistic with the **critical value** of z (known σ) or t (unknown σ) from a table or from Excel. Tests of a proportion are based on the normal distribution (if the sample is large enough, according to a rule of thumb), although in small samples the binomial is required. In any hypothesis test, the **p-value** shows the probability that the test statistic (or one more extreme) would be observed by chance, assuming that H_0 is true. If the p-value is smaller than α, we reject H_0 (i.e., a small p-value indicates a **significant** departure from H_0). A two-tailed test is analogous to a confidence interval seen in the last chapter. Power is greater the further away the true parameter is from the null hypothesis value.

KEY TERMS

alternative hypothesis, *321*	importance, *320*	right-tailed test, *323*
benchmark, *341*	left-tailed test, *323*	significance, *320*
critical value, *331*	level of significance, *326*	statistical hypothesis, *323*
decision rule, *320*	null hypothesis, *321*	test statistic, *330*
hypothesis, *319*	power, *327*	two-tailed test, *323*
hypothesis test, *323*	p-value method, *332*	Type I error, *322*
hypothesis testing, *319*	rejection region, *325*	Type II error, *322*

Commonly Used Formulas in One-Sample Hypothesis Tests

Type I error: $\alpha = P(\text{reject } H_0 \mid H_0 \text{ is true})$

Type II error: $\beta = P(\text{fail to reject } H_0 \mid H_0 \text{ is false})$

Power: $1 - \beta = P(\text{reject } H_0 \mid H_0 \text{ is false})$

Test statistic for sample mean, σ known: $z_{\text{calc}} = \dfrac{\bar{x} - \mu_0}{\dfrac{\sigma}{\sqrt{n}}}$

Test statistic for sample mean, σ unknown: $t_{\text{calc}} = \dfrac{\bar{x} - \mu_0}{\dfrac{s}{\sqrt{n}}}$

Test statistic for sample proportion: $z_{\text{calc}} = \dfrac{p - \pi_0}{\sqrt{\dfrac{\pi_0(1 - \pi_0)}{n}}}$

CHAPTER REVIEW

Note: Questions labeled* are based on optional material from this chapter.

1. (a) List the steps in testing a hypothesis. (b) Why can't a hypothesis ever be proven?

2. (a) Explain the difference between the null hypothesis and the alternative hypothesis. (b) How is the null hypothesis chosen (why is it "null")?

3. (a) Why do we say "fail to reject H_0" instead of "accept H_0"? (b) What does it mean to "provisionally accept a hypothesis"?

4. (a) Define Type I error and Type II error. (b) Give an original example to illustrate.

5. (a) Explain the difference between a left-tailed test, two-tailed test, and right-tailed test. (b) When would we choose a two-tailed test? (c) How can we tell the direction of the test by looking at a pair of hypotheses?

6. (a) Explain the meaning of the rejection region in a decision rule. (b) Why do we need to know the sampling distribution of a statistic before we can do a hypothesis test?

7. (a) Define level of significance. (b) Define power.

8. (a) Why do we prefer low values for α and β? (b) For a given sample size, why is there a trade-off between α and β? (c) How could we decrease both α and β?

9. (a) Why is a "statistically significant difference" not necessarily a "practically important difference"? Give an illustration. (b) Why do statisticians play only a limited role in deciding whether a significant difference requires action?

10. (a) In a hypothesis test for a proportion, when can normality be assumed? *Optional* (b) If the sample is too small to assume normality, what can we do?

11. (a) In a hypothesis test of one mean, what assumptions do we make? (b) When do we use t instead of z? (c) When is the difference between z and t immaterial?

12. (a) Explain what a p-value means. Give an example and interpret it. (b) Why is the p-value method an attractive alternative to specifying α in advance?

13. Why is a confidence interval similar to a two-tailed test?

CHAPTER EXERCISES

Note: Explain answers and show your work clearly.

connect

TYPE I AND II ERROR

9.37 Suppose a potential buyer for your home is ready to purchase but before making their final decision they would like to be assured that the radon level in the home is safe. The EPA recommends remedial action if the radon level is greater than 4.0 pCi/L. You show results of a test stating that the radon level in your home is 1.2 pCi/L. (a) If the individual does purchase your home based on the results of your radon test, which type of error did they expose themselves to? (b) What are the possible consequences?

9.38 Suppose you always reject the null hypothesis, regardless of any sample evidence. (a) What is the probability of Type II error? (b) Why might this be a bad policy?

9.39   Suppose the judge decides to acquit all defendants, regardless of the evidence. (a) What is the probability of Type I error? (b) Why might this be a bad policy?

9.40   High blood pressure, if untreated, can lead to increased risk of stroke and heart attack. A common definition of hypertension is diastolic blood pressure of 90 or more. (a) State the null and alternative hypotheses for a physician who checks your blood pressure. (b) Define Type I and II error. What are the consequences of each? (c) Which type of error is more to be feared, and by whom?

9.41   A nuclear power plant replaces its ID card facility access system cards with a biometric security system that scans the iris pattern of the employee and compares it with a data bank. Users are classified as authorized or unauthorized. (a) State the null and alternative hypotheses. (b) Define Type I and II error. What are the consequences of each? (c) Which is more to be feared, and by whom?

9.42   If the true mean is 50 and we reject the hypothesis that $\mu = 50$, what is the probability of Type II error? *Hint:* This is a trick question.

9.43   If the null hypothesis that $\pi = .50$ is accepted even though the true proportion is .60, what is the probability of Type I error? *Hint:* This is a trick question.

9.44   Pap smears are a test for abnormal cancerous and precancerous cells taken from the cervix. (a) State a pair of hypotheses and then explain the meaning of a false negative and a false positive. (b) Why is the null hypothesis "null"? (c) Who bears the cost of each type of error?

9.45   In a commercially available fingerprint scanner (e.g., for your home or office PC) false acceptances are 1 in 25 million for high-end devices, with false rejection rates of around 3 percent. (a) Define Type I and II error. (b) Why do you suppose the false rejection rate is so high compared with the false acceptance rate? (Data are from *Scientific American* 288, no. 3 [March 2003], p. 98.)

9.46   When told that over a 10-year period a mammogram test has a false positive rate of 50 percent, Bob said, "That means that about half the women tested actually have no cancer." Correct Bob's mistaken interpretation.

TESTS OF MEANS AND PROPORTIONS

9.47   A can of peeled whole tomatoes is supposed to contain an average of 19 ounces of tomatoes (excluding the juice). The actual weight is a normally distributed random variable whose standard deviation is known to be 0.25 ounces. (a) In quality control, would a one-tailed or two-tailed test be used? Why? (b) Explain the consequences of departure from the mean in either direction. (c) Which sampling distribution would you use if samples of four cans are weighed? Why? (d) Set up a two-tailed decision rule for $\alpha = .01$.

9.48   At Ajax Spring Water, a half-liter bottle of soft drink is supposed to contain a mean of 520 ml. The filling process follows a normal distribution with a known process standard deviation of 4 ml. (a) Which sampling distribution would you use if random samples of 10 bottles are to be weighed? Why? (b) Set up hypotheses and a two-tailed decision rule for the correct mean using the 5 percent level of significance. (c) If a sample of 16 bottles shows a mean fill of 515 ml, does this contradict the hypothesis that the true mean is 520 ml?

9.49   On eight Friday quizzes, Bob received scores of 80, 85, 95, 92, 89, 84, 90, 92. He tells Prof. Hardtack that he is really a 90+ performer but this sample just happened to fall below his true performance level. (a) State an appropriate pair of hypotheses. (b) State the formula for the test statistic and show your decision rule using the 1 percent level of significance. (c) Carry out the test. Show your work. (d) What assumptions are required? (e) Use Excel to find the *p*-value and interpret it.   **BobQuiz**

9.50   Faced with rising fax costs, a firm issued a guideline that transmissions of 10 pages or more should be sent by 2-day mail instead. Exceptions are allowed, but they want the average to be 10 or below. The firm examined 35 randomly chosen fax transmissions during the next year, yielding a sample mean of 14.44 with a standard deviation of 4.45 pages. (a) At the .01 level of significance, is the true mean greater than 10? (b) Use Excel to find the right-tail *p*-value.

9.51   A U.S. dime weighs 2.268 grams when minted. A random sample of 15 circulated dimes showed a mean weight of 2.256 grams with a standard deviation of .026 grams. (a) Using $\alpha = .05$, is the mean weight of all circulated dimes lower than the mint weight? State your hypotheses and decision rule. (b) Why might circulated dimes weigh less than the mint specification? (See *Science News* 157, no. 14 [April 1, 2000], p. 216.)

9.52   A coin was flipped 60 times and came up heads 38 times. (a) At the .10 level of significance, is the coin biased toward heads? Show your decision rule and calculations. (b) Calculate a *p*-value and interpret it.

9.53 A sample of 100 one-dollar bills from the Subway cash register revealed that 16 had something written on them besides the normal printing (e.g., "Bob ♥ Mary"). (a) At $\alpha = .05$, is this sample evidence consistent with the hypothesis that 10 percent or fewer of all dollar bills have anything written on them besides the normal printing? Include a sketch of your decision rule and show all calculations. (b) Is your decision sensitive to the choice of α? (c) Find the *p*-value.

9.54 A sample of 100 mortgages approved during the current year showed that 31 were issued to a single-earner family or individual. The historical average is 25 percent. (a) At the .05 level of significance in a right-tailed test, has the percentage of single-earner or individual mortgages risen? Include a sketch of your decision rule and show all work. (b) Is this a close decision? (c) State any assumptions that are required.

9.55 A state weights-and-measures standard requires that no more than 5 percent of bags of Halloween candy be underweight. A random sample of 200 bags showed that 16 were underweight. (a) At $\alpha = .025$, is the standard being violated? Use a right-tailed test and show your work. (b) Find the *p*-value.

9.56 Ages for the 2005 Boston Red Sox pitchers are shown below. (a) Assuming this is a random sample of major league pitchers, at the 5 percent level of significance does this sample show that the true mean age of all American League pitchers is over 30 years? State your hypotheses and decision rule and show all work. (b) If there is a difference, is it important? (c) Find the *p*-value and interpret it. (Data are from http://boston.redsox.mlb.com.)   **RedSox**

Ages of Boston Red Sox Pitchers, October 2005

Arroyo	28	Foulke	33	Mantei	32	Timlin	39
Clement	31	Gonzalez	30	Miller	29	Wakefield	39
Embree	35	Halama	33	Myers	36	Wells	42

9.57 The EPA is concerned about the quality of drinking water served on airline flights. In September 2004, a sample of 158 flights found unacceptable bacterial contamination on 20 flights. (a) At $\alpha = .05$, does this sample show that more than 10 percent of all flights have contaminated water? (b) Find the *p*-value. (Data are from *The Wall Street Journal,* November 10, 2004, p. D1.)

9.58 The Web-based company *Oh Baby! Gifts* has a goal of processing 95 percent of its orders on the same day they are received. If 485 out of the next 500 orders are processed on the same day, would this prove that they are exceeding their goal, using $\alpha = .025$? (See story.news.yahoo.com accessed June 25, 2004.)

9.59 In the Big Ten (the NCAA sports league) a sample showed that only 267 out of 584 freshmen football players graduated within 6 years. (a) At $\alpha = .05$ does this sample contradict the claim that at least half graduate within 6 years? State your hypotheses and decision rule. (b) Calculate the *p*-value and interpret it. (c) Do you think the difference is important, as opposed to significant?

9.60 An auditor reviewed 25 oral surgery insurance claims from a particular surgical office, determining that the mean out-of-pocket patient billing above the reimbursed amount was $275.66 with a standard deviation of $78.11. (a) At the 5 percent level of significance, does this sample prove a violation of the guideline that the average patient should pay no more than $250 out-of-pocket? State your hypotheses and decision rule. (b) Is this a close decision?

9.61 The average service time at a Noodles & Company restaurant was 3.5 minutes in the previous year. Noodles implemented some time-saving measures and would like to know if they have been effective. They sample 20 service times and find the sample average is 3.2 minutes with a sample standard deviation of .4 minutes. Using an $\alpha = .05$, were the measures effective?

9.62 A digital camcorder repair service has set a goal not to exceed an average of 5 working days from the time the unit is brought in to the time repairs are completed. A random sample of 12 repair records showed the following repair times (in days): 9, 2, 5, 1, 5, 4, 7, 5, 11, 3, 7, 2. At $\alpha = .05$ is the goal being met?   **Repair**

9.63 A recent study by the Government Accountability Office found that consumers got correct answers about Medicare only 67 percent of the time when they called 1-800-MEDICARE. (a) At $\alpha = .05$, would a subsequent audit of 50 randomly chosen calls with 40 correct answers suffice to show that the percentage had risen? What is the *p*-value? (b) Is the normality criterion met? (See *The New York Times,* November 7, 2006.)

9.64 Beer shelf life is a problem for brewers and distributors, because when beer is stored at room temperature, its flavor deteriorates. When the average furfuryl ether content reaches 6 μg per liter, a typical consumer begins to taste an unpleasant chemical flavor. At $\alpha = .05$, would the following sample of 12 randomly chosen bottles stored for a month convince you that the mean furfuryl ether content exceeds the taste threshhold? What is the *p*-value? (See *Science News,* December 3, 2005, p. 363.) 🍺 **BeerTaste**

6.53, 5.68, 8.10, 7.50, 6.32, 8.75, 5.98, 7.50, 5.01, 5.95, 6.40, 7.02

PROPORTIONS: SMALL SAMPLES

9.65 An automaker states that its cars equipped with electronic fuel injection and computerized engine controls will start on the first try (hot or cold) 99 percent of the time. A survey of 100 new car owners revealed that 3 had not started on the first try during a recent cold snap. (a) At $\alpha = .025$ does this demonstrate that the automaker's claim is incorrect? (b) Calculate the *p*-value and interpret it. *Hint:* Use MINITAB, or use Excel to calculate the cumulative binomial probability $P(X \geq 3 \mid n = 100, \pi = .01) = 1 - P(X \leq 2 \mid n = 100, \pi = .01)$.

9.66 A quality standard says that no more than 2 percent of the eggs sold in a store may be cracked (not broken, just cracked). In 3 cartons (12 eggs each carton) 2 eggs are cracked. (a) At the .10 level of significance, does this prove that the standard is exceeded? (b) Calculate a *p*-value for the observed sample result. *Hint:* Use Excel to calculate the binomial probability $P(X \geq 2 \mid n = 36, \pi = .02) = 1 - P(X \leq 1 \mid n = 36, \pi = .02)$.

9.67 An experimental medication is administered to 16 people who suffer from migraines. After an hour, 10 say they feel better. Is the medication effective (i.e., is the percent who feel better greater than 50 percent)? Use $\alpha = .10$, explain fully, and show all steps.

9.68 The historical on-time percentage for Amtrak's Sunset Limited is 10 percent. In July 2004, the train was on time 0 times in 31 runs. Has the on-time percentage fallen? Explain clearly. *Hint:* Use Excel to calculate the cumulative binomial probability $P(X \leq 0 \mid n = 31, \pi = .10)$. (Data are from *The Wall Street Journal,* August 10, 2004.)

9.69 After 7 months, none of 238 angioplasty patients who received a drug-coated stent to keep their arteries open had experienced restenosis (re-blocking of the arteries). (a) Use MINITAB to construct a 95 percent binomial confidence interval for the proportion of all angioplasty patients who experience restenosis. (b) Why is it necessary to use a binomial in this case? (c) If the goal is to reduce the occurrence of restenosis to 5 percent or less, does this sample show that the goal is being achieved? (Data are from *Detroit Free Press,* March 18, 2002, p. 1A.)

9.70 (a) A statistical study reported that a drug was effective with a *p*-value of .042. Explain in words what this tells you. (b) How would that compare to a drug that had a *p*-value of .087?

9.71 Bob said, "Why is a small *p*-value significant, when a large one isn't? That seems backwards." Try to explain it to Bob, giving an example to make your point.

SHORT ESSAY

9.72 Read the passage below, and then consider the following scenario. A physician is trying to decide whether to prescribe medication for cholesterol reduction in a 45-year-old female patient. The null hypothesis is that the patient's cholesterol is less than the threshold of treatable hypercholesterolemia. However, a sample of readings over a 2-year time period shows considerable variation, usually below but sometimes above the threshold. (a) Define Type I and Type II error. (b) List the costs of each type of error (in general terms). Who bears the cost of each? (c) How might the patient's point of view differ from the HMO's or doctor's? (d) In what sense is this a business problem? A societal problem? An individual problem?

> Hypercholesterolemia is a known risk factor for coronary artery disease. The risk of death from coronary artery disease has a continuous and graded relation to total serum cholesterol levels higher than 180 mg/dl. However, the ratio of total cholesterol to HDL cholesterol is a better predictor of coronary artery disease than the level of either fraction alone. . . . After menopause, plasma LDL cholesterol concentrations rise to equal, and then to exceed, those of men, at the same time HDL cholesterol concentrations fall slightly. . . . This puts women at equal or greater risk for cardiovascular disease. According to the results of medical trials, there is compelling evidence that a reduction in the level of cholesterol leads to a significant decrease in the rate of cardiovascular events. . . . Therefore, screening for high blood cholesterol is an important clinical intervention. The National Heart, Lung, and Blood Institute . . . recommends that all persons aged 20 and above have a cholesterol determination at least once every five years. . . . Timely identification of high-risk individuals allows consideration of various treatment alternatives. For patients who do not have coronary heart disease or peripheral vascular disease, emphasis should be placed on non-pharmacologic approaches, mainly changes in diet and exercise. Drug therapy should be reserved for those at highest risk of coronary heart disease: men above 35 years of age and postmenopausal women. (Source: www.dakotacare.com.)

LearningStats Unit 09   One-Sample Hypothesis Tests   LS

LearningStats Unit 09 explains the logic of hypothesis testing, gives examples of the most common one-sample hypothesis tests (one mean, one proportion, one variance), and discusses Type I and II error. Your instructor may assign specific modules, or you may decide to check them out because the topic sounds interesting.

Topic	LearningStats Modules
Hypothesis testing	Overview of Hypothesis Testing One-Sample Hypothesis Tests
Common hypothesis tests	One-Sample Tests Do-It-Yourself Simulation Sampling Distribution Examples
Type I error and power	Type I Error p-Value Illustration Power Curves: Examples Power Curves: Do-It-Yourself Power Curve Families: μ Power Curve Families: π
Optional topics	Probability Plots Finite Population Correction
Equations	One-Sample Formulas Sampling Distributions
Tables	Appendix C—Normal Appendix D—Student's t Appendix E—Chi-Square

Key: = PowerPoint   = Word   = Excel

Visual Statistics   VS

Visual Statistics Modules on One-Sample Tests

Module	Module Name
6	VS Visualizing Random Samples
9	VS Visualizing One-Sample Hypothesis Tests

Visual Statistics Modules 6 and 9 (included on your CD) are designed to help you

- Understand variability in samples.
- Learn to distinguish between one-tailed and two-tailed tests.
- Be able to explain the meaning of significance and power.
- Interpret decision rules, critical values, and p-values.
- Know the role of the normality assumption and the effects of violating it.

The worktext (included on the CD in .PDF format) contains lists of concepts covered, objectives of the modules, overviews of concepts, illustrations of concepts, orientations to module features, learning exercises (basic, intermediate, advanced), learning projects (individual, team), self-evaluation quizzes, glossaries of terms, and solutions to self-evaluation quizzes.

Two-Sample Hypothesis Tests

Chapter Learning Objectives

When you finish this chapter you should be able to

- Recognize when a two-sample test for proportions is required.
- Carry out a two-sample test for proportions and know its assumptions.
- Check whether normality may be assumed for two proportions.
- Explain the analogy between confidence intervals and two-tailed tests.
- Recognize when a two-sample test for means is required.
- Choose the correct formulas for a two-sample comparison for means.
- Explain the assumptions underlying the two-sample test of means.
- Know when a two-sample test of means should not be performed.
- Recognize paired data and be able to perform a paired t test.
- List the main characteristics of the F distribution and why it is used.
- Perform a one-tailed or two-tailed test to compare two variances.
- Recognize the assumptions underlying the F test and when they are violated.
- Use one or more computer software packages to do two-sample tests.

The logic and applications of hypothesis testing that you learned in Chapter 9 will continue here, but now we consider two-sample tests. The two-sample test is used to make inferences about the two populations from which the samples were drawn. The use of these techniques is widespread in science and engineering as well as social sciences. Drug companies use sophisticated versions called clinical trials to determine the effectiveness of new drugs, agricultural science continually uses these methods to compare yields to improve productivity, and a wide variety of businesses use them to test or compare things.

What Is a Two-Sample Test?

Two-sample tests compare two sample estimates *with each other,* whereas one-sample tests compare a sample estimate with a nonsample benchmark (a claim or prior belief about a population parameter). Here are some actual two-sample tests from this chapter:

Automotive   A new bumper is installed on selected vehicles in a corporate fleet. During a 1-year test period, 12 vehicles with the new bumper were involved in accidents, incurring mean damage of $1,101 with a standard deviation of $696. During the same year, 9 vehicles with the old bumpers were involved in accidents, incurring mean damage of $1,766 with a standard deviation of $838. Did the new bumper significantly reduce damage? Did it reduce variation?

Marketing   At a matinee performance of *Spider-Man 3,* a random sample of 25 concession purchases showed a mean of $7.29 with a standard deviation of $3.02. For the evening performance a random sample of 25 concession purchases showed a mean of $7.12 with a standard deviation of $2.14. Is there less variation in the evenings?

Safety   In Dallas, some fire trucks were painted yellow (instead of red) to heighten their visibility. During a test period, the fleet of red fire trucks made 153,348 runs and had 20 accidents, while the fleet of yellow fire trucks made 135,035 runs and had 4 accidents. Is the difference in accident rates significant?

Medicine   Half of a group of 18,882 healthy men with no sign of prostate cancer were given an experimental drug called finasteride, while half were given a placebo, based on a random selection process. Participants underwent annual exams and blood tests. Over the next 7 years, 571 men in the placebo group developed prostate cancer, compared with only 435 in the finasteride group. Is the difference in cancer rates significant?

Education   In a certain college class, 20 randomly chosen students were given a tutorial, while 20 others used a self-study computer simulation. On the same 20-point quiz, the tutorial students' mean score was 16.7 with a standard deviation of 2.5, compared with a mean of 14.5 and a standard deviation of 3.2 for the simulation students. Did the tutorial students do better, or is it just due to chance? Is there any significant difference in the degree of variation in the two groups?

Mini Case   10.1

Early Intervention Saves Lives

Statistics is helping U.S. hospitals prove the value of innovative organizational changes to deal with medical crisis situations. At the Pittsburgh Medical Center, "SWAT teams" were shown to reduce patient mortality by cutting red tape for critically ill patients. They formed a Rapid Response Team (RRT) consisting of a critical care nurse, intensive care therapist, and a respiratory therapist, empowered to make decisions without waiting until the patient's doctor could be paged. Statistics were collected on cardiac arrests for two months before and after the RRT concept was implemented. The sample data revealed more than a 50 percent reduction in total cardiac deaths and a decline in average ICU days after cardiac arrest from 163 days to only 33 days after RRT. These improvements were both *statistically significant* and of *practical importance* because of the medical benefits and the large cost savings in hospital care. Statistics played a similar role at the University of California San Francisco Medical Center in demonstrating the value of a new method of expediting treatment of heart attack emergency patients. (See *The Wall Street Journal,* December 1, 2004, p. D1; and "How Statistics Can Save Failing Hearts," *The New York Times,* March 7, 2007, p. C1.)

Basis of Two-Sample Tests

Two-sample tests are especially useful because they possess a built-in point of comparison. You can think of many situations where two groups are to be compared (e.g., before and after, old and new, experimental and control). Sometimes we don't really care about the actual value of the population parameter, but only whether the parameter is the same for both populations. Usually, the null hypothesis is that both samples were drawn from populations with the same parameter value, but we can also test for a given degree of difference.

The logic of two-sample tests is based on the fact that two samples drawn from the *same population* may yield *different estimates* of a parameter due to chance. For example, exhaust emission tests could yield different results for two vehicles of the same type. Only if the two sample statistics differ by more than the amount attributable to chance can we conclude that the samples came from populations with different parameter values, as illustrated in Figure 10.1.

Test Procedure

The testing procedure is like that of one-sample tests. We state our hypotheses, set up a decision rule, insert the sample statistics, and make a decision, or we can use *p-values*. Since the true parameters are unknown, we rely on statistical theory to help us reach a defensible conclusion about our hypotheses. Our decision could be wrong—we could commit a **Type I** or **Type II error**—but at least we can specify our acceptable risk levels. Larger samples are

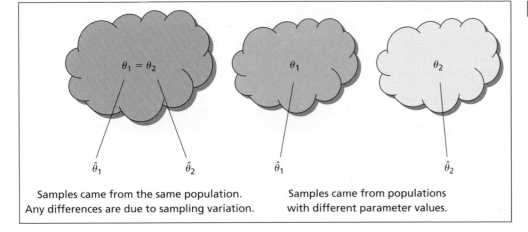

FIGURE 10.1
Same Population or Different?

Samples came from the same population. Any differences are due to sampling variation.

Samples came from populations with different parameter values.

always desirable because they permit us to reduce either Type I error or Type II error (i.e., increase the power of the test) or some combination, as we choose.

Comparing two means is a common business problem. Is the average customer purchase at Starbucks the same on Saturday and Sunday morning? Is the average customer waiting time the same at two different branches of Chase Bank? Do male and female Wal-Mart employees work the same average overtime hours?

Format of Hypotheses

The population means are denoted μ_1 and μ_2. The possible pairs of hypotheses are

Left-Tailed Test	*Two-Tailed Test*	*Right-Tailed Test*
$H_0: \mu_1 \geq \mu_2$	$H_0: \mu_1 = \mu_2$	$H_0: \mu_1 \leq \mu_2$
$H_1: \mu_1 < \mu_2$	$H_1: \mu_1 \neq \mu_2$	$H_1: \mu_1 > \mu_2$

Test Statistic

The **test statistic** is the difference of the sample means divided by its standard error. If the population variances σ_1^2 and σ_2^2 are known (a rarity), we can use the normal distribution. If the variances are estimated using s_1^2 and s_2^2, we must use Student's t (the typical situation). There are three cases, shown in Table 10.1. Although the formulas may appear different, the same reasoning is used in each. Each test statistic divides the difference of sample means by its standard error. All the tests presume independent samples and normal populations, although in practice they are robust to non-normality as long as the samples are not too small and the population is not too skewed.

TABLE 10.1
Test Statistic for Difference of Means

Case 1	*Case 2*	*Case 3*
Known Variances	Unknown Variances, Assumed Equal	Unknown Variances, Assumed Unequal
$z_{calc} = \dfrac{\bar{x}_1 - \bar{x}_2}{\sqrt{\dfrac{\sigma_1^2}{n_1} + \dfrac{\sigma_2^2}{n_2}}}$	$t_{calc} = \dfrac{\bar{x}_1 - \bar{x}_2}{\sqrt{\dfrac{s_p^2}{n_1} + \dfrac{s_p^2}{n_2}}}$ where $s_p^2 = \dfrac{(n_1-1)s_1^2 + (n_2-1)s_2^2}{n_1 + n_2 - 2}$	$t_{calc} = \dfrac{\bar{x}_1 - \bar{x}_2}{\sqrt{\dfrac{s_1^2}{n_1} + \dfrac{s_2^2}{n_2}}}$
For critical value, use normal distribution	For critical value, use Student's t with $n_1 + n_2 - 2$ degrees of freedom	For critical value, use Student's t with Welch's adjusted degrees of freedom (see formula 10.6)

The formulas in Table 10.1 require some calculations, but most of the time you will be using a computer. As long as you have raw data (i.e., the original samples of n_1 and n_2 observations) Excel's Tools > Data Analysis menu handles all three cases, as shown in Figure 10.2. *MegaStat* and *MINITAB* also perform these tests. *LearningStats* also provides a calculator for summarized data (i.e., when you have $\bar{x}_1$, $\bar{x}_2$, s_1, s_2 instead of the n_1 and n_2 data columns).

FIGURE 10.2

Excel's Tools > Data Analysis Menu

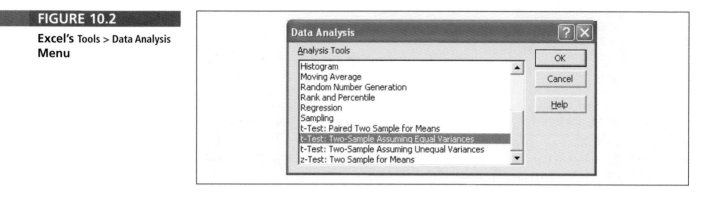

Case 1: Known Variances

In all three cases, the numerator is the *difference* of the sample means and the denominator is the *standard error* of the difference of the means. In *Case 1,* σ_1^2 and σ_2^2 are known (an unlikely situation) so the standard error is the square root of the sum of the variances of $\bar{x}_1$ and $\bar{x}_2$, and we use the normal distribution for the test (assuming a normal population):

(10.1)
$$z_{\text{calc}} = \frac{\bar{x}_1 - \bar{x}_2}{\sqrt{\dfrac{\sigma_1^2}{n_1} + \dfrac{\sigma_2^2}{n_2}}} \qquad \text{(Case 1: known population variances)}$$

Case 2: Unknown Variances, Assumed Equal

In *Case 2,* the variances are unknown (as they usually are) so we must estimate them and use the Student's t distribution. If we assume that the population variances are equal, we can take a weighted average of the sample variances s_1^2 and s_2^2 to create an *estimate* of the common variance. Weights are assigned to s_1^2 and s_2^2 based on their respective degrees of freedom $(n_1 - 1)$ and $(n_2 - 1)$. Because we are pooling the sample variances, the common variance estimate is called the **pooled variance** and is denoted s_p^2. *Case 2* is often called the *pooled* t *test*.

(10.2)
$$s_p^2 = \frac{(n_1 - 1)s_1^2 + (n_2 - 1)s_2^2}{n_1 + n_2 - 2} \qquad \text{(pooled estimate of common variance)}$$

Since the variances are assumed equal, s_p^2 replaces both σ_1^2 and σ_2^2, so the test statistic is

(10.3)
$$t_{\text{calc}} = \frac{\bar{x}_1 - \bar{x}_2}{\sqrt{\dfrac{s_p^2}{n_1} + \dfrac{s_p^2}{n_2}}} \qquad \text{(Case 2: unknown variances, assumed equal)}$$

When the sample variances are pooled, we add their degrees of freedom $(n_1 - 1) + (n_2 - 1)$:

(10.4)
$$\nu = n_1 + n_2 - 2 \qquad \text{(degrees of freedom for pooled } t \text{ test)}$$

Case 3: Unknown Variances, Assumed Unequal

If the unknown variances σ_1^2 and σ_2^2 are assumed *unequal,* we do not pool the variances (a safer assumption than Case 2). Statisticians have shown that under these conditions the distribution of the random variable $\bar{x}_1 - \bar{x}_2$ is no longer certain, a difficulty known as the **Behrens-Fisher problem.** One solution to this problem is the **Welch-Satterthwaite test** which replaces σ_1^2 and σ_2^2 with s_1^2 and s_2^2 in the known variance z formula, but then uses a Student's t test with **Welch's adjusted degrees of freedom**.

$$t_{calc} = \frac{\bar{x}_1 - \bar{x}_2}{\sqrt{\dfrac{s_1^2}{n_1} + \dfrac{s_2^2}{n_2}}} \qquad \text{(unknown variances, assumed unequal)} \qquad \textbf{(10.5)}$$

$$v' = \frac{\left[s_1^2/n_1 + s_2^2/n_2\right]^2}{\dfrac{\left(s_1^2/n_1\right)^2}{n_1 - 1} + \dfrac{\left(s_2^2/n_2\right)^2}{n_2 - 1}} \qquad \text{(Welch's adjusted degrees of freedom)} \qquad \textbf{(10.6)}$$

If the sample sizes are equal, the value of t_{calc} will be the same as in Case 2, although the degrees of freedom may differ. If the variances are similar, Welch's adjusted degrees of freedom v' (i.e., *Case 3*) will be almost the same as the unadjusted degrees of freedom $v = n_1 + n_2 - 2$ (i.e., *Case 2*). Finding Welch's adjusted degrees of freedom requires a tedious calculation, but this is easily handled by Excel, MegaStat, or MINITAB. Welch's adjusted degrees of freedom v' is always between $\min(n_1 - 1, n_2 - 1)$ and $n_1 + n_2 - 2$. To avoid calculating v', a conservative quick rule for degrees of freedom is to use $v^* = \min(n_1 - 1, n_2 - 1)$. The formulas for Case 2 and Case 3 will usually yield the same decision unless the sample sizes and variances differ greatly.

The price of prescription drugs is an ongoing national issue in the United States. Zocor is a common prescription cholesterol-reducing drug prescribed for people who are at risk for heart disease. Table 10.2 shows Zocor prices from 15 randomly selected pharmacies in two states. At $\alpha = .05$, is there a difference in the mean for all pharmacies in Colorado and Texas? From the dot plots shown in Figure 10.3, it seems unlikely that there is a significant difference, but we will do a test of means to see whether our intuition is correct.

EXAMPLE

Drug Prices in Two States

TABLE 10.2	Zocor Prices (30-Day Supply) in Two States Zocor		
Colorado Pharmacies		**Texas Pharmacies**	
City	*Price ($)*	*City*	*Price ($)*
Alamosa	125.05	Austin	145.32
Avon	137.56	Austin	131.19
Broomfield	142.50	Austin	151.65
Buena Vista	145.95	Austin	141.55
Colorado Springs	117.49	Austin	125.99
Colorado Springs	142.75	Dallas	126.29
Denver	121.99	Dallas	139.19
Denver	117.49	Dallas	156.00
Eaton	141.64	Dallas	137.56
Fort Collins	128.69	Houston	154.10
Gunnison	130.29	Houston	126.41
Pueblo	142.39	Houston	114.00
Pueblo	121.99	Houston	144.99
Pueblo	141.30		
Sterling	153.43		
Walsenburg	133.39		
$\bar{x}_1 = \$133.994$		$\bar{x}_2 = \$138.018$	
$s_1 = \$11.015$		$s_2 = \$12.663$	
$n_1 = 16$ pharmacies		$n_2 = 13$ pharmacies	

Source: Public Research Interest Group (www.pirg.org). Surveyed pharmacies were chosen from the telephone directory in 2004. Data used with permission.

FIGURE 10.3   **Zocor Prices from Sampled Pharmacies in Two States**

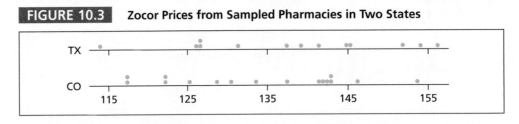

Step 1: State the Hypotheses

To check for a significant difference without regard for its direction, we choose a two-tailed test. The hypotheses to be tested are

$$H_0: \mu_1 = \mu_2$$
$$H_1: \mu_1 \neq \mu_2$$

Step 2: Specify the Decision Rule

We will assume equal variances. For the pooled-variance t test, degrees of freedom are $\nu = n_1 + n_2 - 2 = 16 + 13 - 2 = 27$. From Appendix D we get the two-tail critical value $t = \pm 2.052$. The decision rule is illustrated in Figure 10.4.

FIGURE 10.4   **Two-Tailed Decision Rule for Student's t with $\alpha = .05$ and d.f. = 27**

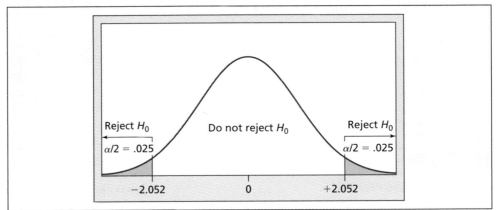

Step 3: Calculate the Test Statistic

The sample statistics are

$$\bar{x}_1 = 133.994 \qquad \bar{x}_2 = 138.018$$
$$s_1 = 11.015 \qquad s_2 = 12.663$$
$$n_1 = 16 \qquad n_2 = 13$$

The pooled variance s_p^2 is

$$s_p^2 = \frac{(n_1 - 1)s_1^2 + (n_2 - 1)s_2^2}{n_1 + n_2 - 2} = \frac{(16 - 1)(11.015)^2 + (13 - 1)(12.663)^2}{16 + 13 - 2} = 138.6737$$

Using s_p^2 the test statistic is

$$t_{calc} = \frac{\bar{x}_1 - \bar{x}_2}{\sqrt{\dfrac{s_p^2}{n_1} + \dfrac{s_p^2}{n_2}}} = \frac{133.994 - 138.018}{\sqrt{\dfrac{138.6737}{16} + \dfrac{138.6737}{13}}} = \frac{-4.024}{4.39708} = -0.915$$

The pooled standard deviation is $s_p = \sqrt{138.6737} = 11.776$. Notice that s_p always lies between s_1 and s_2 (if not, you have an arithmetic error). This is because s_p^2 is an average of s_1^2 and s_2^2.

Step 4: Make the Decision

The test statistic $t_{calc} = -0.915$ does not fall in the rejection region so we cannot reject the hypothesis of equal means. Excel's menu and output are shown in Figure 10.5. Both one-tailed and two-tailed tests are shown.

FIGURE 10.5   Excel's **Tools > Data Analysis** with Unknown but Equal Variances

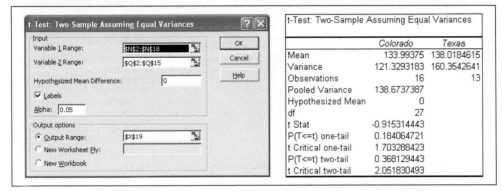

t-Test: Two-Sample Assuming Equal Variances		
	Colorado	*Texas*
Mean	133.99375	138.0184615
Variance	121.3293183	160.3542641
Observations	16	13
Pooled Variance	138.6737387	
Hypothesized Mean	0	
df	27	
t Stat	-0.915314443	
P(T<=t) one-tail	0.184064721	
t Critical one-tail	1.703288423	
P(T<=t) two-tail	0.368129443	
t Critical two-tail	2.051830493	

The *p*-value can be calculated using Excel's two-tail function =TDIST(.915,27,2) which gives $p = .3681$. This large *p*-value says that a result this extreme would happen by chance about 37 percent of the time if $\mu_1 = \mu_2$. The difference in sample means seems to be well within the realm of chance.

The sample variances in this example are similar, so the assumption of equal variances is reasonable. But if we instead use the formulas for *Case 3* (assuming *unequal* variances) the test statistic is

$$t_{calc} = \frac{\bar{x}_1 - \bar{x}_2}{\sqrt{\dfrac{s_1^2}{n_1} + \dfrac{s_2^2}{n_2}}} = \frac{133.994 - 138.018}{\sqrt{\dfrac{(11.015)^2}{16} + \dfrac{(12.663)^2}{13}}} = \frac{-4.024}{4.4629} = -0.902$$

The formula for adjusted degrees of freedom for the Welch-Satterthwaite test is

$$\nu' = \frac{\left[\dfrac{s_1^2}{n_1} + \dfrac{s_2^2}{n_2}\right]^2}{\dfrac{\left(\dfrac{s_1^2}{n_1}\right)^2}{n_1 - 1} + \dfrac{\left(\dfrac{s_2^2}{n_2}\right)^2}{n_2 - 1}} = \frac{\left[\dfrac{(11.015)^2}{16} + \dfrac{(12.663)^2}{13}\right]^2}{\dfrac{\left(\dfrac{(11.015)^2}{16}\right)^2}{16 - 1} + \dfrac{\left(\dfrac{(12.663)^2}{13}\right)^2}{13 - 1}} = 24$$

The adjusted degrees of freedom are rounded to the next lower integer, to be conservative.

For the unequal-variance *t* test with degrees of freedom $\nu' = 24$, Appendix D gives the two-tail critical value $t_{.025} = \pm 2.064$. The decision rule is illustrated in Figure 10.6.

FIGURE 10.6   Two-Tail Decision Rule for Student's *t* with $\alpha = .05$ and d.f. = 24

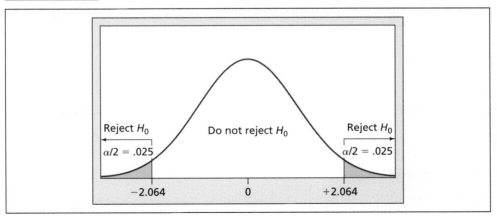

The calculations are best done by computer. Excel's menu and output are shown in Figure 10.7. Both one-tailed and two-tailed tests are shown.

FIGURE 10.7   **Excel's** Tools > Data Analysis **with Unknown but Equal Variances**

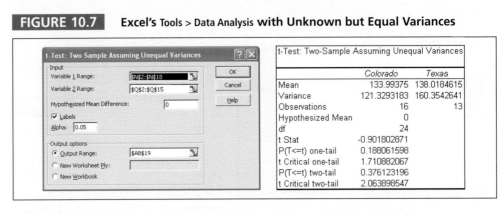

For the Zocor data, either assumption leads to the same conclusion:

Assumption	Test Statistic	d.f.	Critical Value	Decision
Case 2 (equal variances)	$t_{calc} = -0.915$	27	$t_{.025} = \pm2.052$	Don't reject
Case 3 (unequal variances)	$t_{calc} = -0.902$	24	$t_{.025} = \pm2.064$	Don't reject

Which Assumption Is Best?

If the *sample sizes are equal,* the *Case 2* and *Case 3* test statistics will be identical, although the degrees of freedom may differ. If the *variances are similar,* the two tests usually agree. If you have no information about the population variances, then the best choice is *Case 3.* The fewer assumptions you make about your populations, the less likely you are to make a mistake in your conclusions. Case 1 (known population variances) is not explored further here because it is so uncommon in business.

Must Sample Sizes Be Equal?

Unequal sample sizes are common, and the formulas still apply. However, there are advantages to equal sample sizes. We avoid unbalanced sample sizes when possible. But many times, we have to take the samples as they come.

Large Samples

For unknown variances, if both samples are large ($n_1 \geq 30$ and $n_2 \geq 30$) and you have reason to think the population isn't badly skewed (look at the histograms or dot plots of the samples), it is common to use formula 10.7 with Appendix C. Although it usually gives results very close to the "proper" *t* tests, this approach is not conservative (i.e., it may increase Type I risk).

(10.7) $$z_{calc} = \frac{\bar{x}_1 - \bar{x}_2}{\sqrt{\dfrac{s_1^2}{n_1} + \dfrac{s_2^2}{n_2}}}$$ (large samples, symmetric populations)

Caution: Three Issues

Bear in mind three questions when you are comparing two sample means:

- Are the populations skewed? Are there outliers?
- Are the sample sizes large ($n \geq 30$)?
- Is the difference *important* as well as significant?

Skewness or outliers can usually be seen in a histogram or dot plot of each sample. The *t* tests (*Case 2* and *Case 3*) are probably OK in the face of moderate skewness, especially if the samples are large (e.g., sample sizes of at least 30). Outliers are more serious and might require consultation with a statistician. In such cases, you might ask yourself whether a test of means is appropriate. With small samples or skewed data, the mean may not be a very reliable indicator of central tendency, and your test may lack power. In such situations, it may be better merely to describe the samples, comment on similarities or differences in the data, and skip the formal *t*-tests.

Regarding importance, note that a small difference in means or proportions could be significant if the sample size is large, because the standard error gets smaller as the sample size gets larger. So, we must separately ask if the difference is *important*. The answer depends on the data magnitude and the consequences to the decision maker. How large must a price differential be to make it worthwhile for a consumer to drive from *A* to *B* to save 10 percent on a loaf of bread? A DVD player? A new car? Research suggests, for example, that some cancer victims will travel far and pay much for treatments that offer only small improvement in their chances of survival, because life is so precious. But few consumers compare prices or drive far to save money on a gallon of milk or other items that are unimportant in their overall budget.

Mini Case   10.2

Length of Statistics Articles

Are articles in leading statistics journals getting longer? It appears so, based on a comparison of the June 2000 and June 1990 issues of the *Journal of the American Statistical Association* (*JASA*), shown in Table 10.3.

TABLE 10.3	Article Length in *JASA*
June 1990 JASA	**June 2000 JASA**
$\bar{x}_1 = 7.1333$ pages	$\bar{x}_2 = 11.8333$ pages
$s_1 = 1.9250$ pages	$s_2 = 2.5166$ pages
$n_1 = 30$ articles	$n_2 = 12$ articles

Source: *Journal of the American Statistical Association* 85, no. 410, and 95, no. 450.

We will do a left-tailed test at $\alpha = .01$. The hypotheses are

$H_0: \mu_1 \geq \mu_2$

$H_1: \mu_1 < \mu_2$

Since the variances are unknown, we will use a *t* test (both equal and unequal variances) checking the results with Excel. The pooled-variance test (*Case 2*) requires degrees of freedom $v = n_1 + n_2 - 2 = 30 + 12 - 2 = 40$, yielding a left-tail critical value of $t_{.01} = -2.423$. The estimate of the pooled variance is

$$s_p = \sqrt{\frac{(n_1 - 1)s_1^2 + (n_2 - 1)s_2^2}{n_1 + n_2 - 2}} = \sqrt{\frac{(30 - 1)(1.9250)^2 + (12 - 1)(2.5166)^2}{30 + 12 - 2}}$$

$$= \sqrt{4.428333} = 2.10436$$

The test statistic is $t_{\text{calc}} = -6.539$, indicating a very strong rejection of the hypothesis of equal means:

$$t_{\text{calc}} = \frac{\bar{x}_1 - \bar{x}_2}{s_p\sqrt{\frac{1}{n_1} + \frac{1}{n_2}}} = \frac{7.1333 - 11.8333}{(2.10436)\sqrt{\frac{1}{30} + \frac{1}{12}}} = \frac{-4.70000}{0.718776} = -6.539$$

Using the Welch-Sattherwaite t test (assuming unequal variances) the test statistic is

$$t_{calc} = \frac{\bar{x}_1 - \bar{x}_2}{\sqrt{\dfrac{s_1^2}{n_1} + \dfrac{s_2^2}{n_2}}} = \frac{7.1333 - 11.8333}{\sqrt{\dfrac{(1.9250)^2}{30} + \dfrac{(2.5166)^2}{12}}} = \frac{-4.7000}{0.80703} = -5.824$$

The formula for adjusted degrees of freedom for the Welch-Satterthwaite test is

$$\nu' = \frac{\left[\dfrac{s_1^2}{n_1} + \dfrac{s_2^2}{n_2}\right]^2}{\dfrac{\left(\dfrac{s_1^2}{n_1}\right)^2}{n_1 - 1} + \dfrac{\left(\dfrac{s_2^2}{n_2}\right)^2}{n_2 - 1}} = \frac{\left[\dfrac{(1.9250)^2}{30} + \dfrac{(2.5166)^2}{12}\right]^2}{\dfrac{\left(\dfrac{(1.9250)^2}{30}\right)^2}{30 - 1} + \dfrac{\left(\dfrac{(2.5166)^2}{12}\right)^2}{12 - 1}} = 16$$

so the critical value is $t_{.01} = -2.583$. If we use the Quick Rule for degrees of freedom, instead of wading through this tedious calculation, we get $\nu^* = \min(n_1 - 1 \text{ or } n_2 - 1) = \min(30 - 1 \text{ or } 12 - 1) = 11$ or $t_{.01} = -2.718$, which leads to the same conclusion. Regardless of our assumption about variances, we conclude that articles in *JASA* are getting longer. The decision is clear-cut. Our conviction about the conclusion depends on whether these samples are truly representative of *JASA* articles. This question might be probed further, and more articles could be examined. However, this result seems reasonable *a priori*, due to the growing use of graphics and computer simulation that could lengthen the articles. Is a difference of 4.7 pages of practical importance? Well, editors must find room for articles, so if articles are getting longer, journals must contain more pages or publish fewer articles. A difference of 5 pages over 20 or 30 articles might indeed be important.

SECTION EXERCISES

connect

Hint: Show all formulas and calculations, but use the calculator in *LearningStats* Unit 10 to check your work. Calculate the *p*-values using Excel, and show each Excel formula you used (note that Excel's TDIST function requires that you omit the sign if the test statistic is negative).

10.1 Do a two-sample test for equality of means assuming equal variances. Calculate the *p*-value.
 a. Comparison of GPA for randomly chosen college juniors and seniors: $\bar{x}_1 = 3.05$, $s_1 = .20$, $n_1 = 15$, $\bar{x}_2 = 3.25$, $s_2 = .30$, $n_2 = 15$, $\alpha = .025$, left-tailed test.
 b. Comparison of average commute miles for randomly chosen students at two community colleges: $\bar{x}_1 = 15$, $s_1 = 5$, $n_1 = 22$, $\bar{x}_2 = 18$, $s_2 = 7$, $n_2 = 19$, $\alpha = .05$, two-tailed test.
 c. Comparison of credits at time of graduation for randomly chosen accounting and economics students: $\bar{x}_1 = 139$, $s_1 = 2.8$, $n_1 = 12$, $\bar{x}_2 = 137$, $s_2 = 2.7$, $n_2 = 17$, $\alpha = .05$, right-tailed test.

10.2 Repeat the previous exercise, assuming unequal variances. Calculate the *p*-value using Excel, and show the Excel formula you used.

10.3 The average length of stay (LOS) from U.S. short-stay hospitals for a sample of 25 male pneumonia patients was 5.5 days with a standard deviation of 1.2 days. For a sample of 25 females, the average LOS was 5.9 days with a standard deviation of 2.2 days. (a) Assuming equal variances, is there a significant difference at $\alpha = .10$? (b) Calculate the *p*-value using Excel. (See Department of Health and Human Services, *Advance Data from Vital and Health Statistics,* no. 332 [April 9, 2003], p. 13.)

10.4 The average mpg usage for a 2004 Ford Expedition 2WD for a sample of 10 tanks of gas was 17.0 with a standard deviation of 0.8. For a Ford Explorer 2WD, the average mpg usage for a sample of 10 tanks of gas was 18.5 with a standard deviation of 1.0. (a) Assuming equal variances, at $\alpha = .01$, is the true mean mpg lower for the Ford Expedition? (b) Calculate the *p*-value using Excel. (Data are from www.fueleconomy.gov.)

10.5 When the background music was slow, the mean amount of bar purchases for a sample of 17 restaurant patrons was $30.47 with a standard deviation of $15.10. When the background music was fast, the mean amount of bar purchases for a sample of 14 patrons in the same restaurant was $21.62 with a standard deviation of $9.50. (a) Assuming unequal variances, at $\alpha = .01$, is the true mean higher when the music is slow? (b) Calculate the *p*-value using Excel.

10.6   Are women's feet getting bigger? Retailers in the last 20 years have had to increase their stock of larger sizes. Wal-Mart Stores, Inc., and Payless ShoeSource, Inc., have been aggressive in stocking larger sizes, and Nordstrom's reports that its larger sizes typically sell out first. Assuming equal variances, at $\alpha = .025$, do these random shoe size samples of 12 randomly chosen women in each age group show that women's shoe sizes have increased? (See *The Wall Street Journal*, July 17, 2004.)   **ShoeSize1**

| Born in 1980: | 8 | 7.5 | 8.5 | 8.5 | 8 | 7.5 | 9.5 | 7.5 | 8 | 8 | 8.5 | 9 |
| Born in 1960: | 8.5 | 7.5 | 8 | 8 | 7.5 | 7.5 | 7.5 | 8 | 7 | 8 | 7 | 8 |

10.7   Just how "decaffeinated" is decaffeinated coffee? Researchers analyzed 12 samples of two kinds of Starbucks' decaffeinated coffee. The caffeine in a cup of decaffeinated espresso had a mean 9.4 mg with a standard deviation of 3.2 mg, while brewed decaffeinated coffee had a mean of 12.7 mg with a standard deviation of 0.35 mg. Assuming unequal population variances, is there a significant difference in caffeine content between these two beverages at $\alpha = .01$? (Based on McCusker, R. R., *Journal of Analytical Toxicology* 30 [March 2006], pp. 112–114.)

Paired Data

When sample data consist of n matched pairs, a different approach is required. If the *same* individuals are observed twice but under different circumstances, we have a **paired comparison**. For example:

- Fifteen retirees with diagnosed hypertension are assigned a program of diet, exercise, and meditation. A baseline measurement of blood pressure is taken *before* the program begins and again *after* 2 months. Was the program effective in reducing blood pressure?

- Ten cutting tools use lubricant A for 10 minutes. The blade temperatures are taken. When the machine has cooled, it is run with lubricant B for 10 minutes and the blade temperatures are again measured. Which lubricant makes the blades run cooler?

- Weekly sales of Snapple at 12 Wal-Mart stores are compared *before* and *after* installing a new eye-catching display. Did the new display increase sales?

Paired data typically come from a *before-after* experiment. If we treat the data as two independent samples, ignoring the *dependence* between the data pairs, the test is less powerful.

Paired *t* Test

In the **paired *t* test** we define a new variable $d = X_1 - X_2$ as the *difference* between X_1 and X_2. We usually present the n observed differences in column form:

Obs	X_1	X_2	$d = X_1 - X_2$
1	XXX	XXX	XXX
2	XXX	XXX	XXX
3	XXX	XXX	XXX
. . .	. . .	. . .	. . .
. . .	. . .	. . .	. . .
n	XXX	XXX	XXX

The same sample data could also be presented in row form:

Obs	1	2	3	. . .	. . .	n
X_1	XXX	XXX	XXX	. . .	. . .	XXX
X_2	XXX	XXX	XXX	. . .	. . .	XXX
$d = X_1 - X_2$	XXX	XXX	XXX	. . .	. . .	XXX

The mean $\bar{d}$ and standard deviation s_d of the sample of n differences are calculated with the usual formulas for a mean and standard deviation. We call the mean $\bar{d}$ instead of $\bar{x}$ merely to remind ourselves that we are dealing with *differences*.

$$(10.8) \qquad \bar{d} = \frac{\sum\limits_{i=1}^{n} d_i}{n} \qquad \text{(mean of } n \text{ differences)}$$

$$(10.9) \qquad s_d = \sqrt{\sum_{i=1}^{n} \frac{\left(d_i - \bar{d}\right)^2}{n-1}} \qquad \text{(Std. Dev. of } n \text{ differences)}$$

Since the population variance of d is unknown, we will do a paired t test using Student's t with $n-1$ degrees of freedom to compare the sample mean difference $\bar{d}$ with a hypothesized difference μ_d (usually $\mu_d = 0$). The test statistic is really a one-sample t test, just like those in Chapter 9.

$$(10.10) \qquad t_{calc} = \frac{\bar{d} - \mu_d}{\dfrac{s_d}{\sqrt{n}}} \qquad \text{(test statistic for } \textbf{paired samples)}$$

EXAMPLE

Repair Estimates

Repair

An insurance company's procedure in settling a claim under $10,000 for fire or water damage to a home owner is to require two estimates for cleanup and repair of structural damage before allowing the insured to proceed with the work. The insurance company compares estimates from two contractors who most frequently handle this type of work in this geographical area. Table 10.4 shows the 10 most recent claims for which damage estimates were provided by both contractors. At the .05 level of significance, is there a difference between the two contractors?

TABLE 10.4	Damage Repair Estimates ($) for 10 Claims	Repair	
	X_1	X_2	$d = X_1 - X_2$
Claim	Contractor A	Contractor B	Difference
1. Jones, C.	5,500	6,000	−500
2. Smith, R.	1,000	900	100
3. Xia, Y.	2,500	2,500	0
4. Gallo, J.	7,800	8,300	−500
5. Carson, R.	6,400	6,200	200
6. Petty, M.	8,800	9,400	−600
7. Tracy, L.	600	500	100
8. Barnes, J.	3,300	3,500	−200
9. Rodriguez, J.	4,500	5,200	−700
10. Van Dyke, P.	6,500	6,800	−300

$$\bar{d} = -240.00$$
$$s_d = 327.28$$
$$n = 10$$

Step 1: State the Hypotheses

Since we have no reason to be interested in directionality, we will choose a two-tailed test using these hypotheses:

$H_0: \mu_d = 0$

$H_1: \mu_d \neq 0$

Step 2: Specify the Decision Rule

Our test statistic will follow a Student's t distribution with d.f. $= n - 1 = 10 - 1 = 9$, so from Appendix D with $\alpha = .05$ the two-tail critical value is $t_{.025} = \pm 2.262$, as illustrated in

FIGURE 10.8   **Decision Rule for Two-Tailed Paired *t* Test at $\alpha = .05$**

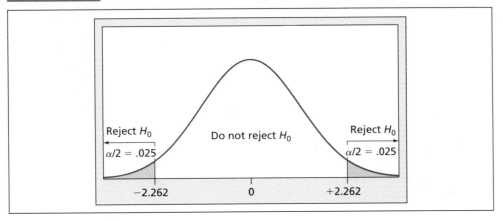

Figure 10.8. The decision rule is

Reject H_0 if $t_{calc} < -2.262$ or if $t_{calc} > +2.262$
Otherwise accept H_0

Step 3: Calculate the Test Statistic
The mean and standard deviation are calculated in the usual way, as shown in Table 10.4, so the test statistic is

$$t_{calc} = \frac{\bar{d} - \mu_d}{\frac{s_d}{\sqrt{n}}} = \frac{-240 - 0}{\left(\frac{327.28}{\sqrt{10}}\right)} = \frac{-240}{103.495} = -2.319$$

Step 4: Make the Decision
Since $t_{calc} = -2.319$ falls in the left-tail critical region (below -2.262), we reject the null hypothesis, and conclude that there is a significant difference between the two contractors. However, it is a *very* close decision.

Excel's Paired Difference Test

The calculations for our repair estimates example are easy in Excel, as illustrated in Figure 10.9. Excel gives you the option of choosing either a one-tailed or two-tailed test, and also shows the *p*-value. For a two-tailed test, the *p*-value is $p = .0456$, which would barely lead to rejection of the hypothesis of zero difference of means at $\alpha = .05$. The borderline *p*-value reinforces our conclusion that the decision is sensitive to our choice of α. MegaStat and MINITAB also provide a paired *t* test.

FIGURE 10.9

Results of Excel's Paired *t* Test at $\alpha = .05$

Data Analysis

Analysis Tools

- Histogram
- Moving Average
- Random Number Generation
- Rank and Percentile
- Regression
- Sampling
- t-Test: Paired Two Sample for Means
- t-Test: Two-Sample Assuming Equal Variances
- t-Test: Two-Sample Assuming Unequal Variances
- z-Test: Two Sample for Means

OK
Cancel
Help

t-Test: Paired Two Sample for Means

	Contractor A	Contractor B
Mean	4690	4930
Variance	7836555.556	9053444.444
Observations	10	10
Pearson Correlation	0.996247386	
Hypothesized Mean Difference	0	
df	9	
t Stat	-2.318963855	
P(T<=t) one-tail	0.022781515	
t Critical one-tail	1.833112923	
P(T<=t) two-tail	0.045563029	
t Critical two-tail	2.262157158	

Analogy to Confidence Interval

A two-tailed test for a zero difference is equivalent to asking whether the confidence interval for the true mean difference μ_d includes zero.

$$(10.11) \qquad \bar{d} \pm t \frac{s_d}{\sqrt{n}} \qquad \text{(confidence interval for difference of paired means)}$$

It depends on the confidence level:

90% confidence ($t = 1.833$): $-429.72 < \mu_d < -50.28$

95% confidence ($t = 2.262$): $-474.12 < \mu_d < -5.88$

99% confidence ($t = 3.250$): $-576.34 < \mu_d < +96.34$

As Figure 10.10 shows, the 99 percent confidence interval includes zero, but the 90 percent and 95 percent confidence intervals do not.

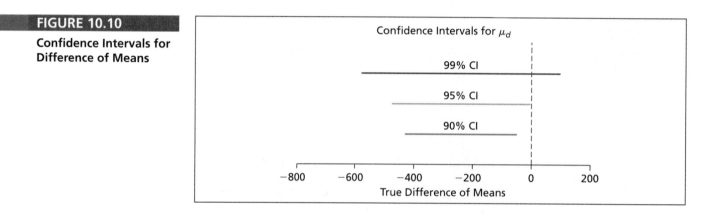

Why Not Treat Paired Data As Independent Samples?

When observations are matched pairs, the paired t test is more powerful, because it utilizes information that is ignored if we treat the samples separately. To show this, let's treat each data column as an **independent sample**. The summary statistics are:

$$\bar{x}_1 = 4{,}690.00 \qquad \bar{x}_2 = 4{,}930.00$$
$$s_1 = 2{,}799.38 \qquad s_2 = 3{,}008.89$$
$$n_1 = 10 \qquad n_2 = 10$$

Assuming equal variances, we get the results shown in Figure 10.11. The p-values (one tail or two-tail) are not even close to being significant at the usual α levels. By ignoring the dependence between the samples, we unnecessarily *sacrifice the power of the test*. Therefore, if the two data columns are paired, we should not treat them independently.

FIGURE 10.11

Excel's Independent Sample *t* Test

t-Test: Two-Sample Assuming Equal Variances		
	Contractor A	Contractor B
Mean	4690	4930
Variance	7836555.6	9053444.4
Observations	10	10
Pooled Variance	8445000	
Hypothesized Mean Difference	0	
df	18	
t Stat	-0.1846700	
P(T<=t) one-tail	0.4277763	
t Critical one-tail	1.7340636	
P(T<=t) two-tail	0.8555526	
t Critical two-tail	2.1009220	

10.8 A new cell phone battery is being considered as a replacement for the current one. Ten college student cell phone users are selected to try each battery in their usual mix of "talk" and "standby" and to record the number of hours until recharge was needed. (a) Do these results show that the new battery has significantly longer life at $\alpha = .05$? State your hypotheses and show all steps clearly. (b) Is the decision close? (c) Are you convinced?   **Battery**

	Bob	May	Deno	Sri	Pat	Alexis	Scott	Aretha	Jen	Ben
New battery	45	41	53	40	43	43	49	39	41	43
Old battery	52	34	40	38	38	44	34	45	28	33

10.9 (a) At $\alpha = .05$, does the following sample show that daughters are taller than their mothers? (b) Is the decision close? (c) Why might daughters tend to be taller than their mothers? Why might they not?   **Height**

Family	Daughter's Height (cm)	Mother's Height (cm)
1	167	172
2	166	162
3	176	157
4	171	159
5	165	157
6	181	177
7	173	174

10.10 An experimental surgical procedure is being studied as an alternative to the old method. Both methods are considered safe. Five surgeons perform the operation on two patients matched by age, sex, and other relevant factors, with the results shown. The time to complete the surgery (in minutes) is recorded. (a) At the 5 percent significance level, is the new way faster? State your hypotheses and show all steps clearly. (b) Is the decision close?   **Surgery**

	Surgeon 1	Surgeon 2	Surgeon 3	Surgeon 4	Surgeon 5
Old way	36	55	28	40	62
New way	29	42	30	32	56

10.11 Blockbuster is testing a new policy of waiving all late fees on DVD rentals using a sample of 10 randomly chosen customers. (a) At $\alpha = .10$, does the data show that the mean number of monthly rentals has increased? (b) Is the decision close? (c) Are you convinced?   **DVDRental**

Customer	No Late Fee	Late Fee
1	14	10
2	12	7
3	14	10
4	13	13
5	10	9
6	13	14
7	12	12
8	10	7
9	13	13
10	13	9

10.12 Below is a random sample of shoe sizes for 12 mothers and their daughters. (a) At $\alpha = .01$, does this sample show that women's shoe sizes have increased? State your hypotheses and show all steps clearly. (b) Is the decision close? (c) Are you convinced? (d) Why might shoe sizes change over time? (See *The Wall Street Journal*, July 17, 2004.)   **ShoeSize2**

	1	2	3	4	5	6	7	8	9	10	11	12
Daughter	8	8	7.5	8	9	9	8.5	9	9	8	7	8
Mother	7	7	7.5	8	8.5	8.5	7.5	7.5	6	8	7	7

10.13 A newly installed automatic gate system was being tested to see if the number of failures in 1,000 entry attempts was the same as the number of failures in 1,000 exit attempts. A random sample of eight delivery trucks was selected for data collection. Do these sample results show that there is a significant difference between entry and exit gate failures? Use $\alpha = .01$.   **Gates**

	Truck 1	Truck 2	Truck 3	Truck 4	Truck 5	Truck 6	Truck 7	Truck 8
Entry failures	43	45	53	56	61	51	48	44
Exit failures	48	51	60	58	58	45	55	50

Mini Case   10.3

Detroit's Weight-Loss Contest

Table 10.5 shows the results of a weight-loss contest sponsored by a local newspaper. Participants came from the East Side and West Side, and were encouraged to compete over a 1-month period. At $\alpha = .01$, was there a significant weight loss? The hypotheses are $H_0: \mu_d \geq 0$ and $H_1: \mu_d < 0$.

TABLE 10.5   **Results of Detroit's Weight-Loss Contest**   **WeightLoss**

Obs	Name	After	Before	Difference
1	Michael M.	202.5	217.0	−14.5
2	Tracy S.	178.0	188.0	−10.0
3	Gregg G.	210.0	225.0	−15.0
4	Boydea P.	157.0	168.0	−11.0
5	Donna I.	169.0	178.0	−9.0
6	Elizabeth C.	173.5	182.0	−8.5
7	Carole K.	163.5	174.5	−11.0
8	Candace G.	153.0	161.5	−8.5
9	Jo Anne M.	170.5	177.5	−7.0
10	Willis B.	336.0	358.5	−22.5
11	Marilyn S.	174.0	181.0	−7.0
12	Tim B.	197.5	210.0	−12.5

$$\bar{d} = -11.375$$
$$s_d = 4.37516$$

Source: *Detroit Free Press*, February 12, 2002, pp. 10H–11H.

The test statistic is over nine standard errors from zero, a highly significant difference:

$$t_{calc} = \frac{\bar{d} - 0}{\frac{s_d}{\sqrt{n}}} = \frac{-11.375 - 0}{\frac{4.37516}{\sqrt{12}}} = -9.006$$

Excel's p-value for the paired t test in Figure 10.12 is $p = .0000$ for a one-tailed test (a significant result at any α). Therefore, the mean weight loss of 11.375 pounds was *significant* at $\alpha = .01$. Moreover, to most people, a weight loss of 11.375 pounds would also be *important*.

FIGURE 10.12 **Excel Output for Paired *t* Test**

t-Test: Paired Two Sample for Means

	After	Before
Mean	190.375	201.75
Variance	2416.4148	2825.0227
Observations	12	12
Hypothesized Mean Diff	0	
df	11	
t Stat	−9.006	
P(T < t) one-tail	0.0000	
t Critical one-tail	2.718	

10.4
COMPARING TWO PROPORTIONS

The test for two proportions is the simplest and perhaps most commonly used two-sample test, because percents are ubiquitous. Is the president's approval rating greater, lower, or the same as last month? Is the proportion of satisfied Dell customers greater than Gateway's? Is the annual nursing turnover percentage at Mayo Clinic higher, lower, or the same as Johns Hopkins? To answer such questions, we would compare two sample proportions.

Testing for Zero Difference: $\pi_1 = \pi_2$

Let the true proportions in the two populations be denoted π_1 and π_2. To compare the two population proportions, the pairs of possible hypotheses are

Left-Tailed Test	*Two-Tailed Test*	*Right-Tailed Test*
$H_0: \pi_1 \geq \pi_2$	$H_0: \pi_1 = \pi_2$	$H_0: \pi_1 \leq \pi_2$
$H_1: \pi_1 < \pi_2$	$H_1: \pi_1 \neq \pi_2$	$H_1: \pi_1 > \pi_2$

Sample Proportions

The sample proportion p_1 is a point estimate of π_1, and the sample proportion p_2 is a point estimate of π_2. A "success" is any event of interest (not necessarily something desirable).

$$p_1 = \frac{x_1}{n_1} = \frac{\text{number of "successes" in sample 1}}{\text{number of items in sample 1}} \qquad \textbf{(10.12)}$$

$$p_2 = \frac{x_2}{n_2} = \frac{\text{number of "successes" in sample 2}}{\text{number of items in sample 2}} \qquad \textbf{(10.13)}$$

Pooled Proportion

If H_0 is true, there is no difference between π_1 and π_2, so the samples can logically be *pooled* or averaged into one "big" sample to estimate the common population proportion:

$$\bar{p} = \frac{x_1 + x_2}{n_1 + n_2} = \frac{\text{number of successes in combined samples}}{\text{combined sample size}} \qquad \textbf{(pooled proportion)} \quad \textbf{(10.14)}$$

Test Statistic

If the samples are large, the difference of proportions $p_1 - p_2$ may be assumed normally distributed. The *test statistic* is the difference of the sample proportions $p_1 - p_2$ divided by the standard error of the difference $p_1 - p_2$. The standard error is calculated by using the pooled proportion. If we are testing the hypothesis that $\pi_1 = \pi_2$, the test statistic is

$$z_{calc} = \frac{p_1 - p_2}{\sqrt{\frac{\bar{p}(1-\bar{p})}{n_1} + \frac{\bar{p}(1-\bar{p})}{n_2}}} \qquad \text{(test statistic for equality of proportions)} \quad \textbf{(10.15)}$$

If you find it easier for computation, the test statistic may also be written

$$(10.16) \quad z_{calc} = \frac{p_1 - p_2}{\sqrt{\bar{p}(1 - \bar{p})\left[\dfrac{1}{n_1} + \dfrac{1}{n_2}\right]}} \quad \text{(test statistic for equality of proportions)}$$

EXAMPLE

DES and Cancer

A study showed 118 instances of breast cancer among 3,033 mothers who used diethyl-stilbestrol (DES), an estrogen-like substance formerly used to prevent miscarriage, compared with 80 cases in 3,033 unexposed women comprising a control group (See Table 10.6). At the .01 level of significance, was the incidence of cancer greater in the DES users?

TABLE 10.6   **Cancer Study Results**

Statistic	DES Takers	Non-DES Takers
Number of cancers	$x_1 = 118$ cancers	$x_2 = 80$ cancers
Number of mothers	$n_1 = 3{,}033$ women	$n_2 = 3{,}033$ women
Cancer rate	$p_1 = \dfrac{118}{3{,}033} = .03891$	$p_2 = \dfrac{80}{3{,}033} = .02638$

Source: *Science News* 126, no. 22 (1984), p. 343.

Step 1: State the Hypotheses
Because it is suspected that DES increases the cancer risk, we will do a right-tailed test for equality of proportions. We test *only at the equality* because rejecting $H_0: \pi_1 = \pi_2$ would imply rejecting the entire class of hypotheses $H_0: \pi_1 \leq \pi_2$. We can state the pair of hypotheses in either of two equivalent ways:

$$H_0: \pi_1 = \pi_2 \quad \text{or} \quad H_0: \pi_1 - \pi_2 = 0$$

$$H_1: \pi_1 > \pi_2 \quad \text{or} \quad H_1: \pi_1 - \pi_2 > 0$$

Step 2: Specify the Decision Rule
At $\alpha = .01$ the right-tail critical value is $z_{.01} = 2.326$, which yields the decision rule

Reject H_0 if $z_{calc} > 2.326$

Otherwise do not reject H_0

The decision rule is illustrated in Figure 10.13. Since Excel uses cumulative left-tail areas, the right-tail critical value $z_{.01} = 2.326$ is obtained using =NORMSINV(.99).

FIGURE 10.13   **Right-Tailed Test for Two Proportions**

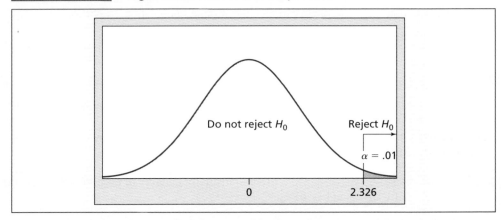

Step 3: Calculate the Test Statistic
The sample proportions indicate that DES-users have a higher incidence of breast cancer (.03891) than non-DES users (.02638). We assume that $\pi_1 = \pi_2$ and see if a contradiction stems from this assumption. Assuming that $\pi_1 = \pi_2$, we can pool the two samples to obtain a **pooled estimate** of the common proportion by dividing the combined number of breast cancer cases by the combined sample size:

$$\bar{p} = \frac{x_1 + x_2}{n_1 + n_2} = \frac{118 + 80}{3{,}033 + 3{,}033} = \frac{198}{6{,}066} = .03264, \text{ or } 3.26\%$$

Assuming normality (i.e., large samples) the test statistic is

$$z_{\text{calc}} = \frac{p_1 - p_2}{\sqrt{\bar{p}(1 - \bar{p})\left[\dfrac{1}{n_1} + \dfrac{1}{n_2}\right]}} = \frac{.03891 - .02638}{\sqrt{.03264(1 - .03264)\left[\dfrac{1}{3{,}033} + \dfrac{1}{3{,}033}\right]}} = 2.746$$

Step 4: Make the Decision
If H_0 were true, the test statistic should be near zero. Since the test statistic ($z_{\text{calc}} = 2.746$) exceeds the critical value ($z_{.01} = 2.326$) we reject the null hypothesis and conclude that $\pi_1 > \pi_2$. Since we are able to reject the hypothesis $\pi_1 = \pi_2$, we can also reject the entire class of hypotheses $\pi_1 \leq \pi_2$ at $\alpha = .01$, that is, DES users have a significantly higher cancer rate than do non-DES users.

Using the *p*-Value

We can find the right-tail area for $z_{\text{calc}} = 2.746$ by using the function =1-NORMSDIST(2.746) in Excel:

$$P(Z > 2.746) = 1 - .9970 = .0030 \qquad \text{(from Excel)}$$

This *p*-value of .003 is the level of significance which would allow us to reject H_0. The *p*-value says that if H_0 were true, a sample result as extreme as ours would happen by chance approximately 3 times in 1,000 decisions. If we don't have Excel, we can obtain the same result from Appendix C-2 even though it requires rounding the *z*-value slightly to two digits:

$$P(Z > 2.75) = 1 - .9970 = .0030 \qquad \text{(from Appendix C-2)}$$

Since the *p*-value (.0030) is less than the chosen level of significance ($\alpha = .01$) we would reject H_0 in a right-tailed test. The advantage of the *p*-value approach is that it gives more information and lets different researchers choose their own α values. For example, the FDA might have a different view of Type I error than a cancer patient. The *p*-value directly shows our chance of Type I error if we reject H_0. *A smaller* p-*value indicates a more significant difference*. Figure 10.14 illustrates the *p*-value.

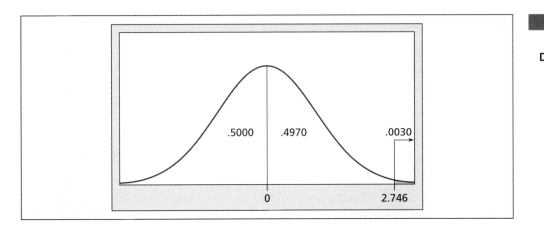

FIGURE 10.14

Right-Tail *p*-Value for DES and Non-DES Users

Checking Normality

We have assumed a normal distribution for the statistic $p_1 - p_2$. This assumption can be checked. For a test of two proportions, the criterion for normality is $n\pi \geq 10$ and $n(1 - \pi) \geq 10$ for *each* sample, using each sample proportion in place of π:

$$n_1 p_1 = (3{,}033)(118/3{,}033) = 118 \quad n_1(1 - p_1) = (3{,}033)(1 - 118/3{,}033) = 2{,}915$$
$$n_2 p_2 = (3{,}033)(80/3{,}033) = 80 \quad n_2(1 - p_2) = (3{,}033)(1 - 80/3{,}033) = 2{,}953$$

The normality requirement is comfortably fulfilled in this case. Ideally, these numbers should exceed 10 by a comfortable margin, as they do in this example. Since the samples are pooled, this guarantees that the pooled proportion $(n_1 + n_2)\bar{p} \geq 10$. Note that when using sample data, the sample size rule of thumb is equivalent to requiring that each sample contains at least 10 "successes" and at least 10 "failures."

If sample sizes do not justify the normality assumption, each sample should be treated as a binomial experiment. Unless you have good computational software, this may not be worthwhile. If the samples are small, the test is likely to have low power.

Must Sample Sizes Be Equal?   No. Although sample sizes happen to be equal in our example, balanced sample sizes are not necessary. Unequal sample sizes are common, and the formulas still apply.

Using Software for Calculations

Given the tedium of the calculations, it is desirable to use software. MegaStat gives you the option of entering sample proportions or the fractions. MINITAB gives you the option of nonpooled proportions, which we will discuss shortly. Figure 10.15 illustrates their data-entry screens using the DES data.

FIGURE 10.15

Two Proportion Tests Using MegaStat and MINITAB

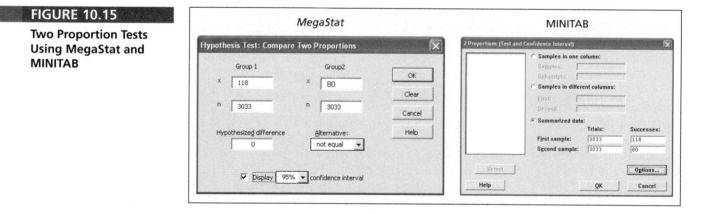

Analogy to Confidence Intervals

Especially for two-tailed tests, the analogy between confidence intervals and two sample hypothesis tests is very strong. We create the confidence interval for $\pi_1 - \pi_2$ *without pooling the samples*. Since the samples are treated separately, we add the variances of the sample proportions to get the variance of $p_1 - p_2$ and take the square root to obtain the *estimated standard error* of $p_1 - p_2$. The confidence interval is

$$(10.17) \quad (p_1 - p_2) \pm z \sqrt{\frac{p_1(1 - p_1)}{n_1} + \frac{p_2(1 - p_2)}{n_2}} \qquad \text{(confidence interval for } \pi_1 - \pi_2\text{)}$$

Plugging in $p_1 = 118/3{,}033$ and $p_2 = 80/3{,}033$ we obtain confidence intervals for $\pi_1 - \pi_2$, shown below (calculations not shown).

Confidence Level	Confidence Interval for $\pi_1 - \pi_2$
90% ($z = \pm 1.645$)	$.00503 < \pi_1 - \pi_2 < .02003$
95% ($z = \pm 1.960$)	$.00359 < \pi_1 - \pi_2 < .02147$
99% ($z = \pm 2.576$)	$.00078 < \pi_1 - \pi_2 < .02428$

All three confidence intervals for the difference of proportions fail to include zero, suggesting rejection of $H_0: \pi_1 - \pi_2 = 0$. These confidence intervals are more vivid if displayed graphically, as in Figure 10.16. Although none of the confidence intervals includes zero, the 99 percent confidence interval *almost* does, so our rejection of $H_0: \pi_1 - \pi_2 = 0$ would be a close call for 99 percent confidence and a two-tailed test.

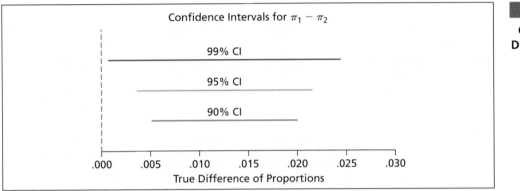

FIGURE 10.16

Confidence Intervals for Difference of Proportions

To test for equal population proportions, you might wonder why we don't just construct a confidence interval for π_1 (as we did in Chapter 8) and then do the same for π_2. If the intervals overlap, would that not suggest that the population proportions are the same? Although intuitively appealing, researchers have found that this method fails to maintain the desired Type I error. So it is better to use formula 10.17 to construct a single confidence interval for the difference $\pi_1 - \pi_2$.*

Mini Case   10.4

How Does Noodles & Company Provide Value to Customers?

Value perception is an important concept for all companies, but is especially relevant for consumer-oriented industries such as retail and restaurants. Most retailers and restaurant concepts periodically make price increases to reflect changes in inflationary items such as cost of goods and labor costs. In 2006, however, Noodles & Company took the opposite approach when it evaluated its value perception through its consumers.

Through rigorous statistical analysis Noodles recognized that a significant percentage of current customers would increase their frequency of visits if the menu items were priced slightly lower. The company evaluated the trade-offs that a price decrease would represent and determined that they would actually be able to increase revenue by reducing price. Despite not advertising this price decrease, the company did in fact see an increase in frequency of visits resulting from the change. To measure the impact, the company statistically evaluated both the increase in frequency as well as customer evaluations of Noodles & Company's value perception. Within a few months, the statistical analysis showed that not only had customer frequency increased by 2–3%, but also that the improved value perception led to an increase in average party size of 2%. Ultimately, the price decrease of roughly 2% led to a total revenue increase of 4–5%.

*See end of chapter reference by Payton, Greenstone, and Schenker (2003).

Hint: Show all formulas and calculations, but use the calculator in *LearningStats* Unit 10 to check your work.

connect

10.14 Find the sample proportions and test statistic for equal proportions. Is the decision close? Find the *p*-value.
  a. Dissatisfied workers in two companies: $x_1 = 40$, $n_1 = 100$, $x_2 = 30$, $n_2 = 100$, $\alpha = .05$, two-tailed test.
  b. Rooms rented at least a week in advance at two hotels: $x_1 = 24$, $n_1 = 200$, $x_2 = 12$, $n_2 = 50$, $\alpha = .01$, left-tailed test.
  c. Home equity loan default rates in two banks: $x_1 = 36$, $n_1 = 480$, $x_2 = 26$, $n_2 = 520$, $\alpha = .05$, right-tailed test.

10.15 Find the test statistic and do the two-sample test for equality of proportions. Is the decision close?
  a. Repeat buyers at two car dealerships: $p_1 = .30$, $n_1 = 50$, $p_2 = .54$, $n_2 = 50$, $\alpha = .01$, left-tailed test.
  b. Honor roll students in two sororities: $p_1 = .45$, $n_1 = 80$, $p_2 = .25$, $n_2 = 48$, $\alpha = .10$, two-tailed test.
  c. First-time Hawaii visitors at two hotels: $p_1 = .20$, $n_1 = 80$, $p_2 = .32$, $n_2 = 75$, $\alpha = .05$, left-tailed test.

10.16 During the period 1990–1998 there were 46 Atlantic hurricanes, of which 19 struck the United States. During the period 1999–2006 there were 70 hurricanes, of which 45 struck the United States. (a) Does this evidence convince you that the percentage of hurricanes that strike the United States is increasing, at $\alpha = .01$? (b) Can normality be assumed? (Data are from *The New York Times,* August 27, 2006, p. 2WK.)

10.17 In 1999, a sample of 200 in-store shoppers showed that 42 paid by debit card. In 2004, a sample of the same size showed that 62 paid by debit card. (a) Formulate appropriate hypotheses to test whether the percentage of debit card shoppers increased. (b) Carry out the test at $\alpha = .01$. (c) Find the *p*-value. (d) Test whether normality may be assumed.

10.18 A survey of 100 mayonnaise purchasers showed that 65 were loyal to one brand. For 100 bath soap purchasers, only 53 were loyal to one brand. (a) Perform a two-tailed test comparing the proportion of brand-loyal customers at $\alpha = .05$. (b) Form a confidence interval for the difference of proportions, without pooling the samples. Does it include zero?

10.19 A 20-minute consumer survey mailed to 500 adults aged 25–34 included a $5 Starbucks gift certificate. The same survey was mailed to 500 adults aged 25–34 without the gift certificate. There were 65 responses from the first group and 45 from the second group. (a) Perform a two-tailed test comparing the response rates (proportions) at $\alpha = .05$. (b) Form a confidence interval for the difference of proportions, without pooling the samples. Does it include zero?

10.20 Is the water on your airline flight safe to drink? It is not feasible to analyze the water on every flight, so sampling is necessary. In August and September 2004, the Environmental Protection Agency (EPA) found bacterial contamination in water samples from the lavatories and galley water taps on 20 of 158 randomly selected U.S. flights. Alarmed by the data, the EPA ordered sanitation improvements, and then tested water samples again in November and December 2004. In the second sample, bacterial contamination was found in 29 of 169 randomly sampled flights. (a) Use a tailed test at $\alpha = .05$ to check whether the percent of all flights with contaminated water was lower in the sample. (b) Find the *p*-value. (c) Discuss the question of significance versus importance in this specific application. (d) Test whether normality may be assumed. (Data are from *The Wall Street Journal,* November 10, 2004, and January 20, 2005.)

10.21 When tested for compliance with Sarbanes-Oxley requirements for financial records and fraud protection, 14 of 180 publicly traded business services companies failed, compared with 7 of 67 computer hardware, software and telecommunications companies. (a) Is this a statistically significant difference at $\alpha = .05$? (b) Can normality be assumed? (Data are from *The New York Times,* April 27, 2005, p. BU5.)

Testing for Nonzero Difference (Optional)

Testing for equality of π_1 and π_2 is a special case of testing for a specified difference D_0 between the two proportions:

Left-Tailed Test	*Two-Tailed Test*	*Right-Tailed Test*
$H_0: \pi_1 - \pi_2 \geq D_0$	$H_0: \pi_1 - \pi_2 = D_0$	$H_0: \pi_1 - \pi_2 \leq D_0$
$H_1: \pi_1 - \pi_2 < D_0$	$H_1: \pi_1 - \pi_2 \neq D_0$	$H_1: \pi_1 - \pi_2 > D_0$

We have shown how to test for $D_0 = 0$, that is, $\pi_1 = \pi_2$. If the hypothesized difference D_0 is nonzero, we do not pool the sample proportions, but instead use the test statistic shown in formula 10.18.

$$z_{calc} = \frac{p_1 - p_2 - D_0}{\sqrt{\dfrac{p_1(1 - p_1)}{n_1} + \dfrac{p_2(1 - p_2)}{n_2}}} \qquad \text{(test statistic for nonzero difference } D_0) \qquad \textbf{(10.18)}$$

A sample of 111 magazine advertisements in *Good Housekeeping* showed 70 that listed a Web site. In *Fortune,* a sample of 145 advertisements showed 131 that listed a Web site. At $\alpha = .025$, does the *Fortune* proportion differ from the *Good Housekeeping* proportion by at least 20 percent? Table 10.7 shows the data.

EXAMPLE

Magazine Ads

TABLE 10.7	Magazine Ads with Web Sites	
Statistic	**Fortune**	**Good Housekeeping**
Number with Web sites	$x_1 = 131$ with Web site	$x_2 = 70$ with Web site
Number of ads examined	$n_1 = 145$ ads	$n_2 = 111$ ads
Proportion	$p_1 = \dfrac{131}{145} = .90345$	$p_2 = \dfrac{70}{111} = .63063$

Source: Project by MBA students Frank George, Karen Orso, and Lincy Zachariah.

Test Statistic

We will do a right-tailed test for $D_0 = .20$. The hypotheses are

$H_0: \pi_1 - \pi_2 \leq .20$

$H_1: \pi_1 - \pi_2 > .20$

The test statistic is

$$z_{calc} = \frac{p_1 - p_2 - D_0}{\sqrt{\dfrac{p_1(1 - p_1)}{n_1} + \dfrac{p_2(1 - p_2)}{n_2}}}$$

$$= \frac{.90345 - .63063 - .20}{\sqrt{\dfrac{.90345(1 - .90345)}{145} + \dfrac{.63063(1 - .63063)}{111}}} = 1.401$$

At $\alpha = .025$ the right-tail critical value is $z_{.025} = 1.960$, so the difference of proportions is insufficient to reject the hypothesis that the difference is .20 or less. The decision rule is illustrated in Figure 10.17.

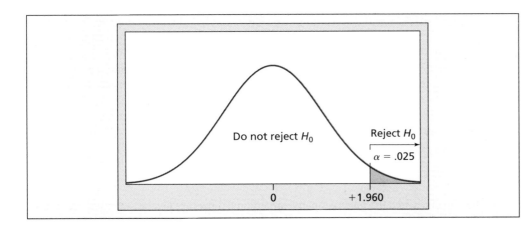

FIGURE 10.17

Right-Tailed Test for Magazine Ads at $\alpha = .025$

FIGURE 10.18

p-Value for Magazine
Proportions Differing by
$D_0 = .20$

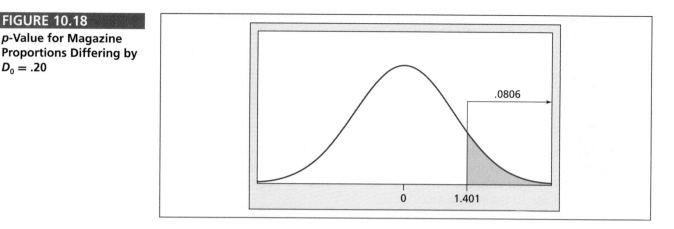

.0806

0   1.401

Calculating the *p*-Value

Using the *p*-value approach, we would insert the test statistic $z_{calc} = 1.401$ into Excel's cumulative normal =1-NORMSDIST(1.401) to obtain a right-tail area of .0806 as shown in Figure 10.18. Since the *p*-value >.025, we would not reject H_0. The conclusion is that the difference in proportions is not greater than .20.

SECTION EXERCISES

connect

Note: Use *LearningStats,* MINITAB, or MegaStat for calculations.

10.22 In 1999, a sample of 200 in-store shoppers showed that 42 paid by debit card. In 2004, a sample of the same size showed that 62 paid by debit card. (a) Formulate appropriate hypotheses to test whether the percentage of debit card shoppers increased by at least 5 percent, using $\alpha = .10$. (b) Find the *p*-value.

10.23 From a telephone log, an executive finds that 36 of 128 incoming telephone calls last week lasted at least 5 minutes. She vows to make an effort to reduce the length of time spent on calls. The phone log for the next week shows that 14 of 96 incoming calls lasted at least 5 minutes. (a) At $\alpha = .05$, has the proportion of 5-minute phone calls declined by at least 10 percent? (b) Find the *p*-value.

10.24 A 30-minute consumer survey mailed to 500 adults aged 25–34 included a $10 gift certificate to Borders. The same survey was mailed to 500 adults aged 25–34 without the gift certificate. There were 185 responses from the first group and 45 from the second group. (a) At $\alpha = .025$, did the gift certificate increase the response rate by at least 20 percent? (b) Find the *p*-value.

Mini Case   10.5

Automated Parking Lot Entry/Exit Gate System

Large universities have many different parking lots. Delivery trucks travel between various buildings all day long to deliver food, mail, and other items. Automated entry/exit gates make travel time much faster for the trucks and cars entering and exiting the different parking lots because the drivers do not have to stop to activate the gate manually. The gate is electronically activated as the truck or car approaches the parking lot.

One large university with two campuses recently negotiated with a company to install a new automated system. One requirement of the contract stated that the proportion of failed gate activations on one campus would be no different from the proportion of failed gate activations on the second campus. (A failed activation was one in which the driver had to manually activate the gate.) The university facilities operations manager designed and conducted a test to establish whether the gate company had violated this requirement of the contract. The university could renegotiate the contract if there was significant evidence showing that the two proportions were different.

The test was set up as a two-tailed test and the hypotheses tested were

$H_0: \pi_1 = \pi_2$

$H_1: \pi_1 \neq \pi_2$

Both the university and the gate company agreed on a 5 percent level of significance. Random samples from each campus were collected. The data are shown in Table 10.8.

TABLE 10.8	Proportion of Failed Gate Activations	
Statistic	**Campus 1**	**Campus 2**
Number of failed activations	$x_1 = 52$	$x_2 = 63$
Sample size (number of entry/exit attempts)	$n_1 = 1{,}000$	$n_2 = 1{,}000$
Proportion	$p_1 = \dfrac{52}{1{,}000} = .052$	$p_2 = \dfrac{63}{1{,}000} = .063$

The pooled proportion is

$$\bar{p} = \frac{x_1 + x_2}{n_1 + n_2} = \frac{52 + 63}{1{,}000 + 1{,}000} = \frac{115}{2{,}000} = .0575$$

The test statistic is

$$z_{\text{calc}} = \frac{p_1 - p_2}{\sqrt{\bar{p}(1-\bar{p})\left[\dfrac{1}{n_1} + \dfrac{1}{n_2}\right]}} = \frac{.052 - .063}{\sqrt{.0575(1 - .0575)\left[\dfrac{1}{1{,}000} + \dfrac{1}{1{,}000}\right]}} = -1.057$$

Using the 5 percent level of significance the critical value is $z_{.025} = 1.96$ so it is clear that there is no significant difference between these two proportions. This conclusion is reinforced by Excel's cumulative normal function =NORMSDIST(−1.057) which gives the area to the left of −1.057 as .1453. Because this is a two-tailed test the *p*-value is .2906.

Was it reasonable to assume normality of the test statistic? Yes, the criterion was met.

$$n_1 p_1 = 1{,}000(52/1{,}000) = 52 \qquad n_1(1 - p_1) = 1{,}000(1 - 52/1{,}000) = 948$$
$$n_2 p_2 = 1{,}000(63/1{,}000) = 63 \qquad n_2(1 - p_2) = 1{,}000(1 - 63/1{,}000) = 937$$

Based on this sample, the university had no evidence to refute the gate company's claim that the failed activation proportions were the same for each campus.

Source: This case was based on a real contract negotiation between a large western university and a private company. The contract was still being negotiated as of the publication of this text.

The business statistician knows that comparing the *variances* may be as important as comparing the *means* of two populations. In manufacturing, smaller variation around the mean would indicate a more reliable product. In finance, smaller variation around the mean would indicate less volatility in asset returns. In services, smaller variation around the mean would indicate more consistency in customer treatment. For example, is the *variance* in Ford Mustang assembly times the same this month as last month? Is the *variability* in customer waiting times the same at two Tim Horton's franchises? Is the *variation* the same for customer concession purchases at a movie theater on Friday and Saturday nights?

10.5
COMPARING TWO VARIANCES

Chapter 10

Format of Hypotheses ●

We may test the null hypothesis against a left-tailed, two-tailed, or right-tailed alternative:

Left-Tailed Test	*Two-Tailed Test*	*Right-Tailed Test*
$H_0: \sigma_1^2 \geq \sigma_2^2$	$H_0: \sigma_1^2 = \sigma_2^2$	$H_0: \sigma_1^2 \leq \sigma_2^2$
$H_1: \sigma_1^2 < \sigma_2^2$	$H_1: \sigma_1^2 \neq \sigma_2^2$	$H_1: \sigma_1^2 > \sigma_2^2$

An equivalent way to state these hypotheses is to look at the *ratio* of the two variances. A ratio near 1 would indicate equal variances.

Left-Tailed Test	*Two-Tailed Test*	*Right-Tailed Test*
$H_0: \dfrac{\sigma_1^2}{\sigma_2^2} \geq 1$	$H_0: \dfrac{\sigma_1^2}{\sigma_2^2} = 1$	$H_0: \dfrac{\sigma_1^2}{\sigma_2^2} \leq 1$
$H_1: \dfrac{\sigma_1^2}{\sigma_2^2} < 1$	$H_1: \dfrac{\sigma_1^2}{\sigma_2^2} \neq 1$	$H_1: \dfrac{\sigma_1^2}{\sigma_2^2} > 1$

The *F* Test

In a left-tailed or right-tailed test, we actually test only at the equality, with the understanding that rejection of H_0 would imply rejecting values more extreme. The test statistic is the ratio of the sample variances. Assuming the populations are normal, the test statistic follows the **F distribution**, named for Ronald A. Fisher (1890–1962), one of the most famous statisticians of all time.

(10.19)

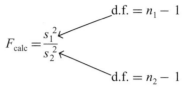

$$F_{calc} = \frac{s_1^2}{s_2^2}$$

d.f. $= n_1 - 1$

d.f. $= n_2 - 1$

If the null hypothesis of equal variances is true, this ratio should be near 1:

$$F_{calc} \approx 1 \qquad \text{(if } H_0 \text{ is true)}$$

If the test statistic F is much less than 1 or much greater than 1, we would reject the hypothesis of equal population variances. The numerator s_1^2 has degrees of freedom $\nu_1 = n_1 - 1$, while the denominator s_2^2 has degrees of freedom $\nu_2 = n_2 - 1$. The F distribution is skewed. Its mean is always greater than 1 and its mode (the "peak" of the distribution) is always less than 1, but both the mean and mode tend to be near 1 for large samples. F cannot be negative, since s_1^2 and s_2^2 cannot be negative. (See *LearningStats* Unit 10 for details.)

Critical Values

Critical values for the **F test** are denoted F_L (left tail) and F_R (right tail). The form of the two-tailed F test is shown in Figure 10.19. Notice that the rejection regions are asymmetric. A right-tail critical value F_R may be found from Appendix F using ν_1 and ν_2 degrees of freedom. It is written

(10.20) $\qquad\qquad F_R = F_{\nu_1, \nu_2} \qquad$ (right-tail critical F)

To obtain a left-tail critical value F_L we reverse the numerator and denominator degrees of freedom, find the critical value from Appendix F, and take its reciprocal:

(10.21) $\qquad F_L = \dfrac{1}{F_{\nu_2, \nu_1}} \qquad$ (left-tail critical F with switched ν_1 and ν_2)

Excel will give F_R using the function =FINV($\alpha/2$, ν_1, ν_2) or F_L using =FINV($1 - \alpha/2$, ν_1, ν_2).

FIGURE 10.19

Critical Values for *F* Test for Variances

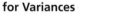

Reject H_0

$\alpha/2$

Do not reject H_0

Reject H_0

$\alpha/2$

0   F_L 1.00 F_R

Illustration: Collision Damage

An experimental bumper was designed to reduce damage in low-speed collisions. This bumper was installed on an experimental group of vans in a large fleet, but not on a control group. At the end of a trial period, accident data showed 12 repair incidents (a "repair incident" is a repair invoice) for the experimental vehicles and 9 repair incidents for the control group vehicles. Table 10.9 shows the dollar cost of the repair incidents.

Source: Unpublished study by
Floyd G. Willoughby and
Thomas W. Lauer, Oakland University.

TABLE 10.9

Repair Cost ($) for Accident Damage 🐝 Damage

Experimental Vehicles	Control Vehicles
1,973	1,185
403	885
509	2,955
2,103	815
1,153	2,852
292	1,217
1,916	1,762
1,602	2,592
1,559	1,632
547	
801	
359	

$\bar{x}_1 = \$1,101.42$ $\bar{x}_2 = \$1,766.11$
$s_1 = \$696.20$ $s_2 = \$837.62$
$n_1 = 12$ incidents $n_2 = 9$ incidents

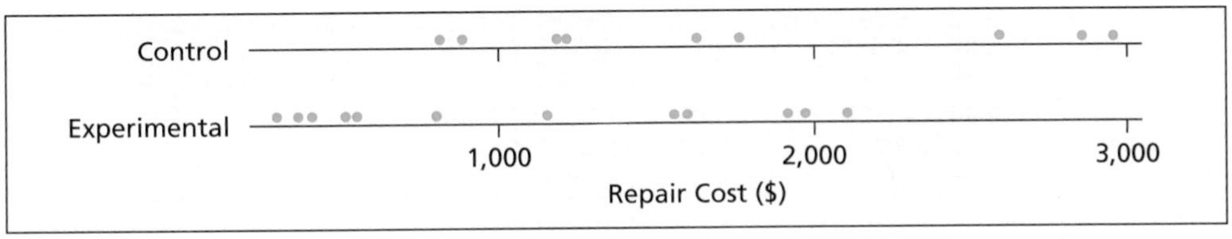

FIGURE 10.20

Dot Plots for Collision Repair Costs 🐝 Damage

The same data set could be used to compare either the means or the variances. A dot plot of the two samples, shown in Figure 10.20, suggests that the new bumper may have reduced the *mean* damage. However, the firm was also interested in whether the *variance* in damage had changed. The null hypothesis is that the variances are the same for the control group and the experimental group. We can use the F test to test the hypothesis of equal variances.

Comparison of Variances: Two-Tailed Test

Do the sample variances support the idea of equal variances in the population? We will perform a two-tailed test.

Step 1: State the Hypotheses For a two-tailed test for equality of variances, the hypotheses are

$H_0: \sigma_1^2 = \sigma_2^2$ or $H_0: \sigma_1^2 / \sigma_2^2 = 1$
$H_1: \sigma_1^2 \neq \sigma_2^2$ $H_1: \sigma_1^2 / \sigma_2^2 \neq 1$

Step 2: Specify the Decision Rule Degrees of freedom for the F test are

Numerator: $v_1 = n_1 - 1 = 12 - 1 = 11$
Denominator: $v_2 = n_2 - 1 = 9 - 1 = 8$

For a two-tailed test, we split the α risk and put $\alpha/2$ in each tail. For $\alpha = .05$ we use Appendix F with $\alpha/2 = .025$. To avoid interpolating, we use the next lower degrees of freedom when the required entry is not found in Appendix F. This conservative practice will not increase the probability of Type I error. For example, since $F_{11,8}$ is not in the table we use $F_{10,8}$, as shown in Figure 10.21.

$$F_R = F_{v_1, v_2} = F_{11,8} \approx F_{10,8} = 4.30 \quad \text{(right-tail critical value)}$$

Alternatively, we could use Excel to get F_R=FINV(.025,11,8)=4.243 and F_L=FINV(.975,11,8)=0.273. To find the left-tail critical value we reverse the numerator and denominator degrees of freedom, find the critical value from Appendix F, and take its reciprocal, as shown in Figure 10.22. (Excel's function=FINV returns a *right-tail* area.)

$$F_L = \frac{1}{F_{v_2, v_1}} = \frac{1}{F_{8,11}} = \frac{1}{3.66} = 0.273 \quad \text{(left-tail critical value)}$$

FIGURE 10.21

Critical Value for Right-Tail F_R for $\alpha/2 = .025$

CRITICAL VALUES OF $F_{.025}$

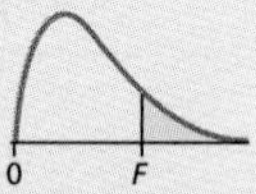

This table shows the 2.5 percent right-tail critical values of F for the stated degrees of freedom (ν).

Denominator Degrees of Freedom (ν_2)	Numerator Degrees of Freedom (ν_1)										
	1	2	3	4	5	6	7	8	9	10	12
1	647.8	799.5	864.2	899.6	921.8	937.1	948.2	956.6	963.3	968.6	976.7
2	38.51	39.00	39.17	39.25	39.30	39.33	39.36	39.37	39.39	39.40	39.41
3	17.44	16.04	15.44	15.10	14.88	14.73	14.62	14.54	14.47	14.42	14.34
4	12.22	10.65	9.98	9.60	9.36	9.20	9.07	8.98	8.90	8.84	8.75
5	10.01	8.43	7.76	7.39	7.15	6.98	6.85	6.76	6.68	6.62	6.52
6	8.81	7.26	6.60	6.23	5.99	5.82	5.70	5.60	5.52	5.46	5.37
7	8.07	6.54	5.89	5.52	5.29	5.12	4.99	4.90	4.82	4.76	4.67
8	7.57	6.06	5.42	5.05	4.82	4.65	4.53	4.43	4.36	4.30	4.20
9	7.21	5.71	5.08	4.72	4.48	4.32	4.20	4.10	4.03	3.96	3.87
10	6.94	5.46	4.83	4.47	4.24	4.07	3.95	3.85	3.78	3.72	3.62
11	6.72	5.26	4.63	4.28	4.04	3.88	3.76	3.66	3.59	3.53	3.43
12	6.55	5.10	4.47	4.12	3.89	3.73	3.61	3.51	3.44	3.37	3.28
13	6.41	4.97	4.35	4.00	3.77	3.60	3.48	3.39	3.31	3.25	3.15
14	6.30	4.86	4.24	3.89	3.66	3.50	3.38	3.29	3.21	3.15	3.05
15	6.20	4.77	4.15	3.80	3.58	3.41	3.29	3.20	3.12	3.06	2.96

FIGURE 10.22

Critical Value for Left-Tail F_L for $\alpha/2 = .025$

CRITICAL VALUES OF $F_{.025}$

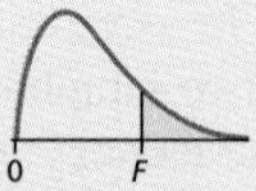

This table shows the 2.5 percent right-tail critical values of F for the stated degrees of freedom (ν).

Denominator Degrees of Freedom (ν_2)	Numerator Degrees of Freedom (ν_1)										
	1	2	3	4	5	6	7	8	9	10	12
1	647.8	799.5	864.2	899.6	921.8	937.1	948.2	956.6	963.3	968.6	976.7
2	38.51	39.00	39.17	39.25	39.30	39.33	39.36	39.37	39.39	39.40	39.41
3	17.44	16.04	15.44	15.10	14.88	14.73	14.62	14.54	14.47	14.42	14.34
4	12.22	10.65	9.98	9.60	9.36	9.20	9.07	8.98	8.90	8.84	8.75
5	10.01	8.43	7.76	7.39	7.15	6.98	6.85	6.76	6.68	6.62	6.52
6	8.81	7.26	6.60	6.23	5.99	5.82	5.70	5.60	5.52	5.46	5.37
7	8.07	6.54	5.89	5.52	5.29	5.12	4.99	4.90	4.82	4.76	4.67
8	7.57	6.06	5.42	5.05	4.82	4.65	4.53	4.43	4.36	4.30	4.20
9	7.21	5.71	5.08	4.72	4.48	4.32	4.20	4.10	4.03	3.96	3.87
10	6.94	5.46	4.83	4.47	4.24	4.07	3.95	3.85	3.78	3.72	3.62
11	6.72	5.26	4.63	4.28	4.04	3.88	3.76	3.66	3.59	3.53	3.43
12	6.55	5.10	4.47	4.12	3.89	3.73	3.61	3.51	3.44	3.37	3.28
13	6.41	4.97	4.35	4.00	3.77	3.60	3.48	3.39	3.31	3.25	3.15
14	6.30	4.86	4.24	3.89	3.66	3.50	3.38	3.29	3.21	3.15	3.05
15	6.20	4.77	4.15	3.80	3.58	3.41	3.29	3.20	3.12	3.06	2.96

As shown in Figure 10.23, the two-tailed decision rule is

Reject H_0 if $F_{calc} < 0.273$ or if $F_{calc} > 4.30$

Otherwise do not reject H_0

Step 3: Calculate the Test Statistic   The test statistic is

$$F_{calc} = \frac{s_1^2}{s_2^2} = \frac{(696.20)^2}{(837.62)^2} = 0.691$$

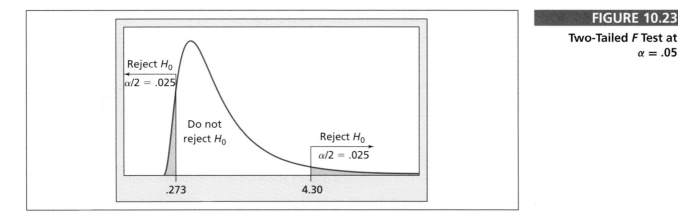

FIGURE 10.23

Two-Tailed *F* Test at
α = .05

Step 4: Make the Decision Since $F_{calc} = 0.691$, we cannot reject the hypothesis of equal variances in a two-tailed test at $\alpha = .05$. In other words, the ratio of the sample variances does not differ significantly from 1. Because Excel's function = FDIST gives a *right-tail* area, the function you use for the *p*-value will depend on the value of F_{calc}:

If $F_{calc} > 1$ Two-tailed *p*-value is =2*FDIST(F_{calc}, df1, df2)

If $F_{calc} < 1$ Two-tailed *p*-value is =2*FDIST(1/F_{calc}, df2, df1)

For the bumper data, $F_{calc} = 0.691$ so Excel's two-tailed *p*-value is =2*FDIST((1/0.691),8,11) = .5575.

Folded *F* Test

We can make the two-tailed test for equal variances into a right-tailed test, so it is easier to look up the critical values in Appendix F. This method requires that we put the *larger observed variance* in the numerator, and then look up the critical value for $\alpha/2$ instead of the chosen α. The test statistic for the folded *F* test is.

$$F_{calc} = \frac{s^2_{larger}}{s^2_{smaller}} \tag{10.22}$$

The larger variance goes in the numerator and the smaller variance in the denominator. *"Larger" refers to the variance (not to the sample size)*. But the hypotheses are the same as for a two-tailed test:

$H_0: \sigma_1^2 = \sigma_2^2$

$H_1: \sigma_1^2 \neq \sigma_2^2$

For the bumper data, the second sample variance ($s_2^2 = 837.62$) is larger than the first sample variance ($s_1^2 = 696.20$) so the folded *F* test statistic is

$$F_{calc} = \frac{s^2_{larger}}{s^2_{smaller}} = \frac{s_2^2}{s_1^2} = \frac{(837.62)^2}{(696.20)^2} = 1.448$$

We must be careful that the degrees of freedom match the variances in the modified *F* statistic. In this case, the second sample variance is larger (it goes in the numerator) so we must reverse the degrees of freedom:

Numerator: $n_2 - 1 = 9 - 1 = 8$

Denominator: $n_1 - 1 = 12 - 1 = 11$

Now we look up the critical value for $F_{8,\,11}$ in Appendix F using $\alpha/2 = .05/2 = .025$:

$$F_{.025} = 3.66$$

Since the test statistic $F_{calc} = 1.448$ does not exceed the critical value $F_{.025} = 3.66$, we cannot reject the hypothesis of equal variances. This is the same conclusion that we reached in the two-tailed test. Since $F_{calc} > 1$, Excel's two-tailed *p*-value is =2*FDIST(1.448,8,11) = .5569 which is the same as in the previous result except for rounding. Anytime you want a two-tailed *F* test, you may use the folded *F* test if you think it is easier.

Comparison of Variances: One-Tailed Test   ————————•

In this case, the firm was interested in knowing whether the new bumper had *reduced* the variance in collision damage cost, so the consultant was asked to do a left-tailed test.

Step 1: State the Hypotheses   The hypotheses for a left-tailed test are

$$H_0: \sigma_1^2 \geq \sigma_2^2$$
$$H_1: \sigma_1^2 < \sigma_2^2$$

Step 2: Specify the Decision Rule   Degrees of freedom for the F test are the same as for a two-tailed test (the hypothesis doesn't affect the degrees of freedom):

Numerator: $\nu_1 = n_1 - 1 = 12 - 1 = 11$

Denominator: $\nu_2 = n_2 - 1 = 9 - 1 = 8$

However, now the entire $\alpha = .05$ goes in the left tail. We reverse the degrees of freedom and find the left-tail critical value from Appendix F as the reciprocal of the table value, as illustrated in Figures 10.24 and 10.25. Notice that the asymmetry of the F distribution causes the left-tail area to be compressed in the horizontal direction.

$$F_L = \frac{1}{F_{\nu_2,\nu_1}} = \frac{1}{F_{8,11}} = \frac{1}{2.95} = 0.339 \qquad \text{(left-tail critical value)}$$

The decision rule is

Reject H_0 if $F_{\text{calc}} < 0.339$

Otherwise do not reject H_0

Step 3: Calculate the Test Statistic   The test statistic is the same as for a two-tailed test (the hypothesis doesn't affect the test statistic):

$$F_{\text{calc}} = \frac{s_1^2}{s_2^2} = \frac{(696.20)^2}{(837.62)^2} = 0.691$$

FIGURE 10.24

Right-Tail F_R for $\alpha = .05$

CRITICAL VALUES OF $F_{.05}$

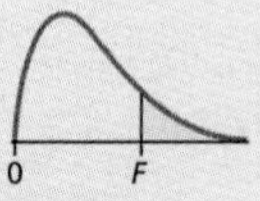

This table shows the 5 percent right-tail critical values of F for the stated degrees of freedom (ν).

Denominator Degrees of Freedom (ν_2)	Numerator Degrees of Freedom (ν_1)										
	1	2	3	4	5	6	7	8	9	10	12
1	161.4	199.5	215.7	224.6	230.2	234.0	236.8	238.9	240.5	241.9	243.9
2	18.51	19.00	19.16	19.25	19.30	19.33	19.35	19.37	19.38	19.40	19.41
3	10.13	9.55	9.28	9.12	9.01	8.94	8.89	8.85	8.81	8.79	8.74
4	7.71	6.94	6.59	6.39	6.26	6.16	6.09	6.04	6.00	5.96	5.91
5	6.61	5.79	5.41	5.19	5.05	4.95	4.88	4.82	4.77	4.74	4.68
6	5.99	5.14	4.76	4.53	4.39	4.28	4.21	4.15	4.10	4.06	4.00
7	5.59	4.74	4.35	4.12	3.97	3.87	3.79	3.73	3.68	3.64	3.57
8	5.32	4.46	4.07	3.84	3.69	3.58	3.50	3.44	3.39	3.35	3.28
9	5.12	4.26	3.86	3.63	3.48	3.37	3.29	3.23	3.18	3.14	3.07
10	4.96	4.10	3.71	3.48	3.33	3.22	3.14	3.07	3.02	2.98	2.91
11	4.84	3.98	3.59	3.36	3.20	3.09	3.01	2.95	2.90	2.85	2.79
12	4.75	3.89	3.49	3.26	3.11	3.00	2.91	2.85	2.80	2.75	2.69
13	4.67	3.81	3.41	3.18	3.03	2.92	2.83	2.77	2.71	2.67	2.60
14	4.60	3.74	3.34	3.11	2.96	2.85	2.76	2.70	2.65	2.60	2.53
15	4.54	3.68	3.29	3.06	2.90	2.79	2.71	2.64	2.59	2.54	2.48

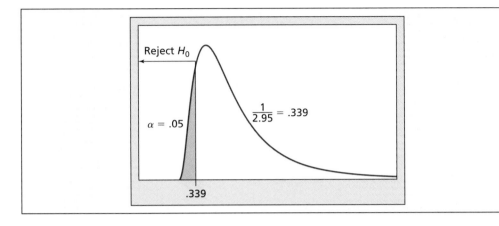

FIGURE 10.25

Left-Tail F_L for $\alpha = .05$

Step 4: Make the Decision   Since the test statistic $F = 0.691$ is not in the critical region, we cannot reject the hypothesis of equal variances in a one-tailed test. The bumpers did not significantly decrease the variance in collision repair cost.

Excel's *F* Test

Excel makes it quite easy to do the F test for variances. Figure 10.26 shows Excel's left-tailed test. One advantage of using Excel is that you also get a *p*-value. For the bumper data, the large *p*-value of .279 indicates that we would face a Type I error risk of about 28 percent if we were to reject H_0. In other words, a sample variance ratio as extreme as $F = 0.691$ would occur by chance about 28 percent of the time if the population variances were in fact equal. The sample evidence does not indicate that the variances differ.

FIGURE 10.26

Excel's *F* Test of Variances

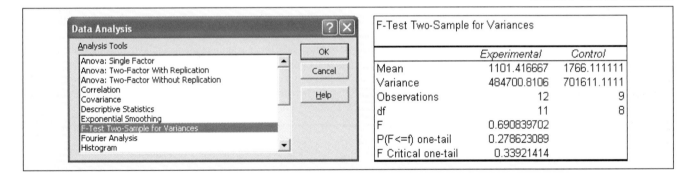

Assumptions of the *F* Test

The F test assumes that the populations being sampled are normal. Unfortunately, the test is rather sensitive to non-normality of the sampled populations. Alternative tests are available, but they tend to be rather complex and nonintuitive. MINITAB reports both the F test and a robust alternative known as *Levene's test* along with their *p*-values. As long as you know how to interpret a *p*-value, you really don't need to know the details of Levene's test. An attractive feature of MINITAB's F test is its graphical display of a confidence interval for each population standard deviation, shown in Figure 10.27. If you are concerned about non-normality, you can test each sample for non-normality by using a probability plot, although these samples are a bit small for normality tests.

Significance versus Importance

The test of means showed a mean difference of $665 per repair incident. That is large enough that it might be important. The incremental cost per vehicle of the new bumper would have to

FIGURE 10.27

MINITAB's Test for Variances

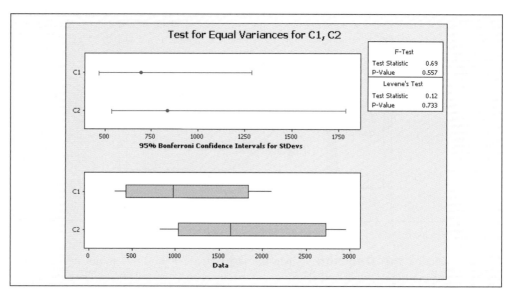

be compared with the present discounted value of the expected annual savings per vehicle over its useful life. In a large fleet of vehicles, the payback period could be calculated. Most firms require that a change pay for itself in a fairly short period of time. *Importance* is a question to be answered ultimately by financial experts, not statisticians.

SECTION EXERCISES

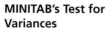

Hint: Use Excel or MegaStat.

10.25 Which samples show unequal variances? Use $\alpha = .05$ in all tests. Show the critical values and degrees of freedom clearly and illustrate the decision rule.
a. $s_1 = 5.1$, $n_1 = 11$, $s_2 = 3.2$, $n_2 = 8$, two-tailed test
b. $s_1 = 221$, $n_1 = 8$, $s_2 = 445$, $n_2 = 8$, left-tailed test
c. $s_1 = 67$, $n_1 = 10$, $s_2 = 15$, $n_2 = 13$, right-tailed test

10.26 Researchers at the Mayo Clinic have studied the effect of sound levels on patient healing and have found a significant association (louder hospital ambient sound level is associated with slower postsurgical healing). Based on the Mayo Clinic's experience, Ardmore Hospital installed a new vinyl flooring that is supposed to reduce the mean sound level (decibels) in the hospital corridors. The sound level is measured at five randomly selected times in the main corridor. (a) At $\alpha = .05$, has the mean been reduced? Show the hypotheses, decision rule, and test statistic. (b) At $\alpha = .05$, has the variance changed? Show the hypotheses, decision rule, and test statistic. (See *Detroit Free Press*, February 2, 2004, p. 8H.) **Decibels**

New Flooring	Old Flooring
42	48
41	51
40	44
37	48
44	52

10.27 A manufacturing process drills holes in sheet metal that are supposed to be .5000 cm in diameter. Before and after a new drill press is installed, the hole diameter is carefully measured (in cm) for 12 randomly chosen parts. At $\alpha = .05$, do these independent random samples prove that the new process has smaller variance? Show the hypotheses, decision rule, and test statistic. *Hint:* Use Excel =FINV(1-α, v_1, v_2) to get F_L. **Diameter**

New drill:	.5005	.5010	.5024	.4988	.4997	.4995
	.4976	.5042	.5014	.4995	.4988	.4992
Old drill:	.5052	.5053	.4947	.4907	.5031	.4923
	.5040	.5035	.5061	.4956	.5035	.4962

10.28 Examine the data below showing the weights (in pounds) of randomly selected checked bags for an airline's flights on the same day. (a) At $\alpha = .05$, is the mean weight of an international bag greater? Show the hypotheses, decision rule, and test statistic. (b) At $\alpha = .05$, is the variance greater for bags on an international flight? Show the hypotheses, decision rule, and test statistic. **Luggage**

International (10 bags)		Domestic (15 bags)		
39	47	29	37	43
54	48	36	33	42
46	28	33	29	32
39	54	34	43	35
69	62	38	39	39

CHAPTER SUMMARY

A **two-sample test** compares samples with each other rather than comparing with a benchmark, as in a one-sample test. For **independent samples,** the comparison of means generally utilizes the Student's *t* distribution, because the population variances are almost always unknown. If the unknown variances are **assumed equal,** we use a **pooled variance** estimate and **add the degrees of freedom.** If the unknown variances are **assumed unequal,** we do not pool the variances and we reduce the degrees of freedom by using **Welch's formula.** The test statistic is the difference of means divided by their standard error. For tests of means or proportions, **equal sample sizes** are desirable, but not necessary. The *t* **test for paired samples** uses the differences of *n* paired observations, thereby being a **one-sample *t* test.** For two proportions, the samples may be **pooled** if the population proportions are assumed equal, and the test statistic is the difference of proportions divided by the standard error, the square root of the sum of the sample variances. For proportions, **normality** may be assumed if both samples are large, that is, if they each contain at least 10 successes and 10 failures. The ***F* test** for equality of **two variances** is named after Sir Ronald Fisher. Its test statistic is the **ratio** of the sample variances. We want to see if the ratio differs significantly from 1. The *F* table shows critical values based on both **numerator** and **denominator** degrees of freedom.

KEY TERMS

Behrens-Fisher problem, *360*
F distribution, *382*
F test, *382*
independent sample, *370*
paired comparison, *367*
paired samples, *368*

paired *t* test, *367*
pooled estimate, *375*
pooled proportion, *373*
pooled variance, *360*
p-values, *358*
test statistic, *359*
two-sample tests, *357*

Type I error, *358*
Type II error, *358*
Welch-Satterthwaite test, *360*
Welch's adjusted degrees of freedom, *361*

Commonly Used Formulas in Two-Sample Hypothesis Tests

Test Statistic (Difference of Means, Equal Variances): $t_{calc} = \dfrac{\bar{x}_1 - \bar{x}_2}{\sqrt{\dfrac{s_p^2}{n_1} + \dfrac{s_p^2}{n_2}}}$

$$\text{d.f.} = n_1 + n_2 - 2$$

$$s_p^2 = \frac{(n_1 - 1)s_1^2 + (n_2 - 1)s_2^2}{n_1 + n_2 - 2}$$

Test Statistic (Difference of Means, Unequal Variances): $t_{calc} = \dfrac{\bar{x}_1 - \bar{x}_2}{\sqrt{\dfrac{s_1^2}{n_1} + \dfrac{s_2^2}{n_2}}}$

$$\text{d.f.} = \frac{\left[s_1^2/n_1 + s_2^2/n_2\right]^2}{\dfrac{\left(s_1^2/n_1\right)^2}{n_1 - 1} + \dfrac{\left(s_2^2/n_2\right)^2}{n_2 - 1}}$$

Test Statistic (Paired Differences): $t_{\text{calc}} = \dfrac{\bar{d} - \mu_d}{\dfrac{s_d}{\sqrt{n}}}$

$$\text{d.f.} = n - 1$$

Test Statistic (Equality of Proportions): $z_{\text{calc}} = \dfrac{p_1 - p_2}{\sqrt{\bar{p}(1 - \bar{p})\left[\dfrac{1}{n_1} + \dfrac{1}{n_2}\right]}}$

$$\bar{p} = \frac{x_1 + x_2}{n_1 + n_2}$$

Confidence Interval for $\pi_1 - \pi_2$: $(p_1 - p_2) \pm z\sqrt{\dfrac{p_1(1 - p_1)}{n_1} + \dfrac{p_2(1 - p_2)}{n_2}}$

Test Statistic (Two Variances): $F_{\text{calc}} = \dfrac{s_1^2}{s_2^2}$

$$\text{d.f.}_1 = n_1 - 1, \ \ \text{d.f.}_2 = n_2 - 1$$

CHAPTER REVIEW

1. (a) Explain why two samples from the same population could appear different. (b) Why do we say that two-sample tests have a built-in point of reference?

2. (a) In a two-sample test of proportions, what is a pooled proportion? (b) Why is the test for normality important for a two-sample test of proportions? (c) What is the criterion for assuming normality of the test statistic?

3. (a) Is it necessary that sample sizes be equal for a two-sample test of proportions? Is it desirable? (b) Explain the analogy between overlapping confidence intervals and testing for equality of two proportions.

4. List the three cases for a test comparing two means. Explain carefully how they differ.

5. Consider *Case 1* (known variances) in the test comparing two means. (a) Why is *Case 1* unusual and not used very often? (b) What distribution is used for the test statistic? (c) Write the formula for the test statistic.

6. Consider *Case 2* (unknown but equal variances) in the test comparing two means. (a) Why is *Case 2* common? (b) What distribution is used for the test statistic? (c) State the degrees of freedom used in this test. (d) Write the formula for the pooled variance and interpret it. (e) Write the formula for the test statistic.

7. Consider *Case 3* (unknown and unequal variances) in the test comparing two means. (a) What complication arises in degrees of freedom for *Case 3*? (b) What distribution is used for the test statistic? (c) Write the formula for the test statistic.

8. (a) Is it ever acceptable to use a normal distribution in a test of means with unknown variances? (b) If we assume normality, what is gained? What is lost?

9. Why is it a good idea to use a computer program like Excel to do tests of means?

10. (a) Explain why the paired *t* test for dependent samples is really a one-sample test. (b) State the degrees of freedom for the paired *t* test. (c) Why not treat two paired samples as if they were independent?

11. Explain how a difference in means could be statistically *significant* but not *important*.

12. (a) Why do we use an *F* test? (b) Where did it get its name? (c) When two population variances are equal, what value would you expect of the *F* test statistic?

13. (a) In an *F* test for two variances, explain how to obtain left- and right-tail critical values. (b) What are the assumptions underlying the *F* test?

Note: For tests on two proportions, two means, or two variances it is a good idea to check your work by using MINITAB, MegaStat, or the *LearningStats* two-sample calculators in Unit 10.

10.29 The top food snacks consumed by adults aged 18–54 are gum, chocolate candy, fresh fruit, potato chips, breath mints/candy, ice cream, nuts, cookies, bars, yogurt, and crackers. Out of a random sample of 25 men, 15 ranked fresh fruit in their top five snack choices. Out of a random sample of 32 women, 22 ranked fresh fruit in their top five snack choices. Is there a difference in the proportion of men and women who rank fresh fruit in their top five list of snacks? (a) State the hypotheses and a decision rule for $\alpha = .10$. (b) Calculate the sample proportions. (c) Find the test statistic and its *p*-value. What is your conclusion? (d) Is normality assured? (Data are from The NPD Group press release, "Fruit #1 Snack Food Consumed by Kids," June 16, 2005.)

10.30 In Dallas, some fire trucks were painted yellow (instead of red) to heighten their visibility. During a test period, the fleet of red fire trucks made 153,348 runs and had 20 accidents, while the fleet of yellow fire trucks made 135,035 runs and had 4 accidents. At $\alpha = .01$, did the yellow fire trucks have a significantly lower accident rate? (a) State the hypotheses. (b) State the decision rule and sketch it. (c) Find the sample proportions and *z* test statistic. (d) Make a decision. (e) Find the *p*-value and interpret it. (f) If statistically significant, do you think the difference is large enough to be important? If so, to whom, and why? (g) Is the normality assumption fulfilled? Explain.

Accident Rate for Dallas Fire Trucks

Statistic	Red Fire Trucks	Yellow Fire Trucks
Number of accidents	$x_1 = 20$ accidents	$x_2 = 4$ accidents
Number of fire runs	$n_1 = 153,348$ runs	$n_2 = 135,035$ runs

Source: *The Wall Street Journal,* June 26, 1995, p. B1.

10.31 Do a larger proportion of college students than young children eat cereal? Researchers surveyed both age groups to find the answer. The results are shown in the table below. (a) State the hypotheses used to answer the question. (b) Using $\alpha = .05$, state the decision rule and sketch it. (c) Find the sample proportions and *z* statistic. (d) Make a decision. (e) Find the *p*-value and interpret it. (f) Is the normality assumption fulfilled? Explain.

Statistic	College Students (ages 18–25)	Young Children (ages 6–11)
Number who eat cereal	$x_1 = 833$	$x_2 = 692$
Number surveyed	$n_1 = 850$	$n_2 = 740$

10.32 A 2005 study found that 202 women held board seats out of a total of 1,195 seats in the Fortune 100 companies. A 2003 study found that 779 women held board seats out of a total of 5,727 seats in the Fortune 500 companies. Treating these as random samples (since board seat assignments change often), can we conclude that Fortune 100 companies have a greater proportion of women board members than the Fortune 500? (a) State the hypotheses. (b) Calculate the sample proportions. (c) Find the test statistic and its *p*-value. What is your conclusion at $\alpha = .05$? (d) If statistically significant, can you suggest factors that might explain the increase? (Data are from *The 2003 Catalyst Census of Women Board Directors of the Fortune 500,* and "Women and Minorities on Fortune 100 Boards," *The Alliance for Board Diversity,* May 17, 2005.)

10.33 A study of the Fortune 100 board of director members showed that there were 36 minority women holding board seats out of 202 total female board members. There were 142 minority men holding board seats out of 993 total male board members. (a) Treating the findings from this study as samples, calculate the sample proportions. (b) Find the test statistic and its *p*-value. (c) At the 5 percent level of significance, is there a difference in the percentage of minority women board directors and minority men board directors? (Data are from "Women and Minorities on Fortune 100 Boards," *The Alliance for Board Diversity,* May 17, 2005.)

10.34 To test his hypothesis that students who finish an exam first get better grades, a professor kept track of the order in which papers were handed in. Of the first 25 papers, 10 received a B or better compared with 8 of the last 24 papers handed in. Is the first group better, at $\alpha = .10$? (a) State your hypotheses and obtain a test statistic and *p*-value. Interpret the results. (b) Are the samples large enough to assure normality? (c) Make an argument that early-finishers should do better. Then make the opposite argument. Which is more convincing?

10.35 How many full-page advertisements are found in a magazine? In an October issue of *Muscle and Fitness,* there were 252 ads, of which 97 were full-page. For the same month, the magazine *Glamour* had 342 ads, of which 167 were full-page. (a) Is the difference significant at $\alpha = .01$? (b) Find the *p*-value. (c) Is normality assured? (d) Based on what you know of these magazines, why might the proportions of full-page ads differ? (Data are from a project by MBA students Amy DeGuire and Don Finney.)

10.36 In Utica, Michigan, 205 of 226 school buses passed the annual safety inspection. In Detroit, Michigan, only 151 of 296 buses passed the inspection. (a) State the hypotheses for a right-tailed test. (b) Obtain a test statistic and *p*-value. (c) Is normality assured? (d) If *significant,* is the difference also large enough to be *important?* (Data are from *Detroit Free Press,* August 19, 2000, p. 8A.)

10.37 After John F. Kennedy, Jr., was killed in an airplane crash at night, a survey was taken, asking whether a noninstrument-rated pilot should be allowed to fly at night. Of 409 New York State residents, 61 said yes. Of 70 aviation experts who were asked the same question, 40 said yes. (a) At $\alpha = .01$, did a larger proportion of experts say yes compared with the general public, or is the difference within the realm of chance? (b) Find the *p*-value and interpret it. (b) Is normality assured? (Data are from www.siena.edu/sri.)

10.38 A ski company in Vail owns two ski shops, one on the east side and one on the west side. Sales data showed that at the eastern location there were 56 pairs of large gloves sold out of 304 total pairs sold. At the western location there were 145 pairs of large gloves sold out of 562 total pairs sold. (a) Calculate the sample proportion of large gloves for each location. (b) At $\alpha = .05$, is there a significant difference in the proportion of large gloves sold? (c) Can you suggest any reasons why a difference might exist? (*Note:* Problem is based on actual sales data).

10.39 Does hormone replacement therapy (HRT) cause breast cancer? Researchers studied women ages 50 to 79 who used either HRT or a dummy pill over a 5-year period. Of the 8,304 HRT women, 245 cancers were reported, compared with 185 cancers for the 8,304 women who got the dummy pill. Assume that the participants were randomly assigned to two equal groups. (a) State the hypotheses for a one-tailed test to see if HRT was associated with increased cancer risk. (b) Obtain a test statistic and *p*-value. Interpret the results. (c) Is normality assured? (d) Is the difference large enough to be important? Explain. (e) What else would you need to know to assess this research? (Data are from *www.cbsnews.com,* accessed June 25, 2003.)

10.40 A sample of high school seniors showed that 18 of 60 who owned PlayStation 3 spent more than an hour a day playing games, compared with 32 of 80 who owned Xbox 360. Is there a significant difference in the population proportions at $\alpha = .10$?

10.41 Does a "follow-up reminder" increase the renewal rate on a magazine subscription? A magazine sent out 760 subscription renewal notices (without a reminder) and got 703 renewals. As an experiment, they sent out 240 subscription renewal notices (with a reminder) and got 228 renewals. (a) At $\alpha = .05$, was the renewal rate higher in the experimental group? (b) Can normality be assumed?

10.42 A study of people in a driving simulator showed that 12 of 24 using a cell phone with a headset (group 1) missed their freeway exit, 3 of 24 talking to a passenger (group 2) missed their freeway exit, and 2 of 48 driving unaccompanied and not talking (group 3) missed their freeway exit. (a) For each sample, construct a 95 percent confidence interval for the true proportion. Do they overlap? So what? (b) Do a two-tailed hypothesis test at $\alpha = .05$ to compare group 1 and group 2. What is your conclusion? (c) Did you find the confidence intervals or the hypothesis test more helpful in visualizing the situation? (d) Is normality assured? (Data are from *The Wall Street Journal,* September 24, 2004, p. B1.)

10.43 In a marketing class, 44 student members of virtual (Internet) project teams (group 1) and 42 members of face-to-face project teams (group 2) were asked to respond on a 1–5 scale to the question: "As compared to other teams, the members helped each other." For group 1 the mean was 2.73 with a standard deviation of 0.97, while for group 2 the mean was 1.90 with a standard deviation of 0.91. At $\alpha = .01$, is the virtual team mean significantly higher? (Data are from Roger W. Berry, *Marketing Education Review* 12, no. 2 [2002], pp. 73–78.)

10.44 Does lovastatin (a cholesterol-lowering drug) reduce the risk of heart attack? In a Texas study, researchers gave lovastatin to 2,325 people and an inactive substitute to 2,081 people (average age 58). After 5 years, 57 of the lovastatin group had suffered a heart attack, compared with 97 for the inactive pill. (a) State the appropriate hypotheses. (b) Obtain a test statistic and *p*-value. Interpret the results at $\alpha = .01$. (c) Is normality assured? (d) Is the difference large enough to be important? (e) What else would medical researchers need to know before prescribing this drug widely? (Data are from *Science News* 153 [May 30, 1998], p. 343.)

10.45 U.S. Vice President Dick Cheney received a lot of publicity after his fourth heart attack. A portable defibrillator was surgically implanted in his chest to deliver an electric shock to restore his heart rhythm whenever another attack was threatening. Researchers at the University of Rochester (NY) Medical Center implanted defibrillators in 742 patients after a heart attack and compared them with 490 similar patients without the implant. Over the next 2 years, 98 of those without defibrillators had died, compared with 104 of those with defibrillators. (a) State the hypotheses for a one-tailed test to see if the defibrillators reduced the death rate. (b) Obtain a test statistic and *p*-value. (c) Is normality assured? (d) Why might such devices not be widely implanted in heart attack patients? (Data are from *Science News* 161 [April 27, 2002], p. 270.)

10.46 To test the hypothesis that students who finish an exam first get better grades, Professor Hardtack kept track of the order in which papers were handed in. The first 25 papers showed a mean score of 77.1 with a standard deviation of 19.6, while the last 24 papers handed in showed a mean score of 69.3 with a standard deviation of 24.9. Is this a significant difference at $\alpha = .05$? (a) State the hypotheses for a right-tailed test. (b) Obtain a test statistic and *p*-value assuming equal variances. Interpret these results. (c) Is the difference in mean scores large enough to be important? (d) Is it reasonable to assume equal variances? (e) Carry out a formal test for equal variances at $\alpha = .05$, showing all steps clearly.

10.47 Has the cost to outsource a standard employee background check changed from 2005 to 2006? A random sample of 10 companies in spring 2005 showed a sample average of $105 with a sample standard deviation equal to $32. A random sample of 10 different companies in spring 2006 resulted in a sample average of $75 with a sample standard deviation equal to $45. (a) Conduct a hypothesis test to test the difference in sample means with a level of significance equal to .05. Assume the population variances are not equal. (b) Discuss why a paired sample design might have made more sense in this case.

10.48 From her firm's computer telephone log, an executive found that the mean length of 64 telephone calls during July was 4.48 minutes with a standard deviation of 5.87 minutes. She vowed to make an effort to reduce the length of calls. The August phone log showed 48 telephone calls whose mean was 2.396 minutes with a standard deviation of 2.018 minutes. (a) State the hypotheses for a right-tailed test. (b) Obtain a test statistic and *p*-value assuming unequal variances. Interpret these results using $\alpha = .01$. (c) Why might the sample data *not* follow a normal, bell-shaped curve? If not, how might this affect your conclusions?

10.49 An experimental bumper was designed to reduce damage in low-speed collisions. This bumper was installed on an experimental group of vans in a large fleet, but not on a control group. At the end of a trial period, accident data showed 12 repair incidents for the experimental group and 9 repair incidents for the control group. Vehicle downtime (in days per repair incident) is shown below. At $\alpha = .05$, did the new bumper reduce downtime? (a) Make stacked dot plots of the data (a sketch is OK). (b) State the hypotheses. (c) State the decision rule and sketch it. (d) Find the test statistic. (e) Make a decision. (f) Find the *p*-value and interpret it. (g) Do you think the difference is large enough to be important? Explain. (Data are from an unpublished study by Floyd G. Willoughby and Thomas W. Lauer, Oakland University.)   **DownTime**

New bumper (12 repair incidents): 9, 2, 5, 12, 5, 4, 7, 5, 11, 3, 7, 1

Control group (9 repair incidents): 7, 5, 7, 4, 18, 4, 8, 14, 13

10.50 Medicare spending per patient in different U.S. metropolitan areas may differ. Based on the sample data below, is the average spending in the northern region significantly less than the average spending in the southern region at the 1 percent level? (a) State the hypotheses and decision rule. (b) Find the test statistic assuming unequal variances. (c) State your conclusion. Is this a strong conclusion? (d) Can you suggest reasons why a difference might exist? (See *The New Yorker* [May 30, 2005], p. 38).

Medicare Spending per Patient (adjusted for age, sex, and race)

Statistic	Northern Region	Southern Region
Sample mean	$3,123	$8,456
Sample standard deviation	$1,546	$3,678
Sample size	14 patients	16 patients

10.51 In a 15-day survey of air pollution in two European capitals, the mean particulate count (micrograms per cubic meter) in Athens was 39.5 with a standard deviation of 3.75, while in London the mean was 31.5 with a standard deviation of 2.25. (a) Assuming equal population variances, does this evidence convince you that the mean particulate count is higher in Athens, at $\alpha = .05$? (b) Are the variances equal or not, at $\alpha = .05$? (Based on *The Economist* 383, no. 8514 [February 3, 2007], p. 58.)

10.52 One group of accounting students took a distance learning class, while another group took the same course in a traditional classroom. At $\alpha = .10$, is there a significant difference in the mean scores listed below? (a) State the hypotheses. (b) State the decision rule and sketch it. (c) Find the test statistic. (d) Make a decision. (e) Use Excel to find the p-value and interpret it.

Exam Scores for Accounting Students

Statistic	Distance	Classroom
Mean scores	$\bar{x}_1 = 9.1$	$\bar{x}_2 = 10.3$
Sample std. dev.	$s_1 = 2.4$	$s_2 = 2.5$
Number of students	$n_1 = 20$	$n_2 = 20$

10.53 Do male and female school superintendents earn the same pay? Salaries for 20 males and 17 females in a certain metropolitan area are shown below. At $\alpha = .01$, were the mean superintendent salaries greater for men than for women? (a) Make stacked dot plots of the sample data (a sketch will do). (b) State the hypotheses. (c) State the decision rule and sketch it. (d) Find the test statistic. (e) Make a decision. (f) Estimate the p-value and interpret it. (g) If statistically significant, do you think the difference is large enough to be important? Explain. **Paycheck**

School Superintendent Pay

Men (n = 20)		Women (n = 17)	
114,000	121,421	94,675	96,000
115,024	112,187	123,484	112,455
115,598	110,160	99,703	120,118
108,400	128,322	86,000	124,163
109,900	128,041	108,000	76,340
120,352	125,462	94,940	89,600
118,000	113,611	83,933	91,993
108,209	123,814	102,181	
110,000	111,280	86,840	
151,008	112,280	85,000	

10.54 The average take-out order size for Ashoka Curry House restaurant is shown. Assuming equal variances, at $\alpha = .05$, is there a significant difference in the order sizes? (a) State the hypotheses. (b) State the decision rule and sketch it. (c) Find the test statistic. (d) Make a decision. (e) Use Excel to find the p-value and interpret it.

Customer Order Size

Statistic	Friday Night	Saturday Night
Mean order size	$\bar{x}_1 = 22.32$	$\bar{x}_2 = 25.56$
Standard deviation	$s_1 = 4.35$	$s_2 = 6.16$
Number of orders	$n_1 = 13$	$n_2 = 18$

10.55 Cash withdrawals (in multiples of $20) at an on-campus ATM for a random sample of 30 Fridays and 30 Mondays are shown following. At $\alpha = .01$, is there a difference in the mean ATM withdrawal on Monday and Friday? (a) Make stacked dot plots of the data (a sketch is OK). (b) State the hypotheses. (c) State the decision rule and sketch it. (d) Find the test statistic. (e) Make a decision. (f) Find the p-value and interpret it. **ATM**

Randomly Chosen ATM Withdrawals ($)

Friday			Monday		
250	10	10	40	30	10
20	10	30	100	70	370
110	20	10	20	20	10
40	20	40	30	50	30
70	10	10	200	20	40
20	20	400	20	30	20
10	20	10	10	20	100
50	20	10	30	40	20
100	20	20	50	10	20
20	60	70	60	10	20

10.56 A sample of 25 concession stand purchases at the May 12 matinee of *Spider-Man 3* showed a mean purchase of $7.29 with a standard deviation of $3.02. For the May 18 evening showing of the same movie, for a sample of 25 purchases the mean was $7.12 with a standard deviation of $2.14. The means appear to be very close, but not the variances. At $\alpha = .05$, is there a difference in variances? Show all steps clearly, including an illustration of the decision rule.

10.57 A ski company in Vail owns two ski shops, one on the west side and one on the east side of Vail. Is there a difference in daily average goggle sales between the two stores? Assume equal variances. (a) State the hypotheses for a two-tailed test. (b) State the decision rule for a level of significance equal to 5 percent and sketch it. (c) Find the test statistic and state your conclusion.

Sales Data for Ski Goggles

Statistic	East Side Shop	West Side Shop
Mean sales	$328	$435
Sample std. dev.	$104	$147
Sample size	28 days	29 days

10.58 A ski company in Vail owns two ski shops, one on the west side and one on the east side of Vail. Ski hat sales data (in dollars) for a random sample of 5 Saturdays during the 2004 season showed the following results. Is there a significant difference in sales dollars of hats between the west side and east side stores at the 5 percent level of significance? (a) State the hypotheses. (b) State the decision rule and sketch it. (c) Find the test statistic and state your conclusion. 🐿 **Hats**

Saturday Sales Data ($) for Ski Hats

Saturday	East Side Shop	West Side Shop
1	548	523
2	493	721
3	609	695
4	567	510
5	432	532

10.59 Emergency room arrivals in a large hospital showed the statistics below for 2 months. At $\alpha = .05$, has the variance changed? Show all steps clearly, including an illustration of the decision rule.

Statistic	October	November
Mean arrivals	177.0323	171.7333
Standard deviation	13.48205	15.4271
Days	31	30

10.60 Here are heart rates for a sample of 30 students before and after a class break. At $\alpha = .05$, was there a significant difference in the mean heart rate? (a) State the hypotheses. (b) State the decision rule and sketch it. (c) Find the test statistic. (d) Make a decision. (e) Estimate the p-value and interpret it.   HeartRate

Heart Rate before and after Class Break

Student	Before	After	Student	Before	After
1	60	62	16	70	64
2	70	76	17	69	66
3	77	78	18	64	69
4	80	83	19	70	73
5	82	82	20	59	58
6	82	83	21	62	65
7	41	66	22	66	68
8	65	63	23	81	77
9	58	60	24	56	57
10	50	54	25	64	62
11	82	93	26	78	79
12	56	55	27	75	74
13	71	67	28	66	67
14	67	68	29	59	63
15	66	75	30	98	82

Note: Thanks to colleague Gene Fliedner for having his evening students take their own pulses before and after the 10-minute class break.

10.61 A certain company will purchase the house of any employee who is transferred out of state and will handle all details of reselling the house. The purchase price is based on two assessments, one assessor being chosen by the employee and one by the company. Based on the sample of eight assessments shown, do the two assessors agree? Use the .01 level of significance, state hypotheses clearly, and show all steps.   HomeValue

Assessments of Eight Homes ($ thousands)

Assessed By	Home 1	Home 2	Home 3	Home 4	Home 5	Home 6	Home 7	Home 8
Company	328	350	455	278	290	285	535	745
Employee	318	345	470	285	310	280	525	765

10.62 Nine homes are chosen at random from real estate listings in two suburban neighborhoods, and the square footage of each home is noted following. At the .10 level of significance, is there a difference between the sizes of homes in the two neighborhoods? State your hypotheses and show all steps clearly.   HomeSize

Size of Homes in Two Subdivisions

Subdivision	Square Footage								
Greenwood	2,320	2,450	2,270	2,200	2,850	2,150	2,400	2,800	2,430
Pinewood	2,850	2,560	2,300	2,100	2,750	2,450	2,550	2,750	3,150

10.63 Two labs produce 1280 × 1024 LCD displays. At random, records are examined for 12 independently chosen hours of production in each lab, and the number of bad pixels per thousand displays is recorded. (a) Assuming equal variances, at the .01 level of significance, is there a difference in the defect rate between the two labs? State your hypotheses and show all steps clearly. (b) At the

.01 level of significance, can you reject the hypothesis of equal variances? State your hypotheses and show all steps clearly.

Defects in Randomly Inspected LCD Displays   🐭 **LCDDefects**

Lab A   422, 319, 326, 410, 393, 368, 497, 381, 515, 472, 423, 355

Lab B   497, 421, 408, 375, 410, 489, 389, 418, 447, 429, 404, 477

10.64 A cognitive retraining clinic assists outpatient victims of head injury, anoxia, or other conditions that result in cognitive impairment. Each incoming patient is evaluated to establish an appropriate treatment program and estimated length of stay. To see if the evaluation teams are consistent, 12 randomly chosen patients are separately evaluated by two expert teams (A and B) as shown. At the .10 level of significance, are the evaluator teams consistent in their estimates? State your hypotheses and show all steps clearly.   🐭 **LengthStay**

Estimated Length of Stay in Weeks

	Patient											
Team	1	2	3	4	5	6	7	8	9	10	11	12
A	24	24	52	30	40	30	18	30	18	40	24	12
B	24	20	52	36	36	36	24	36	16	52	24	16

10.65 Rates of return (annualized) in two investment portfolios are compared over the last 12 quarters. They are considered similar in safety, but portfolio B is advertised as being "less volatile." (a) At $\alpha = .025$, does the sample show that portfolio A has significantly greater variance in rates of return than portfolio B? (b) At $\alpha = .025$, is there a significant difference in the means?   🐭 **Portfolio**

Portfolio A	Portfolio B	Portfolio A	Portfolio B
5.23	8.96	7.89	7.68
10.91	8.60	9.82	7.62
12.49	7.61	9.62	8.71
4.17	6.60	4.93	8.97
5.54	7.77	11.66	7.71
8.68	7.06	11.49	9.91

DO-IT-YOURSELF

10.66 Count the number of two-door vehicles among 50 vehicles from a college or university student parking lot. Use any sampling method you like (e.g., the first 50 you see). Do the same for a grocery store that is not very close to the college or university. At $\alpha = .10$, is there a significant difference in the proportion of two-door vehicles in these two locations? (a) State the hypotheses. (b) State the decision rule and sketch it. (c) Find the sample proportions and z test statistic. (d) Make a decision. (e) Find the p-value and interpret it. (f) Is the normality assumption fulfilled? Explain.

10.67 Choose 40 words at random from this book (use a systematic sampling method, such as every fifth word on every tenth page). Then do the same for a novel of your choice. List the words and count the syllables in each. Find the mean and standard deviation. Is there a significant difference in the number of syllables at the .05 level? If so, is the difference important, as well as significant? To whom, and why? Show all work carefully.

10.68 Choose 100 words at random from this book (use a systematic sampling method, such as every tenth word on every fifth page). Then do the same for a novel of your choice. List the words and count the syllables in each. For each sample, find the proportion of words with more than three syllables. Is there a significant difference in the at the .05 level? How does this analysis differ from the preceding exercise?

10.69 Use the *LearningStats* MBA database for this exercise. Choose either year (1990 or 1998) and sort the data on any variable you wish (sex, GPA, major, etc.). Then split the data into two groups based on the sorted list (e.g., male or female, high GPA or low GPA). For each group, calculate the mean and standard deviation for a quantitative variable of your choice (number of siblings, hours of work, number of traffic tickets, etc.). Test for significant difference of two means, choosing any level of significance you wish. State your hypotheses clearly and tell why you might expect a difference (or not, if none is expected). Show work and explain.

10.70 Use the *LearningStats* MBA database for this exercise. Choose either year (1990 or 1998) and sort the data on any variable you wish (sex, GPA, major, etc.). Then split the data into two groups based on the sorted list (e.g., male or female, high GPA or low GPA). For each group, calculate a proportion of your choice (proportion who read a daily newspaper, proportion who can conduct transactions in a foreign language, etc.). Choose any level of significance you wish. State your hypotheses clearly and tell why you might expect a difference (or not, if none is expected). Show all work and explain fully.

10.71 Use the *LearningStats* miscellaneous data for this exercise. Compare the age at inauguration of the first 21 U.S. presidents (George Washington through Chester Alan Arthur) with the second set of 22 U.S. presidents (Grover Cleveland through George W. Bush). (a) At the .05 level of significance, is there a significant difference in mean age at inauguration? Explain clearly and intrepret the results. (b) At the .05 level of significance, should equal variances be assumed? Explain your reasoning fully.

10.72 Use the *LearningStats* state data for this exercise. Choose a database for any year (1990, 1997, or 2000). (a) Copy three data columns into a new worksheet: State, Income, and Urban%. (b) Sort the data on Urban% and then split the states into two roughly equal groups (low urban, high urban). (c) For each group, calculate the mean and standard deviation for Income and carry out a test for difference of means at $\alpha = .05$. Explain fully. (d) Perform a test for equal variances in the two groups at $\alpha = .05$. Explain fully. (e) Does urbanization seem to be related to income? (f) Make a scatter plot of Urban% and Income. What does it suggest?

10.73 Use the *LearningStats* nations data for this exercise. Choose a database for any year (1995, 1999, or 2002). (a) Copy three data columns into a new worksheet: Nation, BirthRate, and InfMort. (b) Sort the data on BirthRate and then split the nations into two roughly equal groups (low births, high births). (c) For each group, calculate the mean and standard deviation for InfMort and carry out a test for difference of means at $\alpha = .05$. Explain fully. (d) Perform a test for equal variances in the two groups at $\alpha = .05$. Explain fully. (e) Does birth rate seem to be related to infant mortality? (f) Make a scatter plot of BirthRate and InfMort. What does it suggest?

RELATED READINGS

Best, D. J.; and J. C. W. Rayner. "Welch's Approximate Solution for the Behrens-Fisher Problem." *Technometrics* 29 (1987), pp. 205–10.

Payton, Mark E.; Matthew H. Greenstone; and Nathan Schenker. "Overlapping Confidence Intervals or Standard Error Intervals: What Do They Mean in terms of Statistical Significance?" *Journal of Insect Science* 3, no. 34 (October 2003), pp. 1–6.

Posten, H. O. "Robustness of the Two-Sample *t*-Test under Violations of the Homogeneity of Variance Assumption, Part II." *Communications in Statistics—Theory and Methods* 21 (1995), pp. 2169–84.

Scheffé, H. "Practical Solutions of the Behrens-Fisher Problem." *Journal of the American Statistical Association* 65 (1970), pp. 1501–08.

Shoemaker, Lewis F. "Fixing the *F* Test for Equal Variances." *The American Statistician* 57, no. 2 (May 2003), pp. 105–14.

Wang, Y. "Probabilities of the Type I Errors of the Welch Tests for the Behrens-Fisher Problem." *Journal of the American Statistical Association* 66 (1971), pp. 605–08.

LearningStats Unit 10   Two-Sample Hypothesis Tests

LearningStats Unit 10 gives examples of the most common two-sample hypothesis tests (two means, two proportions, two variances) and offers tables of critical values. Your instructor may assign specific modules, or you may pursue those that sound interesting.

Topic	LearningStats Modules
Hypothesis testing	Two-Sample Hypothesis Tests
Common hypothesis tests	Two-Sample Tests Calculator for Two Means Calculator for Two Proportions
Simulations	Two-Sample Generator Paired Data Generator Two-Sample Bootstrap Welch Correction Demo
Case studies	Case—Exam Scores Case—Weight-Loss Paired Data Case—Heart Rate Paired Case—Right-Handed Desks
Equations	Formulas for Two-Sample Tests Sampling Distribution PDFs
Tables	Appendix C—Normal Appendix D—Student's *t* Appendix F—*F* Distribution

Key: = PowerPoint   = Word   = Excel

Visual Statistics

Visual Statistics Modules on Two-Sample Tests

Module	Module Name
10	Visualizing Two-Sample Hypothesis Tests

Visual Statistics Module 10 (included on your CD) is designed to help you

- Become familiar with the sampling distributions used in tests of two means or two variances.
- Understand the relationship between a confidence interval and a two-sample test.
- Be able to explain Type I error, Type II error, and power for two-sample tests.
- Know the assumptions underlying two-sample tests and the effects of violating them.

The worktext (included on the CD in .PDF format) contains lists of concepts covered, objectives of the modules, overviews of concepts, illustrations of concepts, orientations to module features, learning exercises (basic, intermediate, advanced), learning projects (individual, team), self-evaluation quizzes, glossaries of terms, and solutions to self-evaluation quizzes.

EXAM REVIEW QUESTIONS FOR CHAPTERS 8–10

1. Which statement is *not* correct? Explain.
   a. the sample data $x_1, x_2, \ldots, x_n$ will be approximately normal if the sample size n is large.
   b. for a skewed population, the distribution of $\bar{X}$ is approximately normal if n is large.
   c. the expected value of $\bar{X}$ is equal to the true mean μ even if the population is skewed.
2. Match each statement to the correct property of an estimator (unbiased, consistent, efficient):
   a. The estimator "collapses" on the true parameter as n increases.
   b. The estimator has a relatively small variance.
   c. The expected value of the estimator is the true parameter.
3. Concerning confidence intervals, which statement is *most nearly* correct? Why not the others?
   a. We should use z instead of t when n is large.
   b. We use the Student's t distribution when σ is unknown.
   c. Using the Student's t distribution instead of z narrows the confidence interval.
4. A sample of 9 customers in the "quick" lane in a supermarket showed a mean purchase of $14.75 with a standard deviation of $2.10. (a) Find the 95 percent confidence interval for the true mean. (b) Why should you use t instead of z in this case?
5. A sample of 200 customers at a supermarket showed that 28 used a debit card to pay for their purchases. (a) Find the 95 percent confidence interval for the population proportion. (b) Why is it OK to assume normality in this case? (c) What sample size would be needed to estimate the population proportion with 90 percent confidence and an error of $\pm$ .03?
6. Which statement is *incorrect*? Explain.
   a. If $p = .50$ and $n = 100$ the estimated standard error of the sample proportion is .05.
   b. In a sample size calculation for estimating π it is conservative to assume $\pi = .50$.
   c. If $n = 250$ and $p = .07$ it is not safe to assume normality in a confidence interval for π.
7. Given H_0: $\mu \geq 18$ and H_1: $\mu < 18$, we would commit Type I error if we
   a. conclude that $\mu \geq 18$ when the truth is that $\mu < 18$.
   b. conclude that $\mu < 18$ when the truth is that $\mu \geq 18$.
   c. fail to reject $\mu \geq 18$ when the truth is that $\mu < 18$.
8. Which is the correct z value for a two-tailed test at $\alpha = .05$?
   a. $z = \pm 1.645$ b. $z = \pm 1.960$ c. $z = \pm 2.326$
9. The process that produces Sonora Bars (a type of candy) is intended to produce bars with a mean weight of 56 gm. The process standard deviation is known to be 0.77 gm. A random sample of 49 candy bars yields a mean weight of 55.82 gm. (a) State the hypotheses to test whether the mean is smaller than it is supposed to be. (b) What is the test statistic? (c) At $\alpha = .05$, what is the critical value for this test? (d) What is your conclusion?
10. A sample of 16 ATM transactions shows a mean transaction time of 67 seconds with a standard deviation of 12 seconds. (a) State the hypotheses to test whether the mean transaction time exceeds 60 seconds. (b) Find the test statistic. (c) At $\alpha = .025$, what is the critical value for this test? (d) What is your conclusion?
11. Which statement is *correct*? Why not the others?
    a. The level of significance α is the probability of committing Type I error.
    b. As the sample size increases, critical values of $t_{.05}$ increase, gradually approaching $z_{.05}$.
    c. When σ is unknown, it is conservative to use $z_{.05}$ instead of $t_{.05}$ in a hypothesis test for μ.
12. Last month, 85 percent of the visitors to the Sonora Candy Factory made a purchase in the on-site candy shop after taking the factory tour. This month, a random sample of 500 such visitors showed that 435 purchased candy after the tour. The manager said "Good, the percentage of candy-buyers has risen significantly." (a) At $\alpha = .05$, do you agree? (b) Why is it acceptable to assume normality in this test?
13. Weights of 12 randomly-chosen Sonora Bars (a type of candy) from assembly line 1 had a mean weight of 56.25 gm with a standard deviation of 0.65 gm, while the weights of 12 randomly-chosen Sonora Bars from assembly line 2 had a mean weight of 56.75 gm with a standard deviation of 0.55 gm. (a) Find the test statistic to test whether or not the mean population weights are the same for both assembly lines (i.e., that the difference is due to random variation). (b) State the critical value for $\alpha = .05$ and degrees of freedom that you are using. (c) State your conclusion.
14. In a random sample of 200 Colorado residents, 150 had skied at least once last winter. A similar sample of 200 Utah residents revealed that 140 had skied at least once last winter. At $\alpha = .025$, is the percentage significantly greater in Colorado? Explain fully and show calculations.

15. Five students in a large lecture class compared their scores on two exams. "Looks like the class mean was higher on the second exam," Bob said. (a) What kind of test would you use? (b) At $\alpha = .10$, what is the critical value? (c) Do you agree with Bob? Explain.

	Bill	Mary	Sam	Sarah	Megan
Exam 1	75	85	90	65	86
Exam 2	86	81	90	71	89

16. Which statement is *not* correct concerning a *p*-value? Explain.
   a. *Ceteris paribus,* a larger *p*-value makes it more likely that H_0 will be rejected.
   b. The *p*-value shows the risk of Type I error if we reject H_0 when H_0 is true.
   c. In making a decision, we compare the *p*-value with the desired level of significance α.

17. Given $n_1 = 8$, $s_1 = 14$, $n_2 = 12$, $s_2 = 7$. (a) Find the test statistic for a test for equal population variances. (b) At $\alpha = .05$ in a two-tailed test, state the critical value and degrees of freedom.

CHAPTER

Analysis of Variance

Chapter Contents

Chapter Learning Objectives

When you finish this chapter you should be able to

- Use basic ANOVA terminology correctly (e.g., response variable, factors, treatments).
- Use a table or Excel to find critical values for the F distribution.
- Recognize from the data format which type of ANOVA is appropriate.
- Use Excel or another software package to perform ANOVA calculations.
- Explain the assumptions of ANOVA and why they are important.
- Understand and perform Tukey's test for differences in pairs of group means.
- Use the F_{max} or other tests for equal variances in c treatment groups.
- Recognize when higher-order ANOVA models are needed.

You have already learned to compare the means of two samples. In this chapter, you will learn to compare more than two means *simultaneously* and how to trace sources of variation to potential explanatory factors by using **analysis of variance** (commonly referred to as **ANOVA**). Proper *experimental design* can make efficient use of limited data to draw the strongest possible inferences. Although analysis of variance has a relatively short history, it is one of the richest and most thoroughly explored fields of statistics. Originally developed by the English statistician Ronald A. Fisher (1890–1962) in connection with agricultural research (factors affecting crop growth), it was quickly applied in biology and medicine. Because of its versatility, it is now used in engineering, psychology, marketing, and many other areas. In this chapter, we will only illustrate a few kinds of problems where ANOVA may be utilized (see Related Reading if you need to go further).

The Goal: Explaining Variation ●

Analysis of variance seeks to identify *sources of variation* in a numerical *dependent* variable Y (the **response variable**). Variation in the response variable about its mean either is **explained** by one or more categorical *independent* variables (the **factors**) or is **unexplained** (random error):

$$\begin{array}{ccc} \text{Variation in } Y & = \quad \text{Explained Variation} \quad + & \text{Unexplained Variation} \\ \text{(around its mean)} & \text{(due to factors)} & \text{(random error)} \end{array}$$

ANOVA is a *comparison of means*. Each possible value of a factor or combination of factors is a **treatment**. Sample observations within each treatment are viewed as coming from populations with possibly different means. We test whether each factor has a significant effect on Y, and sometimes we test for interaction between factors. The test uses the F distribution, which was introduced in Chapter 10. ANOVA can handle any number of factors, but the researcher often is interested only in a few. Also, data collection costs may impose practical limits on the number of factors or treatments we can choose. This chapter concentrates on the one-factor ANOVA model, which is the most common model used in business.

Illustration: Manufacturing Defect Rates

Figure 11.1 shows a dot plot of daily defect rates for automotive computer chips manufactured at four plant locations. Samples of 10 days' production were taken at each plant. Are the observed differences in the plants' sample mean defect rates merely due to random variation? Or are the observed differences between the plants' defect rates too great to be attributed to chance? This is the kind of question that ANOVA is designed to answer.

FIGURE 11.1

Chip defect rates at four plants. **VS** The treatment means are significantly different (p = .02). Note that the confidence interval for Lee's Bluff falls to the right of the dotted vertical line, which represents the overall mean.

Chapter 12

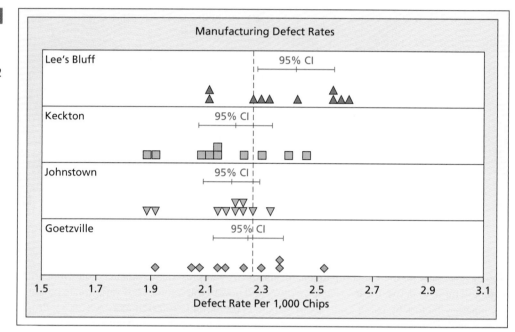

A simple way to state the ANOVA hypothesis is

$H_0: \mu_1 = \mu_2 = \mu_3 = \mu_4$ (mean defect rates are the same at all four plants)

H_1: Not all the means are equal (at least one mean differs from the others)

If we cannot reject H_0, then we conclude that the observations within each treatment or group actually have a common mean μ (represented by a dashed line in Figure 11.1). This one-factor ANOVA model may be visualized as in Figure 11.2.

FIGURE 11.2

ANOVA Model for Chip Defect Rate

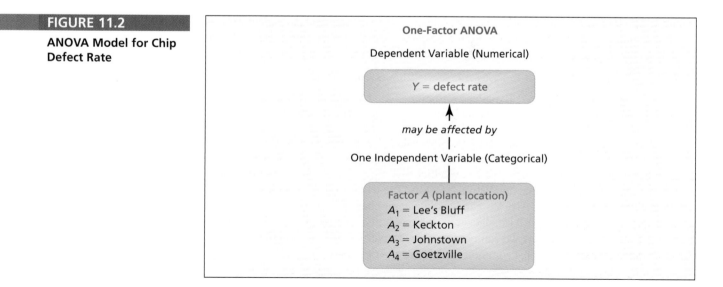

Illustration: Hospital Length of Stay ●────────

To allocate resources and fixed costs correctly, hospital management needs to test whether a patient's length of a stay (LOS) depends on the diagnostic-related group (DRG) code. Consider the case of a bone fracture. LOS is a *numerical* response variable (measured in hours). The hospital organizes the data by using five diagnostic codes for type of fracture (facial, radius or ulna, hip or femur, other lower extremity, all other). Figure 11.3 illustrates the ANOVA model. The hypotheses are:

$H_0: \mu_1 = \mu_2 = \mu_3 = \mu_4 = \mu_5$ (mean length of stay is the same for all five fracture types)

$H_1:$ Not all the means are equal (at least one mean differs from the others)

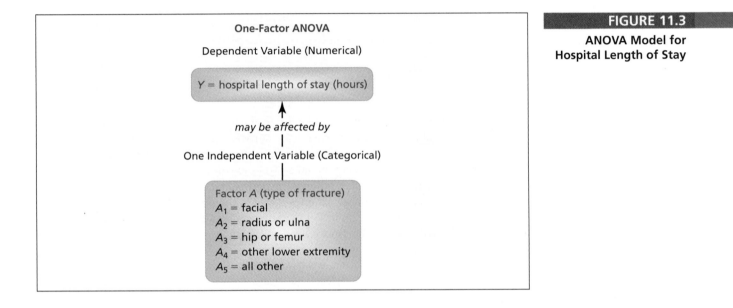

FIGURE 11.3

ANOVA Model for Hospital Length of Stay

Illustration: Automobile Painting ●────────

Paint quality is a major concern of car makers. A key characteristic of paint is its viscosity, a continuous *numerical* variable. Viscosity is to be tested for dependence on application temperature (low, medium, high). Although temperature is a numerical variable, it has been coded into *categories* that represent the test conditions of the experiment. Figure 11.4 illustrates the ANOVA model. The hypotheses are:

$H_0: \mu_1 = \mu_2 = \mu_3$ (mean viscosity is the same for all three temperatures settings)

$H_1:$ Not all the means are equal (at least one mean differs from the others)

ANOVA Assumptions ●────────

Analysis of variance assumes that the

- Observations on Y are independent.
- Populations being sampled are normal.
- Populations being sampled have equal variances.

Fortunately, ANOVA is somewhat robust to departures from the normality and equal variance assumptions. Later in this chapter, you will see tests for equal variances and normality.

FIGURE 11.4

ANOVA Model for Paint Viscosity

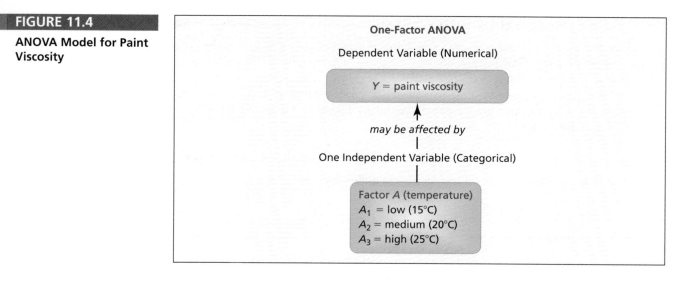

One-Factor ANOVA

Dependent Variable (Numerical)

Y = paint viscosity

may be affected by

One Independent Variable (Categorical)

Factor A (temperature)
A_1 = low (15°C)
A_2 = medium (20°C)
A_3 = high (25°C)

ANOVA Calculations

ANOVA calculations usually are too tedious to do by calculator, so after we choose an ANOVA model and collect the data, we rely on software (e.g., Excel, MegaStat, MINITAB, SPSS) to do the calculations. In some applications (accounting, finance, human resources, marketing) large samples can easily be taken from existing records, while in others (engineering, manufacturing, computer systems) experimental data collection is so expensive that small samples are used. Large samples increase the power of the test, but power also depends on the degree of variation in Y. Lowest power would be in small samples with high variation in Y, and conversely. Specialized software is needed to calculate power for ANOVA experiments.

11.2 ONE-FACTOR ANOVA (COMPLETELY RANDOMIZED MODEL)

Data Format

If we are only interested in comparing the means of c groups (*treatments* or *factor levels*), we have a **one-factor ANOVA.*** This is by far the most common ANOVA model that covers many business problems. The one-factor ANOVA is usually viewed as a comparison between several columns of data, although the data could also be presented in rows. Table 11.1 illustrates the data format for a one-factor ANOVA with c treatments, denoted $A_1, A_2, \ldots, A_c$. The group means are $\bar{y}_1, \bar{y}_2, \ldots, \bar{y}_c$.

TABLE 11.1

Format of One-Factor ANOVA Data

One-Factor ANOVA: Data in Columns

A_1	A_2	...	A_c
y_{11}	y_{12}	...	y_{1c}
y_{21}	y_{22}	...	y_{2c}
y_{31}	y_{32}	...	y_{3c}
...	...	...	...
etc.	etc.	...	etc.
n_1 obs.	n_2 obs.	...	n_c obs.
$\bar{y}_1$	$\bar{y}_2$	...	$\bar{y}_c$

One-Factor ANOVA: Data in Rows

A_1	y_{11}	y_{21}	y_{31}	... etc.	n_1 obs.	$\bar{y}_1$
A_2	y_{12}	y_{22}	y_{32}	... etc.	n_2 obs.	$\bar{y}_2$
...				...	...	...
A_c	y_{1c}	y_{2c}	y_{3c}	... etc.	n_c obs.	$\bar{y}_c$

---

*If subjects (or individuals) are assigned randomly to treatments, then we call this the *completely randomized model.*

Within treatment j we have n_j observations on Y. Sample sizes within each treatment do *not* need to be equal, although there are advantages to having balanced sample sizes. Equal sample size (1) ensures that each treatment contributes equally to the analysis; (2) reduces problems arising from violations of the assumptions (e.g., nonindependent Y values, unequal variances or nonidentical distributions within treatments, or non-normality of Y); and (3) increases the power of the test (i.e., the ability of the test to detect differences in treatment means). The total number of observations is the sum of the sample sizes for each treatment:

$$n = n_1 + n_2 + \cdots + n_c \tag{11.1}$$

Hypotheses to Be Tested

The question of interest is whether the mean of Y varies from treatment to treatment. The hypotheses to be tested are

$H_0: \mu_1 = \mu_2 = \cdots = \mu_c$ (all the treatment means are equal)

H_1: Not all the means are equal (at least one treatment mean is different)

Since one-factor ANOVA is a generalization of the test for equality of two means, why not just compare all possible pairs of means by using repeated two-sample t tests (as in Chapter 10)? Consider our experiment comparing the four manufacturing plant average defect rates. To compare pairs of plant averages we would have to perform six different t tests. If each t test has a Type I error probability equal to .05, then the probability that at least one of those tests results in a Type I error is $1 - (.95)^6 = .2649$. ANOVA tests all the means *simultaneously* and therefore does not inflate our Type I error.

One-Factor ANOVA as a Linear Model

An equivalent way to express the one-factor model is to say that observations in treatment j came from a population with a common mean (μ) plus a treatment effect (A_j) plus random error (ε_{ij}):

$$y_{ij} = \mu + A_j + \varepsilon_{ij} \quad j = 1, 2, \ldots, c \quad \text{and} \quad i = 1, 2, \ldots, n_j \tag{11.2}$$

The random error is assumed to be normally distributed with zero mean and the same variance for all treatments. If we are interested only in what happens to the response for the particular *levels* of the factor that were selected (a **fixed-effects model**), then the hypotheses to be tested are

$H_0: A_1 = A_2 = \cdots = A_c = 0$ (all treatment effects are zero)

H_1: Not all A_j are zero (some treatment effects are nonzero)

If the null hypothesis is true ($A_j = 0$ for all j), then knowing that an observation x came from treatment j does not help explain the variation in Y and the ANOVA model collapses to

$$y_{ij} = \mu + \varepsilon_{ij} \tag{11.3}$$

Group Means

The *mean of each group* is calculated in the usual way by summing the observations in the treatment and dividing by the sample size:

$$\bar{y}_j = \frac{1}{n_j} \sum_{i=1}^{n_j} y_{ij} \tag{11.4}$$

The *overall sample mean* or *grand mean* $\bar{y}$ can be calculated either by summing *all* the observations and dividing by n or by taking a weighted average of the c sample means:

$$\bar{y} = \frac{1}{n} \sum_{j=1}^{c} \sum_{i=1}^{n_j} y_{ij} = \frac{1}{n} \sum_{j=1}^{c} n_j \, \bar{y}_j \tag{11.5}$$

Partitioned Sum of Squares

To understand the logic of ANOVA, consider that for a given observation y_{ij} the following relationship must hold (on the right-hand side we just add and subtract $\bar{y}_j$):

(11.6) $$(y_{ij} - \bar{y}) = (\bar{y}_j - \bar{y}) + (y_{ij} - \bar{y}_j)$$

This says that any deviation of an observation from the grand mean $\bar{y}$ may be expressed in two parts: the deviation of the column mean $(\bar{y}_j)$ from the grand mean $(\bar{y})$, or *between* treatments, and the deviation of the observation (y_{ij}) from its own column mean $(\bar{y}_j)$, or *within* treatments. We can show that this relationship also holds for *sums* of squared deviations, yielding the **partitioned sum of squares**:

(11.7) $$\sum_{j=1}^{c} \sum_{i=1}^{n_j} (y_{ij} - \bar{y})^2 = \sum_{j=1}^{c} n_j(\bar{y}_j - \bar{y})^2 + \sum_{j=1}^{c} \sum_{i=1}^{n_j} (y_{ij} - \bar{y}_j)^2$$

This important relationship may be expressed simply as

(11.8) $$SST = SSA + SSE \qquad \text{(partitioned sum of squares)}$$

Partitioned Sum of Squares

Sum of Squares Total (SST)	=	Sum of Squares between Treatments (SSA)	+	Sum of Squares within Treatments (SSE)
		↑ Explained by Factor A		↑ Unexplained Random Error

If the treatment means do not differ greatly from the grand mean, *SSA* will be small and *SSE* will be large (and conversely). The sums *SSA* and *SSE* may be used to test the hypothesis that the treatment means differ from the grand mean. However, we first divide each sum of squares by its *degrees of freedom* (to adjust for group sizes). The *F test statistic* is the ratio of the resulting **mean squares**. These calculations can be arranged in a worksheet like Table 11.2.

TABLE 11.2

One-Factor ANOVA Table

Source of Variation	Sum of Squares	Degrees of Freedom	Mean Square	F Statistic
Treatment (between groups)	$SSA = \sum_{j=1}^{c} n_j(\bar{y}_j - \bar{y})^2$	$c - 1$	$MSA = \dfrac{SSA}{c-1}$	$F = \dfrac{MSA}{MSE}$
Error (within groups)	$SSE = \sum_{j=1}^{c} \sum_{i=1}^{n_j} (y_{ij} - \bar{y}_j)^2$	$n - c$	$MSE = \dfrac{SSE}{n-c}$	
Total	$SST = \sum_{j=1}^{c} \sum_{i=1}^{n_j} (y_{ij} - \bar{y})^2$	$n - 1$		

The ANOVA calculations are mathematically simple but involve tedious sums. These calculations are almost always done on a computer.* For example, Excel's one-factor ANOVA menu using Tools > Data Analysis is shown in Figure 11.5. MegaStat uses a similar menu.

---

*Detailed step-by-step examples of all ANOVA calculations can be found in the case studies in *LearningStats* Unit 11.

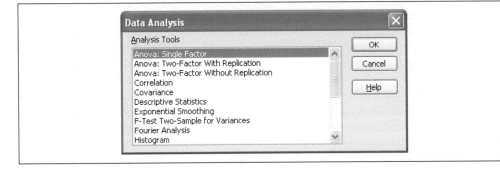

FIGURE 11.5

Excel's ANOVA Menu

Test Statistic

At the beginning of this chapter we described the variation in Y as consisting of explained variation and unexplained variation. To test whether the independent variable explains a significant proportion of the variation in Y, we need to compare the explained (due to treatments) and unexplained (due to error) variation. Recall that the F distribution describes the *ratio of two variances*. Therefore it makes sense that the ANOVA test statistic is the F *test statistic*. The F statistic is the ratio of the variance due to treatments to the variance due to error. MSA is the mean square due to treatments and MSE is the mean square within treatments. Formula 11.9 shows the F statistic and its degrees of freedom.

$$F = \frac{MSA}{MSE} = \frac{\left(\dfrac{SSA}{c-1}\right) \quad\text{d.f.}_1 = c-1 \text{ (numerator)}}{\left(\dfrac{SSE}{n-c}\right) \quad\text{d.f.}_2 = n-c \text{ (denominator)}} \tag{11.9}$$

The test statistic $F = MSA/MSE$ cannot be negative (it's based on sums of squares—see Table 11.2). The F test for equal treatment means is always a right-tailed test. If there is little difference among treatments, we would expect MSA to be near zero because the treatment means $\bar{y}_j$ would be near the overall mean $\bar{y}$. Thus, when F is near zero we would not expect to reject the hypothesis of equal group means. The larger the F statistic, the more we are inclined to reject the hypothesis of equal means. But how large must F be to convince us that the means differ? Just as with a z test or a t test, we need a *decision rule*.

Decision Rule

The F distribution is a right-skewed distribution that starts at zero (F cannot be negative since variances are sums of squares) and has no upper limit (since the variances could be of any magnitude). For ANOVA, the F test is a right-tailed test. For a given level of significance α, we can use Appendix F to obtain the right-tail critical value of F. Alternatively, we can use Excel's function =FINV(α,df$_1$,df$_2$). The decision rule is illustrated in Figure 11.6. This critical value is denoted F_{df_1,df_2} or $F_{c-1,n-c}$.

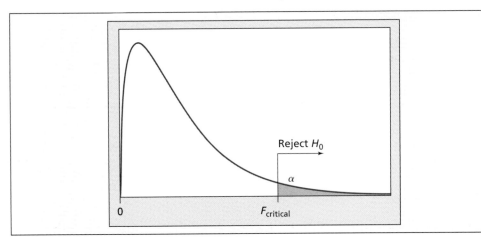

FIGURE 11.6

Decision Rule for an *F* Test

EXAMPLE

Carton Packing

A cosmetics manufacturer's regional distribution center has four workstations that are responsible for packing cartons for shipment to small retailers. Each workstation is staffed by two workers. The task involves assembling each order, placing it in a shipping carton, inserting packing material, taping the carton, and placing a computer-generated shipping label on each carton. Generally, each station can pack 200 cartons a day, and often more. However, there is variability, due to differences in orders, labels, and cartons. Table 11.3 shows the number of cartons packed per day during a recent week. Is the variation among stations within the range attributable to chance, or do these samples indicate actual differences in the means?

TABLE 11.3	Number of Cartons Packed	Cartons		
	Station 1	*Station 2*	*Station 3*	*Station 4*
	236	238	220	241
	250	239	236	233
	252	262	232	212
	233	247	243	231
	239	246	213	213
Sum	1,210	1,232	1,144	1,130
Mean	242.0	246.4	228.8	226.0
St. Dev.	8.515	9.607	12.153	12.884
n	5	5	5	5

As a preliminary step, we plot the data (Figure 11.7) to check for any time pattern and just to visualize the data. We see some potential differences in means, but no obvious time pattern (otherwise we would have to consider observation order as a second factor). We proceed with the hypothesis test.

FIGURE 11.7   **Plot of the Data**

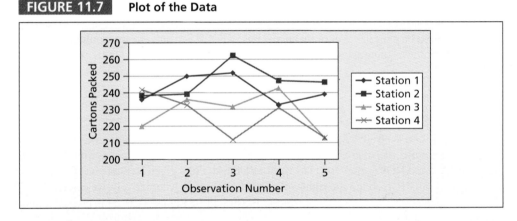

Step 1: State the Hypotheses
The hypotheses to be tested are

H_0: $\mu_1 = \mu_2 = \mu_3 = \mu_4$ (the means are the same)

H_1: Not all the means are equal (at least one mean is different)

Step 2: State the Decision Rule
There are $c = 4$ groups and $n = 20$ observations, so degrees of freedom for the F test are

Numerator: $\text{d.f.}_1 = c - 1 = 4 - 1 = 3$ (between treatments, factor)

Denominator: $\text{d.f.}_2 = n - c = 20 - 4 = 16$ (within treatments, error)

We will use $\alpha = .05$ for the test. The 5 percent right-tail critical value from Appendix F is $F_{3,16} = 3.24$. Instead of Appendix F we could use Excel's function =FINV(0.05,3,16) which yields $F_{.05} = 3.238872$. This decision rule is illustrated in Figure 11.8.

FIGURE 11.8

F Test Using $\alpha = .05$ with $F_{3,16}$

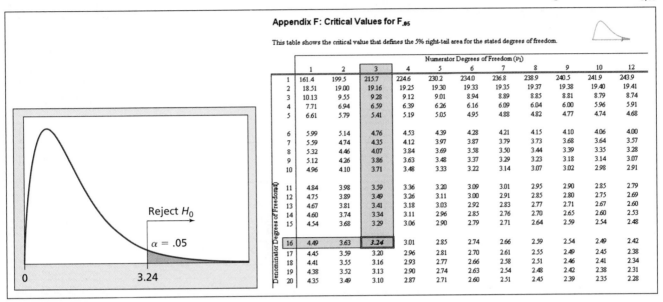

Appendix F: Critical Values for $F_{.05}$

This table shows the critical value that defines the 5% right-tail area for the stated degrees of freedom.

		1	2	3	4	5	6	7	8	9	10	12
	1	161.4	199.5	215.7	224.6	230.2	234.0	236.8	238.9	240.5	241.9	243.9
	2	18.51	19.00	19.16	19.25	19.30	19.33	19.35	19.37	19.38	19.40	19.41
	3	10.13	9.55	9.28	9.12	9.01	8.94	8.89	8.85	8.81	8.79	8.74
	4	7.71	6.94	6.59	6.39	6.26	6.16	6.09	6.04	6.00	5.96	5.91
	5	6.61	5.79	5.41	5.19	5.05	4.95	4.88	4.82	4.77	4.74	4.68
	6	5.99	5.14	4.76	4.53	4.39	4.28	4.21	4.15	4.10	4.06	4.00
	7	5.59	4.74	4.35	4.12	3.97	3.87	3.79	3.73	3.68	3.64	3.57
	8	5.32	4.46	4.07	3.84	3.69	3.58	3.50	3.44	3.39	3.35	3.28
	9	5.12	4.26	3.86	3.63	3.48	3.37	3.29	3.23	3.18	3.14	3.07
	10	4.96	4.10	3.71	3.48	3.33	3.22	3.14	3.07	3.02	2.98	2.91
	11	4.84	3.98	3.59	3.36	3.20	3.09	3.01	2.95	2.90	2.85	2.79
	12	4.75	3.89	3.49	3.26	3.11	3.00	2.91	2.85	2.80	2.75	2.69
	13	4.67	3.81	3.41	3.18	3.03	2.92	2.83	2.77	2.71	2.67	2.60
	14	4.60	3.74	3.34	3.11	2.96	2.85	2.76	2.70	2.65	2.60	2.53
	15	4.54	3.68	3.29	3.06	2.90	2.79	2.71	2.64	2.59	2.54	2.48
	16	4.49	3.63	3.24	3.01	2.85	2.74	2.66	2.59	2.54	2.49	2.42
	17	4.45	3.59	3.20	2.96	2.81	2.70	2.61	2.55	2.49	2.45	2.38
	18	4.41	3.55	3.16	2.93	2.77	2.66	2.58	2.51	2.46	2.41	2.34
	19	4.38	3.52	3.13	2.90	2.74	2.63	2.54	2.48	2.42	2.38	2.31
	20	4.35	3.49	3.10	2.87	2.71	2.60	2.51	2.45	2.39	2.35	2.28

Numerator Degrees of Freedom (v_1)
Denominator Degrees of Freedom (v_2)

Reject H_0

$\alpha = .05$

0   3.24

Step 3: Perform the Calculations

Using Excel for the calculations, we obtain the results shown in Figure 11.9. You can specify the desired level of significance (Excel's default is $\alpha = .05$). Note that Excel labels *SSA* "between groups" and *SSE* "within groups." This is an intuitive and attractive way to describe the variation.

FIGURE 11.9   **Excel's One-Factor ANOVA Results**   **Cartons**

Anova: Single Factor

SUMMARY

Groups	Count	Sum	Average	Variance
Station 1	5	1210	242	72.5
Station 2	5	1232	246.4	92.3
Station 3	5	1144	228.8	147.7
Station 4	5	1130	226	166

ANOVA

Source of Variation	SS	df	MS	F	P-value	F crit
Between Groups	1479.2	3	493.0667	4.121769	0.024124	3.238872
Within Groups	1914	16	119.625			
Total	3393.2	19				

Step 4: Make the Decision

Since the test statistic $F = 4.12$ exceeds the critical value $F_{.05} = 3.24$, we can reject the hypothesis of equal means. Since Excel gives the *p*-value, you don't actually need Excel's critical value. The *p*-value ($p = .024124$) is less than the level of significance ($\alpha = .05$) which confirms that we should reject the hypothesis of equal treatment means. For comparison, Figure 11.10 shows MegaStat's ANOVA table for the same data. The results are the same, although MegaStat rounds things off, highlights significant *p*-values, and gives standard deviations instead of variances for each treatment.

FIGURE 11.10   MegaStat's One-Factor ANOVA Results   Cartons

One factor ANOVA

Mean	n	Std. Dev	
242.0	5	8.51	Station 1
246.4	5	9.61	Station 2
228.8	5	12.15	Station 3
226.0	5	12.88	Station 4
235.8	20	13.36	Total

ANOVA table

Source	SS	df	MS	F	p-value
Treatment	1,479.20	3	493.067	4.12	.0241
Error	1,914.00	16	119.625		
Total	3,393.20	19			

MegaStat provides additional insights by showing a dot plot of observations by group, shown in Figure 11.11. The display includes group means (shown as short horizontal tick marks) and the overall mean (shown as a dashed line). The dot plot suggests that stations 3 and 4 have means below the overall mean, while stations 1 and 2 are above the overall mean.

FIGURE 11.11   Dot Plot of Four Samples   Cartons

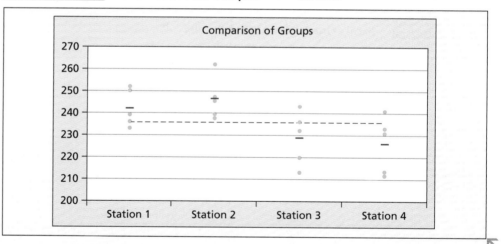

Using MINITAB

MINITAB's output, shown in Figure 11.12, is the same as Excel's except that MINITAB rounds off the results and displays a confidence interval for each group mean, an attractive feature.* In our carton example, the confidence intervals overlap, except possibly stations 2 and 4. But comparing pairs of confidence intervals is not quite the same as what an ANOVA test does, since ANOVA seeks to compare *all* the group means *simultaneously.*

---

*MINITAB and most other statistical packages prefer the data in *stacked* format. Each variable has its own column (e.g., column one contains all the *Y* values, while column two contains group labels like "Station 1"). MINITAB will convert *unstacked* data to *stacked* data for one-factor ANOVA. See *LearningStats* Unit 11 for examples of *stacked* versus *unstacked* data.

FIGURE 11.12

MINITAB's One-Factor ANOVA

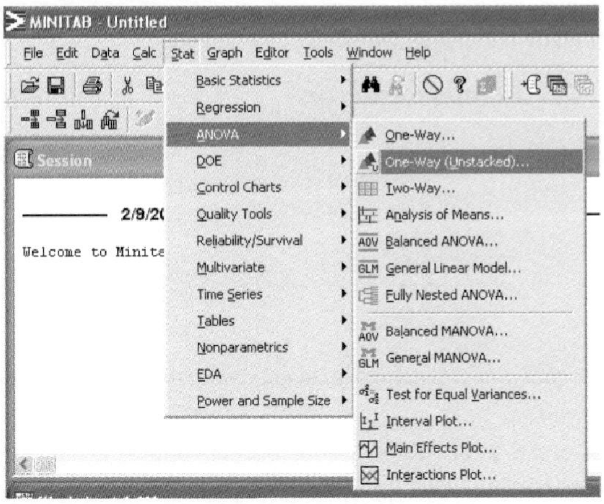

```
MINITAB - Untitled
File Edit Data Calc Stat Graph Editor Tools Window Help
                    Basic Statistics
                    Regression
                    ANOVA          ▸  One-Way...
                    DOE               One-Way (Unstacked)...
Session             Control Charts    Two-Way...
                    Quality Tools     Analysis of Means...
       2/9/20       Reliability/Survival  Balanced ANOVA...
Welcome to Minit    Multivariate      General Linear Model...
                    Time Series       Fully Nested ANOVA...
                    Tables
                    Nonparametrics    Balanced MANOVA...
                    EDA               General MANOVA...
                    Power and Sample Size  Test for Equal Variances...
                                      Interval Plot...
                                      Main Effects Plot...
                                      Interactions Plot...
```

```
One-way ANOVA: Station 1, Station 2, Station 3, Station 4

Source  DF    SS   MS    F     P
Factor   3  1479  493  4.12  0.024
Error   16  1914  120
Total   19  3393

S = 10.94   R-Sq = 43.59%   R-Sq(adj) = 33.02%

                                 Individual 95% CIs For Mean Based on
                                 Pooled StDev
Level      N   Mean   StDev   +---------+---------+---------+---------
Station 1  5  242.00   8.51                      (--------*-------)
Station 2  5  246.40   9.61                        (-------*--------)
Station 3  5  228.80  12.15         (--------*-------)
Station 4  5  226.00  12.88     (-------*--------)
                               +---------+---------+---------+---------
                              216       228       240       252

Pooled StDev = 10.94
```

Instructions: For each data set: (a) State the hypotheses. (b) Use Excel's Tools > Data Analysis (or MegaStat or MINITAB) to perform the one-factor ANOVA, using $\alpha = .05$. (c) State your conclusion about the population means. Was the decision close? (d) Interpret the *p*-value carefully. (e) Include a plot of the data for each group if you are using MegaStat, and confidence intervals for the group means if you are using MINITAB. What do the plots show?

SECTION EXERCISES

connect

11.1   Scrap rates per thousand (parts whose defects cannot be reworked) are compared for 5 randomly selected days at three plants. Does the data prove a significant difference in mean scrap rates?
   ScrapRate

Scrap Rate (Per Thousand Units)

	Plant A	Plant B	Plant C
	11.4	11.1	10.2
	12.5	14.1	9.5
	10.1	16.8	9.0
	13.8	13.2	13.3
	13.7	14.6	5.9

11.2   One particular morning, the length of time spent in the examination rooms is recorded for each patient seen by each physician at an orthopedic clinic. Does the data prove a significant difference in mean times?   **Physicians**

Time in Examination Rooms (minutes)

Physician 1	Physician 2	Physician 3	Physician 4
34	33	17	28
25	35	30	33
27	31	30	31
31	31	26	27
26	42	32	32
34	33	28	33
21		26	40
		29	

11.3   Semester GPAs are compared for seven randomly chosen students in each of four business majors at Oxnard University. Does the data prove a significant difference in mean GPAs?   🐝   **GPA1**

GPA for Randomly Selected Students in Four Business Majors

Accounting	Finance	Human Resources	Marketing
2.48	3.16	2.93	3.54
2.19	3.01	2.89	3.71
2.62	3.07	3.48	2.94
3.15	2.88	3.33	3.46
3.56	3.33	3.53	3.50
2.53	2.87	2.95	3.25
3.31	2.85	3.58	3.20

11.4   Sales of *People* magazine are compared over a 5-week period at four Borders outlets in Chicago. Does the data prove a significant difference in mean weekly sales?   🐝   **Magazines**

Weekly Sales

Store 1	Store 2	Store 3	Store 4
102	97	89	100
106	77	91	116
105	82	75	87
115	80	106	102
112	101	94	100

11.3
MULTIPLE COMPARISONS

Tukey's Test

Besides performing an F test to compare the c means *simultaneously,* we also could ask whether *pairs* of means differ. You might expect to do a t test for two independent means (Chapter 10), or check whether there is overlap in the confidence intervals for each group's mean. But the null hypothesis in ANOVA is that *all* the means are the same, so to maintain the desired overall probability of Type I error, we need to create a *simultaneous confidence interval* for the difference of means based on the *pooled* samples for all c groups at once and then see which pairs exclude zero. For c groups, there are $c(c-1)/2$ distinct pairs of means to be compared.

Several **multiple comparison** tests are available. Their logic is similar. We will discuss only one, called **Tukey's studentized range test** (sometimes called the *HSD* or "honestly significant difference" test). It has good power and is widely used. We will refer to it as *Tukey's test,* named for statistician John Wilder Tukey (1915–2000). This test is available in most statistical packages (but not in Excel's Tools > Data Analysis). It is a two-tailed test for equality of paired means from c groups compared simultaneously and is a natural follow-up when the results of the one-factor ANOVA test show a significant difference in at least one mean. The hypotheses to compare group j with group k are

$H_0: \mu_j = \mu_k$

$H_1: \mu_j \neq \mu_k$

The decision rule is

(11.10) $$\text{Reject } H_0 \text{ if } T_{\text{calc}} = \frac{|\bar{y}_j - \bar{y}_k|}{\sqrt{MSE\left[\dfrac{1}{n_j} + \dfrac{1}{n_k}\right]}} > T_{c,n-c}$$

where $T_{c,n-c}$ is a critical value of the *Tukey test statistic* T_{calc} for the desired level of significance. Table 11.4 shows 5 percent critical values of $T_{c,n-c}$. If the desired degrees of freedom cannot be found, we could interpolate or better yet rely on a computer package like MegaStat to provide the exact critical value. We take *MSE* directly from the ANOVA calculations (see Table 11.2).

				Number of Groups (c)					
$n - c$	2	3	4	5	6	7	8	9	10
5	2.57	3.26	3.69	4.01	4.27	4.48	4.66	4.81	4.95
6	2.45	3.07	3.46	3.75	3.98	4.17	4.33	4.47	4.59
7	2.37	2.95	3.31	3.58	3.79	3.96	4.11	4.24	4.36
8	2.31	2.86	3.20	3.46	3.66	3.82	3.96	4.08	4.19
9	2.26	2.79	3.12	3.36	3.55	3.71	3.84	3.96	4.06
10	2.23	2.74	3.06	3.29	3.47	3.62	3.75	3.86	3.96
15	2.13	2.60	2.88	3.09	3.25	3.38	3.49	3.59	3.68
20	2.09	2.53	2.80	2.99	3.14	3.27	3.37	3.46	3.54
30	2.04	2.47	2.72	2.90	3.04	3.16	3.25	3.34	3.41
40	2.02	2.43	2.68	2.86	2.99	3.10	3.20	3.28	3.35
60	2.00	2.40	2.64	2.81	2.94	3.05	3.14	3.22	3.29
120	1.98	2.37	2.61	2.77	2.90	3.00	3.09	3.16	3.22
∞	1.96	2.34	2.57	2.73	2.85	2.95	3.03	3.10	3.16

TABLE 11.4

Five Percent Critical Values of Tukey Test Statistic*

*Table shows studentized range divided by $\sqrt{2}$ to obtain $T_{c,n-c}$. See R. E. Lund and J. R. Lund, "Probabilities and Upper Quantiles for the Studentized Range," *Applied Statistics* 32 (1983), pp. 204–210.

We will illustrate the Tukey test for the carton-packing data. We assume that a one-factor ANOVA has already been performed and the results showed that at least one mean was significantly different. We will use the *MSE* from the ANOVA. For the carton-packing data there are 4 groups and 20 observations, so $c = 4$ and $n - c = 20 - 4 = 16$. From Table 11.4 we must interpolate between $T_{4,15} = 2.88$ and $T_{4,20} = 2.80$ to get $T_{4,16} = 2.86$. The decision rule for any pair of means is therefore

$$\text{Reject } H_0 \text{ if } T_{calc} = \frac{|\bar{y}_j - \bar{y}_k|}{\sqrt{MSE\left[\dfrac{1}{n_j} + \dfrac{1}{n_k}\right]}} > 2.86$$

There may be a different decision rule for every pair of stations unless the sample sizes n_j and n_k are identical (in our example, the group sizes are the same). For example, to compare groups 2 and 4 the test statistic is

$$T_{calc} = \frac{|\bar{y}_2 - \bar{y}_4|}{\sqrt{MSE\left[\dfrac{1}{n_2} + \dfrac{1}{n_4}\right]}} = \frac{|246.4 - 226.0|}{\sqrt{119.625\left[\dfrac{1}{5} + \dfrac{1}{5}\right]}} = 2.95$$

Since $T_{calc} = 2.95$ exceeds 2.86, we reject the hypothesis of equal means for station 2 and station 4. We conclude that there is a significant difference between the mean output of stations 2 and 4. A similar test must be performed for every possible pair of means.

Using MegaStat

MegaStat includes all six possible comparisons of means, as shown in Figure 11.13. Only stations 2 and 4 differ at $\alpha = .05$. However, if we use the independent sample t test (as in Chapter 10) shown in MegaStat's lower table, we obtain two p-values smaller than $\alpha = .05$ (stations 1, 4 and stations 2, 3) and one that is below $\alpha = .01$ (stations 2, 4). This demonstrates that a *simultaneous* Tukey T test is not the same as comparing individual pairs of means. As noted in Section 11.2, using multiple independent t tests results in a greater probability of making a Type I error. An attractive feature of MegaStat's Tukey test is that it highlights significant results using color-coding for $\alpha = .05$ and $\alpha = .01$, as seen in Figure 11.13.

Tukey simultaneous comparison *t*-values (d.f. = 16)

		Station 4 226.0	Station 3 228.8	Station 1 242.0	Station 2 246.4
Station 4	226.0				
Station 3	228.8	0.40			
Station 1	242.0	2.31	1.91		
Station 2	246.4	2.95	2.54	0.64	

critical values for experimentwise error rate:

0.05	2.86
0.01	3.67

p-values for pairwise *t*-tests

		Station 4 226.0	Station 3 228.8	Station 1 242.0	Station 2 246.4
Station 4	226.0				
Station 3	228.8	.6910			
Station 1	242.0	.0344	.0745		
Station 2	246.4	.0094	.0217	.5337	

Instructions: Use MegaStat, MINITAB, or another software package to perform Tukey's test for significant pairwise differences. Perform the test using both the 5 percent and 1 percent levels of significance.

11.5 Refer to Exercise 11.1. Which pairs of mean scrap rates differ significantly (3 plants)? 🐁 **ScrapRate**

11.6 Refer to Exercise 11.2. Which pairs of mean examination times differ significantly (4 physicians)? 🐁 **Physicians**

11.7 Refer to Exercise 11.3. Which pairs of mean GPAs differ significantly (4 majors)? 🐁 **GPA1**

11.8 Refer to Exercise 11.4. Which pairs of mean weekly sales differ significantly (4 stores)? 🐁 **Magazines**

11.4
TESTS FOR HOMOGENEITY OF VARIANCES

ANOVA Assumptions

Analysis of variance assumes that observations on the response variable are from normally distributed populations that have the same variance. We have noted that few populations meet these requirements perfectly and unless the sample is quite large, a test for normality is impractical. However, we can easily test the assumption of **homogeneous** (equal) **variances**. Although the one-factor ANOVA test is only slightly affected by inequality of variance when group sizes are equal or nearly so, it is still a good idea to test this assumption. In general, surprisingly large differences in variances must exist to conclude that the population variances are unequal.

Hartley's F_{max} Test

If we had only two groups, we could use the *F* test you learned in Chapter 10 to compare the variances. But for *c* groups, a more general test is required. One such test is **Hartley's F_{max} test,** named for statistician H. O. Hartley (1912–1980). The hypotheses are

$H_0: \sigma_1^2 = \sigma_2^2 = \cdots = \sigma_c^2$ (equal variances)

H_1: The σ_j^2 are not all equal (unequal variances)

The test statistic is the ratio of the largest sample variance to the smallest sample variance:

$$F_{max} = \frac{s_{max}^2}{s_{min}^2} \qquad \text{(11.11)}$$

The decision rule is:

Reject H_0 if $F_{max} > F_{critical}$

Critical values of F_{max} may be found in Table 11.5 using degrees of freedom given by

Numerator: $\text{d.f.}_1 = c$

Denominator: $\text{d.f.}_2 = \dfrac{n}{c} - 1$

where n is the total number of observations. This test assumes equal group sizes, so d.f._2 would be an integer. For group sizes that are not drastically unequal, this procedure will still be approximately correct, using the next lower integer if d.f._2 is not an integer. Note that this is *not* the same table as the F table you have used previously.

Denominator d.f.	Numerator d.f. 2	3	4	5	6	7	8	9	10
2	39.0	87.5	142	202	266	333	403	475	550
3	15.4	27.8	39.2	50.7	62.0	72.9	83.5	93.9	104
4	9.60	15.5	20.6	25.2	29.5	33.6	37.5	41.1	44.6
5	7.15	10.8	13.7	16.3	18.7	20.8	22.9	24.7	26.5
6	5.82	8.38	10.4	12.1	13.7	15.0	16.3	17.5	18.6
7	4.99	6.94	8.44	9.7	10.8	11.8	12.7	13.5	14.3
8	4.43	6.00	7.18	8.12	9.03	9.78	10.5	11.1	11.7
9	4.03	5.34	6.31	7.11	7.80	8.41	8.95	9.45	9.91
10	3.72	4.85	5.67	6.34	6.92	7.42	7.87	8.28	8.66
12	3.28	4.16	4.79	5.30	5.72	6.09	6.42	6.72	7.00
15	2.86	3.54	4.01	4.37	4.68	4.95	5.19	5.40	5.59
20	2.46	2.95	3.29	3.54	3.76	3.94	4.10	4.24	4.37
30	2.07	2.40	2.61	2.78	2.91	3.02	3.12	3.21	3.29
60	1.67	1.85	1.96	2.04	2.11	2.17	2.22	2.26	2.30
∞	1.00	1.00	1.00	1.00	1.00	1.00	1.00	1.00	1.00

TABLE 11.5

Critical 5 Percent Values of Hartley's
$$F_{max} = s_{max}^2/s_{min}^2$$

Source: E. S. Pearson and H. O. Hartley, *Biometrika Tables for Statisticians,* 3rd. ed. (Oxford University Press, 1970), p. 202. Copyright © 1970 Oxford University Press. Used with permission.

Using the carton-packing data in Table 11.3, there are 4 groups and 20 total observations, so we have

Numerator: $\text{d.f.}_1 = c = 4$

Denominator: $\text{d.f.}_2 = n/c - 1 = 20/4 - 1 = 5 - 1 = 4$

From Table 11.5 we choose the critical value $F_{max} = 20.6$ using $\text{d.f.}_1 = 4$ and $\text{d.f.}_2 = 4$. The sample statistics (from Excel) for our workstations are

EXAMPLE

Carton Packing: Tukey Test 🐢 **Cartons**

Work Station	n	Mean	Variance
Station 1	15	242.0	72.5
Station 2	17	246.4	92.3
Station 3	15	228.8	147.7
Station 4	12	226.0	166.0

The test statistic is

$$F_{max} = \frac{s_{max}^2}{s_{min}^2} = \frac{166.0}{72.5} = 2.29$$

In this case, we cannot reject the hypothesis of equal variances. Indeed, Table 11.5 makes it clear that unless the sample size is very large, the variance ratio would have to be quite large to reject the hypothesis of equal population variances. If the F_{max} test is significant, we prefer an alternative* to one-factor ANOVA, which does not require this assumption.

Levene's Test

The F_{max} test relies on the assumption of normality in the populations from which the sample observations are drawn. A more robust alternative is **Levene's test,** which does not assume a normal distribution. This test requires a computer package. It is not necessary to discuss the computational procedure except to say that Levene's test is based on the distances of the observations from their sample *medians* rather than their sample *means*. As long as you know how to interpret a *p*-value, Levene's test is easy to use. Figure 11.14 shows MINITAB's output for the test of homogeneity of variance for the carton-packing data using Levene's test, with the added attraction of confidence intervals for each population standard deviation. Since the confidence intervals overlap and the *p*-value (.823) is large, we cannot reject the hypothesis of equal population variances. This confirms that the one-factor ANOVA procedure was appropriate for the carton-packing data.

FIGURE 11.14

MINITAB's Equal-Variance Test   Cartons

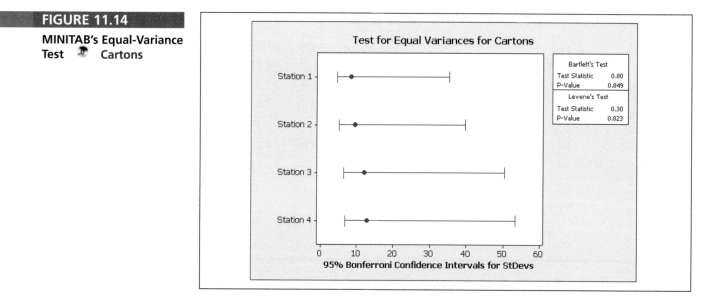

SECTION EXERCISES

connect

Instructions: For each data set, use Hartley's F_{max} test to test the hypothesis of equal variances, using the 5 percent table of critical values from this section and the largest and smallest sample variances from your previous ANOVA. Alternatively, if you have access to MINITAB or another software package, perform Levene's test for equal group variances, discuss the *p*-value, and interpret the graphical display of confidence intervals for standard deviations.

11.9 Refer to Exercise 11.1. Are the population variances the same for scrap rates (3 plants)? **ScrapRate**

11.10 Refer to Exercise 11.2. Are the population variances the same for examination times (4 physicians)? **Physicians**

11.11 Refer to Exercise 11.3. Are the population variances the same for the GPAs (4 majors)? **GPA1**

11.12 Refer to Exercise 11.4. Are the population variances the same for weekly sales (4 stores)? **Magazines**

---

*We could use the nonparametric *Kruskal-Wallis* test from MegaStat or MINITAB.

Mini Case   11.1

Hospital Emergency Arrivals

To plan its staffing schedule, a large urban hospital examined the number of arrivals per day over a 3-month period, as shown in Table 11.6. Each day has 13 observations except Tuesday, which has 14. Data are shown in rows rather than in columns to make a more compact table.

TABLE 11.6   **Number of Emergency Arrivals by Day of the Week**
                    🐜 **Emergency**

Mon	188	175	208	176	179	184	191	194	174	191	198	213	217	
Tue	174	167	165	164	169	164	150	175	178	164	202	175	191	180
Wed	177	169	180	173	182	181	168	165	174	175	174	177	182	
Thu	170	164	190	169	164	170	153	150	156	173	177	183	208	
Fri	177	167	172	185	185	170	170	193	212	171	175	177	209	
Sat	162	184	173	175	144	170	163	157	181	185	199	203	198	
Sun	182	176	183	228	148	178	175	174	188	179	220	207	193	

We perform a one-factor ANOVA to test the model *Arrivals* = *f(Weekday)*. The single factor (*Weekday*) has 7 treatments. The Excel results, shown in Figure 11.15, indicate that *Weekday* does have a significant effect on *Arrivals,* since the test statistic $F = 3.257$ exceeds the 5 percent critical value $F_{6,85} = 2.207$. The *p*-value (.006) indicates that a test statistic this large would arise by chance only about 6 times in 1,000 samples if the hypothesis of equal daily means were true.

FIGURE 11.15

One-Factor ANOVA for Emergency Arrivals and Sample Plot

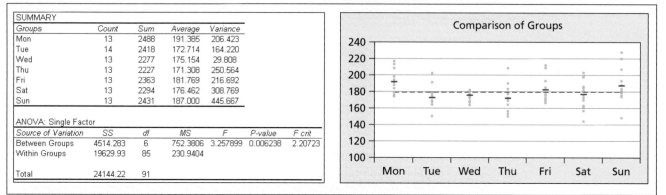

The Tukey multiple comparison test (Figure 11.16) shows that the only pairs of *significantly* different means at $\alpha = .05$ are (*Mon, Tue*) and (*Mon, Thu*). In testing for equal variances, we

FIGURE 11.16   **MegaStat's Tukey Test for $\mu_j - \mu_k$**

Tukey simultaneous comparison *t*-values (d.f. = 84)

		Thu 171.3	Tue 172.2	Wed 175.2	Sat 176.5	Fri 181.8	Sun 187.0	Mon 191.4
Thu	171.3							
Tue	172.2	0.14						
Wed	175.2	0.64	0.50					
Sat	176.5	0.86	0.72	0.22				
Fri	181.8	1.75	1.61	1.10	0.89			
Sun	187.0	2.62	2.48	1.98	1.76	0.87		
Mon	191.4	3.35	3.21	2.71	2.49	1.61	0.73	

critical values for experimentwise error rate:
        0.05   3.03
        0.01   3.59

get conflicting conclusions, depending on which test we use. Hartley's test gives $F_{max} = (445.667)/(29.808) = 14.95$, which exceeds the critical value $F_{7,12} = 6.09$ (note that *Wed* has a *very* small variance). But Levene's test for homogeneity of variances (Figure 11.17) has a p-value of .221, which at $\alpha = .05$ does not allow us to reject the equal-variance assumption that underlies the ANOVA test. When it is available, we prefer Levene's test because it does not depend on the assumption of normality.

FIGURE 11.17   MINITAB Test for Equal Variances   Emergency

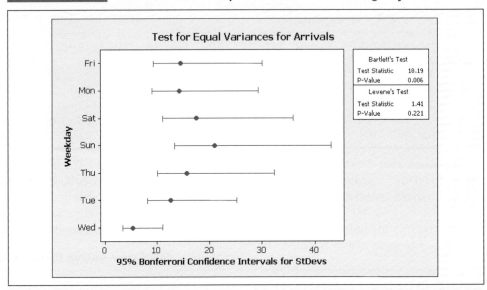

Higher-Order ANOVA Models

Why limit ourselves to one factor? Although complex ANOVA models are beyond the scope of this textbook, the idea of a multifactor ANOVA is not difficult to grasp. Consider the hospital LOS (length of stay) problem from the beginning of this chapter. The mean length of stay might depend not only on fracture type (*Factor A*), but also on the patient's age group (*Factor B*) and gender (*Factor C*). Since ANOVA computations are done by computer, the analysis is no harder than a simple ANOVA. The "catch" is that higher order ANOVA models quickly go beyond Excel's capabilities, so we need a general-purpose statistical package (e.g., MINITAB, SPSS, SAS). We can use the **general linear model** (GLM) for our estimates. Besides allowing more than two factors, GLM permits unbalanced data (unequal sample size within treatments) and complex interactions among factors. GLM can also provide predictions and identify unusual observations, and does not require equal variances (although care must be taken to avoid sparse or empty cells in the data matrix). Consult the *Related Readings* at the end of this chapter if you encounter advanced ANOVA models in your career (or ask your employer to send you to a training class in ANOVA and **experimental design**).

CHAPTER SUMMARY

ANOVA tests whether a numerical dependent variable (**response variable**) is associated with one or more categorical independent variables (**factors**) with several **levels.** Each level or combination of levels is a **treatment. A one-factor ANOVA** compares means in c columns of data. It is a generalization of a two-tailed t test for two independent sample means. Fisher's ***F* statistic** is a ratio of two variances (treatment versus error). It is compared with a right-tailed critical value from an F table or from Excel for appropriate numerator and denominator degrees of freedom. Alternatively, we compare the p-value for the F test statistic with the desired level of significance (p-value less than α is significant). The **Tukey test** compares individual pairs of treatment means. We test for homogeneous variances (an assumption of ANOVA) using **Hartley's F_{max} test** or **Levene's test.** The **general linear model** (GLM) is used when there are more than two factors.

- ANOVA may be helpful even if those who collected the data did not utilize a formal experimental design (often the case in real-world business situations).
- ANOVA calculations are tedious because of the sums required, so computers are generally used.
- One-factor ANOVA is the most common and suffices for many business situations.

- ANOVA is an overall test. To tell which specific pairs of treatment means differ, use the Tukey test.
- Although real-life data may not perfectly meet the normality and equal-variance assumptions, ANOVA is reasonably robust (and alternative tests do exist).

analysis of variance (ANOVA), *403*	Hartley's F_{max} test, *416* homogeneous	partitioned sum of squares, *408*
experimental design, *420*	variances, *416*	response variable, *403*
explained variance, *403*	Levene's test, *418*	treatment, *403*
factors, *403*	mean squares, *408*	Tukey's studentized range
fixed-effects model, *407*	multiple comparison, *414*	test, *414*
general linear model, *420*	one-factor ANOVA, *406*	unexplained variance, *403*

1. Explain each term: (a) explained variation; (b) unexplained variation; (c) factor; (d) treatment.
2. (a) Write the linear model form of one-factor ANOVA. (b) State the hypotheses for a one-factor ANOVA in two different ways.
3. (a) State three assumptions of ANOVA. (b) What do we mean when we say that ANOVA is fairly robust to violations of these assumptions?
4. (a) Sketch the format of a one-factor ANOVA data set (completely randomized model). (b) Must group sizes be the same for one-factor ANOVA? Is it better if they are? (c) Explain the concepts of variation *between treatments* and variation *within treatments*. (d) What is the *F* statistic? (e) State the degrees of freedom for the *F* test in one-factor ANOVA.
5. (a) What is the purpose of the Tukey test? (b) Why can't we just compare all possible pairs of group means using the two-sample *t* test?
6. (a) What does a test for homogeneity of variances tell us? (b) Why should we test for homogeneity of variances? (c) Explain what Hartley's F_{max} test measures. (d) Why might we use Levene's test instead of the F_{max} test?
7. What is the general linear model and why is it useful?

Instructions: You may use Excel, MegaStat, MINITAB, or another computer package of your choice. Attach appropriate copies of the output or capture the screens, tables, and relevant graphs and include them in a written report. Try to state your conclusions succinctly in language that would be clear to a decision maker who is a nonstatistician. Exercises marked * are based on optional material. Answer the following questions, or those your instructor assigns.

a. Choose an appropriate ANOVA model. State the hypotheses to be tested.
b. Display the data visually (e.g., dot plots or MegaStat's line plots). What do the displays show?
c. Do the ANOVA calculations using the computer.
d. State the decision rule for $\alpha = .05$ and make the decision. Interpret the *p*-value.
e. In your judgment, are the observed differences in treatment means (if any) large enough to be of practical importance?
f. Do you think the sample size is sufficient? Explain. Could it be increased? Given the nature of the data, would more data collection be costly?
g. Perform Tukey multiple comparison tests and discuss the results.
h. Perform a test for homogeneity of variances. Explain fully.

11.13 Below are grade point averages for 25 randomly chosen university business students during a recent semester. *Research question:* Are the mean grade point averages the same for students in these four class levels?   GPA2

Grade Point Averages of 25 Business Students

Freshman (5 students)	Sophomore (7 students)	Junior (7 students)	Senior (6 students)
1.91	3.89	3.01	3.32
2.14	2.02	2.89	2.45
3.47	2.96	3.45	3.81
2.19	3.32	3.67	3.02
2.71	2.29	3.33	3.01
	2.82	2.98	3.17
	3.11	3.26	

11.14 The XYZ Corporation is interested in possible differences in days worked by salaried employees in three departments in the financial area. A survey of 23 randomly chosen employees reveals the data shown below. Because of the casual sampling methodology in this survey, the sample sizes are unequal. *Research question:* Are the mean annual attendance rates the same for employees in these three departments? 🐭 **DaysWorked**

Days Worked Last Year by 23 Employees

Department	Days Worked									
Budgets (5 workers)	278	260	265	245	258					
Payables (10 workers)	205	270	220	240	255	217	266	239	240	228
Pricing (8 workers)	240	258	233	256	233	242	244	249		

11.15 Mean output of solar cells of three types are measured six times under random light intensity over a period of 5 minutes, yielding the results shown. *Research question:* Is the mean solar cell output the same for all cell types? 🐭 **SolarWatts**

Solar Cell Output (watts)

Cell Type	Output (watts)					
A	123	121	123	124	125	127
B	125	122	122	121	122	126
C	126	128	125	129	131	128

11.16 In a bumper test, three types of autos were deliberately crashed into a barrier at 5 mph, and the resulting damage (in dollars) was estimated. Five test vehicles of each type were crashed, with the results shown below. *Research question:* Are the mean crash damages the same for these three vehicles? 🐭 **Crash1**

Crash Damage ($)

Goliath	Varmint	Weasel
1,600	1,290	1,090
760	1,400	2,100
880	1,390	1,830
1,950	1,850	1,250
1,220	950	1,920

11.17 The waiting time (in minutes) for emergency room patients with non-life-threatening injuries was measured at four hospitals for all patients who arrived between 6:00 and 6:30 PM on a certain Wednesday. The results are shown below. *Research question:* Are the mean waiting times the same for emergency patients in these four hospitals? 🐭 **ERWait**

Emergency Room Waiting Time (minutes)

Hospital A (5 patients)	Hospital B (4 patients)	Hospital C (7 patients)	Hospital D (6 patients)
10	8	5	0
19	25	11	20
5	17	24	9
26	36	16	5
11		18	10
		29	12
		15	

11.18 The results shown below are mean productivity measurements (average number of assemblies completed per hour) for a random sample of workers at each of three plants. *Research question:* Are the mean hourly productivity levels the same for workers in these three plants? **Productivity**

Hourly Productivity of Assemblers in Plants

Plant	*Finished Units Produced Per Hour*									
A (9 workers)	3.6	5.1	2.8	4.6	4.7	4.1	3.4	2.9	4.5	
B (6 workers)	2.7	3.1	5.0	1.9	2.2	3.2				
C (10 workers)	6.8	2.5	5.4	6.7	4.6	3.9	5.4	4.9	7.1	8.4

11.19 The Environmental Protection Agency (EPA) advocates a maximum arsenic level in water of 10 micrograms per liter. Below are results of EPA tests on randomly chosen wells in a suburban Michigan county. *Research question:* Is the mean arsenic level affected by age of well? **Arsenic**

Arsenic Level in Wells (micrograms per liter)

	Age of Well (years)	
Under 10	***10 to 19***	***20 and Over***
5.4	6.1	6.8
4.3	4.1	5.4
6.1	5.8	5.7
3.4	5.1	4.5
3.7	3.7	5.5
4.3	4.4	4.6
2.4	3.8	3.9
2.9	2.7	2.9
2.7	3.4	4.0

11.20 An MBA director examined GMAT scores for the first ten MBA applicants (assumed to be a random sample of early applicants) for four academic quarters. *Research question:* Do the mean GMAT scores for early applicants differ by quarter? **GMAT**

GMAT Sores of First Ten Applicants

Fall	490	580	440	580	430	420	640	470	530	640
Winter	310	590	730	710	540	450	670	390	500	470
Spring	500	450	510	570	610	490	450	590	640	650
Summer	450	590	710	240	510	670	610	550	540	540

11.21 An ANOVA study was conducted to compare dental offices in six small towns. The response variable was the number of days each dental office was open last year. *Research question:* Is there a difference in the means among these six towns? **DaysOpen**

Dental Clinic Days Open During the Last Year in Six Towns

Chalmers	***Greenburg***	***Villa Nueve***	***Ulysses***	***Hazeltown***
230	194	206	198	214
215	193	200	186	196
221	208	208	206	194
205	198	206	189	190
232		232	181	203
210		208		

11.22 This table shows partial results for a one-factor ANOVA, (a) Calculate the F test statistic. (b) Calculate the p-value using Excel's function =FDIST(F,DF1,DF2). (c) Find the critical value $F_{.05}$ from Appendix F or using Excel's function =FINV(.05,DF1,DF2). (d) Interpret the results.

ANOVA

Source of Variation	SS	df	MS	F	p-value	$F_{.05}$
Between groups	3207.5	3	1069.17			
Within groups	441730	36	12270.28			
Total	444937.5	39				

11.23 Several friends go bowling several times per month. They keep track of their scores over several months. An ANOVA was performed. (a) How could you tell how many friends there were in the sample just from the ANOVA table? Explain. (b) What are your conclusions about bowling scores? Explain, referring either to the *F* test or *p*-value. (c) Do you think the variances can be assumed equal? Explain your reasoning.

SUMMARY

Bowler	Count	Sum	Average	Variance
Mary	15	1856	123.733	77.067
Bill	14	1599	114.214	200.797
Sally	12	1763	146.917	160.083
Robert	15	2211	147.400	83.686
Tom	11	1267	115.182	90.164

ANOVA

Source of Variation	SS	df	MS	F	p-value	F crit
Between Groups	14465.63	4	3616.408	29.8025	0.0000	2.5201
Within Groups	7523.444	62	121.3459			
Total	21989.07	66				

11.24 Are large companies more profitable *per dollar of assets?* The largest 500 companies in the world in 2000 were ranked according to their number of employees, with groups defined as follows: Small = Under 25,000 employees, Medium = 25,000 to 49,999 employees, Large = 50,000 to 99,000 employees, Huge = 100,000 employees or more. An ANOVA was performed using the company's profit-to-assets ratio (percent) as the dependent variable. (a) What is your conclusion about the research question? Explain, referring either to the *F* test or *p*-value. (b) What can you learn from the plots that compare the groups? (c) Do you think the variances can be assumed equal? Explain your reasoning. (d) Perform an F_{max} test to test for unequal variances. (e) Which groups of companies have significantly different means? Explain.

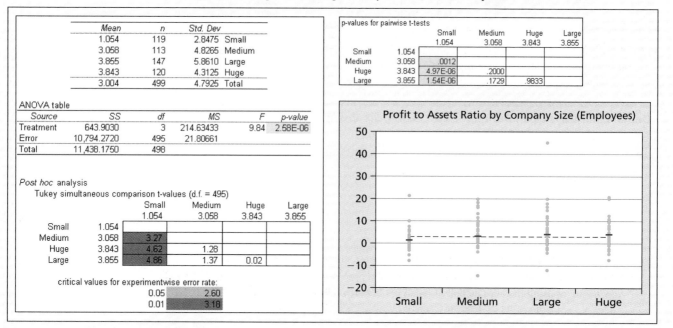

Box, George E.; J. Stuart Hunter; and William G. Hunter. *Statistics for Experimenters.* 2nd ed. John Wiley & Sons, 2005.

Hilbe, Joseph M. "Generalized Linear Models." *The American Statistician* 48, no. 3 (August 1994), pp. 255–65.

Kutner, Michael H.; Christopher Nachtsheim; John Neter; and William Li. *Applied Linear Statistical Models.* 5th ed. McGraw-Hill, 2005.

Miller, Rupert G. *Simultaneous Statistical Inference.* 2nd ed. Springer-Verlag, 1981.

Montgomery, Douglas C. *Design and Analysis of Experiments.* 5th ed. John Wiley & Sons, 2000.

Nelson, Peter R.; Peter S. Wludyka; and Karen A. F. Copeland. *The Analysis of Means: A Graphical Method for Comparing Means, Rates, and Proportions.* SIAM, 2005.

RELATED READINGS

LearningStats Unit 11   Analysis of Variance   LS

LearningStats Unit 11 gives examples of the three most common ANOVA tests (one-factor, two-factor, full factorial), including a simulation and tables of critical values. Your instructor may assign specific modules, or you may pursue those that sound interesting.

Topic	LearningStats Modules
Overview	One-Factor ANOVA Two-Factor ANOVA ANOVA Case Studies
Format and Excel examples	Examples: ANOVA Tests Stacked versus Unstacked Data
Simulation	One-Factor ANOVA ANOVA Data Set Generator
Case studies	One Factor: Car Braking and Noise Two Factors: Car Braking and Noise Two-Factor Replicated: ATM Data Student Project: Call Center Times One Factor: Drug Prices (details) Two Factors: Car Noise (details) Two-Factor Replicated: Braking (details)
General linear model	Insurance Claims Case Study
Tables	Appendix F—Critical Values of *F*

Key: = PowerPoint   = Word   = Excel

Visual Statistics   VS

Visual Statistics Modules on Analysis of Variance

Module	Module Name
12	VS Visualizing Analysis of Variance

Visual Statistics Module 12 (included on your CD) is designed to help you

- Become familiar with situations in which one-factor ANOVA is applicable.
- Understand how much difference must exist between groups to be detected using an *F* test.
- Appreciate the role of sample size in determining power.
- Know the ANOVA assumptions and the effects of violating them.

The worktext (included on the CD in .PDF format) contains lists of concepts covered, objectives of the modules, overviews of concepts, illustrations of concepts, orientations to module features, learning exercises (basic, intermediate, advanced), learning projects (individual, team), self-evaluation quizzes, glossaries of terms, and solutions to self-evaluation quizzes.

Simple Regression

Chapter Contents

Chapter Learning Objectives

When you finish this chapter you should be able to

- Calculate and test a correlation coefficient for significance.

- Explain the OLS method and use the formulas for the slope and intercept.

- Fit a simple regression on an Excel scatter plot.

- Perform regression by using Excel and another package such as MegaStat.

- Interpret confidence intervals for regression coefficients.

- Test hypotheses about the slope and intercept by using t tests.

- Find and interpret the coefficient of determination R^2 and standard error s_{yx}.

- Interpret the ANOVA table and use the F test for a regression.

- Distinguish between confidence and prediction intervals.

- Identify unusual residuals and high-leverage observations.

- Test the residuals for non-normality, heteroscedasticity, and autocorrelation.

- Explain the role of data conditioning and data transformations.

Up to this point, our study of the discipline of statistical analysis has primarily focused on learning how to describe and make inferences about single variables. It is now time to learn how to describe and summarize relationships *between* variables. Businesses of all types can be quite complex. Understanding how different variables in our business processes are related to each other helps us predict and, hopefully, improve our business performance.

Examples of quantitative variables that might be related to each other include: spending on advertising and sales revenue, produce delivery time and percentage of spoiled produce, premium and regular gas prices, preventive maintenance spending and manufacturing productivity rates. It may be that with some of these pairs there is one variable that we would like to be able to *predict* such as sales revenue, percentage of spoiled produce, and productivity rates. But first we must learn how to *visualize, describe,* and *quantify* the relationships between variables such as these.

Chapter 14

Visual Displays

Analysis of **bivariate data** (i.e., two variables) typically begins with a **scatter plot** that displays each observed data pair (x_i, y_i) as a dot on an *X-Y* grid. This diagram provides a visual indication of the strength of the relationship or association between the two random variables. This simple display requires no assumptions or computation. A scatter plot is typically the precursor to more complex analytical techniques. Figure 12.1 shows a scatter plot comparing the price per gallon of regular unleaded gasoline to the price per gallon of premium gasoline.

We look at scatter plots to get an initial idea of the relationship between two random variables. Is there an evident pattern to the data? Is the pattern linear or nonlinear? Are there data points that are not part of the overall pattern? We would characterize the fuel price relationship as linear (although not perfectly linear) and positive (as diesel prices increase, so do regular unleaded prices). We see one pair of values set slightly apart from the rest, above and to the right. This happens to be the state of Hawaii.

FIGURE 12.1

Fuel Prices

FuelPrices

Source: AAA Fuel Gauge Report,
May 27, 2007, www.fuelgaugereport.com

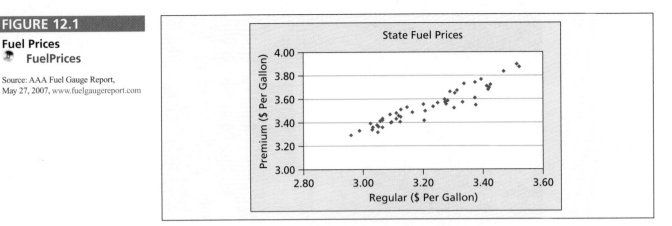

Correlation Coefficient

A visual display is a good first step in analysis but we would also like to quantify the strength of the association between two variables. Therefore, accompanying the scatter plot is the **sample correlation coefficient** (also called the Pearson correlation coefficient.) This statistic measures the degree of linearity in the relationship between X and Y and is denoted r. Its range is $-1 \le r \le +1$. When r is near 0 there is little or no linear relationship between X and Y. An r-value near $+1$ indicates a strong positive relationship, while an r-value near -1 indicates a strong negative relationship.

$$(12.1) \qquad r = \frac{\sum_{i=1}^{n}(x_i - \bar{x})(y_i - \bar{y})}{\sqrt{\sum_{i=1}^{n}(x_i - \bar{x})^2}\sqrt{\sum_{i=1}^{n}(y_i - \bar{y})^2}} \qquad \text{(sample correlation coefficient)}$$

To simplify the notation here and elsewhere in this chapter, we define three terms called **sums of squares**:

$$(12.2) \quad SS_{xx} = \sum_{i=1}^{n}(x_i - \bar{x})^2 \qquad SS_{yy} = \sum_{i=1}^{n}(y_i - \bar{y})^2 \qquad SS_{xy} = \sum_{i=1}^{n}(x_i - \bar{x})(y_i - \bar{y})$$

Using this notation, the formula for the sample correlation coefficient can be written

$$(12.3) \qquad r = \frac{SS_{xy}}{\sqrt{SS_{xx}}\sqrt{SS_{yy}}} \qquad \text{(sample correlation coefficient)}$$

Excel Tip

To calculate a sample correlation coefficient, use Excel's function =CORREL(array1,array2) where array1 is the range for X and array2 is the range for Y. Data may be in rows or columns. Arrays must be the same length.

The correlation coefficient for the variables shown in Figure 12.1 is $r = .947$, which is not surprising. We would expect to see a strong linear positive relationship between state regular unleaded gasoline prices and premium gasoline prices. Figure 12.2 shows prototype scatter plots. We see that a correlation of .500 implies a great deal of random variation, and even a correlation of .900 is far from "perfect" linearity. The last scatter plot shows $r = .00$ despite an obvious *curvilinear* relationship between X and Y. This illustrates the fact that a correlation coefficient only measures the degree of *linear* relationship between X and Y.

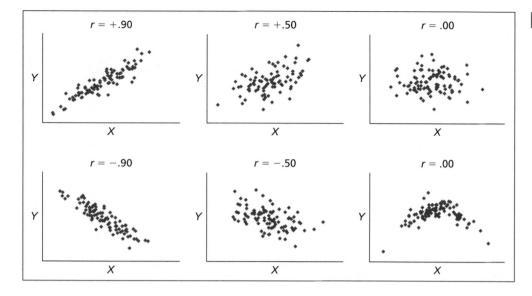

FIGURE 12.2

Scatter Plots Showing Various Correlation Coefficient Values

Correlation analysis has many business applications. For example:

- Financial planners study correlations between asset classes over time, in order to help their clients diversify their portfolios.
- Marketing analysts study correlations between customer online purchases in order to develop new Web advertising strategies.
- Human resources experts study correlations between measures of employee performance in order to devise new job-training programs.

Tests for Significance

The sample correlation coefficient r is an estimate of the **population correlation coefficient** ρ (the Greek letter *rho*). There is no flat rule for a "high" correlation because sample size must be taken into consideration. There are two ways to test a correlation coefficient for significance. To test the hypothesis H_0: $\rho = 0$, the test statistic is

$$t_{\text{calc}} = r\sqrt{\frac{n-2}{1-r^2}} \qquad \text{(test for zero correlation)} \qquad (12.4)$$

We compare this t test statistic with a critical value of t for a one-tailed or two-tailed test from Appendix D using $\nu = n - 2$ degrees of freedom and any desired α. After calculating the *t statistic*, we can find its *p*-value by using Excel's function =TDIST(t,deg_freedom,tails). MINITAB directly calculates the *p*-value for a two-tailed test without displaying the *t* statistic.

In its admission decision process, a university's MBA program examines an applicant's cumulative undergraduate GPA, as well as the applicant's GPA in the last 60 credits taken. They also examine scores on the GMAT (Graduate Management Aptitude Test), which has both verbal and quantitative components. Figure 12.3 shows two scatter plots with sample correlation coefficients for 30 MBA applicants randomly chosen from 1,961 MBA applicant records at a public university in the Midwest. Is the correlation ($r = .8296$) between cumulative and last 60 credit GPA statistically significant? Is the correlation ($r = .4356$) between verbal and quantitative GMAT scores statistically significant?

EXAMPLE

MBA Applicants
MBA

Step 1: State the Hypotheses
We will use a two-tailed test for significance at $\alpha = .05$. The hypotheses are

H_0: $\rho = 0$
H_1: $\rho \neq 0$

FIGURE 12.3

Scatter Plots for 30 MBA Applicants   🐟   **MBA**

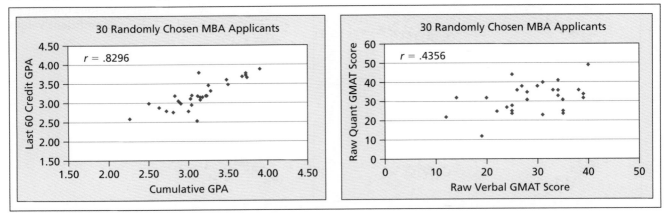

Step 2: Specify the Decision Rule

For a two-tailed test using $v = n - 2 = 30 - 2 = 28$ degrees of freedom, Appendix D gives $t_{.025} = 2.048$. The decision rule is

Reject H_0 if $t_{calc} > 2.048$ or if $t_{calc} < -2.048$.

This rule is the same for testing the correlation between either pair of variables since the number of paired observations is the same.

Step 3: Calculate the Test Statistic

To calculate the test statistic we first need to find the values for r. Using Excel's function =CORREL(array1,array2) we find $r = .8296$ for the variables *Cumulative GPA* and *Last 60 Credit GPA*. We find $r = .4356$ for the variables *Quant GMAT* and *Verbal GMAT*. We must then calculate two values of t_{calc}. For GPA,

$$t_{calc} = r \sqrt{\frac{n-2}{1-r^2}} = .8296 \sqrt{\frac{30-2}{1-(.8296)^2}} = 7.862$$

and for GMAT score,

$$t_{calc} = r \sqrt{\frac{n-2}{1-r^2}} = .4356 \sqrt{\frac{30-2}{1-(.4356)^2}} = 2.561$$

Step 4: Make a Decision

Both test statistic values ($t_{calc} = 7.862$ and $t_{calc} = 2.561$) exceed the critical value $t_{.025} = 2.048$, so we reject the hypothesis of zero correlation at $\alpha = .05$ in both cases. Notice that t_{calc} is much greater for the GPA variables, leading to a stronger rejection of zero correlation than in the case of the GMAT score variables.

We can also find the *p*-value for each test using the Excel function =TDIST(t,deg_freedom,tails). For example, for the two-tailed *p*-value for GPA, =TDIST(7.862,28,2) = .0000 and for the two-tailed *p*-value for GMAT score, =TDIST(2.561,28,2) = .0161. We would reject $\rho = 0$ in both cases since $p < .05$.

Mini Case   12.1

Alumni Giving

Private universities (and, increasingly, public ones) rely heavily on alumni donations. Do highly selective universities have more loyal alumni? Figure 12.4 shows a scatter plot of freshman acceptance rates against percent of alumni who donate at 115 nationally ranked U.S. universities (those that offer a wide range of undergraduate, master's, and doctoral degrees). The correlation coefficient, calculated in Excel by using Tools > Data Analysis > Correlation is $r = -.6248$. This negative correlation suggests that more competitive universities

FIGURE 12.4   **Scatter Plot for Acceptance Rates and Alumni Giving**

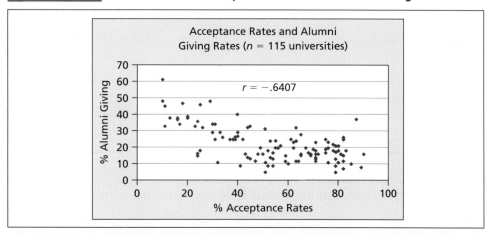

(lower acceptance rate) have more loyal alumni (higher percentage contributing annually). But is the correlation statistically significant?

Since we have a prior hypothesis of an inverse relationship between X and Y, we choose a left-tailed test:

H_0: $\rho \geq 0$

H_1: $\rho < 0$

With $v = n - 2 = 115 - 2 = 113$ degrees of freedom, for $\alpha = .05$, we use Excel's *two-tailed* function =TINV(0.10,113) to obtain the *one-tail* critical value $t_{.05} = 1.65845$. Since we are doing a left-tailed test, the critical value is $t_{.05} = -1.65845$. The t test statistic is

$$t_{\text{calc}} = r\sqrt{\frac{n-2}{1-r^2}} = (-.6407)\sqrt{\frac{115-2}{1-(-.6407)^2}} = -8.871$$

Since the test statistic $t_{\text{calc}} = -8.871$ is less than the critical value $t_{.05} = -1.65845$, we conclude that the true correlation is negative. We can use Excel's function =TDIST(8.871,113,1) to obtain $p = .0000$.

See *U.S. News & World Report*, August 30, 2004, pp. 94–96.

Critical Value for Correlation Coefficient

An equivalent approach is to calculate a critical value for the correlation coefficient. First, look up the critical value of t from Appendix D with $v = n - 2$ degrees of freedom for either a one-tailed or two-tailed test, with the α you choose. Then, the critical value of the correlation coefficient, r_{critical}, is

$$r_{\text{critical}} = \frac{t}{\sqrt{t^2 + n - 2}} \qquad \text{(critical value for a correlation coefficient)} \qquad \textbf{(12.5)}$$

An advantage of this method is that you get a benchmark for the correlation coefficient. Its disadvantage is that there is no *p*-value and it is inflexible if you change your mind about α. MegaStat uses this method, giving two-tail critical values for $\alpha = .05$ and $\alpha = .01$.

When the t table is unavailable, a quick two-tailed test for significance of a correlation at $\alpha = .05$ is

$$|r| > 2/\sqrt{n} \qquad \text{(quick 5\% rule for significance)} \qquad \textbf{(12.6)}$$

This quick rule is derived from formula 12.5 by inserting 2 in place of t. It is based on the fact that two-tail t-values for $\alpha = .05$ usually are not far from 2, as you can verify from Appendix D. This quick rule is exact for $v = 60$ and works reasonably well as long as n is not too small. It is illustrated in Table 12.1.

Table 12.1 shows that, as sample size increases, the critical value of r becomes smaller. Thus, in very large samples, even very small correlations could be "significant." In a larger sample, smaller values of the sample correlation coefficient can be considered "significant." While

TABLE 12.1

Quick 5 Percent Critical Value for Correlation Coefficients

Sample Size	Quick Rule	Quick $r_{critical}$	Actual $r_{critical}$
$n = 25$	$\lvert r \rvert > \dfrac{2}{\sqrt{25}}$	.400	.396
$n = 50$	$\lvert r \rvert > \dfrac{2}{\sqrt{50}}$	.283	.279
$n = 100$	$\lvert r \rvert > \dfrac{2}{\sqrt{100}}$	.200	.197
$n = 200$	$\lvert r \rvert > \dfrac{2}{\sqrt{200}}$	.141	.139

a larger sample does give a better estimate of the true value of ρ, a larger sample does *not* mean that the correlation is stronger nor does its increased *significance* imply increased *importance*.

Tip

In large samples, small correlations may be significant, even though the scatter plot shows little evidence of linearity. Thus, a *significant* correlation may lack practical *importance*.

EXAMPLE

Using $r_{critical}$ to Find Significant Correlation

States

This example illustrates how MegaStat tests for significant correlation. Eight cross-sectional variables were selected from the *LearningStats* state database (50 states):

Burglary	Burglary rate per 100,000 population
Age65%	Percent of population aged 65 and over
Income	Personal income per capita in current dollars
Unem	Unemployment rate, civilian labor force
SATQ	Average SAT quantitative test score
Cancer	Death rate per 100,000 population due to cancer
Unmar	Percent of total births by unmarried women
Urban%	Percent of population living in urban areas

For $n = 50$ states we have $v = n - 2 = 50 - 2 = 48$ degrees of freedom. From Appendix D and using α's of .05 and .01, the two-tail critical values for Student's t are $t_{.025} = 2.011$ and $t_{.005} = 2.682$. MegaStat calculates $r_{critical}$ using formula 12.5.

For $\alpha = .05$,

$$r_{critical} = \frac{t_{.025}}{\sqrt{t_{.025}^2 + n - 2}} = \frac{2.011}{\sqrt{(2.011)^2 + 50 - 2}} = .279$$

and for $\alpha = .01$,

$$r_{critical} = \frac{t_{.005}}{\sqrt{t_{.005} + n - 2}} = \frac{2.682}{\sqrt{(2.682)^2 + 50 - 2}} = .361$$

Figure 12.5 shows MegaStat's correlation matrix for these eight cross-sectional variables. The critical values are shown and significant correlations are highlighted. Four are significant at $\alpha = .01$ and seven more at $\alpha = .05$. In a two-tailed test, the sign of the correlation is of no interest, but the sign does reveal the direction of the association. For example, there is a strong positive correlation between *Cancer* and *Age65%*, and between *Urban%* and *Income*. This says that states with older populations have higher cancer rates and that states with a greater degree of urbanization tend to have higher incomes. The negative correlation between *Burglary* and *Income* says that states with higher incomes tend to have fewer burglaries. Although no cause-and-effect is posited, such correlations naturally invite speculation about causation.

FIGURE 12.5 MegaStat's Correlation Matrix for State Data 🐟 States

	Burglary	Age65%	Income	Unem	SATQ	Cancer	Unmar	Urban%
Burglary	1.000							
Age65%	−.120	1.000						
Income	−.345	−.088	1.000					
Unem	.340	−.280	−.326	1.000				
SATQ	−.179	.105	−.273	−.138	1.000			
Cancer	−.085	.867	−.091	−.151	−.044	1.000		
Unmar	.595	.125	−.291	.420	−.207	.283	1.000	
Urban%	.210	−.030	.646	−.098	−.341	−.031	.099	1.000

50 sample size   ±.279 critical value .05 (two-tail)
±.361 critical value .01 (two-tail)

Note that each cell on the diagonal is equal to 1.000 because each variable is perfectly correlated with itself.

12.1 For each sample, do a test for zero correlation. (a) Use Appendix D to find the critical value of t_α.
(b) State the hypotheses about ρ. (c) Perform the t test and report your decision. (d) Find the critical value of r_α and use it to perform the same hypothesis test.

a. $r = +.45$, $n = 20$, $\alpha = .05$, two-tailed test
b. $r = -.35$, $n = 30$, $\alpha = .10$, two-tailed test
c. $r = +.60$, $n = 7$, $\alpha = .05$, right-tailed test
d. $r = -.30$, $n = 61$, $\alpha = .01$, left-tailed test

SECTION EXERCISES

connect·

Instructions for Exercises 12.2 and 12.3: (a) Make an Excel scatter plot. What does it suggest about
the population correlation between X and Y? (b) Make an Excel worksheet to calculate SS_{xx}, SS_{yy}, and
SS_{xy}. Use these sums to calculate the sample correlation coefficient. Check your work by using Excel's
function =CORREL(array1,array2). (c) Use Appendix D to find $t_{.025}$ for a two-tailed test for zero correlation
at $\alpha = .05$. (d) Calculate the t test statistic. Can you reject $\rho = 0$? (e) Use Excel's function
=TDIST(t,deg_freedom,tails) to calculate the two-tail p-value.

12.2 Part-Time Weekly Earnings ($) by College Students 🐟 WeekPay

Hours Worked (X)	Weekly Pay (Y)
10	93
15	171
20	204
20	156
35	261

12.3 Data Set Telephone Hold Time (min.) for Concert Tickets 🐟 CallWait

Operators (X)	Wait Time (Y)
4	385
5	335
6	383
7	344
8	288

Instructions for Exercises 12.4–12.6: (a) Make a scatter plot of the data. What does it suggest about the
correlation between X and Y? (b) Use Excel, MegaStat, or MINITAB to calculate the correlation coefficient. (c) Use Excel or Appendix D to find $t_{.025}$ for a two-tailed test at $\alpha = .05$. (d) Calculate the t test
statistic. (e) Can you reject $\rho = 0$?

12.4   Moviegoer Spending ($) on Snacks   Movies

Age (X)	Spent (Y)
30	2.85
50	6.50
34	1.50
12	6.35
37	6.20
33	6.75
36	3.60
26	6.10
18	8.35
46	4.35

12.5   Portfolio Returns on Selected Mutual Funds   Portfolio

Last Year (X)	This Year (Y)
11.9	15.4
19.5	26.7
11.2	18.2
14.1	16.7
14.2	13.2
5.2	16.4
20.7	21.1
11.3	12.0
−1.1	12.1
3.9	7.4
12.9	11.5
12.4	23.0
12.5	12.7
2.7	15.1
8.8	18.7
7.2	9.9
5.9	18.9

12.6   Number of Orders and Shipping Cost ($)   ShipCost

Orders (X)	Ship Cost (Y)
1,068	4,489
1,026	5,611
767	3,290
885	4,113
1,156	4,883
1,146	5,425
892	4,414
938	5,506
769	3,346
677	3,673
1,174	6,542
1,009	5,088

12.7   (a) Use Excel, MegaStat, or MINITAB to calculate a matrix of correlation coefficients. (b) Calculate the critical value of r_α. (c) Highlight the correlation coefficients that lead you to reject $\rho = 0$ in a two-tailed test. (d) What conclusions can you draw about rates of return?

Average Annual Returns for 12 Home Construction Companies				Construction
Company Name	*1-Year*	*3-Year*	*5-Year*	*10-Year*
Beazer Homes USA	50.3	26.1	50.1	28.9
Centex	23.4	33.3	40.8	28.6
D.R. Horton	41.4	42.4	52.9	35.8
Hovnanian Ent	13.8	67.0	73.1	33.8
KB Home	46.1	38.8	35.3	24.9
Lennar	19.4	39.3	50.9	36.0
M.D.C. Holdings	48.7	41.6	53.2	39.7
NVR	65.1	55.7	74.4	63.9
Pulte Homes	36.8	42.4	42.1	27.9
Ryland Group	30.5	46.9	59.0	33.3
Standard Pacific	33.0	39.5	44.2	27.8
Toll Brothers	72.6	46.2	49.1	29.9

Source: *The Wall Street Journal*, February 28, 2005. *Note:* Data are intended for educational purposes only.

Mini Case   12.2

Do Loyalty Cards Promote Sales Growth?

A business can achieve sales growth by increasing the number of new customers. Another way is by increasing business from existing customers. Loyal customers visit more often, thus contributing to sales growth. Loyalty cards are used by many companies to foster positive relationships with their customers. Customers carry a card that records the number of purchases or visits they make. They are rewarded with a free item or discount after so many visits. But do these loyalty cards provide incentive to repeat customers to visit more often? Surprisingly, Noodles & Company found out that this wasn't happening in some markets. After several years of running a loyalty card program without truly measuring their impact on the business, in 2005, Noodles performed a correlation analysis on the variables "Sales Growth Percentage" and "Loyalty Card Sales Percentage". The results showed that in some markets there was no significant correlation, meaning the loyalty cards weren't associated with increased sales revenue. However, in other markets there was actually *a statistically significant negative correlation.* In other words, loyalty cards were associated with a decrease in sales growth. Why? Ultimately, the free visits that customers had earned were replacing visits that they would have otherwise paid full price for. Moreover, the resources the company was devoting to the program were taking away from more proven sales building techniques, such as holding non-profit fundraisers or tastings for local businesses. Based on this analysis, Noodles & Company made the decision to discontinue their loyalty card program and focused on other approaches to building loyal customers.

What Is Regression?   12.2
                                                                              SIMPLE
                                                                            REGRESSION

Correlation coefficients and scatter plots provide clues about relationships among variables and may suffice for some purposes. But often, the analyst would like to model the relationship for prediction purposes. For example, a business might hypothesize that

- Advertising expenditures predict quarterly sales revenue.
- Number of dependents predicts employee prescription drug expenses.
- Apartment size predicts monthly rent.

- Number of diners predicts business lunch expense.
- Assembly line speed predicts number of product defects.

A **simple regression** model specifies one *dependent* variable (sometimes called the *response*) and one *independent* variable (sometimes called the *predictor*). Only the dependent variable (not the independent variable) is treated as a random variable. After these relationships are estimated, the business can explore policy questions such as:

- How much extra sales will be generated, on average, by a $1 million increase in advertising expenditures? What would expected sales be with no advertising?
- How much do prescription drug costs per employee rise, on average, with each extra dependent? What would be the expected cost if the employee had no dependents?
- How much extra rent, on average, is paid per extra square foot?
- How much extra luncheon cost, on average, is generated by each additional member of the group? How much could be saved by restricting luncheon groups to three persons?
- If the assembly line speed is increased by 20 units per hour, what would happen to the mean number of product defects?

Interpreting a Fitted Regression

The intercept and slope of a **fitted regression** can provide useful information. For example:

$Sales = 268 + 7.37\ Ads$

Each extra $1 million of advertising will generate $7.37 million of sales on average. The firm would average $268 million of sales with zero advertising. However, the intercept may not be meaningful because $Ads = 0$ may be outside the range of observed data.

$DrugCost = 410 + 550\ Dependents$

Each extra dependent raises the mean annual prescription drug cost by $550. An employee with zero dependents averages $410 in prescription drugs.

$Rent = 150 + 1.05\ SqFt$

Each extra square foot adds $1.05 to monthly apartment rent. The intercept is not meaningful because no apartment can have $SqFt = 0$.

$Cost = 15.22 + 19.96\ Persons$

Each additional diner increases the mean dinner cost by $19.96. The intercept is not meaningful because $Persons = 0$ would not be observable.

$Defects = 3.2 + 0.045\ Speed$

Each unit increase in assembly line speed adds an average of 0.045 defects per million. The intercept is not meaningful since zero assembly line speed implies no production at all.

When we propose a regression model, we have a causal mechanism in mind, but cause-and-effect is not proven by a simple regression. We should not read too much into a fitted equation.

Prediction Using Regression

One of the main uses of regression is to make predictions. Once we have a fitted regression equation that shows the estimated relationship between X (the independent variable) and Y (the dependent variable), we can plug in any value of X to obtain the prediction for Y. For example:

Sales $= 268 + 7.37$ *Ads*	If the firm spends \$10 million on advertising, its expected sales would be \$341.7 million, that is, *Sales* $= 268 + 7.37(10) = 341.7$.
DrugCost $= 410 + 550$ *Dependents*	If an employee has four dependents, the expected annual drug cost would be \$2,610, that is, *DrugCost* $= 410 + 550(4) = 2,610$.
Rent $= 150 + 1.05$ *SqFt*	The expected rent on an 800 square foot apartment is \$990, that is, *Rent* $= 150 + 1.05(800) = 990$.
Cost $= 15.22 + 19.96$ *Persons*	The expected cost of dinner for two couples would be \$95.06, that is, *Cost* $= 15.22 + 19.96(4) = 95.06$.
Defects $= 3.2 + 0.045$ *Speed*	If 100 units per hour are produced, the expected defect rate is 7.7 defects per million, that is, *Defects* $= 3.2 + 0.045(100) = 7.7$.

12.8   (a) Interpret the slope of the fitted regression *Sales* $= 842 - 37.5$ *Price*. (b) If *Price* $= 20$, what is the prediction for *Sales*? (c) Would the intercept be meaningful if this regression represents DVD sales at Blockbuster?

12.9   (a) Interpret the slope of the fitted regression *HomePrice* $= 125,000 + 150$ *SquareFeet*. (b) What is the prediction for *HomePrice* if *SquareFeet* $= 2,000$? (c) Would the intercept be meaningful if this regression applies to home sales in a certain subdivision?

Models and Parameters

The model's *unknown parameters* are denoted by Greek letters β_0 (the **intercept**) and β_1 (the **slope**). The *assumed* model for a linear relationship is

$$y_i = \beta_0 + \beta_1 x_i + \varepsilon_i \qquad \text{(assumed linear relationship)} \qquad \textbf{(12.7)}$$

This relationship is assumed to hold for all observations ($i = 1, 2, \ldots, n$). Inclusion of a random error ε_i is necessary because other unspecified variables may also affect Y and also because there may be measurement error in Y. The error is not observable. We assume that the error term ε_i is a normally distributed random variable with mean 0 and standard deviation σ. Thus, the regression model actually has three unknown parameters: β_0, β_1, and σ. From the sample, we estimate the **fitted model** and use it to predict the *expected* value of Y for a given value of X:

$$\hat{y}_i = b_0 + b_1 x_i \qquad \text{(fitted linear regression model)} \qquad \textbf{(12.8)}$$

Roman letters denote the *fitted coefficients* b_0 (the estimated intercept) and b_1 (the estimated slope). For a given value x_i the *fitted* value (or estimated value) of the dependent variable is $\hat{y}_i$. (You can read this as "y-hat".) The difference between the observed value y_i and the fitted value $\hat{y}_i$ is the **residual** and is denoted e_i. A residual will always be calculated as the observed value minus the estimated value.

$$e_i = y_i - \hat{y}_i \qquad \text{(residual)} \qquad \textbf{(12.9)}$$

The residuals may be used to estimate σ, the standard deviation of the errors.

Estimating a Regression Line by Eye

From a scatter plot, you can visually estimate the slope and intercept, as illustrated in Figure 12.6. In this graph, the approximate slope is 10 and the approximate intercept (when $X = 0$) is around 15 (i.e., $\hat{y}_i = 15 + 10x_i$). This method, of course, is inexact. However, experiments suggest that people are pretty good at "eyeball" line fitting. You intuitively try to adjust the line so as to ensure that the residuals sum to zero (i.e., the positive residuals offset the negative residuals) and to ensure that no other values for the slope or intercept would give a better "fit."

"Eyeball" Regression Line Fitting

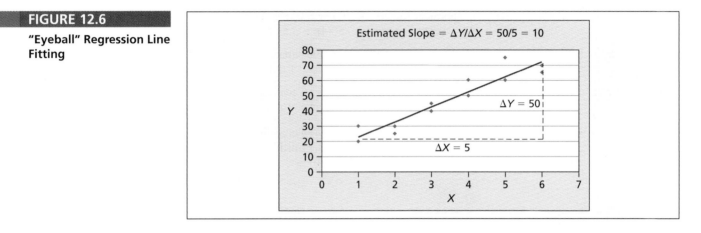

Fitting a Regression on a Scatter Plot in Excel

A more precise method is to let Excel do the estimates. We enter observations on the independent variable $x_1, x_2, \ldots, x_n$ and the dependent variable $y_1, y_2, \ldots, y_n$ into separate columns, and let Excel fit the regression equation.* The easiest way to find the equation of the regression line is to have Excel add the line onto a scatter plot, using the following steps:

- Step 1:   Highlight the data columns.
- Step 2:   Click on Insert and choose Scatter to create a graph.
- Step 3:   Click on the scatter plot points to select the data.
- Step 4:   Right-click and choose Add Trendline.
- Step 5:   Choose Options and check Display equation on chart.

The menus are shown in Figure 12.7. (The R-squared statistic is actually the correlation coefficient squared. It tells us what proportion of the variation in Y is explained by X. We will more fully define R^2 in section 12.4.) Excel will choose the regression coefficients so as to produce a good fit. In this case, Excel's fitted regression $\hat{y}_i = 13 + 9.857x_i$ is close to our "eyeball" regression equation.

FIGURE 12.7

Excel's Trendline Menus

---

*Excel calls its regression equation a "trendline," although actually that would refer to a time-series trend.

Illustration: Piper Cheyenne Fuel Consumption   Cheyenne

Table 12.2 shows a sample of fuel consumption and flight hours for five legs of a cross-country test flight in a Piper Cheyenne, a twin-engine piston business aircraft. Figure 12.8 displays the Excel graph and its fitted regression equation.

Flight Hours	Fuel Used (lbs.)
2.3	145
4.2	258
3.6	219
4.7	276
4.9	283

TABLE 12.2

Piper Cheyenne Fuel Usage

Source: *Flying* 130, no. 4 (April 2003), p. 99.

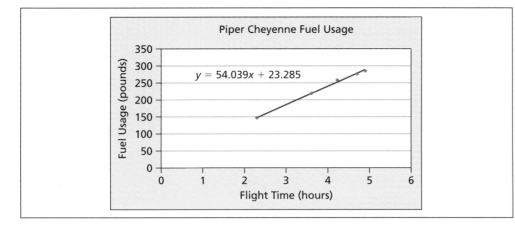

FIGURE 12.8

Fitted Regression

Slope Interpretation   The fitted regression is $\hat{y} = 23.285 + 54.039x$. The slope ($b_1 = 54.039$) says that for each additional hour of flight, the Piper Cheyenne consumed about 54 pounds of fuel (1 gallon $\approx$ 6 pounds). This estimated slope is a *statistic,* since a different sample might yield a different estimate of the slope. Bear in mind also that the sample size is very small.

Intercept Interpretation   The intercept ($b_0 = 23.295$) suggests that even if the plane is not flying ($X = 0$) some fuel would be consumed. However, the intercept has little meaning in this case, not only because zero flight hour makes no logical sense, but also because extrapolating to $X = 0$ is beyond the range of the observed data.

Regression Caveats

- The "fit" of the regression does *not* depend on the sign of its slope. The sign of the fitted slope merely tells whether X has a positive or negative association with Y.
- View the intercept with skepticism unless $X = 0$ is logically possible and was actually observed in the data set.
- Regression does not demonstrate cause-and-effect between X and Y. A good fit only shows that X and Y vary together. Both could be affected by another variable or by the way the data are defined.

12.10   The regression equation *NetIncome* $= 2,277 + .0307$ *Revenue* was fitted from a sample of 100 leading world companies (variables are in millions of dollars). (a) Interpret the slope. (b) Is the intercept meaningful? Explain. (c) Make a prediction of *NetIncome* when *Revenue* $= 50,000$. (Data are from www.forbes.com and *Forbes* 172, no. 2 [July 21, 2003], pp. 108–110.)   **Global100**

SECTION EXERCISES

connect

12.11 The regression equation *HomePrice* $= 51.3 + 2.61$ *Income* was fitted from a sample of 34 cities in the eastern United States. Both variables are in thousands of dollars. *HomePrice* is the median selling price of homes in the city, and *Income* is median family income for the city. (a) Interpret the slope. (b) Is the intercept meaningful? Explain. (c) Make a prediction of *HomePrice* when *Income* = 50 and also when *Income* = 100. (Data are from *Money Magazine* 32, no. 1 [January 2004], pp. 102–103.)   **HomePrice1**

12.12 The regression equation *Credits* $= 15.4 - .07$ *Work* was fitted from a sample of 21 statistics students. *Credits* is the number of college credits taken and *Work* is the number of hours worked per week at an outside job. (a) Interpret the slope. (b) Is the intercept meaningful? Explain. (c) Make a prediction of *Credits* when *Work* = 0 and when *Work* = 40. What do these predictions tell you?   **Credits**

12.13 Below are fitted regressions for Y = asking price of a used vehicle and X = the age of the vehicle. The observed range of X was 1 to 8 years. The sample consisted of all vehicles listed for sale in a particular week in 2005. (a) Interpret the slope of each fitted regression. (b) Interpret the intercept of each fitted regression. Does the intercept have meaning? (c) Predict the price of a 5-year-old Chevy Blazer. (d) Predict the price of a 5-year-old Chevy Silverado. (Data are from *AutoFocus* 4, Issue 38 (Sept. 17–23, 2004) and are for educational purposes only.)   **CarPrices**

Chevy Blazer: *Price* $= 16,189 - 1,050$ *Age* ($n = 21$ vehicles, observed X range was 1 to 8 years).

Chevy Silverado: *Price* $= 22,951 - 1,339$ *Age* ($n = 24$ vehicles, observed X range was 1 to 10 years).

12.14 These data are for a sample of 10 college students who work at weekend jobs in restaurants. (a) Fit an "eyeball" regression equation to this scatter plot of Y = tips earned last weekend and X = hours worked. (b) Interpret the slope. (c) Interpret the intercept. Would the intercept have meaning in this example?

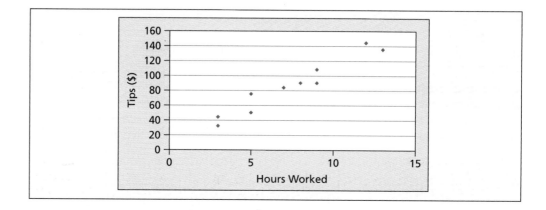

12.15 These data are for a sample of 10 different vendors in a large airport. (a) Fit an "eyeball" regression equation to this scatter plot of Y = bottles of Evian water sold and X = price of the water. (b) Interpret the slope. (c) Interpret the intercept. Would the intercept have meaning in this example?

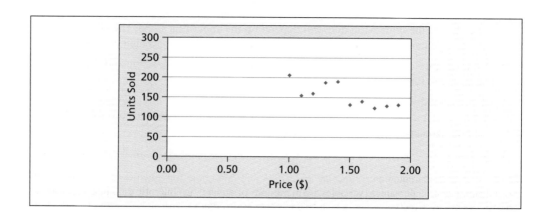

Slope and Intercept

The **ordinary least squares** method (or **OLS** method for short) is used to estimate a regression so as to ensure the best fit. "Best" fit in this case means that we have selected the slope and intercept so that our residuals are as small as possible. However, it is a characteristic of the OLS estimation method that the residuals around the regression line always sum to zero. That is, the positive residuals exactly cancel the negative ones:

$$\sum_{i=1}^{n}(y_i - \hat{y}_i) = 0 \quad \text{(OLS residuals always sum to zero)} \quad \textbf{(12.10)}$$

Therefore to work with an equation that has a nonzero sum we square the residuals, just as we squared the deviations from the mean when we developed the equation for variance back in Chapter 4. The fitted coefficients b_0 and b_1 are chosen so that the fitted linear model $\hat{y}_i = b_0 + b_1 x_i$ has the smallest possible sum of squared residuals (*SSE*):

$$SSE = \sum_{i=1}^{n}(y_i - \hat{y}_i)^2 = \sum_{i=1}^{n}(y_i - b_0 - b_1 x_i)^2 \quad \text{(sum to be minimized)} \quad \textbf{(12.11)}$$

This is an optimization problem that can be solved for b_0 and b_1 by using Excel's Solver Add-In. However, we can also use calculus (see derivation in *LearningStats* Unit 12) to solve for b_0 and b_1.

$$b_1 = \frac{\sum_{i=1}^{n}(x_i - \bar{x})(y_i - \bar{y})}{\sum_{i=1}^{n}(x_i - \bar{x})^2} \quad \text{(OLS estimator for slope)} \quad \textbf{(12.12)}$$

$$b_0 = \bar{y} - b_1\bar{x} \quad \text{(OLS estimator for intercept)} \quad \textbf{(12.13)}$$

If we use the notation for sums of squares (see formula 12.2), then the OLS formula for the slope can be written

$$b_1 = \frac{SS_{xy}}{SS_{xx}} \quad \text{(OLS estimator for slope)} \quad \textbf{(12.14)}$$

These formulas require only a few spreadsheet operations to find the means, deviations around the means, and their products and sums. They are built into Excel and many calculators. The OLS formulas give unbiased and consistent estimates* of β_0 and β_1. *The OLS regression line always passes through the point $(\bar{x}, \bar{y})$ for any data, as illustrated in Figure 12.9.*

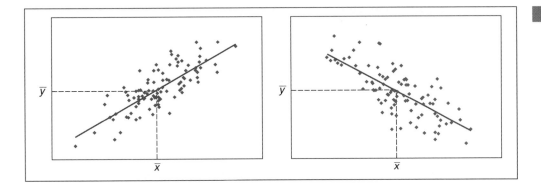

FIGURE 12.9

OLS Regression Line Always Passes Through $(\bar{x}, \bar{y})$.

---

*Recall from Chapter 9 that an unbiased estimator's expected value is the true parameter and that a consistent estimator approaches ever closer to the true parameter as the sample size increases.

Illustration: Exam Scores and Study Time

Table 12.3 shows study time and exam scores for 10 students. The worksheet in Table 12.4 shows the calculations of the sums needed for the slope and intercept. Figure 12.10 shows a fitted regression line. The vertical line segments in the scatter plot show the differences between the actual and fitted exam scores (i.e., residuals). The OLS residuals always sum to zero. We have:

$$b_1 = \frac{SS_{xy}}{SS_{xx}} = \frac{519.50}{264.50} = 1.9641 \qquad \text{(fitted slope)}$$

$$b_0 = \bar{y} - b_1\bar{x} = 70.1 - (1.9641)(10.5) = 49.477 \qquad \text{(fitted intercept)}$$

TABLE 12.3

Study Time and Exam Scores ExamScores

Student	Study Hours	Exam Score
Tom	1	53
Mary	5	74
Sarah	7	59
Oscar	8	43
Cullyn	10	56
Jaime	11	84
Theresa	14	96
Knut	15	69
Jin-Mae	15	84
Courtney	19	83
Sum	105	701
Mean	$\bar{x} = 10.5$	$\bar{y} = 70.1$

TABLE 12.4

Worksheet for Slope and Intercept Calculations ExamScores

Student	x_i	y_i	$x_i - \bar{x}$	$y_i - \bar{y}$	$(x_i - \bar{x})(y_i - \bar{y})$	$(x_i - \bar{x})^2$
Tom	1	53	−9.5	−17.1	162.45	90.25
Mary	5	74	−5.5	3.9	−21.45	30.25
Sarah	7	59	−3.5	−11.1	38.85	12.25
Oscar	8	43	−2.5	−27.1	67.75	6.25
Cullyn	10	56	−0.5	−14.1	7.05	0.25
Jaime	11	84	0.5	13.9	6.95	0.25
Theresa	14	96	3.5	25.9	90.65	12.25
Knut	15	69	4.5	−1.1	−4.95	20.25
Jin-Mae	15	84	4.5	13.9	62.55	20.25
Courtney	19	83	8.5	12.9	109.65	72.25
Sum	105	701	0	0	$SS_{xy} = 519.50$	$SS_{xx} = 264.50$
Mean	$\bar{x} = 10.5$	$\bar{y} = 70.1$				

FIGURE 12.10

Scatter Plot with Fitted Line and Residuals Shown as Vertical Line Segments

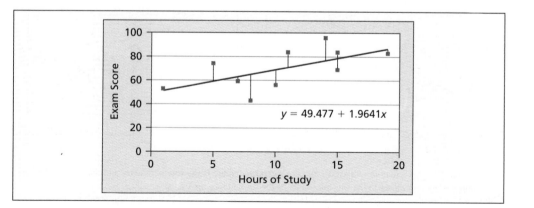

$y = 49.477 + 1.9641x$

Interpretation   The fitted regression $Score = 49.477 + 1.9641\, Study$ says that, on average, each additional hour of study yields a little less than 2 additional exam points (the slope). A student who did not study ($Study = 0$) would expect a score of about 49 (the intercept). In this example, the intercept is meaningful because zero study time not only is possible (though hopefully uncommon) but also was almost within the range of observed data. The scatter plot shows an imperfect fit, since not all of the variation in exam scores can be explained by study time. The remaining *unexplained* variation in exam scores reflects other factors (e.g., previous night's sleep, class attendance, test anxiety). We can use the fitted regression equation $\hat{y}_i = 1.9641 x_i + 49.477$ to find each student's *expected* exam score. Each prediction is a *conditional mean,* given the student's study hours. For example:

Student and Study Time	Expected Exam Score
Oscar, 8 hours	$\hat{y}_i = 49.48 + 1.964\,(8) = 65.19$ (65 to nearest integer)
Theresa, 14 hours	$\hat{y}_i = 49.48 + 1.964\,(14) = 76.98$ (77 to nearest integer)
Courtney, 19 hours	$\hat{y}_i = 49.48 + 1.964\,(19) = 86.79$ (87 to nearest integer)

Oscar's actual exam score was only 43, so he did worse than his predicted score of 65. Theresa scored 96, far above her predicted score of 77. Courtney, who studied the longest (19 hours), scored 83, fairly close to her predicted score of 87. These examples show that study time is not a perfect predictor of exam scores.

Assessing Fit

In a regression, we seek to explain the variation in the dependent variable around its mean. We express the *total variation* as a sum of squares (denoted *SST*):

$$SST = \sum_{i=1}^{n} (y_i - \bar{y})^2 \quad \text{(total sum of squares)} \quad \text{(12.15)}$$

Now we split the total variation into two parts:

SST	=	SSR	+	SSE
(*total* variation around the mean)		(variation explained by the *regression*)		(unexplained or *error* variation)

The *explained variation* in *Y* (denoted *SSR*) is the sum of the squared differences between the conditional mean $\hat{y}_i$ (conditioned on a given value x_i) and the unconditional mean $\bar{y}$ (same for all x_i):

$$SSR = \sum_{i=1}^{n} (\hat{y}_i - \bar{y})^2 \quad (\text{*regression* sum of squares, explained}) \quad \text{(12.16)}$$

The *unexplained variation* in *Y* (denoted *SSE*) is the sum of *squared* residuals, sometimes referred to as the **error sum of squares.***

$$SSE = \sum_{i=1}^{n} (y_i - \hat{y}_i)^2 \quad (\text{*error* sum of squares, unexplained}) \quad \text{(12.17)}$$

If the fit is good, *SSE* will be relatively small compared to *SST*. If each observed data value y_i is exactly the same as its estimate $\hat{y}_i$ (i.e., a perfect fit), then *SSE* will be zero. There is no upper limit on *SSE*. Table 12.5 shows the calculation of *SSE* for the exam scores.

Coefficient of Determination

Since the magnitude of *SSE* is dependent on sample size and on the units of measurement (e.g., dollars, kilograms, ounces) we need a *unit-free* benchmark. The **coefficient of determination**

---

*But bear in mind that the residual e_i (observable) is not the same as the true error ε_i (unobservable).

TABLE 12.5			Calculations of Sums of Squares			ExamScores	
Student	**Hours** x_i	**Score** y_i	**Estimated Score** $\hat{y}_i = 1.9641x_i + 49.477$	**Residual** $y_i - \hat{y}_i$	$(y_i - \hat{y}_i)^2$	$(\hat{y}_i - \bar{y})^2$	$(y_i - \bar{y})^2$
Tom	1	53	51.441	1.559	2.43	348.15	292.41
Mary	5	74	59.298	14.702	216.15	116.68	15.21
Sarah	7	59	63.226	−4.226	17.86	47.25	123.21
Oscar	8	43	65.190	−22.190	492.40	24.11	734.41
Cullyn	10	56	69.118	−13.118	172.08	0.96	198.81
Jaime	11	84	71.082	12.918	166.87	0.96	193.21
Theresa	14	96	76.974	19.026	361.99	47.25	670.81
Knut	15	69	78.939	−9.939	98.78	78.13	1.21
Jin-Mae	15	84	78.939	5.061	25.61	78.13	193.21
Courtney	19	83	86.795	−3.795	14.40	278.72	166.41
					SSE $= 1{,}568.57$	*SSR* $= 1{,}020.34$	*SST* $= 2{,}588.90$

or R^2 is a measure of *relative fit* based on a comparison of *SSR* and *SST*. Excel calculates this statistic automatically. It may be calculated in either of two ways:

$$(12.18) \qquad R^2 = 1 - \frac{SSE}{SST} \quad \text{or} \quad R^2 = \frac{SSR}{SST}$$

The range of the coefficient of determination is $0 \le R^2 \le 1$. The highest possible R^2 is 1 because, if the regression gives a perfect fit, then $SSE = 0$:

$$R^2 = 1 - \frac{SSE}{SST} = 1 - \frac{0}{SST} = 1 - 0 = 1 \quad \text{if } SSE = 0 \text{ (perfect fit)}$$

The lowest possible R^2 is 0 because, if knowing the value of X does not help predict the value of Y, then $SSE = SST$:

$$R^2 = 1 - \frac{SSE}{SST} = 1 - \frac{SST}{SST} = 1 - 1 = 0 \quad \text{if } SSE = SST \text{ (worst fit)}$$

For the exam scores, the coefficient of determination is

$$R^2 = 1 - \frac{SSE}{SST} = 1 - \frac{1{,}568.57}{2{,}588.90} = 1 - .6059 = .3941$$

Because a coefficient of determination always lies in the range $0 \le R^2 \le 1$, it is often expressed as a *percent of variation explained*. Since the exam score regression yields $R^2 = .3941$, we could say that X (hours of study) "explains" 39.41 percent of the variation in Y (exam scores). On the other hand, 60.59 percent of the variation in exam scores is *not* explained by study time. The *unexplained variation* reflects factors not included in our model (e.g., reading skills, hours of sleep, hours of work at a job, physical health, etc.) or just plain random variation. Although the word "explained" does not necessarily imply causation, in this case we have *a priori* reason to believe that causation exists, that is, that increased study time improves exam scores.

Tip

In a simple regression, R^2 is the square of the correlation coefficient r. Thus, if $r = .50$ then $R^2 = .25$. For this reason, MegaStat (and some textbooks) denotes the coefficient of determination as r^2 instead of R^2. In this textbook, the uppercase notation R^2 is used to indicate the difference in their definitions. It is tempting to think that a low R^2 indicates that the model is not useful. Yet in some applications (e.g., predicting crude oil future prices) even a slight improvement in predictive power can translate into millions of dollars.

Instructions for Exercises 12.16 and 12.17: (a) Make an Excel worksheet to calculate SS_{xx}, SS_{yy}, and SS_{xy} (the same worksheet you used in Exercises 12.2 and 12.3). (b) Use the formulas to calculate the slope and intercept. (c) Use your estimated slope and intercept to make a worksheet to calculate SSE, SSR, and SST. (d) Use these sums to calculate the R^2. (e) To check your answers, make an Excel scatter plot of X and Y, select the data points, right-click, select Add Trendline, select the Options tab, and choose Display equation on chart and Display R-squared value on chart.

12.16   Part-Time Weekly Earnings by College Students   WeekPay

Hours Worked (X)	Weekly Pay (Y)
10	93
15	171
20	204
20	156
35	261

12.17   Seconds of Telephone Hold Time for Concert Tickets   CallWait

Operators On Duty (X)	Wait Time (Y)
4	385
5	335
6	383
7	344
8	288

Instructions for Exercises 12.18–12.20: (a) Use Excel to make a scatter plot of the data. (b) Select the data points, right-click, select Add Trendline, select the Options tab, and choose Display equation on chart and Display R-squared value on chart. (c) Interpret the fitted slope. (d) Is the intercept meaningful? Explain. (e) Interpret the R^2.

12.18   Portfolio Returns (%) on Selected Mutual Funds   Portfolio

Last Year (X)	This Year (Y)
11.9	15.4
19.5	26.7
11.2	18.2
14.1	16.7
14.2	13.2
5.2	16.4
20.7	21.1
11.3	12.0
−1.1	12.1
3.9	7.4
12.9	11.5
12.4	23.0
12.5	12.7
2.7	15.1
8.8	18.7
7.2	9.9
5.9	18.9

12.19   Number of Orders and Shipping Cost   ShipCost

Orders (X)	($) Ship Cost (Y)
1,068	4,489
1,026	5,611
767	3,290
885	4,113
1,156	4,883
1,146	5,425
892	4,414
938	5,506
769	3,346
677	3,673
1,174	6,542
1,009	5,088

12.20   Moviegoer Spending on Snacks   Movies

Age (X)	($) Spent (Y)
30	2.85
50	6.50
34	1.50
12	6.35
37	6.20
33	6.75
36	3.60
26	6.10
18	8.35
46	4.35

12.5
TESTS FOR
SIGNIFICANCE

Standard Error of Regression

A measure of overall fit is the **standard error** of the estimate, denoted s_{yx}:

(12.19)
$$s_{yx} = \sqrt{\frac{SSE}{n-2}} \qquad \text{(standard error)}$$

If the fitted model's predictions are perfect ($SSE = 0$), the standard error s_{yx} will be zero. In general, a smaller value of s_{yx} indicates a better fit. For the exam scores, we can use SSE from Table 12.5 to find s_{yx}:

$$s_{yx} = \sqrt{\frac{SSE}{n-2}} = \sqrt{\frac{1,568.57}{10-2}} = \sqrt{\frac{1,568.57}{8}} = 14.002$$

The standard error s_{yx} is an estimate of σ (the standard deviation of the unobservable errors). Because it measures overall fit, the standard error s_{yx} serves somewhat the same function as the coefficient of determination. However, unlike R^2, the magnitude of s_{yx} depends on the units of measurement of the dependent variable (e.g., dollars, kilograms, ounces) and on the data magnitude. For this reason, R^2 is often the preferred measure of overall fit because its scale is always 0 to 1. The main use of the standard error s_{yx} is to construct confidence intervals.

Confidence Intervals for Slope and Intercept

Once we have the standard error s_{yx}, we construct confidence intervals for the coefficients from the formulas shown below. Excel, MegaStat, and MINITAB find them automatically.

(12.20)
$$s_{b_1} = \frac{s_{yx}}{\sqrt{\sum_{i=1}^{n}(x_i - \bar{x})^2}} \qquad \text{(standard error of slope)}$$

$$s_{b_0} = s_{yx} \sqrt{\frac{1}{n} + \frac{\bar{x}^2}{\sum_{i=1}^{n}(x_i - \bar{x})^2}} \qquad \text{(standard error of intercept)} \qquad \textbf{(12.21)}$$

For the exam score data, plugging in the sums from Table 12.4, we get

$$s_{b_1} = \frac{s_{yx}}{\sqrt{\sum_{i=1}^{n}(x_i - \bar{x})^2}} = \frac{14.002}{\sqrt{264.50}} = 0.86095$$

$$s_{b_0} = s_{yx} \sqrt{\frac{1}{n} + \frac{\bar{x}^2}{\sum_{i=1}^{n}(x_i - \bar{x})^2}} = 14.002 \sqrt{\frac{1}{10} + \frac{(10.5)^2}{264.50}} = 10.066$$

These standard errors are used to construct confidence intervals for the true slope and intercept, using Student's t with $\nu = n - 2$ degrees of freedom and any desired confidence level. Some software packages (e.g., Excel and MegaStat) provide confidence intervals automatically, while others do not (e.g., MINITAB).

$$b_1 - t_{n-2}s_{b_1} \le \beta_1 \le b_1 + t_{n-2}s_{b_1} \qquad \text{(CI for true slope)} \qquad \textbf{(12.22)}$$

$$b_0 - t_{n-2}s_{b_0} \le \beta_0 \le b_0 + t_{n-2}s_{b_0} \qquad \text{(CI for true intercept)} \qquad \textbf{(12.23)}$$

For the exam scores, degrees of freedom are $n - 2 = 10 - 2 = 8$, so from Appendix D we get $t_{n-2} = 2.306$ for 95 percent confidence. The 95 percent confidence intervals for the coefficients are

Slope

$$b_1 - t_{n-2}s_{b_1} \le \beta_1 \le b_1 + t_{n-2}s_{b_1}$$

$$1.9641 - (2.306)(0.86101) \le \beta_1 \le 1.9641 + (2.306)(0.86101)$$

$$-0.0213 \le \beta_1 \le 3.9495$$

Intercept

$$b_0 - t_{n-2}s_{b_0} \le \beta_0 \le b_0 + t_{n-2}s_{b_0}$$

$$49.477 - (2.306)(10.066) \le \beta_0 \le 49.477 + (2.306)(10.066)$$

$$26.26 \le \beta_0 \le 72.69$$

These confidence intervals are fairly wide. The width of any confidence interval can be reduced by obtaining a larger sample, partly because the t-value would shrink (toward the normal z-value) but mainly because the standard errors shrink as n increases. For the exam scores, the slope includes zero, suggesting that the true slope could be zero.

Hypothesis Tests

Is the true slope different from zero? This is an important question because if $\beta_1 = 0$, then X does not influence Y and the regression model collapses to a constant β_0 plus a random error term:

Initial Model	*If $\beta_1 = 0$*	*Then*
$y_i = \beta_0 + \beta_1 x_i + \varepsilon_i$	$y_i = \beta_0 + (0)x_i + \varepsilon_i$	$y_i = \beta_0 + \varepsilon_i$

We could also test for a zero intercept. For either coefficient, we use a t test with $\nu = n - 2$ degrees of freedom. The hypotheses and their test statistics are:

Coefficient	*Hypotheses*	*Test Statistic*	
Slope	$H_0: \beta_1 = 0$ $H_1: \beta_1 \ne 0$	$t_{calc} = \dfrac{b_1 - 0}{s_{b_1}}$	**(12.24)**
Intercept	$H_0: \beta_0 = 0$ $H_1: \beta_0 \ne 0$	$t_{calc} = \dfrac{b_0 - 0}{s_{b_0}}$	**(12.25)**

Usually we are interested in testing whether the parameter is equal to zero as shown here, but you may substitute another value in place of 0 if you wish. The critical value of t_{n-2} is obtained from Appendix D or from Excel's function =TDIST(t,deg_freedom, tails) where tails is 1 (one-tailed test) or 2 (two-tailed test). Often, the researcher uses a two-tailed test as the starting point, because rejection in a two-tailed test always implies rejection in a one-tailed test (but not vice versa).

Useful Fact

The test for zero slope is the same as the test for zero correlation. That is, the t test for zero slope (formula 12.24) will always yield *exactly* the same t_{calc} as the t test for zero correlation (formula 12.4).

Test for Zero Slope: Exam Scores ExamScores

For the exam scores, we would anticipate a positive slope (i.e., more study hours should improve exam scores) so we will use a right-tailed test:

Hypotheses	Test Statistic	Critical Value	Decision
$H_0: \beta_1 \leq 0$ $H_1: \beta_1 > 0$	$t_{calc} = \dfrac{b_1 - 0}{s_{b_1}} = \dfrac{1.9641 - 0}{0.86095} = 2.281$	$t_{.05} = 1.860$	Reject H_0 (i.e., slope is positive)

We can reject the hypothesis of a zero slope in a right-tailed test. (We would be unable to do so in a two-tailed test because the critical value of our t statistic would be 2.306.) Once we have the test statistic for the slope or intercept, we can find the p-value by using Excel's function =TDIST(t, deg_freedom, tails). The p-value method is preferred by researchers, because it obviates the need for prior specification of α.

Parameter	Excel Function	p-Value
Slope	=TDIST(2.281,8,1)	.025995 (right-tailed test)

Using Excel: Exam Scores ExamScores

These calculations are normally done by computer (we have demonstrated the calculations only to illustrate the formulas). The Excel menu to accomplish these tasks is shown in Figure 12.11. The resulting output, shown in Figure 12.12, can be used to verify our calculations. Excel always does two-tailed tests, so you must halve the p-value if you need a one-tailed test. You may specify the confidence level, but Excel's default is 95 percent confidence.

FIGURE 12.11

Excel's Regression Menu

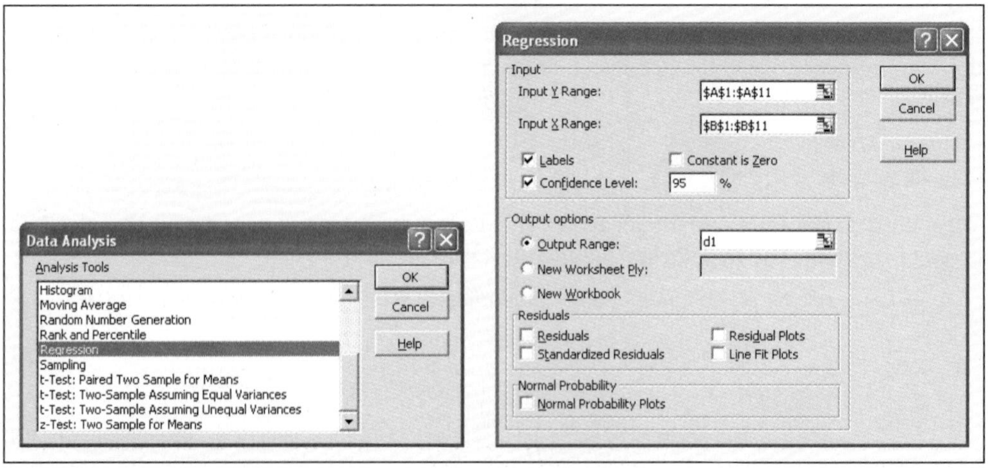

FIGURE 12.12

Excel's Regression Results for Exam Scores

SUMMARY OUTPUT

Regression Statistics

Multiple R	0.627790986
R Square	0.394121523
Adjusted R Square	0.318386713
Standard Error	14.00249438
Observations	10

Variable	Coefficient	Standard Error	t Stat	P-value	Lower 95%	Upper 95%
Intercept	49.47712665	10.06646125	4.915047	0.001171	26.26381038	72.69044293
Study Hours	1.964083176	0.86097902	2.281221	0.051972	−0.021339288	3.94950564

Tip

Avoid checking the Constant is Zero box in Excel's menu. This would force the intercept through the origin, changing the model drastically. Leave this option to the experts.

Using MegaStat: Exam Scores ExamScores

Figure 12.13 shows MegaStat's menu, and Figure 12.14 shows MegaStat's regression output for this data. The output format is similar to Excel's, except that MegaStat highlights coefficients that differ significantly from zero at $\alpha = .05$ in a two-tailed test.

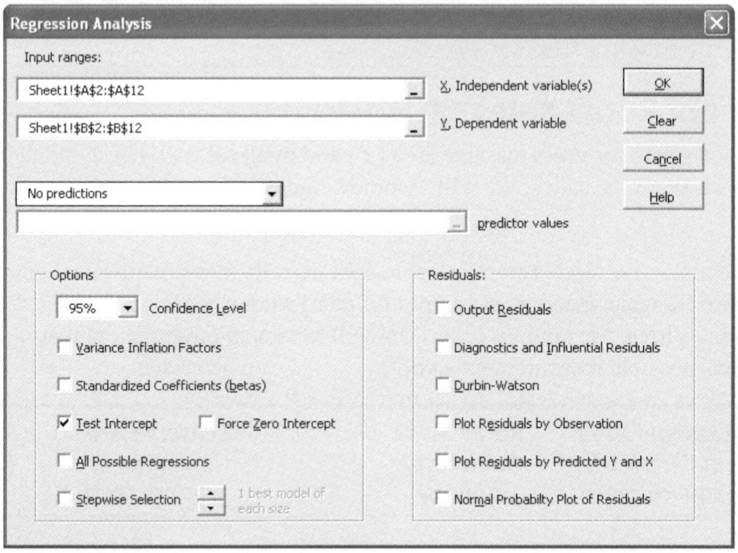

FIGURE 12.13

MegaStat's Regression Menu

FIGURE 12.14

MegaStat's Regression Results for Exam Scores

Regression Analysis

r^2	0.394	n	10	
r	0.628	k	1	
Std. Error	14.002	Dep. Var.	Exam Score	

Regression output confidence interval

variables	coefficients	std. error	t (df = 8)	p-value	95% lower	95% upper
Intercept	49.4771	10.0665	4.915	.0012	26.2638	72.6904
Study Hours	1.9641	0.8610	2.281	.0520	−0.0213	3.9495

Using MINITAB: Exam Scores 🐁 ExamScores ─────────────●

Figure 12.15 shows MINITAB's regression menus, and Figure 12.16 shows MINITAB's regression output for this data. MINITAB gives you the same general output as Excel, but with strongly rounded results.*

FIGURE 12.15

MINITAB's Regression Menus

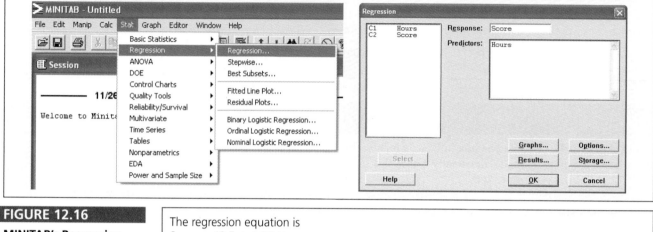

FIGURE 12.16

MINITAB's Regression Results for Exam Scores

The regression equation is
Score = 49.5 + 1.96 Hours

Predictor	Coef	SE Coef	T	P
Constant	49.48	10.07	4.92	0.001
Hours	1.9641	0.8610	2.28	0.052

S = 14.00   R-Sq = 39.4%   R-Sq(adj) = 31.8%

Application: Retail Sales 🐁 RetailSales ─────────────●

Table 12.6 shows data for gross leasable area (X) and retail sales (Y) in shopping malls in $n = 24$ randomly chosen U.S. states. We will assume a linear relationship between X and Y:

$$Sales = \beta_0 + \beta_1\, Area + \varepsilon_i$$

We anticipate a positive slope (more leasable area permits more retail sales) and an intercept near zero (zero leasable space would imply no retail sales). Since retail sales do not depend solely on leasable area, the random error term will reflect all other factors that influence retail sales as well as possible measurement error.

TABLE 12.6

Leasable Area and Retail Sales 🐁 **RetailSales**

State	Leasable Area (millions of square feet)	Retail Sales (billions of dollars)	State	Leasable Area (millions of square feet)	Retail Sales (billions of dollars)
AK	8	3.3	MT	10	3.0
AR	41	10.2	ND	10	3.2
AZ	150	36.8	NM	32	9.1
CA	755	182.8	NY	266	65.2
CO	125	35.3	OH	270	59.9
FL	488	144.5	OK	63	17.8
IL	282	63.4	RI	24	5.6
KS	62	16.7	SD	8	1.9
MA	123	35.7	TX	410	127.0
MI	155	37.0	VA	187	47.9
MN	76	20.7	VT	9	2.8
MO	129	33.0	WI	82	21.7

*You may have noticed that both Excel and MINITAB calculated something called "adjusted R-Square." For a simple regression, this statistic is of little interest, but in the next chapter it becomes important.

Based on the scatter plot and Excel's fitted linear regression, displayed in Figure 12.17, the linear model seems justified. The very high R^2 says that *Area* "explains" about 98 percent of the variation in *Sales*. Although it is reasonable to assume causation between *Area* and *Sales* in this model, the high R^2 alone does not prove cause-and-effect.

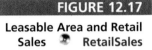

FIGURE 12.17

Leasable Area and Retail Sales **RetailSales**

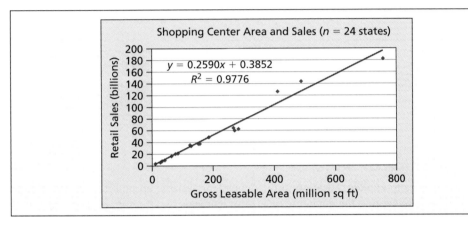

Using MegaStat For a more detailed look, we examine MegaStat's regression output for this data, shown in Figure 12.18. On average, each extra million square feet of leasable space yields an extra \$259 billion in retail sales ($b_1 = .2590$). The slope is nonzero in MegaStat's two-tail test ($t = 30.972$) as indicated by its tiny p-value ($p = 1.22 \times 10^{-19}$). MegaStat's yellow highlight indicates that the slope differs significantly from zero at $\alpha = .01$, and the narrow confidence interval for the slope (0.2417 to 0.2764) does not enclose zero. We conclude that this sample result (non-zero slope) did not arise by chance—rarely will you see such small p-values (except perhaps in time series data). But the intercept ($b_0 = 0.3852$) does not differ significantly from zero ($p = .8479$, $t = 0.194$) and the confidence interval for the intercept (-3.7320 to $+4.5023$) includes zero. These conclusions are in line with our prior expectations.

FIGURE 12.18

MegaStat Regression Results for Retail Sales **RetailSales**

Regression output					Confidence Interval	
Variables	*Coefficients*	*Std. Error*	*t (df = 26)*	*p-value*	*95% lower*	*95% upper*
Intercept	0.3852	1.9853	0.194	.8479	−3.7320	4.5023
Area	0.2590	0.0084	30.972	1.22E-19	0.2417	0.2764

Tip

The test for zero slope always yields a t statistic that is identical to the test for zero correlation coefficient. Therefore, it is not necessary to do both tests. Since regression output always includes a t-test for the slope, that is the test we usually use.

12.21 A regression was performed using data on 32 NFL teams in 2003. The variables were $Y =$ current value of team (millions of dollars) and $X =$ total debt held by the team owners (millions of dollars). (a) Write the fitted regression equation. (b) Construct a 95 percent confidence interval for the slope. (c) Perform a right-tailed t test for zero slope at $\alpha = .05$. State the hypotheses clearly. (d) Use Excel to find the p-value for the t statistic for the slope. (Data are from *Forbes* 172, no. 5, pp. 82–83.) **NFL**

SECTION EXERCISES

connect

variables	*coefficients*	*std. error*
Intercept	557.4511	25.3385
Debt	3.0047	0.8820

12.22 A regression was performed using data on 16 randomly selected charities in 2003. The variables were Y = expenses (millions of dollars) and X = revenue (millions of dollars). (a) Write the fitted regression equation. (b) Construct a 95 percent confidence interval for the slope. (c) Perform a right-tailed t test for zero slope at $\alpha = .05$. State the hypotheses clearly. (d) Use Excel to find the p-value for the t statistic for the slope. (Data are from *Forbes* 172, no. 12, p. 248, and www.forbes.com.) ✎ **Charities**

variables	coefficients	std. error
Intercept	7.6425	10.0403
Revenue	0.9467	0.0936

12.6
ANALYSIS OF VARIANCE: OVERALL FIT

Decomposition of Variance

A regression seeks to explain variation in the dependent variable around its mean. A simple way to see this is to express the deviation of y_i from its mean $\bar{y}$ as the sum of the deviation of y_i from the regression estimate $\hat{y}_i$ plus the deviation of the regression estimate $\hat{y}_i$ from the mean $\bar{y}$:

(12.26) $\qquad y_i - \bar{y} = (y_i - \hat{y}_i) + (\hat{y}_i - \bar{y})$ $\qquad$ (adding and subtracting $\hat{y}_i$)

It can be shown that this same decomposition also holds for the *sums of squares:*

(12.27) $\qquad \displaystyle\sum_{i=1}^{n}(y_i - \bar{y})^2 = \sum_{i=1}^{n}(y_i - \hat{y}_i)^2 + \sum_{i=1}^{n}(\hat{y}_i - \bar{y})^2$ $\qquad$ (sums of squares)

This *decomposition of variance* may be written as

$$
\begin{array}{ccccc}
SST & = & SSE & + & SSR \\
(\textit{total variation} & & (\textit{unexplained} & & (\textit{variation explained} \\
\textit{around the mean}) & & \textit{or error variation}) & & \textit{by the regression})
\end{array}
$$

F Statistic for Overall Fit

To test a regression for overall significance, we use an F test to compare the explained (SSR) and unexplained (SSE) sums of squares. We divide each sum by its respective degrees of freedom to obtain *mean squares* (MSR and MSE). The F statistic is the ratio of these two mean squares. Calculations of the F statistic are arranged in a table called the *analysis of variance* or ANOVA table (see Table 12.7). The ANOVA table also contains the sums required to calculate $R^2 = SSR/SST$. An ANOVA table is provided automatically by any regression software (e.g., Excel, MegaStat).

TABLE 12.7

ANOVA Table for a Simple Regression

Source of Variation	Sum of Squares	df	Mean Square	F	Excel p-value
Regression (explained)	$SSR = \displaystyle\sum_{i=1}^{n}(\hat{y}_i - \bar{y})^2$	1	$MSR = \dfrac{SSR}{1}$	$F_{calc} = \dfrac{MSR}{MSE}$	=FDIST(F_{calc},1, n−2)
Residual (unexplained)	$SSE = \displaystyle\sum_{i=1}^{n}(y_i - \hat{y}_i)^2$	n − 2	$MSE = \dfrac{SSE}{n-2}$		
Total	$SST = \displaystyle\sum_{i=1}^{n}(y_i - \bar{y})^2$	n − 1			

The formula for the F test statistic is:

$$F_{calc} = \frac{MSR}{MSE} = \frac{SSR/1}{SSE/(n-2)} = (n-2)\frac{SSR}{SSE} \qquad (F \text{ statistic for simple regression}) \quad (12.28)$$

The F statistic reflects both the sample size and the ratio of SSR to SSE. For a given sample size, a larger F statistic indicates a better fit (larger SSR relative to SSE), while F close to zero indicates a poor fit (small SSR relative to SSE). The F statistic must be compared with a critical value $F_{1,n-2}$ from Appendix F for whatever level of significance is desired, and we can find the p-value by using Excel's function =FDIST(F_{calc},1,n−2). Software packages provide the p-value automatically.

Figure 12.19 shows MegaStat's ANOVA table for the exam scores. The F statistic is

$$F_{calc} = \frac{MSR}{MSE} = \frac{1020.3412}{196.0698} = 5.20$$

From Appendix F the critical value of $F_{1,8}$ at the 5 percent level of significance would be 5.32, so the exam score regression is not quite significant at $\alpha = .05$. The p-value of .052 says a sample such as ours would be expected about 52 times in 1,000 samples if X and Y were unrelated. In other words, if we reject the hypothesis of no relationship between X and Y, we face a Type I error risk of 5.2 percent. This p-value might be called *marginally significant*.

EXAMPLE

Exam Scores:
F Statistic

ExamScores

FIGURE 12.19 **MegaStat's ANOVA Table for Exam Data**

ANOVA table

Source	SS	df	MS	F	p-value
Regression	1,020.3412	1	1,020.3412	5.20	.0520
Residual	1,568.5588	8	196.0698		
Total	2,588.9000	9			

From the ANOVA table, we can calculate the standard error from the mean square for the residuals:

$$s_{yx} = \sqrt{MSE} = \sqrt{196.0698} = 14.002 \qquad (\text{standard error for exam scores})$$

Tip

In a simple regression, the F test always yields the same p-value as a two-tailed t test for zero slope, which in turn always gives the same p-value as a two-tailed test for zero correlation. The relationship between the test statistics is $F_{calc} = t_{calc}^2$.

SECTION EXERCISES

connect

12.23 Below is a regression using X = home price (000), Y = annual taxes (000), n = 20 homes. (a) Write the fitted regression equation. (b) Write the formula for each t statistic and verify the t statistics shown below. (c) State the degrees of freedom for the t tests and find the two-tail critical value for t by using Appendix D. (d) Use Excel's function =TDIST(t, deg_freedom, tails) to verify the p-value shown for each t statistic (slope, intercept). (e) Verify that $F = t^2$ for the slope. (f) In your own words, describe the fit of this regression.

R²   0.452
Std. Error 0.454
n   12

ANOVA table

Source	SS	df	MS	F	p-value
Regression	1.6941	1	1.6941	8.23	.0167
Residual	2.0578	10	0.2058		
Total	3.7519	11			

Regression output   confidence interval

variables	coefficients	std. error	t (df =10)	p-value	95% lower	95% upper
Intercept	1.8064	0.6116	2.954	.0144	0.4438	3.1691
Slope	0.0039	0.0014	2.869	.0167	0.0009	0.0070

12.24 Below is a regression using X average price, $Y =$ units sold, $n = 20$ stores. (a) Write the fitted regression equation. (b) Write the formula for each t statistic and verify the t statistics shown below. (c) State the degrees of freedom for the t tests and find the two-tail critical value for t by using Appendix D. (d) Use Excel's function =TDIST(t, deg_freedom, tails) to verify the p-value shown for each t statistic (slope, intercept). (e) Verify that $F = t^2$ for the slope. (f) In your own words, describe the fit of this regression.

R²   0.200
Std. Error 26.128
n   20

ANOVA table

Source	SS	df	MS	F	p-value
Regression	3,080.89	1	3,080.89	4.51	.0478
Residual	12,288.31	18	682.68		
Total	15,369.20	19			

Regression output   confidence interval

variables	coefficients	std. error	t (df =18)	p-value	95% lower	95% upper
Intercept	614.9300	51.2343	12.002	.0000	507.2908	722.5692
Slope	−109.1120	51.3623	−2.124	.0478	−217.0202	−1.2038

Instructions for Exercises 12.25–12.27: (a) Use Excel's Tools > Data Analysis > Regression (or MegaStat or MINITAB) to obtain regression estimates. (b) Interpret the 95 percent confidence interval for the slope. Does it contain zero? (c) Interpret the t test for the slope and its p-value. (d) Interpret the F statistic. (e) Verify that the p-value for F is the same as for the slope's t statistic, and show that $t^2 = F$. (f) Describe the fit of the regression.

12.25 **Portfolio Returns (%) on Selected Mutual Funds (*n* = 17 funds)** 🔊 Portfolio

Last Year (X)	This Year (Y)
11.9	15.4
19.5	26.7
11.2	18.2
14.1	16.7
14.2	13.2
5.2	16.4
20.7	21.1
11.3	12.0
−1.1	12.1
3.9	7.4
12.9	11.5
12.4	23.0
12.5	12.7
2.7	15.1
8.8	18.7
7.2	9.9
5.9	18.9

12.26 **Number of Orders and Shipping Cost (*n* = 12 orders)** 🔊 ShipCost

Orders (X)	($) Ship Cost (Y)
1,068	4,489
1,026	5,611
767	3,290
885	4,113
1,156	4,883
1,146	5,425
892	4,414
938	5,506
769	3,346
677	3,673
1,174	6,542
1,009	5,088

12.27 **Moviegoer Spending on Snacks (*n* = 10 purchases)** 🔊 Movies

Age (X)	$ Spent (Y)
30	2.85
50	6.50
34	1.50
12	6.35
37	6.20
33	6.75
36	3.60
26	6.10
18	8.35
46	4.35

Mini Case   12.3

Airplane Cockpit Noise   Cockpit

Career airline pilots face the risk of progressive hearing loss, due to the noisy cockpits of most jet aircraft. Much of the noise comes not from engines but from air roar, which increases at high speeds. To assess this workplace hazard, a pilot measured cockpit noise at randomly selected points during the flight by using a handheld meter. Noise level (in decibels) was measured in seven different aircraft at the first officer's left ear position using a handheld meter. For reference, 60 dB is a normal conversation, 75 is a typical vacuum cleaner, 85 is city traffic, 90 is a typical hair dryer, and 110 is a chain saw. Table 12.8 shows 61 observations on cockpit noise (decibels) and airspeed (knots indicated air speed, KIAS) for a Boeing 727, an older type of aircraft lacking design improvements in newer planes.

TABLE 12.8   Cockpit Noise Level and Airspeed for B-727 ($n = 61$)   Cockpit

Speed	Noise	Speed	Noise	Speed	Noise	Speed	Noise	Speed	Noise	Speed	Noise
250	83	380	93	340	90	330	91	350	90	272	84.5
340	89	380	91	340	91	360	94	380	92	310	88
320	88	390	94	380	96	370	94.5	310	88	350	90
330	89	400	95	385	96	380	95	295	87	370	91
346	92	400	96	420	97	395	96	280	86	405	93
260	85	405	97	230	82	365	91	320	88	250	82
280	84	320	89	340	91	320	88	330	90		
395	92	310	88.5	250	86	250	85	320	88		
380	92	250	82	320	89	250	82	340	89		
400	93	280	87	340	90	320	88	350	90		
335	91	320	89	320	90	305	88	270	84		

The scatter plot in Figure 12.20 suggests that a linear model provides a reasonable description of the data. The fitted regression shows that each additional knot of airspeed increases the noise level by 0.0765 dB. Thus, a 100-knot increase in airspeed would add about 7.65 dB of noise. The intercept of 64.229 suggests that if the plane were not flying ($KIAS = 0$) the noise level would be only slightly greater than a normal conversation.

FIGURE 12.20   Scatter Plot of Cockpit Noise Data Courtesy of Capt. R. E. Hartl (ret) of Delta Airlines.

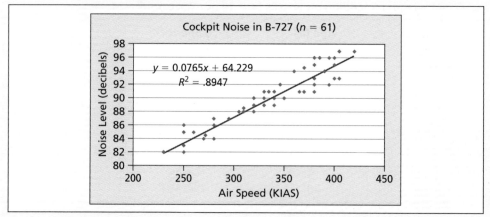

The regression results in Figure 12.21 show that the fit is very good ($R^2 = .895$) and that the regression is highly significant ($F = 501.16$, $p < .001$). Both the slope and intercept have *p*-values below .001, indicating that the true parameters are nonzero. Thus, the regression is significant, as well as having practical value.

FIGURE 12.21   **Regression Results of Cockpit Noise**

Regression Analysis

r^2	0.895	n	61	
r	0.946	k	1	
Std. Error	1.292	Dep. Var.	**Noise**	

ANOVA table

Source	SS	df	MS	F	p-value
Regression	836.9817	1	836.9817	501.16	1.60E-30
Residual	98.5347	59	1.6701		
Total	935.5164	60			

Regression output   confidence interval

variables	coefficients	std. error	t (df = 59)	p-value	95% lower	95% upper
Intercept	64.2294	1.1489	55.907	8.29E-53	61.9306	66.5283
Speed	0.0765	0.0034	22.387	1.60E-30	0.0697	0.0834

How to Construct an Interval Estimate for *Y*

12.7
CONFIDENCE
AND
PREDICTION
INTERVALS
FOR Y

The regression line is an estimate of the *conditional mean* of *Y* (i.e., the expected value of *Y* for a given value of *X*). But the estimate may be too high or too low. To make this *point estimate* more useful, we need an *interval estimate* to show a range of likely values. To do this, we insert the x_i value into the fitted regression equation, calculate the estimated $\hat{y}_i$, and use the formulas shown below. The first formula gives a **confidence interval** for the conditional mean of *Y*, while the second is a **prediction interval** for individual values of *Y*. The formulas are similar, except that prediction intervals are wider because *individual Y* values vary more than the *mean* of *Y*.

$$\hat{y}_i \pm t_{n-2} s_{yx} \sqrt{\frac{1}{n} + \frac{(x_i - \bar{x})^2}{\sum\limits_{i=1}^{n} (x_i - \bar{x})^2}} \qquad \text{(confidence interval for mean of } Y) \qquad \textbf{(12.29)}$$

$$\hat{y}_i \pm t_{n-2} s_{yx} \sqrt{1 + \frac{1}{n} + \frac{(x_i - \bar{x})^2}{\sum\limits_{i=1}^{n} (x_i - \bar{x})^2}} \qquad \text{(prediction interval for individual } Y) \qquad \textbf{(12.30)}$$

Let's use formula 12.30 to predict the exam score for a student who studies 4 hours, using the regression model developed in Section 12.4. What is the 95 percent prediction interval? The student's predicted exam score (see Table 12.5) would be $\hat{y} = 1.9641 (4) + 49.477 = 57.333$. For 95 percent confidence with $d.f. = n - 2 = 10 - 2 = 8$ we use $t_{.025} = 2.306$. Using the sums from Table 12.4, the 95 percent prediction interval is:

$$57.333 \pm (2.306)(14.002)\sqrt{1 + \frac{1}{10} + \frac{(4 - 10.5)^2}{264.5}} \quad \text{or } 57.33 \pm 36.24$$

FIGURE 12.22

MegaStat's Confidence and Prediction Intervals

Regression Analysis ☒

Input ranges:

'Exam Scores'!$C$6:$C$15 ⬇ X, Independent variable(s) [OK]

'Exam Scores'!$D$6:$D$15 ⬇ Y, Dependent variable [Clear]

[Cancel]

Type in predictor values ▼ [Help]

0 2 4 6 8 10 12 14 16 18 20 predictor values

Options
- 95% ▼ Confidence Level
- ☐ Variance Inflation Factors
- ☐ Standardized Coefficients (betas)
- ☑ Test Intercept ☐ Force Zero Intercept
- ☐ All Possible Regressions
- ☐ Stepwise Selection ⬆⬇ 1 best model of each size

Residuals:
- ☐ Output Residuals
- ☐ Diagnostics and Influential Residuals
- ☐ Durbin-Watson
- ☐ Plot Residuals by Observation
- ☐ Plot Residuals by Predicted Y and X
- ☐ Normal Probabilty Plot of Residuals

Predicted values for Exam Scores

		95% Confidence Intervals		95% Prediction Intervals	
X	Predicted	lower	upper	lower	upper
0	49.477	26.264	72.690	9.709	89.245
2	53.405	33.681	73.130	15.568	91.243
4	57.333	40.877	73.790	21.092	93.575
6	61.262	47.694	74.829	26.237	96.286
8	65.190	53.836	76.543	30.962	99.417
10	69.118	58.859	79.377	35.238	102.998
12	73.046	62.410	83.682	39.050	107.043
14	76.974	64.623	89.325	42.403	111.546
16	80.902	65.952	95.853	45.320	116.485
18	84.831	66.775	102.886	47.836	121.826
20	88.759	67.311	110.207	49.995	127.523

This very wide interval says that we cannot make precise predictions of the exam score for a student who studies 4 hours. This is not surprising since the fit for the exam score data ($R^2 = .3941$) was not very high. Prediction intervals are more precise when R^2 is high.

Interval width varies with the value of x_i, being narrowest when x_i is near its mean (note that when $x_i = \bar{x}$ the last term under the square root disappears completely). For some data sets, the degree of narrowing near $\bar{x}$ is almost indiscernible, while for other data sets it is quite pronounced. These calculations are usually done by computer (see Figure 12.22). Both MegaStat and MINITAB, for example, will let you type in the x_i values and will give both confidence and prediction intervals *only* for that x_i value, but you must make your own graphs.

Two Illustrations: Exam Scores and Retail Sales

☞ **ExamScores** ☞ **RetailSales** ─────────────────────●

Since there will be a different interval for every X value, it is helpful to see confidence and prediction intervals over the entire range of X. Figure 12.23 shows confidence and prediction intervals for exam scores and retail sales. The contrast between the two graphs is striking. Confidence and prediction intervals for exam scores are wide and clearly narrower for X values near the mean. The prediction bands for exam scores for large X values (e.g., $X = 20$ hours of study) even extend above 100 points (presumably the upper limit for an exam

FIGURE 12.23

Confidence and Prediction Intervals Illustrated

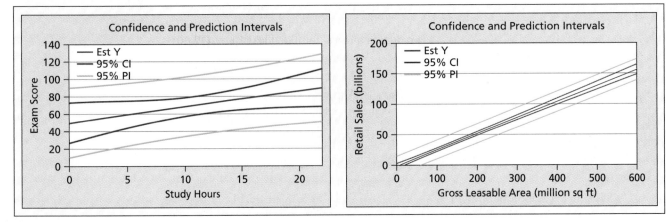

score). In contrast, the intervals for retail sales appear narrow and only slightly wider for X values below or above the mean. While the prediction bands for retail sales seem narrow, they still represent billions of dollars (e.g., for $X = 500$ the retail sales prediction interval has a width of about $33 billion). This shows that a high R^2 does not guarantee precise predictions.

Quick Rules for Confidence and Prediction Intervals ●

Because the confidence interval formulas are complex enough to discourage their use, we are motivated to consider approximations. When x_i is not too far from $\bar{x}$, the last term under the square root is small and might be ignored. As a further simplification, we might ignore $1/n$ in the individual Y formula (if n is large, then $1/n$ will be small). These simplifications yield the quick confidence and prediction intervals shown below. If you want a *really* quick 95 percent interval, you can plug in $t = 2$ (since most 95 percent t-values are not far from 2).

$$\hat{y}_i \pm t_{n-2} \frac{s_{yx}}{\sqrt{n}} \qquad \text{(quick confidence interval for mean of } Y) \qquad \textbf{(12.31)}$$

$$\hat{y}_i \pm t_{n-2} s_{yx} \qquad \text{(quick prediction interval for individual } Y) \qquad \textbf{(12.32)}$$

These quick rules lead to constant width intervals and are *not* conservative (i.e., the resulting intervals will be somewhat too narrow). They work best for large samples and when X is near its mean. They are questionable when X is near either extreme of its range. Yet they often are close enough to convey a general idea of the accuracy of your predictions. Their purpose is just to give a quick answer without getting lost in unwieldy formulas.

Three Important Assumptions ●

Recall that the dependent variable is a random variable that has an error component, ε_i. The OLS method makes several assumptions about the random error term ε_i. Although ε_i is unobservable, clues may be found in the residuals e_i. Three important assumptions can be tested:

- Assumption 1: The errors are normally distributed.
- Assumption 2: The errors have constant variance (i.e., they are *homoscedastic*).
- Assumption 3: The errors are independent (i.e., they are *nonautocorrelated*).

Since we cannot observe the error ε_i we must rely on the residuals e_i from the fitted regression for clues about possible violations of these assumptions. Regression residuals often violate one or more of these assumptions. Fortunately, regression is fairly robust in the face of moderate violations of these assumptions. We will examine each violation, explain its consequences, show how to check it, and discuss possible remedies.

Non-Normal Errors ●

Non-normality of errors is usually considered a mild violation, since the regression parameter estimates b_0 and b_1 and their variances remain unbiased and consistent. The main ill consequence is that confidence intervals for the parameters may be untrustworthy, because the normality assumption is used to justify using Student's t to construct confidence intervals. However, if the sample size is large (say, $n > 30$), the confidence intervals should be OK. An exception would be if outliers exist, posing a serious problem that cannot be cured by large sample size.

Histogram of Residuals   A simple way to check for non-normality is to make a histogram of the residuals. You can use either plain residuals or **standardized residuals**. A *standardized residual* is obtained by dividing each residual by its standard error. Histogram shapes will be the same, but standardized residuals offer the advantage of a predictable scale (between -3 and $+3$ unless there are outliers). A simple "eyeball test" can usually reveal outliers or serious asymmetry. Figure 12.24 shows a standardized residual histogram for

12.8
VIOLATIONS OF ASSUMPTIONS

FIGURE 12.24

**Cockpit Noise Residuals
(Histogram)**
 Cockpit

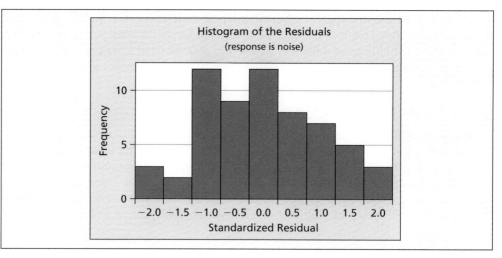

Mini Case 12.2. There are no outliers and the histogram is roughly symmetric, albeit possibly platykurtic (i.e., flatter than normal).

Normal Probability Plot Another visual test for normality is the probability plot. It is produced as an option by MINITAB and MegaStat. The hypotheses are

H_0: Errors are normally distributed

H_1: Errors are not normally distributed

If the null hypothesis is true, the residual probability plot should be linear. For example in Figure 12.25 we see slight deviations from linearity at the lower and upper ends of the residual probability plot for Mini Case 12.2 (cockpit noise). But overall, the residuals seem to be consistent with the hypothesis of normality. There are more tests for normality, but the histogram and probability plot suffice for most purposes.

FIGURE 12.25

**Cockpit Noise Residuals
(Normal Probability Plot)**

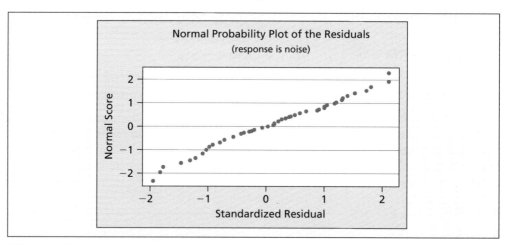

What to Do About Non-Normality? First, consider trimming outliers—but only if they clearly are mistakes. Second, can you increase the sample size? If so, it will help assure asymptotic normality of the estimates. Third, you could try a logarithmic transformation of both X and Y. However, this is a new model specification which may require advice from a professional statistician. We will discuss data transformations later in this chapter. Fourth, you could do nothing—just be aware of the problem.

Tip

Non-normality is not considered a major violation, so don't worry too much about it *unless* you have major outliers.

Heteroscedastic Errors (Nonconstant Variance) ————————•

The regression should fit equally well for all values of X. If the error magnitude is constant for all X, the errors are **homoscedastic** (the ideal condition). If the errors increase or decrease with X, they are **heteroscedastic**. Although the OLS regression parameter estimates b_0 and b_1 are still unbiased and consistent, their estimated variances are biased and are neither efficient nor asymptotically efficient. In the most common form of heteroscedasticity, the variances of the estimators are likely to be understated, resulting in overstated t statistics and artificially narrow confidence intervals. Your regression estimates may thus seem more significant than is warranted.

Tests for Heteroscedasticity For a simple regression, you can see heteroscedasticity on the XY scatter plot, but a more general visual test is to plot the residuals against X. Ideally, there is no pattern in the residuals as we move from left to right:

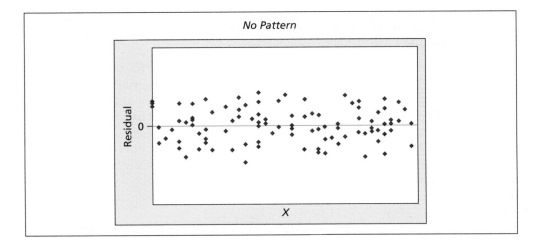

Notice that the residuals *always* have a mean of zero. Although many patterns of nonconstant variance might exist, the "fan-out" pattern (increasing residual variance) is most common:

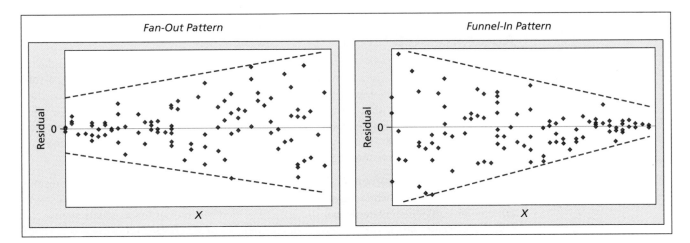

Residual plots provide a fairly sensitive "eyeball test" for heteroscedasticity. The residual plot is therefore considered an important tool in the statistician's diagnostic kit. The hypotheses are

H_0: Errors have constant variance (homoscedastic)

H_1: Errors have nonconstant variance (heteroscedastic)

Figure 12.26 shows a residual plot for Mini Case 12.2 (cockpit noise). In the residual plot, we see residuals of the same magnitude as we look from left to right. A random pattern like this

FIGURE 12.26

Cockpit Noise Residual Plot

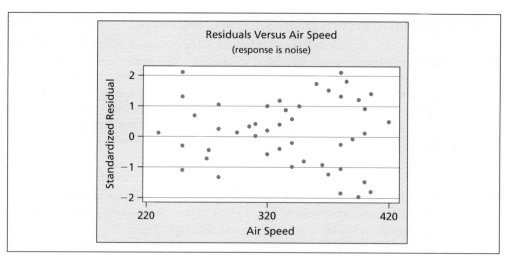

is consistent with the hypothesis of homoscedasticity (constant variance), although some observers might see a hint of a "fan-out" pattern.

What to Do About Heteroscedasticity?   Heteroscedasticity may arise in economic time-series data if X and Y increase in magnitude over time, causing the errors also to increase. In financial data (e.g., GDP) heteroscedasticity can sometimes be reduced by expressing the data in constant dollars (dividing by a price index). In cross-sectional data (e.g., total crimes in a state) heteroscedasticity may be mitigated by expressing the data in relative terms (e.g., per capita crime). A more general approach to reducing heteroscedasticity is to transform both X and Y (e.g., by taking logs). However, this is a new model specification, which requires a reverse transformation when making predictions of Y. This approach will be considered later in this chapter.

Tip

Although it can widen the confidence intervals for the coefficients, heteroscedasticity does not bias the estimates. At this stage of your training, it is sufficient just to recognize its existence.

Autocorrelated Errors

Autocorrelation is a pattern of nonindependent errors, mainly found in time-series data.* In a time-series regression, each residual e_t should be independent of its predecessors $e_{t-1}, e_{t-2}, \ldots, e_{t-n}$. Violations of this assumption can show up in different ways. In the simple model of *first-order autocorrelation* we would find that e_t is correlated with the prior residual e_{t-1}. The OLS estimators b_0 and b_1 are still unbiased and consistent, but their estimated variances are biased in a way that typically leads to confidence intervals that are too narrow and t statistics that are too large. Thus, the model's fit may be overstated.

Runs Test for Autocorrelation   *Positive* autocorrelation is indicated by runs of residuals with the *same* sign, while *negative autocorrelation* is indicated by runs of residuals with *alternating* signs. Such patterns can sometimes be seen in a plot of the residuals against the order of data entry. In the *runs test,* we count the number of sign reversals (i.e., how often does the residual plot cross the zero centerline?). If the pattern is random, the number of sign changes should be approximately $n/2$. Fewer than $n/2$ centerline crossings would suggest positive autocorrelation, while more than $n/2$ centerline crossings would suggest negative autocorrelation. For example, if $n = 50$, we would expect about 25 centerline crossings. In the first illustration, there are only 11 crossings (positive autocorrelation) while in the second illustration there are 36 crossings (negative autocorrelation). Positive autocorrelation is

---

*Cross-sectional data may exhibit autocorrelation, but typically it is an artifact of the order of data entry.

common in economic time-series regressions, due to the cyclical nature of the economy. It is harder to envision logical reasons for negative autocorrelation, and in fact it is rarely observed.

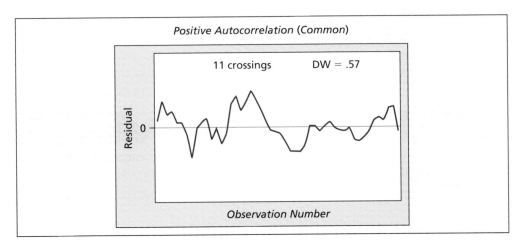

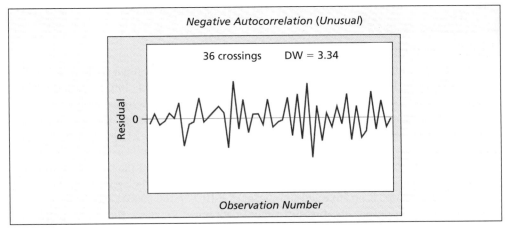

Durbin-Watson Test   The most widely used test for autocorrelation is the **Durbin-Watson test**. The hypotheses are

H_0: Errors are nonautocorrelated

H_1: Errors are autocorrelated

The Durbin-Watson test statistic for autocorrelation is

$$DW = \frac{\sum_{t=2}^{n} (e_t - e_{t-1})^2}{\sum_{t=1}^{n} e_t^2} \qquad \text{(Durbin-Watson test statistic)} \qquad \textbf{(12.33)}$$

When there is no autocorrelation, the DW statistic will be near 2, though its range is from 0 to 4. For a formal hypothesis test, a special table is required. For now, we simply note that in general

$DW < 2$ suggests positive autocorrelation (common).

$DW \approx 2$ suggests no autocorrelation (ideal).

$DW > 2$ suggests negative autocorrelation (rare).

What to Do About Autocorrelation?   A cure for first-order time-series autocorrelation is to transform both variables. A very simple transformation is the *method of first differences* in which both variables are redefined as *changes:*

$\Delta x_t = x_t - x_{t-1}$ (change in X from period $t - 1$ to period t)

$\Delta y_t = y_t - y_{t-1}$ (change in Y from period $t - 1$ to period t)

Then we regress ΔY against ΔX. This transformation can easily be done in a spreadsheet by subtracting each cell from its predecessor and then re-running the regression. One observation is lost, since the first observation has no predecessor. The method of first differences has logical appeal, since there is little conceptual difference between regressing taxes against income and regressing the *change in taxes* against the *change in income*. The new slope should be the same as in the original model but the new intercept should be zero. You will learn about more general transformations, favored by researchers, if you study econometrics.

Tip

Although it can widen the confidence intervals for the coefficients, autocorrelation does not bias the estimates. At this stage of your training, it is sufficient just to recognize when you have autocorrelation.

Mini Case   12.4

Exports and Imports   Exports

We often see headlines about the persistent imbalance in U.S. foreign trade (e.g., "U.S. Trade Deficit Sets Record," *International Herald Tribune,* March 14, 2007). But when U.S. imports increase, other nations acquire dollar balances which economists predict will lead to increased purchases of U.S. goods and services, thereby increasing U.S. exports (i.e., trade imbalances are supposed to be self-correcting). Figure 12.27 shows a regression based on U.S. exports and imports for 1959–2005. To reduce autocorrelation (these are time-series data) the model regresses the *change* in exports against the *change* in imports for each period ($n = 46$ years). The fitted model is $\Delta Exports = 5.2849 + 0.5193\,\Delta Imports$. As expected, the slope is positive and significant ($t = 10.277, p < .0001$) and the fit is fairly good ($R^2 = .7059$) despite the first-differences data transformation. But the slope ($b_1 = 0.5193$) indicates that the change in exports is only about half the change in imports, so the trade imbalance remains a puzzle. An economist would perhaps want to examine the role of exchange rate inflexibility vis-à-vis China or other factors, in constructing a more complex model.

FIGURE 12.27   **Excel Scatter Plot and Regression**

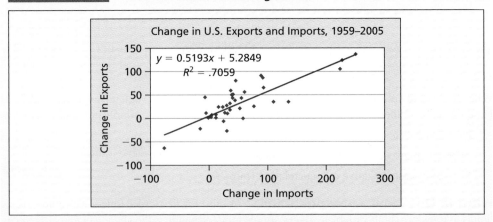

The residuals appear normal (the probability plot in Figure 12.28 is roughly linear with no obvious outliers) and homoscedastic (Figure 12.29 shows no pattern in the plot of residuals against predicted *Y*). But autocorrelation still appears to be a problem (Figure 12.30 shows 9 centerline crossings in the residual plot over time, and has a Durbin-Watson statistic $DW = 0.78$, which suggests positive autocorrelation).

FIGURE 12.28   **Residual Test for Non-Normality**

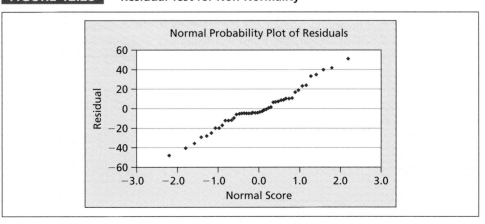

FIGURE 12.29   **Residual Test for Heteroscedasticity**

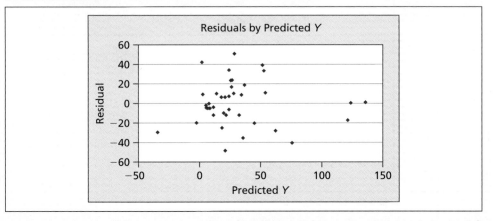

FIGURE 12.30   **Residual Test for Autocorrelation**

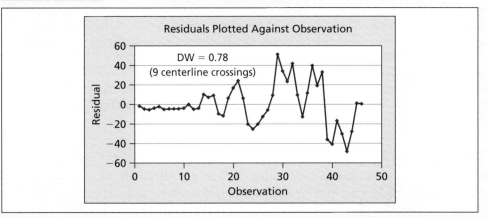

12.9
UNUSUAL OBSERVATIONS

In a regression, we look for observations that are unusual. An observation could be unusual because its Y-value is poorly predicted by the regression model (*unusual residual*) or because its unusual X-value greatly affects the regression line (*high leverage*). Tests for unusual residuals and high leverage are important diagnostic tools in evaluating the fitted regression.

Standardized Residuals: Excel

Excel's Tools > Data Analysis > Regression provides residuals as an option, as shown in Figure 12.31. Since every regression may have different Y units (e.g., stock price in dollars, shipping time in days) it is helpful to *standardize* the residuals by dividing each residual by its standard error. As a rule of thumb (the Empirical Rule) any *standardized residual* whose absolute value is 2 or more is unusual, and any residual whose absolute value is 3 or more would be considered an outlier. Excel obtains its "standardized residuals" by dividing each residual by the standard deviation of the column of residuals. This procedure is not quite correct, as explained below, but generally suffices to identify unusual residuals. Using the Empirical Rule, there are no unusual standardized residuals in Figure 12.31.

FIGURE 12.31

Excel's Exam Score Regression with Residuals **ExamScores**

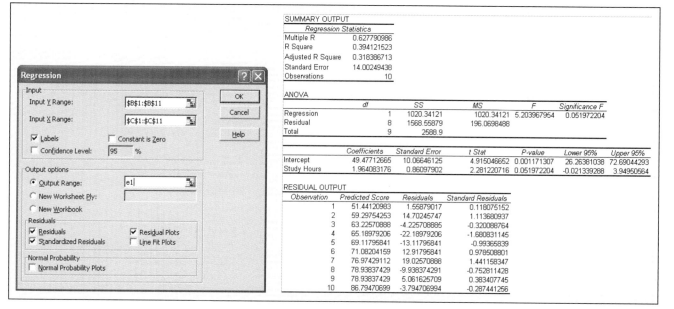

Studentized Residuals: MINITAB

MINITAB gives you the same general output as Excel, but with rounded results and more detailed residual information. Its menus are shown in Figure 12.32. MINITAB uses **studentized residuals**, obtained by dividing each residual by its *true standard error*. This calculation requires a unique adjustment for each residual, based on the observation's distance from the mean. Studentized residuals usually are close to Excel's "standardized" residuals. MINITAB's results confirm that there are no unusual residuals in the exam score regression. An attractive feature of MINITAB is that actual and fitted Y-values are displayed (Excel shows only the fitted Y-values). MINITAB also gives the standard error for the mean of Y (the output column labeled SE Fit), which you can multiply by $t_{\alpha/2}$ to get the confidence interval width.

Studentized Residuals: MegaStat

MegaStat gives you the same general output as Excel and MINITAB. Its regression menu is shown in Figure 12.33. Like MINITAB, it offers studentized residuals, as well as several other residual diagnostics that we will discuss shortly. Also like MINITAB, MegaStat rounds off things to make the output more readable. It also highlights significant items.

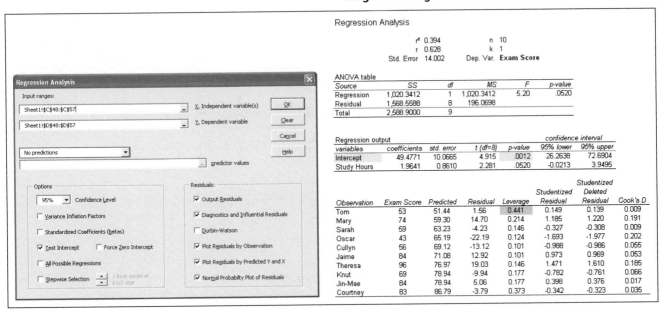

FIGURE 12.32

MINITAB's Regression with Residuals   **ExamScores**

Regression Analysis: Score versus Hours

The regression equation is
Score = 49.5 + 1.96 Hours

Predictor	Coef	SE Coef	T	P
Constant	49.48	10.07	4.92	0.001
Hours	1.9641	0.8610	2.28	0.052

S = 14.0025   R-Sq = 39.4%   R-Sq(adj) = 31.8%

Analysis of Variance

Source	DF	SS	MS	F	P
Regression	1	1020.3	1020.3	5.20	0.052
Residual Error	8	1568.6	196.1		
Total	9	2588.9			

Obs	Hours	Score	Fit	SE Fit	Residual	St Resid
1	1.0	53.00	51.44	9.30	1.56	0.15
2	5.0	74.00	59.30	6.48	14.70	1.18
3	7.0	59.00	63.23	5.36	-4.23	-0.33
4	8.0	43.00	65.19	4.92	-22.19	-1.69
5	10.0	56.00	69.12	4.45	-13.12	-0.99
6	11.0	84.00	71.08	4.45	12.92	0.97
7	14.0	96.00	76.97	5.36	19.03	1.47
8	15.0	69.00	78.94	5.88	-9.94	-0.78
9	15.0	84.00	78.94	5.88	5.06	0.40
10	19.0	83.00	86.79	8.55	-3.79	-0.34

Regression - Results

Control the Display of Results
- Display nothing
- Regression equation, table of coefficients, s, R-squared, and basic analysis of variance
- In addition, sequential sums of squares and the unusual observations in the table of fits and residuals
- In addition, the full table of fits and residuals

Help   OK   Cancel

FIGURE 12.33

MegaStat's Regression with Residuals   **ExamScores**

Regression Analysis

r^2	0.394	n	10
r	0.628	k	1
Std. Error	14.002	Dep. Var.	**Exam Score**

ANOVA table

Source	SS	df	MS	F	p-value
Regression	1,020.3412	1	1,020.3412	5.20	.0520
Residual	1,568.5588	8	196.0698		
Total	2,588.9000	9			

Regression output

variables	coefficients	std. error	t (df=8)	p-value	confidence interval 95% lower	95% upper
Intercept	49.4771	10.0665	4.915	.0012	26.2638	72.6904
Study Hours	1.9641	0.8610	2.281	.0520	-0.0213	3.9495

Observation	Exam Score	Predicted	Residual	Leverage	Studentized Residual	Studentized Deleted Residual	Cook's D
Tom	53	51.44	1.56	0.441	0.149	0.139	0.009
Mary	74	59.30	14.70	0.214	1.185	1.220	0.191
Sarah	59	63.23	-4.23	0.146	-0.327	-0.308	0.009
Oscar	43	65.19	-22.19	0.124	-1.693	-1.977	0.202
Cullyn	56	69.12	-13.12	0.101	-0.988	-0.986	0.055
Jaime	84	71.08	12.92	0.101	0.973	0.969	0.053
Theresa	96	76.97	19.03	0.146	1.471	1.610	0.185
Knut	69	78.94	-9.94	0.177	-0.782	-0.761	0.066
Jin-Mae	84	78.94	5.06	0.177	0.398	0.376	0.017
Courtney	83	86.79	-3.79	0.373	-0.342	-0.323	0.035

Regression Analysis

Input ranges:

Sheet1!$C$48:$C$57   X, Independent variable(s)   OK

Sheet1!$D$48:$D$57   Y, Dependent variable   Clear

No predictions   Cancel

   predictor values   Help

Options
- 95% Confidence Level
- Variance Inflation Factors
- Standardized Coefficients (betas)
- ✓ Test Intercept □ Force Zero Intercept
- All Possible Regressions
- Stepwise Selection

Residuals:
- ✓ Output Residuals
- ✓ Diagnostics and Influential Residuals
- Durbin-Watson
- ✓ Plot Residuals by Observation
- ✓ Plot Residuals by Predicted Y and X
- ✓ Normal Probability Plot of Residuals

Leverage and Influence

A high **leverage** statistic indicates that the observation is far from the mean of X. Such observations have great influence on the regression estimates, because they are at the "end of the lever." Figure 12.34 illustrates this concept. One individual worked 65 hours, while the others worked between 12 and 42 hours. This individual will have a big effect on the slope estimate, because he is so far above the mean of X. Yet this highly leveraged data point is *not* an outlier (i.e., the fitted regression line comes very close to the data point, so its residual will be small). The leverage for observation i is denoted h_i and is calculated as

$$h_i = \frac{1}{n} + \frac{(x_i - \bar{x})^2}{\sum_{i=1}^{n}(x_i - \bar{x})^2} \qquad (12.34)$$

FIGURE 12.34

Illustration of High Leverage   Leverage

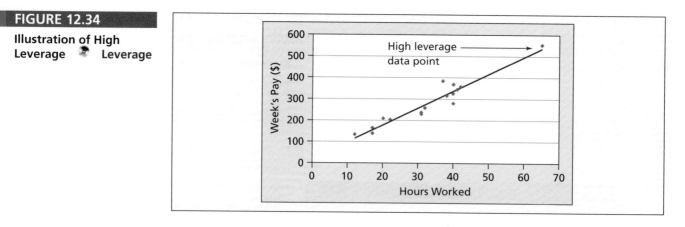

As a rule of thumb, a leverage statistic that exceeds $4/n$ is unusual (note that if $x_i = \bar{x}$ the leverage statistic h_i is $1/n$ so the rule of thumb is just four times this value).

EXAMPLE

Exam Scores: Leverage and Influence

ExamScores

We see from Figure 12.35 that two data points (Tom and Courtney) are likely to have high leverage because Tom studied for only 1 hour (far below the mean) while Courtney studied for 19 hours (far above the mean). Using the information in Table 12.4 (p. 442) we can calculate their leverages:

$$h_{Tom} = \frac{1}{10} + \frac{(1 - 10.5)^2}{264.50} = .441 \qquad \text{(Tom's leverage)}$$

$$h_{Courtney} = \frac{1}{10} + \frac{(19 - 10.5)^2}{264.50} = .373 \qquad \text{(Courtney's leverage)}$$

FIGURE 12.35   **Scatter Plot for Exam Data**   **ExamScores**

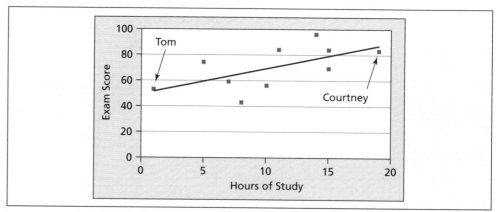

By the quick rule, both exceed $4/n = 4/10 = .400$, so these two observations are *influential*. Yet despite their high leverages, the regression fits Tom's and Courtney's actual exam scores well, so their *residuals* are not unusual. This illustrates that *high leverage* and *unusual residuals* are two different concepts.

Studentized Deleted Residuals

Unusual residuals give important clues about the model's adequacy. MegaStat also shows *studentized deleted residuals*—yet another way to identify unusual residuals. The calculation is equivalent to re-running the regression n times, with each observation omitted in turn, and re-calculating the studentized residuals. Further details are reserved for an advanced statistics class, but interpretation is simple. A studentized deleted residual whose absolute value is 2 or more may be considered unusual, and one whose absolute value is 3 or more is an outlier (applying the usual Empirical Rule).

Mini Case   12.5

Body Fat 🐟 BodyFat

Is waistline a good predictor of body fat? Table 12.9 shows a random sample of 50 men's weights (pounds) and girths (centimeters). Figure 12.36 suggests that a linear regression is appropriate, and the MegaStat output in Figure 12.37 shows that the regression is highly significant ($F = 97.68$, $t = 9.883$, $p = .0000$).

MegaStat's table of residuals, shown in Figure 12.38, highlights four unusual observations. Observations 5, 45, and 50 have high leverage values (exceeding $4/n = 4/50 = .08$)

TABLE 12.9   Abdomen Measurement and Body Fat ($n = 50$ men)

Girth	Fat%	Girth	Fat%	Girth	Fat%	Girth	Fat%
99.1	19.0	78.0	7.3	93.0	18.1	95.0	21.6
76.0	8.4	83.2	13.4	76.0	13.7	86.0	8.8
83.1	9.2	85.6	22.3	106.1	28.1	90.6	19.5
88.5	21.8	90.3	20.2	109.3	23.0	105.5	31.0
118.0	33.6	104.5	16.8	104.3	30.8	79.4	10.4
104.3	31.7	95.6	18.4	100.5	16.5	*126.2*	33.1
79.5	6.4	103.1	27.7	77.9	7.4	98.0	20.2
108.8	24.6	89.9	17.4	101.6	18.2	95.5	21.9
81.9	4.1	104.0	26.4	99.7	25.1	73.7	11.2
76.6	12.8	95.3	11.3	96.7	16.1	86.4	10.9
88.7	12.3	105.0	27.1	95.8	30.2	*122.1*	45.1
90.9	8.5	83.5	17.2	104.8	25.4		
89.0	26.0	86.7	10.7	92.4	25.9		

Data are from a larger sample of 252 men in Roger W. Johnson, *Journal of Statistics Education* 4, No. 1 (1996).

FIGURE 12.36   Body Fat Regression

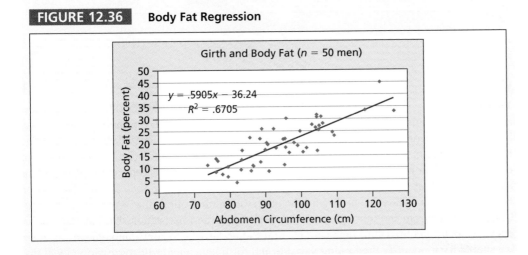

FIGURE 12.37 **Body Fat Scatter Plot**

Regression Analysis

r^2	0.671	n	50
r	0.819	k	1
Std. Error	5.086	Dep. Var.	Fat%1

ANOVA table

Source	SS	df	MS	F	p-value
Regression	2,527.1190	1	2,527.1190	97.68	3.71E-13
Residual	1,241.8162	48	25.8712		
Total	3,768.9352	49			

Regression output — confidence interval

variables	coefficients	std. error	t (df = 48)	p-value	95% lower	95% upper
Intercept	−36.2397	5.6690	−6.393	6.28E-08	−47.6379	−24.8415
Abdomen	0.5905	0.0597	9.883	3.71E-13	0.4704	0.7107

because their abdomen measurements (italicized and boldfaced in Table 12.9) are far from the mean. Observation 37 has a large studentized deleted residual (actual body fat of 30.20 percent is much greater than the predicted 20.33 percent). "Well-behaved" observations are omitted because they are not unusual according to any of the diagnostic criteria (leverage, studentized residual, or studentized deleted residual).

FIGURE 12.38 **Unusual Body Fat Residuals**

Observation	Fat%1	Predicted	Residual	Leverage	Studentized Residual	Studentized Deleted Residual
5	33.60	33.44	0.16	0.099	0.033	0.032
37	30.20	20.33	9.87	0.020	1.960	2.022
45	33.10	38.28	−5.18	0.162	−1.114	−1.116
50	45.10	35.86	9.24	0.128	1.945	2.005

12.10 OTHER REGRESSION PROBLEMS

Outliers

We have mentioned outliers under the discussion of non-normal residuals. However, outliers are the source of many other woes, including loss of fit. What causes outliers? An outlier may be an error in recording the data. If so, the observation should be deleted. But how can you tell? Impossible or bizarre data values are *prima facie* reasons to discard a data value. For example, in a sample of body fat data, one adult man's weight was reported as 205 pounds and his height as 29.5 inches (probably a typographical error that should have been 69.5 inches). It is reasonable to discard the observation on grounds that it represents a population different from the other men. An outlier may be an observation that has been influenced by an unspecified "lurking" variable that should have been controlled but wasn't. If so, we should try to identify the lurking variable and formulate a *multiple* regression model that includes the lurking variable(s) as predictors.

Model Misspecification

If a relevant predictor has been omitted, then the model is *misspecified*. Instead of simple regression, you should use *multiple regression*. Such a situation is so common that it is almost a warning against relying on simple regression, since we usually can think of more than one explanatory variable. As you will see in the next chapter, multiple regression is computationally easy because the computer does all the work. In fact, most computer packages just call it "regression" regardless of the number of predictors.

Ill-Conditioned Data

Variables in the regression should be of the same general order of magnitude, and most people take steps intuitively to make sure this is the case (**well-conditioned data**). Unusually large or small data (called **ill-conditioned**) can cause loss of regression accuracy or can create awkward estimates with exponential notation. Consider the data in Table 12.10 for 30 randomly selected large companies (only a few of the 30 selected are shown in this table). The table shows two ways of displaying the same data, but with the decimal point changed. Figures 12.39 and 12.40

Company	Net Income in Thousands	Revenue in Thousands	Net Income in Millions	Revenue in Millions
Allstate	1,714,000	30,142,000	1,714	30,142
American Int'l Group	5,493,000	70,272,000	5,493	70,272
Barclays	3,348,000	26,565,000	3,348	26,565
⋮	⋮	⋮	⋮	⋮
Volkswagen Group	2,432,000	84,707,000	2,432	84,707
Wachovia	3,693,000	23,455,000	3,693	23,455
Walt Disney	1,024,000	26,255,000	1,024	26,255

TABLE 12.10

Net Income and Revenue for Selected Global 100 Companies Global30

Source: www.forbes.com and *Forbes* 172, no. 2 (July 21, 2003), pp. 108–110.

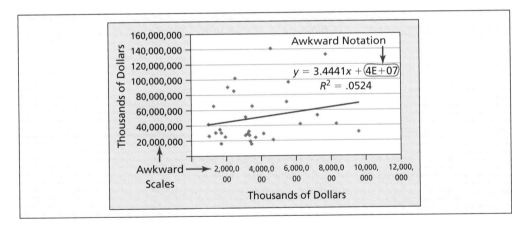

FIGURE 12.39

Ill-Conditioned Data

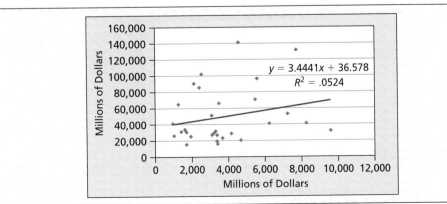

FIGURE 12.40

Well-Conditioned Data

show Excel scatter plots with regression lines. Their appearance is the same, but the first graph has disastrously crowded axis labels. The graphs have the same slope and R^2, but the first regression has an unintelligible intercept (4E+07).

Awkwardly small numbers may also require adjustment. For example, the number of automobile thefts per capita in the United States in 1990 was 0.004207. However, this statistic is easier to work with if it is reported "per 100,000 population" as 420.7. Worst of all would be to mix very large data with very small data. For example, in 1999 the per capita income in New York was $27,546 and the number of active physicians per capita was 0.00395. To avoid mixing magnitudes, we can redefine the variables as per capita income in thousands of dollars (27.546) and the number of active physicians per 10,000 population (39.5).

Tip

Adjust the magnitude of your data *before* running the regression.

Spurious Correlation 🐟 Prisoners

In a **spurious correlation**, two variables appear related because of the way they are defined. For example, consider the hypothesis that a state's spending on education is a linear function of its prison population. Such a hypothesis seems absurd, and we would expect the regression to be insignificant. But if the variables are defined as *totals* without adjusting for population, we will observe significant correlation. This phenomenon is called the *size effect* or the *problem of totals*. Table 12.11 shows selected data, first with the variables as *totals* and then as adjusted for population.

TABLE 12.11

State Spending on Education and State and Federal Prisoners 🐟 **Prisoners**

Source: *Statistical Abstract of the United States, 2001.*

| | | Using Totals | | Using Per Capita Data | |
State	Total Population (millions)	K–12 Spending ($ billions)	No. of Prisoners (thousands)	K–12 Spending per Capita ($)	Prisoners per 1,000 Pop.
Alabama	4.447	4.52	24.66	1,016	5.54
Alaska	0.627	1.33	3.95	2,129	6.30
⋮	⋮	⋮	⋮	⋮	⋮
Wisconsin	5.364	8.48	20.42	1,580	3.81
Wyoming	0.494	0.76	1.71	1,543	3.47

Figure 12.41 shows that, contrary to expectation, the regression on totals gives a very strong fit to the data. Yet Figure 12.42 shows that if we divide by population and adjust the decimals, the fit is nonexistent and the slope is indistinguishable from zero. The spurious

FIGURE 12.41

Spurious Model Using Totals

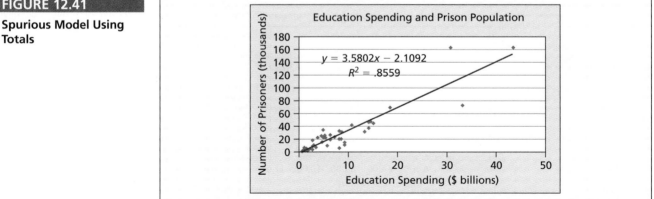

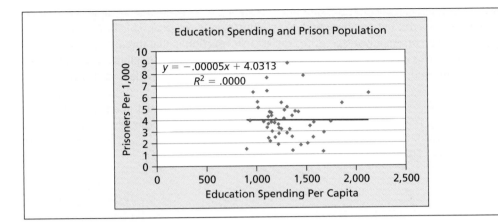

FIGURE 12.42

Better Model: Per Capita Data

correlation arose merely because both variables reflect the size of a state's population. For example, New York and California lie far to the upper right on the first scatter plot because they are populous states, while smaller states like South Dakota and Delaware are near the origin.

Model Form and Variable Transforms   MPG

Sometimes a relationship cannot be modeled using a linear regression. For example, Figure 12.43 shows fuel efficiency (city MPG) and engine size (horsepower) for a sample of 93 vehicles with a nonlinear model form fitted by Excel. This is one of several nonlinear forms offered by Excel (there are also logarithmic and exponential functions). Figure 12.44 shows an

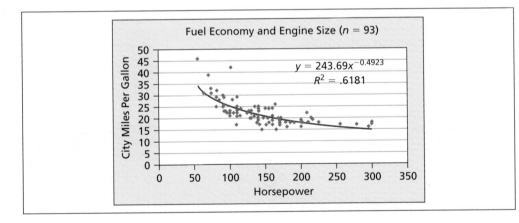

FIGURE 12.43

Nonlinear Regression

Source: Robin H. Lock, *Journal of Statistics Education* 1, no. 1 (1993).

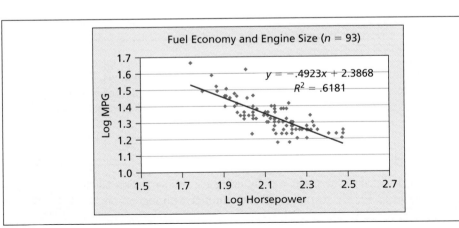

FIGURE 12.44

After Log Transform

alternative, which is a linear regression after taking *logarithms* of each variable. These logarithms are in base 10, but any base will do (scientists prefer base *e*). This is an example of a **variable transform**. An advantage of the **log transformation** is that it reduces heteroscedasticity and improves the normality of the residuals, especially when dealing with totals (the *size problem* mentioned earlier). But log transforms will not work if any data values are zero or negative.

Excel makes it easy to fit all sorts of regression models. But fit is only one criterion for evaluating a regression model. Since nonlinear or transformed models might be hard to justify or explain to others, the principle of *Occam's Razor* (choosing the simplest explanation that fits the facts) favors linear regression, unless there are other compelling factors.

Time Series Trend

A special case of bivariate regression is the **fitted linear trend** model for time series data whose form is $\hat{y}_t = b_0 + b_1 x_t$. The following notation is used:

y_t is the value of the time-series in period t.

t is an index denoting the time period ($t = 1, 2, \ldots, n$).

n is the number of time periods.

$y_1, y_2, \ldots, y_n$ is the data set for analysis.

When x represents time, we use the subscript "t" instead of "i" in the regression model. A linear trend is useful for a time-series that grows or declines by the same amount (b_1) in each period, as shown in Figure 12.45. It is the simplest trend model, and may suffice for short-run forecasting. It is generally preferred in business as a baseline forecasting model unless there are compelling reasons to consider a more complex model.

FIGURE 12.45

Linear Trend Models

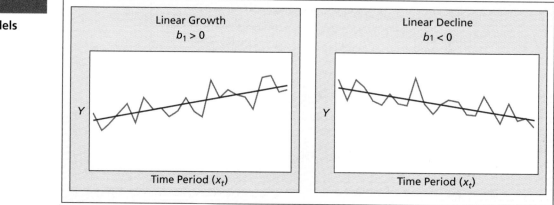

Illustration: Linear Trend

In recent years, the number of U.S. franchised new car dealerships has been declining, due to phasing out of low-volume dealerships and consolidation of market areas. What has been the average annual decline? Based on the line graph in Figure 12.46, the linear model seems appropriate to describe this trend. The slope of Excel's fitted trend indicates that, on average, 235 dealerships are being lost annually.

Linear Trend Calculations

The linear trend is fitted in the usual way by using the ordinary least squares formulas, as illustrated in Table 12.12. Since you are already familiar with regression, we will only point

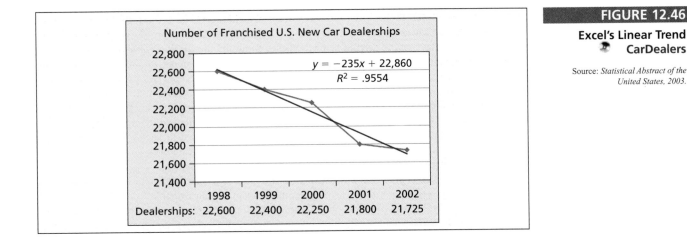

FIGURE 12.46

Excel's Linear Trend
🖙 **CarDealers**

Source: *Statistical Abstract of the United States, 2003.*

TABLE 12.12

Sums for Least Squares Calculations

Year	x_t	y_t	$x_t - \bar{x}$	$y_t - \bar{y}$	$(x_t - \bar{x})^2$	$(x_t - \bar{x})(y_t - \bar{y})$
1998	1	22,600	−2	445	4	−890
1999	2	22,400	−1	245	1	−245
2000	3	22,250	0	95	0	0
2001	4	21,800	1	−355	1	−355
2002	5	21,725	2	−430	4	−860
Sum	15	110,775	0	0	10	−2,350
Mean	3	22,155	0	0	2	−470

out the use of the index $x_t = 1, 2, 3, 4, 5$ for the calculations (instead of using the years 1998, 1999, 2000, 2001, 2002). We use this time index to simplify the calculations and keep the data magnitudes under control (Excel uses this method too).

$$\text{Slope:} \quad b_1 = \frac{\sum_{t=1}^{n}(x_t - \bar{x})(y_t - \bar{y})}{\sum_{t=1}^{n}(x_t - \bar{x})^2} = \frac{-2,350}{10} = -235$$

$$\text{Intercept:} \quad b_0 = \bar{y} - b\bar{x} = 22,155 - (-235)(3) = 22,860$$

Interpreting a Linear Trend

The *slope* of the fitted trend $x_t = 22,860 - 235x_t$ says that we expect to lose 235 dealerships each year $(dy_t/dx_t = -235)$. The *intercept* is the "starting point" for the time-series in period $t = 0$ (year 1997); that is, $y_0 = 22,860 - 235(0) = 22,860$.

Forecasting a Linear Trend ●

We can make a forecast for any future year by using the fitted model $y_t = 22,860 - 235t$. In the car dealer example, the fitted trend equation is based on only 5 years' data, so we should be wary of extrapolating very far ahead:

For 2003 $(t = 6)$: $y_6 = 22,860 - 235(6) = 21,450$

For 2004 $(t = 7)$: $y_7 = 22,860 - 235(7) = 21,215$

For 2005 $(t = 8)$: $y_8 = 22,860 - 235(8) = 20,980$

CHAPTER SUMMARY

The **sample correlation coefficient** r measures linear association between X and Y, with values near 0 indicating a lack of linearity while values near -1 (negative correlation) or $+1$ (positive correlation) suggest linearity. The **t test** is used to test hypotheses about the **population correlation** ρ. In **simple regression** there is an assumed linear relationship between the independent variable X (the **predictor**) and the dependent variable Y (the **response**). The slope (β_1) and intercept (β_0) are unknown **parameters** that are estimated from a sample. **Residuals** are the differences between **observed** and **fitted** Y-values. The **ordinary least squares** (OLS) method yields **regression coefficients** for the slope (b_1) and intercept (b_0) that minimize the sum of squared residuals. The **coefficient of determination** (R^2) measures the overall fit of the regression, with R^2 near 1 signifying a good fit and R^2 near 0 indicating a poor fit. The **F statistic** in the **ANOVA table** is used to test for significant overall regression, while the **t statistics** (and their p-values) are used to test hypotheses about the slope and intercept. The **standard error** of the regression is used to create **confidence intervals** or **prediction intervals** for Y. Regression assumes that the errors are normally distributed, independent random variables with constant variance σ^2. **Residual tests** identify possible **violations** of assumptions (**non-normality, autocorrelation, heteroscedasticity**). Data values with high **leverage** (unusual X-values) have strong influence on the regression. Unusual **standardized residuals** indicate cases where the regression gives a poor fit. **Ill-conditioned** data may lead to **spurious** correlation or other problems. **Data transforms** may help, but they also change the **model specification.**

KEY TERMS

autocorrelation, *462*
bivariate data, *427*
coefficient of determination,
   R^2, *443–444*
confidence interval, *457*
Durbin-Watson test, *463*
error sum of squares, *443*
fitted linear trend *474*
fitted model, *437*
fitted regression, *436*
heteroscedastic, *461*
homoscedastic, *461*

ill-conditioned data, *471*
intercept, *437*
leverage, *467*
log transformation, *474*
non-normality, *459*
ordinary least squares (OLS), *441*
population correlation
   coefficient, ρ, *429*
prediction interval, *457*
residual, *437*
sample correlation
   coefficient, r, *428*

scatter plot, *427*
simple regression, *436*
slope, *437*
spurious correlation, *472*
standard error, *446*
standardized residuals, *459*
studentized residuals, *466*
sums of squares, *428*
t statistic, *429*
variable transform, *474*
well-conditioned data, *471*

Commonly Used Formulas in Simple Regression

Sample correlation coefficient:
$$r = \frac{\sum_{i=1}^{n}(x_i - \bar{x})(y_i - \bar{y})}{\sqrt{\sum_{i=1}^{n}(x_i - \bar{x})^2}\sqrt{\sum_{i=1}^{n}(y_i - \bar{y})^2}}$$

Test statistic for zero correlation: $t_{\text{calc}} = r\sqrt{\dfrac{n-2}{1-r^2}}$

True regression line: $y_i = \beta_0 + \beta_1 x_i + \varepsilon_i$

Fitted regression line: $\hat{y}_i = b_0 + b_1 x_i$

Slope of fitted regression:
$$b_1 = \frac{\sum_{i=1}^{n}(x_i - \bar{x})(y_i - \bar{y})}{\sum_{i=1}^{n}(x_i - \bar{x})^2}$$

Intercept of fitted regression: $b_0 = \bar{y} - b_1\bar{x}$

Sum of squared residuals: $SSE = \sum_{i=1}^{n}(y_i - \hat{y}_i)^2 = \sum_{i=1}^{n}(y_i - b_0 - b_1 x_i)^2$

Coefficient of determination:
$$R^2 = 1 - \frac{\sum_{i=1}^{n}(y_i - \hat{y}_i)^2}{\sum_{i=1}^{n}(y_i - \bar{y})^2} = 1 - \frac{SSE}{SST}$$

Standard error of the estimate:
$$s_{yx} = \sqrt{\frac{\sum_{i=1}^{n}(y_i - \hat{y}_i)^2}{n-2}} = \sqrt{\frac{SSE}{n-2}}$$

Standard error of the slope: $s_{b_1} = \dfrac{s_{yx}}{\sqrt{\sum\limits_{i=1}^{n}(x_i - \bar{x})^2}}$

t test for zero slope: $t_{calc} = \dfrac{b_1 - 0}{s_{b_1}}$

Confidence interval for true slope: $b_1 - t_{n-2}s_{b_1} \le \beta_1 \le b_1 + t_{n-2}s_{b_1}$

Confidence interval for conditional mean of Y: $\hat{y}_i \pm t_{n-2}s_{yx}\sqrt{\dfrac{1}{n} + \dfrac{(x_i - \bar{x})^2}{\sum\limits_{i=1}^{n}(x_i - \bar{x})^2}}$

Prediction interval for Y: $\hat{y}_i \pm t_{n-2}s_{yx}\sqrt{1 + \dfrac{1}{n} + \dfrac{(x_i - \bar{x})^2}{\sum\limits_{i=1}^{n}(x_i - \bar{x})^2}}$

CHAPTER REVIEW

1. (a) How does correlation analysis differ from regression analysis? (b) What does a correlation coefficient reveal? (c) State the quick rule for a significant correlation and explain its limitations. (d) What sums are needed to calculate a correlation coefficient? (e) What are the two ways of testing a correlation coefficient for significance?

2. (a) What is a simple regression model? (b) State three caveats about regression. (c) What does the random error component in a regression model represent? (d) What is the difference between a regression residual and the true random error?

3. (a) Explain how you fit a regression to an Excel scatter plot. (b) What are the limitations of Excel's scatter plot fitted regression?

4. (a) Explain the logic of the ordinary least squares (OLS) method. (b) How are the least squares formulas for the slope and intercept derived? (c) What sums are needed to calculate the least squares estimates?

5. (a) Why can't we use the sum of the residuals to assess fit? (b) What sums are needed to calculate R^2? (c) Name an advantage of using the R^2 statistic instead of the standard error s_{yx} to measure fit. (d) Why do we need the standard error s_{yx}?

6. (a) Explain why a confidence interval for the slope or intercept would be equivalent to a two-tailed hypothesis test. (b) Why is it especially important to test for a zero slope?

7. (a) What does the F statistic show? (b) What is its range? (c) What is the relationship between the F test and the t tests for the slope and correlation coefficient?

8. (a) For a given X, explain the distinction between a confidence interval for the conditional mean of Y and a prediction interval for an individual Y-value. (b) Why is the individual prediction interval wider? (c) Why are these intervals narrowest when X is near its mean? (d) When can quick rules for these intervals give acceptable results, and when not?

9. (a) What is a residual? (b) What is a standardized residual and why is it useful? (c) Name two alternative ways to identify unusual residuals.

10. (a) When does a data point have high leverage (refer to the scatter plot)? (b) Name one test for unusual leverage.

11. (a) Name three assumptions about the random error term in the regression model. (b) Why are the residuals important in testing these assumptions?

12. (a) What are the consequences of non-normal errors? (b) Explain two tests for non-normality. (c) What can we do about non-normal residuals?

13. (a) What is heteroscedasticity? Identify its two common forms. (b) What are its consequences? (c) How do we test for it? (d) What can we do about it?

14. (a) What is autocorrelation? Identify two main forms of it. (b) What are its consequences? (c) Name two ways to test for it. (d) What can we do about it?

15. (a) Why might there be outliers in the residuals? (b) What actions could be taken?

16. (a) What is ill-conditioned data? How can it be avoided? (b) What is spurious correlation? How can it be avoided?

17. (a) What is a log transform? (b) What are its advantages and disadvantages?

CHAPTER EXERCISES

connect

Instructions: Choose one or more of the data sets *A–J* below, or as assigned by your instructor. Choose the dependent variable (the *response variable* to be "explained") and the independent variable (the *predictor* or *explanatory variable*) as you judge appropriate. Use a spreadsheet or a statistical package (e.g., MegaStat or MINITAB) to obtain the fitted regression and required graphs. Write your answers to exercises 12.28 through 12.43 (or those assigned by your instructor) in a concise report, labeling your answers to each question. Insert tables and graphs in your report as appropriate. You may work with a partner if your instructor allows it.

12.28 Are the variables cross-sectional data or time-series data?

12.29 How do you imagine the data were collected?

12.30 Is the sample size sufficient to yield a good estimate? If not, do you think more data could easily be obtained, given the nature of the problem?

12.31 State your *a priori* hypothesis about the sign of the slope. Is it reasonable to suppose a cause and effect relationship?

12.32 Make a scatter plot of *Y* against *X*. Discuss what it tells you.

12.33 Use Excel's Add Trendline feature to fit a linear regression to the scatter plot. Is a linear model credible?

12.34 Interpret the slope. Does the intercept have meaning, given the range of the data?

12.35 Use Excel, MegaStat, or MINITAB to fit the regression model, including residuals and standardized residuals.

12.36 (a) Does the 95 percent confidence interval for the slope include zero? If so, what does it mean? If not, what does it mean? (b) Do a two-tailed *t* test for zero slope at $\alpha = .05$. State the hypotheses, degrees of freedom, and critical value for your test. (c) Interpret the *p*-value for the slope. (d) Which approach do you prefer, the *t* test or the *p*-value? Why? (e) Did the sample support your hypothesis about the sign of the slope?

12.37 (a) Based on the R^2 and ANOVA table for your model, how would you assess the fit? (b) Interpret the *p*-value for the *F* statistic. (c) Would you say that your model's fit is good enough to be of practical value?

12.38 Study the table of residuals. Identify as *outliers* any standardized residuals that exceed 3 and as *unusual* any that exceed 2. Can you suggest any reasons for these unusual residuals?

12.39 (a) Make a histogram (or normal probability plot) of the residuals and discuss its appearance. (b) Do you see evidence that your regression may violate the assumption of normal errors?

12.40 Inspect the residual plot to check for heteroscedasticity and report your conclusions.

12.41 Is an autocorrelation test appropriate for your data? If so, perform one or more tests of the residuals (eyeball inspection of residual plot against observation order, runs test, and/or Durbin-Watson test).

12.42 Use MegaStat or MINITAB to generate 95 percent confidence and prediction intervals for various *X*-values.

12.43 Use MegaStat or MINITAB to identify observations with high leverage.

DATA SET A Median Income and Median Home Prices in Selected Eastern Cities (*n* = 34 cities)   HomePrice1

City	Income	Home
Alexandria, VA	59.976	290.000
Bernards Twp., NJ	112.435	279.900
Brentwood, TN	107.866	338.250
⋮	⋮	⋮
Sugarland Run, VA	103.350	278.250
Sully, VA	92.942	290.000
Wellington, FL	76.076	230.000

Source: *Money Magazine* 32, no. 1 (January, 2004), pp. 102–103.

Note: Values are in thousands of dollars. Data are for educational purposes only.

DATA SET B Employees and Revenue in Large Automotive Companies in 1999 (*n* = 24 companies)   CarFirms

Company	Employees	Revenue
BMW	119.9	35.9
DaimlerChrysler	441.5	154.6
Dana	86.4	12.8
⋮	⋮	⋮
TRW	78.0	11.9
Volkswagen	297.9	76.3
Volvo	70.3	26.8

Source: Project by statistics students Paul Ruskin, Kristy Bielewski, and Linda Stengel.

Note: Employees are in thousands and *Revenue* is in billions.

DATA SET C Estimated and Actual Length of Stay in Months (*n* = 16 patients) Hospital

Patient	ELOS	ALOS
1	10.5	10
2	4.5	2
3	7.5	4
⋮	⋮	⋮
14	6	10
15	7.5	7
16	3	5.5

Source: Records of a hospital outpatient cognitive retraining clinic.

Note: ELOS used a 42-item assessment instrument combined with expert team judgment. Patients had suffered head trauma, stroke, or other medical conditions affecting cognitive function.

DATA SET D Single-Engine Aircraft Performance (*n* = 52 airplanes) Airplanes

Mfgr/Model	Cruise	TotalHP
AMD CH 2000	100	116
Beech Baron 58	200	600
Beech Baron 58P	241	650
⋮	⋮	⋮
Sky Arrow 650 TC	98	81
Socata TB20 Trinidad	163	250
Tiger AG-5B	143	180

Source: New and used airplane reports in *Flying* (various issues).

Note: Cruise is in knots (nautical miles per hour). Data are for educational purposes only and should not be used as a guide to aircraft performance. *TotalHP* is total horse power.

DATA SET E Ages and Weights of 31 Randomly Chosen U.S. Nickels (*n* = 31 nickels) Nickels

Obs	Age (yrs)	Weight (gm)
1	2	5.043
2	15	4.893
3	22	4.883
⋮	⋮	⋮
29	21	4.927
30	1	5.035
31	16	4.983

Source: As an independent project, a statistics student weighed randomly-chosen circulated nickels on a scale whose accuracy is 0.001 gram.

Note: Coin age is the difference between the measurement year and the mint year.

DATA SET F U.S. Annual Percent Inflation in Prices of Commodities and Services (*n* = 47 years) Inflation

Year	Commodities%	Services%
1960	0.9	3.4
1961	0.6	1.7
1962	0.9	2.0
⋮	⋮	⋮
2004	2.3	2.9
2005	3.6	3.3
2006	2.4	3.8

Source: *Economic Report of the President, 2007.*

Note: Data are year-to-year percent changes in the Consumer Price Index (CPI) in these two categories.

DATA SET G Mileage and Vehicle Weight (*n* = 43 vehicles) MPG

Vehicle	City MPG	Weight
Acura CL	20	3450
Accura TSX	23	3320
BMW 3-Series	19	3390
⋮	⋮	⋮
Toyota Sienna	19	4120
Volkswagen Jetta	34	3045
Volvo C70	20	3690

Source: *Consumer Reports New Car Buying Guide 2003–2004* (Consumers Union, 2003).

Note: Sample is the first vehicle on every 5th page starting at page 40. Data are for statistical education only and should not be viewed as a guide to vehicle performance.

DATA SET H Pasta Sauce Per Gram Total Calories and Fat Calories (*n* = 20 products) Pasta

Product	Cal/gm	Fat Cal/gm
Barilla Roasted Garlic & Onion	0.64	0.20
Barilla Tomato & Basil	0.56	0.12
Classico Tomato & Basil	0.40	0.08
⋮	⋮	⋮
Ragu Roasted Garlic	0.70	0.19
Ragu Traditional	0.56	0.20
Sutter Home Tomato & Garlic	0.64	0.16

Source: Independent project by statistics students Donna Bennett, Nicole Cook, Latrice Haywood, and Robert Malcolm.

Note: Data are intended for educational purposes only and should not be viewed as a nutrition guide.

DATA SET I	Electric Bills and Consumption for a Residence (n = 24 months) ☂ Electric	
Month	Usage (kWh)	Avg Temp (F°)
1	436	62
2	464	71
3	446	76
⋮	⋮	⋮
22	840	25
23	867	38
24	606	48

Source: Electric bills for a residence and NOAA weather data.

DATA SET J	Life Expectancy and Birth Rates (n = 153 nations) ☂ BirthRates	
Nation	Life Expectancy	Birth rate
Afghanistan	46.6	41.03
Albania	72.1	18.59
Algeria	70.2	22.34
⋮	⋮	⋮
Yemen	60.6	43.30
Zambia	37.4	41.01
Zimbabwe	36.5	24.59

Source: Central Intelligence Agency, *The World Factbook, 2003.*

12.44 Researchers found a correlation coefficient of $r = .50$ on personality measures for identical twins. A reporter interpreted this to mean that "the environment orchestrated one-half of their personality differences." Do you agree with this interpretation? Discuss. (See *Science News* 140 [December 7, 1991], p. 377.)

12.45 A study of the role of spreadsheets in planning in 55 small firms defined $Y =$ "satisfaction with sales growth" and $X =$ "executive commitment to planning." Analysis yielded an overall correlation of $r = .3043$. Do a two-tailed test for zero correlation at $\alpha = .025$.

12.46 In a study of stock prices from 1970 to 1994, the correlation between Nasdaq closing prices on successive days (i.e., with a 1-day lag) was $r = .13$ with a t statistic of 5.47. Interpret this result. (See David Nawrocki, "The Problems with Monte Carlo Simulation," *Journal of Financial Planning* 14, no. 11 [November 2001], p. 96.)

12.47 Regression analysis of free throws by 29 NBA teams during the 2002–2003 season revealed the fitted regression $Y = 55.2 + .73X$ ($R^2 = .874$, $s_{yx} = 53.2$) where $Y =$ total free throws made and $X =$ total free throws attempted. The observed range of X was from 1,620 (New York Knicks) to 2,382 (Golden State Warriors). (a) Find the expected number of free throws made for a team that shoots 2,000 free throws. (b) Do you think that the intercept is meaningful? *Hint:* Make a scatter plot and let Excel fit the line. (c) Use the quick rule to make a 95 percent prediction interval for Y when $X = 2,000$. ☂ **FreeThrows**

12.48 In the following regression, $X =$ weekly pay, $Y =$ income tax withheld, and $n = 35$ McDonald's employees. (a) Write the fitted regression equation. (b) State the degrees of freedom for a two-tailed test for zero slope, and use Appendix D to find the critical value at $\alpha = .05$. (c) What is your conclusion about the slope? (d) Interpret the 95 percent confidence limits for the slope. (e) Verify that $F = t^2$ for the slope. (f) In your own words, describe the fit of this regression.

R^2	0.202
Std. Error	6.816
n	35

ANOVA table

Source	SS	df	MS	F	p-value
Regression	387.6959	1	387.6959	8.35	.0068
Residual	1,533.0614	33	46.4564		
Total	1,920.7573	34			

Regression output					confidence interval	
variables	coefficients	std. error	t (df = 33)	p-value	95% lower	95% upper
Intercept	30.7963	6.4078	4.806	.0000	17.7595	43.8331
Slope	0.0343	0.0119	2.889	.0068	0.0101	0.0584

12.49 In the following regression, $X =$ monthly maintenance spending (dollars), $Y =$ monthly machine downtime (hours), and $n = 15$ copy machines. (a) Write the fitted regression equation. (b) State the degrees of freedom for a two-tailed test for zero slope, and use Appendix D to find the critical value at $\alpha = .05$. (c) What is your conclusion about the slope? (d) Interpret the 95 percent confidence limits for the slope. (e) Verify that $F = t^2$ for the slope. (f) In your own words, describe the fit of this regression.

R^2	0.370
Std. Error	286.793
n	15

ANOVA table

Source	SS	df	MS	F	p-value
Regression	628,298.2	1	628,298.2	7.64	.0161
Residual	1,069,251.8	13	82,250.1		
Total	1,697,550.0	14			

Regression output

variables	coefficients	std. error	t (df = 13)	p-value	confidence interval 95% lower	95% upper
Intercept	1,743.57	288.82	6.037	.0000	1,119.61	2,367.53
Slope	−1.2163	0.4401	−2.764	.0161	−2.1671	−0.2656

12.50 In the following regression, $X =$ total assets (\$ billions), $Y =$ total revenue (\$ billions), and $n = 64$ large banks. (a) Write the fitted regression equation. (b) State the degrees of freedom for a two-tailed test for zero slope, and use Appendix D to find the critical value at $\alpha = .05$. (c) What is your conclusion about the slope? (d) Interpret the 95 percent confidence limits for the slope. (e) Verify that $F = t^2$ for the slope. (f) In your own words, describe the fit of this regression.

R^2	0.519
Std. Error	6.977
n	64

ANOVA table

Source	SS	df	MS	F	p-value
Regression	3,260.0981	1	3,260.0981	66.97	1.90E-11
Residual	3,018.3339	62	48.6828		
Total	6,278.4320	63			

Regression output

variables	coefficients	std. error	t (df = 62)	p-value	confidence interval 95% lower	95% upper
Intercept	6.5763	1.9254	3.416	.0011	2.7275	10.4252
X1	0.0452	0.0055	8.183	1.90E-11	0.0342	0.0563

12.51 Do stock prices of competing companies move together? Below are daily closing prices of two computer services firms (IBM = International Business Machines Corporation, EDS = Electronic Data Systems Corporation). (a) Calculate the sample correlation coefficient (e.g., using Excel or MegaStat). (b) At $\alpha = .01$ can you conclude that the true correlation coefficient is greater than zero? (c) Make a scatter plot of the data. What does it say? (Data are from Center for Research and Security Prices, University of Chicago.) **StockPrices**

Daily Closing Price ($) of Two Stocks in October and November 2004 ($n = 42$ days)

Date	IBM	EDS
9/1/04	84.22	19.31
9/2/04	84.57	19.63
9/3/04	84.39	19.19
⋮	⋮	⋮
10/27/04	90.00	21.26
10/28/04	89.50	21.41
10/29/04	89.75	21.27

12.52 Below are percentages for *annual sales growth* and *net sales attributed to loyalty card usage* at 74 Noodles & Company restaurants. (a) Make a scatter plot. (b) Find the correlation coefficient and interpret it. (c) Test the correlation coefficient for significance, clearly stating the degrees of freedom. (d) Does it appear that loyalty card usage is associated with increased sales growth? **LoyaltyCard**

Annual Sales Growth (%) and Loyalty Card Usage (% of Net Sales) ($n = 74$ restaurants)

Store	Growth%	Loyalty%
1	−8.3	2.1
2	−4.0	2.5
3	−3.9	1.7
⋮	⋮	⋮
72	20.8	1.1
73	25.5	0.6
74	28.8	1.8

Source: Noodles & Company

12.53 Below are fertility rates (average children born per woman) in 15 EU nations for 2 years. (a) Make a scatter plot. (b) Find the correlation coefficient and interpret it. (c) Test the correlation coefficient for significance, clearly stating the degrees of freedom. (Data are from the World Health Organization.) **Fertility**

Fertility Rates for EU Nations ($n = 15$)

Nation	1990	2000
Austria	1.5	1.3
Belgium	1.6	1.5
Denmark	1.6	1.7
⋮	⋮	⋮
Spain	1.4	1.1
Sweden	2.0	1.4
U.K.	1.8	1.7

12.54 Consider the following prices and accuracy ratings for 27 stereo speakers. (a) Make a scatter plot of accuracy rating as a function of price. (b) Calculate the correlation coefficient. At $\alpha = .05$, does the correlation differ from zero? (c) In your own words, describe the scatter plot. (Data are from *Consumer Reports* 68, no. 11 [November 2003], p. 31. Data are intended for statistical education and not as a guide to speaker performance.) **Speakers**

Price and Accuracy of Selected Stereo Speakers (n = 27)

Brand and Model	Type	Price ($)	Accuracy
BIC America Venturi DV62si	Shelf	200	91
Bose 141	Shelf	100	86
Bose 201 Series V	Shelf	220	89
⋮	⋮	⋮	⋮
Sony SS-MB350H	Shelf	100	92
Sony SS-MF750H	Floor	280	91
Sony SS-X30ED	Shelf	500	83

12.55 Choose *one* of these three data sets. (a) Make a scatter plot. (b) Let Excel estimate the regression line, with fitted equation and R^2. (c) Describe the fit of the regression. (d) Write the fitted regression equation and interpret the slope. (e) Do you think that the estimated intercept is meaningful? Explain.

Commercial Real Estate (X = floor space, sq. ft.; Y = assessed value, $000) (n = 15)
Assessed

Assessed	Size
1,796	4,790
1,544	4,720
2,094	5,940
⋮	⋮
1,678	4,880
710	1,620
678	1,820

Sasnak Co. Salaries (X = employee age; Y = employee salary, $000) (n = 23)
Salaries

Employee	Age	Salary
Mary	23	28.6
Frieda	31	53.3
Alicia	44	73.8
⋮	⋮	⋮
Marcia	54	75.8
Ellen	44	79.8
Iggy	36	70.2

Poway Big Homes, Ltd. (X = home size, sq. ft.; Y = selling price, $000) (n = 20)
HomePrice2

SqFt	Price
3,570	861
3,410	740
2,690	563
⋮	⋮
3,020	720
2,320	575
3,130	785

12.56 Regression was employed to establish the effects of childhood exposure to lead. The effective sample size was about 122 subjects. The independent variable was the level of dentin lead (parts per million). Below are regressions using various dependent variables. (a) Calculate the *t* statistic for each slope. (b) From the *p*-values, which slopes differ from zero at $\alpha = .01$? (c) Do you feel that cause and effect can be assumed? *Hint:* Do a Web search for information about effects of childhood lead exposure. (Data are from H. L. Needleman et al., *The New England Journal of Medicine* 322, no. 2 [January 1990], p. 86.)

Dependent Variable	R^2	Estimated Slope	Std Error	p-value
Highest grade achieved	.061	−0.027	0.009	.008
Reading grade equivalent	.121	−0.070	0.018	.000
Class standing	.039	−0.006	0.003	.048
Absence from school	.071	4.8	1.7	.006
Grammatical reasoning	.051	0.159	0.062	.012
Vocabulary	.108	−0.124	0.032	.000
Hand-eye coordination	.043	0.041	0.018	.020
Reaction time	.025	11.8	6.66	.080
Minor antisocial behavior	.025	−0.639	0.36	.082

12.57 Below are recent financial ratios for a random sample of 20 integrated health care systems. *Operating Margin* is total revenue minus total expenses divided by total revenue plus net operating profits. *Equity Financing* is fund balance divided by total assets. (a) Make a scatter plot of $Y =$ operating margin and $X =$ equity financing (both variables are in percent). (b) Use Excel to fit the regression, with fitted equation and R^2. (c) In your own words, describe the fit. (Data are from *Hospitals & Health Networks* 71, no. 6 [March 20, 1997], pp. 48–49. Copyright © 1997 by Health Forum, Inc. Used with permission. Data are intended for statistical education and not as a guide to financial performance.) 🏥 **HealthCare**

Financial Ratios for Selected Health Care Systems ($n = 20$)

Name of Health Care System	Operating Margin	Equity Financing
Albert Einstein Healthcare Network	3.89	35.58
Alliant Health Systems	8.23	59.68
Baptist Memorial Health Care System	2.56	40.48
⋮	⋮	⋮
OSF Healthcare Network	4.75	54.21
Samaritan Health System	0.00	59.73
Scottsdale Memorial Health System	10.79	46.21

12.58 Consider the following data on 20 chemical reactions, with $Y =$ chromatographic retention time (seconds) and $X =$ molecular weight (gm/mole). (a) Make a scatter plot. (b) Use Excel to fit the regression, with fitted equation and R^2. (c) In your own words, describe the fit. (Data provided by John Seeley of Oakland University.) 🧪 **Chemicals**

Retention Time and Molecular Weight ($n = 20$)

Name	Retention Time	Molecular Weight
alpha-pinene	234.50	136.24
cyclopentene	95.27	68.12
p-diethylbenzene	284.00	134.22
⋮	⋮	⋮
pentane	78.00	72.15
isooctane	136.90	114.23
hexane	106.00	86.18

12.59 A common belief among faculty is that teaching ratings are lower in large classes. Below are MINITAB results from a regression using $Y =$ mean student evaluation of the professor and $X =$ class size for 364 business school classes taught during the 2002–2003 academic year. Ratings are on a scale of 1 (lowest) to 5 (highest). (a) What do these regression results tell you about the relationship between class size and faculty ratings? (b) Is a bivariate model adequate? If not, suggest additional predictors to be considered.

Predictor	Coef	SE Coef	T	P
Constant	4.18378	0.07226	57.90	0.000
Enroll	0.000578	0.002014	0.29	0.774

$S = 0.5688$ R-Sq = 0.0%   R-Sq(adj) = 0.0%

12.60 Below are revenue and profit (both in $ billions) for nine large entertainment companies. (a) Make a scatter plot of profit as a function of revenue. (b) Use Excel to fit the regression, with fitted equation and R^2. (c) In your own words, describe the fit. (Data are from *Fortune* 149, no. 7 [April 5, 2005], p. F-50.)   **Entertainment**

Revenue and Profit of Entertainment Companies (n = 9)

Company	Revenue	Profit
AMC Entertainment	1.792	−0.020
Clear Channel Communication	8.931	1.146
Liberty Media	2.446	−0.978
⋮	⋮	⋮
Univision Communications	1.311	0.155
Viacom	26.585	1.417
Walt Disney	27.061	1.267

12.61 Below are fitted regressions based on used vehicle ads. Observed ranges of X are shown. The assumed regression model is *AskingPrice* = f(*VehicleAge*). (a) Interpret the slopes. (b) Are the intercepts meaningful? Explain. (c) Assess the fit of each model. (d) Is a bivariate model adequate to explain vehicle prices? If not, what other predictors might be considered? (Data are from *Detroit's AutoFocus* 4, Issue 38 [September 17–23, 2004]. Data are for educational purposes only and should not be viewed as a guide to vehicle prices.)

Vehicle	n	Intercept	Slope	R^2	Min Age	Max Age
Ford Explorer	31	22,252	−2,452	.643	2	6
Ford F-150 Pickup	43	26,164	−2,239	.713	1	37
Ford Mustang	33	21,308	−1,691	.328	1	10
Ford Taurus	32	13,160	−906	.679	1	14

12.62 Below are results of a regression of Y = average stock returns (in percent) as a function of X = average price/earnings ratios for the period 1949–1997 (49 years). Separate regressions were done for various holding periods (sample sizes are therefore variable). (a) Summarize what the regression results tell you. (b) Would you anticipate autocorrelation in this type of data? Explain. (Data are from Ruben Trevino and Fiona Robertson, "P/E Ratios and Stock Market Returns," *Journal of Financial Planning* 15, no. 2 [February 2002], p. 78.)

Holding Period	Intercept	Slope	t	R^2	p
1-Year	28.10	−0.92	1.86	.0688	.0686
2-Year	26.11	−0.86	2.57	.1252	.0136
5-Year	20.67	−0.57	2.99	.1720	.0046
8-Year	24.73	−0.94	6.93	.5459	.0000
10-Year	24.51	−0.95	8.43	.6516	.0000

12.63 Adult height is somewhat predictable from average height of both parents. For females, a commonly used equation is *YourHeight* = *ParentHeight* − 2.5 while for males the equation is *YourHeight* = *ParentHeight* + 2.5. (a) Test these equations on yourself (or on somebody else). (b) How well did the equations predict your height? (c) How do you suppose these equations were derived? Note: Heights are in inches.

12.64 (a) Make an attractive, well-labeled time-series line chart for JetBlue's revenue. (b) Describe the trend (if any) and discuss possible causes. (c) Fit a linear trend to the data, using Excel's option to display the fitted trend line and R^2 Statistic. (d) Make a forecast for 2007. (e) How well does the linear trend describe the data?   **JetBlue**

JetBlue Airlines Revenue, 2002–2006 (millions)

Year	Revenue
2002	635
2003	998
2004	1,265
2005	1,701
2006	2,363

Source: *Standard & Poor's Stock Reports,* February 2007.

12.65 (a) Plot U.S. petroleum imports on a graph. (b) Describe the trend (if any) and discuss possible causes. (c) Fit a linear trend. (c) Interpret the fitted trend equation, explaining the implications. (d) Make a projection for 2010. Do you believe it? (e) Does the linear trend describe the data well? (f) To whom is this issue relevant? *Note:* Time increments are 5 years, so use $t = 11$ for the 2010 forecast. 🐞 **Petroleum**

U.S. Annual Petroleum Imports, 1960–2005 (billions of barrels)

Year	Imports	Year	Imports
1960	664	1985	1,850
1965	901	1990	2,926
1970	1,248	1995	3,225
1975	2,210	2000	4,194
1980	2,529	2005	4,937

Source: www.eia.doe.gov.

LearningStats Unit 12   Regression I [LS]

LearningStats Unit 12 covers correlation and simple regression. It includes demonstrations of the least squares method, regression formulas, effects of model form and range of X, confidence and prediction intervals, violations of assumptions, and examples of student projects. Your instructor may assign specific modules, or you may decide to check them out because the topic sounds interesting.

Topic	LearningStats Modules
Correlation	Overview of Correlation Correlation Analysis
Regression	Overview of Simple Regression Using Excel for Regression
Ordinary least squares estimators	Least Squares Method Demonstration Doing Regression Calculations Effect of Model Form Effect of X Range
Confidence and prediction intervals	Confidence and Prediction Intervals Calculations for Confidence Intervals Superimposing Many Fitted Regressions
Violations of assumptions	Non-Normal Errors Heteroscedastic Errors Autocorrelated Errors Cochrane-Orcutt Transform
Formulas	Derivation of OLS Estimators Formulas for Significance Tests
Student presentations	Birth Rates Effects of Urbanization
Tables of critical values	Appendix D—Student's t Appendix F—F Distribution

Key: 🅲 = PowerPoint   🅦 = Word   🅧 = Excel

Visual Statistics

Visual Statistics Modules on Describing Data

Module	Module Name
14	**VS** Bivariate Data Analysis
15	**VS** Simple Regression
16	**VS** Regression Assumptions
18	**VS** Regression Models

Visual Statistics modules 14, 15, 16, and 18 (included on your CD) are designed with the following objectives:

Module 14

- Become familiar with ways to display bivariate data.
- Understand measures of association in bivariate data.
- Be able to interpret regression statistics and assess their significance.

Module 15

- Understand OLS terminology.
- Understand how sample size, standard error, and range of X affect estimation accuracy.
- Understand confidence intervals for $E(y|x)$ and prediction intervals for $y|x$.

Module 16

- Learn the regression assumptions required to ensure desirable properties for OLS estimators.
- Learn to recognize violations of the regression assumptions.
- Be able to identify the effects of assumption violations.

Module 18

- Know the common variable transformations and their purposes.
- Learn the effects of variable transformations on the fitted regression and statistics of fit.
- Understand polynomial models.

The worktext chapter (included on the CD in .PDF format) contains a list of concepts covered, objectives of the module, overview of concepts, illustration of concepts, orientation to module features, learning exercises (basic, intermediate, advanced), learning projects (individual, team), self-evaluation quiz, glossary of terms, and solutions to self-evaluation quiz.

Multiple Regression

Chapter Learning Objectives

When you finish this chapter you should be able to

- Use a fitted multiple regression equation to make predictions.

- Interpret the R^2 and perform an *F* test for overall significance.

- Test individual predictors for significance.

- Interpret confidence intervals for regression coefficients.

- Detect multicollinearity and assess its effects.

- Identify unusual residuals and outliers by using standardized residuals.

- Interpret tests for leverage.

- Analyze the residuals to check for violations of regression assumptions.

- Explain the role of data conditioning and data transformations.

Bivariate or Multivariate?

Multiple regression extends bivariate regression to include several independent variables (or *predictors*). Everything you learned about *bivariate regression* is a special case of multiple regression. The interpretation of multiple regression is similar, except that two-dimensional *X-Y* scatter plots are of limited value in higher-dimensional models. Since all calculations are done by computer, there is no extra computational burden. In fact, statisticians make no distinction between bivariate and multivariate regression—they just call it *regression*.

Multiple regression is required when a single-predictor model is inadequate to describe the true relationship between the dependent variable *Y* (the response variable) and its potential predictors ($X_1, X_2, X_3, \ldots$). Adding predictors is more than a matter of "improving the fit." Rather, it is a question of specifying a correct model. Omission of relevant predictors (*model misspecification*) can cause biased estimates and misleading results. A low R^2 in a bivariate regression model does not necessarily mean that *X* and *Y* are unrelated, but may simply indicate that the model is incorrectly specified.

Chapter 17

Limitations of Bivariate Regression

- Often simplistic (multiple relationships usually exist).
- Biased estimates if relevant predictors are omitted.
- Lack of fit does not show that *X* is unrelated to *Y* if the true model is multivariate.

Since multiple predictors usually are relevant, bivariate regression is only used when there is a compelling need for a simple model, or when other predictors have only modest effects and a single logical predictor "stands out" as doing a very good job all by itself.

Regression Terminology

The **response variable** (*Y*) is a random variable that is assumed to be related to the *k* **predictors** ($X_1, X_2, \ldots, X_k$) by a linear equation called the *population regression model:*

$$Y = \beta_0 + \beta_1 X_1 + \beta_2 X_2 + \cdots + \beta_k X_k + \varepsilon \tag{13.1}$$

489

Each value of Y is assumed to differ from the *conditional mean* $E(Y) = \beta_0 + \beta_1 X_1 + \beta_2 X_2 + \cdots + \beta_k X_k$ by a *random error* ε representing everything that is not part of the model. The unknown regression coefficients $\beta_0, \beta_1, \beta_2, \ldots, \beta_k$ are *parameters* and are denoted by Greek letters. Each coefficient β_j shows the change in the expected value of Y for a unit change in X_j while holding everything else constant (*ceteris paribus*). The errors are assumed to be unobservable, independent random disturbances that are normally distributed with zero mean and constant variance, that is, $\varepsilon \sim N(0, \sigma^2)$. Under these assumptions, the ordinary least squares (OLS) estimation method yields unbiased, consistent, efficient estimates of the unknown parameters. The *sample estimates* of the regression coefficients are denoted by Roman letters $b_0, b_1, b_2, \ldots, b_k$. The *predicted* value of the response variable is denoted $\hat{Y}$ and is calculated by inserting the values of the predictors into the *fitted regression equation:*

(13.2)
$$\hat{Y} = b_0 + b_1 X_1 + b_2 X_2 + \cdots + b_k X_k \qquad \text{(predicted value of } Y)$$

In this chapter, we will not show formulas for the estimated coefficients $b_0, b_1, b_2, \ldots, b_k$ because they entail matrix algebra. All regressions are fitted by computer software (Excel, MegaStat, MINITAB, etc.) utilizing the appropriate formulas.

Figure 13.1 illustrates the idea of a multiple regression model. Some of the proposed predictors may be useful, while others may not. We won't know until the regression is actually fitted. If an estimated coefficient has a positive (+) sign, then higher X values are associated with higher Y values, and conversely if an estimated coefficient has a negative sign.

In a bivariate regression (one predictor) the fitted regression is a *line*, while in multiple regression (more than one predictor) the fitted regression is a *surface* or *plane* as illustrated in Figure 13.2. If there are more than two predictors, no diagram can be drawn, and the fitted regression is represented by a hyperplane.

FIGURE 13.1

Visualizing a Multiple Regression

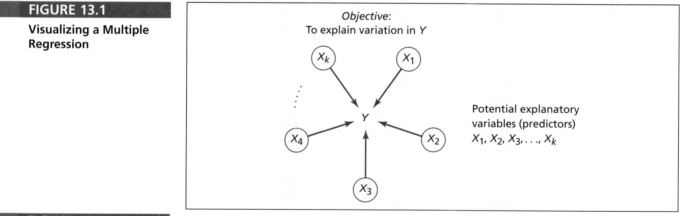

FIGURE 13.2

Fitted Regression: Bivariate versus Multivariate

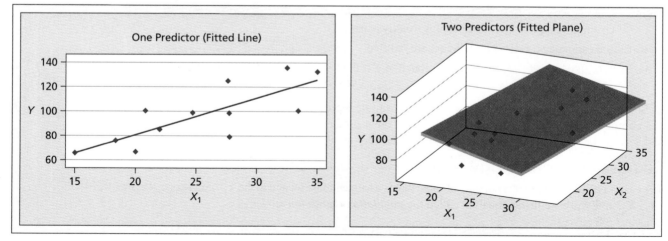

Data Format

To obtain a fitted regression we need n observed values of the response variable Y and its proposed predictors $X_1, X_2, \ldots, X_k$. A multivariate data set is a single column of Y-values and k columns of X-values. The form of this $n \times k$ matrix of observations is shown in Figure 13.3.

Response	Predictors			
Y	X_1	X_2	$\ldots$	X_k
y_1	x_{11}	x_{12}	$\ldots$	x_{1k}
y_2	x_{21}	x_{22}	$\ldots$	x_{2k}
$\vdots$	$\vdots$	$\vdots$	$\vdots$	$\vdots$
y_n	x_{n1}	x_{n2}	$\ldots$	x_{nk}

FIGURE 13.3

Data for a Multiple Regression

In Excel's Tools > Data Analysis > Regression you are required to have the X data in contiguous columns. However, MegaStat and MINITAB permit nonadjacent columns of X data. Flexibility in choosing data columns is useful if you decide to omit one or more X data columns and re-run the regression (e.g., to seek parsimony).

Illustration: Home Prices

Table 13.1 shows sales of 30 new homes in an upscale development. Although the selling price of a home (the *response variable*) may depend on many factors, we will examine three potential *explanatory variables.*

Definition of Variable	Short Name
Y = selling price of a home (thousands of dollars)	*Price*
X_1 = home size (square feet)	*SqFt*
X_2 = lot size (thousand square feet)	*LotSize*
X_3 = number of bathrooms	*Baths*

Using short variable names instead of Y and X we may write the regression model in an intuitive form:

$$Price = \beta_0 + \beta_1\ SqFt + \beta_2\ LotSize + \beta_3\ Baths + \varepsilon$$

| | | Characteristics of 30 New Homes | | | | NewHomes | | | **TABLE 13.1** | |

Home	Price	SqFt	LotSize	Baths	Home	Price	SqFt	LotSize	Baths
1	505.5	2,192	16.4	2.5	16	675.1	3,076	19.8	3.0
2	784.1	3,429	24.7	3.5	17	710.4	3,259	20.8	3.5
3	649.0	2,842	17.7	3.5	18	674.7	3,162	19.4	4.0
4	689.8	2,987	20.3	3.5	19	663.6	2,885	23.2	3.0
5	709.8	3,029	22.2	3.0	20	606.6	2,550	20.2	3.0
6	590.2	2,616	20.8	2.5	21	758.9	3,380	19.6	4.5
7	643.3	2,978	17.3	3.0	22	723.7	3,131	22.5	3.5
8	789.7	3,595	22.4	3.5	23	621.8	2,754	19.2	2.5
9	683.0	2,838	27.4	3.0	24	622.4	2,710	21.6	3.0
10	544.3	2,591	19.2	2.0	25	631.3	2,616	20.8	2.5
11	822.8	3,633	26.9	4.0	26	574.0	2,608	17.3	3.5
12	637.7	2,822	23.1	3.0	27	863.8	3,572	29.0	4.0
13	618.7	2,994	20.4	3.0	28	652.7	2,924	21.8	2.5
14	619.3	2,696	22.7	3.5	29	844.2	3,614	25.5	3.5
15	490.5	2,134	13.4	2.5	30	629.9	2,600	24.1	3.5

Logic of Variable Selection

Before doing the estimation, it is desirable to state our hypotheses about the sign of the coefficients in the model. In so doing, we force ourselves to think about our motives for including each predictor, instead of just throwing predictors into the model willy-nilly. Sometimes, of course, we may include a predictor as a "wild card" without any clear expectation about its sign. In the home price example, each predictor is expected to contribute positively to the selling price.

Predictor	Anticipated Sign	Reasoning
SqFt	>0	Larger homes cost more to build and give greater utility to the buyer.
LotSize	>0	Larger lots are desirable for privacy, gardening, and play.
Baths	>0	Additional baths give more utility to the purchaser with a family.

Explicit *a priori* reasoning about cause-and-effect permits us to compare the regression estimates with our expectation and to recognize any surprising results that may occur. However, we would not abandon a predictor whose relevance is grounded solidly in existing theory or common sense simply because it was not a "significant" predictor of Y.

Fitted Regression

A regression can be fitted by using Excel, MegaStat, MINITAB, or any other statistical package. Using the sample of $n = 30$ home sales, we obtain the fitted regression and its statistics of fit (R^2 is the coefficient of determination, SE is the standard error):

$$Price = -28.85 + 0.171\ SqFt + 6.78\ LotSize + 15.53\ Baths\ (R^2 = .956,\ SE = 20.31)$$

The intercept is not meaningful, since there can be no home with $SqFt = 0$, $LotSize = 0$, and $Baths = 0$. Each additional square foot seems to add about 0.171 (i.e., $171, since $Price$ is measured in thousands of dollars) to the average selling price, *ceteris paribus*. The coefficient of $LotSize$ implies that, on average, each additional thousand square feet of lot size adds 6.78 (i.e., $6,780) to the selling price. The coefficient of $Baths$ says that, on average, each additional bathroom adds 15.53 (i.e., $15,530) to the selling price. Although the three-predictor model's fit ($R^2 = .956$) is good, its standard error (20.31 or $20,310) suggests that prediction intervals will be rather wide.

Predictions from a Fitted Regression

We can use the fitted regression model to make predictions for various assumed predictor values. For example, what would be the expected selling price of a 2,800 square foot home with 2-1/2 baths on a lot with 18,500 square feet? In the fitted regression equation, we simply plug in $SqFt = 2800$, $LotSize = 18.5$, and $Baths = 2.5$ to get the predicted selling price:

$$SqFt = 2800 \qquad LotSize = 18.5 \qquad Baths = 2.5$$

$$Price = -28.85 + 0.171\ (2800) + 6.78\ (18.5) + 15.53\ (2.5) = 614.23\ \text{or}\ \$614,230$$

Although we could plug in any desired values of the predictors (*SqFt, LotSize, Baths*) it is risky to use predictor values outside the predictor value ranges in the data set used to estimate the fitted regression. For example, it would be risky to choose *SqFt* = 4000 since no home this large was seen in the original data set. Although the prediction might turn out to be reasonable, we would be extrapolating beyond the range of observed data.

Common Misconceptions about Fit

A common mistake is to assume that the model with the best fit is preferred. Sometimes a model with a low R^2 may give useful predictions, while a model with a high R^2 may conceal problems. Fit is only one criterion for assessing a regression. For example, a bivariate model using only *SqFt* as a predictor does a pretty good job of predicting *Price* and has an attractive simplicity:

$$Price = 15.47 + 0.222 \; SqFt \; (R^2 = .914, SE = 27.28)$$

Should we perhaps prefer the simpler model? The principle of **Occam's Razor** says that a complex model that is only slightly better may not be preferred if a simpler model will do the job. However, in this case the three-predictor model is not very complex and is based on solid *a priori* logic.

Principle of Occam's Razor

When two explanations are otherwise equivalent, we prefer the simpler, more parsimonious one.

Also, a high R^2 only indicates a good fit for the observed data set ($i = 1, 2, \ldots, n$). If we wanted to use the fitted regression equation to predict *Y* from a different set of *X*'s, the fit might not be the same. For this reason, if the sample is large enough, a statistician likes to use half the data to *estimate* the model and the other half to *test* the model's predictions.

Regression Modeling

The choice of predictors and model form (e.g., linear or nonlinear) are tasks of *regression modeling*. To begin with, we restrict our attention to predictors that meet the test of *a priori* logic, to avoid endless "data shopping." Naturally, we want predictors that are significant in "explaining" the variation in *Y* (i.e., predictors that improve the "fit"). But we also prefer predictors that add new information, rather than mirroring one another.

For example, we would expect that *LotSize* and *SqFt* are related (a bigger house may require a bigger lot) and likewise *SqFt* and *Baths* (a bigger house is likely to require more baths). If so, there may be overlap in their contributions to explaining *Price*. Closely related predictors can introduce instability in the regression estimates. If we include too many predictors, we violate the principle of Occam's Razor, which favors simple models, *ceteris paribus*. In this chapter, you will see how these criteria can be used to develop and assess regression models.

Four Criteria for Regression Assessment

- **Logic**   Is there an *a priori* reason to expect a causal relationship between the predictors and the response variable?

- **Fit**   Does the *overall* regression show a significant relationship between the predictors and the response variable?

- **Parsimony**   Does *each predictor* contribute significantly to the explanation? Are some predictors not worth the trouble?

- **Stability**   Are the predictors related to one another so strongly that regression estimates become erratic?

13.1   Observations are taken on net revenue from sales of a certain plasma TV at 50 retail outlets. The regression model was Y = net revenue (thousands of dollars), X_1 = shipping cost (dollars per unit), X_2 = expenditures on print advertising (thousands of dollars), X_3 = expenditure on electronic media ads (thousands), X_4 = rebate rate (percent of retail price). (a) Write the fitted regression equation. (b) Interpret each coefficient. (c) Would the intercept be likely to have meaning in this regression? (d) Use the fitted equation to make a prediction for *NetRevenue* when *ShipCost* = 10, *PrintAds* = 50, *WebAds* = 40, and *Rebate%* = 15.   ● **PlasmaTV**

Predictor	Coefficient
Intercept	4.306
ShipCost	−0.082
PrintAds	2.265
WebAds	2.498
Rebate%	16.697

13.2   Observations are taken on sales of a certain mountain bike in 30 sporting goods stores. The regression model was Y = total sales (thousands of dollars), X_1 = display floor space (square meters), X_2 = competitors' advertising expenditures (thousands of dollars), X_3 = advertised price (dollars per unit). (a) Write the fitted regression equation. (b) Interpret each coefficient. (c) Would the intercept seem to have meaning in this regression? (d) Make a prediction for *Sales* when *FloorSpace* = 80, *CompetingAds* = 100, and *Price* = 1,200.   ● **Bikes**

Predictor	Coefficient
Intercept	1225.44
FloorSpace	11.52
CompetingAds	−6.935
Price	−0.1496

13.2

ASSESSING OVERALL FIT

As in bivariate regression, there is one residual for every observation in a multiple regression:

$$e_i = y_i - \hat{y}_i \qquad \text{for } i = 1, 2, \ldots, n$$

Figure 13.4 illustrates the residual for one data value in a two-predictor regression. Each expected value of Y is a point on the fitted regression plane for a given pair of X values (x_1, x_2). The residual is the vertical distance from the actual Y_i value for those particular X values (x_1, x_2) to $E(Y_i)$. Just as in bivariate regression, we use the sum of squared residuals (*SSE*) as a measure of "fit" of the model.

FIGURE 13.4

Residual in Two-Predictor Model

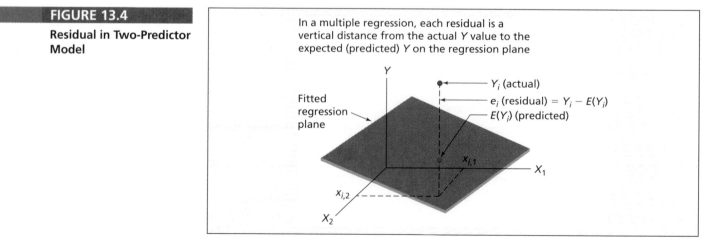

In a multiple regression, each residual is a vertical distance from the actual Y value to the expected (predicted) Y on the regression plane

Y_i (actual)

e_i (residual) = $Y_i - E(Y_i)$

$E(Y_i)$ (predicted)

F Test for Significance

Overall fit of a regression is assessed using the **F test**. For a regression with k predictors, the hypotheses to be tested are

H_0: All the true coefficients are zero ($\beta_1 = \beta_2 = \cdots = \beta_k = 0$)

H_1: At least one of the coefficients is nonzero

The basis for the F test is the **ANOVA table**, which decomposes variation of the response variable around its mean into two parts:

SST	=	SSR	+	SSE
Total variation		Explained by regression		Unexplained error

$$\sum_{i=1}^{n}(y_i - \bar{y})^2 = \sum_{i=1}^{n}(\hat{y}_i - \bar{y})^2 + \sum_{i=1}^{n}(y_i - \hat{y}_i)^2 \tag{13.3}$$

SSE is the sum of the squared residuals, just as it was in a simple regression (Chapter 12) except now each predicted value $\hat{y}_i$ is based on a fitted regression equation with k predictors. The ANOVA calculations for a k-predictor model can be summarized in a table like Table 13.2.

TABLE 13.2

ANOVA Table Format

Source of Variation	Sum of Squares	df	Mean Square	F	Excel p-Value
Regression (explained)	$SSR = \sum_{i=1}^{n}(\hat{y}_i - \bar{y})^2$	k	$MSR = \dfrac{SSR}{k}$	$F_{calc} = \dfrac{MSR}{MSE}$	=FDIST(F_{calc}, k, n − k−1)
Residual (unexplained)	$SSE = \sum_{i=1}^{n}(y_i - \hat{y}_i)^2$	$n - k - 1$	$MSE = \dfrac{SSE}{n - k - 1}$		
Total	$SST = \sum_{i=1}^{n}(y_i - \bar{y})^2$	$n - 1$			

After simplifying the ratios in Table 13.2, the formula for the F test statistic is:

$$F_{calc} = \frac{MSR}{MSE} = \frac{\sum_{i=1}^{n}(\hat{y}_i - \bar{y})^2}{\sum_{i=1}^{n}(y_i - \hat{y}_i)^2}\left(\frac{n - k - 1}{k}\right) \tag{13.4}$$

MINITAB and MegaStat will do all the calculations and print the ANOVA table. Table 13.3 shows the ANOVA table for the home price regression with $n = 30$ observations and $k = 3$ predictors.

TABLE 13.3

ANOVA Results for Three-Predictor Home Price Regression

Source	Sum of Squares	d.f.	Mean Square	F	p-value
Regression	232,450	3	77,483	187.92	.0000
Error	10,720	26	412.32		
Total	243,170	29			

The hypotheses to be tested are

H_0: All the coefficients are zero ($\beta_1 = \beta_2 = \beta_3 = 0$)

H_1: At least one coefficient is nonzero

Calculation of the sums SSR, SSE, and SST would be tedious without the computer. The F test statistic is $F_{calc} = MSR/MSE = 77,483/412.32 = 187.92$. Degrees of freedom are $k = 3$ for the numerator and $n - k - 1 = 30 - 3 - 1 = 26$ for the denominator. For $\alpha = .05$, Appendix F gives a critical value of $F_{3,26} = 2.98$, so the regression clearly is significant overall. MINITAB and MegaStat calculate the p-value ($p = .000$) for the F statistic. Alternatively, we can also use Excel's function =FDIST(187.92,3,26) to verify the p-value ($p = .000$).

Coefficient of Determination (R^2)

The most common measure of overall fit is the **coefficient of determination** or R^2, which is based on the ANOVA table's sums of squares. It can be calculated in two ways by using the error sum of squares (SSE), regression sum of squares (SSR), and total sum of squares (SST). The formulas are illustrated using the three-predictor regression of home prices.

$$(13.5) \qquad R^2 = 1 - \frac{SSE}{SST} = 1 - \frac{\sum_{i=1}^{n}(y_i - \hat{y}_i)^2}{\sum_{i=1}^{n}(y_i - \bar{y}_i)^2} = 1 - \frac{10,720}{243,170} = 1 - .044 = .956$$

or equivalently

$$(13.6) \qquad R^2 = \frac{SSR}{SST} = \frac{\sum_{i=1}^{n}(\hat{y}_i - \bar{y}_i)^2}{\sum_{i=1}^{n}(y_i - \bar{y}_i)^2} = \frac{232,450}{243,170} = .956$$

For the home price data, the R^2 statistic indicates that 95.6 percent of the variation in selling price is "explained" by our three predictors. While this indicates a very good fit, there is still some unexplained variation. Adding more predictors can *never* decrease the R^2, and generally will raise R^2. However, when R^2 already is high, there is not a lot of room for improvement.

Adjusted R^2

In multiple regression, it is generally possible to raise the coefficient of determination R^2 by including additional predictors. This may tempt you to imagine that we should always include many predictors to get a "better fit." To discourage this tactic (called *overfitting* the model) an adjustment can be made in the R^2 statistic to penalize the inclusion of useless predictors. The **adjusted coefficient of determination** using n observations and k predictors is

$$(13.7) \qquad R^2_{adj} = 1 - (1 - R^2)\left(\frac{n - 1}{n - k - 1}\right) \qquad \text{(adjusted } R^2\text{)}$$

R^2_{adj} is always less than or equal to R^2. As you add predictors, R^2 cannot decline, and generally will rise. But R^2_{adj} may rise, remain the same, or fall, depending on whether the added predictors increase R^2 sufficiently to offset the penalty. If R^2_{adj} is substantially smaller than R^2, it suggests that the model contains useless predictors. For the home price data with three predictors, both statistics are similar ($R^2 = .956$ and $R^2_{adj} = .951$), which suggests that the model does not contain useless predictors.

$$R^2_{adj} = 1 - (1 - .956)\left(\frac{30 - 1}{30 - 3 - 1}\right) = .951$$

There is no fixed rule of thumb for comparing R^2 and R^2_{adj}. A smaller gap between R^2 and R^2_{adj} indicates a more parsimonious model. A large gap would suggest that if some weak predictors were deleted, a leaner model would be obtained without losing very much predictive power.

How Many Predictors?

One way to prevent overfitting the model is to limit the number of predictors based on the sample size. A conservative rule (**Evans' Rule**) suggests that n/k should be at least 10 (i.e., at least 10 observations per predictor). A more relaxed rule (**Doane's Rule**) suggests that n/k be only at least 5 (i.e., at least 5 observations per predictor). For the home price regression with $n = 30$ and $k = 3$ example, $n/k = 30/3 = 10$ so either guideline is met.

Evans' Rule (*conservative*): $n/k \geq 10$ (at least 10 observations per predictor)

Doane's Rule (*relaxed*): $n/k \geq 5$ (at least 5 observations per predictor)

These rules are merely suggestions. Technically, a regression is possible as long as the sample size exceeds the number of predictors. But when n/k is small, the R^2 no longer gives a reliable indication of fit. Sometimes, researchers must work with small samples that cannot be enlarged. For example, a start-up business selling health food might have only 12 observations on quarterly sales. Should they attempt a regression model to predict sales using four predictors (advertising, product price, competitor prices, and population density)? Although $n = 12$ and $k = 3$ would violate even the lax guideline ($n/k = 12/4 = 3$), the firm might feel that an imperfect analysis is better than none at all.

13.3   Refer to the ANOVA table for this regression. (a) State the degrees of freedom for the F test for overall significance. (b) Use Appendix F to look up the critical value of F for $\alpha = .05$. (c) Calculate the F statistic. Is the regression significant overall? (d) Calculate R^2 and R^2_{adj}, showing your formulas clearly.   **PlasmaTV**

Source	d.f.	SS	MS
Regression	4	259,412	64,853
Error	45	224,539	4,990
Total	49	483,951	

13.4   Refer to the ANOVA table for this regression. (a) State the degrees of freedom for the F test for overall significance. (b) Use Appendix F to look up the critical value of F for $\alpha = .05$. (c) Calculate the F statistic. Is the regression significant overall? (d) Calculate R^2 and R^2_{adj}, showing your formulas clearly.   **Bikes**

Source	d.f.	SS	MS
Regression	3	1,196,410	398,803
Error	26	379,332	14,590
Total	29	1,575,742	

Hypothesis Tests

Each estimated coefficient shows the change in the conditional mean of Y associated with a one-unit change in an explanatory variable, holding the other explanatory variables constant. We are usually interested in testing each fitted coefficient to see whether it is significantly different from zero. If there is an *a priori* reason to anticipate a particular direction of association, we could choose a right-tailed or left-tailed test. For example, we would expect *SqFt* to have a positive effect on *Price,* so a right-tailed test might be used. However, the default choice is a two-tailed test because, if the null hypothesis can be rejected in a two-tailed test, it can also be rejected in a one-tailed test at the same level of significance.

Hypothesis Tests for Coefficient of Predictor X_j

Left-Tailed Test	*Two-Tailed Test*	*Right-Tailed Test*
$H_0: \beta_j = 0$	$H_0: \beta_j = 0$	$H_0: \beta_j = 0$
$H_1: \beta_j < 0$	$H_1: \beta_j \neq 0$	$H_1: \beta_j > 0$

13.3

PREDICTOR SIGNIFICANCE

Chapter 17

Tip

Software packages like Excel, MegaStat, or MINITAB report only two-tail *p*-values because, if you can reject H_0 in a two-tailed test, you can also reject H_0 in a one-tailed test at the same α.

If we cannot reject the hypothesis that a coefficient is zero, then the corresponding predictor does not contribute to the prediction of Y. For example, consider a three-predictor model:

$$Y = \beta_0 + \beta_1 X_1 + \beta_2 X_2 + \beta_3 X_3 + \varepsilon$$

Does X_2 help us to predict Y? To find out, we might choose a two-tailed test:

$H_0: \beta_2 = 0$ (X_2 is *not* related to Y)
$H_1: \beta_2 \neq 0$ (X_2 *is* related to Y)

If we are unable to reject H_0, the term involving X_2 will drop out:

$$Y = \beta_0 + \beta_1 X_1 + \boxed{0 X_2} + \beta_3 X_3 + \varepsilon \qquad (X_2 \text{ term drops out if } \beta_2 = 0)$$

and the regression will collapse to a *two-variable* model:

$$Y = \beta_0 + \beta_1 X_1 + \beta_3 X_3 + \varepsilon$$

Test Statistic

Rarely would a fitted coefficient be *exactly* zero, so we use a t test to test whether the difference from zero* is *significant*. For predictor X_j the test statistic for k predictors is Student's t with $n - k - 1$ degrees of freedom. To test for a zero coefficient, we take the ratio of the fitted coefficient b_j to its standard error s_j:

(13.8) $\qquad t_{\text{calc}} = \dfrac{b_j - 0}{s_j} \qquad$ (test statistic for coefficient of predictor X_j)

We can use Appendix D to find a critical value of t for a chosen level of significance α, or we could find the p-value for the t statistic using Excel's function =TDIST(t, deg_freedom, tails). All computer packages report the t statistic and the p-value for each predictor, so we actually do not need tables. To test for a zero coefficient, we could alternatively construct a confidence interval for the true coefficient β_j, and see whether the interval includes zero. Excel and MegaStat show a confidence interval for each coefficient, using this form:

(13.9) $\quad b_j - t_{n-k-1} s_j \leq \beta_j \leq b_j + t_{n-k-1} s_j \qquad$ (95% confidence interval for coefficient β_j)

MegaStat allows 99, 95, or 90 percent confidence intervals, while in Excel you can enter any confidence level you wish. All calculations are provided by Excel, so you only have to know how to interpret the results.

Tip

Checking to see whether the confidence interval includes zero is equivalent to a two-tailed test of $H_0: \beta_j = 0$.

Regression output contains many statistics, but some of them are especially important in getting the "big picture." Figure 13.5 shows a typical regression printout ($Y =$ car theft rate in the 50 states) with certain key features circled and comments that a statistician might make (you will learn about VIFs shortly).

---

*You needn't use 0 in the t test. For example, if you want to know whether an extra square foot adds at least $200 to a home's selling price, you would use 200 instead of 0 in the formula for the test statistic. However, $\beta = 0$ is the default hypothesis in Excel and other statistical packages.

FIGURE 13.5

**Typical Regression
Output**

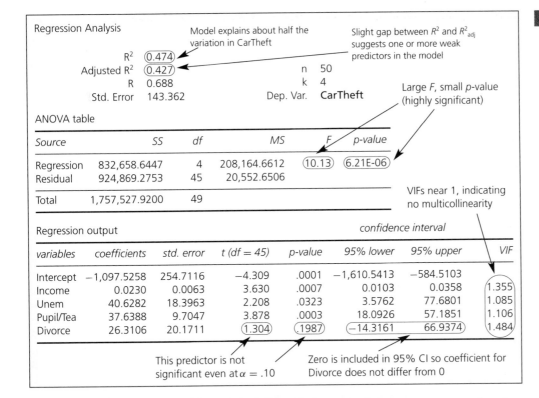

Figure 13.6 shows MegaStat's fitted regression for the three-predictor model, including a table of estimated coefficients, standard errors, *t* statistics, and *p*-values. MegaStat computes two-tail *p*-values, as do most statistical packages. Notice that 0 is within the 95 percent confidence interval for *Baths,* while the confidence intervals for *SqFt* and *LotSize* do not include 0. This suggests that the hypothesis of a zero coefficient can be rejected for *SqFt* and *LotSize* but not for *Baths.*

There are four estimated coefficients (counting the intercept). For reasons stated previously, the intercept is of no interest. For the three predictors, each *t* test uses $n - k - 1$ degrees of freedom. Since we have $n = 30$ observations and $k = 3$ predictors, we have $n - k - 1 = 30 - 3 - 1 = 26$ degrees of freedom. From Appendix D we can obtain two-tailed critical values of *t* for α equal to .10, .05, or .01 ($t_{.05} = 1.706$, $t_{.025} = 2.056$, and $t_{.005} = 2.779$). However, since *p*-values are provided, we do not really need these critical values.

$$SqFt: t_{calc} = 0.1709/0.01545 = 11.06 \ (p = .0000)$$
$$LotSize: t_{calc} = 6.778/1.421 = 4.77 \ (p = .0001)$$
$$Baths: t_{calc} = 15.535/9.208 = 1.69 \ (p = .1036)$$

The coefficients of *SqFt* and *LotSize* differ significantly from zero at any common α because their *p*-values are practically zero. The coefficient of *Baths* is not quite significant at $\alpha = .10$. Based on the *t*-values, we conclude that *SqFt* is a very strong predictor of *Price,* followed closely by *LotSize,* while *Baths* is of marginal significance.

EXAMPLE

Home Prices

FIGURE 13.6   **MegaStat's Regression for Home Prices (three predictors)**

Regression output					confidence interval	
variables	coefficients	std. error	t(df = 26)	p-value	95% lower	95% upper
Intercept	−28.8477	29.7115	−0.971	0.3405	−89.9206	32.2251
SqFt	0.1709	0.0154	11.064	0.0000	0.1392	0.2027
LotSize	6.7777	1.4213	4.769	0.0001	3.8562	9.6992
Baths	15.5347	9.2083	1.687	0.1036	−3.3932	34.4626

13.5 Observations are taken on net revenue from sales of a certain plasma TV at 50 retail outlets. The regression model was Y = net revenue (thousands of dollars), X_1 = shipping cost (dollars per unit), X_2 = expenditures on print advertising (thousands of dollars), X_3 = expenditure on electronic media ads (thousands), X_4 = rebate rate (percent of retail price). (a) Calculate the t statistic for each coefficient to test for $\beta = 0$. (b) Look up the critical value of Student's t in Appendix D for a two-tailed test at $\alpha = .01$. Which coefficients differ significantly from zero? (c) Use Excel to find the p-value for each coefficient. ⚡ **PlasmaTV**

Predictor	Coefficient	SE
Intercept	4.310	70.82
ShipCost	−0.0820	4.678
PrintAds	2.265	1.050
WebAds	2.498	0.8457
Rebate%	16.697	3.570

13.6 Observations are taken on sales of a certain mountain bike in 30 sporting goods stores. The regression model was Y = total sales (thousands of dollars), X_1 = display floor space (square meters), X_2 = competitors' advertising expenditures (thousands of dollars), X_3 = advertised price (dollars per unit). (a) Calculate the t statistic for each coefficient to test for $\beta = 0$. (b) Look up the critical value of Student's t in Appendix D for a two-tailed test at $\alpha = .01$. Which coefficients differ significantly from zero? (c) Use Excel to find the p-value for each coefficient. ⚡ **Bikes**

Predictor	Coefficient	SE
Intercept	1225.4	397.3
FloorSpace	11.522	1.330
CompetingAds	−6.935	3.905
Price	−0.14955	0.08927

13.4 CONFIDENCE INTERVALS FOR Y

Standard Error

Another important measure of fit is the **standard error (SE) of the regression**, derived from the sum of squared residuals (SSE) for n observations and k predictors:

$$(13.10) \quad SE = \sqrt{\frac{\sum_{i=1}^{n}(y_i - \hat{y}_i)^2}{n-k-1}} = \sqrt{\frac{SSE}{n-k-1}} \quad \text{(standard error of the regression)}$$

The standard error is measured in the same units as the response variable Y (dollars, square feet, etc). A smaller SE indicates a better fit. If all predictions were perfect (i.e., if $y_i = \hat{y}_i$ for all observations), then SE would be zero. However, perfect predictions are unlikely.

EXAMPLE

Home Prices II

From the ANOVA table for the three-predictor home price model we obtain $SSE = 10,720$, so

$$SE = \sqrt{\frac{SSE}{n-k-1}} = \sqrt{\frac{10,720}{30-3-1}} = 20.31$$

$SE = 20.31$ (i.e., $20,310 since Y is measured in thousands of dollars) suggests that the model has room for improvement, despite its good fit ($R^2 = .956$). Forecasters find the standard error more useful than R^2 because SE tells more about the *practical utility* of the forecasts, especially when it is used to make confidence or prediction intervals.

Approximate Confidence and Prediction Intervals for *Y* ———•

We can use the standard error to create approximate confidence or prediction intervals for values of $X_1, X_2, \ldots, X_k$ that are not far from their respective means.* Although these approximate intervals somewhat understate the interval widths, they are helpful when you only need a general idea of the accuracy of your model's predictions.

$$\hat{y}_i \pm t_{n-k-1} \frac{SE}{\sqrt{n}} \qquad \text{(approximate confidence interval for conditional mean of } Y \text{)}$$

$$\text{(13.11)}$$

$$\hat{y}_i \pm t_{n-k-1} SE \qquad \text{(approximate prediction interval for individual } Y\text{-value)} \qquad \text{(13.12)}$$

For home prices using the three-predictor model ($SE = 20.31$) the 95 percent confidence interval would require $n - k - 1 = 30 - 3 - 1 = 26$ degrees of freedom. From Appendix D we obtain $t_{.025} = 2.056$ so the *approximate* intervals are

EXAMPLE

Home Prices III

$$\hat{y}_i \pm (2.056) \frac{20.31}{\sqrt{30}} = \hat{y}_i \pm 7.62 \qquad \text{(95\% confidence interval for conditional mean)}$$

$$\hat{y}_i \pm (2.056)(20.31) = \hat{y}_i \pm 41.76 \qquad \text{(95\% prediction interval for individual home price)}$$

Exact 95 percent confidence and prediction intervals for a home with $SqFt = 2{,}950$, $LotSize = 21$, and $Baths = 3$ (these values are very near the predictor means for our sample) are $\hat{y}_i \pm 8.55$ and $\hat{y}_i \pm 42.61$, respectively. Thus, our *approximate* intervals are not conservative (i.e., slightly too narrow). Nonetheless, the approximate intervals provide a ballpark idea of the accuracy of the model's predictions. Despite its good fit ($R^2 = .956$) we see that the three-predictor model's predictions are far from perfect. For example, the 95 percent prediction interval for an individual home price is $\pm\$41{,}760$.

Quick 95 Percent Confidence and Prediction Interval for *Y* ———•

The *t*-values for a 95 percent confidence level are typically near 2 (as long as *n* is not too small). This suggests quick interval, without using a *t* table:

$$\hat{y}_i \pm 2\frac{SE}{\sqrt{n}} \qquad \text{(quick 95\% confidence interval for conditional mean of } Y \text{)} \qquad \text{(13.13)}$$

$$\hat{y}_i \pm 2SE \qquad \text{(quick 95\% prediction interval for individual } Y\text{-value)} \qquad \text{(13.14)}$$

These quick formulas are suitable only for rough calculations when you lack access to regression software or *t* tables (e.g., when taking a statistics exam).

13.7 A regression of accountants' starting salaries in a large firm was estimated using 40 new hires and five predictors (college GPA, gender, score on CPA exam, years' prior experience, size of graduating class). The standard error was $3,620. Find the approximate width of a 95 percent prediction interval for an employee's salary, assuming that the predictor values for the individual are near the means of the sample predictors. Would the quick rule give similar results?

13.8 An agribusiness performed a regression of wheat yield (bushels per acre) using observations on 25 test plots with four predictors (rainfall, fertilizer, soil acidity, hours of sun). The standard error was 1.17 bushels. Find the approximate width of a 95 percent prediction interval for wheat yield, assuming that the predictor values for a test plot are near the means of the sample predictors. Would the quick rule give similar results?

SECTION EXERCISES

connect

---

*The exact formulas for a confidence or prediction interval for $\mu_{Y|X}$ or Y require matrix algebra. If you need exact intervals, you should use MegaStat or a similar computer package. You must specify the value of *each predictor* for which the confidence interval or prediction is desired.

Mini Case 13.1

Birth Rates and Life Expectancy 🐤 BirthRates1

Table 13.4 shows the birth rate (Y = births per 1,000 population), life expectancy (X_1 = life expectancy at birth), and literacy (X_2 = percent of population that can read and write) for a random sample of 49 world nations.

TABLE 13.4 Birth Rates, Life Expectancy, and Literacy in Selected World Nations

Nation	BirthRate	LifeExp	Literate
Albania	18.59	72.1	93
Algeria	22.34	70.2	62
Australia	12.71	80.0	100
⋮	⋮	⋮	⋮
Yemen	43.30	60.6	38
Zambia	41.01	37.4	79
Zimbabwe	24.59	36.5	85

FIGURE 13.7 MegaStat's Output for Birth Rate Data

Regression Analysis: Birth Rates

R^2	0.743	n	49
Adjusted R^2	0.732	k	2
Std. Error	5.190	Dep. Var.	**BirthRate**

ANOVA table

Source	SS	df	MS	F	p-value
Regression	3,578.2364	2	1,789.1182	66.42	0.0000
Residual	1,239.1479	46	26.9380		
Total	4,817.3843	48			

Regression output — confidence interval

variables	coefficients	std. error	t(df = 46)	p-value	95% lower	95% upper
Intercept	65.8790	3.8513	17.106	0.0000	58.1268	73.6312
LifeExp	−0.3618	0.0666	−5.431	0.0000	−0.4960	−0.2277
Literate	−0.2330	0.0415	−5.610	0.0000	−0.3166	−0.1494

From Figure 13.7, the fitted regression equation is *BirthRate* = 65.9 − 0.362 *LifeExp* − 0.233 *Literate,* which says, *ceteris paribus,* that one year's increase in *LifeExp* is associated with 0.362 fewer babies per 1,000 persons, while one extra percent of *Literate* is associated with 0.233 fewer babies per 1,000 persons. The coefficient of determination is fairly high (R^2 = .743) and the overall regression is significant (F_{calc} = 66.42, p = .000). Since both predictors are significant (t_{calc} = −5.431 and t_{calc} = −5.610, p-values near .000) the evidence favors the hypothesis that birth rates tend to fall as nations achieve higher life expectancy and greater literacy. Although cause-and-effect is unproven, the conclusions are consistent with what we know about nutrition, health, and education.

Source: Central Intelligence Agency, *The World Factbook, 2003.*

What Is a Binary Predictor?

Chapter 19

We cannot directly include a *categorical* variable (qualitative data) as a predictor in a regression, because regression requires *numerical* data (quantitative data). But through simple data coding, we can convert categorical data into useful predictors. A **binary predictor** has two values, denoting the presence or absence of a condition (usually coded 0 and 1). Statisticians like to use intuitive names for the binary variable. For example:

For *n* Graduates from an MBA Program

$Employed = 1$ (if the individual is currently employed)

$Employed = 0$ (otherwise)

For *n* Quarters of Sales Data

$Recession = 1$ (if the sales data is for a recession year)

$Recession = 0$ (otherwise)

For *n* Business Schools

$AACSB = 1$ (if the school is accredited by the AACSB)

$AACSB = 0$ (otherwise)

For *n* States

$West = 1$ (if the state is west of the Mississippi)

$West = 0$ (otherwise)

Binary predictors are easy to create and are extremely important, because they allow us to capture the effects of nonquantitative (categorical) variables such as gender (female, male) or stock fund type (load, no-load). Such variables are also called **dummy** or **indicator variables**.

Tip

Name the binary variable for the characteristic that is present when the variable is 1 (e.g., *Male*) so that others can immediately see what the "1" stands for.

Effects of a Binary Predictor

A binary predictor is sometimes called a **shift variable** because it shifts the regression plane up or down. Suppose that we have a two-predictor fitted regression $Y = b_0 + b_1 X_1 + b_2 X_2$ where X_1 is a binary predictor. Since the only values that X_1 can take on are either 0 or 1, its contribution to the regression is either b_1 or nothing, as seen in this example:

If $X_1 = 0$, then $Y = b_0 + b_1(0) + b_2 X_2$, so $Y = b_0 + b_2 X_2$.

If $X_1 = 1$, then $Y = b_0 + b_1(1) + b_2 X_2$, so $Y = (b_0 + b_1) + b_2 X_2$.

The slope of the regression plane on the X_2-axis (b_2) is the same, regardless of the value of X_1, but the intercept either is b_0 (when $X_1 = 0$) or $b_0 + b_1$ (when $X_1 = 1$).

For example, suppose we have a fitted regression of fuel economy based on a sample of 43 cars:

$$MPG = 39.5 - 0.00463 \, Weight + 1.51 \, Manual$$

where

$Weight =$ vehicle curb weight as tested (pounds)

$Manual = 1$ if manual transmission, 0 if automatic

If *Manual* = 0, then

$$MPG = 39.5 - 0.00463 \, Weight + 1.51(0)$$

$$= 39.5 - 0.00463 \, Weight$$

If *Manual* = 1, then

$$MPG = 39.5 - 0.00463 \, Weight + 1.51(1)$$

$$= 41.01 - 0.00463 \, Weight$$

Thus, the binary variable shifts the intercept, leaving the slope unchanged. The situation is illustrated in Figure 13.8. In this case, we see that, although a manual transmission raises *MPG* slightly (by 1.51 miles per gallon, on average) the change in the intercept is rather small (i.e., manual transmission did not have a very large effect). A different sample could, of course, yield a different result. Many experts feel that the choice of automatic versus manual transmission makes very little difference in fuel economy today.

FIGURE 13.8

Binary Shift Variable Illustrated

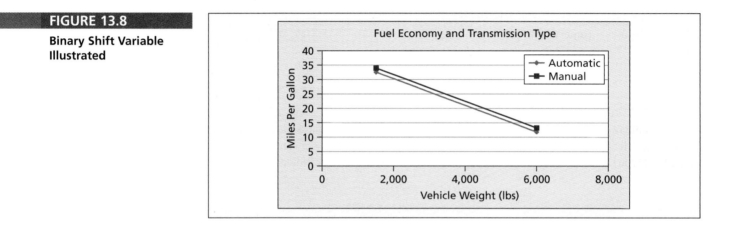

Testing a Binary for Significance

We test the degree of significance of the binary predictor just as we would test any other predictor, using a *t* test. In multiple regression, binary predictors require no special treatment.

EXAMPLE

Subdivision Home Prices

OakKnoll

We know that location is an important determinant of home price. But how can we include "location" in a regression? The answer is to code it as a binary predictor. Table 13.5 shows 20 home sales in two different subdivisions, Oak Knoll and Hidden Hills. We create a binary predictor, arbitrarily designating *OakKnoll* = 1 if the home is in the Oak Knoll subdivision, and *OakKnoll* = 0 otherwise. We then do an ordinary regression, shown in Figure 13.9.

The model has a rather good fit ($R^2 = .922$) and is significant overall ($F_{calc} = 100.94$, $p = .0000$). Both predictors have a significant effect on *Price* at $\alpha = .05$, although *SqFt* ($t_{calc} = 14.008$, $p = .0000$) is a much stronger predictor than *OakKnoll* ($t_{calc} = 2.340$, $p = .0317$). The fitted coefficient of *OakKnoll* tells us that, on average, a home in the Oak Knoll subdivision sells for 33.538 more than a home in Hidden Hills (i.e., $33,538 since *Price* is in thousands of dollars). Rounded off a bit, the fitted regression equation is *Price* = 10.6 + 0.199 *SqFt* + 33.5 *OakKnoll*. The intercept ($t_{calc} = 0.237$, $p = .8154$) does not differ significantly from zero, as can also be seen from the 95 percent confidence interval for the intercept (which includes zero).

TABLE 13.5	Home Prices with Binary Predictor OakKnoll			
Obs	Price ($000)	SqFt	OakKnoll	Subdivision
1	615.6	3,055	0	Hidden Hills
2	557.4	2,731	0	Hidden Hills
3	472.6	2,515	0	Hidden Hills
4	595.3	3,011	0	Hidden Hills
5	696.9	3,267	1	Oak Knoll
6	409.2	2,061	1	Oak Knoll
7	814.2	3,842	1	Oak Knoll
8	592.4	2,777	1	Oak Knoll
9	695.5	3,514	0	Hidden Hills
10	495.3	2,145	1	Oak Knoll
11	488.4	2,277	1	Oak Knoll
12	605.4	3,200	0	Hidden Hills
13	635.7	3,065	0	Hidden Hills
14	654.8	2,998	0	Hidden Hills
15	565.6	2,875	0	Hidden Hills
16	642.2	3,000	0	Hidden Hills
17	568.9	2,374	1	Oak Knoll
18	686.5	3,393	1	Oak Knoll
19	724.5	3,457	0	Hidden Hills
20	749.7	3,754	0	Hidden Hills

FIGURE 13.9	Oak Knoll Regression for 20 Home Sales

Regression Analysis: Subdivision Binary (n = 20)

R^2	0.922			
Adjusted R^2	0.913		n	20
R	0.960		k	2
Std. Error	29.670		Dep. Var.	Price (000)

ANOVA table

Source	SS	df	MS	F	p-value
Regression	177,706.7957	2	88,853.3979	100.94	.0000
Residual	14,964.9538	17	880.2914		
Total	192,671.7495	19			

Regression output   confidence interval

variables	coefficients	std. error	t(df = 17)	p-value	95% lower	95% upper
Intercept	10.6185	44.7725	0.237	.8154	−83.8433	105.0803
SqFt	0.1987	0.0142	14.008	0.0000	0.1688	0.2286
OakKnoll	33.5383	14.3328	2.340	.0317	3.2986	63.7780

More Than One Binary

A variable like gender (male, female) requires only one binary predictor (e.g., *Male*) because *Male* = 0 would indicate a female. But what if we need several binary predictors to code the data? This occurs when the number of categories to be coded exceeds two. For example, we might have home sales in five subdivisions, or quarterly Wal-Mart profits, or student GPA by class level:

Home sales by subdivision: *OakKnoll, HiddenHills, RockDale, Lochmoor, KingsRidge*

Wal-Mart profit by quarter: *Qtr1, Qtr2, Qtr3, Qtr4*

GPA by class level: *Freshman, Sophomore, Junior, Senior, Master's, Doctoral*

Each category is a binary variable denoting the presence (1) or absence (0) of the characteristic of interest. For example:

Freshman = 1 if the student is a freshman, 0 otherwise

Sophomore = 1 if the student is a sophomore, 0 otherwise

Junior = 1 if the student is a junior, 0 otherwise

Senior = 1 if the student is a senior, 0 otherwise

Master's = 1 if the student is a master's candidate, 0 otherwise

Doctoral = 1 if the student is a PhD candidate, 0 otherwise

But if there are c categories (assuming they are mutually exclusive and collectively exhaustive), we need only $c - 1$ binaries to code each observation. This is equivalent to omitting any *one* of the categories. This is possible because the $c - 1$ remaining binary values uniquely determine the remaining binary. For example, Table 13.6 shows that we could omit the last binary column without losing any information. Since only one column can be 1 and the other columns must be 0, the following relation holds:

$$Freshman + Sophomore + Junior + Senior + Master's + Doctoral = 1$$

that is,

$$Doctoral = 1 - Freshman - Sophomore - Junior - Senior - Master's$$

TABLE 13.6						
Why We Need Only $c - 1$ Binaries to Code c Categories						

Name	*Freshman*	*Sophomore*	*Junior*	*Senior*	*Master's*	*Doctoral*
Jaime	0	0	1	0	0	0
Fritz	0	1	0	0	0	0
Mary	0	0	0	0	0	1
Jean	0	0	0	1	0	0
Otto	0	0	0	0	1	0
Gail	1	0	0	0	0	0
etc.	...	...	...	...	...	...

That Mary is a doctoral student can be inferred from the fact that 0 appears in all the other columns. Since Mary is *not* in any of the other five categories, she must be in the sixth category:

$$Doctoral = 1 - 0 - 0 - 0 - 0 - 0 = 1$$

There is nothing special about the last column; we could have omitted any other column instead. Similarly, we might omit the *KingsRidge* data column from home sales data, since a home that is not in one of the first four subdivisions must be *KingsRidge*. We could omit the *Qtr4* column from the Wal-Mart time series, since if an observation is not from the first, second, or third quarter, it must be from *Qtr4*:

Home sales: *OakKnoll, HiddenHills, RockDale, Lochmoor, ~~KingsRidge~~*

Wal-Mart profit: *Qtr1, Qtr2, Qtr3, ~~Qtr4~~*

Again, there is nothing special about omitting the last category. We can omit any single binary instead. The omitted binary becomes the base reference point for the regression; that is, it is part of the intercept. No information is lost.

What If I Forget to Exclude One Binary?

If you include all c binaries for c categories, you will introduce a serious problem for the regression estimation, because one column in the X data matrix will then be a perfect linear combination of the other column(s). The least squares estimation would then fail because the data matrix would be singular (i.e., would have no inverse). MINITAB automatically checks for such a situation and omits one of the offending predictors, but it is safer to decide for yourself which binary to exclude. Excel merely gives an error.

Mini Case   13.2

Age or Gender Bias?   🐟 Oxnard

We can't use simple *t* tests to compare employee groups based on gender or age or job classification because they fail to take into account relevant factors such as education and experience. A simplistic salary equity study that fails to account for such control variables would be subject to criticism. Instead, we can use binary variables to study the effects of age, experience, gender, and education on salaries within a corporation. Gender and education can be coded as binary variables, and age can be forced into a binary variable that defines older employees explicitly, rather than assuming that age has a linear effect on salary.

Table 13.7 shows salaries for 25 employees in the advertising department at Oxnard Petro, Ltd. As an initial step in a salary equity study, the human resources consultant performed a linear regression using the proposed model $Salary = \beta_0 + \beta_1\ Male + \beta_2\ Exper + \beta_3\ Ovr50 + \beta_4\ MBA$. *Exper* is the employee's experience in years; *Salary* is in thousands of dollars. Binaries are used for gender (*Male* = 0, 1), age (*Ovr50* = 0, 1), and MBA degree (*MBA* = 0, 1). Can we reject the hypothesis that the coefficients of *Male* and *Ovr50* are zero? If so, it would suggest salary inequity based on gender and/or age.

TABLE 13.7   Salaries of Advertising Staff of Oxnard Petro, Ltd.

Obs	Employee	Salary	Male	Exper	Ovr50	MBA
1	Mary	28.6	0	0	0	1
2	Frieda	53.3	0	4	0	1
3	Alicia	73.8	0	12	0	0
4	Tom	26.0	1	0	0	0
5	Nicole	77.5	0	19	0	0
6	Xihong	95.1	1	17	0	0
7	Ellen	34.3	0	1	0	1
8	Bob	63.5	1	9	0	0
9	Vivian	96.4	0	19	0	0
10	Cecil	122.9	1	31	0	0
11	Barry	63.8	1	12	0	0
12	Jaime	111.1	1	29	1	0
13	Wanda	82.5	0	12	0	1
14	Sam	80.4	1	19	1	0
15	Saundra	69.3	0	10	0	0
16	Pete	52.8	1	8	0	0
17	Steve	54.0	1	2	0	1
18	Juan	58.7	1	11	0	0
19	Dick	72.3	1	14	0	0
20	Lee	88.6	1	21	0	0
21	Judd	60.2	1	10	0	0
22	Sunil	61.0	1	7	0	0
23	Marcia	75.8	0	18	0	0
24	Vivian	79.8	0	19	0	0
25	Igor	70.2	1	12	0	0

The coefficients in Figure 13.10 suggest that, *ceteris paribus,* a male (*Male* = 1) makes $3,013 more on average than a female. However, the coefficient of *Male* does not differ significantly from zero even at $\alpha = .10$ ($t_{calc} = 0.86, p = .399$). The evidence for age discrimination is a little stronger. Although an older employee (*Ovr50* = 1) makes $8,598 less than others, on average, the *p*-value for *Ovr50* ($t_{calc} = -1.36, p = .189$) is not convincing at $\alpha = .10$. The coefficient of MBA indicates that, *ceteris paribus,* MBA degree holders earn

FIGURE 13.10   **MINITAB Results for Oxnard Salary Equity Study**

The regression equation is
Salary = 28.9 + 3.01 Male − 8.60 Ovr50 + 3.02 Exper + 9.59 MBA

Predictor	Coef	SE Coef	T	P
Constant	28.878	4.925	5.86	0.000
Male	3.013	3.496	0.86	0.399
Ovr50	−8.598	6.324	−1.36	0.189
Exper	3.0190	0.2499	12.08	0.000
MBA	9.587	5.003	1.92	0.070

S = 7.44388   R-Sq = 91.3%   R-Sq(adj) = 89.6%

$9,587 more than others, and the coefficient differs from zero at $\alpha = .10$ ($t_{calc} = 1.92, p = .070$). Salaries at Oxnard Petro are dominated by *Exper* ($t_{calc} = 12.08, p = .000$). Each additional year of experience adds $3,019, on average, to an employee's salary. The regression is significant overall ($F_{calc} = 52.62, p = .000$) and has a good fit ($R^2 = .913$). Although the sample fails Evans' 10:1 ratio test for n/k, it passes Doane's 5:1 ratio test. A more complete equity study might consider additional predictors.

Regional Binaries

One very common use of binaries is to code regions. Figure 13.11 shows how the 50 states of the United States could be divided into four regions by using these binaries:

Midwest = 1 if state is in the Midwest, 0 otherwise

Neast = 1 if state is in the Northeast, 0 otherwise

Seast = 1 if state is in the Southeast, 0 otherwise

West = 1 if state is in the West, 0 otherwise

FIGURE 13.11

Four Regional Binaries

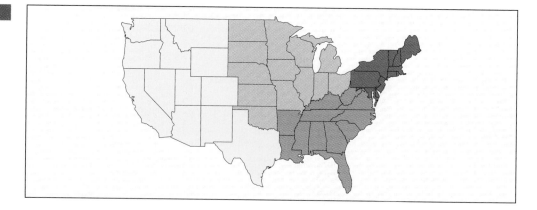

These are the same regional binaries that are used in the *LearningStats* state databases (cross-sectional data). For example, we can use regression to analyze the U.S. voting patterns in the 2000 U.S. presidential election. Binary predictors could permit us to analyze the effects of region (a qualitative variable) on voting patterns.

Mini Case   13.3

Regional Voting Patterns   Election2000

Table 13.8 shows abbreviated data for the 50 U.S. states from the *LearningStats* 2000 database. There are four regional binaries. Arbitrarily, we omit the *Seast* column, which becomes the baseline for the regression to examine a hypothesis about the effects of population age, urbanization, college graduation rates, unionization, and region on voting patterns in the 2000 U.S. presidential election. The dependent variable (*Bush%*) is the percentage vote for George W. Bush, and the proffered hypothesis to be investigated is

$$Bush\% = \beta_0 + \beta_1 \, Age65\% + \beta_2 \, Urban\% + \beta_3 \, ColGrad\% + \beta_4 \, Union\%$$

$$+ \, \beta_5 \, Midwest + \beta_6 \, Neast + \beta_7 \, West$$

								Omitted	
State	**Bush%**	**Age65%**	**Urban%**	**ColGrad%**	**Union%**	**Midwest**	**Neast**	**Seast**	**West**
AL	56.5	13.0	69.9	20.4	9.6	0	0	1	0
AK	58.6	5.7	41.5	28.1	21.9	0	0	0	1
AZ	51.0	13.0	88.2	24.6	6.4	0	0	0	1
AR	51.3	14.0	49.9	18.4	5.8	0	0	1	0
CA	41.7	10.6	96.7	27.5	16.0	0	0	0	1
CO	50.8	9.7	83.9	34.6	9.0	0	0	0	1
CT	38.4	13.8	95.6	31.6	16.3	0	1	0	0
⋮	⋮	⋮	⋮	⋮	⋮	⋮	⋮	⋮	⋮
etc.	etc.	etc.	etc.	etc.	etc.	etc.	etc.	etc.	etc.

Characteristics of U.S. States in 2000 Election — TABLE 13.8

The fitted regression shown in Figure 13.12 has four quantitative predictors and three binaries. The regression is significant overall ($F_{calc} = 22.92$, $p = .000$). It suggests that, *ceteris paribus,* the percent of voters choosing Bush was lower in states with older citizens, greater urbanization, higher percentage of college graduates, and more unionization. The Bush vote was, *ceteris paribus,* significantly higher in the Midwest ($t_{calc} = 2.79$, $p = .008$) and, to a lesser extent, in the West ($t_{calc} = 1.87$, $p = .069$). The coefficient of *Neast* suggests less Bush support in the Northeast ($t_{calc} = -0.65$, $p = .522$) but the coefficient of *Neast* is not statistically significant (perhaps masked by quantitative variables such as *Urban%* and *Union%*, which tend to distinguish the northeastern states). Using regional binaries allows us to analyze the effects of these *qualitative* factors. Those who say statistics can only deal with numbers must think again.

FIGURE 13.12 **MINITAB Output for Voting Patterns**

```
The regression equation is
Bush% = 94.6 − 1.29 Age65% − 0.0983 Urban% − 0.582 ColGrad% − 0.728 Union%
        + 5.67 Midwest − 1.61 Neast + 3.75 West

Predictor       Coef      SE Coef       T        P      VIF
Constant       94.550      7.525      12.56    0.000
Age65%         −1.2869     0.4010     −3.21    0.003    1.6
Urban%         −0.09827    0.03476    −2.83    0.007    1.4
ColGrad%       −0.5815     0.1933     −3.01    0.004    1.9
Union%         −0.7281     0.1327     −5.49    0.000    1.5
Midwest         5.671      2.034       2.79    0.008    2.2
Neast          −1.606      2.490      −0.65    0.522    2.9
West            3.748      2.007       1.87    0.069    2.2

S = 4.28656    R-Sq = 79.3%    R-Sq(adj) = 75.8%

Analysis of Variance

Source           DF        SS        MS        F        P
Regression        7     2948.11    421.16    22.92    0.000
Residual Error    42     771.73     18.37
Total             49    3719.84
```

13.6
MULTICOLLINEARITY

Chapter 17

What Is Multicollinearity?

When the independent variables $X_1, X_2, \ldots, X_m$ are intercorrelated instead of being independent, we have a condition known as **multicollinearity**. If only two predictors are correlated, we have **collinearity**. Almost any data set will have some degree of correlation among the predictors. The depth of our concern would depend on the *degree* of multicollinearity.

Variance Inflation

Multicollinearity does not bias the least squares estimates or the predictions for Y, but it does induce *variance inflation*. When predictors are strongly intercorrelated, the variances of their estimated coefficients tend to become inflated, widening the confidence intervals for the true coefficients $\beta_1, \beta_2, \ldots, \beta_k$ and making the t statistics less reliable. It can thus be difficult to identify the separate contribution of each predictor to "explaining" the response variable, due to the entanglement of their roles. Consequences of variance inflation can range from trivial to severe. In the most extreme case, when one X data column is an exact linear function of one or more other X data columns, the least squares estimation will fail.* That could happen, for example, if you inadvertently included the same predictor twice, or if you forgot to omit one of the c binaries used to code c attribute categories. Some software packages (e.g., MINITAB) will check for perfect multicollinearity and will remove one of the offending predictors, but don't count on it.

Variance inflation generally does not cause major problems, and some researchers suggest that it is best ignored except in extreme cases. However, it is a good idea to investigate the degree of multicollinearity in the regression model. There are several ways to do this.

Correlation Matrix

To check whether any two predictors are correlated (*collinearity*) we can inspect the **correlation matrix** for all predictors using Excel's function =CORREL(XData) or MegaStat's Correlation Matrix or MINITAB's Stat > Basic Statistics > Correlation. The correlation matrix for the home price data (see Table 13.1) is shown in Figure 13.13. The response variable (*Price*) is not included, since collinearity *among the predictors* is the condition we are investigating. Cells above the diagonal are redundant and hence are not shown. Correlations that differ from zero at $\alpha = .05$ are highlighted by MegaStat. In this example, all three predictors are significantly correlated, which is not an unusual situation in regression modeling. *Baths* and *LotSize* are strongly correlated with *SqFt*, which is logical. *Baths* and *LotSize* are also positively correlated, but less strongly.

Significant predictor correlations do not *per se* indicate a serious problem. **Klein's Rule** (see Related Reading) suggests that we should worry about the stability of the regression coefficient estimates only when a predictor correlation exceeds the multiple correlation coefficient R (i.e., the square root of R^2). For the home price regression shown in Figure 13.14, none of the predictor correlations exceeds the multiple correlation coefficient ($R = .978$), so the confidence intervals and t tests should be reliable.

FIGURE 13.13

Correlation Matrix for Home Prices Data ($n = 30$) NewHomes

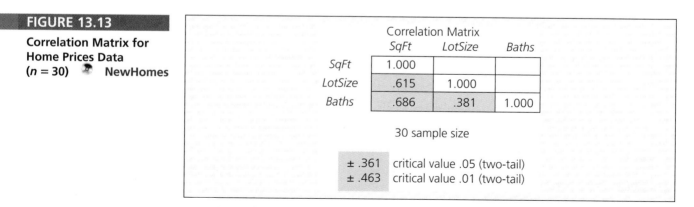

Correlation Matrix			
	SqFt	LotSize	Baths
SqFt	1.000		
LotSize	.615	1.000	
Baths	.686	.381	1.000

30 sample size

± .361   critical value .05 (two-tail)
± .463   critical value .01 (two-tail)

*If the X data matrix has no inverse, we cannot solve for the OLS estimates.

FIGURE 13.14

**Regression for Home
Prices (*n* = 30)
NewHomes**

Regression Analysis

		Klein's Rule for		
R^2	0.956	collinearity test		
Adjusted R^2	0.951		n	30
R	0.978		k	3
Std. Error	20.306		Dep. Var.	**Price**

Regression output   *confidence interval*

variables	coefficients	std. error	t (df = 26)	p-value	95% lower	95% upper
Intercept	−28.8477	29.7115	−0.971	.3405	−89.9206	32.2251
SqFt	0.1709	0.0154	11.064	2.48E-11	0.1392	0.2027
LotSize	6.7777	1.4213	4.769	.0001	3.8562	9.6992
Baths	15.5347	9.2083	1.687	.1036	−3.3932	34.4626

Quick Rule

A sample correlation whose absolute value exceeds $2/\sqrt{n}$ probably differs significantly from zero in a two-tailed test at $\alpha = .05$. This quick rule applies to samples that are not too small (say, 20 or more). However, Klein's Rule says not to worry unless correlation between any two predictors also exceeds the overall multiple correlation coefficient R.

Variance Inflation Factor (VIF)

Although the matrix scatter plots and correlation matrix are easy to understand, they only show correlations between *pairs* of predictors (e.g., X_1 and X_2). A general test for multi-collinearity should reveal more complex relationships *among* predictors. For example, X_2 might be a linear function of X_1, X_3, and X_4 even though its pairwise correlation with each is not very large.

$$X_1 = f(X_2, X_3, \ldots, X_k) \quad \rightarrow \quad R_1^2$$
$$X_2 = f(X_1, X_3, \ldots, X_k) \quad \rightarrow \quad R_2^2$$
$$\vdots$$
$$X_k = f(X_1, X_2, \ldots, X_{k-1}) \quad \rightarrow \quad R_k^2$$

The **variance inflation factor (VIF)** for each predictor provides a more comprehensive test. For a given predictor X_j the VIF is defined as

$$VIF_j = \frac{1}{1 - R_j^2} \tag{13.15}$$

where R_j^2 is the coefficient of determination when predictor j is regressed against *all* the other predictors (excluding Y). If predictor j is unrelated to the other predictors, its R_j^2 will be 0 and its VIF will be 1 (an ideal situation that will rarely be seen with actual data). Some possible situations are:

R_j^2	VIF_j	Interpretation
0.00	$\frac{1}{1 - R_j^2} = \frac{1}{1 - 0.00} = 1.0$	No variance inflation
0.50	$\frac{1}{1 - R_j^2} = \frac{1}{1 - 0.50} = 2.0$	Mild variance inflation
0.90	$\frac{1}{1 - R_j^2} = \frac{1}{1 - 0.90} = 10.0$	Strong variance inflation
0.99	$\frac{1}{1 - R_j^2} = \frac{1}{1 - 0.99} = 100.0$	Severe variance inflation

There is no limit on the magnitude of a VIF. Some researchers suggest that when a VIF exceeds 10, there is cause for concern, or even removal of predictor j from the model. But that rule of thumb is perhaps too conservative. A VIF of 10 says that the other predictors "explain" 90 percent of the variation in predictor j. While a VIF of 10 shows that predictor j is strongly related to the other predictors, it is not necessarily indicative of instability in the least squares estimates. Removing a relevant predictor is a step that should not be taken lightly, for it could result in misspecification of the model. A better way to think of it is that a large VIF is a warning to consider whether predictor j really belongs in the model.

Are Coefficients Stable?

Evidence of instability would be when X_1 and X_2 have a high pairwise correlation with Y, yet one or both predictors have insignificant t statistics in the fitted multiple regression. Another symptom would be if X_1 and X_2 are positively correlated with Y, yet one of them has a negative slope in the multiple regression. As a general test, you can try dropping a collinear predictor from the regression and watch what happens to the fitted coefficients in the re-estimated model. If they do not change very much, multicollinearity was probably not a concern. If dropping one collinear predictor causes sharp changes in one or more of the remaining coefficients in the model, then your multicollinearity may be causing instability. Keep in mind that a predictor must be significantly different from zero in order to say that it "changed" in the re-estimation.

Both MegaStat and MINITAB will calculate variance inflation factors, but you must request it as an option. Their VIF menu options are shown in Figures 13.15 and 13.16.

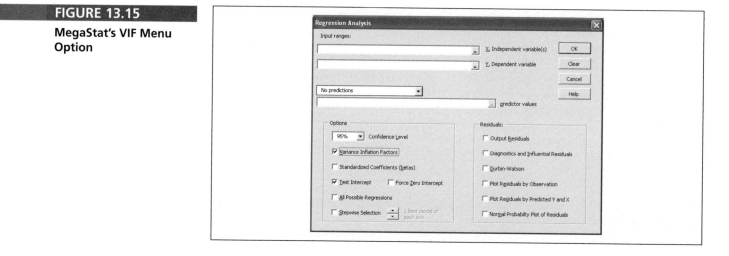

FIGURE 13.15

MegaStat's VIF Menu Option

FIGURE 13.16

MINITAB's VIF Menu Option

Mini Case 13.4

Regional Voting Patterns 🐭 Election2000

Mini Case 13.3 investigated a hypothesis about predictors for the percentage vote for George W. Bush in each of the 50 states. The proffered model was $Bush\% = \beta_0 + \beta_1\ Age65\% + \beta_2\ Urban\% + \beta_3\ ColGrad\% + \beta_4\ Union\% + \beta_5\ Midwest + \beta_6\ Neast + \beta_7\ West$. Table 13.9 and Figure 13.17 show the correlation matrix and matrix plot for the predictors (binary predictors omitted from the scatter plots). The quick rule for $n = 50$ says that a correlation is significant if it exceeds $2/\sqrt{n} = 2/\sqrt{50} = 0.28$. By this rule, a majority of the predictor correlations are significant at $\alpha = .05$ (shaded cells in table). However, none is close to the multiple correlation coefficient ($R = .890$) so by Klein's Rule we should not worry.

TABLE 13.9 Correlation Matrix for 2000 Election Predictors 🐭 Election2000

	Age65%	Urban%	ColGrad%	Union%	Midwest	Neast	Seast
Urban%	−0.030						
ColGrad%	−0.204	0.406					
Union%	0.006	0.342	0.308				
Midwest	0.237	−0.140	−0.031	0.088			
Neast	0.230	0.266	0.439	0.335	−0.315		
Seast	0.073	−0.109	−0.454	−0.482	−0.333	−0.298	
West	−0.513	−0.006	0.057	0.063	−0.370	−0.331	−0.350

FIGURE 13.17 MINITAB's Matrix Scatter Plot for 2000 Election Predictors

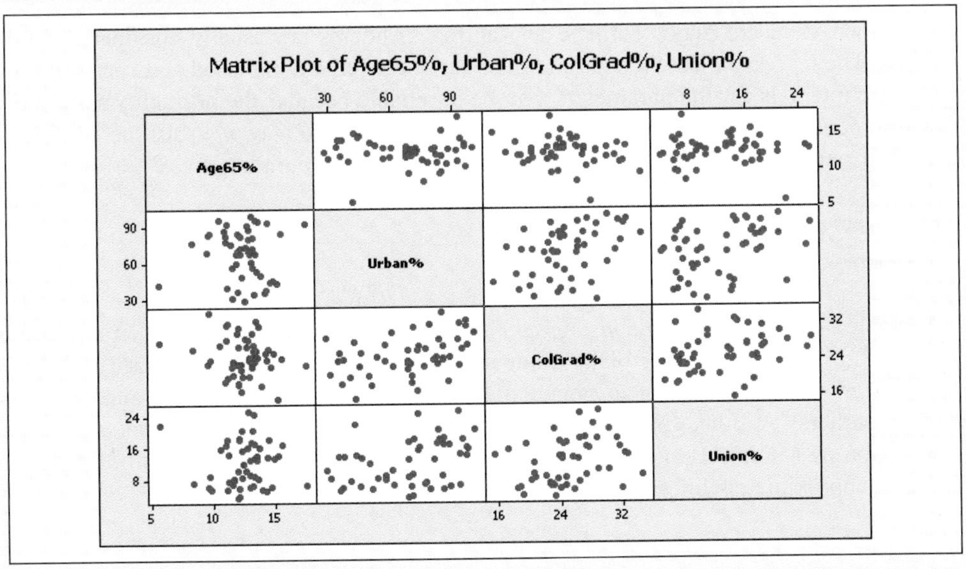

Despite the significant correlations between certain predictors, Figure 13.18 shows that for the election data no VIF exceeds 10 and the overall mean VIF is small. Thus, the confidence intervals should be reliable.

FIGURE 13.18   MegaStat's VIFs for Election Study   🐝   **Election2000**

variables	coefficients	std. error	t(df = 42)	p-value	95% lower	95% upper	VIF
Regression output					confidence interval		
Intercept	94.5502	7.5254	12.564	0.0000	79.3633	109.7370	
Age65%	−1.2869	0.4010	−3.210	0.0025	−2.0961	−0.4777	1.555
Urban%	−0.0983	0.0348	−2.827	0.0072	−0.1684	−0.0281	1.361
ColGrad%	−0.5815	0.1933	−3.008	0.0044	−0.9716	−0.1914	1.853
Union%	−0.7281	0.1327	−5.485	0.0000	−0.9960	−0.4602	1.517
Midwest	5.6715	2.0340	2.788	0.0079	1.5666	9.7763	2.166
Neast	−1.6063	2.4902	−0.645	0.5224	−6.6318	3.4191	2.896
West	3.7483	2.0071	1.868	0.0688	−0.3022	7.7988	2.210

13.7
VIOLATIONS OF ASSUMPTIONS

Chapter 16

Recall that the least squares method makes several assumptions about random errors ε_i. Although ε_i is unobservable, clues may be found in the residuals e_i. We routinely test three important assumptions:

- *Assumption* 1: The errors are normally distributed.
- *Assumption* 2: The errors have constant variance (i.e., they are homoscedastic).
- *Assumption* 3: The errors are independent (i.e., they are nonautocorrelated).

Regression residuals often violate one or more of these assumptions. The consequences may be mild, moderate, or severe, depending on various factors. **Residual tests** for violations of regression assumptions are routinely provided by regression software. These tests were discussed in detail in Sections 12.8 and 12.9. We briefly review each assumption.

Non-Normal Errors

Except when there are major outliers, non-normal residuals are usually considered a mild violation. The regression coefficients and their variances remain unbiased and consistent, but confidence intervals for the parameters may be unreliable because the normality assumption is used to construct them. However, if the sample size is large (say, $n > 30$) the confidence intervals generally are OK unless serious outliers exist. The hypotheses are:

H_0: Errors are normally distributed

H_1: Errors are not normally distributed

A simple "eyeball test" of the *histogram of residuals* can usually reveal outliers or serious asymmetry. You can use either plain residuals or standardized (i.e., studentized) residuals. Standardized residuals offer the advantage of a predictable scale (between −3 and +3 unless there are outliers). Another visual test for normality is the *probability plot,* which is produced as an option by MINITAB and MegaStat. If the null hypothesis is true, the probability plot should be approximately linear.

Nonconstant Variance (Heteroscedasticity)

The regression should fit equally well for all values of X. If the error variance is constant, the errors are *homoscedastic*. If the error variance is nonconstant, the errors are *heteroscedastic*. This violation is potentially serious. Although the least squares regression parameter estimates are still unbiased and consistent, their estimated variances are biased and are neither efficient nor asymptotically efficient. In the most common form of heteroscedasticity, the variances of the estimators are likely to be understated, resulting in overstated *t* statistics and artificially narrow confidence intervals. In a multiple regression, a visual test for constant variance can be performed by examining scatter plots of the residuals against each predictor or against the fitted *Y*-values. Ideally, there will be no pattern and the vertical spread (residual variance) will be similar regardless of the *X*-values. The hypotheses are:

H_0: Errors have constant variance (homoscedastic)

H_1: Errors have nonconstant variance (heteroscedastic)

In a multiple regression, to avoid looking at all *k* residual plots (one for each predictor) we usually just examine the plot of residuals against the predicted *Y*-values. Although many patterns of nonconstant variance might exist, the "fan-out" pattern of increasing variance is most common (see Figure 13.19). The zero line appears more or less in the center of the residual plot, since the residuals always sum to zero (see *LearningStats* Unit 13 for details).

FIGURE 13.19

Heteroscedastic Residual Plots

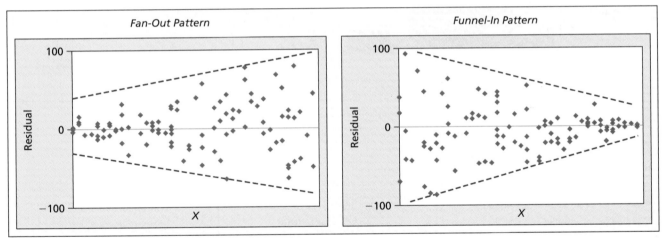

Mini Case 13.5

Non-Normality and Heteroscedasticity HeartDeaths

Figure 13.20 shows MINITAB regression diagnostics for a regression model of heart deaths in all 50 U.S. states for the year 2000. The dependent variable is *Heart* = heart deaths per 100,000 population and the three predictors are *Age65%* = percent of population age 65 and over, *Income* = per capita income in thousands of dollars, and *Black%* = percent of population that is African American.

The histogram is arguably bell-shaped. Since the residuals have been standardized, we can see that there are no outliers (more than 3 standard errors from zero). The probability plot reveals slight deviations from linearity at the lower and upper ends, but overall the plot is consistent with the hypothesis of normality. For an overall test for heteroscedasticity, we

FIGURE 13.20

MINITAB Diagnostics for Heart Death Regression

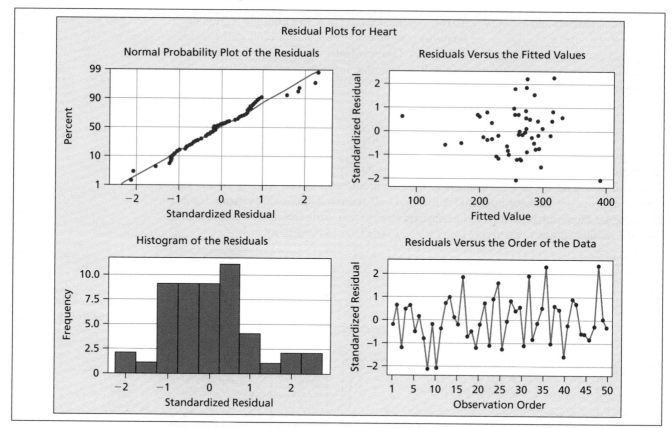

FIGURE 13.21

MINITAB Residual Plots for Heart Death Regression

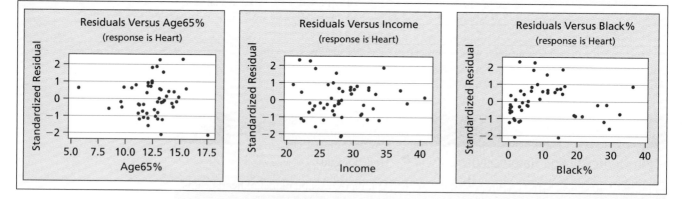

can look at the plot of residuals against the fitted *Y*-values in Figure 13.20. It shows no clear pattern, so we are disinclined to suspect heteroscedasticity. But we should also examine residual plots against each predictor. The residual plots for the three predictors (Figure 13.21) show no pronounced consistent "fan-out" or "funnel-in" pattern, thereby favoring the hypothesis of homoscedasticity (constant variance).

Autocorrelation (Optional)

If you are working with time-series data, you need to be aware of the possibility of *autocorrelation,* a pattern of nonindependent errors that violates the regression assumption that each error is independent of its predecessor. Cross-sectional data may exhibit autocorrelation, but usually it is an artifact of the order of data entry and so may be ignored. When the errors in a regression are autocorrelated, the least squares estimators of the coefficients are still unbiased and consistent. However, their estimated variances are biased in a way that typically leads to confidence intervals that are too narrow and *t* statistics that are too large. Thus, the model's fit may be overstated. The hypotheses are:

H_0: Errors are nonautocorrelated

H_1: Errors are autocorrelated

Since the true errors are unobservable, we rely on the residuals $e_1, e_2, \ldots, e_n$ for evidence of autocorrelation. The most common test for autocorrelation is the Durbin-Watson test. Using e_t to denote the *t*th residual (assuming you are working with time-series data) the Durbin-Watson test statistic for autocorrelation is

$$DW = \frac{\sum_{t=2}^{n}(e_t - e_{t-1})^2}{\sum_{t=1}^{n} e_t^2} \qquad \text{(Durbin-Watson test statistic)} \qquad \textbf{(13.16)}$$

If you study econometrics or forecasting, you will use a special table to test the DW statistic for significance. For now, simply note that the DW statistic lies between 0 and 4. When the null hypothesis is true (no autocorrelation) the DW statistic will be near 2, while DW < 2 would suggest *positive* autocorrelation and DW > 2 would suggest *negative* autocorrelation. For cross-sectional data, we usually ignore the DW statistic.

Unusual Observations

Several tests for unusual observations are routinely provided by regression software. An observation may be unusual for two reasons: (1) because the fitted model's prediction is poor (*unusual residuals*), or (2) because one or more predictors may be having a large influence on the regression estimates (*unusual leverage*). Unusual observations may be highlighted (MegaStat), displayed separately and marked (MINITAB), or not indicated at all (Excel).

To check for unusual residuals, we can simply inspect the residuals to find instances where the model does not predict well. For example, the model might fit well in Alabama but not in Alaska. We apply the Empirical Rule (standardized residuals more than 2 SE from zero are *unusual,* while residuals more than 3 SE from zero are outliers).

Unusual Residuals   MegaStat highlights unusual residuals in blue, while MINITAB marks them with an "R." As explained in Chapter 12, different software packages may use different definitions for "standardized" or "studentized" residuals, but usually they give similar indications of "unusual" residuals. For example, in Figure 13.22 the last two columns of the printout can be interpreted the same even though there are slight differences in the values.

Unusual Leverage   To check for unusual leverage, we look at the *leverage statistic* for each observation. It shows how far the predictors are from their means. As you saw in Chapter 12 (Section 12.8) such observations potentially have great influence on the regression estimates, because they are at the "end of the lever." For n observations and k predictors, any observation whose leverage statistic exceeds $2(k + 1)/n$ is highlighted in green by MegaStat, while MINITAB marks it with an "X."

FIGURE 13.22

MegaStat Output for Heart Death Regression

Regression Analysis: Heart Deaths per 100,000

R^2	0.779		
Adjusted R^2	0.764	n	50
R	0.883	k	3
Std. Error	27.422	Dep. Var.	**Heart**

ANOVA table

Source	SS	df	MS	F	p-value
Regression	121,809.5684	3	40,603.1895	54.00	0.0000
Residual	34,590.3558	46	751.9643		
Total	156,399.9242	49			

Regression output — confidence interval

variables	coefficients	std. error	t(df = 46)	p-value	95% lower	95% upper	VIF
Intercept	−37.0813	39.2007	−0.946	0.3491	−115.9882	41.8256	
Age65%	24.2509	2.0753	11.686	0.0000	20.0736	28.4282	1.018
Income	−1.0800	0.9151	−1.180	0.2440	−2.9220	0.7620	1.012
Black%	2.2682	0.4116	5.511	0.0000	1.4398	3.0967	1.013

Unusual Observations

Observation	Heart	Predicted	Residual	Leverage	Studentized Residual	Studentized Deleted Residual
AK	90.90	76.62	14.28	0.304	0.624	0.620
CT	278.10	274.33	3.77	0.208	0.154	0.153
FL	340.40	392.45	−52.05	0.177	−2.092	−2.176
HI	203.30	259.06	−55.76	0.037	−2.072	−2.152
MS	337.20	316.02	21.18	0.223	0.876	0.874
OK	335.40	274.87	60.53	0.047	2.261	2.372
UT	130.80	145.05	−14.25	0.172	−0.571	−0.567
WV	377.50	317.55	59.95	0.108	2.315	2.436

Mini Case

13.6

Unusual Observations 🖱 HeartDeaths

Figure 13.22 shows MegaStat's regression results for a regression model of heart deaths in the 50 U.S. states for the year 2000 (variables are drawn from the *LearningStats* state database). The response variable is *Heart* = heart deaths per 100,000 population, with predictors *Age65%* = percent of population age 65 and over, *Income* = per capita income in thousands of dollars, and *Black%* = percent of population classified as African American. The fitted regression is

$$Heart = -37.1 + 24.3\ Age65\% - 1.08\ Income + 2.27\ Black\%$$

Age65% has the anticipated positive sign and is highly significant, and similarly for *Black%*. Income has a negative sign but is not significant even at $\alpha = .10$. The regression overall is significant ($F = 54.00, p = .0000$). The R^2 shows that the predictors explain 77.9 percent of the variation in *Heart* among the states. The adjusted R^2 is 76.4 percent, indicating that no unhelpful predictors are present. Since this is cross-sectional data, the DW statistic was not requested.

Figure 13.22, lists eight unusual observations (the other 42 states are not unusual). Five states (AK, CT, FL, MS, UT), are highlighted because they have unusual *leverage*—a leverage statistic that exceeds $2(k + 1)/n = (2)(3 + 1)/50 = 0.16$, One or more predictors for these states must differ greatly from the mean of that predictor, but only by inspecting the X data columns (*Age65%, Income,* or *Black%*) could we identify their unusual X values. Four states are highlighted because they have unusual *residuals*—a gap of at least two standard deviations (studentized residuals) between actual and predicted *Heart* values. FL and HI are more than 2 standard deviations lower than predicted, while OK and WV are more than 2 standard deviations higher than predicted. One state, FL, is unusual with respect to both residual and leverage.

Outliers

An outlier may be due to an error in recording the data. If so, the observation should be deleted. But how can you tell? Impossible or truly bizarre data values are apparent reasons to discard an observation. For example, a realtor's database of recent home sales in a million-dollar neighborhood contained this observation:

Price	BR	Bath	Basement	Built	SqFeet	Garage
95,000	4	3	Y	2001	4,335	Y

The price is probably a typographical error. Even if the price were correct, it would be reasonable to discard the observation on grounds that is represents a different population than the other homes (e.g., a "gift" sale by a wealthy parent to a newlywed couple).

Missing Predictors

An outlier may also be an observation that has been influenced by an unspecified "lurking" variable that should have been controlled but wasn't. In this case, we should try to identify the lurking variable and formulate a multiple regression model that includes both predictors. For example, a model such as $Y =$ home price, $X_1 =$ square feet, and $X_2 =$ lot size might give poor predictions unless we add one or more neighborhood binary predictors (you can probably think of areas where a large house on a large lot might command a poor price).

Ill-Conditioned Data

All variables in the regression should be of the same general order of magnitude (not too small, not too large). If your coefficients come out in exponential notation (e.g., 7.3154 E+06), you probably should adjust the decimal point in one or more variables to a convenient magnitude, as long as you treat all the values in the same data column consistently. Decimal adjustments need not be the same for all data columns.

Significance in Large Samples

Statistical significance may not imply *practical importance*. In a large sample, we can obtain very large t statistics with low p-values for our predictors when, in fact, their effect on Y is very slight. There is an old saying in statistics that you can make anything significant if you get a large enough sample. In medical research, where thousands of patients are enrolled in clinical trials, this is a familiar problem. It can become difficult in such models to figure out which variables are really *important*.

Model Specification Errors

If you estimate a linear model when actually a nonlinear model is required, or when you omit a relevant predictor, you have a *misspecified model*. To detect misspecification you can:

- Plot the residuals against estimated Y (should be no discernable pattern).
- Plot the residuals against actual Y (should be no discernable pattern).
- Plot the fitted Y against the actual Y (should be a 45-degree line).

What are the cures for misspecification? Start by looking for a missing relevant predictor, seek a model with a better theoretical basis, or redefine your variables.

Missing Data

If many values in a data column are missing, we might want to discard that variable. If a *Y* data value is missing, we discard the entire observation. If any *X* data values are missing, the conservative action is to discard the entire observation. However, since discarding an entire observation would mean losing other good information, statisticians have developed procedures for imputing missing values, such as using the mean of the *X* data column or by a regression procedure to "fit" the missing *X*-value from the complete observations. Imputing missing values requires specialized software and expert statistical advice.

Binary Dependent Variable

We have seen that binary predictors pose no special problem. However, when the response variable *Y* is binary (0, 1) the least squares estimation method no longer is appropriate. Specialized regression methods such as logit and probit are called for. MINITAB and other software packages handle this situation easily, but a different interpretation is required. See *LearningStats* Unit 20 for a case study with binary *Y*.

Stepwise and Best Subsets Regression

It may have occurred to you that there ought to be a way to automate the task of fitting the "best" regression using *k* predictors. The *stepwise regression* procedure uses the power of the computer to fit the best model using 1, 2, 3, . . . , *k* predictors. For example, aerospace engineers had a large data set of 469 observations on *Thrust* (takeoff thrust of a jet turbine) along with seven potential predictors (*TurbTemp, AirFlow, TurbSpeed, OilTemp, OilPres, RunTime, ThermCyc*). In the absence of a theoretical model, a stepwise regression was run, with the results shown in Figure 13.23. Only *p*-values are shown for each predictor, along with R^2, R^2_{adj}, and standard error. You can easily assess the effect of adding more predictors. In this example, most *p*-values are tiny due to the large *n*. While stepwise regression is an efficient way to identify the "best" model for each number of predictors (1, 2, . . . , *k*), it is appropriate only when there is no theoretical model that specifies which predictors *should* be used. A further degree of automation of the regression task is to perform *best subsets* regression using all possible combinations of predictors. This option is offered by many computer packages, but is not recommended because it yields too much output and too little additional insight.

FIGURE 13.23

MegaStat's Stepwise Regression of Turbine Data 🐢 **Turbines**

Regression Analysis—Stepwise Selection displaying the best model of each size

469 observations
Thrust is the dependent variable

				p-values for the coefficients						
Nvar	TurbTemp	Airflow	TurbSpeed	OilTemp	OilPres	RunTime	ThermCyc	s	Adj R²	R²
1		.0000						12.370	.252	.254
2		.0000			.0004			12.219	.270	.273
3	.0003	.0000					.0005	12.113	.283	.287
4		.0000		.0081	.0000		.0039	12.041	.291	.297
5	.0010	.0000		.0009	.0003		.0006	11.914	.306	.314
6	.0010	.0000	.1440	.0037	.0005		.0010	11.899	.308	.317
7	.0008	.0000	.1624	.0031	.0007	.2049	.0006	11.891	.309	.319

Multivariate regression extends bivariate regression to include multiple **predictors** of the **response variable.** Criteria to judge a fitted regression model include **logic, fit, parsimony,** and **stability.** Using too many predictors violates the principle of **Occam's Razor,** which favors a simpler model if it is adequate. If the R^2 differs greatly from R^2_{adj}, the model may contain unhelpful predictors. The ANOVA table and *F* **test** measure overall significance, while the *t* **test** is used to test hypotheses about individual predictors. A **confidence interval** for each unknown **parameter** is equivalent to a two-tailed hypothesis test for $\beta = 0$. The **standard error** of the regression is used to create **confidence intervals** or **prediction intervals** for *Y*. A **binary predictor** (also called a **dummy variable** or an **indicator**) has value 1 if the condition of interest is present, 0 otherwise. For *c* categories, we only include $c - 1$ binaries or the regression will fail. **Collinearity** (correlation between *two* predictors) is detected in the **correlation matrix,** while **multicollinearity** (when a predictor depends on *several* other predictors) is identified from the **variance inflation factor** (VIF) for each predictor. Regression assumes that the errors are normally distributed, independent random variables with constant variance. **Residual tests** identify possible **non-normality, autocorrelation,** or **heteroscedasticity.**

adjusted coefficient of
   determination R^2_{adj}, *496*
ANOVA table, *495*
binary predictor, *503*
coefficient of determination
   (R^2), *496*
collinearity, *510*
correlation matrix, *510*
Doane's Rule, *496*
dummy variable, *503*

Evans' Rule, *496*
fit, *493*
F test, *495*
indicator variable, *503*
Klein's Rule, *510*
logic, *493*
multicollinearity, *510*
multiple regression, *489*
Occam's Razor, *493*
parsimony, *493*

predictors, *489*
residual tests, *514*
response variable, *489*
shift variable, *503*
stability, *493*
standard error (SE) of the
   regression, *500*
variance inflation factor
   (VIF), *511*

Commonly Used Formulas

Population regression model for *k* predictors: $Y = \beta_0 + \beta_1 X_1 + \beta_2 X_2 + \cdots + \beta_k X_k + \varepsilon$

Fitted regression equation for *k* predictors: $\hat{Y} = b_0 + b_1 X_1 + b_2 X_2 + \cdots + b_k X_k$

Residual for *i*th observation: $e_i = y_i - \hat{y}_i$ (for $i = 1, 2, \ldots, n$)

ANOVA sums: $SST = SSR + SSE$

SST (total sum of squares): $\displaystyle\sum_{i=1}^{n}(y_i - \bar{y})^2$

SSR (regression sum of squares): $\displaystyle\sum_{i=1}^{n}(\hat{y}_i - \bar{y})^2$

SSE (error sum of squares): $\displaystyle\sum_{i=1}^{n}(y_i - \hat{y}_i)^2$

MSR (regression mean square): $MSR = SSR/k$

MSE (error mean square): $MSE = SSE/(n - k - 1)$

F test statistic for overall significance: $F_{calc} = MSR/MSE$

Coefficient of determination: $R^2 = 1 - \dfrac{SSE}{SST}$ or $R^2 = \dfrac{SSR}{SST}$

Adjusted R^2: $R^2_{adj} = 1 - (1 - R^2)\left(\dfrac{n-1}{n-k-1}\right)$

Test statistic for coefficient of predictor X_j: $t_{calc} = \dfrac{b_j - 0}{s_j}$ where s_j is the standard error of b_j

Confidence interval for coefficient β_j: $b_j - t_{n-k-1}s_j \le \beta_j \le b_j + t_{n-k-1}s_j$

Estimated standard error of the regression: $SE = \sqrt{\dfrac{\displaystyle\sum_{i=1}^{n}(y_i - \hat{y}_i)^2}{n - k - 1}} = \sqrt{\dfrac{SSE}{n - k - 1}}$

Approximate confidence interval for $E(Y/X)$: $\hat{y}_i \pm t_{n-k-1}\dfrac{SE}{\sqrt{n}}$

Approximate prediction interval for Y: $\hat{y}_i \pm t_{n-k-1} SE$

Variance inflation factor for predictor j: $VIF_j = \dfrac{1}{1 - R_j^2}$

Evans' Rule (conservative): $n/k \geq 10$ (10 observations per predictor)

Doane's Rule (relaxed): $n/k \geq 5$ (5 observations per predictor)

CHAPTER REVIEW

1. (a) List two limitations of bivariate regression. (b) Why is estimating a multiple regression model just as easy as bivariate regression?

2. (a) What does ε represent in the regression model? (b) What assumptions do we make about ε? What is the distinction between Greek letters (β) and Roman letters (b) in representing a regression equation?

3. (a) Describe the format of a multiple regression data set. (b) Why is it a good idea to write down our *a priori* reasoning about a proposed regression?

4. (a) Why does a higher R^2 not always indicate a good model? (b) State the principle of Occam's Razor. (c) List four criteria for assessing a regression model.

5. (a) What is the role of the F test in multiple regression? (b) How is the F statistic calculated from the ANOVA table? (c) Why are tables rarely needed for the F test?

6. (a) Why is testing H_0: $\beta = 0$ a very common test for a predictor? (b) How many degrees of freedom do we use in a t test for an individual predictor's significance?

7. (a) Explain why a confidence interval for a predictor coefficient is equivalent to a two-tailed test of significance. (b) Why are t tables rarely needed in performing significance tests?

8. (a) What does a coefficient of determination (R^2) measure? (b) When R^2 and R_{adj}^2 differ considerably, what does it indicate?

9. State some guidelines to prevent inclusion of too many predictors in a regression.

10. (a) State the formula for the standard error of the regression. (b) Why is it sometimes preferred to R^2 as a measure of "fit"? (c) What is the formula for a quick prediction interval for individual Y-values? (d) When you need an exact prediction, what must you do?

11. (a) What is a binary predictor? (b) Why is a binary predictor sometimes called a "shift variable"? (c) How do we test a binary predictor for significance?

12. If we have c categories for an attribute, why do we only use $c - 1$ binaries to represent them in a fitted regression?

13. (a) What is multicollinearity? (b) What are its potential consequences? (c) Why is it a matter of degree? (d) Why might it be ignored?

14. (a) How does multicollinearity differ from collinearity? (b) Explain how we can use the correlation matrix to test for collinearity. (c) State a quick rule to test for significant collinearity in a correlation matrix. (d) What is Klein's Rule?

15. (a) State the formula for a variance inflation factor (VIF) for a predictor. (b) Why does the VIF provide a more general test for multicollinearity than a correlation matrix or a matrix plot? (c) State a rule of thumb for detecting strong variance inflation.

16. If multicollinearity is severe, what might its symptoms be?

17. (a) How can we detect an unusual residual? An outlier? (b) How can we identify an influential observation?

18. (a) Name two ways to detect non-normality of the residuals. (b) What are the potential consequences of this violation? (c) What remedies might be appropriate?

19. (a) Name two ways to detect heteroscedastic residuals. (b) What are the potential consequences of this violation? (c) What remedies might be appropriate?

20. (a) Name two ways to detect autocorrelated residuals. (b) What are the potential consequences of this violation? (c) What remedies might be appropriate?

21. (a) What is a lurking variable? How might it be inferred? (b) What are ill-conditioned data?

CHAPTER EXERCISES

connect

Instructions for Data Sets: Choose one of the data sets $A - J$ below or as assigned by your instructor. Only the first three and last three observations are shown for each data set (files are on the CD). In each data set, the dependent variable (*response*) is the first variable. Choose the independent variables (*predictors*) as you judge appropriate. Use a spreadsheet or a statistical package (e.g., MegaStat or MINITAB) to perform the necessary regression calculations and to obtain the required graphs. Write a concise report answering questions 13.9 through 13.25 (or a subset of these questions assigned by your instructor). Label sections of your report to correspond to the questions. Insert tables and graphs in your report as appropriate. You may work with a partner if your instructor allows it.

13.9   Is this cross-sectional data or time-series data? What is the unit of observation (e.g., firm, individual, year)?

13.10 Are the X and Y data well-conditioned? If not, make any transformations that may be necessary and explain.

13.11 State your *a priori* hypotheses about the sign ($+$ or $-$) of each predictor and your reasoning about cause and effect. Would the intercept have meaning in this problem? Explain.

13.12 Does your sample size fulfill Evans' Rule ($n/k \geq 10$) or at least Doane's Rule ($n/k \geq 5$)?

13.13 Perform the regression and write the estimated regression equation (round off to 3 or 4 significant digits for clarity). Do the coefficient signs agree with your *a priori* expectations?

13.14 Does the 95 percent confidence interval for each predictor coefficient include zero? What conclusion can you draw? *Note:* Skip this question if you are using MINITAB, since predictor confidence intervals are not shown.

13.15 Do a two-tailed t test for zero slope for each predictor coefficient at $\alpha = .05$. State the degrees of freedom and look up the critical value in Appendix D (or from Excel).

13.16 (a) Which p-values indicate predictor significance at $\alpha = .05$? (b) Do the p-values support the conclusions you reached from the t tests? (c) Do you prefer the t test or the p-value approach? Why?

13.17 Based on the R^2 and ANOVA table for your model, how would you describe the fit?

13.18 Use the standard error to construct an *approximate* prediction interval for Y. Based on the width of this prediction interval, would you say the predictions are good enough to have practical value?

13.19 (a) Generate a correlation matrix for your predictors. Round the results to three decimal places. (b) Based on the correlation matrix, is collinearity a problem? What rules of thumb (if any) are you using?

13.20 (a) If you did not already do so, re-run the regression requesting variance inflation factors (VIFs) for your predictors. (b) Do the VIFs suggest that multicollinearity is a problem? Explain.

13.21 (a) If you did not already do so, request a table of standardized residuals. (b) Are any residuals *outliers* (three standard errors) or *unusual* (two standard errors)?

13.22 If you did not already do so, request leverage statistics. Are any observations influential? Explain.

13.23 If you did not already do so, request a histogram of standardized residuals and/or a normal probability plot. Do the residuals suggest non-normal errors? Explain.

13.24 If you did not already do so, request a plot of residuals versus the fitted Y. Is heteroscedasticity a concern?

13.25 If you are using time-series data, perform one or more tests for autocorrelation (visual inspection of residuals plotted against observation order, runs test, Durbin-Watson test). Is autocorrelation a concern?

DATA SET A   **Mileage and Other Characteristics of Randomly Selected Vehicles**
($n = 43$, $k = 4$) 🚗   **Mileage**

Obs	Vehicle	City	Length	Width	Weight	Japan
1	Acura CL	20	192	69	3,450	1
2	Accura TSX	23	183	59	3,320	1
3	BMW 3-Series	19	176	69	3,390	0
⋮	⋮	⋮	⋮	⋮	⋮	⋮
41	Toyota Sienna	19	200	77	4,120	1
42	Volkswagen Jetta	34	172	68	3,045	0
43	Volvo C70	20	186	72	3,690	0

City = EPA miles per gallon in city driving, *Length* = vehicle length (inches), *Width* = vehicle width (inches), *Weight* = weight (pounds), *Japan* = 1 if carmaker is Japanese, 0 otherwise.

Source: *Consumer Reports New Car Buying Guide 2003–2004* (Consumers Union, 2003). Sampling methodology was to select the vehicle on every fifth page starting at page 40. Data are intended for purposes of statistical education and should not be viewed as a guide to vehicle performance.

DATA SET B   **Noodles & Company Sales, Seating, and Demographic Data (n = 74, k = 5)**   Noodles2

Obs	Sales/SqFt	Seats-Inside	Seats-Patio	MedIncome	MedAge	BachDeg%
1	702	66	18	45.2	34.4	31
2	210	69	16	51.9	41.2	20
3	365	67	10	51.4	40.3	24
⋮	⋮	⋮	⋮	⋮	⋮	⋮
72	340	63	28	60.9	43.5	21
73	401	72	15	73.8	41.6	29
74	327	76	24	64.2	31.4	15

Sales/SqFt = sales per square foot of floor space, *Seats-Inside* = number of interior seats, *Seats-Patio* = number of outside seats. The three demographic variables refer to a three-mile radius of the restaurant: *MedIncome* = median family income, *MedAge* = median age, and *BachDeg%* = percentage of population with at least a bachelor's degree.

Source: Noodles & Company.

DATA SET C   **Assessed Value of Small Medical Office Buildings (n = 32, k = 5)**   Assessed

Obs	Assessed	Floor	Offices	Entrances	Age	Freeway
1	1796	4790	4	2	8	0
2	1544	4720	3	2	12	0
3	2094	5940	4	2	2	0
⋮	⋮	⋮	⋮	⋮	⋮	⋮
30	1264	3580	3	2	27	0
31	1162	3610	2	1	8	1
32	1447	3960	3	2	17	0

Assessed = assessed value (thousands of dollars), *Floor* = square feet of floor space, *Offices* = number of offices in the building, *Entrances* = number of customer entrances (excluding service doors), *Age* = age of the building (years), *Freeway* = 1 if within one mile of freeway, 0 otherwise.

DATA SET D   **Changes in Consumer Price Index, Capacity Utilization, Changes in Money Supply Components, and Unemployment (n = 41, k = 4)**   Money

Year	ChgCPI	CapUtil	ChgM1	ChgM2	Unem
1966	2.9	91.1	2.5	4.6	3.8
1967	3.1	87.2	6.6	9.3	3.8
1968	4.2	87.1	7.7	8.0	3.6
⋮	⋮	⋮	⋮	⋮	⋮
2004	2.7	76.6	5.3	5.8	5.5
2005	3.4	78.8	−0.2	4.0	5.1
2006	3.2	80.4	−0.5	5.3	4.6

ChCPI = percent change in the Consumer Price Index (CPI) over previous year, *CapUtil* = percent utilization of manufacturing capacity in current year, *ChgM1* = percent change in currency and demand deposits (M1) over previous year, *ChgM2* = percent change in small time deposits and other near-money (M2) over previous year, *Unem* = civilian unemployment rate in percent.

Source: *Economic Report of the President, 2007.* These variables are selected from *LearningStats* (Time-Series Data).

DATA SET E   College Graduation Rate and Selected Characteristics of U.S. States
(n = 50, k = 8)   ColGrads

State	ColGrad%	Dropout	EdSpend	Urban	Age	Femlab	Neast	Seast	West
AL	15.6	35.3	3,627	60.4	33.0	51.8	0	1	0
AK	23.0	31.6	8,330	67.5	29.4	64.9	0	0	1
AZ	20.3	27.5	4,309	87.5	32.2	55.6	0	0	1
⋮	⋮	⋮	⋮	⋮	⋮	⋮	⋮	⋮	⋮
WV	12.3	22.7	4,911	36.1	35.4	44.2	0	1	0
WI	17.7	15.8	5,871	65.7	32.9	63.1	0	0	0
WY	18.8	21.4	5,723	65.0	32.0	61.8	0	0	1

ColGrad% = percent of state population with a college degree, *Dropout* = percent of high school students who do not graduate, *EdSpend* = per capita spending on K–12 education, *Urban* = percent of state population living in urban areas, *Age* = median age of state's population, *FemLab* = percent of adult females who are in the labor force, *Neast* = 1 if state is in the Northeast, 0 otherwise, *Seast* = 1 if state is in the Southeast, 0 otherwise, *West* = 1 if state is in the West, 0 otherwise.

Source: *Statistical Abstract of the United States, 1990.* These variables are selected from *LearningStats* (States).

DATA SET F   Characteristics of Selected Piston Aircraft (n = 55, k = 4)
CruiseSpeed

Obs	Mfgr/Model	Cruise	Year	TotalHP	NumBlades	Turbo
1	Cessna Turbo Stationair TU206	148	1981	310	3	1
2	Cessna 310 R	194	1975	570	3	0
3	Piper 125 Tri Pacer	107	1951	125	2	0
⋮	⋮	⋮	⋮	⋮	⋮	⋮
53	OMF Aircraft Symphony	128	2002	160	2	0
54	Liberty XL-2	132	2003	125	2	0
55	Piper 6X	148	2004	300	3	0

Cruise = best cruise speed (knots indicated air speed) at 65–75 percent power, *Year* = year of manufacture, *TotalHP* = total horsepower (both engines if twin), *NumBlades* = number of propeller blades, *Turbo* = 1 if turbocharged, 0 otherwise.

Source: *Flying Magazine* (various issues). Data are for educational purposes only and not as a guide to performance. These variables are selected from *LearningStats* (Technology Data).

DATA SET G   Characteristics of Randomly Chosen Hydrocarbons (n = 35, k = 7)   Retention

Obs	Name	Ret	MW	BP	RI	H1	H2	H3	H4	H5
1	2,4,4-trimethyl-2-pentene	153.57	112.215	105.06	1.4135	0	1	0	0	0
2	1,5-cyclooctadiene	237.56	108.183	150.27	1.4905	0	0	0	1	0
3	methylcyclohexane	153.57	98.188	101.08	1.4206	0	0	1	0	0
⋮	⋮	⋮	⋮	⋮	⋮	⋮	⋮	⋮	⋮	⋮
33	ethylbenzene	209.700	106.170	136.000	1.4950	0	0	0	0	1
34	m-ethyl toluene	247.800	120.194	161.480	1.4941	0	0	0	0	1
35	3-methylhexane	132.320	100.204	92.000	1.3861	1	0	0	0	0

Ret = Chromatographic retention time (seconds), *MW* = molecular weight (gm/mole), *BP* = boiling point in °C, *RI* = refractive index (dimensionless), *Class* = hydrocarbon class (*H1* = acyclic saturated, *H2* = acyclic unsaturated, *H3* = cyclic saturated, *H4* = cyclic unsaturated, *H5* = aromatic).

Source: Data are courtesy of John Seeley of Oakland University. This is a 50 percent sample of the full data set found in *LearningStats* (Technology Data).

DATA SET H Price and Percent Metal Content of Recovered Metal ($n = 33$, $k = 6$)
  Metals

Obs	Price/lb	Al	Si	Cr	Ti	Zn	Pb
1	0.87000	94.2248	0.6079	0.1203	0.0327	0.2316	0.0000
2	0.89240	91.5803	0.2496	0.1006	0.0213	0.1094	0.0594
3	0.91526	91.4810	0.1850	0.1031	0.0227	0.0793	0.0691
⋮	⋮	⋮	⋮	⋮	⋮	⋮	⋮
31	0.94350	94.3890	0.3646	0.0904	0.0321	0.0640	0.0249
32	0.94490	93.9500	0.3001	0.0832	0.0281	0.0697	0.0265
33	0.94790	94.1019	0.2813	0.0915	0.0259	0.1443	0.0290

Each observation shows the selling price per pound and percent metal content of one shipment of metal alloy recovered and processed by a metal recovery firm. Al = percent aluminum, Si = percent silicon, Cr = percent chromium, Ti = percent titanium, Zn = percent zinc, Pb = percent lead.

Source: Confidential.

DATA SET I Body Fat and Personal Measurements for Males ($n = 50$, $k = 8$)   BodyFat2

Obs	Fat%	Age	Weight	Height	Neck	Chest	Abdomen	Hip	Thigh
1	12.6	23	154.25	67.75	36.2	93.1	85.2	94.5	59.0
2	6.9	22	173.25	72.25	38.5	93.6	83.0	98.7	58.7
3	24.6	22	154.00	66.25	34.0	95.8	87.9	99.2	59.6
⋮	⋮	⋮	⋮	⋮	⋮	⋮	⋮	⋮	⋮
48	6.4	39	148.50	71.25	34.6	89.8	79.5	92.7	52.7
49	13.4	45	135.75	68.50	32.8	92.3	83.4	90.4	52.0
50	5.0	47	127.50	66.75	34.0	83.4	70.4	87.2	50.6

$Fat\%$ = percent body fat, Age = age (yrs.), $Weight$ = weight (lbs.), $Height$ = height (in.), $Neck$ = neck circumference (cm), $Chest$ = chest circumference (cm), $Abdomen$ = abdomen circumference (cm), Hip = hip circumference (cm), $Thigh$ = thigh circumference (cm).

Data are a subsample of 252 males analyzed in Roger W. Johnson (1996), "Fitting Percentage of Body Fat to Simple Body Measurements," *Journal of Statistics Education* 4, no. 1.

DATA SET J Used Vehicle Prices ($n = 637$, $k = 4$)   Vehicles

Obs	Model	Price	Age	Car	Truck	SUV
1	Astro GulfStream Conversion	12,988	3	0	0	0
2	Astro LS 4.3L V6	5,950	9	0	0	0
3	Astro LS V6	19,995	4	0	0	0
⋮	⋮	⋮	⋮	⋮	⋮	⋮
635	DC 300M Autostick	10,995	6	1	0	0
636	DC 300M Special Edition	22,995	1	1	0	0
637	GM 3500 4×4 w/8ft bed and plow	17,995	5	0	1	0

$Price$ = asking price ($), Age = vehicle age (yrs), Car = 1 if passenger car, 0 otherwise, $Truck$ = 1 if truck, 0 otherwise, SUV = 1 if sport utility vehicle, 0 otherwise. (*Van* is the omitted fourth binary).

Source: *Detroit AutoFocus* 4, Issue 38 (Sept. 17–23, 2004). Data are for educational purposes only and should not be used as a guide to depreciation.

GENERAL EXERCISES

13.26 In a model of Ford's quarterly revenue $TotalRevenue = \beta_0 + \beta_1\, CarSales + \beta_2\, TruckSales + \beta_3\, SUVSales + \varepsilon$, the three predictors are measured in number of units sold (not dollars). (a) Interpret each slope. (b) Would the intercept be meaningful? (c) What factors might be reflected in the error term? Explain.

13.27 In a study of paint peel problems, a regression was suggested to predict defects per million (the response variable). The intended predictors were supplier (four suppliers, coded as binaries) and substrate (four materials, coded as binaries). There were 11 observations. Explain why regression is impractical in this case, and suggest a remedy.

13.28 A hospital emergency room analyzed $n = 17{,}664$ hourly observations on its average occupancy rates using six binary predictors representing days of the week and two binary predictors representing the 8-hour work shift (12 A.M.–8 A.M., 8 A.M.–4 P.M., 4 P.M.–12 A.M.) when the data were collected. The fitted regression equation was $AvgOccupancy = 11.2 + 1.19\,Mon - 0.187\,Tue - 0.785\,Wed - 0.580$ $Thu - 0.451\,Fri - 0.267\,Sat - 4.58\,Shift1 - 1.65\,Shift2$ ($SE = 6.18$, $R^2 = .094$, $R^2_{adj} = .093$). (a) Why did the analyst use only six binaries for days when there are 7 days in a week? (b) Why did the analyst use only two work shift binaries when there are three work shifts? (c) Which is the busiest day? (d) Which is the busiest shift? (e) Interpret the intercept. (f) Assess the regression's fit.

13.29 Using test data on 20 types of laundry detergent, an analyst fitted a regression to predict *CostPerLoad* (average cost per load in cents per load) using binary predictors *TopLoad* (1 if washer is a top-loading model, 0 otherwise) and *Powder* (if detergent was in powder form, 0 otherwise). Interpret the results. (Data are from *Consumer Reports* 68, no. 8 [November 2003], p. 42.)   🦈 **Laundry**

R²	0.117			
Adjusted R²	0.006	n	19	
R	0.341	k	2	
Std. Error	5.915	Dep. Var.	**Cost Per Load**	

ANOVA table

Source	SS	df	MS	F	p-value
Regression	73.8699	2	36.9350	1.06	.3710
Residual	559.8143	16	34.9884		
Total	633.6842	18			

Regression output   confidence interval

variables	coefficients	std. error	t(df = 16)	p-value	95% lower	95% upper
Intercept	26.0000	4.1826	6.216	1.23E-05	17.1333	34.8667
Top-Load	−6.3000	4.5818	−1.375	.1881	−16.0130	3.4130
Powder	−0.2714	2.9150	−0.093	.9270	−6.4509	5.9081

13.30 A researcher used stepwise regression to create regression models to predict *BirthRate* (births per 1,000) using five predictors: *LifeExp* (life expectancy in years), *InfMort* (infant mortality rate), *Density* (population density per square kilometer), *GDPCap* (Gross Domestic Product per capita), and *Literate* (literacy percent). Interpret these results.   🦈 **BirthRates2**

Regression Analysis—Stepwise Selection (best model of each size)

153   observations
BirthRate is the dependent variable

p-values for the coefficients

Nvar	LifeExp	InfMort	Density	GDPCap	Literate	s	Adj R²	R²
1		.0000				6.318	.722	.724
2		.0000			.0000	5.334	.802	.805
3		.0000		.0242	.0000	5.261	.807	.811
4	.5764	.0000		.0311	.0000	5.273	.806	.812
5	.5937	.0000	.6289	.0440	.0000	5.287	.805	.812

13.31 A sports enthusiast created an equation to predict *Victories* (the team's number of victories in the National Basketball Association regular season play) using predictors *FGP* (team field goal percentage), *FTP* (team free throw percentage), *Points* = (team average points per game), *Fouls* (team average number of fouls per game), *TrnOvr* (team average number of turnovers per game), and *Rbnds* (team average number of rebounds per game). The fitted regression was $Victories = -281 + 523\,FGP + 3.12\,FTP + 0.781\,Points - 2.90\,Fouls + 1.60\,TrnOvr + 0.649\,Rbnds$ ($R^2 = .802$, $F = 10.80$, $SE = 6.87$). The strongest predictors were *FGP* ($t = 4.35$) and *Fouls* ($t = -2.146$). The other predictors were only marginally significant and *FTP* and *Rbnds* were not significant. The matrix of correlations is shown below. At the time of this analysis, there were 23 NBA teams. (a) Do the regression coefficients make sense? (b) Is the intercept meaningful? Explain. (c) Is the sample size a problem (using Evans' Rule or Doane's Rule)? (d) Why might collinearity account for the lack of significance of some predictors? (Data are from a research project by MBA student Michael S. Malloy.)

	FGP	FTP	Points	Fouls	TrnOvr	Rbnds
FGP	1.000					
FTP	−0.039	1.000				
Points	0.475	0.242	1.000			
Fouls	−0.014	0.211	0.054	1.000		
TrnOvr	0.276	0.028	0.033	0.340	1.000	
Rbnds	0.436	0.137	0.767	−0.032	0.202	1.000

13.32 An expert witness in a case of alleged racial discrimination in a state university school of nursing introduced a regression of the determinants of *Salary* of each professor for each year during an 8-year period ($n = 423$) with the following results, with dependent variable *Salary* and predictors *Year* (year in which the salary was observed), *YearHire* (year when the individual was hired), *Race* (1 if individual is black, 0 otherwise), and *Rank* (1 if individual is an assistant professor, 0 otherwise). Interpret these results.

Variable	Coefficient	t	p
Intercept	−3,816,521	−29.4	.000
Year	1,948	29.8	.000
YearHire	−826	−5.5	.000
Race	−2,093	−4.3	.000
Rank	−6,438	−22.3	.000
$R^2 = 0.811$		$R^2_{adj} = 0.809$	$s = 3,318$

13.33 Analysis of a Detroit Marathon ($n = 1,015$ men, $n = 150$ women) produced the regression results shown below, with dependent variable *Time* (the marathon time in minutes) and predictors *Age* (runner's age), *Weight* (runner's weight in pounds), *Height* (runner's height in inches), and *Exp* (1 if runner had prior marathon experience, 0 otherwise). (a) Interpret the coefficient of *Exp*. (b) Does the intercept have any meaning? (c) Why do you suppose squared predictors were included? (d) Plug in your own *Age, Height, Weight,* and *Exp* to predict your own running time. Do you believe it? (Data courtesy of Detroit Striders.)

	Men ($n = 1,015$)		Women ($n = 150$)	
Variable	Coefficient	t	Coefficient	t
Intercept	−366		−2,820	
Age	−4.827	−6.1	−3.593	−2.5
Age^2	0.07671	7.1	0.05240	2.6
Weight	−1.598	−1.9	3.000	0.7
Weight^2	0.008961	3.4	−0.004041	−2.0
Height	24.65	1.5	96.13	1.6
Height^2	−0.2074	−1.7	−0.8040	−1.8
Exp	−41.74	−17.0	−28.65	−4.3
	$R^2 = 0.423$		$R^2 = 0.334$	

13.34 Using test data on 43 vehicles, an analyst fitted a regression to predict *CityMPG* (miles per gallon in city driving) using as predictors *Length* (length of car in inches), *Width* (width of car in inches), and *Weight* (weight of car in pounds). Interpret the results. Do you see evidence that some predictors were unhelpful? **CityMPG**

R²	0.682			
Adjusted R²	0.658	n	43	
R	0.826	k	3	
Std. Error	2.558	Dep. Var.	**CityMPG**	

ANOVA table

Source	SS	df	MS	F	p-value
Regression	547.3722	3	182.4574	27.90	8.35E-10
Residual	255.0929	39	6.5408		
Total	802.4651	42			

Regression output — confidence interval

variables	coefficients	std. error	t(df = 39)	p-value	95% lower	95% upper	VIF
Intercept	39.4492	8.1678	4.830	.0000	22.9283	55.9701	
Length (in)	−0.0016	0.0454	−0.035	.9725	−0.0934	0.0902	2.669
Width (in)	−0.0463	0.1373	−0.337	.7379	−0.3239	0.2314	2.552
Weight (lbs)	−0.0043	0.0008	−5.166	.0000	−0.0060	−0.0026	2.836

13.35 A researcher used stepwise regression to create regression models to predict *CarTheft* (thefts per 1000) using four predictors: *Income* (per capita income), *Unem* (unemployment percent), *Pupil/Tea* (pupil-to-teacher ratio), and *Divorce* (divorces per 1,000 population) for the 50 U.S. states. Interpret these results. **CarTheft**

Regression Analysis—Stepwise Selection (best model of each size)

50 observations
CarTheft is the dependent variable

p-values for the coefficients

Nvar	Income	Unem	Pupil/Tea	Divorce	Std. Err	Adj R²	R²
1			.0004		167.482	.218	.234
2	.0018		.0000		152.362	.353	.379
3	.0013	.0157	.0001		144.451	.418	.454
4	.0007	.0323	.0003	.1987	143.362	.427	.474

RELATED READINGS

Evans, Martin G. "The Problem of Analyzing Multiplicative Composites." *American Psychologist,* January 1991, p. 675 (Evans' Rule).

Kennedy, Peter. *A Guide to Econometrics.* 5th ed. MIT Press, 2003, p. 132 (Klein's Rule).

Kutner, Michael H.; Christopher J. Nachtsheim; and John Neter. *Applied Linear Regression Models.* 4th ed. McGraw-Hill/Irwin, 2004.

Ryan, Thomas P. *Modern Regression Methods.* Wiley, 1996.

LearningStats Unit 13   Multiple Regression   LS

LearningStats Unit 13 illustrates uses of multiple regression, assessing fit (e.g., R^2 and R^2_{adj}), tests for significance (e.g., ANOVA, *t* tests), and model adequacy (e.g., residual tests). Binary predictors and tests for nonlinearity are illustrated. Special attention is given to the issue of multicollinearity and its effects on tests for significance of individual predictors. Your instructor may assign specific modules, or you may pursue those that sound interesting.

Topic	*LearningStats Modules*
Multiple regression overview	Multiple Regression Overview Violations of Assumptions
Using Excel and MINITAB	Regression Using Excel Regression Using MINITAB
Simulation	Effects of Collinearity Effects of Multicollinearity Salary Data Modeling
Case studies	Binary Predictors Variance Inflation Stepwise Regression Squared Predictors
Student presentations	Murder Rates Birth Weight Cancer Deaths Birth Rates Car Theft
Student reports	Income Per Capita Teen Moms by State Student Worksheets
Formulas	Useful Regression Formulas
Tables	Appendix D—Student's *t* Appendix F—Critical Values of *F*

Key: = PowerPoint   = Word   = Excel

Visual Statistics

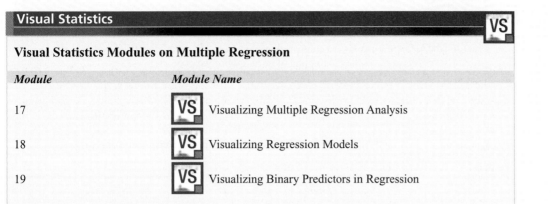

Visual Statistics Modules on Multiple Regression

Module	Module Name
17	Visualizing Multiple Regression Analysis
18	Visualizing Regression Models
19	Visualizing Binary Predictors in Regression

Visual Statistics Modules 17, 18, and 19 (included on your CD) are designed to help you:

- Recognize and use the terminology of multiple regression.
- Be able to perform significance tests and interpret confidence intervals for model parameters.
- Understand the importance of data conditioning and the potential effects of ill-conditioned data.
- Detect multicollinearity and recognize its common symptoms.
- Learn when a model may be overfitted and why that can be a problem.
- Use visual displays to check residuals for non-normality, autocorrelation, and heteroscedasticity.
- Know the commonly used variable transformations and their purposes.
- Understand how to use polynomial models and interaction tests.
- Be able to interpret regressions with intercept binaries or slope binaries.

The worktext (included on the CD in .PDF format) contains lists of concepts covered, objectives of the modules, overviews of concepts, illustrations of concepts, orientations to module features, learning exercises (basic, intermediate, advanced), learning projects (individual, team), self-evaluation quizzes, glossaries of terms, and solutions to self-evaluation quizzes.

1. Which statement is *correct* concerning one-factor ANOVA? Why not the others?
   a. The ANOVA is a test to see whether the variances of c groups are the same.
   b. In ANOVA, the k groups are compared two at a time, not simultaneously.
   c. ANOVA depends on the assumption of normality of the populations sampled.

2. Which statement is *incorrect?* Explain.
   a. We need a Tukey test because ANOVA doesn't tell *which* group means differ.
   b. Hartley's F_{max} test is needed to determine whether the means of the groups differ.
   c. ANOVA assumes equal variances in the k groups being compared.

3. Given the following ANOVA table, find the F statistic and the critical value of $F_{.05}$.

Source	Sum of Squares	df	Mean Square	F
Treatment	744.00	4		
Error	751.50	15		
Total	1,495.50	19		

4. Which statement is correct? Why not the others?
   a. A sample correlation $r = +.40$ indicates a stronger linear relationship than $r = -.60$.
   b. When using the least squares method, the residuals always sum to zero.
   c. A very small standard error would indicate a poor fit in the regression.

5. Given a sample correlation coefficient $r = .373$ with $n = 30$, can you reject the hypothesis $\rho = 0$ for the population at $\alpha = .01$? Explain, stating the critical value you are using in the test.

6. Which statement is *incorrect?* Explain.
   a. Correlation uses a t-test with $n-2$ degrees of freedom.
   b. Correlation analysis assumes that X is independent and Y is dependent.
   c. Correlation analysis is a test for the degree of linearity between X and Y.

7. Based on the information in this ANOVA table, the coefficient of determination R^2 is
   a. 0.499   b. 0.501   c. 0.382

ANOVA Table

Source	Sum of Squares	df	Mean Square	F	p-Value
Regression	158.3268	1	158.3268	24.88	0.00004
Residual	159.0806	25	6.3632		
Total	317.4074	26			

8. In a test of the regression model $Y = \beta_0 + \beta_1 X$ with 27 observations, what is the critical value of t to test the hypothesis that $\beta_1 = 0$ using $\alpha = .05$ in a two-tailed test?
   a. 1.960   b. 2.060   c. 1.708

9. Which statement is *correct* for a bivariate regression? Why not the others?
   a. A 95% confidence interval (CI) for the mean of Y is wider than the 95% CI for the predicted Y.
   b. A confidence interval for the predicted Y is widest when $X = \bar{x}$.
   c. The t test for zero slope always gives the same t_{calc} as the correlation test for $\rho = 0$.

10. Tell if each statement is *true* or *false* for a bivariate regression. If false, explain.
    a. If the standard error is $s_{yx} = 3,207$ then a residual $e_i = 4,327$ would be an outlier.
    b. In a regression with $n = 50$ then a leverage statistic $h_i = .10$ indicates unusual leverage.
    c. A decimal change is often used to improve data conditioning.

11. For a multiple regression, which statement is *true?* Why not the others?
    a. Evans' Rule suggests at least 10 observations for each predictor.
    b. The t_{calc} in a test for significance of a binary predictor can have only two values.
    c. Occam's Razor says we must prefer bivariate regression because it is simple.

12. For a multiple regression, which statement is *false?* Explain.
    a. If $R^2 = .752$ and $R^2_{adj} = .578$, the model probably has at least one weak predictor.
    b. R^2_{adj} can exceed R^2 if the model contains some very strong predictors.
    c. Deleting a predictor could increase the R^2_{adj} but will not increase R^2.

13. Which *predictor coefficients* differ significantly from zero at $\alpha = .05$?
    a. X3 and X5   b. X5 only   c. all but X1 and X3

	Coefficients	Std. Error	Lower 95%	Upper 95%
Intercept	22.47427	6.43282	9.40122	35.54733
X1	−0.243035	0.162983	−0.574256	0.088186
X2	0.187555	0.278185	−0.377784	0.752895
X3	−0.339730	0.063168	−0.468102	−0.211358
X4	0.001902	0.008016	−0.014389	0.018193
X5	1.602511	0.723290	0.132609	3.072413

14. Which predictors differ significantly from zero at $\alpha = .05$?
    a. X3 only   b. X4 only   c. both X3 and X4

	Coefficients	Std. Error	p-Value
Intercept	23.3015	4.1948	0.0000
X1	−0.227977	0.178227	0.2100
X2	0.218970	0.300784	0.4719
X3	−0.343658	0.059742	0.0000
X4	1.588353	0.742737	0.0402

15. In this regression with $n = 40$, which *predictor* differs significantly from zero at $\alpha = .01$?
    a. X2   b. X3   c. X5

	Coefficients	Std. Error
Intercept	3.210610	0.918974
X1	−0.034719	0.023283
X2	0.026794	0.039741
X3	−0.048533	0.009024
X4	0.000272	0.001145
X5	0.228930	0.103327

Chi-Square Tests

Chapter Learning Objectives

When you finish this chapter you should be able to

- Recognize a contingency table (cross-tabulation of frequencies).
- Find degrees of freedom and use the chi-square table of critical values.
- Perform a chi-square test for independence on a contingency table.
- Perform a goodness-of-fit (GOF) test for a uniform distribution.

Not all information pertaining to business can be summarized numerically. We are often interested in answers to questions such as: Do employees in different age groups choose different types of health plans? Do consumers prefer red, yellow, or blue package lettering on our bread bags? Does the name of our new lawn mower influence how we perceive the quality? Answers to questions such as these are not measurements on a numerical scale. Rather, the variables that we are interested in learning about may be *categorical* or *ordinal*. Health plans are categorized by the way services are paid, so the variable *health plan* might have four different categories: Catastrophic, HMO (health maintenance organization), POS (point of service), and CDHP (consumer-driven health plan). The variable *package lettering color* would have categories red, yellow, and blue, and the variable *perceived quality* might have categories excellent, satisfactory, and poor.

We can collect observations on these variables to answer the types of questions posed either by surveying our customers and employees or by conducting carefully designed experiments. Once our data have been collected we summarize by tallying response frequencies on a table that we call a *contingency table*. A **contingency table** is a cross-tabulation of *n* paired observations into categories. Each cell shows the count of observations that fall into the category defined by its row and column heading.

14.1
CHI-SQUARE TEST FOR INDEPENDENCE

Chapter 14

EXAMPLE

Web Pages (4 × 3 Table)

As online shopping has grown, opportunity has also grown for personal data collection and invasion of privacy. Mainstream online retailers have policies known as "privacy disclaimers" that define the rules regarding their uses of information collected, the customer's right to refuse third-party promotional offers, and so on. You can access these policies through a Web link, found either on the Web site's home page, on the order page (i.e., as you enter your credit card information), on a client Web page, or on some other Web page. In the United States, such links are voluntary, while in the European Union (EU) they are mandated by law. Location of the privacy disclaimer is considered to be a measure of the degree of consumer protection (the farther the link is from the home page, the less likely it is to be noticed). Marketing researchers did a survey of 291 Web sites in three nations (France,

U.K., U.S.) and obtained the *contingency table* shown here as Table 14.1. Is location of the privacy disclaimer *independent* of the Web site's nationality? This question can be answered by using a test based on the frequencies in this contingency table.

TABLE 14.1   **Privacy Disclaimer Location and Web Site Nationality**   WebSites

	Nationality of Web Site			
Location of Disclaimer	France	U.K.	U.S.	Row Total
Home page	56	68	35	159
Order page	19	19	28	66
Client page	6	10	16	32
Other page	12	9	13	34
Col Total	93	106	92	291

Source: Calin Gurau, Ashok Ranchhod, and Claire Gauzente, "To Legislate or Not to Legislate: A Comparative Exploratory Study of Privacy/Personalisation Factors Affecting French, UK, and US Web Sites," *Journal of Consumer Marketing* 20, no. 7 (2003), p. 659. Used with permission, Emerald Group Publishing Limited.

Table 14.2 illustrates the terminology of a contingency table. Variable A has r levels (rows) and variable B has c levels (columns) so we call this an $r \times c$ contingency table. Each cell shows the observed frequency f_{jk} in row j and column k.

TABLE 14.2

Table of Observed Frequencies

	Variable B				
Variable A	1	2	...	c	Row Total
1	f_{11}	f_{12}	...	f_{1c}	R_1
2	f_{21}	f_{22}	...	f_{2c}	R_2
⋮	⋮	⋮	⋮	⋮	⋮
r	f_{r1}	f_{r2}	...	f_{rc}	R_r
Col Total	C_1	C_2	...	C_c	n

Chi-Square Test

In a test of independence for an $r \times c$ contingency table, the hypotheses are:

H_0: Variable A is independent of variable B

H_1: Variable A is not independent of variable B

To test these hypotheses, we use the **chi-square test** *for independence,* developed by Karl Pearson (1857–1936). It is a test based on *frequencies.* It measures the association between the two variables A and B in the contingency table. The chi-square test for independence is a distribution-free test. The only operation performed is classifying the n data pairs into r rows (variable A) and c columns (variable B), and then comparing the **observed frequency** f_{jk} in each cell of the contingency table with the **expected frequency** e_{jk} under the assumption of independence. The chi-square test statistic measures the *relative* difference between expected and observed frequencies:

(14.1)
$$\chi^2_{\text{calc}} = \sum_{j=1}^{r} \sum_{k=1}^{c} \frac{[f_{jk} - e_{jk}]^2}{e_{jk}}$$

If the two variables are **independent**, then f_{jk} should be close to e_{jk}, leading to a chi-square test statistic near zero. Conversely, large differences between f_{jk} and e_{jk} will lead to a large chi-square test statistic. The chi-square test statistic cannot be negative (due to squaring) so it is always a right-tailed test. If the test statistic is far enough in the right tail, we will reject the hypothesis of independence. Squaring each difference removes the sign, so it doesn't matter whether e_{jk} is greater than or less than f_{jk}. Each squared difference is expressed *relative to* e_{jk}.

Chi-Square Distribution

The test statistic is compared with a critical value from the **chi-square probability distribution**. It has one parameter v called **degrees of freedom**. For the $r \times c$ contingency table, the degrees of freedom are:

$$v = \text{degrees of freedom} = (r-1)(c-1) \qquad \textbf{(14.2)}$$

where

  r = the number of rows in the contingency table

  c = the number of columns in the contingency table

The parameter v is the number of non-redundant cells in the contingency table (see *LearningStats* Unit 15 "Degrees of Freedom" for further explanation). There is a different chi-square distribution for each value of v. Appendix E contains critical values for right-tail areas of the chi-square distribution. Its mean is v and its variance is $2v$. As illustrated in Figure 14.1, all chi-square distributions are skewed to the right, but become more symmetric as v increases. For $v = 1$ the distribution is discontinuous near the origin. As v increases the shape begins to resemble a normal, bell-shaped curve. However, for any contingency table you are likely to encounter, degrees of freedom will not be large enough to assume normality.

FIGURE 14.1

Various Chi-Square Distributions

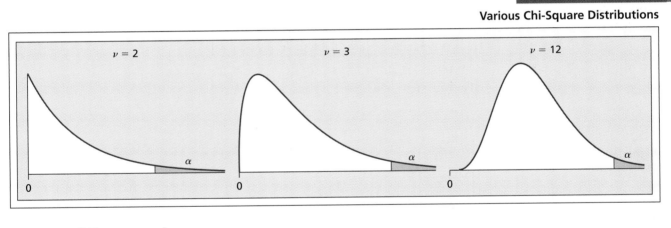

Expected Frequencies

Assuming that H_0 is true, the expected frequency of row j and column k is

$$e_{jk} = R_j C_k / n \qquad \text{(expected frequency in row } j \text{ and column } k) \qquad \textbf{(14.3)}$$

where

  R_j = total for row j ($j = 1, 2, \ldots, r$)

  C_k = total for column k ($k = 1, 2, \ldots, c$)

  n = sample size (or number of responses)

This formula for expected frequencies stems from the definition of independent events (see Chapter 5). When two events are independent, their *joint* probability is the product of their marginal probabilities, so for a cell in row j and column k the joint probability would be $(R_j/n)(C_k/n)$. To get the expected cell frequency, we multiply this joint probability by the sample size n to obtain $e_{jk} = R_j C_k / n$. The e_{jk} always sum to the same row and column frequencies as the observed frequencies. Expected frequencies will not, in general, be integers.

Illustration of the Chi-Square Calculations ————————•

We will illustrate the chi-square test by using the Web page frequencies from the contingency table (Table 14.1). We follow the usual five-step hypothesis testing procedure:

Step 1: State the Hypotheses   For the Web page example, the hypotheses are:

H_0: Privacy disclaimer location is independent of Web site nationality

H_1: Privacy disclaimer location is dependent on Web site nationality

Step 2: Specify the Decision Rule   For the Web page contingency table, we have $r = 4$ rows and $c = 3$ columns, so degrees of freedom are $v = (r - 1)(c - 1) = (4 - 1)(3 - 1) = 6$. We will choose $\alpha = .05$ for the test. Figure 14.2 shows that the right-tail critical value from Appendix E with $v = 6$ is $\chi^2_{.05} = 12.59$. This critical value could also be obtained from Excel using =CHIINV(.05,6).

FIGURE 14.2

Critical Value of Chi-Square from Appendix E

Appendix E: Critical Values for Chi-Square

This table shows the critical value that defines the specified area for the stated degrees of freedom (v).

		Left Tail Area					Right Tail Area			
v	0.005	0.01	0.025	0.05	0.10	0.10	0.05	0.025	0.01	0.005
1	0.000	0.000	0.001	0.004	0.016	2.706	3.841	5.024	6.635	7.879
2	0.010	0.020	0.051	0.103	0.211	4.605	5.991	7.378	9.210	10.60
3	0.072	0.115	0.216	0.352	0.584	6.251	7.815	9.348	11.34	12.84
4	0.207	0.297	0.484	0.711	1.064	7.779	9.488	11.14	13.28	14.86
5	0.412	0.554	0.831	1.145	1.610	9.236	11.07	12.83	15.09	16.75
6	0.676	0.872	1.237	1.635	2.204	10.64	12.59	14.45	16.81	18.55
7	0.989	1.239	1.690	2.167	2.833	12.02	14.07	16.01	18.48	20.28
8	1.344	1.646	2.180	2.733	3.490	13.36	15.51	17.53	20.09	21.95
9	1.735	2.088	2.700	3.325	4.168	14.68	16.92	19.02	21.67	23.59
10	2.156	2.558	3.247	3.940	4.865	15.99	18.31	20.48	23.21	25.19

For $\alpha = .05$ in this right-tailed test, the decision rule is:

Reject H_0 if $\chi^2_{calc} > 12.59$

Otherwise do no reject H_0

The decision rule is illustrated in Figure 14.3.

FIGURE 14.3

Right-Tailed Chi-Square Test for $v = 6$

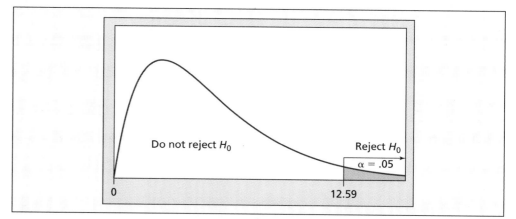

Do not reject H_0

Reject H_0

$\alpha = .05$

0

12.59

Step 3: Calculate the Expected Frequencies   The expected frequency in row j and column k is $e_{jk} = R_j C_k / n$. The calculations are illustrated in Table 14.3. The expected frequencies (lower part of Table 14.3) must sum to the same row and column frequencies at the observed frequencies (upper part of Table 14.3).

Step 4: Calculate the Test Statistic   The chi-square test statistic is

$$\chi^2_{calc} = \sum_{j=1}^{r}\sum_{k=1}^{c} \frac{[f_{jk} - e_{jk}]^2}{e_{jk}} = \frac{(56 - 50.81)^2}{50.81} + \cdots + \frac{(13 - 10.75)^2}{10.75}$$

$$= 0.53 + \cdots + 0.47 = 17.54$$

| Observed and Expected Frequencies | WebSites | | | **TABLE 14.3** |

Observed Frequencies

Location	France	UK	USA	Row Total
Home	56	68	35	159
Order	19	19	28	66
Client	6	10	16	32
Other	12	9	13	34
Col Total	93	106	92	291

Expected Frequencies (assuming independence)

Location	France	UK	USA	Row Total
Home	$(159 \times 93)/291 = 50.81$	$(159 \times 106)/291 = 57.92$	$(159 \times 92)/291 = 50.27$	159
Order	$(66 \times 93)/291 = 21.09$	$(66 \times 106)/291 = 24.04$	$(66 \times 92)/291 = 20.87$	66
Client	$(32 \times 93)/291 = 10.23$	$(32 \times 106)/291 = 11.66$	$(32 \times 92)/291 = 10.12$	32
Other	$(34 \times 93)/291 = 10.87$	$(34 \times 106)/291 = 12.38$	$(34 \times 92)/291 = 10.75$	34
Col Total	93	106	92	291

Even for this simple problem, the calculations are too lengthy to show in full. In fact, few would choose to do the calculations of the expected frequencies and chi-square test statistic without a spreadsheet. Fortunately, any statistical package will do a chi-square test. MegaStat's setup and output are shown in Figure 14.4. As you can see, MegaStat's calculations are arranged in a tabular form.

FIGURE 14.4

MegaStat's Chi-Square Test for Web Page Data

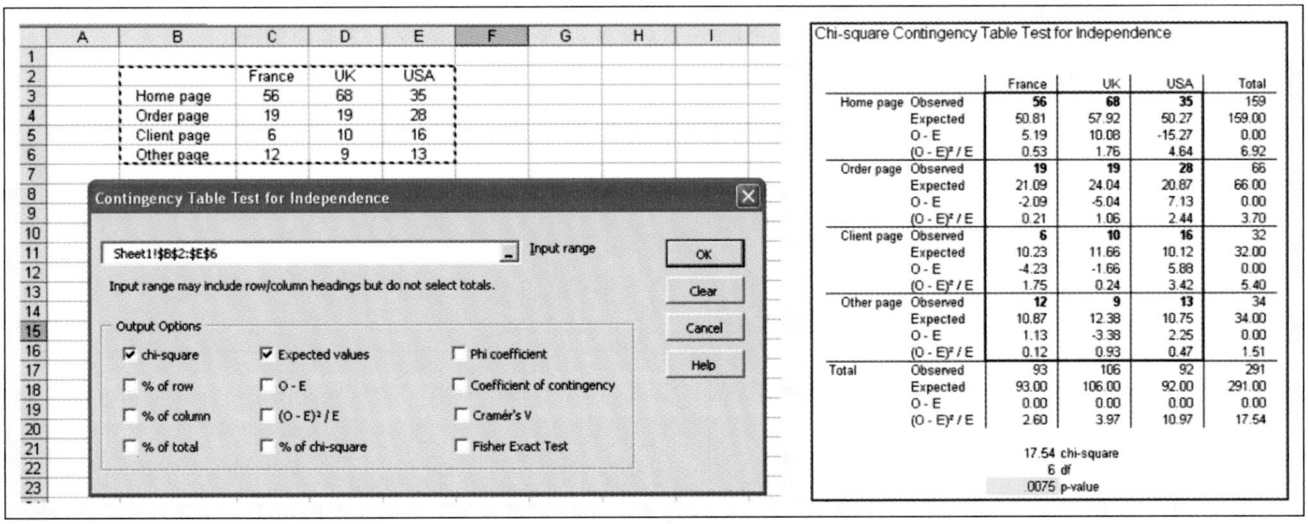

Step 5: Make the Decision Since the test statistic $\chi^2_{calc} = 17.54$ exceeds 12.59, we conclude that the observed differences between expected and observed frequencies differ significantly at $\alpha = .05$. The *p*-value (.0075) indicates that H_0 should be rejected at $\alpha = .05$. You can obtain this same *p*-value using Excel's function =CHIDIST(χ^2, v) or in this case =CHIDIST(17.54,6), which gives a right-tail area of .0075. This *p*-value indicates that privacy disclaimer location is *not* independent of nationality at $\alpha = .05$, based on this sample of 291 Web sites.

Discussion   MegaStat rounds things off for display purposes, though it maintains full internal accuracy in the calculations (as you must, if you do these calculations by hand). Differences between observed and expected frequencies O–E must sum to zero across each row and down each column. If you are doing these calculations by hand, check these sums (if they are not zero, you have made an error). From Figure 14.4 we see that only three cells (column 3, rows 1, 2, and 3) contribute a majority (4.64, 2.44, 3.42) of the chi-square sum (17.54). The hypothesis of independence fails largely because of these three cells.

EXAMPLE

*Night Flying
(2 × 2 Table)*

After the accident in which U.S. Senator John F. Kennedy, Jr., died while piloting his airplane at night from New York to Cape Cod, a random telephone poll was taken in which 409 New Yorkers were asked, "Should private pilots be allowed to fly at night without an instrument rating?" The same question was posed to 70 aviation experts. Results are shown in Table 14.4. The totals exclude those who had "No Opinion" (1 expert and 25 general public).

TABLE 14.4   **Should Noninstrument Rated Pilots Fly at Night?**   🐦   **Pilots**

Opinion	Experienced Pilots	General Public	Row Total
Yes	40	61	101
No	29	323	352
Col Total	69	384	453

Source: Siena College Research Institute.

The hypotheses are:

H_0: Opinion is independent of aviation expertise

H_1: Opinion is not independent of aviation expertise

The test results from MegaStat are shown in Figure 14.5. Degrees of freedom are $v = (r - 1)(c - 1) = (2 - 1)(2 - 1) = 1$. Appendix E shows that the critical value of chi-square for $\alpha = .005$ is 7.879. Since the test statistic $\chi^2 = 59.80$ greatly exceeds 7.879, we firmly reject the hypothesis. The *p*-value (.0000) confirms that opinion is *not* independent of aviation experience.

FIGURE 14.5   **MegaStat Chi-Square Test with $v = 1$**

Chi-square Contingency Table Test for Independence

	Col 1	Col 2	Total
Row 1 Observed	**40**	**61**	101
Expected	14.38	85.62	101.00
O − E	24.62	−24.62	0.00
$(O − E)^2/E$	39.39	7.08	46.47
Row 2 Observed	**29**	**323**	352
Expected	53.62	298.38	352.00
O − E	−24.62	24.62	0.00
$(O − E)^2/E$	11.30	2.03	13.33
Total Observed	69	384	453
Expected	69.00	384.00	453.00
O − E	0.00	0.00	0.00
$(O − E)^2/E$	50.69	9.11	59.80

59.80	chi-square
1	df
1.05E-14	p-value

Small Expected Frequencies

The chi-square test is unreliable if the *expected* frequencies are too small. As you can see from the formula for the test statistic, when e_{jk} in the denominator is small, the chi-square statistic may be inflated. A commonly used rule of thumb known as **Cochran's Rule** requires that $e_{jk} > 5$ for all cells. Another rule of thumb says that up to 20 percent of the cells may have $e_{jk} < 5$. Statisticians generally become quite nervous when $e_{jk} < 2$, and there is agreement that a chi-square test is infeasible if $e_{jk} < 1$ in any cell. Computer packages may offer warnings or refuse to proceed when expected frequencies are too small. When this happens, it may be possible to salvage the test by combining adjacent rows or columns to enlarge the expected frequencies. In the Web page example, all the expected frequencies are safely greater than 5.

Cross-Tabulating Raw Data

Chi-square tests for independence are quite flexible. Although most often used with nominal data such as gender (male, female), we can also analyze quantitative variables (such as salary) by coding them into categories (e.g., under \$25,000; \$25,000 to \$50,000; \$50,000 and over). Open-ended classes are acceptable. We can mix data types as required (nominal, ordinal, interval, ratio) by defining the bins appropriately. Few statistical tests are so versatile. Continuous data may be classified into any categories that make sense. To tabulate a continuous variable into two classes, we would make the cut at the median. For three bins, we would use the 33rd and 67th percentiles as cutpoints. For four bins, we would use the 25th, 50th, and 75th percentiles as cutpoints. We prefer classes that yield approximately equal frequencies for each cell to help protect against small expected frequencies (recall that Cochran's Rule requires expected frequencies be at least 5). Our bin choices are limited when we have integer data with a small range (e.g., a Likert scale with responses 1, 2, 3, 4, 5), but we can still define classes however we wish (e.g., 1 or 2, 3, 4 or 5).

EXAMPLE

Doctors and Infant Mortality   **Doctors**

Let $X =$ doctors per 100,000 residents of a state, and $Y =$ infant deaths per 1,000 births in the state. We might reasonably hypothesize that states with more doctors relative to population would have lower infant mortality, but do they? We are reluctant to assume normality and equal variances, so we prefer to avoid a *t* test. Instead, we hypothesize:

H_0: Infant mortality rate is independent of doctors per 100,000 population
H_1: Infant mortality rate is not independent of doctors per 100,000 population

Depending on how we form the contingency table, we could get different results. Figure 14.6 shows 2×2 and 3×3 tables created using Visual Statistics. Each table shows both actual and expected frequencies assuming the null hypothesis. Neither *p*-value indicates a very strong relationship. Since we cannot reject H_0 at any customary level of significance, we conclude that doctors and infant mortality are not strongly related. A *multivariate* regression model might be the next step, to explore other predictors (e.g., per capita income, per capita Medicaid spending, percent of college graduates) that might be related to infant mortality in a state.

FIGURE 14.6   **Visual Statistics Contingency Tables**

2×2 Table
Doctors Per 100,000

Infant Deaths Per 1,000	Low	High	Total
High	15/13.0	11/13.0	26
Low	10/12.0	14/12.0	24
Total	25	25	50

Chi-square test statistic = 1.282 (p = .258)

3×3 Table
Doctors Per 100,000

Infant Deaths Per 1,000	Low	Med	High	Total
High	8/5.4	4/5.4	4/5.1	16
Med	4/5.4	6/5.4	6/5.1	16
Low	5/6.1	7/6.1	6/5.8	18
Total	17	17	16	50

Chi-square test statistic = 2.762 (p = .598)

Why Do a Chi-Square Test on Numerical Data?

Why would anyone convert numerical data (X, Y) into categorical data in order to make a contingency table and do a chi-square test? Why not use the (X, Y) data to calculate a correlation coefficient or fit a regression? Here are three reasons:

- The researcher may believe there is a relationship between X and Y, but does not want to make an assumption about its form (linear, curvilinear, etc.) as required in a regression.

- There are outliers or other anomalies that prevent us from assuming that the data came from a normal population. Unlike correlation and regression, the chi-square test does *not* require any normality assumptions.

- The researcher has numerical data for one variable but not the other. A chi-square test can be used if we convert the numerical variable into categories.

3-Way Tables and Higher

There is no conceptual reason to limit ourselves to two-way contingency tables comparing two variables. However, such tables become rather hard to visualize, even when they are "sliced" into a series of 2-way tables. A table comparing three variables can be visualized as a *cube* or as a stack of tiled 2-way contingency tables. Major computer packages (SAS, SPSS, and others) permit 3-way contingency tables. For four or more variables, there is no physical analog to aid us, and their cumbersome nature would suggest analytical methods other than chi-square tests.

SECTION EXERCISES

connect

Instructions: For each exercise, include MegaStat or Excel exhibits to support your chi-square calculations. (a) State the hypotheses. (b) Show how the degrees of freedom are calculated for the contingency table. (c) Using the level of significance specified in the exercise, find the critical value of chi-square from Appendix E or from Excel's function =CHIINV(alpha, deg_freedom). (d) Carry out the calculations for a chi-square test for independence and draw a conclusion. (e) Which cells of the contingency table contribute the most to the chi-square test statistic? (f) Are any of the expected frequencies too small? (g) Interpret the *p*-value. If necessary, you can calculate the *p*-value using Excel's function =CHIDIST(test statistic, deg_freedom).

14.1 In a study of how managers attempt to manage earnings, researchers analyzed a sample of 515 earnings-management attempts from a survey of experienced auditors. The frequency of effects is summarized in the table shown. *Research question:* At $\alpha = .01$, is the effect on earnings independent of the approach used? (Data are from Mark W. Nelson, John A. Elliott, and Robin L. Tarpley, "How Are Earnings Managed? Examples from Auditors," *Accounting Horizons,* Supplement, 2003, pp. 17–35.) 🐛 **Earnings**

Current-Period Income Effect of Four Earnings Management Approaches

Approach Used	Increase	Decrease	No Clear Effect	Row Total
Expenses and Other Losses	133	113	23	269
Revenue and Other Gains	86	20	8	114
Business Combinations	12	22	33	67
Other Approaches	41	4	20	65
Col Total	272	159	84	515

14.2 Teenagers make up a large percentage of the market for clothing. Below are data on running shoe ownership in four world regions (excluding China). *Research question:* At $\alpha = .01$, does this sample show that running shoe ownership depends on world region? (See J. Paul Peter and Jerry C. Olson, *Consumer Behavior and Marketing Strategy,* 9th ed. [McGraw-Hill, 2004], p. 64.) 🐛 **Running**

Running Shoe Ownership in World Regions

Owned By	U.S.	Europe	Asia	Latin America	Row Total
Teens	80	89	69	65	303
Adults	20	11	31	35	97
Col Total	100	100	100	100	400

14.3 Students applying for admission to an MBA program must submit scores from the GMAT test, which includes a verbal and a quantitative component. Shown here are raw scores for 100 randomly chosen MBA applicants at a Midwestern, public, AACSB-accredited business school. *Research question:* At $\alpha = .005$, is the quantitative score independent of the verbal score? **GMAT**

Verbal	Quantitative			Row Total
	Under 25	25 to 35	35 or More	
Under 25	25	9	1	35
25 to 35	4	28	18	50
35 or More	1	3	11	15
Col Total	30	40	30	100

14.4 Computer abuse by employees is an ongoing worry to businesses. A study revealed the data shown below. *Research question:* At $\alpha = .01$, is the frequency of disciplinary action independent of the abuser's level of privilege? (Data are from Detmar W. Straub and William D. Nance, "Discovering and Disciplining Computer Abuse in Organizations," *MIS Quarterly* 14, no. 1 [March 1990], pp. 45–60.) **Abuse**

Computer Abuse Incidents Cross-Tabulated by Privilege and Punishment

Level of Privilege	Disciplined	Not Disciplined	Row Total
Low	20	11	31
Medium	42	3	45
High	33	3	36
Col Total	95	17	112

14.5 Marketing researchers prepared an advance notification card announcing an upcoming mail survey and describing the purpose of their research. Half the target customers received the prenotification, followed by the survey. The other half received only the survey. The survey return rates are shown below. *Research question:* At $\alpha = .025$, is return rate independent of prenotification? (Data are from Paul R. Murphy, Douglas R. Dalenberg, and James M. Daley, "Improving Survey Responses with Postcards," *Industrial Marketing Management* 19, no. 4 [November 1990], pp. 349–355.) **Advance**

Cross-Tabulation of Returns by Notification

Pre-Notified?	Returned	Not Returned	Row Total
Yes	39	155	194
No	22	170	192
Col Total	61	325	386

Mini Case   14.1

Student Work and Car Age

Do students work longer hours to pay for newer cars? This hypothesis was tested using data from a 2001 survey of introductory business statistics students at a large commuter university campus. The survey contained these two fill-in-the-blank questions:

About how many hours per week do you expect to work at an outside job this semester?

What is the age (in years) of the car you usually drive?

The contingency table shown in Table 14.5 summarizes the responses of 162 students. Very few students worked less than 15 hours, and a majority worked 25 hours or more. Most drove cars less than 3 years old, although a few drove cars 10 years old or more. Neither variable was normally distributed (and there were outliers) so a chi-square test was preferable to a correlation or regression model. The hypotheses to be tested are:

H_0: Car age is independent of work hours

H_1: Car age is not independent of work hours

TABLE 14.5   **Frequency Classification for Work Hours and Car Age**   🐟 **CarAge**

Hours of Outside Work Per Week	Age of Car Usually Driven				Row Total
	Less than 3	3 to 6	6 to 10	10 or More	
Under 15	9	8	8	4	29
15 to 25	34	17	11	9	71
25 or More	28	20	8	6	62
Col Total	71	45	27	19	162

Figure 14.7 shows MegaStat's analysis of the 3 × 4 contingency table. Two expected frequencies (upper right) are below 5, so Cochran's Rule is not quite met. MegaStat has

FIGURE 14.7   **MegaStat's Analysis of Car Age Data**

Chi-square Contingency Table Test for Independence

		Less than 3	3 to 6	6 to 10	10 or More	Total
Under 15	Observed	**9**	**8**	**8**	**4**	29
	Expected	12.71	8.06	4.83	3.40	29.00
	O − E	−3.71	−0.06	3.17	0.60	0.00
	$(O-E)^2/E$	1.08	0.00	2.07	0.11	3.26
15 to 25	Observed	**34**	**17**	**11**	**9**	71
	Expected	31.12	19.72	11.83	8.33	71.00
	O − E	2.88	−2.72	−0.83	0.67	0.00
	$(O-E)^2/E$	0.27	0.38	0.06	0.05	0.76
25 or More	Observed	**28**	**20**	**8**	**6**	62
	Expected	27.17	17.22	10.33	7.27	62.00
	O − E	0.83	2.78	−2.33	−1.27	0.00
	$(O-E)^2/E$	0.03	0.45	0.53	0.22	1.22
Total	Observed	71	45	27	19	162
	Expected	71.00	45.00	27.00	19.00	162.00
	O − E	0.00	0.00	0.00	0.00	0.00
	$(O-E)^2/E$	1.38	0.82	2.66	0.38	5.24

5.24	chi-square
6	df
.5132	p-value

highlighted these cells to call attention to this concern. But the most striking feature of this table is that almost all of the actual frequencies are very close to the frequencies expected under the hypothesis of independence, leading to a very small chi-square test statistic (5.24). The test requires six degrees of freedom, i.e. $\nu = (r-1)(c-1) = (3-1)(4-1) = 6$. From Appendix E we obtain the right-tail critical value $\chi^2_{.10} = 10.64$ at $\alpha = .10$. Even at this rather weak level of significance, we cannot reject H_0. MegaStat's *p*-value (.5132) says that a test statistic of this magnitude could arise by chance more than half the time in samples from a population in which the two variables really were independent. Hence, the data lend no support to the hypothesis that students work longer hours to support newer cars.

Purpose of the Test

A **goodness-of-fit test** (or GOF test) is used to help you decide whether your sample resembles a particular kind of population. The chi-square test can be used to compare sample frequencies with any probability distribution. Tests for goodness-of-fit are easy to understand, but until spreadsheets came along, the calculations were tedious. Today, computers make it easy, and tests for departure from normality or any other distribution are routine. We will first illustrate the GOF test using the most general type of distribution. A **multinomial distribution** is defined by any k probabilities $\pi_1, \pi_2, \ldots, \pi_k$ that sum to one. You can apply this same technique for the three familiar distributions we have already studied (uniform, Poisson, and normal). Although there are many tests for goodness-of-fit, the chi-square test is attractive because it is versatile and easy to understand.

14.2
CHI-SQUARE TESTS FOR GOODNESS-OF-FIT

Chapter 13

Example of Multinomial GOF Test: M&M Colors

According to the "official" M&M Web site* the distribution of M&M colors is:

Brown (13%)   Red (13%)   Blue (24%)
Orange (20%)   Yellow (16%)   Green (14%)

But do bags of M&Ms shipped to retailers actually follow this distribution? We will use a sample of four bags of candy and conduct a chi-square GOF test. We will assume the distribution is the same as stated on the Web site *unless the sample shows us otherwise.*

Hypotheses

The hypotheses are:

H_0: $\pi_{\text{brown}} = .13$, $\pi_{\text{red}} = .13$, $\pi_{\text{blue}} = .24$, $\pi_{\text{orange}} = .20$, $\pi_{\text{yellow}} = .16$, $\pi_{\text{green}} = .14$

H_1: At least one of the π's differs from the hypothesized value

To test these hypotheses, statistics students opened four bags of M&Ms ($n = 220$ pieces) and counted the number of each color, with the results shown in Table 14.6. We assign an index to

Color	Official π_j	Observed f_j	Expected $e_j = n \times \pi_j$	$f_j - e_j$	$(f_j - e_j)^2/e_j$
Brown	0.13	38	28.6	+9.4	3.0895
Red	0.13	30	28.6	+1.4	0.0685
Blue	0.24	44	52.8	−8.8	1.4667
Orange	0.20	52	44.0	+8.0	1.4545
Green	0.16	30	35.2	−5.2	0.7682
Yellow	0.14	26	30.8	−4.8	0.7481
Sum	1.00	220	220.0	0.0	$\chi^2_{\text{calc}} = 7.5955$

TABLE 14.6

Hypothesis Test of M&M Proportions
MM

*The official Web site for M&M candies is http://us.mms.com/us/about/products/milkchocolate/. These proportions were taken from their Web site during June 2006.

each of the six colors ($j = 1, 2, \ldots, 6$) and define:

$f_j =$ the actual frequency of M&Ms of color j

$e_j =$ the expected frequency of M&Ms of color j assuming that H_0 is true

Each expected frequency (e_j) is calculated by multiplying the sample size (n) by the hypothesized proportion (π_j). We can now calculate a chi-square test statistic that compares the actual and expected frequencies:

(14.4)
$$\chi^2_{calc} = \sum_{j=1}^{c} \frac{[f_j - e_j]^2}{e_j}$$

If the proposed distribution gives a good fit to the sample, the chi-square statistic will be near zero because f_j and e_j will be approximately equal. Conversely, if f_j and e_j differ greatly, the chi-square statistic will be large. It is always a right-tail test. We will reject H_0 if the test statistic exceeds the chi-square critical value chosen from Appendix E. For any GOF test, the rule for degrees of freedom is:

(14.5)
$$\nu = c - m - 1$$

where c is the number of classes used in the test and m is the number of parameters estimated.

Results of the Test

Table 14.6 summarizes the calculations in a worksheet. No parameters were estimated ($m = 0$) and we have six classes ($c = 6$), so degrees of freedom are:

$$\nu = c - m - 1 = 6 - 0 - 1 = 5$$

From Appendix E, the critical value of chi-square for $\alpha = .01$ is $\chi^2_{.01} = 15.09$. Since the test statistic $\chi^2_{calc} = 7.5955$ (from Table 14.6) is smaller than the critical value, we cannot reject the hypothesis that the M&M's color distribution is as stated on the M&M Web site. Notice that the f_j and e_j *always* sum exactly to the sample size ($n = 220$ in this example) and the differences $f_j - e_j$ must sum to zero. If not, you have made a mistake in your calculations—a useful way to check your work.

Small Expected Frequencies

Goodness-of-fit tests may lack power in small samples. Further, small expected frequencies tend to inflate the χ^2 test statistic because e_j is in the denominator of formula 14.4. The minimum necessary sample size depends on the type of test being employed. As a guideline, a chi-square goodness-of-fit test should be avoided if $n < 25$ (some experts would suggest a higher number). Cochran's Rule that expected frequencies should be at least 5 (i.e., all $e_j \geq 5$) also provides a guideline, although some experts would weaken the rule to require only $e_j \geq 2$. In the M&M example, the expected frequencies are all large, so there is no reason to doubt the test.

GOF Tests for Other Distributions

We can also use the chi-square GOF test to compare a sample of data with a familiar distribution such as the uniform, Poisson, or normal. We would state the hypotheses as below:

H_0: The population follows a _____ distribution.

H_1: The population doesn't follow a _____ distribution.

The blank may contain the name of any theoretical distribution. Assuming that we have n observations, we group the observations into c classes and then find the *chi-square test statistic* using formula 14.4. In a GOF test, if we use sample data to *estimate* the distribution's parameters then our degrees of freedom would be as follows:

(14.6)   **Uniform:** $\nu = c - m - 1 = c - 0 - 1 = c - 1$ (no parameters are estimated)

(14.7)   **Poisson:** $\nu = c - m - 1 = c - 1 - 1 = c - 2$ (if λ is estimated)

(14.8)   **Normal:** $\nu = c - m - 1 = c - 2 - 1 = c - 3$ (if μ and σ are estimated)

Uniform Distribution

The uniform goodness-of-fit test is a special case of the multinomial in which every value has the same chance of occurrence. Uniform data-generating situations are rare, but some data *must* be from a **uniform distribution**, such as winning lottery numbers or random digits generated by a computer for random sampling. Another use of the uniform distribution is as a worst case scenario for an unknown distribution whose range is specified in a what-if analysis.

The chi-square test for a uniform distribution is a generalization of the test for equality of two proportions. The hypotheses are:

$H_0: \pi_1 = \pi_2 = \cdots = \pi_c = 1/c$

H_1: Not all the π_j are equal

The chi-square test compares all c groups *simultaneously.* Each discrete outcome should have probability $1/c$, so the test is very easy to perform. Evidence against H_0 would consist of sample frequencies that were not the same for all categories.

Classes need not represent numerical values. For example, we might compare the total number of items scanned per hour by four supermarket checkers (Bob, Frieda, Sam, and Wanda). The uniform test is quite versatile. For numerical variables, bins do not have to be of equal width and can be open-ended. For example, we might be interested in the ages of X-ray machines in a hospital (under 2 years, 2 to 5 years, 5 to 10 years, 10 years and over). In a uniform population, each category would be expected to have $e_j = n/c$ observations, so the calculation of expected frequencies is simple.

Uniform GOF Test: Grouped Data

The test is easiest if data are already tabulated into groups, which saves us the effort of defining the groups. For example, one year, a certain state had 756 traffic fatalities. Table 14.7 suggests that fatalities are not uniformly distributed by day of week, being higher on weekends. Can we reject the hypothesis of a uniform distribution, say, at $\alpha = .005$? The hypotheses are:

H_0: Traffic fatalities are uniformly distributed by day of the week

H_1: Traffic fatalities are not uniformly distributed by day of the week

Day	f_j	e_j	$f_j - e_j$	$(f_j - e_j)^2$	$(f_j - e_j)^2/e_j$
Sun	121	108	13	169	1.565
Mon	96	108	−12	144	1.333
Tue	91	108	−17	289	2.676
Wed	92	108	−16	256	2.370
Thu	96	108	−12	144	1.333
Fri	122	108	14	196	1.815
Sat	138	108	30	900	8.333
Total	756	756	0		$\chi^2_{calc} = 19.426$

TABLE 14.7

Traffic Fatalities by Day of Week   Traffic

Source: Based on www-nrd.nhtsa.dot.gov.

Under H_0 the expected frequency for each weekday is $e_j = n/c = 756/7 = 108$. The expected frequencies happen to be integers, although this is not true in general. Since no parameters were estimated ($m = 0$) to form the seven classes ($c = 7$) the chi-square test will have $v = c - m - 1 = 7 - 0 - 1 = 6$ degrees of freedom. From Appendix E the critical value of chi-square for the 1 percent level of significance is $\chi^2_{.01} = 16.81$, so the hypothesis of a rectangular or uniform population can be rejected. The *p*-value (.0035) can be obtained from the Excel function =CHIDIST(19.426,6). The *p*-value tells us that such a sample result would occur by chance only about 35 times in 10,000 samples. There is a believable underlying causal mechanism at work (e.g., people may drink and drive more often on weekends).

Data-Generating Situations

"Fishing" for a good-fitting model is inappropriate. Instead, we visualize *a priori* the characteristics of the underlying *data-generating process*. It is undoubtedly true that the most common GOF test is for the normal distribution, simply because so many parametric tests assume normality, and that assumption must be tested. Also, the normal distribution may be used as a default benchmark for any mound-shaped data that has centrality and tapering tails, as long as you have reason to believe that a constant mean and variance would be reasonable (e.g., weights of circulated dimes). However, you would not consider a Poisson distribution for continuous data (e.g., gasoline price per liter) or certain integer variables (e.g., exam scores) because a Poisson model only applies to integer data on arrivals or rare, independent events (e.g., number of paint defects per square meter). We remind you of this because software makes it possible to fit inappropriate distributions all too easily.

Mixtures: A Problem

Your sample may not resemble any known distribution. One common problem is *mixtures*. A sample may have been created by more than one data-generating process superimposed on top of one another. For example, adult heights of either sex would follow a normal distribution, but a combined sample of both genders will be bimodal, and its mean and standard deviation may be unrepresentative of either sex. Obtaining a good fit is not *per se* sufficient justification for assuming a particular model. Each probability distribution has its own logic about the nature of the underlying process, so we must also examine the data-generating situation and be convinced that the proposed model is both logical *and* empirically apt.

Eyeball Tests

A simple "eyeball" inspection of the histogram or dot plot may suffice to rule out a hypothesized population. For example, if the sample is strongly bimodal or skewed, or if outliers are present, we would anticipate a poor fit to a normal distribution. The shape of the histogram can give you a rough idea whether a normal distribution is a likely candidate for a good fit. You can be fairly sure that a formal test will agree with what your common sense tells you, as long as the sample size is not too small.

Yet a limitation of eyeball tests is that we may be unsure just how much variation is expected for a given sample size. If anything, the human eye is overly sensitive, causing us to commit α error (rejecting a true null hypothesis) too often. People are sometimes unduly impressed by a small departure from the hypothesized distribution, when actually it is within chance. We will see examples of this.

SECTION EXERCISES

connect

14.6 Advertisers need to know which age groups are likely to see their ads. Purchasers of 120 copies of *Cosmopolitan* are shown by age group. (a) Make a bar chart and describe it. (b) Assuming a uniform distribution on age groups, calculate expected frequencies for each class. (c) Perform the chi-square test for a uniform distribution. At $\alpha = .01$, does this sample contradict the assumption that readership is uniformly distributed among these six age groups? (See J. Paul Peter and Jerry C. Olson, *Consumer Behavior and Marketing Strategy,* 9th ed. [McGraw-Hill, 2004], p. 300.)
🐦 **Cosmo**

Purchaser Age	Units Sold
18–24	38
25–34	28
35–44	19
45–54	16
55–64	10
65+	9
Total	120

14.7   One-year sales volume of four similar 20-oz. beverages on a college campus is shown. (a) Make a bar chart and describe it. (b) Assuming a uniform distribution on each begerage type, calculate expected frequencies for each class. (c) Perform the chi-square test for a uniform distribution. At $\alpha = .05$, does this sample contradict the assumption that sales are the same for each beverage?
🍹 **Frapp**

Beverage	Sales (Cases)
Frappuccino Coffee	18
Frappuccino Mocha	23
Frappuccino Vanilla	23
Frappuccino Caramel	20
Total	84

14.8   In a three-digit lottery, each of the three digits is supposed to have the same probability of occurrence (counting initial blanks as zeros, e.g., 32 is treated as 032). The table shows the frequency of occurrence of each digit for 90 consecutive daily three-digit drawings. (a) Make a bar chart and describe it. (b) Calculate expected frequencies for each class. (c) Perform the chi-square test for a uniform distribution. At $\alpha = .05$, can you reject the hypothesis that the digits are from a uniform population? 🍹 **Lottery3**

Digit	Frequency
0	33
1	17
2	25
3	30
4	31
5	28
6	24
7	25
8	32
9	25
Total	270

CHAPTER SUMMARY

A **chi-square test of independence** requires an $r \times c$ **contingency table** that has r rows and c columns. Degrees of freedom for the chi-square test will be $(r - 1)(c - 1)$. In this test, the **observed frequencies** are compared with the **expected frequencies** under the hypothesis of independence. The test assumes categorical data (attribute data) but can also be used with numerical data grouped into classes. **Cochran's Rule** requires that expected frequencies be at least 5 in each cell, although this rule is often relaxed. A test for **goodness-of-fit (GOF)** uses the chi-square statistic to decide whether a sample is from a specified distribution (e.g., multinomial, uniform, Poisson, normal). The **parameters** of the fitted distribution (e.g., the mean) may be specified *a priori,* but more often are estimated from the sample. Degrees of freedom for the GOF test are $c - m - 1$ where c is the number of categories and m is the number of parameters estimated.

KEY TERMS

chi-square probability distribution, *537*
chi-square test, *536*
Cochran's Rule, *541*

contingency table, *535*
degrees of freedom, *537*
expected frequency, *536*
goodness-of-fit test, *545*

independent, *536*
multinomial distribution, *545*
observed frequency, *536*
uniform distribution, *547*

Commonly Used Formulas ●

Chi-Square Test for Independence

Test statistic for independence in a contingency table with r rows

and c columns: $\chi^2_{calc} = \sum_{j=1}^{r} \sum_{k=1}^{c} \frac{[f_{jk} - e_{jk}]^2}{e_{jk}}$

Degrees of freedom for a contingency table with r rows and c columns: $v = (r - 1)(c - 1)$

Expected frequency in row j and column k: $e_{jk} = R_j C_k / n$

Chi-Square Test for Goodness-of-Fit

Test statistic for observed frequencies in c classes under an hypothesized distribution

H_0 (e.g., uniform, Poisson, normal): $\chi_{calc}^2 = \sum_{j=1}^{c} \frac{[f_j - e_j]^2}{e_j}$

where

f_j = the observed frequency in class j

e_j = the expected frequency in class j

Degrees of freedom for the chi-square GOF test: $v = c - m - 1$

where

c = the number of classes used in the test

m = the number of parameters estimated

Expected frequency in class j assuming a uniform distribution with c classes: $e_j = n/c$

CHAPTER REVIEW

1. (a) What are the hypotheses in a chi-square test for independence? (b) Why do we call it a test of frequencies? (c) What distribution is used in this test? (d) How do we calculate the degrees of freedom for an $r \times c$ contingency table?

2. How do we calculate the expected frequencies for each cell of the contingency table?

3. What is Cochran's Rule, and why is it needed? Why do we call it a "rule of thumb"?

4. (a) What are the hypotheses for a GOF test? (b) Explain how a chi-square GOF test is carried out in general.

5. What is the general formula for degrees of freedom in a chi-square GOF test?

6. (a) In a uniform GOF test, how do we calculate the expected frequencies? (b) Why is the test easier if the data are already grouped?

CHAPTER EXERCISES

connect

Instructions: In all exercises, include MegaStat, Excel, or MINITAB exhibits to support your calculations. State the hypotheses, show how the degrees of freedom are calculated, find the critical value of chi-square from Appendix E or from Excel's function =CHIINV(alpha, deg_freedom), and interpret the *p*-value. Tell whether the conclusion is sensitive to the level of significance chosen, identify cells that contribute the most to the chi-square test statistic, and check for small expected frequencies. If necessary, you can calculate the *p*-value by using Excel's function =CHIDIST(test statistic,deg_freedom).

14.9   Employees of Axolotl Corporation were sampled at random from pay records and asked to complete an anonymous job satisfaction survey, yielding the tabulation shown. *Research question:* At $\alpha = .05$, is job satisfaction independent of pay category?   **Employees**

Pay Type	Satisfied	Neutral	Dissatisfied	Total
Salaried	20	13	2	35
Hourly	135	127	58	320
Total	155	140	60	355

14.10 Sixty-four students in an introductory college economics class were asked how many credits they had earned in college, and how certain they were about their choice of major. *Research question:* At $\alpha = .01$, is the degree of certainty independent of credits earned?   **Certainty**

Credits Earned	Very Uncertain	Somewhat Certain	Very Certain	Row Total
0–9	12	8	3	23
10–59	8	4	10	22
60 or more	1	7	11	19
Col Total	21	19	24	64

14.11 To see whether students who finish an exam first get the same grades as those who finish later, a professor kept track of the order in which papers were handed in. Of the first 25 papers, 10 received a "B" or better compared with 8 of the last 24 papers handed in. *Research question:* At $\alpha = .10$, is the grade independent of the order handed in? **Grades**

Grade	Earlier Hand-In	Later Hand-In	Row Total
"B" or better	10	8	18
"C" or worse	15	16	31
Col Total	25	24	49

14.12 From 74 of its restaurants, Noodles & Company managers collected data on per-person sales and the percent of sales due to "potstickers" (a popular food item). Both numerical variables failed tests for normality, so they tried a chi-square test. Each variable was converted into ordinal categories (low, medium, high) using cutoff points that produced roughly equal group sizes. *Research question:* At $\alpha = .05$, is per-person spending independent of percent of sales from potstickers? **Noodles**

	Potsticker % of Sales			
Per person Spending	Low	Medium	High	Row Total
Low	14	7	3	24
Medium	7	15	6	28
High	3	4	15	22
Col Total	24	26	24	74

14.13 A Web-based anonymous survey of students asked for a self-rating on proficiency in a language other than English and the student's frequency of newspaper reading. *Research question:* At $\alpha = .10$, is frequency of newspaper reading independent of foreign language proficiency? **WebSurvey**

	Daily Newspaper Reading			
Non-English Proficiency	Never	Occasionally	Regularly	Row Total
None	4	13	5	22
Slight	11	45	9	65
Moderate	6	33	7	46
Fluent	5	19	1	25
Col Total	26	110	22	158

14.14 A student team examined parked cars in four different suburban shopping malls. One hundred vehicles were examined in each location. *Research question:* At $\alpha = .05$, does vehicle type vary by mall location? (Data are from a project by MBA students Steve Bennett, Alicia Morais, Steve Olson, and Greg Corda.) **Vehicles**

Vehicle Type	Somerset	Oakland	Great Lakes	Jamestown	Row Total
Car	44	49	36	64	193
Minivan	21	15	18	13	67
Full-sized Van	2	3	3	2	10
SUV	19	27	26	12	84
Truck	14	6	17	9	46
Col Total	100	100	100	100	400

14.15 Choose either 2 × 2 contingency table shown below (males *or* females). *Research question:* At $\alpha = .005$, is smoking independent of race? (Smoking rates are from *Statistical Abstract of the United States, 2001,* pp. 16 and 12, applied to hypothetical samples of 500.) **Smoking**

Smoking by Race for Males Aged 18–24

Race	Smoker	Nonsmoker	Row Total
White	145	280	425
Black	15	60	75
Col Total	160	340	500

Smoking by Race for Females Aged 18–24

Race	Smoker	Nonsmoker	Row Total
White	116	299	415
Black	7	78	85
Col Total	123	377	500

14.16 High levels of cockpit noise in an aircraft can damage the hearing of pilots who are exposed to this hazard for many hours. A Boeing 727 co-pilot collected 61 noise observations using a handheld sound meter. Noise level is defined as "Low" (under 88 decibels), "Medium" (88 to 91 decibels), or "High" (92 decibels or more). There are three flight phases (Climb, Cruise, Descent). *Research question:* At $\alpha = .05$, is the cockpit noise level independent of flight phase? (Data are from Capt. Robert E. Hartl, retired.) **Noise**

Noise Level	Climb	Cruise	Descent	Row Total
Low	6	2	6	14
Medium	18	3	8	29
High	1	3	14	18
Col Total	25	8	28	61

14.17 Forecasters' interest rate predictions over the period 1982–1990 were studied to see whether the predictions corresponded to what actually happened. The 2 × 2 contingency table below shows the frequencies of actual and predicted interest rate movements. *Research question:* At $\alpha = .10$, is the actual change independent of the predicted change? (Data are from R. A. Kolb and H. O. Steckler, "How Well Do Analysts Forecast Interest Rates?" *Journal of Forecasting* 15, no. 15 [1996], pp. 385–394.) **Forecasts**

Forecasted Change	Rates Fell	Rates Rose	Row Total
Rates would fall	7	12	19
Rates would rise	9	6	15
Col Total	16	18	34

14.18 In a study of childhood asthma, 4,317 observations were collected on education and smoking during pregnancy, shown in the 4 × 3 contingency table below. *Research question:* At $\alpha = .005$, is smoking during pregnancy independent of education level? (Data are from Michael Weitzman and Deborah Klein Walker, "Maternal Smoking and Asthma," *Pediatrics* 85, no. 4 [April 1990], p. 507.)   **Pregnancy**

Education	No Smoking	$<\frac{1}{2}$ Pack	$\geq\frac{1}{2}$ Pack	Row Total
<High School	641	196	196	1,033
High School	1,370	290	270	1,930
Some College	635	68	53	756
College	550	30	18	598
Col Total	3,196	584	537	4,317

14.19 Two contingency tables below show return on investment (ROI) and percent of sales growth over the previous 5 years for 85 U.S. firms. ROI is defined as percentage of return on a combination of stockholders' equity (both common and preferred) plus capital from long-term debt including current maturities, minority stockholders' equity in consolidated subsidiaries, and accumulated deferred taxes and investment tax credits. *Research question:* At $\alpha = .05$, is ROI independent of sales growth? Would you expect it to be? Do the two tables (2 × 2 and 3 × 3) agree? Are small expected frequencies a problem? (Data are adapted from a research project by MBA student B. J. Oline.)   **ROI**

2 × 2 Cross-Tabulation of Companies

ROI	Low Growth	High Growth	Row Total
Low ROI	24	16	40
High ROI	14	31	45
Col Total	38	47	85

3 × 3 Cross-Tabulation of Companies

ROI	Low Growth	Medium Growth	High Growth	Row Total
Low ROI	9	12	7	28
Medium ROI	6	14	7	27
High ROI	1	12	17	30
Col Total	16	38	31	85

14.20 Can people really identify their favorite brand of cola? Volunteers tasted Coca-Cola Classic, Pepsi, Diet Coke, and Diet Pepsi, with the results shown below. *Research question:* At $\alpha = .05$, is the correctness of the prediction different for the two types of cola drinkers? Could *you* identify your favorite brand in this kind of test? (Data are from *Consumer Reports* 56, no. 8 [August 1991], p. 519.)   **Cola**

Correct?	Regular Cola	Diet Cola	Row Total
Yes, got it right	7	7	14
No, got it wrong	12	20	32
Col Total	19	27	46

14.21 A survey of randomly chosen new students at a certain university revealed the data below concerning the main reason for choosing this university instead of another. *Research question:* At $\alpha = .01$, is the main reason for choosing the university independent of student type?   **Students**

New Student	Tuition	Location	Reputation	Row Total
Freshmen	50	30	35	115
Transfers	15	29	20	64
MBAs	5	20	60	85
Col Total	70	79	115	264

14.22 A survey of 189 statistics students asked the age of car usually driven and the student's political orientation. The car age was a numerical variable, which was converted into ordinal categories. *Research question:* At $\alpha = .10$, are students' political views independent of the age of car they usually drive? 🎣 **Politics**

	Age of Car Usually Driven			
Politics	Under 3	3–6	7 or More	Row Total
Liberal	19	12	13	44
Middle-of-Road	33	31	28	92
Conservative	16	24	13	53
Col Total	68	67	54	189

14.23 Here is a table showing the season in which the first 36 U.S. presidents died. *Research question:* At $\alpha = .10$, can you reject the hypothesis that presidents' deaths are uniformly distributed by season? (Data are from *The World Almanac and Book of Facts, 2002,* pp. 545–556.) 🎣 **Presidents-A**

Month of Demise	Deaths
January–March	11
April–June	9
July–September	10
October–December	6
Total	36

14.24 Prof. Green's multiple-choice exam had 50 questions with the distribution of correct answers shown below. *Research question:* At $\alpha = .05$, can you reject the hypothesis that Green's exam answers came from a uniform population? 🎣 **Correct**

Correct Answer	Frequency
A	8
B	8
C	9
D	11
E	14
Total	50

14.25 Oxnard Kortholt, Ltd., employs 50 workers. During the last year, the company noted the number of visits with health care professionals (doctor, emergency, home) for each of its employees. U.S. national averages are shown. *Research question:* At $\alpha = .05$, do Oxnard employees differ significantly from the national percent distribution? (National averages are from *The World Almanac and Book of Facts, 2005* [World Almanac Education Group, Inc., 2005], p. 180.) 🎣 **Oxnard**

Health Care Visits	National Average (%)	Oxnard Employees (%)
No visits	16.5	4
1–3 visits	45.8	20
4–9 visits	24.4	15
10 or more visits	13.3	11
Total	100.0	50

14.26 In a four-digit lottery, each of the four digits is supposed to have the same probability of occurrence. The table shows the frequency of occurrence of each digit for 89 consecutive daily four-digit drawings. *Research question:* At $\alpha = .01$, can you reject the hypothesis that the digits are from a uniform population? Why do the frequencies add to 356? 🖭 **Lottery4**

Digit	Frequency
0	39
1	27
2	35
3	39
4	35
5	35
6	27
7	42
8	36
9	41
Total	356

14.27 A student rolled a supposedly fair die 60 times, resulting in the distribution of dots shown. *Research question:* At $\alpha = .10$, can you reject the hypothesis that the die is fair? 🖭 **Dice**

			Number of Dots				
	1	*2*	*3*	*4*	*5*	*6*	*Total*
Frequency	7	14	9	13	7	10	60

RELATED READING

Bowman, K. O.; and L. R. Shenton. "Omnibus Test Contours for Departures from Normality Based on β_1 and β_2." *Biometrika* 62, no. 2 (1975), pp. 243–50.

Conover, William J. "Some Reasons for Not Using the Yates Continuity Correction on 2×2 Contingency Tables." *Journal of the American Statistical Association* 69 (1974), pp. 374–76.

D'Agostino, Ralph B.; and Michael A. Stephens. *Goodness-of-Fit Techniques.* Marcel Dekker, 1986.

Haber, Michael. "A Comparison of Some Continuity Corrections for the Chi-Squared Test on 2×2 Tables." *Journal of the American Statistical Association* 75, no. 371 (1980), pp. 510–14.

Mantel, Nathan. "The Continuity Correction." *The American Statistician* 30, no. 2 (May 1976), pp. 103–104.

Thode, Henry C., Jr. *Testing for Normality.* Marcel Dekker, 2002.

LearningStats Unit 15   Chi-Square Tests

LearningStats Unit 15 explains the chi-square test for independence in contingency tables and illustrates goodness-of-fit tests for uniform, Poisson, and normal distributions. Attention is also given to other tests for normality based on ECDF plots. Your instructor may assign a specific module, but you can work on the others if they sound interesting.

Topic	LearningStats Modules
Overview	▣ Chi-Square Test for Independence ▣ Goodness-of-Fit Tests
Chi-square tests on contingency tables	▨ Effects of Table Size ▨ Simulation and Type I Error ▨ Using Raw Data
Goodness-of-fit tests	▨ Normal and Uniform Tests ▨ Uniform Tests: Choosing Letters ▨ Uniform Tests: World Series Runs ▨ ECDF Plots Illustrated ▨ Probability Plots: A Simulation ▨ CDF Normality Test ▨ Degrees of Freedom ▨ How Big a Sample ▤ Student GOF Project
@Risk Projects	▨ Table of Chi-Square Critical Values

Key: ▣ = PowerPoint   ▤ = Word   ▨ = Excel

Visual Statistics

VS

Visual Statistics Goodness-of-Fit and Independence Tests

Module	Module Name
13	VS Visualizing Goodness-of-Fit Tests
14	VS Visualizing Bivariate Data Analysis

Visual Statistics Modules 13 and 14 (included on your CD) are designed to help you

- Know how to use and interpret a chi-square test for independence in cross-tabulated data.
- Recognize characteristics of data-generating situations that suggest appropriate distributions to fit.
- Interpret common data displays that may reveal whether a specified distribution is appropriate.
- Learn how the chi-square goodness-of-fit test works and how class formation affects it.
- Recognize limitations of the chi-square goodness-of-fit test and alternatives that are available.
- Use visual and analytical ECDF-based tests for goodness-of-fit and compare them with chi-square.

The worktext (included on the CD in .PDF format) contains a list of concepts covered, objectives of the module, overview of concepts, illustration of concepts, orientation to module features, learning exercises (basic, intermediate, advanced), learning projects (individual, team), self-evaluation quiz, glossary of terms, and solutions to self-evaluation quiz.

APPENDIX A

EXACT BINOMIAL PROBABILITIES

n	X	.01	.02	.05	.10	.15	.20	.30	.40	.50	.60	.70	.80	.85	.90	.95	.98	.99
2	0	.9801	.9604	.9025	.8100	.7225	.6400	.4900	.3600	.2500	.1600	.0900	.0400	.0225	.0100	.0025	.0004	.0001
	1	.0198	.0392	.0950	.1800	.2550	.3200	.4200	.4800	.5000	.4800	.4200	.3200	.2550	.1800	.0950	.0392	.0198
	2	.0001	.0004	.0025	.0100	.0225	.0400	.0900	.1600	.2500	.3600	.4900	.6400	.7225	.8100	.9025	.9604	.9801
3	0	.9703	.9412	.8574	.7290	.6141	.5120	.3430	.2160	.1250	.0640	.0270	.0080	.0034	.0010	.0001	—	—
	1	.0294	.0576	.1354	.2430	.3251	.3840	.4410	.4320	.3750	.2880	.1890	.0960	.0574	.0270	.0071	.0012	.0003
	2	.0003	.0012	.0071	.0270	.0574	.0960	.1890	.2880	.3750	.4320	.4410	.3840	.3251	.2430	.1354	.0576	.0294
	3	—	—	.0001	.0010	.0034	.0080	.0270	.0640	.1250	.2160	.3430	.5120	.6141	.7290	.8574	.9412	.9703
4	0	.9606	.9224	.8145	.6561	.5220	.4096	.2401	.1296	.0625	.0256	.0081	.0016	.0005	.0001	—	—	—
	1	.0388	.0753	.1715	.2916	.3685	.4096	.4116	.3456	.2500	.1536	.0756	.0256	.0115	.0036	.0005	—	—
	2	.0006	.0023	.0135	.0486	.0975	.1536	.2646	.3456	.3750	.3456	.2646	.1536	.0975	.0486	.0135	.0023	.0006
	3	—	—	.0005	.0036	.0115	.0256	.0756	.1536	.2500	.3456	.4116	.4096	.3685	.2916	.1715	.0753	.0388
	4	—	—	—	.0001	.0005	.0016	.0081	.0256	.0625	.1296	.2401	.4096	.5220	.6561	.8145	.9224	.9606
5	0	.9510	.9039	.7738	.5905	.4437	.3277	.1681	.0778	.0313	.0102	.0024	.0003	.0001	—	—	—	—
	1	.0480	.0922	.2036	.3281	.3915	.4096	.3602	.2592	.1563	.0768	.0284	.0064	.0022	.0005	—	—	—
	2	.0010	.0038	.0214	.0729	.1382	.2048	.3087	.3456	.3125	.2304	.1323	.0512	.0244	.0081	.0011	.0001	—
	3	—	.0001	.0011	.0081	.0244	.0512	.1323	.2304	.3125	.3456	.3087	.2048	.1382	.0729	.0214	.0038	.0010
	4	—	—	.0005	.0022	.0064	.0284	.0768	.1563	.2592	.3602	.4096	.3915	.3281	.2036	.0922	.0480
	5	—	—	—	—	.0001	.0003	.0024	.0102	.0313	.0778	.1681	.3277	.4437	.5905	.7738	.9039	.9510
6	0	.9415	.8858	.7351	.5314	.3771	.2621	.1176	.0467	.0156	.0041	.0007	.0001	—	—	—	—	—
	1	.0571	.1085	.2321	.3543	.3993	.3932	.3025	.1866	.0938	.0369	.0102	.0015	.0004	.0001	—	—	—
	2	.0014	.0055	.0305	.0984	.1762	.2458	.3241	.3110	.2344	.1382	.0595	.0154	.0055	.0012	.0001	—	—
	3	—	.0002	.0021	.0146	.0415	.0819	.1852	.2765	.3125	.2765	.1852	.0819	.0415	.0146	.0021	.0002	—
	4	—	—	.0001	.0012	.0055	.0154	.0595	.1382	.2344	.3110	.3241	.2458	.1762	.0984	.0305	.0055	.0014
	5	—	—	—	.0001	.0004	.0015	.0102	.0369	.0938	.1866	.3025	.3932	.3993	.3543	.2321	.1085	.0571
	6	—	—	—	—	—	.0001	.0007	.0041	.0156	.0467	.1176	.2621	.3771	.5314	.7351	.8858	.9415
7	0	.9321	.8681	.6983	.4783	.3206	.2097	.0824	.0280	.0078	.0016	.0002	—	—	—	—	—	—
	1	.0659	.1240	.2573	.3720	.3960	.3670	.2471	.1306	.0547	.0172	.0036	.0004	.0001	—	—	—	—
	2	.0020	.0076	.0406	.1240	.2097	.2753	.3177	.2613	.1641	.0774	.0250	.0043	.0012	.0002	—	—	—
	3	—	.0003	.0036	.0230	.0617	.1147	.2269	.2903	.2734	.1935	.0972	.0287	.0109	.0026	.0002	—	—
	4	—	—	.0002	.0026	.0109	.0287	.0972	.1935	.2734	.2903	.2269	.1147	.0617	.0230	.0036	.0003	—
	5	—	—	—	.0002	.0012	.0043	.0250	.0774	.1641	.2613	.3177	.2753	.2097	.1240	.0406	.0076	.0020
	6	—	—	—	—	.0001	.0004	.0036	.0172	.0547	.1306	.2471	.3670	.3960	.3720	.2573	.1240	.0659
	7	—	—	—	—	—	—	.0002	.0016	.0078	.0280	.0824	.2097	.3206	.4783	.6983	.8681	.9321
8	0	.9227	.8508	.6634	.4305	.2725	.1678	.0576	.0168	.0039	.0007	.0001	—	—	—	—	—	—
	1	.0746	.1389	.2793	.3826	.3847	.3355	.1977	.0896	.0313	.0079	.0012	.0001	—	—	—	—	—
	2	.0026	.0099	.0515	.1488	.2376	.2936	.2965	.2090	.1094	.0413	.0100	.0011	.0002	—	—	—	—
	3	.0001	.0004	.0054	.0331	.0839	.1468	.2541	.2787	.2188	.1239	.0467	.0092	.0026	.0004	—	—	—
	4	—	—	.0004	.0046	.0185	.0459	.1361	.2322	.2734	.2322	.1361	.0459	.0185	.0046	.0004	—	—
	5	—	—	—	.0004	.0026	.0092	.0467	.1239	.2188	.2787	.2541	.1468	.0839	.0331	.0054	.0004	.0001
	6	—	—	—	—	.0002	.0011	.0100	.0413	.1094	.2090	.2965	.2936	.2376	.1488	.0515	.0099	.0026
	7	—	—	—	—	—	.0001	.0012	.0079	.0313	.0896	.1977	.3355	.3847	.3826	.2793	.1389	.0746
	8	—	—	—	—	—	—	.0001	.0007	.0039	.0168	.0576	.1678	.2725	.4305	.6634	.8508	.9227
9	0	.9135	.8337	.6302	.3874	.2316	.1342	.0404	.0101	.0020	.0003	—	—	—	—	—	—	—
	1	.0830	.1531	.2985	.3874	.3679	.3020	.1556	.0605	.0176	.0035	.0004	—	—	—	—	—	—
	2	.0034	.0125	.0629	.1722	.2597	.3020	.2668	.1612	.0703	.0212	.0039	.0003	—	—	—	—	—
	3	.0001	.0006	.0077	.0446	.1069	.1762	.2668	.2508	.1641	.0743	.0210	.0028	.0006	.0001	—	—	—
	4	—	—	.0006	.0074	.0283	.0661	.1715	.2508	.2461	.1672	.0735	.0165	.0050	.0008	—	—	—
	5	—	—	—	.0008	.0050	.0165	.0735	.1672	.2461	.2508	.1715	.0661	.0283	.0074	.0006	—	—
	6	—	—	—	.0001	.0006	.0028	.0210	.0743	.1641	.2508	.2668	.1762	.1069	.0446	.0077	.0006	.0001
	7	—	—	—	—	—	.0003	.0039	.0212	.0703	.1612	.2668	.3020	.2597	.1722	.0629	.0125	.0034
	8	—	—	—	—	—	—	.0004	.0035	.0176	.0605	.1556	.3020	.3679	.3874	.2985	.1531	.0830
	9	—	—	—	—	—	—	—	.0003	.0020	.0101	.0404	.1342	.2316	.3874	.6302	.8337	.9135

π

n	X	.01	.02	.05	.10	.15	.20	.30	.40	.50	.60	.70	.80	.85	.90	.95	.98	.99
10	0	.9044	.8171	.5987	.3487	.1969	.1074	.0282	.0060	.0010	.0001	—	—	—	—	—	—	—
	1	.0914	.1667	.3151	.3874	.3474	.2684	.1211	.0403	.0098	.0016	.0001	—	—	—	—	—	—
	2	.0042	.0153	.0746	.1937	.2759	.3020	.2335	.1209	.0439	.0106	.0014	.0001	—	—	—	—	—
	3	.0001	.0008	.0105	.0574	.1298	.2013	.2668	.2150	.1172	.0425	.0090	.0008	.0001	—	—	—	—
	4	—	—	.0010	.0112	.0401	.0881	.2001	.2508	.2051	.1115	.0368	.0055	.0012	.0001	—	—	—
	5	—	—	.0001	.0015	.0085	.0264	.1029	.2007	.2461	.2007	.1029	.0264	.0085	.0015	.0001	—	—
	6	—	—	—	.0001	.0012	.0055	.0368	.1115	.2051	.2508	.2001	.0881	.0401	.0112	.0010	—	—
	7	—	—	—	—	.0001	.0008	.0090	.0425	.1172	.2150	.2668	.2013	.1298	.0574	.0105	.0008	.0001
	8	—	—	—	—	—	.0001	.0014	.0106	.0439	.1209	.2335	.3020	.2759	.1937	.0746	.0153	.0042
	9	—	—	—	—	—	—	.0001	.0016	.0098	.0403	.1211	.2684	.3474	.3874	.3151	.1667	.0914
	10	—	—	—	—	—	—	—	.0001	.0010	.0060	.0282	.1074	.1969	.3487	.5987	.8171	.9044
12	0	.8864	.7847	.5404	.2824	.1422	.0687	.0138	.0022	.0002	—	—	—	—	—	—	—	—
	1	.1074	.1922	.3413	.3766	.3012	.2062	.0712	.0174	.0029	.0003	—	—	—	—	—	—	—
	2	.0060	.0216	.0988	.2301	.2924	.2835	.1678	.0639	.0161	.0025	.0002	—	—	—	—	—	—
	3	.0002	.0015	.0173	.0852	.1720	.2362	.2397	.1419	.0537	.0125	.0015	.0001	—	—	—	—	—
	4	—	.0001	.0021	.0213	.0683	.1329	.2311	.2128	.1208	.0420	.0078	.0005	.0001	—	—	—	—
	5	—	—	.0002	.0038	.0193	.0532	.1585	.2270	.1934	.1009	.0291	.0033	.0006	—	—	—	—
	6	—	—	—	.0005	.0040	.0155	.0792	.1766	.2256	.1766	.0792	.0155	.0040	.0005	—	—	—
	7	—	—	—	—	.0006	.0033	.0291	.1009	.1934	.2270	.1585	.0532	.0193	.0038	.0002	—	—
	8	—	—	—	—	.0001	.0005	.0078	.0420	.1208	.2128	.2311	.1329	.0683	.0213	.0021	.0001	—
	9	—	—	—	—	—	.0001	.0015	.0125	.0537	.1419	.2397	.2362	.1720	.0852	.0173	.0015	.0002
	10	—	—	—	—	—	—	.0002	.0025	.0161	.0639	.1678	.2835	.2924	.2301	.0988	.0216	.0060
	11	—	—	—	—	—	—	—	.0003	.0029	.0174	.0712	.2062	.3012	.3766	.3413	.1922	.1074
	12	—	—	—	—	—	—	—	—	.0002	.0022	.0138	.0687	.1422	.2824	.5404	.7847	.8864
14	0	.8687	.7536	.4877	.2288	.1028	.0440	.0068	.0008	.0001	—	—	—	—	—	—	—	—
	1	.1229	.2153	.3593	.3559	.2539	.1539	.0407	.0073	.0009	.0001	—	—	—	—	—	—	—
	2	.0081	.0286	.1229	.2570	.2912	.2501	.1134	.0317	.0056	.0005	—	—	—	—	—	—	—
	3	.0003	.0023	.0259	.1142	.2056	.2501	.1943	.0845	.0222	.0033	.0002	—	—	—	—	—	—
	4	—	.0001	.0037	.0349	.0998	.1720	.2290	.1549	.0611	.0136	.0014	—	—	—	—	—	—
	5	—	—	.0004	.0078	.0352	.0860	.1963	.2066	.1222	.0408	.0066	.0003	—	—	—	—	—
	6	—	—	—	.0013	.0093	.0322	.1262	.2066	.1833	.0918	.0232	.0020	.0003	—	—	—	—
	7	—	—	—	.0002	.0019	.0092	.0618	.1574	.2095	.1574	.0618	.0092	.0019	.0002	—	—	—
	8	—	—	—	—	.0003	.0020	.0232	.0918	.1833	.2066	.1262	.0322	.0093	.0013	—	—	—
	9	—	—	—	—	—	.0003	.0066	.0408	.1222	.1963	.2290	.1720	.0998	.0349	.0037	.0001	—
	10	—	—	—	—	—	—	.0014	.0136	.0611	.1549	.2290	.2501	.2056	.1142	.0259	.0023	.0003
	11	—	—	—	—	—	—	.0002	.0033	.0222	.0845	.1943	.2501	.2912	.2570	.1229	.0286	.0081
	12	—	—	—	—	—	—	—	.0005	.0056	.0317	.1134	.2501	.2912	.2570	.1229	.0286	.0081
	13	—	—	—	—	—	—	—	.0001	.0009	.0073	.0407	.1539	.2539	.3559	.3593	.2153	.1229
	14	—	—	—	—	—	—	—	—	.0001	.0008	.0068	.0440	.1028	.2288	.4877	.7536	.8687
16	0	.8515	.7238	.4401	.1853	.0743	.0281	.0033	.0003	—	—	—	—	—	—	—	—	—
	1	.1376	.2363	.3706	.3294	.2097	.1126	.0228	.0030	.0002	—	—	—	—	—	—	—	—
	2	.0104	.0362	.1463	.2745	.2775	.2111	.0732	.0150	.0018	.0001	—	—	—	—	—	—	—
	3	.0005	.0034	.0359	.1423	.2285	.2463	.1465	.0468	.0085	.0008	—	—	—	—	—	—	—
	4	—	.0002	.0061	.0514	.1311	.2001	.2040	.1014	.0278	.0040	.0002	—	—	—	—	—	—
	5	—	—	.0008	.0137	.0555	.1201	.2099	.1623	.0667	.0142	.0013	—	—	—	—	—	—
	6	—	—	.0001	.0028	.0180	.0550	.1649	.1983	.1222	.0392	.0056	.0002	—	—	—	—	—
	7	—	—	—	.0004	.0045	.0197	.1010	.1889	.1746	.0840	.0185	.0012	.0001	—	—	—	—
	8	—	—	—	.0001	.0009	.0055	.0487	.1417	.1964	.1417	.0487	.0055	.0009	.0001	—	—	—
	9	—	—	—	—	.0001	.0012	.0185	.0840	.1746	.1889	.1010	.0197	.0045	.0004	—	—	—
	10	—	—	—	—	—	.0002	.0056	.0392	.1222	.1983	.1649	.0550	.0180	.0028	.0001	—	—
	11	—	—	—	—	—	—	.0013	.0142	.0667	.1623	.2099	.1201	.0555	.0137	.0008	—	—
	12	—	—	—	—	—	—	.0002	.0040	.0278	.1014	.2040	.2001	.1311	.0514	.0061	.0002	—
	13	—	—	—	—	—	—	—	.0008	.0085	.0468	.1465	.2463	.2285	.1423	.0359	.0034	.0005
	14	—	—	—	—	—	—	—	.0001	.0018	.0150	.0732	.2111	.2775	.2745	.1463	.0362	.0104
	15	—	—	—	—	—	—	—	—	.0002	.0030	.0228	.1126	.2097	.3294	.3706	.2363	.1376
	16	—	—	—	—	—	—	—	—	—	.0003	.0033	.0281	.0743	.1853	.4401	.7238	.8515

APPENDIX B

EXACT POISSON PROBABILITIES

X	λ 0.1	0.2	0.3	0.4	0.5	0.6	0.7	0.8	0.9	1.0	1.1	1.2	1.3	1.4	1.5
0	.9048	.8187	.7408	.6703	.6065	.5488	.4966	.4493	.4066	.3679	.3329	.3012	.2725	.2466	.2231
1	.0905	.1637	.2222	.2681	.3033	.3293	.3476	.3595	.3659	.3679	.3662	.3614	.3543	.3452	.3347
2	.0045	.0164	.0333	.0536	.0758	.0988	.1217	.1438	.1647	.1839	.2014	.2169	.2303	.2417	.2510
3	.0002	.0011	.0033	.0072	.0126	.0198	.0284	.0383	.0494	.0613	.0738	.0867	.0998	.1128	.1255
4	—	.0001	.0003	.0007	.0016	.0030	.0050	.0077	.0111	.0153	.0203	.0260	.0324	.0395	.0471
5	—	—	—	.0001	.0002	.0004	.0007	.0012	.0020	.0031	.0045	.0062	.0084	.0111	.0141
6	—	—	—	—	—	—	.0001	.0002	.0003	.0005	.0008	.0012	.0018	.0026	.0035
7	—	—	—	—	—	—	—	—	—	.0001	.0001	.0002	.0003	.0005	.0008
8	—	—	—	—	—	—	—	—	—	—	—	—	.0001	.0001	.0001

X	λ 1.6	1.7	1.8	1.9	2.0	2.1	2.2	2.3	2.4	2.5	2.6	2.7	2.8	2.9	3.0
0	.2019	.1827	.1653	.1496	.1353	.1225	.1108	.1003	.0907	.0821	.0743	.0672	.0608	.0550	.0498
1	.3230	.3106	.2975	.2842	.2707	.2572	.2438	.2306	.2177	.2052	.1931	.1815	.1703	.1596	.1494
2	.2584	.2640	.2678	.2700	.2707	.2700	.2681	.2652	.2613	.2565	.2510	.2450	.2384	.2314	.2240
3	.1378	.1496	.1607	.1710	.1804	.1890	.1966	.2033	.2090	.2138	.2176	.2205	.2225	.2237	.2240
4	.0551	.0636	.0723	.0812	.0902	.0992	.1082	.1169	.1254	.1336	.1414	.1488	.1557	.1622	.1680
5	.0176	.0216	.0260	.0309	.0361	.0417	.0476	.0538	.0602	.0668	.0735	.0804	.0872	.0940	.1008
6	.0047	.0061	.0078	.0098	.0120	.0146	.0174	.0206	.0241	.0278	.0319	.0362	.0407	.0455	.0504
7	.0011	.0015	.0020	.0027	.0034	.0044	.0055	.0068	.0083	.0099	.0118	.0139	.0163	.0188	.0216
8	.0002	.0003	.0005	.0006	.0009	.0011	.0015	.0019	.0025	.0031	.0038	.0047	.0057	.0068	.0081
9	—	.0001	.0001	.0001	.0002	.0003	.0004	.0005	.0007	.0009	.0011	.0014	.0018	.0022	.0027
10	—	—	—	—	—	.0001	.0001	.0001	.0002	.0002	.0003	.0004	.0005	.0006	.0008
11	—	—	—	—	—	—	—	—	—	—	.0001	.0001	.0001	.0002	.0002
12	—	—	—	—	—	—	—	—	—	—	—	—	—	—	.0001

X	λ 3.1	3.2	3.3	3.4	3.5	3.6	3.7	3.8	3.9	4.0	4.1	4.2	4.3	4.4	4.5
0	.0450	.0408	.0369	.0334	.0302	.0273	.0247	.0224	.0202	.0183	.0166	.0150	.0136	.0123	.0111
1	.1397	.1304	.1217	.1135	.1057	.0984	.0915	.0850	.0789	.0733	.0679	.0630	.0583	.0540	.0500
2	.2165	.2087	.2008	.1929	.1850	.1771	.1692	.1615	.1539	.1465	.1393	.1323	.1254	.1188	.1125
3	.2237	.2226	.2209	.2186	.2158	.2125	.2087	.2046	.2001	.1954	.1904	.1852	.1798	.1743	.1687
4	.1733	.1781	.1823	.1858	.1888	.1912	.1931	.1944	.1951	.1954	.1951	.1944	.1933	.1917	.1898
5	.1075	.1140	.1203	.1264	.1322	.1377	.1429	.1477	.1522	.1563	.1600	.1633	.1662	.1687	.1708
6	.0555	.0608	.0662	.0716	.0771	.0826	.0881	.0936	.0989	.1042	.1093	.1143	.1191	.1237	.1281
7	.0246	.0278	.0312	.0348	.0385	.0425	.0466	.0508	.0551	.0595	.0640	.0686	.0732	.0778	.0824
8	.0095	.0111	.0129	.0148	.0169	.0191	.0215	.0241	.0269	.0298	.0328	.0360	.0393	.0428	.0463
9	.0033	.0040	.0047	.0056	.0066	.0076	.0089	.0102	.0116	.0132	.0150	.0168	.0188	.0209	.0232
10	.0010	.0013	.0016	.0019	.0023	.0028	.0033	.0039	.0045	.0053	.0061	.0071	.0081	.0092	.0104
11	.0003	.0004	.0005	.0006	.0007	.0009	.0011	.0013	.0016	.0019	.0023	.0027	.0032	.0037	.0043
12	.0001	.0001	.0001	.0002	.0002	.0003	.0003	.0004	.0005	.0006	.0008	.0009	.0011	.0013	.0016
13	—	—	—	—	.0001	.0001	.0001	.0001	.0002	.0002	.0002	.0003	.0004	.0005	.0006
14	—	—	—	—	—	—	—	—	—	.0001	.0001	.0001	.0001	.0001	.0002
15	—	—	—	—	—	—	—	—	—	—	—	—	—	—	.0001

λ

X	4.6	4.7	4.8	4.9	5.0	5.1	5.2	5.3	5.4	5.5	5.6	5.7	5.8	5.9	6.0
0	.0101	.0091	.0082	.0074	.0067	.0061	.0055	.0050	.0045	.0041	.0037	.0033	.0030	.0027	.0025
1	.0462	.0427	.0395	.0365	.0337	.0311	.0287	.0265	.0244	.0225	.0207	.0191	.0176	.0162	.0149
2	.1063	.1005	.0948	.0894	.0842	.0793	.0746	.0701	.0659	.0618	.0580	.0544	.0509	.0477	.0446
3	.1631	.1574	.1517	.1460	.1404	.1348	.1293	.1239	.1185	.1133	.1082	.1033	.0985	.0938	.0892
4	.1875	.1849	.1820	.1789	.1755	.1719	.1681	.1641	.1600	.1558	.1515	.1472	.1428	.1383	.1339
5	.1725	.1738	.1747	.1753	.1755	.1753	.1748	.1740	.1728	.1714	.1697	.1678	.1656	.1632	.1606
6	.1323	.1362	.1398	.1432	.1462	.1490	.1515	.1537	.1555	.1571	.1584	.1594	.1601	.1605	.1606
7	.0869	.0914	.0959	.1002	.1044	.1086	.1125	.1163	.1200	.1234	.1267	.1298	.1326	.1353	.1377
8	.0500	.0537	.0575	.0614	.0653	.0692	.0731	.0771	.0810	.0849	.0887	.0925	.0962	.0998	.1033
9	.0255	.0281	.0307	.0334	.0363	.0392	.0423	.0454	.0486	.0519	.0552	.0586	.0620	.0654	.0688
10	.0118	.0132	.0147	.0164	.0181	.0200	.0220	.0241	.0262	.0285	.0309	.0334	.0359	.0386	.0413
11	.0049	.0056	.0064	.0073	.0082	.0093	.0104	.0116	.0129	.0143	.0157	.0173	.0190	.0207	.0225
12	.0019	.0022	.0026	.0030	.0034	.0039	.0045	.0051	.0058	.0065	.0073	.0082	.0092	.0102	.0113
13	.0007	.0008	.0009	.0011	.0013	.0015	.0018	.0021	.0024	.0028	.0032	.0036	.0041	.0046	.0052
14	.0002	.0003	.0003	.0004	.0005	.0006	.0007	.0008	.0009	.0011	.0013	.0015	.0017	.0019	.0022
15	.0001	.0001	.0001	.0001	.0002	.0002	.0002	.0003	.0003	.0004	.0005	.0006	.0007	.0008	.0009
16	—	—	—	—	—	.0001	.0001	.0001	.0001	.0001	.0002	.0002	.0002	.0003	.0003
17	—	—	—	—	—	—	—	—	—	—	.0001	.0001	.0001	.0001	.0001

λ

X	6.1	6.2	6.3	6.4	6.5	6.6	6.7	6.8	6.9	7.0	7.1	7.2	7.3	7.4	7.5
0	.0022	.0020	.0018	.0017	.0015	.0014	.0012	.0011	.0010	.0009	.0008	.0007	.0007	.0006	.0006
1	.0137	.0126	.0116	.0106	.0098	.0090	.0082	.0076	.0070	.0064	.0059	.0054	.0049	.0045	.0041
2	.0417	.0390	.0364	.0340	.0318	.0296	.0276	.0258	.0240	.0223	.0208	.0194	.0180	.0167	.0156
3	.0848	.0806	.0765	.0726	.0688	.0652	.0617	.0584	.0552	.0521	.0492	.0464	.0438	.0413	.0389
4	.1294	.1249	.1205	.1162	.1118	.1076	.1034	.0992	.0952	.0912	.0874	.0836	.0799	.0764	.0729
5	.1579	.1549	.1519	.1487	.1454	.1420	.1385	.1349	.1314	.1277	.1241	.1204	.1167	.1130	.1094
6	.1605	.1601	.1595	.1586	.1575	.1562	.1546	.1529	.1511	.1490	.1468	.1445	.1420	.1394	.1367
7	.1399	.1418	.1435	.1450	.1462	.1472	.1480	.1486	.1489	.1490	.1489	.1486	.1481	.1474	.1465
8	.1066	.1099	.1130	.1160	.1188	.1215	.1240	.1263	.1284	.1304	.1321	.1337	.1351	.1363	.1373
9	.0723	.0757	.0791	.0825	.0858	.0891	.0923	.0954	.0985	.1014	.1042	.1070	.1096	.1121	.1144
10	.0441	.0469	.0498	.0528	.0558	.0588	.0618	.0649	.0679	.0710	.0740	.0770	.0800	.0829	.0858
11	.0244	.0265	.0285	.0307	.0330	.0353	.0377	.0401	.0426	.0452	.0478	.0504	.0531	.0558	.0585
12	.0124	.0137	.0150	.0164	.0179	.0194	.0210	.0227	.0245	.0263	.0283	.0303	.0323	.0344	.0366
13	.0058	.0065	.0073	.0081	.0089	.0099	.0108	.0119	.0130	.0142	.0154	.0168	.0181	.0196	.0211
14	.0025	.0029	.0033	.0037	.0041	.0046	.0052	.0058	.0064	.0071	.0078	.0086	.0095	.0104	.0113
15	.0010	.0012	.0014	.0016	.0018	.0020	.0023	.0026	.0029	.0033	.0037	.0041	.0046	.0051	.0057
16	.0004	.0005	.0005	.0006	.0007	.0008	.0010	.0011	.0013	.0014	.0016	.0019	.0021	.0024	.0026
17	.0001	.0002	.0002	.0002	.0003	.0003	.0004	.0004	.0005	.0006	.0007	.0008	.0009	.0010	.0012
18	—	.0001	.0001	.0001	.0001	.0001	.0001	.0002	.0002	.0002	.0003	.0003	.0004	.0004	.0005
19	—	—	—	—	—	—	.0001	.0001	.0001	.0001	.0001	.0001	.0001	.0002	.0002
20	—	—	—	—	—	—	—	—	—	—	—	—	.0001	.0001	.0001

λ

X	8.0	8.5	9.0	9.5	10.0	11.0	12.0	13.0	14.0	15.0	16.0	17.0	18.0	19.0	20.0
0	.0003	.0002	.0001	.0001	—	—	—	—	—	—	—	—	—	—	—
1	.0027	.0017	.0011	.0007	.0005	.0002	.0001	—	—	—	—	—	—	—	—
2	.0107	.0074	.0050	.0034	.0023	.0010	.0004	.0002	.0001	—	—	—	—	—	—
3	.0286	.0208	.0150	.0107	.0076	.0037	.0018	.0008	.0004	.0002	.0001	—	—	—	—
4	.0573	.0443	.0337	.0254	.0189	.0102	.0053	.0027	.0013	.0006	.0003	.0001	.0001	—	—
5	.0916	.0752	.0607	.0483	.0378	.0224	.0127	.0070	.0037	.0019	.0010	.0005	.0002	.0001	.0001
6	.1221	.1066	.0911	.0764	.0631	.0411	.0255	.0152	.0087	.0048	.0026	.0014	.0007	.0004	.0002
7	.1396	.1294	.1171	.1037	.0901	.0646	.0437	.0281	.0174	.0104	.0060	.0034	.0019	.0010	.0005
8	.1396	.1375	.1318	.1232	.1126	.0888	.0655	.0457	.0304	.0194	.0120	.0072	.0042	.0024	.0013
9	.1241	.1299	.1318	.1300	.1251	.1085	.0874	.0661	.0473	.0324	.0213	.0135	.0083	.0050	.0029
10	.0993	.1104	.1186	.1235	.1251	.1194	.1048	.0859	.0663	.0486	.0341	.0230	.0150	.0095	.0058
11	.0722	.0853	.0970	.1067	.1137	.1194	.1144	.1015	.0844	.0663	.0496	.0355	.0245	.0164	.0106
12	.0481	.0604	.0728	.0844	.0948	.1094	.1144	.1099	.0984	.0829	.0661	.0504	.0368	.0259	.0176
13	.0296	.0395	.0504	.0617	.0729	.0926	.1056	.1099	.1060	.0956	.0814	.0658	.0509	.0378	.0271
14	.0169	.0240	.0324	.0419	.0521	.0728	.0905	.1021	.1060	.1024	.0930	.0800	.0655	.0514	.0387
15	.0090	.0136	.0194	.0265	.0347	.0534	.0724	.0885	.0989	.1024	.0992	.0906	.0786	.0650	.0516
16	.0045	.0072	.0109	.0157	.0217	.0367	.0543	.0719	.0866	.0960	.0992	.0963	.0884	.0772	.0646
17	.0021	.0036	.0058	.0088	.0128	.0237	.0383	.0550	.0713	.0847	.0934	.0963	.0936	.0863	.0760
18	.0009	.0017	.0029	.0046	.0071	.0145	.0255	.0397	.0554	.0706	.0830	.0909	.0936	.0911	.0844
19	.0004	.0008	.0014	.0023	.0037	.0084	.0161	.0272	.0409	.0557	.0699	.0814	.0887	.0911	.0888
20	.0002	.0003	.0006	.0011	.0019	.0046	.0097	.0177	.0286	.0418	.0559	.0692	.0798	.0866	.0888
21	.0001	.0001	.0003	.0005	.0009	.0024	.0055	.0109	.0191	.0299	.0426	.0560	.0684	.0783	.0846
22	—	.0001	.0001	.0002	.0004	.0012	.0030	.0065	.0121	.0204	.0310	.0433	.0560	.0676	.0769
23	—	—	—	.0001	.0002	.0006	.0016	.0037	.0074	.0133	.0216	.0320	.0438	.0559	.0669
24	—	—	—	—	.0001	.0003	.0008	.0020	.0043	.0083	.0144	.0226	.0328	.0442	.0557
25	—	—	—	—	—	.0001	.0004	.0010	.0024	.0050	.0092	.0154	.0237	.0336	.0446
26	—	—	—	—	—	—	.0002	.0005	.0013	.0029	.0057	.0101	.0164	.0246	.0343
27	—	—	—	—	—	—	.0001	.0002	.0007	.0016	.0034	.0063	.0109	.0173	.0254
28	—	—	—	—	—	—	—	.0001	.0003	.0009	.0019	.0038	.0070	.0117	.0181
29	—	—	—	—	—	—	—	.0001	.0002	.0004	.0011	.0023	.0044	.0077	.0125
30	—	—	—	—	—	—	—	—	.0001	.0002	.0006	.0013	.0026	.0049	.0083
31	—	—	—	—	—	—	—	—	—	.0001	.0003	.0007	.0015	.0030	.0054
32	—	—	—	—	—	—	—	—	—	.0001	.0001	.0004	.0009	.0018	.0034
33	—	—	—	—	—	—	—	—	—	—	.0001	.0002	.0005	.0010	.0020
34	—	—	—	—	—	—	—	—	—	—	—	.0001	.0002	.0006	.0012
35	—	—	—	—	—	—	—	—	—	—	—	—	.0001	.0003	.0007
36	—	—	—	—	—	—	—	—	—	—	—	—	.0001	.0002	.0004
37	—	—	—	—	—	—	—	—	—	—	—	—	—	.0001	.0002
38	—	—	—	—	—	—	—	—	—	—	—	—	—	—	.0001
39	—	—	—	—	—	—	—	—	—	—	—	—	—	—	.0001

APPENDIX

C-1

STANDARD NORMAL AREAS

Example: $P(0 < z < 1.96) = .4750$

This table shows the normal area between 0 and z.

z	.00	.01	.02	.03	.04	.05	.06	.07	.08	.09
0.0	.0000	.0040	.0080	.0120	.0160	.0199	.0239	.0279	.0319	.0359
0.1	.0398	.0438	.0478	.0517	.0557	.0596	.0636	.0675	.0714	.0753
0.2	.0793	.0832	.0871	.0910	.0948	.0987	.1026	.1064	.1103	.1141
0.3	.1179	.1217	.1255	.1293	.1331	.1368	.1406	.1443	.1480	.1517
0.4	.1554	.1591	.1628	.1664	.1700	.1736	.1772	.1808	.1844	.1879
0.5	.1915	.1950	.1985	.2019	.2054	.2088	.2123	.2157	.2190	.2224
0.6	.2257	.2291	.2324	.2357	.2389	.2422	.2454	.2486	.2517	.2549
0.7	.2580	.2611	.2642	.2673	.2704	.2734	.2764	.2794	.2823	.2852
0.8	.2881	.2910	.2939	.2967	.2995	.3023	.3051	.3078	.3106	.3133
0.9	.3159	.3186	.3212	.3238	.3264	.3289	.3315	.3340	.3365	.3389
1.0	.3413	.3438	.3461	.3485	.3508	.3531	.3554	.3577	.3599	.3621
1.1	.3643	.3665	.3686	.3708	.3729	.3749	.3770	.3790	.3810	.3830
1.2	.3849	.3869	.3888	.3907	.3925	.3944	.3962	.3980	.3997	.4015
1.3	.4032	.4049	.4066	.4082	.4099	.4115	.4131	.4147	.4162	.4177
1.4	.4192	.4207	.4222	.4236	.4251	.4265	.4279	.4292	.4306	.4319
1.5	.4332	.4345	.4357	.4370	.4382	.4394	.4406	.4418	.4429	.4441
1.6	.4452	.4463	.4474	.4484	.4495	.4505	.4515	.4525	.4535	.4545
1.7	.4554	.4564	.4573	.4582	.4591	.4599	.4608	.4616	.4625	.4633
1.8	.4641	.4649	.4656	.4664	.4671	.4678	.4686	.4693	.4699	.4706
1.9	.4713	.4719	.4726	.4732	.4738	.4744	.4750	.4756	.4761	.4767
2.0	.4772	.4778	.4783	.4788	.4793	.4798	.4803	.4808	.4812	.4817
2.1	.4821	.4826	.4830	.4834	.4838	.4842	.4846	.4850	.4854	.4857
2.2	.4861	.4864	.4868	.4871	.4875	.4878	.4881	.4884	.4887	.4890
2.3	.4893	.4896	.4898	.4901	.4904	.4906	.4909	.4911	.4913	.4916
2.4	.4918	.4920	.4922	.4925	.4927	.4929	.4931	.4932	.4934	.4936
2.5	.4938	.4940	.4941	.4943	.4945	.4946	.4948	.4949	.4951	.4952
2.6	.4953	.4955	.4956	.4957	.4959	.4960	.4961	.4962	.4963	.4964
2.7	.4965	.4966	.4967	.4968	.4969	.4970	.4971	.4972	.4973	.4974
2.8	.4974	.4975	.4976	.4977	.4977	.4978	.4979	.4979	.4980	.4981
2.9	.4981	.4982	.4982	.4983	.4984	.4984	.4985	.4985	.4986	.4986
3.0	.49865	.49869	.49874	.49878	.49882	.49886	.49889	.49893	.49896	.49900
3.1	.49903	.49906	.49910	.49913	.49916	.49918	.49921	.49924	.49926	.49929
3.2	.49931	.49934	.49936	.49938	.49940	.49942	.49944	.49946	.49948	.49950
3.3	.49952	.49953	.49955	.49957	.49958	.49960	.49961	.49962	.49964	.49965
3.4	.49966	.49968	.49969	.49970	.49971	.49972	.49973	.49974	.49975	.49976
3.5	.49977	.49978	.49978	.49979	.49980	.49981	.49981	.49982	.49983	.49983
3.6	.49984	.49985	.49985	.49986	.49986	.49987	.49987	.49988	.49988	.49989
3.7	.49989	.49990	.49990	.49990	.49991	.49991	.49992	.49992	.49992	.49992

APPENDIX

C-2

CUMULATIVE STANDARD NORMAL DISTRIBUTION

Example: $P(z < -1.96) = .0250$

This table shows the normal area less than z.

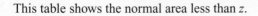

z	.00	.01	.02	.03	.04	.05	.06	.07	.08	.09
−3.7	.00011	.00010	.00010	.00010	.00009	.00009	.00008	.00008	.00008	.00008
−3.6	.00016	.00015	.00015	.00014	.00014	.00013	.00013	.00012	.00012	.00011
−3.5	.00023	.00022	.00022	.00021	.00020	.00019	.00019	.00018	.00017	.00017
−3.4	.00034	.00032	.00031	.00030	.00029	.00028	.00027	.00026	.00025	.00024
−3.3	.00048	.00047	.00045	.00043	.00042	.00040	.00039	.00038	.00036	.00035
−3.2	.00069	.00066	.00064	.00062	.00060	.00058	.00056	.00054	.00052	.00050
−3.1	.00097	.00094	.00090	.00087	.00084	.00082	.00079	.00076	.00074	.00071
−3.0	.00135	.00131	.00126	.00122	.00118	.00114	.00111	.00107	.00104	.00100
−2.9	.0019	.0018	.0018	.0017	.0016	.0016	.0015	.0015	.0014	.0014
−2.8	.0026	.0025	.0024	.0023	.0023	.0022	.0021	.0021	.0020	.0019
−2.7	.0035	.0034	.0033	.0032	.0031	.0030	.0029	.0028	.0027	.0026
−2.6	.0047	.0045	.0044	.0043	.0041	.0040	.0039	.0038	.0037	.0036
−2.5	.0062	.0060	.0059	.0057	.0055	.0054	.0052	.0051	.0049	.0048
−2.4	.0082	.0080	.0078	.0075	.0073	.0071	.0069	.0068	.0066	.0064
−2.3	.0107	.0104	.0102	.0099	.0096	.0094	.0091	.0089	.0087	.0084
−2.2	.0139	.0136	.0132	.0129	.0125	.0122	.0119	.0116	.0113	.0110
−2.1	.0179	.0174	.0170	.0166	.0162	.0158	.0154	.0150	.0146	.0143
−2.0	.0228	.0222	.0217	.0212	.0207	.0202	.0197	.0192	.0188	.0183
−1.9	.0287	.0281	.0274	.0268	.0262	.0256	.0250	.0244	.0239	.0233
−1.8	.0359	.0351	.0344	.0336	.0329	.0322	.0314	.0307	.0301	.0294
−1.7	.0446	.0436	.0427	.0418	.0409	.0401	.0392	.0384	.0375	.0367
−1.6	.0548	.0537	.0526	.0516	.0505	.0495	.0485	.0475	.0465	.0455
−1.5	.0668	.0655	.0643	.0630	.0618	.0606	.0594	.0582	.0571	.0559
−1.4	.0808	.0793	.0778	.0764	.0749	.0735	.0721	.0708	.0694	.0681
−1.3	.0968	.0951	.0934	.0918	.0901	.0885	.0869	.0853	.0838	.0823
−1.2	.1151	.1131	.1112	.1093	.1075	.1056	.1038	.1020	.1003	.0985
−1.1	.1357	.1335	.1314	.1292	.1271	.1251	.1230	.1210	.1190	.1170
−1.0	.1587	.1562	.1539	.1515	.1492	.1469	.1446	.1423	.1401	.1379
−0.9	.1841	.1814	.1788	.1762	.1736	.1711	.1685	.1660	.1635	.1611
−0.8	.2119	.2090	.2061	.2033	.2005	.1977	.1949	.1922	.1894	.1867
−0.7	.2420	.2389	.2358	.2327	.2296	.2266	.2236	.2206	.2177	.2148
−0.6	.2743	.2709	.2676	.2643	.2611	.2578	.2546	.2514	.2483	.2451
−0.5	.3085	.3050	.3015	.2981	.2946	.2912	.2877	.2843	.2810	.2776
−0.4	.3446	.3409	.3372	.3336	.3300	.3264	.3228	.3192	.3156	.3121
−0.3	.3821	.3783	.3745	.3707	.3669	.3632	.3594	.3557	.3520	.3483
−0.2	.4207	.4168	.4129	.4090	.4052	.4013	.3974	.3936	.3897	.3859
−0.1	.4602	.4562	.4522	.4483	.4443	.4404	.4364	.4325	.4286	.4247
−0.0	.5000	.4960	.4920	.4880	.4841	.4801	.4761	.4721	.4681	.4641

This table shows the normal area less than z.

z	.00	.01	.02	.03	.04	.05	.06	.07	.08	.09
0.0	.5000	.5040	.5080	.5120	.5160	.5199	.5239	.5279	.5319	.5359
0.1	.5398	.5438	.5478	.5517	.5557	.5596	.5636	.5675	.5714	.5753
0.2	.5793	.5832	.5871	.5910	.5948	.5987	.6026	.6064	.6103	.6141
0.3	.6179	.6217	.6255	.6293	.6331	.6368	.6406	.6443	.6480	.6517
0.4	.6554	.6591	.6628	.6664	.6700	.6736	.6772	.6808	.6844	.6879
0.5	.6915	.6950	.6985	.7019	.7054	.7088	.7123	.7157	.7190	.7224
0.6	.7257	.7291	.7324	.7357	.7389	.7422	.7454	.7486	.7517	.7549
0.7	.7580	.7611	.7642	.7673	.7704	.7734	.7764	.7794	.7823	.7852
0.8	.7881	.7910	.7939	.7967	.7995	.8023	.8051	.8078	.8106	.8133
0.9	.8159	.8186	.8212	.8238	.8264	.8289	.8315	.8340	.8365	.8389
1.0	.8413	.8438	.8461	.8485	.8508	.8531	.8554	.8577	.8599	.8621
1.1	.8643	.8665	.8686	.8708	.8729	.8749	.8770	.8790	.8810	.8830
1.2	.8849	.8869	.8888	.8907	.8925	.8944	.8962	.8980	.8997	.9015
1.3	.9032	.9049	.9066	.9082	.9099	.9115	.9131	.9147	.9162	.9177
1.4	.9192	.9207	.9222	.9236	.9251	.9265	.9279	.9292	.9306	.9319
1.5	.9332	.9345	.9357	.9370	.9382	.9394	.9406	.9418	.9429	.9441
1.6	.9452	.9463	.9474	.9484	.9495	.9505	.9515	.9525	.9535	.9545
1.7	.9554	.9564	.9573	.9582	.9591	.9599	.9608	.9616	.9625	.9633
1.8	.9641	.9649	.9656	.9664	.9671	.9678	.9686	.9693	.9699	.9706
1.9	.9713	.9719	.9726	.9732	.9738	.9744	.9750	.9756	.9761	.9767
2.0	.9772	.9778	.9783	.9788	.9793	.9798	.9803	.9808	.9812	.9817
2.1	.9821	.9826	.9830	.9834	.9838	.9842	.9846	.9850	.9854	.9857
2.2	.9861	.9864	.9868	.9871	.9875	.9878	.9881	.9884	.9887	.9890
2.3	.9893	.9896	.9898	.9901	.9904	.9906	.9909	.9911	.9913	.9916
2.4	.9918	.9920	.9922	.9925	.9927	.9929	.9931	.9932	.9934	.9936
2.5	.9938	.9940	.9941	.9943	.9945	.9946	.9948	.9949	.9951	.9952
2.6	.9953	.9955	.9956	.9957	.9959	.9960	.9961	.9962	.9963	.9964
2.7	.9965	.9966	.9967	.9968	.9969	.9970	.9971	.9972	.9973	.9974
2.8	.9974	.9975	.9976	.9977	.9977	.9978	.9979	.9979	.9980	.9981
2.9	.9981	.9982	.9982	.9983	.9984	.9984	.9985	.9985	.9986	.9986
3.0	.99865	.99869	.99874	.99878	.99882	.99886	.99889	.99893	.99896	.99900
3.1	.99903	.99906	.99910	.99913	.99916	.99918	.99921	.99924	.99926	.99929
3.2	.99931	.99934	.99936	.99938	.99940	.99942	.99944	.99946	.99948	.99950
3.3	.99952	.99953	.99955	.99957	.99958	.99960	.99961	.99962	.99964	.99965
3.4	.99966	.99968	.99969	.99970	.99971	.99972	.99973	.99974	.99975	.99976
3.5	.99977	.99978	.99978	.99979	.99980	.99981	.99981	.99982	.99983	.99983
3.6	.99984	.99985	.99985	.99986	.99986	.99987	.99987	.99988	.99988	.99989
3.7	.99989	.99990	.99990	.99990	.99991	.99991	.99992	.99992	.99992	.99992

APPENDIX D

STUDENT'S *t* CRITICAL VALUES

This table shows the *t*-value that defines the area for the stated degrees of freedom (ν).

	Confidence Level						Confidence Level			
	.80	.90	.95	.98	.99		.80	.90	.95	.98	.99
	Significance Level for Two-Tailed Test						Significance Level for Two-Tailed Test				
	.20	.10	.05	.02	.01		.20	.10	.05	.02	.01
	Significance Level for One-Tailed Test						Significance Level for One-Tailed Test				
ν	.10	.05	.025	.01	.005	ν	.10	.05	.025	.01	.005
1	3.078	6.314	12.706	31.821	63.656	36	1.306	1.688	2.028	2.434	2.719
2	1.886	2.920	4.303	6.965	9.925	37	1.305	1.687	2.026	2.431	2.715
3	1.638	2.353	3.182	4.541	5.841	38	1.304	1.686	2.024	2.429	2.712
4	1.533	2.132	2.776	3.747	4.604	39	1.304	1.685	2.023	2.426	2.708
5	1.476	2.015	2.571	3.365	4.032	40	1.303	1.684	2.021	2.423	2.704
6	1.440	1.943	2.447	3.143	3.707	41	1.303	1.683	2.020	2.421	2.701
7	1.415	1.895	2.365	2.998	3.499	42	1.302	1.682	2.018	2.418	2.698
8	1.397	1.860	2.306	2.896	3.355	43	1.302	1.681	2.017	2.416	2.695
9	1.383	1.833	2.262	2.821	3.250	44	1.301	1.680	2.015	2.414	2.692
10	1.372	1.812	2.228	2.764	3.169	45	1.301	1.679	2.014	2.412	2.690
11	1.363	1.796	2.201	2.718	3.106	46	1.300	1.679	2.013	2.410	2.687
12	1.356	1.782	2.179	2.681	3.055	47	1.300	1.678	2.012	2.408	2.685
13	1.350	1.771	2.160	2.650	3.012	48	1.299	1.677	2.011	2.407	2.682
14	1.345	1.761	2.145	2.624	2.977	49	1.299	1.677	2.010	2.405	2.680
15	1.341	1.753	2.131	2.602	2.947	50	1.299	1.676	2.009	2.403	2.678
16	1.337	1.746	2.120	2.583	2.921	55	1.297	1.673	2.004	2.396	2.668
17	1.333	1.740	2.110	2.567	2.898	60	1.296	1.671	2.000	2.390	2.660
18	1.330	1.734	2.101	2.552	2.878	65	1.295	1.669	1.997	2.385	2.654
19	1.328	1.729	2.093	2.539	2.861	70	1.294	1.667	1.994	2.381	2.648
20	1.325	1.725	2.086	2.528	2.845	75	1.293	1.665	1.992	2.377	2.643
21	1.323	1.721	2.080	2.518	2.831	80	1.292	1.664	1.990	2.374	2.639
22	1.321	1.717	2.074	2.508	2.819	85	1.292	1.663	1.988	2.371	2.635
23	1.319	1.714	2.069	2.500	2.807	90	1.291	1.662	1.987	2.368	2.632
24	1.318	1.711	2.064	2.492	2.797	95	1.291	1.661	1.985	2.366	2.629
25	1.316	1.708	2.060	2.485	2.787	100	1.290	1.660	1.984	2.364	2.626
26	1.315	1.706	2.056	2.479	2.779	110	1.289	1.659	1.982	2.361	2.621
27	1.314	1.703	2.052	2.473	2.771	120	1.289	1.658	1.980	2.358	2.617
28	1.313	1.701	2.048	2.467	2.763	130	1.288	1.657	1.978	2.355	2.614
29	1.311	1.699	2.045	2.462	2.756	140	1.288	1.656	1.977	2.353	2.611
30	1.310	1.697	2.042	2.457	2.750	150	1.287	1.655	1.976	2.351	2.609
31	1.309	1.696	2.040	2.453	2.744	∞	1.282	1.645	1.960	2.326	2.576
32	1.309	1.694	2.037	2.449	2.738						
33	1.308	1.692	2.035	2.445	2.733						
34	1.307	1.691	2.032	2.441	2.728						
35	1.306	1.690	2.030	2.438	2.724						

Note: As *n* increases, critical values of Student's *t* approach the *z*-values in the last line of this table. A common rule of thumb is to use *z* when *n* > 30, but that is *not* conservative.

APPENDIX

E

CHI-SQUARE CRITICAL VALUES

This table shows the critical value for the tail areas for the stated degrees of freedom (ν).

Left   Right

	Left-Tail Area					Right-Tail Area				
ν	.005	.01	.025	.05	.10	.10	.05	.025	.01	.005
1	0.000	0.000	0.001	0.004	0.016	2.706	3.841	5.024	6.635	7.879
2	0.010	0.020	0.051	0.103	0.211	4.605	5.991	7.378	9.210	10.60
3	0.072	0.115	0.216	0.352	0.584	6.251	7.815	9.348	11.34	12.84
4	0.207	0.297	0.484	0.711	1.064	7.779	9.488	11.14	13.28	14.86
5	0.412	0.554	0.831	1.145	1.610	9.236	11.07	12.83	15.09	16.75
6	0.676	0.872	1.237	1.635	2.204	10.64	12.59	14.45	16.81	18.55
7	0.989	1.239	1.690	2.167	2.833	12.02	14.07	16.01	18.48	20.28
8	1.344	1.647	2.180	2.733	3.490	13.36	15.51	17.53	20.09	21.95
9	1.735	2.088	2.700	3.325	4.168	14.68	16.92	19.02	21.67	23.59
10	2.156	2.558	3.247	3.940	4.865	15.99	18.31	20.48	23.21	25.19
11	2.603	3.053	3.816	4.575	5.578	17.28	19.68	21.92	24.73	26.76
12	3.074	3.571	4.404	5.226	6.304	18.55	21.03	23.34	26.22	28.30
13	3.565	4.107	5.009	5.892	7.041	19.81	22.36	24.74	27.69	29.82
14	4.075	4.660	5.629	6.571	7.790	21.06	23.68	26.12	29.14	31.32
15	4.601	5.229	6.262	7.261	8.547	22.31	25.00	27.49	30.58	32.80
16	5.142	5.812	6.908	7.962	9.312	23.54	26.30	28.85	32.00	34.27
17	5.697	6.408	7.564	8.672	10.09	24.77	27.59	30.19	33.41	35.72
18	6.265	7.015	8.231	9.390	10.86	25.99	28.87	31.53	34.81	37.16
19	6.844	7.633	8.907	10.12	11.65	27.20	30.14	32.85	36.19	38.58
20	7.434	8.260	9.591	10.85	12.44	28.41	31.41	34.17	37.57	40.00
21	8.034	8.897	10.28	11.59	13.24	29.62	32.67	35.48	38.93	41.40
22	8.643	9.542	10.98	12.34	14.04	30.81	33.92	36.78	40.29	42.80
23	9.260	10.20	11.69	13.09	14.85	32.01	35.17	38.08	41.64	44.18
24	9.886	10.86	12.40	13.85	15.66	33.20	36.42	39.36	42.98	45.56
25	10.52	11.52	13.12	14.61	16.47	34.38	37.65	40.65	44.31	46.93
26	11.16	12.20	13.84	15.38	17.29	35.56	38.89	41.92	45.64	48.29
27	11.81	12.88	14.57	16.15	18.11	36.74	40.11	43.19	46.96	49.65
28	12.46	13.56	15.31	16.93	18.94	37.92	41.34	44.46	48.28	50.99
29	13.12	14.26	16.05	17.71	19.77	39.09	42.56	45.72	49.59	52.34
30	13.79	14.95	16.79	18.49	20.60	40.26	43.77	46.98	50.89	53.67
31	14.46	15.66	17.54	19.28	21.43	41.42	44.99	48.23	52.19	55.00
32	15.13	16.36	18.29	20.07	22.27	42.58	46.19	49.48	53.49	56.33
33	15.82	17.07	19.05	20.87	23.11	43.75	47.40	50.73	54.78	57.65
34	16.50	17.79	19.81	21.66	23.95	44.90	48.60	51.97	56.06	58.96
35	17.19	18.51	20.57	22.47	24.80	46.06	49.80	53.20	57.34	60.27
36	17.89	19.23	21.34	23.27	25.64	47.21	51.00	54.44	58.62	61.58
37	18.59	19.96	22.11	24.07	26.49	48.36	52.19	55.67	59.89	62.88
38	19.29	20.69	22.88	24.88	27.34	49.51	53.38	56.90	61.16	64.18
39	20.00	21.43	23.65	25.70	28.20	50.66	54.57	58.12	62.43	65.48
40	20.71	22.16	24.43	26.51	29.05	51.81	55.76	59.34	63.69	66.77
50	27.99	29.71	32.36	34.76	37.69	63.17	67.50	71.42	76.15	79.49
60	35.53	37.48	40.48	43.19	46.46	74.40	79.08	83.30	88.38	91.95
70	43.28	45.44	48.76	51.74	55.33	85.53	90.53	95.02	100.4	104.2
80	51.17	53.54	57.15	60.39	64.28	96.58	101.9	106.6	112.3	116.3
90	59.20	61.75	65.65	69.13	73.29	107.6	113.1	118.1	124.1	128.3
100	67.33	70.06	74.22	77.93	82.36	118.5	124.3	129.6	135.8	140.2

APPENDIX

F

CRITICAL VALUES OF $F_{.10}$

This table shows the 10 percent right-tail critical values of F for the stated degrees of freedom (ν).

Denominator Degrees of Freedom (ν_2)	Numerator Degrees of Freedom (ν_1)										
	1	2	3	4	5	6	7	8	9	10	12
1	39.86	49.50	53.59	55.83	57.24	58.20	58.91	59.44	59.86	60.19	60.71
2	8.53	9.00	9.16	9.24	9.29	9.33	9.35	9.37	9.38	9.39	9.41
3	5.54	5.46	5.39	5.34	5.31	5.28	5.27	5.25	5.24	5.23	5.22
4	4.54	4.32	4.19	4.11	4.05	4.01	3.98	3.95	3.94	3.92	3.90
5	4.06	3.78	3.62	3.52	3.45	3.40	3.37	3.34	3.32	3.30	3.27
6	3.78	3.46	3.29	3.18	3.11	3.05	3.01	2.98	2.96	2.94	2.90
7	3.59	3.26	3.07	2.96	2.88	2.83	2.78	2.75	2.72	2.70	2.67
8	3.46	3.11	2.92	2.81	2.73	2.67	2.62	2.59	2.56	2.54	2.50
9	3.36	3.01	2.81	2.69	2.61	2.55	2.51	2.47	2.44	2.42	2.38
10	3.29	2.92	2.73	2.61	2.52	2.46	2.41	2.38	2.35	2.32	2.28
11	3.23	2.86	2.66	2.54	2.45	2.39	2.34	2.30	2.27	2.25	2.21
12	3.18	2.81	2.61	2.48	2.39	2.33	2.28	2.24	2.21	2.19	2.15
13	3.14	2.76	2.56	2.43	2.35	2.28	2.23	2.20	2.16	2.14	2.10
14	3.10	2.73	2.52	2.39	2.31	2.24	2.19	2.15	2.12	2.10	2.05
15	3.07	2.70	2.49	2.36	2.27	2.21	2.16	2.12	2.09	2.06	2.02
16	3.05	2.67	2.46	2.33	2.24	2.18	2.13	2.09	2.06	2.03	1.99
17	3.03	2.64	2.44	2.31	2.22	2.15	2.10	2.06	2.03	2.00	1.96
18	3.01	2.62	2.42	2.29	2.20	2.13	2.08	2.04	2.00	1.98	1.93
19	2.99	2.61	2.40	2.27	2.18	2.11	2.06	2.02	1.98	1.96	1.91
20	2.97	2.59	2.38	2.25	2.16	2.09	2.04	2.00	1.96	1.94	1.89
21	2.96	2.57	2.36	2.23	2.14	2.08	2.02	1.98	1.95	1.92	1.87
22	2.95	2.56	2.35	2.22	2.13	2.06	2.01	1.97	1.93	1.90	1.86
23	2.94	2.55	2.34	2.21	2.11	2.05	1.99	1.95	1.92	1.89	1.84
24	2.93	2.54	2.33	2.19	2.10	2.04	1.98	1.94	1.91	1.88	1.83
25	2.92	2.53	2.32	2.18	2.09	2.02	1.97	1.93	1.89	1.87	1.82
26	2.91	2.52	2.31	2.17	2.08	2.01	1.96	1.92	1.88	1.86	1.81
27	2.90	2.51	2.30	2.17	2.07	2.00	1.95	1.91	1.87	1.85	1.80
28	2.89	2.50	2.29	2.16	2.06	2.00	1.94	1.90	1.87	1.84	1.79
29	2.89	2.50	2.28	2.15	2.06	1.99	1.93	1.89	1.86	1.83	1.78
30	2.88	2.49	2.28	2.14	2.05	1.98	1.93	1.88	1.85	1.82	1.77
40	2.84	2.44	2.23	2.09	2.00	1.93	1.87	1.83	1.79	1.76	1.71
50	2.81	2.41	2.20	2.06	1.97	1.90	1.84	1.80	1.76	1.73	1.68
60	2.79	2.39	2.18	2.04	1.95	1.87	1.82	1.77	1.74	1.71	1.66
120	2.75	2.35	2.13	1.99	1.90	1.82	1.77	1.72	1.68	1.65	1.60
200	2.73	2.33	2.11	1.97	1.88	1.80	1.75	1.70	1.66	1.63	1.58
∞	2.71	2.30	2.08	1.94	1.85	1.77	1.72	1.67	1.63	1.60	1.55

Denominator Degrees of Freedom (v_2)	Numerator Degrees of Freedom (v_1)										
	15	20	25	30	35	40	50	60	120	200	∞
1	61.22	61.74	62.05	62.26	62.42	62.53	62.69	62.79	63.06	63.17	63.32
2	9.42	9.44	9.45	9.46	9.46	9.47	9.47	9.47	9.48	9.49	9.49
3	5.20	5.18	5.17	5.17	5.16	5.16	5.15	5.15	5.14	5.14	5.13
4	3.87	3.84	3.83	3.82	3.81	3.80	3.80	3.79	3.78	3.77	3.76
5	3.24	3.21	3.19	3.17	3.16	3.16	3.15	3.14	3.12	3.12	3.11
6	2.87	2.84	2.81	2.80	2.79	2.78	2.77	2.76	2.74	2.73	2.72
7	2.63	2.59	2.57	2.56	2.54	2.54	2.52	2.51	2.49	2.48	2.47
8	2.46	2.42	2.40	2.38	2.37	2.36	2.35	2.34	2.32	2.31	2.29
9	2.34	2.30	2.27	2.25	2.24	2.23	2.22	2.21	2.18	2.17	2.16
10	2.24	2.20	2.17	2.16	2.14	2.13	2.12	2.11	2.08	2.07	2.06
11	2.17	2.12	2.10	2.08	2.06	2.05	2.04	2.03	2.00	1.99	1.97
12	2.10	2.06	2.03	2.01	2.00	1.99	1.97	1.96	1.93	1.92	1.90
13	2.05	2.01	1.98	1.96	1.94	1.93	1.92	1.90	1.88	1.86	1.85
14	2.01	1.96	1.93	1.91	1.90	1.89	1.87	1.86	1.83	1.82	1.80
15	1.97	1.92	1.89	1.87	1.86	1.85	1.83	1.82	1.79	1.77	1.76
16	1.94	1.89	1.86	1.84	1.82	1.81	1.79	1.78	1.75	1.74	1.72
17	1.91	1.86	1.83	1.81	1.79	1.78	1.76	1.75	1.72	1.71	1.69
18	1.89	1.84	1.80	1.78	1.77	1.75	1.74	1.72	1.69	1.68	1.66
19	1.86	1.81	1.78	1.76	1.74	1.73	1.71	1.70	1.67	1.65	1.63
20	1.84	1.79	1.76	1.74	1.72	1.71	1.69	1.68	1.64	1.63	1.61
21	1.83	1.78	1.74	1.72	1.70	1.69	1.67	1.66	1.62	1.61	1.59
22	1.81	1.76	1.73	1.70	1.68	1.67	1.65	1.64	1.60	1.59	1.57
23	1.80	1.74	1.71	1.69	1.67	1.66	1.64	1.62	1.59	1.57	1.55
24	1.78	1.73	1.70	1.67	1.65	1.64	1.62	1.61	1.57	1.56	1.53
25	1.77	1.72	1.68	1.66	1.64	1.63	1.61	1.59	1.56	1.54	1.52
26	1.76	1.71	1.67	1.65	1.63	1.61	1.59	1.58	1.54	1.53	1.50
27	1.75	1.70	1.66	1.64	1.62	1.60	1.58	1.57	1.53	1.52	1.49
28	1.74	1.69	1.65	1.63	1.61	1.59	1.57	1.56	1.52	1.50	1.48
29	1.73	1.68	1.64	1.62	1.60	1.58	1.56	1.55	1.51	1.49	1.47
30	1.72	1.67	1.63	1.61	1.59	1.57	1.55	1.54	1.50	1.48	1.46
40	1.66	1.61	1.57	1.54	1.52	1.51	1.48	1.47	1.42	1.41	1.38
50	1.63	1.57	1.53	1.50	1.48	1.46	1.44	1.42	1.38	1.36	1.33
60	1.60	1.54	1.50	1.48	1.45	1.44	1.41	1.40	1.35	1.33	1.29
120	1.55	1.48	1.44	1.41	1.39	1.37	1.34	1.32	1.26	1.24	1.19
200	1.52	1.46	1.41	1.38	1.36	1.34	1.31	1.29	1.23	1.20	1.15
∞	2.71	1.49	1.42	1.38	1.34	1.32	1.30	1.26	1.24	1.17	1.13

CRITICAL VALUES OF $F_{.05}$

This table shows the 5 percent right-tail critical values of F for the stated degrees of freedom (v).

Denominator Degrees of Freedom (v_2)	Numerator Degrees of Freedom (v_1)										
	1	2	3	4	5	6	7	8	9	10	12
1	161.4	199.5	215.7	224.6	230.2	234.0	236.8	238.9	240.5	241.9	243.9
2	18.51	19.00	19.16	19.25	19.30	19.33	19.35	19.37	19.38	19.40	19.41
3	10.13	9.55	9.28	9.12	9.01	8.94	8.89	8.85	8.81	8.79	8.74
4	7.71	6.94	6.59	6.39	6.26	6.16	6.09	6.04	6.00	5.96	5.91
5	6.61	5.79	5.41	5.19	5.05	4.95	4.88	4.82	4.77	4.74	4.68
6	5.99	5.14	4.76	4.53	4.39	4.28	4.21	4.15	4.10	4.06	4.00
7	5.59	4.74	4.35	4.12	3.97	3.87	3.79	3.73	3.68	3.64	3.57
8	5.32	4.46	4.07	3.84	3.69	3.58	3.50	3.44	3.39	3.35	3.28
9	5.12	4.26	3.86	3.63	3.48	3.37	3.29	3.23	3.18	3.14	3.07
10	4.96	4.10	3.71	3.48	3.33	3.22	3.14	3.07	3.02	2.98	2.91
11	4.84	3.98	3.59	3.36	3.20	3.09	3.01	2.95	2.90	2.85	2.79
12	4.75	3.89	3.49	3.26	3.11	3.00	2.91	2.85	2.80	2.75	2.69
13	4.67	3.81	3.41	3.18	3.03	2.92	2.83	2.77	2.71	2.67	2.60
14	4.60	3.74	3.34	3.11	2.96	2.85	2.76	2.70	2.65	2.60	2.53
15	4.54	3.68	3.29	3.06	2.90	2.79	2.71	2.64	2.59	2.54	2.48
16	4.49	3.63	3.24	3.01	2.85	2.74	2.66	2.59	2.54	2.49	2.42
17	4.45	3.59	3.20	2.96	2.81	2.70	2.61	2.55	2.49	2.45	2.38
18	4.41	3.55	3.16	2.93	2.77	2.66	2.58	2.51	2.46	2.41	2.34
19	4.38	3.52	3.13	2.90	2.74	2.63	2.54	2.48	2.42	2.38	2.31
20	4.35	3.49	3.10	2.87	2.71	2.60	2.51	2.45	2.39	2.35	2.28
21	4.32	3.47	3.07	2.84	2.68	2.57	2.49	2.42	2.37	2.32	2.25
22	4.30	3.44	3.05	2.82	2.66	2.55	2.46	2.40	2.34	2.30	2.23
23	4.28	3.42	3.03	2.80	2.64	2.53	2.44	2.37	2.32	2.27	2.20
24	4.26	3.40	3.01	2.78	2.62	2.51	2.42	2.36	2.30	2.25	2.18
25	4.24	3.39	2.99	2.76	2.60	2.49	2.40	2.34	2.28	2.24	2.16
26	4.23	3.37	2.98	2.74	2.59	2.47	2.39	2.32	2.27	2.22	2.15
27	4.21	3.35	2.96	2.73	2.57	2.46	2.37	2.31	2.25	2.20	2.13
28	4.20	3.34	2.95	2.71	2.56	2.45	2.36	2.29	2.24	2.19	2.12
29	4.18	3.33	2.93	2.70	2.55	2.43	2.35	2.28	2.22	2.18	2.10
30	4.17	3.32	2.92	2.69	2.53	2.42	2.33	2.27	2.21	2.16	2.09
40	4.08	3.23	2.84	2.61	2.45	2.34	2.25	2.18	2.12	2.08	2.00
50	4.03	3.18	2.79	2.56	2.40	2.29	2.20	2.13	2.07	2.03	1.95
60	4.00	3.15	2.76	2.53	2.37	2.25	2.17	2.10	2.04	1.99	1.92
120	3.92	3.07	2.68	2.45	2.29	2.18	2.09	2.02	1.96	1.91	1.83
200	3.89	3.04	2.65	2.42	2.26	2.14	2.06	1.98	1.93	1.88	1.80
∞	2.71	3.84	3.00	2.60	2.37	2.21	2.10	2.01	1.94	1.88	1.83

Denominator Degrees of Freedom (ν_2)	Numerator Degrees of Freedom (ν_1)										
	15	20	25	30	35	40	50	60	120	200	∞
1	245.9	248.0	249.3	250.1	250.7	251.1	251.8	252.2	253.3	253.7	254.3
2	19.43	19.45	19.46	19.46	19.47	19.47	19.48	19.48	19.49	19.49	19.50
3	8.70	8.66	8.63	8.62	8.60	8.59	8.58	8.57	8.55	8.54	8.53
4	5.86	5.80	5.77	5.75	5.73	5.72	5.70	5.69	5.66	5.65	5.63
5	4.62	4.56	4.52	4.50	4.48	4.46	4.44	4.43	4.40	4.39	4.37
6	3.94	3.87	3.83	3.81	3.79	3.77	3.75	3.74	3.70	3.69	3.67
7	3.51	3.44	3.40	3.38	3.36	3.34	3.32	3.30	3.27	3.25	3.23
8	3.22	3.15	3.11	3.08	3.06	3.04	3.02	3.01	2.97	2.95	2.93
9	3.01	2.94	2.89	2.86	2.84	2.83	2.80	2.79	2.75	2.73	2.71
10	2.85	2.77	2.73	2.70	2.68	2.66	2.64	2.62	2.58	2.56	2.54
11	2.72	2.65	2.60	2.57	2.55	2.53	2.51	2.49	2.45	2.43	2.41
12	2.62	2.54	2.50	2.47	2.44	2.43	2.40	2.38	2.34	2.32	2.30
13	2.53	2.46	2.41	2.38	2.36	2.34	2.31	2.30	2.25	2.23	2.21
14	2.46	2.39	2.34	2.31	2.28	2.27	2.24	2.22	2.18	2.16	2.13
15	2.40	2.33	2.28	2.25	2.22	2.20	2.18	2.16	2.11	2.10	2.07
16	2.35	2.28	2.23	2.19	2.17	2.15	2.12	2.11	2.06	2.04	2.01
17	2.31	2.23	2.18	2.15	2.12	2.10	2.08	2.06	2.01	1.99	1.96
18	2.27	2.19	2.14	2.11	2.08	2.06	2.04	2.02	1.97	1.95	1.92
19	2.23	2.16	2.11	2.07	2.05	2.03	2.00	1.98	1.93	1.91	1.88
20	2.20	2.12	2.07	2.04	2.01	1.99	1.97	1.95	1.90	1.88	1.84
21	2.18	2.10	2.05	2.01	1.98	1.96	1.94	1.92	1.87	1.84	1.81
22	2.15	2.07	2.02	1.98	1.96	1.94	1.91	1.89	1.84	1.82	1.78
23	2.13	2.05	2.00	1.96	1.93	1.91	1.88	1.86	1.81	1.79	1.76
24	2.11	2.03	1.97	1.94	1.91	1.89	1.86	1.84	1.79	1.77	1.73
25	2.09	2.01	1.96	1.92	1.89	1.87	1.84	1.82	1.77	1.75	1.71
26	2.07	1.99	1.94	1.90	1.87	1.85	1.82	1.80	1.75	1.73	1.69
27	2.06	1.97	1.92	1.88	1.86	1.84	1.81	1.79	1.73	1.71	1.67
28	2.04	1.96	1.91	1.87	1.84	1.82	1.79	1.77	1.71	1.69	1.66
29	2.03	1.94	1.89	1.85	1.83	1.81	1.77	1.75	1.70	1.67	1.64
30	2.01	1.93	1.88	1.84	1.81	1.79	1.76	1.74	1.68	1.66	1.62
40	1.92	1.84	1.78	1.74	1.72	1.69	1.66	1.64	1.58	1.55	1.51
50	1.87	1.78	1.73	1.69	1.66	1.63	1.60	1.58	1.51	1.48	1.44
60	1.84	1.75	1.69	1.65	1.62	1.59	1.56	1.53	1.47	1.44	1.39
120	1.75	1.66	1.60	1.55	1.52	1.50	1.46	1.43	1.35	1.32	1.26
200	1.72	1.62	1.56	1.52	1.48	1.46	1.41	1.39	1.30	1.26	1.19
∞	2.71	1.67	1.57	1.51	1.46	1.42	1.39	1.35	1.32	1.22	1.17

CRITICAL VALUES OF $F_{.025}$

This table shows the 2.5 percent right-tail critical values of F for the stated degrees of freedom (v).

Denominator Degrees of Freedom (v_2)	Numerator Degrees of Freedom (v_1)										
	1	2	3	4	5	6	7	8	9	10	12
1	647.8	799.5	864.2	899.6	921.8	937.1	948.2	956.6	963.3	968.6	976.7
2	38.51	39.00	39.17	39.25	39.30	39.33	39.36	39.37	39.39	39.40	39.41
3	17.44	16.04	15.44	15.10	14.88	14.73	14.62	14.54	14.47	14.42	14.34
4	12.22	10.65	9.98	9.60	9.36	9.20	9.07	8.98	8.90	8.84	8.75
5	10.01	8.43	7.76	7.39	7.15	6.98	6.85	6.76	6.68	6.62	6.52
6	8.81	7.26	6.60	6.23	5.99	5.82	5.70	5.60	5.52	5.46	5.37
7	8.07	6.54	5.89	5.52	5.29	5.12	4.99	4.90	4.82	4.76	4.67
8	7.57	6.06	5.42	5.05	4.82	4.65	4.53	4.43	4.36	4.30	4.20
9	7.21	5.71	5.08	4.72	4.48	4.32	4.20	4.10	4.03	3.96	3.87
10	6.94	5.46	4.83	4.47	4.24	4.07	3.95	3.85	3.78	3.72	3.62
11	6.72	5.26	4.63	4.28	4.04	3.88	3.76	3.66	3.59	3.53	3.43
12	6.55	5.10	4.47	4.12	3.89	3.73	3.61	3.51	3.44	3.37	3.28
13	6.41	4.97	4.35	4.00	3.77	3.60	3.48	3.39	3.31	3.25	3.15
14	6.30	4.86	4.24	3.89	3.66	3.50	3.38	3.29	3.21	3.15	3.05
15	6.20	4.77	4.15	3.80	3.58	3.41	3.29	3.20	3.12	3.06	2.96
16	6.12	4.69	4.08	3.73	3.50	3.34	3.22	3.12	3.05	2.99	2.89
17	6.04	4.62	4.01	3.66	3.44	3.28	3.16	3.06	2.98	2.92	2.82
18	5.98	4.56	3.95	3.61	3.38	3.22	3.10	3.01	2.93	2.87	2.77
19	5.92	4.51	3.90	3.56	3.33	3.17	3.05	2.96	2.88	2.82	2.72
20	5.87	4.46	3.86	3.51	3.29	3.13	3.01	2.91	2.84	2.77	2.68
21	5.83	4.42	3.82	3.48	3.25	3.09	2.97	2.87	2.80	2.73	2.64
22	5.79	4.38	3.78	3.44	3.22	3.05	2.93	2.84	2.76	2.70	2.60
23	5.75	4.35	3.75	3.41	3.18	3.02	2.90	2.81	2.73	2.67	2.57
24	5.72	4.32	3.72	3.38	3.15	2.99	2.87	2.78	2.70	2.64	2.54
25	5.69	4.29	3.69	3.35	3.13	2.97	2.85	2.75	2.68	2.61	2.51
26	5.66	4.27	3.67	3.33	3.10	2.94	2.82	2.73	2.65	2.59	2.49
27	5.63	4.24	3.65	3.31	3.08	2.92	2.80	2.71	2.63	2.57	2.47
28	5.61	4.22	3.63	3.29	3.06	2.90	2.78	2.69	2.61	2.55	2.45
29	5.59	4.20	3.61	3.27	3.04	2.88	2.76	2.67	2.59	2.53	2.43
30	5.57	4.18	3.59	3.25	3.03	2.87	2.75	2.65	2.57	2.51	2.41
40	5.42	4.05	3.46	3.13	2.90	2.74	2.62	2.53	2.45	2.39	2.29
50	5.34	3.97	3.39	3.05	2.83	2.67	2.55	2.46	2.38	2.32	2.22
60	5.29	3.93	3.34	3.01	2.79	2.63	2.51	2.41	2.33	2.27	2.17
120	5.15	3.80	3.23	2.89	2.67	2.52	2.39	2.30	2.22	2.16	2.05
200	5.10	3.76	3.18	2.85	2.63	2.47	2.35	2.26	2.18	2.11	2.01
∞	2.71	5.02	3.69	3.12	2.79	2.57	2.41	2.29	2.19	2.11	2.05

Denominator Degrees of Freedom (v_2)	Numerator Degrees of Freedom (v_1)										
	15	20	25	30	35	40	50	60	120	200	∞
1	984.9	993.1	998.1	1001	1004	1006	1008	1010	1014	1016	1018
2	39.43	39.45	39.46	39.46	39.47	39.47	39.48	39.48	39.49	39.49	39.50
3	14.25	14.17	14.12	14.08	14.06	14.04	14.01	13.99	13.95	13.93	13.90
4	8.66	8.56	8.50	8.46	8.43	8.41	8.38	8.36	8.31	8.29	8.26
5	6.43	6.33	6.27	6.23	6.20	6.18	6.14	6.12	6.07	6.05	6.02
6	5.27	5.17	5.11	5.07	5.04	5.01	4.98	4.96	4.90	4.88	4.85
7	4.57	4.47	4.40	4.36	4.33	4.31	4.28	4.25	4.20	4.18	4.14
8	4.10	4.00	3.94	3.89	3.86	3.84	3.81	3.78	3.73	3.70	3.67
9	3.77	3.67	3.60	3.56	3.53	3.51	3.47	3.45	3.39	3.37	3.33
10	3.52	3.42	3.35	3.31	3.28	3.26	3.22	3.20	3.14	3.12	3.08
11	3.33	3.23	3.16	3.12	3.09	3.06	3.03	3.00	2.94	2.92	2.88
12	3.18	3.07	3.01	2.96	2.93	2.91	2.87	2.85	2.79	2.76	2.73
13	3.05	2.95	2.88	2.84	2.80	2.78	2.74	2.72	2.66	2.63	2.60
14	2.95	2.84	2.78	2.73	2.70	2.67	2.64	2.61	2.55	2.53	2.49
15	2.86	2.76	2.69	2.64	2.61	2.59	2.55	2.52	2.46	2.44	2.40
16	2.79	2.68	2.61	2.57	2.53	2.51	2.47	2.45	2.38	2.36	2.32
17	2.72	2.62	2.55	2.50	2.47	2.44	2.41	2.38	2.32	2.29	2.25
18	2.67	2.56	2.49	2.44	2.41	2.38	2.35	2.32	2.26	2.23	2.19
19	2.62	2.51	2.44	2.39	2.36	2.33	2.30	2.27	2.20	2.18	2.13
20	2.57	2.46	2.40	2.35	2.31	2.29	2.25	2.22	2.16	2.13	2.09
21	2.53	2.42	2.36	2.31	2.27	2.25	2.21	2.18	2.11	2.09	2.04
22	2.50	2.39	2.32	2.27	2.24	2.21	2.17	2.14	2.08	2.05	2.01
23	2.47	2.36	2.29	2.24	2.20	2.18	2.14	2.11	2.04	2.01	1.97
24	2.44	2.33	2.26	2.21	2.17	2.15	2.11	2.08	2.01	1.98	1.94
25	2.41	2.30	2.23	2.18	2.15	2.12	2.08	2.05	1.98	1.95	1.91
26	2.39	2.28	2.21	2.16	2.12	2.09	2.05	2.03	1.95	1.92	1.88
27	2.36	2.25	2.18	2.13	2.10	2.07	2.03	2.00	1.93	1.90	1.85
28	2.34	2.23	2.16	2.11	2.08	2.05	2.01	1.98	1.91	1.88	1.83
29	2.32	2.21	2.14	2.09	2.06	2.03	1.99	1.96	1.89	1.86	1.81
30	2.31	2.20	2.12	2.07	2.04	2.01	1.97	1.94	1.87	1.84	1.79
40	2.18	2.07	1.99	1.94	1.90	1.88	1.83	1.80	1.72	1.69	1.64
50	2.11	1.99	1.92	1.87	1.83	1.80	1.75	1.72	1.64	1.60	1.55
60	2.06	1.94	1.87	1.82	1.78	1.74	1.70	1.67	1.58	1.54	1.48
120	1.94	1.82	1.75	1.69	1.65	1.61	1.56	1.53	1.43	1.39	1.31
200	1.90	1.78	1.70	1.64	1.60	1.56	1.51	1.47	1.37	1.32	1.23
∞	2.71	1.83	1.71	1.63	1.57	1.52	1.48	1.43	1.39	1.27	1.21

CRITICAL VALUES OF $F_{.01}$

This table shows the 1 percent right-tail critical values of F for the stated degrees of freedom (ν).

Denominator Degrees of Freedom (ν_2)	Numerator Degrees of Freedom (ν_1)										
	1	2	3	4	5	6	7	8	9	10	12
1	4052	4999	5404	5624	5764	5859	5928	5981	6022	6056	6107
2	98.50	99.00	99.16	99.25	99.30	99.33	99.36	99.38	99.39	99.40	99.42
3	34.12	30.82	29.46	28.71	28.24	27.91	27.67	27.49	27.34	27.23	27.05
4	21.20	18.00	16.69	15.98	15.52	15.21	14.98	14.80	14.66	14.55	14.37
5	16.26	13.27	12.06	11.39	10.97	10.67	10.46	10.29	10.16	10.05	9.89
6	13.75	10.92	9.78	9.15	8.75	8.47	8.26	8.10	7.98	7.87	7.72
7	12.25	9.55	8.45	7.85	7.46	7.19	6.99	6.84	6.72	6.62	6.47
8	11.26	8.65	7.59	7.01	6.63	6.37	6.18	6.03	5.91	5.81	5.67
9	10.56	8.02	6.99	6.42	6.06	5.80	5.61	5.47	5.35	5.26	5.11
10	10.04	7.56	6.55	5.99	5.64	5.39	5.20	5.06	4.94	4.85	4.71
11	9.65	7.21	6.22	5.67	5.32	5.07	4.89	4.74	4.63	4.54	4.40
12	9.33	6.93	5.95	5.41	5.06	4.82	4.64	4.50	4.39	4.30	4.16
13	9.07	6.70	5.74	5.21	4.86	4.62	4.44	4.30	4.19	4.10	3.96
14	8.86	6.51	5.56	5.04	4.69	4.46	4.28	4.14	4.03	3.94	3.80
15	8.68	6.36	5.42	4.89	4.56	4.32	4.14	4.00	3.89	3.80	3.67
16	8.53	6.23	5.29	4.77	4.44	4.20	4.03	3.89	3.78	3.69	3.55
17	8.40	6.11	5.19	4.67	4.34	4.10	3.93	3.79	3.68	3.59	3.46
18	8.29	6.01	5.09	4.58	4.25	4.01	3.84	3.71	3.60	3.51	3.37
19	8.18	5.93	5.01	4.50	4.17	3.94	3.77	3.63	3.52	3.43	3.30
20	8.10	5.85	4.94	4.43	4.10	3.87	3.70	3.56	3.46	3.37	3.23
21	8.02	5.78	4.87	4.37	4.04	3.81	3.64	3.51	3.40	3.31	3.17
22	7.95	5.72	4.82	4.31	3.99	3.76	3.59	3.45	3.35	3.26	3.12
23	7.88	5.66	4.76	4.26	3.94	3.71	3.54	3.41	3.30	3.21	3.07
24	7.82	5.61	4.72	4.22	3.90	3.67	3.50	3.36	3.26	3.17	3.03
25	7.77	5.57	4.68	4.18	3.85	3.63	3.46	3.32	3.22	3.13	2.99
26	7.72	5.53	4.64	4.14	3.82	3.59	3.42	3.29	3.18	3.09	2.96
27	7.68	5.49	4.60	4.11	3.78	3.56	3.39	3.26	3.15	3.06	2.93
28	7.64	5.45	4.57	4.07	3.75	3.53	3.36	3.23	3.12	3.03	2.90
29	7.60	5.42	4.54	4.04	3.73	3.50	3.33	3.20	3.09	3.00	2.87
30	7.56	5.39	4.51	4.02	3.70	3.47	3.30	3.17	3.07	2.98	2.84
40	7.31	5.18	4.31	3.83	3.51	3.29	3.12	2.99	2.89	2.80	2.66
50	7.17	5.06	4.20	3.72	3.41	3.19	3.02	2.89	2.78	2.70	2.56
60	7.08	4.98	4.13	3.65	3.34	3.12	2.95	2.82	2.72	2.63	2.50
120	6.85	4.79	3.95	3.48	3.17	2.96	2.79	2.66	2.56	2.47	2.34
200	6.76	4.71	3.88	3.41	3.11	2.89	2.73	2.60	2.50	2.41	2.27
∞	2.71	6.63	4.61	3.78	3.32	3.02	2.80	2.64	2.51	2.41	2.32

Denominator Degrees of Freedom (v_2)	Numerator Degrees of Freedom (v_1)										
	15	20	25	30	35	40	50	60	120	200	∞
1	6157	6209	6240	6260	6275	6286	6302	6313	6340	6350	6366
2	99.43	99.45	99.46	99.47	99.47	99.48	99.48	99.48	99.49	99.49	99.50
3	26.87	26.69	26.58	26.50	26.45	26.41	26.35	26.32	26.22	26.18	26.13
4	14.20	14.02	13.91	13.84	13.79	13.75	13.69	13.65	13.56	13.52	13.47
5	9.72	9.55	9.45	9.38	9.33	9.29	9.24	9.20	9.11	9.08	9.02
6	7.56	7.40	7.30	7.23	7.18	7.14	7.09	7.06	6.97	6.93	6.88
7	6.31	6.16	6.06	5.99	5.94	5.91	5.86	5.82	5.74	5.70	5.65
8	5.52	5.36	5.26	5.20	5.15	5.12	5.07	5.03	4.95	4.91	4.86
9	4.96	4.81	4.71	4.65	4.60	4.57	4.52	4.48	4.40	4.36	4.31
10	4.56	4.41	4.31	4.25	4.20	4.17	4.12	4.08	4.00	3.96	3.91
11	4.25	4.10	4.01	3.94	3.89	3.86	3.81	3.78	3.69	3.66	3.60
12	4.01	3.86	3.76	3.70	3.65	3.62	3.57	3.54	3.45	3.41	3.36
13	3.82	3.66	3.57	3.51	3.46	3.43	3.38	3.34	3.25	3.22	3.17
14	3.66	3.51	3.41	3.35	3.30	3.27	3.22	3.18	3.09	3.06	3.01
15	3.52	3.37	3.28	3.21	3.17	3.13	3.08	3.05	2.96	2.92	2.87
16	3.41	3.26	3.16	3.10	3.05	3.02	2.97	2.93	2.84	2.81	2.76
17	3.31	3.16	3.07	3.00	2.96	2.92	2.87	2.83	2.75	2.71	2.66
18	3.23	3.08	2.98	2.92	2.87	2.84	2.78	2.75	2.66	2.62	2.57
19	3.15	3.00	2.91	2.84	2.80	2.76	2.71	2.67	2.58	2.55	2.49
20	3.09	2.94	2.84	2.78	2.73	2.69	2.64	2.61	2.52	2.48	2.42
21	3.03	2.88	2.79	2.72	2.67	2.64	2.58	2.55	2.46	2.42	2.36
22	2.98	2.83	2.73	2.67	2.62	2.58	2.53	2.50	2.40	2.36	2.31
23	2.93	2.78	2.69	2.62	2.57	2.54	2.48	2.45	2.35	2.32	2.26
24	2.89	2.74	2.64	2.58	2.53	2.49	2.44	2.40	2.31	2.27	2.21
25	2.85	2.70	2.60	2.54	2.49	2.45	2.40	2.36	2.27	2.23	2.17
26	2.81	2.66	2.57	2.50	2.45	2.42	2.36	2.33	2.23	2.19	2.13
27	2.78	2.63	2.54	2.47	2.42	2.38	2.33	2.29	2.20	2.16	2.10
28	2.75	2.60	2.51	2.44	2.39	2.35	2.30	2.26	2.17	2.13	2.07
29	2.73	2.57	2.48	2.41	2.36	2.33	2.27	2.23	2.14	2.10	2.04
30	2.70	2.55	2.45	2.39	2.34	2.30	2.25	2.21	2.11	2.07	2.01
40	2.52	2.37	2.27	2.20	2.15	2.11	2.06	2.02	1.92	1.87	1.81
50	2.42	2.27	2.17	2.10	2.05	2.01	1.95	1.91	1.80	1.76	1.69
60	2.35	2.20	2.10	2.03	1.98	1.94	1.88	1.84	1.73	1.68	1.60
120	2.19	2.03	1.93	1.86	1.81	1.76	1.70	1.66	1.53	1.48	1.38
200	2.13	1.97	1.87	1.79	1.74	1.69	1.63	1.58	1.45	1.39	1.28
∞	2.71	2.04	1.88	1.77	1.70	1.64	1.59	1.52	1.47	1.32	1.25

Solutions to Odd-Numbered Exercises

CHAPTER 1

1.5 a. Statistics summarizes data.
b. Statistics tells us how large a sample to take.

1.7 a. Most would prefer the graph, but both are clear.
b. The number of salads sold reached a maximum in May and decreased steadily toward the end of 2005.

1.11 a. All combinations have same chance of winning so method did not "work."
b. No, same as any other six numbers.

1.13 A reduction of .2% may not seem important to the individual customer, but from the company's perspective it could be significant depending on how many customers they have.

1.17 a. Analyze the 80 responses but make no conclusions about nonrespondents.
b. No, study seems too flawed.
c. Suggest a new well-designed survey with response incentive.

1.19 a. Attendance, study time, ability level, interest level, instructor's ability, prerequisites.
b. Reverse causation? Good students make better decisions about their health.
c. No, causation is not shown.

1.21 A major problem is that we don't know number of students in each major.
a. Likely fewer philosophy majors to begin with.
b. Likely more engineers want an MBA, so they take it.
c. Causation not shown. Physics may differ from marketing majors (e.g., math skills).
d. The GMAT is just an indicator of academic skills.

1.23 a. "Its R^2 value is quite close to 1, indicating it is a good fit to the actual data. I feel that G.E. is one of the most respected corporations in the world because of its strong management and name recognition. Its valuable assets make it poised for steady growth over the next decade."
b. "If a country's unemployment rate is too high, it could cause a downturn in their economy's structure."
c. "This forecast is very unlikely, because you cannot have a negative number of people unemployed."
d. "This is not a well-designed graph because the title is too long and there are no labels on the axes."
e. "This graph has no clear border to give a sense of containment. It is dealing with three separate pieces of information. In this graph, the same data is presented, but in a deceptive manner. The sources do not contain enough detail."

CHAPTER 2

2.1 Observation—single data point. Variable—characteristic of an individual that takes on various values.

2.3 a. categorical   b. categorical   c. discrete numerical
d. continuous numerical   e. continuous numerical
f. continuous numerical   g. continuous numerical

2.7 a. ratio   b. ordinal   c. nominal   d. interval
e. ratio   f. ordinal

2.11 a. cross-sectional   b. time series
c. time series   d. cross-sectional

2.13 a. time series   b. cross-sectional
c. time series   d. cross-sectional

2.15 a. Census   b. Sample   c. Sample   d. Census

2.17 a. Sample   b. Census   c. Sample   d. Census

2.19 a. Convenience   b. Systematic   c. Judgment or biased

2.25 a. Telephone or Web.   b. Direct observation.
c. Interview, Web, or mail.   d. Interview or Web.

2.27 Version 1: Most would say yes. Version 2: More varied responses.

2.29 a. Continuous numerical   b. Categorical
c. Discrete numerical   d. Discrete numerical
e. Continuous numerical

2.33 Q1 Categorical, nominal   Q2 Continuous, ratio
Q3 Continuous, ratio   Q4 Discrete, ratio
Q5 Categorical, ordinal   Q6 Categorical, interval
Q7 Discrete, ratio   Q8 Continuous, ratio
Q9 Discrete, ratio   Q10 Categorical, ordinal
Q11 Continuous, ratio   Q12 Discrete, ratio
Q13 Categorical, ordinal   Q14 Categorical, nominal
Q15 Categorical, ordinal

2.35 a. statistic   b. parameter
c. statistic   d. parameter

2.37 a. Number of employees or industry.
b. Firms may differ in size, etc.
c. Under representation of chemical companies.

2.39 Use mail or telephone. Census not possible.

2.41 a. Cluster sampling   b. Finite   c. Yes

2.43 a. Cluster sampling.
b. Yes, if selected stores had the same supplier.

2.45 a. Census   b. Sample   c. Sample   d. Census

2.47 a. Internet Survey.   b. Telephone Survey.
c. Random Sample of tax returns.   d. Statistic based on sales, not a sample.   e. Extrapolated from government population surveys.

2.49 a. Cluster sampling, neighborhoods are natural clusters.
b. Impractical if potential gain is small.
c. Picking a day near a holiday with light trash.

2.51 a. systematic.   b. simple random sample.
c. systematic or simple random sample.
d. simple random sample or systematic.   e. stratified.

2.53 a. Income, store type
b. Simple random sample

2.55 a. No   b. Systematic

2.57 Convenience. Cost and Time.

2.59 Education and income could affect who uses the no-call list.
a. They won't reach those who purchase such services.
Same response for b and c.

Surveys and Scales

2.61 a. Ordinal.   b. Intervals are equal.

2.63 a. Rate the effectiveness of this professor. 1—Excellent
to 5—Poor.
b. Rate your satisfaction with the President's economic
policy. 1—Very Satisfied to 5—Very dissatisfied.
c. How long did you wait to see your doctor? Less than
15 minutes, between 15 and 30 minutes, between
30 minutes and 1 hour, more than 1 hour.

2.67 a. Likert

CHAPTER 3

3.1 Approximately symmetric with typical values around 25.

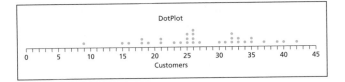

3.3 Sarah's calls are shorter.

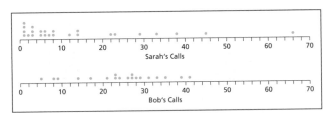

3.5 Sturges' Rule suggests about 6 bins. Slight right skew.

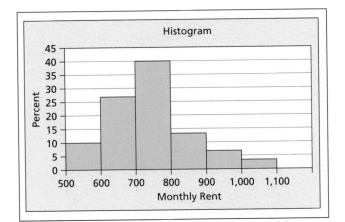

3.7 a. 7 bins, width = 5, Sturges' Rule = 6 bins
b. 8 bins, width = 10, Sturges' Rule = 6 or 7 bins
c. 10 bins, width = 0.15, Sturges' Rule = 9 bins
d. 8 bins, width = 0.01, Sturges' Rule = 8 bins

3.9 Declining at a declining rate.

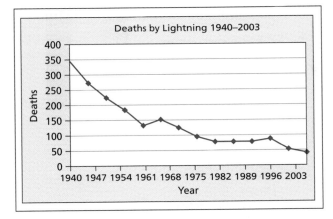

3.11 a. Line chart is clear but not attention-getting.

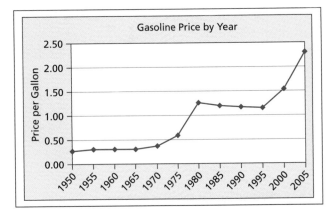

b. Bar chart displays a more dramatic increase.

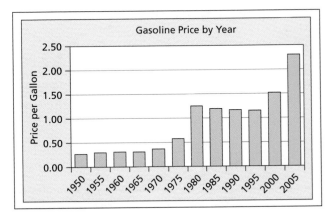

3.13 Chart is fairly easy to interpret as long as the data values are displayed.

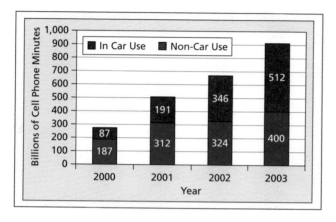

3.15 a. To show more detail, you could start the graph at (20,20).
b. There is a moderate positive linear relationship.

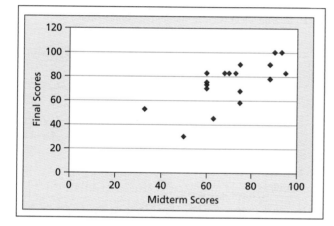

3.17 a. To show more detail, you could start the graph at (.80,100).
b. There is a moderate negative linear relationship.

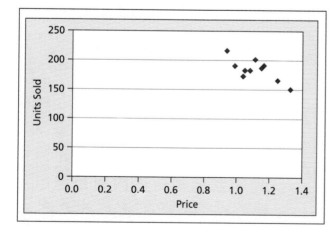

3.19 a. Default pie is clear, but rather small (can be dragged larger).
b. Visually strong, but harder to read due to rotation.
c. Clear, easy to read.

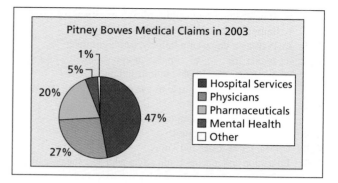

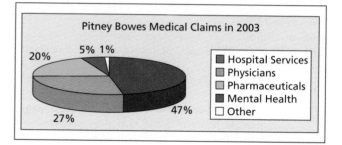

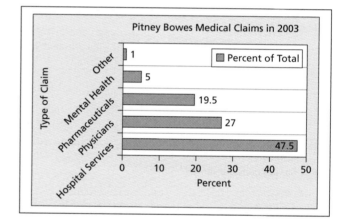

3.21 a.

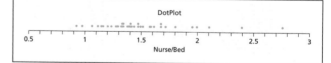

b.

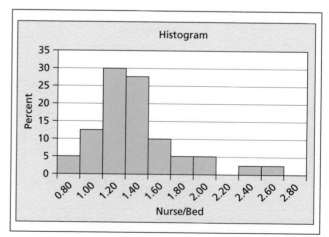

c. Skewed to the right. Half of the data values are between 1.2 and 1.6.

3.23 a. MegaStat's dotplot.

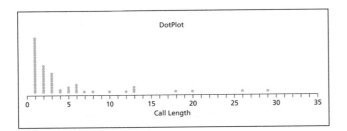

b. MegaStat's histogram.

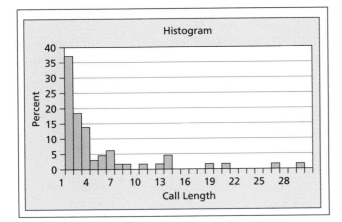

c. Heavily skewed to the right. Central tendency approximately 3 minutes.

3.25

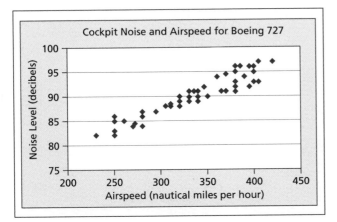

3.27 a. Horizontal bar chart with 3D visual effect.
   b. Strengths: Good proportions and no distracting pictures. Weaknesses: No labels on X and Y axes, title unclear, 3D effect does not add to presentation.
   c. Vertical bar chart without visual effect and label on X axis.

3.29 a. Pictograph. b. Pictures distracting, implies irresponsibility, does show source of data. c. Take out pictures, show a simple line chart.

3.31 a. Exploded pie chart.
   b. Strengths: Information complete, colorful. Weaknesses: Hard to assess differences in size of pie slices.
   c. Sorted column chart with OPEC and non-OPEC countries color coded.

3.33 a. Bar Chart using pictures for bars.
   b. Strengths: Visually appealing; good summary data. Weaknesses: Difficult to assess differences; uses area trick.
   c. Use plain bar chart.

3.35 a.

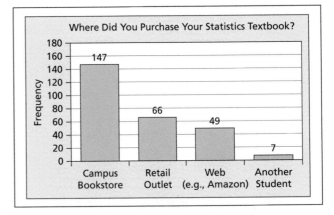

b. Yes, pie chart could be used.

3.37 a.

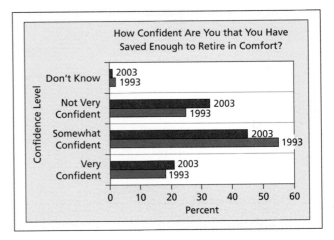

b. Yes, a vertical column chart would also work.

3.39 a.

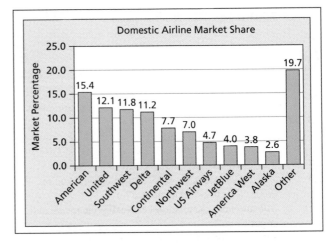

b. Yes, a pie chart could be used.

3.41 a.

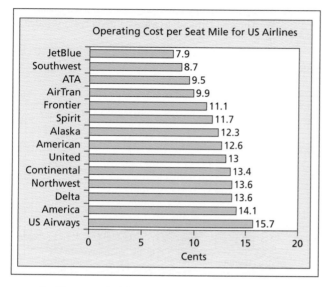

b. Yes, a vertical bar chart could be used. But a table may be clearest, because the large quantity of data tends to clutter the graphs.

3.43 a.

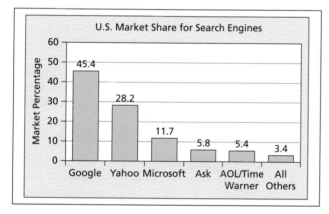

b. Yes, a pie chart would work.

3.45 a. Bar chart.

b. Yes, but so many categories might make it hard to read.

CHAPTER 4

4.1 a. mean = 2.83, median = 1.5, mode = 0.

b. mean = 68.33, median = 72, mode = 40.

c. mean = 3.044, median = 3.03, no mode.

4.3 a. $\bar{x} = 27.34$, median = 26, mode = 26.

b. No, $\bar{x}$ is greater than the median and mode.

c. Slightly skewed right.

d. Choose mean or median because data is quantitative.

4.5 b. $\bar{x} = 4.48$, median = 2, mode = 1.

c. No, $\bar{x} >$ median > mode.

e. Skewed right.

4.7 a. TRIMMEAN(A1:A50,.2). b. 5. c. 10.

4.9 a. $\bar{x} = 27.34$, midrange = 25.50, geometric mean = 26.08, 10% trimmed mean = 27.47.

b. The measures are all close, especially the mean and trimmed mean.

4.11 a. $\bar{x} = 4.48$, midrange = 15.0, geometric mean = 2.6, 10% trimmed mean = 3.13.

b. No, the midrange is much greater than the other three measures.

c. The data is skewed right.

d. Mean and geometric mean describe the central tendency better than the other two, but also affected by skewness.

4.13 a. Sample A: $\bar{x} = 7$, $s = 1$. Sample B: $\bar{x} = 62$, $s = 1$. Sample C: $\bar{x} = 1001$, $s = 1$.

b. The standard deviation is not a function of the mean.

4.15 a. Stock A: $CV = 21.43\%$. Stock B: $CV = 8.32\%$. Stock C: $CV = 36.17\%$.

b. Directly comparing standard deviation would not be helpful in this case because the means have different magnitudes.

4.17 $s = 5.87$, $MAD = 3.92$.

4.19 a. $z = 2.4$. b. $z = 1$. c. $z = 0.6$.

4.21 b. 18 ($z = 2.30$) and 20 ($z = 2.64$) are unusual observations. 26 ($z = 3.67$) and 29 ($z = 4.18$) are outliers.

c. 87.7% lie within 1 standard deviation and 93.8% lie within 2 standard deviations. 87.7% is much greater than the 68% specified by the empirical rule. The distribution does not appear normal.

d. Yes.

4.23 a. $Q_1 = 1$, $Q_3 = 5$. The middle 50% of the calls last between 1 and 5 minutes.

b. *Midhinge* = 3. Calls typically last 3 minutes.

c. The data are heavily skewed to the right.

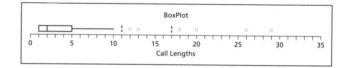

4.25

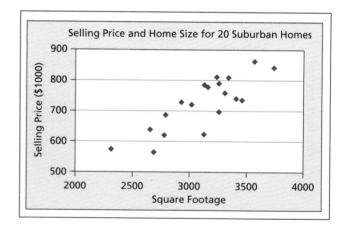

4.27 a.

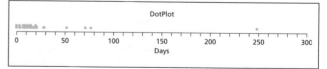

The distribution is heavily skewed right.

b. $\bar{x} = 26.71$, median = 14.5, mode = 11, and midrange = 124.5.

c. $Q_1 = 7.75$, $Q_3 = 20.25$, *Midhinge* = 14, and $CQV = 44.64\%$.

d. The geometric mean is only valid for data greater than zero.
e. The median because the data is quantitative and heavily skewed right.

4.29 a. Stock funds: $\bar{x} = 1.329$, median $= 1.22$, mode $= 0.99$. Bond funds: $\bar{x} = 0.875$, median $= 0.85$, mode $= 0.64$.
b. The central tendency of stock fund expense ratios is higher than bond funds.
c. Stock funds: $s = 0.5933$, $CV = 44.65\%$. Bond funds: $s = 0.4489$, $CV = 51.32\%$. The stock funds have less variability relative to the mean.
d. Stock funds: $Q_1 = 1.035$, $Q_3 = 1.565$, $Midhinge = 1.3$. Bond funds: $Q_1 = 0.64$, $Q_3 = 0.99$, $Midhinge = 0.815$. Stock funds have higher expense ratios in general than bond funds.

4.31 a.

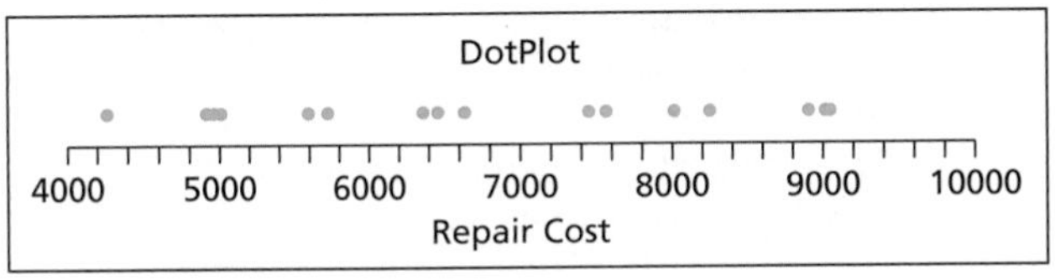

b. mean = 6807, median = 6,646.
c. Not skewed.
d. There is no mode.

4.33 a.

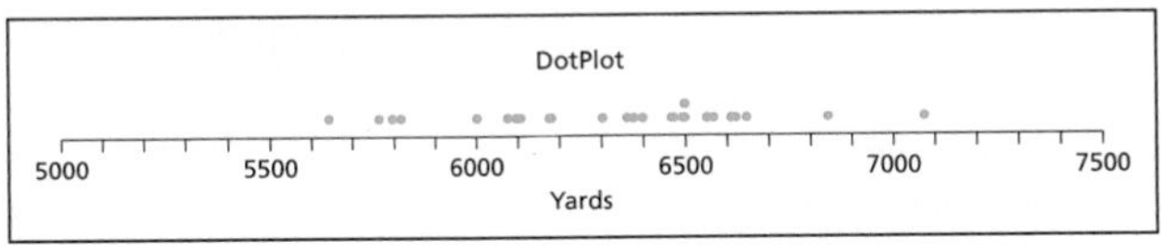

The dot plot shows that most of the data are centered around 6500 yards. The distribution is skewed to the left.
b. $\bar{x} = 6{,}335.52$, median $= 6{,}400.0$, mode $= 6{,}500.0$, and midrange $= 6{,}361.5$.
c. Best: Median because data is quantitative and skewed left. Worst: Mode worst because the data is quantitative and very few values repeat themselves.
d. This data is not highly skewed. The geometric mean works well for skewed data.

4.35 a. Male: $Midhinge = 177$, $CQV = 2.82\%$. Female: $Midhinge = 163.5$, $CQV = 2.75\%$. These statistics are appropriate because we have specific percentiles but not the entire data set.
b. Yes, height percentiles do change. The population is slowly increasing in height.

4.37 a. $\bar{x} = 3012.44$, median $= 2{,}550.5$. There is no value for the mode.
b. The typical cricket club's income is approximately £2.5 million.

4.39 a.

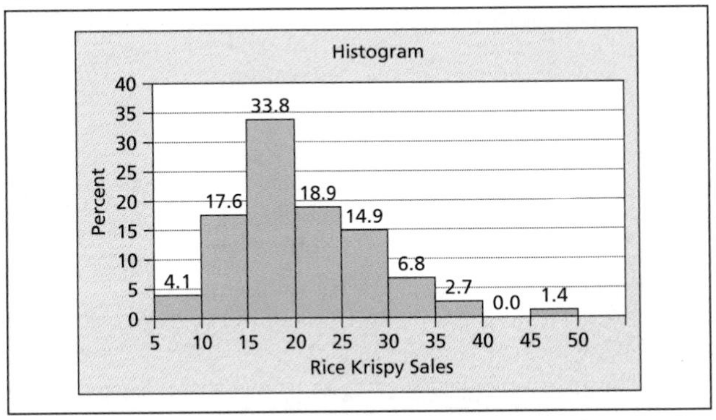

b. mean = 20.12, median = 18.5, mode = 16.
c. standard deviation = 7.64.
d. One possible outlier at 49 (store 22).

4.41 a. Tuition Plans: $CV = 42.86\%$, S&P 500: $CV = 122.48\%$.
b. The CV shows *relative* risk for each investment.
c. While the tuition plans have a lower return, there is less risk of losing your investment than if you had invested in stocks.

4.43 a. $Midrange = 0.855$. b. The methods for estimating the mean and standard deviation are based on a normal distribution. c. Normal assumption reasonable.

4.45 a. The distribution is skewed to the right.
b. This makes sense, most patrons would keep books about 10 days with a few keeping them much longer.

4.47 a. Reasonable to expect the distribution is skewed right.
b. Mode < median < mean.

4.49 a. Would expect mean to be close in value to the median, or slightly higher. b. Life span would have normal distribution. If skewed, more likely skewed right than left. Life span is bounded below by zero, but is unbounded in the positive direction.

4.51 a. It is the midrange, not the median.
b. The midrange is influenced by outliers. Salaries tend to be skewed to the right. Community should use the median.

4.53 a. and c.

	Week 1	*Week 2*	*Week 3*	*Week 4*
mean	50.00	50.00	50.00	50.00
sample standard deviation	10.61	10.61	10.61	10.61
median	50.00	52.00	56.00	47.00

b. Based on the mean and standard deviation, it appears that the distributions are the same.

d.

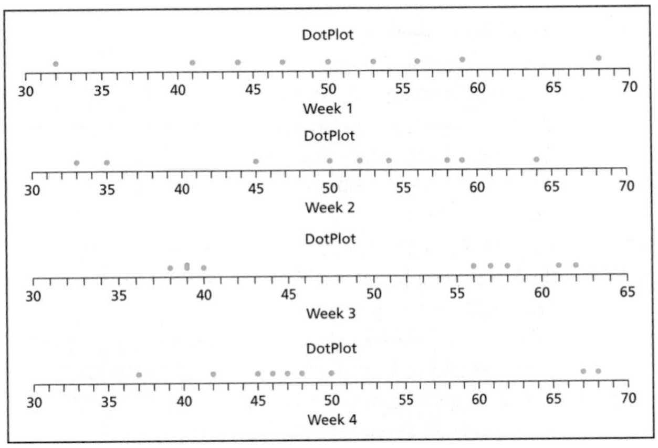

e. Based on the medians and dotplots, distributions are quite different.

4.57   a.

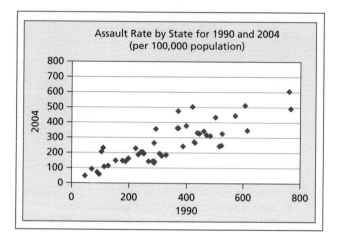

b. $r = .8332$.

c. The rates are positively correlated.

d. 1990: mean = 331.92, median = 3.7, mode = 286.
2004: mean = 256.6, median = 232, mode = 143.

CHAPTER 5

5.1   a. S = {(V,B), (V,E), (V,O), (M,B), (M,E), (M,O), (A,B), (A,E), (A,O)}

b. Events are not equally likely. Border's probably carries more books than other merchandise.

5.3   a. S = {(L,B), (L,B'), (R,B), (R,B')}

b. Events are not equally likely. More right handed people than left handed people.

5.5   a. Expert opinion of stock brokers or empirical.

b. From historical data of IPOs or based on judgments.

5.7   a. Empirical.

b. Historical data of past launches.

5.9   a. Subjective.   b. Expert judgment by NASA.

5.11   a. Not mutually exclusive.

b. Mutually exclusive.

c. Not mutually exclusive.

5.13   a. $P(A \cup B) = .4 + .5 - .05 = .85$.

b. $P(A \mid B) = .05/.50 = .10$.

c. $P(B \mid A) = .05/.4 = .125$.

5.15   a. $P(S) = .217$.   b. $P(S') = .783$.

c. Odds in favor of S: $.217/.783 = .277$.

d. Odds against S: $.783/.217 = 3.61$

5.17   a. $X = 1$ if the drug is approved, 0 otherwise.

b. $X = 1$ if batter gets a hit, 0 otherwise.

c. $X = 1$ if breast cancer detected, 0 otherwise.

5.19   a. $P(S') = 1 - .246$. There is a 75.4% chance that a female aged 18–24 is a nonsmoker.

b. $P(S \cup C) = .246 + .830 - .232 = .014$. There is an 84.4% chance that a female aged 18–24 is a smoker or is Caucasian.

c. $P(S \mid C) = .232/.830 = .2795$. Given that the female aged 18–24 is a Caucasian, there is a 27.95% chance that they are a smoker.

d. $P(S \cap C') = P(S) - P(S \cap C) = .246 - .232 = .014$. $P(S \mid C') = .014/.17 = .0824$. Given that the female ages 18–24 is *not* Caucasian, there is an 8.24% chance that she smokes.

5.21 $P(A \mid B) = P(A \cap B)/P(B) = .05/.50 = .10$ No, A and B are not independent because $P(A \mid B) \neq P(A)$.

5.23   a. $P(V \cup M) = .73 + .18 - .03 = .88$.

b. $P(V \cap M) \neq P(V)P(M)$ therefore V and M are not independent.

5.25   "Five nines" reliability means $P(not\ failing) = .99999$. $P(power\ system\ failure) = 1 - (.05)^3 = .999875$. The system does not meet the test.

5.27   a. $P(D) = .5064$.   b. $P(R) = .1410$.

c. $P(D \cap R) = .0513$.   d. $P(D \cup R) = .5962$.

e. $P(R \mid D) = .1013$.   f. $P(R \mid P) = .1628$.

5.29   *Gender* and *Major* are not independent. For example, $P(A \cap F) = .22$. $P(A)P(F) = .245$. Because the values are not equal, the events are not independent.

5.31   a. 5040   b. 8.718×10^{10} c. 1.198×10^{100}.

5.33   a. $26^6 = 308,915,776$.   b. $36^6 = 2,176,782,336$.

c. $32^6 = 1,073,741,824$.

5.35   a. $10^6 = 1,000,000$.

b. $10^5 = 100,000$.   c. $10^6 = 1,000,000$

5.37   a. $7! = 5,040$ ways.   b. No, too many!

5.39   a. $_8C_3 = 56$.   b. $_8C_5 = 56$.

c. $_8C_1 = 8$.   d. $_8C_8 = 1$.

5.45   a. An empirical probability using response frequencies from the survey.

b. Odds for failure: $.44/.56 = .786$ or 11 to 14.

5.47   No, the law of large numbers says that the larger the sample, the closer our sample results will be to the true value. If Tom Brookens increases his times "at bat" he'll get closer and closer to his true batting average, which is probably close to .176.

5.49   a. Empirical or subjective.

b. Most likely estimated by interviewing ER doctors.

c. The sample could have been small, not representative of all doctors.

5.51   a. Subjective.

b. Simulated experiment using a computer model.

c. The estimate is probably not very accurate. Results highly dependent on the simulation and data in the model.

5.53   a. Empirical or subjective.

b. Observation or survey.

c. The estimate is probably not very accurate. Observation is difficult and survey results may be biased.

5.57   Odds against an Acura Integra being stolen = $.987/.013 = 76$ to 1.

5.59   P(Detroit Wins) = $1/51 = .0196$. P(New Jersey Wins) = $1/6 = .1667$.

5.61   a. $26^3 10^3 = 17,576,000$.

b. $36^6 = 2,176,782,336$.

c. 0 and 1 might be disallowed since they are similar in appearance to letters like O and I.

d. Yes, 2.2 billion unique plates should be enough.

e. $34^6 = 1,544,804,416$.

5.63 $(7)(6)(5) = 210$.

5.65   No, $P(A)P(B) \neq .05$.

5.67   a. Having independent back up power for computers might have eliminated delayed flights.

b. If the cost due to delayed/cancelled flights, weighted by the risk of a power outage, is greater than \$100,000, then the airline can justify the expenditure.

5.69 Assuming independence, P(3 cases won out of next 3) = $.7^3 = .343$.

5.71 a. i. .4825 ii. .25 iii. .115 iv. .19 v. .64 vi. .3316 vii. .09 viii. .015 ix. .0325.
   b. Yes, the vehicle type and mall location are dependent.

5.73 a. i. .5588 ii. .5294 iii. .3684 iv. .4000 v. .1765 vi. .2059.
   b. No, P(A−) = .4705 and P(A− | F−) = .3684. Interest rates moved down 47% of the time and yet the forecasters predictions of a decline showed a 37% accuracy rate.

CHAPTER 6

6.1 Only A is a PDF since $P(x)$ sum to 1.

6.3 $E(X) = 2.25, V(X) = 1.6875, \sigma = 1.299$, right-skewed.

6.5 $E(X) = 1000(.01) + (0)(.999) = \$10$, add \$25, charges \$35.

6.7 $E(X) = 250(.3) + 950(.3) + 0(.4) = \$360$ million.

6.9 a. $\mu = (20 + 60)/2 = 40$, $\sigma = \sqrt{[(60 - 20 + 1)^2 - 1]/12} = 11.83$.
   b. $P(X \geq 40) = .525, P(X \geq 30) = .775$.

6.11 a. $\mu = (1 + 31)/2 = 16$, $\sigma = \sqrt{[(31 - 1 + 1)^2 - 1]/12} = 8.944$.
   b. Yes, if conception is random.

6.13 Answers may vary.
   a. 1 = correct, 0 = incorrect.
   b. 1 = insured, 0 = uninsured.
   c. 1 = busy, 0 = not busy.
   d. 1 = lost weight, 0 no weight loss.

6.15 a. $\mu = 0.8, \sigma = 0.8485$ b. $\mu = 4, \sigma = 1.5492$
   c. $\mu = 6, \sigma = 1.7321$ d. $\mu = 27, \sigma = 1.6432$
   e. $\mu = 56, \sigma = 4.0988$ f. $\mu = 16, \sigma = 1.7888$

6.17 a. $P(X \leq 3) = .9437$
   b. $P(X > 7) = 1 - P(X \leq 7) = .0547$
   c. $P(X < 3) = P(X \leq 2) = .0705$
   d. $P(X \leq 10) = .00417$

6.19 a. $P(X = 0) = .10737$ b. $P(X \geq 2) = .62419$
   c. $P(X < 3) = .67780$ d. $\mu = n\pi = (10)(.2) = 2$
   e. $\sigma = \sqrt{(10)(.2)(1 - .2)} = 1.2649$ g. Skewed right.

6.21 a. $P(X = 0) = .0916$.   b. $P(X \geq 2) = .6276$.
   c. $P(X < 4) = .9274$.   d. $P(X = 5) = .0079$.

6.23 a. $\lambda = 1, \mu = 1.0, \sigma = 1$
   b. $\lambda = 2, \mu = 2.0, \sigma = 1.414$
   c. $\lambda = 4, \mu = 4.0, \sigma = 2.0$ d. $\lambda = 9, \mu = 9.0, \sigma = 3$
   e. $\lambda = 12, \mu = 12.0, \sigma = 3.464$

6.25 a. $\lambda = 4.3, P(X \leq 3) = .37715$
   b. $\lambda = 5.2, P(X > 7) = .15508$
   c. $\lambda = 2.7, P(X < 3) = .49362$
   d. $\lambda = 11.0, P(X \leq 10) = .45989$

6.27 a. $P(X \geq 1) = .8173$.   b. $P(X = 0) = .1827$.
   c. $P(X > 3) = .0932$.

6.29 a. Add-ons are ordered independently.
   b. $P(X \geq 2) = .4082$.   c. $P(X = 0) = .2466$.

6.31* Let $\lambda = n\pi = (500)(.003) = 1.5$
   a. $P(X \geq 2) = 1 - .55783 = .44217$
   b. $P(X \leq 4) = .93436$ c. Large n and small π.
   d. Yes, $n \geq 20$ and $\pi \leq .05$

6.33* a. Set $\lambda = \mu = (200)(.03) = 6$
   b. $\sigma = \sqrt{(200)(.03)(1 - .03)} = 2.412$

c. $P(X \geq 10) = 1 - .91608 = .08392$
d. $P(X \leq 4) = .28506$
e. n is too large without Excel.
f. Yes, $n \geq 20$ and $\pi \leq .05$.

6.35 a. $E(X) = 2.3$.
   b. $P(X = 0) \approx .1003, P(X > 2) = .4040$.

6.37 $E(X) = (100)(1/6) + (-15)(5/6) = 16.67 - 12.50 = \$4.17$.

6.39 a. $\mu = (1 + 44)/2 = 22.5$, $\sigma = \sqrt{[(44 - 1 + 1)^2 - 1]/12} = 12.698$.
   b. What was n? Histogram shape?

6.41 a. $\pi = .80$ (answers will vary).
   b. $\pi = .300$ (answers will vary).
   c. $\pi = .50$ (answers will vary).
   d. $\pi = .80$ (answers will vary).
   e. One trial may influence the next.

6.43 a. $P(X = 5) = .59049$ b. $P(X = 4) = .32805$
   c. Strongly right-skewed

6.45 a. $P(X = 0) = .06250$
   b. $P(X \geq 2) = 1 - .31250 = .68750$
   c. $P(X \leq 2) = .68750$ d. Symmetric.

6.47 a. =BINOMDIST(3,20,0.3,0)
   b. =BINOMDIST(7,50,0.1,0)
   c. =BINOMDIST(6,80,0.05,1)
   d. =1−BINOMDIST(29,120,0.2,1)

6.49 a. $P(X = 0) = .48398$
   b. $P(X \geq 3) = 1 - P(X \leq 2) = 1 - .97166 = .02834$
   c. $\mu = n\pi = (10)(.07) = 0.7$ defaults

6.51 Binomial with $n = 16, \pi = .8$:
   a. $P(X \geq 10) = 1 - P(X \leq 9) = 1 - .02666 = .97334$.
   b. $P(X < 8) = P(X \leq 7) = .00148$.

6.53 Let X = number of no shows. Then:
   a. If $n = 10$ and $\pi = .10$, then $P(X = 0) = .34868$.
   b. If $n = 11$ and $\pi = .10$, then $P(X \geq 1) = 1 - P(X = 0) = 1 - .31381 = .68619$.
   c. If they sell 11 seats, not more than 1 will be bumped.
   d. If X = number who show ($\pi = .90$). Using = 1 − BINOMDIST(9, n, .9,TRUE) we find that $n = 13$ will ensure that $P(X \geq 10) \geq .95$.

6.55 a. Calls to the fire station may be dependent events.
   b. Answers will vary.

6.57 a. $P(X = 5) = .0872$.
   b. $P(X \leq 5) = .9349$.
   c. $\lambda = 14$ arrivals/5 minute interval.   d. Independence.

6.59 a. Assume independent cancellations.
   b. $P(X = 0) = .22313$ c. $P(X = 1) = .33470$
   d. $P(X > 2) = 1 - .80885 = .19115$
   e. $P(X \geq 5) = 1 - .98142 = .01858$

6.61 a. Assume independent defects with $\lambda = 2.4$.
   b. $P(X = 0) = .09072$ c. $P(X = 1) = .21772$
   d. $P(X \leq 1) = .30844$

6.63 P(at least one rogue wave in 5 days) = $1 - P(X = 0) = .9892$.

6.65 a. Assume independent crashes.
   b. $P(X \geq 1) = 1 - .13534 = .86466$
   c. $P(X < 5) = P(X \leq 4) = .94735$
   d. Skewed right.

6.67* a. Set $\lambda = n\pi = (200)(.02) = 4$.
   b. $P(X = 0) = .01832$ c. $P(X = 1) = .07326$
   d. $P(X = 0) = .01759$ from =BINOMDIST(0,200,0.02,0)
   $P(X = 1) = .07179$ from =BINOMDIST(1,200,0.02,0)
   e. Yes, $n \geq 20$ and $\pi \leq .05$.

6.69* a. $E(X) = 6.4$.
    b. $P(X < 10) = .8858$, $P(X > 5) = .6163$.

CHAPTER 7

Note: Using Appendix C or Excel will lead to somewhat different answers.

7.1 a. D   b. C   c. C

7.3 a. Area $= bh = (1)(.25) = .25$, so not a PDF (area is not 1).
    b. Area $= bh = (4)(.25) = 1$, so could be a PDF (area is 1).
    c. Area $= \frac{1}{2}bh = \frac{1}{2}(2)(2) = 2$, so not a PDF (area is not 1).

7.5 a. $\mu = (0 + 10)/2 = 5, \sigma = \sqrt{\dfrac{(10 - 0)^2}{12}} = 2.886751$.

    b. $\mu = (200 + 100)/2 = 150, \sigma = \sqrt{\dfrac{(200 - 100)^2}{12}} = 28.86751$.

    c. $\mu = (1 + 99)/2 = 50, \sigma = \sqrt{\dfrac{(99 - 1)^2}{12}} = 28.29016$.

7.7 A point has no area in a continuous distribution so $<$ or $\leq$ yields the same result.

7.9 Means and standard deviations differ (X axis scales are different) and so do $f(x)$ heights.

7.11 For samples from a *normal distribution* we expect about 68.26% within $\mu \pm 1\ \sigma$, about 95.44% within $\mu \pm 2\ \sigma$, and about 99.73% within $\mu \pm 3\ \sigma$.

7.13 Using Appendix C-1:
    a. $P(0 < Z < 0.50) = .1915$
    b. $P(-0.50 < Z < 0) = P(0 < Z < 0.50) = .1915$.
    c. $P(Z > 0) = .5000$.
    d. Probability of any point is 0.

7.15 Using Appendix C-1:
    a. $P(Z < 2.15) - P(Z < -1.22) = .9842 - .1112 = .8730$
    b. $P(Z < 2.00) - P(Z < -3.00) = .9772 - .00135 = .97585$ c. $P(Z < 2.00) = .9772$
    d. Probability of any point is 0.

7.17 a. $P(X < 300) = P(Z < 0.71) = .7611$
    b. $P(X > 250) = 1 - P(Z < 2.86) = .9979$
    c. $P(275 < X < 310) = P(Z < 1.43) - P(Z < -1.07) = .9236 - .1423 = .7813$

7.19 $P(X \geq 24) = P(Z \geq 1.92) = 1 - .9726 = .0274$.

7.21 a. $Z = 1.282, X = 13.85$.   b. $Z = 0, X = 10.00$.
    c. $Z = 1.645, X = 14.94$.   d. $Z = -0.842, X = 7.47$.
    e. $Z = -1.282, X = 6.15$.
    f. $Z = \pm 0.675, X = 7.98, 12.03$.
    g. $Z = 1.476, X = 14.43$.
    h. $Z = \pm 1.960, X = 4.12, 15.88$.
    i. $Z = -1.476, X = 5.572$.

7.23 a. $Z = (8.0 - 6.9)/1.2 = 0.92$, so $P(Z < 0.92) = .8212$ (82 percentile). Not that common but not unlikely.
    b. $Z = 1.282, X = 8.44$ lbs
    c. $Z = \pm 1.960, X = 4.55$ lbs to 9.25 lbs

7.25 $P(X \leq X_L) = .25$ and $P(X \geq X_U) = .25$. Solve for X_L and X_U using $z = \pm 0.67$. $X_L = 18$ and $X_U = 21$. The middle 50% of occupied beds falls between 18 and 21.

7.27 a. $P(X < 110) =$NORMDIST(110,100,15,TRUE) $= .74751$
    b. $P(Z < 2.00) =$NORMDIST(2,0,1,TRUE) $= .97725$
    c. $P(X < 5{,}000) =$NORMDIST(5000,6000,1000,TRUE) $= .15866$ d. $P(X < 450) =$NORMDIST (450,600,100,TRUE) $= .06681$

7.29 a. $=$NORMINV(0.1,360,9) $= 348.466$
    b. $=$NORMINV(0.32,360,9) $= 355.791$
    c. $=$NORMINV(0.75,360,9) $= 366.070$
    d. $=$NORMINV(0.9,360,9) $= 371.534$
    e. $=$NORMINV(0.999,360,9) $= 387.812$
    f. $=$NORMINV(0.9999,360,9) $= 393.472$

7.31 a. $=$NORMSINV(RAND())
    b. $\mu = 0$ and $\sigma = 1$ (answers will vary)
    c. $\mu = 0$ and $\sigma = 1$ (answers will vary)

7.33 Normality OK since $n\pi = (1000)(.07) = 70 \geq 10$, $n(1 - \pi) = (1000)(.93) = 930 \geq 10$. Set $\mu = n\pi = 70$ and $\sigma = \sqrt{n\pi(1 - \pi)} = 8.0684571$.
    a. $P(X < 50) = P(Z < -2.54) = .0055$ (using $X = 49.5$)
    b. $P(X > 100) = P(Z > 3.78) = 1 - P(Z \leq 3.78) = 1 - .99992 = .00008$ (using $X = 100.5$)

7.35 Normality OK. Set $\mu = 180, \sigma = 4.242641$.
    a. $P(X \geq 175) = P(Z \geq -1.30) = 1 - P(Z \leq 1.30) = 1 - .0968 = .9032$ (using $X = 174.5$)
    b. $P(X < 190) = P(Z \leq 2.24) = .9875$ (using $X = 189.5$)

7.37 Set $\mu = \lambda = 28$ and $\sigma = \sqrt{28} = 5.2915$.
    a. $P(X > 35) = 1 - P(Z \leq 1.42) = 1 - .9222 = .0788$ (using $X = 35.5$)
    b. $P(X < 25) = P(Z \leq -0.66) = .2546$ (using $X = 24.5$)
    c. $\lambda = 28 \geq 10$, so OK to use normal.
    d. .0823 and .2599. Yes, it is good.

7.39 a. $P(X > 7) = e^{-\lambda x} = e^{-(0.3)(7)} = e^{-2.1} = .1225$
    b. $P(X < 2) = 1 - e^{-\lambda x} = 1 - e^{-(0.3)(2)} = 1 - e^{-0.6} = 1 - .5488 = .4512$

7.41 $\lambda = 2.1$ alarms/minute or $\lambda = 0.035$ alarms/second.
    a. $P(X < 60) = 1 - e^{-\lambda x} = 1 - e^{-(0.035)(60)} = 1 - .1225 = .8775$
    b. $P(X > 30) = e^{-\lambda x} = e^{-(0.035)(30)} = .3499$
    c. $P(X \geq 45) = e^{-\lambda x} = e^{-(0.035)(45)} = .2070$

7.43 a. $P(X > 30\ \text{sec}) = .2466$.   b. $P(X \leq 15\ \text{sec}) = .5034$.
    c. $P(X > 1\ \text{min}) = .0608$.

7.45 $\lambda = 4.2$ orders/hour or $\lambda = .07$ orders/minute.
    a. Set $e^{-\lambda x} = .50$, take natural log, $x = 0.165035$ hr (9.9 min).
    b. Set $e^{-\lambda x} = .25$, take natural log, $x = 0.33007$ hr (19.8 min).
    c. Set $e^{-\lambda x} = .10$, take natural log, $x = 0.548235$ hr (32.89 min).

7.47 MTBE $= 20$ min/order so $\lambda = 1/$MTBE $= 1/20$ orders/min.
    a. Set $e^{-\lambda x} = .50$, take natural log, $x = 13.86$ min.
    b. Distribution is very right-skewed.
    c. Set $e^{-\lambda x} = .25$, take natural log, $x = 27.7$ min.

7.49 a. D   b. C   c. C

7.51 a. $\mu = (25 + 65)/2 = 45$ b. $\sigma = 11.54701$
    c. $P(X > 45) = (65 - 45)/(65 - 25) = 0.5$
    d. $P(X > 55) = (65 - 55)/(65 - 25) = 0.25$
    e. $P(30 < X < 60) = (60 - 30)/(65 - 25) = 0.75$

7.53 a. Right-skewed (zero low bound, high outliers likely).
    b. Right-skewed (zero low bound, high outliers likely).
    c. Normal.
    d. Normal.

7.55 a. $=$NORMSDIST(1) $= .8413$, 84th percentile.
    b. $=$NORMSDIST(2.57) $= .9949$, 99th percentile.
    c. $=$NORMSDIST(-1.714) $= .0433$, 4th percentile.

7.57 a. $=$NORMINV(0.5,450,80) $= 450$
    b. $=$NORMINV(0.25,450,80) $= 396.04$
    c. $=$NORMINV(0.9,450,80) $= 552.52$

d. =NORMINV(0.2,450,80) = 382.67
e. =NORMINV(0.95,450,80) = 581.59
f. =NORMINV(0.25,450,80) to
=NORMINV(0.75,450,80) or 396.04 to 503.95
g. =NORMINV(0.2,450,80) = 382.67
h. =NORMINV(0.025,450,80) to
=NORMINV(0.975,450,80) or 293.20 to 606.80
i. =NORMINV(0.99,450,80) = 636.11

7.59 a. =1−NORMDIST(130,115,20,TRUE) = .2266
b. =NORMDIST(100,115,20,TRUE) = .2266
c. =NORMDIST(91,115,20,TRUE) = .1151

7.61 a. $P(28 < X < 32) = P(X < 32) − P(X < 28) = .8413 −$ .1587 = .6826
b. $P(X < 28) = .1587$
c. 75% of 30 is 22.5, so $P(X < 22.5) = P(Z < −3.75) =$ .00009

7.63 $P(1.975 < X < 2.095) = P(−2.00 < Z < +2.00) = .9544$, so 4.55% will not meet specs.

7.65 Using Excel (answers with continuity correction in parentheses):
a. $P(X > 50) = P(Z > .78) = .2177 (.2086)$
b. $P(X < 29) = P(Z < −.54) = .2946 (.2836)$
c. $P(40 < X < 50) = P(X < 50) − P(X < 40) = .2223$ (.2190)
d. Normal distribution assumed.

7.67 a. $P(X < 90) = $ NORMDIST(90,84,10,TRUE) = .7257
b. Normal distribution assumed.

7.69 a. $P(X > 5200) = 1−$NORMDIST(5200,4905,355,TRUE) = 0.2030

7.71 a. 5.3% below John.   b. 69.2% below Mary.
c. 96.3% below Zak.   d. 99.3% below Frieda.

7.73 Probability of making it to the airport in 54 minutes or less is .5000 for A and .0228 for B, so use route A. Probability of making it to the airport in 60 minutes or less is .8413 for A and .5000 for B, so use route A. Probability of making it to the airport in 66 minutes or less is the same for routes A and B.
a. $P(X < 54)$ Route A: =NORMDIST(54,54,6,TRUE) = .5000
Route B: =NORMDIST(54,60,3,TRUE) =.0228
b. $P(X < 60)$ Route A: =NORMDIST(60,54,6,TRUE) = .8413
Route B: =NORMDIST(60,60,3,TRUE) = .5000
c. $P(X < 66)$ Route A: =NORMDIST(66,54,6,TRUE) = .9772
Route B: =NORMDIST(66,60,3,TRUE) = .9772

7.75 =NORMINV(.20) = −0.842, so $x = \mu + z\sigma = 12.5 +$ (−0.842)(1.2) = 11.49 inches

7.77 For any normal distribution, $P(X > \mu) = .5$ or $P(X < \mu) = .5$. Assuming independent events:
a. Probability that both exceed the mean is (.5)(.5) = .25
b. Probability that both are less than the mean is (.5)(.5) = .25
c. Probability that one is above and one is less than the mean is (.5)(.5) = .25 but there are two combinations that yield this, so the likelihood is: .25 + .25 = .50.
d. $P(X = \mu) = 0$ for any continuous random variable.

7.79 Normality OK since $n\pi \geq 10$ and $n(1 − \pi) \geq 10$. Set $\mu = n\pi = (.25)(100) = 25$ and $\sigma = $ SQRT(.25*100* (1 − .25)) = 4.3301. Then $P(X < 19.5) =$NORMDIST (19.5,25,4.3301,1) = .1020.

7.81 Set $\mu = n\pi = (.25)(100) = 25$ and $\sigma = $ SQRT(.25*100* (1 − .25)) = 4.3301.

a. $z = $ NORMSINV(.95) = 1.645 so $x = \mu + z\sigma = 25 +$ 1.645(4.3301) = 32.12
b. $z = $ NORMSINV(.99) = 2.326 so $x = \mu + z\sigma = 25 +$ 2.326(4.3301) = 35.07
c. Q1 = NORMINV(0.25,25,4.3301) = 22.08
Q2 = NORMINV(0.5, 25,4.3301) = 25.00
Q3 = NORMINV(0.75, 25,4.3301) = 27.92

7.83 Set $\mu = n\pi = (.02)(1500) = 30$ and $\sigma = $ SQRT(.02* 1500*(1 − .02)) = 5.4222. Then
a. $P(X > 24.5) = 1 − P(X < 24.5) =$ 1−NORMDIST(24.5,30,5.4222,1) = .8448
b. $P(X > 40.5) = 1 − P(X < 40.5) =$ 1−NORMDIST(40.5, 30,5.4222,1) = .0264

7.85 a. $P(X > 100{,}000$ hrs.$) = .2397$.
b. $P(X \leq 50{,}000$ hrs.$) = .5105$.
c. $P(50{,}000 \leq X \leq 80{,}000) = .6811 −.5105 = .1706$.

7.87 a. $P(X \leq 3$ min$) = .6321$.
b. The distribution is skewed right so the mean is greater than the median.

7.89 a. 5.75, 4.55, 5.55, 5.45
b. Yes, if scores were normally distributed.

CHAPTER 8

8.1 a. 16
b. 8
c. 4

8.3 a. (4.0252, 4.0448)   b. (4.0330, 4.0370)
c. both are outside expected range

8.5 a. (11.06, 16.94)   b. (33.68, 40.33)
c. (115.12, 126.88)

8.9 a. 2.262, 2.2622
b. 2.602, 2.6025
c. 1.678, 1.6779

8.11 a. (33.01, 58.31)
b. Increase n or decrease 95%.

8.13 a. (742.20, 882.80)

8.15 a. (81.87, 88.13) for Exam 1, (82.79, 94.41) for Exam 2, (73.34, 78.66) for Exam 3.
b. Exams 1 and 2 overlap.   c. Unknown σ.

8.17 a. .062   b. .0877   c. .1216

8.19 a. (.2556, .4752)   b. Yes, normal.

8.21 a. (.0166, .0794)   b. Yes, normal.

8.23 a. 0.1507, 0.3199   b. Yes, normal.

8.25 25

8.27 97 assuming $\sigma = 25 = R/4$

8.29 385

8.31 a. 1692   b. Stratify (e.g., income)

8.33 a. 2401   b. Stratify (e.g., age)

8.35 a. Uneven wear.   b. (0.8332, 0.8355)
c. Normality.   d. 95

8.37 a. (29.443, 39.634)   b. Varying methods
c. Raisin clumps

8.39 a. (19.25, 20.69)   b. Small n.

8.41 a. (33.013, 58.315)   b. Outliers
c. 119   d. (21.26, 40.14)

8.43 a. (29.078, 29.982)   b. Yes   c. 116

8.45 a. (48.515, 56.965)   b. Outliers   c. 75

8.47 a. (.125, .255)   b. Yes   c. 463

8.49 136

8.51 a. (.258, .322)   b. Yes

8.53 a. (.595, .733)   b. No

8.55 a. margin of error = .035 for 95% CI   b. Greater
8.57 a. (.393, .527)   b. Yes
8.59 a. No   b. (.0044, .0405)
8.61 a. (.914, 1.006)   b. Severity of effect.
　　　 c. Use binomial.   d. (.863, .995) from MINITAB
8.63 .04 for 95% CI.

CHAPTER 9

9.1 a. Reject in lower tail.   b. Reject in both tails.
　　　c. Reject in upper tail.
9.3 a. Type I error: Admit even though no heart attack. Type II error: Fail to admit when there is a heart attack.
　　　b. Type I error: Allow a landing even though there is enough fuel. Type II error: Fail to let the plane land when there is not enough fuel.
　　　c. Type I error: Go to Staples even though there is enough ink. Type II error: Don't go to Staples and run out of ink.
9.5 a. H_0: Employee not using drugs.
　　　　H_1: Employee is using drugs.
　　　b. Type I error: Test positive for drugs when not using. Type II error: Test negative for drugs when using.
　　　c. Employees fear Type I, while employers fear both for legal reasons.
9.7 a. $z = 1.50$, p-value = .1336.
　　　b. $z = -2.0$, p-value = .0228.
　　　c. $z = 3.75$, p-value = .0001
9.9 p-value = .0062. The mean weight is heavier than it should be.
9.11 a. Reject H_0 if $z > 1.96$ or $z < -1.96$.
　　　b. $z = 0.78$. Fail to reject H_0.
9.13 $z = 3.26$, p-value = .0006.
9.15 a. p-value = .0836.   b. p-value = .0316.
　　　c. p-value = .0391.
9.17 a. $t = 1.5$, p-value = .1544.
　　　b. $t = -2.0$, p-value = .0285.
　　　c. $t = 3.75$, p-value = .0003.
9.19 H_0: $\mu \geq 400$ H_1: $\mu < 400$. Reject H_0 if p-value is less than .10. The p-value = 0.0525, therefore reject H_0. Decision is close at $\alpha = 0.05$, could be important to a large contractor.
9.21 a. p-value = .0097. Reject H_0.
9.23 a. p-value = .1079. Fail to reject H_0.
　　　b. (3.226, 3.474) includes 3.25
9.25 a. $z = 2.0$, p-value = .046.
　　　b. $z = 1.90$, p-value = .971.
　　　c. $z = 1.14$, p-value = .127.
9.27 a. No.   b. No.   c. Yes.
9.29 a. H_0: $\pi = .997$ versus H_1: $\pi < .997$. Reject H_0 if the p-value is less than 0.05.
　　　b. Yes.
　　　c. Type I error: Throw away a good syringe. Type II error: Keep a bad syringe.
　　　d. p-value = .1401 ($z = -1.08$)
　　　e. Type II increases.
9.31 a. H_0: $\pi = .50$ versus H_1: $\pi > 0.50$. If the p-value is less than .05, reject H_0.
　　　b. p-value = .0228.
　　　c. Yes, cost could be high if call volume is large.
9.33 p-value ≈ 0. More than half support the ban.
9.35 a. p-value = .143. Standard is being met.
　　　b. Less than five defects observed, cannot assume normality.

9.37 a. Type II
　　　b. Possible exposure to radon.
9.39 a. P(Type I error) = 0.
　　　b. You increase the P(Type II error).
9.41 a. H_0: User is authorized.
　　　　H_1: User is unauthorized.
　　　b. Type I error: Scanner fails to admit an authorized user. Type II error: Scanner admits an unauthorized user.
　　　c. Type II is feared by the public.
9.43 P(Type I error) = 0.
9.45 a. Type I: deny access to authorized user, Type II: allow access to an unauthorized user.
　　　b. The consequences of a false rejection are less serious than a false authorization.
9.47 a. A two-tailed test.
　　　b. Overfill is unnecessary while underfill is illegal.
　　　c. Normal (known σ).
　　　d. Reject if $z > 2.576$ or if $z < -2.576$.
9.49 a. H_0: $\mu \geq 90$
　　　　H_1: $\mu < 90$
　　　b. Student's t.
　　　c. $t = -0.92$. Fail to reject H_0.
　　　d. At least a symmetric population.
　　　e. p-value = .1936.
9.51 a. H_0: $\mu \geq 2.268$
　　　　H_1: $\mu < 2.268$
　　　　If the p-value is less than .05 reject H_0.
　　　　p-value = .0478. Reject H_0.
　　　b. Usage wears them down.
9.53 p-value = .0228. Reject H_0.
9.55 p-value = .0258. Fail to reject (close decision) H_0.
9.57 p-value = .1327. Fail to reject H_0.
9.59 p-value = .0193. Reject H_0. Important to players and universities.
9.61 Yes, $z = -3.35$, p-value = .0004.
9.63 a. Yes, $z = 195$, p-value = .0253.   b. Yes.
9.65 p-value = .0794. Fail to reject H_0.
9.67 H_0: $\pi = .50$ vs. H_1: $\pi > .50$. $P(X \geq 10 \mid n = 16, \pi = .5) = .2272$. Fail to reject H_0.
9.69 a. (0, .0154)
　　　b. $np < 10$.
　　　c. Goal is being achieved.

CHAPTER 10

Note: Results from Excel except as noted (may not agree with Appendix C, D, or E due to rounding or use of exact d.f.).

10.1 a. H_0: $\mu_1 \geq \mu_2$, H_1: $\mu_1 < \mu_2$, $t = -2.148$, df = 28, $t_{.025} = -2.048$, p-value = .0202, so reject H_0.
　　　b. H_0: $\mu_1 = \mu_2$, H_1: $\mu_1 \neq \mu_2$, $t = -1.595$, df = 39, $t_{.05} = \pm2.023$, p-value = .1188, so can't reject H_0.
　　　c. H_0: $\mu_1 \leq \mu_2$, H_1: $\mu_1 > \mu_2$, $t = 1.935$, df = 27, $t_{.05} = 1.703$, p-value = .0318, so reject H_0.
10.3 a. H_0: $\mu_1 = \mu_2$, H_1: $\mu_1 \neq \mu_2$, $t = -0.798$, df = 48, $t_{.05} = \pm1.677$, can't reject H_0.
　　　b. p-value = .4288. Difference is not significant.
10.5 a. H_0: $\mu_1 \leq \mu_2$, H_1: $\mu_1 > \mu_2$, $t = 1.902$, df = 29, $t_{.01} = 2.462$, can't reject H_0.
　　　b. p-value = .0336. Would be significant at $\alpha = .05$.
10.7 H_0: $\mu_1 = \mu_2$ vs. H_1: $\mu_1 \neq \mu_2$, $t = -3.55$, df = 11, p-value = .0045. Reject H_0.

10.9 H_0: $\mu_d \le 0$, H_1: $\mu_d > 0$, $t = 1.93$, df $= 6$, and p-value $= .0509$, so can't quite reject H_0 at $\alpha = .05$.

10.11 H_0: $\mu_d \le 0$, H_1: $\mu_d > 0$, $t = 2.86$, df $= 9$, and p-value $= .0094$, so reject H_0 at $\alpha = .10$.

10.13 H_0: $\mu_d = 0$, H_1: $\mu_d \ne 0$, $t = -1.71$, df $= 7$, and p-value $= .1307$, so can't reject H_0 at $\alpha = .01$.

10.15 a. H_0: $\pi_1 \ge \pi_2$, H_1: $\pi_1 < \pi_2$, $\bar p = .4200$, $z = -2.431$, $z_{.01} = -2.326$, p-value $= .0075$, so reject at $\alpha = .01$.
b. H_0: $\pi_1 = \pi_2$, H_1: $\pi_1 \ne \pi_2$, $\bar p = .37500$, $z = 2.263$, $z_{.05} = \pm1.645$, p-value $= .0237$, reject at $\alpha = .10$.
c. H_0: $\pi_1 \ge \pi_2$, H_1: $\pi_1 < \pi_2$, $\bar p = .25806$, $z = -1.706$, $z_{.05} = -1.645$, p-value $= .0440$, reject at $\alpha = .05$.

10.17 a. H_0: $\pi_1 \ge \pi_2$, H_1: $\pi_1 < \pi_2$, $\bar p = .26000$, $z = -2.280$.
b. $z_{.01} = -2.326$, can't reject at $\alpha = .01$ (close decision).
c. p-value $= .0113$
d. Normality OK since $n_1 p_1 = 42$, $n_2 p_2 = 62$, both exceed 10.

10.19 a. H_0: $\pi_1 = \pi_2$, H_1: $\pi_1 \ne \pi_2$, $\bar p = .11$, $z = 2.021$, $z_{.025} = \pm1.960$ ($p = .0432$) so reject at $\alpha = .05$ (close decision).
b. $(.0013, .0787)$, does not include zero

10.21 a. $p_1 = .07778$, $p_2 = .10448$, H_0: $\pi_1 = \pi_2$, H_1: $\pi_1 \ne \pi_2$, $\bar p = .08502$, $z = -0.669$, critical value is $z_{.025} = 1.960$, and p-value $= .5036$, so cannot reject at $\alpha = .05$.
b. Normality not OK since $n_1 p_1 = 14$ but $n_2 p_2 = 7$.

10.23 a. $p_1 = .28125$, $p_2 = .14583$, $\bar p = .22321$, H_0: $\pi_1 - \pi_2 \le .10$, H_1: $\pi_1 - \pi_2 > .10$, $z = 0.630$, and critical value is $z_{.05} = 1.645$.
b. p-value $= .2644$, cannot reject at $\alpha = .05$

10.25 a. H_0: $\sigma_1^2 = \sigma_2^2$ versus $\sigma_1^2 \ne \sigma_2^2$. Reject H_0 if $F > 4.76$ or $F < .253$. ($v_1 = 10$, $v_2 = 7$.) $F = 2.54$ so we fail to reject the null hypothesis.
b. H_0: $\sigma_1^2 = \sigma_2^2$ versus $\sigma_1^2 < \sigma_2^2$. Reject H_0 if $F < .264$ ($v_1 = 7$, $v_2 = 7$). $F = .247$ so we reject the null hypothesis.
c. H_0: $\sigma_1^2 = \sigma_2^2$ versus $\sigma_1^2 > \sigma_2^2$. Reject H_0 if $F > 2.80$ ($v_1 = 9$, $v_2 = 12$). $F = 19.95$ so we reject the null hypothesis.

10.27 H_0: $\sigma_1^2 = \sigma_2^2$ versus $\sigma_1^2 < \sigma_2^2$. Reject H_0 if $F < .3549$ ($v_1 = 11$, $v_2 = 11$). $F = .103$ so we reject the null hypothesis. The new drill has a reduced variance.

10.29 a. H_0: $\pi_M = \pi_W$ versus H_1: $\pi_M \ne \pi_W$. Reject the null hypothesis if $z < -1.645$ or $z > 1.645$.
b. $p_M = .60$ and $p_W = .6875$.
c. $z = -.69$, p-value $= .492$. The sample does not show a significant difference in proportions.
d. Normality can be assumed because both $n_1 p_1 > 10$ and $n_2 p_2 > 10$.

10.31 a. H_0: $\pi_1 \le \pi_2$, H_1: $\pi_1 > \pi_2$ b. Reject if $z > z_{.05} = 1.645$.
c. $p_1 = .98000$, $p_2 = .93514$, $\bar p = .95912$, $z = 4.507$.
d. Reject at $\alpha = .05$.   e. p-value $= .0000$.
f. Normality is OK since $n_1(1 - \pi_1) = 17$ and $n_2(1 - \pi_2) = 48$ both > 10.

10.33 a. H_0: $\pi_1 = \pi_2$, H_1: $\pi_1 \ne \pi_2$
b. $p_1 = .17822$, $p_2 = .14300$, $\bar p = .14895$, $z = 1.282$, p-value $= .2000$. Since z is within ±1.960 for a two-tail test at $\alpha = .05$ and p-value exceeds $.05$, we fail to reject H_0.

10.35 a. H_0: $\pi_1 = \pi_2$, H_1: $\pi_1 \ne \pi_2$, $p_1 = .38492$, $p_2 = .48830$, $\bar p = .44444$, $z = -2.506$. Since z does not exceed ±2.576, we cannot reject H_0.
b. Two-tailed p-value $= .0122$.

c. Normality OK since $n_1 p_1 = 97$, $n_2 p_2 = 167$ both exceed 10.
d. Gender interests may imply different marketing strategies.

10.37 a. H_0: $\pi_1 \ge \pi_2$, H_1: $\pi_1 < \pi_2$, $p_1 = .14914$, $p_2 = .57143$, $\bar p = .21086$, $z = -8.003$. Since $z < -2.326$, we conclude that pilots are more likely to approve of night-flying without non-instrument rating.
b. Left-tailed p-value $= .0000$.
c. Normality assumption OK since $n_1 p_1 = 61$, $n_2(1 - p_2) = 30$ both exceed 10.

10.39 a. H_0: $\pi_1 \le \pi_2$, H_1: $\pi_1 > \pi_2$, $p_1 = .02850$, $p_2 = .02229$, $\bar p = .02589$, $z = 2.932$. Reject H_0 since $z > 2.326$.
b. Right-tailed p-value $= .0017$.
c. Normality OK since $n_1 p_1 = 245$, $n_2 p_2 = 185$ both exceed 10.
d. Not a large difference, but life is important.
e. Were smoking, diet, exercise, etc. considered?

10.41 a. H_0: $\pi_1 = \pi_2$ versus H_1: $\pi_1 < \pi_2$. Reject the null hypothesis if $z < -1.645$ or p-value $< .05$. p-value $= .0914$, fail to reject H_0.   b. Yes, normality is met.

10.43 a. H_0: $\mu_1 \le \mu_2$, H_1: $\mu_1 > \mu_2$. Assuming equal variances, $t = 4.089$ with d.f. $= 84$. Since the p-value is $.0000$, reject H_0 at $\alpha = .01$.

10.45 a. H_0: $\pi_1 \ge \pi_2$, H_1: $\pi_1 < \pi_2$, $p_1 = .1402$, $p_2 = .2000$, $\bar p = .16396$.
b. $z = -2.777$ and left-tailed p-value $= .0027$. Since $z < -2.326$, reject H_0.
c. Normality OK since $n_1 p_1 = 104$, $n_2 p_2 = 98$ both exceed 10.
d. Many people can't afford them or lack insurance to pay for them.

10.47 a. H_0: $\mu_1 \le \mu_2$, H_1: $\mu_1 > \mu_2$. Assuming unequal variances, $t = 1.718$ with $v = 16$ (using Welch's adjustment). Since the p-value is $.0525$, we fail to reject H_0 at $\alpha = .05$.
b. If we had looked at the same firm in each year, the test would have more power.

10.49 a. Dot plots suggest that the new bumper has less downtime, but variation is similar.

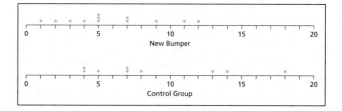

b. H_0: $\mu_1 \le \mu_2$, H_1: $\mu_1 > \mu_2$.
c. Assuming equal variances, reject H_0 if $t < -1.729$ with df $= 19$.
d. $\bar x_1 = 5.917$, $s_1 = 3.423$, $\bar x_2 = 8.889$, $s_2 = 4.961$, $s_p^2 = 17.148$, $t = 1.63$, p-value $= .0600$, so fail to reject H_0 at $\alpha = .05$.

10.51 a. H_0: $\mu_1 \le \mu_2$ vs. H_1: $\mu_1 > \mu_2$, $t = 7.08$, $df = 28$, p-value ≈ 0. Reject H_0.
b. H_0: $\sigma_1^2 = \sigma_2^2$ versus $\sigma_1^2 \ne \sigma_2^2$. Reject H_0 if $F < .3357$ or $F > 2.9786$ ($v_1 = 14$, $v_2 = 14$). $F = 2.778$ so we fail to reject the null hypothesis.

10.53 a. Dot plots suggest that the means differ and variances differ (outlier in men's salaries).

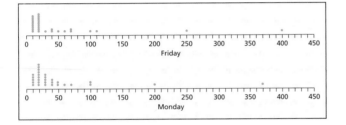

b. $H_0: \mu_1 \le \mu_2, H_1: \mu_1 > \mu_2$.
c. Reject H_0 if $t > 2.438$ with df $= 35$.
d. $\bar{x}_1 = 117,853, s_1 = 10,115, \bar{x}_2 = 98,554$, $s_2 = 14,541, s_p^2 = 152,192,286, t = 4.742$.
e. Reject H_0 at $\alpha = .01$. Men are paid significantly more.
f. p-value $= .0000$. Unlikely result if H_0 is true.
g. Yes, the large difference suggests gender discrimination.

10.55 a. Dot plots show strong skewness, but means could be similar.

b. $H_0: \mu_1 = \mu_2, H_1: \mu_1 \ne \mu_2$. Assume equal variances.
c. Reject H_0 if $t > 2.663$ or if $t < -2.663$ with df $= 58$.
d. $\bar{x}_1 = 50.333, s_1 = 81.684, \bar{x}_2 = 50.000, s_2 = 71.631$, $s_p^2 = 5,901.667$. Since $t = .017$ we cannot reject H_0.
e. p-value $= .9866$. Sample result well within chance range.
10.57 a. $H_0: \mu_1 = \mu_2, H_1: \mu_1 \ne \mu_2$.
b. For equal variances, df $= 55$, reject H_0 if $t < -2.004$.
c. Since $t = -3.162$ ($p = .0025$) we reject H_0 at $\alpha = .05$. Mean sales are lower on the east side.
10.59 $H_0: \sigma_1^2 = \sigma_2^2, H_1: \sigma_1^2 \ne \sigma_2^2$, df$_1 = 30$, df$_2 = 29$. For $\alpha/2 = .025$ $F_R = F_{30,29} = 2.09$, and $F_L = 1/F_{29,30} \cong 1/F_{25,30} = 1/2.12 = .47$. Test statistic is $F = (13.482)^2/(15.427)^2 = 0.76$, so we can't reject H_0.
10.61 $H_0: \mu_d = 0$ vs. $H_1: \mu_d \ne 0$. $t = -0.87$. p-value $= .4154$ (from MegaStat). Fail to reject the null hypothesis.
10.63 a. $H_0: \mu_1 = \mu_2$ vs. $H_1: \mu_1 \ne \mu_2, t = -1.10, df = 22$, p-value $= .2839$. Fail to reject H_0.
b. $H_0: \sigma_1^2 = \sigma_2^2$ versus $\sigma_1^2 \ne \sigma_2^2$. Reject H_0 if $F < .1880$ or $F > 5.320$ ($v_1 = 11, v_2 = 11$). $F = 2.59$ so we fail to reject the null hypothesis.
10.65 a. $H_0: \sigma_1^2 \le \sigma_2^2, H_1: \sigma_1^2 > \sigma_2^2$, df$_1 = 11$, df$_2 = 11$. For a right-tail test at $\alpha = .025$, Appendix F gives $F_R = F_{11,11} \cong F_{10,11} = 3.53$. The test statistic is $F = (2.9386)^2/(0.9359)^2 = 9.86$, so conclude that Portfolio A has a greater variance than Portfolio B.
b. These are independent samples. $H_0: \mu_1 = \mu_2, H_1: \mu_1 \ne \mu_2$. $\bar{x}_1 = 8.5358, s_1 = 2.9386, \bar{x}_2 = 8.1000, s_2 = .9359$, Assuming unequal variances with df $= 13$ (with Welch's adjustment) we get $t = 0.49$ with p-value $= .6326$, so we cannot reject H_0 at $\alpha = .025$.

CHAPTER 11

11.1 a. $H_0: \mu_A = \mu_B = \mu_C, H_1$: Not all means are equal.
b. One-factor, $F = 5.31$, p-value $= .0223$.
c. Reject H_0 at $\alpha = .05$.
d. Plant B mean likely higher, Plant C lower.

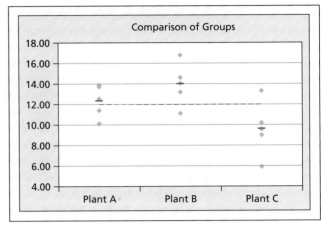

11.3 a. $H_0: \mu_1 = \mu_2 = \mu_3 = \mu_4, H_1$: Not all equal.
b. One-factor $F = 3.52$, p-value $= .0304$.
c. Reject H_0 at $\alpha = .05$. GPAs not the same.
d. Marketing and HR likely higher, accounting and finance lower.
11.5 Only Plant B and Plant C differ at $\alpha = .05$ ($t = 3.23$) using MegaStat Tukey test.
11.7 Only marketing and accounting differ at $\alpha = .05$ (Tukey $t = 3.00$).
11.9 $F_{max} = 7.027/2.475 = 2.839$. Critical value from Table 11.5 = 15.5 (df$_1 = c = 3$, df$_2 = n/c - 1 = 4$). Fail to reject equal variances.
11.11 $F_{max} = 8.097$. Critical value from Table 11.5 = 10.4 (df$_1 = c = 4$, df$_2 = n/c - 1 = 6$). Fail to reject null.
11.13 a. $H_0: \mu_1 = \mu_2 = \mu_3 = \mu_4, H_1$: Not all the means are equal.
b. Graph shows mean Freshmen GPA is lower than overall mean.
c. $F = 2.36$ ($p = .1000$), fail to reject H_0 at $\alpha = .05$, No significant difference among GPAs.
d. Reject H_0 if $F > F_{3,21} = 3.07$.
e. Differences in mean grades large enough (.4 to .7) to matter, but not significant, so cannot be considered important.
f. Large variances within groups and small samples rob the test of power, suggests larger sample within each group.
g. Tukey confirms no significant difference in any pairs of means.
h. $F_{max} = (0.6265)^2/(0.2826)^2 = 4.91$ which is less than Hartley's critical value 13.7 with df$_1 = c = 4$ and df$_2 = n/c - 1 = 5$, so conclude equal variances.
11.15 a. $H_0: \mu_1 = \mu_2 = \mu_3, H_1$: Not all means are equal.
b. Graph suggests Type B a bit lower, C higher than the overall mean.
c. $F = 9.44$ ($p = .0022$) so there is a significant difference in mean cell outputs.
d. Reject H_0 if $F > F_{2,15} = 3.68$.
e. Small differences in means, but could be important in a large solar cell array.
f. Sounds like a controlled experiment and variances are small, so a small sample suffices.

g. Tukey test shows that C differs from B at $\alpha = .01$ and from A at $\alpha = .05$.

h. $F_{max} = (4.57)/(4.00) = 1.14$, less than Hartley's 10.8 with $df_1 = c = 3$ and $df_2 = n/c - 1 = 5$, conclude equal variances.

11.17 a. $H_0: \mu_1 = \mu_2 = \mu_3 = \mu_4, H_1$: Not all means equal.

b. Graph shows B higher, D lower.

c. $F = 1.79$ ($p = .1857$) so at $\alpha = .05$ no significant difference in mean waiting times.

d. Reject H_0 if $F > F_{3,18} = 3.16$.

e. Differences in means might matter to patient, but not significant so can't be considered important.

f. Variances large, samples small, so test has low power.

g. Tukey test shows no significant differences in pairs of means.

h. $F_{max} = (11.90)^2/(6.74)^2 = 3.121$, less than the Hartley's 20.6 with $df_1 = c = 4$ and $df_2 = n/c - 1 = 4$ so conclude equal variances.

11.19 a. $H_0: \mu_1 = \mu_2 = \mu_3; H_1$: Not all means equal.

b. Graph suggests levels higher for older wells.

c. $F_{calc} = 1.31$ ($p = .2882$) so fail to reject H_0.

d. Reject H_0 if $F_{calc} > 3.4028$ at $\alpha = .05$.

e. Differences not significant, not important.

f. Could increase sample size but would increase costs.

g. Tukey test shows no significant differences.

h. $F_{max} = (1.244432)^2/(1.125956)^2 = 1.221516$, does not exceed Hartley's 6.00 with $df_1 = 3$ and $df_2 = 8$. Conclude equal variances.

11.21 a. $H_0: \mu_1 = \mu_2 = \mu_3 = \mu_4 = \mu_5; H_1$: Not all means equal.

b. Graph suggests that Chalmers is higher and Ulysses is lower.

c. $F_{calc} = 6.19$ ($p = .0019$) so reject H_0. There are significant differences in means.

d. Reject H_0 if $F_{calc} > F_{4,21} = 2.84$ at $\alpha = .05$.

e. Significant and probably important to clients.

f. Sample may be limited by number of clinics in each town.

g. Chalmers differs from all except Villa Nueve, while other means do not differ significantly.

h. $F_{max} = (11.171)^2/(6.850)^2 = 2.659$ does not exceed Hartley's $H_{crit} = 25.2$ with $df_1 = c = 5$ and $df_2 = n/c - 1 = 26/5 - 1 = 4$ so conclude equal variances.

11.23 a. Between Groups $df_1 = 4$ and $df_1 = c - 1$ so $c = 5$ bowlers.

b. p-value 0.000, reject null, conclude there is difference.

c. Sample variances 83.66 to 200.797, $F_{max} = 200.797/83.66 = 2.40$. Hartley's test, $df_1 = c = 5$ and $df_2 = n/c - 1 = 67/5 - 1 = 12$, critical value is 5.30. Not enough variation to reject null hypothesis of homogeneity.

CHAPTER 12

12.1 For each sample: $H_0: \rho = 0$ vs. $H_1: \rho \neq 0$

Sample	df	r	t	t_α	r_α	Decision
a	18	.45	2.138	2.101	.444	Reject
b	28	−.35	−1.977	1.701	.306	Reject
c	5	.6	1.677	2.015	.669	Fail to Reject
d	59	−.3	−2.416	2.39	.297	Reject

12.3 b. −.7328   c. $t_{.025} = 3.183$

d. $t = -1.865$, Fail to reject.   e. p-value $= .159$

12.5 b. .531   c. 2.131   d. 2.429   e. ±.482

f. Yes, reject.

12.7 a.

	1-Year	3-Year	5-Year	10-Year
1-Year	1.000			
3-Year	−.095	1.000		
5-Year	.014	.771	1.000	
10-Year	.341	.463	.746	1.000

b. $r_{.05} = .576$.

c. Significant positive correlation between years 3 and 5 and 5 and 10.

12.9 a. Each additional sf increases price $150.   b. $425,000.

c. No.

12.11 a. Earning an extra $1,000 raises home price by $2610.

b. No.   c. $181,800, $312,300.

12.13 a. Blazer: Each year reduces price by $1050. Silverado: each year reduces price by $1339.

b. Intercept could indicate price of new car.

c. $10,939.

d. $15,895

12.15 a. Units Sold $= 300 - 150*$Price (answers will vary).

b. $1 increase in price decreases units sold by 150.

c. No.

12.17 b. Wait Time $= 458 - 18.5$ Operators.

d. $R^2 = .5369$.

12.19 $y = -31.19 + 4.9322x, R^2 = .6717$.

12.21 a. $y = 557.45 + 3.00x$

b. (1.2034, 4.806)

c. $H_0: \beta_1 \leq 0$ vs. $H_1: \beta_1 > 0$, p-value $= .0009$, Reject H_0.

12.23 a. $y = 1.8064 + .0039x$

b. intercept: $1.8064/.6116 = 2.954$, slope: $.0039/.0014 = 2.786$ (may be off due to rounding).

c. $df = 10, t_{.025} = \pm 2.228$.

12.25 a. $y = 11.1549 + 0.458x$

b. (0.0561, 0.8598). Interval does not contain zero, slope is greater than zero.

c. t test p-value $= .0282$. Conclusion: slope is greater than zero.

d. F statistic p-value $= .0282$. Conclusion: significant relationship between variables.

e. $5.90 = (2.429)^2$

12.27 a. $y = 6.9609 - 0.053x$

b. (−0.1946, 0.0886). Interval does contain zero, slope is not significantly different from zero.

c. t test p-value $= .4133$. Conclusion: slope is not significantly different from zero.

d. F statistic p-value $= .4133$. Conclusion: No significant relationship between variables.

e. $0.74 = (-0.863)^2$

12.45 $t_{critical} = 2.3069$ (from Excel). From sample: $t = 2.3256$. Reject H_0.

12.47 a. 1515.2.

b. No.

c. (1406.03, 1624.37).

12.49 a. $y = 1743.57 - 1.2163x$.

b. $df = 13$. $t_{critical} = 2.160$.

c. Slope is significantly different from zero.

d. $(-2.1671, -0.2656)$. Interval indicates slope is significantly less than zero.

e. $7.64 = (-2.764)^2$

12.51 a. $r = .6771$

b. From sample: $t = 5.8193$. $t_{.01} = 2.423$. Reject H_0.

12.53 b. $r = .749$

c. $df = 13$. $r_{.05} = .514$. Reject H_0.

12.57 b. $y = -4.2896 + 0.171x$, $R^2 = .2474$. Fit is poor.

12.59 a. No significant relationship between variables. (p-value $= .774$).

b. No, study time and class level could be predictors. (Answers will vary.)

12.61 a. The negative slope means that as age increases, price decreases.

b. Intercepts could be asking price of a new car.

c. The fit is good for the Explorer, Pickup, and Taurus.

d. Additional predictors: condition of car, mileage.

12.65 a. Steady upward trend.

b. Growing population, bigger cars, rising world demand.

c. Linear: $y_t = 39.667 + 441.59t$ ($R^2 = .9188$).

d. Forecast for 2010: Linear: $y_{11} = 4897$. Believable, given continued role of oil in the U.S. economy.

e. Yes, R^2 is high. Should see a continued increase in imports.

f. Consumers, producers, government, refiners (i.e., all of us).

CHAPTER 13

13.1 a. *Net Revenue* $= 4.31 - 0.082 ShipCost + 2.265\ PrintAds + 2.498 WebAds + 16.7 Rebate\%$

b. Positive coefficients indicate an increase in net revenue; negative coefficients indicate a decrease in net revenue.

c. The intercept is meaningless.

d. 467.16

13.3 a. df are 4 (numerator) and 45 (denominator).

b. $F_{.05} = 2.61$.

c. $F = 12.997$. Yes, overall regression is significant.

d. $R^2 = .536$. $R^2_{adj} = .495$.

13.5 a. and c. See Table.

Predictor	Coef	SE	t-value	p-value
Intercept	4.31	70.82	0.0608585	0.9517414
ShipCost	−0.082	4.678	−0.0175289	0.9860922
PrintAds	2.265	1.05	2.1571429	0.0363725
WebAds	2.498	0.8457	2.9537661	0.0049772
Rebate%	16.697	3.57	4.6770308	.0003

b. $t_{critical} = 2.69$. WebAds and Rebate% differ significantly from zero.

13.7 $\hat{y}_i \pm 2.032(3620)$: $\hat{y}_i \pm 7355.84$.

Quick Rule $\hat{y}_i \pm 2SE$: $\hat{y}_i \pm 7240$.

13.27 The sample size is too small relative to number of predictors

13.29 Overall regression not significant (F statistic p-value $= .371$), $R^2 = 0.117$ indicates poor fit. Conclusion: No apparent relationship between cost per load and predictors type of washer and type of detergent used.

13.31 a. Coefficients make sense, except for TrnOvr, which would be expected to be negative.

b. No.

c. With 6 predictors, should have minimum of 30 observations. We have only 23 so sample is small.

d. Rebounds and points highly correlated.

13.33 a. Experience lowers the predicted finish time.

b. No.

c. If the relationship is not strictly linear, it can make sense to include a squared predictor, such as seen here.

13.35 The first three predictors (*Income, Unem, Pupil/Tea*) are significant at $\alpha = .05$, but adding the fourth predictor (*Divorce*) yields a weak p-value (.1987) and R^2 and R^2_{adj} barely improve when *Divorce* is added.

CHAPTER 14

14.1 a. H_0: *Earnings* are independent of *Approach*

b. Degrees of Freedom $= (r - 1)(c - 1) = (4 - 1)(3 - 1) = 6$

c. CHIINV(.01,6) $= 16.81$

d. Test statistic is 127.57 ($p = .0000$) so reject null at $\alpha = .01$.

e. *No Clear Effect* and *Business Combinations* contributes the most.

f. All expected frequencies exceed 5.

g. p-value is near zero (observed difference not due to chance).

14.3 a. H_0: *Verbal* and *Quantitative* are independent

b. Degrees of Freedom $= (r - 1)(c - 1) = (3 - 1)(3 - 1) = 4$

c. CHIINV(.005,4) $= 14.86$

d. Test statistic is 55.88 ($p = .0000$), reject null at $\alpha = .005$.

e. *Under 25* and *Under 25* contributes the most.

f. Expected frequency is less than 5 in two cells.

g. p-value is nearly zero (observed difference not due to chance).

14.5 a. H_0: *Return Rate* and *Notification* are independent

b. Degrees of Freedom $= (r - 1)(c - 1) = (2 - 1)(2 - 1) = 1$

c. CHIINV(.025,1) $= 5.024$

d. Test statistic is 5.42 ($p = .0199$), reject null at $\alpha = .025$.

e. *Returned* and *No* contribute the most.

f. All expected frequencies exceed 5.

g. p-value is less than .025 (observed difference did not arise by chance).

h. $z = 2.33$ (p-value $= .0199$ for two-tailed test).

14.7 a. Bars are similar in length. Vanilla and Mocha are the leading flavors.

b. If uniform, $e_j = 84/4 = 21$ for each flavor.

c. Test statistic is 0.86 with d.f. $= 4 - 1 = 3$ (p-value $= .8358$). Chi-square critical value for $\alpha = .05$ is 7.815, so sample does not contradict the hypothesis that sales are the same for each beverage.

14.9 Is *Satisfaction* independent of *Pay Category?* For d.f. $= (r - 1)(c - 1) = (3 - 1)(2 - 1) = 2$, critical value is CHIINV(.05,2) $= 5.991$. Test statistic is 4.54 ($p = .1032$), cannot reject the null at $\alpha = .05$. *Salaried* and *Dissatisfied* contributes the most. All expected frequencies exceed 5. The p-value suggests that observed difference would arise by chance 103 times in 1,000 samples if the two variables really were independent, which is not very convincing.

14.11 Is *Grade* independent of *Hand-In Order?* For d.f. =
$(r-1)(c-1) = (2-1)(2-1) = 1$, critical value
CHIINV(.10,1) = 2.706. Test statistic is 0.23 ($p = .6284$)
so cannot reject the null at $\alpha = .10$. *"B" or Better* and
Later Hand-In contributes the most. All expected frequencies exceed 5. For a two-tailed test of proportions, $p_1 =$
.4000, $p_2 = .3333$, $\bar{p} = .3673$, $z = 0.48$ (*p*-value $= .6284$)
which agrees with the chi-square test.

14.13 a. Is *Reading* independent of *Language?* For d.f. =
$(r-1)(c-1) = (3-1)(4-1) = 6$ the critical value
is CHIINV (.10,6) = 10.64. Test statistic is 4.14
($p = .6577$) so we cannot reject the null at $\alpha = .10$. Four
cells (each corner) have expected frequencies below 5.

14.15 Is *Smoking* independent of *Race?* For d.f. =
$(r-1)(c-1) = (2-1)(2-1) = 1$, critical value is
CHIINV(.005,1) = 7.879. For males, test statistic is 5.84
($p = .0157$), can't reject the null at $\alpha = .005$. For females,
test statistic is 14.79 ($p = .0001$) so reject the null at $\alpha =$
.005. *Black* and *Smoker* contributes the most in each test.
All expected frequencies exceed 5. The two-tailed test of
proportions agrees.

14.17 For d.f. $= (r-1)(c-1) = (2-1)(2-1) = 1$, critical
value CHIINV(.10,1) = 2.706, test statistic is 1.80 ($p =$
.1792) so fail to reject the null at $\alpha = .10$. The lower left
cell contributes most. All expected frequencies exceed 5.

The two-tailed test of proportions ($z = 1.342$) agrees with
the chi-square test. Interestingly, the relationship seems to
be inverse (i.e., rates tend to rise when they are predicted
to fall).

14.19 For the 2×2 table, d.f. = 1, critical value is
CHIINV(.05,1) = 3.841, test statistic is 7.15 ($p = .0075$)
so reject null at $\alpha = .05$. For the 3×3 table, d.f. = 4,
critical value is CHIINV(.05,4) = 13.28, test statistic is
12.30 ($p = .0153$), so reject null at $\alpha = .05$. All expected
frequencies exceed 5.

14.21 With d.f. $= (r-1)(c-1) = (3-1)(3-1) = 4$, the
critical value is CHIINV(.01,4) = 2.706. The test statistic
is 54.18 ($p = .0000$) so we reject the null at $\alpha = .01$. All
expected frequencies exceed 5.

14.23 If uniform, all expected frequencies would be 9. For d.f. =
$4 - 1 = 3$, critical value is CHIINV(.10,3) = 6.251,
test statistic is 1.556 ($p = .6695$) so cannot reject the
hypothesis of a uniform (it is logical to expect no
pattern).

14.25 For d.f. $= 4 - 1 = 3$, critical value is CHIINV(.05,3) =
7.815, test statistic is 6.045 ($p = .1095$) so we cannot
reject hypothesis that Oxnard follows U.S. distribution.

14.27 For d.f. $= 6 - 1 = 5$, critical value is CHIINV(.10,5) =
9.236, test statistic is 4.40 ($p = .4934$) so we can't reject
the hypothesis that the die is fair.

Answers to Exam Review Questions

CHAPTERS 1–4

1. a. inferential;   b. descriptive;   c. inferential
2. c. independent judgment is needed
3. b. anecdotal data ($n = 1$)
4. a. numerical;   b. categorical;   c. numerical
5. a. ratio (true zero);   b. ordinal;   c. nominal
6. a. continuous;   b. continuous;   c. discrete
7. a. convenience;   b. simple random;   c. systematic
8. c. random numbers have no bias
9. a. Likert only if distances have meaning
10. a. sampling error cannot be eliminated
11. bimodal, no outliers, Sturges $k \cong 6$
12. c. range is $-1 \le r \le +1$
13. a. small n and sum to 100%
14. $\bar{x} = 12$, $s = 5.701$, CV = 47.5%
15. $\bar{x} = 59.3$, median = 58.5, modes 55, 58, 62 (not unique), mean or median best
16. a. slight positive correlation;
    b. $r = 0.5656$ (not very linear)

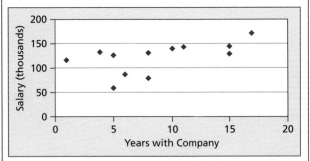

17. b. GEOMEAN(Data) requires all $x_i > 0$
18. a. $z = (x - \mu)/\sigma = (81 - 52)/15 = 1.93$ (not an outlier)
19. b. log scales are less familiar to most

CHAPTERS 5–7

1. a. empirical; b. subjective; c. classical
2. a. 40/200 = .20;   b. 50/90 = .5556;
   c. 100/200 = .50
3. no, since $P(A)P(B) = (.30)(.70) = .21 \ne P(A \cap B) = .25$
4. b. would be true if $P(A \cap B) = 0$

5. c. $U(a, b)$ has two parameters
6. c. $.60(1000) + .30(2000) + .10(5000) = 1700$
7. a. .2565;   b. .4562;   c. .7576;
   d. Poisson, $\lambda = 2.5$
8. a. .1468;   b. .0563;   c. .7969;
   d. binomial, $n = 8$, $\pi = .20$
9. a. $\mu = n\pi = (50)(.30) = 15$;
   b. $\sigma = \sqrt{n\pi(1 - \pi)} = \sqrt{(50)(.30)(.70)} = 3.24$
10. a. binomial ($n = 8$ trials, π unknown)
    b. Poisson (arrivals, λ unknown);
    c. discrete uniform ($a = 0$, $b = 9$)
11. c. = RAND() is a uniform variate
12. a. points have no area, hence no probability
13. b. normal CDF has lazy S shape
14. Using Appendix C:
    a. $P(Z > 1.14) = .1271$;
    b. $P(-.71 < Z < +0.71) = .5222$;
    c. $P(Z < 0) = .5000$.
    Using Excel:
    a. .1265;   b. .5249;   c. .5000
15. Using Table 7.9:
    a. $\mu + 1.645\sigma = 70 + 1.645(7) = 81.52$;
    b. $\mu - 1.282\sigma = 70 - 1.282(7) = 61.03$;
    c. $\mu + 0.675\sigma = 70 + 0.675(7) = 74.73$
16. a. gives cumulative left tail area
17. Using $\lambda = 1.2$:
    a. $P(X < 1.5) = 1 - e^{-\lambda x} = 1 - e^{(-1.2)(1.5)} = .8347$;
    b. $P(X > 0.5) = e^{-\lambda x} = e^{(-1.2)(0.5)} = .5488$;
    c. $P(X > 1) - P(X > 2) = e^{(-1.2)(1)} - e^{(-1.2)(2)} = .3012 - .0907 = .2105$ (if X is expressed in minutes)
18. Using $\lambda = 1.2$:
    a. Solve $e^{-\lambda x} = .05$ to get $x = 2.496$ min (149.8 sec);
    b. Solve $e^{-\lambda x} = .75$ to get $x = 0.2397$ min (14.38 sec);
    c. MTBE $= 1/\lambda = (1/1.2) = 0.83$ min (50 sec)
19. a. This is a correct rule of thumb (set $\mu = \lambda$ and $\sigma = \sqrt{\lambda}$)

CHAPTERS 8–10

1. a. CLT applies to $\overline{X}$. Sample *data* may not be normal.
2. a. consistent;   b. efficient;   c. unbiased
3. b. It is conservative to use t *whenever* σ is unknown, regardless of n.
4. a. d.f. $= n - 1 = 8$, $t_{.025} = 2.306$, so $\bar{x} \pm t \frac{s}{\sqrt{n}}$
   gives $13.14 < \mu < 16.36$;
   b. Unknown σ.

5. a. $n = 200, z = 1.96, p = 28/200 = .14,$
   so $p \pm z\sqrt{\frac{p(1-p)}{n}}$ gives $.092 < \pi < .188;$

  b. $np = 28 > 10;$

  c. Using $z = 1.645$ and $E = \pm.03$ the formula
   $n = \left(\frac{z}{E}\right)^2 \pi(1-\pi)$ gives $n = 363$ (using $p = .14$ for π
   from preliminary sample) or $n = 752$ (using $\pi = .50$ if
   we want to be very conservative)

6. c. Normality OK since $np = 17.5 > 10.$

7. b. Type I error is rejecting a true $H_0.$

8. b. $z_{.025} = \pm1.960$

9. a. $H_0 : \mu \geq 56, H_1 : \mu < 56;$

  b. Using $\bar{x} = 55.82, \sigma = 0.75$ (known), and $n = 49,$ we get
   $z_{calc} = \frac{\bar{x}-\mu_0}{\sigma/\sqrt{n}} = -1.636;$

  c. $z_{.05} = -1.645;$

  d. fail to reject (but a very close decision)

10. a. $H_0 : \mu \leq 60, H_1 : \mu > 60;$

  b. Using $\bar{x} = 67, s = 12,$ and $n = 16,$ we get $t_{calc} = \frac{\bar{x}-\mu_0}{s/\sqrt{n}}$
   $= 2.333;$

  c. For d.f. $= n - 1 = 15, t_{.025} = 2.131;$ d. reject

11. a. $\alpha = P(\text{reject } H_0 \mid H_0 \text{ is true})$

12. a. $H_0 : \pi \leq .85, H_1 : \pi > .85, p = 435/500 = .87,$
   $z_{calc} = \frac{p-\pi_0}{\sqrt{\frac{\pi_0(1-\pi_0)}{n}}} = 1.252, z_{.05} = 1.645,$ not a
   significant increase;

  b. $n\pi_0 = (500)(.85) = 425 > 10$ and
   $n(1 - \pi_0) = (500)(.15) = 75 > 10$

13. a. independent samples, unknown variances, $t_{calc} = -2.034$
   (regardless whether equal or unequal variances assumed);

  b. two-tailed test, $t_{.025} = \pm1.717$ (if equal variances
   assumed, d.f. $= 22$) or $t_{.025} = \pm1.721$ (if unequal
   variances assumed, d.f. $= 21$);

  c. reject $H_0 : \mu_1 = \mu_2$ in favor of $H_1 : \mu_1 \neq \mu_2.$

14. a. $H_0 : \pi_1 \leq \pi_2, H_1 : \pi_1 > \pi_2, p_1 = 150/200 = .75,$
   $p_2 = 140/200 = .70, \bar{p} = .725,$
   $z_{calc} = 1.120, z_{.025} = 1.96$
   Colorado not significantly greater

15. a. paired t-test;

  b. d.f. $= n - 1 = 5 - 1 = 4,$ left-tailed test, $t_{.10} = -1.533$

  c. $t_{calc} = -1.251,$ fail to reject, second exam not significantly greater

16. a. Reject if *small p*-value

17. a. $F_{calc} = s_1^2/s_2^2 = (14^2)/(7^2) = 4.00;$

  b. $\alpha/2 = .05/2 = .025, F_L = 1/(5.12) = 0.195$
   (d.f. $= 6, 7$) and $F_R = 5.70$ (d.f. $= 7, 6$) or folded
   F-test, $F_{.025} = 5.70,$ fail to reject $H_0 : \sigma_1^2 = \sigma_2^2.$

CHAPTERS 11-13

1. a. In ANOVA, each population is assumed normal.

2. b. Hartley's F_{max} test compares variances (not means).

3. $F_{calc} = (744/4)/(751.5/15) = 3.71, F_{4,15} = 3.06$

4. c. Small standard error shows a good fit.

5. Two-tailed test, $t_{calc} = 2.127,$ d.f. $= 28, t_{.005} = 2.763,$ fail
   to reject.

6. b. In correlation analysis, neither variable is assumed
   dependent.

7. a. $R^2 = SSR/SST = (158.3268)/(317.4074) = .4988.$

8. b. d.f. $= n - 2 = 25, t_{.025} = 2.060$

9. a, c. Both formulas give the same $t_{calc}.$

10. a. false (residual is within $\pm1s_{yx}$);

  b. true;

  c. true

11. a. Evans' Rule suggests $n/k \geq 10.$

12. b. $R_{adj}^2 \leq R^2$ always, big difference would suggest weak
   predictors

13. a. because their 95% CIs do not include zero.

14. c. p-value $< .05$ for X_3 (clearly) and X_4 (barely)

15. d.f. $= 38, t_{.005} = \pm2.712,$ so only X_3 is significant
   ($t_{calc} = -5.378$)

PHOTO CREDITS

INDEX

Page numbers followed by *n* indicate material found in notes.

CUMULATIVE STANDARD NORMAL DISTRIBUTION

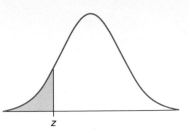

This table shows the normal area less than z. Example: $P(z < -1.96) = .0250$

z	.00	.01	.02	.03	.04	.05	.06	.07	.08	.09
-3.7	.00011	.00010	.00010	.00010	.00009	.00009	.00008	.00008	.00008	.00008
-3.6	.00016	.00015	.00015	.00014	.00014	.00013	.00013	.00012	.00012	.00011
-3.5	.00023	.00022	.00022	.00021	.00020	.00019	.00019	.00018	.00017	.00017
-3.4	.00034	.00032	.00031	.00030	.00029	.00028	.00027	.00026	.00025	.00024
-3.3	.00048	.00047	.00045	.00043	.00042	.00040	.00039	.00038	.00036	.00035
-3.2	.00069	.00066	.00064	.00062	.00060	.00058	.00056	.00054	.00052	.00050
-3.1	.00097	.00094	.00090	.00087	.00084	.00082	.00079	.00076	.00074	.00071
-3.0	.00135	.00131	.00126	.00122	.00118	.00114	.00111	.00107	.00104	.00100
-2.9	.0019	.0018	.0018	.0017	.0016	.0016	.0015	.0015	.0014	.0014
-2.8	.0026	.0025	.0024	.0023	.0023	.0022	.0021	.0021	.0020	.0019
-2.7	.0035	.0034	.0033	.0032	.0031	.0030	.0029	.0028	.0027	.0026
-2.6	.0047	.0045	.0044	.0043	.0041	.0040	.0039	.0038	.0037	.0036
-2.5	.0062	.0060	.0059	.0057	.0055	.0054	.0052	.0051	.0049	.0048
-2.4	.0082	.0080	.0078	.0075	.0073	.0071	.0069	.0068	.0066	.0064
-2.3	.0107	.0104	.0102	.0099	.0096	.0094	.0091	.0089	.0087	.0084
-2.2	.0139	.0136	.0132	.0129	.0125	.0122	.0119	.0116	.0113	.0110
-2.1	.0179	.0174	.0170	.0166	.0162	.0158	.0154	.0150	.0146	.0143
-2.0	.0228	.0222	.0217	.0212	.0207	.0202	.0197	.0192	.0188	.0183
-1.9	.0287	.0281	.0274	.0268	.0262	.0256	**.0250**	.0244	.0239	.0233
-1.8	.0359	.0351	.0344	.0336	.0329	.0322	.0314	.0307	.0301	.0294
-1.7	.0446	.0436	.0427	.0418	.0409	.0401	.0392	.0384	.0375	.0367
-1.6	.0548	.0537	.0526	.0516	.0505	.0495	.0485	.0475	.0465	.0455
-1.5	.0668	.0655	.0643	.0630	.0618	.0606	.0594	.0582	.0571	.0559
-1.4	.0808	.0793	.0778	.0764	.0749	.0735	.0721	.0708	.0694	.0681
-1.3	.0968	.0951	.0934	.0918	.0901	.0885	.0869	.0853	.0838	.0823
-1.2	.1151	.1131	.1112	.1093	.1075	.1056	.1038	.1020	.1003	.0985
-1.1	.1357	.1335	.1314	.1292	.1271	.1251	.1230	.1210	.1190	.1170
-1.0	.1587	.1562	.1539	.1515	.1492	.1469	.1446	.1423	.1401	.1379
-0.9	.1841	.1814	.1788	.1762	.1736	.1711	.1685	.1660	.1635	.1611
-0.8	.2119	.2090	.2061	.2033	.2005	.1977	.1949	.1922	.1894	.1867
-0.7	.2420	.2389	.2358	.2327	.2296	.2266	.2236	.2206	.2177	.2148
-0.6	.2743	.2709	.2676	.2643	.2611	.2578	.2546	.2514	.2483	.2451
-0.5	.3085	.3050	.3015	.2981	.2946	.2912	.2877	.2843	.2810	.2776
-0.4	.3446	.3409	.3372	.3336	.3300	.3264	.3228	.3192	.3156	.3121
-0.3	.3821	.3783	.3745	.3707	.3669	.3632	.3594	.3557	.3520	.3483
-0.2	.4207	.4168	.4129	.4090	.4052	.4013	.3974	.3936	.3897	.3859
-0.1	.4602	.4562	.4522	.4483	.4443	.4404	.4364	.4325	.4286	.4247
-0.0	.5000	.4960	.4920	.4880	.4841	.4801	.4761	.4721	.4681	.4641